MW01658516

THE * simple bible

The Bible that reads the way you **talk.**

Simple, straightforward, easy to understand, and easy to finish.

The Simple Bible

Published by Simple Bibles

Charleston, SC

www.SimpleBibles.com

This Bible is a simplified, contemporary-language version of the Holy Bible, written with clarity and accessibility in mind. It is designed for new believers, young adults, and readers of all ages seeking a version that reads the way they speak and can be completed in 30 days.

Unless otherwise indicated, all Scripture in this book has been adapted and simplified from public domain Bible translations (such as the American Standard Version, World English Bible, and King James Version) and rewritten in contemporary language, with limited metaphors, symbolisms, and poetic language.

ISBN: 979-8-9993534-0-5

First Edition

Printed in the United States of America

Design and layout by Hayek-Saleeby

Cover image by Hayek-Saleeby

Typeset in Garamond 9 pt

Formatted for 6" x 9" print edition

A portion of proceeds from this book may be donated to outreach ministries and organizations focused on making the Bible accessible to new readers around the world.

For permission or inquiries, contact:

contact@simplebibles.com

Table of Contents

Old Testament

New Testament

Introduction

The Simple Bible was created to solve a problem many readers—both new and experienced—have faced for years: the Bible is often intimidating to start, difficult to understand, and hard to finish.

This is not a summary, abridgment, or study guide. It's a full paraphrase of the Bible, written in direct, modern, everyday language so readers can clearly understand what they're reading—without needing a commentary, a dictionary, or internet research.

Every book was rewritten verse by verse from public domain source texts, ensuring that the message, meaning, and structure remain intact. The focus was on clarity, flow, and comprehension—cutting out or limiting metaphors, symbolic and poetic language that often gets in the way of understanding and avoiding outdated phrasing that makes passages harder to follow.

It's written for the modern reader—for the new believer, the returning Christian, the person who has tried reading the Bible before but gave up, and even for those who've been in church for years but want something straightforward and easy to grasp. It's written at a sixth-grade reading level for maximum clarity but designed with adults in mind. Whether you're 12, 32, or 62, this is for anyone who wants to read the Bible and finally understand Scripture.

This Bible was designed with two priorities:
1. Make it easy to read — using plain, direct language in every verse.
2. Make it easy to finish — by laying it out with clean formatting, generous spacing, and structured flow, so that each chapter feels readable and never overwhelming.

The structure is intentional to reduce visual fatigue and create a smoother reading experience. Chapters and verses are formatted to make it easy to track your place without feeling like you're reading dense walls of text. Unlike most—where verses can blur into long paragraphs or confusing footnotes—this format was built to guide the eye and support retention.

The wording follows a strict standard: it simplifies without removing meaning. In some cases, verses may appear to be combined when the flow or meaning demanded it. No content meaning was skipped or removed; all core messages, details, and facts remain intact. Any differences in verse counts across chapters are purely structural and were made for clarity—not to change or leave anything out.

This Bible is not a replacement for traditional translations. It's an entry point—a foundation. A Bible that can be picked up and read from start to finish without confusion or burnout. And for those who may want to later move on to a more traditional or formal Bible and study format, this version provides a strong foundation to build on—without needing to decode what every passage "might" mean.

Whether this is your first Bible or your tenth, the goal was simple:
To give you a version of the Bible that you can actually read, understand, and finish.

30-Day Bible Reading Journey

Spend 30–45 minutes each day. Use this guide to stay on track.

Day 1 [ ] Genesis 1 – Genesis 36

Day 2 [ ] Genesis 37 – Exodus 10

Day 3 [ ] Exodus 11 – Exodus 34

Day 4 [ ] Exodus 35 – Leviticus 20

Day 5 [ ] Leviticus 21 – Numbers 12

Day 6 [ ] Numbers 13 – Deuteronomy 4

Day 7 [ ] Deuteronomy 5 – Joshua 18

Day 8 [ ] Joshua 19 – Judges 17

Day 9 [ ] Judges 18 – 1 Samuel 15

Day 10 [ ] 1 Samuel 16 – 2 Samuel 18

Day 11 [ ] 2 Samuel 19 – 1 Kings 14

Day 12 [ ] 1 Kings 15 – 2 Kings 12

Day 13 [ ] 2 Kings 13 – 2 Chronicles 8

Day 14 [ ] 2 Chronicles 9 – Nehemiah 3

Day 15 [ ] Nehemiah 4 – Job 3

Day 16 [ ] Job 4 – Psalms 16

Day 17 [ ] Psalms 17 – Psalms 81

Day 18 [ ] Psalms 82 – Proverbs 10

Day 19 [ ] Proverbs 11 – Isaiah 3

Day 20 [ ] Isaiah 4 – Isaiah 47

Day 21 [ ] Isaiah 48 – Jeremiah 9

Day 22 [ ] Jeremiah 10 – Jeremiah 41

Day 23 [ ] Jeremiah 42 – Ezekiel 12

Day 24 [ ] Ezekiel 13 – Ezekiel 41

Day 25 [ ] Ezekiel 42 – Daniel 12

Day 26 [ ] Hosea 1 – Zechariah 9

Day 27 [ ] Zechariah 10 – Matthew 13

Day 28 [ ] Matthew 14 – Luke 9

Day 29 [ ] Luke 10 – John 19

Day 30 [ ] John 20 – Revelation 22

Thank You

Thank you for allowing us to be part of your journey.
Whether this is your first time reading the Bible or a fresh start,
we're honored that you chose to begin here.
May these pages bring truth, clarity, peace, hope, and strength for the road ahead—
and give you the confidence to keep going, one page at a time.

Old Testament

– Genesis –

God creates the world, humanity falls, and God begins His plan through Abraham's family.

Genesis 1

1. First God made the heaven and earth—everything you see and don't see.
2. God made everything from nothing. The earth was a shapeless, empty, watery wasteland. Everything was dark, but God's Spirit was everywhere.
3. God said, "Let there be light," and light appeared.
4. God saw the light and liked it. He separated light from darkness.
5. He named the light Day and the darkness Night. This was the first day—morning and evening.
6. God said, "Let there be sky," and the sky appeared to separate the water.
7. God placed the sky above the waters.
8. He named the sky Heaven. This was the second day.
9. God said, "Let land appear and separate the water."
10. He named the land Earth and the water Oceans. God liked what He made.
11. God said, "Let grass, plants, and fruit trees grow," and they did.
12. God saw the grass, the many kinds of plants, and fruit trees, and He said it was good.
13. This was the third day.
14. God said, "Let lights shine in the sky to divide day from night and mark seasons, days, and years."
15. "Let the lights in Heaven shine on Earth."
16. God made two main lights: one bright for the day, one dim for the night. He also made the stars.
17. God placed them in the sky to light the earth.
18. They helped separate day from night. God saw it was good.
19. This was the fourth day.
20. God created fish to live in water and birds to fly under Heaven.
21. He made all kinds of sea animals, big and small, and many kinds of birds. God liked what He created.
22. God gave them power to have babies and fill the skies and oceans.
23. This was the fifth day.
24. God said, "Let there be animals on land—cattle, reptiles, bugs, and more."
25. He made all kinds of animals, and many varieties of each. God liked what He created.
26. Then God said, "Let's make man in our image to be like us. Let man rule over all other creatures and the earth."
27. So God made man and woman in His image.
28. He blessed them and told them to have children and fill the earth. He gave them power over all animals.
29. God said people could eat from all fruit trees.
30. He told animals to eat plants.
31. God looked at all He had made that day (day 6) and liked it.

Genesis 2

1. Heaven and Earth were completely finished.
2. On day 7, God stopped working.
3. He blessed day 7 and made it holy because He rested from all His work.
4. This is how God made the heavens and the earth.
5. God made man before rain, before plants were growing in the garden. The land was still dry.
6. Water came up from the ground and watered the land.

7. God made man from dust and breathed life into him. Man became a living person.
8. God planted a garden in Eden and put the man there.
9. He made beautiful trees and fruit trees. In the middle were the Tree of Life and the Tree of Knowledge of Good and Evil.
10. A river flowed out of Eden and split into four rivers.
11. The first was the Pishon, flowing around Havilah where gold is found.
12. That gold is pure. There's also bdellium and onyx.
13. The second river is the Gihon, flowing around the land of Cush.
14. The third is the Hiddekel (Tigris), east of Asshur. The fourth is the Perath (Euphrates).
15. God put the man in Eden to take care of it.
16. God said, "You can eat from any tree—
17. except the Tree of Knowledge of Good and Evil. If you eat from it, you will die."
18. God said, "It's not good for man to be alone. I'll make a helper for him."
19. God made all animals and birds from dirt. He brought them to the man to name.
20. The man named all the animals but didn't find a good helper.
21. God made the man fall into deep sleep. He took one of his ribs.
22. From it, God made a woman and brought her to the man.
23. The man said, "This is part of me—bone of my bones, flesh of my flesh. I'll call her woman."
24. This is why a man leaves his parents and joins with his wife, and they become one.
25. The man and woman were both naked, but not ashamed.

Genesis 3

1. The snake was tricky. He asked the woman, "Did God really say you can't eat from any tree?"
2. The woman said, "We can eat from all trees—
3. except the one in the middle. God said not to eat or touch it, or we'll die."
4. The snake said, "You won't die!
5. God knows if you eat it, you'll understand good and evil and be like Him."
6. The woman saw the fruit looked good. She ate it and gave some to the man.
7. Their eyes opened, and they realized they were naked. They sewed leaves to cover themselves.
8. That evening, they heard God walking and hid.
9. God called, "Where are you?"
10. The man said, "I was afraid because I was naked, so I hid."
11. God said, "Who told you that? Did you eat the fruit from the tree I told you not to?"
12. The man said, "The woman gave it to me."
13. God asked the woman, "What have you done?" She said, "The snake tricked me."
14. God said to the snake, "You are cursed. You'll crawl on your belly.
15. You and the woman will be enemies. Her child will crush your head, and you'll strike his heel."
16. To the woman, God said, "Childbirth will hurt. You'll want your husband, and he'll rule over you."
17. To the man, God said, "You listened to your wife and ate the fruit. Now the ground is cursed.
18. You'll get thorns and weeds.
19. You'll work hard until you die and return to the dust."

20. The man named his wife Eve because she would be the mother of all people.
21. God made clothes from animal skins for them.
22. God said, "Now man knows good and evil. We must not let him eat from the Tree of Life."
23. So God sent them out of Eden to farm the ground.
24. He placed angels and a flaming sword to guard the Tree of Life.

Genesis 4

1. Adam and Eve had a son, Cain. Then another named Abel.
2. Abel took care of sheep. Cain farmed the land.
3. Cain brought some crops as a gift to God.
4. Abel brought the best of his sheep. God accepted Abel's gift,
5. but not Cain's. Cain got angry.
6. God said, "Why are you angry?
7. If you do right, you'll be accepted. If not, sin is waiting at the door. It wants to control you, but you must rule over it."
8. Cain told Abel to go out to the field. Then he killed him.
9. God asked Cain, "Where is Abel?" Cain said, "I don't know. Am I his babysitter?"
10. God said, "What have you done? Your brother's blood cries out from the ground.
11. Now the ground is cursed.
12. It won't grow food for you. You'll wander the earth."
13. Cain said, "My punishment is too much!
14. I'll be a homeless wanderer. People will kill me."
15. God said, "No. If anyone kills you, I'll punish them seven times." Then He marked Cain to protect him.
16. Cain left and lived in the land of Nod, east of Eden.
17. Cain's wife had a son, Enoch. Cain built a city and named it after Enoch. 18–22. His family grew. They made tents, played music, and worked with bronze and iron.
18. Lamech said, "I killed a man for hurting me.
19. If Cain is avenged 7 times, I will be 77 times."
20. Adam and Eve had another son, Seth.
21. Seth's son was Enosh. Then people began to worship God again.

Genesis 5

1. This is the family line that started with Adam. When God made people, He made them like Himself.
2. He made them male and female and gave them His blessing.
3. Adam was 130 when he had Seth.
4. He lived 800 more years and had other children.
5. He died at 930 years old.
6. Seth was 105 when he had Enosh.
7. He lived 807 more years and had other children.
8. He died at 912 years old.
9. Enosh was 90 when he had Kenan.
10. He lived 815 more years and had other children.
11. He died at 905 years old.
12. Kenan was 70 when he had Mahalalel.
13. He lived 840 more years and had other children.
14. He died at 910 years old.
15. Mahalalel was 65 when he had Jared.

16. He lived 830 more years and had other children.
17. He died at 895 years old.
18. Jared was 162 when he had Enoch.
19. He lived 800 more years and had other children.
20. He died at 962 years old.
21. Enoch was 65 when he had Methuselah.
22. He walked closely with God for 300 more years and had other children.
23. He lived 365 years total.
24. Then he disappeared—God took him away. He didn't die.
25. Methuselah was 187 when he had Lamech.
26. He lived 782 more years and had other children.
27. He died at 969 years old.
28. Lamech was 182 when he had a son.
29. He named him Noah, saying, "This boy will comfort us from the hard work caused by the curse on the ground."
30. Lamech lived 595 more years and had other children.
31. He died at 777 years old.
32. Noah was 500 years old when he had Shem, Ham, and Japheth.

Genesis 6

1. After time, the population grew, and more couples were having daughters.
2. The sons of God saw the daughters of men were beautiful. They picked the ones they liked and made them their wives.
3. The Lord said, "I won't let man live forever. Man will now die. From now on, man will live only 120 years."
4. Giants called Nephilim lived on the earth then. When the sons of God had children with human women, their kids became strong famous heroes.
5. God saw people were evil. They were always thinking bad things.
6. God was sorry He made humans. His heart was hurt.
7. God said, "I will wipe out every human and animal I made. I regret making them."
8. But God liked Noah.
9. Noah was a good man who obeyed God. He had 3 sons: Shem, Ham, and Japheth.
10. The world became full of evil and violence.
11. God saw it was corrupt. Everyone was doing bad things.
12. God told Noah, "I'm going to destroy everyone and the earth.
13. Build a big boat using cypress wood. Make rooms and cover it with tar inside and out.
14. Make the boat 450 feet long, 75 feet wide, and 45 feet high.
15. Put a window near the top and a door on the side. Make 3 decks—bottom, middle, and top.
16. I will send a flood to destroy everything alive.
17. But I will make a promise with you.
18. You, your wife, your sons, and their wives will go on the boat.
19. Bring 2 of every living animal—male and female—into the boat to stay alive.
20. Birds, animals, crawling things—2 of each kind will come to you.
21. Store food for you and the animals."
22. Noah did everything God told him to do.

Genesis 7

1. Then God told Noah, "Get on the boat with your family. You are the only good people left."

2. "Bring 7 males and 7 females of every clean animal. Bring 1 male and 1 female of every unclean animal.
3. Bring 7 male and 7 female birds so they survive."
4. "In 7 days, I'll make it rain for 40 days and nights. Everything on earth will die."
5. Noah did what God told him.
6. He was 600 years old when the flood came.
7. Noah and his family got on the boat.
8. Animals, clean and unclean, birds, and crawling things
9. all came to the boat in pairs, just as God had said.
10. After 7 days, the flood started.
11. On the 17th day of the 2nd month, water burst from underground, and heavy rain came from the sky.
12. It rained for 40 days and nights.
13. That same day, Noah and his family entered the boat.
14. All kinds of animals, birds, and creatures joined them.
15. Two of each kind came to Noah, male and female.
16. They entered as God commanded, and God shut the door.
17. The flood covered the earth for 40 days. Water lifted the boat high above the ground.
18. Water got deeper and deeper. The boat floated safely.
19. All the tall mountains were covered.
20. Water rose 22 feet above the highest mountain.
21. Everything died—people, animals, birds, and crawling things.
22. Everything that breathed air died.
23. Only Noah and those with him on the boat were safe.
24. Water covered the earth for 150 days.

Genesis 8

1. God didn't forget Noah or the animals. He sent a wind to dry the land.
2. Rain stopped falling, and water from underground stopped rising.
3. After 150 days, the water started going down.
4. On the 17th day of the 7th month, the boat rested on the mountains of Ararat.
5. The water kept going down. By the 10th month, mountaintops could be seen.
6. After 40 days, Noah opened the window he had made.
7. He sent out a raven. It flew back and forth until the ground dried.
8. He sent out a dove to see if the water had gone down.
9. The dove couldn't find a place to land, so it came back. Noah reached out and brought it in.
10. He waited 7 more days and sent the dove again.
11. The dove returned with a fresh olive leaf. Noah knew the water had gone down.
12. He waited 7 more days and sent the dove again. This time, it didn't come back.
13. On the 1st day of the 1st month, Noah was 601. He opened the roof and saw the ground was dry.
14. By the 27th day of the 2nd month, the earth was dry.
15. God said,
16. "Leave the boat, you and your family.
17. Bring out the animals so they can have babies and fill the earth."
18. Noah, his family, and all the animals came out.
19. Noah built an altar and offered clean animals and birds to God.

20. God liked the offering. He said, "I will never again curse the ground because of man.
21. As long as earth lasts, there will be seasons, day and night, planting and harvest."

Genesis 9

1. God blessed Noah and his sons. He said, "Have kids and fill the earth."
2. "All animals will fear you. You are over them."
3. "You can eat meat, just like plants.
4. But don't eat meat with blood in it."
5. "If someone kills another person, they will be punished.
6. If you take a life, your life will be taken. People are made in God's image."
7. "Now go fill the earth again."
8. God made a promise to Noah,
9. "This is my promise to you and your family
10. and every living thing."
11. "I will never destroy all life with a flood again."
12. God said, "This rainbow is the sign of my promise.
13. I will put it in the sky.
14. When I see it,
15. I will remember my promise to never destroy the earth with a flood."
16. "The rainbow will remind Me of my promise."
17. God said this to Noah.
18. Noah's sons were Shem, Ham, and Japheth. Ham was the father of Canaan.
19. From these 3 sons, the whole world was repopulated.
20. Noah became a farmer and planted a vineyard.
21. He drank too much wine and got drunk. He lay naked inside his tent.
22. Ham saw his father naked and told his brothers. That's why Noah cursed Ham's son, Canaan.
23. Shem and Japheth took a blanket and covered their father without looking.
24. When Noah woke up, he found out what Ham had done.
25. He said, "Canaan is cursed! He will be a slave to his brothers."
26. "Praise the Lord, the God of Shem. Canaan will be his servant."
27. "May God give land to Japheth. He will live in Shem's tents. Canaan will be his slave."
28. Noah lived 350 more years after the flood.
29. He died at 950 years old.

Genesis 10

1. This is the family tree of Noah's sons: Shem, Ham, and Japheth.
2. Japheth's sons: Gomer, Magog, Madai, Javan, Tubal, Meshech, and Tiras.
3. Gomer's sons: Ashkenaz, Riphath, and Togarmah.
4. Javan's sons: Elishah, Tarshish, Kittim, and Dodanim.
5. These people spread to different lands, each with their own language.
6. Ham's sons: Cush, Mizraim, Put, and Canaan.
7. Cush's sons: Seba, Havilah, Sabtah, Raamah, and Sabteca. Raamah's sons: Sheba and Dedan.
8. Cush had Nimrod. He became a powerful man.
9. He was a strong hunter before the Lord.
10. His kingdom began in Babel, Erech, Accad, and Calneh in Shinar.
11. From there, he went to Assyria and built Nineveh, Rehoboth-Ir, Calah,
12. and Resen (between Nineveh and Calah).

13. Mizraim had Ludim, Anamim, Lehabim, Naphtuhim,
14. Pathrusim, Casluhim (from whom the Philistines came), and Caphtorim.
15. Canaan had Sidon (his firstborn), Heth,
16. the Jebusites, Amorites, Girgashites,
17. Hivites, Arkites, Sinites,
18. Arvadites, Zemarites, and Hamathites. These families spread out later.
19. Canaan's land was from Sidon to Gerar and Gaza, and to Sodom, Gomorrah, Admah, and Zeboiim, as far as Lasha.
20. These were Ham's sons by land, language, tribe, and nation.
21. Shem's older brother was Japheth. Shem had sons too.
22. Shem's sons: Elam, Asshur, Arphaxad, Lud, and Aram.
23. Aram's sons: Uz, Hul, Gether, and Mash.
24. Arphaxad had Shelah. Shelah had Eber.
25. Eber had two sons: Peleg (during his time the earth was divided), and Joktan.
26. Joktan's sons: Almodad, Sheleph, Hazarmaveth, Jerah,
27. Hadoram, Uzal, Diklah,
28. Obal, Abimael, Sheba,
29. Ophir, Havilah, and Jobab. They lived in the eastern mountains.
30. Their land stretched from Mesha toward Sephar.
31. These were Shem's sons by family, language, land, and nation.
32. These are the families of Noah's sons. From them, the nations spread across the earth after the flood by tribe, language, and land.

Genesis 11

1. Everyone on earth spoke the same language.
2. As people moved east, they found a flat land in Shinar and settled there.
3. They said, "Let's make bricks and bake them well." They used bricks instead of stone and tar instead of cement.
4. Then they said, "Let's build a city and a tall tower that reaches heaven. Let's make a name for ourselves so we won't be scattered."
5. God came down to look at the city and tower people were building.
6. God said, "These people are united with one language. This is just the beginning. Soon they'll do anything they want."
7. "Let's go down and confuse their language so they can't understand each other."
8. So God scattered them all over the earth, and they stopped building the city.
9. That's why it was called Babel—because God confused their language and scattered them.

Genesis 12

1. God told Abram, "Leave your country, your family, and your father's house. I'll show you where to go."
2. "I'll make your family into a great nation. I'll bless you and make your name famous."
3. "I'll bless those who bless you and curse those who curse you. All families on earth will be blessed because of you."
4. Abram was 75 years old when he left Haran with his wife Sarai, nephew Lot, and all their things.
5. They traveled to Canaan.
6. Abram passed through Shechem and camped near the oak tree of Moreh. Canaanites lived there then.
7. There God told Abram, "I'll give this land to your kids." Abram built an altar there.
8. Then he moved to the hills east of Bethel and pitched his tent between

Bethel and Ai. He built another altar and prayed.

9. Abram kept moving south toward the Negev.
10. There was a famine, so Abram went to Mizraim to stay there for a while.
11. He told Sarai, "You are beautiful.
12. If the Mizraim people see you, they'll kill me and take you."
13. "Please say you are my sister. That way I'll be safe, and they'll treat me well."
14. When they got to Mizraim, everyone noticed Sarai's beauty.
15. Pharaoh's men saw her and told Pharaoh. She was taken to Pharaoh's palace.
16. Pharaoh gave Abram gifts—sheep, cattle, donkeys, servants, and camels.
17. But God sent plagues to Pharaoh's house because of Sarai.
18. Pharaoh called Abram and said, "Why did you lie? Why didn't you say she was your wife?"
19. "Why did you say she was your sister? Take your wife and go!"
20. Pharaoh ordered his men to send Abram, Sarai, and everything they had away.

Genesis 13

1. Abram left Mizraim with Sarai, Lot, and all their stuff.
2. Abram was rich—he had silver, gold, and livestock.
3. He traveled back to Bethel, where he had camped before, between Bethel and Ai.
4. There he had built an altar and prayed to God.
5. Lot, who was traveling with him, also had herds, tents, and workers.
6. The land couldn't support both of them—they had too many animals.
7. Their workers started arguing. (At that time, the Canaanites and Perizzites lived there too.)
8. Abram said to Lot, "Let's not fight. We're family.
9. The land is wide. You choose where to go. If you go left, I'll go right. If you go right, I'll go left."
10. Lot looked around and saw the Jordan Valley. It looked like Eden, like Mizraim—lush and green.
11. So Lot picked the Jordan Valley and moved east. They split up.
12. Abram stayed in Canaan. Lot lived near the cities in the valley and pitched his tent near Sodom.
13. The people of Sodom were very evil.
14. After Lot left, God said to Abram, "Look in every direction—north, south, east, and west.
15. I will give you and your children all this land forever."
16. "Your family will be large too many to count—like trying to count dust."
17. "Walk the land. I'm giving it to you."
18. Abram moved to Hebron and lived near the oak trees of Mamre. He built an altar to God there.

Genesis 14

1. Kings Amraphel of Shinar, Arioch of Ellasar, Chedorlaomer of Elam, and Tidal of Goiim
2. went to war against kings Bera of Sodom, Birsha of Gomorrah, Shinab of Admah, Shemeber of Zeboiim, and the king of Bela (also called Zoar).
3. These 5 kings joined forces in the Valley of Siddim (the Salt Sea).
4. For 12 years they served Chedorlaomer, but in year 13 they rebelled.
5. In year 14, Chedorlaomer and his allies defeated the Rephaim in Ashteroth-karnaim, Zuzim in Ham, Emim in Shaveh-kiriathaim,

6. and Horites in Seir. Then they went to El-paran near the desert.

7. They returned to En-mishpat (Kadesh), conquered Amalekites and Amorites in Hazazon-tamar.

8. The 5 kings came to fight them in the Valley of Siddim.

9. They battled Chedorlaomer and his allies.

10. The valley had many tar pits. The kings of Sodom and Gomorrah fled and fell there. The rest ran to the hills.

11. The winners took everything from Sodom and Gomorrah, including food and supplies.

12. They also captured Lot, Abram's nephew, who lived in Sodom.

13. One man escaped and told Abram. Abram lived near the trees of Mamre the Amorite, who was his ally.

14. Abram heard Lot was taken and gathered 318 trained men. He chased the enemies as far as Dan.

15. At night, Abram and his men attacked and beat them, chasing them to Hobah, north of Damascus.

16. Abram brought back Lot, all the goods, women, and people.

17. After the win, the king of Sodom came to meet Abram in the Valley of Shaveh (King's Valley).

18. Melchizedek, king of Salem and priest of God Most High, brought bread and wine.

19. He blessed Abram and said, "God Most High made heaven and earth and helped you win."

20. Abram gave Melchizedek a tenth of everything.

21. The king of Sodom said, "Give me the people, and you can keep the goods."

22. Abram said, "I promised God I wouldn't take anything—not even a thread or sandal strap—

23. so you can't say you made me rich."

24. "Let my allies Aner, Eshcol, and Mamre take their share."

Genesis 15

1. After all this, God spoke to Abram in a vision: "Don't be afraid. I will protect you and reward you."

2. Abram said, "But God, what good is a reward? I don't have kids. My servant Eliezer from Damascus will get everything."

3. "You haven't given me a child, so a servant will inherit."

4. God said, "No. Your own son will inherit."

5. God took Abram outside and said, "Look at the sky. Count the stars if you can. That's how many children you'll have."

6. Abram believed God, and God accepted him as good because of his faith.

7. God said, "I brought you from Ur to give you this land."

8. Abram asked, "How do I know I'll really get it?"

9. God said, "Bring me a 3-year-old cow, goat, and ram, plus a dove and young pigeon."

10. Abram brought them, cut the animals in half, and placed them across from each other. He didn't cut the birds.

11. Birds tried to eat the animals, but Abram chased them away.

12. As the sun set, Abram fell into deep sleep. He felt afraid and a heavy darkness came.

13. God said, "Your kids will live in a land that isn't theirs. They'll be slaves for 400 years there in Egypt.

14. But I will punish the nation that enslaves them, and they will leave with great wealth."

15. "You will die in peace at an old age.

16. After 4 generations, your people will return here."

17. After dark, a smoking fire pot and flaming torch passed between the animal pieces.
18. That day, God made a promise with Abram: "I give this land to your children—from the river of Mizraim to the Euphrates—
19. including land of the Kenites, Kenizzites, Kadmonites,
20. Hittites, Perizzites, Rephaim,
21. Amorites, Canaanites, Girgashites, and Jebusites."

Genesis 16

1. Sarai still hadn't had a child, but she had a maid named Hagar from Mizraim.
2. Sarai said to Abram, "God hasn't given me children. Sleep with my maid. Maybe we can have a child through her." Abram agreed.
3. After living in Canaan for 10 years, Sarai gave Hagar to Abram as a wife.
4. Abram slept with Hagar and she got pregnant. When Hagar knew she was pregnant, she looked down on Sarai.
5. Sarai said to Abram, "This is your fault! I gave you my maid, and now she disrespects me. May God judge between us."
6. Abram said, "She's your maid. Do what you want." So Sarai treated Hagar so badly that Hagar ran away.
7. God's angel found Hagar near a spring in the desert on the way to Shur.
8. He said, "Hagar, Sarai's maid, where are you coming from and where are you going?" She said, "I'm running away from Sarai."
9. The angel said, "Go back to Sarai and obey her."
10. He said, "You will have many children—too many to count."
11. He said, "You are pregnant and will have a son. Name him Ishmael because God has heard your cry."
12. "Your son will be wild and free. He will fight with everyone, and everyone will fight him. He will live apart from his relatives."
13. Hagar called God "The One Who Sees Me." She said, "I have seen the one who sees me."
14. That's why the spring is called Beer-lahai-roi. It's between Kadesh and Bered.
15. Hagar had a son and named him Ishmael.
16. Abram was 86 years old when Ishmael was born.

Genesis 17

1. When Abram was 99, God said, "I am God. Live the right way and do what's good."
2. "I'm making a promise with you. You'll have many children."
3. Abram bowed with his face to the ground.
4. God said, "You'll be the father of many nations."
5. "Your name will be Abraham, not Abram, because I'm making you a father of many nations."
6. "You'll have many descendants—even kings."
7. "This promise is for you and your descendants forever: I will be your God."
8. "I will give you and your children the land of Canaan forever."
9. God said, "You and your children must keep this promise."
10. "Every male must be circumcised to show this promise."
11. "Cut the skin from the tip of your penis. That's the sign of the promise."
12. "Do this to every baby boy when he's 8 days old. Do it to everyone born in your home or bought with money."

13. "This includes servants and anyone not related by blood."
14. "If a male isn't circumcised, he is breaking the promise and must be removed."
15. "Your wife's name will be Sarah, not Sarai."
16. "I will bless her and give her a son. She will be the mother of nations and kings."
17. Abraham laughed and said to himself, "How can I have a son at 100? And Sarah at 90?"
18. He said to God, "Please let Ishmael be the one you bless."
19. God said, "No. Sarah will have your son, and you'll name him Isaac. I'll keep my promise with him."
20. "I'll bless Ishmael too. He will have 12 sons and become a great nation."
21. "But my promise is with Isaac, who Sarah will have next year."
22. Then God left Abraham.
23. That day, Abraham circumcised himself, Ishmael, and every male in his house.
24. Abraham was 99 when he was circumcised.
25. Ishmael was 13.
26. They were both circumcised that same day.
27. Every man in Abraham's house was circumcised too.

Genesis 18

1. God appeared to Abraham by the trees of Mamre while he sat at his tent's entrance in the heat of the day.
2. Abraham looked up and saw 3 men. He ran to them, bowed,
3. and said, "Please stay with me.
4. Let me wash your feet and bring you food. Then you can go." They said, "Yes."
5. Abraham hurried into the tent and told Sarah to make bread.
6. He ran to pick a young cow and had a servant cook it.
7. He gave them meat, butter, and milk, and stood by while they ate.
8. They asked, "Where is your wife Sarah?" Abraham said, "She's in the tent."
9. One said, "I'll return next year, and Sarah will have a son." Sarah heard from inside the tent.
10. Abraham and Sarah were very old. Sarah couldn't have children anymore.
11. Sarah laughed and thought, "I'm too old to have a child."
12. God said to Abraham, "Why did Sarah laugh? Is anything too hard for God? I will return next year and she will have a son."
13. Sarah was afraid and lied, saying, "I didn't laugh." But God said, "Yes, you did."
14. The men left and looked toward Sodom. Abraham walked with them.
15. God said, "Should I hide my plans from Abraham?
16. I've chosen him to become a great nation and teach his family to do what's right."
17. "Sodom and Gomorrah are very evil. I will go see for myself."
18. The men left, but Abraham stayed with God.
19. Abraham asked, "Will you destroy the good people with the bad?"
20. "What if there are 50 good people?"
21. God said, "I won't destroy the city if I find 50 good people."
22. Abraham said, "What if there are 45?" God said, "I won't destroy it."
23. "What about 40?" God said, "I won't destroy it."
24. "30?" "I won't destroy it."
25. "20?" "I won't destroy it."

26. "What if there are 10?" God said, "I won't destroy it if I find 10."
27. Then God left and Abraham went home.

Genesis 19

1. Two angels came to Sodom at night. Lot was at the gate and greeted them.
2. He said, "Come stay at my house." They said, "No, we'll sleep outside."
3. Lot insisted, so they came in. He made them dinner and bread.
4. Before they slept, the men of Sodom surrounded the house.
5. They yelled, "Bring out the men who came to you. We want to have sex with them."
6. Lot went out and shut the door behind him.
7. Desperate and knowing it was wrong he said, "Don't do this evil thing."
8. "I have two virgin daughters. Do what you want with them, but don't sleep with these men."
9. They yelled, "Get out of the way! We'll treat you worse than them!" They pushed Lot and tried to break the door.
10. The angels pulled Lot inside and shut the door.
11. They blinded the men outside so they couldn't find the door.
12. The angels said, "Do you have family here? Get them out now.
13. We're going to destroy this place. The cries against it are loud, and God sent us to destroy it."
14. Lot told his sons-in-law, but they thought he was joking.
15. At dawn, the angels said, "Hurry! Take your wife and daughters or you'll die!"
16. Lot waited, so the angels grabbed their hands and led them out.
17. One said, "Run for your lives! Don't look back! Run to the hills!"
18. Lot said, "Please, not the hills!
19. Let me go to the little town of Zoar and live there."
20. The angel said, "Okay, go. I won't destroy Zoar."
21. Lot reached Zoar, and the sun was rising.
22. Then God sent fire on Sodom and Gomorrah.
23. He destroyed everything and everyone in the valley.
24. Lot's wife looked back and turned into a salt pillar.
25. Early in the morning, Abraham looked and saw smoke rising.
26. God saved Lot but destroyed the cities.
27. Lot left Zoar and lived in a cave with his daughters.
28. The older daughter said, "There are no men left. Let's get Dad drunk and sleep with him so we can have kids."
29. They got him drunk and slept with him—first the older, then the younger.
30. Both daughters became pregnant by Lot.
31. The older daughter had a son named Moab.
32. The younger had a son named Ben-Ammi.

Genesis 20

1. Abraham moved to Gerar.
2. He said Sarah was his sister, so King Abimelech took her.
3. That night, God came to Abimelech in a dream and said, "You're going to die! She's a married woman."
4. Abimelech hadn't touched her and said, "I didn't know! He said she was his sister."
5. God said, "I know you didn't mean to. That's why I stopped you.
6. Give her back. Abraham is a prophet and will pray for you."

7. If you don't, you and your people will die."
8. Abimelech got up early and told his servants. They were scared.
9. He called Abraham and said, "What have you done to us? Why would you lie and put us in danger?"
10. Abraham said, "I thought no one here feared God. I was afraid."
11. "She really is my sister—my father's daughter but not my mother's."
12. "I asked her to say she's my sister wherever we go."
13. Abimelech gave Abraham sheep, cattle, and servants.
14. He gave Sarah back and said, "Live anywhere you want."
15. To Sarah, he said, "I'm giving your brother 1,000 pieces of silver to show you're innocent."
16. Abraham prayed, and God healed Abimelech, his wife, and his maids so they could have children again.

Genesis 21

1. God kept his promise to Sarah.
2. She became pregnant and had a son for Abraham, just like God said.
3. They named him Isaac.
4. When Isaac was 8 days old, Abraham circumcised him, as God told him.
5. Abraham was 100 years old when Isaac was born.
6. Sarah said, "God made me laugh. Everyone who hears will laugh with me."
7. "Who would have said Abraham and I would have a child? But I had a son for him!"
8. When Isaac grew old enough to eat food, Abraham had a big party.
9. Sarah saw Ishmael (Hagar's son) playing with Isaac.
10. She told Abraham, "Send away that slave woman and her son. He won't share Isaac's inheritance."
11. This upset Abraham because Ishmael was his son too.
12. But God said, "Don't be upset. Listen to Sarah. Isaac is the one I chose."
13. "I'll also make a nation from Ishmael, because he's your son too."
14. Early the next morning, Abraham gave Hagar food and water and sent her away with Ishmael.
15. They wandered in the desert of Beersheba.
16. When the water ran out, Hagar put Ishmael under a bush and sat away from him. She cried.
17. God heard the boy. An angel said, "Hagar, don't be afraid. God heard him."
18. "Go pick him up. I'll make him a great nation."
19. God helped her see a well. She filled the water and gave it to Ishmael.
20. God was with him as he grew up. He lived in the desert and became a skilled archer.
21. He lived in the desert of Paran. His mother got him a wife from Mizraim.
22. Abimelech and his army commander said to Abraham, "God is with you.
23. Promise not to lie to me or my kids. Be kind like I've been to you."
24. Abraham said, "I promise."
25. But Abraham told Abimelech, "Your men took my well."
26. Abimelech said, "I didn't know about it until now."
27. Abraham gave Abimelech sheep and cattle to seal their agreement.
28. He set aside 7 female lambs.
29. Abimelech asked, "What are these for?"
30. Abraham said, "I'm giving them so you know I dug this well."

31. They called the place Beersheba.
32. They made a deal, and Abimelech went back to the land of the Philistines.
33. Abraham planted a tree in Beersheba and worshiped God there.
34. Abraham stayed in the land of the Philistines for a long time.

Genesis 22

1. God tested Abraham. He said, "Here I am."
2. God said, "Take your only son Isaac to Moriah. I'll show you a mountain to offer him as a sacrifice on."
3. Abraham got up early, cut wood, took two servants and Isaac, and left.
4. On the third day, he saw the mountain.
5. He told the servants, "Stay here. Isaac and I will worship and come back."
6. Abraham gave Isaac the wood and carried fire and a knife himself.
7. Isaac asked, "Where's the lamb for the offering?"
8. Abraham said, "God will provide."
9. When they got there, Abraham built an altar, tied Isaac, and laid him on it.
10. He picked up the knife to kill him.
11. An angel called from heaven, "Abraham!" He said, "Here I am."
12. The angel said, "Don't hurt him. Now I know you fear God."
13. Abraham saw a ram caught in a bush and sacrificed it instead.
14. He named the place "God Will Provide."
15. The angel called again and said,
16. "Because you didn't hold back your only son,
17. I'll bless you with many descendants—more than stars or sand.
18. All nations will be blessed through them because you obeyed me."
19. Abraham and Isaac went back to the servants and returned to Beersheba.
20. Later Abraham heard Milcah had sons for Nahor:
21. Uz, Buz, Kemuel,
22. Kesed, Hazo, Pildash, Jidlaph, and Bethuel.
23. Bethuel became Rebekah's father.
24. Nahor also had sons by Reumah: Tebah, Gaham, Tahash, and Maacah.

Genesis 23

1. Sarah lived to be 127 years old.
2. She died in Kiriath-arba (Hebron in Canaan), and Abraham mourned.
3. He asked the Hethites,
4. "I'm a stranger here. Please sell me land to bury my wife."
5. They replied, "You are respected. Choose any grave you want."
6. Abraham stood and said,
7. "Please ask Ephron son of Zohar to sell me his cave at Machpelah for full price."
8. Ephron was there and said,
9. "No, my lord. I'll give you the cave and field."
10. Abraham bowed and said,
11. "Please take my money. I want to pay."
12. Ephron said, "The land is worth 400 silver coins, but take it and bury your wife."
13. Abraham agreed and paid him.
14. The field and cave became Abraham's legal property.
15. He buried Sarah there, in Machpelah near Mamre (Hebron).

Genesis 24

1. Abraham was very old. God had blessed him in every way.

2. He said to his chief servant, "Swear to me you won't get a wife for Isaac from Canaan.
3. Go to my homeland and family to find him a wife."
4. The servant asked, "What if she won't come? Should I take Isaac there?"
5. Abraham said, "No. God will send an angel to help you. But if she won't come, you're free."
6. The servant swore.
7. He took 10 camels and gifts and went to Nahor's town in Mesopotamia.
8. He stopped at a well outside the city in the evening.
9. He prayed, "God, help me find the right woman for Isaac."
10. "If she offers me and my camels water, let her be the one."
11. Rebekah came out with a jar.
12. She was very pretty and unmarried. She went down to the spring to fill her jar.
13. The servant asked, "Can I have a drink?"
14. She said, "Yes," and gave him water.
15. Then she said, "I'll get water for your camels too."
16. She ran to get more water until all the camels drank.
17. The servant watched silently.
18. He gave her a gold nose ring and bracelets and asked, "Who's your father?"
19. She said, "I'm Bethuel's daughter. We have room for you to stay."
20. The servant bowed and thanked God.
21. Rebekah ran to tell her family.
22. Her brother Laban ran to meet the servant.
23. He said, "Come stay with us."
24. The servant came in, unloaded the camels, and they ate.
25. He said, "I'm Abraham's servant. God led me here to find a wife for Isaac."
26. He told the whole story.
27. Laban and Bethuel said, "This is from God. Take Rebekah."
28. The servant gave gifts and spent the night.
29. The next day he said, "Let me go back."
30. They asked if Rebekah could stay a while, but she agreed to leave.
31. They blessed her and sent her off.
32. Isaac was in the Negev.
33. He saw the camels coming.
34. Rebekah saw him and asked, "Who is that man?"
35. The servant said, "That's Isaac."
36. She covered her face with a veil.
37. The servant told Isaac everything.
38. Isaac married Rebekah and loved her. He was comforted after Sarah's death.

Genesis 25

1. Abraham married Keturah.
2. She had Zimran, Jokshan, Medan, Midian, Ishbak, and Shuah.
3. Jokshan's sons were Sheba and Dedan.
4. Midian's sons were Ephah, Epher, Hanoch, Abida, and Eldaah.
5. Abraham gave everything to Isaac.
6. He gave gifts to Keturah's sons and sent them east.
7. Abraham lived 175 years.
8. He died at a good old age.
9. Isaac and Ishmael buried him in the cave of Machpelah near Mamre.
10. That's where Sarah was buried.
11. After Abraham died, God blessed Isaac. Isaac lived near Beer-lahai-roi.
12. These are Ishmael's sons:
13. Nebaioth, Kedar, Adbeel, Mibsam,

14. Mishma, Dumah, Massa,
15. Hadad, Tema, Jetur, Naphish, and Kedemah.
16. These were 12 tribal leaders.
17. Ishmael lived 137 years.
18. He died and his family lived from Havilah to Shur near Mizraim.
19. This is Isaac's story.
20. Isaac was 40 when he married Rebekah.
21. She couldn't have kids, so Isaac prayed. God helped her.
22. She had twins.
23. God said, "Two nations are in you. The older will serve the younger."
24. She gave birth to Esau and Jacob.
25. Esau was red and hairy. Jacob grabbed Esau's heel.
26. Isaac was 60 when they were born.
27. Esau grew up to be a hunter. Jacob stayed home.
28. Isaac loved Esau. Rebekah loved Jacob.
29. One day, Jacob made stew. Esau came home hungry.
30. Esau said, "I'm starving. Give me some stew."
31. Jacob said, "Trade me your rights as the firstborn."
32. Esau said, "I'm dying anyway. What good are my rights?"
33. Jacob made him swear. Then gave him stew and bread.
34. Esau ate, drank, and left. He didn't care about his birthright.

Genesis 26

1. There was a famine in the land, like during Abraham's time. Isaac went to Abimelek, king of the Philistines, in Gerar.
2. God said, "Don't go to Mizraim. Stay where I tell you.
3. Live here. I will be with you and bless you. I will give this land to you and your children.
4. I will give you as many kids as stars. They will get this land. Everyone on earth will be blessed through them.
5. This is because Abraham obeyed me."
6. So Isaac stayed in Gerar.
7. The men there asked about his wife. Isaac said, "She is my sister," because he was scared they would kill him for Rebekah, who was very beautiful.
8. After a while, Abimelek saw Isaac being romantic with Rebekah.
9. Abimelek said, "She is your wife! Why did you lie?" Isaac said, "I was afraid they'd kill me."
10. Abimelek said, "What if someone had slept with her? You could've made us guilty!"
11. Then Abimelek warned everyone not to touch Isaac or Rebekah.
12. Isaac planted crops and that year got 100 times more than he planted. God blessed him.
13. Isaac became rich and kept getting richer.
14. He had many animals and servants. The Philistines were jealous.
15. They filled the wells Abraham's servants had dug.
16. Abimelek said, "Leave us. You're too powerful."
17. Isaac left and camped in the Gerar Valley.
18. He reopened the wells Abraham had dug.
19. Isaac's men dug and found water.
20. The Gerar herders argued over it. So Isaac named the well Esek (meaning "argument").
21. They dug another well. There was more fighting. He named it Sitnah (meaning "opposition").

22. He dug again. No one argued. He named it Rehoboth (meaning "room") and said, "Now God has given us space to grow."
23. Isaac went to Beersheba.
24. That night God said, "I am the God of Abraham. Don't be afraid. I am with you and will bless you."
25. Isaac built an altar, prayed, set up his tent, and his servants dug a well.
26. Abimelek came with his men.
27. Isaac said, "Why are you here? You told me to leave."
28. They said, "We see God is with you. Let's make peace."
29. "Promise not to hurt us, like we didn't hurt you."
30. Isaac made a feast and they ate and drank.
31. They made peace the next morning.
32. Later, Isaac's servants told him, "We found water!"
33. He named the well Shibah. The city is called Beersheba.

Genesis 27

1. Isaac was old and couldn't see. He called Esau and said, "My son." Esau said, "Here I am."
2. Isaac said, "I'm old. I could die any day.
3. Go hunt and make me food I like. Then I'll bless you before I die."
4. Rebekah heard this. When Esau left,
5. She told Jacob, "Your father plans to bless Esau.
6. Do what I say.
7. Go get two goats. I'll cook food he loves.
8. You take it to him so he'll bless you instead."
9. Jacob said, "Esau is hairy, I'm not. He'll know I'm tricking him and curse me."
10. Rebekah said, "Let the curse be on me. Just do it."
11. Jacob got the goats. Rebekah cooked the food.
12. She put Esau's clothes on Jacob and goat skins on his hands and neck.
13. She gave him the food and bread.
14. Jacob went to Isaac and said, "Father." Isaac said, "Who are you?"
15. Jacob said, "I'm Esau. I did what you said. Eat and bless me."
16. Isaac asked, "How did you find it so fast?" Jacob said, "God helped me."
17. Isaac said, "Come close so I can feel you."
18. Isaac touched him and said, "The voice is Jacob's, but the hands are Esau's."
19. He asked again, "Are you really Esau?" Jacob said, "Yes."
20. Isaac ate the food and drank the wine.
21. Then he said, "Come kiss me."
22. Jacob kissed him. Isaac smelled his clothes and blessed him:
23. "You smell like a field God has blessed.
24. God will give you good crops, wine, and rain.
25. Nations will serve you. Be the ruler of your family.
26. Those who curse you will be cursed. Those who bless you will be blessed."
27. After Jacob left, Esau came with food.
28. He said, "Father, sit up and eat so you can bless me."
29. Isaac said, "Who are you?" Esau said, "I'm your son, Esau."
30. Isaac shook and said, "Then who just brought me food and got the blessing?"
31. Esau cried out, "Bless me too!"
32. Isaac said, "Your brother tricked me and took your blessing."

33. Esau said, "Isn't he rightly named Jacob (which means 'deceiver')? He took my birthright and now my blessing!"
34. He begged, "Please bless me too!"
35. Isaac said, "I already made him your master."
36. Esau cried and said, "Don't you have any blessing left?"
37. Isaac said, "You will live away from rich land,
38. You'll live by your sword and serve your brother.
39. But one day, you'll break free."
40. Esau hated Jacob and said, "I'll kill him after Dad dies."
41. Rebekah heard and told Jacob, "Your brother plans to kill you."
42. She said, "Go to my brother Laban in Haran.
43. Stay there until Esau calms down.
44. I'll send for you when it's safe."
45. Rebekah told Isaac, "I'm tired of these local women. If Jacob marries one, I'll die."

Genesis 28

1. Isaac called Jacob, blessed him, and said, "Don't marry a Canaanite woman.
2. Go to Paddan-Aram to marry one of your uncle Laban's daughters."
3. "May God bless you with many children and make you into a great nation.
4. May He give you the land He promised Abraham."
5. Isaac sent Jacob away. He went to Paddan-Aram to Laban, Rebekah's brother.
6. Esau saw Isaac blessed Jacob and sent him away to get a wife.
7. He saw Jacob obeyed and went to Paddan-Aram.
8. Esau knew his Canaanite wives upset his parents.
9. So he married Mahalath, Ishmael's daughter.
10. Jacob left Beersheba and went to Haran.
11. He stopped for the night and used a stone for a pillow.
12. He dreamed of a ladder reaching heaven, with angels going up and down.
13. God stood above it and said, "I am the God of Abraham and Isaac. I will give you this land."
14. "You will have many children, like dust on the ground. Everyone on earth will be blessed through your family."
15. "I am with you and will bring you back to this land. I won't leave you."
16. Jacob woke up and said, "God is here, and I didn't know it!"
17. He was afraid and said, "This is God's house—the gate of heaven."
18. Early in the morning, he took the stone and set it up as a marker.
19. He named the place Bethel. Before, it was called Luz.
20. Jacob made a promise: "If God protects me and gives me food and clothes,
21. and brings me back home safely,
22. then He will be my God. I will give Him a tenth of everything He gives me."

Genesis 29

1. Jacob continued his journey and saw a well in a field.
2. Three flocks of sheep were lying near it.
3. A big stone covered the well.
4. When all the flocks came, the stone was rolled away and the sheep were watered.

5. Jacob asked the shepherds, "Where are you from?" They said, "Haran."
6. He asked, "Do you know Laban?" They said, "Yes."
7. He asked, "Is he doing well?" They said, "Yes, and his daughter Rachel is coming."
8. Jacob said, "It's still early. Water the sheep and take them back to pasture."
9. They said, "We can't until all the flocks come."
10. While they were talking, Rachel came with her father's sheep.
11. When Jacob saw her, he rolled the stone away and watered the sheep.
12. Then he kissed Rachel and cried.
13. He told her he was Rebekah's son. She ran to tell her father.
14. Laban welcomed him and said, "You're family!"
15. After a month, Laban said, "You shouldn't work for free. What should I pay you?"
16. Laban had two daughters: Leah, the older, and Rachel, the younger.
17. Leah had weak eyes, but Rachel was beautiful.
18. Jacob loved Rachel and said, "I'll work 7 years to marry her."
19. Laban said, "It's better to give her to you than a stranger."
20. Jacob worked 7 years, but it felt like days because he loved her.
21. He said, "Give me my wife now."
22. Laban had a feast.
23. At night, he gave Leah to Jacob instead of Rachel.
24. He also gave Leah his servant Zilpah.
25. In the morning, Jacob saw it was Leah! He said, "Why did you trick me?"
26. Laban said, "It's our custom to marry off the older daughter first.
27. Finish this wedding week. Then you can marry Rachel too—if you work another 7 years."
28. Jacob agreed. He married Rachel a week later.
29. Laban gave Rachel his servant Bilhah.
30. Jacob loved Rachel more than Leah and worked 7 more years.
31. God saw Leah was not loved and let her have children. Rachel had none.
32. Leah had a son and named him Reuben. "God saw my pain," she said.
33. She had another son, Simeon. "God heard I'm unloved."
34. She had a third son, Levi. "Now my husband will love me."
35. She had a fourth son, Judah. "Now I will praise God." Then she stopped having kids.

Genesis 30

1. Rachel saw she had no children and got jealous. She told Jacob, "Give me children or I'll die!"
2. Jacob got angry. "I'm not God!" he said.
3. Rachel said, "Take my servant Bilhah. She'll have kids for me."
4. Bilhah had a son. Rachel named him Dan. "God judged in my favor."
5. Bilhah had another son. Rachel named him Naphtali. "I've had a great struggle and won."
6. Leah saw she wasn't having more kids. She gave her servant Zilpah to Jacob.
7. Zilpah had a son. Leah named him Gad. "What luck!"
8. Zilpah had another son. Leah named him Asher. "I'm happy. Women will call me happy."
9. During wheat harvest, Reuben brought mandrakes to Leah. Rachel asked for some.
10. Leah said, "You took my husband. Now you want my son's mandrakes?"

11. Rachel said, "Jacob can sleep with you tonight if I get the mandrake plants."
12. That night, Leah met Jacob and said, "You must sleep with me."
13. She became pregnant and had a fifth son. She named him Issachar.
14. Then she had a sixth son, Zebulun.
15. Later, she had a daughter, Dinah.
16. God remembered Rachel. She became pregnant.
17. She had a son and named him Joseph. "May God give me another son."
18. Jacob told Laban, "Let me go home."
19. Laban said, "Stay. I've been blessed because of you."
20. Jacob said, "I worked hard. Let me leave with my family."
21. Laban asked, "What should I pay you?" Jacob said,
22. "Let me take the speckled and spotted sheep and goats. That's my pay."
23. Laban agreed.
24. That day, Laban took away all the speckled and spotted animals and gave them to his sons.
25. Jacob used branches to help strong animals produce speckled babies.
26. He didn't use this trick with the weak ones.
27. Jacob became very rich with many animals, servants, camels, and donkeys.

Genesis 31

1. Jacob heard Laban's sons say he stole everything and got rich from their father's things.
2. Jacob saw that Laban didn't treat him the same anymore.
3. God told Jacob, "Go back home. I'll be with you."
4. Jacob called Rachel and Leah to the field.
5. He said, "Your father doesn't like me anymore, but God is with me.
6. You know I worked hard for your father.
7. He cheated me and changed my pay ten times, but God protected me.
8. If he said, 'You get the spotted animals,' then they were all spotted. If he said, 'You get the striped ones,' they were all striped.
9. That's how God gave me all his animals.
10. I had a dream during mating season and saw the animals were spotted and striped.
11. An angel said, 'Jacob!' I said, 'Here I am.'
12. He said, 'Look at the animals. I saw what Laban did to you.
13. I'm the God of Beth-el, where you prayed. Go back to your home.'
14. Rachel and Leah said, "We have no share in our father's stuff.
15. He treats us like strangers and sold us.
16. So everything God took from him is ours and our kids'. Do what God said."
17. Jacob got his family and animals and left.
18. He took all he owned from Paddan-aram to Canaan.
19. Rachel stole her father's idols.
20. Jacob didn't tell Laban he was leaving.
21. He ran away, crossed the Euphrates, and headed toward the hill country of Gilead.
22. After 3 days, Laban heard Jacob was gone.
23. He chased him for 7 days and caught him in Gilead.
24. God told Laban in a dream, "Don't say anything good or bad to Jacob."
25. Laban found Jacob and set up camp.
26. He said, "Why did you run off? Why steal my daughters like captives?

27. You didn't let me say goodbye.
28. You didn't let me kiss my kids and grandkids.
29. I could hurt you, but God told me not to say anything.
30. Why did you steal my idols?"
31. Jacob said, "I was scared you'd take your daughters.
32. I didn't take your idols. If you find them, kill the person."
33. Laban searched Jacob's tents but didn't find them.
34. Rachel hid them in a camel's saddle and sat on it.
35. She said, "Sorry, I can't stand up. I'm on my period." Laban didn't find the idols.
36. Jacob got angry and said, "What did I do wrong?
37. You searched everything. Find one thing that's yours.
38. I worked for you 20 years. Your animals never miscarried.
39. I paid for every lost animal.
40. I suffered in the heat and cold.
41. I worked 14 years for your daughters, 6 for your animals. You changed my pay 10 times.
42. If God hadn't been with me, you'd have sent me away with nothing. But God saw my hard work and gave judgment last night."

Genesis 32

1. On his way home, Jacob saw God's angels.
2. He said, "This is God's army" and named the place Mahanaim.
3. Jacob sent messengers to Esau in Edom.
4. He said, "Tell Esau, 'I've been with Laban. I have animals and servants. I hope you'll be kind to me.'"
5. The messengers came back and said, "Esau is coming with 400 men."
6. Jacob got scared and split his people and animals into two groups.
7. He thought, "If Esau attacks one, the other can escape."
8. He prayed, "God of my fathers, you told me to come back and you'd be good to me.
9. I don't deserve your kindness. I left with only a walking stick. Now I have two camps.
10. Please save me from Esau. I'm scared he'll kill us.
11. You promised to be good to me and give me many descendants."
12. He stayed the night and prepared gifts for Esau:
13. 200 female goats, 20 males, 200 sheep, 20 rams,
14. 30 camels with babies, 40 cows, 10 bulls, 20 donkeys.
15. He told his servants to go ahead with the gifts in groups.
16. He said, "If Esau asks, say, 'They're gifts from Jacob. He's coming behind us.'"
17. Jacob said, "I'll try to calm Esau with gifts first."
18. That night, he sent his family across the stream and was left alone.
19. A man came and wrestled with him all night.
20. When the man saw he couldn't win, he touched Jacob's hip and dislocated it.
21. He said, "Let me go." Jacob said, "Not until you bless me."
22. He asked, "What's your name?" Jacob said, "Jacob."
23. He said, "You'll now be called Israel, because you wrestled with God and people and won."
24. Jacob said, "What's your name?" He said, "Why ask?" Then he blessed him.

25. Jacob named the place Peniel, "I saw God and lived."
26. The sun rose as he left, limping.

Genesis 33

1. Jacob looked up and saw Esau coming with 400 men. He split his kids among Leah, Rachel, and the two servants.
2. He put the servants and their kids first, then Leah and her kids, and Rachel with Joseph last.
3. Jacob walked ahead and bowed to the ground seven times as he came near Esau.
4. Esau ran to him, hugged him, and kissed him. They both cried.
5. Esau saw the women and kids and asked, "Who are they?" Jacob said, "The children God gave me."
6. The servant women came with their kids and bowed.
7. Then Leah and her kids came and bowed. Last, Rachel and Joseph came and bowed.
8. Esau asked, "What's with all the animals I met?" Jacob said, "A gift for you to be kind to me."
9. Esau said, "I have enough. Keep it."
10. Jacob said, "Please take it. Seeing your face is like seeing God smile at me.
11. Take the gift. God has been good to me, and I have plenty." Esau took it.
12. Esau said, "Let's travel together."
13. Jacob said, "The kids and animals are slow. If we push them, they'll die.
14. You go ahead. I'll come later."
15. Esau said, "Then let me leave some men to help." Jacob said, "That's not needed."
16. Esau went to Seir.
17. Jacob went to Sukkoth. He built a house and made shelters for his animals.
18. Then he went to Shechem in Canaan and camped outside the city.
19. He bought the land from Hamor's sons for 100 silver coins.
20. He set up an altar and called it El Elohe Yisrael.

Genesis 34

1. Dinah, Leah's daughter, went to visit some local girls.
2. Shechem, the son of Hamor the Hivite, saw her, grabbed her, and hurt her badly.
3. He liked her and wanted to marry her.
4. He told his father, "Get me this girl as a wife."
5. Jacob heard what happened but stayed quiet until his sons came in from the fields.
6. Hamor came to talk with Jacob.
7. Jacob's sons were angry. They were shocked because Shechem had done a terrible thing to their sister.
8. Hamor said, "My son really wants to marry your daughter Dinah.
9. Let's marry off each other's daughters and live together.
10. You can own land here and do business."
11. Shechem said, "I'll give anything you want. Just let me marry her."
12. "Name your price. I'll pay it."
13. Jacob's sons lied because Shechem had hurt Dinah.
14. They said, "We can't give our sister to a man who isn't circumcised.
15. If all your men get circumcised, then we'll give her to you.
16. But if not, we'll take her and leave."
17. Hamor and Shechem liked the idea.
18. Shechem didn't wait. He was well-liked in town.

19. He and his dad told the men, "These people are peaceful. Let's live together.
20. If we all get circumcised, their daughters and animals will be ours."
21. Every man in the city agreed and got circumcised.
22. Three days later, when they were still in pain, Simeon and Levi took swords and killed every man in the city.
23. They killed Hamor and Shechem and took Dinah from the house.
24. Jacob's sons looted the city to get back at what was done to Dinah.
25. They took sheep, cows, donkeys, and everything in the houses.
26. Jacob said to Simeon and Levi, "You've made us look bad. The Canaanites will hate us and kill us."
27. They said, "Should we have just let him treat our sister like that?"

Genesis 35

1. God said to Jacob, "Go to Beth-el and live there. Build an altar where I appeared to you."
2. Jacob told his family, "Get rid of idols. Wash and change clothes."
3. "We're going to Beth-el. I'll build an altar to the God who helped me."
4. They gave Jacob all their idols and earrings. He buried them under a tree near Shechem.
5. As they traveled, God made people afraid, so no one attacked them.
6. They reached Luz (now Beth-el).
7. Jacob built an altar and called the place El-beth-el.
8. Rebekah's nurse, Deborah, died and was buried under a tree called Allon-bacuth.
9. God appeared again and blessed Jacob.
10. God said, "Your name is Jacob, but now you will be called Israel."
11. He said, "I am God Almighty. Have many children. Nations and kings will come from you.
12. I will give you this land, like I promised Abraham and Isaac."
13. Then God left him.
14. Jacob set up a stone and poured wine and oil on it.
15. He named the place Beth-el.
16. They left Beth-el. Rachel had a hard time giving birth.
17. She had great pain but gave birth to a son.
18. As she died, she named him Ben-oni. Jacob called him Benjamin.
19. Rachel died and was buried near Ephrath (Bethlehem).
20. Jacob set up a stone on her grave.
21. Israel moved on and camped near Migdal-eder.
22. While he lived there, Reuben slept with Bilhah, his father's servant. Israel found out.
23. Jacob had 12 sons:
24. Leah's sons: Reuben, Simeon, Levi, Judah, Issachar, Zebulun.
25. Rachel's sons: Joseph and Benjamin.
26. Rachel's servant Bilhah's sons: Dan and Naphtali.
27. Leah's servant Zilpah's sons: Gad and Asher.
28. Jacob came home to his father Isaac in Mamre (near Hebron).
29. Isaac lived 180 years.
30. He died and was buried by Esau and Jacob.

Genesis 36

Esau's Family

1. This is Esau's family, also known as Edom.
2. Esau had three wives from Canaan:

3. Adah, daughter of Elon the Hittite.
4. Oholibamah, daughter of Anah and granddaughter of Zibeon the Hivite.
5. Basemath, daughter of Ishmael and sister of Nebaioth.
6. Adah's son was Eliphaz.
7. Basemath's son was Reuel.
8. Oholibamah had Jeush, Jalam, and Korah.
9. These sons were born in Canaan.
10. Esau took his family, animals, and everything he owned and moved away from Jacob.
11. The land couldn't support both of them together.
12. Esau lived in the hill country of Seir.
13. Esau is also called Edom.
14. These are the names of Esau's sons and grandsons:
15. Eliphaz's sons: Teman, Omar, Zepho, Gatam, and Kenaz.
16. Eliphaz also had Amalek by his servant Timna.
17. Reuel's sons: Nahath, Zerah, Shammah, and Mizzah.
18. These are the chiefs from Esau's family in Edom.
19. Oholibamah's sons were also chiefs.
20. These are the Horites living in Seir before Esau: Lotan, Shobal, Zibeon, Anah, Dishon, Ezer, and Dishan.
21. Lotan's sons: Hori and Hemam.
22. Lotan's sister was Timna.
23. Shobal's sons: Alvan, Manahath, Ebal, Shepho, and Onam.
24. Zibeon's sons: Aiah and Anah.
25. Anah's son was Dishon.
26. Dishon's sons: Hemdan, Eshban, Ithran, and Keran.
27. Ezer's sons: Bilhan, Zaavan, and Akan.
28. Dishan's sons: Uz and Aran.
29. These were the Horite chiefs in Seir.
30. Later kings ruled Edom before Israel had a king.
31. These kings ruled in Edom:
32. Bela son of Beor in Dinhabah.
33. Jobab son of Zerah from Bozrah.
34. Husham from the land of the Temanites.
35. Hadad son of Bedad from Avith.
36. Samlah from Masrekah.
37. Shaul from Rehoboth.
38. Baal-hanan son of Achbor.
39. Hadar ruled in Pau. His wife was Mehetabel.
40. These were the chiefs descended from Esau.

Genesis 37

Joseph and His Brothers

1. Jacob lived in Canaan.
2. Joseph was 17 and helped care for the sheep with his half-brothers.
3. Joseph gave bad reports about his brothers to Jacob.
4. Jacob loved Joseph most and gave him a special coat.
5. His brothers hated him and wouldn't speak nicely to him.
6. Joseph had a dream and told his brothers.
7. He said, "We were tying bundles of grain, and mine stood up while yours bowed down."
8. His brothers said, "Do you think you'll rule over us?"
9. Joseph had another dream: "The sun, moon, and 11 stars bowed to me."
10. He told his father, who said, "Will your mother and I bow to you too?"
11. His brothers were jealous, but Jacob kept thinking about it.
12. One day Jacob sent Joseph to check on his brothers near Shechem.

13. Joseph found them in Dothan.
14. They saw him coming and said, "Let's kill him."
15. Reuben said, "Don't kill him. Throw him in a pit." He planned to rescue him later.
16. They took Joseph's coat and threw him in a dry pit.
17. Then they saw Ishmaelite traders coming.
18. Judah said, "Let's sell him instead of killing him."
19. They sold Joseph for 20 silver coins.
20. Reuben came back and saw Joseph was gone.
21. They dipped his coat in goat blood.
22. They gave it to Jacob, who thought a wild animal killed Joseph.
23. Jacob tore his clothes and cried for many days.
24. Meanwhile, the traders sold Joseph in Egypt to Potiphar.

Genesis 38

Judah and Tamar

1. Judah left his brothers and stayed with Hirah in Adullam.
2. He married a Canaanite woman, the daughter of Shua.
3. She had three sons: Er, Onan, and Shelah.
4. Judah got a wife named Tamar for Er.
5. But Er was evil, so God killed him.
6. Judah told Onan to marry Tamar and have children for his brother.
7. Onan didn't want to, so he spilled his seed and God killed him too.
8. Judah said, "Wait until Shelah grows up."
9. Tamar waited but Judah didn't give her Shelah.
10. She dressed like a prostitute and waited by the road.
11. Judah didn't know it was her and asked to sleep with her.
12. She asked for his seal, cord, and staff as a promise.
13. She got pregnant.
14. Judah sent a goat to pay her but couldn't find her.
15. Three months later, Judah heard Tamar was pregnant. He said, "Burn her!"
16. She showed his seal and staff. Judah said, "She's more right than I am."
17. She had twins: Perez and Zerah.

Genesis 39

Joseph in Egypt

1. Joseph was sold to Potiphar in Egypt.
2. God was with Joseph, and he succeeded.
3. Potiphar saw God helped Joseph, so he trusted him.
4. Joseph became his top helper and ran the whole house.
5. God blessed everything Potiphar owned.
6. Joseph was good-looking. Potiphar's wife wanted him.
7. She said, "Sleep with me."
8. He said, "No! I won't sin against God or your husband."
9. She asked him every day, but he kept saying no.
10. One day they were alone. She grabbed his cloak. He ran out, leaving it.
11. She screamed and lied, saying Joseph tried to hurt her.
12. Potiphar believed her and put Joseph in prison.
13. But God was still with Joseph.
14. The prison warden liked him and put him in charge.
15. God made everything Joseph did succeed.

Genesis 40

Joseph Helps in Prison

1. Later, Pharaoh's wine server and baker made him angry.
2. He put them in prison with Joseph.
3. They had dreams, and Joseph saw they were upset.
4. He said, "Tell me your dreams. God will help me understand."
5. The wine server said, "I saw a vine with three branches. It budded, blossomed, and made grapes. I squeezed them into Pharaoh's cup."
6. Joseph said, "In three days, Pharaoh will give you your job back.
7. Please remember me and help me get out of here."
8. The baker said, "I saw three baskets of bread on my head. Birds ate from the top basket."
9. Joseph said, "In three days, Pharaoh will hang you."
10. Three days later was Pharaoh's birthday. He gave the wine server his job back.
11. He hanged the baker.
12. But the wine server forgot about Joseph.

Genesis 41

Joseph Explains Pharaoh's Dreams

1. Two years later, Pharaoh had a dream.
2. He was standing by the Nile River.
3. Seven fat, healthy cows came out of the river and ate grass.
4. Then seven thin, sick cows came out and stood next to them.
5. The thin cows ate the fat cows.
6. Then Pharaoh woke up.
7. He went back to sleep and had another dream.
8. He saw seven full, good heads of grain on one stalk.
9. Then seven thin, dried-out heads of grain grew after them.
10. The thin heads swallowed the good heads.
11. Pharaoh woke up and realized it was just a dream.
12. In the morning, he was worried. He called all the magicians and wise men.
13. No one could explain the dream.
14. Then the wine server remembered Joseph.
15. He said, "When I was in prison, a young Hebrew man explained our dreams."
16. Pharaoh sent for Joseph. They cleaned him up and brought him in.
17. Pharaoh said, "I had a dream no one can explain. I heard you can explain dreams."
18. Joseph said, "I can't, but God will tell you what it means."
19. Pharaoh told Joseph the dreams.
20. Joseph said, "Both dreams mean the same thing.
21. God is telling you what He's going to do.
22. The seven fat cows and good heads of grain mean seven good years.
23. The seven thin cows and bad heads mean seven years of hunger.
24. There will be seven good years, then seven bad years so bad no one will remember the good ones.
25. You dreamed twice because God has set this to happen soon.
26. Choose a wise man to be in charge of the land.
27. Store food during the seven good years so Egypt won't starve during the bad years."
28. Pharaoh said, "Who else has God's wisdom like this man?"
29. He made Joseph second in command over all Egypt.

30. He gave Joseph a royal ring, fine clothes, and a gold chain.
31. He gave him a new name: Zaphenath-paneah, and a wife: Asenath.
32. Joseph was 30 years old.
33. He traveled through Egypt and stored food during the good years.
34. He saved so much it couldn't be counted.
35. Joseph had two sons: Manasseh and Ephraim.
36. Then the seven bad years came, and people everywhere were hungry.
37. But Egypt had food.
38. People came from all over to buy from Joseph.

Genesis 42

Joseph's Brothers Go to Egypt for Food

1. Jacob heard there was food in Egypt.
2. He told his sons, "Why are you standing around? Go buy food so we don't die."
3. So ten brothers went.
4. Jacob didn't send Benjamin, afraid something might happen to him.
5. The brothers arrived in Egypt and bowed before Joseph.
6. Joseph knew who they were, but they didn't recognize him.
7. He pretended to be a stranger and spoke harshly.
8. He asked, "Where are you from?" They said, "From Canaan to buy food."
9. Joseph remembered his dreams and said, "You are spies!"
10. They said, "No! We're honest men.
11. We are all brothers. The youngest stayed home. One is gone."
12. Joseph said, "I'll test you. One of you must go get your brother.
13. The rest will stay here in prison."
14. He locked them up for three days.
15. On the third day, Joseph said, "If you're honest, one will stay here. The rest go get your brother."
16. They said to each other, "This is happening because of what we did to Joseph."
17. Reuben said, "I told you not to hurt him!"
18. Joseph turned away and cried.
19. He picked Simeon to stay in prison.
20. He gave them food and put their money back in their bags.
21. On the way home, one opened his bag and saw the money.
22. They were scared and said, "What is God doing to us?"
23. They told Jacob everything.
24. Jacob said, "You want to take Benjamin too? Joseph is gone. Simeon is gone. No!"
25. Reuben said, "If I don't bring Benjamin back, you can kill my sons."
26. Jacob said, "My son will not go with you."

Genesis 43

The Brothers Return with Benjamin

1. The food ran out, so Jacob said, "Go back to Egypt."
2. Judah said, "We can't go unless we take Benjamin.
3. The man warned us."
4. Jacob said, "Why did you tell him you had a brother?"
5. They said, "He asked about our family."
6. Judah said, "I'll take care of Benjamin. If I don't bring him back, blame me forever."
7. Jacob agreed and told them to bring gifts and double the money.
8. He prayed for mercy.

9. They arrived in Egypt and stood before Joseph.
10. Joseph saw Benjamin and told his servant, "Prepare a meal. These men will eat with me."
11. The brothers were afraid. They thought they were in trouble over the money.
12. They explained to the servant, but he said, "Don't worry. Your God gave you treasure."
13. He brought out Simeon.
14. They washed and prepared the gifts.
15. When Joseph came, they gave him the gifts and bowed.
16. He asked about their father.
17. He saw Benjamin and said, "Is this your youngest brother?"
18. He rushed away and cried.
19. Then he washed his face and served food.
20. They were seated in order by age and were amazed.
21. Joseph gave Benjamin five times more food. They ate and drank together.

Genesis 44

Joseph Tests His Brothers

1. Joseph told his servant, "Fill their bags with food. Put each man's money back.
2. Put my silver cup in the youngest one's bag."
3. At dawn, they left.
4. Joseph sent his servant after them.
5. He asked, "Why did you steal my master's cup?"
6. The brothers said, "We didn't! If you find it, kill the guilty one."
7. Each man opened his bag.
8. The cup was in Benjamin's bag.
9. They tore their clothes and returned to the city.
10. Joseph said, "What have you done?"
11. Judah said, "God has found our guilt. We are your slaves."
12. Joseph said, "Only the one with the cup will stay. The rest may go."
13. Judah begged, "Please let me stay instead of Benjamin.
14. If I go back without him, my father will die of sadness."
15. "I promised to protect him. Please let me take his place."

Genesis 45

Joseph Reveals Who He Is

1. Joseph couldn't hold back anymore.
2. He sent everyone else out and cried loudly.
3. He said to his brothers, "I am Joseph! Is my father still alive?"
4. They were shocked and afraid.
5. Joseph said, "Don't be upset. God sent me here to save lives.
6. There are still five more years of famine.
7. God made me a leader in Egypt.
8. Go bring my father here quickly.
9. Tell him everything you saw and hurry back."
10. He hugged Benjamin and cried.
11. Then he hugged his other brothers and cried too.
12. Pharaoh heard the news and was pleased.
13. He gave them wagons and supplies to move the family.
14. Joseph gave clothes to everyone, but gave Benjamin extra.
15. He also gave gifts for their father.
16. He said, "Don't fight on the way back."
17. They returned to Canaan and told Jacob, "Joseph is alive!"

18. Jacob was shocked but believed them when he saw the wagons.
19. He said, "I will go see him before I die."

Genesis 46

Jacob Goes to Egypt

1. Jacob packed everything and went to Beersheba. He gave sacrifices to God.
2. That night, God spoke in a dream and said, "Jacob!" He answered, "I'm here."
3. God said, "I am the God of your father. Don't be afraid to go to Egypt. I will make your family a great nation there.
4. I will go with you and bring you back. Joseph will be with you when you die."
5. Jacob left Beersheba. His sons put him, their kids, and their wives in the wagons Pharaoh gave.
6. They took all their things and went to Egypt.
7. Jacob took all his children and grandchildren.
8. These are the names of Jacob's family who went:
9. Reuben and his sons: Hanoch, Pallu, Hezron, and Carmi.
10. Simeon's sons: Jemuel, Jamin, Ohad, Jakin, Zohar, and Shaul.
11. Levi's sons: Gershon, Kohath, and Merari.
12. Judah's sons: Er, Onan, Shelah, Perez, and Zerah. (Er and Onan died in Canaan.) Perez had Hezron and Hamul.
13. Issachar's sons: Tola, Puah, Jashub, and Shimron.
14. Zebulun's sons: Sered, Elon, and Jahleel.
15. These were Leah's children and grandchildren—33 people total.
16. Gad's sons: Zephon, Haggi, Shuni, Ezbon, Eri, Arodi, and Areli.
17. Asher's sons: Imnah, Ishvah, Ishvi, Beriah, and their sister Serah. Beriah had Heber and Malkiel.
18. These were Zilpah's children and grandchildren—16 total.
19. Rachel's sons: Joseph and Benjamin.
20. Joseph's sons in Egypt were Manasseh and Ephraim.
21. Benjamin's sons: Bela, Beker, Ashbel, Gera, Naaman, Ehi, Rosh, Muppim, Huppim, and Ard.
22. These were Rachel's children—14 total.
23. Dan's son: Hushim.
24. Naphtali's sons: Jahzeel, Guni, Jezer, and Shillem.
25. These were Bilhah's children—7 total.
26. Jacob had 66 children and grandchildren go with him.
27. With Joseph's family in Egypt, the total was 70.
28. Jacob sent Judah ahead to meet Joseph.
29. Joseph met his father and hugged him a long time while crying.
30. Jacob said, "Now I can die because I've seen you."
31. Joseph told his family, "I'll tell Pharaoh you're shepherds and have come from Canaan."
32. "Say you've always been shepherds so you can live in Goshen, away from Egyptians."

Genesis 47

Jacob and His Family Settle in Egypt

1. Joseph told Pharaoh, "My father and brothers are here with their animals in Goshen."
2. He brought five of his brothers to meet Pharaoh.
3. Pharaoh asked, "What do you do?" They said, "We're shepherds."
4. They said, "There's no food in Canaan. Please let us stay in Goshen."

5. Pharaoh said to Joseph, "They can live there. If any are good workers, put them in charge of my animals."
6. Joseph brought Jacob to meet Pharaoh.
7. Pharaoh asked Jacob, "How old are you?"
8. Jacob said, "I'm 130. My life has been short and hard."
9. Then Jacob blessed Pharaoh and left.
10. Joseph gave his family land in Goshen and enough food.
11. The famine was bad. People ran out of money and came to Joseph.
12. They said, "Buy us and our land so we can eat."
13. Joseph gave them food in exchange for their animals.
14. When they had no animals left, they gave their land.
15. Joseph made the people slaves of Pharaoh.
16. Only the priests kept their land because Pharaoh gave them food.
17. Joseph said, "You belong to Pharaoh now. I'll give you seeds. Give one-fifth of the crops to Pharaoh."
18. They agreed and thanked Joseph.
19. Israel lived in Egypt and grew in number.
20. Jacob lived 17 more years and died at 147.
21. When he was close to death, he said to Joseph, "Promise to bury me in Canaan."
22. Joseph promised. Jacob bowed and thanked God.

Genesis 48

Jacob Blesses Joseph's Sons

1. Joseph heard Jacob was sick and brought Manasseh and Ephraim.
2. Jacob sat up in bed when he saw them.
3. He said, "God appeared to me and promised to make my family great."
4. "Now I'm claiming your two sons as mine."
5. "Any other children you have will be yours."
6. Joseph brought his sons close.
7. Jacob hugged and kissed them.
8. He said, "I didn't think I'd see you again—and now I've seen your kids too!"
9. He put Ephraim on his right and Manasseh on his left.
10. But Jacob crossed his hands and gave the bigger blessing to Ephraim.
11. Joseph tried to switch their hands.
12. Jacob said, "I know. Manasseh will be great, but Ephraim will be even greater."
13. He blessed them both.
14. Then Jacob said, "God will bring you back to Canaan.
15. And Joseph, I give you an extra part of the land."

Genesis 49

Jacob Blesses His Sons

1. Jacob called all his sons.
2. He said, "Listen, I'll tell you what will happen in the future."
3. "Reuben, you're my firstborn, but you won't be first anymore. You dishonored me."
4. "Simeon and Levi, you are violent. You used swords in anger."
5. "I will scatter your descendants."
6. "Judah, your brothers will praise you. You will lead them. Kings will come from you."
7. "Zebulun will live near the sea."
8. "Issachar will work hard but be forced to serve."

9. “Dan will judge his people and be like a snake that bites.”
10. “I trust God to save us.”
11. “Gad will be attacked but fight back.”
12. “Asher will have rich food.”
13. “Naphtali is like a deer—fast and free.”
14. “Joseph is strong and blessed by God. He helped others even when hated.”
15. “Benjamin is like a wolf—he attacks in the morning and divides the food at night.”
16. These were the blessings for Jacob’s sons.
17. Then Jacob told them, “Bury me with my fathers in Canaan.”
18. “I buried Abraham and Sarah, and Isaac and Rebekah there. I buried Leah there too.”
19. When Jacob finished talking, he died.

Genesis 50

Joseph Buries His Father

1. Joseph cried and kissed Jacob.
2. He had him embalmed. It took 40 days.
3. The Egyptians mourned for 70 days.
4. Joseph asked Pharaoh’s permission to bury Jacob in Canaan.
5. Pharaoh agreed.
6. Joseph and his brothers, along with officials and servants, went to Canaan.
7. They left children and animals in Goshen.
8. A large group with chariots and soldiers went too.
9. They mourned deeply at Atad.
10. They buried Jacob in the cave at Machpelah, near Mamre.
11. Then everyone returned to Egypt.
12. Joseph’s brothers were afraid he’d hurt them.
13. They said, “Dad said to forgive us.”
14. Joseph cried and said, “Don’t be afraid. I’m not God.”
15. “You meant to hurt me, but God used it for good.”
16. “I’ll take care of you and your children.”
17. Joseph lived 110 years.
18. He saw his grandchildren.
19. Before he died, he said, “God will help you return to Canaan.”
20. “When that happens, take my bones with you.”
21. Joseph died and was embalmed and placed in a coffin in Egypt.

– Exodus –

God frees the Israelites from Egypt and gives them the Law at Mount Sinai.

Exodus 1

1. These are the names of Jacob’s sons who came to Egypt with their families:
2. Reuben, Simeon, Levi, Judah,
3. Issachar, Zebulun, Benjamin,
4. Dan, Naphtali, Gad, and Asher.
5. In total, Jacob had 70 family members in Egypt, including Joseph.
6. Joseph and his brothers died, along with their whole generation.
7. But the Israelites had many children and became very strong. The land was full of them.
8. Then a new king came to power in Egypt. He didn’t know Joseph.
9. He said, “Look, the Israelites are more numerous and stronger than us.”
10. “We must stop them from growing. If war comes, they might join our enemies and leave the country.”
11. So the Egyptians forced them into slavery and made them build the cities of Pithom and Rameses.

12. But the more they were mistreated, the more they grew. The Egyptians began to fear them.
13. So they were even more cruel to them.
14. They made the Israelites' lives bitter with hard work in brick-making and farming.
15. Then the king told the Hebrew midwives, Shiphrah and Puah,
16. "When you help Hebrew women give birth, if it's a boy, kill him. If it's a girl, let her live."
17. But the midwives respected God and let the boys live.
18. The king asked them, "Why did you let the boys live?"
19. They said, "Hebrew women are strong. They give birth before we get there."
20. God was kind to the midwives, and the people kept growing stronger.
21. Because the midwives respected God, He gave them families.
22. Then Pharaoh ordered all his people, "Throw every Hebrew baby boy into the Nile, but let the girls live."

Exodus 2

1. A man and woman from the tribe of Levi got married.
2. She had a baby boy and hid him for three months.
3. When she couldn't hide him anymore, she put him in a basket and placed it by the river.
4. His sister watched to see what would happen.
5. Pharaoh's daughter came to bathe and saw the basket. She sent her maid to get it.
6. She opened it, saw the crying baby, and felt sorry for him. "This is a Hebrew baby," she said.
7. The baby's sister asked, "Should I find a Hebrew woman to nurse the baby for you?"
8. "Yes," said the princess. So she got the baby's mother.
9. Pharaoh's daughter said, "Take care of him for me, and I'll pay you." So the mother did.
10. When the child was older, she took him to Pharaoh's daughter. He became her son. She named him Moses, saying, "I pulled him out of the water."
11. When Moses grew up, he saw an Egyptian hurting a Hebrew slave.
12. He looked around, killed the Egyptian, and hid the body.
13. The next day, he saw two Hebrews fighting. "Why are you hitting each other?" he asked.
14. The man said, "Who made you our boss? Are you going to kill me too?" Moses got scared and thought, "People know what I did."
15. Pharaoh heard and tried to kill Moses, but Moses ran to Midian and sat by a well.
16. A priest in Midian had seven daughters. They came to get water for their animals.
17. Some shepherds chased them away, but Moses helped them and watered their flock.
18. When they got home, their father Reuel said, "Why are you back so soon?"
19. They said, "An Egyptian saved us and got water for our animals."
20. Reuel asked, "Where is he? Go invite him to eat."
21. Moses agreed to stay with them, and Reuel gave him his daughter Zipporah to marry.
22. She had a son. Moses named him Gershom, saying, "I've been a stranger in a strange land."
23. Years passed. The king of Egypt died. The Israelites cried out to God for help.
24. God heard them and remembered his promise to Abraham, Isaac, and Jacob.

25. God saw their suffering and was ready to help.

Exodus 3

1. Moses was taking care of Jethro's sheep and led them to Mount Sinai.
2. There, an angel of God appeared in a burning bush that didn't burn up.
3. Moses said, "This is strange. Why doesn't it burn?"
4. God saw Moses coming closer and called, "Moses! Moses!" He answered, "Here I am."
5. God said, "Don't come closer. Take off your sandals. This is HOLY GROUND."
6. "I'm the God of your father, Abraham, Isaac, and Jacob." Moses hid his face, afraid to look.
7. God said, "I see my people suffering in Egypt. I hear their cries.
8. I've come to rescue them and bring them to a good land, where many nations live now.
9. I've seen how badly the Egyptians treat them.
10. So I'm sending you to Pharaoh to bring my people out."
11. Moses said, "Who am I to do that?"
12. God said, "I'll be with you. This will be the sign: you'll worship me on this mountain after you leave Egypt."
13. Moses asked, "What if they ask your name?"
14. God said, "I AM WHO I AM. Tell them 'I AM' sent me."
15. God also said, "Tell them the LORD, the God of their ancestors, sent you. That's my name forever."
16. "Go gather the elders and say, 'God has seen what Egypt did to you.'
17. I'll rescue you and take you to the land of the Canaanites and others, a land with milk and honey.
18. They'll listen. Then go to Pharaoh and say, 'Let us go three days into the desert to worship.'
19. But Pharaoh won't let you go unless forced.
20. So I'll punish Egypt with miracles. Then he'll let you go.
21. I'll make the Egyptians kind to you. You won't leave empty-handed.
22. Each woman will ask her Egyptian neighbor for silver, gold, and clothes. You'll take them with you."

Exodus 4

1. Moses asked, "What if they don't believe me?"
2. God said, "What's in your hand?" "A staff," Moses said.
3. "Throw it down," God said. It turned into a snake, and Moses backed away.
4. "Pick it up by the tail," God said. Moses did, and it became a staff again.
5. "This sign will show them I sent you."
6. "Now put your hand in your robe." He did, and it came out white with disease.
7. "Put it back." He did, and it was healed.
8. "If they don't believe the first sign, maybe they'll believe the second.
9. If not, take water from the Nile and pour it on the ground. It'll turn to blood."
10. Moses said, "Lord, I'm not good with words. I get nervous and mess up."
11. God said, "Who made your mouth? I did.
12. Now go. I'll help you speak."
13. But Moses said, "Please send someone else."
14. God got angry. "Your brother Aaron can speak well. He's already coming to see you.
15. Tell him what to say. I'll help both of you speak.

16. He'll speak for you. You'll speak through him like I speak through you.
17. Take your staff with you to do the miracles."
18. Moses went back to Jethro and said, "Please let me go to Egypt to see my family." Jethro said, "Go in peace."
19. God told Moses, "Go back to Egypt. The people who wanted to kill you are dead."
20. Moses took his wife and sons, put them on a donkey, and went back to Egypt with God's staff.
21. God said, "When you go to Pharaoh, show him the miracles, but I'll harden his heart so he won't let the people go.
22. Say, 'This is what God says: Israel is my firstborn son.
23. Let him go worship me. If you don't, I'll kill your firstborn son.'"
24. On the way, God came to kill Moses.
25. Zipporah took a sharp stone, circumcised their son, and touched Moses's feet with the skin. "You're a husband of blood," she said.
26. So God let him live. She said that was because of the circumcision.
27. God told Aaron, "Go meet Moses in the desert." He met him at the mountain and hugged him.
28. Moses told Aaron everything God had said and showed him the miracles.
29. They gathered the elders of Israel.
30. Aaron told them what God said, and Moses showed them the miracles.
31. The people believed. When they heard that God had seen their suffering, they bowed down and worshiped.

Exodus 5

1. Moses and Aaron told Pharaoh, "The Lord says: Let my people go so they can worship me in the desert."
2. Pharaoh said, "Who is the Lord? Why should I obey him? I don't know him, and I won't let Israel go."
3. They said, "The God of the Hebrews met with us. Let us go three days into the desert to offer sacrifices. If we don't, he may punish us."
4. Pharaoh said, "Moses and Aaron, why are you stopping the people from working? Get back to work!"
5. "There are so many people, and now you want to stop their labor?"
6. That same day, Pharaoh gave orders to the slave drivers and the Israelite bosses.
7. "Don't give them any more straw to make bricks. They must get it themselves.
8. But they still have to make the same number of bricks. They're lazy, that's why they want to worship their God.
9. Make the work harder so they won't listen to lies."
10. So the slave drivers told the people, "Pharaoh says no more straw will be given to you."
11. "Go find your own straw, but you must still make the same number of bricks."
12. So the people went all over Egypt to find straw.
13. The slave drivers shouted at them to make just as many bricks as before.
14. The Israelite leaders were beaten and asked, "Why haven't you made enough bricks like before?"
15. The Israelite leaders went to Pharaoh and said, "Why are you treating us this way?"
16. "We're not given any straw, yet we're told to make bricks, and we're beaten. It's your people's fault, not ours."
17. Pharaoh said, "You're lazy! That's why you say, 'Let us go worship.'"
18. "Now get back to work! No straw, but still the same number of bricks!"

19. The leaders knew they were in trouble when told not to reduce the daily bricks.
20. As they left Pharaoh, they found Moses and Aaron waiting.
21. They said, "May God punish you. You've made Pharaoh hate us. You gave him a reason to kill us!"
22. Moses prayed, "Lord, why did you bring this trouble? Why did you send me?"
23. "Ever since I spoke to Pharaoh, things got worse. You haven't helped at all."

Exodus 6

1. God told Moses, "Now you'll see what I'll do. Pharaoh will be forced to let them go."
2. God said, "I am the Lord."
3. "I appeared to Abraham, Isaac, and Jacob as God Almighty, but not by my name, the Lord."
4. "I promised to give them the land of Canaan."
5. "I've heard the Israelites crying and I remember my promise."
6. "Tell them: I am the Lord. I'll free you from Egypt with great power."
7. "I'll make you my people. I'll be your God. You'll know I saved you."
8. "I'll give you the land I promised to Abraham, Isaac, and Jacob. I am the Lord."
9. Moses told the Israelites, but they didn't listen. They were too discouraged.
10. Then the Lord said to Moses,
11. "Tell Pharaoh to let the Israelites go."
12. Moses said, "The Israelites won't listen to me. Why would Pharaoh? I'm a poor speaker."
13. But the Lord told Moses and Aaron to bring the people out of Egypt.
14. Here are the family leaders: Reuben's sons—Hanoch, Pallu, Hezron, and Carmi.
15. Simeon's sons—Jemuel, Jamin, Ohad, Jachin, Zohar, and Shaul.
16. Levi lived 137 years. His sons were Gershon, Kohath, and Merari.
17. Gershon's sons were Libni and Shimei.
18. Kohath lived 133 years. His sons were Amram, Izhar, Hebron, and Uzziel.
19. Merari's sons were Mahli and Mushi.
20. Amram lived 137 years. He married Jochebed, and they had Aaron and Moses.
21. Izhar's sons were Korah, Nepheg, and Zichri.
22. Uzziel's sons were Mishael, Elzaphan, and Sithri.
23. Aaron married Elisheba. They had Nadab, Abihu, Eleazar, and Ithamar.
24. Korah's sons were Assir, Elkanah, and Abiasaph.
25. Eleazar married one of Putiel's daughters. They had a son named Phinehas.
26. These are the men God chose to bring the Israelites out of Egypt.
27. Moses and Aaron spoke to Pharaoh about freeing the Israelites.
28. When the Lord spoke to Moses in Egypt,
29. He said, "Tell Pharaoh everything I say."
30. Moses said, "I'm not a good speaker. Why would Pharaoh listen?"

Exodus 7

1. The Lord said, "Moses, I've made you like God to Pharaoh, and Aaron will be your prophet."
2. "Tell Aaron what I say. He'll tell Pharaoh to let my people go."
3. "I'll harden Pharaoh's heart so I can do many miracles."

4. "Pharaoh won't listen, so I'll punish Egypt and bring my people out."
5. "Then the Egyptians will know I am the Lord."
6. Moses and Aaron did what God told them.
7. Moses was 80 and Aaron was 83 when they spoke to Pharaoh.

A Staff Turns into a Snake

8. The Lord said to Moses and Aaron,
9. "If Pharaoh asks for a miracle, tell Aaron to throw down his staff. It will become a snake."
10. They did this. Aaron threw down his staff, and it became a snake.
11. Pharaoh called his magicians. They did the same trick.
12. Each threw down a staff, and they turned into snakes. But Aaron's snake ate theirs.
13. Still, Pharaoh's heart was hard, and he wouldn't listen.

The Nile Turns to Blood

14. The Lord said, "Pharaoh's heart is stubborn. He refuses to let the people go."
15. "Meet him in the morning at the Nile. Bring your staff."
16. "Say: The Lord says, 'Let my people go to worship me.' But you won't listen."
17. "Now I'll show you I am the Lord. I'll strike the Nile, and it'll turn to blood."
18. "The fish will die, and the river will stink. No one will drink it."
19. God told Moses to have Aaron raise the staff over all the water. Every bit of water will turn to blood.
20. Aaron did it, and all the water turned to blood—even in jars.
21. The fish died, and the water smelled. The people couldn't drink it.
22. The magicians did the same trick, so Pharaoh stayed stubborn.
23. He went home and didn't care.
24. The Egyptians dug around the river to find drinking water.
25. Seven days passed after the Lord struck the Nile.

Exodus 8

1. The Lord said, "Go to Pharaoh and say: Let my people go so they can worship me."
2. "If you don't, I'll send frogs all over your land."
3. "They'll be in your palace, your bed, your ovens, and everywhere."
4. "They'll jump on you, your people, and your officials."
5. God said, "Tell Aaron to stretch out his staff over the water and bring up frogs."
6. Aaron did, and frogs covered the land.
7. The magicians did the same thing and brought frogs too.
8. Pharaoh begged Moses and Aaron, "Ask the Lord to take away the frogs. Then I'll let the people go."
9. Moses said, "When should I ask God to remove them?" Pharaoh said, "Tomorrow."
10. Moses said, "Alright. Then you'll know there's no one like the Lord."
11. "The frogs will leave your homes and stay only in the Nile."
12. Moses prayed to God about the frogs.
13. God did what Moses asked. The frogs died in homes, yards, and fields.
14. They were piled up, and the land smelled terrible.
15. But when Pharaoh saw relief, he changed his mind again.

Gnats

16. God said, "Tell Aaron to hit the ground with his staff. Dust will turn to gnats."
17. Aaron struck the ground, and gnats covered people and animals.

18. The magicians tried to do the same, but couldn't.
19. They told Pharaoh, "This is God's power!" But Pharaoh stayed stubborn.

Flies

20. God said, "In the morning, tell Pharaoh: Let my people go to worship me."
21. "If not, I'll send swarms of flies everywhere—in homes and all over Egypt."
22. "But no flies will be in Goshen, where my people live. Then you'll know I'm Lord."
23. "I'll show a clear difference between your people and mine."
24. The Lord sent huge swarms of flies that ruined Egypt.
25. Pharaoh said, "Go sacrifice to your God—but do it here in Egypt."
26. Moses said, "We can't. Our sacrifices would offend Egyptians."
27. "We must go three days into the desert, like God said."
28. Pharaoh said, "Fine, go—but not far. And pray for me."
29. Moses said, "I'll pray, but don't lie to us again."
30. Moses prayed.
31. God removed every fly.
32. But Pharaoh hardened his heart again.

Exodus 9

1. God said, "Tell Pharaoh: Let my people go to worship me."
2. "If you don't,
3. God will strike all your animals—horses, cows, sheep, and goats—with a deadly disease."
4. "But none of Israel's animals will die."
5. "Tomorrow it will happen."
6. God did it. All Egyptian animals died, but not one of Israel's animals did.
7. Pharaoh checked—and it was true. But he stayed stubborn.

Sores

8. God told Moses and Aaron, "Take ashes from a furnace and toss them in the air in front of Pharaoh."
9. "They'll become dust and cause painful sores on people and animals."
10. Moses tossed the ashes, and sores broke out on everyone.
11. The magicians couldn't stand before Moses—they had sores too.
12. But God hardened Pharaoh's heart again.

Hailstorm

13. God told Moses, "In the morning, tell Pharaoh: Let my people go to worship me."
14. "This time, I'll punish you too. Then you'll know there's no one like me."
15. "I could've wiped you out already."
16. "But I let you live to show my power."
17. "But you still refuse to obey."
18. "So tomorrow I'll send the worst hailstorm Egypt has ever seen."
19. "Bring in your people and animals. If they stay outside, they'll die."
20. Some officials believed and brought their animals inside.
21. Others ignored the warning and left them out.
22. God said, "Moses, raise your hand toward the sky. Hail will fall on everything outside."
23. Moses raised his staff. Thunder, lightning, and hail came down hard.
24. It was the worst storm Egypt had ever seen.
25. It destroyed crops, trees, animals, and people outside.
26. But it didn't hail in Goshen, where the Israelites lived.
27. Pharaoh said, "I've sinned! The Lord is right. We're wrong."

28. "Please ask God to stop the thunder and hail. I'll let you go."
29. Moses said, "I'll pray. Then you'll know the earth belongs to God."
30. "But I know you and your officials still don't fear him."
31. (The flax and barley were destroyed because they ripened early.)
32. (The wheat was safe because it ripens later.)
33. Moses prayed, and the storm stopped.
34. But Pharaoh sinned again. He and his officials hardened their hearts.
35. He still wouldn't let the people go.

Exodus 10

1. God said, "Go to Pharaoh. I've hardened his heart so I can do more miracles."
2. "Then your kids will know what I did in Egypt, and they'll know I am the Lord."
3. Moses and Aaron said, "How long will you refuse to obey God? Let his people go."
4. "If not, tomorrow locusts will cover the land."
5. "They'll eat everything left after the hail—even the trees."
6. "They'll fill every home. Nothing like it has ever happened before." Moses then left.
7. Pharaoh's officials said, "Let them go! Don't you see Egypt is ruined?"
8. Pharaoh asked, "Who exactly is going?"
9. Moses said, "Everyone—young, old, and all our animals."
10. Pharaoh said, "No way! Only the men can go!" And he kicked them out.
11. (He meant only the men could go.)
12. God said, "Raise your hand so locusts will come and eat everything left."
13. Moses did. A wind blew all night and brought locusts in the morning.
14. They covered the land completely—more than ever before.
15. They ate everything green. Nothing was left on the trees or in the fields.
16. Pharaoh rushed to Moses and said, "I've sinned!
17. Please forgive me this once and ask God to take away this disaster!"
18. Moses prayed.
19. God sent a strong wind that blew the locusts into the sea. Not one was left.
20. But Pharaoh stayed stubborn.
21. God said, "Raise your hand. Darkness will cover Egypt—a darkness they can feel."
22. Moses did. Deep darkness covered Egypt for 3 days.
23. No one could see or move. But the Israelites had light.
24. Pharaoh said, "Go worship—but leave your animals here."
25. Moses said, "No. We need animals for worship, and we don't know which ones until we get there."
26. "We must take everything."
27. God hardened Pharaoh's heart again.
28. Pharaoh shouted, "Get out! Don't come back! If I see you again, you'll die!"
29. Moses said, "Fine. You'll never see me again."

Exodus 11

1. God said to Moses, "I'll bring one more plague on Egypt. After that, Pharaoh will force you to leave."
2. "Tell the people to ask the Egyptians for silver and gold."
3. The Egyptians respected the Israelites. Moses was honored by everyone.

4. Moses said, "This is what God says: Around midnight, I'll go through Egypt."
5. "Every firstborn son will die—from Pharaoh's son to the lowest servant's son. Even the firstborn animals will die."
6. "There will be loud crying everywhere in Egypt like never before."
7. "But not even a dog will bark at the Israelites. Then you'll know God makes a difference between Egypt and Israel."
8. "Your people will beg me to leave. Then I'll go." And Moses left Pharaoh angry.
9. God said, "Pharaoh won't listen, so I can do more miracles."
10. Moses and Aaron did all these miracles, but God made Pharaoh stubborn.

Exodus 12

1. God told Moses and Aaron in Egypt,
2. "This month will be your first month of the year."
3. "Tell everyone: On the 10th day, each family must pick a lamb or young goat."
4. "If a family is too small, they can share with neighbors."
5. "Choose a one-year-old male with no defects."
6. "Take care of it until the 14th day, then kill it at twilight."
7. "Put some of its blood on the doorframe of your house."
8. "Eat the meat that night, roasted with bread without yeast and bitter herbs."
9. "Don't eat it raw or boiled—roast it whole."
10. "Don't leave leftovers. Burn any leftovers the next morning."
11. "Eat quickly, dressed and ready to go. This is the Lord's Passover."
12. "That night I'll go through Egypt and kill every firstborn person and animal. I'll punish the gods of Egypt."
13. "The blood on your doors will be a sign. I'll pass over your house and not hurt you."
14. "Remember this day forever. Celebrate it every year."
15. "Eat no yeast for 7 days. Remove yeast from your homes. Anyone who eats it will be cut off."
16. "On the 1st and 7th days, meet to worship. No work except preparing food."
17. "Celebrate this every year. It's the day I brought you out of Egypt."
18. "Eat no yeast from the evening of the 14th to the evening of the 21st."
19. "No yeast anywhere. Anyone who eats it will be cut off, even visitors."
20. "Eat only bread without yeast."
21. Moses said, "Pick a lamb and kill it for Passover."
22. "Use a branch to put its blood on your doorframe. Stay inside until morning."
23. "When God sees the blood, He won't let the destroyer enter your home."
24. "Obey these rules forever."
25. "When you enter the new land, keep this tradition."
26. "When your kids ask what it means,"
27. "Tell them it's the Passover sacrifice. God passed over our homes in Egypt." The people bowed and worshiped.
28. They did everything God told Moses and Aaron.

The Death of the Firstborn

29. At midnight, God killed all the firstborn in Egypt—from Pharaoh's son to the prisoner's son—even the animals' firstborn.
30. Pharaoh, his officials, and all Egypt woke up crying. Every home had someone dead.

Israel Escapes Egypt

31. Pharaoh called Moses and Aaron and said, "Leave now, you and your people. Go worship."
32. "Take your animals—and bless me."
33. The Egyptians begged them to leave. "If you don't, we'll all die!"
34. So they left quickly, carrying their dough before it rose.
35. The Israelites asked for silver, gold, and clothes—just like Moses said.
36. God made the Egyptians give them everything they asked.
37. They left Rameses and walked to Succoth—about 600,000 men, plus women and children.
38. Other people went too, along with lots of animals.
39. They baked flat bread, since they had no time to prepare food.
40. They had lived in Egypt for 430 years.
41. On the last day of the 430th year, they all left Egypt.
42. That night, God kept His promise, and now they must honor Him every year.

Passover Instructions

43. God said, "No foreigner may eat the Passover meal."
44. "But if a slave is circumcised, he can eat it."
45. "Visitors and hired workers may not eat it."
46. "Eat it in one house. Don't take any meat outside or break its bones."
47. "All Israel must celebrate it."
48. "If a visitor wants to join, all males in his home must be circumcised first."
49. "This law is the same for everyone—Israelites and non-Israelites."
50. The people obeyed everything God said.
51. That very day, God brought them out of Egypt.

Exodus 13

1. God said to Moses,
2. "Give me every firstborn son and male animal. They belong to me."

Festival of Unleavened Bread

3. Moses told the people, "Remember this day! You were freed from Egypt. Don't eat bread with yeast."
4. "Today, in the month of Abib, you are leaving."
5. "When God brings you to the land of the Canaanites and others, keep this tradition."
6. "For 7 days, eat bread without yeast. On the 7th day, celebrate the Lord."
7. "No yeast is allowed in your land."
8. "Tell your kids: We do this because God brought us out of Egypt."
9. "It's a reminder on your hand and forehead that God saved you."
10. "Do this every year at the same time."

Rules for Firstborn Sons

11. "When you enter the promised land,"
12. "Give God every firstborn son and male animal."
13. "Buy back every firstborn donkey with a lamb—or break its neck. Also buy back your firstborn sons."
14. "When your child asks, 'What does this mean?' say, 'God rescued us with His power.'"
15. "When Pharaoh refused to let us go, God killed every firstborn in Egypt. That's why we give Him our firstborn animals and buy back our sons."
16. "It's like a mark on your hand and forehead to remind you of God's power."

God Leads His People

17. When Pharaoh let them go, God didn't take them through the land of the Philistines, even though it was shorter. God said, "They might change their minds if they see war."

18. So God led them through the desert toward the Red Sea. The Israelites left ready for battle.
19. Moses took Joseph's bones with him. Joseph had made them promise to do that.
20. They left Succoth and camped at Etham near the desert.
21. God led them in a cloud during the day and fire at night so they could travel anytime.
22. The cloud and fire never left them.

Exodus 14

1. God said to Moses,
2. "Tell the Israelites to camp near the Red Sea across from Baal-Zephon."
3. "Pharaoh will think you're lost and trapped."
4. "I'll harden his heart, and he'll chase you. But I'll defeat him, and everyone will know I am the Lord." The people obeyed.
5. When Pharaoh heard they left, he and his officials changed their minds. "Why did we let them go?"
6. He got his chariot ready and took his army.
7. He took 600 of his best chariots and many others with commanders.
8. God made Pharaoh stubborn, and he chased the Israelites, who had left proudly.
9. The Egyptians caught up to them near the sea.
10. When the Israelites saw them coming, they were scared and cried to God.
11. They said to Moses, "Why did you bring us here to die? Were there no graves in Egypt?"
12. "We told you to leave us alone. Being slaves was better than dying here!"
13. Moses said, "Don't be afraid. Stand still and watch God save you today."
14. "God will fight for you. Just stay calm."
15. God said, "Why are you crying to me? Tell the people to move forward."
16. "Raise your staff and stretch your hand over the sea to divide it so they can walk on dry ground."
17. "I'll harden the Egyptians' hearts so they follow. I'll defeat them to show my power."
18. "Then they'll know I am the Lord."
19. The angel of God moved from in front of Israel's camp to behind it. The cloud moved too.
20. It came between the Israelites and Egyptians. It was dark for Egypt but gave light to Israel all night.
21. Moses raised his hand, and God sent a strong wind that pushed back the sea all night, turning it into dry land.
22. The Israelites walked through with walls of water on both sides.
23. The Egyptians followed them in.
24. Early in the morning, God looked down and confused the Egyptians.
25. He made their chariot wheels fall off. "Let's run!" they said. "God is fighting for them!"
26. God said to Moses, "Stretch your hand over the sea again."
27. Moses did, and the sea returned to normal. The Egyptians tried to run, but God swept them into the sea.
28. The water covered the army. Not one survived.
29. But the Israelites walked safely on dry ground with walls of water beside them.
30. That day God saved Israel from Egypt, and they saw the Egyptians' bodies on the shore.
31. When they saw God's power, they trusted Him and Moses.

Exodus 15

1. Moses and the Israelites sang, "I'll sing to the Lord! He threw the horse and rider into the sea."
2. "The Lord is my strength and my song. He saved me. I will praise Him."
3. "The Lord is a warrior. His name is the Lord."
4. "He threw Pharaoh's army into the sea. His best officers drowned."
5. "The water covered them. They sank like stones."
6. "Your powerful hand, Lord, crushed the enemy."
7. "Your anger burned them up like straw."
8. "At your breath, the water piled up. The sea stood like walls."
9. "The enemy said, 'I'll chase and catch them, take their things, and kill them.'"
10. "But you blew, and the sea covered them. They sank like lead."
11. "Lord, who is like you? Holy, powerful, and full of wonders?"
12. "You lifted your hand, and the earth swallowed them."
13. "You led your people with love and power."
14. "The nations heard and trembled."
15. "Leaders of Edom and Moab shook with fear. People in Canaan lost courage."
16. "Fear fell on them. You protected your people as they passed through."
17. "You'll bring them to your holy mountain, your special place."
18. "The Lord will rule forever!"

The Song of Miriam

19. After God drowned Pharaoh's army,
20. Miriam led the women with tambourines and dancing.
21. She sang, "Sing to the Lord! He threw horse and rider into the sea!"

Bitter Water Made Good

22. Moses led the people into the desert. For 3 days they had no water.
23. They found water at Marah, but it was too bitter to drink.
24. The people complained, "What will we drink?"
25. Moses prayed, and God showed him a piece of wood. He threw it in the water, and it became good. God gave them rules and tested them there.
26. God said, "If you obey me, I won't punish you like I did Egypt. I am the Lord who heals you."
27. They came to Elim, where there were 12 springs and 70 palm trees. They camped there.

Exodus 16

1. One month after leaving Egypt, the Israelites left Elim and entered the desert.
2. They complained to Moses and Aaron.
3. "We wish we died in Egypt where we had food. Now we'll starve here!"
4. God said, "I'll send bread from heaven. Each day, gather only what you need. I'm testing them."
5. "On the 6th day, gather twice as much."
6. Moses and Aaron said, "Tonight you'll know God brought you out."
7. "In the morning, you'll see His power. Your complaints are really against Him."
8. Moses added, "God will give meat tonight and bread in the morning."
9. Moses told Aaron, "Call everyone. God heard their complaints."
10. As Aaron spoke, they looked and saw God's glory in a cloud.
11. God told Moses,
12. "I've heard them. Tonight they'll eat meat. Tomorrow morning, bread. Then they'll know I'm the Lord."

13. That evening, quail came and covered the camp. In the morning, dew lay on the ground.
14. When the dew dried, thin flakes were left—like frost.
15. They asked, "What is it?" Moses said, "It's the bread God gave you."
16. "Gather what you need—about two quarts per person."
17. Some gathered more, some less.
18. But everyone had enough.
19. Moses said, "Don't save any for the next day."
20. Some didn't listen. The extra grew worms and smelled bad. Moses was angry.
21. Every morning they gathered what they needed. When the sun got hot, it melted.
22. On the 6th day, they gathered twice as much. The leaders asked Moses why.
23. Moses said, "Tomorrow is a rest day, God's Sabbath. Bake today. Save leftovers for tomorrow."
24. They saved it, and it didn't smell or grow worms.
25. Moses said, "Eat it today. There's no food in the field on the Sabbath."
26. "Gather for 6 days, but not on the 7th."
27. Some people went out anyway but found nothing.
28. God said, "Why won't they follow my rules?"
29. "I gave you rest. That's why I send enough on the 6th day."
30. So they rested on the 7th day.
31. They called the food manna. It was white and tasted like honey wafers.
32. Moses said, "God says to save some manna for the future to remember how He fed you."
33. Moses told Aaron, "Put a jar of manna in the place of worship."
34. Aaron did as God commanded.
35. They ate manna for 40 years until they reached Canaan.
36. (A jar held about 2 quarts.)

Exodus 17

1. The Israelites left the desert and moved from place to place, as God told them. They camped at Rephidim, but there was no water.
2. They argued with Moses, "Give us water!" Moses said, "Why are you testing God?"
3. They kept complaining, "Why did you bring us out of Egypt just to die of thirst?"
4. Moses prayed, "What should I do? They're about to stone me!"
5. God said, "Take your staff and some leaders and walk ahead of the people."
6. "I'll be at the rock on Mount Sinai. Hit the rock, and water will come out." Moses did, and the leaders saw it.
7. Moses named the place Massah and Meribah, because the people complained and tested God by saying, "Is God really with us?"

Israel Defeats the Amalekites

8. At Rephidim, the Amalekites attacked.
9. Moses told Joshua, "Pick men to fight. Tomorrow, I'll stand on the hill with God's staff."
10. Joshua fought while Moses, Aaron, and Hur climbed the hill.
11. When Moses raised his hands, Israel won. When he lowered them, Amalek won.
12. Moses got tired. Aaron and Hur gave him a rock to sit on and held up his arms. His hands stayed raised until sunset.
13. So Joshua won the battle.
14. God told Moses, "Write this down and tell Joshua. I'll erase Amalek's name."

15. Moses built an altar called "The Lord is My Banner."
16. He said, "God will fight Amalek forever."

Exodus 18

1. Jethro, Moses' father-in-law, heard how God rescued Israel.
2. Moses had sent his wife and sons to stay with Jethro.
3. One son was named Gershom ("Foreigner"),
4. and the other Eliezer ("God is my helper").
5. Jethro brought them to Moses at the mountain of God.
6. He sent a message saying they were coming.
7. Moses greeted Jethro, bowed, kissed him, and they talked in a tent.
8. Moses told him everything God had done to save them.
9. Jethro was happy and thankful.
10. He said, "Praise God for saving you!"
11. "Now I know the Lord is greater than all gods!"
12. Jethro gave an offering. Aaron and the leaders joined him to eat with God.

Moses Gets Help

13. The next day, Moses spent all day solving people's problems.
14. Jethro asked, "Why do you do this alone all day?"
15. Moses said, "People come to me to ask what God wants."
16. "I help them with their arguments and teach them God's rules."
17. Jethro said, "This isn't good. You'll wear out yourself and the people."
18. "You need help."
19. "Listen to me—God will guide you. You speak for the people to God."
20. "Teach them His rules and how to live."
21. "Pick honest, wise men who respect God. Put them in charge of groups of 10, 50, 100, and 1,000."
22. "They'll handle small problems. Bring only the hard ones to you."
23. "If you do this, you'll be able to keep going, and people will be happy."
24. Moses listened to Jethro's advice.
25. He chose good men and made them leaders.
26. They handled small cases and brought the hard ones to Moses.
27. Then Moses let Jethro go home.

Exodus 19

1. Two months after leaving Egypt, the Israelites reached the Sinai Desert.
2. They camped at the base of Mount Sinai.
3. Moses climbed the mountain to meet God. God told him, "Speak to the people of Israel."
4. "Tell them I saved you from Egypt and brought you here."
5. "If you obey me, you'll be my special people."
6. "You'll be my holy nation and priests."
7. Moses told the elders everything God said.
8. The people answered, "We will do everything God says." Moses gave their answer to God.
9. God said, "I'll come in a thick cloud so the people can hear me and trust you."
10. God told Moses, "Tell the people to get ready today and tomorrow. Have them wash their clothes."
11. "Be ready on the third day. I'll come down on Mount Sinai."
12. "Put a boundary around the mountain. No one must touch it. If they do, they'll die."

13. "Anyone who touches it must be stoned or shot. People and animals must stay back."

14. Moses went down and told the people to get ready. They washed their clothes.

15. He told them, "Be ready in three days. Don't have sex before then."

God Comes to Mount Sinai

16. On the third day, there was thunder, lightning, a thick cloud, and a loud trumpet. The people were afraid.

17. Moses led them out to meet God at the mountain.

18. The mountain was covered in smoke because God came down in fire. It shook violently.

19. The trumpet got louder. Moses spoke, and God answered with thunder.

20. God came down to the top of the mountain and called Moses up.

21. God said, "Go warn the people not to cross the boundary or they'll die."

22. "Even the priests must be careful and holy."

23. Moses said, "They won't cross. You told us to mark the boundary."

24. God said, "Go down and bring Aaron back with you. But no one else must come near."

25. So Moses went down and told the people.

Exodus 20

The Ten Commandments

1. God gave these commands:

2. "I am the Lord your God. I brought you out of Egypt."

3. "Don't worship any other gods but me."

4. "Don't make or worship idols of anything in the sky, earth, or sea."

5. "I'm a jealous God. If you reject me, your children and grandchildren will be punished."

6. "But I'll show love to thousands who love me and obey me."

7. "Don't misuse my name. I'll punish anyone who does."

8. "Keep the Sabbath day holy."

9. "Work for six days,

10. but the seventh day is for rest. Don't work. That includes you, your family, workers, and animals."

11. "I made everything in six days and rested on the seventh. That's why I blessed the Sabbath."

12. "Respect your father and mother so you can live a long life in the land I give you."

13. "Don't murder."

14. "Don't cheat on your husband or wife."

15. "Don't steal."

16. "Don't lie about others."

17. "Don't want what belongs to someone else—not their house, wife, workers, animals, or anything they own."

18. The people saw lightning, heard thunder and a loud trumpet, and saw smoke on the mountain. They were scared.

19. They told Moses, "You talk to us. Don't let God speak or we'll die."

20. Moses said, "Don't be afraid. God came to test you so you'll obey Him."

21. The people stayed back while Moses went near the dark cloud where God was.

Worship and Altars

22. God told Moses, "Tell the people: You saw me speak to you from heaven."

23. "Don't make idols of silver or gold."

24. "Build an altar from dirt and offer sheep or cattle. I'll bless the place where I'm worshiped."

25. "If you use stones, don't shape them with tools. That ruins them."

26. "Don't build steps to the altar. People might see up your clothes."

Exodus 21

Laws About People

1. These are the rules to give the people:
2. "If you buy a Hebrew slave, he serves for 6 years. In the 7th year, he's free."
3. "If he was single, he leaves single. If he was married, his wife leaves too."
4. "If his master gave him a wife and they had kids, the wife and kids stay with the master."
5. "If the man says, 'I love my family and don't want to leave,'"
6. "The master takes him to court, then pierces his ear. He'll serve for life."
7. "If a man sells his daughter as a servant, she doesn't go free the same way."
8. "If the man who bought her doesn't marry her or treat her right, he must let her go."
9. "If he chooses her for his son, she must be treated like a daughter."
10. "If he marries someone else, he must still provide her food, clothes, and love."
11. "If he doesn't, she's free to leave."

Laws About Violence

12. "If someone kills a person on purpose, they must be put to death."
13. "If it was an accident, they can run to a safe place."
14. "But if they planned it, take them away and punish them."
15. "Anyone who hits their parents must be killed."
16. "Anyone who kidnaps must be killed—whether they still have the person or already sold them."
17. "Anyone who curses their parents must be killed."
18. "If people fight and one hits the other with a rock or stick but doesn't die,
19. the one who hit him must pay for missed work and take care of him until he's better."
20. "If someone beats their slave and the slave dies, they must be punished."
21. "But if the slave lives a few days, there's no punishment—the slave was their property."
22. "If two men fight and hit a pregnant woman and she gives birth early but isn't hurt, the one who hit her must pay what the husband demands."
23. "But if she or the baby dies, it's life for life,
24. eye for eye, tooth for tooth,
25. hand for hand, foot for foot, burn for burn, wound for wound, bruise for bruise."
26. "If a man knocks out a slave's eye or
27. tooth, the slave is free."
28. "If your bull kills someone, kill the bull. Don't eat its meat. The owner is not blamed."
29. "But if the bull did this before and the owner didn't stop it, and it kills someone, both the bull and the owner must be killed or pay money."
30. "If a payment is made, the owner must pay whatever is decided."
31. "This rule applies if the bull kills a son or daughter too."
32. "If a bull kills a slave, the owner must pay 30 silver coins and the bull is killed."

Laws About Property

33. "If someone leaves a hole open and another person's animal falls in and dies,
34. the owner of the hole must pay for it and keep the dead animal."
35. "If someone's bull kills another's bull, sell both and split the money and meat."

36. "But if the bull had done this before and the owner did nothing, he must pay full price and keep the dead one."

Exodus 22

More Laws

1. "If someone steals an ox or sheep and kills or sells it, they must pay back 5 oxen for 1, or 4 sheep for 1."
2. "If a thief is caught breaking in at night and is killed, it's not murder."
3. "But if it happens during the day, it is murder."
4. "If the thief is caught alive, they must pay back double."
5. "If someone lets their animals eat in someone else's field, they must pay back with the best of their own field."
6. "If a fire spreads and burns a field, the one who started it must pay for the damage."
7. "If someone gives you money or stuff to keep safe and it gets stolen, the thief must pay double."
8. "If the thief isn't found, the person who was keeping it must swear they didn't steal it."
9. "In any dispute over property, both people must go to court."
10. "If someone gives you an animal to watch and it dies or is hurt and no one saw it,
11. you must swear before God that you didn't harm it."
12. "But if it was stolen, the keeper must pay back the owner."
13. "If the animal was killed by a wild animal, bring the body as proof. No payment needed."
14. "If you borrowed something and it broke or the animal died, you must pay for it."
15. "Unless the owner was there, then you don't have to pay."

Laws About People and Morals

16. "If a man sleeps with a woman who's not married, he must pay her family and marry her."
17. "If her father refuses, he must still pay the bride price."
18. "Don't let sorcerers live."
19. "Anyone who has sex with animals must be killed."
20. "Don't worship other gods. You must be destroyed if you do."
21. "Don't be mean to foreigners—you were once foreigners too."
22. "Don't hurt widows or orphans."
23. "If you do and they cry to me, I'll hear them."
24. "I'll get angry and kill you. Then your wives and children will be widows and orphans."
25. "If you lend money to poor people, don't act like a greedy lender. Don't charge interest."
26. "If you take a poor person's coat as a promise, return it before night. It's all they have to sleep in."
27. "If they cry to me, I'll hear them. I am kind."
28. "Don't curse God or your leaders."
29. "Give me the first of your harvest and animals."
30. "Give me the firstborn of your cattle and sheep after seven days."
31. "You belong to me. Don't eat animals killed by wild animals. Feed it to dogs."

Exodus 23

1. "Don't tell lies in court. Don't help a guilty person by lying."
2. "Don't follow a crowd in doing wrong. Even in court, do what's right, not what others do."
3. "Don't favor a poor person in court just because they're poor."
4. "If you find your enemy's animal wandering, bring it back."

5. "If your enemy's donkey has fallen, help lift it up."
6. "Don't cheat poor people in court."
7. "Stay far away from lies. Don't kill innocent people. I won't let guilty people go free."
8. "Don't take bribes. They make people ignore what's right."
9. "Don't treat foreigners badly. You were foreigners in Egypt."

Sabbath and Rest

10. "Plant and harvest your fields for six years,
11. but in the seventh year, leave them alone. Let the poor and wild animals eat what's left."
12. "Work six days, but rest on the seventh. Let your workers and animals rest too."
13. "Obey everything I've said. Don't even speak the names of other gods."

Three Festivals

14. "Celebrate three festivals each year in my honor."
15. "First, the Festival of Unleavened Bread. For seven days, eat bread without yeast, just like I told you. Do this every spring, because that's when you left Egypt. Don't come to me empty-handed."
16. "Second, the Festival of Harvest when you bring the first crops you've grown."
17. "Third, the Festival of Final Harvest at the end of the year."
18. "Don't offer bread with yeast along with animal sacrifices. Don't save the fat from a sacrifice overnight."
19. "Bring the best of your first harvest to God's house. Don't boil a baby goat in its mother's milk."

God's Angel Will Lead You

20. "I'm sending an angel to protect you and lead you to the land I've prepared."
21. "Listen to him. Don't make him angry. He speaks for me."
22. "If you obey him, I'll be enemies to your enemies."
23. "My angel will go ahead of you and defeat the people living there."
24. "Don't worship their gods. Destroy their idols completely."
25. "Worship only me. I'll give you food, water, and health."
26. "No women will miscarry or be childless. I'll give you a full life."
27. "I'll scare your enemies and make them run."
28. "I'll send hornets to drive out the people ahead of you."
29. "But I won't do it all at once, or wild animals will take over."
30. "I'll do it little by little until your numbers grow."
31. "I'll set your borders from the Red Sea to the sea of the Philistines, from the desert to the Euphrates River."
32. "Don't make peace with them or their gods."
33. "Don't let them live in your land, or they'll lead you to sin."

Exodus 24

1. God said to Moses, "Bring Aaron, Nadab, Abihu, and 70 leaders. Worship from a distance."
2. "Only you, Moses, may come close. The others must stay back."
3. Moses told the people all of God's laws. They said, "We will obey everything."
4. Moses wrote it all down. He built an altar with 12 stone pillars—one for each tribe.
5. Young men gave burnt offerings and peace offerings.
6. Moses put half the blood in bowls and splashed the other half on the altar.

7. He read the Book of the Covenant. The people said, "We will do everything God said."
8. Moses sprinkled the blood on the people and said, "This blood shows the promise God made with you."

Moses Goes Up the Mountain

9. Moses, Aaron, Nadab, Abihu, and the 70 leaders went up.
10. They saw God! Under His feet was something like blue glass.
11. God didn't harm them. They saw Him and ate a meal together.
12. God said, "Come up the mountain. I'll give you stone tablets with the law I've written."
13. Moses and his helper Joshua went up the mountain.
14. Moses told the leaders, "Wait here. Aaron and Hur are in charge while I'm gone."
15. Moses climbed higher into the cloud that covered the mountain.
16. God's glory stayed there for six days. On the seventh day, God called to Moses.
17. To the people, God's glory looked like fire on the mountain.
18. Moses went into the cloud and stayed there for 40 days and 40 nights.

Exodus 25

Offerings and Instructions for the Tabernacle

1. God told Moses,
2. "Tell the Israelites to bring me gifts. Anyone who wants to may give."
3. "Collect gold, silver, bronze,
4. blue, purple, and red yarn, fine linen, goat hair,
5. ramskins dyed red, fine leather, acacia wood,
6. olive oil for the lamps, spices for oil and incense,
7. onyx stones and other gems for the priest's clothes."
8. "Tell them to build a holy place for me, and I'll live among them."
9. "Follow the exact plan I give you for the tent and everything in it."

The Ark of the Covenant

10. "Make an Ark (a wooden chest) from acacia wood—3¾ feet long, 2¼ feet wide and high."
11. "Cover it inside and out with gold. Make a gold strip around it."
12. "Cast four gold rings and attach them to the corners."
13. "Make poles from acacia wood and cover them with gold."
14. "Put the poles through the rings so you can carry the Ark."
15. "Never remove the poles."
16. "Put inside the Ark the tablets with my law."
17. "Make a lid of pure gold—3¾ feet long, 2¼ feet wide."
18. "Make two gold cherubim (angel figures) on the lid."
19. "One on each end, facing each other with wings spread upward."
20. "Their wings should cover the lid."
21. "Put the lid on top of the Ark and the tablets inside."
22. "That's where I'll meet with you and speak to you."

The Table for Bread

23. "Make a table of acacia wood—3 feet long, 1½ feet wide and high."
24. "Cover it with gold and put a gold strip around it."
25. "Add a frame and a gold border."
26. "Make four gold rings for the legs."
27. "Put the rings near the corners for the carrying poles."
28. "Make poles of acacia wood, covered in gold."

29. "Make gold dishes, bowls, pitchers, and jars."
30. "Always keep the sacred bread on the table."

The Lampstand

31. "Make a gold lampstand with six branches—three on each side."
32. "Shape it like a tree with almond flowers and buds."
33. "Each branch should have three flower cups."
34. "The main stem should have four cups too."
35. "One cup under each pair of branches."
36. "It must all be made from one piece of gold."
37. "Make seven lamps and set them on top to shine forward."
38. "Use pure gold for the tools too—wick trimmers and trays."
39. "Use 75 pounds of pure gold in total."
40. "Follow the exact pattern I showed you on the mountain."

Exodus 26

The Tent (Tabernacle)

1. "Make ten curtains of fine linen with blue, purple, and red yarn. Sew cherubim designs into them."
2. "Each curtain should be 42 feet long and 6 feet wide."
3. "Sew five together to make one large piece. Do the same with the other five."
4. "Add loops of blue cloth to the edge of each large piece."
5. "Make 50 loops on each edge."
6. "Make 50 gold hooks to join the two large pieces together into one tent."

Goat Hair Covering

7. "Make 11 curtains from goat hair for a covering over the tent."
8. "Each one should be 45 feet long and 6 feet wide."
9. "Sew five together, and the other six together. Fold the sixth one over the front."
10. "Make 50 loops on the edges of each set."
11. "Make 50 bronze hooks to join them."
12. "Let the extra part hang over the back and sides."
13. "It should cover the tent completely."
14. "Add more coverings made of red ram skins and fine leather."

Frames for the Tent

15. "Make wooden frames to hold up the tent."
16. "Each frame is 15 feet tall and 2¼ feet wide."
17. "Each has two pegs at the bottom to stand upright."
18. "Make 20 frames for the south side,"
19. "with 40 silver bases—two under each frame."
20. "Do the same for the north side."
21. (Same number of bases.)
22. "Make six frames for the west side (the back),
23. plus two more for the corners."
24. "Join the corner frames tightly."
25. "In total, 8 frames and 16 silver bases."
26. "Make crossbars from acacia wood."
27. "Five for each side and five for the back."
28. "Run one bar halfway up the middle."
29. "Cover the frames and bars with gold. Put gold rings on the frames for the bars to fit into."
30. "Set up the tent exactly like I showed you."

The Curtain Inside

31. "Make a curtain of blue, purple, and red yarn and fine linen with cherubim sewn into it."
32. "Hang it on four gold-covered posts with gold hooks and silver bases."
33. "Hang the curtain to separate the Holy Place from the Most Holy Place."
34. "Put the Ark behind it. That's the Most Holy Place."
35. "Put the table and lampstand outside the curtain."
36. "Make another curtain for the tent entrance. Use blue, purple, and red yarn with fine linen."
37. "Hang it on five gold-covered posts with gold hooks and bronze bases."

Exodus 27

The Altar and Courtyard

1. "Make an altar of acacia wood—7½ feet square and 4½ feet high."
2. "Make horns on the corners from the same wood. Cover it all with bronze."
3. "Make bronze buckets, shovels, bowls, forks, and firepans."
4. "Make a bronze grating with a bronze ring at each corner."
5. "Put the grating halfway up the altar."
6. "Make poles of acacia wood covered with bronze."
7. "Put them through the rings to carry the altar."
8. "Make it hollow, like a box, just like I showed you."

The Courtyard

9. "Make a courtyard around the tent. On the south side, put up curtains 150 feet long made of fine linen."
10. "Use 20 posts with bronze bases and silver hooks."
11. "Do the same for the north side."
12. "For the west side, make curtains 75 feet long with 10 posts and bases."
13. "Same for the east side."
14. "On each side of the gate, make curtains 22½ feet long with three posts and bases."
15. (Repeat for the other side.)
16. "Make the entrance curtain 30 feet wide using blue, purple, red yarn, and fine linen. Use four posts and bases."
17. "All posts around the courtyard must have silver hooks, silver tops, and bronze bases."
18. "The courtyard is 150 feet long, 75 feet wide, and 7½ feet high, with fine linen curtains and bronze bases."
19. "Make all tools for the tent out of bronze."

The Oil for the Lamp

20. "Tell the Israelites to bring pure olive oil to keep the lamp burning always."
21. "Aaron and his sons will keep the lamp lit from evening to morning. Do this forever."

Exodus 28

Special Clothes for the Priests

1. "Have your brother Aaron and his sons serve as priests: Aaron, Nadab, Abihu, Eleazar, and Ithamar."
2. "Make special clothes for Aaron to show his honor and beauty."
3. "Tell skilled workers to make these clothes for him to wear as he serves me."
4. "These are the clothes: a chestpiece, an ephod, a robe, a woven shirt, a turban, and a sash. Make them for Aaron and his sons."
5. "Use gold, blue, purple, red yarn, and fine linen."

The Ephod

6. "Make the ephod from gold, blue, purple, red yarn, and fine linen."
7. "It should have shoulder straps on each side."

8. "Make a fancy waistband from the same materials."
9. "Take two onyx stones and carve the names of the sons of Israel."
10. "Six names on one stone, six on the other."
11. "Carve them like a seal and put them in gold settings."
12. "Attach them to the shoulder straps. They will remind me of Israel when Aaron wears them."
13. "Make gold frames
14. and two braided chains of pure gold to attach to the frames."

The Chestpiece for Decisions

15. "Make a chestpiece for decision-making, like the ephod, using gold, blue, purple, red yarn, and fine linen."
16. "It should be square—9 inches by 9 inches—and folded in half."
17. "Decorate it with 4 rows of gemstones: first row—ruby, topaz, beryl;
18. second row—turquoise, sapphire, emerald;
19. third row—jacinth, agate, amethyst;
20. fourth row—chrysolite, onyx, jasper. Mount them in gold."
21. "Each stone represents one of the 12 tribes."
22. "Make two braided gold chains for it."
23. "Add two gold rings to the top corners."
24. "Attach the chains to the rings
25. and to the ephod's shoulder pieces."
26. "Add two more rings to the lower corners of the chestpiece
27. and two more on the ephod near the waistband."
28. "Tie them together with a blue cord so the chestpiece stays in place."
29. "When Aaron wears it, he carries the names of Israel over his heart."
30. "Put the Urim and Thummim inside the chestpiece. They help make decisions."

Other Priestly Clothes

31. "Make a robe for the ephod entirely from blue cloth."
32. "Make a hole at the top for his head and stitch around it so it won't tear."
33. "Decorate the bottom with blue, purple, and red yarn shaped like pomegranates, and gold bells between them."
34. "The bells and pomegranates should go all the way around."
35. "Aaron will wear this robe. The bells will ring when he enters and leaves the holy place, so he won't die."
36. "Make a gold medallion and carve 'Holy to the Lord' on it."
37. "Tie it to the turban with a blue cord."
38. "It shows that Aaron is holy and can carry the people's sins."
39. "Make a woven shirt, a turban, and a sash of fine linen."
40. "Make clothes, sashes, and caps for Aaron's sons to show their honor."
41. "Dress them, anoint them with oil, and make them priests."
42. "Make linen underwear for them to cover their bodies from waist to thigh."
43. "They must wear them when they go into the tent or they'll be guilty and die. This rule lasts forever."

Exodus 29

Setting the Priests Apart

1. "This is how you must make Aaron and his sons holy to serve me as priests: Take a young bull and two perfect rams.
2. Make bread and cakes without yeast using fine flour and olive oil.
3. Put them in a basket and bring them with the bull and the two rams.

4. Bring Aaron and his sons to the entrance of the tent and wash them."
5. "Dress Aaron in the shirt, robe, ephod, chestpiece, and sash.
6. Put the turban and gold medallion on his head."
7. "Anoint him by pouring oil on his head."
8. "Dress his sons in shirts, sashes, and caps."
9. "This shows they are priests. This rule lasts forever."

The Offerings

10. "Bring the bull. Aaron and his sons must place their hands on its head.
11. Kill it before the Lord.
12. Put its blood on the altar's horns and pour the rest at the base.
13. Burn its fat, liver, and kidneys on the altar.
14. Burn the rest outside the camp—it's a sin offering."
15. "Then take one ram. Have them place their hands on it.
16. Kill it and splash its blood on the altar.
17. Cut it in pieces, wash the inner parts, and burn it all on the altar."
18. "It's a burnt offering to the Lord—a sweet smell."
19. "Take the second ram. They must lay their hands on it too.
20. Kill it, and put some blood on Aaron's and his sons' right ears, thumbs, and big toes.
21. Sprinkle oil and blood on them and their clothes. This makes them holy."
22. "Take the fat, tail, inner parts, liver, kidneys, and right thigh.
23. Add bread, cakes, and wafers from the basket.
24. Put all this in their hands and wave it before the Lord."
25. "Take it back and burn it on the altar. It pleases the Lord."
26. "The priest will keep the breast part as his share.
27. The thigh and breast are gifts to the priests from Israel's peace offerings."
28. "This will always belong to the priests."
29. "Aaron's holy clothes must be passed down to his sons when they become priests."
30. "The new priest must wear them for seven days."
31. "Cook the ram's meat in a holy place."
32. "Aaron and his sons will eat it and the bread.
33. No one else may eat it. It's holy."
34. "Burn anything left until morning."
35. "Do all this for seven days to make them priests."
36. "Each day, offer a bull to cleanse the altar.
37. Do this for seven days to make the altar holy. Then it will be most holy."

Daily Offerings

38. "Every day, offer two one-year-old lambs.
39. One in the morning and one at sunset."
40. "With each lamb, offer flour mixed with oil and a drink offering."
41. "Do the same at sunset."
42. "This must be done forever at the entrance of the tent. That's where I'll meet you."
43. "I'll speak to you there."
44. "I will make the tent and the altar holy. I'll make Aaron and his sons holy to serve me."
45. "I'll live among the Israelites."
46. "They'll know I am the Lord their God who brought them out of Egypt to live with them."

Exodus 30

More Instructions for Worship

1. "Make an altar for burning incense. Use acacia wood."
2. "It must be 18 inches square and 3 feet tall, with horns on each corner made from the same wood."
3. "Cover it with pure gold—top, sides, and horns. Add a gold strip around it."
4. "Make two gold rings for the sides to hold the poles."
5. "Make the poles from acacia wood covered in gold."
6. "Put the altar in front of the curtain that hides the Ark, where I'll meet with you."
7. "Every morning, Aaron must burn sweet incense when he lights the oil lamps."
8. "He must do the same at sunset. This must happen every day, forever."
9. "Don't offer any other incense, burnt offerings, grain offerings, or drink offerings on this altar."
10. "Once a year, Aaron must put blood on its horns to make it pure. This will make it holy to the Lord."

Money for the Tent

11. God told Moses,
12. "When you count the Israelites, each one must give a payment to the Lord to stay safe."
13. "Everyone 20 or older must pay half a shekel as an offering to the Lord."
14. "Rich or poor, everyone pays the same amount."
15. "Use this money to take care of the Tent of Meeting. It helps pay for your lives."

The Wash Basin

16. God said,
17. "Make a bronze washbasin with a bronze stand. Put it between the tent and the altar. Fill it with water."
18. "Aaron and his sons must wash their hands and feet before going into the tent or offering a sacrifice."
19. "If they don't, they'll die."
20. "This is a rule forever."

Special Oil

21. God said,
22. "Take these spices: myrrh, cinnamon, sweet cane,
23. cassia, and olive oil."
24. "Make a special anointing oil like a perfumer would make."
25. "Use it to anoint the tent, Ark,
26. table, lampstand, incense altar,
27. altar of burnt offering, and washbasin."
28. "This will make them holy."
29. "Anoint Aaron and his sons to serve me."
30. "This oil is holy. Use it for generations to come."
31. "Never pour it on anyone else or make any like it."
32. "Anyone who copies it must be cut off from the people."

Special Incense

33. God said, "Make holy incense using equal amounts of gum resin, onycha, galbanum, and pure frankincense."
34. "Grind it into powder and use it as holy incense."
35. "Put some in front of the Ark, where I'll meet you. It is very holy."
36. "Don't make any for yourself to smell."
37. "Anyone who does must be cut off."

Exodus 31

Workers and the Sabbath

1. God said to Moses,
2. "I have chosen Bezalel from the tribe of Judah."
3. "I filled him with wisdom and skill to design all kinds of things."
4. "He can work with gold, silver, bronze,

5. cut stones, carve wood, and do all kinds of crafts."
6. "I have given him a helper, Oholiab from the tribe of Dan. I gave special skills to others too."
7. "They will build the tent, the Ark, the lid, the furniture,
8. the table, lampstand, incense altar,
9. altar of burnt offering, washbasin,
10. clothes for the priests,
11. oil, and incense—everything I commanded you."

The Sabbath Day

12. God said to Moses,
13. "Tell the Israelites to keep the Sabbath. It's a sign between us forever."
14. "Keep it holy. Anyone who works on it must die."
15. "Work six days, rest on the seventh. Whoever works on the Sabbath must be put to death."
16. "This rule lasts forever."
17. "It's a sign forever. God made everything in six days and rested on the seventh."
18. When God finished speaking, He gave Moses two stone tablets with the commandments written by God's own hand.

Exodus 32

The Gold Calf

1. When the people saw Moses was gone a long time, they said to Aaron, "Make us a god to lead us. We don't know what happened to Moses."
2. Aaron said, "Give me your gold earrings."
3. Everyone gave him their gold.
4. He melted it and made a golden calf. The people said, "This is the god who brought us out of Egypt!"
5. Aaron built an altar and said, "Tomorrow we'll have a festival for the Lord."
6. The next morning they brought offerings. They ate, drank, and partied wildly.
7. God said to Moses, "Go down! The people you brought from Egypt have sinned."
8. "They made a golden calf and are worshiping it."
9. "They are stubborn.
10. Let me destroy them and make a new nation from you."
11. Moses begged God, "Please don't be angry! You saved them from Egypt."
12. "Don't let Egypt say you brought them out just to kill them."
13. "Remember your promise to Abraham, Isaac, and Jacob."
14. So God changed His mind and didn't destroy them.
15. Moses went down the mountain with the two stone tablets God wrote on.
16. God Himself had made and written on them.
17. Joshua heard shouting and said, "There's war in the camp!"
18. Moses said, "That's not war. It's singing."
19. When Moses saw the calf and dancing, he got angry and broke the tablets.
20. He burned the calf, ground it to powder, mixed it with water, and made the people drink it.
21. He said to Aaron, "What did they do to make you do this?"
22. Aaron said, "Don't be mad. You know these people are evil."
23. "They told me to make a god because you were gone too long."
24. "So I took their gold, threw it in the fire, and out came this calf!"
25. Moses saw the people were out of control.

26. He shouted, “Who is on the Lord’s side? Come here!” The Levites came.
27. He told them, “God says: Go through the camp and kill your brothers and neighbors.”
28. They did, and about 3,000 people died.
29. Moses said, “Today you showed you belong to the Lord.”
30. The next day, Moses told the people, “You have sinned badly. I’ll try to ask God to forgive you.”
31. Moses prayed, “They made a gold god. Please forgive them.”
32. “But if you won’t, then erase my name from your book.”
33. God said, “I’ll erase the names of those who sin.
34. Now go, and I’ll send my angel ahead. But I’ll punish them later.”
35. God punished them with a plague for making the calf.

Exodus 33

God’s Promise and Moses Talks with God

1. God told Moses, “Leave this place. Go to the land I promised Abraham, Isaac, and Jacob.”
2. “I’ll send an angel ahead to drive out the other nations.”
3. “But I won’t go with you, or I might destroy you because you’re stubborn.”
4. The people were sad and took off their jewelry.
5. God said, “If I go with you, I might destroy you. Take off your jewelry and I’ll decide what to do.”
6. So they stopped wearing jewelry from then on.

The Meeting Tent

7. Moses pitched a tent outside the camp where he talked to God.
8. When he went to the tent, the people stood at their doors and watched.
9. A cloud came down to the tent as God spoke with Moses.
10. The people bowed and worshiped.
11. God talked to Moses like a friend. Afterward, Joshua stayed behind in the tent.

Moses Asks for God’s Presence

12. Moses said, “You told me to lead the people, but you haven’t told me who will go with me.”
13. “If you’re pleased with me, show me your ways so I may know you better.”
14. God said, “I will go with you and give you rest.”
15. Moses said, “If you don’t go with us, don’t send us.”
16. “How will anyone know you’re with us unless you go?”
17. God said, “I will do what you ask. I know you by name.”
18. Moses said, “Show me your glory.”
19. God said, “I will show my goodness and speak my name. I have mercy on whom I choose.”
20. “But you can’t see my face and live.”
21. “Stand on this rock.
22. When my glory passes by, I’ll cover you with my hand.
23. Then I’ll remove my hand, and you’ll see my back, but not my face.”

Exodus 34

New Tablets and God’s Covenant

1. God said, “Cut two new stone tablets like the ones you broke. I’ll write the same words.”
2. “Be ready in the morning. Come alone up the mountain.”
3. “No one else can come. No animals near the mountain.”
4. Moses cut two tablets and climbed Mount Sinai early the next day.

5. God came in a cloud and called out His name.
6. He said, "I am the Lord, kind and patient, full of love and truth.
7. I forgive evil but punish the guilty down to their grandchildren."
8. Moses bowed and worshiped.
9. He said, "Please stay with us, even though we're stubborn. Forgive us and make us your people."
10. God said, "I'm making a promise with you. I'll do amazing things no one has seen before."
11. "Obey me, and I'll drive out the other nations."
12. "Don't make peace with them or you'll fall into sin."
13. "Destroy their idols and altars."
14. "Worship only me. I'm a jealous God."
15. "Don't make deals with them. They'll invite you to eat food offered to idols."
16. "You'll marry their daughters and follow their false gods."
17. "Don't make idols."
18. "Celebrate the Festival of Unleavened Bread for seven days in spring."
19. "The firstborn of every animal belongs to me."
20. "Buy back your firstborn sons. Don't come to me empty-handed."
21. "Work six days, rest on the seventh—even during planting or harvest."
22. "Celebrate the Festival of Harvest and the Festival of Final Harvest."
23. "All men must appear before me three times a year."
24. "I'll protect your land when you go."
25. "Don't offer bread with yeast or keep leftover Passover meat until morning."
26. "Bring the best of your first crops. Don't cook a goat in its mother's milk."
27. God said, "Write down everything I've told you. This is my covenant."
28. Moses stayed on the mountain for 40 days and nights without food or water. God wrote the Ten Commandments again.
29. When Moses came down, his face was shining because he had been with God.
30. The people were afraid to come near.
31. Moses called them over. Aaron and the leaders came first.
32. Then everyone came, and Moses gave them God's message.
33. After speaking, Moses put a veil over his face.
34. He removed it when talking to God and then told the people what God said.
35. They saw his shining face, and he wore the veil until he went to speak with God again.

Exodus 35

Instructions for the Sabbath and the Tabernacle

1. Moses gathered everyone and said, "This is what the Lord told us to do."
2. "Work for six days, but rest on the seventh—it's holy. Anyone who works on the Sabbath must be put to death."
3. "Don't even light a fire in your homes on the Sabbath."

Offerings for the Tabernacle

4. Moses said, "Bring an offering to the Lord. Everyone who wants to can give."
5. "Bring gold, silver, and bronze;
6. blue, purple, and red yarn; fine linen and goat hair;
7. red-dyed ram skins and fine leather;
8. olive oil, spices, and incense;
9. onyx and other gems for the priest's clothes."
10. "Anyone with skill should help build everything God commanded:

11. the tent, its coverings, hooks, and frames;
12. the Ark, poles, lid, and curtain;
13. the table and items on it; the lampstand and tools;
14. the altar of incense and oils;
15. the altar for burnt offerings, the washbasin,
16. the curtains, stakes, and ropes;
17. the special clothes for the priests;
18. and all the items for worship."

The People Give

19. The people left.
20. Everyone who wanted to help brought gifts for God.
21. Men and women brought jewelry, earrings, rings, and necklaces.
22. Others brought yarn, linen, goat hair, leather, and skins.
23. People also gave silver, bronze, and wood.
24. Skilled women spun yarn and linen.
25. Women with special skill spun goat hair.
26. Leaders brought onyx stones and other gems.
27. They also gave spices and oil for the lamps and incense.
28. Everyone who wanted to give did so freely.

Bezalel and Oholiab

29. Moses said, "God has chosen Bezalel of the tribe of Judah.
30. He gave him wisdom and skill to design things
31. using gold, silver, bronze,
32. stone, wood, and more.
33. God also gave him and Oholiab the ability to teach others.
34. They can work with cloth, yarn, carving, and all kinds of crafts."

Exodus 36

Skilled Workers Begin the Work

1. Bezalel, Oholiab, and other skilled workers did everything God commanded.
2. Moses called them to start the work. They were eager to help.
3. Moses gave them all the offerings the people had brought.
4. Each morning, more gifts came.
5. The workers told Moses, "The people are giving too much!"
6. Moses said, "Stop bringing more." So the people stopped.
7. They had more than enough for the job.

Building the Tabernacle

8. Skilled workers made ten curtains with cherubim using blue, purple, and red yarn and fine linen.
9. Each curtain was the same size—42 feet long, 6 feet wide.
10. They joined five curtains together in two sets.
11. Blue loops were added to the edges of each set.
12. There were 50 loops on each end.
13. They made 50 gold hooks to join the sets into one tent.

Goat Hair Covering

14. They made 11 goat hair curtains.
15. Each was 45 feet long and 6 feet wide.
16. They joined five together and then six.
17. 50 loops were added to each set.
18. They used 50 bronze hooks to join the sets.
19. Then they made two more coverings: one of red-dyed ram skins and one of fine leather.

Wooden Frames

20. They made upright frames from acacia wood.

21. Each frame was 15 feet tall and 2¼ feet wide.
22. Each frame had two pegs at the bottom.
23. They made 20 frames for the south side
24. with 40 silver bases.
25. 20 more for the north side,
26. also with 40 bases.
27. Six frames were made for the west side.
28. Two extra corner frames were added.
29. They were joined tightly at the top.
30. Eight frames with 16 silver bases.

Crossbars

31. They made five wooden crossbars for each side—north,
32. south, and west (rear side of Tent)
33. The middle bar ran halfway up the frames.
34. All the wood was covered with gold.
35. They made gold rings to hold the bars.

The Inside Curtain

36. They made a curtain of blue, purple, and red yarn with cherubim.
37. It hung from four gold-covered posts with silver bases.

The Entrance Curtain

38. They made another curtain for the entrance using blue, purple, and red yarn and fine linen.
39. It hung on five posts with gold hooks and bronze bases.

Exodus 37

Building the Ark, Table, Lampstand, and Altar

1. Bezalel made the Ark from acacia wood—3¾ feet long, 2¼ feet wide and high.
2. He covered it inside and out with gold and added a gold strip around it.
3. He made four gold rings and put them on the corners.
4. He made poles of acacia wood, covered them with gold,
5. and put them through the rings to carry the Ark.
6. He made a pure gold lid for the Ark, same size.
7. He made two cherubim of gold,
8. one on each end.
9. The cherubim faced each other with wings spread out above the lid.

The Table

10. He made a table of acacia wood—3 feet long, 1½ feet wide, 2¼ feet high.
11. He covered it with gold and added a gold strip around it.
12. He made a frame and border with gold.
13. He made four gold rings for the corners.
14. He made poles of acacia wood, covered them in gold,
15. and put them in the rings to carry the table.
16. He made gold plates, bowls, pitchers, and jars for drink offerings.

The Lampstand

17. He made a lampstand of pure gold, hammered from one piece.
18. It had six branches—three on each side.
19. Each branch had three flower cups shaped like almond blossoms.
20. The main stem had four cups.
21. One cup was under each pair of branches.
22. It was all one piece of gold.
23. He made seven lamps and gold tools to care for the lamps.
24. It took 75 pounds of pure gold.

The Altar of Incense

25. He made an incense altar of acacia wood—1½ feet square and 3 feet high.
26. He covered it with pure gold—top, sides, and horns—and added a gold strip around it.
27. He made two gold rings for the sides to hold the poles.
28. He made the poles of acacia wood covered with gold.
29. He made the holy anointing oil and the pure incense from special spices.

Exodus 38

Finishing the Altar, Washbasin, Courtyard, and Inventory

1. Bezalel made the altar for burnt offerings from acacia wood—7½ feet wide and long, 4½ feet high.
2. He made horns on each corner from the same wood, covered it all with bronze.
3. He made bronze tools: buckets, shovels, bowls, forks, and firepans.
4. He made a bronze grate under the ledge, halfway up.
5. He cast four bronze rings for the corners to hold poles.
6. He made poles from acacia wood, covered them with bronze,
7. and used them to carry the altar. He made it hollow like a box.

The Washbasin

8. He made a bronze washbasin with a bronze stand from mirrors given by women who served at the tent entrance.

The Courtyard

9. He made a courtyard. The south side had linen curtains 150 feet long
10. with 20 bronze posts and silver hooks and bands.
11. The north side was the same.
12. The west side was 75 feet long with 10 posts.
13. The east side was also 75 feet wide.
14. One side of the gate had a 22½-foot curtain with three posts,
15. the other side was the same.
16. All the curtains were made of fine linen.
17. The bases were bronze; the tops and hooks were silver.
18. The gate curtain was 30 feet wide, made with blue, purple, red yarn and linen, woven by skilled workers.
19. It had four posts and bronze bases, with silver hooks.
20. All tent pegs were bronze.

Inventory of Materials

21. Moses told Ithamar, son of Aaron, to keep a record of everything used.
22. Bezalel made everything just as God commanded.
23. Oholiab helped with the design and needlework.
24. The gold used for the work weighed 2,193 pounds.
25. The silver collected from the people was 7,544 pounds—
26. about 1/5 ounce per man, 603,550 men in total.
27. 100 silver bases were made from it—75 pounds each.
28. The rest was used for hooks, tops, and bands for the posts.
29. The bronze weighed 5,310 pounds.
30. It was used for bases, the altar, tools,
31. the posts around the courtyard, and the entrance curtain.

Exodus 39

Making the Priest's Clothes

1. They made special clothes for serving in the holy place, just as God commanded Moses.

The Ephod

2. They made the ephod with gold, blue, purple, red yarn, and linen.
3. Gold was hammered into thin strips and woven into the fabric.
4. 4- 5. It had shoulder straps and a belt, made from the same materials.
5. Onyx stones were set in gold, with names of Israel's sons.
6. The stones were attached to the shoulder straps.

The Chestpiece

7. The chestpiece was made like the ephod—gold, blue, purple, red yarn, and linen.
8. It was square and folded double, 9 inches by 9 inches.
9. They placed four rows of stones:
10. First row—ruby, topaz, beryl;
11. second—turquoise, sapphire, emerald;
12. third—jacinth, agate, amethyst;
13. fourth—chrysolite, onyx, jasper. Each had a tribe's name.
14. They made braided gold chains for it.
15. 16 - 17. They made gold rings and connected them to the ephod and chestpiece.
16. Blue cords tied it securely to the ephod.

Other Clothes

17. They made a blue robe for the ephod.
18. It had a strong collar to keep it from tearing.
19. Around the bottom were pomegranate-shaped yarn decorations
20. and gold bells.
21. The bells and pomegranates went all the way around.
22. They made linen shirts for Aaron and his sons,
23. a turban, caps, and linen underclothes,
24. a sash made with colorful yarn.
25. They made a gold medallion that said "Holy to the Lord."
26. They tied it to the turban with a blue cord.

Work Completed

27. The work on the tent was finished. They did everything as God commanded.
28. They brought everything to Moses: the tent, its parts,
29. coverings, curtain,
30. Ark, Mercy Seat (lid)
31. table, utensils and the bread of the Presence,
32. pure gold lampstand,
33. gold altar, oil, incense,
34. bronze alter, washbasin, courtyard, and ropes—
35. everything needed for the Meeting Tent.
36. Clothes for priest Aaron and his sons, and the holy garments.
37. The Israelites did all the work exactly as God told Moses.
38. Moses inspected everything. He saw it was done right, so he blessed them.

Exodus 40

Setting Up the Tabernacle

1. God told Moses,
2. "Set up the tabernacle on the first day of the first month."
3. "Put the Ark in place and hang the curtain."
4. "Bring in the table, arrange the items, set up the lampstand, and light the lamps."
5. "Place the gold altar and hang the entrance curtain."
6. "Put the altar for burnt offerings in front of the entrance."
7. "Put the washbasin between the tent and altar and fill it with water."

8. "Set up the courtyard and hang its entrance curtain."
9. "Anoint the tabernacle and everything in it with oil to make it holy."
10. "Anoint the altar and tools to make them most holy."
11. "Anoint the washbasin and stand."
12. "Bring Aaron and his sons. Wash them."
13. "Put on Aaron's holy clothes and anoint him as priest."
14. "Do the same for his sons. This will be a lasting rule."
15. "They will be anointed and serve as priests forever."

The Tabernacle Is Set Up

16. Moses did everything just as God commanded.
17. On the first day of the first month, they set it up.
18. Moses built the tent: bases, frames, crossbars, and posts.
19. He spread out the coverings as God said.
20. He put the tablets in the Ark, added poles and the lid.
21. He brought the Ark into the tent and hung the curtain to hide it.

22-23. He set up the table with bread.

24. He placed the lampstand in the tent on the south side.
25. and set up the lamps, as the Lord commanded him.
26. He put the gold altar in front of the curtain
27. and burned incense.
28. He hung the entrance curtain.
29. He placed the altar outside and made burnt offerings.
30. He put the washbasin between the tent and altar.
31. Moses, Aaron, and his sons washed there.
32. They washed whenever they entered the tent or approached the altar, as the Lord commanded.
33. Moses put up the courtyard and the entrance curtain. He finished the work.

God's Glory Fills the Tabernacle

34. Then the cloud covered the tent, and God's glory filled it.
35. Moses couldn't enter because of the cloud.
36. When the cloud lifted, the people moved forward.
37. If it didn't lift, they stayed put.
38. The cloud was over the tent by day, and fire was in it at night for all to see—throughout their journey.

– Leviticus –

God gives laws about worship, purity, and sacrifices to help Israel live as His holy people.

Leviticus 1

Burnt Offerings

1. The Lord spoke to Moses from the Meeting Tent.
2. "Tell the Israelites: When you bring me an offering, use a cow, sheep, or goat.
3. If it's a cow, it must be a young, healthy male. Bring it to the entrance of the Tent to be accepted.
4. Lay your hand on its head. It will be accepted to take away your sin.
5. Kill the bull before the Lord. The priests must splash its blood on all sides of the altar.
6. Skin the bull and cut it into pieces.
7. The priests will put firewood on the altar and start the fire.
8. Then they will place the pieces, including the head and fat, on the fire.
9. Wash the organs and legs. The priest will burn it all. The smell pleases the Lord.

10. If it's a sheep or goat, it must be a healthy male.
11. Kill it on the north side of the altar. The priests will splash its blood on all sides.
12. Cut it into pieces. The priest will place them, including the head and fat, on the fire.
13. Wash the organs and legs. The priest will burn everything. The smell pleases the Lord.
14. If it's a bird, bring a turtledove or young pigeon.
15. The priest will bring it to the altar, twist off its head, and burn it. The blood must be drained on the side of the altar.
16. He must remove the feathers and insides and throw them in the ashes on the east side of the altar.
17. He will tear the bird open by its wings, but not fully apart, and burn it whole. The smell pleases the Lord.

Leviticus 2

Grain Offerings

1. If you give a grain offering, use fine flour. Pour oil on it and add incense.
2. Bring it to the priests. He'll take a handful with oil and incense and burn it. The smell pleases the Lord.
3. The rest belongs to the priests. It is very holy.
4. If you bake it, use fine flour with oil. It can be thin loaves or flat cakes.
5. If you cook it on a griddle, make it from fine flour mixed with oil.
6. Break it into pieces and pour oil on it.
7. If it's cooked in a pan, use fine flour and oil.
8. Bring your grain offering to the priests. He will take it to the altar.
9. He will burn part of it to please the Lord.
10. The rest belongs to the priests. It is holy.
11. Don't use yeast or honey in offerings that are burned.
12. You can offer yeast and honey as firstfruits, but not on the altar.
13. Add salt to every offering. Don't forget it. It shows your promise with God.
14. If you give a firstfruit grain offering, roast the crushed heads of grain.
15. Add oil and incense.
16. The priest will burn part of the crushed grain with oil and incense. It pleases the Lord.

Leviticus 3

Fellowship Offerings

1. If you bring a fellowship offering using a cow, it must be healthy.
2. Lay your hand on its head and kill it at the entrance. The priests will splash its blood on the altar.
3. Offer the fat near the organs,
4. both kidneys, and the fat on them. Remove the liver.
5. The priest will burn it on top of the burnt offering. It pleases the Lord.
6. If your offering is a sheep, it must be healthy.
7. If it's a male or female sheep, lay your hand on its head and kill it.
8. The priests will splash the blood on the altar.
9. Offer the fat, the whole tail, and the fat near the organs.
10. Include the kidneys and liver fat.
11. The priest will burn it. It pleases the Lord.
12. If your offering is a goat,
13. lay your hand on its head and kill it. The priests will splash the blood on the altar.
14. Offer the fat near the organs,

15. both kidneys, and the fat on them. Remove the liver fat.
16. The priest will burn it. It pleases the Lord.
17. This rule lasts forever: never eat fat or blood.

Leviticus 4

Sin Offerings

1. The Lord said to Moses,
2. "Tell the people: If someone sins by accident and breaks a command,
3. and it's the high priest who sins, he must bring a young bull to the Lord.
4. He must bring it to the entrance of the Meeting Tent, lay his hand on it, and kill it.
5. The priest must take some of its blood into the Meeting Tent.
6. Dip his finger in the blood and sprinkle it seven times toward the curtain in front of the Lord.
7. Put some blood on the altar horns inside the Meeting Tent. Pour the rest at the base of the altar for burnt offerings.
8. Then remove all the fat,
9. the kidneys, and the liver fat.
10. Just like in the fellowship offering, burn it on the altar.
11. Take the rest of the bull—hide, meat, and guts—
12. and burn it all outside the camp. It must be burned completely.
13. If the whole community sins by accident,
14. they must bring a young bull when they find out.
15. The leaders will lay their hands on it, then kill it before the Lord.
16. The priest will take some blood into the Meeting Tent,
17. dip his finger, and sprinkle it seven times in front of the curtain.
18. He will put some blood on the altar horns in the Meeting Tent and pour the rest at the base of the altar for burnt offerings.
19. Remove all the fat and burn it.
20. Just like with the high priest's bull, it will make them forgiven.
21. Then take the bull outside the camp and burn it, just like before.
22. If a leader sins by accident,
23. he must bring a healthy male goat when he finds out.
24. Lay his hand on it and kill it at the place where burnt offerings are killed.
25. The priest will put blood on the altar horns and pour the rest at the base.
26. Burn the fat like a fellowship offering. This will make him forgiven.
27. If an ordinary person sins by accident,
28. he must bring a healthy female goat when he finds out.
29. Lay his hand on it and kill it at the place where burnt offerings are killed.
30. The priest will put blood on the altar horns and pour the rest at the base.
31. Burn the fat. The Lord will forgive him.
32. If he brings a lamb instead, it must be healthy.
33. Lay his hand on it and kill it at the place for burnt offerings.
34. The priest will put blood on the altar horns and pour the rest at the base.
35. Remove the fat and burn it like the fellowship offering. The Lord will forgive him.

Leviticus 5

More Sin Offerings

1. If you see something wrong and don't speak up, you are guilty.
2. If you touch something unclean, even by accident, you are guilty.

3. If you make a promise and forget it, you are guilty.
4. If you realize you sinned,
5. you must admit what you did wrong.
6. Bring a female sheep or goat for the sin. The priest will ask God to forgive you.
7. If you can't afford that, bring two doves or pigeons. One is for sin, the other for a burnt offering.
8. The priest will kill the sin bird first, twisting its neck but not pulling it off.
9. Sprinkle some blood on the altar and pour the rest at the base.
10. Then burn the second bird for the burnt offering. You will be forgiven.
11. If you can't afford birds, bring 2 cups of fine flour. Don't add oil or incense.
12. The priest will take a handful and burn it.
13. The rest belongs to the priest. You will be forgiven.
14. The Lord said to Moses,
15. "If someone breaks a holy rule by accident, they must bring a healthy ram as a penalty."
16. "They must also pay back what was taken and add an extra fifth. Give it to the priest."
17. "If someone sins by breaking a command, even if they don't know, they are guilty and must be punished."
18. "Bring a healthy ram. The priest will ask God to forgive you."
19. "It is a penalty offering. You are guilty before the Lord."

Leviticus 6

More Rules for Offerings

1. The Lord told Moses,
2. "If someone lies about something they stole or kept or found,
3. or lies about a promise,
4. they are guilty and must return what was taken."
5. "They must also add one-fifth extra and give it to the owner."
6. "Then they must bring a healthy ram to the priest."
7. "The priest will ask God to forgive them. Then they'll be forgiven."

Burnt Offerings

8. The Lord told Moses,
9. "Tell the priests: The burnt offering must stay on the altar fire all night."
10. "In the morning, the priest must wear linen clothes, clean up the ashes, and put them beside the altar."
11. "Then change clothes and take the ashes outside the camp."
12. "Keep the altar fire burning—it must never go out."
13. "Add wood every morning and burn offerings on it."

Grain Offerings

14. "These are the rules for grain offerings: Aaron's sons must bring it to the altar."
15. "The priest will take a handful and burn it. The smell pleases the Lord."
16. "The rest belongs to the priests. It must be eaten without yeast in the holy area."
17. "It is holy. Don't bake it with yeast."
18. "Only male priests may eat it. It is a lasting rule."

20. Priest's Grain Offering

19. The Lord told Moses,
20. "When a priest is anointed, he must offer a grain offering of 4 cups of flour—half in the morning, half in the evening."
21. "Cook it in a pan with oil and break it into pieces. Offer it to the Lord."
22. "Another priest must offer it if the first one dies. Burn it all."
23. "No one is to eat it."

Sin Offerings

21. The Lord told Moses,
22. "The sin offering must be killed at the same place as the burnt offering."
23. "The priest who offers it may eat it in the holy area."
24. "Anything that touches the meat becomes holy. If blood splashes on clothes, wash them in the holy area."
25. "If it's cooked in a clay pot, break the pot. If in a bronze pot, clean and rinse it."
26. "Only male priests may eat it. It is holy."
27. "But if the blood is taken into the Meeting Tent, the meat must not be eaten. Burn it."

Leviticus 7

Rules for Offerings

1. "These are the rules for the penalty offering. It is very holy.
2. Kill it where burnt offerings are killed. Splash its blood on the altar.
3. Offer all the fat—the tail, fat near organs,
4. kidneys, and liver fat.
5. Burn it all on the altar."
6. "Only male priests may eat it in the holy area."
7. "The sin and penalty offering are alike. The priest who offers it keeps the meat."
8. "The priest also keeps the skin of any burnt offering he makes."
9. "Every grain offering cooked in a pan belongs to the priest who offers it."
10. "But all priests share offerings not baked."

Fellowship Offerings

11. "These are the rules for fellowship offerings."
12. "If you bring it to give thanks, add bread without yeast and with oil, and flat bread brushed with oil."
13. "Also bring yeast bread with your offering."
14. "One piece goes to the priest. The rest belongs to the one giving the offering."
15. "Eat all the meat the same day. Don't save any."
16. "If it's for a vow or gift, eat it the same day and the next.
17. But burn anything left on the third day."
18. "If you eat it on the third day, it won't be accepted. It will be unclean."
19. "Don't eat meat that touches anything unclean. Burn it."
20. "Anyone who eats unclean meat is guilty and must be cut off."
21. "Anyone who touches something unclean and then eats fellowship meat must be cut off."

Don't Eat Fat or Blood

22. The Lord told Moses,
23. "Tell the people: Don't eat fat from cows, sheep, or goats.
24. You may use fat from dead animals, but don't eat it.
25. If you eat it, you will be cut off."
26. "Don't eat blood from any animal or bird."
27. "Anyone who does will be cut off."

Portions for Priests

28. The Lord told Moses,
29. "When you bring a fellowship offering, give part to the Lord."
30. "Bring it yourself. The fat and breast go to the Lord."
31. "The priest burns the fat. The breast belongs to Aaron and his sons."
32. "Give the right thigh to the priest."
33. "It goes to the one who offered the blood and fat."

34. "I have given the breast and thigh from Israel's offerings to the priests forever."

35. "This is what they get for serving me at the Meeting Tent."

36. "I gave it to them on the day they were anointed. This is a lasting rule."

Summary of Offerings

37. "These are the rules for burnt, grain, sin, penalty, ordination, and fellowship offerings."

38. "The Lord gave them to Moses on Mount Sinai to tell the Israelites."

Leviticus 8

Aaron and His Sons Are Made Priests

1. The Lord said to Moses,

2. "Bring Aaron and his sons, the clothes, oil, the bull, two rams, and the basket of bread."

3. "Call everyone to the Meeting Tent."

4. Moses did as the Lord said. Everyone came and stood at the entrance.

5. Moses said, "This is what the Lord has told us to do."

6. He washed Aaron and his sons with water.

7. He dressed Aaron in the robe, belt, and ephod.

8. He put on the chestpiece and Urim and Thummim.

9. He put the turban and the gold crown on his head.

10. Moses poured oil on the Meeting Tent and everything in it to make it holy.

11. He sprinkled oil on the altar and its tools, the washbasin, and its stand.

12. He poured oil on Aaron's head to make him holy.

13. He dressed Aaron's sons with robes, belts, and caps.

14. Moses brought the bull for the sin offering. Aaron and his sons laid hands on its head.

15. Moses killed it. He put blood on the altar horns and poured the rest at the base.

16. He burned the fat and organs.

17. He burned the rest outside the camp.

18. He brought the ram for the burnt offering. They laid hands on it.

19. He killed it and splashed the blood on all sides of the altar.

20. He cut it into pieces and burned them all.

21. He washed the organs and legs and burned them too. It was a burnt offering that pleased the Lord.

22. He brought the second ram, the ordination ram. They laid hands on it.

23. Moses killed it. He put blood on Aaron's right ear, thumb, and big toe.

24. He did the same for Aaron's sons.

25. He burned the fat, tail, organs, kidneys, and liver fat.

26. He took bread from the basket and placed it with the fat and thigh.

27. He put it all in Aaron's hands and his sons' hands to offer to the Lord.

28. Then Moses burned it all on the altar.

29. He gave the breast to himself, as the Lord commanded.

30. He sprinkled oil and blood on Aaron and his sons and their clothes.

31. He told them, "Boil the meat at the Meeting Tent entrance and eat it with the bread.

32. Burn what's left."

33. "Stay at the entrance for 7 days until your time of service is complete."

34. "This is what the Lord commanded, so you will be forgiven."

35. "Stay day and night at the Meeting Tent entrance."

36. Aaron and his sons did everything the Lord told them.

Leviticus 9

Aaron Begins His Work

1. On the 8th day, Moses called Aaron, his sons, and the elders.
2. He said, "Bring a bull for a sin offering and a ram for a burnt offering."
3. "Tell the people to bring a male goat, a calf, and a lamb for burnt offerings, plus an ox and ram for peace offerings and a grain offering."
4. "The Lord will appear to you today."
5. They brought everything to the Meeting Tent.
6. Moses said, "This is what God commands. If you obey, His glory will appear."
7. He told Aaron, "Come to the altar. Offer your sin and burnt offerings to be forgiven."
8. Aaron offered the bull for his sin.
9. His sons gave him the blood. He dipped his finger in it and put it on the altar horns. He poured the rest at the base.
10. He burned the fat and organs.
11. He burned the rest of the bull outside the camp.
12. Then he offered the burnt offering.
13. His sons gave him the pieces, and he burned them.
14. He washed the organs and legs and burned them too.
15. Then he brought the people's offering—the goat for sin—and killed it.
16. He offered the burnt offering as ordered.
17. He brought the grain offering, took a handful, and burned it.
18. He killed the ox and ram for peace offerings. His sons gave him the blood, and he splashed it on the altar.
19. He gave them the fat and organs.
20. They laid it on top of the breast meat, and Aaron burned it.
21. He waved the breast and right thigh as an offering.
22. Aaron raised his hands and blessed the people. He came down from the altar.
23. Moses and Aaron went into the Meeting Tent, then came out and blessed the people. God's glory appeared.
24. Fire came from the Lord and burned the offering. The people shouted and fell face down.

Leviticus 10

Nadab and Abihu Die

1. Aaron's sons Nadab and Abihu used their own fire and burned incense. This was not what God told them to do.
2. So God sent fire and killed them.
3. Moses said, "This is what God meant: 'I must be treated as holy.'" Aaron stayed silent.
4. Moses told Mishael and Elzaphan, "Come get the bodies and carry them outside the camp."
5. They came and carried them out in their clothes.
6. Moses told Aaron and his other sons, "Don't tear your clothes or mourn. Don't leave the Meeting Tent or you will die. Let the people mourn."
7. "You must stay near the Meeting Tent because you were anointed."
8. The Lord said to Aaron,
9. "You and your sons must never drink wine or alcohol when entering the Meeting Tent, or you will die."
10. "You must know the difference between clean and unclean."
11. "Teach the people all the Lord's commands."
12. Moses told Aaron and his sons, "Eat the grain offering beside the altar. It's holy."

13. "Eat it in the holy place. It's your share."
14. "You and your families may eat the breast and thigh in a clean place."
15. "These parts were given to you by the people."
16. Moses looked for the goat of the sin offering and found it was burned. He got angry with Eleazar and Ithamar.
17. He asked, "Why didn't you eat it in the holy place? It was holy and for your forgiveness."
18. "Its blood wasn't taken into the Meeting Tent, so you should've eaten it."
19. Aaron said, "Today they offered their sin and burnt offerings, but with what happened, would the Lord have accepted it?"
20. Moses heard this and was satisfied.

Leviticus 11

Clean and Unclean Animals

1. The Lord told Moses and Aaron,
2. "Tell the people: These are the animals you can eat from those on the land."
3. "You may eat animals that have split hooves and chew their food again."

4-6. "Don't eat camels, rock badgers, or rabbits. They chew food again but don't have split hooves."

7. "Don't eat pigs. They have split hooves but don't chew food again."
8. "Don't eat their meat or touch their dead bodies. They are unclean."
9. "You may eat animals in water that have fins and scales."
10. "Don't eat things in water without fins and scales. They are unclean."
11. "Don't eat or touch them."
12. "They are unclean."
13. "These birds are unclean: eagles, vultures,
14. black vultures,
15. kites, falcons,
16. ravens,
17. owls, seagulls, hawks,
18. screech owls, cormorants,
19. storks, herons, hoopoes, and bats."
20. "Don't eat flying insects that walk on four legs."

21-22. "You may eat winged insects with jointed legs for hopping—like locusts and grasshoppers."

23. "All other flying insects are unclean."
24. "If you touch any of these dead animals, you become unclean."
25. "If you carry their body, you must wash your clothes and stay unclean until evening."
26. "Animals with only one clean feature are unclean."
27. "Animals that walk on paws are unclean. Don't touch their bodies."
28. "Wash your clothes and stay unclean until evening."
29. "These crawling animals are unclean: weasels, rats, lizards,
30. geckos, monitors, wall lizards, skinks, and chameleons."
31. "Whoever touches their bodies is unclean until evening."
32. "If any fall on something, it becomes unclean—like clothes, clay pots, or tools."
33. "Clay pots must be broken."
34. "Food or drink touched by these animals becomes unclean."
35. "If any part of their body falls on an oven, break it."
36. "Water springs and wells remain clean, but anything they touch becomes unclean."
37. "If one falls on seeds, the seeds stay clean."
38. "But if the seeds are wet, they become unclean."

39. "If a clean animal dies, anyone who touches it becomes unclean."
40. "Whoever eats it must wash their clothes and stay unclean until evening."
41. "Don't eat any crawling animal. They are unclean."
42. "Don't eat animals that crawl on their belly or walk on many legs."
43. "Don't make yourselves unclean."
44. "I am the Lord. Be holy because I am holy."
45. "I brought you out of Egypt. Be holy."
46. "These are the rules for animals, birds, water creatures, and crawlers."
47. "They help you know what is clean and unclean."

Leviticus 12

Rules for New Mothers

1. The Lord told Moses,
2. "Tell the people: A woman is unclean for 7 days after giving birth to a boy, just like during her monthly time."
3. "On day 8, the boy must be circumcised."
4. "Then the mother must wait 33 more days to be fully clean."
5. "If she has a girl, she is unclean for 14 days, then waits 66 days."
6. "After this, she must bring a year-old lamb for a burnt offering and a dove or pigeon for a sin offering to the priest at the Meeting Tent."
7. "The priest will offer them to make her clean. She will be forgiven."
8. "If she can't afford a lamb, bring two doves or two pigeons."

Leviticus 13

Skin Diseases and Mold

1. The Lord told Moses and Aaron,
2. "If someone has a sore, rash, or spot, they must be brought to Aaron or a priest."
3. "The priest will examine the sore. If the hair has turned white and the sore goes deep, it's a skin disease. The person is unclean."
4. "If the sore is only on the surface, isolate them for 7 days."
5. "Check again on day 7. If it hasn't spread, isolate them 7 more days."
6. "If it hasn't spread after 14 days, it's just a rash. They are clean."
7. "But if it spreads, the person is unclean."
8. "Let the priest decide."
9. "If someone has a skin disease,
10. and the sore is white with raw skin,
11. it's an old infection. The person is unclean."
12. "If the disease spreads all over the body,
13. the person is clean. It has become all white."
14. "But if raw flesh appears, they are unclean."
15. "The priest must declare them unclean."
16. "If the raw turns white again, they must return to the priest."
17. "If it's turned white, they are clean."
18. "If someone has a boil that heals,
19. but leaves a white spot or red patch,
20. the priest must check it. If hair turns white and it goes deep, it's a disease."
21. "If it's just on the surface and not spreading, it's only a scar."
22. "If it spreads, it's a disease."
23. "If it stays the same, it's just a scar."
24. "If a person gets a burn and it turns red or white,
25. and the hair turns white or it goes deep, it's a disease."

26. "If it's just on the surface, it's only a burn scar."
27. "If it spreads, it's a disease."
28. "If it stays the same, it's just a scar."
29. "If someone has a sore on the head or beard,
30. and the hair is thin and yellow, it's a disease."
31. "If there's no yellow hair or spreading, isolate them for 7 days."

32-34. "Check on day 7. If it hasn't spread and no yellow hair, shave the area and isolate again."

35. "If after 14 days it hasn't spread, it's clean."
36. "If it spreads, it's a disease."
37. "The priest doesn't need to look for yellow hair—it's already unclean."
38. "If the sore doesn't spread and black hair grows, the person is clean."
39. "If white spots appear on the skin,
40. and they are dull, it's not a disease."
41. "A bald man is clean."
42. "If he loses hair in the front, he is still clean."
43. "But if a red sore appears on the bald area, it's a disease."
44. "The priest must check."
45. "If the sore is red and deep, he is unclean."
46. "He must wear torn clothes, keep his hair messy, cover his mouth, and shout 'Unclean! Unclean!'"
47. "He must live alone outside the camp."
48. "If mold appears in clothing made of wool or linen,
49. or woven fabric or leather,
50. and the spot is green or red,
51. the priest must isolate it for 7 days."
52. "If the mold has spread, it is unclean."
53. "The item must be burned."
54. "If it hasn't spread,
55. wash it and isolate it 7 more days."
56. "If the mold is still there, burn it."
57. "If the mold fades, cut out the spot."
58. "If it comes back, burn it."
59. "If not, wash it again and it is clean."
60. "These are the rules for clothing with mold."

Leviticus 14

Cleaning a Person or House with a Skin Disease

1. The Lord told Moses,
2. "These are the rules for someone healed from a skin disease. They must be brought to the priest."
3. "The priest goes outside the camp to check the person. If they are healed,
4. the priest will order two clean birds, cedar wood, red yarn, and hyssop."
5. "One bird is killed over a bowl of fresh water.
6. Dip the live bird, wood, yarn, and hyssop in the blood and water."
7. "Sprinkle the person seven times. Let the live bird go free."
8. "The person must wash their clothes, shave, and bathe. Then they can enter the camp but stay outside their tent for 7 days."
9. "On day 7, they must shave everything again and bathe."
10. "On day 8, bring two lambs and a year-old ewe, plus grain and oil."
11. "The priest presents them at the entrance of the Meeting Tent."
12. "He offers one lamb as a guilt offering with oil."
13. "He kills the lamb where the sin offering is killed."
14. "He puts blood on the person's right ear, thumb, and big toe."
15. "He pours some oil into his hand,

16. dips his finger in it, and sprinkles it seven times before the Lord."
17. "He puts oil on the person's right ear, thumb, and big toe—on top of the blood."
18. "He puts the rest on the person's head."
19. "He makes a sin offering to forgive the person."
20. "He also offers the burnt and grain offerings. The person is clean."
21. "If the person is poor, they may bring one lamb, some flour with oil, and two doves or pigeons."
22. "One bird is for sin and the other for a burnt offering."
23. "Bring it all to the priest on day 8 at the Meeting Tent."
24. "The priest makes the guilt offering and offers oil to the Lord."
25. "He puts the blood on the right ear, thumb, and big toe."
26. "He pours oil into his hand,
27. sprinkles it seven times,
28. and puts it on the person like before."
29. "The rest goes on their head."
30. "He sacrifices the birds."
31. "One for sin, one for burnt. The person is forgiven and clean."
32. "These are the rules for people who are poor and healed."
33. The Lord told Moses and Aaron,
34. "When you enter Canaan, I may send mold into a house."
35. "The owner must tell the priest, 'It looks unclean.'"
36. "Before checking, the priest empties the house."
37. "If the mold is green or red and deep,
38. the priest locks the house for 7 days."
39. "He checks it again. If it spread,
40. the stones must be removed and thrown outside the camp."
41. "Scrape the walls and throw away the dust."
42. "Replace the stones and plaster."
43. "If the mold comes back,
44. it is unclean. Tear down the house."
45. "Take the materials outside the camp."
46. "Anyone who goes inside is unclean until evening."
47. "Anyone who sleeps or eats there must wash clothes."
48. "If the mold hasn't spread, the house is clean."
49. "To clean it, use two birds, cedar wood, red yarn, and hyssop."
50. "Kill one bird over fresh water."
51. "Dip the live bird, wood, yarn, and hyssop in the blood and sprinkle it seven times."
52. "This will clean the house."
53. "Let the live bird go free."
54. "These are the rules for skin diseases, rashes, mold,
55. clothing, and houses.
56. These help know what is clean or unclean."

Leviticus 15

Rules About Body Fluids

1. The Lord told Moses and Aaron,
2. "If a man has a discharge, he is unclean."
3. "Whether it flows or is blocked, he is still unclean."
4. "Anything he lies or sits on becomes unclean."
5. "Whoever touches it must wash clothes, bathe, and stay unclean until evening."
6. "Same rule for anyone who sits where he sat."
7. "Whoever touches him must wash and stay unclean."

8. "If he spits on someone, they are unclean."
9. "Any saddle he sits on is unclean."
10. "Touching anything under him makes you unclean."
11. "If he touches someone without washing, that person is unclean."
12. "Clay pots he touches must be broken. Wood items must be washed."
13. "When the discharge ends, wait 7 days and wash."
14. "On day 8, bring two birds to the priest at the Meeting Tent."
15. "He will sacrifice them for forgiveness."
16. "If a man has a release of semen, he must wash and stay unclean until evening."
17. "Clothes or blankets touched must be washed."
18. "If a man and woman have sex, they must wash and are unclean until evening."
19. "If a woman bleeds during her period, she is unclean for 7 days."
20. "Anything she lies or sits on is unclean."
21. "Anyone who touches it must wash and stay unclean."
22. "Same rule for sitting on her seat."
23. "Touching her bed makes you unclean until evening."
24. "If a man has sex with her, he is unclean for 7 days."
25. "If bleeding lasts longer than normal, she is unclean the whole time."
26. "Everything she touches is unclean."
27. "Whoever touches her must wash and stay unclean."
28. "When bleeding stops, wait 7 days and wash."
29. "On day 8, bring two birds to the priest at the Meeting Tent."
30. "He will offer them for forgiveness."
31. "Keep the people from becoming unclean or they will die for making my holy place unclean."
32. "These are the rules for men and women with discharges or during a woman's period."
33. "Also for men who have a release and women who bleed outside their period."

Leviticus 16

The Day of Atonement (Yom Kippur)

1. After Aaron's two sons died, the Lord said,
2. "Tell Aaron not to enter the Most Holy Place anytime he wants. I appear in a cloud over the lid."
3. "He must bring a bull for sin and a ram for burnt offering."
4. "He must wear holy linen clothes and wash before putting them on."
5. "From the people, take two male goats for sin and one ram for burnt offering."
6. "Aaron offers the bull for his own sin."
7. "Bring the two goats to the Meeting Tent entrance."
8. "Cast lots—one for the Lord, one for the scapegoat."
9. "Sacrifice the goat for the Lord."
10. "The scapegoat is sent into the wilderness."
11. "Aaron sacrifices the bull for his sins."
12. "He takes burning coals and incense inside the veil."
13. "He puts incense on the fire so the smoke covers the Ark."
14. "He sprinkles bull's blood on the front and top of the Ark."
15. "Then he kills the goat for the people's sin and sprinkles its blood the same way."
16. "He makes the holy place clean from people's sins."

17. "No one else can enter the Meeting Tent."
18. "He also puts blood on the altar horns."
19. "He sprinkles it seven times to make it clean."
20. "When finished, he places both hands on the scapegoat's head."
21. "He confesses all sins and sends it into the desert."
22. "The goat carries the sins away."
23. "Aaron goes into the Meeting Tent, removes his clothes,
24. bathes, and puts on his regular clothes."
25. "He offers his and the people's burnt offerings."
26. "The man who released the goat must wash and change clothes before returning."
27. "The bull and goat's remains must be burned outside the camp."
28. "The person who burns them must wash and change clothes."
29. "Celebrate this every year. Don't eat or work. It's a lasting rule."
30. "On this day, you will be made clean from all your sins."
31. "It is a holy day of rest."
32. "The priest will do this each year for people's sins."
33. "He makes everything clean: the holy tent, altar, priests, and people."
34. "This rule lasts forever."

Leviticus 17

Rules About Sacrifices and Blood

1. The Lord told Moses,
2. "Tell Aaron, his sons, and all the Israelites these rules."
3. "If anyone kills a cow, sheep, or goat
4. and doesn't bring it to the Meeting Tent, they are guilty of murder. They must be cut off."
5. "They must bring the animal to the priest at the Meeting Tent to be offered to the Lord."
6. "The priest will splash the blood on the altar and burn the fat. This pleases the Lord."
7. "They must not offer sacrifices to goat idols anymore. This rule lasts forever."
8. "Anyone offering a burnt or peace offering
9. must bring it to the Meeting Tent. If not, they must be cut off."
10. "If anyone eats blood, I will turn against them and cut them off."
11. "Life is in the blood. I gave it to you to make you clean through sacrifices."
12. "That's why no one may eat blood."
13. "If you hunt an animal or bird, drain the blood and cover it with dirt."
14. "Blood is life. Don't eat it."
15. "If you eat meat from a dead or torn animal, wash and stay unclean until evening."
16. "If not, you are guilty."

Leviticus 18

Don't Follow Bad Customs

1. The Lord told Moses,
2. "Tell the Israelites: I am the Lord your God.
3. Don't live like the Egyptians or Canaanites. Don't follow their ways."
4. "Obey my laws."
5. "Follow my commands and you will live."
6. "Don't have sex with close family."
7. "Don't have sex with your mother."
8. "Don't have sex with your stepmother."

9. "Don't have sex with your sister or half-sister."
10. "Don't have sex with your granddaughter."
11. "Don't have sex with your stepsister."
12. "Don't have sex with your aunt."
13. "Don't have sex with your father's sister."
14. "Don't have sex with your uncle's wife."
15. "Don't have sex with your daughter-in-law."
16. "Don't have sex with your brother's wife."
17. "Don't have sex with a woman and her daughter or granddaughter."
18. "Don't marry a woman and her sister while both are alive."
19. "Don't have sex with a woman during her period."
20. "Don't sleep with another man's wife."
21. "Don't give your children to Molech."
22. "Don't have sex with another man."
23. "Don't have sex with animals."
24. "Don't make yourselves unclean like the other nations."
25. "They made the land unclean, and I punished them."
26. "Obey my laws."
27. "All these sins are what made the land unclean."
28. "If you do the same, the land will reject you too."
29. "Anyone who does these things must be cut off."
30. "Obey me and don't follow their evil customs."

Leviticus 19

Be Holy

1. The Lord told Moses,
2. "Tell the people: Be holy, because I am holy."
3. "Respect your parents and keep the Sabbath."
4. "Don't worship idols."
5. "If you bring a peace offering, do it the right way."
6. "Eat it the same day or next. Burn leftovers on day 3."
7. "If you eat it after that, it's wrong."
8. "Anyone who does must be cut off."
9. "Leave some crops for the poor and foreigners."
10. "Don't pick every grape. Leave some for the poor."
11. "Don't steal or lie."
12. "Don't use my name to lie or swear."
13. "Don't cheat or rob anyone."
14. "Don't make fun of the deaf or blind."
15. "Judge fairly. Don't favor the rich or poor."
16. "Don't spread gossip. Don't let someone die if you can help."
17. "Don't hate others. Correct them if needed."
18. "Don't try to get even. Love others like yourself."
19. "Obey my rules: Don't mix animals, seeds, or fabrics."
20. "If a slave woman is promised to a man and sleeps with someone else, punish them, but not with death."
21. "Bring a ram to the Meeting Tent."
22. "The priest will offer it and you will be forgiven."
23. "Don't eat fruit from a new tree for three years."
24. "On year four, give the fruit to the Lord."
25. "Eat it on year five."
26. "Don't eat meat with blood or use magic."

27. "Don't shave your head or beard in strange ways."
28. "Don't cut your body or get tattoos for the dead."
29. "Don't make your daughter a prostitute."
30. "Keep the Sabbath and respect my holy place."
31. "Don't go to witches or fortune-tellers."
32. "Stand up for the elderly."
33. "Don't be mean to foreigners."
34. "Love them like yourself."
35. "Be honest in business."
36. "Use fair weights and measures."
37. "Obey all my rules."

Leviticus 20

Punishments for Sin

1. The Lord told Moses,
2. "Tell the people: If anyone gives their child to Molech, they must die."
3. "I will turn against them."
4. "If people ignore it,
5. I will turn against their whole family."
6. "If someone goes to witches, I will turn against them."
7. "Be holy, because I am your God."
8. "Obey my laws."
9. "Anyone who curses their parents must die."
10. "If a man sleeps with another man's wife, they both must die."
11. "If a man sleeps with his stepmother, they both must die."
12. "If a man sleeps with his daughter-in-law, they both must die."
13. "If a man sleeps with another man, they must die."
14. "If a man marries a woman and her mother, all must be burned."
15. "If a man has sex with an animal, kill both him and the animal."
16. "If a woman does, kill them both."
17. "If someone sleeps with a sibling, they are guilty."
18. "If a man sleeps with a woman during her period, they are unclean."
19. "Don't have sex with your aunt or uncle's wife."
20. "Don't sleep with your uncle's wife."
21. "Don't sleep with your sister-in-law."
22. "Obey my laws so the land won't throw you out."
23. "Don't follow the ways of the nations I'm removing."
24. "I've given you the land. Be different from them."
25. "Separate clean and unclean animals."
26. "You must be holy because I, the Lord, am holy."
27. "Anyone who uses magic or talks to spirits must be put to death."

Leviticus 21

Rules for Priests

1. The Lord told Moses, "Tell the priests: Don't make yourselves unclean by touching a dead body."
2. "Except for close family: mother, father, son, daughter, brother,
3. or an unmarried sister still living at home."
4. "Don't make yourself unclean for relatives by marriage."
5. "Don't shave your head, trim your beard weirdly, or cut your body."
6. "Be holy. You offer food to the Lord, so don't dishonor His name."
7. "Don't marry a woman who is a prostitute or divorced."
8. "Stay holy, because you offer food to God."

9. "If a priest's daughter becomes a prostitute, she brings shame and must be burned."
10. "The high priest must not let his hair go messy or tear his clothes."
11. "He must not go near a dead body—not even for family."
12. "He must stay near the Meeting Tent and not leave."
13. "He must marry a virgin."
14. "Not a widow, divorced woman, or prostitute."
15. "He must keep his children pure."
16. The Lord said to Moses,
17. "Tell Aaron: If a priest has a defect, he can't offer food to God."
18. "No one who is blind, lame, deformed,
19. has a broken foot or hand,
20. a hunchback, dwarf, eye problem, skin disease, or damaged genitals—
21. may not serve at the altar."
22. "He may eat the holy food
23. but may not go near the curtain or altar."
24. Moses told this to Aaron and his sons.

Leviticus 22

More Rules for Priests

1. The Lord told Moses,
2. "Tell Aaron and his sons to treat my holy gifts with respect."
3. "If a priest touches something unclean, he must not eat the holy food or he will be cut off."
4. "If a priest has a skin disease or discharge, he may not eat the holy food until he is clean."
5. "If he touches something dead,
6. or something unclean, he stays unclean until evening and must wash."
7. "Then he may eat the holy food."
8. "He must not eat anything found dead or torn by animals."
9. "They must obey these rules or they'll be guilty."
10. "No one outside a priest's family may eat the holy food."
11. "But a slave bought by a priest may eat it."
12. "If a priest's daughter marries a non-priest, she may not eat holy food."
13. "But if she becomes a widow or is divorced and has no children, she may return and eat again."
14. "If someone eats the holy food by mistake, they must pay back the amount plus 20%."
15. "The people must not treat holy offerings as unclean."
16. "If they do, they will be guilty."
17. The Lord told Moses,
18. "Tell Aaron, his sons, and all the people: If you bring an offering to the Lord,
19. it must be a healthy male animal."
20. "Don't bring anything with a defect."
21. "Peace offerings must be perfect to be accepted."
22. "Don't offer animals that are blind, injured, or have sores."
23. "You may give one with a short or long leg, but not as a vow."
24. "Don't offer animals whose parts were damaged or removed."
25. "Don't accept damaged animals from foreigners."
26. The Lord told Moses,
27. "A newborn animal must stay with its mother for 7 days. On day 8, it can be offered."
28. "Don't kill a mother and baby animal on the same day."
29. "If you bring a thank offering, do it the right way."

30. "Eat it the same day. Don't leave leftovers."
31. "Obey my commands."
32. "Don't dishonor my holy name."
33. "I brought you out of Egypt. I am the Lord."

Leviticus 23

The Lord's Special Days

1. The Lord told Moses,
2. "Tell the people: These are my special days. You must rest and worship."
3. "Work for six days, but the seventh day is a Sabbath. Don't work. It's for worship."
4. "These are my festivals:"
5. "Passover starts on the 14th day of the first month at sunset."
6. "The Festival of Unleavened Bread begins the next day. Eat bread without yeast for 7 days."
7. "Rest on the first day and meet together."
8. "Bring offerings each day. Rest again on the seventh day."
9. The Lord told Moses,
10. "When you enter the land and harvest crops, bring the first bundle to the priest."
11. "He will lift it up to me the day after the Sabbath."
12. "Also bring a year-old lamb as a burnt offering."
13. "Bring flour and oil for a grain offering, and wine for a drink offering."
14. "Don't eat any grain until you bring this offering."
15. "Count 7 full weeks from the day after the Sabbath."
16. "On day 50, bring a new grain offering."
17. "Bring two loaves of bread made with yeast from your homes."
18. "Also bring seven lambs, one bull, and two rams. These are burnt offerings."
19. "Bring a goat for a sin offering and two lambs for a peace offering."
20. "The priest will lift them up to the Lord."
21. "Rest on this day. It's a lasting rule."
22. "Leave some crops in your field for the poor and foreigners."
23. The Lord told Moses,
24. "On the first day of the seventh month, rest and blow trumpets."
25. "Bring offerings and don't work."
26. The Lord told Moses,
27. "On the 10th day of the seventh month is the Day of Atonement."
28. "Rest and bring offerings. Don't work."
29. "Anyone who doesn't fast must be cut off."
30. "Anyone who works must be removed."
31. "This rule lasts forever."
32. "It's a day of complete rest. Start at sunset the day before."
33. The Lord told Moses,
34. "The Festival of Shelters begins on the 15th day of the seventh month. It lasts 7 days."
35. "Rest and meet on the first day."
36. "Bring offerings for 7 days. On day 8, rest and meet again."
37. "These are my special days. Bring burnt, grain, peace, and drink offerings."
38. "These are in addition to your regular offerings."
39. "On the 15th day, after the harvest, celebrate for 7 days."
40. "Take palm branches and other leaves. Celebrate with joy."

41. "Do this each year. It's a lasting rule."
42. "Live in shelters for 7 days."
43. "This reminds you that I made Israel live in shelters when I brought them out of Egypt."
44. Moses told the people about these special days.

Leviticus 24

More Laws and a Warning

1. The Lord told Moses,
2. "Tell the people to bring pure olive oil to keep the lamp burning."
3. "Aaron must keep it lit in the Meeting Tent every night."
4. "He will set up the lamps on the gold lampstand."
5. "Take fine flour and bake 12 loaves."
6. "Put them in two stacks of six on the gold table."
7. "Add pure incense to each stack. It's a gift to me."
8. "Every Sabbath, replace the bread. It belongs to Aaron and his sons."
9. "They will eat it in the holy place."
10. A man with an Israelite mother and Egyptian father got in a fight.
11. He cursed God's name. The people brought him to Moses. His mother was Shelomith.
12. They kept him under guard until the Lord gave a ruling.
13. The Lord told Moses,
14. "Take the man outside the camp. Everyone who heard him must touch his head. Then the people must stone him."
15. "Anyone who curses God must be punished."
16. "Anyone who curses my name must be stoned."
17. "Anyone who kills a person must die."
18. "Anyone who kills an animal must pay for it."
19. "If you hurt someone, you will be hurt the same way:
20. an eye for an eye, a tooth for a tooth."
21. "Kill anyone who kills another person."
22. "These laws are the same for everyone."
23. Moses told the people. They took the man outside and stoned him.

Leviticus 25

The Sabbath Year and Year of Freedom

1. The Lord told Moses on Mount Sinai,
2. "Tell the people: When you enter the land, let it rest every 7th year."
3. "Plant your fields and harvest for 6 years."
4. "In year 7, don't plant or prune. Let the land rest."
5. "Don't harvest what grows on its own."
6. "The land's food is for everyone: you, your workers, your animals."
7. "Count 7 Sabbath years—49 years."
8. "On the 10th day of the 7th month, blow a trumpet."
9. "Make the 50th year holy. Free everyone and return land to its owner."
10. "Don't plant or harvest."
11. "Eat only what grows on its own."
12. "Everyone must return to their land."
13. "Be fair when selling or buying."
14. "Prices depend on years left until the 50th year."
15. "More years means a higher price; fewer years means lower."
16. "Don't cheat each other."
17. "Obey my laws, and you'll live safely."
18. "You'll eat well and live without fear."

19. "If you ask, 'What will we eat in year 7?'
20. I'll bless you with three times more in year 6."
21. "You'll eat from it until new crops grow."
22. "The land belongs to me. You are just my guests."
23. "You must give land back in the 50th year."
24. "If someone becomes poor and sells land, a family member can buy it back."
25. "If he gets rich, he can buy it back himself."
26. "Pay for the years left."
27. "If not, it returns to him in the 50th year."
28. "If you sell a house in a walled city, you have 1 year to buy it back."
29. "If not, it stays with the buyer."
30. "Homes in villages can always be bought back and return in the 50th year."
31. "Levites can always buy back their homes."
32. "Their houses go back to them in the 50th year."
33. "Levite fields must never be sold. They belong to them forever."
34. "If someone becomes poor, help them like a neighbor."
35. "Don't charge interest or try to profit."
36. "Don't charge for food or loans."
37. "I am the Lord who brought you from Egypt."
38. "If an Israelite becomes your slave, don't treat them harshly."
39. "They must serve you until the 50th year."
40. "Then they and their children are free."
41. "They are my servants, not to be sold as slaves."
42. "Don't be cruel."
43. "You may have slaves from other nations,
44. including people born in your land."
45. "They can be passed down, but don't treat Israelites like that."
46. "If a foreigner gets rich and buys an Israelite,
47. their family can buy them back."
48. "Or they can buy their own freedom."
49. "Count the years left and pay fairly."
50. "Pay based on time left."
51. "If few years remain, pay less."
52. "Don't treat them harshly."
53. "If not bought back, they go free in the 50th year."
54. "All Israelites are my servants."

Leviticus 26

Blessings and Punishments

1. "Don't make idols or statues. Don't bow down to them. I am the Lord."
2. "Respect my Sabbaths and honor my holy place. I am the Lord."
3. "If you obey my rules,
4. I will send rain, and crops will grow.
5. You'll have more than enough food and live safely.
6. I'll bring peace. No wild animals or enemies will hurt you.
7. You will defeat your enemies.
8. Five of you will chase a hundred. A hundred will chase ten thousand.
9. I'll bless you and give you many children.
10. You'll still have food left over when the new harvest comes.
11. I will live among you.
12. I will walk with you and be your God.
13. I brought you out of Egypt. You are free."

14. "But if you disobey me and ignore my commands,
15. and reject my rules,
16. I will punish you with fear, disease, and hunger.
17. Your enemies will defeat you.
18. If you still don't listen, I'll punish you 7 times more.
19. I'll break your pride and stop the rain.
20. Your land won't grow crops."
21. "If you keep disobeying,
22. I'll send wild animals. They'll kill your children and animals."
23. "If that doesn't change you,
24. I'll punish you 7 more times.
25. I'll send enemies with swords and diseases.
26. You'll be so hungry that 10 women will bake bread in one oven."
27. "If you still won't listen,
28. I'll punish you 7 more times with anger.
29. You'll be so hungry you'll eat your own children."
30. "I'll destroy your places of worship.
31. Your cities will be empty.
32. The land will become a waste."
33. "I'll scatter you in other nations."
34. "Then the land will enjoy its Sabbaths while you're gone.
35. It will rest every year you ignored."
36. "Those who survive will live in fear in foreign lands.
37. They'll panic even when no one chases them."
38. "You will be lost among other nations.
39. You'll waste away for your sins."
40. "But if you admit your sins and your ancestors' sins,
41. and if you humble yourselves,
42. I will remember my promise to Abraham, Isaac, and Jacob.
43. The land will rest, but I won't forget you.
44. Even if you are in enemy lands, I won't reject you.
45. I will remember my promise. I am the Lord."
46. These are the laws God gave Moses for the Israelites.

Leviticus 27

Promises and Payments to the Lord

1. The Lord told Moses,
2. "Tell the people: If anyone makes a special promise to give something to me, here are the values:"
3. "A man 20–60 years old = 50 silver coins."
4. "A woman = 30 silver coins."
5. "A boy 5–20 years = 20 coins. A girl = 10 coins."
6. "A child 1 month to 5 years: boy = 5 coins, girl = 3 coins."
7. "A man 60+ = 15 coins. A woman = 10 coins."
8. "If someone is too poor, the priest will decide a fair amount."
9. "If the promise is an animal, it becomes holy and can't be changed.
10. If you try to switch animals, both become holy."
11. "If it's an unclean animal,
12. the priest will decide its value.
13. If you want it back, add 20%."
14. "If someone gives a house to the Lord, the priest will set its value.
15. To buy it back, pay 20% more."
16. "If someone gives part of their land, its value depends on how much seed it needs.
17. If it's promised during the Year of Freedom, it keeps full value.

18. Later promises are worth less."
19. "If you want the land back, add 20%."
20. "If not, it stays holy forever."
21. "In the Year of Freedom, it goes to the priests."
22. "If you give land you bought,
23. the priest will set its value and you pay that amount.
24. In the Year of Freedom, the land goes back to the original owner."
25. "Use the Temple standard for all money."
26. "You can't promise a firstborn animal—it already belongs to the Lord."
27. "If it's unclean, you may buy it back with 20% added."
28. "Anything devoted to the Lord can't be sold or bought back. It's very holy."
29. "Anyone set apart for destruction must die."
30. "Give one-tenth of all crops to the Lord. It's holy."
31. "If you want to keep it, add 20%."
32. "Every tenth animal belongs to the Lord."
33. "Don't choose the best or worst. Once picked, it's holy."
34. These are the commands the Lord gave Moses for the Israelites.

–Numbers –

Israel wanders in the wilderness for 40 years due to disobedience but prepares to enter the Promised Land.

Numbers 1

The People of Israel Are Counted

1. On the first day of the second month, one year after leaving Egypt, the Lord spoke to Moses in the Meeting Tent in the Sinai Desert.
2. He said, "Count every man in Israel by name, family, and household."
3. "You and Aaron must list all men 20 years and older who can serve in the army."
4. "Each tribe's leader must help you."
5. These are the men who will help: from Reuben, Elizur son of Shedeur;
6. from Simeon, Shelumiel son of Zurishaddai;
7. from Judah, Nahshon son of Amminadab;
8. from Issachar, Nethanel son of Zuar;
9. from Zebulun, Eliab son of Helon;
10. from Joseph's sons: Ephraim, Elishama son of Ammihud; Manasseh, Gamaliel son of Pedahzur;
11. from Benjamin, Abidan son of Gideoni;
12. from Dan, Ahiezer son of Ammishaddai;
13. from Asher, Pagiel son of Okran;
14. from Gad, Eliasaph son of Deuel;
15. from Naphtali, Ahira son of Enan.
16. These men were leaders chosen from the people.
17. Moses and Aaron took them,
18. and gathered all Israel on the first day of the second month. The men 20 years or older were listed by name and family,
19. just as the Lord commanded. They were counted in the Sinai Desert.

20–21. Reuben: 46,500

22–23. Simeon: 59,300

24–25. Gad: 45,650

26–27. Judah: 74,600

28–29. Issachar: 54,400

30–31. Zebulun: 57,400

32–33. Ephraim: 40,500

34–35. Manasseh: 32,200

36–37. Benjamin: 35,400

38–39. Dan: 62,700

40–41. Asher: 41,500

42–43. Naphtali: 53,400

44. These men were counted by Moses, Aaron, and the 12 leaders.
45. All Israelite men 20 years or older were counted by family.
46. Total: 603,550 men.
47. The Levites were not included.
48. The Lord told Moses:
49. "Don't count the Levites with the rest of Israel."
50. "They must take care of the Meeting Tent and everything in it."
51. "They will take it down and set it up. Anyone else who comes near must die."
52. "All tribes must camp under their own flags."
53. "The Levites will camp around the Meeting Tent to protect it."
54. The Israelites did everything the Lord told Moses.

Numbers 2

Setting Up the Camp

1. The Lord told Moses and Aaron:
2. "The Israelites must camp around the Meeting Tent, under their own flag, not too close."
3. On the east: Judah's camp, led by Nahshon son of Amminadab.
4. Judah's army: 74,600
5. Next to them: Issachar, led by Nethanel son of Zuar.
6. Issachar's army: 54,400
7. Next: Zebulun, led by Eliab son of Helon.
8. Zebulun's army: 57,400
9. These 186,400 men go first.
10. On the south: Reuben's camp, led by Elizur son of Shedeur.
11. Reuben's army: 46,500
12. Next: Simeon, led by Shelumiel son of Zurishaddai.
13. Simeon's army: 59,300
14. Next: Gad, led by Eliasaph son of Deuel.
15. Gad's army: 45,650
16. These 151,450 men go second.
17. The Levites and the Meeting Tent travel next, in the center, with each group under its flag.
18. On the west: Ephraim's camp, led by Elishama son of Ammihud.
19. Ephraim's army: 40,500
20. Next: Manasseh, led by Gamaliel son of Pedahzur.
21. Manasseh's army: 32,200
22. Next: Benjamin, led by Abidan son of Gideoni.
23. Benjamin's army: 35,400
24. These 108,100 men go third.
25. On the north: Dan's camp, led by Ahiezer son of Ammishaddai.
26. Dan's army: 62,700
27. Next: Asher, led by Pagiel son of Okran.
28. Asher's army: 41,500
29. Next: Naphtali, led by Ahira son of Enan.
30. Naphtali's army: 53,400
31. These 157,600 men go last.
32. Total men counted for the army: 603,550
33. The Levites were not counted.
34. The Israelites followed all the Lord's commands.

Numbers 3

The Levites' Job

1. This is the family of Aaron and Moses when the Lord spoke to Moses at Mount Sinai.
2. Aaron's sons were Nadab, Abihu, Eleazar, and Ithamar.
3. They were chosen and anointed as priests.
4. Nadab and Abihu died before the Lord when they offered unauthorized fire. They had no sons. Eleazar and Ithamar served as priests under Aaron.
5. The Lord said to Moses,
6. "Bring the tribe of Levi to help Aaron the priest.
7. They must serve him and take care of the Meeting Tent."
8. "They must be responsible for all its items and help with all the work."
9. "Give the Levites to Aaron. They are his helpers."
10. "Only Aaron and his sons may serve as priests. Anyone else who tries must be put to death."
11. The Lord also said to Moses,
12. "I have chosen the Levites instead of the firstborn sons from every Israelite family. The Levites are mine.
13. Every firstborn belongs to me. On the day I killed the firstborn in Egypt, I claimed all Israel's firstborn as mine. The Levites now belong to me."
14. The Lord told Moses in the Sinai Desert,
15. "Count all Levite males one month old or older by family and clan."
16. Moses obeyed the Lord and counted them.
17. Levi's sons were Gershon, Kohath, and Merari.
18. Gershon's sons were Libni and Shimei.
19. Kohath's sons were Amram, Izhar, Hebron, and Uzziel.
20. Merari's sons were Mahli and Mushi. These were Levi's clans.
21. The Gershon clans were the Libnites and the Shimeites.
22. There were 7,500 males one month old or older.
23. They camped on the west side of the Meeting Tent.
24. The leader of the Gershonites was Eliasaph son of Lael.
25. Their job was to take care of the Tent coverings,
26. curtains, entrance screen, and ropes for the Tent.
27. Kohath's clans were the Amramites, Izharites, Hebronites, and Uzzielites.
28. There were 8,600 males one month old or older.
29. They camped on the south side of the Meeting Tent.
30. The leader of the Kohathites was Elizaphan son of Uzziel.
31. They were in charge of the ark, the table, the lampstand, the altars, the tools, and the curtain.
32. Eleazar, Aaron's son, was in charge of all the Levites and of everything in the Meeting Tent.
33. Merari's clans were the Mahlites and Mushites.
34. There were 6,200 males one month old or older.
35. Their leader was Zuriel son of Abihail. They camped on the north side of the Tent.
36. They were in charge of the Tent's frames, crossbars, posts, bases, and all tools,
37. as well as the courtyard posts, bases, ropes, and pegs.
38. Moses, Aaron, and his sons camped on the east side of the Meeting Tent. They guarded it for the people. Anyone else who came near was to be put to death.
39. The total number of Levite males one month old or older was 22,000.

40. The Lord said to Moses, "Count every firstborn Israelite male one month old or older, and list their names."

41. "The Levites will take the place of the firstborn sons. Their animals will replace the firstborn animals. The Levites belong to me."

42. Moses did what the Lord said.

43. The total number of firstborn males one month old or older was 22,273.

44. The Lord told Moses,

45. "Use the Levites to replace the firstborn Israelites. Use their animals for the firstborn animals."

46. "There are 273 more firstborn sons than Levites.

47. Collect 5 silver coins for each extra son.

48. Give the money to Aaron and his sons."

49. Moses collected the money from the 273 extra firstborn sons.

50. He collected 1,365 silver coins.

51. Moses gave the money to Aaron and his sons, just as the Lord commanded.

Numbers 4

Jobs for the Levite Men

1. The Lord said to Moses and Aaron,

2. "Count the Kohath men, ages 30–50, who can work in the Meeting Tent."

3-4. "This is their job: to take care of the most holy things."

5. "When the camp moves, Aaron and his sons must cover the ark with the curtain.

6. Then cover it with leather and a blue cloth, and insert the carrying poles."

7-8. "Cover the table and its things with a blue cloth, then leather, and insert the poles."

9-10. "Wrap the lampstand and all its tools in blue cloth, then leather, and carry it."

11. "Cover the gold altar with blue cloth and leather, then insert the poles."

12. "Wrap all the tools used for worship and place them on a cloth and cover with leather."

13. "Clean the bronze altar, then cover it with purple cloth."

14. "Place its tools on it, cover it with leather, and insert the poles."

15. "When everything is packed, the Kohath men will carry it. But they must not touch any holy object or they will die."

16. "Eleazar, Aaron's son, is in charge of the oil, incense, grain offerings, and all holy items."

17. The Lord told Moses and Aaron,

18. "Don't let the Kohath families die for getting too close to the holy things."

19. "Aaron and his sons must cover everything before the Kohath men come."

20. "They must not see the holy items or they will die."

21. The Lord said to Moses,

22-23. "Count the Gershon men, ages 30–50, who can work."

24. "They will carry the Tent's curtains,

25. coverings, entrance curtain,

26. courtyard curtains and ropes, and tools."

27. "Aaron and his sons will direct all their work."

28. "These are the jobs for the Gershon families."

29-30. "Count the Merari men, ages 30–50."

31. "They will carry the Tent's frames, bars, posts, bases,

32. courtyard posts and bases, ropes, and pegs."

33. "Ithamar, Aaron's son, is in charge of them."

34. Moses, Aaron, and the leaders counted the Kohath men.
35. They counted 2,750 men,
36. ages 30–50, able to work.
37. These were the Kohath men assigned to carry holy things.
38. They counted the Gershon men.
39. 2,630 men, ages 30–50.
40. These were their assigned jobs.
41. They counted the Merari men.
42. 3,200 men, ages 30–50.
43. These were their assigned jobs.
44. The total number of Levites working in the Meeting Tent
45. from ages 30–50 was 8,580 men.
46. Each one had a job, just as the Lord told Moses.

Numbers 5

Keep the Camp Clean

1. The Lord told Moses,
2. "Send anyone with a skin disease or body discharge outside the camp.
3. This includes both men and women. Don't let them stay in the camp."
4. The Israelites did what the Lord said.
5. The Lord told Moses,
6. "Tell the people: If anyone sins and breaks trust with the Lord,
7. they must admit their sin and pay back what they took, plus 20%."
8. "If there is no one to pay back, give it to the priest."
9. "The priest also receives any gift that is given to the Lord."
10. "Whatever is given belongs to the priest."
11. The Lord told Moses,
12. "Tell the people: If a man thinks his wife has cheated on him,
13. but there are no witnesses and she wasn't caught,
14. and he gets jealous,
15. he must bring her to the priest with a grain offering. No oil or incense."
16. "The priest will make her stand before the Lord."
17. "He will mix holy water with dust from the floor of the Meeting Tent."
18. "The woman must loosen her hair. The priest gives her bitter water to drink and reminds her of the curse."
19. "He will say: 'If you didn't cheat, this water won't hurt you.'
20. 'But if you did,
21. may the Lord make your body sick.'
22. 'May this water cause your belly to swell and make you sick.' She must say, 'Amen.'"
23. "The priest writes the curse on a scroll and washes it off into the water.
24. Then he gives her the water to drink."
25. "He will offer her grain to remember her sin."
26. "He will burn a handful of it and give her the water."
27. "If she cheated, the water will make her very sick. She will never have children.
28. If she didn't, she won't get sick and can have children."
29. "This is the law about jealousy."
30. "If a man gets jealous, he must follow this law."
31. "The man is not guilty. The woman must face the result."

Numbers 6

Special Vows to God

1. The Lord told Moses,
2. "Tell the people: If a man or woman makes a special vow to serve me, they become a Nazirite."

3. "They must not drink wine, vinegar, or anything made from grapes.
4. They must not eat grapes or raisins."
5. "They must not cut their hair during the vow."
6. "They must stay away from dead bodies,
7. even their parents or siblings."
8. "They are set apart for the Lord."
9. "If someone dies suddenly near them, they must shave their head seven days later."
10. "On day 8, they must bring two birds to the priest."
11. "One is for sin, the other for a burnt offering. The priest makes them clean again."
12. "They must start the vow over. Bring a young lamb for a guilt offering. The days before don't count."
13. "When the vow is done, bring the person to the Meeting Tent.
14. Bring a male lamb, a female lamb, a ram,
15. bread without yeast, oil cakes, and grain and drink offerings."
16. "The priest offers them all to the Lord."
17. "The ram is for peace. The priest burns the grain offering and pours the drink offering."
18. "The person must shave their head and put the hair on the fire under the peace offering."
19. "The priest gives them the boiled shoulder of the ram, a cake, and bread."
20. "He lifts them up before the Lord. After that, the person may drink wine."
21. "This is the law of the Nazirite. They must bring what they promised."
22. The Lord told Moses,
23. "Tell Aaron and his sons: This is how you bless the people."
24. 'May the Lord bless you and keep you.
25. May He smile on you and be kind to you.
26. May He look on you with favor and give you peace.'
27. "Put my name on the people, and I will bless them."

Numbers 7

Offerings for the Tent

1. Moses finished setting up the Meeting Tent, and he anointed and made everything holy.
2. The leaders of Israel, heads of the tribes, brought offerings.
3. They brought six carts and twelve oxen—one cart from every two leaders, and one ox each.
4. The Lord told Moses,
5. "Accept them for the Levites. Use them to do the work."
6. Moses gave the carts and oxen to the Levites.
7. He gave two carts and four oxen to the Gershonites.
8. He gave four carts and eight oxen to the Merarites.
9. The Kohathites got none because they carried the holy things on their shoulders.
10. The leaders brought gifts for the altar's dedication.
11. The Lord said, "Let each leader bring their offering on a different day."
12. Day 1: Nahshon son of Amminadab from Judah.
13. His offering: a silver plate (3.4 pounds), a silver bowl (1.7 pounds), both with flour and oil,
14. a gold dish (4 ounces) with incense,
15. one young bull, one ram, and one male lamb for a burnt offering,
16. one male goat for sin,

17. and two oxen, five rams, five goats, five male lambs for a peace offering.

18–23. Day 2: Nethanel from Issachar – same offering.

24–29. Day 3: Eliab from Zebulun – same offering.

30–35. Day 4: Elizur from Reuben – same offering.

36–41. Day 5: Shelumiel from Simeon – same offering.

42–47. Day 6: Eliasaph from Gad – same offering.

48–53. Day 7: Elishama from Ephraim – same offering.

54–59. Day 8: Gamaliel from Manasseh – same offering.

60–65. Day 9: Abidan from Benjamin – same offering.

66–71. Day 10: Ahiezer from Dan – same offering.

72–77. Day 11: Pagiel from Asher – same offering.

78–83. Day 12: Ahira from Naphtali – same offering.

84. These were the gifts from the leaders for the altar:

85. 12 silver plates and 12 silver bowls, weighing 60 pounds in total.

86. 12 gold dishes with incense, 3 pounds total.

87. 12 bulls, 12 rams, 12 lambs for burnt offerings.

88. 12 goats for sin offerings.

89. When Moses entered the Meeting Tent, he heard the Lord speaking to him from above the Ark.

Numbers 8

Setting Up the Lamp and Levites

1. The Lord told Moses,
2. "Tell Aaron: Set up the seven lamps so they shine forward."
3. Aaron did what the Lord said.
4. The lampstand was made of hammered gold, just like the Lord showed Moses.
5. The Lord said to Moses,
6. "Make the Levites clean."
7. "Sprinkle them with water. Shave their bodies and wash their clothes."
8. "They must bring a young bull and grain offering. Bring a second bull for a sin offering."
9. "Bring the Levites to the Meeting Tent."
10. "Have the people place their hands on them."
11. "Aaron will present them as a gift to the Lord."
12. "The Levites must lay their hands on the bulls. Offer one for sin and the other for burnt."
13. "Set the Levites apart."
14. "They now belong to me instead of the firstborn sons."
15. "After that, they can serve at the Meeting Tent."
16. "I chose them instead of the firstborns."
17. "Every firstborn is mine since I struck down Egypt's firstborns."
18. "I took the Levites instead."
19. "They help Aaron so there is no disaster when people come near me."
20. Moses, Aaron, and the Israelites did everything the Lord said.
21. The Levites made themselves clean.
22. Then they went to work at the Meeting Tent.
23. The Lord told Moses,
24. "Levites may serve from age 25 to 50."
25. "After 50, they must stop working."
26. "They may help, but not do the work."

Numbers 9

Passover and the Cloud

1. In the first month of the second year, the Lord told Moses in the Sinai Desert,

2-3. "Tell the people to celebrate Passover on the 14th day at sunset."

4. Moses told the people, and they obeyed.

5. They celebrated Passover as God commanded.

6. Some men were unclean because of a dead body, so they couldn't join.

7. They asked Moses, "Why can't we give our offering?"

8. Moses said, "Wait. I'll ask the Lord."

9. The Lord said,

10. "If someone is unclean or far away,

11. they may celebrate Passover a month later, on the 14th day of the second month."

12. "They must follow all the same rules."

13. "But if someone skips it without a reason, they must be cut off."

14. "Foreigners must follow the same Passover rules too."

15. On the day the Tent was set up, a cloud covered it. At night it looked like fire.

16. This happened every day.

17. When the cloud lifted, the people moved.

18. When it stayed, they stayed.

19. If it stayed long, they obeyed and waited.

20. Sometimes it stayed only a few days.

21. Or overnight.

22. Whether long or short, they obeyed the Lord.

23. They followed the Lord's command given through Moses.

Numbers 10

Silver Trumpets and Leaving Sinai

1. The Lord told Moses,

2. "Make two silver trumpets. Use them to call the people and start moving."

3. "When both are blown, everyone must gather at the Meeting Tent."

4. "If only one is blown, just the leaders come."

5. "When you blow a warning sound, the east camps move out."

6. "Blow again, and the south camps move out."

7. "But when you gather the people, blow without a warning sound."

8. "Only the priests can blow the trumpets. This is a rule forever."

9. "Blow them when you go to war, and I will help you."

10. "Also blow them during festivals and sacrifices. It will remind me to bless you."

11. On the 20th day of the second month, the cloud lifted from the Tent.

12. The people left Sinai and followed the cloud.

13. It was their first time moving with the Lord's command.

14. Judah's army led the way led by Nahshon.

15. Issachar's army was led by Nethanel.

16. Zebulun's army was led by Eliab.

17. The Tent was taken down, and the Gershon and Merari families carried it.

18. Reuben's army moved next led by Elizur.

19. Simeon's army was led by Shelumiel.

20. Gad's army was led by Eliasaph.

21. The Kohath family carried the holy items. The Tent was set up before they arrived.

22. Ephraim's army moved next led by Elishama.

23. Manasseh's army was led by Gamaliel.

24. Benjamin's army was led by Abidan.

25. Dan's army went last led by Ahiezer.
26. Asher's army was led by Pagiel.
27. Naphtali's army was led by Ahira.
28. This was the order of travel.
29. Moses said to Hobab, "Come with us. The Lord will bless you."
30. But Hobab said, "No, I'll go back home."
31. Moses said, "Please don't leave. You know the desert well."
32. "If you come, the Lord's blessings will be for you too."
33. They left Sinai and traveled for three days. The Ark went ahead to find a place to rest.
34. The cloud stayed over them by day.
35. When the Ark moved, Moses said, "Rise, Lord! Scatter your enemies!"
36. When it rested, he said, "Return, Lord, to your people!"

Numbers 11

Complaining and Quail

1. The people complained, and the Lord got angry. Fire burned around the camp.
2. The people cried to Moses. He prayed, and the fire stopped.
3. They called the place Taberah, which means "burning."
4. Some foreigners with them wanted meat, and the Israelites joined in. They cried, "We want meat!"
5. "We remember fish, cucumbers, melons, leeks, onions, and garlic in Egypt!"
6. "Now we have nothing but manna!"
7. Manna was like coriander seed and looked like sap.
8. People gathered it, grounded it, and cooked it. It tasted like baked goods with oil.
9. It fell at night with the dew.
10. Moses heard the people crying at their tents. The Lord was angry, and Moses was upset.
11. He asked, "Why did you give me this burden?"
12. "Did I give birth to these people?"
13. "Where can I get meat for all of them?"
14. "I can't do this alone!"
15. "If this is how it will be, just kill me now."
16. The Lord said, "Choose 70 elders to help you."
17. "I will take some of your spirit and give it to them. They will help carry the load."
18. "Tell the people: 'Get ready for meat. You will eat it for a whole month.'"
19. "Not just one day or two…"
20. "You will eat until you're sick of it, because you rejected me."
21. Moses said, "There are 600,000 men! Where will we get that much meat?"
22. "Even if we caught all the fish or killed all the animals?"
23. The Lord said, "Is my power too small? You'll see what I do."
24. Moses told the people what God said. He gathered 70 leaders.
25. The Lord gave them the spirit, and they began to prophesy.
26. Two men stayed in the camp—Eldad and Medad—and they prophesied too.
27. A young man ran to Moses and said, "They are prophesying in the camp!"
28. Joshua said, "Stop them!"
29. Moses replied, "Are you jealous for me? I wish all God's people had the Spirit."
30. Moses and the elders returned to the camp.
31. The Lord sent a wind with quail. Birds fell all around the camp.

32. The people gathered quail all day, night, and next day.
33. But while they were still eating, the Lord got angry and struck them with a plague.
34. They called the place Kibroth Hattaavah, meaning "graves of craving."
35. Then they moved to Hazeroth and camped.

Numbers 12

Miriam and Aaron Complain

1. Miriam and Aaron spoke against Moses because he married a Cushite woman.
2. They said, "Has the Lord only spoken through Moses? What about us?" The Lord heard them.
3. Moses was the humblest man on earth.
4. The Lord told Moses, Aaron, and Miriam to come to the Meeting Tent.
5. The Lord came down in a cloud and called Aaron and Miriam.
6. He said, "When I speak to prophets, I use dreams."
7. "But Moses is different. He is faithful in my house."
8. "I speak to him face to face. Why weren't you afraid to speak against him?"
9. The Lord was angry and left.
10. When the cloud lifted, Miriam got leprosy and turned like snow. Aaron turned and saw her.
11. Aaron said to Moses, "Please forgive us for our foolish sin.
12. Don't let her die like this."
13. Moses prayed, "Lord, please heal her!" and He did.
14. The Lord said, "If her father spit in her face, she'd be ashamed for seven days. Keep her outside the camp for seven days."
15. Miriam stayed outside the camp for seven days. The people didn't move until she returned.
16. After that, they left Hazeroth and camped in the Desert of Paran.

Numbers 13

Spies Check Out Canaan

1. The Lord told Moses,
2. "Send one man from each tribe to explore Canaan."
3. So Moses sent 12 men as the Lord commanded.
4. From Reuben: Shammua
5. From Simeon: Shaphat
6. From Judah: Caleb
7. From Issachar: Igal
8. From Ephraim: Hoshea (Joshua)
9. From Benjamin: Palti
10. From Zebulun: Gaddiel
11. From Manasseh: Gaddi
12. From Dan: Ammiel
13. From Asher: Sethur
14. From Naphtali: Nahbi
15. From Gad: Geuel
16. Moses gave Hoshea the new name Joshua.
17. He told them, "Go into Canaan. Check the land."
18. "See if the people are strong or weak, many or few."
19. "See if the land is good or bad, and what towns they live in."
20. "See if the soil is rich or poor. Bring back some fruit." It was the season for grapes.
21. The men went as far as Hebron.
22. Hebron had giants: Ahiman, Sheshai, and Talmai.

23. At the Valley of Eshkol, they gathered a huge cluster of grapes. Two men carried it.
24. They also picked pomegranates and figs.
25. After 40 days, they returned.
26. They gave their report to Moses, Aaron, and the people.
27. They said, "The land is good! It has lots of fruit."
28. "But the people are strong, and the cities are big and walled."
29. "Giants live there! Amalekites, Hittites, Jebusites, Amorites, and Canaanites are everywhere."
30. Caleb said, "We can take the land!"
31. But the others said, "No, they are stronger than us."
32. They gave a bad report. "The land eats up people!"
33. "We saw giants there. We felt like grasshoppers."

Numbers 14

The People Refuse to Go

1. That night, everyone cried out loud.
2. They complained, "We should have died in Egypt or the desert!"
3. "Why is the Lord bringing us here to die?"
4. "Let's choose a new leader and go back to Egypt."
5. Moses and Aaron fell to the ground.
6. Joshua and Caleb tore their clothes.
7. They said, "The land is very good!"
8. "If the Lord is with us, He will give it to us."
9. "Don't rebel or be afraid. The Lord is with us!"
10. But the people talked about stoning them. Then the Lord's glory appeared.
11. The Lord said to Moses, "How long will they not trust me?"
12. "I will strike them down and start over with you."
13. Moses said, "But the Egyptians will hear,
14. and tell others You brought us out but couldn't finish."

15-16. "If You kill them now, people will say You weren't strong enough so you killed them."

17. "Please show your great love."
18. "You are slow to anger and full of mercy."
19. "Please forgive them."
20. The Lord said, "I forgive them.

21-22. But I promise: all who saw my glory and still disobeyed will not enter the land."

23. "None of them will see it."
24. "But Caleb has a different spirit. He followed me fully. He will enter the land."
25. "Now go back to the desert. The Amalekites and Canaanites are ahead."
26. The Lord told Moses and Aaron,
27. "How long will these people keep complaining?"
28. "Tell them: As I live, you'll get what you said."
29. "You said you'd die in the desert—and you will."
30. "None of you will enter the land, except Caleb and Joshua."
31. "But your children will go in."
32. "You will die in the desert."
33. "Your kids will wander 40 years for your sin."
34. "One year for each of the 40 days you explored."
35. "You will die here."
36. The men who gave the bad report
37. were struck dead by a plague.
38. Only Joshua and Caleb survived.

39. Moses told this to the people, and they mourned.
40. In the morning, they tried to go into the land anyway.
41-42. Moses said, "Why are you disobeying? Don't go! The Lord isn't with you."
43. "Your enemies will win."
44. But they went anyway.
45. The Amalekites and Canaanites attacked and beat them badly.

Numbers 15

Rules for Offerings and Sin

1. The Lord told Moses,
2. "Tell the people: When you enter the land,
3. bring offerings with your burnt or vow offerings."
4. "The one offering must bring grain and mix it with oil.
5. and wine with the sacrifice."

6-7. "For a ram, bring more flour, oil, and wine."
8-9. "For a bull, bring even more."
10. "This is the food offering. It's a sweet smell to the Lord."
11-12. "Do this for every animal you offer."
13. "All native Israelites must do this."
14-15. "Foreigners must follow the same rules."
16. "There is one law for everyone."
17. The Lord said to Moses,
18. "When you eat food in the new land,
19. give the Lord the first part."
20. "Offer a loaf from the first grain."
21. "Give the first of your flour to the Lord always."
22. "If the community sins by mistake,
23. they must follow this rule:
24. bring a young bull, grain offering, and goat."
25. "The priest will offer them, and they will be forgiven."
26. "This is for all the people, including foreigners."
27. "If one person sins by mistake, bring a female goat."
28. "The priest will offer it, and the person will be forgiven."
29. "Same rule for foreigners."
30. "But if someone sins on purpose, they must be cut off."
31. "They rejected the Lord and must be punished."
32. One day a man was caught gathering sticks on the Sabbath.
33. He was taken to Moses and Aaron.
34. They kept him under guard.
35. The Lord said, "He must die."
36. So the people stoned him outside the camp.
37. The Lord told Moses,
38. "Tell the people to sew tassels on their clothes with a blue cord."
39. "They will remind you to obey my commands."
40. "Then you will be holy."
41. "I am the Lord who brought you out of Egypt. I am your God."

Numbers 16

Korah's Rebellion

1. Korah, Dathan, Abiram, and On led a rebellion.
2. They gathered 250 leaders and confronted Moses.
3. They said, "You've taken too much power. Everyone is holy! Why do you lead us?"
4. Moses fell face down and prayed.

5. He said, "Tomorrow the Lord will show who is holy."
6. "Korah and his men—bring incense pans."
7. "The Lord will choose the true leader."
8. Moses said to Korah,
9. "Isn't it enough that God chose you Levites to serve at the Meeting Tent?"
10. "Now you want the priesthood too?"
11. "You are really complaining against God, not me."
12. Moses called Dathan and Abiram, but they said,
13. "You brought us out of a good land to die in the desert!"
14. "You didn't give us land or fields. We won't come!"
15. Moses got very angry and said, "Don't accept their offering, Lord!"
16. Moses told Korah, "Come tomorrow with your followers."
17. "Bring your incense pans."
18. They did.
19. Korah gathered everyone at the Meeting Tent entrance. Then God's glory appeared.
20. The Lord said to Moses and Aaron,
21. "Move away. I will destroy them all now."
22. They fell face down and said, "Please don't punish everyone!"
23. The Lord said,
24. "Tell everyone to move away from Korah, Dathan, and Abiram's tents."
25. Moses went to them.
26. He said, "Leave these wicked men. Don't touch anything of theirs."
27. Everyone moved away.
28. Moses said, "This is how you'll know the Lord sent me and it's not my idea-
29. If these men die normally, then God did not send me."
30. "But if the ground opens up and swallows them, you'll know they sinned against God."
31. Right after Moses finished speaking, the ground split open.
32. It swallowed Korah, everyone in his rebellion, their families, and everything they owned.
33. They went down alive into the earth, and it closed over them.
34. Everyone ran away, shouting, "The earth might swallow us too!"
35. Then fire from the Lord burned up the 250 men offering incense.
36. The Lord told Moses,
37. "Tell Eleazar to collect the incense pans from the fire."
38. "They are holy. Hammer them into a covering for the altar."
39. Eleazar did this.
40. This was to remind everyone not to act like Korah.
41. The next day, the people complained again. "You killed God's people!"
42. As they gathered, the cloud covered the Tent and God's glory appeared.
43. Moses and Aaron went to the Meeting Tent.
44. The Lord said,
45. "Move away from the people. I will destroy them now." Moses and Aaron fell face down.
46. Moses told Aaron, "Take your incense and go quickly to make peace."
47. Aaron ran with incense.
48. He stood between the living and the dead. The plague stopped.
49. 14,700 people died, plus those in Korah's group.
50. Aaron returned to Moses at the Meeting Tent. The plague had stopped.

Numbers 17

Aaron's Staff Grows

1. The Lord told Moses,
2. "Take a staff from each tribe, 12 total. Write each name on it.
3. Write Aaron's name on the staff for Levi."
4. "Place them in the Meeting Tent in front of the Ark."
5. "I will make one staff grow buds. That will stop the people from complaining."
6. Moses told the people. Each leader gave him a staff.
7. Moses put them in the Tent before the Lord.
8. The next day, Aaron's staff had sprouted! It had buds, flowers, and almonds.
9. Moses brought out the staffs. Each leader took their own.
10. The Lord said, "Put Aaron's staff back in front of the Ark. It will be a warning to stop complaints."
11. Moses obeyed.
12. The people said, "We're going to die!"
13. "Anyone who goes near the Lord's holy place dies!"

Numbers 18

Duties and Support for Priests and Levites

1. The Lord told Aaron, "You and your sons are responsible for the holy place and altar."
2. "Bring the rest of the Levites to help you."
3. "They can serve, but not go near the holy things."
4. "They must guard the Tent and help you."
5. "You must protect the holy place so my anger doesn't come again."
6. "I chose the Levites to help you."
7. "Only you and your sons may serve as priests."
8. The Lord told Aaron, "You may have the offerings the people bring to me. They are holy."
9. "You may eat the most holy offerings."
10. "Only males may eat them, and only in a holy place."
11. "You may also have the gifts lifted to the Lord. Your family may eat them."
12. "You may have the best oil, wine, and grain offerings."
13. "Everything first harvested belongs to you."
14. "Everything set apart to the Lord is yours."
15. "Every firstborn animal or child belongs to me, but people and unclean animals must be bought back."
16. "Pay five silver coins to buy back people."
17. "But don't buy back firstborn cows, sheep, or goats. They must be offered."
18. "The meat is yours, like the peace offerings."
19. "These offerings are a lasting gift to you and your family."
20. The Lord said, "You won't get land in Israel. I am your share."
21. "The Levites will get a tenth of everything from the people."
22. "No one else may go near the Meeting Tent or they will die."
23. "Only Levites may do the Tent work. This rule lasts forever."
24. "The Levites will get tithes instead of land."
25. The Lord told Moses,
26. "Tell the Levites to give a tenth of the tithes they receive to the Lord."
27. "It will count as your own offering."
28. "Give it to Aaron the priest."

29. "It must be the best part."
30. "After giving the best part, the rest is yours."
31. "You may eat it anywhere—it's your pay."
32. "As long as you give the best part, you won't be guilty."

Numbers 19

Water That Makes You Clean

1. The Lord told Moses and Aaron,
2. "Tell the people to bring a perfect red cow with no defects and that has never worked."
3. "Give it to Eleazar. Take it outside the camp and kill it there."
4. "Eleazar must sprinkle its blood seven times toward the Meeting Tent."
5. "Burn the whole cow, including skin, meat, blood, and waste."
6. "Throw cedar wood, hyssop, and red cloth into the fire."
7. "The priest must wash his clothes, bathe, and be unclean until evening."
8. "The man who burns it must also wash and be unclean until evening."
9. "Someone clean must collect the ashes and store them outside the camp. They are used for cleaning sin."
10. "The person who collects the ashes must wash and be unclean until evening."
11. "Anyone who touches a dead body is unclean for seven days."
12. "They must wash with the special water on day 3 and day 7 or they stay unclean."
13. "If they don't do it, they remain guilty and must be cut off."
14. "This is the law: if someone dies in a tent, everyone in the tent is unclean seven days."
15. "Any open jar without a lid is also unclean."
16. "If you touch a dead body, bone, or grave, you are unclean seven days."
17. "To be clean, mix ashes from the cow with water."
18. "A clean person dips hyssop in it and sprinkles it on the unclean person, tent, and everything inside."
19. "Do this on day 3 and 7. Then they must wash and be clean at evening."
20. "If someone refuses, they must be cut off. They stayed unclean."
21. "This is a lasting rule."
22. "Anything touched by an unclean person also becomes unclean."

Numbers 20

Water from a Rock

1. In the first month, the people arrived at Kadesh. Miriam died and was buried there.
2. There was no water, so the people argued with Moses.

3-4. "Why did you bring us here to die?"

5. "There's no grain, figs, grapes, or water!"
6. Moses and Aaron went to the Meeting Tent and fell facedown. God's glory appeared.
7. The Lord said,
8. "Take your staff. You and Aaron must speak to the rock, and it will give water."
9. Moses took the staff.
10. He and Aaron gathered the people and said, "Must we bring you water from this rock?"
11. Moses hit the rock twice. Water poured out.
12. The Lord said, "You didn't listen to me, I told you to speak to the rock, not hit it. Because of this you won't enter the Promise Land."
13. This place was called Meribah, because the people complained.

14. Moses sent messengers to the king of Edom: "Please let us pass through your land."
15. "We were slaves in Egypt, but God saved us."
16. "We won't go through fields or drink your water."
17. "We'll stay on the main road."
18. Edom said, "No. If you try, we'll attack."
19. Israel said, "We'll pay for any water we use."
20. Edom said no again and sent a large army.
21. So Israel turned away.
22. They left Kadesh and came to Mount Hor.
23. The Lord said,
24. "Aaron will die here. He won't enter the land because you disobeyed me."
25. "Take Aaron and Eleazar up the mountain."
26. "Take off Aaron's priest clothes and put them on Eleazar." Aaron will die there."
27. Moses did as the Lord said.
28. Aaron died there. Moses and Eleazar came down.
29. The people mourned Aaron for 30 days.

Numbers 21

Snakes and Victories

1. The king of Arad heard Israel was coming and attacked, taking some prisoners.
2. Israel made a promise to the Lord: "If You help us win, we will destroy their towns."
3. The Lord helped them win. They destroyed the towns and named the place Hormah.
4. They traveled around Edom. The people grew impatient.
5. They said, "Why did you bring us here? There's no food or water, and we hate this manna!"
6. The Lord sent poisonous snakes. Many died.
7. The people said, "We sinned! Pray to God to take the snakes away." Moses prayed.
8. The Lord said, "Make a snake and put it on a pole. Whoever looks at it will live."
9. Moses made a bronze snake and put it on a pole. Anyone who looked at it lived.
10. The Israelites traveled and camped at Oboth.
11. Then they camped at Iye Abarim.
12. Then at Zered Valley.
13. Then across the Arnon River, which is the border of Moab.
14. This is written in the Book of the Wars of the Lord: "...Waheb and the Arnon River..."
15. "...and the slopes to Ar..."
16. From there they went to Beer. God said, "I will give them water."
17. The people sang: "Spring up, O well!"
18. The leaders dug the well with staffs.
19. They traveled to Mattanah,
20. then to Nahaliel, then to Bamoth, then to the valley near Pisgah.
21. Israel sent messengers to King Sihon:
22. "Let us pass through. We won't touch your land."
23. But Sihon refused and fought Israel.
24. Israel won and took his land.
25. They captured all the cities and lived there.
26. Heshbon was his capital.
27. A song was sung: "Come to Heshbon, rebuilt by Sihon!"
28. "Fire came from Heshbon and burned Ar of Moab!"

29. "Woe to Moab! Sihon defeated them!"
30. "We destroyed their towns!"
31. Israel lived in the land of the Amorites.
32. They sent spies to Jazer, captured it, and drove out the Amorites.
33. Then they went to Bashan. King Og came to fight.
34. The Lord said, "Don't be afraid. I've given him to you."
35. Israel won and took his land.

Numbers 22

Balaam and the Donkey

1. The Israelites camped in Moab, across from Jericho.
2. King Balak of Moab saw what Israel did to the Amorites.
3. Moab was afraid because there were so many Israelites.
4. Moab said to the Midian leaders, "Israel will destroy everything around us."
5. Balak sent messengers to Balaam, a prophet, to ask for help.
6. "Come curse these people for me. Maybe I can beat them."
7. The messengers brought money and told Balaam what Balak said.
8. Balaam said, "Stay the night. I will ask God."
9. God asked, "Who are these men?"

10-11. Balaam said, "King Balak wants me to curse Israel."

12. God said, "Don't go with them. Don't curse the people. They are blessed."
13. Balaam told them, "Go home. God said no."
14. They told Balak, "Balaam won't come."
15. Balak sent more important leaders.

16-17. They said, "Please come. I'll reward you greatly."

18-19. Balaam said, "Even if I got a palace of gold, I can only say what God allows. Stay tonight. I'll ask again."

20. That night God said, "You may go, but say only what I tell you."
21. Balaam got up, saddled his donkey, and went.
22. God was angry. The angel of the Lord stood in his path.
23. The donkey saw the angel with a sword and turned into a field. Balaam hit it.
24. The angel stood on a narrow path.
25. The donkey pressed against a wall and crushed Balaam's foot. He hit it again.
26. The angel stood in a narrow place with no room to turn.
27. The donkey lay down. Balaam hit it again.
28. Then the Lord made the donkey talk. "What have I done to deserve this?"
29. Balaam said, "You've made me look foolish! I wish I could kill you!"
30. The donkey said, "Haven't I always been your donkey? Have I ever done this before?" Balaam said, "No."
31. Then the Lord let Balaam see the angel. Balaam bowed down.
32. The angel said, "Why did you hit your donkey? It saved your life."
33. "I would have killed you and let the donkey live."
34. Balaam said, "I have sinned. I didn't know you were there. I'll go back."
35. The angel said, "Go, but say only what I tell you."
36. Balak met Balaam.
37. "Why didn't you come the first time?"
38. Balaam said, "I can only say what God tells me."
39. They went to a city called Kiriath Huzoth.
40. Balak sacrificed cattle and sheep and gave some to Balaam.

41. The next day, Balak took him to a high place to see part of the Israelite camp.

Numbers 23

Balaam Blesses Israel

1. Balaam said, "Build seven altars. Prepare seven bulls and seven rams."
2. Balak did it.
3. Balaam said, "Stay here. I will go talk to God."
4. God met Balaam. Balaam said, "I built the altars."
5. God gave Balaam a message.
6. He returned to Balak, who was standing with his leaders.
7. Balaam spoke: "Balak brought me to curse Jacob."
8. "But I can't curse what God hasn't cursed."
9. "I see them from the mountain. They live apart from others."
10. "They are too many to count. Let me die like them—right with God!"
11. Balak said, "What are you doing? I brought you to curse them, not bless them!"
12. Balaam said, "I can only say what God tells me."
13. Balak said, "Let's try another place."
14. He took Balaam to a mountain where he could see part of the Israelites.
15. Balaam said, "Build seven altars and offer seven bulls and seven rams."
16. The Lord met Balaam again and gave him a message.
17. Balaam returned to Balak.
18. He said: "God is not human. He doesn't lie."
19. "If He speaks, He does it. If He promises, He keeps it."
20. "He told me to bless Israel. I can't change that."
21. "God is with them. He is their King."
22. "God brought them out of Egypt. They are strong."
23. "No curse or magic works against them."
24. "They rise up like lions and don't rest until they win."
25. Balak said, "If you won't curse them, don't bless them either!"
26. Balaam said, "I must speak only what God says."
27. Balak said, "Come, I'll try one more place."
28. He took Balaam to Mount Peor.
29. Balaam said, "Build seven altars again."
30. Balak did as Balaam said.

Numbers 24

Balaam's Final Blessings

1. Balaam saw that the Lord wanted to bless Israel. He didn't try magic this time.
2. He saw the Israelites camped by tribes, and God's Spirit came on him.
3. He said: "This is the message of Balaam."
4. "God opened my eyes. I see clearly."
5. "Your tents are beautiful, Israel!"
6. "You're like valleys, gardens, and trees by the water."
7. "Your king is strong. You'll defeat your enemies."
8. "God brought them from Egypt. They are powerful."
9. "They're like lions. Whoever blesses them will be blessed. Whoever curses them will be cursed."

10-11. Balak got angry. "Go home! I wanted to reward you, but God kept you from it."

12-13. Balaam said, "Didn't I say I could only speak what God tells me?"

14. "Before I go home, I will tell you what Israel will do in the future."

15. He said: "This is Balaam's message."
16. "I see clearly what God shows me."
17. "I see someone coming. A star will rise from Jacob. He will crush Moab and defeat enemies."
18. "Edom and Seir will be conquered. Israel will win."
19. "A ruler will rise from Jacob and destroy cities."
20. He saw Amalek and said, "They were first among nations, but they will be destroyed."
21. He saw the Kenites and said, "Your home is strong, but you will be taken away."
22. "Assyria will carry you off."
23. He said, "Who can survive unless God allows it?"
24. "Ships from the west will attack Assyria and Eber. But they too will be destroyed."
25. Then Balaam left and returned home. Balak also went his way.

Numbers 25

Sin at Peor

1. While Israel stayed in Shittim, the men started sinning with Moabite women.
2. The women invited them to worship their gods. The men ate and bowed down to the idols.
3. Israel joined in worshiping Baal of Peor. The Lord was very angry.
4. The Lord said to Moses, "Take all the leaders and kill them in public."
5. Moses told the judges, "Kill everyone who joined Baal of Peor."
6. Then an Israelite man brought a Midianite woman into the camp in front of Moses and the people, while they were crying at the Meeting Tent.
7. Phinehas, son of Eleazar, saw this. He grabbed a spear,
8. went into the man's tent, and killed them both. This stopped the plague.
9. But 24,000 people had already died.
10. The Lord praised Phinehas and told Moses,
11. "Phinehas stopped my anger. He cared about my honor."
12. "So I make a peace agreement with him.
13. He and his family will always be priests."
14. The man killed was Zimri from the tribe of Simeon.
15. The woman was Cozbi, daughter of Zur, a Midianite leader.
16. The Lord said to Moses,
17. "Attack the Midianites.
18. They tricked you at Peor and caused the plague."

Numbers 26

Second Census

1. After the plague, the Lord said to Moses and Eleazar,
2. "Count all men 20 years or older, by tribe."
3. So Moses and Eleazar counted them on the plains of Moab.
4. These are the Israelites who came from Egypt:

5–51. (Tribe-by-tribe count summarized below)

Reuben: 43,730

Simeon: 22,200

Gad: 40,500

Judah: 76,500

Issachar: 64,300

Zebulun: 60,500

Manasseh: 52,700

Ephraim: 32,500

Benjamin: 45,600

Dan: 64,400

Asher: 53,400

Naphtali: 45,400

Total: 601,730 men.

52. The Lord said to Moses,
53. "Divide the land among the tribes by size."
54. "Big tribes get more land, small tribes get less."
55. "Use lots to decide which part each tribe gets."
56. Each tribe's land will be chosen by lot.

57–62. The Levites were counted too. Total: 23,000 males one month or older. They got no land.

63. These were counted by Moses and Eleazar in Moab.
64. None were in the first count at Sinai,
65. because the Lord said they would die in the desert. Only Caleb and Joshua survived.

Numbers 27

Daughters Ask for Land & Joshua Chosen

1. Five daughters of Zelophehad (from Manasseh) came to Moses: Mahlah, Noah, Hoglah, Milcah, and Tirzah.
2. They stood at the Meeting Tent with the leaders.
3. They said, "Our father died in the desert. He had no sons."
4. "Why should his name disappear? Let us have land like sons."
5. Moses asked the Lord.
6. The Lord said,
7. "The daughters are right. Give them land.
8. If a man has no son, give land to his daughter.
9. If no daughter, then to his brothers.
10. If no brothers, to his uncles.
11. If no uncles, then to his closest relative."
12. The Lord told Moses, "Go to the mountain and see the land I'm giving Israel.
13. After you see it, you will die like Aaron.
14. You didn't trust me at Meribah."
15. Moses said,
16. "Lord, please choose a new leader
17. to guide the people so they are not like sheep without a shepherd."
18. The Lord said, "Choose Joshua. He has the Spirit. Lay your hand on him.
19. Bring him before Eleazar and the people."
20. "Give him some of your authority so people listen to him."
21. "He will get guidance through Eleazar, who asks me using the Urim."
22. Moses did as the Lord said.
23. He laid hands on Joshua and gave him the job.

Numbers 28

Daily, Weekly, and Monthly Offerings

1. The Lord told Moses,
2. "Tell the Israelites: Bring my offerings at the right times. They are my food, and I am pleased by them."
3. "Each day, offer two lambs a year old with no defects—one in the morning,
4. one in the evening.
5. Also bring flour mixed with oil.
6. This is a daily burnt offering that began at Mount Sinai.
7. Pour out a drink offering of wine with it."
8. "Offer the second lamb in the evening, just like the morning one."
9. "On the Sabbath, offer two more lambs and grain offerings.
10. This is the weekly Sabbath offering."

11. "On the first day of each month, offer two bulls, one ram, and seven lambs.
12. Bring grain and drink offerings with each.
13–14. Use flour and oil and wine with every animal.
15. Also offer one goat for sin."

Passover and Other Festivals

16. "Celebrate Passover on the 14th day of the first month.
17. On the 15th day, celebrate the Festival of Unleavened Bread. Eat bread with no yeast for 7 days.
18. Meet on the first day and do no work.
19. Bring offerings: two bulls, one ram, and seven lambs.
20–23. Add grain and drink offerings.
24. Don't use your regular daily offering—bring this one instead.
25. Do this each of the 7 days.
26. Meet on the seventh day and don't work."
27. "On the day of first fruits (when you bring your first grain to the Lord),
28. bring two bulls, one ram, and seven lambs.
29–30. Add grain and drink offerings.
31. All must be perfect animals."

Numbers 29

More Festivals and Offerings

1. "On the first day of the seventh month, blow trumpets. Don't work.
2. Bring a burnt offering: one bull, one ram, seven lambs.
3–6. Add grain, drink, and sin offerings."
7. "On the tenth day (Day of Atonement), don't eat or work.
8. Offer one bull, one ram, and seven lambs.
9–11. Add all grain, drink, and sin offerings."
12. "On the 15th day (Festival of Shelters), don't work. Celebrate for 7 days.
13. On day 1: 13 bulls, two rams, 14 lambs.
14–16. Add grain, drink, and sin offerings."
17. "Day 2: 12 bulls, two rams, 14 lambs.
18–19. Add offerings."
20. "Day 3: 11 bulls, two rams, 14 lambs.
21–22. Add offerings."
23. "Day 4: 10 bulls, two rams, 14 lambs.
24–25. Add offerings."
26. "Day 5: 9 bulls, two rams, 14 lambs.
27–28. Add offerings."
29. "Day 6: 8 bulls, two rams, 14 lambs.
30–31. Add offerings."
32. "Day 7: 7 bulls, two rams, 14 lambs.
33–34. Add offerings."
35. "Day 8: a special meeting. Don't work. Offer one bull, one ram, 7 lambs.
36–38. Add offerings."
39. "These are extra offerings for festivals. Keep doing your daily and monthly offerings.
40. Moses told all this to the Israelites."

Numbers 30

Keeping Promises to God

1. Moses told the leaders:
2. "If a man makes a promise to the Lord, he must keep it."
3. "If a young woman makes a promise while living at home,
4. and her father says nothing, the promise stands.
5. But if her father says no, the promise is canceled."
6. "If a woman makes a promise after she marries,
7. and her husband says nothing, the promise stands.

8. But if he stops her, the promise is canceled."
9. "If a widow or divorced woman makes a promise, she must keep it."
10. "If a wife makes a promise,
11. and her husband says nothing, it stands.
12. But if he cancels it, it's canceled."
13. "A husband may cancel any promise that causes suffering."
14. "If he waits too long, the promise stands."
15. "If he cancels it later, he is guilty."
16. These are the rules the Lord gave Moses about promises made by women to the Lord.

Numbers 31

Israel Fights Midian

1. The Lord told Moses,
2. "Take revenge on the Midianites. Then you will die."
3. Moses told the people, "Get ready to fight Midian."
4. "Send 1,000 men from each tribe."
5. So 12,000 men went to war.
6. Moses sent them with Phinehas and the holy tools, including trumpets.
7. They fought Midian and killed all the men.
8. They killed the kings and Balaam too.
9. They captured the women, children, animals, and riches.
10. They burned the cities and camps.
11. They brought everything back to Moses, Eleazar, and the rest of the people.
12. They brought the prisoners and goods to the camp near the Jordan River.
13. Moses, Eleazar, and the leaders went out to meet them.
14. Moses was angry and said,
15. "Why did you let the women live?
16. They led us to sin at Peor."
17. "Kill every boy and woman who has slept with a man.
18. Keep the girls who haven't."
19. "Stay outside the camp seven days. If you touched a dead body, you're unclean."
20. "Purify all clothes, leather, and wood."
21. Eleazar said,
22. "Gold, silver, bronze, iron, tin, and lead must be cleaned with fire.
23. Then wash them with the special water.
24. On day 7, wash your clothes and you'll be clean."
25. The Lord told Moses,
26. "Count all the people and animals taken in battle."
27. "Divide it equally between the soldiers and the rest of the people."
28. "Take a tax from the soldiers: one out of every 500 animals."
29. "Give that to Eleazar."
30. "From the people's half, take one out of every 50 and give it to the Levites."
31. Moses and Eleazar did what God said.

32–35. Total: 675,000 sheep, 72,000 cattle, 61,000 donkeys, and 32,000 girls.

36–47. They divided it all and gave God's share to Eleazar and the Levites.

48. The army leaders came to Moses and said,
49. "We counted the soldiers—no one died!"
50. "We're giving gold as a gift to the Lord."

51–54. Moses and Eleazar accepted the gold and brought it to the Meeting Tent.

Numbers 32

Two Tribes Settle Early

1. The tribes of Reuben and Gad had lots of animals. They saw the land east of the Jordan was perfect.
2. They said to Moses,

3–4. "This land is great for animals."

5. "Let us have it. Don't make us cross the Jordan."
6. Moses said, "Should your brothers go to war while you stay here?"
7. "You're discouraging the others."
8. "This is what your ancestors did when I sent them to spy out the land."
9. "They made the people afraid."

10–11. "So God said they would die in the desert."

12. "Only Caleb and Joshua were faithful."
13. "God made Israel wander for 40 years."
14. "Now you're doing the same thing!"
15. "If you turn from God, He'll leave us here even longer!"
16. They replied, "We'll build homes for our families and pens for our animals."
17. "Then we'll go help the others take their land.
18. "We won't rest until they all have land too."
19. "We want our share on this side of the Jordan."
20. Moses said, "If you keep your promise and fight,

21–22. and help everyone, then you can return here and settle.

23. But if not, you will be sinning—and God will punish you."
24. "Build what you need, then get ready."
25. They said, "We will do what you command."

26–27. "Our wives and kids will stay, but our men will fight."

28. Moses told Eleazar, Joshua, and the leaders.
29. "If they fight and help, give them this land.
30. If not, they must settle west of the Jordan."
31. The men agreed.
32. "We will go fight and obey the Lord."
33. So Moses gave the land to Reuben, Gad, and half of Manasseh.

34–38. They rebuilt and renamed cities.

39–42. Some of Manasseh's people also captured nearby towns and lived there.

Numbers 33

A List of Places Traveled

1. These are the places Israel traveled after leaving Egypt, led by Moses and Aaron.
2. Moses wrote down each place they camped as God guided them.
3. They left Rameses on the 15th day of the first month—the day after Passover.
4. The Egyptians were burying their dead when God struck them.

5–49. (Summary: List of all places the Israelites camped. Includes over 40 stops, like Rameses, Marah, Sinai, Kadesh, and the plains of Moab near the Jordan.)

50. The Lord told Moses in Moab,
51. "Tell the people: When you cross the Jordan,
52. destroy all idols and pagan places.
53. Take the land—I'm giving it to you."
54. "Divide it fairly by tribe size."
55. "If you don't remove the people, they'll be trouble and cause pain."
56. "And I'll do to you what I planned to do to them."

Numbers 34

Borders and Leaders for the Promised Land

1. The Lord told Moses,
2. "Tell the Israelites: This is the land I'm giving you in Canaan."
3. "The southern border will be from the Desert of Zin along Edom and end at the Dead Sea.
4. It will turn south of Scorpion Pass and go to Zin, ending at Kadesh Barnea.
5. Then it goes to the Brook of Egypt and ends at the Mediterranean Sea."
6. "The western border is the Mediterranean Sea."
7. "The northern border starts at the Mediterranean Sea and goes to Mount Hor,
8. then to Lebo Hamath and Zedad,
9. to Ziphron and ends at Hazar Enan."
10. "The eastern border goes from Hazar Enan to Shepham,
11. down to Riblah on the east side of Ain,
12. and ends at the Dead Sea."
13. Moses said, "This is the land you will get. Nine and a half tribes will receive it."
14. "Reuben, Gad, and half of Manasseh already got their land on the east side of the Jordan."
15. "They got land east of Jericho."
16. The Lord said,
17. "Here are the leaders who will divide the land: Eleazar the priest and Joshua."
18. "Pick one leader from each tribe."
19. These are their names: Caleb son of Jephunneh, from Judah;
20. Shemuel son of Ammihud, from Simeon;
21. Elidad son of Kislon, from Benjamin;
22. Bukki son of Jogli, from Dan;
23. Hanniel son of Ephod, from Joseph;
24. Kemuel son of Shiphtan, from Ephraim;
25. Elizaphan son of Parnak, from Zebulun;
26. Paltiel son of Azzan, from Issachar;
27. Ahihud son of Shelomi, from Asher;
28. Pedahel son of Ammihud, from Naphtali.
29. These men were chosen to divide the land.

Numbers 35

Towns for Levites and Cities of Safety

1. The Lord told Moses in the plains of Moab,
2. "Tell the people: When you get the land, give towns to the Levites."
3. "They will live in the towns and use the fields for animals."
4. "The land around the towns will be used for animals, gardens, and storage."
5. "Measure 1,000 cubits (about half a mile) in each direction from the town."
6. "Give the Levites 48 towns in total, including 6 cities of safety."
7. "The total is 48 towns for the Levites."
8. "Big tribes will give more, small tribes will give less."
9. The Lord told Moses,
10. "Tell the people: When you cross into Canaan,
11. choose six cities of safety."
12. "They will protect people who kill someone by accident."
13. "There must be six total—
14. three on the east side of the Jordan and three in Canaan."
15. "They are for Israelites, foreigners, and visitors."
16. "If someone uses an iron tool to kill, it's murder—they must die.

17–18. Same with stone or wood tools.

19. The victim's family may carry out the punishment."

20–21. "If it was on purpose with hate, it's murder—put them to death."

22–23. "But if it was an accident,

24. a judge will decide.

25. If innocent, the person must stay in a city of safety until the high priest dies."

26. "If they leave the city early,

27. the family can kill them without guilt."

28. "They must stay in the city until the high priest dies. Then they are free."

29. "This law is forever."

30. "One witness is not enough for a death sentence.

31. Don't accept money to save a murderer—they must die.

32. Don't let someone buy their way out of a city of safety."

33. "Murder pollutes the land. Only the killer's death can clean it."

34. "Don't make the land unclean. I live there with you."

Numbers 36

Property Rules for Zelophehad's Daughters

1. Leaders from the Manasseh tribe came to Moses.
2. They said, "The Lord gave land to Zelophehad's daughters.
3. If they marry men from other tribes, that land will leave our tribe."
4. "In the Year of Freedom, the land will move to another tribe."
5. Moses gave God's answer:
6. "The daughters may marry anyone, but only from their own tribe."
7. "That way, land stays in the family and tribe.
8. Every daughter with land must marry in her tribe."
9. "No land may be transferred between tribes."
10. So the daughters of Zelophehad obeyed.
11. Mahlah, Tirzah, Hoglah, Milcah, and Noah married cousins from their own tribe.
12. This kept the land in the tribe of Manasseh.
13. These are the commands the Lord gave Moses for the Israelites in the plains of Moab near the Jordan across from Jericho.

–Deuteronomy –

Moses gives final speeches and repeats God's laws before Israel enters the land.

Deuteronomy 1

Moses Reminds Israel About the Journey

1. These are the words Moses spoke to all Israel in the desert east of the Jordan.
2. It takes 11 days to go from Horeb to Kadesh Barnea by Mount Seir.
3. On the first day of the eleventh month, Moses told the people what the Lord had commanded.
4. This was after they defeated King Sihon of the Amorites and King Og of Bashan.
5. In Moab, Moses began to explain the law:
6. "The Lord said at Horeb, 'You have stayed here long enough.
7. Go to the hill country, the land of the Amorites, and everywhere else I promised.
8. I have given you this land. Go and take it, as I promised your ancestors.'"
9. I told you, "I can't carry all your problems by myself.

10. There are too many of you—the Lord has made you grow.
11. May the Lord give you a thousand times more and bless you!
12. But I can't solve all your arguments alone.
13. Choose wise and understanding men from your tribes, and I'll make them your leaders."
14. You agreed with my plan.
16. So I chose leaders for each tribe and gave them jobs.
17. I told the judges: "Be fair. Listen to everyone—Israelite or foreigner.
18. Don't favor anyone. Bring hard cases to me."
19. I told you everything you needed to do.
20. Then we left Horeb and traveled through the desert to Kadesh Barnea.
21. I said, "The land the Lord promised us is right in front of us.
22. Go and take it! Don't be afraid."
23. You asked me to send men to explore the land first.
24. I agreed and chose 12 men—one from each tribe.
25. They went into the hill country and came to the Valley of Eshkol.
26. They brought back fruit and said, "It's a good land!"
27. But you refused to go.
28. You complained and said, "The Lord hates us! He brought us here to die!"
29. "The people are taller and stronger than us. Their cities are huge!"
30. I told you, "Don't be afraid.
31. The Lord will fight for you like He did in Egypt.
32. He carried you like a father carries his child.
33. But you didn't trust Him."
34. "He went ahead of you to show the way and gave you light at night and a cloud by day."
35. The Lord heard your complaints and got angry.
36. He said, "None of this generation will see the land I promised,
37. except Caleb. He followed me with his whole heart."
38. The Lord was also angry with me and said I couldn't go in either.
39. But Joshua will lead you. Encourage him.
40. Your children, who didn't know right from wrong, will enter the land.
41. But you must turn back into the desert."
42. You said, "We've sinned! We'll go fight now!"
43. But the Lord warned, "Don't go! I won't be with you."
44. You didn't listen and went anyway.
45. The Amorites attacked and chased you like bees.
46. You cried to the Lord, but He didn't listen.
47. So you stayed in Kadesh a long time.

Deuteronomy 2

More of the Journey

1. Then we turned around and went back into the desert toward the Red Sea.
2. The Lord said,
3. "You've wandered long enough. Now go north."
4. "Pass through Seir, the land of your relatives, the people of Esau. They will be afraid, but don't bother them.
5. Don't fight them. I gave them their land, and it won't be yours."
6. Buy food and water from them.

7. The Lord has blessed you. He has watched over you for 40 years in the desert.
8. So we passed by our relatives, the people of Esau, and traveled along the desert road.
9. The Lord said, "Don't bother the Moabites. I gave Ar to them, not you."
10. (The Emites once lived there. They were strong and tall.)
11. (They were like the Anakites and called Rephaites too.)
12. (The Horites once lived in Seir, but Esau's people drove them out.)
13. The Lord said, "Cross the Zered Valley." So we did.
14. It had been 38 years since we left Kadesh, and all the fighting men had died.
15. The Lord was against them until they were all gone.
16. After they died,
17. the Lord said,
18. "You are about to pass through Moab."
19. "Don't fight the Ammonites. I gave that land to them."
20. (That land also used to belong to Rephaites.)
21. (They were tall and strong, but the Lord helped the Ammonites defeat them.)
22. (He did the same for Esau's people in Seir.)
23. (The Caphtorites defeated the Avvites and took their land.)
24. The Lord said, "Get ready to cross the Arnon Valley. I'm giving you Sihon's land."
25. "All the nations will be afraid of you."
26. I sent messengers to Sihon with peaceful words.
27. I said, "Let us pass through your land.
28. We'll buy food and water.
29. Just like we did with Esau's people and the Moabites."
30. But Sihon refused because the Lord made him stubborn so we could defeat him.
31. The Lord said, "I've given Sihon's land to you. Take it!"
32. Sihon came out to fight us.
33. The Lord gave him to us. We won.
34. We captured his towns and destroyed everyone, even the children.
35. We took the animals and valuables.
36. We defeated every town from Aroer to Gilead.
37. But we did not go near Ammon, just as the Lord told us.

Deuteronomy 3

More Victories

1. Then we turned and went toward Bashan. King Og came to fight us.
2. The Lord said, "Don't be afraid. I will help you just like with Sihon."
3. So we defeated Og, his sons, and all his army.
4. We took all his cities—60 in total.
5. These cities had strong walls and gates.
6. We destroyed them all, just like we did to Sihon's towns.
7. We kept the animals and riches.
8. We took land from both kings east of the Jordan.
9. (Mount Hermon was called Sirion by the Sidonians and Senir by the Amorites.)
10. We took all the towns from Gilead to Bashan.
11. Og was the last of the Rephaites. His bed was 13 feet long!
12. I gave Reuben and Gad the land from Aroer to Gilead.
13. I gave half of Bashan to half of Manasseh's tribe.

14. Jair's family took the towns in Bashan and named them after himself.
15. I gave Gilead to Makir.
16. The land from Gilead to the Arnon River went to Reuben and Gad.
17. Their border was the Jordan River.
18. I told the tribes, "The Lord gave you this land, but your fighting men must help your brothers."
19. "Your families can stay here,
20. but you must help until everyone has land."
21. I told Joshua, "You saw what God did to these kings. He will do the same in Canaan."
22. "Don't be afraid. The Lord will fight for you."
23. I begged the Lord,
24. "Lord, you've shown your power. Let me see the land."
25. "Let me go across the Jordan."
26. But the Lord was angry and said, "That's enough. Don't ask again."
27. "Go to the top of Pisgah and look at the land."
28. "Appoint Joshua to lead the people."
29. So we stayed in the valley near Beth Peor.

Deuteronomy 4

Obey God's Laws

1. Moses said, "Israel, listen to God's laws. Obey them so you can live and take the land."
2. "Don't add to or take away from these laws."
3. "You saw what God did at Baal Peor. He destroyed the people who followed false gods."
4. "But you who stayed faithful are still alive."
5. "I've taught you all the laws the Lord gave me."
6. "Obey them. Other nations will see your wisdom and say, 'These people are wise!'"

7-8. "What other nation has a God so close or laws so fair?"

9. "Be careful. Don't forget what you've seen. Teach it to your children."
10. "Remember when you stood before the Lord at Horeb. He said, 'Gather the people. I'll teach them to respect me.'"
11. "You stood at the mountain, covered in fire and clouds."
12. "You heard God speak, but didn't see Him."
13. "He gave you the Ten Commandments on two stone tablets."
14. "And He told me to teach you the rest."
15. "Be careful. You didn't see a shape when God spoke.

16-18. Don't make idols of people, animals, birds, or fish.

19. Don't worship the sun, moon, or stars. God gave those to all people, not just you."
20. "God rescued you from Egypt to be His people."
21. "God was angry with me and said I couldn't enter the land."
22. "But you will cross the Jordan. I won't."
23. "Don't forget your agreement with God. Don't make idols."
24. "God is like fire. He's a jealous God."
25. "If you have kids and grandkids, don't forget God or make idols."
26. "If you do, you won't live long in the land. You'll be destroyed."
27. "God will scatter you. Only a few will survive."
28. "You'll worship man-made gods that can't speak or hear."
29. "But if you look for God with all your heart, you will find Him."

30. "In trouble, you'll turn back to Him."
31. "God is kind. He won't forget His promise."
32. "Has anything this great ever happened before?"
33. "Did any other people hear God speak and live?"
34. "Did any god take a nation out of another with miracles like God did in Egypt?"
35. "God showed you this so you'd know He is the only God."
36. "He let you hear His voice and see His fire."
37. "Because He loved your ancestors, He chose you."
38. "He helped you beat stronger nations and gave you their land."
39. "Know this: there is no other God in heaven or earth."
40. "Obey His rules so you and your kids will live long in the land."
41. Moses chose three cities east of the Jordan as safe places.
42. If someone killed by accident, they could run there for safety:
43. Bezer, Ramoth, and Golan.
44. These are the laws Moses gave the Israelites.
45. They were given after leaving Egypt,
46. east of the Jordan in Moab,
47. after they defeated King Sihon.

48–49. The land stretched from Aroer to Mount Pisgah.

Deuteronomy 5

The Ten Commandments Repeated

1. Moses said, "Israel, listen to these laws. Learn them and obey them."
2. "God made an agreement with us at Horeb."
3. "It wasn't just for our ancestors—it's for us too."
4. "God spoke to you face-to-face from the fire."
5. "I stood between you and God because you were afraid."
7. "God said: I am the Lord who brought you out of Egypt."
8. "Don't have any other gods."
9. "Don't make or worship idols of anything in heaven, on earth, or in the sea."
10. "I, the Lord, am a jealous God. I punish those who hate me but love those who love me."
11. "Don't misuse my name."
12. "Keep the Sabbath day holy, as I commanded."
13. "Work for six days,
14. but rest on the seventh. This is for everyone, even animals."
15. "Remember, you were slaves in Egypt and God gave you rest."
16. "Honor your father and mother so you'll live long."
17. "Don't murder."
18. "Don't commit adultery."
19. "Don't steal."
20. "Don't lie about others."
21. "Don't want what belongs to others—not their house, spouse, or anything else."
22. "God spoke these words to the whole nation from the fire. He wrote them on two stone tablets."
23. "When you heard His voice, you came to me afraid."
24. "You said, 'We've heard God speak and lived!'
25. 'But if He keeps speaking, we might die!'
26. 'No one has ever heard God speak like this and lived.'
27. 'You go talk to God. Then tell us what He says.'"

28. "The Lord said, 'I heard the people. They are right.'
30. 'I wish they would always fear me and obey.'
31. 'Tell them to go back to their tents.'
32. 'But you stay. I'll give you all my laws to teach them.'"
33. "So obey God. Don't turn left or right."
34. "Follow His path and you'll live long and do well."

Deuteronomy 6

Love the Lord

1. These are the laws the Lord told me to teach you.
2. Fear God and obey His commands, so you and your kids will live long.
3. Listen and obey, and you'll have a good life in the land.
4. The Lord is our God—the only God.
5. Love Him with all your heart, soul, and strength.
6. Keep these words in your heart.
7. Teach them to your children. Talk about them at home, on the road, at bedtime, and in the morning.
8. Tie them on your hands and heads as reminders.
9. Write them on your doors and gates.
10. When God gives you homes, cities, and things you didn't build,
11. and you have plenty of food,
12. don't forget the Lord who rescued you from Egypt.
13. Respect the Lord. Serve only Him and make promises in His name.
14. Don't follow other gods.
15. The Lord gets angry if you do, and you'll be destroyed.
16. Don't test God like you did at Massah.
17. Obey His commands and do what's right.
18. Then you'll live well in the land He promised.
19. He will help you defeat your enemies.
20. When your kids ask why we obey God's laws,
21. tell them, "We were slaves in Egypt,
22. but God did great miracles,
23. and brought us to this land."
24. "He gave us these laws to protect us and help us live."
25. "If we obey, God will see us as right."

Deuteronomy 7

Destroy False Gods

1. The Lord will bring you into the land and remove seven nations stronger than you.
2. He will help you defeat them. Destroy them completely. Don't make peace treaties.
3. Don't marry them.
4. They will turn your children away from God. Then the Lord will be angry and destroy you.
5. Break down their altars, smash their stones, cut down their poles, and burn their idols.
6. You are special to the Lord. He chose you out of all the people on earth.
7. He didn't choose you because you were the biggest nation—you were the smallest.
8. He chose you because He loves you and keeps His promises.
9. Know this: the Lord is God. He keeps His promises to those who love and obey Him.
10. But He punishes those who hate Him.
11. So obey His commands.
12. If you obey, God will keep His promise and bless you.

13. He will love you, bless your children, give you good crops and animals.
14. You'll be more blessed than other nations.
15. He will keep you healthy and protect you from diseases.
16. Destroy all the people the Lord gives you. Don't worship their gods—they are a trap.
17. Don't say, "They're too strong for us."
18. Remember what God did to Pharaoh and Egypt.
19. You saw the signs and miracles. He will do the same again.
20. He will send fear on them until they're gone.
21. Don't be afraid—God is powerful and with you.
22. He will remove them slowly so wild animals don't take over.
23. He will defeat them.
24. He will put their kings in your hands.
26. Burn their idols. Don't keep any gold or silver from them.
27. Don't bring any of their cursed things into your home, or you'll be cursed too.

Deuteronomy 8

Don't Forget God

1. Obey every command so you will live and enter the land.
2. Remember how God led you in the desert for 40 years to test your heart.
3. He made you hungry, then gave you manna to teach you that people need more than bread—they need God's words.
4. Your clothes didn't wear out. Your feet didn't swell.
5. God was teaching you like a parent teaches a child.
6. So respect and obey Him.
7. You're entering a good land with streams, springs, and water.
8. It has wheat, barley, vines, figs, pomegranates, oil, and honey.
9. You'll have plenty of food and lack nothing.
10. When you eat and are full, thank the Lord.
11. Don't forget God or stop obeying Him.
12. When you have plenty—houses, animals, silver, and gold—
13. don't become proud and forget He rescued you from Egypt.
14. He led you through a dangerous desert with snakes and scorpions.
15. He gave you manna to humble you and test you for your good.
16. Don't say, "I did all this by myself!"
17. Remember—it is God who gives you power to be successful.
18. If you forget Him and follow other gods,
19. you will be destroyed like other nations.

Deuteronomy 9

God Wins the Battles

1. Israel, listen: You will cross the Jordan and defeat nations stronger and taller than you.
2. Their cities have high walls. Their people are giants.
3. But God will go ahead of you like a fire. He will destroy them.
4. Don't say, "God gave us this land because we're good." No! These nations are evil.
5. You are not getting this land because you are good, but because they are wicked and God keeps His promise to your ancestors.

6. Understand this: You are stubborn, and God is not giving you the land because you deserve it.
7. Remember how you kept disobeying God since you left Egypt.
8. At Mount Horeb, you made God angry enough to destroy you.
9. I went up the mountain to get the stone tablets. I stayed 40 days and nights with no food or water.
10. God gave me the tablets with the Ten Commandments.
11. After 40 days, He gave them to me.
12. He said, "Go down. The people have sinned. They made an idol."
13. "They are stubborn."
14. "Let me destroy them and make a great nation from you."
15. I went down with the tablets. The mountain was on fire.
16. I saw your sin—you made a gold calf!
17. I threw down the tablets and broke them.
18. Then I lay before the Lord 40 days and nights with no food or water.
20. I was afraid God would destroy you, but He listened to me.
21. He was also angry with Aaron and wanted to destroy him, but I prayed for him too.
22. I burned and crushed the calf and threw the powder into the stream.
23. At Taberah, Massah, and Kibroth Hattaavah, you also made God angry.
24. At Kadesh Barnea, He told you to take the land, but you didn't trust or obey Him.
25. You've been rebellious ever since I've known you.
26. I lay before the Lord 40 days and nights. I begged Him not to destroy you.
27. I said, "Lord, don't destroy your people. You saved them with great power.
28. Remember Abraham, Isaac, and Jacob. Don't look at their sin.
29. The nations will say, 'God wasn't strong enough to give them the land.'"
30. "But they are Your people—You brought them out of Egypt with great strength."

Deuteronomy 10

What God Wants From You

1. God told me, "Make two new stone tablets and a wooden chest.
2. I'll write the same commands on them."
3. So I made a chest and brought up two tablets.
4. God wrote the same Ten Commandments and gave them to me.
5. I put them in the chest, and they are still there.
6. (The Israelites moved from Beeroth to Moserah. Aaron died there. His son Eleazar became priest.)
7. (Then they traveled to Gudgodah, then to Jotbathah.)
8. (The Lord chose the Levites to carry the chest, serve at the Meeting Tent, and bless the people.)
9. (That's why Levites don't get land—the Lord is their inheritance.)
10. I stayed on the mountain 40 days and nights, just like before. The Lord listened and didn't destroy you.
11. He said, "Go lead the people. They will take the land I promised."
12. Now, Israel, what does God want from you? Respect Him, follow His ways, love Him, and obey His commands.
13. These commands are for your own good.
14. Everything in heaven and earth belongs to God.
15. But He chose you out of all people to be His own.

16. So open your hearts and stop being stubborn.
17. The Lord is the greatest God. He doesn't play favorites or take bribes.
18. He defends orphans, widows, and loves foreigners.
19. So you must love foreigners too—you were foreigners in Egypt.
20. Respect the Lord. Serve only Him.
21. He is your God. He did great and amazing things for you.
22. Your ancestors were only 70 people, but now you are as many as the stars in the sky.

Deuteronomy 11

Love and Obey God

1. Love the Lord and always obey His laws.
2. You saw what God did—you saw His greatness and power.
3. You saw the signs and miracles in Egypt.
4. You saw Him destroy Pharaoh's army in the sea.
5. You saw what He did in the desert.
6. You saw the earth open and swallow Dathan and Abiram for rebelling.
7. You saw all these great things the Lord did.
8. So obey His commands and be strong. Then you'll live in the land and win battles.
9. You'll live long in the land He promised your ancestors.
10. Egypt was hard—you had to water the land yourself.
11. But the new land has rain, hills, and valleys.
12. The Lord cares for it and watches over it all year.
13. If you love God and serve Him,
14. He'll send rain for your crops.
15. You'll have food for yourselves and your animals.
16. Don't turn away and worship other gods.
17. If you do, He will stop the rain, and you'll starve.
18. Keep these words in your heart. Tie them to your hands and heads.
19. Teach them to your kids. Talk about them at home, outside, morning, and night.
20. Write them on your doors and gates.
21. Then you and your children will live long in the land.
23. If you love God and obey Him,
24. He will help you defeat strong nations.
25. Every place you step will be yours.
26. No one will stand against you—God will make them afraid.
27. I give you a choice: a blessing or a curse.
28. A blessing if you obey God.
29. A curse if you disobey and follow other gods.
30. When you enter the land, say the blessings from Mount Gerizim and the curses from Mount Ebal.
31. These mountains are on the west side of the Jordan near Gilgal.
32. You are crossing the Jordan to take the land.
33. Obey all the laws I've given you today.

Deuteronomy 12

Only Worship God's Way

1. These are the laws to follow in the land the Lord is giving you.
2. Destroy all the places where the other nations worshiped their gods—on hills, mountains, and under trees.
3. Smash their altars and idols. Burn them and erase their names.
4. Don't worship God in those ways.

5. Go to the place the Lord chooses. That is where you must worship.
6. Bring your offerings there—your sacrifices, tithes, gifts, and special promises.
7. Celebrate there with your families. Be happy with the blessings God gave you.
8. Don't worship any way you want.
9. You haven't yet reached the peaceful land God is giving you.
10. But when you get there and live safely,
11. then bring everything to the place the Lord chooses.
12. Celebrate there with your families, including Levites who live among you.
13. Don't offer sacrifices just anywhere.
14. Only in the place God chooses.
15. You may eat meat anywhere in your towns, just like wild deer or animals.
16. But don't eat the blood—pour it out on the ground.
17. Don't eat tithes or offerings at home.
18. Eat them only at the place God chooses. Share with Levites and be happy.
19. Don't forget the Levites—they have no land.
20. When God increases your land, you may eat meat whenever you want.
21. If the Lord's chosen place is far, you may eat meat in your town.
22. Eat it like you would deer or antelope.
23. But don't eat the blood—it has life.
24. Pour it out on the ground.
25. Don't eat it, so you and your children will do well.
26. Bring only your holy offerings to God's chosen place.
27. Offer them on the altar. Pour out the blood and eat the meat.
28. Obey all these laws, so you and your children will be blessed.
29. When God removes the other nations,
30. don't ask, "How did they worship?" Don't copy them.
31. Don't worship God their way—they did evil things like burning their own children!
32. Do only what God commands. Don't add or take away from it.

Deuteronomy 13

Don't Follow False Prophets

1. If a prophet or dreamer gives you a sign or miracle,
2. and says, "Let's follow other gods,"
3. don't listen. God is testing you to see if you really love Him.
4. Follow the Lord, respect Him, obey Him, and stay close to Him.
5. That prophet must be put to death for trying to turn you away from God.
6. If your brother, child, wife, or best friend secretly says, "Let's follow other gods,"
7. gods that no one in Israel has ever worshipped,
8. don't listen or show mercy.
9. Report them, and they must be punished.
10. Throw the first stone, then all the people must help.
11. All Israel will hear and be afraid to do this evil again.
12. If you hear that people in a town are turning others away from God,
13. saying, "Let's follow other gods,"
14. you must check the facts carefully.
15. If it's true, destroy the whole town.
16. Burn everything. Don't keep anything for yourself.
17. God will turn away from His anger and show you mercy again.
18. He will bless you if you obey Him and do what is right.

Deuteronomy 14

Clean and Unclean Food

1. Don't cut yourself or shave your head for the dead.
2. You are God's special people. He chose you out of all nations.
3. Don't eat anything unclean.

4–5. You may eat these animals: ox, sheep, goat, deer, and similar ones.

6. Only eat animals that chew the cud and have split hooves.
7. Don't eat camels, rabbits, or pigs.
8. Don't touch their dead bodies.
9. You may eat fish with fins and scales.
10. Don't eat anything without fins or scales.
11. You may eat clean birds.

12–18. Don't eat eagles, vultures, owls, hawks, or bats.

19. Don't eat insects with wings.
20. But you may eat clean flying insects.
21. Don't eat anything that dies on its own. You may give it to a foreigner.
22. Don't cook a young goat in its mother's milk.

Tithes

23. Set aside a tenth of your crops every year.
24. Eat it before the Lord at the place He chooses.
25. If it's too far,
26. turn your tithe into money.
27. Use the money to buy food and drinks, then celebrate with your family.
28. Don't forget the Levites—they have no land.
29. Every third year, store your tithe in your town.
30. Give it to Levites, foreigners, orphans, and widows. Then God will bless you.

Deuteronomy 15

The Year to Cancel Debts

1. Every seven years, cancel all debts.
2. If someone owes you money, forgive it.
3. You may still collect from foreigners.
4. No one in Israel should be poor.
5. If you obey God, He will bless you.
6. You will lend to other nations, but not borrow. You'll rule others, not be ruled.
7. Don't be selfish. Help poor people in your town.
8. Be generous.
9. Don't hold back just because the seventh year is near. God will see and be angry.
10. Give freely. God will bless you.
11. There will always be poor people—so be kind and give to them.

Freeing Slaves

12. If a fellow Israelite becomes your slave, free them in the seventh year.
13. Don't let them leave empty-handed.
14. Give generously from your flocks and fields.
15. Remember—you were slaves in Egypt, and God saved you.
16. If the slave loves you and wants to stay,
17. pierce their ear to show they belong to you. Then they can stay forever.
18. Don't be upset about freeing your slave. They served you well.

Firstborn Animals

19. Set aside all firstborn male animals for the Lord.
20. Don't work your firstborn ox or shear your firstborn sheep.
21. Eat them with your family at the place God chooses.
22. If the animal has a defect, don't offer it to God.

23. You may eat it at home, like deer or antelope.
24. But never eat the blood—pour it out on the ground.

Deuteronomy 16

Special Festivals

1. Celebrate Passover in the first month because that's when God brought you out of Egypt.
2. Offer the Passover sacrifice at the place God chooses.
3. Don't eat bread with yeast—only eat flat bread for seven days to remember when you left Egypt fast.
4. Don't keep any yeast for those seven days. Don't save any meat until morning.
5. Don't offer the sacrifice in just any town.
6. Offer it at sunset at the place God chooses.
7. Cook and eat it there, then return home in the morning.
8. On the seventh day, have a special meeting and don't work.
9. Count seven weeks from when you start harvesting.
10. Then celebrate the Festival of Weeks. Bring an offering from what you earned.
11. Celebrate with your family, the Levites, foreigners, orphans, and widows at the place God chooses.
12. Remember—you were once slaves in Egypt. Follow these rules.
13. Celebrate the Festival of Shelters for seven days after the harvest.
14. Be happy with your family and everyone in your town.
15. God will bless your work, so celebrate with joy.
16. Three times a year, all men must go to the place God chooses for these festivals: Passover, Weeks, and Shelters. Don't come empty-handed.
17. Each person should give as much as they can, based on how God has blessed them.

Judges and Justice

18. Choose judges and officers for every town. They must judge fairly.
19. Don't show favoritism or take bribes. Bribes twist justice.
20. Always do what is right so you can live and stay in the land.
21. Don't plant trees or poles near the altar for false gods.
22. Don't set up sacred stones—God hates them.

Deuteronomy 17

Judges, Kings, and Justice

1. Don't offer animals with defects—they're not acceptable to God.
2. If someone worships other gods,
3. like the sun, moon, or stars,
4. and it's true after checking,
5. stone that person to death.
6. There must be two or three witnesses—never just one.
7. The witnesses must throw the first stones.
8. If a case is too hard to decide, go to the priests and judges at the Meeting Tent.
9. Ask for their decision.
10. Do exactly what they say.
11. Follow their instructions carefully.
12. If someone refuses to listen, they must die. Remove the evil.
13. Everyone will hear and be afraid to disobey.
14. When you ask for a king, like other nations,
15. choose someone God approves—an Israelite, not a foreigner.

16. The king must not collect many horses or send people back to Egypt for them.
17. He must not have many wives or too much silver and gold.
18. He must write a copy of these laws and read and obey them daily.
19. This will help him respect God and obey the laws.
20. Then he won't think he's better than others and will rule for a long time.

Deuteronomy 18

Priests, Levites, and Prophets

1. The Levites and priests won't get land. Their share is the Lord's offerings.
2. They live off what the Lord gives them.
3. This is what priests get: the shoulder, cheeks, and stomach from sacrifices.
4. They also get the first grain, wine, oil, and wool.
5. God chose them to serve Him always.
6. A Levite may move to another town and still serve at the Meeting Tent.
7. He can work there just like the other Levites.
8. He gets the same share of food, plus anything his family gave him.
9. Don't copy the evil practices of the nations you drive out.

10-11. Don't sacrifice your children, tell fortunes, use magic, or talk to spirits.

12. God hates these things. That's why He's removing those nations.
13. Be faithful to the Lord.
14. Those nations listen to fortune-tellers—but not you.
15. God will send you a prophet like me. You must listen to him.
16. You asked for this at Mount Horeb when you were afraid to hear God speak again.
17. God said, "They are right.
18. I will raise up a prophet like you, and I will put my words in his mouth."
19. Anyone who doesn't listen to that prophet will be punished.
20. A false prophet who speaks in God's name or speaks for other gods must die.
21. If you wonder, "How do we know if a message is really from God?"
22. If it doesn't come true, it's not from God. Don't be afraid of that prophet.

Deuteronomy 19

Cities of Safety and Fair Trials

1. When God gives you land,
2. choose three cities to be safe places.
3. Make good roads to them. Divide the land into three parts, so anyone can reach a city fast.
4. These cities are for people who kill someone by accident.
5. For example, if two people cut wood and the ax head flies off and kills someone, the one who caused it can run to a safe city.
6. This keeps angry relatives from chasing and killing someone who didn't mean to hurt anyone.
7. That's why I command you to set up three cities.
8. If God gives you more land,
9. and you keep His laws,
10. then set up three more cities. This keeps innocent people from being killed.
11. But if someone hates another and kills them on purpose,
12. bring that person back from the city and punish him.
13. Don't feel sorry for a murderer—remove the evil from Israel.
14. Don't move your neighbor's boundary markers.

15. One witness isn't enough to prove someone guilty. It must be two or three.
16. If someone gives a false witness,
17. both people must stand before the priests and judges.
18. The judges must check carefully. If the witness lied,
19. give the liar the same punishment they tried to give the other person.
21. People will hear about it and be afraid.
22. Don't show pity—life for life, eye for eye, tooth for tooth.

Deuteronomy 20

Rules for War

1. When you go to war and see big armies, don't be afraid. God is with you.
2. Before the battle, the priest must speak to the army.

3-4. He'll say, "Don't be afraid. God will help you win."

5. The officers will say, "Did anyone build a new house and not live in it? Go home."
6. "Did anyone plant a vineyard but not enjoy it? Go home."
7. "Did anyone get engaged but not marry yet? Go home."
8. "Is anyone scared? Go home."
9. After that, leaders will pick commanders for the army.
10. When you come to a city, offer peace first.
11. If they agree, they will serve you.
12. If they refuse, attack them.
13. Kill all the men.
14. Keep the women, children, animals, and valuables.
15. This is for cities far away.
16. For cities in the land God gives you, destroy everything.
17. Destroy the Hittites, Amorites, Canaanites, Perizzites, Hivites, and Jebusites.
18. If you don't, they'll teach you to sin.
19. When attacking a city, don't destroy trees with fruit.
20. But you may cut down trees that don't give fruit.

Deuteronomy 21

Other Laws for Justice and Mercy

1. If someone is killed and no one knows who did it,
2. the leaders must measure to the closest town.
3. The leaders of that town must take a young cow that never worked,
4. and break its neck in a valley.
5. Then the priests come and pray.
6. The leaders wash their hands over the cow,
7. and say, "We didn't do this or see it happen."
8. "Lord, forgive Your people. Don't blame us for this death."
9. Then they will be forgiven.

10-11. If you go to war and see a beautiful woman and want to marry her,

12. take her home. She must shave her head and cut her nails.
13. She must mourn her family for one month. Then you can marry her.
14. If you don't want her later, let her go free. Don't treat her like a slave.
15. If a man has two wives and loves one more, and both have sons,
16. he must give the firstborn son his proper share, even if he's from the wife he doesn't love.
17. The firstborn son gets double the share because he is the first sign of strength.
18. If a son is stubborn and won't obey his parents,

19. they must bring him to the town leaders.
20. They will say, "Our son won't listen. He's wild and a drunk."
21. Then all the men must stone him. Remove the evil. Everyone will hear and be afraid.
23. If someone is guilty and put to death, and their body is hung on a tree, don't leave the body overnight.
24. Bury it the same day. Anyone hung on a tree is under God's curse. Don't make the land unclean.

Deuteronomy 22

Kindness and Respect

1. If you see your neighbor's ox or sheep wandering off, don't ignore it—take it back.
2. If you don't know who owns it, keep it safe until they come looking for it.
3. Do the same with anything your neighbor loses.
4. If you see their animal fall, help them lift it up.
5. Men must not dress like women, and women must not dress like men. God doesn't like that.
6. If you find a bird's nest on the ground or in a tree, don't take the mother with the babies.
7. You may take the babies, but let the mother go so things go well for you.
8. When you build a new house, put a fence on the roof so no one falls off and dies.
9. Don't plant two kinds of seeds in the same field.
10. Don't plow with an ox and a donkey together.
11. Don't wear clothes made of both wool and linen.
12. Sew tassels on the corners of your cloak.

Marriage Rules

13-14. If a man marries a woman and then says she's not a virgin,

15. her parents must bring proof to the town leaders.

16-17. Her father must say, "This man lied about my daughter."

18. The leaders must punish the man.
19. He must pay her father and stay married to her for life.
20. But if the charge is true,
21. the woman must be punished by stoning at her father's house. She sinned in Israel.
22. If a man sleeps with a married woman, both must be killed.
23. If a man sleeps with a promised virgin in town, both must die.
24. The woman didn't scream, and the man did wrong.
25. But if it happens in a field, only the man dies.
26. The woman did nothing wrong.
27. She had no one to help her.
28. If a man sleeps with a virgin who is not promised to anyone,
29. he must pay her father and marry her for life.
30. A man must not marry his father's wife.

Deuteronomy 23

Staying Pure in God's Camp

1. A man with crushed private parts may not enter the Lord's assembly.
2. A child born from a forbidden relationship may not enter either.
3. No Ammonite or Moabite may join the assembly—not even after ten generations.
4. They didn't give you food or water when you left Egypt and tried to hire Balaam to curse you.

5. But God turned the curse into a blessing.
6. Don't make peace with them.
7. Don't hate Edomites or Egyptians. You lived in their land.
8. Their grandchildren may join the assembly.
9. When you camp for war, stay pure.
10. If someone becomes unclean, leave the camp until evening.
11. Then bathe and return at sunset.
13. Keep a place outside the camp to use the bathroom.
13. Carry a shovel to cover your waste.
14. God walks in your camp, so keep it clean.
15. If a slave runs to you for safety, don't return them.
16. Let them live wherever they choose. Don't treat them badly.
17. Don't allow temple prostitution—man or woman.
18. Don't bring money earned that way into God's house. He hates it.
19. Don't charge interest to other Israelites.
20. You may charge foreigners, but not each other. Then God will bless you.
21. If you promise something to God, keep it.
22. But if you don't promise, that's okay.
23. Keep your word if you do.
24. You may eat grapes from your neighbor's vineyard, but don't take any home.
25. You may pick grain with your hands, but don't use a tool to harvest it.

Deuteronomy 24

Fairness in Daily Life

1. If a man divorces his wife, he must give her written papers and send her away.
2. If she marries someone else,
3. and that second husband divorces her or dies,
4. her first husband can't marry her again. That would be wrong.
5. A man who just got married must stay home for one year to make his wife happy.
6. Don't take someone's millstones as a loan. That would be like taking away their food.
7. If someone kidnaps an Israelite and sells them, the kidnapper must be killed. Remove the evil.
8. Follow the priest's rules for skin diseases.
9. Remember what God did to Miriam.
10. If you lend something, don't go into the borrower's house to get it.
11. Wait outside until they bring it out.
12. If they are poor,
13. give back their coat before sunset so they can sleep in it.
14. Don't cheat poor workers, whether they are Israelites or foreigners.
15. Pay them daily, before sunset.
16. Parents must not be punished for their children's sins, and children not for their parents'. Only the guilty person should be punished.
17. Don't be unfair to foreigners or orphans. Don't take a widow's coat as a loan.
18. Remember—you were slaves in Egypt, and God rescued you.
19. If you forget some grain in your field, leave it for the poor, foreigners, orphans, and widows.
20. Do the same with your olives.
21. And with your grapes.
22. Remember—you were slaves in Egypt. That's why you must do this.

Deuteronomy 25

Fair Rules for Everyone

1. If two people argue, the judges must decide who is right and who is wrong.
2. If the guilty one must be beaten,
3. give no more than 40 lashes. Too many would be shameful.
4. Don't stop an ox from eating while it works.
5. If a man dies and has no son, his brother must marry the widow.
6. Their first son will carry the dead brother's name.
7. If the brother refuses,
8. the leaders will talk to him. If he still says no,
9. the woman will take off his sandal and spit in his face.
10. His family will be called "The Unsandaled Family."
11. If two men fight and a wife grabs the other man to help her husband,
12. cut off her hand. Don't feel sorry for her.
13. Don't carry two sets of weights—one big and one small.
14. Don't cheat with different measurements.
15. Be honest so you can live long.
16. God hates cheaters.
17. Remember what the Amalekites did.
18. They attacked when you were tired and weak.
19. When God gives you peace, erase their name forever. Don't forget.

Deuteronomy 26

First Fruits and Tithes

1. When you enter the land God gives you,
2. bring your first crops to Him in a basket.
3. Go to the priest and say, "I bring the first crops from the land God gave me."
4. The priest will set the basket before the altar.
5. Then say, "My ancestor was a poor wanderer. He went to Egypt,
6. but the Egyptians made us slaves.
7. We cried to God,
8. and He saved us with power and miracles.
9. He brought us here to a rich and good land.
10. Now I give the first of the crops You gave me."
11. Then celebrate with your family and with the Levites and foreigners.
12. Every third year, give your tithe to the Levites, orphans, and widows.
13. Say, "I have given it just like You said. I didn't use it for anything wrong."
14. "I obeyed You. Please bless us."
15. "Look down from heaven and bless the land You gave us."
16. Today, God commands you to obey His laws with all your heart.
17. You have promised to follow Him.
18. He has chosen you to be His special people.
20. He will make you the most praised and honored nation. You will belong to Him.

Deuteronomy 27

Set Up Stones and Speak the Curses

1. Moses and the leaders told the people, "Obey all the laws we give you today."
2. "When you cross the Jordan, set up large stones and cover them with plaster.
3. Write all the laws on them. This will be in the land God is giving you."

4. "Set them up on Mount Ebal. Build an altar there."
5. "Use stones that haven't been shaped with tools.
6. Offer sacrifices to God on the altar."
7. "Eat and celebrate together."
8. "Write all these laws clearly on the stones."
9. Moses and the priests said, "Israel, be quiet and listen. Today you have become God's people.
10. So obey Him and keep His commands."
11. That day Moses gave these commands:
12. "When you cross the Jordan, six tribes will stand on Mount Gerizim to bless the people: Simeon, Levi, Judah, Issachar, Joseph, and Benjamin.
13. The other six will stand on Mount Ebal to say the curses: Reuben, Gad, Asher, Zebulun, Dan, and Naphtali."
14. The Levites will speak loudly to all the people:
15. "Cursed is anyone who makes or worships idols." All the people must say, "Amen."
16. "Cursed is anyone who dishonors their parents." All say, "Amen."
17. "Cursed is anyone who moves a boundary marker." All say, "Amen."
18. "Cursed is anyone who leads the blind the wrong way." All say, "Amen."
19. "Cursed is anyone who mistreats foreigners, orphans, or widows." All say, "Amen."
21. "Cursed is anyone who sleeps with his father's wife." All say, "Amen."
22. "Cursed is anyone who sleeps with an animal." All say, "Amen."
23. "Cursed is anyone who sleeps with his sister." All say, "Amen."
24. "Cursed is anyone who sleeps with his mother-in-law." All say, "Amen."
25. "Cursed is anyone who kills secretly." All say, "Amen."
26. "Cursed is anyone who takes money to hurt innocent people." All say, "Amen."
27. "Cursed is anyone who doesn't obey these laws." All say, "Amen."

Deuteronomy 28

Blessings for Obedience, Curses for Disobedience

1. If you obey the Lord fully, He will bless you more than any other nation.
2. All these blessings will come to you:
3. You'll be blessed in cities and in fields.
4. Your children, crops, and animals will be blessed.
5. Your baskets and food will be blessed.
6. You'll be blessed when you come in and go out.
7. Your enemies will run from you.
8. God will bless your work and barns.
9. He will make you His holy people.
10. Other nations will see you belong to God and respect you.
11. He will give you many children, animals, and crops.
12. He will send rain and bless all your work. You'll lend it to others but borrow from no one.
13. You'll be the head, not the tail, if you obey.
14. But don't turn from God's commands or follow other gods.
15. If you disobey, these curses will come:
16. You'll be cursed in cities and in fields.
17. Your baskets and food will be cursed.
18. Your children, crops, and animals will be cursed.
19. You'll be cursed when you come in and go out.
20. Everything you do will fail until you are destroyed.
21. God will send diseases.

22. He will strike you with sickness, fever, and drought.
23. The sky will be like bronze and the ground like iron.
24. Rain will turn to dust.
25. You'll lose battles.
26. Your bodies will be food for birds and animals.
28. God will give you the same diseases Egypt had.
29. He will confuse and blind you.
30. You'll feel around like a blind person. You won't succeed.
31. You'll marry, but someone else will take your wife.
31. Your animals will be stolen.
32. Your children will be taken and you'll be helpless.
33. Strangers will take your crops.
34. You'll go crazy from what you see.
35. You'll get a painful skin disease that won't heal.
36. God will take you and your king to a nation you don't know.
37. You'll become a joke to other nations.
38. You'll plant but harvest little.
39. You'll have vineyards but no wine.
40. Your olive trees won't give oil.
41. Your children will be taken away.
42. Insects will destroy your trees and crops.
43. Strangers among you will rise above you.
44. You'll borrow but not lend.
45. All these curses will chase you until you're gone.
46. These signs will stay with you and your descendants.
47. It's because you didn't serve God with joy.
48. So you'll serve your enemies in hunger, thirst, and fear.
49. A foreign nation will attack you quickly like an eagle.
50. They won't care about young or old.
51. They'll eat your animals and crops.
52. They'll destroy your towns.
53. You'll be so hungry you'll eat your own children.
54. The gentlest man will become selfish.
55. He won't share even with his own family.
56. The gentlest woman will turn cruel.
57. She won't share food with her own baby.
58. If you don't obey all of God's words,
59. He will send terrible sickness.
60. You'll get the same diseases Egypt had.
61. You'll get every kind of sickness not even written here.
62. You'll become few.
63. Just as God loved to bless you, He will now destroy you.
64. He will scatter you to other nations.
65. You'll find no peace—only fear and sadness.
66. You'll always worry.
67. You'll say, "I wish it were evening" in the morning, and "I wish it were morning" in the evening.
68. You'll be sent back to Egypt, but no one will buy you.

Deuteronomy 29

Agreement with God

1. These are the words of the agreement God made with Israel in Moab, not the one at Mount Sinai.

2-3. Moses told the people, "You saw what God did in Egypt—great miracles and wonders.

4. But God hasn't let you fully understand yet.

5. He led you 40 years in the desert. Your clothes and sandals didn't wear out.
6. You didn't eat bread or drink wine, so you'd know God is your Lord."
7. "You defeated Sihon and Og and took their land.
8. You gave it to Reuben, Gad, and half of Manasseh's tribe.
9. Obey this agreement so you will succeed.
10. Everyone is standing here today—leaders, tribes, men, women, children, and foreigners—
11. even workers who cut wood and carry water.
12. You are entering an agreement with God.
13. He is making you His people today.
14. This promise isn't just for you,
15. but also for your future children."

16-17. "You saw the evil and idols in Egypt.

18. Make sure no one here secretly worships other gods.
19. Don't say, 'I'll be fine even if I disobey.' God will punish that.
20. God won't forgive them. He'll be angry and curse them.
21. Their name will be erased.
22. Later generations and foreigners will ask, 'Why did this land become ruined?'
23. The land will be dry and dead like Sodom and Gomorrah.
24. People will say, 'It's because they left the Lord's agreement.'
25. 'They followed other gods.'
26. That's why God was angry.
27. He punished them and removed them from the land."
28. "God has secrets we don't know, but we must obey the things He has shown us."

Deuteronomy 30

Return to God

1. When all these blessings and curses happen, think about them.
2. If you return to God and obey Him,
3. He will be kind and bring you back from exile.
4. Even if you are far away.
5. He'll bring you back to the land, and you'll have more than before.
6. He will change your heart so you will love Him with all your heart and live.
7. God will put these curses on your enemies.
8. You will obey God again.
9. He will bless your children, animals, and land.
10. This will happen if you obey God and keep His laws.
11. These commands are not too hard or too far away.
12. They're not up in the sky.
13. They're not across the sea.
14. They are very near—already in your heart and mouth.
16. Today I give you a choice: life and good, or death and evil.
17. If you love and obey God, you'll live and be blessed.
18. But if you turn away and worship other gods,
19. you will be destroyed.
20. I call heaven and earth to witness: I offer you life or death, blessings or curses. Choose life!
21. Love and obey God. Then you and your children will live in the land He promised.

Deuteronomy 31

Moses Chooses Joshua

1. Moses said,

2. "I'm 120 years old and can't lead you anymore. God said I won't cross the Jordan."
3. "But God will go ahead of you. Joshua will lead you."
4. "God will destroy the nations, like He did to Sihon and Og."
5. "You will defeat them. Do what God commands."
6. "Be strong and brave. God is with you. He won't leave you."
7. Moses told Joshua in front of everyone, "Be strong and brave. You will lead the people into the land. God will be with you."
8. "God will go ahead of you. Don't be afraid."
9. Moses wrote down the law and gave it to the priests and leaders.
10. He said, "Every 7 years, during the Festival of Shelters,
11. read this law to all the people at the Meeting Tent."
12. "Gather everyone—men, women, children, and foreigners."
13. "Teach your children to obey so they will fear God."
14. God said, "It's time for you to die. Call Joshua. I will give him instructions."
15. God appeared in a cloud at the Meeting Tent.
16. God said, "After you die, the people will worship other gods. I'll be angry and leave them."
17. "They'll be in trouble, and I won't help them.
18. They will suffer because they turned away from Me."
19. "Write down this song. Teach it to the people as a warning."
20. "They'll eat well and still turn from Me to idols."
21. "This song will remind them when trouble comes."
22. Moses wrote the song that day and taught it to the Israelites.
23. God told Joshua, "Be strong and brave. You will lead the people into the land."
24. When Moses finished writing the law,
25. he gave it to the Levites who carried the chest.
26. He said, "Put this book next to the chest of the agreement. It will be a witness."
27. "I know you are stubborn and rebellious."
28. "Bring everyone here so I can tell them what will happen after I die."
29. "I know you will disobey and make God angry."

Deuteronomy 32

The Song of Moses

1. Listen, heavens and earth, to my words.
2. Let my words fall like rain and dew.
3. I will praise God's name. He is great!
4. He is the Rock. He is perfect and fair.
5. But His people have been unfaithful.
6. Is this how you treat God? He made you and gave you life.
7. Remember the old days. Ask your parents and leaders to tell you.
8. God gave nations their land and set their borders.
9. But His own people, Israel, are His special share.
10. He found them in a desert and cared for them.
11. Like an eagle, He protected and taught them to fly.
12. God alone led them—no other gods helped.
13. He gave them rich land with plenty of food.
14. He gave them milk, meat, grain, and wine.

15. But they became fat and lazy. They rejected God.
16. They made Him angry by worshiping idols.
17. They sacrificed to demons, not to God.
18. They forgot the One who gave them life.
19. God saw this and was angry.
20. He said, "I will turn away and see what happens to them."
21. "They made Me jealous with false gods, so I'll make them jealous with a foolish nation."
22. "My anger burns like fire and will destroy the land."
23. "I will send disasters on them."
24. "They will die from hunger, sickness, and wild animals."
25. "Outside, they'll die by sword; inside, by fear."
26. "I would have destroyed them completely,
27. but enemies might think they won by their own power."
28. "Israel has no understanding.
29. If they were wise, they would obey and be safe."
30. "One enemy can chase a thousand because God is not with you."
31. "Our enemies know their gods are weak."
32. "Their ways are evil and bitter."
33. "Their wine is poison."
34. "But I am watching and will act at the right time."
35. "I will punish them. Their fall will come fast."
36. "God will help His people when they have nothing left."
37. "He will ask, 'Where are their fake gods now?'"
38. "Let those idols save them—if they can!"
39. "I am the only God. I can kill and give life."
40. "I lift My hand and promise: I live forever!"
41. "I will strike My enemies."
42. "Their land will be filled with blood."
43. "He will avenge His people and forgive His land."
44. Moses and Joshua taught the people this song.
45. When Moses finished,
46. he said, "Take these words seriously. Teach them to your children."
47. "They are not just words. They are your life. Obey them to live long in the land."
48. That same day, God told Moses,
49. "Go up Mount Nebo and look at the land I'm giving Israel.
50. Then you will die,
51. because you broke faith with Me at Meribah.
52. You can see the land, but you will not enter it."

Deuteronomy 33

Moses Blesses the Tribes

1. Before he died, Moses blessed the people of Israel.
2. He said, "God came with His holy ones and gave His law to us."
3. "He loves His people. They listen to His words."
4. "Moses gave us the law. It belongs to all of us."
5. "He was our leader when the tribes gathered."
6. "Let Reuben live and grow strong."
7. "Bless Judah. Help him fight and return safely."
8. "Let Levi teach and serve. You tested them and they passed."

9. "They obeyed You above their own families."
10. "They teach Your law and offer sacrifices."
11. "Bless their work and defeat their enemies."
12. "Let Benjamin be loved by God and rest safely beside Him."
13. "Bless Joseph with the best land and many gifts."
14. "Give him rich crops and full harvests."
15. "Let his land be beautiful and full."
16. "Let his brothers respect him."
17. "He is like a bull with great horns—he will win many battles."
18. "Bless Zebulun and Issachar. Rejoice in your travels and work."
19. "They will call others to worship and share riches."
20. "Bless Gad. He is strong like a lion."
21. "He chose the best land and led with justice."
22. "Dan is like a young lion."
23. "Naphtali is full of favor and receives God's blessings."
24. "Asher is blessed with many children and strength."
25. "You will always have what you need."
26. "There is no god like the Lord! He rides the skies to help you."
27. "He is your safe home. He destroys your enemies."
28. "You will live in safety with plenty of food and rain."
29. "You are blessed, Israel! God saves you. He is your shield and sword. You will win!"

Deuteronomy 34

Moses Dies

1. Moses climbed Mount Nebo and looked across the land.

2-3. He saw all the tribes and regions.

4. God said, "This is the land I promised. You may see it, but you won't enter."
5. Moses died there, just as God said.
6. God buried him in Moab, but no one knows the exact place.
7. Moses was 120 years old. He was strong and could still see clearly.
8. The people mourned him for 30 days.
9. Joshua was full of wisdom because Moses laid hands on him. The people obeyed him.
10. No prophet in Israel was ever like Moses.
11. He knew God face to face.
12. He did powerful signs and miracles in Egypt and before all of Israel.

– Joshua –

Joshua leads Israel to conquer Canaan and divide the land among the tribes.

Joshua 1

Joshua Becomes Leader of Israel

1. After Moses died, the Lord spoke to Joshua.
2. He said, "Moses is dead. Now you must lead the Israelites across the Jordan River into the land I'm giving all of you."
3. I promised Moses this land. Wherever you go, it will belong to you.
4. From the southern desert to the Lebanon mountains, from the Euphrates River to the Mediterranean Sea, including all the land of the Hittites.
5. No one will defeat you. I'll be with you like I was with Moses. I won't leave or fail you.
6. Be strong and brave. You will give the people the land I promised their ancestors.

7. Be strong and brave. Obey all the laws Moses gave you. Don't turn away from them. Then you'll succeed.

8. Read the laws every day. Think about them day and night. Obey them, and you will do well.

9. I'm telling you again: Be strong and brave. Don't be afraid or give up. I am the Lord your God, and I will be with you wherever you go.

The Eastern Tribes Promise to Help

10. Joshua told the leaders of the people,

11. "Go through the camp and tell everyone to get food ready. In a few days, we will cross the Jordan River and take the land the Lord is giving us."

12. Then Joshua spoke to the tribes of Reuben, Gad, and half the tribe of Manasseh.

13. He said, "Remember what Moses told you. The Lord is giving you this land east of the Jordan River as your home.

14. Your wives, children, and animals can stay here. But your soldiers must cross ahead of the others and help them.

15. Help them take the land the Lord is giving them. Then you can return and live here in the land the Lord promised you."

16. They answered Joshua, "We will do everything you say and go wherever you send us.

17. We obeyed Moses, and we'll obey you too. May the Lord be with you like He was with Moses.

18. Anyone who refuses to obey you will be put to death. Be strong and brave!"

Joshua 2

Rahab Helps the Israelite Spies

1. Joshua secretly sent two spies to Jericho. They stayed at the house of a woman named Rahab.

2. Someone told the king of Jericho that Israelite spies had come.

3. So the king sent a message to Rahab: "Bring out the men staying at your house. They came to spy on us."

4. But Rahab had hidden them. She said, "Yes, they were here, but I didn't know where they were from.

5. They left at sunset just before the gate closed. I don't know where they went. If you hurry, you might catch them."

6. But she had taken them up to her roof and hidden them under some flax.

7. The king's men chased them toward the Jordan River. As soon as they left, the gate was shut.

8. Before the spies went to sleep, Rahab came to talk to them.

9. She said, "We know the Lord gave you this land. Everyone here is scared of you.

10. We heard how the Lord dried up the Red Sea so you could leave Egypt, and how you defeated the two Amorite kings, Sihon and Og.

11. After we heard that, we lost all courage. Your God is the true God in heaven and on earth.

12. Please promise me, in the Lord's name, that you'll be kind to me and my family like I was kind to you.

13. Save me, my parents, my brothers and sisters, and all their families. Don't let us die."

14. The men said, "We promise to keep you safe. May the Lord punish us if we break our word. But don't tell anyone what we are doing."

15. Rahab's house was part of the city wall, so she let them down with a rope through the window.

16. She told them, "Hide in the hills for three days. After the king's men stop searching, you can go."

17. The spies said, "We won't keep our promise unless,

18. when we come back, you tie this red rope in your window and keep all your family inside the house.

19. If anyone leaves your house and is killed, it's not our fault. But if anyone inside is hurt, we're responsible.
20. If you tell anyone what we've done, our promise is broken."
21. Rahab agreed and tied the red rope in her window.
22. The spies hid in the hills for three days. The king's men searched everywhere but didn't find them.
23. Then the spies returned to Joshua and told him everything that happened.
24. They said, "The Lord has given us the whole land. Everyone there is terrified of us."

Joshua 3

The Israelites Cross the Jordan River

1. Early the next morning, Joshua and the Israelites left the Acacia Grove and camped by the Jordan River.
2. Three days later, the leaders went through the camp
3. and told the people, "When you see the priests carrying the Ark of the Covenant, follow them.
4. They will guide you because you've never been here before. Stay about half a mile behind them. Don't go too close."
5. Joshua said to the people, "Make yourselves clean and ready. Tomorrow the Lord will do miracles among you."
6. Then he told the priests, "Pick up the Ark and go ahead of the people." So they did.
7. The Lord said to Joshua, "Today I will show everyone that I am with you, just like I was with Moses."
8. "Tell the priests carrying the Ark to go stand in the river when they reach the edge."
9. Joshua told the people, "Come listen to what the Lord your God says."
10. He said, "Today you will know that the living God is with you. He will force out the Canaanites, Hittites, Hivites, Perizzites, Girgashites, Amorites, and Jebusites."
11. "The Ark of the Lord will go ahead of you into the Jordan River."
12. "Choose 12 men, one from each tribe."
13. "When the priests step into the water, the river will stop flowing and pile up in a heap."
14. The people left their camp to cross the Jordan. The priests carrying the Ark walked ahead of them.
15. It was harvest season, and the river was flooding. But when the priests stepped into the water,
16. the water stopped! It piled up far away near the town of Adam. The water flowing to the Dead Sea stopped completely, and the people crossed near Jericho.
17. The priests stood on dry ground in the middle of the river while the people crossed safely.

Joshua 4

The People Build a Stone Reminder

1. After everyone crossed, the Lord said to Joshua,
2. "Choose 12 men, one from each tribe.
3. Tell them to take 12 stones from the middle of the river, where the priests stood, and put them where you'll camp tonight."
4. So Joshua called the 12 men,
5. and told them, "Go into the river in front of the Ark. Each man must pick up one stone and carry it out.
6. These stones will remind your children what happened here.
7. Tell them, 'The Jordan River stopped when the Ark crossed. These stones remind us of that.'"
8. The men did exactly what Joshua told them. They took 12 stones and brought them to the camp.

9. Joshua also set up 12 stones in the river where the priests were standing. The stones are still there today.

The Israelites Camp at Gilgal

10. The priests stayed in the river until the people had finished crossing, just like the Lord told Joshua.
11. After everyone crossed, the priests followed them with the Ark.
12. The men from Reuben, Gad, and half of Manasseh crossed ahead, like Moses had said.
13. About 40,000 soldiers crossed, ready for battle, in front of the Lord.
14. That day the Lord honored Joshua in front of all Israel. From then on, they respected him like they did Moses.
15. Then the Lord told Joshua,
16. "Tell the priests to come out of the river."
17. So Joshua told them.
18. When the priests stepped out, the water started flowing again, just like before.
19. On the 10th day of the 1st month, the Israelites crossed the Jordan and camped at Gilgal, east of Jericho.
20. Joshua set up the 12 stones from the river at Gilgal.
21. Then he told the people, "One day your kids will ask, 'What do these stones mean?'
22. Tell them, 'We crossed the Jordan River on dry land.'
23. The Lord dried up the Jordan just like He dried the Red Sea,
24. so everyone on earth would know how powerful He is. You should respect the Lord your God forever."

Joshua 5

The Enemy Kings Get Scared

1. The Amorite and Canaanite kings heard that the Lord dried up the Jordan River. They were so scared they didn't even try to fight.

Israel Gets Ready for Passover

2. Then the Lord told Joshua, "Make flint knives and circumcise the men again."
3. So Joshua made the knives and did it at a place called Haaraloth Hill.
4. This was needed because all the men who left Egypt had died in the desert.
5. They had been circumcised, but the boys born in the desert had not.
6. The Israelites wandered 40 years until all the men who had disobeyed the Lord died. They weren't allowed to enter the promised land.
7. So Joshua circumcised their sons, the new generation.
8. After that, they stayed in camp until they healed.
9. Then the Lord said, "Today I've removed the shame of Egypt from you." That's why the place is called Gilgal.
10. On the 14th day of that month, the Israelites celebrated Passover at Gilgal.
11. The next day, they ate bread without yeast and roasted grain from the land.
12. After that, the manna stopped. They never saw it again. From then on, they ate the food from Canaan.

Joshua Meets the Lord's Commander

13. While Joshua was near Jericho, he saw a man with a sword. He asked, "Are you on our side or theirs?"
14. The man said, "Neither. I'm the commander of the Lord's army." Joshua bowed down and said, "What do you want to tell me?"
15. The man said, "Take off your sandals. You are on holy ground." So Joshua did.

Joshua 6

The Walls of Jericho Fall Down

1. Jericho's gates were locked to keep the Israelites out. No one went in or out.
2. The Lord said to Joshua, "I'm giving Jericho, its king, and soldiers to you.
3. March around the city once a day for 6 days with your army.
4. Have 7 priests blow trumpets in front of the Ark. On the 7th day, march around the city 7 times.
5. When you hear one long blast, everyone must shout. Then the walls will fall, and your army can go straight in."
6. So Joshua told the priests, "Carry the Ark, and 7 of you blow your horns."
7. Then he told the army, "March ahead of the Ark and blow your horns."
8. The 7 priests started marching and blowing their horns, with the Ark behind them.
9. Some soldiers went ahead of the priests, and others followed behind the Ark.
10. But Joshua said, "Don't shout or talk until I say so."
11. They marched once around the city, then camped for the night.
12. The next morning, Joshua got up early, and they did the same thing.
13. The priests and soldiers marched with the Ark, blowing their horns.
14. They marched once around the city again on the second day. They did the same thing for 6 days.
15. On the 7th day, they got up early and marched around the city 7 times.
16. After the 7th time, the priests blew the horns, and Joshua shouted, "Shout! The Lord has given you the city!
17. Everything in the city must be destroyed as an offering to the Lord. Only Rahab and her family will be saved because she protected our spies.
18. Don't take anything or you'll bring trouble on all of Israel.
19. Silver, gold, bronze, and iron must be put in the Lord's treasury."
20. When the priests blew the trumpets, the people shouted. The walls fell, and the people ran in and took the city.
21. They destroyed everything—men, women, kids, animals—everyone.
22. Joshua told the two spies, "Go get Rahab and her family."
23. The spies brought Rahab and all her family to safety outside the camp.
24. Then they burned the city, but saved the gold, silver, bronze, and iron for the Lord.
25. Joshua let Rahab and her family live because she helped the spies. Her family still lived in Israel.
26. Joshua said, "Anyone who rebuilds this city will be cursed. They'll lose their first son when they lay the foundation, and their last son when they finish the gates."
27. The Lord was with Joshua, and everyone in the land heard about him.

Joshua 7

Achan Disobeys the Lord

1. The Lord had said not to take anything from Jericho, but Achan, from the tribe of Judah, didn't listen and took some things. So the Lord was angry with all the Israelites.
2. Joshua sent men to spy on the town of Ai, east of Bethel.
3. They returned and said, "We don't need the whole army. Just send 2,000 or 3,000 men. The town is small."
4. So about 3,000 men went—but they were defeated.
5. The people of Ai chased them and killed about 36 Israelites. The others ran away terrified.
6. Joshua and the leaders tore their clothes, fell face-down in front of the Ark, and stayed there all day. They put dust on their heads.

7. Joshua cried, "Lord, why did you bring us across the river just to let us be killed? We should've stayed on the other side!
8. Now what do I say after we've run from our enemies?
9. The Canaanites will hear and destroy us. Then what will happen to your great name?"

The Lord Explains the Defeat

10. The Lord said, "Get up! Why are you lying on the ground?
11. Israel has sinned. They broke my command and took what was supposed to be destroyed. They lied and hid it.
12. That's why Israel can't win. I won't help you unless you get rid of what was stolen.
13. Tell the people to make themselves clean. Tomorrow I will show who sinned.
14. In the morning, bring everyone by tribes. I'll pick the tribe, then the family, then the man.
15. The man who stole will be burned along with everything he owns. He disobeyed me and brought shame to Israel."

Achan is Found and Punished

16. Early the next morning, Joshua brought the tribes, and the tribe of Judah was chosen.
17. Then the family of Zerah was chosen, and then the family of Zabdi.
18. Finally, Achan was picked.
19. Joshua said, "Tell the truth. What did you do?"
20. Achan said, "I sinned. I saw a beautiful robe, silver, and a gold bar. I wanted them, so I took them and buried them under my tent."
21. (continued) "The silver is buried deepest."
22. Joshua sent men to check. They found everything under Achan's tent.
23. They brought it to Joshua and laid it out before the Lord.
24. Then Joshua and the Israelites took Achan, the stolen items, his sons and daughters, his animals, his tent—everything—to the Valley of Trouble.
25. Joshua said, "You brought trouble on us. Now the Lord will bring trouble on you." Then all the Israelites stoned them and burned their bodies and belongings.
26. They piled stones over the spot, which are still there today. After that, the Lord was no longer angry.

Joshua 8

Israel Destroys Ai

1. The Lord told Joshua, "Don't be afraid. Take your whole army and attack Ai. I'll help you win. You can keep the animals and goods this time. Set up an ambush behind the city."
2. So Joshua chose 30,000 strong soldiers and sent them out at night.
3. He told them,
4. "Hide behind the city. Stay close and be ready.
5. I'll lead the main army to the front of Ai. When they come out, we'll run away like last time.
6. They'll chase us and leave the city.
7. Then you come out and take it. The Lord will give it to you.
8. Burn the city, just as the Lord said."
9. So they went and hid behind Ai. Joshua stayed in camp that night.
10. Early the next morning, Joshua and his army marched toward Ai.
11. They camped north of the city, with a valley between them.
12. Joshua sent 5,000 more soldiers to hide west of the city.
13. The city was surrounded: the main army to the north, the others to the

west. That night Joshua went into the valley.

14. When the king of Ai saw them, he and his men rushed out to fight. He didn't know about the ambush.
15. Joshua and his army pretended to retreat.
16. All the men of Ai chased them, leaving the city open.
17. Not a single man stayed behind. The city was wide open.

Ai is Burned and Destroyed

18. Then the Lord said, "Point your sword at Ai. I'm giving it to you."
19. As soon as Joshua did, the soldiers in hiding ran into the city and set it on fire.
20. The men of Ai looked back and saw smoke rising. They had nowhere to run.
21. Joshua and his men stopped running and attacked.
22. The soldiers who had burned the city came out and joined the fight. The men of Ai were trapped and killed.
23. Only the king was taken alive.
24. After killing all the men outside, Israel went into the city and killed everyone inside.
25. That day, 12,000 people in Ai died.
26. Joshua kept his sword raised until all the people were gone.
27. Israel took the animals and valuables for themselves, just as the Lord said.
28. Joshua burned the city. It still lies in ruins today.
29. He hung the king's body on a tree until evening. Then it was taken down and buried under a pile of rocks.

Joshua Reads the Law to the People

30. Joshua built an altar to the Lord on Mount Ebal.
31. He used stones that had not been cut with tools, just like Moses had said. He offered sacrifices on it.
32. Joshua copied the laws of Moses onto the stones while everyone watched.
33. All the Israelites—men, women, children, and foreigners—stood on both sides of the Ark. Half were near Mount Gerizim and half near Mount Ebal, just like Moses said.
34. Then Joshua read every word of the Law, including the blessings and curses.
35. He read it all to everyone, including women, children, and foreigners living among them.

Joshua 9

The People of Gibeon Trick Israel

1. The kings west of the Jordan heard what had happened—those from the hills, valleys, and coast all the way to Lebanon.
2. They joined together to fight Joshua and the Israelites.
3. But the people of Gibeon had a different idea. They had heard what happened to Jericho and Ai.
4. So they decided to trick Israel. They loaded worn-out bags and old wineskins on their donkeys.
5. They wore old, patched sandals and clothes. Their bread was dry and moldy.
6. They went to Joshua at Gilgal and said, "We've come from far away. Please make a peace treaty with us."
7. The Israelites said, "You might live nearby. We can't make a treaty with you."
8. But the Gibeonites said, "We are your servants." Joshua asked, "Who are you? Where are you from?"
9. They said, "We're from a faraway land. We heard about your God and what He did in Egypt.
10. And we heard about the two Amorite kings east of the Jordan—Sihon and Og."

11. "So our leaders told us to come and ask for peace. We brought this bread—it was fresh when we left.
12. Now it's dry and moldy.
13. Our wineskins were new, now they're cracked. Our clothes and sandals are worn out from the trip."
14. The Israelites checked their supplies, but didn't ask the Lord what to do.
15. So Joshua made a peace treaty with them and promised not to hurt them. The leaders agreed with an oath.
16. Three days later, the Israelites found out the truth—they lived nearby!
17. So the Israelites went to their cities: Gibeon, Kephirah, Beeroth, and Kiriath-Jearim.
18. But they didn't attack them because of the peace treaty. The people complained to the leaders.
19. But the leaders said, "We made a promise in the Lord's name. We can't break it.
20. If we harm them, the Lord will punish us. We must let them live."
21. They said, "They can live, but they will cut wood and carry water for us." That's how they kept the promise.
22. Then Joshua said to the Gibeonites, "Why did you lie to us and say you were from far away?
23. Now you are cursed. You will always be our servants—woodcutters and water carriers for the house of God."
24. They said, "We were afraid. The Lord told Moses to destroy everyone here. We didn't want to die."
25. "Now we are in your hands. Do what seems right to you."
26. So Joshua let them live but made them serve as workers.
27. From then on, they were woodcutters and water carriers for Israel and the altar of the Lord.

Joshua 10

Joshua Commands the Sun to Stop

1. King Adoni-Zedek of Jerusalem heard what Joshua did to Jericho and Ai. He also heard that Gibeon had made peace with Israel.
2. He and his people were scared. Gibeon was a large city with strong warriors.
3. So he sent messages to four other kings: Hoham of Hebron, Piram of Jarmuth, Japhia of Lachish, and Debir of Eglon.
4. He said, "Come help me attack Gibeon. They made peace with Israel."
5. The five kings and their armies joined forces and attacked Gibeon.
6. The Gibeonites sent a message to Joshua at Gilgal: "Don't abandon us! Come quickly and help us!"
7. So Joshua and his army marched all night to Gibeon.
8. The Lord said, "Don't be afraid. I will help you win. None of them will stand against you."
9. Joshua surprised the enemy with a night attack.
10. The Lord made them panic. Israel chased and defeated them all the way to Azekah and Makkedah.
11. As they ran away, the Lord sent a hailstorm from the sky. More men died from hailstones than from swords.
12. Then Joshua prayed, "Sun, stand still over Gibeon! Moon, stay over the Valley of Aijalon!"
13. The sun and moon stopped until Israel won. This is written in the Book of Jashar. The sun stayed up for a whole day during battle.
14. There had never been a day like it before or since. The Lord answered a man's prayer and fought for Israel.
15. Then Joshua and the army returned to the camp at Gilgal.

Joshua Captures the Five Kings

16. The five kings ran and hid in a cave at Makkedah.
17. Joshua was told they were found.
18. He said, "Roll stones in front of the cave and put guards there.
19. But don't stop fighting. Chase your enemies and don't let them escape."
20. Joshua and the Israelites killed many of them. Some ran away to their cities.
21. Then everyone returned safely to Joshua. No one dared speak against Israel after that.
22. Joshua said, "Open the cave and bring out the five kings."
23. So they brought out the kings of Jerusalem, Hebron, Jarmuth, Lachish, and Eglon.
24. Joshua called his commanders and said, "Put your feet on their necks." They did.
25. Joshua said, "Don't be afraid or give up. Be strong and brave. This is what the Lord will do to all your enemies."
26. Then Joshua killed the five kings and hung them on trees until sunset.
27. At sunset, he took them down and threw their bodies into the cave and covered it with stones.

Joshua Defeats More Cities

28. That same day, Joshua captured Makkedah and killed the king and everyone there.
29. Then they went to Libnah and attacked it.
30. The Lord gave them the city. They killed the king and everyone there.
31. Then they attacked Lachish.
32. The Lord gave it to them, and they destroyed it the next day.
33. King Horam of Gezer came to help Lachish, but Joshua's army killed him and all his men.
34. Then Joshua went to Eglon and attacked it.
35. They captured and destroyed it in one day.
36. Then they went to Hebron.
37. They captured the city and nearby villages, killed the king and everyone there.
38. Then they went to Debir.
39. They captured it and nearby villages, killed the king and everyone there—just like they did to the other cities.
40. Joshua took the whole land—the hill country, the lowlands, and the slopes. He killed all the kings and people, just as the Lord commanded.
41. He conquered the land from Kadesh-Barnea to Gaza and from Goshen to Gibeon.
42. Joshua won all these battles in one trip, because the Lord fought for Israel.
43. Then Joshua and all Israel returned to their camp at Gilgal.

Joshua 11

Joshua Captures Cities in the North

1. When King Jabin of Hazor heard what happened, he sent messages to King Jobab of Madon, the king of Shimron, the king of Achshaph,
2. and to the kings in the northern hills, the Jordan Valley south of Lake Galilee, the foothills, and the coast near Dor.
3. He also called the Canaanite kings in the east and west, the Amorites, Hittites, Perizzites, and Jebusites in the hills, and the Hivites near Mount Hermon in Mizpah.
4. These kings brought huge armies, as many soldiers as grains of sand, with lots of horses and chariots.
5. They all joined together and camped at the Waters of Merom to fight Israel.
6. But the Lord told Joshua, "Don't be afraid. Tomorrow at this time, I'll let you defeat them. Cripple their horses and burn their chariots."

7. So Joshua and his whole army surprised them at the Waters of Merom and attacked.
8. The Lord helped Israel win. They chased the enemy all the way to Greater Sidon, Misrephoth-maim, and the valley near Mizpah. No one survived.
9. Joshua did everything the Lord told him. He crippled their horses and burned their chariots.
10. Then Joshua turned back and captured Hazor, killing its king. Hazor was the most powerful city at that time.
11. They killed everyone there and burned the city.
12. Joshua also captured all the other cities and killed their kings and people, just as Moses had commanded.
13. But the Israelites didn't burn cities built on mounds—except Hazor.
14. They took all the valuables and animals but killed everyone in the cities.
15. The Lord told Moses, Moses told Joshua, and Joshua did everything exactly as he was told.

Joshua Takes All the Land

16. Joshua took the whole land—the hills, the Negev, all of Goshen, the lowlands, the Arabah, and the Israelite mountains with their valleys.
17. He took the land from Mount Halak near Seir to Baal Gad in the Lebanon Valley below Mount Hermon. He captured and killed all the kings.
18. It took a long time to fight all those kings.
19. Only the people of Gibeon made peace with Israel. All the others were defeated.
20. The Lord made them stubborn so they would fight Israel and be completely destroyed without mercy, just as He told Moses.
21. During that time, Joshua also destroyed the Anakim giants living in the hill country—at Hebron, Debir, and Anab.
22. None of the Anakim were left in Israel's land, except a few in Gaza, Gath, and Ashdod.
23. Joshua took the whole land, just as the Lord told Moses. He divided it among the tribes of Israel. After that, the land had peace.

Joshua 12

Kings Defeated by Moses and Joshua

1. These are the kings the Israelites defeated east of the Jordan River, from the Arnon Valley to Mount Hermon, including the Jordan Valley.
2. King Sihon of the Amorites lived in Heshbon. He ruled from Aroer on the edge of the Arnon River Valley to the Jabbok River, which was the border of the Ammonites. He ruled half of Gilead.
3. He also ruled the Jordan Valley from the Sea of Galilee to the Dead Sea, including the road to Beth-jeshimoth and the slopes of Pisgah.
4. They also defeated King Og of Bashan, one of the last Rephaites, who lived in Ashtaroth and Edrei.
5. He ruled Mount Hermon, Salekah, all of Bashan to the borders of Geshur and Maacah, and half of Gilead to the border of King Sihon.
6. Moses and the Israelites defeated these two kings, and Moses gave their land to the tribes of Reuben, Gad, and half of Manasseh.

Kings Defeated by Joshua

7. These are the kings Joshua and the Israelites defeated west of the Jordan River, from Baal Gad in the Lebanon Valley to Mount Halak near Seir. Joshua gave this land to the tribes of Israel.
8. The land included the hills, valleys, Arabah, mountain slopes, deserts, and the land of the Hittites, Amorites, Canaanites, Perizzites, Hivites, and Jebusites.

9. The king of Jericho, the king of Ai (near Bethel),
10. the king of Jerusalem, the king of Hebron,
11. the king of Jarmuth, the king of Lachish,
12. the king of Eglon, the king of Gezer,
13. the king of Debir, the king of Geder,
14. the king of Hormah, the king of Arad,
15. the king of Libnah, the king of Adullam,
16. the king of Makkedah, the king of Bethel,
17. the king of Tappuah, the king of Hepher,
18. the king of Aphek, the king of Lasharon,
19. the king of Madon, the king of Hazor,
20. the king of Shimron-meron, the king of Acshaph,
21. the king of Taanach, the king of Megiddo,
22. the king of Kedesh, the king of Jokneam in Carmel,
23. the king of Dor (in Naphoth-dor), the king of Goyim in Gilgal,
24. and the king of Tirzah. In total, 31 kings were defeated.

Joshua 13

Land Still Not Taken

1. Joshua was now very old. The Lord said, "You are old, and there is still a lot of land that hasn't been taken.
2. This includes all the land of the Philistines and the Geshurites,
3. from the Shihor River near Egypt to the border of Ekron, including the five Philistine rulers in Gaza, Ashdod, Ashkelon, Gath, and Ekron, and the land of the Avvites
4. in the south. It also includes all the Canaanite land from Arah (of the Sidonians) to Aphek, to the border of the Amorites,
5. and the land of the Gebalites and all of Lebanon from Baal Gad below Mount Hermon to Lebo Hamath.
6. I will force out all the people in the hills from Lebanon to Misrephoth-maim, including the Sidonians. Just give this land to Israel like I told you.
7. So divide this land among the nine tribes and the half-tribe of Manasseh."

Land East of the Jordan River

8. Moses already gave land east of the Jordan River to the tribes of Reuben, Gad, and half of Manasseh.
9. Their land started at Aroer near the Arnon Valley, including the city in the valley and the flatlands from Medeba to Dibon.
10. It also included all the towns ruled by King Sihon of Heshbon, all the way to the Ammonite border.
11. It included Gilead, and the land of the Geshurites and Maacathites, Mount Hermon, and all of Bashan to Salekah—
12. all the land ruled by King Og of Bashan, who lived in Ashtaroth and Edrei. He was the last of the Rephaites. Moses defeated him and forced them out.
13. But the Israelites did not force out the Geshurites and Maacathites. They still live in Israel today.

Why Levi Got No Land

14. Moses didn't give land to the tribe of Levi. Instead, the Lord gave them the offerings brought to the altar.

Land Given to the Tribe of Reuben

15. Moses gave land to the tribe of Reuben.
16. Their land started at Aroer near the Arnon Valley, including the town in the valley and the whole flatland past Medeba.

17. It included Heshbon and towns on the flatlands: Dibon, Bamoth-baal, Beth-baal-meon,

18. Jahaz, Kedemoth, Mephaath,

19. Kiriathaim, Sibmah, Zereth-shahar on the hill in the valley,

20. Beth-peor, the slopes of Pisgah, and Beth-jeshimoth.

21. This was all the land of King Sihon of Heshbon, whom Moses defeated along with the leaders of Midian: Evi, Rekem, Zur, Hur, and Reba.

22. The Israelites also killed Balaam son of Beor, who used magic to tell the future.

23. The western border was the Jordan River. This land and its towns were given to the tribe of Reuben.

Land Given to the Tribe of Gad

24. Moses gave land to the tribe of Gad.

25. Their land included Jazer, all the towns of Gilead, and half the land of the Ammonites to Aroer, near Rabbah.

26. It went from Heshbon to Ramath-mizpah and Betonim, and from Mahanaim to Debir.

27. In the valley, it included Beth-haram, Beth-nimrah, Succoth, Zaphon, and the rest of King Sihon's kingdom, all the way to the Sea of Galilee.

28. This land and its towns were given to the tribe of Gad.

Land Given to Half of Manasseh

29. Moses gave land to half the tribe of Manasseh.

30. Their land started at Mahanaim and included all of Bashan, all the land ruled by King Og, and all 60 towns of Jair in Bashan.

31. It also included half of Gilead and the cities of Ashtaroth and Edrei. This land was given to the descendants of Makir son of Manasseh.

32. These were the lands Moses gave while in Moab, east of the Jordan River.

33. Moses didn't give any land to the Levites. The Lord himself was their gift, just as he promised.

Joshua 14

Land West of the Jordan

1. The rest of the land in Canaan was divided by Eleazar the priest, Joshua, and the leaders of Israel.

2. The land for the nine and a half tribes was given by drawing lots, as the Lord had commanded.

3. Moses had already given land east of the Jordan to the other two and a half tribes. He gave no land to the Levites.

4. The tribe of Joseph had two parts: Manasseh and Ephraim. The Levites got no land—only towns and pasturelands.

5. So the Israelites divided the land just like the Lord told Moses.

Caleb Asks for His Land

6. The tribe of Judah came to Joshua at Gilgal. Caleb son of Jephunneh said, "You know what the Lord told Moses about you and me at Kadesh-barnea.

7. I was 40 when Moses sent me to spy on the land. I gave an honest report.

8. The others made the people afraid, but I stayed loyal to the Lord.

9. Moses promised that the land I walked on would belong to me and my descendants forever, because I obeyed the Lord completely.

10. That was 45 years ago. Now I am 85, and the Lord has kept me alive.

11. I'm still strong—just as strong as when Moses sent me. I can still fight and travel.

12. So please give me the hill country the Lord promised. You know the Anakim live there in strong cities. But with the Lord's help, I will drive them out."

13. So Joshua blessed Caleb and gave him the town of Hebron.

14. Hebron still belongs to Caleb's family because he obeyed the Lord fully.
15. Hebron used to be called Kiriath-arba, named after Arba, the greatest man among the Anakim. After this, the land had peace.

Joshua 15

Land Given to Judah

1. The tribe of Judah got land that reached the border of Edom, all the way south into the Zin Desert.
2. The southern border started at the south end of the Dead Sea,
3. went south of Scorpion Pass into the Zin Desert, past Kadesh-barnea, then up to Hezron and turned toward Addar and Karka.
4. It continued to Azmon and joined the River of Egypt, ending at the Mediterranean Sea. That was the southern border.
5. The eastern border was the Dead Sea, all the way up to the Jordan River inlet. The northern border began there.
6. It went to Beth-hoglah, then north of Beth-arabah to the Stone of Bohan (Reuben's son).
7. From there it went through the Valley of Achor to Debir, turned north to Gilgal (across from Adummim), then to the springs of En-shemesh and En-rogel.
8. It went up the Valley of Hinnom, south of the Jebusite city (Jerusalem), to the top of the hill west of Hinnom Valley and north of Rephaim Valley.
9. From there it went to the spring of Nephtoah and the cities on Mount Ephron, then turned to Baalah (also called Kiriath-jearim).
10. It circled west to Mount Seir, ran along the north slope of Mount Jearim (Kesalon), down to Beth-shemesh, and over to Timnah.
11. It went north of Ekron, turned toward Shikkeron, passed Mount Baalah, and ended at Jabneel and the Mediterranean Sea.
12. The western border was the Mediterranean coastline. This was the land given to Judah.

Caleb's Land

13. Joshua gave Caleb some land in Judah, just like the Lord commanded. He gave him Hebron, also called Kiriath-arba (named after Arba, ancestor of the Anakites).
14. Caleb drove out three Anakite men: Sheshai, Ahiman, and Talmai.
15. Then he went to fight the people in Debir (also called Kiriath-sepher).
16. Caleb said, "Whoever captures Kiriath-sepher can marry my daughter Achsah."
17. His nephew Othniel (son of Kenaz, Caleb's brother) captured it. So Caleb let him marry Achsah.
18. When they got married, Achsah asked her father for some land. She got off her donkey, and Caleb said, "What do you want?"
19. She said, "You gave me desert land. Please give me springs of water too." So Caleb gave her the upper and lower springs.

Cities in Judah's Land

20. These are the cities that belonged to Judah's tribe.
21. In the far south near Edom: Kabzeel, Eder, Jagur,
22. Kinah, Dimonah, Adadah,
23. Kedesh, Hazor, Ithnan,
24. Ziph, Telem, Bealoth,
25. Hazor-hadattah, Kerioth-hezron (also called Hazor),
26. Amam, Shema, Moladah,
27. Hazar-gaddah, Heshmon, Beth-pelet,
28. Hazar-shual, Beersheba, Biziothiah,
29. Baalah, Iim, Ezem,
30. Eltolad, Kesil, Hormah,

31. Ziklag, Madmannah, Sansannah,
32. Lebaoth, Shilhim, Ain, and Rimmon—29 cities with their villages.
33. In the lowlands: Eshtaol, Zorah, Ashnah,
34. Zanoah, En-gannim, Tappuah, Enam,
35. Jarmuth, Adullam, Socoh, Azekah,
36. Shaaraim, Adithaim, Gederah, and Gederothaim—14 cities with their villages.
37. Zenan, Hadashah, Migdal-gad,
38. Dilean, Mizpeh, Joktheel,
39. Lachish, Bozkath, Eglon,
40. Cabbon, Lahmam, Kitlish,
41. Gederoth, Beth-dagon, Naamah, and Makkedah—16 cities with their villages.
42. Libnah, Ether, Ashan,
43. Iphtah, Ashnah, Nezib,
44. Keilah, Achzib, and Mareshah—9 cities with their villages.
45. Ekron and its towns and villages.
46. From Ekron to the sea, all towns near Ashdod with their villages.
47. Ashdod and Gaza, with their towns and villages, as far as the River of Egypt and the Mediterranean Sea.
48. In the hill country: Shamir, Jattir, Socoh,
49. Dannah, Kiriath-sannah (Debir),
50. Anab, Eshtemoh, Anim,
51. Goshen, Holon, and Giloh—11 cities with their villages.
52. Arab, Dumah, Eshan,
53. Janim, Beth-tappuah, Aphekah,
54. Humtah, Kiriath-arba (Hebron), and Zior—9 cities with their villages.
55. Maon, Carmel, Ziph, Juttah,
56. Jezreel, Jokdeam, Zanoah,
57. Kain, Gibeah, and Timnah—10 cities with their villages.
58. Halhul, Beth-zur, Gedor,
59. Maarath, Beth-anoth, and Eltekon—6 cities with their villages.
60. Kiriath-baal (Kiriath-jearim) and Rabbah—2 cities with their villages.
61. In the desert: Beth-arabah, Middin, Secacah,
62. Nibshan, Salt City, and En-gedi—6 cities with their villages.

Jebusites in Jerusalem

63. The tribe of Judah could not drive out the Jebusites living in Jerusalem. They still live there with Judah's people to this day.

Joshua 16

Land Given to Ephraim

1. The land for Joseph's descendants started at the Jordan River near Jericho and went through the desert into the hill country to Bethel.
2. From Bethel (also called Luz), it went to Ataroth, where the Arkites lived.
3. Then it went west to Japhletite territory, then to Lower Beth-horon and to Gezer, ending at the Mediterranean Sea.
4. So the tribes of Ephraim and Manasseh (Joseph's sons) got their land.

Ephraim's Borders and Towns

5. This is the land given to the families of Ephraim: Their border went from Ataroth-addar on the east to Upper Beth-horon,
6. then to the Mediterranean Sea. From Micmethath on the north, it curved east past Taanath-shiloh to Janoah.
7. It went down from Janoah to Ataroth and Naarah, touched Jericho, and ended at the Jordan River.
8. From Tappuah, the border went west to the Kanah River and ended at the Mediterranean Sea. This was their land.
9. Ephraim also had towns and villages inside Manasseh's land.

10. But they didn't drive out the Canaanites in Gezer. So the Canaanites still live there today, but they became forced labor.

Joshua 17

Land for the Tribe of Manasseh

1. This was the land given to the tribe of Manasseh (Joseph's first son). Makir, Manasseh's oldest son and father of Gilead, was a great warrior. He received Gilead and Bashan.
2. The rest of Manasseh's sons got land, divided by their families: Abiezer, Helek, Asriel, Shechem, Hepher, and Shemida.
3. Zelophehad, son of Hepher, had no sons—only daughters: Mahlah, Noah, Hoglah, Milcah, and Tirzah.
4. They went to Eleazar the priest, Joshua, and the leaders. They said, "The Lord told Moses to give us land just like the sons." So they were given land, just like their uncles.
5. Manasseh got ten parts of land west of the Jordan, plus Gilead and Bashan on the east.
6. This happened because Manasseh's daughters received land like the sons. Gilead was for the rest of the tribe.

Borders of Manasseh's Land

7. Manasseh's western border went from Asher to Micmethath near Shechem. Then it went south to the people of Tappuah.
8. The land around Tappuah belonged to Manasseh, but the town of Tappuah, on the border, belonged to Ephraim.
9. The border went down to the Kanah River. Towns south of the river belonged to Ephraim, even though they were in Manasseh's land.
10. So the land south of the river was Ephraim's, and the north side was Manasseh's. The border ended at the Mediterranean Sea.
11. Manasseh also had towns in Issachar and Asher, including Beth-shan, Ibleam, Dor, Endor, Taanach, and Megiddo, and their nearby villages.
12. But the people of Manasseh couldn't take these towns, and the Canaanites stayed.
13. Later, when Israel grew stronger, they forced the Canaanites to work for them but didn't drive them out.

Joseph's Tribes Want More Land

14. The people of Joseph (Ephraim and Manasseh) asked Joshua, "Why did you only give us one part of land? We're a large tribe because the Lord has blessed us."
15. Joshua said, "If you're so many, go into the forest and clear land in the hill country of the Perizzites and Rephaites."
16. They said, "The hill country isn't enough. The Canaanites in the valley have iron chariots—both in Beth-shan and in the Jezreel Valley."
17. Joshua told the tribes of Joseph, "You are many and strong. You will have more than one share.
18. The forested hill country will be yours. Clear it and take it. The Canaanites may be strong with iron chariots, but you will drive them out."

Joshua 18

The Remaining Land is Divided

1. All the Israelites gathered at Shiloh and set up the tent of the Lord's presence. The land was now mostly under their control.
2. But seven tribes still had not received their land.
3. Joshua said, "Why are you waiting? Go take the land the Lord gave you!
4. Choose three men from each tribe. I'll send them to map out the land, then they'll return to me.

5. They'll divide it into seven parts. Judah will keep the land in the south. Joseph will keep their land in the north.
6. After the land is mapped, I'll cast lots to see which tribe gets what part."
7. "The Levites don't get land. The tribes of Gad, Reuben, and half of Manasseh already got their land east of the Jordan, which Moses gave them."

Land Surveyed and Divided

8. The men left to map the land. Joshua told them, "Walk through the land, write down what you see, then return to me. I will cast lots for you here at Shiloh."
9. The men traveled through the land and wrote down the layout of the seven parts. Then they went back to Joshua at Shiloh.
10. There, Joshua cast lots in the presence of the Lord and gave each tribe its land.

Land Given to Benjamin

11. The tribe of Benjamin was the first to receive land by lot. Their land was between Judah and Joseph.
12. The northern border went from the Jordan River, up to Jericho, and west into the hills, ending at the desert of Beth-aven.
13. From there it went to Luz (Bethel), down to Ataroth-addar near the hill south of Lower Beth-horon.
14. Then it turned south along the west side to Kiriath-baal (also called Kiriath-jearim), a town of Judah. That was the western border.
15. The southern border started near Kiriath-jearim and went west to the spring of Nephtoah.
16. It went down to the foot of the hill near the Valley of Hinnom, north of Rephaim Valley, and down into Hinnom Valley, south of the Jebusite city (Jerusalem). Then it went to En-rogel.
17. From there it curved north to En-shemesh, passed Geliloth (across from Adummim), down to the Stone of Bohan (Reuben's son),
18. continued to the north slope of Beth-arabah, down to the Jordan Valley,
19. and ended at the north bay of the Dead Sea, near the Jordan River inlet. That was the southern border.
20. The eastern border was the Jordan River. This was the land of Benjamin.

Towns in Benjamin's Land

21. These were the towns in Benjamin's land: Jericho, Beth-hoglah, Emek-keziz,
22. Beth-arabah, Zemaraim, Bethel,
23. Avvim, Parah, Ophrah,
24. Kephar-ammoni, Ophni, and Geba—12 towns with their villages.
25. Gibeon, Ramah, Beeroth,
26. Mizpah, Kephirah, Mozah,
27. Rekem, Irpeel, Taralah,
28. Zela, Haeleph, Jebus (Jerusalem), Gibeah, and Kiriath—14 towns with their villages. This was Benjamin's land.

Joshua 19

Land Given to Simeon

1. The second lot went to the tribe of Simeon. Their land was inside Judah's land.
2. They got Beersheba, Sheba, Moladah,
3. Hazar-shual, Balah, Ezem,
4. Eltolad, Bethul, Hormah,
5. Ziklag, Beth-marcaboth, Hazar-susah,
6. Beth-lebaoth, and Sharuhen—13 towns with villages.
7. Also Ain, Rimmon, Ether, and Ashan—4 towns with villages.
8. These towns and villages reached as far as Baalath-beer (Ramah of the Negev). This was Simeon's land.
9. Their land came from Judah's share because Judah had too much. That's why Simeon's land was inside Judah's.

Land Given to Zebulun

10. The third lot went to Zebulun. Their border started at Sarid,

11. went west to Maralah, Dabbesheth, and near Jokneam.

12. It turned east to Kisloth-tabor, went to Daberath, and up to Japhia.

13. Then it continued to Gath-hepher, Eth-kazin, Rimmon, and turned toward Neah.

14. It circled around to Hannathon and ended at the valley of Iphtahel.

15. They got 12 towns and villages, including Kattath, Nahalal, Shimron, Idalah, and Bethlehem.

16. This was Zebulun's land.

Land Given to Issachar

17. The fourth lot went to Issachar.

18. They got Jezreel, Kesulloth, Shunem,

19. Hapharaim, Shion, Anaharath,

20. Rabbith, Kishion, Ebez,

21. Remeth, En-gannim, En-haddah, and Beth-pazzez.

22. The border touched Tabor, Shahazumah, and Beth-shemesh, and ended at the Jordan River—16 towns and villages.

23. This was Issachar's land.

Land Given to Asher

24. The fifth lot went to Asher.

25. They got Helkath, Hali, Beten, Achshaph,

26. Allammelech, Amad, and Mishal. The border touched Carmel and Shihor-libnath.

27. It turned east to Beth-dagon, touched Zebulun and the Valley of Iphtahel, and went north to Beth-emek and Neiel, then to Cabul.

28. It included Ebron, Rehob, Hammon, and Kanah all the way to Sidon.

29. The border reached Ramah and the strong city of Tyre, turned to Hosah, and ended at the sea near Akzib.

30. Also included were Ummah, Aphek, and Rehob—22 towns with villages.

31. This was Asher's land.

Land Given to Naphtali

32. The sixth lot went to Naphtali.

33. Their border started at Heleph, passed Zaanannim, Adami-nekeb, and Jabneel to Lakkum, and ended at the Jordan River.

34. It went west to Aznoth-tabor, passed Hukkok, and touched Zebulun, Asher, and the Jordan River on the east.

35. Their towns included Ziddim, Zer, Hammath, Rakkath, Chinnereth,

36. Adamah, Ramah, Hazor,

37. Kedesh, Edrei, En-hazor,

38. Iron, Migdal-el, Horem, Beth-anath, and Beth-shemesh—19 towns with villages.

39. This was Naphtali's land.

Land Given to Dan

40. The seventh lot went to Dan.

41. Their towns were Zorah, Eshtaol, Ir-shemesh,

42. Shaalabbin, Aijalon, Ithlah,

43. Elon, Timnah, Ekron,

44. Eltekeh, Gibbethon, Baalath,

45. Jehud, Bene-berak, Gath-rimmon,

46. Me-jarkon, and Rakkon with the area near Joppa.

47. Dan's border was too small, so they attacked Leshem, captured it, renamed it Dan, and lived there.

48. This was Dan's land.

Land Given to Joshua

49. After dividing the land, the Israelites gave Joshua his own town.

50. He chose Timnath-serah in the hill country of Ephraim. He built the town and lived there.

51. These land divisions were made by Eleazar the priest, Joshua, and the leaders at Shiloh. They cast lots before

the Lord at the entrance of the meeting tent. This finished dividing the land.

Joshua 20

Cities of Safety

1. The Lord said to Joshua,
2. "Tell the people to choose the cities of safety I told Moses about.
3. If someone kills a person by accident, they can run to one of these cities and be safe from anyone wanting revenge.
4. They must go to the city gate and tell the leaders what happened. If accepted, they can enter and live there.
5. If the dead person's family tries to get them, don't hand them over. The death wasn't planned.
6. They must stay in the city until they stand trial and until the high priest dies. Then they may return home."
7. They chose Kedesh in Galilee (Naphtali), Shechem (Ephraim), and Hebron (Judah).
8. East of the Jordan, they chose Bezer (Reuben), Ramoth (Gad), and Golan (Manasseh).
9. These cities were for Israelites and any foreigners living with them. Anyone who killed someone by accident could run there and stay safe until judged.

Joshua 21

Towns for the Levites

1. The leaders of the Levite families came to Eleazar the priest, Joshua, and the other leaders.
2. At Shiloh in Canaan, they said, "The Lord told Moses to give us towns to live in, with land for our animals."
3. So the Israelites gave them towns and pastures from their own land, just as the Lord had said.
4. The families of Kohath (from Levi's tribe) got land first. The priests (from Aaron's family) got 13 towns in Judah, Simeon, and Benjamin.
5. The other Kohath families got 10 towns from Ephraim, Dan, and half of Manasseh.
6. The Gershon families got 13 towns from Issachar, Asher, Naphtali, and half of Manasseh in Bashan.
7. The Merari families got 12 towns from Reuben, Gad, and Zebulun.
8. These towns and pastures were given by drawing lots, just as the Lord had commanded through Moses.

Towns for the Priests

9. These are the towns given to the priests (from Aaron's family) in Judah and Simeon:
10. They were from the Kohath clan.
11. They got Hebron (also called Kiriath-arba) in Judah's hill country, with land around it.
12. But the fields and villages around Hebron were given to Caleb.
13. The priests got Hebron (a city of safety), Libnah,
14. Jattir, Eshtemoa,
15. Holon, Debir,
16. Ain, Juttah, and Beth-shemesh—9 towns from Judah and Simeon.
17. From Benjamin they got Gibeon, Geba,
18. Anathoth, and Almon—4 towns.
19. So the priests got 13 towns in all.

Towns for the Other Kohath Families

20. The other Kohath families got towns from Ephraim.
21. They got Shechem (a city of safety) in the hill country, Gezer,
22. Kibzaim, and Beth-horon—4 towns.
23. From Dan: Eltekeh, Gibbethon,
24. Aijalon, and Gath-rimmon—4 towns.
25. From half of Manasseh: Taanach and Gath-rimmon—2 towns.

26. These Kohath families got 10 towns total.

Towns for the Gershon Families

27. From the other half of Manasseh: Golan (a city of safety) and Beeshterah—2 towns.
28. From Issachar: Kishion, Daberath,
29. Jarmuth, and En-gannim—4 towns.
30. From Asher: Mishal, Abdon,
31. Helkath, and Rehob—4 towns.
32. From Naphtali: Kedesh (a city of safety), Hammoth-dor, and Kartan—3 towns.
33. These Gershon families got 13 towns total.

Towns for the Merari Families

34. From Zebulun: Jokneam, Kartah,
35. Dimnah, and Nahalal—4 towns.
36. From Reuben: Bezer, Jahaz,
37. Kedemoth, and Mephaath—4 towns.
38. From Gad: Ramoth (a city of safety), Mahanaim,
39. Heshbon, and Jazer—4 towns.
40. The Merari families got 12 towns total.

Total Towns for the Levites

41. In all, the Levites got 48 towns with pastures.
42. Each town had land around it for animals.
43. So the Lord gave Israel all the land He promised their ancestors. They took it and lived in it.
44. The Lord gave them peace with all their enemies. No one could stand against them.
45. Every promise the Lord made came true—not one failed.

Joshua 22

Eastern Tribes Return Home

1. Joshua called together the tribes of Reuben, Gad, and half of Manasseh.
2. He said, "You obeyed everything Moses and I told you.
3. You stayed and helped your brothers all this time.
4. Now the Lord has given them rest, so you can go home—to the land Moses gave you on the east side of the Jordan.
5. But keep obeying the law Moses gave you. Love and serve the Lord with all your heart."
6. Then Joshua blessed them and sent them home.
7. Moses had given land to half of Manasseh in Bashan, and Joshua gave land to the other half west of the Jordan. He blessed them and sent them home.
8. He said, "Go back with all your riches—lots of animals, silver, gold, bronze, and iron. Share it with the rest of your tribe."

An Altar by the Jordan

9. The men of Reuben, Gad, and half of Manasseh left the rest of Israel at Shiloh and went home to Gilead.
10. When they reached the Jordan, they built a large altar near it.
11. The rest of Israel heard about it and said, "The eastern tribes built an altar! That's rebellion!"
12. So they gathered to go to war against them.
13. They sent Phinehas (son of the priest Eleazar) to talk to them,
14. along with 10 leaders—one from each western tribe.
15. They said,
16. "Why did you build this altar? Are you turning against the Lord?
17. Remember what happened at Peor? We're still suffering from that sin.
18. And now you're rebelling again?
19. If your land is unclean, come live with us in the Lord's land where the meeting tent is. But don't turn against the Lord by building your own altar.

20. Remember Achan? His sin caused trouble for all of us!"
21. The eastern tribes answered:
22. "The Lord knows the truth, and Israel should know too. If we built this altar to rebel, then let God punish us.
23. If we made it to offer sacrifices, may God judge us.
24. No! We built it so future generations wouldn't say we don't belong to the Lord.
25. We were afraid your descendants might reject ours, saying, 'You have no share in the Lord.'
26. So we built this altar—not for sacrifices,
27. but as a reminder that we worship the Lord just like you do.
28. If anyone says we don't belong, we'll point to this altar as proof.
29. We'd never turn from the Lord or build another altar. Only the Lord's altar near the meeting tent is right."
30. Phinehas and the leaders were happy with the answer.
31. Phinehas said, "Now we know the Lord is with us and you didn't sin."
32. They returned to Canaan and gave the people the good news.
33. Everyone was glad and praised God. They didn't go to war.
34. The eastern tribes named the altar "Proof Between Us"—a reminder that they serve the Lord.

Joshua 23

Joshua's Goodbye Speech

1. A long time passed. The Lord had given Israel peace from all its enemies. Joshua was very old.
2. He called all the leaders and said, "I'm very old now.
3. You've seen everything the Lord has done for you. He fought for you.
4. I gave you land from the nations we defeated. There are still some nations left.
5. The Lord your God will force them out. You'll take their land, just like He promised.
6. Be strong. Obey everything in the Law of Moses. Don't turn away from it.
7. Don't mix with the nations left around you. Don't even say their gods' names. Don't worship them.
8. Stay close to the Lord your God, like you've done until now.
9. The Lord has driven out great and powerful nations. No one has defeated you.
10. One of you can chase a thousand, because the Lord fights for you.
11. So love the Lord your God.
12. But if you turn away and join the people who remain,
13. know this: The Lord won't drive them out. They'll be a trap and a thorn in your side until you're destroyed.
14. I'm about to die. You know in your heart that everything the Lord promised has come true.
15. But if you disobey, all the bad things He warned about will happen too.
16. If you break your promise and worship other gods, the Lord will be angry and destroy you."

Joshua 24

Joshua Reminds the People

1. Joshua gathered all the tribes at Shechem. He called the leaders to stand before God.
2. Joshua said, "This is what the Lord says: Long ago, your ancestors, including Abraham's father Terah, lived beyond the Euphrates River and worshiped other gods.
3. I took Abraham from that land and gave him many descendants.

4. I gave him Isaac. To Isaac, I gave Jacob and Esau. I gave Esau the hill country. Jacob and his family went to Egypt.
5. I sent Moses and Aaron. I made Egypt suffer and brought your people out.
6. When you left Egypt and reached the Red Sea, the Egyptians chased you.
7. You cried to me, and I put darkness between you and them. I drowned them in the sea. You saw it happen. Then you lived in the desert a long time.
8. I brought you to the land of the Amorites. They fought you, but I gave you victory.
9. Balak, king of Moab, tried to fight you by asking Balaam to curse you.
10. But I didn't let Balaam curse you. I made him bless you.
11. You crossed the Jordan and came to Jericho. The people of Jericho fought you, as did others. But I gave you victory.
12. I sent hornets to drive them out. You didn't win by your swords or strength.
13. I gave you land, cities, and vineyards you didn't work for."

Serve the Lord

14. "So respect the Lord. Serve Him with all your heart. Throw away the gods your ancestors worshiped. Serve only the Lord.
15. But if you don't want to serve Him, choose today who you will serve—the
16. old gods or the gods of the land you live in. But I and my family will serve the Lord."
17. The people said, "We would never stop serving the Lord!
18. He brought us and our families out of Egypt. He protected us and did great miracles.
19. He gave us this land. We will serve Him because He is our God."
20. Joshua said, "You can't serve the Lord if you sin. He is holy and won't forgive if you turn away.
21. If you leave Him and serve other gods, He will turn against you and destroy you."
22. But the people said, "No! We will serve the Lord."
23. Joshua said, "You are witnesses to your own choice." They said, "Yes, we are."
24. He said, "Then throw away your idols and give your hearts fully to the Lord."
25. The people said, "We will serve and obey the Lord."
26. Joshua made an agreement with them that day and gave them laws and rules.
27. He wrote them in the book of God's Law. Then he set up a large stone under the tree near the Lord's meeting tent.
28. Joshua said, "This stone has heard everything the Lord said. It will remind you not to lie to your God."
29. Then Joshua sent everyone home.

Joshua Dies

30. After all this, Joshua died at age 110.
31. They buried him in his land at Timnath-serah in the hill country of Ephraim.
32. Israel served the Lord all the days of Joshua and the elders who outlived him—those who saw what the Lord had done.
33. They also buried Joseph's bones at Shechem, in the land Jacob had bought.
34. Eleazar the priest died too. He was buried at Gibeah, in land given to his son Phinehas.

– Judges –

Israel repeatedly turns from God, faces oppression, and is rescued by leaders called judges.

Judges 1

Judah and Simeon Fight the Canaanites

1. After Joshua died, the Israelites asked the Lord, "Who should go first to fight the Canaanites?"
2. The Lord said, "Judah will go first. I'm giving them the land."
3. The men of Judah said to Simeon, "Come fight with us, and we'll help you later." So Simeon went with them.
4. Judah attacked, and the Lord gave them victory over the Canaanites and Perizzites. They killed 10,000 men at Bezek.
5. They found Adoni-Bezek there, fought him, and beat the Canaanites and Perizzites.
6. Adoni-Bezek tried to run away, but they caught him and cut off his thumbs and big toes.
7. Adoni-Bezek said, "I did the same to 70 kings. Now God is punishing me." They took him to Jerusalem, and he died there.
8. Judah attacked Jerusalem, captured it, killed everyone, and burned it down.
9. Then they went to fight the Canaanites in the hills, desert, and foothills.
10. They fought the Canaanites in Hebron (once called Kiriath-Arba) and defeated Sheshai, Ahiman, and Talmai.
11. From there, they attacked Debir (once called Kiriath-Sepher).
12. Caleb said, "Whoever captures Kiriath-Sepher can marry my daughter Achsah."
13. Caleb's nephew Othniel captured it, so Caleb gave him his daughter Achsah.
14. When Achsah came to Othniel, she asked for land. As she got off her donkey, Caleb asked, "What do you want?"
15. She said, "This land is dry. Please give me water springs." So Caleb gave her both the upper and lower springs.
16. The Kenites (Moses's father-in-law's family) moved from Jericho with Judah and lived in the desert of Judah, near Arad.
17. Judah and Simeon attacked the Canaanites in Zephath and destroyed the city. They renamed it Hormah.
18. Judah also took Gaza, Ashkelon, and Ekron and the land around them.
19. The Lord helped Judah take the hill country, but they couldn't drive out the people in the valleys because they had iron chariots.
20. Hebron was given to Caleb, just like Moses promised. Caleb drove the Anakite families out there.

Benjamin Doesn't Take Jerusalem

21. But the tribe of Benjamin didn't drive out the Jebusites living in Jerusalem. So they still live there with the Benjaminites today.

Ephraim and Manasseh Take Bethel

22. The descendants of Joseph attacked Bethel, and the Lord helped them.
23. They sent spies to look at Bethel (once called Luz).
24. The spies saw a man leaving the city and said, "Show us how to get in, and we won't hurt you."
25. He showed them a way in, and they killed everyone except him and his family.
26. He later moved to the land of the Hittites and built a city named Luz, which still exists today.

Israel Doesn't Remove All the Canaanites

27. Manasseh didn't drive out the people in Beth-Shan, Taanach, Dor, Ibleam, or Megiddo. The Canaanites stayed there.
28. When Israel grew stronger, they made the Canaanites work for them, but didn't remove them.
29. Ephraim didn't remove the Canaanites in Gezer, so they lived together.

30. Zebulun didn't remove the Canaanites in Kitron or Nahalol but made them work for them.
31. Asher didn't remove the people in Acco, Sidon, Ahlab, Akzib, Helbah, Aphek, or Rehob.
32. So Asher lived among the Canaanites.
33. Naphtali didn't remove the people in Beth-Shemesh or Beth-Anath. They lived with the Canaanites but made them work.
34. The Amorites forced the tribe of Dan into the hills and didn't let them live in the valley.
35. The Amorites stayed in Mount Heres, Aijalon, and Shaalbim. But when the descendants of Joseph grew stronger, they made the Amorites work for them.
36. The border of the Amorites ran from Scorpion Pass to Sela and beyond.

Judges 2

The Angel of the Lord Speaks

1. The angel of the Lord went from Gilgal to Bokim and said, "I brought you out of Egypt and gave you this land.
2. I told you not to make deals with the people here. I said to tear down their altars. But you didn't obey me.
3. So now I won't drive them out. They'll be a trap, and their gods will tempt you."
4. When the angel finished speaking, the people cried loudly.
5. That's why the place was called Bokim. They offered sacrifices there to the Lord.

Joshua Dies

6. After Joshua sent the people away, they went to take their land.
7. As long as Joshua and the elders lived, the people served the Lord.
8. Joshua died at age 110.
9. He was buried in Timnath-heres in Ephraim's hill country.
10. After that generation died, the next generation didn't know the Lord or what He had done.

Israel Turns Away From God

11. The Israelites sinned and worshiped Baal.
12. They forgot the Lord who saved them from Egypt. They followed other gods.
13. They turned away from the Lord and worshiped Baal and Ashtoreth.
14. So the Lord was angry and let enemies defeat them.
15. They lost every battle because the Lord wasn't with them.
16. Then the Lord sent judges to save them from their enemies.
17. But they didn't listen. They worshiped other gods instead.
18. When a judge was alive, the Lord helped them win. But after the judge died,
19. they became worse than before—following and worshiping other gods.
20. The Lord was angry and said, "These people broke the promise their ancestors made.
21. I won't drive out the nations Joshua left.
22. I'll use them to test Israel, to see if they obey me."
23. So the Lord let those nations stay.

Judges 3

Nations Left to Test Israel

1. These are the nations the Lord left to test Israel:
2. He wanted Israel to learn how to fight.
3. The nations were the Philistines, the Canaanites, the Sidonians, and the Hivites living in the hills and Lebanon.
4. They tested Israel, to see if they'd obey God's commands.

5. The Israelites lived with these people and
6. married their sons and daughters. They worshiped their gods.

Othniel, the First Judge

7. The Israelites did evil and forgot the Lord.
8. So He let King Cushan-rishathaim of Aram defeat them. Israel served him for 8 years.
9. Then they cried to the Lord, and He sent Othniel to save them.
10. The Lord's Spirit was with Othniel. He became Israel's leader and won the war.
11. The land had peace for 40 years. Then Othniel died.

Ehud, the Second Judge

12. Israel sinned again. So the Lord let King Eglon of Moab defeat them.
13. Eglon got help from the Ammonites and Amalekites. They took Jericho.
14. Israel served Eglon for 18 years.
15. They cried to the Lord, and He sent Ehud. He was left-handed.
16. Ehud made a short sword and hid it on his right leg.
17. He brought gifts to Eglon, who was very fat.
18. After giving the gifts, Ehud sent the men home.
19. But he turned back and said, "I have a secret message." So the king sent everyone out.
20. Ehud came close as the king sat alone. Ehud said, "I have a message from God." Eglon stood up.
21. Ehud pulled the sword from his right side and stabbed him in the belly.
22. The handle went in with the blade, and Eglon's fat closed around it. Ehud left the sword inside.
23. He closed the doors and left.
24. The servants returned later and found the doors locked. They thought the king was using the bathroom.
25. They waited so long they became embarrassed. Then they unlocked the doors and found him dead.
26. Ehud had escaped while they waited.
27. When he reached Israel's land, he blew a trumpet. The Israelites followed him.
28. He said, "Follow me! The Lord has given us victory!" They blocked the Jordan River crossings.
29. They killed 10,000 strong Moabite men.
30. Moab was defeated, and the land had peace for 80 years.

Shamgar, the Third Judge

31. After Ehud, Shamgar became judge. He killed 600 Philistines with an ox stick and saved Israel.

Judges 4

Deborah Leads Israel

1. After Ehud died, Israel sinned again.
2. So the Lord let King Jabin of Hazor rule over them. His army commander was Sisera.
3. Sisera had 900 iron chariots and made Israel suffer for 20 years.
4. Deborah, a prophet and judge, led Israel at that time.
5. She sat under a palm tree, and the people came to her for help.
6. She called Barak and said, "The Lord commands you to take 10,000 men and fight Sisera.
7. God will bring Sisera to the river and give you victory."
8. Barak said, "I'll go only if you come too."
9. Deborah said, "I'll go, but the Lord will let a woman defeat Sisera instead of you."

10. So Barak gathered the army, and Deborah went with him.
11. Heber the Kenite had moved away and camped by Kedesh.
12. Sisera heard Barak had gone to Mount Tabor.
13. He brought all 900 chariots and his army to the Kishon River.
14. Deborah said, "Go now! The Lord is with you!" So Barak attacked.
15. The Lord confused Sisera's army. They ran away, and Sisera left his chariot and fled.
16. Barak chased the army and killed every soldier.
17. Sisera ran to the tent of Jael, the wife of Heber, because they had peace.
18. Jael went out and said, "Come in. Don't be afraid." So Sisera entered, and she covered him with a blanket.
19. He said, "Please give me water." She gave him milk instead.
20. He said, "Stand at the door. If anyone comes, say I'm not here."
21. Then Jael took a tent peg and hammer, and while he slept, she drove the peg through his head and killed him.
22. When Barak came, Jael said, "Come, I'll show you the man you're looking for."
23. That day, God gave Israel victory over King Jabin.
24. Israel grew stronger and finally destroyed him.

Judges 5

Deborah and Barak's Song

1. That day, Deborah and Barak sang this song:
2. "Praise the Lord! The leaders and people of Israel volunteered to fight.
3. Listen, kings and rulers! I will sing to the Lord.
4. Lord, when you came from Seir, from Edom's land, the earth shook and the skies poured rain.
5. The mountains shook before the Lord, the God of Israel.
6. In Shamgar's and Jael's time, roads were empty. Travelers took side paths.
7. Villages in Israel were abandoned until I, Deborah, arose to lead.
8. When new gods were chosen, war came. Not a shield or spear was found among 40,000 in Israel.
9. My heart is with the leaders and people who volunteered. Praise the Lord!
10. Tell this, you who ride donkeys, sit in fancy seats, or walk on the road.
11. Hear them sing at the wells—the Lord's victories in Israel!
12. Wake up, Deborah! Sing! Get up, Barak! Lead your captives away!
13. The survivors came down to fight. The Lord sent heroes.
14. Some came from Ephraim, Benjamin, Makir, and Zebulun.
15. The leaders from Issachar were with Deborah. Barak followed them.
16. But why did you stay among the sheep pens, listening to flutes?
17. Gilead stayed across the Jordan. Dan stayed on his ships. Asher stayed by the sea.
18. But Zebulun and Naphtali risked their lives in battle.
19. Kings came and fought, but not for treasure.
20. Stars fought from heaven.
21. The Kishon River swept them away. March on, my soul, with courage!
22. Horses pounded the ground as they ran.
23. Curse Meroz, said the angel of the Lord, because they didn't help.
24. Jael is blessed above all women.

25. Sisera asked for water. She gave him milk.
26. She used a hammer and peg. She crushed his head.
27. He sank and died at her feet.
28. Sisera's mother looked out the window. She wondered why his chariot was late.
29. Her servant said, "Maybe they're dividing the goods—clothes and women."
30. (continued) "A prize for each man, colorful robes for Sisera."
31. Lord, may your enemies die like Sisera, but may your people rise like the sun." Then the land had peace for 40 years.

Judges 6

Midian Oppresses Israel

1. Israel sinned again. So the Lord let Midian rule for 7 years.
2. The Midianites were so cruel that the Israelites hid in caves and mountains.
3. Every time Israel planted crops, the Midianites, Amalekites, and others attacked.
4. They ruined the land, stole crops and animals, and left nothing.
5. They came like locusts—too many to count.
6. Israel was starving, so they cried out to the Lord.
7. The Lord sent a prophet who said,
8. "God brought you out of Egypt,
9. saved you from your enemies,
10. and told you not to worship the gods of the Amorites. But you didn't listen."

The Angel Visits Gideon

11. The angel of the Lord sat under a tree. Gideon was hiding while threshing wheat.
12. The angel said, "The Lord is with you, brave warrior!"
13. Gideon said, "If the Lord is with us, why are we suffering? Where are the miracles?"
14. The Lord said, "Go save Israel. I am sending you."
15. Gideon said, "How? My family is the weakest, and I'm the least important."
16. The Lord said, "I will be with you. You will defeat Midian."
17. Gideon said, "Give me a sign."
18. He asked the Lord to wait while he brought an offering.
19. Gideon prepared meat and bread and brought it to the angel.
20. The angel said, "Put the food on the rock and pour broth over it." Gideon obeyed.
21. The angel touched it with his staff, and fire consumed the offering. Then the angel disappeared.
22. Gideon said, "Oh no! I saw the angel of the Lord face-to-face!"
23. But the Lord said, "Don't be afraid. You won't die."
24. Gideon built an altar there and called it "The Lord is Peace." It still stands in Ophrah.

Gideon Destroys the Altar of Baal

25. That night, the Lord told Gideon, "Tear down your father's altar to Baal and the Asherah pole next to it.
26. Build an altar to the Lord and sacrifice a bull using the wood from the pole."
27. Gideon obeyed, but he did it at night because he was afraid.
28. In the morning, the people saw the altar was gone and asked, "Who did this?"
29. After asking around, they found out Gideon did it.
30. They told his father, "Bring your son out. He must die!"
31. But his father said, "If Baal is real, let him defend himself."

32. From then on, Gideon was called Jerub-Baal, meaning "Let Baal fight him."

Gideon Prepares for Battle

33. The Midianites and others camped in the valley.
34. The Spirit of the Lord came on Gideon. He blew a trumpet and called others to join him.
35. He sent messengers to many tribes, and they followed him.
36. Gideon said to God, "If you'll help me win,
37. I'll lay a wool fleece on the ground. If it's wet but the ground is dry, I'll know you'll help."
38. The next morning, the fleece was wet, and the ground was dry.
39. Gideon said, "Don't be angry, but let me test once more. This time, make the fleece dry and the ground wet."
40. That night, God did it. The fleece was dry, and the ground was wet.

Judges 7

Gideon's Small Army Wins

1. Gideon and his men camped near the spring of Harod.
2. The Lord said, "You have too many men. If you win now, Israel will brag.
3. Tell anyone who's afraid to go home." So 22,000 left, and 10,000 stayed.
4. The Lord said, "Still too many. Take them to the water."
5. The Lord told Gideon to keep only the men who drank by cupping their hands.
6. 300 men did that. The rest knelt to drink.
7. The Lord said, "Use the 300. I will help you win."
8. Gideon kept the 300 and sent the rest home.
9. That night, the Lord said, "Go to the Midianite camp. I will help you win.
10. If you're afraid, take your servant Purah and listen to what they say."
11. So Gideon and Purah went to the enemy camp.
12. The valley was filled with Midianites, Amalekites, and others—like locusts, with too many camels to count.
13. Gideon heard a man tell his friend a dream: "A loaf of bread rolled into our camp and knocked down a tent."
14. The friend said, "That's Gideon! God will help him defeat us!"
15. Gideon worshiped God, then returned and said, "Get up! The Lord has given us victory!"
16. He divided the 300 men into 3 groups, gave them trumpets and jars with torches inside.
17. He said, "Watch me. Do what I do."
18. "When I blow my trumpet, you blow yours and shout, 'For the Lord and Gideon!'"
19. They reached the camp at night. They blew trumpets and broke the jars.
20. Each group held torches in one hand and trumpets in the other and shouted, "For the Lord and Gideon!"
21. The enemy ran in panic.
22. The Lord made them fight each other. They fled toward Beth-shittah.
23. Israel chased them.
24. Gideon sent messengers to cut off their escape at the river.
25. They captured and killed the Midianite leaders Oreb and Zeeb. They brought their heads to Gideon.

Judges 8

Gideon Defeats Midian's Kings

1. The men of Ephraim asked Gideon, "Why didn't you call us to fight?" They were angry.

2. Gideon said, "What I did isn't better than what you did. You caught Oreb and Zeeb."
3. "God gave them to you. Why be angry with me?" That calmed them down.
4. Gideon and his 300 men crossed the Jordan River, tired but still chasing the enemy.
5. He asked the people of Succoth, "Please give my men bread. We're chasing Zebah and Zalmunna."
6. But the leaders of Succoth said, "Why help you? You haven't caught them yet."
7. Gideon said, "When I do, I'll come back and punish you with thorns."
8. Then he went to Peniel and asked the same thing. They said no too.
9. He told them, "When I return, I'll tear down your tower."
10. Zebah and Zalmunna were in Karkor with 15,000 men left. 120,000 had already died.
11. Gideon attacked from a surprise route.
12. The enemy ran. He caught the two kings and scared the whole army.
13. Gideon returned from the battle.
14. He captured a young man from Succoth who listed all 77 leaders.
15. Gideon showed the list to the men of Succoth and said, "You refused to help."
16. Then he punished the leaders with thorns.
17. He tore down the tower of Peniel and killed the men there.
18. He asked the two kings, "What did the men at Tabor look like?" They said, "They looked like you."
19. Gideon said, "They were my brothers. If you had spared them, I wouldn't kill you."
20. He told his son Jether to kill them, but the boy was afraid.
21. The kings said, "Do it yourself." So Gideon killed them and took their royal necklaces.

Israel Wants Gideon as King

22. The Israelites said, "Rule over us—you and your sons."
23. Gideon said, "No. The Lord will rule over you."
24. But he asked for gold earrings.
25. They gave him 43 pounds of gold, plus jewelry and purple robes.
26. Gideon made a gold ephod (a priest's garment) and put it in Ophrah. The people worshiped it, which became a trap.
27. Midian was defeated, and Israel had peace for 40 years.

Gideon Dies

28. Gideon went home.
29. He had 70 sons because he had many wives.
30. He also had a concubine in Shechem who had a son named Abimelech.
31. Gideon died at age 110 and was buried in Ophrah.
32. After he died, Israel turned away from God again and worshiped Baal.
33. They forgot the Lord who saved them.
34. And they didn't show kindness to Gideon's family.

Judges 9

Abimelech Becomes King

1. Abimelech, Gideon's son, went to his mother's family in Shechem.
2. He said, "Would you rather have 70 rulers or just me, your relative?"
3. His uncles supported him.
4. They gave him 2 pounds of silver, and he hired thugs.
5. He went to Ophrah and killed his 70 brothers on one stone. Only Jotham escaped.

6. Then the people of Shechem made Abimelech king.
7. When Jotham heard, he stood on Mount Gerizim and shouted:
8. "The trees wanted a king. They asked the olive tree,
9. but it said no—it wanted to keep making oil.
10. The fig tree and grapevine also said no.
11. Finally, they asked the thornbush.
12. The thornbush said, 'If you really want me, come find shade in my thorns. If not, fire will come from me and burn you all.'
13. Jotham said, "If you made Abimelech king honestly, then fine.
14. But remember, my father risked his life for you.
15. Now you've killed his sons and made Abimelech king just because he's your relative.
16. If that was right, then enjoy him. If not, may fire destroy you all."
17. Then Jotham ran away to Beer and hid.

Abimelech's Downfall

18. Abimelech ruled for 3 years.
19. Then God caused trouble between Abimelech and Shechem.
20. This was to punish him for killing his brothers.
21. The people of Shechem set ambushes in the hills.
22. A man named Gaal moved to Shechem, and the people trusted him.
23. They had a festival, got drunk, and cursed Abimelech.
24. Gaal said, "Why should we serve Abimelech? Let me lead!"
25. Zebul, the city leader, heard and got angry.
26. He secretly warned Abimelech.
27. He said, "Come at night and set an ambush."
28. "In the morning, attack when Gaal comes out."
29. Abimelech and his men did exactly that.
30. Gaal stood at the gate, and Abimelech came from hiding.
31. Gaal saw them and said, "Men are coming down the mountain!" Zebul said, "That's just shadows."
32. Gaal said, "No! People are coming from many places!"
33. Zebul said, "Why aren't you talking now? Go fight!"
34. Gaal and his men fought but lost.
35. They ran back, and many died.
36. Abimelech stayed in Arumah. Zebul chased Gaal out.
37. The next day, people went to the fields.
38. Abimelech hid men and attacked.
39. He and his troops killed many and took the city.
40. He destroyed it and scattered salt over the land.
41. The leaders hid in the temple tower.
42. Abimelech heard about it
43. and cut branches from trees. He told his men to do the same.
44. They stacked the branches around the tower and burned it. Everyone inside died—about 1,000 people.
45. Then he went to Thebez and surrounded it.
46. But there was a strong tower. Everyone ran inside.
47. Abimelech went to set it on fire.
48. But a woman dropped a heavy stone on his head and cracked his skull.
49. He told his helper, "Kill me, so no one says a woman killed me." So the helper stabbed him, and he died.
50. When the Israelites saw he was dead, they went home.
51. God punished Abimelech for his evil.

52. God also punished the people of Shechem for their sins.

Judges 10

Tola and Jair

1. Tola became the next judge. He saved Israel.
2. He led for 23 years, then died and was buried in Shamir.
3. After him, Jair became judge. He led Israel for 22 years.
4. He had 30 sons who rode 30 donkeys and ruled 30 towns, called Havvoth-jair.
5. Jair died and was buried in Kamon.

Israel Turns Away Again

6. Israel sinned again. They worshiped Baal, Ashtoreths, and gods of Aram, Sidon, Moab, Ammon, and the Philistines.
7. The Lord was angry and let the Philistines and Ammonites defeat them.
8. They crushed Israel for 18 years—especially east of the Jordan.
9. The Ammonites also crossed the Jordan to fight Judah, Benjamin, and Ephraim.
10. Israel cried out, "We have sinned! We left you for other gods."
11. The Lord said, "Didn't I save you from Egypt, the Amorites, Ammon, and Philistines,
12. from the Sidonians, Amalekites, and Maonites?
13. But you left me again.
14. Go ask your new gods to save you!"
15. The Israelites said, "We have sinned. Punish us, but please save us!"
16. They threw out the false gods and served the Lord. He couldn't ignore their suffering.
17. The Ammonites gathered their army.
18. The Israelites camped at Mizpah and asked, "Who will lead us against Ammon?"

Judges 11

Jephthah Becomes Leader

1. Jephthah was a strong warrior. His father was Gilead, and his mother was a prostitute.
2. Gilead's other sons drove Jephthah away and said, "You won't inherit anything. You're not from our mother."
3. So Jephthah left and lived in Tob. He gathered a group of rough men who followed him.
4. Later, the Ammonites made war with Israel.
5. The elders of Gilead went to find Jephthah.
6. They said, "Come lead us in battle against Ammon."
7. Jephthah said, "You hated me and threw me out. Why come now?"
8. They said, "That's why we're here. Come fight, and you can lead us all."
9. Jephthah said, "If I return and the Lord gives me victory, will I really be your leader?"
10. They said, "Yes. The Lord is our witness."
11. Jephthah went with them, and they made him their leader at Mizpah.
12. Jephthah sent messengers to the king of Ammon: "Why are you attacking our land?"
13. The king said, "Israel took our land from the Arnon River to the Jabbok and the Jordan. Give it back."
14. Jephthah sent another message:
15. "Israel didn't take Moab or Ammon's land.
16. When we left Egypt, we stayed in the desert.

17. We asked Edom and Moab for passage, but they said no.
18. So we stayed away and camped near the Arnon River.
19. We asked King Sihon of the Amorites to pass through his land.
20. He refused and fought us.
21. The Lord helped us defeat him, and we took his land.
22. From the Arnon to the Jabbok, it belonged to him, not you.
23. So if the Lord gave us this land, why should we return it to you?
24. You keep what your god Chemosh gives you. We'll keep what the Lord gave us.
25. Are you better than Balak, Moab's king? He never fought us.
26. Israel has lived here 300 years. Why try to take it now?
27. I haven't wronged you, but you are doing wrong by attacking. The Lord will decide who's right."
28. But the Ammonite king didn't listen.

Jephthah's Promise

29. The Spirit of the Lord came on Jephthah. He traveled through Gilead and Mizpah, then attacked Ammon.
30. He made a promise: "Lord, if you help me win,
31. I will give you whatever comes out of my house to meet me. I'll offer it as a sacrifice."
32. Jephthah attacked the Ammonites.
33. He crushed them and took 20 towns. It was a big victory.
34. When he went home, his daughter came out dancing. She was his only child.
35. He cried, "Oh no, my daughter! You've crushed me. I made a promise to God."
36. She said, "Keep your promise. God gave you victory."
37. She asked for two months to go into the hills with her friends and cry because she'd never marry.
38. He agreed.
39. She returned, and Jephthah kept his promise to God. He gave her up as a sacrifice, just like he said. She never married.
40. Each year, Israel's women remembered her for four days.

Judges 12

Jephthah Defeats Ephraim

1. The men of Ephraim said, "Why didn't you call us to fight Ammon? We'll burn your house!"
2. Jephthah said, "I did ask, but you didn't come.
3. So I risked my life, and the Lord gave me victory. Why come now to fight me?"
4. Then Jephthah called the men of Gilead, and they fought Ephraim.
5. They captured the Jordan River crossings. If an Ephraimite tried to cross,
6. they'd ask him to say 'Shibboleth.' If he said 'Sibboleth,' they knew he was from Ephraim and killed him. 42,000 died.
7. Jephthah led Israel for 6 years, then died and was buried in Gilead.

Ibzan, Elon, and Abdon

8. After Jephthah, Ibzan led Israel.
9. He had 30 sons and 30 daughters. He married them into other families. He led for 7 years.
10. He died and was buried in Bethlehem.
11. After him, Elon from Zebulun led Israel for 10 years.
12. He died and was buried in Aijalon.
13. Then Abdon led Israel. He had 40 sons and 30 grandsons who rode 70 donkeys.
14. He led Israel for 8 years.

15. He died and was buried in Pirathon in Ephraim.

Judges 13

Samson's Birth Is Promised

1. Israel sinned again, so the Lord let the Philistines rule for 40 years.
2. A man named Manoah lived in Zorah. His wife couldn't have children.
3. The angel of the Lord appeared to her and said, "You can't have kids now, but you will.
4. Don't drink wine or eat anything unclean.
5. You will have a son. Don't cut his hair. He'll be a Nazirite and save Israel from the Philistines."
6. She told her husband, "A man of God visited me. He looked like an angel. I didn't ask who he was, and he didn't say.
7. He said I'll have a son and must not drink wine or eat anything unclean."
8. Manoah prayed, "Lord, please send him back to teach us what to do."
9. God answered, and the angel came again to his wife in the field.
10. She ran to get Manoah.
11. He asked the angel, "Are you the man who spoke to my wife?" The angel said, "Yes."
12. Manoah asked, "What should we do when the boy is born?"
13. The angel said, "Your wife must do everything I told her.
14. She must not eat or drink anything unclean."
15. Manoah said, "Stay while we prepare food."
16. The angel said, "Even if you prepare it, I won't eat it. But offer it as a sacrifice to the Lord."
17. Manoah asked, "What's your name, so we can honor you?"
18. The angel said, "Why do you ask? It's a mystery."
19. Manoah offered a goat and grain offering.
20. As the flame rose, the angel went up in it. Manoah and his wife fell to the ground.
21. They realized it was the angel of the Lord.
22. Manoah said, "We will die! We saw God!"
23. But his wife said, "If the Lord wanted to kill us, He wouldn't have accepted our offering."
24. She had a son and named him Samson. He grew, and the Lord blessed him.
25. The Spirit of the Lord began to move in him while he was in Mahaneh-dan.

Judges 14

Samson Marries a Philistine Woman

1. Samson went to Timnah and saw a Philistine woman.
2. He told his parents, "I saw a woman in Timnah. I want to marry her."
3. They said, "Can't you marry someone from Israel?" But Samson said, "She's the one I want."
4. His parents didn't know the Lord was using this to create a fight with the Philistines.
5. As Samson and his parents went to Timnah, a young lion came at him.
6. The Spirit of the Lord gave Samson power, and he tore the lion apart with his bare hands. He didn't tell his parents.
7. He met the woman and liked her.
8. Later, he returned to marry her. He saw the lion's body and found bees and honey inside.
9. He ate the honey and gave some to his parents but didn't say where it came from.

10. His father arranged the marriage. Samson held a party, as young men did.
11. When the Philistines saw him, they brought 30 men to be with him.
12. Samson said, "I have a riddle. If you can solve it in 7 days, I'll give you 30 shirts and robes.
13. If not, you give me 30." They agreed.
14. He said, "Out of the eater came something to eat. Out of the strong came something sweet." They couldn't figure it out.
15. On day 4, they told Samson's wife, "Get the answer or we'll burn you and your family."
16. She cried to Samson, "You don't love me! You won't tell me the riddle!"
17. She cried every day. On the 7th day, he told her. She told the men.
18. They said, "What's sweeter than honey? What's stronger than a lion?" Samson said, "You wouldn't know unless you plowed with my heifer."
19. The Spirit of the Lord came on him. He went to Ashkelon, killed 30 men, and gave their clothes to the winners. Then he went home angry.
20. His wife was given to his best man.

Judges 15

Samson Gets Revenge

1. Later, Samson brought a goat to visit his wife. But her father wouldn't let him in.
2. He said, "I thought you hated her, so I gave her to your friend. Take her sister instead."
3. Samson said, "Now I have a good reason to hurt the Philistines."
4. He caught 300 foxes, tied their tails in pairs with torches,
5. and lit them. The foxes ran through the fields, burning grain, vineyards, and olive trees.
6. The Philistines asked, "Who did this?" They were told it was Samson. So they burned his wife and her father.
7. Samson said, "Because you did that, I won't stop until I get revenge."
8. He attacked them and killed many. Then he hid in a cave at Etam Rock.
9. The Philistines camped in Judah.
10. The people asked, "Why are you here?" They said, "We want Samson."
11. Judah sent 3,000 men to Samson and said, "Don't you know the Philistines rule us?"
12. They said, "We came to tie you up and hand you over." Samson said, "Swear you won't kill me yourselves."
13. They said, "We won't. We'll just tie you." They tied him and brought him from the cave.
14. As he reached the camp, the Spirit of the Lord came on him. The ropes snapped.
15. He found a donkey's jawbone and killed 1,000 men.
16. He said, "With a donkey's jawbone, I made heaps of them. I killed 1,000 men."
17. Then he threw it away. The place was named Ramath-lehi.
18. Samson was very thirsty and cried to the Lord, "You gave me victory. Now I might die of thirst!"
19. God made water come out of a hollow in the ground. Samson drank and was refreshed. The place was called En-hakkore.
20. Samson led Israel for 20 years while the Philistines ruled.

Judges 16

Samson and Delilah

1. Samson went to Gaza and spent the night with a prostitute.
2. The people said, "He's here!" So they waited to attack him at dawn.

3. But Samson got up at midnight, lifted the city gate, and carried it to a hill near Hebron.
4. Later, he fell in love with Delilah in the Valley of Sorek.
5. The Philistine leaders told her, "Find out his secret. We'll each give you 1,100 silver coins."
6. Delilah asked, "What makes you so strong? How can you be tied up?"
7. Samson said, "If I'm tied with 7 fresh bowstrings, I'll be weak."
8. They brought her the strings.
9. She hid men in the room and tied him up. Then she shouted, "Samson! The Philistines are here!" But he snapped the strings easily.
10. She said, "You lied! Tell me the truth."
11. He said, "Tie me with new ropes."
12. She did, and shouted again. But he broke free.
13. She said, "You keep lying! Tell me!" He said, "Weave my hair into a loom."
14. She did, and shouted again. He pulled the loom apart.
15. She said, "You say you love me, but you lie. You won't share your secret."
16. She nagged him every day until he was sick of it.
17. He finally said, "I've never cut my hair. I'm a Nazirite. If my hair is cut, I'll lose my strength."
18. Delilah knew he told the truth. She told the leaders.
19. She made him sleep on her lap and had someone shave his hair. His strength left him.
20. She shouted, "Samson! The Philistines are here!" He got up but didn't know the Lord had left him.
21. They captured him, gouged out his eyes, and made him grind grain in prison.
22. But his hair started to grow again.

Samson's Final Act

23. The Philistine leaders held a big party to praise their god Dagon.
24. They said, "Dagon gave us victory over Samson."
25. They brought Samson out to entertain them and made him stand between pillars.
26. Samson asked the servant to let him lean on the pillars.
27. The building was full of people—about 3,000 on the roof.
28. Samson prayed, "Lord, remember me. Give me strength one more time so I can take revenge."
29. He pushed against the two center pillars.
30. He said, "Let me die with the Philistines!" He pushed, and the building collapsed. He killed more people in his death than in his life.
31. His family took his body and buried him in Zorah. He led Israel for 20 years.

Judges 17

Micah's Idols

1. A man named Micah lived in the hill country of Ephraim.
2. He said to his mom, "You cursed whoever stole your 1,100 silver coins. I took them. Here they are." She said, "May the Lord bless you, my son."

3-4. He gave her the money. She used 200 coins to make a silver idol and image. These were kept in Micah's house.

5. Micah had a shrine. He made more idols and appointed one of his sons as a priest.
6. At that time, Israel had no king. Everyone did whatever they wanted.
7. A young Levite from Bethlehem in Judah left to find a new place to live.
8. He came to Micah's house while traveling.

9. Micah asked, "Where are you from?" He said, "I'm a Levite from Bethlehem. I'm looking for a place to stay."
10. Micah said, "Live with me. I'll pay you and give you food and clothes."
11. The Levite agreed. He became like a son to Micah.
12. Micah made him priest.
13. Micah said, "Now the Lord will bless me. I have a Levite as my priest."

Judges 18

The Tribe of Dan Looks for Land

1. Israel had no king. The tribe of Dan hadn't yet received land.
2. They sent five men to explore and find land. They stayed at Micah's house.
3. They heard the Levite's voice and asked, "What are you doing here?"
4. He said, "Micah hired me. I'm his priest."
5. They said, "Ask God if our journey will be successful."
6. The priest said, "Go in peace. The Lord is with you."
7. The men found Laish. The people there felt safe and had no enemies.

8-9. They returned to their tribe and said, "Let's attack. The land is great!"

10. "God has given it to us."
11. So 600 men from Dan left for battle.
12. They camped near Kiriath-jearim.
13. From there, they went to Micah's house.
14. The five scouts said, "There's a shrine and idols here. You know what to do."
15. They went to the Levite and asked how he was.
16. The 600 men stood outside the gate.
17. The five went in and took the idols and ephod. The Levite asked, "What are you doing?"
18. They said, "Be quiet. Come with us. Be a priest for our tribe. Isn't that better?"
19. The priest was glad. He took the idols and went with them.
20. They left, with children, animals, and belongings in front.
21. Micah's neighbors chased them and caught up.
22. They shouted, and the men of Dan turned around.
23. Micah said, "You took my gods and my priest. What do I have left?"
24. Dan's men said, "Don't argue or we'll attack you."
25. Micah saw he couldn't win and went home.
26. Dan took Laish. They killed the people and burned the town.
27. No one came to help. The town was far from others and had no allies.
28. They rebuilt it and named it Dan.
29. They set up the idols. Jonathan (a descendant of Moses) and his sons became priests for Dan.
30. They used the idols the whole time God's house was in Shiloh.

Judges 19

A Levite and His Concubine

1. In those days, Israel had no king. A Levite lived in the hill country of Ephraim. He had a concubine from Bethlehem.
2. She was unfaithful and went back to her father's house.
3. After 4 months, the Levite went to bring her back. He spoke kindly, and she agreed to return.
4. Her father welcomed him.
5. He stayed 3 days, then got ready to leave. But her father said, "Stay and eat."
6. So they stayed.

7. The next day, the same thing happened.
8. On the fifth day, the Levite again prepared to leave, but the father delayed him.
9. Later that day, the Levite said, "We must leave now."
10. He wouldn't stay another night. They passed Jerusalem and went to Gibeah in Benjamin's territory.
11. It was late, and his servant said, "Let's stay in Jerusalem."

12-13. But the Levite said, "No, we won't stay in a non-Israelite city. We'll go to Gibeah."

14. So they went to Gibeah. No one invited them in.
15. They sat in the town square.

16-17. An old man from Ephraim saw them and said, "Where are you going?"

18. The Levite said, "We're traveling from Bethlehem to Ephraim. No one has offered us a place to stay."
19. "We have food for our animals and bread and wine for us."
20. The old man said, "Come stay with me. Don't sleep in the square."
21. He took them to his house and gave their donkeys food. They ate and drank.
22. While they were relaxing, some wicked men surrounded the house. They shouted, "Send out the man so we can abuse him!"
23. The old man said, "Don't do this evil thing. He's my guest."
24. "Take my virgin daughter and his concubine instead."
25. But the men wouldn't listen. So the Levite sent out his concubine. They abused her all night.
26. At dawn, she collapsed at the door.
27. In the morning, the Levite opened the door and found her lying there.
28. He said, "Get up. Let's go." But she didn't move.
29. He put her on his donkey and went home. Then he cut her body into 12 pieces and sent them to the tribes of Israel.
30. Everyone who saw it said, "Nothing like this has ever happened! We must speak up and act!"

Judges 20

Israel Prepares for War

1. All the Israelites—from every tribe—gathered before the Lord at Mizpah.
2. The leaders of all the tribes came together.
3. The people of Benjamin heard about the meeting. The Israelites said, "Tell us what happened."
4. The Levite said, "I came to Gibeah with my concubine.
5. The men there surrounded the house and attacked. They raped her until she died.
6. I cut her body into pieces and sent them to each tribe.
7. All of you must decide what to do."
8. The people said, "None of us will go home until justice is done."
9. They agreed to choose men to fight.
10. They would punish Gibeah for this evil.
11. All Israel agreed to act together.
12. They sent messengers to the tribe of Benjamin: "Give us the wicked men of Gibeah so we can punish them."
13. But Benjamin refused and prepared to fight.

14-15. They gathered 26,000 soldiers, plus 700 from Gibeah.

16. Among them were 700 left-handed men who could sling a stone and hit a hair.
17. Israel had 400,000 soldiers.

18. They went to Bethel and asked God, "Who should go first?" God said, "Judah."

19-20. The next day, they attacked Gibeah.

21. But Benjamin's army killed 22,000 Israelites.

22. The Israelites encouraged each other and fought again.

23. They wept and asked God, "Should we fight again?" God said, "Yes."

24. They fought the second day,

25. but Benjamin killed 18,000 more.

26. All the Israelites wept and fasted. They offered sacrifices to the Lord.

27. They asked God what to do.

28. The priest Phinehas asked, and the Lord said, "Go. Tomorrow I will give you victory."

29. Israel set an ambush around Gibeah.

30. On the third day, they attacked as before.

31. Benjamin came out and started killing Israelites again, about 30 men.

32. They said, "We're winning again!" But the Israelites were pulling them away from the city.

33. The main army turned and attacked.

34. 10,000 men fought hard near Gibeah.

35. The Lord gave Israel the victory. They killed 25,100 Benjaminites.

36. The Israelites pulled back to lure the enemy.

37. The hidden men rushed into Gibeah and set it on fire.

38. The signal was a big cloud of smoke.

39. When the Benjaminites saw the smoke, they knew they had been tricked.

40. They turned back and saw the city burning.

41. The Israelites turned and attacked.

42. Benjamin tried to escape, but they were trapped.

43. They were surrounded and defeated.

44. 18,000 died.

45. The rest ran toward the desert, but 5,000 more were killed at the roads.

46. In total, 25,000 Benjamin men died.

47. Only 600 escaped to hide at Rimmon Rock for four months.

48. Israel destroyed the towns and people of Benjamin, even animals and everything they found.

Judges 21

Wives for the Tribe of Benjamin

1. The Israelites had promised, "No one will give a daughter to Benjamin in marriage."
2. They went to Bethel and cried before God.
3. They said, "Why did one tribe disappear from Israel?"
4. The next day, they offered sacrifices.
5. They asked, "Did any tribe fail to meet with us?"
6. They felt sorry for Benjamin, their brothers.
7. They said, "How can we give them wives? We made a promise not to."
8. They learned that no one from Jabesh-gilead had come.
9. They counted the people and saw no one from that town.
10. So they sent 12,000 soldiers to kill everyone there except young women.
11. They killed every man, woman, and child—except the virgins.
12. They found 400 virgins and brought them to the camp.
13. Then they offered peace to Benjamin.
14. The 600 men returned, and the 400 women were given to them. But that wasn't enough.
15. The people felt sorry for Benjamin.
16. The leaders said, "What can we do? We need more wives."

17-18. "Benjamin must survive. But we can't break our promise."

19. They said, "Every year, there's a festival to the Lord at Shiloh."

20. "Tell the men to hide in the vineyards.

21. When the girls come out to dance, grab one and run to Benjamin's land."

22. "If the girls' fathers complain, we'll say, 'Let them go. This is how we saved Benjamin.'"

23. So the men did that. Each grabbed a girl and took her home.

24. Then the Israelites went home to their tribes and land.

25. In those days, Israel had no king, and everyone did whatever they wanted.

– Ruth –

A Moabite woman named Ruth shows loyalty and becomes an ancestor of King David.

Ruth 1

Ruth Stays with Naomi

1. During the time of the judges, there was a food shortage. A man from Bethlehem took his wife and two sons to live in Moab.

2. The man was Elimelech. His wife was Naomi. Their sons were Mahlon and Kilion. They were from Bethlehem.

3. Elimelech died, and Naomi was left with her sons.

4. Her sons married Moabite women—Orpah and Ruth. After 10 years,

5. both sons died. Naomi was left alone.

6. Naomi heard that the Lord had blessed Judah with food, so she prepared to return home.

7. She and her daughters-in-law started the journey back.

8. Naomi said, "Go home to your mothers. May the Lord be kind to you, like you were to me and my sons.

9. May He help you find new husbands." She kissed them, and they cried.

10. They said, "We want to go with you to your people."

11. But Naomi said, "Go home. Why come with me? I have no more sons.

12. I'm too old to marry again. Even if I had sons now,

13. would you wait for them to grow up? No. It's harder for me than for you. The Lord is against me."They cried again. Orpah kissed Naomi and left, but Ruth stayed.

14. Naomi said, "Orpah went back to her people and gods. Go with her."

15. But Ruth said, "Don't ask me to leave. I'll go where you go, live where you live. Your people are my people, and your God is my God.

16. I'll die where you die and be buried there. May God punish me if I ever leave you."

17. Naomi saw that Ruth wouldn't change her mind, so she stopped asking.

18. They traveled to Bethlehem. When they arrived, the town was excited. The women said, "Is this Naomi?"

19. She said, "Don't call me Naomi. Call me Marah. God has made my life bitter.

20. I had everything, and now I have nothing. The Lord has made me suffer."

21. Naomi returned from Moab with Ruth. They arrived in Bethlehem at the start of barley harvest.

Ruth 2

Ruth Meets Boaz

1. Naomi's husband had a rich relative named Boaz.

2. Ruth said, "Let me go gather leftover grain behind someone kind." Naomi said, "Go, my daughter."

3. Ruth went to pick up grain and ended up in Boaz's field.

4. Boaz arrived and greeted the workers. They replied, "The Lord bless you!"
5. Boaz asked his foreman, "Who is that young woman?"
6. He said, "She's the one who came with Naomi from Moab.
7. She asked to gather grain and has been working since morning."
8. Boaz said to Ruth, "Stay here in my field. Work with my women.
9. Follow them closely. I told the men not to bother you. When thirsty, drink from our jars."
10. Ruth bowed and said, "Why are you so kind to me, a foreigner?"
11. Boaz said, "I know all you've done for Naomi. You left your family to live with strangers.
12. May God reward you for trusting Him."
13. She said, "I hope I continue to please you. You've been very kind to me."
14. At lunch, Boaz invited her to eat. She sat with the workers. He gave her roasted grain. She ate and saved some.
15. As she went back to work, Boaz told his men, "Let her gather from the bundles. Don't yell at her.
16. Drop extra stalks for her. Don't stop her."
17. Ruth worked until evening. She gathered almost 25 pounds of barley.
18. She carried it to Naomi and gave her the leftover food.
19. Naomi asked, "Where did you work? God bless the man who noticed you!" Ruth said, "His name is Boaz."
20. Naomi said, "The Lord bless him! He's one of our closest relatives."
21. Ruth said, "He told me to stay with his workers until harvest is over."
22. Naomi said, "Good. Stay in his field. You'll be safe there."
23. So Ruth worked with Boaz's women through barley and wheat harvest, and lived with Naomi.

Ruth 3

Naomi's Plan for Ruth

1. Naomi said, "My daughter, I must find you a good home.
2. Boaz is our relative, and you've worked with his women. Tonight he'll be at the threshing floor.
3. Wash, put on perfume, and wear nice clothes. Don't let him see you until he's done eating and drinking.
4. Watch where he lies down. Then go lie at his feet. He'll tell you what to do."
5. Ruth said, "I'll do everything you say."
6. She went and did as Naomi told her.
7. After Boaz ate and drank, he lay down. Ruth quietly uncovered his feet and lay down.
8. At midnight, Boaz woke up and was surprised to find a woman there.
9. He said, "Who are you?" She said, "I'm Ruth. Marry me since you are my family protector."
10. Boaz said, "God bless you. You didn't chase younger men.
11. Don't worry. I'll do what you ask. Everyone knows you're a good woman.
12. It's true I'm a close relative, but there's someone closer.
13. Stay here tonight. If he wants to marry you, good. If not, I will. Sleep here until morning."
14. She lay at his feet until morning but left before anyone saw her. He said, "No one must know a woman was here."
15. He said, "Hold out your shawl." He filled it with six measures of barley. She carried it back to the city.
16. Naomi asked, "How did it go?" Ruth told her everything.
17. She said, "He gave me this barley and said not to come back empty-handed."

18. Naomi said, "Wait. He will settle this today."

Ruth 4

Boaz Marries Ruth

1. Boaz went to the town gate. The close relative passed by, and Boaz said, "Come sit down."
2. Boaz also gathered 10 town leaders as witnesses.
3. Boaz said, "Naomi is selling Elimelech's land.
4. You have the first right to buy it. If not, I will." The man said, "I'll buy it."
5. Boaz said, "If you buy the land, you must marry Ruth to keep the family name."
6. The man said, "Then I can't. You buy it."
7. In those days, a sandal was removed to make the deal legal.
8. The man gave Boaz his sandal and said, "You buy it."
9. Boaz said, "You are witnesses. I've bought everything from Naomi—Elimelech's, Kilion's, and Mahlon's land.
10. I will marry Ruth so the family name stays with the land. You are witnesses."
11. The leaders said, "We are witnesses. May the Lord bless your wife like
12. Rachel and Leah. May you be famous in Bethlehem.
13. May your children be like those of Perez, son of Tamar and Judah."
14. Boaz married Ruth. The Lord let her have a son.
15. The women said, "Praise the Lord! He has given Naomi someone to care for her. May this child be famous."
16. "He will take care of you. Your daughter-in-law loves you and is better than seven sons."
17. Naomi held the baby and cared for him.
18. The women said, "Naomi has a son!" They named him Obed. He was Jesse's father and David's grandfather.
19. These are the family roots: Perez was the father of Hezron,
20. Hezron was the father of Ram, and Ram was the father of Amminadab.
21. Amminadab was the father of Nahshon. Nahshon was the father of Salmon.
22. Salmon was the father of Boaz. Boaz was the father of Obed.
23. Obed was the father of Jesse, and Jesse was the father of David.

– 1 Samuel –

Israel transitions from judges to kings; Saul becomes king, but David is chosen by God.

1 Samuel 1

Hannah Asks God for a Baby

1. A man named Elkanah lived in Ramah, in the hill country of Ephraim. He was the son of Jeroham, grandson of Elihu, great-grandson of Tohu, and great-great-grandson of Zuph.
2. He had two wives, Hannah and Peninnah. Peninnah had kids, but Hannah didn't.
3. Every year Elkanah went to Shiloh to worship and offer sacrifices to the Lord. Eli's sons, Hophni and Phinehas, were the priests there.
4. When Elkanah gave his sacrifice, he gave some meat to Peninnah and her kids.
5. But he gave Hannah extra because he loved her, even though she had no kids.
6. Peninnah made fun of Hannah all the time because she had no children.
7. This happened every year when they went to the Lord's house. Peninnah teased her so badly that Hannah cried and wouldn't eat.

8. Her husband said, "Hannah, why are you crying? Why won't you eat? Aren't I better than ten sons?"

9. After they ate and drank, Hannah stood up. Eli the priest was sitting by the temple door.

10. Hannah was very sad. She cried and prayed to the Lord.

11. She made a promise: "Lord, if you see how sad I am and give me a son, I will give him to you for his whole life. And he will never cut his hair."

12. As she prayed, Eli watched her.

13. Her lips were moving, but her voice was quiet. Eli thought she was drunk.

14. He said, "How long will you stay drunk? Stop drinking!"

15. Hannah said, "I'm not drunk. I'm very upset and have been praying to the Lord. I haven't had any wine or beer."

16. "Don't think I'm a bad woman. I've been praying because I'm so sad."

17. Eli said, "Go in peace. May God give you what you asked for."

18. She said, "Thank you for being kind." Then she ate and wasn't sad anymore.

Samuel Is Born

19. The next morning they worshiped, then went home. Elkanah slept with

20. Hannah, and God remembered her prayer.

21. Later she had a baby boy and named him Samuel. She said, "I asked God for him."

Hannah Gives Samuel to the Lord

22. The next year Elkanah went to give his yearly offering and keep his promise.

23. But Hannah didn't go. She told her husband, "When the child is weaned, I'll take him to the Lord, and he will stay there forever."

24. Elkanah said, "Do what you think is best. Stay home until he's ready. May God help you keep your promise." So she stayed home and nursed her son.

25. When he was weaned, she took him to the Lord's house in Shiloh. She also brought a 3-year-old bull, some flour, and wine.

26. They sacrificed the bull and brought the boy to Eli.

27. She said, "Sir, I'm the woman who stood here praying to the Lord.

28. I prayed for this child, and the Lord gave me what I asked for.

29. Now I give him to the Lord. He will belong to the Lord all his life." Then Samuel worshiped the Lord there.

1 Samuel 2

Hannah's Prayer

1. Hannah prayed, "My heart is happy because of the Lord. He made me strong. Now I smile at my enemies because of what God has done."

2. "No one is holy like the Lord. No one else is God. No one is strong like him."

3. "Stop talking proud. The Lord knows everything and judges what people do."

4. "Soldiers lose their weapons, but weak people become strong."

5. "People who had plenty are now poor, and the hungry have enough. The woman with no children has seven, but the woman with many is now sad."

6. "The Lord gives life and takes it away. He brings people down to the grave and lifts them up again."

7. "The Lord makes people poor or rich. He brings them low or lifts them up."

8. "He lifts the poor from the dirt and the needy from the trash. He gives them places of honor. The earth belongs to the Lord."

9. "He protects his faithful people. The wicked will be lost in darkness. Strength alone won't save anyone."

10. "The Lord destroys his enemies. He speaks from heaven and judges the earth. He gives strength to his king."

Samuel Stays with Eli

11. Elkanah went home, but Samuel stayed and served the Lord under Eli.

Eli's Sons Sin

12. Eli's sons were evil and didn't respect the Lord.
13. When someone gave a sacrifice, the priest's helper would come with a fork while the meat was cooking.
14. He would stick the fork into the pot, and whatever came out was taken for the priest. That's how they treated everyone.
15. Even before the fat was burned, the helper would demand raw meat.
16. If someone said, "Burn the fat first," the helper would say, "No, give it now, or I'll take it by force."
17. These young men sinned badly. They disrespected the Lord's offerings.

Hannah Visits Samuel

18. Samuel served the Lord, wearing a priest's robe.
19. Every year his mother brought him a new robe when she came with her husband.
20. Eli blessed Elkanah and Hannah, saying, "May God give you more children for the one you gave him." Then they went home.
21. The Lord blessed Hannah. She had three more sons and two daughters. Samuel grew up serving the Lord.

Eli Warns His Sons

22. Eli was very old and heard what his sons were doing, even sleeping with women at the temple.
23. He said, "Why are you doing these evil things?"
24. "Stop, my sons. This is a bad report."
25. "If someone sins against another, God can help. But who helps if someone sins against God?" But his sons didn't listen because God had decided to punish them.

God Sends a Message to Eli

26. Samuel kept growing and was liked by God and people.
27. A man of God came to Eli and said, "Didn't I show myself to your family in Egypt?"
28. "I chose them to be my priests, offer sacrifices, and wear special robes. I gave them the offerings."
29. "Why do you disrespect my sacrifices? Why do you honor your sons more than me by letting them steal the best parts?"
30. "I promised your family would always serve me. But now I say—those who honor me, I will honor. Those who don't, I will reject."
31. "Your family won't grow old.
32. You'll see trouble, and your family will be jealous of others.
33. I'll spare one man, but only to make him sad. Your family will die young."
34. "As a sign, your two sons, Hophni and Phinehas, will die on the same day."
35. "Then I will choose a faithful priest to do my will. His family will serve my chosen king."
36. "Anyone left in your family will beg that priest for food and work."

1 Samuel 3

God Calls Samuel

1. Samuel served God under Eli. God's messages were rare then.
2. One night, Eli, who was almost blind, was sleeping.
3. Samuel was sleeping in the Lord's house near the Ark.
4. God called, "Samuel!" He answered, "Here I am."
5. He ran to Eli and said, "Here I am. Did you call me?" Eli said, "I didn't call you. Go back to bed."

6. God called again. Samuel went to Eli. "Did you call me?" Eli said, "No, go back to bed."
7. Samuel didn't know God's voice yet.
8. God called a third time. Samuel went again. Then Eli realized God was calling him.
9. Eli said, "Go lie down. If he calls, say, 'Speak, Lord. I'm listening.'" So Samuel went back.
10. God came and called again, "Samuel! Samuel!" Samuel said, "Speak. I'm listening."
11. God said, "I will do something in Israel that will shock everyone."
12. "I will punish Eli's family just like I said."
13. "I told him I would judge his family forever because he let his sons sin."
14. "Their sin will never be forgiven, even with sacrifices."
15. Samuel stayed in bed until morning, then opened the temple doors. He was afraid to tell Eli.
16. Eli called him, "Samuel, my son." He said, "Here I am."
17. Eli said, "Tell me what God said. Don't hide anything or he'll punish you."
18. So Samuel told him everything. Eli said, "He is the Lord. Let him do what's best."

God Helps Samuel

19. God was with Samuel as he grew. Everything Samuel said came true.
20. All of Israel knew Samuel was God's prophet.
21. God kept appearing in Shiloh and spoke to Samuel there.

1 Samuel 4

The Ark Is Taken

1. Samuel's message spread through Israel. The Israelites went to fight the Philistines. They camped at Ebenezer. The Philistines camped at Aphek.
2. The Philistines attacked and killed 4,000 Israelites.
3. The leaders said, "Why did God let this happen? Let's bring the Ark of the Covenant to the battle. It will save us."
4. They got the Ark from Shiloh. Eli's sons, Hophni and Phinehas, brought it.
5. When the Ark arrived, the Israelites shouted so loud the ground shook.
6. The Philistines heard and asked, "What's all the shouting?" They learned the Ark had come.
7. They were scared. "A god is in their camp! We've never seen this before."
8. "Who can save us from their powerful gods? These are the gods who struck Egypt with plagues."
9. "Be brave, Philistines! If we don't fight, we'll be their slaves like they were ours."
10. The Philistines fought hard and won. They killed 30,000 Israelites. The rest ran away.
11. The Ark was taken, and Hophni and Phinehas died.

Eli Dies

12. A man from Benjamin ran to Shiloh with his clothes torn and dirt on his head.
13. Eli was sitting by the road, nervous about the Ark. When the man entered the city and told what happened, the people cried out.
14. Eli asked, "What's all the noise?" The man hurried to tell him.
15. Eli was 98 and blind.
16. The man said, "I came from the battle today." Eli asked, "What happened?"
17. He said, "Israel lost. Many died. Your sons died. And the Ark was taken."
18. When he mentioned the Ark, Eli fell backward off his chair, broke his neck, and died. He was old and heavy and had judged Israel 40 years.

Ichabod Is Born

19. Eli's daughter-in-law, Phinehas's wife, was pregnant. When she heard the news, she went into labor.
20. As she was dying, the women said, "Don't worry. You had a son!" But she didn't respond.
21. She named him Ichabod, meaning "Where is the glory?" because the Ark was taken and her husband and father-in-law died.
22. She said, "The glory has left Israel, because the Ark was taken."

1 Samuel 5

God Sends Trouble to the Philistines

1. After the Philistines took the Ark, they brought it from Ebenezer to Ashdod.
2. They put it in Dagon's temple beside Dagon's statue.
3. The next morning, Dagon had fallen face down in front of the Ark. They put him back.
4. The next day, Dagon had fallen again. This time, his head and hands broke off. Only his body was left.
5. That's why Dagon's priests still don't step on the threshold of his temple.
6. The Lord punished the people in Ashdod and nearby towns with painful tumors.
7. The people said, "The God of Israel is punishing us and our god Dagon. We must get rid of the Ark!"
8. The rulers met and said, "Move the Ark to Gath." So they did.
9. But then the Lord struck Gath with tumors too. People panicked.
10. They sent the Ark to Ekron. But when it arrived, the people screamed, "They're trying to kill us!"
11. The rulers met again. "Send the Ark back to Israel before we all die!" Everyone was terrified.
12. People who didn't die got tumors, and the people cried out for help.

1 Samuel 6

The Philistines Return the Ark

1. The Ark stayed in Philistine land for 7 months.
2. The Philistines called their priests and asked, "What should we do with the Ark? How can we send it back?"
3. They said, "Don't send it back without a gift. Send a guilt offering and maybe God will stop punishing you."
4. They asked, "What should we send?" The answer: "5 gold tumors and 5 gold rats—one for each Philistine ruler."
5. "Make the gold rats and tumors to match what hurt you. Show honor to Israel's God. Maybe he will stop punishing you."
6. "Don't be stubborn like Egypt and Pharaoh. They let the Israelites go after God punished them."
7. "Get a new cart and two cows that just had calves and haven't pulled anything before. Tie them to the cart. Take their calves back home."
8. "Put the Ark on the cart, with a box beside it holding the gold items."
9. "Watch. If the cows go to Beth-Shemesh, then God punished us. If not, it was just bad luck."
10. They did as told. They tied the cows and took the calves away.
11. They put the Ark and the gold gifts on the cart.
12. The cows went straight to Beth-Shemesh. The rulers followed them to the border.
13. The people of Beth-Shemesh were harvesting wheat and shouted for joy when they saw the Ark.
14. The cart stopped in Joshua's field. They used the wood and cows for a burnt offering.

15. The Levites put the Ark and gold box on a big rock. The people gave more sacrifices that day.
16. The 5 Philistine rulers watched and then returned to Ekron.
17. The 5 gold tumors were from the cities of Ashdod, Gaza, Ashkelon, Gath, and Ekron.
18. The gold rats matched all 5 cities and their nearby villages. The big rock is still in Joshua's field today.

God Punishes Those Who Look Inside the Ark

19. The Lord killed 70 men in Beth-Shemesh because they looked inside the Ark. The people were very sad.
20. They said, "Who can stand near this holy God? Where can we send the Ark?"
21. So they sent messengers to Kiriath-Jearim: "The Philistines gave the Ark back. Come get it!"

1 Samuel 7

The Ark Is Taken to Kiriath-Jearim

1. The men of Kiriath-Jearim came and got the Ark. They took it to Abinadab's house on a hill. They chose his son Eleazar to guard it.
2. The Ark stayed there for 20 years. The people of Israel missed the Lord.

Israel Turns Back to God

3. Samuel told the people, "If you really want to follow God, get rid of your idols. Worship only the Lord. He will save you from the Philistines."
4. So they got rid of their idols and worshiped only the Lord.
5. Samuel said, "Bring everyone to Mizpah. I will pray for you."
6. At Mizpah, the people poured out water to the Lord, fasted, and admitted their sins. Samuel became their judge there.

The Philistines Attack Again

7. When the Philistines heard the Israelites gathered at Mizpah, they sent their army to attack. The Israelites were afraid.
8. They begged Samuel, "Pray to the Lord to save us!"
9. Samuel sacrificed a lamb and prayed. God answered him.
10. As the Philistines came to attack, God sent thunder that scared them. Israel defeated them.
11. The Israelites chased and killed them all the way to Beth-Car.
12. Samuel set up a stone and named it Ebenezer, saying, "The Lord has helped us this far."
13. The Philistines didn't attack again while Samuel lived. God protected Israel.
14. Israel got back the towns the Philistines had taken and lived in peace with the Amorites.

Samuel Leads Israel

15. Samuel led Israel for the rest of his life.
16. Each year he traveled to Bethel, Gilgal, and Mizpah to judge the people.
17. He always returned to Ramah, where he lived and judged Israel. He also built an altar there.

1 Samuel 8

Israel Wants a King

1. When Samuel got old, he made his sons judges in Israel.
2. His sons were Joel and Abijah. They judged in Beersheba.
3. But they didn't live right. They took bribes and made unfair decisions.
4. So the leaders of Israel met with Samuel at Ramah.
5. They said, "You're old, and your sons aren't like you. We want a king to lead us, like other nations."

6. Samuel didn't like this, so he prayed to God.
7. The Lord said, "Listen to them. They're not rejecting you—they're rejecting me as their king."
8. "Ever since I brought them from Egypt, they've turned from me. Now they're doing the same to you."
9. "Give them a king, but warn them what a king will do."
10. So Samuel told the people what the Lord said.
11. "This is what the king will do: He'll take your sons for his army—some to drive chariots, ride horses, or run in front of them."
12. "Some will be officers, others will farm his land or make weapons."
13. "He'll take your daughters to make perfume, cook, and bake."
14. "He'll take your best fields, vineyards, and olive groves and give them to his servants."
15. "He'll take a tenth of your grain and grapes for his officials."
16. "He'll take your servants and best animals."
17. "He'll take a tenth of your flocks. You will become his slaves."
18. "One day you'll cry out for help from the king you wanted, but God won't help you."
19. But the people refused to listen. "No! We want a king!"
20. "We want to be like other nations, with a king to lead and fight for us."
21. Samuel told God what the people said.
22. God said, "Give them a king." So Samuel sent everyone home.

1 Samuel 9

Saul Meets Samuel

1. A man named Kish lived in Benjamin. He was the son of Abiel, grandson of Zeror, great-grandson of Becorath, and great-great-grandson of Aphiah.
2. His son Saul was the tallest and most handsome man in Israel.
3. Kish lost some donkeys and told Saul, "Take a servant and go find them."
4. Saul and the servant searched all over but didn't find them.
5. When they got to Zuph, Saul said, "Let's go home. My dad is probably more worried about us now than the donkeys."
6. The servant said, "Wait! There's a respected man of God in town. Let's ask him. Maybe he can help us."
7. Saul said, "But we have nothing to give him. No food, nothing."
8. The servant said, "I have a small silver coin. I'll give it to him."
9. In those days, people called prophets "seers."
10. Saul said, "Good idea. Let's go." So they went to the town.
11. On the way, they met girls getting water and asked, "Is the seer here?"
12. The girls said, "Yes! He's ahead of you. Hurry! He's here for today's sacrifice."
13. "You'll find him before he goes to eat. No one eats until he blesses the food."
14. As they entered town, Samuel was coming out to go to the place of worship.
15. God had told Samuel the day before,
16. "Tomorrow I'll send you a man from Benjamin. Anoint him as ruler. He will save my people from the Philistines. I've heard their cries."
17. When Samuel saw Saul, God said, "That's him! He will rule my people."
18. Saul went to Samuel and asked, "Where is the seer's house?"
19. Samuel said, "I'm the seer. Come with me. We'll eat today, and tomorrow I'll tell you everything and send you home."

20. "Don't worry about the donkeys. They've been found. And Israel's hope is now on you and your family."
21. Saul said, "But I'm from the tribe of Benjamin—the smallest tribe. And my family is the least important. Why are you saying this?"

Saul Eats with Samuel

22. Samuel took Saul and the servant to the dining hall and gave them the best seats.
23. Samuel told the cook, "Bring the special portion I set aside."
24. The cook brought it, and Samuel said, "Eat! This was saved just for you." So Saul ate with Samuel.
25. Afterward, they went to Samuel's house and talked on the roof.
26. The next morning, Samuel called to Saul, "Get up! It's time to go."
27. As they neared the edge of town, Samuel said, "Send your servant ahead. I need to give you a message from God."

1 Samuel 10

Samuel Anoints Saul

1. Samuel took a flask of oil, poured it on Saul's head, kissed him, and said, "God has made you king of Israel."
2. "Today, you'll meet two men near Rachel's tomb. They'll say your donkeys were found, and now your dad is worried about you."
3. "Then you'll meet three men near the tree at Tabor. One will have three goats, another three loaves of bread, and another wine."
4. "They'll greet you and give you two loaves. Take them."
5. "Then you'll go to Gibeah. There you'll meet prophets playing music."
6. "The Spirit of the Lord will come on you. You'll prophesy with them and become a different person."
7. "When that happens, do whatever you think is right. God is with you."
8. "Go ahead of me to Gilgal. I'll meet you there to offer sacrifices. Wait seven days until I come."

Everything Happens Just as Samuel Said

9. As Saul left, God changed his heart. Everything happened that day as Samuel said.
10. When Saul got to Gibeah, he met the prophets. The Spirit of God came on him, and he prophesied.
11. People who knew him were shocked. "Is Saul now a prophet?"
12. Someone said, "Can anyone be a prophet? Is Saul really one?" That's why people say, "Is Saul also a prophet?"
13. After that, Saul went to the worship place.
14. Saul's uncle asked him and his servant, "Where did you go?" Saul said, "To find the donkeys. When we couldn't, we went to Samuel."
15. His uncle asked, "What did Samuel say?"
16. Saul said, "He told us the donkeys were found." But he didn't say anything about becoming king.

Saul Is Chosen Publicly

17. Samuel called all Israel to meet with God at Mizpah.
18. He said, "God says: I rescued you from Egypt and your enemies.
19. But you rejected me and asked for a king. Now come forward by tribes and families."
20. Samuel had all the tribes come forward. The tribe of Benjamin was chosen.
21. Then the family of Matri was chosen, then Saul son of Kish. But he was missing.
22. They asked God, "Where is he?" God said, "He's hiding in the supplies."

23. They found him and brought him out. He stood taller than anyone else.

24. Samuel said, "Here is the man the Lord has chosen. There's no one like him!" The people shouted, "Long live the king!"

25. Samuel explained the rules of kingship and wrote them in a book. Then he sent the people home.

26. Saul went back to Gibeah with brave men whose hearts God had touched.

27. But some troublemakers said, "How can this man save us?" They didn't respect him and gave no gifts. But Saul stayed quiet.

1 Samuel 11

Saul Saves Jabesh-Gilead

1. Nahash the Ammonite attacked and surrounded Jabesh-Gilead. The men said, "Make a peace deal, and we'll serve you."

2. Nahash said, "Only if I gouge out everyone's right eye to shame Israel."

3. The leaders said, "Give us 7 days to ask for help. If no one helps, we'll surrender."

4. When messengers came to Saul's town and told the people, everyone cried.

5. Saul was coming in from the field with his oxen and asked, "What's wrong? Why is everyone crying?" They told him what happened.

6. Then God's Spirit came on Saul, and he got very angry.

7. He cut up two oxen and sent the pieces across Israel with a warning: "Anyone who doesn't join Saul and Samuel will lose their oxen like this." Everyone was afraid of the Lord and came together.

8. At Bezek, Saul counted 300,000 men from Israel and 30,000 from Judah.

9. They told the messengers, "Tell Jabesh-Gilead: You'll be rescued tomorrow by noon." The people were happy.

10. The next day, the men of Jabesh said, "We will surrender tomorrow. Do whatever you want."

11. Saul split his army into 3 groups and attacked before sunrise. They beat the Ammonites so badly that the survivors ran away alone.

Saul Is Made King

12. The people said, "Where are those who doubted Saul? Let's kill them!"

13. But Saul said, "No one will die today. The Lord rescued Israel!"

14. Then Samuel said, "Let's go to Gilgal and make Saul king."

15. They all went to Gilgal. They made Saul king before the Lord and celebrated with sacrifices and joy.

1 Samuel 12

Samuel's Goodbye Speech

1. Samuel said, "I listened to you and gave you a king."

2. "Now your king leads you. I'm old and gray, and my sons are here. I've been your leader since I was young."

3. "Here I am. Have I taken anything from you—money, animals, bribes? Tell me, and I'll pay it back."

4. They said, "No. You've been honest."

5. Samuel said, "The Lord and your king are witnesses that I've done no wrong." They said, "Yes."

6. Samuel said, "It was God who chose Moses and Aaron and brought your families out of Egypt."

7. "Now stand still while I remind you of all God has done for you and your ancestors."

8. "When Jacob's family was in Egypt and cried for help, God sent Moses and Aaron, who led them out."

9. "But they forgot the Lord, so he let their enemies defeat them."

10. "Then they cried, 'We sinned! We worshiped other gods! Save us and we'll follow you!'"

11. "God sent Gideon, Bedan, Jephthah, and me to save you. And you were safe."

12. "But when you saw Nahash coming, you asked for a king—even though God was already your king."

13. "Now here's the king you wanted. God gave him to you."

14. "If you obey God, then both you and your king will be blessed."

15. "But if you disobey, God will punish you like he did before."

16. "Now watch what the Lord will do."

17. "It's the dry season—you never get rain now. But I'll ask God to send thunder and rain to show how wrong you were to ask for a king."

18. Samuel prayed. God sent thunder and rain. The people were scared of God and Samuel.

19. They said, "Please pray so we won't die! We've sinned by asking for a king."

20. Samuel said, "Don't be afraid. You've sinned, but don't turn from God. Keep serving him."

21. "Don't follow useless idols—they can't help you."

22. "God won't leave you, because you are his people and that would hurt his name."

23. "I won't sin by stopping my prayers. I'll keep teaching you what's right."

24. "Respect God, serve him with all your heart, and remember what he's done for you."

25. "But if you keep doing evil, you and your king will be destroyed."

1 Samuel 13

Saul Disobeys God

1. Saul was 30 when he became king. He ruled for 42 years.

2. He chose 3,000 soldiers—2,000 stayed with him, and 1,000 with Jonathan. The rest went home.

3. Jonathan attacked the Philistine camp at Geba. News spread fast. Saul blew a trumpet, and everyone heard: "Saul attacked the Philistines! Now we're in trouble!"

4. Everyone gathered at Gilgal to join Saul.

5. The Philistines brought a huge army—3,000 chariots, 6,000 horsemen, and so many soldiers they were like sand on a beach. They camped at Michmash.

6. The Israelites saw they were in danger, so they hid in caves, bushes, and wells.

7. Some ran across the Jordan River, but Saul stayed in Gilgal. His men were afraid.

8. Saul waited 7 days, just like Samuel told him, but Samuel didn't come. So Saul's men started to leave.

9. Saul said, "Bring me the offerings," and he made the burnt offering himself.

10. As soon as he finished, Samuel arrived. Saul went out to greet him.

11. Samuel said, "What did you do?" Saul answered, "My troops were leaving, you didn't come, and the Philistines were ready to attack.

12. I was scared and hadn't prayed to God yet, so I made the offering."

13. Samuel said, "You acted foolishly. You didn't obey God. If you had, your kingdom would've lasted forever."

14. "But now your kingdom won't last. God has chosen someone else who obeys him."

15. Then Samuel left. Saul counted the soldiers—only 600 were left.

Israel Has No Weapons

16. Saul, Jonathan, and their men stayed at Gibeah. The Philistines were at Michmash.

17. The Philistines sent 3 groups of raiders—one toward Ophrah,

18. one toward Beth-Horon, and one toward the valley near Zeboim.

19. There were no blacksmiths in Israel, because the Philistines banned them. They didn't want Israel to make swords or spears.

20. So Israelites had to go to the Philistines to sharpen tools.

21. They charged money to sharpen plows, hoes, and axes.

22. On the day of battle, only Saul and Jonathan had swords. No one else did.

23. A Philistine guard was posted at the pass near Michmash.

1 Samuel 14

Jonathan Attacks the Philistines

1. One day, Jonathan said to his armor-bearer, "Let's go to the Philistine camp." He didn't tell his dad.

2. Saul and 600 men were sitting under a pomegranate tree in Gibeah.

3. With them was Ahijah the priest, wearing the priest's robe. He was Eli's great-grandson. No one knew Jonathan had left.

4. Jonathan had to climb between two cliffs to reach the Philistines. One cliff was Bozez, the other Seneh.

5. One cliff faced north toward Michmash, the other south toward Geba.

6. Jonathan said, "Let's go. Maybe God will help us. He can win with many or few."

7. His armor-bearer said, "Do what you think is best. I'm with you."

8. Jonathan said, "We'll let them see us.

9. If they say, 'Wait, we're coming,' we'll stay.

10. If they say, 'Come up, we'll go'. That will be God's sign that we'll win."

11. The Philistines saw them and said, "Look! Hebrews are crawling out of their holes!"

12. They shouted, "Come up here! We'll teach you a lesson!" Jonathan said, "Follow me! God is giving us victory!"

13. He climbed up, and his helper followed. Jonathan attacked from the front and his helper from behind.

14. In that first attack, they killed about 20 men in a small field.

15. Panic spread through the Philistine camp. The ground shook. Everyone was terrified.

Israel Defeats the Philistines

16. Saul's watchmen saw the Philistines running everywhere.

17. Saul said, "Count the troops. Who's missing?" They counted and saw Jonathan and his helper were gone.

18. Saul said to Ahijah, "Bring the Ark of God." (It was there at the time.)

19. As Saul talked to the priest, the panic grew. Saul said, "Stop! Forget the Ark."

20. Saul and his men ran to battle. The Philistines were confused and fighting each other.

21. Some Hebrews had been helping the Philistines. Now they switched sides to help Israel.

22. Other Israelites hiding in the hills heard the Philistines were running, so they joined the fight.

23. God saved Israel that day, and the battle moved past Beth-Aven.

Saul's Rash Oath

24. The Israelite soldiers were tired because Saul had said, "No one can eat until I get revenge." So no one ate all day.

25. They entered a forest and saw honey on the ground.

26. But no one ate it because of Saul's command.

27. Jonathan didn't hear the command. He dipped his stick into the honey and ate some. He felt better.

28. Someone said, "Your dad said we'd be cursed if we ate today. That's why we're weak."
29. Jonathan said, "My dad caused trouble. Look how I feel after just a little honey!
30. If we had eaten, we could've beaten more Philistines."
31. That day they fought from Michmash to Aijalon. The people were exhausted.
32. They took animals from the enemy and ate the meat without draining the blood.
33. Someone told Saul, "The people are sinning by eating blood!" Saul said, "That's wrong. Bring a big stone."
34. He told everyone, "Bring your animals. Kill them here and drain the blood." So they did.
35. Saul built an altar to the Lord. It was his first one.

Jonathan Is Saved

36. Saul said, "Let's keep attacking at night." The men said, "Okay," but the priest said, "Ask God first."
37. Saul asked, "Should I attack? Will you help us win?" But God didn't answer.
38. Saul said, "Someone sinned today. Let's find out who."
39. "Even if it's my son Jonathan, he must die." But no one said a word.
40. Saul said, "You stand over there. Jonathan and I will stand here." They agreed.
41. Saul prayed, and God showed that Jonathan was the one.
42. Saul said, "Tell me what you did." Jonathan said, "I ate a little honey."
43. "So now I must die."
44. Saul said, "Yes. You will die!"
45. But the people said, "Jonathan saved Israel! He must not die! Not a hair on his head will fall." So they rescued him.
46. Saul stopped fighting, and the Philistines went home.

Saul's Battles and Family

47. Saul fought enemies all around: Moab, Ammon, Edom, Zobah, and the Philistines.
48. He defeated the Amalekites too.
49. Saul's sons were Jonathan, Ishvi, and Malchishua. His daughters were Merab and Michal.
50. His wife was Ahinoam. His army commander was Abner, his uncle's son.
51. Saul's dad and Abner's dad were both sons of Abiel.
52. Israel fought the Philistines often. Saul recruited every strong man he saw.

1 Samuel 15

Saul Disobeys God Again

1. Samuel told Saul, "God made you king. Now listen to his message."
2. "God says: I will punish the Amalekites for attacking Israel after Egypt."
3. "Destroy everything—men, women, kids, babies, animals."
4. Saul gathered 210,000 soldiers and went to attack.
5. He set an ambush in the valley.
6. He told the Kenites, "Leave now. You were kind to us. Don't die with the Amalekites." So they left.
7. Saul attacked from Havilah to Shur.
8. He captured King Agag alive but killed everyone else.
9. But Saul and his men kept the best animals. They only destroyed what they didn't want.

God Rejects Saul

10. God told Samuel,
11. "I regret making Saul king. He disobeyed me." Samuel was so upset he cried all night.
12. Early next morning, Samuel went to find Saul. Someone said, "He's in Carmel building a monument to himself."

13. When Samuel found him, Saul said, "I obeyed the Lord!"
14. Samuel said, "Then why do I hear cows and sheep?"
15. Saul said, "We kept the best animals to offer to God. We destroyed everything else."
16. Samuel said, "Stop. Listen to what God told me last night."
17. "You used to think you were nobody, but God made you king."
18. "He told you to destroy the Amalekites completely.
19. Why didn't you obey? Why did you keep the loot?"
20. Saul said, "I did obey! I destroyed everyone except King Agag.
21. The people saved the best animals to sacrifice to God."
22. Samuel said, "Does God want sacrifices more than obedience? No! Obeying is better than sacrifice.
23. Rebellion is like witchcraft. Stubbornness is like worshiping idols. You rejected God's command, so he rejects you as king."
24. Saul said, "I sinned. I was afraid of the people, so I gave in.
25. Please forgive me and come with me to worship."
26. Samuel said, "No. You rejected God. Now God rejects you."
27. As Samuel turned to go, Saul grabbed his robe and it tore.
28. Samuel said, "God has torn the kingdom from you and given it to someone better."
29. "God does not lie or change his mind."
30. Saul said, "I've sinned. But please honor me in front of the leaders. Come with me."
31. So Samuel went with him, and Saul worshiped God.
32. Samuel said, "Bring me Agag." Agag came thinking he would be spared.
33. Samuel said, "Your sword made mothers childless—now your mother will be childless." Then he killed Agag.
34. Samuel went to Ramah. Saul went to his home in Gibeah.
35. Samuel never saw Saul again, but he mourned him. God was sorry he made Saul king.

1 Samuel 16

God Chooses David

1. God said, "How long will you mourn for Saul? I've rejected him. Go to Jesse in Bethlehem. I've chosen one of his sons to be king."
2. Samuel said, "If Saul hears, he'll kill me." God said, "Take a cow and say, 'I've come to sacrifice.'"
3. "Invite Jesse. I'll show you what to do."
4. Samuel went. The town leaders were scared. "Do you come in peace?"
5. He said, "Yes. I came to sacrifice. Clean yourselves and come." He also invited Jesse and his sons.
6. When he saw Eliab, Samuel thought, "This must be the one!"
7. But God said, "No. I don't look at the outside. I look at the heart."
8. Jesse brought in Abinadab. Samuel said, "Nope."
9. Then Shammah. Samuel said, "Not him either."
10. Jesse brought 7 sons, but God didn't choose any.
11. Samuel asked, "Are these all?" Jesse said, "There's the youngest. He's watching sheep." Samuel said, "Send for him."
12. David came. He was handsome and healthy. God said, "That's him! Anoint him!"
13. Samuel anointed David. God's Spirit came on him from that day on. Samuel went back to Ramah.

David Plays Music for Saul

14. God's Spirit left Saul. An evil spirit tormented him.
15. His servants said, "Let's find someone who plays the harp to help you."
16. "When the spirit comes, he'll play and you'll feel better."
17. Saul said, "Find someone good."
18. A servant said, "I know Jesse's son David. He plays well, is brave, speaks well, and the Lord is with him."
19. Saul sent messengers to Jesse: "Send me your son David."
20. Jesse sent David with gifts.
21. David came to Saul and served him. Saul liked him and made him his armor-bearer.
22. Saul asked Jesse to let David stay.
23. When the evil spirit came, David played his harp. Saul felt better, and the spirit left.

1 Samuel 17

Goliath Challenges Israel

1. The Philistines got ready for battle and camped at Ephes-Dammim.
2. Saul and the Israelites camped in Elah Valley.
3. The Philistines stood on one hill, the Israelites on another. A valley was between them.
4. Goliath came out from the Philistines. He was over 9 feet tall.
5. He wore a bronze helmet and armor that weighed 125 pounds.
6. He had bronze leg armor and carried a bronze javelin.
7. His spear was thick like a weaver's rod, and the tip weighed 15 pounds. A soldier carried his shield.
8. Goliath shouted, "Why are you lining up to fight? I'm a Philistine, and you are Saul's servants! Pick a man to fight me."
9. "If he kills me, we'll serve you. But if I kill him, you'll serve us."
10. "I challenge Israel! Send someone to fight me!"
11. Saul and the Israelites were terrified.

David Hears Goliath's Challenge

12. Jesse was from Bethlehem and had eight sons. He was old.
13. His three oldest sons—Eliab, Abinadab, and Shimea—were in Saul's army.
14. David was the youngest. The three oldest were at war.
15. David went back and forth from Saul to take care of his father's sheep.
16. Goliath came out and shouted every morning and evening for 40 days.
17. Jesse said, "David, take this food to your brothers."
18. "Also take these cheeses to their commander. See how they're doing and bring something back."
19. His brothers were with Saul in the valley, fighting the Philistines.
20. David left early, gave the supplies to a helper, and went to the battle lines.
21. The armies lined up against each other.
22. David left his things with the supply guard and ran to his brothers.
23. As he talked with them, Goliath came out and shouted like before. David heard him.
24. The Israelites ran away scared.
25. They said, "This man keeps taunting Israel. The king will reward whoever kills him with money, his daughter, and no taxes."
26. David asked, "What's the reward for killing this man? Who does this Philistine think he is to insult God's army?"
27. They repeated the reward.
28. David's oldest brother Eliab got angry and said, "Why are you here? Shouldn't

you be watching the sheep? You just want to watch the battle!"

29. David said, "What did I do? I just asked a question."
30. He turned to others and asked again. They gave the same answer.
31. People told Saul what David said. Saul sent for him.
32. David said, "Don't worry! I'll fight him!"
33. Saul said, "You can't. You're just a boy, and he's a warrior."
34. David said, "I take care of my father's sheep. When a lion or bear comes,
35. I grab it and kill it."
36. "I've killed lions and bears. I'll kill this Philistine too for insulting God's army!"
37. "God saved me from lions and bears. He'll save me now!" Saul said, "Go. God be with you."

David Fights Goliath

38. Saul gave David his armor.
39. David tried to walk in it but said, "I can't wear this." He took it off.
40. He took his stick, picked 5 smooth stones, put them in his bag, and walked toward Goliath with his sling.
41. Goliath walked out with his shield-bearer.
42. He saw David and made fun of him for being young and good-looking.
43. Goliath said, "Am I a dog that you come at me with a stick?" He cursed David.
44. "Come here! I'll feed you to the birds and animals!"
45. David said, "You come with a sword and spear. I come with the name of the Lord, the God you insulted."
46. "Today God will give you to me. I'll kill you and cut off your head. I'll feed your army to the birds. Everyone will know God is real!"
47. "Everyone here will know God doesn't need swords to win. This is God's battle, and He will defeat you!"
48. Goliath came forward. David ran to him.
49. David took a stone, slung it, and hit Goliath in the forehead. Goliath fell face down.
50. David killed him with a sling and a stone. No sword was needed.
51. David ran over, took Goliath's sword, and cut off his head. The Philistines ran away.
52. Israel and Judah shouted and chased them to Gath and Ekron. Dead Philistines were everywhere.
53. The Israelites returned and took the enemy's things.
54. David took Goliath's head to Jerusalem and kept his weapons.
55. Saul watched David and asked Abner, "Whose son is that?" Abner said, "I don't know."
56. Saul said, "Find out."
57. After David killed Goliath, Abner brought him to Saul. He still had Goliath's head.
58. Saul asked, "Who's your father?" David said, "Jesse from Bethlehem."

1 Samuel 18

David and Jonathan Become Friends

1. After talking with Saul, David and Jonathan became best friends.
2. Saul didn't let David go home anymore.
3. Jonathan made a promise to David because he loved him.
4. He gave David his robe, armor, sword, bow, and belt.
5. David succeeded in everything Saul asked him to do. So Saul made him a high officer. Everyone was happy.

Saul Gets Jealous

6. When David and the army returned, women came out singing and dancing.
7. They sang: "Saul has killed thousands, and David tens of thousands!"
8. This made Saul angry. "They credit David with more than me! What's next—he'll take the kingdom?"
9. From that day on, Saul watched David closely.
10. The next day, an evil spirit from God came on Saul. He raved inside his house while David played the harp.
11. Saul had a spear and threw it, saying, "I'll pin David to the wall!" But David escaped twice.
12. Saul was afraid of David because the Lord had left him and was now with David.
13. So he made David a commander over 1,000 soldiers.
14. David kept succeeding because the Lord was with him.
15. Saul was afraid of David's success.
16. But everyone in Israel and Judah loved David because he led the army well.

Saul Tries to Trick David

17. Saul said, "You can marry my daughter Merab—if you fight my battles." But he was really hoping David would be killed in battle.
18. David said, "I'm not worthy to be the king's son-in-law."
19. But when it was time to marry Merab, she was given to someone else.
20. Saul's other daughter, Michal, loved David. Saul was happy.
21. He thought, "She will trap him, and the Philistines will kill him." So he told David, "You can marry her."
22. Saul told his servants, "Tell David the king likes him. You should be his son-in-law."
23. The servants told David. He said, "You think it's easy to marry the king's daughter? I'm poor and unimportant."
24. The servants told Saul what David said.
25. Saul said, "Tell David I don't want money—just 100 Philistine foreskins." He thought David would die trying.
26. David liked the idea. Before time ran out,
27. David and his men killed 200 Philistines. He gave their foreskins to Saul, and Saul gave Michal to David.
28. Saul saw that the Lord was with David and that Michal loved him.
29. Saul was even more afraid and stayed David's enemy for life.
30. The Philistines kept fighting. David won more battles than any of Saul's officers. He became very famous.

1 Samuel 19

Saul Tries to Kill David

1. Saul told Jonathan and his servants to kill David. But Jonathan liked David a lot.
2. He warned David, "My father wants to kill you. Go hide somewhere tomorrow morning."
3. "I'll go out with my father in the field. I'll talk to him about you and tell you what he says."
4. Jonathan spoke well of David to Saul: "David hasn't done anything wrong. He's helped you a lot."
5. "He risked his life to kill Goliath. You were happy about it. Don't hurt someone innocent."
6. Saul listened. He said, "You're right. I won't kill him."
7. Jonathan told David what happened and brought him back to Saul. Everything was good again.
8. War broke out again. David fought and won.

9. But an evil spirit from God came on Saul again. He was sitting with his spear, and David was playing music.
10. Saul tried to pin David to the wall, but David escaped. He ran away that night.
11. Saul sent men to watch David's house and kill him in the morning. Michal warned David, "You must escape tonight or you'll be killed."
12. She helped David escape through a window.
13. Then she put a statue in his bed, put goat hair on its head, and covered it with a blanket.
14. When Saul's men came, she said, "He's sick."
15. Saul said, "Bring him to me in his bed so I can kill him."
16. When they came, they saw the statue.
17. Saul said to Michal, "Why did you trick me?" She said, "He said he'd kill me if I didn't help."
18. David ran to Samuel in Ramah and told him everything. They went to Naioth and stayed there.
19. Saul heard, "David is at Naioth in Ramah."
20. He sent men to capture David, but they began to prophesy.
21. Saul sent more men, and the same thing happened.
22. Then Saul went himself. God's Spirit came on him too, and he prophesied all the way to Naioth.
23. He took off his clothes and lay on the ground all day and night, prophesying. That's why people say, "Is Saul also a prophet?"

1 Samuel 20

David and Jonathan Make a Plan

1. David left Naioth and asked Jonathan, "What did I do wrong? Why does your dad want to kill me?"
2. Jonathan said, "He won't kill you. He tells me everything."
3. David said, "He knows we're close. That's why he's hiding it. I swear—I'm in danger."
4. Jonathan said, "I'll do whatever you need."
5. David said, "Tomorrow is the New Moon feast. I'll hide in the field for three days.
6. If Saul asks, say, 'David went home for a family sacrifice.'
7. If he's okay with it, I'm safe. If he gets mad, he wants to kill me."
8. "If I've done wrong, you kill me. Don't turn me in to Saul."
9. Jonathan said, "Never! I'll tell you if I learn anything bad."
10. David asked, "How will you tell me?"
11. Jonathan said, "Let's go out to the field." They went together.
12. Jonathan said, "I promise—if I learn anything from my dad, I'll tell you."
13. "If he wants to hurt you, I'll warn you to get away. May God punish me if I don't."
14. "Promise me that if I die, you'll always be kind to my family."
15. "Even when God destroys your enemies, don't forget my family."
16. So they made a promise that David would protect Jonathan's family.
17. Jonathan loved David as much as himself.
18. He said, "Tomorrow you'll be missed.
19. On the third day, go to the same hiding place.
20. I'll shoot three arrows as if I'm practicing.
21. I'll send a boy to get them. If I say, 'The arrows are near you,' then it's safe.
22. If I say, 'They're beyond you,' then run, because God wants you gone."

23. "Remember this promise between us."

Jonathan Warns David

24. David hid in the field. Saul sat down for the New Moon feast.
25. He sat where he always did. Jonathan and Abner were there, but David's seat was empty.
26. Saul said nothing, thinking David might be unclean.
27. The next day, David's seat was still empty. Saul asked Jonathan, "Why didn't David come?"
28. Jonathan said, "He asked to go to Bethlehem for a family event."
29. "His brother asked him to come, so I let him go."
30. Saul got angry. "You're siding with David! You bring shame to yourself and your mother!"
31. "As long as David lives, you'll never be king! Go get him!"
32. Jonathan asked, "Why should he die? What did he do?"
33. Saul threw a spear at him. Jonathan knew Saul wanted to kill David.
34. Jonathan left the table angry and didn't eat. He was upset his father wanted to kill his friend.

David and Jonathan Say Goodbye

35. The next morning, Jonathan went to the field with a young boy.
36. He said, "Run and find the arrows I shoot." As the boy ran, Jonathan shot an arrow beyond him.
37. The boy ran to the arrow.
38. Jonathan shouted, "The arrow is beyond you!"
39. The boy didn't understand what it meant. Only Jonathan and David knew.
40. Jonathan gave the boy his bow and arrows and sent him home.
41. David came out and bowed three times. They hugged and cried.
42. Jonathan said, "Go in peace. We made a promise with God. He will always be between us and our families." David left, and Jonathan went home.

1 Samuel 21

David Visits the Priest

1. David went to Nob and saw Ahimelek the priest. Ahimelek was scared and asked, "Why are you alone?"
2. David said, "The king sent me on a secret mission. I told my men to meet me later."
3. "Do you have any food?"
4. The priest said, "I only have holy bread—but your men must be clean."
5. David said, "We haven't been with women. We are clean."
6. So the priest gave him the holy bread because there was no other bread.
7. One of Saul's servants, Doeg the Edomite, was there.
8. David asked, "Do you have a sword?"
9. The priest said, "The only one here is Goliath's sword." David said, "Give it to me. There's none like it."

David Hides with the Philistines

10. David ran to Achish, the king of Gath.
11. The Philistine officials said, "Isn't this David, the one they sing about? 'Saul killed thousands, and David tens of thousands'?"
12. David was afraid of Achish.
13. So he acted insane—scribbled on doors and drooled.
14. Achish said, "Why bring a madman to me?"
15. "I have enough crazy people already!"

1 Samuel 22

1. David left Gath and hid in a cave at Adullam. His family and others joined him.

2. People who were in trouble, in debt, or unhappy came too. He became their leader. About 400 men were with him.
3. David went to Mizpah in Moab and asked the king, "Can my parents stay here until I know what God wants me to do?"
4. So they stayed with the king while David was hiding.
5. A prophet named Gad told David, "Don't stay in the cave. Go to Judah." So David went to Hereth forest.

Saul Kills the Priests

6. Saul heard that David was found. He was sitting under a tree with his spear, surrounded by servants.
7. He said, "Why are you all against me? Did David promise you land or power?"
8. "Why didn't anyone tell me Jonathan helped David? You're all traitors!"
9. Doeg the Edomite said, "I saw David at Nob talking to Ahimelek the priest.
10. Ahimelek asked God for him, gave him food, and gave him Goliath's sword."
11. Saul sent for Ahimelek and his family. They all came.
12. Saul said, "Why did you help David?"
13. "You gave him food and a sword and asked God for him. You helped him rebel!"
14. Ahimelek said, "David is loyal! He's your son-in-law and your top soldier. I always help him."
15. "I didn't know anything about a rebellion."
16. Saul said, "You will die, Ahimelek. You and your family."
17. He told his guards to kill the priests, but they refused.
18. So Saul told Doeg, "You do it." Doeg killed 85 priests that day.
19. Then he killed everyone in Nob—men, women, kids, babies, and animals.
20. Only one son of Ahimelek escaped—Abiathar. He ran to David.
21. He told David what Saul did.
22. David said, "I knew Doeg would tell Saul. I'm responsible for their deaths."
23. "Stay with me. Saul wants to kill you too, but I'll protect you."

1 Samuel 23

David Saves Keilah

1. David heard the Philistines were attacking Keilah and stealing grain.
2. He asked God, "Should I go fight them?" God said, "Yes."
3. David's men said, "We're scared already—fighting the Philistines sounds worse!"
4. David asked God again. God said, "Go. I'll help you win."
5. David and his men fought and won. They saved Keilah.

Saul Comes After David

6. When Abiathar fled to David, he brought the priest's vest.
7. Saul heard David was in Keilah. He said, "God has trapped him in a city with gates."
8. He called his army to surround the city.
9. David heard Saul was coming. He told Abiathar, "Bring the vest."
10. He prayed, "Lord, Saul is coming to destroy the city because of me.
11. Will the leaders give me to him?" God said, "Yes."
12. So David and his 600 men left.
13. Saul found out David had escaped and didn't attack.
14. David hid in the wilderness. Saul searched every day, but God didn't let him find David.

Jonathan Encourages David

15. David was hiding in Horesh and heard Saul was looking for him.

16. Jonathan found him and said,
17. "Don't be afraid. My father won't find you. You will be king, and I'll be second to you."
18. They made a promise before God. Then Jonathan went home.

The People of Ziph Betray David

19. People from Ziph told Saul, "David is hiding in our area."
20. "Come down, and we'll help you catch him."
21. Saul said, "God bless you! You're loyal."
22. "Go find out exactly where he is and who's with him."
23. "Then come back, and I'll go with you."
24. They left. David was in the desert near Maon.
25. Saul went there too. When David heard, he went farther into the desert.
26. Saul was on one side of a mountain, David on the other. Saul was closing in.
27. But a messenger came and said, "The Philistines are attacking!"
28. So Saul left David to fight the Philistines. That's why the place is called Rock of Escape.
29. David went to hide in En Gedi.

1 Samuel 24

David Spares Saul's Life

1. After Saul returned from fighting the Philistines, someone said, "David is in En Gedi."
2. Saul took 3,000 men to search for David near the wild goat rocks.
3. He went into a cave to use the bathroom. David and his men were hiding deep inside.
4. His men whispered, "This is your chance! God has given you Saul!" David quietly cut off a piece of Saul's robe.
5. But afterward, David felt bad.
6. He said, "I shouldn't harm the one God chose."
7. He stopped his men from attacking Saul. Saul left the cave.
8. David came out and shouted, "My lord the king!" Saul turned, and David bowed.
9. David said, "Why do you listen to people who say I want to hurt you?"
10. "Today you saw I could've killed you, but I didn't."
11. "Here's the piece of your robe I cut. I'm not trying to hurt you."
12. "God will judge between us. But I won't harm you."
13. "As the saying goes: 'Bad things come from bad people.' I won't hurt you."
14. "Why are you chasing me? I'm just a flea or a dead dog."
15. "Let God decide between us. Let Him fight for me and save me."
16. Saul said, "Is that your voice, David?" He cried.
17. "You are a better man than me. You treated me kindly when I tried to hurt you."
18. "You could've killed me but didn't."
19. "Who lets an enemy go free like this?"
20. "Now I know you will be king, and Israel will be strong under you."
21. "Promise not to kill my family or erase my name."
22. David promised. Saul went home. David stayed in his stronghold.

1 Samuel 25

Samuel Dies

1. Samuel died, and all Israel gathered to mourn him. They buried him at his home in Ramah. David moved to the Desert of Paran.

David and Nabal

2. A rich man named Nabal lived in Maon. He owned land in Carmel and had 1,000 goats and 3,000 sheep.
3. Nabal was rude and mean. His wife Abigail was wise and beautiful.
4. David heard Nabal was shearing sheep.
5. He sent 10 men to greet Nabal politely.
6. David told them to say, "Peace to you, your family, and everything you own."
7. "We didn't harm your shepherds in Carmel. Ask them—they'll agree."
8. "Please be kind to us. We come on a good day. Give us whatever you can."
9. David's men gave the message and waited.
10. Nabal said, "Who is David? Who is this son of Jesse? Many servants run away from their masters."
11. "Why should I give my food to people I don't know?"
12. David's men returned and told him everything.
13. David said, "Get your swords!" About 400 men went with him. 200 stayed with the supplies.
14. A servant told Abigail, "David's men were kind to us, but Nabal insulted them."
15. "They protected us day and night."
16. "Please do something before it's too late."
17. "Nabal is so mean no one can talk to him."
18. Abigail quickly packed bread, wine, meat, grain, raisins, and figs on donkeys.
19. She told her servants, "Go ahead. I'll follow." She didn't tell Nabal.
20. As she rode her donkey, she met David and his men.
21. David had just said, "We protected Nabal's stuff for nothing. He paid us back with evil."
22. "I swear—by morning, none of Nabal's men will be alive!"
23. Abigail got off her donkey and bowed before David.
24. She said, "Please let me take the blame."
25. "My husband is foolish—his name means 'fool.' Don't listen to him."
26. "God has kept you from killing. Let your enemies end up like Nabal."
27. "Please accept this gift."
28. "Forgive me. God will give you a strong house because you fight His battles."
29. "Even if someone tries to kill you, God will protect you."
30. "One day God will make you ruler of Israel."
31. "Don't let this be a burden or regret. When God blesses you, remember me."
32. David said, "Praise God for sending you today."
33. "Thank you for stopping me. You saved me from doing wrong."
34. "If you hadn't come, none of Nabal's men would be alive by morning."
35. David accepted her gifts and said, "Go home in peace. I listened to you."
36. Abigail returned to Nabal. He was partying and very drunk, so she said nothing.
37. In the morning, she told him what happened. He had a stroke and couldn't move.
38. Ten days later, God struck him dead.
39. David said, "Praise God! He judged Nabal and kept me from doing wrong." Then he sent a message asking Abigail to marry him.
40. His servants gave her the message.
41. She bowed and said, "I'll gladly be his servant."

42. She quickly got ready, rode a donkey, and followed David's men with her servants.
43. David also married Ahinoam from Jezreel.
44. Saul had given his daughter Michal, David's wife, to another man named Palti.

1 Samuel 26

David Spares Saul Again

1. The people of Ziph told Saul, "David is hiding on Hakilah Hill."
2. Saul took 3,000 men to find him.
3. He camped beside the road near Hakilah. David was hiding in the desert.
4. David sent spies and confirmed Saul was there.
5. David went to Saul's camp and saw where Saul and his general Abner were sleeping.
6. David asked, "Who will come with me into Saul's camp?" Abishai said, "I will."
7. They snuck in at night. Saul was sleeping with his spear stuck in the ground beside him. Abner and the guards were asleep.
8. Abishai said, "God has handed your enemy to you. Let me pin him to the ground with one stab."
9. David said, "No! Don't kill him. No one can hurt God's chosen king and be innocent."
10. "God will deal with him—maybe he'll die in battle."
11. "But I won't hurt him. Just take his spear and water jar."
12. So they took the spear and jar and left. No one woke up because God made them sleep deeply.
13. David stood on a hill far away and called to Saul's camp.
14. He shouted to Abner, "Aren't you going to answer me?"
15. "You failed! You didn't protect your king. Someone came to kill him."
16. "You deserve to die for not guarding him. Look! Where's his spear and water jar?"
17. Saul said, "Is that you, David?" David said, "Yes, my king."
18. "Why are you chasing me? What have I done wrong?"
19. "If God sent you, I'll offer a sacrifice. If it's people lying about me, may God punish them."
20. "Why are you chasing me like I'm a flea or a bird?"
21. Saul said, "I've sinned. Come back. I won't hurt you. I was wrong."
22. David said, "Here's your spear. Let someone come get it."
23. "God rewards those who do right. I didn't kill you today even though I could."
24. "Just as I valued your life, may God value mine and save me."
25. Saul said, "Bless you, David. You'll do great things." Then Saul went home, and David went his way.

1 Samuel 27

1. David thought, "One day Saul will catch me. I'll be safer in Philistine land."
2. So he went to Gath with 600 men and their families.
3. He and his men stayed with King Achish of Gath.
4. Saul stopped looking for him.
5. David said to Achish, "Let me live in one of your towns, not in the city with you."
6. So Achish gave him Ziklag. That's why it belongs to Judah's kings.
7. David lived in Philistine land for 1 year and 4 months.

8. David and his men raided nearby groups: the Geshurites, Girzites, and Amalekites.

9. He killed everyone and took animals and supplies back to Achish.

10. When Achish asked, "Where did you raid today?" David would say, "The desert near Judah."

11. David didn't let anyone live to tell the truth.

12. Achish trusted David and thought, "He's made his own people hate him. Now he'll stay here and be my servant for life."

1 Samuel 28

1. The Philistines gathered their army to fight Israel. Achish told David, "You and your men must fight with me."

2. David said, "You'll see what I can do." Achish said, "Good! I'll make you my personal guard for life."

3. Samuel had died, and all Israel mourned him. He was buried in Ramah. Saul had removed all fortune-tellers and mediums from the land.

4. The Philistines camped at Shunem. Saul gathered Israel and camped at Gilboa.

5. When Saul saw the Philistine army, he was afraid and trembled with fear.

6. He asked the Lord what to do, but God didn't answer—no dreams, no priests, and no prophets.

7. Saul told his servants, "Find me a woman who talks to spirits so I can ask her what to do." They said, "There's one in Endor."

8. Saul disguised himself, wore different clothes, and went at night with two men to visit the woman. He told her, "Talk to a spirit for me and bring up the person I ask."

9. The woman said, "You know Saul banned this! Are you trying to get me killed?"

10. Saul promised, "As surely as the Lord lives, you won't be punished."

11. She asked, "Who should I bring up?" Saul said, "Bring up Samuel."

12. When she saw Samuel, she screamed. She said, "Why did you trick me? You're Saul!"

13. The king said, "Don't be afraid. What do you see?" She said, "I see a spirit coming up from the ground."

14. Saul asked, "What does he look like?" She said, "An old man wearing a robe." Saul knew it was Samuel and bowed down.

15. Samuel said, "Why did you disturb me?" Saul said, "I'm in trouble. The Philistines are coming, and God won't answer me. So I called you."

16. Samuel said, "Why ask me if God has left you?"

17. "The Lord has done what He said. He took the kingdom from you and gave it to David."

18. "You didn't obey God or destroy the Amalekites. That's why this is happening."

19. "The Lord will let the Philistines defeat Israel. You and your sons will die tomorrow."

20. Saul fell flat on the ground, afraid of Samuel's words and weak from not eating.

21. The woman came and saw he was terrified. She said, "You listened to me. Now let me give you food so you can eat and get strength."

22. He said, "No, I won't eat." But his men and the woman begged him.

23. He listened and got up and sat on the bed.

24. She had a fat calf, quickly cooked it, and baked bread without yeast.

25. She brought the food to Saul and his men. They ate, then left that night.

1 Samuel 29

1. The Philistines gathered their army at Aphek. The Israelites camped near Jezreel.
2. The Philistine commanders marched by in groups. David and his men were at the back with Achish.
3. The commanders asked, "Why are these Hebrews here?" Achish said, "This is David, the servant of Saul. He's been with me for years and has never done anything wrong."
4. But the commanders got angry and said, "Send him back! He might turn on us during battle to win favor with Saul."
5. "Isn't this the one they sing about: 'Saul killed thousands, and David tens of thousands'?"
6. Achish called David and said, "As surely as God lives, you've been loyal. I trust you. But the other commanders don't want you to fight."
7. "Go back peacefully. Don't upset them."
8. David said, "What have I done? Why can't I fight your enemies?"
9. Achish said, "I know you've done nothing wrong. But the commanders don't trust you."
10. "So leave early in the morning with your men."
11. David and his men got up early and left. The Philistines went on to Jezreel.

1 Samuel 30

1. Three days later, David and his men arrived at Ziklag. They found it burned down. The Amalekites had raided it.
2. They had taken the women and children, but they didn't kill anyone.
3. David and his men saw the burned town and their families gone.
4. They cried loudly until they had no strength left.
5. David's wives, Ahinoam and Abigail, were also taken.
6. David was very upset. The men blamed him and talked about killing him. But David trusted the Lord for strength.
7. He said to Abiathar the priest, "Bring the priest's vest." Abiathar brought it.
8. David asked God, "Should I chase the attackers? Will I catch them?" God said, "Chase them. You will catch them and rescue everyone."
9. David and 600 men went after them. When they reached a stream, 200 men stayed behind—they were too tired to go on.
10. David kept going with 400 men.
11. They found an Egyptian in a field and gave him food and water.
12. He hadn't eaten or drunk anything for 3 days. They gave him more food and raisins. Then he felt better.
13. David asked, "Who are you? Where are you from?" He said, "I'm an Egyptian servant. My master is an Amalekite. He left me behind when I got sick."
14. "We raided the southern area and burned Ziklag."
15. David said, "Will you lead us to them?" The man said, "Promise not to kill me or return me to my master, and I'll take you there."
16. He led David to the Amalekites, who were eating, drinking, and dancing with all the stuff they took.
17. David attacked them from that evening until the next night. None escaped, except 400 young men who rode away on camels.
18. David rescued everyone, including his two wives.
19. Nothing was missing—young or old, sons or daughters, or anything else. David got everything back.
20. He also took all their flocks. His men said, "This is David's reward!"

21. David returned to the 200 tired men who stayed at the stream. They came out to greet him.
22. But some mean men in David's group said, "They didn't fight, so they get nothing but their families."
23. David said, "No! What we won today came from God. We will all share alike."
24. "The one who stayed behind will get the same as the one who fought."
25. From then on, David made that a rule in Israel.
26. David also sent some of the plunder to leaders in Judah, saying, "Here's a gift from the enemies of the Lord."
27. He sent gifts to cities where he and his men had stayed: Bethel, Ramoth-Negev, Jattir,
28. Aroer, Siphmoth, Eshtemoa,
29. Rakal, Jerahmeelite towns, Kenite towns,
30. Hormah, Bor Ashan, Athak,
31. and Hebron. David sent gifts to all the places he and his men had traveled.

1 Samuel 31

1. The Philistines fought Israel. The Israelites ran and many died on Mount Gilboa.
2. The Philistines chased Saul and killed his sons Jonathan, Abinadab, and Malchishua.
3. The battle was fierce. Saul was badly wounded by archers.
4. He said to his armor-bearer, "Kill me before the enemy does." But the armor-bearer was too afraid. So Saul took his own sword and fell on it.
5. When the armor-bearer saw that Saul was dead, he killed himself too.
6. So Saul, his three sons, and his men all died that day.
7. When the Israelites saw what happened, they ran. The Philistines took over their towns.
8. The next day, the Philistines found Saul and his sons on the battlefield.
9. They cut off Saul's head and took his armor. They sent the news all over their land.
10. They put his armor in the temple of their gods and hung his body on the wall of Beth Shan.
11. When the people of Jabesh-Gilead heard what the Philistines had done to Saul,
12. their bravest men traveled all night and took down the bodies of Saul and his sons. They brought them back to Jabesh and burned them there.
13. Then they buried the bones under a tree and fasted for seven days.

– 2 Samuel –

David rules Israel, unites the tribes, but sins and faces the consequences.

2 Samuel 1

1. After Saul died, David came back from fighting the Amalekites and stayed in Ziklag for two days.
2. On the third day, a man from Saul's army came with torn clothes and dust on his head. He bowed to David.
3. David asked, "Where did you come from?" He said, "I escaped from Israel's camp."
4. David asked, "What happened?" He said, "Our army ran away. Many died. Saul and Jonathan are dead."
5. David asked, "How do you know they're dead?"
6. He said, "I was on Mount Gilboa. I saw Saul leaning on his spear. Enemy chariots were coming."
7. "Saul saw me and called to me. I said, 'What do you want?'"

8. "He asked, 'Who are you?' I said, 'I'm an Amalekite.'"
9. "Then he said, 'Kill me. I'm dying and in pain.'"
10. "So I killed him because I knew he wouldn't live. I took his crown and armband and brought them to you."
11. David and his men tore their clothes.
12. They cried and didn't eat until evening. They were sad for Saul, Jonathan, and the people who died.
13. David asked the man, "Where are you from?" He said, "I'm an Amalekite, a foreigner."
14. David asked, "Why weren't you afraid to kill the Lord's chosen king?"
15. Then David told a soldier, "Kill him." The soldier killed him.
16. David said, "You caused your own death. You admitted killing the king."

David's Song About Saul and Jonathan

17. David made a song to honor Saul and Jonathan.
18. He said to teach it to Judah. It was written in the Book of Jashar.
19. "Our heroes died on the hills! The mighty have fallen!
20. Don't tell it in Gath or Ashkelon, or the enemy women will laugh.
21. Let no rain fall on Gilboa's hills. The shields there are ruined. Saul's shield is left dirty.
22. Jonathan's arrows killed. Saul's sword didn't miss.
23. Saul and Jonathan were loved and respected. They were brave in life and in death.
24. Women of Israel, cry for Saul. He gave you fine clothes and gold.
25. The mighty have fallen! Jonathan is dead on the hills.
26. I cry for you, Jonathan. We loved each other deeply.
27. The mighty have fallen! Their weapons are gone!"

2 Samuel 2

David Becomes King of Judah

1. David asked the Lord, "Should I go to a town in Judah?" God said, "Yes." David asked, "Which one?" God said, "Hebron."
2. So David went there with his wives Ahinoam and Abigail.
3. His men and their families also moved to the towns near Hebron.
4. The men of Judah came and made David their king. They told David the men of Jabesh Gilead had buried Saul.
5. David sent a message to those men: "God bless you for being kind to Saul and burying him."
6. "May God reward you. I will also be kind to you."
7. "Saul is dead, and Judah has made me king. Be strong and brave."

Ishbosheth Becomes King of Israel

8. Abner, the commander of Saul's army, made Saul's son Ishbosheth king in Mahanaim.
9. He ruled over Gilead, Jezreel, Ephraim, Benjamin, and all Israel.
10. Ishbosheth was 40 years old and ruled for two years. But Judah followed David.
11. David ruled Judah from Hebron for 7 years and 6 months.

War Between David and Ishbosheth

12. Abner led Ishbosheth's army to Gibeon.
13. Joab, David's commander, met him there with David's men. They sat by a pool, facing each other.
14. Abner said, "Let our men fight for sport." Joab agreed.
15. So 12 men from each side fought.
16. Each grabbed the other and stabbed him. All died. The place was called Field of Daggers.
17. A fierce battle started. David's men defeated Abner's army.

18. Joab's brothers Abishai and Asahel were there. Asahel was fast like a wild deer.
19. He chased Abner and wouldn't stop.
20. Abner looked back and asked, "Is that you, Asahel?" He said, "Yes."
21. Abner said, "Turn back and fight someone else." But Asahel kept chasing him.
22. Abner said again, "Stop! I don't want to kill you. Then I'd face your brother Joab."
23. But Asahel didn't stop, so Abner stabbed him with the back of his spear. Asahel died. Everyone who came to that spot stopped.
24. Joab and Abishai kept chasing Abner. At sunset, they reached the hill of Ammah.
25. Abner's men regrouped and stood on the hill.
26. Abner shouted, "Should we keep fighting? When will you stop chasing us?"
27. Joab said, "If you hadn't spoken, we would've kept chasing until morning."
28. Joab blew the trumpet. His men stopped fighting.
29. Abner and his men marched all night and crossed the Jordan to Mahanaim.
30. Joab stopped chasing and counted his men. Nineteen were missing plus Asahel.
31. David's men had killed 360 of Abner's men.
32. They buried Asahel in Bethlehem. Then Joab and his men returned to Hebron by sunrise.

2 Samuel 3

1. The war between Saul's family and David's family lasted a long time. David's side grew stronger. Saul's side grew weaker.
2. David had sons while he was in Hebron. His first son was Amnon, by Ahinoam.
3. His second was Kileab, by Abigail. His third was Absalom, by Maacah, daughter of Talmai.
4. His fourth was Adonijah, by Haggith. His fifth was Shephatiah, by Abital.
5. His sixth was Ithream, by Eglah. All were born in Hebron.

Abner Joins David

6. As the war continued, Abner grew stronger in Saul's house.
7. Saul had a concubine named Rizpah. Ishbosheth said to Abner, "Why did you sleep with her?"
8. Abner got angry and said, "Am I a dog's head? I've helped you! Now you accuse me?"
9. "God will punish me if I don't help David get the kingdom, just like God promised."
10. "I will make David king over all Israel."
11. Ishbosheth was afraid and didn't say anything else.
12. Abner sent messengers to David: "Make a deal with me, and I'll bring all Israel to you."
13. David said, "I'll agree, but only if you bring back my wife Michal."
14. David sent messengers to Ishbosheth: "Give me my wife. I paid for her with 100 Philistine foreskins."
15. So Ishbosheth took her from her husband Paltiel.
16. Paltiel followed her, crying, until Abner told him to go home. He left.
17. Abner spoke to the elders of Israel: "You wanted David before. Now make him king—God chose him to save you."
18. Abner also talked to the tribe of Benjamin and went to tell David everything.
19. David gave him a feast.

20. Abner said, "I'll bring all Israel to you, and they will make you king." Then he left in peace.

Joab Kills Abner

21. Joab came back and heard Abner had been there and left in peace.
22. Joab went to David and said, "Why did you let him go? He's spying on you!"
23. Then Joab left and sent messengers to bring Abner back. David didn't know.
24. When Abner returned, Joab took him aside and stabbed him in the stomach. Abner died—Joab did this to get revenge for his brother Asahel.
25. David heard and said, "I'm innocent of Abner's death!"
26. "May Joab's family suffer for this. Let them always have sickness, weakness, or trouble."
27. Joab and Abishai killed Abner to avenge Asahel.
28. David told everyone, "Tear your clothes, wear sackcloth, and mourn." David walked behind Abner's body.
29. They buried Abner in Hebron. David cried loudly at the grave.
30. The king sang a song: "Should Abner have died like a fool?"
31. "You weren't tied up, but you died anyway." All the people cried.
32. The people tried to give David food, but he said, "May God punish me if I eat before sunset."
33. Everyone liked what he said.
34. That day, the people knew David hadn't wanted Abner to die.
35. David said, "A great man died today.
36. I am weak, even though I'm king. Joab and his brother are too strong. May God punish them for their crime."

2 Samuel 4

1. When Ishbosheth heard Abner was dead, he and. all of Israel was scared.
2. Two of Saul's commanders, Baanah and Recab, were brothers from Beeroth.
3. The people of Beeroth had moved to Gittaim and lived there.
4. Saul's son Jonathan had a son named Mephibosheth. He was five when Saul and Jonathan died. While running his nurse dropped him. That crippled him.
5. Recab and Baanah came to Ishbosheth's house at noon while he was resting.
6. They went inside as if to get wheat and stabbed him in the stomach.
7. They entered the bedroom, killed him, cut off his head, and ran away.
8. They brought the head to David in Hebron and said, "Look! Saul's son is dead. God gave you victory!"
9. David said, "I once punished someone who said Saul was dead and thought he was bringing good news.
10. I had him killed in Ziklag.
11. Now you've killed an innocent man in his house and on his bed. Shouldn't I punish you?"
12. David told his men to kill them. They cut off their hands and feet and hung their bodies near the pool in Hebron. They buried Ishbosheth's head in Abner's tomb.

2 Samuel 5

David Becomes King Over All Israel

1. The tribes of Israel came to David and said, "We are your people.
2. Even when Saul was king, you led us in battle. God said you would be our shepherd and ruler."
3. David made an agreement with the leaders, and they made him king.
4. David was 30 years old when he became king. He ruled for 40 years.
5. He ruled Judah in Hebron for 7½ years and all Israel from Jerusalem for 33 years.

David Captures Jerusalem

6. David and his men went to Jerusalem, where the Jebusites lived. They said, "You'll never get in here—even the blind and lame can stop you!"
7. But David captured the fortress of Zion. It became the City of David.
8. David said, "Attack through the water tunnel. I hate the blind and lame." That's why people say, "The blind and lame can't enter the palace."
9. David lived in the fortress and called it the City of David. He built around it.
10. David became more powerful because God was with him.

David's Palace and Family

11. King Hiram of Tyre sent messengers with cedar wood, builders, and stone workers. They built David a palace.
12. David knew God had made him king and lifted Israel for their sake.
13. David took more wives and had more sons and daughters in Jerusalem.
14. His sons were Shammua, Shobab, Nathan, Solomon,
15. Ibhar, Elishua, Nepheg, Japhia,
16. Elishama, Eliada, and Eliphelet.

David Defeats the Philistines

17. When the Philistine's heard David was king, they came to find him. David went to his stronghold.
18. The Philistines spread out in the Valley of Rephaim.
19. David asked God, "Should I attack? Will you help me win?" God said, "Yes, go. You will win."
20. David went to Baal Perazim and defeated them. He said, "God broke through my enemies like a flood." That's why the place was named Baal Perazim.
21. The Philistines left their idols there, and David's men took them.
22. The Philistines came again to the valley.
23. David asked God again. God said, "Don't go straight at them. Circle behind and attack near the trees.
24. When you hear marching in the treetops, attack. That means I've gone ahead of you."
25. David did what God said and defeated the Philistines all the way to Gezer.

2 Samuel 6

1. David gathered 30,000 of Israel's best soldiers.
2. He and his men went to get the Ark of God from Baalah. The Ark is called by the name of the Lord, who sits on the throne above it.
3. They put the Ark on a new cart and brought it from Abinadab's house. Uzzah and Ahio were guiding the cart.
4. Ahio walked in front, and Uzzah walked beside the Ark.
5. David and the others were celebrating with all kinds of instruments.
6. When they reached the threshing floor, the oxen stumbled, and Uzzah reached out to steady the Ark.
7. God was angry. Uzzah had touched the Ark, so God killed him.
8. David was upset that God had punished Uzzah like that. He named the place Perez Uzzah.
9. David was afraid of God that day. He said, "How can I bring the Ark to me?"
10. He didn't take the Ark to his city. Instead, he put it in the house of Obed-Edom.
11. The Ark stayed there for three months, and God blessed Obed-Edom and his family.
12. Someone told David, "God has blessed Obed-Edom's house because of the Ark." So David went to bring the Ark to Jerusalem with joy.
13. After the men carrying the Ark walked six steps, David sacrificed a bull and a calf.

14. David danced with all his strength while wearing a linen robe.
15. He and everyone brought the Ark to Jerusalem with shouting and trumpets.
16. As the Ark entered the city, Saul's daughter Michal looked out the window and saw David dancing. She didn't respect him.
17. They placed the Ark in a special tent David had set up. He offered sacrifices.
18. Then he blessed the people in God's name.
19. He gave everyone bread, meat, and cakes. Then they went home.
20. When David got home, Michal said, "You acted like a fool, dancing in front of servant girls!"
21. David said, "I danced for the Lord, who chose me instead of your father."
22. "I'll be even more humble if it honors God. The servant girls you mentioned will still respect me."
23. Michal never had children after that.

2 Samuel 7

1. After David was settled in his house, and God gave him peace from his enemies,
2. He said to Nathan the prophet, "I live in a house of cedar, but God's Ark is in a tent!"
3. Nathan said, "Do whatever you have in mind. God is with you."
4. But that night, God told Nathan,
5. "Tell David: You won't build me a house.
6. I've never lived in a house since bringing Israel out of Egypt. I moved from tent to tent."
7. "I never asked anyone to build me a house."
8. "Tell David: I took you from the pasture to lead Israel.
9. I've been with you and made you famous.
10. I'll give my people a home. They won't be bothered or attacked anymore.
11. I'll give you peace. And I will build a house for you—a royal family line."
12. "When you die, I'll raise up one of your sons to rule.
13. He will build a house for me, and his kingdom will last forever.
14. I will be his father, and he will be my son. If he does wrong, I'll correct him,
15. but I won't take my love from him like I did with Saul."
16. "Your family and kingdom will last forever."
17. Nathan told David everything God said.

David's Prayer

18. David went and sat before the Lord and said, "Who am I, Lord, that you brought me this far?"
19. "You've said great things about my future family too."
20. "What more can I say? You know me completely."
21. "You've done all this because it's your will. You are great, Lord!"
22. "There is no one like you. There is no other God."
23. "You saved Israel, your people, and made them yours forever."
24. "You made Israel your people, and you became their God."
25. "Now keep your promise to me and my family forever."
26. "Then people will praise you and say, 'The Lord is God over Israel.' And my family will be strong forever."
27. "You let me pray this because you told me your plan."
28. "You are God, and your promises are true."
29. "Please bless my family so they will always serve you. Let your blessing be on us forever."

2 Samuel 8

1. David defeated the Philistines and took control of their capital.
2. He also defeated Moab and made the people lie down in rows. He spared every third row. The rest became his servants.
3. David beat Hadadezer, king of Zobah, as he tried to take control of the Euphrates River.
4. David captured 1,700 charioteers and 20,000 foot soldiers. He disabled most of the horses, keeping only enough for 100 chariots.
5. The Arameans from Damascus came to help Hadadezer, but David killed 22,000 of them.
6. He put soldiers in Aram. The Arameans became his servants and paid tribute. God helped David win wherever he went.
7. David took the gold shields from Hadadezer's officers.
8. He also took a lot of bronze from his cities.
9. When the king of Hamath heard David defeated Hadadezer,
10. he sent his son Joram to give gifts and congratulate David. Joram brought silver, gold, and bronze.
11. David gave all the silver and gold to the Lord, just like he did with the other treasures he got from other nations.
12. This included things from Edom, Moab, Ammon, Philistia, and Amalek.
13. David became famous after defeating 18,000 Edomites.
14. He put soldiers all through Edom, and they became his servants. God helped David everywhere.
15. David ruled fairly over Israel.
16. Joab led the army. Jehoshaphat kept the records.
17. Zadok and Ahimelek were priests. Seraiah was the royal secretary.
18. Benaiah led the royal guards. David's sons were his officials.

2 Samuel 9

1. David asked, "Is anyone from Saul's family still alive? I want to be kind to them for Jonathan's sake."
2. A servant named Ziba had served Saul's family. David called for him.
3. David asked, "Is anyone left from Saul's family?" Ziba said, "Jonathan has a son who is crippled."
4. David asked, "Where is he?" Ziba said, "He lives in Lo Debar with Makir."
5. So David sent for him.
6. Mephibosheth, Jonathan's son and Saul's grandson, came to David and bowed. David said, "Mephibosheth!" He said, "I'm your servant."
7. David said, "Don't be afraid. I will be kind to you for your father Jonathan. I'll give you all the land that belonged to Saul, and you'll eat at my table every day."
8. Mephibosheth bowed and said, "Why are you kind to someone like me?"
9. David told Ziba, "I've given Saul's land to his grandson.
10. You and your sons will farm it for him. But he will eat at my table." Ziba had 15 sons and 20 servants.
11. Ziba said, "I will do everything you ask." David said, "Mephibosheth will eat at my table like one of my sons."
12. Mephibosheth had a young son named Mica. Ziba's household served him.
13. Mephibosheth lived in Jerusalem and always ate at the king's table. He was crippled in both feet.

2 Samuel 10

1. After the Ammonite king died, his son Hanun became king.

2. David said, "I'll show kindness to Hanun like his father showed me." He sent men to comfort Hanun.
3. But Hanun's advisors said, "Do you think David really wants to honor your father? His men are here to spy and take over."
4. So Hanun shaved off half of each man's beard, cut off their robes at the hips, and sent them away.
5. When David heard, he told them to stay in Jericho until their beards grew back.
6. The Ammonites knew they had made David mad. So they hired 20,000 Aramean soldiers, 1,000 from the king of Maakah, and 12,000 from Tob.
7. David sent Joab and his army to fight.
8. The Ammonites lined up at the city gate. The hired Aramean soldiers stood in the field.
9. Joab saw they were trapped from both sides, so he picked the best troops to fight the Arameans.
10. He put his brother Abishai in charge of the rest to fight the Ammonites.
11. Joab said, "If the Arameans are too strong for me, come help. If the Ammonites are too strong for you, I'll help."
12. "Be brave and fight for our people and cities. May God do what He thinks is best."
13. Joab and his men attacked the Arameans, and they ran away.
14. When the Ammonites saw this, they also ran. Joab returned to Jerusalem.
15. The Arameans regrouped.
16. Hadadezer brought more troops from beyond the river. Shobach led them.
17. David heard and gathered all Israel. They crossed the Jordan and prepared to fight.
18. The Arameans ran again. David killed 700 charioteers and 40,000 foot soldiers. He also killed their commander, Shobach.
19. The kings who had helped Hadadezer made peace with Israel and served David. The Arameans were too afraid to help the Ammonites again.

2 Samuel 11

1. In the spring, when kings go to war, David sent Joab and his army to attack the Ammonites. But David stayed in Jerusalem.
2. One evening, David walked on his rooftop and saw a beautiful woman bathing.
3. He asked who she was. Someone said, "She is Bathsheba, the wife of Uriah the Hittite."
4. David sent messengers to get her. She came, and he slept with her. Then she went home.
5. She sent word to David: "I'm pregnant."
6. David sent Joab a message: "Send Uriah to me." Joab did.
7. David asked how the battle was going.
8. Then he said to Uriah, "Go home and rest." David even sent a gift.
9. But Uriah slept at the palace door with the servants.
10. When David heard, he asked, "Why didn't you go home?"
11. Uriah said, "The Ark, Israel, and Judah are in tents. My commander and soldiers are camping in the open. I won't go home and relax."
12. David said, "Stay one more day."
13. David got him drunk that evening, but Uriah still didn't go home.
14. The next morning, David sent a letter to Joab with Uriah.
15. The letter said, "Put Uriah at the front of the worst fighting. Then pull back so he's killed."
16. Joab followed the order. Uriah was placed where the battle was fiercest.

17. Uriah was killed, along with other Israelite soldiers.
18. Joab sent a report to David.
19. He told the messenger, "Tell the king everything.
20. If he gets angry and asks, 'Why did you go so close to the wall?'
21. Then say, 'Uriah the Hittite is dead.'"
22. The messenger told David everything Joab said.
23. He said, "They came out and fought us. We pushed them back to the gate.
24. Archers shot from the wall. Some of our men died. Uriah is also dead."
25. David said, "Tell Joab not to worry. These things happen in war. Keep fighting."
26. When Bathsheba heard Uriah was dead, she mourned for him.
27. After the mourning was over, David brought her to his house. She became his wife and had his son. But the Lord was not pleased with what David had done. David slept with another man's wife then had the man killed in battle.

2 Samuel 12

1. The Lord sent Nathan to David. Nathan said, "There were two men—one rich and one poor.
2. The rich man had lots of sheep and cattle.
3. The poor man had only one little lamb. He raised it like a child. It ate from his plate and drank from his cup."
4. "One day, the rich man had a guest. He didn't take one of his own animals. Instead, he took the poor man's lamb and served it as food."
5. David was very angry. He said, "That man deserves to die!
6. He must pay back four lambs for the one he took."
7. Nathan said, "You are that man. The Lord says: I made you king, saved you from Saul, gave you everything."
8. "I gave you wives, power, and more. If that wasn't enough, I would have given you even more."
9. "Why did you disobey me and kill Uriah? You took his wife!"
10. "Because of this, your family will always have trouble. You took another man's wife in secret,
11. but I will punish you in front of everyone. Someone close to you will take your wives."
12. "You sinned in secret, but I will punish you in the open."
13. David said, "I have sinned against the Lord." Nathan said, "God forgives you. You won't die.
14. But your son will die because you gave God's enemies a reason to insult Him."
15. Then Nathan left. The baby became very sick.
16. David prayed and refused to eat. He lay on the floor.
17. His servants tried to get him up, but he wouldn't eat.
18. On the seventh day, the baby died. David's servants were afraid to tell him.
19. David saw them whispering and asked, "Is the child dead?" They said, "Yes."
20. David got up, washed, changed clothes, and worshiped God. Then he ate.
21. His servants said, "You fasted while the child was alive but ate after he died?"
22. David said, "I hoped God might save him. But now he's gone, and I can't bring him back."
23. "I'll go to him someday, but he won't come back to me."
24. David comforted Bathsheba. She had another son and named him Solomon. The Lord loved him.

25. God sent word through Nathan to name him Jedidiah, which means "loved by the Lord."
26. Joab attacked the Ammonite city of Rabbah and captured part of it.
27. He told David, "Come take the final part of the city, or it will be named after me."
28. David gathered the army, attacked the city, and won.
29. He took the crown from the enemy king—it weighed 75 pounds and had gems. David wore it.
30. He took a lot of treasure.
31. He made the people work with saws, picks, and bricks. David did this in all the cities. Then he returned to Jerusalem.

2 Samuel 13

1. David's son Amnon fell in love with his half-sister Tamar, Absalom's sister.
2. He wanted her so badly that he made himself sick. She was a virgin, so he couldn't be with her.
3. Amnon had a clever friend named Jonadab.
4. Jonadab said, "Why are you so sad every day?" Amnon said, "I'm in love with Tamar."
5. Jonadab said, "Pretend you're sick. When your dad visits, ask him to send Tamar to feed you."
6. So Amnon pretended to be sick. When David came, he asked for Tamar.
7. David sent Tamar to Amnon's house to cook for him.
8. She made bread while he watched.
9. She served it, but he refused to eat. He said, "Send everyone out." Then he told Tamar, "Bring the food to my room."
10. She brought it to him.
11. He grabbed her and said, "Come sleep with me."
12. She said, "No, don't do this! That's evil in Israel!
13. You'll ruin me and yourself. Ask the king—he might let us marry."
14. But Amnon refused to listen. He forced himself on her.
15. Afterward, he hated her more than he loved her before. He told her to leave.
16. She said, "No! Sending me away is worse!" But he threw her out.
17. He told a servant, "Get her out and lock the door."
18. Tamar wore a special robe. She tore it, put ashes on her head, and left crying.
19. Her brother Absalom asked, "Did Amnon hurt you? Stay quiet for now—he's your brother."
20. Tamar lived in Absalom's house, very sad.
21. When David heard, he was angry, but he didn't punish Amnon.
22. Absalom said nothing to Amnon, but he hated him.

Absalom Gets Revenge

23. Two years later, Absalom had a big sheep-shearing event and invited all the king's sons.
24. He invited the king too. David said no.
25. Absalom said, "Then let Amnon come." David asked, "Why?"
26. Absalom insisted. So David sent Amnon and his other sons.
27. Absalom told his men, "When Amnon is drunk, kill him. Don't be afraid—I order it."
28. The servants killed Amnon. The other sons ran away.
29. A servant told David, "Absalom killed all your sons!"
30. David tore his clothes and lay on the ground.
31. But Jonadab said, "Only Amnon is dead. Absalom planned this for two years."

32. "All your other sons are safe."
33. Just then, the king's sons arrived, crying. David and his men cried too.
34. Absalom ran away to his grandfather, the king of Geshur.
35. He stayed there for three years.
36. David missed Absalom very much but didn't bring him back.

2 Samuel 14

1. Joab knew the king missed Absalom.
2. He got a wise woman from Tekoa and told her what to say.
3. She went to David and bowed.
4. She said, "Help me, king!"
5. David said, "What's wrong?" She said, "I'm a widow. My husband is dead."
6. "I had two sons. One killed the other during a fight."
7. "Now the family wants to kill the one who's left."
8. David said, "Go home. I'll take care of it."
9. She said, "Let the blame be on me."
10. David said, "If anyone bothers you, bring him to me."
11. She said, "Promise by God that my son won't be harmed." David said, "As surely as the Lord lives, not a hair on his head will fall."
12. She said, "Can I say one more thing?" David said, "Go ahead."
13. She said, "Why don't you bring your son Absalom back? You're doing the same thing I just told you about."
14. "We all die eventually. But God gives second chances."
15. "I came because people are afraid. I hope the king will help."
16. "Maybe the king will stop those trying to destroy me."
17. "You are wise like an angel of God."
18. David said, "Did Joab tell you to say this?" She said, "Yes."
19. "You are as wise as an angel."
20. David told Joab, "Bring Absalom back."
21. Joab bowed and thanked the king.
22. He went to Geshur and brought Absalom home.
23. But David said, "He must stay in his house. I don't want to see him."
24. Absalom lived in Jerusalem for two years but never saw the king.
25. Absalom was very handsome and praised for his looks.
26. He had thick hair and cut it once a year. It weighed about five pounds.
27. He had three sons and a daughter named Tamar, who was very beautiful.
28. After two years, Absalom wanted to see the king.
29. He asked Joab to help, but Joab ignored him.
30. So Absalom set Joab's field on fire to get his attention.
31. Joab asked, "Why did you burn my field?"
32. Absalom said, "I want to see the king. If I've done wrong, let him punish me."
33. Joab went to the king. David sent for Absalom. Absalom came and bowed, and the king kissed him.

2 Samuel 15

1. Absalom got a chariot, horses, and 50 men to run ahead of him.
2. He stood by the city gate and called out to anyone coming with a problem for the king.
3. He'd say, "You're right, but the king won't listen."
4. Then he'd say, "If I were the judge, I'd help you."

5. People bowed to him, but Absalom reached out and hugged them.
6. He did this to all the Israelites and won their hearts.
7. After four years, Absalom said, "Let me go to Hebron to keep a promise to God."
8. He had said, "If God brings me back to Jerusalem, I'll worship Him in Hebron."
9. David said, "Go in peace." So Absalom went.
10. He sent secret messengers through Israel, saying, "When the trumpet blows, shout, 'Absalom is king!'"
11. He took 200 men with him who didn't know what was happening.
12. He sent for Ahithophel, David's advisor. His followers grew stronger.
13. A messenger told David, "Absalom has won the hearts of Israel."
14. David said, "Let's run! If we stay, we'll all be killed."
15. His officials said, "We'll go wherever you go."
16. David left with everyone except ten concubines to care for the palace.
17. They stopped at the edge of the city.
18. All his men passed by, including the Cherethites, Pelethites, and 600 men from Gath.
19. David said to Ittai of Gath, "Go back and stay with the new king. You're new here."
20. "Why should you follow me? Go back."
21. Ittai said, "As surely as the Lord lives, I'll go wherever you go."
22. David said, "Then come." So Ittai and his family went with David.
23. Everyone cried loudly as the king crossed the Kidron Valley and headed to the wilderness.
24. Zadok and Levites brought the Ark. Abiathar offered sacrifices.
25. David said, "Take the Ark back to the city. If God is pleased, He'll bring me back."
26. "If not, let Him do what He wants."
27. David said to Zadok, "Go back in peace. You and Abiathar stay there with your sons."
28. "I'll wait at the river until I get news from you."
29. Zadok and Abiathar took the Ark back to Jerusalem.
30. David walked up the Mount of Olives, crying and barefoot. People followed, also crying.
31. Someone told David, "Ahithophel is helping Absalom." David prayed, "Lord, make his advice foolish."
32. When David reached the top, Hushai met him with torn clothes and dust on his head.
33. David said, "If you come with me, you'll slow me down.
34. But go back and say to Absalom, 'I'll serve you.' Then you can help defeat Ahithophel's advice."
35. "Zadok and Abiathar the priests will be there too. Tell them what you hear."
36. "Their sons will bring me messages."
37. So Hushai went back to Jerusalem just as Absalom arrived.

2 Samuel 16

1. When David passed the hilltop, Ziba met him with donkeys, food, and wine.
2. David asked, "Why are you here?" Ziba said, "The donkeys are for your family, bread and fruit for your men, and wine for the tired."
3. David asked, "Where is Mephibosheth?" Ziba said, "He stayed. He thinks the kingdom will come back to Saul's family."
4. David said, "Then everything that belonged to Mephibosheth is now yours." Ziba said, "Thank you, my king!"

Shimei Curses David

5. As David reached Bahurim, a man named Shimei from Saul's family came out. He cursed and threw stones at David and his men.
6. He yelled, "Get out, murderer!
7. God is punishing you for what you did to Saul's family. Now your son is taking your kingdom!"
8. Abishai said, "Why let this dog curse you? Let me kill him."
9. David said, "Leave him alone. Maybe God told him to curse me."
10. "If my own son wants to kill me, why not this man?"
11. "Maybe God will see my pain and bless me."
12. So David and his men kept walking, and Shimei followed, cursing and throwing stones.
13. They finally reached a place to rest.

Absalom Takes Over

14. Absalom and his army entered Jerusalem. Ahithophel was with him.
15. Hushai came to Absalom and said, "Long live the king!"
16. Absalom asked, "Is this how you treat your friend David?"
17. Hushai said, "I will serve the one chosen by the Lord and the people."
18. "I will serve you like I served your father."
19. Absalom said to Ahithophel, "What should I do now?"
20. He said, "Sleep with your father's concubines. Then all Israel will know you have taken his place."
21. So they set up a tent on the roof, and Absalom slept with the concubines.
22. In those days, Ahithophel's advice was considered as good as God's word.

2 Samuel 17

1. Ahithophel said, "Let me take 12,000 men and chase David tonight.
2. I'll surprise him while he's tired. Everyone will run, and I'll kill David.
3. Then I'll bring everyone back safely."
4. Absalom and his leaders liked this plan.
5. But Absalom said, "Call Hushai and hear his advice too."
6. Hushai came, and Absalom said, "This is Ahithophel's plan. What do you think?"
7. Hushai said, "That's not a good plan."
8. "You know David and his men are strong and angry like a wild bear. He won't stay with the troops—he's probably hiding in a cave."
9. "If your men lose, everyone will panic.
10. Even the bravest will be scared if the rumor spreads that David won."
11. "I suggest waiting and gathering all Israel. Then attack him together."
12. "We'll find him and crush him like dew on the ground."
13. "If he hides in a city, we'll drag the city into the valley."
14. Absalom and the others liked Hushai's advice better because God planned to defeat Ahithophel's plan.

Hushai Sends a Warning

15. Hushai told the priests, "Tell David not to spend the night at the river crossing. Cross over tonight."
16. Jonathan and Ahimaaz were hiding at En Rogel. A servant girl brought them the message.
17. But a boy saw them and told Absalom. The two ran to a house and hid in a well.
18. The woman covered the well and spread grain over it.
19. Absalom's men came and asked, "Where are the two men?" She said, "They crossed the river." They looked and left.

20. After they were gone, the men came out and ran to tell David.
21. They said, "Cross the river now!" So David and everyone crossed during the night.
22. When Ahithophel saw his plan wasn't followed, he went home and hanged himself.
23. David reached Mahanaim. Absalom crossed the Jordan with his army.
24. Absalom made Amasa his army commander.
25. They camped in Gilead.
26. When David arrived at Mahanaim, Shobi, Makir, and Barzillai brought supplies—
27. beds, bowls, clay pots, wheat, barley, flour, roasted grain, beans, and lentils—
28. honey, curds, sheep, and cheese. They said, "The people are tired, hungry, and thirsty."

2 Samuel 18

1. David counted his men and put commanders over them.
2. He divided them into three groups under Joab, Abishai, and Ittai. David said, "I'll go with you."
3. But the men said, "Don't go! If we run or die, the enemy won't care. You're worth 10,000 of us. Stay in the city and help from there."
4. David said, "I'll do what you think is best." He stood at the gate as the troops marched out.
5. He told Joab, Abishai, and Ittai, "Be gentle with Absalom for my sake." All the troops heard.
6. David's army fought Absalom's army in the forest.
7. David's men won. Twenty thousand died.
8. The battle spread everywhere. The forest killed more than the sword that day.
9. Absalom met David's men while riding his mule. His hair got caught in a tree, and he was left hanging as the mule ran away.
10. A soldier saw him and told Joab, "Absalom is hanging in a tree!"
11. Joab said, "Why didn't you kill him? I'd have given you silver and a belt!"
12. The man said, "Even for silver, I wouldn't harm the king's son. We all heard him say, 'Be gentle with Absalom.'"
13. "If I had killed him, you'd let me take the blame!"
14. Joab said, "I'm not waiting." He took three spears and stabbed Absalom in the heart.
15. Ten of Joab's men finished him off.
16. Joab blew the trumpet. The troops stopped fighting.
17. They threw Absalom's body in a pit in the forest and covered it with rocks. The Israelites ran home.
18. Absalom had built a monument to himself, saying, "I have no son to carry my name." He named it after himself.

David Hears the News

19. Ahimaaz said, "Let me run and tell the king." Joab said, "No, not today."
20. "Someone else can bring the news, since the king's son is dead."
21. Joab sent a man from Cush.
22. Ahimaaz asked again. Joab said, "Why? You won't get a reward."
23. But Ahimaaz insisted. Joab said, "Fine, go." Ahimaaz took a different route and arrived first.
24. David was waiting at the gate. A lookout saw a man running.
25. The watchman said, "Someone's coming." The king said, "If he's alone, it's good news."
26. Then the lookout saw a second runner.

27. He said, "The first one runs like Ahimaaz." David said, "He brings good news."
28. Ahimaaz said, "All is well! God gave you victory!"
29. David asked, "Is Absalom safe?" Ahimaaz said, "I saw a lot happening, but I don't know."
30. David said, "Stand here."
31. The Cushite arrived and said, "You've won!"
32. David asked, "Is Absalom safe?" The man said, "May all your enemies end up like him."
33. David was heartbroken. He cried, "My son Absalom! I wish I had died instead of you!"

2 Samuel 19

1. Everyone heard that the king was crying for Absalom.
2. The joy of victory turned into sadness.
3. The soldiers came back quietly, like they were ashamed.
4. The king cried, "My son Absalom!"
5. Joab went to the king and said, "You've made your men feel ashamed.
6. You care more about your enemies than your friends! Your army saved your life."
7. "Go speak kindly to your men, or they'll all leave you."
8. So David went to the gate, and the people came to him.

David Returns to Jerusalem

9. The tribes of Israel argued,
10. "The king saved us from our enemies. He left when Absalom took over, but now Absalom is dead. Why haven't we brought the king back?"
11. David sent word to Judah: "Why are you last to bring me back?"
12. "You're my relatives. Why delay?"
13. He told Amasa, "You'll be my new army commander."
14. This won the hearts of Judah, and they sent word to the king to return.
15. David went back and stopped at the Jordan River. Judah came to meet him.

16-17 Shimei, the man who had cursed David, came with others to ask forgiveness.

18. He begged, "Don't remember what I did."
19. Abishai said, "Shouldn't he be killed for cursing God's king?"
20. David said, "Why are you talking about killing today? No one will die."
21. "You won't die," he told Shimei.

Mephibosheth Meets David

22. Mephibosheth came to meet David. He hadn't washed or trimmed his beard since David left.
23. David asked, "Why didn't you come with me?"
24. Mephibosheth said, "Ziba tricked me and lied about me."
25. "You are like an angel to me. Do what you think is best."
26. David said, "You and Ziba will split the land."
27. Mephibosheth said, "He can have it all—I'm just glad you're safe."

Barzillai Says Goodbye

28. Barzillai, an old man, came to help David.
29. David said, "Come with me to Jerusalem. I'll take care of you."
30. Barzillai said, "I'm 80. I don't need fancy things. Let me go home and die near my family."
31. "But take my servant Chimham instead." David agreed.
32. They crossed the Jordan, and David kissed Barzillai goodbye.
33. All Israel and Judah escorted the king across the river.

34. But the Israelites complained, "Why did Judah get to bring the king back without us?"
35. The people argued loudly over the king.

2 Samuel 20

1. A man named Sheba, from Benjamin, blew a trumpet and said, "We don't want David! Go home, Israel!"
2. So the Israelites left David. But Judah stayed loyal.
3. David returned to Jerusalem and put the ten concubines in a guarded house. He took care of them but didn't visit them again.
4. David told Amasa, "Get the army in three days."
5. Amasa took too long.
6. David told Abishai, "Take the troops. Don't let Sheba escape."
7. Joab's men, the royal guards, and others went after him.
8. At Gibeon, Amasa came to meet them. Joab stabbed him with a sword.
9. Amasa died, and Joab took command.
10. A soldier stood by the body, but the men slowed down.
11. So he dragged Amasa off the road and covered him. Then everyone followed Joab.
12. They chased Sheba to a city called Abel.
13. They built a ramp and tried to break the city wall.
14. A wise woman shouted, "Talk to Joab!"
15. She asked, "Why are you trying to destroy our city?"
16. Joab said, "Sheba is hiding here. Give him to me and we'll leave."
17. She said, "His head will be thrown over the wall."
18. She told the people. They killed Sheba and threw his head out.
19. Joab blew the trumpet, and everyone went home. Joab returned to Jerusalem.
20. Joab was in charge of the army.
21. Benaiah led the royal guards. Jehoshaphat kept records.
22. Sheva was the secretary. Zadok and Abiathar were priests.
23. Ira the Jairite was David's priest.

2 Samuel 21

1. There was a famine for 3 years. David asked God why. God said, "It's because Saul killed the Gibeonites."
2. The Gibeonites weren't Israelites, but Israel had promised to protect them. Saul broke that promise.
3. David asked the Gibeonites, "What can I do to make things right?"
4. They said, "We don't want money or revenge on Israel. We want justice."
5. They said, "Saul tried to wipe us out."
6. "Give us 7 of Saul's sons so we can hang them before the Lord." David said, "Okay."
7. He spared Mephibosheth, Jonathan's son.
8. He gave them two sons of Rizpah and five sons of Saul's daughter Merab.
9. The Gibeonites killed them. They were hung during the harvest.
10. Rizpah spread a cloth on a rock and guarded the bodies. She kept animals and birds away until rain came.
11. David heard what Rizpah did.

12-13.He got the bones of Saul and Jonathan and gathered the bones of the men the Gibeonites killed.

14. They buried them in Saul's family tomb. Then, God ended the famine.

More Battles With Giants

15. The Philistines fought Israel again. David got tired.
16. A giant named Ishbi-Benob tried to kill him. But Abishai rescued David and killed the giant.
17. David's men said, "You can't fight with us anymore. We don't want to lose our king."
18. In another battle, Sibbecai killed a giant.
19. Elhanan killed Goliath's brother, who had a huge spear.
20. In another fight, a man with six fingers on each hand and foot came to fight.
21. Jonathan, David's nephew, killed him.
22. These four giants were from Gath. David and his men killed them.

2 Samuel 22

1. David sang this song to the Lord after God saved him from all his enemies and Saul:
2. "The Lord is my rock, my fortress, my protector.
3. My God is my shield and my safe place.
4. I called to God, and He saved me.
5. I was surrounded by danger.
6. Death tried to trap me.
7. I called to the Lord, and He heard me.
8. The earth shook, and smoke came from God's nose.
9. Fire came from His mouth.
10. He bent the sky and came down.
11. He flew on angels.
12. He hid in darkness.
13. Bright light flashed before Him.
14. God thundered from heaven.
15. He sent lightning and scattered enemies.
16. The sea opened when God spoke.
17. God reached down and pulled me out.
18. He saved me from strong enemies.
19. They attacked when I was weak, but God helped me.
20. He brought me to a safe place.
21. God rewarded me for doing right.
22. I followed His ways.
23. I obeyed His commands.
24. I lived right.
25. So God blessed me.
26. God is kind to the kind.
27. He is pure to the pure, and tricky to the crooked.
28. He saves the humble and brings down the proud.
29. God gives me light.
30. With Him, I can face any army.
31. God's way is perfect. His word is true.
32. Who is God except the Lord?
33. God gives me strength.
34. He makes me fast and sure.
35. He trains me for battle.
36. He protects me.
37. He makes my path smooth.
38. I chased my enemies and won.
39. I crushed them.
40. God made me strong.
41. My enemies ran.
42. They called for help, but no one came.
43. I beat them like dust.
44. God saved me and made me ruler.
45. Foreigners obey me.
46. They lose heart and run.
47. The Lord lives! He is my rock and Savior!
48. He gives me victory.
49. He saved me from my enemies.
50. I praise You, Lord!

51. You give victory to Your king and show love to David forever."

2 Samuel 23

1. These are David's last words: "God chose me and made me strong.
2. God's Spirit spoke through me.
3. God said, 'A good ruler must be fair and respect God.
4. He is like morning light after rain.'
5. God made an agreement with me that will last forever.
6. Evil people are like thorns—useless and dangerous.
7. They must be burned."

David's Best Warriors

8. These are the names of David's top warriors: First was Josheb-Basshebeth. He killed 800 men with his spear in one battle.
9. Next was Eleazar. He fought the Philistines when the others ran away.
10. He kept fighting until his hand was stuck to his sword.
11. Then came Shammah. He stood in a field of lentils while everyone else ran. He killed many Philistines.
12. God gave him a great victory.
13. One time, three of the 30 top warriors visited David during harvest. He was hiding in a cave.
14. The Philistines were in Bethlehem.
15. David said, "I wish I had water from the well in Bethlehem."
16. The three men broke through enemy lines, got the water, and brought it back. But David didn't drink it.
17. He said, "I can't drink this—it's like their blood." He poured it out to God.

More Great Warriors

18. Abishai was Joab's brother. He killed 300 men and became famous.
19. He was the leader of the 30 warriors but wasn't one of the top three.
20. Benaiah killed two great warriors from Moab. He also killed a lion and an Egyptian giant.
21. The Egyptian had a big spear, but Benaiah used only a club and still won.
22. He was just as famous as the other warriors.
23. David put him in charge of his royal guards.
24. Other top warriors included Asahel (Joab's brother), Elhanan,
25. Shammah, Helez,
26. Ira, Abiezer,
27. Mebunnai, Zalmon,
28. Maharai, Heled,
29. Ittai, Benaiah,
30. Hiddai, Abialbon,
31. Azmaveth, Eliahba,
32. Jonathan, Shammah's brother,
33. Ahiam, Eliphelet,
34. Eliam, Hezro,
35. Paarai, Igal,
36. Bani, Zelek,
37. Naharai, Ira,
38. Gareb, and Uriah the Hittite. In total, there were 37 warriors.

2 Samuel 24

1. God was angry with Israel again. David decide to count the people without God's permission.
2. David told Joab, "Count the people in all of Israel and Judah."
3. Joab said, "Why do this? May God give you many people, but why count them?"
4. But the king insisted. Joab and the army officers went out.
5. They traveled through all the land.

6. They went to many cities and regions.
7. After 9 months and 20 days, they returned to Jerusalem.
8. Joab said, "There are 800,000 men in Israel and 500,000 in Judah."
9. David felt guilty. He said, "Lord, I sinned. Please forgive me."
10. The next morning, God sent the prophet Gad.
11. Gad told David, "Choose one punishment:
12. Three years of famine, three months of fleeing enemies, or three days of plague."
13. David said, "Let God decide. He is merciful."
14. So God sent a plague. 70,000 people died.
15. The angel was about to destroy Jerusalem, but God stopped him.
16. The angel stood at the threshing floor of Araunah.
17. David said, "Punish me and my family, not the people."
18. Gad told David, "Build an altar on Araunah's threshing floor."
19. David obeyed.
20. Araunah saw David coming and bowed.
21. David said, "I need to buy your threshing floor to build an altar so the plague will stop."
22. Araunah said, "Take it! Use my oxen and wood for the altar."
23. He gave it all to the king.
24. But David said, "I will not offer to God something that cost me nothing." He paid 50 silver coins.
25. He built the altar and gave offerings. God answered his prayer, and the plague stopped.

– 1 Kings –

Solomon builds the Temple, but after his reign, the kingdom splits into Israel and Judah.

1 Kings 1

1. King David was old and always cold, no matter how many blankets he had.
2. His servants said, "Let's find a young woman to take care of you and keep you warm."
3. They searched for a beautiful young woman and found Abishag from Shunem.
4. She cared for the king and kept him warm, but they didn't sleep together.

Adonijah Tries to Become King

5. Adonijah, David's son, said, "I will be king!" He got chariots, horses, and 50 men to run in front of him.
6. David never corrected Adonijah. Adonijah was very handsome and born after Absalom.
7. He asked Joab and Abiathar the priest to help him, and they agreed.
8. But Zadok the priest, Benaiah, Nathan the prophet, Shimei, Rei, and David's guards did not join him.
9. Adonijah invited his brothers and officials to a feast near En-rogel. He killed many animals for a sacrifice.
10. But he didn't invite Nathan, Benaiah, David's guards, or Solomon.
11. Nathan went to Bathsheba, Solomon's mom, and said, "Did you hear Adonijah made himself king, and David doesn't know?"
12. "If you want to save your life and Solomon's, follow my plan."
13. "Go to David and say, 'You promised that Solomon would be king. Why is Adonijah king?'"
14. "While you're talking, I'll come in and confirm it."
15. Bathsheba went to David. He was in bed, and Abishag was caring for him.

16. Bathsheba bowed. David said, "What do you want?"
17. She said, "You promised that our son Solomon would be king."
18. "But Adonijah made himself king, and you didn't know."
19. "He had a big feast and invited the army and priests. But not Solomon."
20. "All Israel is waiting to hear who the next king is."
21. "If you don't act, Solomon and I will be treated like criminals when you die."
22. While she was talking, Nathan arrived.
23. They told the king, and Nathan came in and bowed.
24. He said, "Did you make Adonijah king?"
25. "He had a big feast and the people are shouting, 'Long live King Adonijah!'"
26. "But he didn't invite me, Zadok, Benaiah, or Solomon."
27. "Did you approve this without telling us who would be king?"

Solomon Becomes King

28. David said, "Call Bathsheba." She came in and stood before him.
29. David said, "As surely as the Lord lives,
30. Solomon will be king today, just like I promised."
31. Bathsheba bowed and said, "May the king live forever!"
32. David said, "Call Zadok, Nathan, and Benaiah." They came.
33. David said, "Put Solomon on my mule and take him to Gihon."
34. "Anoint him king there. Blow the trumpet and shout, 'Long live King Solomon!'"
35. "Bring him back, and he will sit on my throne and rule Israel and Judah."
36. Benaiah said, "Amen! May the Lord confirm it!"
37. "May Solomon's reign be even greater than yours."
38. So Zadok, Nathan, Benaiah, and the guards took Solomon on David's mule to Gihon.
39. Zadok anointed Solomon with oil from the sacred tent. They blew the trumpet, and everyone shouted, "Long live King Solomon!"
40. They marched back celebrating with flutes. The ground shook from the noise.
41. Adonijah and his guests heard the noise as they finished eating. Joab asked, "What's happening in the city?"
42. Jonathan, son of Abiathar, arrived. Adonijah said, "You must have good news."
43. Jonathan said, "No! King David made Solomon king."
44. "Zadok, Nathan, and Benaiah went with him. He rode the king's mule."
45. "They anointed him king at Gihon. Now everyone is celebrating."
46. "Solomon sits on the royal throne."
47. "The king's officials blessed David and said, 'May Solomon's reign be even greater!' David bowed from his bed."
48. "He said, 'Praise the Lord! I got to see my son become king today.'"
49. Adonijah's guests were terrified and ran away.
50. Adonijah was scared of Solomon. He ran to the altar and held its corners.
51. Solomon was told, "Adonijah is scared and wants you to promise not to kill him."
52. Solomon said, "If he behaves, he will live. But if he does wrong, he will die."
53. Solomon sent for him. Adonijah came and bowed. Solomon said, "Go home."

1 Kings 2

1. David knew he was about to die. He told Solomon,

2. "I am going to die soon. Be strong and act like a man.
3. Obey God's commands. Do what He says. Then you will succeed in everything."
4. "God promised, 'If your sons follow me, one of them will always be king.'"
5. "You know Joab killed two army commanders, Abner and Amasa. He acted like it was war, but it wasn't.
6. Be wise. Don't let him die in peace."
7. "Be kind to Barzillai's sons. Let them eat at your table. They helped me when I ran from Absalom."
8. "Shimei cursed me when I ran away. I swore not to kill him.
9. But now you must deal with him. Don't let him die peacefully."

David Dies—Solomon Rules

10. David died and was buried in Jerusalem.
11. He was king for 40 years—7 in Hebron and 33 in Jerusalem.
12. Solomon became king, and his rule was strong.

Solomon Handles His Enemies

13. Adonijah asked Bathsheba to speak to Solomon for him.
14. She said, "Go ahead."
15. He said, "I thought I'd be king, but God chose Solomon.
16. Please ask Solomon to let me marry Abishag."
17. Bathsheba agreed to speak to Solomon.
18. She went to him, and he stood to greet her and had a seat brought for her.
19. She said, "Adonijah has one request: give him Abishag as a wife."
20. Solomon said, "Why not give him the kingdom too? He tried to take the throne."
21. Solomon swore, "God is my witness—Adonijah will die today."
22. He sent Benaiah to kill him.

Abiathar Removed

23. Solomon told Abiathar the priest, "Go to your land. You deserve death, but I won't kill you because you carried the Ark and suffered with my father."
24. So Solomon removed Abiathar, just like God had said would happen to Eli's family.

Joab Is Killed

25. Joab heard this and ran to the altar for safety.
26. Solomon was told, "Joab's at the altar."
27. Solomon sent Benaiah to kill him.
28. Joab said, "I will die here."
29. Solomon said, "Do as he says."
30. Benaiah killed Joab and buried him.
31. This removed the guilt of Joab's murders from David's family.
32. Joab killed innocent men. Now God has punished him.
33. David's family will have peace.
34. Solomon made Benaiah commander of the army.
35. He made Zadok the new priest.

Shimei Breaks His Promise

36. Solomon told Shimei, "Build a house in Jerusalem. Don't leave or you'll die."
37. Shimei agreed.
38. But three years later, two of his servants ran away. Shimei left Jerusalem to find them.
39. Solomon heard and called for him.
40. He said, "You swore you'd stay. Why did you leave?"
41. "You disobeyed and now you will die."
42. Solomon told Benaiah to kill Shimei.
43. So the kingdom was firmly in Solomon's hands.

1 Kings 3

1. Solomon made a peace deal with Egypt and married Pharaoh's daughter.

2. The people were still offering sacrifices at hilltop altars because the temple wasn't built yet.
3. Solomon loved God and followed David's ways, except he still used the hill altars.
4. He went to Gibeon to offer 1,000 sacrifices.
5. That night, God appeared in a dream and said, "Ask for anything."
6. Solomon said, "You were kind to my father. He was honest and faithful.
7. Now I'm king, but I'm young and don't know what to do.
8. I lead your people, and they are too many to count.
9. Give me wisdom to know right from wrong."
10. God was happy Solomon asked for this.
11. God said, "You didn't ask for riches or long life. You asked for wisdom.
12. I will give you wisdom like no one before or after you.
13. I will also give you wealth and honor.
14. If you follow me, I'll give you a long life."
15. Solomon woke up and went to Jerusalem to worship.

Solomon Shows Wisdom

16. Two women came to Solomon. One said,
17. "We live in the same house. I had a baby, then she did.
18. One night, her baby died. She switched babies while I slept.
19. In the morning, I saw the dead baby wasn't mine."
20. The other woman said, "No! The living baby is mine."
21. They argued in front of the king.
22. Solomon said, "Bring me a sword."
23. He said, "Cut the baby in two. Give half to each."
24. The real mother cried, "No! Let her have him, just don't kill him."
25. The other woman said, "Cut him in two."
26. Solomon said, "Give the baby to the first woman. She is the real mother."
27. Everyone heard about it and saw that Solomon had God's wisdom.

1 Kings 4

1. Solomon ruled over all Israel.
2. These were his top officials: Azariah was priest.
3. Elihoreph and Ahijah kept records. Jehoshaphat was historian.
4. Benaiah led the army. Zadok and Abiathar were priests.
5. Azariah managed the governors. Zabud was the king's advisor.
6. Ahishar handled the palace. Adoniram was in charge of workers.
7. Solomon had 12 governors. Each supplied the palace for one month a year.
8. These were their areas:
9. Ben-Hur (Ephraim), Ben-Deker (Makaz, Shaalbim),
10. Ben-Hesed (Arubboth), Ben-Abinadab (Naphath-Dor),
11. Baana (Taanach and Megiddo),
12. Ben-Geber (Ramoth-Gilead),
13. Ahinadab (Mahanaim),
14. Ahimaaz (Naphtali),
15. Baana (Asher and Aloth),
16. Jehoshaphat (Issachar),
17. Shimei (Benjamin),
18. Geber (Gilead).
19. These men brought food to the king's court.
20. Judah and Israel were so many they couldn't be counted. They were happy and well fed.

21. Solomon ruled all the land from the Euphrates to Egypt.
22. Each day, Solomon's palace used: 150 bushels of flour, 300 of meal,
23. 10 cattle, 20 pasture cattle, 100 sheep, plus deer, gazelles, and birds.
24. Solomon ruled all nearby kingdoms and had peace on every side.
25. The people lived safely under their vines and fig trees.
26. Solomon had 4,000 stalls for chariot horses and 12,000 horses.
27. The governors provided food each month.
28. They brought barley and straw for the horses.
29. God gave Solomon great wisdom—more than anyone.
30. His wisdom was greater than all the men of the East and Egypt.
31. He was wiser than anyone, including Ethan and Heman.
32. He wrote 3,000 proverbs and 1,005 songs.
33. He knew all about plants, animals, birds, and fish.
34. People from every nation came to hear Solomon's wisdom.

1 Kings 5

1. King Hiram of Tyre heard Solomon became king, and he sent messengers to him. He had always been friends with David.
2. Solomon sent back a message:
3. "You know my father couldn't build God's temple because of constant wars.
4. Now God has given me peace, and I'm ready to build the temple.
5. God promised David his son would build it. That's me."
6. "Please send cedar trees from Lebanon. My men will help your workers. I'll pay them whatever you ask."
7. Hiram was happy and said, "Praise God for giving David a wise son!"
8. Hiram agreed to send cedar and pine logs.
9. He said, "My workers will cut the logs and float them by sea to wherever you want. You can take them from there."
10. Solomon gave Hiram 100,000 bushels of wheat and 110,000 gallons of oil every year.
11. God gave Solomon wisdom, and there was peace between the two kings.
12. They made a treaty.
13. Solomon forced 30,000 men to work.
14. He sent 10,000 per month to Lebanon in shifts—one month there, two months home.
15. He had 70,000 workers and 80,000 stone cutters in the mountains.
16. He had 3,300 supervisors.
17. The workers cut huge stones for the temple foundation.
18. Solomon's and Hiram's builders and men from Gebal worked together and prepared all the materials.

1 Kings 6

1. Solomon began building the Lord's temple 480 years after Israel left Egypt. It was the 4th year of his reign.
2. The temple was 90 feet long, 30 feet wide, and 45 feet high.
3. The front porch was 30 feet wide and 15 feet deep.
4. He put narrow windows in the temple.
5. He built side rooms all around it.
6. The bottom rooms were 7½ feet wide, the middle were 9 feet, and the top were 10½ feet.
7. The stones were cut at the quarry, so no hammers or tools were heard at the temple site.

8. The entrance to the bottom rooms was on the south side. Stairs led up to the higher levels.
9. He built the roof with cedar beams and boards.
10. He built the side rooms and attached them to the temple.
11. God said to Solomon:
12. "If you follow me and obey my laws, I will keep my promise to your father David.
13. I will live among my people and never leave them."
14. Solomon finished building the temple.
15. Inside, he lined the walls and ceiling with cedar wood. The floor was covered in pine.
16. He built a 30-foot-long inner room at the back—it was the Most Holy Place.
17. The main room in front of it was 60 feet long.
18. Everything was covered in cedar with no stone showing.
19. He prepared the Most Holy Place to hold the Ark of the Covenant.
20. The inner room was 30 feet long, wide, and high. He covered it in pure gold.
21. He also covered the altar in cedar and gold.
22. Everything was gold—even the altar inside the Most Holy Place.
23. He made two olive wood cherub angels, each 15 feet tall, for the inner room.
24. Each wing was 7½ feet, 15 feet across total.
25. Both angels were the same size.
26. They were both 15 feet tall.
27. They were placed in the inner room, side by side, with wings touching wall to wall.
28. He covered them in gold.
29. All the temple walls had carvings of angels, palm trees, and flowers.
30. Even the floor was covered in gold.

31-32. The inner room doors were made of olive wood and carved with angels and flowers. They were covered in gold.

33. The outer doors were made of pine with similar carvings and gold.
34. They had two folding panels.
35. The carvings were all over, and everything was gold.
36. He built an inner courtyard with three layers of stone and one layer of cedar beams.
37. He started building in the fourth year of his reign.
38. He finished in the eleventh year, after seven years of work.

1 Kings 7

1. Solomon took 13 years to build his palace.
2. He built the Palace of the Forest of Lebanon. It was 150 feet long, 75 feet wide, and 45 feet high.
3. It had cedar beams on 45 pillars, 15 in each row.
4. There were three rows of windows.
5. The doors and frames matched the windows.
6. He built a hall with columns, 75 feet long and 45 feet wide, with a roof.
7. He built a throne room to judge people. It was lined with cedar.
8. His own living quarters were behind that hall and similar in design.
9. All the buildings were made with huge stones, cut and polished, from foundation to roof.
10. The foundation had large stones up to 15 feet long.
11. The upper stones were also large and expensive.
12. The palace courtyard matched the temple courtyard with three layers of cut stone and one of cedar.

Hiram Makes Bronze Items

13. Solomon brought Hiram from Tyre.
14. Hiram's mother was from the tribe of Naphtali. His father was from Tyre. Hiram was very skilled in bronze work.
15. He made two bronze pillars, each 27 feet tall and 18 feet around.
16. He made bronze capitals (tops) 7½ feet tall for each pillar.
17. The tops had nets of chains and decorations.
18. There were 200 pomegranates in rows around the capitals.
19. The tops were shaped like lilies.
20. The decorations were on top of the pillars.
21. He placed the pillars at the temple entrance—one on the right named Jakin, and one on the left named Boaz.
22. The tops looked like lilies. That finished the pillars.

More Bronze Work

23. He made a huge bronze bowl, called the Sea. It was 15 feet wide, 7½ feet tall, and 45 feet around.
24. It had two rows of decorations.
25. It stood on 12 bronze bulls—3 facing each direction.
26. The bowl was 3 inches thick and held 11,000 gallons of water.
27. He made 10 bronze stands with wheels. Each was 6 feet long, wide, and high.

28-29 The sides had frames with carvings of lions, bulls, and angels.

30. Each had four wheels and bronze axles.
31. The top opening was 18 inches wide.
32. The wheels were 27 inches tall.
33. They were made like chariot wheels.
34. There were handles at the corners.
35. The top was 18 inches tall, and the sides were decorated.
36. Hiram carved angels, lions, and palm trees into the metal.
37. All 10 stands were made the same.
38. He made 10 bronze basins, each holding 220 gallons. They sat on the stands.
39. Five were placed on the south side of the temple, five on the north. The big bronze bowl was placed in the southeast corner.
40. Hiram also made pots, shovels, and bowls. He finished all the bronze work. 41–45. He made everything: the pillars, bowls, stands, decorations, and all temple items.
41. He made them in the plain of the Jordan using clay molds.
42. Solomon didn't weigh the bronze—it was too much to measure.
43. He also made all the gold items for the temple: the altar, table,
44. lampstands, flowers, lamps, and tongs.
45. He made bowls, wick trimmers, sprinkling dishes, pans, and firepans—all pure gold.
46. When Solomon finished, he stored everything his father had given for the temple's treasures.

1 Kings 8

1. Solomon called all the leaders of Israel to bring the Ark to the temple.
2. Everyone came in the seventh month during the festival.
3. The priests carried the Ark,
4. along with the sacred tent and all holy items.
5. Solomon and the people sacrificed many animals.
6. The priests put the Ark in the Most Holy Place under the wings of the angels.
7. The angels' wings spread over the Ark and its poles.

8. The poles were so long they could be seen from the Holy Place.
9. Inside the Ark were the two stone tablets Moses put there.
10. When the priests left, a cloud filled the temple.
11. The priests couldn't work because God's glory filled the temple.
12. Solomon said, "God said He would live in a dark cloud.
13. But I've built a beautiful house for You to live in forever."
14. Solomon turned to bless the people.
15. He said, "Praise God! He kept His promise to my father David."
16. "God said, 'I didn't choose a city for a temple before, but I chose David to lead Israel.'"
17. "David wanted to build a temple,
18. but God said, 'You wanted to, and that's good,
19. but your son will build it.'"
20. "Now that has happened. I've built the temple,
21. and placed the Ark of the Covenant inside."

Solomon's Prayer

22. Solomon stood and lifted his hands toward heaven.
23. He prayed, "God, there is no one like You. You keep Your promises.
24. You kept Your promise to David.
25. Now keep Your promise to always have one of his sons rule if they obey You.
26. Let Your word come true."
27. "But how can You live here? Even the heavens can't hold You."
28. "Still, please hear my prayer.
29. Keep Your eyes on this temple. Listen when we pray here.
30. Hear us when we pray toward this place. Forgive us."
31. "If someone is wronged and swears an oath,
32. judge fairly between guilty and innocent."
33. "If we lose in battle because we sinned, forgive us when we turn back and pray here."
34. "Hear from heaven and forgive us."
35. "If there's no rain because we sinned, and we pray toward this temple, forgive us and send rain."
36. "Teach us to live right."
37. "If there's famine, plague, or enemy attacks,
38. hear our prayers and help each person.
39. You know every heart."
40. "Then people will respect and follow You."
41. "When foreigners come to pray,
42. because they heard of Your power,
43. hear them and help them so all people will know You."

44-45. "If we go to war and pray toward this temple, hear our prayers and help us."

46. "If we sin and are taken captive,

47-48. and we are sorry and pray toward this temple,

49. then hear and forgive us.
50. Forgive the people. Help them with their enemies."
51. "We are Your people, whom You brought out of Egypt."
52. "Please listen to our prayers."
53. "You chose us from all nations."

Solomon Blesses the People

54. Solomon ended his prayer and blessed the people.
55. He said,
56. "Praise God! He gave rest to His people and kept His promises.
57. May He stay with us and never leave.

58. May He help us follow Him.
59. May He hear our prayers day and night.
60. Then everyone will know He is the only God.
61. Be faithful and follow Him."

Sacrifices and Celebration

62. Solomon and the people gave sacrifices.
63. They gave 22,000 cattle and 120,000 sheep.
64. Solomon made the temple courtyard holy.
65. They celebrated for 14 days.
66. On the 15th day, Solomon sent the people home happy and thankful.

1 Kings 9

1. After Solomon finished the temple and his palace,
2. God appeared to him again.
3. God said, "I heard your prayer. I chose this temple.
4. If you obey Me like David, I'll keep My promise.
5. One of your sons will always be king."
6. "But if you or your sons turn away,
7. I will destroy this temple. People will mock it.
8. They'll ask, 'Why did this happen?'
9. The answer will be, 'They left God and worshiped other gods.'"

Solomon's Agreement with Hiram

10. After 20 years of building the temple and palace,
11. Solomon gave Hiram 20 towns as payment.
12. Hiram visited them and was not pleased.
13. He said, "What kind of towns are these?"
14. But he still gave Solomon gold.

Solomon's Work Projects

15. Solomon used forced labor for the temple, palace, and walls of Jerusalem.
16. Pharaoh had attacked Gezer and given it to Solomon as a wedding gift.

17-18. Solomon rebuilt Gezer and other cities.

19. He built cities for storage and chariots.

20-21. He made non-Israelite people do hard labor.

22. Israelites were soldiers and leaders.
23. There were 550 supervisors.
24. Pharaoh's daughter moved into her palace.
25. Solomon offered sacrifices three times a year.

26-27. He also built ships and had Hiram's men help him sail them.

28. They brought back 31 tons of gold.

1 Kings 10

1. The Queen of Sheba heard about Solomon and came to test him with hard questions.
2. She brought spices, gold, and jewels. She asked him everything on her mind.
3. Solomon answered all her questions.
4. She was amazed by his wisdom, palace, and servants.
5. She said, "Everything I heard is true!
6. But I didn't believe it until I saw it myself.
7. You're even wiser than I was told.
8. Your people are lucky to hear your wisdom every day.
9. Praise God for putting you here to rule fairly."
10. She gave Solomon gold, spices, and jewels. No one ever gave so many spices again.
11. Hiram's ships also brought gold, wood, and jewels.

12. Solomon used the wood for the temple and instruments.
13. Solomon gave the Queen whatever she wanted. Then she went home.

Solomon's Wealth

14. Solomon received 25 tons of gold every year,
15. not counting what traders and kings gave him.
16. He made 200 large shields of gold,
17. and 300 smaller ones.
18. He made a huge throne of ivory covered in gold.

19-20. It had six steps and lion statues.

21. Everything in his palace was gold. Silver was not valuable.
22. His ships brought gold, silver, ivory, apes, and peacocks.
23. Solomon was the richest and wisest king on earth.
24. Kings from everywhere came to hear his wisdom.
25. They brought silver, gold, clothes, weapons, spices, horses, and mules every year.
26. Solomon had 1,400 chariots and 12,000 horses.
27. Silver was as common as stones in Jerusalem.
28. Horses were imported from Egypt.
29. Chariots and horses were also sold to other kings.

1 Kings 11

1. Solomon loved many foreign women, including Moabite, Ammonite, Edomite, Sidonian, and Hittite women who worshipped other gods.
2. God had warned Israel, "Don't marry them. They will turn your heart to their gods." But Solomon loved them anyway.
3. He had 700 wives and 300 concubines. They turned his heart away.
4. When Solomon was old, they made him follow other gods. He was not fully loyal to God like David was.
5. He worshiped Astarte and Milcom.
6. Solomon did evil. He didn't follow God completely.
7. He even built altars for Chemosh and Molech.
8. He did the same for his other wives, who burned incense and sacrificed to their gods.
9. God was angry. He had appeared to Solomon twice
10. and warned him not to follow other gods. But Solomon disobeyed.
11. So God said, "Because you've done this, I will take the kingdom from you and give it to someone else.
12. But not while you live—for the sake of David, I'll take it from your son.
13. I won't take the whole kingdom. I'll leave one tribe for David's sake and for Jerusalem."

Enemies Rise Against Solomon

14. God raised up Hadad the Edomite to be Solomon's enemy.
15. When David fought Edom, Joab killed all the men.
16. Joab stayed there for 6 months.
17. But Hadad escaped to Egypt.
18. Pharaoh gave him land and food.
19. He liked Hadad and even gave him a wife from his own family.
20. She had a son named Genubath.
21. When Hadad heard David and Joab were dead, he wanted to go back to Edom.
22. Pharaoh asked, "Why go back?" Hadad said, "Let me go."

Another Enemy: Rezon

23. God also raised up Rezon, another enemy.
24. He led a gang and ruled Damascus.

25. He hated Israel all through Solomon's reign.

Jeroboam Rebels

26. Jeroboam was one of Solomon's officials. He was strong and hardworking.
27. Solomon gave him charge of workers from the tribe of Joseph.
28. One day the prophet Ahijah met him outside.
29. He tore his own cloak into 12 pieces.
30. He said, "Take 10 pieces. God says, 'I am taking 10 tribes from Solomon.
31. I'll give them to you. He can keep one for David's sake.'
32. 'Solomon has turned away and worshiped other gods.'
33. 'But if you obey Me, I will be with you and give you a lasting kingdom.'"
34. "I won't take it from Solomon, but from his son."
35. Solomon tried to kill Jeroboam, but he ran to Egypt.
36. He stayed there until Solomon died.
37. The rest of Solomon's story is written in the Book of the Acts of Solomon.
38. Solomon ruled for 40 years.
39. He died and was buried in Jerusalem. His son Rehoboam became king.

1 Kings 12

1. Rehoboam went to Shechem. Everyone came to make him king.
2. Jeroboam heard and came back from Egypt.
3. The people said to Rehoboam,
4. "Your father made life hard. Lighten our load, and we'll serve you."
5. Rehoboam said, "Come back in three days."
6. He asked the older men for advice. They said,
7. "Be kind, and the people will serve you forever."
8. But he ignored them and asked his young friends.
9. They said,
10. "Tell them, 'My little finger is thicker than my father's waist.
11. My father was hard, but I'll be harder. I'll punish you even more.'"
12. Jeroboam and the people came back.
13. Rehoboam was harsh and rejected the wise advice.
14. He said, "My father was tough. I'll be tougher."
15. This was God's plan to carry out what He told Jeroboam.
16. The people of Israel said, "Forget David! Let's go home!"
17. Only Judah stayed with Rehoboam.
18. Rehoboam sent Adoniram to collect taxes, but Israel stoned him.
19. Rehoboam ran back to Jerusalem.
20. The people made Jeroboam king.
21. Rehoboam gathered Judah and Benjamin to fight Israel.
22. But God told Shemaiah the prophet,
23. "Tell Rehoboam: Don't fight your brothers. Go home."
24. They listened and went home.

Jeroboam Leads Israel

25. Jeroboam ruled from Shechem, then built up Penuel.

26-27. He thought, "If the people keep going to Jerusalem, they'll go back to Rehoboam."

28. So he made two gold calves and said, "These are your gods who brought you out of Egypt."
29. He put one in Bethel and the other in Dan.
30. This was a big sin. People worshiped the calves.

31. He built temples on hills and chose priests who weren't Levites.
32. He created a new festival on the 15th day of the 8th month.
33. He made sacrifices in Bethel and copied what happened in Judah.

1 Kings 13

1. A prophet from Judah came to Bethel with a message from God.
2. He shouted, "A son named Josiah will destroy these altars!"
3. He said, "This altar will break apart. Ashes will spill out."
4. King Jeroboam heard and pointed at the prophet, saying, "Grab him!"
5. But the king's hand froze, and he couldn't pull it back.
6. The altar split, and ashes spilled out—just like the prophet said.
7. Jeroboam begged, "Please pray for me." The prophet did, and the king's hand was healed.
8. The king said, "Come eat with me."
9. But the prophet said, "No. God told me not to eat or drink here or go back the way I came."
10. So he left another way.

The Old Prophet's Trick

11. An old prophet in Bethel heard what happened.
12. His sons told him, and he went after the man of God.
13. He found him sitting under a tree and said, "Come eat with me."
14. The man said, "God told me not to eat or drink here."
15. The old prophet lied and said, "God told me to bring you back."
16. So the man of God went back and ate with him.
17. While they were eating, God gave the old prophet a real message.
18. He said, "You disobeyed God. You won't be buried in your family tomb."
19. After eating, the man left.
20. A lion attacked and killed him. His body lay by the road.
21. The lion and the donkey stood next to it.
22. People saw it and told the old prophet.
23. He went and found the body, the lion, and the donkey.
24. He put the body on the donkey and took it home.
25. He cried and said, "He disobeyed God."
26. He buried him and said, "When I die, bury me next to him.
27. What he said from God will come true."
28. But Jeroboam didn't change. He kept making priests for the hill altars.
29. This sin led to the downfall of his kingdom.

1 Kings 14

1. Jeroboam's son Abijah got sick.
2. Jeroboam told his wife, "Put on a disguise and go to the prophet Ahijah in Shiloh."
3. "Bring ten loaves of bread, cakes, and honey. Ask him what will happen to our son."
4. She went to Ahijah's house. He was old and blind.
5. But God told him, "Jeroboam's wife is coming in disguise. She'll ask about her son."
6. When she came in, Ahijah said, "Come in, Jeroboam's wife. Why are you pretending?"
7. "I have bad news.
8. God made Jeroboam king but he has done more evil than anyone before him."

9. "He turned away from God and made idols."

10. "So God will punish his family. All the males will die."

11. "Dogs will eat those who die in the city. Birds will eat those who die in the country."

12. "Your son will die when you get home."

13. "He's the only good one in your family, so God will let him be buried."

14. "God will raise up a new king to destroy your family."

15. "Israel will be punished like a reed blowing in the water."

16. "This is because of Jeroboam's sin."

17. Jeroboam's wife went home. As she walked in the door, her son died.

18. They buried him, just like God said.

19. The rest of Jeroboam's story is written in the Book of the Kings of Israel.

20. He ruled 22 years and was buried. His son Nadab became king.

Rehoboam Rules in Judah

21. Rehoboam was 41 years old when he became king. He ruled Judah for 17 years.

22. Judah did evil and made God angry.

23. They built altars and idols.

24. There were male shrine prostitutes in the land. They followed the evil ways of the nations God had removed.

25. In Rehoboam's 5th year, King Shishak of Egypt attacked Jerusalem.

26. He took all the treasures from the temple and palace, including the gold shields.

27. Rehoboam made bronze shields to replace them.

28. Guards carried them when he went to the temple.

29. The rest of Rehoboam's story is written in the Book of the Kings of Judah.

30. There was war between Rehoboam and Jeroboam the whole time.

31. Rehoboam died and was buried. His son Abijah became king.

1 Kings 15

1. In Jeroboam's 18th year, Abijah became king of Judah.

2. He ruled for 3 years.

3. He did wrong like his father. He wasn't fully faithful to God.

4. But God kept Jerusalem safe for David's sake.

5. David obeyed God in everything, except in the case of Uriah.

6. There was war between Abijah and Jeroboam.

7. The rest of Abijah's story is written in the Book of the Kings of Judah.

8. He died, and his son Asa became king.

King Asa of Judah

9. In Jeroboam's 20th year, Asa became king of Judah.

10. He ruled 41 years.

11. Asa did what was right like David.

12. He removed shrine prostitutes and idols.

13. He removed his grandmother as queen because she made an idol. He destroyed it.

14. Asa didn't remove all the high places, but he was faithful to God.

15. He brought silver and gold to the temple.

16. Asa and Baasha (king of Israel) were always at war.

17. Baasha blocked Judah's border.

18. Asa took gold and silver from the temple and palace and sent it to Ben-Hadad of Aram.

19. He said, "Break your treaty with Baasha and help me."

20. Ben-Hadad agreed and attacked Israel's cities.
21. Baasha stopped building and left.
22. Asa made Judah take the building materials and use them to build Geba and Mizpah.
23. The rest of Asa's story is in the Book of the Kings of Judah. He had foot problems in old age.
24. Asa died and was buried. His son Jehoshaphat became king.

Nadab Rules Israel

25. In Asa's 2nd year, Nadab (Jeroboam's son) became king of Israel.
26. He ruled 2 years and did evil like his father.
27. Baasha killed him and became king.
28. He killed Nadab and Jeroboam's whole family.
29. This fulfilled God's promise to destroy Jeroboam's family.
30. Jeroboam sinned and led Israel into sin.
31. The rest of Nadab's story is in the Book of the Kings of Israel.
32. There was war between Asa and Baasha.
33. In Asa's 3rd year, Baasha became king and ruled Israel 24 years.
34. He did evil like Jeroboam.

1 Kings 16

1. God sent Jehu the prophet to speak against Baasha:
2. "I made you king, but you sinned like Jeroboam and led the people into sin.
3. So I will destroy your family."
4. "Dogs will eat those who die in the city. Birds will eat those who die in the fields."
5. The rest of Baasha's story is in the Book of the Kings of Israel.
6. He died, and his son Elah became king.
7. God's message through Jehu came true because of Baasha's evil.

Elah and Zimri

8. In Asa's 26th year, Elah became king and ruled Israel for 2 years.
9. His servant Zimri, a commander, plotted against him.
10. While Elah was drunk, Zimri killed him.
11. Zimri became king and killed all of Baasha's family.
12. This fulfilled God's warning.
13. Baasha sinned and made Israel sin.
14. The rest of Elah's story is in the Book of the Kings of Israel.

Zimri's Short Rule

15. In Asa's 27th year, Zimri ruled for only 7 days.
16. The army heard he had killed the king and made Omri king.
17. Omri's army went to attack Zimri.
18. Zimri saw he would lose, so he set fire to the palace and died.
19. He died because of his sins.
20. The rest of his story is in the Book of the Kings of Israel.

Omri Becomes King

21. Half the people followed Omri. The other half followed Tibni.
22. Omri's side won. Tibni died, and Omri became king.
23. He ruled for 12 years.
24. He bought a hill and built the city of Samaria.
25. Omri did evil, worse than any king before him.
26. He followed Jeroboam's sins and led Israel to do the same.
27. The rest of Omri's story is in the Book of the Kings of Israel.
28. He died, and his son Ahab became king.

King Ahab of Israel

29. In Asa's 38th year, Ahab became king of Israel. He ruled 22 years.

30. Ahab did more evil than any king before him.

31. He married Jezebel and worshiped Baal.

32. He built a temple and altar for Baal.

33. He made an idol and angered God more than any king before him.

34. During Ahab's time, Hiel rebuilt Jericho. He lost his oldest and youngest sons doing it, just as God had said.

1 Kings 17

1. Elijah said to Ahab, "There won't be rain for years—only when I say so."

2. God told Elijah,

3. "Go hide near the Kerith Brook."

4. "You'll drink from the brook, and I'll send ravens to bring you food."

5. Elijah did what God said.

6. Ravens brought him bread and meat morning and night. He drank from the brook.

7. After a while, the brook dried up because there was no rain.

8. God said,

9. "Go to Zarephath. A widow there will give you food."

10. Elijah went. He saw a widow and said, "Please get me water—and some bread too."

11-12. She said, "I have only a little flour and oil. I was going to make one last meal for my son and me, then we'll die."

13. Elijah said, "Don't be afraid. Make me a small loaf first, then make some for you and your son.

14. God says your flour and oil won't run out until it rains again."

15. She did what Elijah said. They had food every day.

16. Her jar never emptied—just as God promised.

17. Later, her son got sick and died.

18. She said, "Did you come to punish me and kill my son?"

19. Elijah took the boy upstairs and laid him on the bed.

20. He cried to God, "Why did You let this boy die?"

21. He stretched out over the boy three times and said, "Lord, bring him back!"

22. God answered, and the boy came back to life.

23. Elijah gave him back to his mother.

24. She said, "Now I know you speak God's truth!"

1 Kings 18

1. After three years, God told Elijah, "Go show yourself to Ahab. I'll send rain."

2. Elijah went. Meanwhile, the famine was very bad.

3. Ahab called Obadiah, a servant who feared God.

4. Obadiah had hidden 100 prophets in caves when Jezebel tried to kill them.

5. Ahab told him, "Let's search for grass so we can keep the animals alive."

6. They split up to look.

7. Obadiah saw Elijah and bowed.

8. Elijah said, "Go tell Ahab I'm here."

9. Obadiah said, "What did I do wrong? Ahab will kill me!"

10. "He's searched everywhere for you."

11. "If I leave, God might move you somewhere else. Then Ahab will kill me."

12-13. "I've always followed God. Didn't you hear I hid prophets from Jezebel?"

14. "Now you want me to tell Ahab you're here? He'll kill me!"

15. Elijah said, "I promise I'll see Ahab today."

16. Obadiah told Ahab. Ahab went to meet Elijah.
17. Ahab said, "Is that you, the one causing trouble?"
18. Elijah said, "You're the troublemaker! You turned from God and followed Baal."
19. "Gather the people and 450 Baal prophets on Mount Carmel."
20. Ahab did it.
21. Elijah said to the people, "How long will you go back and forth? If God is real, follow Him. If Baal is, follow him." The people were silent.
22. Elijah said, "I'm the only prophet left. Baal has 450.
23. Bring two bulls. They'll prepare one and I'll prepare one.
24. Call on your god. I'll call on mine. The God who answers with fire is real." The people agreed.
25. Elijah said, "You go first."
26. They prayed to Baal from morning till noon—nothing happened.
27. Elijah said, "Maybe he's sleeping or busy. Shout louder!"
28. They shouted and cut themselves until they bled.
29. They kept going till evening—but no one answered.
30. Elijah said, "Come here." He rebuilt God's altar.
31. He used 12 stones for the 12 tribes.
32. He dug a trench around the altar.
33. He placed wood and the bull on it.
34. He said, "Pour water over everything—three times."
35. Water soaked the altar and filled the trench.
36. Elijah prayed, "Show them You are the true God!"
37. "Answer me so they'll turn back to You."
38. Fire from God burned the offering, the wood, the stones, the dirt, and the water.
39. The people fell down and said, "God is real!"
40. Elijah said, "Grab the prophets of Baal!" They were taken to the river and killed.
41. Elijah told Ahab, "Get ready. I hear rain coming."
42. Ahab left. Elijah climbed the mountain and prayed.
43. He sent his servant to look—nothing. He sent him seven times.
44. On the seventh time, the servant said, "There's a small cloud."
45. Soon, the sky turned black, and it rained hard. Ahab rode to Jezreel.
46. God gave Elijah strength. He ran ahead of Ahab all the way to Jezreel.

1 Kings 19

1. Ahab told Jezebel everything Elijah did.
2. She sent a message: "By this time tomorrow, you'll be dead like those prophets."
3. Elijah ran for his life and went to Beersheba. He left his servant there
4. and went alone into the desert. He sat under a bush and said, "God, take my life!"
5. He lay down and slept. An angel touched him and said, "Get up and eat."
6. He saw bread and water. He ate and went back to sleep.
7. The angel came again and said, "Eat more or the journey will be too much."
8. He ate and traveled 40 days to Mount Horeb.
9. He stayed in a cave. God asked, "What are you doing here?"

10. Elijah said, "I've worked hard for You, but everyone else turned away. Now they want to kill me."
11. God said, "Go stand outside." A powerful wind came—but God wasn't in the wind.
12. Then an earthquake—but God wasn't in it. Then a fire—but still no God. Then a quiet whisper.
13. Elijah heard it and covered his face. God said again, "What are you doing here?"
14. Elijah gave the same answer.
15. God said, "Go back. Anoint Hazael as king of Aram,
16. Jehu as king of Israel, and Elisha to take your place."
17. "Anyone who escapes Hazael will be caught by Jehu. Those who escape Jehu will face Elisha."
18. "I still have 7,000 in Israel who never worshiped Baal."
19. Elijah found Elisha plowing with 12 oxen. Elijah put his cloak on him.
20. Elisha ran after him and said, "Let me say goodbye to my family." Elijah said, "Go ahead."
21. Elisha killed the oxen, cooked them, and gave the food to the people. Then he followed Elijah and became his helper.

1 Kings 20

1. King Ben-Hadad of Aram gathered 32 kings and their armies to attack Samaria.
2. He sent a message to King Ahab:
3. "Your silver, gold, wives, and children now belong to me."
4. Ahab said, "Everything I have is yours."
5. Ben-Hadad sent another message:
6. "Tomorrow, I'll send men to take anything they want from your palace."
7. Ahab called his leaders. They said, "Don't listen or agree."
8. Ahab told the messengers, "I agreed to the first message, but not this one."
9. They told Ben-Hadad.
10. Ben-Hadad said, "I'll destroy your city until there's nothing left."
11. Ahab replied, "Don't brag before the battle starts."
12. Ben-Hadad was drinking with the kings. He said, "Get ready to attack."
13. A prophet told Ahab, "God will help you win, so you'll know He is Lord."
14. Ahab asked, "Who will fight?" The prophet said, "The young officers will lead."
15. Ahab gathered 232 officers and 7,000 soldiers.
16. They attacked while Ben-Hadad was drunk.
17. His scouts reported, "Men are coming out of Samaria."
18. Ben-Hadad said, "Capture them alive—no matter why they came."
19. The young officers attacked.
20. Each one killed a man. Aram's army ran away. Israel chased them.
21. Ahab led the charge and won.
22. The prophet said, "Prepare for another attack next spring."
23. Aram's advisors said, "Israel's God is a mountain god. Let's fight them on the plains."
24. "Replace the kings with commanders.
25. Build a strong army and fight again."
26. In spring, Ben-Hadad came back to Aphek.
27. Israel's army was small, like two little flocks. Aram's army filled the countryside.
28. A man of God said, "God will let Israel win again, so you know He rules everywhere."

29. The two armies camped for seven days. On the seventh day, they fought.
30. Israel killed 100,000 Arameans. The rest ran, but a wall fell on 27,000 more.
31. Ben-Hadad hid. His men said, "Let's ask Ahab for mercy."
32. They wore sackcloth and begged. Ahab said, "Is he still alive? He's my brother."
33. They took it as a good sign and said, "Yes, he's your brother." Ahab said, "Bring him."
34. Ben-Hadad said, "I'll return your cities." Ahab made a treaty and let him go.
35. A prophet told another man, "Hit me!" But he refused.
36. The prophet said, "You disobeyed God. You'll be killed by a lion." It happened.
37. He asked someone else, who hit him.
38. The prophet put on a disguise.
39. He told the king, "I was told to guard a man. He escaped."
40. Ahab said, "You must pay for that."
41. The prophet removed his disguise. Ahab recognized him.
42. The prophet said, "God told you to kill Ben-Hadad. Now you'll die instead."
43. Ahab went home angry and upset.

1 Kings 21

1. Naboth had a vineyard next to Ahab's palace.
2. Ahab said, "Sell me your vineyard. I'll give you a better one or pay money."
3. Naboth said, "No. God says I must keep my family land."
4. Ahab went home angry and refused to eat.
5. Jezebel asked, "Why are you upset?"
6. He told her.
7. She said, "You're the king! I'll get the vineyard for you."
8. She wrote letters in Ahab's name and sent them to city leaders.
9. She said, "Call a fast. Accuse Naboth of cursing God and the king. Then kill him."

10-11. The leaders followed her plan.

12. They had Naboth stoned to death.
13. They told Jezebel, "Naboth is dead."
14. She said to Ahab, "Go take the vineyard. He's dead."

15-16. Ahab took the land.

17. God told Elijah,
18. "Go to Ahab. He took Naboth's land."
19. Say, "You killed him and stole his land. Now dogs will lick your blood where Naboth died."
20. Ahab said, "So, you found me." Elijah said, "Yes, and God will punish you."
21. "Your family will be wiped out like Jeroboam's and Baasha's.
22. Dogs will eat Jezebel.

23-24. Your family will die and not be buried."

25. Ahab was the most evil king. He followed Jezebel's wicked ways.
26. He worshiped idols like the Amorites.
27. When Ahab heard this, he tore his clothes, wore sackcloth, and fasted.
28. God said to Elijah,
29. "Ahab humbled himself. I won't punish him now. His son will face it instead."

1 Kings 22

1. There was peace for three years between Israel and Aram.
2. In the third year, Jehoshaphat king of Judah visited Ahab.
3. Ahab said, "Ramoth-Gilead belongs to us. Let's take it back from Aram."

4. He asked Jehoshaphat, "Will you fight with me?" He said, "Yes. We're like one army."
5. But he added, "First, ask God."
6. Ahab called 400 prophets. They said, "Go! God will help you win."
7. Jehoshaphat asked, "Isn't there a real prophet of the Lord?"
8. Ahab said, "There's Micaiah, but I hate him. He only says bad things about me."
9. Jehoshaphat said, "Don't say that."
10. The kings sat in royal robes, and the prophets kept saying, "You will win!"
11. One prophet made iron horns and said, "You will crush Aram!"
12. All the prophets agreed.
13. A messenger told Micaiah, "Everyone is saying victory. You should too."
14. Micaiah said, "I will only say what God tells me."
15. Ahab asked him, "Should we go to Ramoth-Gilead?" Micaiah said, "Go ahead. You'll win."
16. Ahab said, "Tell the truth."
17. Micaiah said, "I saw Israel scattered like sheep. God said, 'They have no shepherd.'"
18. Ahab said, "See? He always says bad things."
19. Micaiah said, "I saw God on His throne. He asked, 'Who will trick Ahab into going to battle and dying?'"
20. A spirit said, "I will do it."
21. God said, "Go ahead."
22. "That spirit made your prophets lie."
23. Zedekiah hit Micaiah and said, "Which way did God's Spirit go when He left me?"
24. Micaiah said, "You'll find out when you hide in fear."
25. Ahab said, "Put him in jail and feed him little until I return."
26. Micaiah said, "If you return alive, God didn't speak through me."
27. The kings went to Ramoth-Gilead.
28. Ahab wore a disguise. Jehoshaphat wore his robes.
29. The Aramean king told his chariot commanders, "Only fight the king of Israel."
30. When they saw Jehoshaphat, they thought he was Ahab. But he shouted, and they backed off.
31. A random soldier shot an arrow, and it hit Ahab between his armor plates.
32. He said, "I'm wounded. Get me out!"
33. The battle got worse. Ahab stayed in his chariot all day and died that night.
34. His body was taken to Samaria.
35. They washed his chariot, and dogs licked the blood—just as God said.
36. The rest of Ahab's story is written in the Book of the Kings of Israel.
37. Ahab died, and his son Ahaziah became king.

Jehoshaphat and Ahaziah

38. Jehoshaphat ruled Judah for 25 years.
39. He followed God like his father Asa.
40. He didn't remove all the hill altars.
41. He made peace with Israel's king.
42. His story is written in the Book of the Kings of Judah.
43. He removed the male shrine prostitutes.
44. At that time Edom had no king.
45. Jehoshaphat built ships, but they never sailed.
46. Ahaziah wanted to partner with him, but Jehoshaphat said no.
47. Jehoshaphat died, and his son Jehoram became king.
48. Ahaziah ruled Israel for 2 years.
49. He did evil like his parents.
50. He worshiped Baal and angered God.

– 2 Kings –

Both kingdoms fall into sin, leading to exile—Israel to Assyria, Judah to Babylon.

2 Kings 1

1. After Ahab died, Moab rebelled against Israel.
2. King Ahaziah fell from his upstairs balcony and got hurt. He sent messengers to ask Baalzebub, the god of Ekron, if he would get better.
3. But an angel told Elijah, "Go meet the messengers and ask, 'Is there no God in Israel? Is that why you're going to Baalzebub?'"
4. "Tell the king, 'You'll never leave your bed. You will die.'" So Elijah went.
5. The messengers came back early. The king asked, "Why are you back so soon?"
6. They said, "A man told us to return and say, 'Is there no God in Israel? Why send men to Baalzebub? Because of this, you will die.'"
7. The king asked, "Who was it? What did he look like?"
8. They said, "He was hairy and wore a leather belt." The king said, "It was Elijah from Tishbe!"
9. So the king sent an officer with 50 men to get Elijah. They found him on a hill. The officer said, "Man of God, the king says, 'Come down.'"
10. Elijah said, "If I'm a man of God, let fire fall from heaven and kill you all." Fire came down and killed them.
11. The king sent another officer with 50 men. He said, "Man of God, come down now!"
12. Elijah said, "If I'm a man of God, let fire fall from heaven and kill you." Fire came down again and killed them.
13. The king sent a third officer with 50 men. This one knelt down and begged, "Please spare our lives."
14. "Fire killed the first two groups. Please have mercy on us."
15. God told Elijah, "Go with him. Don't be afraid." So Elijah went to the king.
16. He told the king, "Because you asked Baalzebub instead of God, you'll never leave your bed. You will die."
17. So Ahaziah died. Since he had no son, his brother Joram became king during the second year of King Jehoram of Judah.
18. Everything else Ahaziah did is written in the Book of the Kings of Israel.

2 Kings 2

1. God was about to take Elijah to heaven in a whirlwind. Elijah and Elisha were walking together.
2. Elijah said, "Stay here." But Elisha said, "No, I'm going with you."
3. At Bethel, some prophets said, "Did you know God will take your teacher today?" Elisha said, "Yes. Don't talk about it."
4. Elijah said again, "Stay here." Elisha said, "No, I'm going with you."
5. At Jericho, other prophets said the same thing. Elisha said, "Yes, I know. Be quiet."
6. Elijah said, "Stay here." Elisha said, "I will not leave you."
7. Fifty prophets watched from a distance as they stood by the Jordan River.
8. Elijah rolled up his coat and hit the water. The river split, and they walked across on dry ground.
9. Elijah asked, "What do you want before I go?" Elisha said, "Give me a double portion of your spirit."
10. Elijah said, "If you see me go, you'll get it. If not, you won't."
11. As they walked, a chariot of fire appeared, and Elijah went up to heaven in a whirlwind.
12. Elisha saw it and shouted, "My teacher!" Then Elijah was gone.

13. Elisha picked up Elijah's coat and went back.
14. He hit the water with it and said, "Where is the God of Elijah?" The water split, and he crossed.
15. The prophets watching said, "Elijah's spirit is on Elisha!"
16. They said, "Let us search for Elijah." Elisha said, "Don't go."
17. They insisted, so 50 men searched for 3 days but didn't find him.
18. They came back, and Elisha said, "Didn't I tell you not to go?"
19. The people of Jericho said, "Our water is bad."
20. Elisha said, "Bring me a new bowl with salt."
21. He threw the salt in the spring and said, "God has healed this water."
22. The water stayed clean from then on.
23. Elisha went to Bethel. Some boys mocked him and said, "Go away, baldy!"
24. He cursed them. Two bears came out and attacked 42 boys.
25. Then Elisha went to Mount Carmel and returned to Samaria.

2 Kings 3

1. Joram became king of Israel in Jehoshaphat's 18th year. He ruled for 12 years.
2. He did evil but not as bad as his parents. He removed Baal's altar.
3. But he still followed the sinful ways of Jeroboam.
4. Mesha, king of Moab, had paid Israel in sheep and wool.
5. But when Ahab died, he rebelled.
6. King Joram called all Israel to fight.
7. He asked King Jehoshaphat of Judah, "Will you help?" He said, "Yes. We'll go together."
8. Joram said, "We'll go through the desert of Edom."
9. They marched for 7 days and ran out of water.
10. Joram said, "God brought us here to die!"
11. Jehoshaphat asked, "Is there a prophet of God here?" A servant said, "Elisha is here."
12. Jehoshaphat said, "Let's go see him."
13. Elisha said to Joram, "Go ask your false prophets." Joram said, "No, God brought us here."
14. Elisha said, "If I didn't respect Jehoshaphat, I wouldn't talk to you."
15. "Bring me someone to play music." As music played, God spoke to Elisha.
16. He said, "Dig ditches in this valley.
17. You won't see wind or rain, but the valley will fill with water."
18. "God will also help you beat Moab."
19. "You'll destroy cities, cut trees, block springs, and ruin land."
20. The next morning, water came from Edom and filled the valley.
21. The Moabites saw the water and thought it was blood.
22. They said, "The kings fought each other. Let's take the loot!"
23. But Israel attacked and chased them.
24. They ruined towns, fields, trees, and springs.
25. Only Kir Hareseth was left. Moab's army tried to defend it.
26. The king of Moab tried to break through to the Edomites but failed.
27. He sacrificed his oldest son on the wall. Everyone was shocked. Israel left and went home.

2 Kings 4

1. A widow of a prophet cried to Elisha, "My husband died. A man is coming to take my sons as slaves."

2. Elisha said, "What do you have?" She said, "Only a small jar of oil."
3. He said, "Borrow lots of empty jars from your neighbors."
4. "Go inside, shut the door, and pour oil into the jars."
5. She did it. Her sons brought jars, and she filled them.
6. She said, "Bring another." They said, "No more." Then the oil stopped.
7. She told Elisha. He said, "Sell the oil, pay your debt, and live off the rest."
8. Elisha went to Shunem. A woman there gave him food.
9. She said to her husband, "This is a holy man. Let's make him a room."
10. They built him a room with a bed, table, chair, and lamp.
11. One day Elisha went to his room to rest.
12. He asked his servant Gehazi, "Ask the woman from Shunem to come here."
13. He asked the woman, "Can I do anything for you?" She replied, "No, I have everything I need here."
14. He asked Gehazi, "What can I do for her?" Gehazi replied, "She has no son, and her husband is old."
15. Then Elisha said, "Call her back." She came and stood at the doorway.
16. Elisha said, "This time next year, you'll be holding your son." She said, "No, don't lie to me!"
17. But she became pregnant and had a son, just as Elisha had said.
18. Years later, the boy went out to the field to see his father.
19. He said, "My head hurts!" His father told a servant to carry him home.
20. The boy sat on his mother's lap until noon, then died.
21. She laid him on Elisha's bed and shut the door.
22. She told her husband, "Send me a servant and a donkey. I need to see Elisha."
23. He said, "Why today?" She said, "It's okay."
24. She saddled the donkey and told the servant, "Don't slow down unless I say so."
25. She went to Mount Carmel. Elisha saw her coming and told Gehazi,
26. "Run to meet her and ask, 'Is everything okay with you, your husband, and your son?'" She said, "Everything's fine."
27. But when she reached Elisha, she grabbed his feet. Gehazi tried to push her away, but Elisha said, "Leave her alone—she's upset. God hasn't told me why."
28. She said, "Did I ask for a son? Didn't I say, 'Don't give me false hope'?"
29. Elisha said to Gehazi, "Take my staff and go. Don't stop to talk. Lay the staff on the boy's face."
30. But the woman said, "I won't leave you." So Elisha went with her.
31. Gehazi went ahead and laid the staff on the boy, but nothing happened. He went back and told Elisha.
32. Elisha arrived and went to the room. The boy was dead.
33. He shut the door and prayed.
34. He lay on the boy—mouth to mouth, eyes to eyes, hands to hands. The boy's body grew warm.
35. Elisha got up and walked around, then lay down again. The boy sneezed seven times and opened his eyes.
36. Elisha said, "Call the woman." She came, and he said, "Take your son."
37. She bowed to the ground, picked up her son, and left.

Elisha Feeds Many People

38. Elisha went back to Gilgal. There was a famine. He told a servant to make stew.

39. One man picked wild gourds and added them to the pot without knowing if they were safe.

40. When the men ate it, they shouted, "There's poison in the stew!" They couldn't eat it.

41. Elisha said, "Bring some flour." He added it to the pot and said, "Serve it now." The stew was safe.

42. A man brought Elisha 20 loaves of bread and some grain. Elisha said, "Feed the people."

43. His servant said, "How can I feed 100 men with this?" Elisha said, "God says it will be enough, and there will be leftovers."

44. He served it. Everyone ate and had food left over—just like God said.

2 Kings 5

1. Naaman was a great army commander from Aram. He was brave but had a skin disease.

2. Arameans had taken a young Israelite girl. She served Naaman's wife.

3. The girl said, "If only my master saw the prophet in Israel—he could heal him."

4. Naaman told the king, who said, "Go. I'll write a letter to Israel's king."

5. Naaman took the letter, silver, gold, and clothes.

6. The letter said, "I'm sending Naaman. Please heal him."

7. The king of Israel tore his clothes and said, "Am I God? He's trying to start a fight!"

8. Elisha heard and said, "Send Naaman to me. He'll know there's a prophet in Israel."

9. Naaman went to Elisha's house.

10. Elisha sent a messenger: "Wash seven times in the Jordan River to be healed."

11. Naaman was angry. "I thought he'd wave his hand and heal me."

12. "Aren't our rivers better?" He left in anger.

13. His servants said, "If he told you to do something hard, you would. Why not do this easy thing?"

14. Naaman went and dipped in the Jordan seven times. His skin became clean like a child's.

15. He returned and said, "Now I know there's no God but Israel's God. Please take a gift."

16. Elisha said, "I won't take anything." Naaman begged, but Elisha refused.

17. Naaman said, "Let me take some dirt from Israel to worship God."

18. "Please forgive me when I have to bow in my king's temple."

19. Elisha said, "Go in peace." Naaman left.

20. Gehazi, Elisha's servant, said, "Naaman brought gifts. I'll go get something."

21. He ran after Naaman and lied, saying, "My master sent me. We need silver and clothes."

22. Naaman gave him twice as much.

23. Gehazi took it and hid it.

24. Then he went in and stood before Elisha. Elisha said, "Where did you go?"

25. Gehazi said, "Nowhere."

26. Elisha said, "I saw what you did. You took silver and clothes. Now Naaman's disease will stay with you and your family forever."

27. Gehazi left with skin disease—his skin was white like snow.

2 Kings 6

1. The prophets said to Elisha, "The place where we meet is too small."

2. "Let's go to the Jordan River and get wood to build a new place." Elisha said, "Go."

3. One of them said, "Please come with us." Elisha said, "Okay."
4. They went and started cutting trees.
5. One man's axe head fell into the river. He shouted, "Oh no! I borrowed that axe!"
6. Elisha said, "Where did it fall?" The man showed him. Elisha threw in a stick, and the iron axe floated.
7. Elisha said, "Pick it up." The man reached in and took it.

Elisha Stops the Syrian Army

8. The king of Syria was at war with Israel. He told his army where to hide.
9. Elisha warned Israel's king, "Don't go near that place—the Syrians are there."
10. The king of Israel warned the people. This happened many times.
11. The Syrian king was angry and said, "Which one of you is spying for Israel?"
12. One officer said, "It's not us. Elisha tells Israel's king what you say—even in your bedroom!"
13. The king said, "Find out where he is, so I can capture him." They said, "He's in Dothan."
14. The king sent a large army at night. They surrounded the city.
15. Elisha's servant got up early and saw the army. He said, "What do we do?"
16. Elisha said, "Don't be afraid. We have more with us than they do."
17. Elisha prayed, "God, open his eyes." The servant saw horses and chariots of fire all over the hills.
18. As the enemy came closer, Elisha prayed, "God, make them blind." God made them blind.
19. Elisha told them, "This isn't the right place. Follow me." He led them to Samaria.
20. When they got to Samaria, Elisha said, "God, open their eyes." They saw they were trapped.
21. The king of Israel asked, "Should I kill them?"
22. Elisha said, "No. Give them food and water, then send them home."
23. The king fed them and sent them back. After that, the Syrians stopped raiding Israel.

King Ben-Hadad Attacks Samaria

24. Later, King Ben-Hadad of Syria gathered his army and attacked Samaria.
25. The city was under siege, and food ran out. A donkey's head cost 80 silver coins, and a small bowl of dove droppings cost 5.
26. As the king walked by the city wall, a woman cried, "Help me, my king!"
27. The king said, "If God won't help you, how can I? I don't have food or wine."
28. He asked, "What's wrong?" She said, "This woman said, 'Let's eat your son today and mine tomorrow.'"
29. "So we ate my son. But the next day, she hid hers."
30. When the king heard that, he tore his clothes. The people saw he was wearing sackcloth underneath.
31. He shouted, "God strike me dead if I don't have Elisha killed today!"
32. Elisha was at home with some leaders. He said, "The king is sending a man to kill me. Don't open the door."
33. While he was speaking, the man arrived and said, "This disaster is from God. Why should we wait on Him any longer?"

2 Kings 7

1. Elisha said, "God says: Tomorrow, 10 pounds of wheat or 20 pounds of barley will cost just one silver coin in Samaria."
2. The king's officer said, "That's impossible—even if God made food fall from the sky!" Elisha said, "You'll see it, but you won't eat it."

The Syrian Army Runs Away

3. Four men with skin disease were sitting by the city gate. They said, "Why stay here and die?"
4. "If we go in the city, we'll starve. If we stay here, we'll die. Let's go to the Syrian camp. If they let us live, great. If they kill us, we die anyway."
5. At dusk, they went to the Syrian camp—but no one was there!
6. God made the Syrians hear sounds of chariots and soldiers. They thought Israel had hired other armies to attack.
7. So they ran away at night, leaving tents, horses, and supplies behind.
8. The four men entered the camp, ate, drank, and took silver, gold, and clothes. They hid it all.
9. Then they said, "This isn't right. We have good news! If we wait, we'll be punished. Let's tell the king."
10. They told the city guards, "We went to the Syrian camp. It's empty. Everything is still there!"
11. The guards told the palace.
12. The king got up and said, "It's a trap. The Syrians are hiding in the fields, waiting to attack."
13. One officer said, "Let's send five men to check. We have nothing to lose."
14. They took two chariots and followed the Syrian path.
15. They found clothes and supplies thrown everywhere—the Syrians had run away.
16. The people rushed out and took everything. Just as Elisha said, 10 pounds of wheat or 20 pounds of barley cost one silver coin.
17. The king had put the officer at the gate, but the crowd trampled him. He died.
18. It happened just as Elisha said.
19. The officer who said, "Even if God sent food from the sky…"
20. He saw the food but never got to eat it—he was trampled.

2 Kings 8

1. Elisha told the woman whose son he had raised, "Leave the country. A famine is coming for seven years."
2. She and her family went to Philistine land.
3. After seven years, she came back and asked the king for her land.
4. The king was talking to Gehazi about Elisha's miracles.
5. Gehazi said, "Elisha raised a boy from the dead." Just then, the woman came to ask for her land.
6. The king asked her about it. She told him everything. The king gave her land back and all profits from seven years.

Ben-Hadad's Death

7. Elisha went to Damascus. King Ben-Hadad was sick. He heard Elisha was there.
8. He sent Hazael with gifts to ask, "Will I recover?"
9. Hazael brought the gifts and asked.
10. Elisha said, "Tell him he will recover—but God says he will die."
11. Elisha stared at Hazael and began to cry.
12. Hazael asked, "Why are you crying?" Elisha said, "Because I know you will hurt Israel and kill people."
13. Hazael said, "I'm just a servant. How could I do that?" Elisha said, "God showed me—you will be king."
14. Hazael left. Ben-Hadad asked, "What did he say?" Hazael said, "You'll recover."
15. But the next day, Hazael smothered him and became king.

Jehoram Becomes King of Judah

16. Jehoram, son of Jehoshaphat, became king of Judah.

17. He ruled eight years.
18. He was married to Ahab's daughter and did evil like Ahab's family.
19. But God didn't destroy Judah, because of His promise to David.
20. During Jehoram's time, Edom rebelled.
21. Jehoram tried to fight them but failed.
22. Edom stayed free. Libnah also rebelled.
23. The rest of Jehoram's story is in the book of Judah's kings.
24. He died, and his son Ahaziah became king.

Ahaziah Rules Judah

25. Ahaziah became king of Judah.
26. He was 22 years old and ruled one year.
27. He followed Ahab's family and did evil. His mother was Ahab's daughter.
28. He joined Israel's king Joram in a war against Syria. Joram was wounded.
29. Ahaziah went to visit him in Jezreel.

2 Kings 9

1. Elisha called a young prophet and said, "Get ready, take this jar of oil, and go to Ramoth Gilead."
2. "Find Jehu, son of Jehoshaphat, grandson of Nimshi. Take him to a private room."
3. "Pour oil on his head and say, 'God makes you king of Israel.' Then open the door and run!"
4. So the young prophet went to Ramoth Gilead.
5. He found the army officers meeting and said, "I have a message for you." Jehu asked, "Which one of us?" He said, "You."
6. They went inside. The prophet poured oil on Jehu and said, "God makes you king over His people, Israel."
7. "You must destroy Ahab's family. Jezebel will be punished for killing God's prophets and servants."
8. "Kill every male in Ahab's family—young and old, slave and free."
9. "God will wipe out his family, like He did with Jeroboam and Baasha."
10. "Dogs will eat Jezebel in Jezreel. She won't be buried." Then the prophet ran out.
11. Jehu went back to the others. They asked, "Is everything okay? What did that crazy guy say?" Jehu said, "You know how they are."
12. They said, "Tell us the truth!" Jehu said, "He said God anointed me king of Israel."
13. They quickly put their robes on the steps under him, blew a trumpet, and shouted, "Jehu is king!"

Jehu Kills Joram and Ahaziah

14. Jehu planned against Joram, who had been fighting Syria at Ramoth Gilead.
15. Joram had gone back to Jezreel to heal from his wounds. Jehu said, "If you want me as king, don't let anyone run to Jezreel with news."
16. Jehu rode in his chariot to Jezreel. Joram and King Ahaziah of Judah were both there.
17. A guard on the tower in Jezreel saw Jehu's group coming. He said, "I see riders." Joram said, "Send someone to ask if they come in peace."
18. A rider asked Jehu, "Do you come in peace?" Jehu said, "What do you know about peace? Get behind me." The watchman said, "He didn't come back."
19. So Joram sent another rider. He also asked, "Do you come in peace?" Jehu said, "What do you know about peace? Get behind me."
20. The watchman said, "He didn't return either. And the leader drives like Jehu—fast and wild!"
21. Joram said, "Get my chariot." He and Ahaziah rode out and met Jehu at Naboth's field.

22. Joram asked, "Do you come in peace, Jehu?" Jehu said, "How can there be peace when your mother Jezebel does evil and witchcraft?"

23. Joram turned his chariot and yelled, "Run, Ahaziah!"

24. Jehu shot Joram with an arrow. It hit his heart. Joram collapsed in his chariot.

25. Jehu said, "Throw his body on Naboth's field, just as God said would happen."

26. "God said He saw Naboth and his sons killed. Now this is the payback."

27. When Ahaziah saw this, he ran toward Beth Haggan. Jehu chased him and said, "Shoot him too!" They hit him in his chariot near Ibleam. He escaped to Megiddo but died there.

28. His men brought him to Jerusalem and buried him with his ancestors.

Jezebel's Death

29. This happened in the 11th year of Joram's rule.

30. Jezebel heard Jehu was coming. She put on makeup, fixed her hair, and looked out the window.

31. When Jehu arrived, she shouted, "Have you come in peace, Zimri, you traitor?"

32. Jehu looked up and said, "Who is on my side?" Two or three eunuchs looked down.

33. Jehu said, "Throw her down!" They threw her out the window. Her blood splattered on the wall and horses. Jehu ran over her with his horse.

34. He went inside and ate and drank. Then he said, "Take care of that cursed woman. She was a king's daughter."

35. They went to bury her, but found only her skull, feet, and hands.

36. They went back and told Jehu. He said, "That's what God said would happen: Dogs will eat Jezebel at Jezreel."

37. "Her body will be like trash in the field—no one will even know it was her."

2 Kings 10

1. Ahab had 70 sons in Samaria. Jehu sent letters to the city leaders and guardians.

2. The letter said, "Pick the best son of Ahab, make him king, and fight for his family."

3. But they were afraid and said, "If two kings couldn't beat Jehu, how can we?"

4. So they sent a message to Jehu: "We are your servants. We won't make anyone king. Do whatever you think is best."

5. Jehu wrote back, "If you're on my side, bring me the heads of Ahab's sons by tomorrow."

6. The city leaders had the 70 sons and killed them. They put the heads in baskets and sent them to Jezreel.

7. Jehu said, "Put them in two piles at the gate until morning."

8. In the morning, Jehu said, "I killed Joram. But who killed all these?

9. Just like God promised through Elijah, every word has come true."

10. Jehu then killed everyone left from Ahab's family—officials, friends, and priests—no one was left alive.

11. On the way to Samaria, Jehu stopped at Beth Eked.

12. He met some relatives of King Ahaziah of Judah. He asked, "Who are you?" They said, "We're family of Ahaziah."

13. Jehu said, "Take them alive!" They were captured and killed—42 men.

14. Jehu continued his journey and met Jehonadab. He asked, "Do you support me?"

15. Jehonadab said, "Yes." Jehu said, "Come with me."

16. Jehu said, "See how strong I serve God." They rode together.

17. When Jehu reached Samaria, he killed everyone left from Ahab's family.

18. Then Jehu called the people and said, "Ahab served Baal a little. I will serve him a lot!"

19. "Call all Baal's prophets and priests. Don't let anyone be missing!"
20. They came. Jehu said, "We're having a big sacrifice to Baal."
21. The temple was packed.
22. Jehu told the guards, "Don't let anyone leave."
23. Jehu and Jehonadab went in and said, "Make sure only Baal worshipers are here."
24. They went to make sacrifices. Jehu placed 80 soldiers outside.
25. Jehu said, "Kill them all! Don't let anyone escape!" They killed everyone inside.
26. They destroyed the temple and burned it.
27. They turned it into a bathroom—it stayed that way.
28. Jehu wiped out Baal worship in Israel.
29. But he still followed Jeroboam's sins with the golden calves.
30. God said, "You did what I asked. Your family will rule for four generations."
31. But Jehu didn't fully follow God's laws.
32. At that time, God began reducing Israel's power.
33. King Hazael defeated them in many areas.
34. Everything else Jehu did is written in the history of Israel's kings.
35. Jehu died and was buried in Samaria. His son Jehoahaz became king.
36. Jehu ruled Israel for 28 years.

2 Kings 11

1. When Athaliah, Ahaziah's mother, saw her son was dead, she killed all the royal family.
2. But Jehosheba hid Joash, Ahaziah's son, in a bedroom. She kept him safe for six years.
3. Joash stayed hidden in the temple while Athaliah ruled.
4. In the 7th year, Jehoiada the priest gathered the temple guards.
5. He said, "One-third of you guard the king's house,
6. one-third guard the gate, and
7. one-third guard the temple.
8. Stay near the king with weapons ready."
9. The guards did what Jehoiada said.
10. Jehoiada gave them King David's spears and shields.
11. The guards stood around the king.
12. Jehoiada brought out Joash, put a crown on him, gave him the law, and anointed him king. Everyone clapped and shouted, "Long live the king!"
13. Athaliah heard the noise and ran to the temple.
14. She saw the boy crowned and shouted, "Treason!"
15. Jehoiada said, "Don't kill her in the temple. Take her out and kill anyone who follows her."
16. They took her out and killed her near the palace gate.
17. Jehoiada made a covenant between God, the king, and the people.
18. The people tore down Baal's temple and killed the priest.
19. Jehoiada placed guards at the temple.
20. Everyone was happy. The city was quiet.
21. Joash was 7 years old when he became king.

2 Kings 12

1. Joash became king in the 7th year of Jehu's rule. He ruled for 40 years.
2. Joash did what was right because Jehoiada the priest guided him.
3. But the hilltop altars were not removed. People still made sacrifices there.

4. Joash told the priests, "Use the temple money to fix the building."
5. But by the 23rd year, the priests hadn't repaired the temple.
6. So Joash called Jehoiada and the priests and said, "Why aren't you fixing the temple?"
7. He told them to stop collecting money and hand it over to workers.
8. The priests agreed.
9. Jehoiada made a chest with a hole in the lid and placed it near the altar.
10. When it filled up, the king's secretary and the high priest counted it.
11. They gave the silver to supervisors who paid the workers.
12. The workers repaired the temple—builders, carpenters, stone masons.
13. No silver was used to make items like bowls or trumpets—only for building repairs.
14. The workers were honest and did their jobs well.
15. Money from guilt and sin offerings still went to the priests.
16. Hazael, king of Aram, attacked and captured Gath. Then he moved toward Jerusalem.
17. Joash gave him all the treasures from the temple and palace to stop the attack.
18. Hazael left Jerusalem.
19. Everything else Joash did is written in the Book of the Kings of Judah.
20. His own servants made a plan and killed him at Beth Millo.
21. His son Amaziah became king.

2 Kings 13

1. Jehoahaz became king of Israel in the 23rd year of King Joash of Judah. He ruled 17 years.
2. He did evil like Jeroboam. He led Israel into sin.
3. God was angry and let King Hazael of Syria defeat them.
4. Jehoahaz begged God for help. God listened and saw Israel's suffering.
5. God sent a leader to save them. They were free from Syria but still sinned.
6. They kept the idol poles in Samaria.
7. Jehoahaz only had 50 horsemen, 10 chariots, and 10,000 soldiers left. Syria had destroyed the rest.
8. Everything else Jehoahaz did is in the history book of Israel's kings.
9. He died and was buried. His son Jehoash became king.

King Jehoash of Israel

10. Jehoash became king in the 37th year of King Joash of Judah. He ruled Israel 16 years.
11. He did evil like Jeroboam. He kept Israel sinning.
12. His story is in the history book of Israel's kings.
13. He died and was buried in Samaria. His son Jeroboam became king.

Elisha's Final Days

14. Elisha got sick and was dying. Jehoash went to see him and cried, "My father! My father!"
15. Elisha said, "Get a bow and arrows."
16. Jehoash got them. Elisha put his hands on the king's hands.
17. Elisha said, "Open the east window and shoot." He shot. Elisha said, "That's God's arrow of victory! You will defeat Syria!"
18. Then Elisha said, "Hit the ground with the arrows." The king hit it three times, then stopped.
19. Elisha was upset and said, "You should have hit five or six times. Then you'd have won completely. Now you'll only win three times."
20. Elisha died and was buried. Later, a dead man was thrown into his grave.

When the body touched Elisha's bones, the man came back to life.

21. Hazael had oppressed Israel all Jehoahaz's life.
22. But God had mercy because of His promises to Abraham, Isaac, and Jacob. He did not destroy them.
23. After Hazael died, his son Ben-Hadad became king.
24. Jehoash took back cities from Ben-Hadad that his father had taken. He won three times—just as Elisha said.

2 Kings 14

1. Amaziah became king of Judah in the 2nd year of Jehoash, king of Israel.
2. He was 25 and ruled 29 years. His mother was Jehoaddin.
3. Amaziah did what was right but not as well as David. He followed his father Joash's ways.
4. He didn't remove the hilltop altars. People still made sacrifices there.
5. When he was strong as king, he killed the men who murdered his father.
6. But he didn't kill their children, as God's law said: Only those guilty should die.
7. He defeated 10,000 Edomites and took the city of Sela, renaming it Joktheel.
8. Amaziah sent a message to Jehoash of Israel: "Let's meet in battle!"
9. Jehoash replied, "A thornbush said to a cedar tree, 'Give me your daughter.' Then a wild animal trampled the bush.
10. You beat Edom, but don't get proud. Stay home or you'll be defeated."
11. Amaziah didn't listen. They met in battle at Beth Shemesh.
12. Judah lost. The army ran home.
13. Jehoash captured Amaziah, tore down a big part of Jerusalem's wall,
14. and took gold, silver, treasures, and hostages. He went back to Samaria.
15. The rest of Jehoash's story is in the king's history book.
16. He died, and his son Jeroboam became king.

Amaziah's End

17. Amaziah lived 15 more years after Jehoash died.
18. His story is in the history book of Judah's kings.
19. People made a plan to kill him in Jerusalem, so he fled to Lachish. They killed him there.
20. His body was brought back and buried in Jerusalem.
21. Then the people made his 16-year-old son Azariah king.

Jeroboam II Becomes King of Israel

22. Jeroboam became king in the 15th year of Amaziah. He ruled 41 years.
23. He did evil like the first Jeroboam.
24. He expanded Israel's borders, just as God had said through Jonah.
25. God saw Israel was weak, with no help.
26. He did not want to wipe them out. He used Jeroboam to save them.
27. The rest of Jeroboam's story is in the history book.
28. He died and was buried in Samaria. His son Zechariah became king.

2 Kings 15

1. Azariah became king of Judah in Jeroboam's 27th year.
2. He was 16 years old and ruled 52 years. His mother was Jecoliah.
3. He did what was right like his father.
4. But the hilltop altars stayed. People still made sacrifices there.
5. God made Azariah sick with a skin disease. He lived alone, and his son Jotham governed.
6. His story is in Judah's history book.
7. He died, and Jotham became king.

Zechariah Rules Israel

8. Zechariah became king in Azariah's 38th year. He ruled only six months.
9. He did evil like Jeroboam.
10. Shallum killed him in front of people and became king.
11. His story is in the king's history book.
12. God had said to Jehu, "Your family will rule for four generations." That came true.

Shallum Rules Israel

13. Shallum ruled one month.
14. Menahem attacked and killed him, then became king.
15. Shallum's story is in the king's history book.

Menahem's Reign

16. Menahem attacked Tiphsah and ripped open pregnant women.
17. He ruled Israel 10 years.
18. He did evil like Jeroboam.
19. King Pul of Assyria attacked. Menahem gave him silver to leave.
20. He taxed the people 50 silver coins each.
21. His story is in the king's history book.
22. He died, and his son Pekahiah became king.

Pekahiah's Reign

23. Pekahiah became king in Azariah's 50th year. He ruled two years.
24. He did evil like Jeroboam.
25. Pekah, one of his officers, killed him in Samaria and became king.

Pekah's Reign

26. Pekah became king in Azariah's 52nd year. He ruled 20 years.
27. He did evil like Jeroboam.
28. King Tiglath-Pileser of Assyria took many cities and people.
29. Hoshea killed Pekah and became king.
30. Pekah's story is in the king's history book.

Jotham's Reign in Judah

31. Jotham became king in Pekah's 2nd year.
32. He was 25 years old and ruled 16 years. His mother was Jerusha.
33. He did what was right, like his father Uzziah.
34. But the hilltop altars stayed.
35. His story is in the history book.
36. At that time, God let Syria and Israel start attacking Judah.
37. Jotham died, and his son Ahaz became king.

2 Kings 16

1. In the 17th year of King Pekah of Israel, Ahaz became king of Judah.
2. He was 20 years old and ruled 16 years. He did not follow God like David.
3. He followed the evil ways of Israel. He even burned his son as a sacrifice.
4. He offered sacrifices at high places, hills, and under trees.
5. King Rezin of Syria and King Pekah of Israel attacked Jerusalem, but couldn't win.
6. Rezin took back Elath and forced the Jews out. Syrians lived there instead.
7. Ahaz sent a message to Tiglath-Pileser of Assyria: "Help me! I'm your servant."
8. He sent silver and gold from the temple and palace as a gift.
9. Tiglath-Pileser attacked and captured Damascus. He took the people to Kir and killed Rezin.
10. Ahaz went to meet him in Damascus. He saw an altar there and sent a design of it to Uriah the priest.
11. Uriah built the altar just like the king wanted.

12. When Ahaz returned, he offered sacrifices on it.
13. He offered burnt and grain offerings, poured out drinks, and splashed blood on it.
14. He moved the bronze altar and put the new altar in its place.
15. He told Uriah, "Use the new altar for sacrifices. I'll use the bronze altar to ask God questions."
16. Uriah obeyed.
17. Ahaz took things from the temple and broke them. He removed the bronze stand and the water basin.
18. He changed the temple's entrance to please the Assyrian king.
19. The rest of Ahaz's story is written in Judah's history book.
20. Ahaz died and was buried. His son Hezekiah became king.

2 Kings 17

1. Hoshea became king of Israel in Ahaz's 12th year. He ruled 9 years.
2. He sinned against God, but not as bad as past kings.
3. Shalmaneser of Assyria came and made Hoshea pay tribute.
4. Hoshea stopped paying and asked Egypt for help. Assyria found out and put him in prison.
5. Assyria attacked and surrounded Samaria for 3 years.
6. In Hoshea's 9th year, Assyria captured Samaria. The Israelites were taken to Assyria.
7. This happened because Israel sinned against God.
8. They followed the customs of other nations and the evil kings of Israel.
9. They secretly did wrong things and built high places in their towns.
10. They set up altars and poles on every hill and under trees.
11. They burned incense and did evil things, making God angry.
12. They worshiped idols, even though God said not to.
13. God sent prophets to warn them: "Turn from evil and obey Me!"
14. But they refused and were stubborn.
15. They ignored God's laws and promises. They followed worthless idols and became worthless.
16. They turned away from God and worshiped Baal and stars.
17. They burned their children, did magic, and angered God.
18. God was very angry and removed Israel from His land. Only Judah was left.
19. But Judah also sinned and didn't obey God.
20. So God rejected all of Israel.
21. He had separated them from Judah and let Jeroboam lead them. Jeroboam led them into sin.
22. Israel kept sinning and didn't stop.
23. So God removed them, just like He warned.
24. Then the king of Assyria brought people from other nations to live in Samaria.
25. They didn't worship God, so He sent lions to attack them.
26. The king was told, "These people don't know Israel's God."
27. He said, "Send a priest to teach them."
28. A priest came and taught them about God.
29. But each nation kept worshiping its own gods too.
30. They set up idols and shrines in Samaria.
31. They even burned children as sacrifices.
32. They also worshiped God but chose their own priests.

33. They feared God and worshiped other gods too.
34. They didn't follow God's laws or commands.
35. God made a covenant with Israel: "Don't worship other gods."
36. "Only worship Me. I brought you out of Egypt."
37. "Follow My laws and commands."
38. "Don't forget the covenant I made with you."
39. "Worship Me only, and I'll protect you."
40. But they didn't listen.
41. They kept doing what their ancestors did. They worshiped God—but also idols.

2 Kings 18

1. Hezekiah became king of Judah in Hoshea's 3rd year.
2. He was 25 years old and ruled 29 years. His mother was Abijah.
3. He did what was right, like David.
4. He removed altars, broke the idol poles, and smashed the bronze snake Moses made. People had been worshiping it.
5. Hezekiah trusted God more than any king before or after.
6. He followed God and kept His commands.
7. God was with him, and he succeeded in everything. He rebelled against Assyria and didn't serve them.
8. He defeated the Philistines everywhere.
9. In Hezekiah's 4th year, Assyria attacked Samaria.
10. After 3 years, Assyria captured it.
11. The Israelites were taken to Assyria because they didn't obey God.
12. They didn't keep His laws.

Assyria Threatens Jerusalem

13. In Hezekiah's 14th year, King Sennacherib of Assyria attacked Judah and took many cities.
14. Hezekiah said, "I'll pay whatever you ask."
15. He gave him silver from the temple and palace.
16. He even removed gold from the temple doors and gave it away.
17. The Assyrian king sent three officials with a large army to Jerusalem. They stood at the water tunnel.
18. They called out for King Hezekiah. Three of his men went out to talk.
19. The Assyrian commander said, "Tell Hezekiah: 'What are you trusting in?'"
20. "You say you have plans and power. But you trust in Egypt!"
21. "Egypt is like a broken stick. If you lean on it, it breaks and hurts you."
22. "You might say, 'We trust God.' But didn't Hezekiah remove His altars?"
23. "Make a deal with my king. I'll give you 2,000 horses—if you can find riders!"
24. "You can't beat even one of my lowest officers."
25. "Do you think I attacked Judah without God? God told me to!"
26. Hezekiah's men said, "Speak Aramaic, not Hebrew. The people are listening."
27. The commander said, "My message is for everyone—they'll suffer too."
28. He shouted, "Listen to the king of Assyria!"
29. "Don't let Hezekiah fool you. He can't save you."
30. "Don't trust him when he says, 'God will help us.'"
31. "Make peace and come out. You'll eat from your own fields."
32. "Later, I'll move you to a new land full of good things."

33. "Has any god ever saved a nation from Assyria?"
34. "Where are the gods of Hamath and Arpad?"
35. "No god saved Samaria. Why would your God save Jerusalem?"
36. But the people stayed silent. They didn't say a word.
37. Hezekiah's men tore their clothes and told him everything.

2 Kings 19

1. When Hezekiah heard the news, he tore his clothes, wore sackcloth, and went to the temple.
2. He sent Eliakim, Shebna, and priests to talk to the prophet Isaiah.
3. They said, "Today is full of pain and shame. We are helpless, like a woman who can't give birth.
4. Assyria has insulted God. Maybe God heard them. Please pray for us."
5. When Isaiah heard their message,
6. he said, "Tell the king: God says don't be afraid of their words.
7. I'll make the king of Assyria hear a rumor. He'll return home and be killed there."
8. The Assyrian chief went back and found the king fighting at Libnah.
9. He heard that the king of Ethiopia was coming to attack. So he sent a letter to Hezekiah:
10. "Don't trust your God. He can't save you from me.
11. Look at what we've done to other nations.
12. Their gods didn't save them—Gozan, Haran, Rezeph, or Telassar.
13. What happened to the kings of Hamath, Arpad, Sepharvaim, Hena, and Ivvah?"

Hezekiah's Prayer

14. Hezekiah took the letter to the temple and laid it before God.
15. He prayed, "Lord, You sit above the angels. You rule all nations. You made heaven and earth.
16. Please hear me. See how Sennacherib insults You.
17. It's true—Assyria has destroyed many countries.
18. They burned their gods, but they were just wood and stone.
19. Please save us, so all nations will know You are the only true God."

God's Answer Through Isaiah

20. Isaiah sent this message to Hezekiah: "God says, I've heard your prayer.
21. This is what God says about the king of Assyria: The people laugh at him and shake their heads.
22. Who did he insult? He insulted Me, the Holy God of Israel.
23. He sent messengers to mock Me, saying he'd conquer mountains.
24. He said he'd drink strange waters and dry up rivers.
25. But I planned all of this long ago.
26. That's why cities were weak and easy to take.
27. I know where he goes, and when he rages against Me.
28. Because of his anger, I'll put a hook in his nose and make him go back home.
29. Here's your sign: This year you'll eat what grows by itself. Next year too. In the third year, plant crops again.
30. A few people will survive and grow strong again.
31. A group will escape from Jerusalem. God has decided it.
32. The king of Assyria will not enter this city, shoot arrows, or build ramps.
33. He will return home by the same way he came.

34. I will defend Jerusalem for My sake and for David's sake."
35. That night, an angel killed 185,000 in the Assyrian camp. In the morning, they were all dead.
36. So King Sennacherib of Assyria left and went home to Nineveh.
37. While worshiping in his god's temple, his sons killed him and ran away. His son Esarhaddon became king.

2 Kings 20

1. Hezekiah got very sick. Isaiah told him, "God says: Put your house in order. You will die."
2. Hezekiah turned to the wall and prayed.
3. He cried, "Lord, I've served You with all my heart. Please remember." He wept.
4. Before Isaiah left the palace, God said,
5. "Go back and tell Hezekiah: I heard your prayer and saw your tears. I'll heal you.
6. In 3 days, you'll go to the temple. I'll give you 15 more years and protect Jerusalem from Assyria."
7. Isaiah said, "Put a fig paste on the boil." They did, and he got better.
8. Hezekiah asked, "What's the sign that I'll be healed?"
9. Isaiah said, "God will give you a sign: The shadow on the steps will go forward or backward."
10. Hezekiah said, "Going forward is normal. Let it go backward."
11. Isaiah prayed, and the shadow moved back 10 steps.
12. The king of Babylon sent letters and gifts to Hezekiah because he heard he was sick.
13. Hezekiah showed the messengers everything—his treasures and weapons.
14. Isaiah asked, "Who were they?" Hezekiah said, "Men from Babylon."
15. "What did they see?" "Everything," Hezekiah said.
16. Isaiah said, "God says everything will be taken to Babylon.
17. Nothing will be left.
18. Even your own sons will be taken and made servants in Babylon."
19. Hezekiah said, "God's word is good." He thought, "At least there will be peace in my time."
20. Everything else Hezekiah did is written in Judah's history book.
21. He died, and his son Manasseh became king.

2 Kings 21

1. Manasseh was 12 when he became king. He ruled 55 years.
2. He did evil and followed the nations God had removed.
3. He rebuilt altars his father tore down. He made idols and worshiped stars.
4. He built altars in God's temple.
5. He put altars for stars in both temple courtyards.
6. He burned his son as a sacrifice, used magic, and talked to spirits. God was very angry.
7. He put an idol in God's temple, even though God said, "This is where I'll live forever."
8. "If Israel obeys Me, they'll stay in this land."
9. But they didn't listen. Manasseh led them to do worse things than other nations.
10. God spoke through prophets:
11. "Manasseh has done terrible things, worse than the Amorites. He led Judah into sin.
12. I'll bring such disaster that people will hear about it and tremble.
13. I'll wipe out Jerusalem like a dirty dish.

14. I'll turn away from My people. They've made Me angry."
15. "They've done evil again and again."
16. Manasseh killed many innocent people.
17. The rest of his story is in the king's history book.
18. He died and was buried. His son Amon became king.

Amon's Short Rule

19. Amon was 22 when he became king. He ruled 2 years.
20. He did evil like his father.
21. He worshiped idols just like Manasseh.
22. He turned away from God.
23. His own servants made a plan and killed him.
24. But the people killed the assassins and made his son Josiah king.

2 Kings 22

1. Josiah was 8 years old when he became king. He ruled for 31 years in Jerusalem. His mother was Jedidah.
2. Josiah did what pleased God. He followed the example of David.

The Book of Law Is Found

3. In his 18th year, Josiah sent Shaphan the secretary to the temple.
4. He said, "Go to Hilkiah the priest. Have him collect all the money from the people."
5. "Give it to the men fixing the temple so they can pay the workers."
6. "Buy wood and stone to make repairs."
7. "We don't need to check the money. The workers are honest."
8. Hilkiah said, "I found the Book of the Law in the temple." He gave it to Shaphan, who read it.
9. Shaphan returned to the king and said, "The workers used the money like you said."
10. Then he said, "Hilkiah gave me a book." And he read it to the king.
11. When the king heard the words, he tore his clothes.
12. He told Hilkiah, Shaphan, and others,
13. "Ask God about this book. We have disobeyed it. God must be angry."
14. They went to Huldah the prophetess. She lived in Jerusalem.
15. She said, "Tell the man who sent you:
16. God says, 'I will destroy this city and its people.'
17. 'They turned away from Me and worshiped other gods.'"
18. "But tell the king: God says,
19. 'Because your heart was soft, and you were sorry, I heard you.'"
20. "You will die in peace. You won't see the disaster I will bring."

2 Kings 23

1. The king gathered all the leaders of Judah and Jerusalem.
2. He went to the temple with the people and read the Book of the Law to everyone.
3. He stood by the pillar and promised to obey God with all his heart and soul. The people agreed.

Josiah Cleans Up the Land

4. Josiah told the priests to remove all idols from the temple.
5. He fired the priests who burned incense to false gods.
6. He took the idol pole out of the temple and burned it.
7. He tore down the rooms used by shrine prostitutes.
8. He brought back priests from other cities.
9. Those priests didn't serve at the altar in Jerusalem, but they ate unleavened bread.

10. Josiah destroyed Topheth, where people sacrificed their children.
11. He removed horses and chariots used to worship the sun.
12. He tore down altars made by kings of Judah on the palace roof.
13. He destroyed altars Solomon had made for other gods.
14. He broke the stone idols and cut down the idol poles.
15. He burned the altar in Bethel that Jeroboam had built.
16. He saw tombs nearby, took out the bones, and burned them on the altar.
17. He saw another tomb and asked, "Whose is that?" They said, "A prophet who warned about this."
18. Josiah said, "Leave it alone."
19. He tore down all altars in Israel's cities too.
20. He killed the idol priests and burned their bones on the altars. Then he returned to Jerusalem.

The Passover Is Celebrated

21. Josiah told the people, "Celebrate the Passover like the law says."
22. It had not been done like that since the time of the judges.
23. This Passover was in Josiah's 18th year.

Josiah's Other Changes

24. Josiah removed mediums, idols, and other evil things.
25. No king before or after him loved God like Josiah did.
26. But God was still angry with Judah for Manasseh's sins.
27. He said, "I will also remove Judah, like I did Israel. I will reject Jerusalem and the temple."
28. Josiah's other deeds are written in the kings' history book.
29. In his time, Pharaoh Neco came to fight. Josiah tried to stop him and was killed.
30. His servants brought his body back to Jerusalem. The people made his son Jehoahaz king.

Jehoahaz Becomes King

31. Jehoahaz was 23 when he became king. He ruled 3 months. His mother was Hamutal.
32. He did evil in God's eyes.
33. Pharaoh Neco put him in prison and made Judah pay silver and gold.
34. Neco made Eliakim king and changed his name to Jehoiakim. He took Jehoahaz to Egypt, where he died.
35. Jehoiakim taxed the people to pay the money Neco demanded.

Jehoiakim Rules

36. Jehoiakim was 25 when he became king. He ruled 11 years. His mother was Zebidah.
37. He did evil in God's eyes.

2 Kings 24

1. In Jehoiakim's time, Babylon's king Nebuchadnezzar attacked. Jehoiakim served him 3 years, then rebelled.
2. God sent Babylonian, Aramean, Moabite, and Ammonite raiders to punish Judah.
3. This happened because of Manasseh's evil.
4. He filled Jerusalem with innocent blood, and God would not forgive.
5. The rest of Jehoiakim's story is in Judah's history book.
6. He died, and his son Jehoiachin became king.

Jehoiachin Rules Judah

7. Egypt didn't attack anymore. Babylon controlled the land.
8. Jehoiachin was 18 when he became king. He ruled 3 months. His mother was Nehushta.
9. He did evil in God's eyes.
10. Babylon's army surrounded Jerusalem.

11. King Nebuchadnezzar came during the siege.
12. Jehoiachin surrendered. Babylon took him, his family, and officials.
13. He took treasures from the temple and palace and broke the gold items Solomon made.
14. He took 10,000 people—leaders, warriors, and craftsmen.
15. Only poor people were left.
16. He took Jehoiachin to Babylon, along with his family and nobles.
17. Nebuchadnezzar made Jehoiachin's uncle Mattaniah king, changing his name to Zedekiah.

Zedekiah's Rule

18. Zedekiah was 21 when he became king. He ruled 11 years. His mother was Hamutal.
19. He did evil like Jehoiakim.
20. God was angry with Jerusalem and Judah. Zedekiah rebelled against Babylon.

2 Kings 25

1. In the 9th year of Zedekiah's reign, on the 10th day of the 10th month, King Nebuchadnezzar of Babylon came and attacked Jerusalem. He surrounded it and built ramps against the walls.
2. The city was under siege until the 11th year of Zedekiah's rule.
3. On the 9th day of the 4th month, there was no food left in the city.
4. That night, a hole was made in the city wall. The soldiers and King Zedekiah escaped through the gate by the king's garden. They ran toward the Jordan Valley.
5. But the Babylonian army chased them and caught Zedekiah on the plains of Jericho. His soldiers ran away.
6. They took Zedekiah to King Nebuchadnezzar at Riblah and judged him there.
7. They killed Zedekiah's sons while he watched. Then they blinded him, tied him up with bronze chains, and took him to Babylon.

Jerusalem Is Destroyed

8. On the 7th day of the 5th month, in Nebuchadnezzar's 19th year, his official Nebuzaradan came to Jerusalem.
9. He burned the temple, the palace, and every important building.
10. His army tore down all the walls around the city.
11. Nebuzaradan took away all the people still in the city and those who had surrendered.
12. But he left behind some poor people to work the fields and vineyards.
13. The Babylonians broke the bronze pillars, carts, and the large bronze bowl called the Sea. They took the bronze to Babylon.
14. They also took the pots, shovels, snuffers, dishes, and all bronze tools used in the temple.
15. They took the incense burners and bowls made of pure gold and silver.
16. The bronze from the two pillars, the Sea, and the carts was too heavy to measure.
17. Each pillar was 27 feet tall. The bronze top was 4.5 feet high and decorated with chains and pomegranates.

The People Taken Away

18. Nebuzaradan also took the chief priest Seraiah, the assistant priest Zephaniah, and three temple guards.
19. From the city, he took a commander, five officials close to the king, the army commander's secretary, and 60 other men.
20. He brought them to the king of Babylon at Riblah.
21. The king had them killed there. So Judah was taken away from its land.

Gedaliah Made Governor

22. King Nebuchadnezzar made Gedaliah governor of the people left in Judah.
23. When the army commanders heard Gedaliah was in charge, they came to him.
24. Gedaliah said, "Don't be afraid. Stay here and serve Babylon. Everything will be fine."
25. But in the 7th month, Ishmael killed Gedaliah and the men with him.
26. All the people, from the least to the greatest, ran to Egypt because they were afraid of Babylon.

Jehoiachin Released

27. In the 37th year of Jehoiachin's exile, King Evil-Merodach of Babylon released him.
28. He spoke kindly to Jehoiachin and gave him a special seat above the other captive kings.
29. Jehoiachin was allowed to take off his prison clothes and eat at the king's table for the rest of his life.
30. Every day, the king gave him money for his food until the day he died.

– 1 Chronicles –

Retells David's reign and Israel's history with a focus on temple worship.

1 Chronicles 1

Family Records from Adam to David

The Descendants of Adam

1. Adam's family line was: Adam, Seth, Enosh,
2. Kenan, Mahalalel, Jared,
3. Enoch, Methuselah, Lamech.
4. Then came Noah and his sons: Shem, Ham, and Japheth.

Japheth's Descendants

5. Japheth's sons were: Gomer, Magog, Madai, Javan, Tubal, Meshech, and Tiras.
6. Gomer's sons were: Ashkenaz, Riphath, and Togarmah.
7. Javan's sons were: Elishah, Tarshish, Kittim, and Rodanim.

Ham's Descendants

8. Ham's sons were: Cush, Mizraim, Put, and Canaan.
9. Cush's sons were: Seba, Havilah, Sabtah, Raamah, and Sabteca. Raamah's sons were: Sheba and Dedan.
10. Cush was also the father of Nimrod, the first strong warrior on earth.
11. Mizraim was the father of the Ludites, Anamites, Lehabites, and Naphtuhites,
12. Pathrusites, Casluhites (where the Philistines came from), and Caphtorites.
13. Canaan's oldest son was Sidon. He also had a son named Heth.
14. Canaan's other descendants were the Jebusites, Amorites, and Girgashites,
15. Hivites, Arkites, and Sinites,
16. Arvadites, Zemarites, and Hamathites.

Shem's Descendants

17. Shem's sons were: Elam, Asshur, Arphaxad, Lud, and Aram. Aram's sons were: Uz, Hul, Gether, and Meshech.
18. Arphaxad's son was Shelah, and Shelah's son was Eber.
19. Eber had two sons. One was named Peleg, because people were divided then. Peleg's brother was Joktan.
20. Joktan's sons were: Almodad, Sheleph, Hazarmaveth, Jerah,
21. adoram, Uzal, Diklah,
22. Obal, Abimael, Sheba,
23. Ophir, Havilah, and Jobab. All these were Joktan's sons.

The Family Line from Shem to Abraham

24. Shem's line continued through: Arphaxad, Shelah,
25. Eber, Peleg, Reu,
26. Serug, Nahor, Terah,
27. And Abram, who was later called Abraham.

Abraham's Descendants

28. Abraham had two sons: Isaac and Ishmael.
29. Ishmael's sons were: Nebaioth (the oldest), Kedar, Adbeel, Mibsam,
30. Mishma, Dumah, Massa, Hadad, and Tema,
31. Jetur, Naphish, and Kedemah. These were Ishmael's sons.
32. Abraham also had sons with Keturah: Zimran, Jokshan, Medan, Midian, Ishbak, and Shuah. Jokshan's sons were: Sheba and Dedan.
33. Midian's sons were: Ephah, Epher, Hanoch, Abida, and Eldaah. All these were Abraham's descendants through Keturah.

Isaac's Descendants

34. Abraham's son Isaac had two sons: Esau and Israel.

Esau's Descendants

35. Esau's sons were: Eliphaz, Reuel, Jeush, Jalam, and Korah.
36. Eliphaz's sons were: Teman, Omar, Zephi, Gatam, and Kenaz. (Amalek was born to Eliphaz by Timna.)
37. Reuel's sons were: Nahath, Zerah, Shammah, and Mizzah.

The People of Seir

38. Seir's sons were: Lotan, Shobal, Zibeon, Anah, Dishon, Ezer, and Dishan.
39. Lotan's sons were: Hori and Homam. Lotan's sister was Timna.
40. Shobal's sons were: Alvan, Manahath, Ebal, Shepho, and Onam. Zibeon's sons were: Aiah and Anah.
41. Anah's son was Dishon. Dishon's sons were: Hemdan, Eshban, Ithran, and Keran.
42. Ezer's sons were: Bilhan, Zaavan, and Jaakan. Dishan's sons were: Uz and Aran.

The Kings of Edom

43. These were the kings who ruled Edom before Israel had kings: Bela son of Beor (his city was Dinhabah).
44. When Bela died, Jobab son of Zerah from Bozrah became king.
45. When Jobab died, Husham from the land of the Temanites became king.
46. When Husham died, Hadad son of Bedad became king. He defeated Midian in Moab. His city was Avith.
47. When Hadad died, Samlah from Masrekah became king.
48. When Samlah died, Shaul from Rehoboth by the River became king.
49. When Shaul died, Baal-Hanan son of Acbor became king.
50. When Baal-Hanan died, Hadad became king. His city was Pai. His wife was Mehetabel, daughter of Matred and granddaughter of Me-Zahab.

The Leaders of Edom

51. When Hadad died, the leaders of Edom were: Timna, Alvah, Jetheth,
52. Oholibamah, Elah, Pinon,
53. Kenaz, Teman, Mibzar,
54. Magdiel, and Iram.

1 Chronicles 2

The Descendants of Israel

1. Israel's sons were: Reuben, Simeon, Levi, Judah, Issachar, Zebulun,
2. Dan, Joseph, Benjamin, Naphtali, Gad, and Asher.

Judah's Descendants

3. Judah's sons were: Er, Onan, and Shelah. Their mother was Bathshua from Canaan. Er did wrong, so God put him to death.
4. Judah had two more sons with Tamar: Perez and Zerah. Judah had five sons total.
5. Perez's sons were: Hezron and Hamul.
6. Zerah's sons were: Zimri, Ethan, Heman, Calcol, and Dara—five total.
7. Carmi's son was Achar, who disobeyed God and brought trouble to Israel.
8. Ethan's son was Azariah.
9. Hezron's sons were: Jerahmeel, Ram, and Caleb.
10. Ram's son was Amminadab. Amminadab's son was Nahshon, a leader of Judah.
11. Nahshon's son was Salmon. Salmon's son was Boaz.
12. Boaz's son was Obed. Obed's son was Jesse.
13. Jesse's sons were: Eliab (the oldest), Abinadab, Shimea,
14. Nethanel, Raddai,
15. Ozem, and David (the youngest).
16. Jesse's daughters were Zeruiah and Abigail. Zeruiah's sons were Abishai, Joab, and Asahel—three sons.
17. Abigail's son was Amasa. Amasa's father was Jether, an Ishmaelite.

Hezron's Family

18. Caleb (son of Hezron) had children with Azubah. Her sons were Jesher, Shobab, and Ardon.
19. After Azubah died, Caleb married Ephrath, and she had a son named Hur.
20. Hur's son was Uri. Uri's son was Bezalel.
21. Hezron later married the daughter of Makir (father of Gilead) when he was 60. They had a son named Segub.
22. Segub's son was Jair, who ruled 23 towns in Gilead.
23. The people of Geshur and Aram took Jair's towns, including Kenath and 60 nearby villages. All of them belonged to Makir's family.
24. After Hezron died, Caleb married Ephrath again. She had a son named Ashhur, who started the town of Tekoa.

Jerahmeel's Family (Hezron's Oldest Son)

25. Jerahmeel's sons were: Ram (his oldest), Bunah, Oren, Ozem, and Ahijah.
26. Jerahmeel had another wife named Atarah. She had a son named Onam.
27. Ram's sons were: Maaz, Jamin, and Eker.
28. Onam's sons were: Shammai and Jada. Shammai's sons were: Nadab and Abishur.
29. Abishur's wife was Abihail. Their sons were Ahban and Molid.
30. Nadab's sons were: Seled and Appaim. Seled died without children.
31. Appaim's son was Ishi. Ishi's son was Sheshan. Sheshan's son was Ahlai.
32. Jada (Shammai's brother) had sons: Jether and Jonathan. Jether died without children.
33. Jonathan's sons were: Peleth and Zaza. These were all Jerahmeel's descendants.
34. Sheshan had no sons, only daughters. He gave one daughter to his Egyptian servant Jarha to marry.
35. They had a son named Attai.
36. Attai's son was Nathan. Nathan's son was Zabad.
37. Zabad's son was Ephlal. Ephlal's son was Obed.
38. Obed's son was Jehu. Jehu's son was Azariah.
39. Azariah's son was Helez. Helez's son was Eleasah.

40. Eleasah's son was Sismai. Sismai's son was Shallum.

41. Shallum's son was Jekamiah. Jekamiah's son was Elishama.

Caleb's Family (Brother of Jerahmeel)

42. Caleb's oldest son was Mesha, father of Ziph. Caleb also had a son named Mareshah, father of Hebron.

43. Hebron's sons were: Korah, Tappuah, Rekem, and Shema.

44. Shema was the father of Raham. Raham was the father of Jorkeam. Rekem was the father of Shammai.

45. Shammai's son was Maon. Maon was the father of Beth Zur.

46. Caleb had a servant wife named Ephah. Her sons were Haran, Moza, and Gazez. Haran's son was Gazez.

47. Jahdai's sons were: Regem, Jotham, Geshan, Pelet, Ephah, and Shaaph.

48. Caleb had another servant wife named Maacah. Her sons were Sheber and Tirhanah.

49. Maacah also had: Shaaph (who started Madmannah), Sheva (who started Macbenah and Gibea). Caleb's daughter was Achsah.

50. These were Caleb's descendants: Hur (first son of Caleb's wife Ephrathah), who started Bethlehem.

51. Hur's sons were: Shobal (who started Kiriath Jearim),

52. Salma (who started Bethlehem), and Hareph (who started Beth Gader).

53. Shobal's family included: Haroeh and half the people of Manahath,

54. and the families living in Kiriath Jearim: Ithrites, Puthites, Shumathites, and Mishraites. From these came the Zorathites and Eshtaolites.

55. Salma's descendants included the people of Bethlehem, Netophah, Atroth-Beth Joab, and the families of scribes who lived in Jabez. These scribes were from the Tirathite, Shimeathite, and Sucathite families. They were from the Kenite group that came from Hammath and were ancestors of the Recab people.

1 Chronicles 3

David's Family

1. David had sons while he lived in Hebron. His first son was Amnon. His mother was Ahinoam from Jezreel. His second son was Daniel. His mother was Abigail from Carmel.

2. The third was Absalom, son of Maacah (daughter of Talmai, king of Geshur). The fourth was Adonijah, son of Haggith.

3. The fifth was Shephatiah, son of Abital. The sixth was Ithream, son of Eglah (David's wife).

4. These six sons were born in Hebron, where David ruled for 7½ years. He ruled another 33 years in Jerusalem.

5. In Jerusalem, David had more sons: Shimea, Shobab, Nathan, and Solomon. Their mother was Bathsheba, daughter of Ammiel.

6. David also had Ibhar, Elishua, Elpelet,

7. Nogah, Nepheg, Japhia,

8. Elishama, Eliada, and Eliphelet—nine sons in total from Jerusalem.

9. These were all David's sons. He also had sons with his servant wives. His daughter was Tamar.

Solomon's Family Line

10. Solomon's son was Rehoboam. Rehoboam's son was Abijah. Abijah's son was Asa. Asa's son was Jehoshaphat.

11. Jehoshaphat's son was Jehoram. Jehoram's son was Ahaziah. Ahaziah's son was Joash.

12. Joash's son was Amaziah. Amaziah's son was Azariah. Azariah's son was Jotham.

13. Jotham's son was Ahaz. Ahaz's son was Hezekiah. Hezekiah's son was Manasseh.

14. Manasseh's son was Amon. Amon's son was Josiah.

15. Josiah's sons were: Johanan (the oldest), Jehoiakim, Zedekiah, and Shallum.

16. Jehoiakim's sons were: Jehoiachin and Zedekiah.

Jehoiachin's Family

17. These were the sons of Jehoiachin, who was taken as a prisoner: Shealtiel,

18. Malchiram, Pedaiah, Shenazzar, Jekamiah, Hoshama, and Nedabiah.

19. Pedaiah's sons were: Zerubbabel and Shimei. Zerubbabel's sons were: Meshullam and Hananiah. Their sister was Shelomith.

20. Zerubbabel also had five more sons: Hashubah, Ohel, Berechiah, Hasadiah, and Jushab-Hesed.

21. Hananiah's sons were: Pelatiah and Jeshaiah. Jeshaiah's son was Rephaiah. Rephaiah's son was Arnan. Arnan's son was Obadiah. Obadiah's son was Shecaniah.

22. Shecaniah's son was Shemaiah. Shemaiah had five sons: Hattush, Igal, Bariah, Neariah, and Shaphat.

23. Neariah had three sons: Elioenai, Hizkiah, and Azrikam.

24. Elioenai had seven sons: Hodaviah, Eliashib, Pelaiah, Akkub, Johanan, Delaiah, and Anani.

1 Chronicles 4

The Descendants of Judah

1. Judah's sons were: Perez, Hezron, Karmi, Hur, and Shobal.

2. Shobal's son Reaiah was the father of Jahath. Jahath's sons were Ahumai and Lahad. These were the families of Zorath.

3. These were Etam's sons: Jezreel, Ishma, and Idbash. Their sister was Hazzelelponi.

4. Penuel was the father of Gedor. Ezer was the father of Hushah. These were sons of Hur, the oldest son of Ephrathah and founder of Bethlehem.

5. Ashhur, the father of Tekoa, had two wives, Helah and Naarah.

6. Naarah had Ahuzzam, Hepher, Temeni, and Haahashtari. These were Naarah's sons.

7. Helah's sons were Zereth, Zohar, and Ethnan.

8. Koz was the father of Anub, Zobebah, and the families of Aharhel, son of Harum.

The Prayer of Jabez

9. Jabez was more respected than his brothers. His mother named him Jabez because she said, "I gave birth in pain."

10. Jabez prayed to the God of Israel. He said, "Please bless me. Give me more land. Stay with me and keep me safe from harm." And God gave him what he asked for.

More Descendants of Judah

11. Kelub, Shuhah's brother, had a son named Mehir, who was the father of Eshton.

12. Eshton was the father of Beth-Rapha, Paseah, and Tehinnah (founder of Ir-Nahash). These were the people of Recah.

13. Kenaz's sons were Othniel and Seraiah. Othniel's son was Hathath.

14. Meonothai had a son named Ophrah. Seraiah had a son named Joab. He started the Valley of Craftsmen.

15. Caleb (Jephunneh's son) had sons: Iru, Elah, and Naam. Elah's son was Kenaz.

16. Jehallelel's sons were Ziph, Ziphah, Tiria, and Asarel.

17. Ezrah's sons were Jether, Mered, Epher, and Jalon. Mered's wife was Pharaoh's daughter Bithiah. She had Miriam, Shammai, and Ishbah, who founded Eshtemoa.

18. Mered's other wife, a woman from Judah, gave birth to Jered (father of

Gedor), Heber (father of Soco), and Jekuthiel (father of Zanoah).

19. Hodiah's wife (sister of Naham) had Keilah (father of the Garmite) and Eshtemoa the Maacathite.

20. Shimon's sons were Amnon, Rinnah, Ben-Hanan, and Tilon. Ishi's sons were Zoheth and Ben-Zoheth.

21. Shelah, Judah's son, had Er (father of Lecah), Laadah (father of Mareshah), and the families who made fine linen in Beth-Ashbea.

22. They were Jokim, men of Kozeba, Joash, and Saraph, who ruled in Moab and Jashubi-Lehem. These stories are very old.

23. They were potters. They lived in Netaim and Gederah. They worked for the king and lived there.

The Descendants of Simeon

24. Simeon's sons were: Nemuel, Jamin, Jarib, Zerah, and Shaul.

25. Shaul's son was Shallum. His son was Mibsam. His son was Mishma.

26. Mishma's son was Hammuel. His son was Zaccur. His son was Shimei.

27. Shimei had 16 sons and 6 daughters. But his brothers didn't have many children. Their families didn't grow as much.

28. They lived in Beersheba, Moladah, Hazar-Shual,

29. Bilhah, Ezem, Tolad,

30. Bethuel, Hormah, Ziklag,

31. Beth-Markaboth, Hazar-Susim, Beth-Biri, and Shaaraim. These towns belonged to them during David's rule.

32. Their nearby villages were Etam, Ain, Rimmon, Token, and Ashan—five towns in all.

33. They also had many small towns around these places. This was where they lived. All these names were written in their records.

34. They also had leaders named: Meshobab, Jamlech, Joshah (son of Amaziah),

35. Joel, Jehu (son of Joshibiah, grandson of Seraiah, great-grandson of Asiel),

36. Elioenai, Jaakobah, Jeshohaiah, Asaiah, Adiel, Jesimiel, Benaiah,

37. and Ziza (son of Shiphi, grandson of Allon, great-grandson of Jedaiah, from Shimri and Shemaiah).

38. These men were family leaders. Their families grew and became large.

39. They went to the edge of Gedor, east of the valley, to look for pasture for their sheep.

40. They found good, rich pasture. The land was peaceful and safe. Ham's people had lived there before.

41. During the time of King Hezekiah of Judah, these men fought the people living there. They destroyed them completely and lived in their land. There's no record of those people left.

42. Some from Simeon's group—500 men—went to Mount Seir with these leaders: Pelatiah, Neariah, Rephaiah, and Uzziel (sons of Ishi).

43. They killed the remaining Amalekites who had survived. They still live there today.

1 Chronicles 5

The Family of Reuben

1. Reuben was Israel's oldest son. But because he slept with his father's wife, he lost his rights as the firstborn. Those rights were given to the sons of Joseph.

2. Even though Judah's family became the most powerful, and kings came from Judah, the birthright belonged to Joseph.

3. Reuben's sons were: Hanoch, Pallu, Hezron, and Carmi.

4. Joel was a descendant of Reuben. Joel's son was Shemaiah, then Gog, then Shimei,

5. Then Micah, Reaiah, Baal,
6. And Beerah. He was a leader in Reuben's family and was taken away by King Tiglath-Pileser of Assyria.
7. These were the family leaders of Reuben. Their names were recorded during the time of King Jotham of Judah and King Jeroboam of Israel.
8. They lived in Aroer and as far as Nebo and Baal Meon.
9. They also lived to the east, near the edge of the desert that reaches the Euphrates River, because they had many animals in Gilead.
10. During Saul's reign, they fought the Hagrites and defeated them. They lived in the Hagrites' land after that.

The Family of Gad

11. The family of Gad lived next to Reuben in Bashan, as far as Salekah.
12. Joel was their leader, followed by Shapham, Janai, and Shaphat.
13. They had relatives in seven towns: Michael, Meshullam, Sheba, Jorai, Jacan, Zia, and Eber.
14. These men were all descendants of Abihail son of Huri, grandson of Jaroah, and also from Gilead, Michael, Jeshishai, Jahdo, and Buz.
15. Ahi, son of Abdiel and grandson of Guni, was the family's main leader.
16. They lived in Gilead, Bashan, and all the nearby towns and fields as far as Sharon.
17. All these names were written in family records during the rule of King Jotham of Judah and King Jeroboam of Israel.

War Against the Hagrites

18. The families of Reuben, Gad, and half of Manasseh had 44,760 trained warriors. They used shields, swords, bows, and were ready for battle.
19. They fought the Hagrites and the people of Jetur, Naphish, and Nodab.
20. They asked God for help during the war, and He helped them because they trusted Him. They won the battle.
21. They took 50,000 camels, 250,000 sheep, 2,000 donkeys, and 100,000 people as captives.
22. Many of the enemy were killed because God fought for Israel. After that, the families lived in the land.

The Half Family of Manasseh

23. The half-family of Manasseh lived in the land from Bashan to Baal Hermon, Senir, and Mount Hermon. Their population grew.
24. Their leaders were: Epher, Ishi, Eliel, Azriel, Jeremiah, Hodaviah, and Jahdiel. They were strong warriors and respected men.
25. But they sinned against God. They worshiped the gods of the people whom God had destroyed before them
26. So God let King Pul and King Tiglath-Pileser of Assyria take them away. They were taken to Halah, Habor, Hara, and the Gozan River, where they still live today.

1 Chronicles 6

The Family of Levi

1. Levi's sons were: Gershon, Kohath, and Merari.
2. Kohath's sons were: Amram, Izhar, Hebron, and Uzziel.
3. Amram's children were Aaron, Moses, and Miriam. Aaron's sons were Nadab, Abihu, Eleazar, and Ithamar.
4. Eleazar's son was Phinehas. Phinehas's son was Abishua.
5. Abishua's son was Bukki. Bukki's son was Uzzi.
6. Uzzi's son was Zerahiah. Zerahiah's son was Meraioth.
7. Meraioth's son was Amariah. Amariah's son was Ahitub.
8. Ahitub's son was Zadok. Zadok's son was Ahimaaz.

9. Ahimaaz's son was Azariah. Azariah's son was Johanan.

10. Johanan's son was Azariah, who served as priest in the temple Solomon built in Jerusalem.

11. Azariah's son was Amariah. Amariah's son was Ahitub.

12. Ahitub's son was Zadok. Zadok's son was Shallum.

13. Shallum's son was Hilkiah. Hilkiah's son was Azariah.

14. Azariah's son was Seraiah. Seraiah's son was Jehozadak.

15. Jehozadak went into exile when the Lord sent Judah and Jerusalem away by the hand of Nebuchadnezzar.

The Other Families of Levi

16. Levi's sons were Gershon, Kohath, and Merari.

17. Gershon's sons were Libni and Shimei.

18. Kohath's sons were Amram, Izhar, Hebron, and Uzziel.

19. Merari's sons were Mahli and Mushi. These were the families of Levi by name.

20. Gershon's line: Libni, Jahath, Zimmah,

21. Joah, Iddo, Zerah, and Jeatherai.

22. Kohath's line: Amminadab, Korah, Assir,

23. Elkanah, Ebiasaph, Assir,

24. Tahath, Uriel, Uzziah, and Shaul.

25. Elkanah's sons were Amasai and Ahimoth.

26. Elkanah's line: Elkanah, Zophai, Nahath,

27. Eliab, Jeroham, and Elkanah. Then came Samuel.

28. Samuel's sons were Joel (the oldest) and Abijah.

29. Merari's line: Mahli, Libni, Shimei, Uzzah,

30. Shimea, Haggiah, and Asaiah.

The Levites Who Served with Music

31. These are the men David chose to lead music at the Lord's house after the sacred chest was placed there.

32. They served with music in the tent of meeting until Solomon built the temple. They continued their duties as planned.

33. These are the men who served, listed by family:
Heman led the music. He was son of Joel, son of Samuel,

34. son of Elkanah, son of Jeroham, son of Eliel, son of Toah,

35. son of Zuph, son of Elkanah, son of Mahath, son of Amasai,

36. son of Elkanah, son of Joel, son of Azariah, son of Zephaniah,

37. son of Tahath, son of Assir, son of Ebiasaph, son of Korah,

38. son of Izhar, son of Kohath, son of Levi, son of Israel.

More Singers

39. Heman's relative Asaph served at his right side. He was son of Berechiah, son of Shimea,

40. son of Michael, son of Baaseiah, son of Malchijah,

41. son of Ethni, son of Zerah, son of Adaiah,

42. son of Ethan, son of Zimmah, son of Shimei,

43. son of Jahath, son of Gershon, son of Levi.

44. On Heman's left side was Ethan, from Merari's family. He was son of Kishi, son of Abdi, son of Malluk,

45. son of Hashabiah, son of Amaziah, son of Hilkiah,

46. son of Amzi, son of Bani, son of Shemer,

47. son of Mahli, son of Mushi, son of Merari, son of Levi.

48. Their fellow Levites were assigned to do other work in the tent of the Lord's house.

Aaron's Descendants Who Served as Priests

49. Aaron and his sons gave offerings on the altar and in the temple. They did all the holy work and made sacrifices to forgive sins for the people of Israel.

50. This is Aaron's line: Eleazar, Phinehas, Abishua,

51. Bukki, Uzzi, Zerahiah,

52. Meraioth, Amariah, Ahitub,

53. Zadok, and Ahimaaz.

Where the Levite Families Lived

54. These were the places where Aaron's family lived. They got these towns in Judah because of the special job they had.

55. They were given Hebron in Judah and the land around it.

56. But the fields and villages were given to Caleb (son of Jephunneh).

57. Aaron's family got Hebron (a city of safety), Libnah, Jattir, Eshtemoa,

58. Hilen, Debir,

59. Ashan, and Beth Shemesh.

60. From the tribe of Benjamin they received Geba, Alemeth, and Anathoth—13 towns total.

61. The rest of the Kohath family got 10 towns from half the family of Manasseh.

Where Other Levites Lived

62. The Gershon family got 13 towns from Issachar, Asher, Naphtali, and Manasseh in Bashan.

63. The Merari family got 12 towns from Reuben, Gad, and Zebulun.

64. The Israelites gave all these towns to the Levites.

65. The tribes gave the Levites towns with fields from Judah, Simeon, and Benjamin.

Town Assignments by Family

66. Some Kohath families got towns from Ephraim.

67. In Ephraim, they got Shechem (a city of safety), Gezer,

68. Jokmeam, Beth Horon,

69. Aijalon, and Gath Rimmon.

70. From half of Manasseh's family, they got Aner and Bileam.

More Towns for Levite Families

71. The Gershon families got Golan (a city of safety) and Ashtaroth in Bashan from half of Manasseh's family.

72. From Issachar they got Kedesh, Daberath,

73. Ramoth, and Anem.

74. From Asher they got Mashal, Abdon,

75. Hukok, and Rehob.

76. From Naphtali they got Kedesh in Galilee (a city of safety), Hammoth Dor, and Kartan.

Towns for Merari's Family

77. The rest of the Levites (from Merari's family) got Jokneam, Kartah,

78. Rimmon, and Tabor from Zebulun.

79. From Reuben they got Bezer, Jahaz,

80. Kedemoth, and Mephaath.

81. From Gad they got Ramoth in Gilead, Mahanaim, Heshbon, and Jazer.

1 Chronicles 7

The Family of Issachar

1. Issachar's sons were: Tola, Puah, Jashub, and Shimron—four sons.

2. Tola's sons were: Uzzi, Rephaiah, Jeriel, Jahmai, Ibsam, and Shemuel. They were leaders in their families and strong warriors. In David's time, 22,600 men from their families were counted.

3. Uzzi's son was Izrahiah. His sons were: Michael, Obadiah, Joel, and Isshiah. All five were family leaders.

4. They had many soldiers—36,000—because they had many wives and children.
5. The total number of fighting men in all Issachar's families was 87,000, listed in their records.

The Family of Benjamin

6. Benjamin's sons were: Bela, Beker, and Jediael—three sons.
7. Bela's sons were: Ezbon, Uzzi, Uzziel, Jerimoth, and Iri—five leaders and strong soldiers. 22,034 men were listed from Bela's family.
8. Beker's sons were: Zemirah, Joash, Eliezer, Elioenai, Omri, Jerimoth, Abijah, Anathoth, and Alemeth.
9. These were family leaders. 20,200 fighting men were listed from them.
10. Jediael's son was Bilhan. Bilhan's sons were: Jeush, Benjamin, Ehud, Kenaanah, Zethan, Tarshish, and Ahishahar.
11. They were family leaders and strong soldiers. 17,200 were listed as ready to fight.
12. Shuppim and Huppim were sons of Ir. Hushim was the son of Aher.

The Family of Naphtali

13. Naphtali's sons were: Jahziel, Guni, Jezer, and Shillem. They were descendants of Bilhah.

The Family of Manasseh

14. Manasseh's sons by his Aramean slave wife were Asriel and Makir (father of Gilead).
15. Makir found a wife for his son Huppim and named his other son Shuppim. His sister's name was Maacah. Another son, Zelophehad, had only daughters.
16. Maacah, Makir's wife, had a son and named him Peresh. His brother was Sheresh. Peresh's sons were Ulam and Rakem.
17. Ulam's son was Bedan. These were the sons of Gilead (son of Makir, son of Manasseh).
18. Gilead's sister Hammoleketh had Ishhod, Abiezer, and Mahlah.
19. Shemida's sons were: Ahian, Shechem, Likhi, and Aniam.

The Family of Ephraim

20. Ephraim's sons were: Shuthelah, Bered, Tahath, Eleadah, Tahath,
21. Zabad, and Shuthelah. Ephraim's sons Ezer and Elead were killed trying to steal cattle from people in Gath.
22. Their father Ephraim mourned a long time, and his family came to comfort him.
23. Later, he and his wife had a son, and Ephraim named him Beriah because of the trouble they had.
24. Beriah's daughter was Sheerah. She built Lower and Upper Beth Horon and Uzzen Sheerah.
25. Ephraim's son was Rephah. His line was: Resheph, Telah, Tahan,
26. Ladan, Ammihud, Elishama,
27. Nun, and Joshua.
28. Their land included: Bethel, Naaran (to the east), Gezer and Shechem (to the west), and towns as far as Ayyah.
29. They also had towns near Manasseh's land: Beth Shan, Taanach, Megiddo, and Dor. These towns were where Joseph's family lived.

The Family of Asher

30. Asher's sons were: Imnah, Ishvah, Ishvi, and Beriah. Their sister was Serah.
31. Beriah's sons were: Heber and Malkiel (father of Birzaith).
32. Heber had sons: Japhlet, Shomer, and Hotham. He also had a daughter named Shua.
33. Japhlet's sons were: Pasach, Bimhal, and Ashvath.
34. Shomer's sons were: Ahi, Rohgah, Hubbah, and Aram.
35. Hotham's sons were: Zophah, Imna, Shelesh, and Amal.

36. Zophah's sons were: Suah, Harnepher, Shual, Beri, Imrah,
37. Bezer, Hod, Shamma, Shilshah, Ithran, and Beera.
38. Jether's sons were: Jephunneh, Pispa, and Ara.
39. Ulla's sons were: Arah, Hanniel, and Rizia.
40. All these were from Asher's family. They were family leaders, strong warriors, and respected men. They were ready for battle. 26,000 of them were listed in the family records.

1 Chronicles 8

The Family of Benjamin

1. Benjamin's first son was Bela. His other sons were Ashbel, Aharah,
2. Nohah, and Rapha—five sons in total.
3. Bela's sons were: Addar, Gera, Abihud,
4. Abishua, Naaman, Ahoah,
5. Gera, Shephuphan, and Huram.
6. Ehud's sons were family leaders in Geba, but they were taken away to Manahath.
7. Ehud's sons were Naaman, Ahijah, and Gera. Gera led them into exile and had sons: Uzza and Ahihud.

The Descendants of Shaharaim

8. Shaharaim divorced his wives Hushim and Baara. Later, in Moab,
9. He had sons with Hodesh. Their names were Jobab, Zibia, Mesha, Malcam,
10. Jeuz, Sakia, and Mirmah. These were his sons, all family leaders.
11. He also had sons with his first wife Hushim: Abitub and Elpaal.

The Descendants of Elpaal

12. Elpaal's sons were: Eber, Misham, and Shemed (who built Ono and Lod with nearby towns).
13. Beriah and Shema were leaders of the families in Aijalon. They drove out the people of Gath.
14. Beriah's sons were: Ahio, Shashak, and Jeremoth.
15. Elpaal's other sons were: Zebadiah, Arad, Eder,
16. Michael, Ishpah, and Joha—seven sons in total.
17. Beriah's other sons were: Zebadiah, Meshullam, Hizki, Heber,
18. Ishmerai, Izliah, and Jobab—seven sons in total.
19. Shimei's sons were: Jakim, Zikri, Zabdi,
20. Elienai, Zillethai, Eliel,
21. Adaiah, Beraiah, and Shimrath—sons of Shimei.
22. Ishpan's sons were: Shashak, Jeremoth,
23. Zebadiah, Arad, Eder,
24. Michael, Ishpah, and Joha.
25. Jeroham's sons were: Elioenai, Zillethai, Eliel,
26. Adaiah, Beraiah, and Shimrath.

The Descendants of Shimhi and Shashak

27. Shimei's sons were: Shamsherai, Shehariah, Athaliah,
28. Jaareshiah, Elijah, and Zikri—seven sons in total.
29. Jeroham's family lived in Gibeon. His wife's name was Maacah.
30. His first son was Abdon, then Zur, Kish, Baal, Nadab,
31. Gedor, Ahio, and Zecher.
32. Mikloth was the father of Shimeah. They lived near their relatives in Jerusalem.

The Family of King Saul

33. Ner was the father of Kish. Kish was the father of Saul. Saul's sons were Jonathan, Malki-Shua, Abinadab, and Esh-Baal.

34. Jonathan's son was Merib-Baal. Merib-Baal's son was Micah.
35. Micah's sons were: Pithon, Melek, Tarea, and Ahaz.
36. Ahaz's son was Jehoaddah. Jehoaddah's sons were: Alemeth, Azmaveth, and Zimri. Zimri's son was Moza.
37. Moza's son was Binea. His son was Raphah. His son was Eleasah. His son was Azel.
38. Azel had six sons. Their names were: Azrikam, Bokeru, Ishmael, Sheariah, Obadiah, and Hanan.
39. Azel's brother Eshek had three sons: Ulam, Jeush, and Eliphelet.
40. Ulam's sons were strong warriors who used bows well. They had many sons and grandsons—150 total. All these men were from Benjamin's family.

1 Chronicles 9

The People Who Returned

1. All Israel was listed in family records. These records were kept in the book of the kings of Israel. The people of Judah were taken away to Babylon because they sinned.
2. The first people to return and live again in their towns were Israelites, priests, Levites, and temple helpers.
3. Some people from Judah, Benjamin, Ephraim, and Manasseh lived in Jerusalem.
4. These were the leaders from Judah's family: Uthai (son of Ammihud, grandson of Omri, great-grandson of Imri, from Bani), and from Perez's family.
5. Asaiah, the oldest son of the Shelanite family, lived in Jerusalem.
6. From Zerah's family: Jeuel and 690 others.
7. From Benjamin's family: Sallu (son of Meshullam, grandson of Hodaviah, great-grandson of Hassenuah),
8. Ibneiah (son of Jeroham), Elah (son of Uzzi, son of Mikri), and Meshullam (son of Shephatiah, son of Reuel, son of Ibnijah).
9. These men were family leaders. There were 956 total from Benjamin's family living in Jerusalem.

The Priests Who Returned

10. From the priests: Jedaiah, Jehoiarib, Jakin,
11. Azariah (son of Hilkiah, grandson of Meshullam, great-grandson of Zadok, from Ahitub's family, who served in God's temple),
12. Adaiah (son of Jeroham, son of Pashhur, son of Malkijah), and Maasai (son of Adiel, son of Jahzerah, son of Meshullam, son of Meshillemith, son of Immer).
13. These priests were family leaders. There were 1,760 total who were able and trusted to work at the temple.

The Levites Who Returned

14. From the Levites: Shemaiah (son of Hasshub, son of Azrikam, son of Hashabiah, from Merari's family),
15. Bakbakkar, Heresh, Galal, and Mattaniah (son of Mica, son of Zikri, son of Asaph),
16. Obadiah (son of Shemaiah, son of Galal, son of Jeduthun), and Berekiah (son of Asa, son of Elkanah), who lived in the villages of the Netophathites.

The Gatekeepers Who Returned

17. The gatekeepers were: Shallum, Akkub, Talmon, Ahiman, and their brothers. Shallum was their leader.
18. They guarded the King's Gate on the east side and had done so since being gatekeepers for the Levite camp.
19. Shallum (son of Kore, son of Ebiasaph, son of Korah) and his relatives from the Korahite family were in charge of guarding the entrances to the temple. Their ancestors had guarded the Lord's camp.

20. Phinehas (son of Eleazar) had been in charge of them before, and God was with him.

21. Zechariah (son of Meshelemiah) guarded the gate at the temple entrance.

22. A total of 212 men were chosen to guard the gates. They were listed in the family records. David and Samuel had put them in charge.

23. They and their sons guarded the gates of the Lord's temple.

24. There were guards on all four sides—east, west, north, and south.

25. Their relatives from the villages came in shifts to help them guard for seven days at a time.

26. The four head guards were Levites. They were trusted to be in charge of the rooms and storerooms in God's temple.

27. They stayed around the temple because they had to guard it and open the gates every morning.

The Levite Workers

28. Some of them were in charge of the temple's special items. They counted the items when they were taken out and returned.

29. Others were responsible for the other furniture and tools. They checked everything.

30. Some Levites were in charge of mixing the spices used for the holy oil.

31. Mattithiah (from the Kohathite family and oldest son of Shallum) made the bread offered to God every Sabbath.

32. Some of their brothers, from the Kohathites, were in charge of preparing the special bread placed before the Lord every week.

33. These Levites were the singers. They lived in rooms at the temple and were free from other jobs because they sang day and night.

34. These were the family leaders of the Levites. They were listed in the records and lived in Jerusalem.

The Family of King Saul

35. Jeiel (father of Gibeon) lived in Gibeon. His wife's name was Maacah.

36. His oldest son was Abdon, then Zur, Kish, Baal, Ner, Nadab,

37. Gedor, Ahio, Zechariah, and Mikloth.

38. Mikloth was the father of Shimeam. They all lived near their relatives in Jerusalem.

39. Ner was the father of Kish. Kish was the father of Saul. Saul's sons were Jonathan, Malki-Shua, Abinadab, and Esh-Baal.

40. Jonathan's son was Merib-Baal. Merib-Baal's son was Micah.

41. Micah's sons were: Pithon, Melek, Tahrea, and Ahaz.

42. Ahaz was the father of Jarah. Jarah's sons were Alemeth, Azmaveth, and Zimri. Zimri's son was Moza.

43. Moza's son was Binea. His son was Rephaiah. His son was Eleasah. His son was Azel.

44. Azel had six sons. Their names were: Azrikam, Bokeru, Ishmael, Sheariah, Obadiah, and Hanan. These were Azel's sons.

1 Chronicles 10

The Death of Saul

1. The Philistines fought Israel. The Israelites ran away and many died on Mount Gilboa.

2. The Philistines chased Saul and killed his sons: Jonathan, Abinadab, and Malki-Shua.

3. The battle was heavy around Saul. Archers hit him, and he was badly wounded.

4. Saul told his armor-bearer, "Pull out your sword and kill me, so these enemies don't come and hurt me." But

the man was too afraid. So Saul took his own sword and fell on it.

5. When the armor-bearer saw Saul was dead, he also fell on his sword and died.
6. So Saul, his three sons, and all his men died that day.
7. When the Israelites nearby saw the army had lost and Saul was dead, they left their towns and ran. The Philistines moved in and lived there.
8. The next day, the Philistines found Saul and his sons' bodies on the ground.
9. They took Saul's armor and cut off his head. They sent messengers to tell the good news to their idols and people.
10. They put Saul's armor in the temple of their gods and hung his head in the temple of Dagon.
11. When the people of Jabesh Gilead heard what the Philistines had done to Saul,
12. All the brave men went and got the bodies of Saul and his sons. They brought them to Jabesh and buried them under a tree. Then they fasted for seven days.
13. Saul died because he was not faithful to God. He didn't obey God's commands and even asked for advice from a witch.
14. He didn't ask God for help. So God killed him and gave the kingdom to David.

1 Chronicles 11

David Becomes King

1. All the Israelites came to David at Hebron and said, "We are your own people."
2. "Even before, when Saul was king, you were the one who led us in battle. The Lord said you would be our leader."
3. David made a promise to the leaders at Hebron. They made him king as the Lord had said.
4. David and his men went to Jerusalem (called Jebus). The people there, the Jebusites, told David, "You can't come in here!" But David captured the city.
5. David took the fortress of Zion, now called the City of David.
6. David had said, "Whoever attacks first will be commander." Joab did, so he became commander.
7. David lived in the fortress and named it the City of David.
8. He built the city around it. Joab repaired the rest.
9. David became more powerful because God was with him.

David's Top Warriors

10. These were the leaders of David's strongest warriors. They helped make him king.
11. Jashobeam was the top warrior. He used a spear to kill 300 men at one time.
12. Next was Eleazar.
13. He fought beside David in a field of barley. When everyone else ran, they stayed and won the battle.
14. God gave them a great victory.
15. Once, three of the top warriors went to David at the cave of Adullam. The Philistines were camped in the valley.
16. David was in a stronghold, and Philistine soldiers were in Bethlehem.
17. David said, "I wish I had water from the well near the Bethlehem gate."
18. The three warriors broke through the enemy lines, got water from the well, and brought it back to David. But David refused to drink it.
19. He said, "This water is like the blood of the men who risked their lives." So he poured it out to the Lord.
20. Abishai, Joab's brother, was also a top warrior. He killed 300 men with his spear.
21. He was the most famous of the three but was not as great as the first three.

22. Benaiah was a brave man from Kabzeel. He did great things. He killed two strong Moabite men.
23. He also went into a snowy pit and killed a lion.
24. He killed a giant Egyptian man using the man's own spear.
25. He was as famous as the three but not quite equal to them. David made him the head of his bodyguards.
26. Other great warriors were: Asahel (Joab's brother), Elhanan (son of Dodo),
27. Shammoth from Harod, Helez from Pelon,
28. Ira from Tekoa, Abiezer from Anathoth,
29. Sibbekai from Hushah, Ilai from Ahoah,
30. Maharai from Netophah, Heled (son of Baanah),
31. Ithai (son of Ribai from Gibeah in Benjamin), Benaiah from Pirathon,
32. Hurai from Nahale Gaash, Abiel from Arabah,
33. Azmaveth from Bahurim, Eliahba from Shaalbon,
34. The sons of Hashem from Gizon, Jonathan (son of Shagee from Harar),
35. Ahiam (son of Sakar from Harar), Eliphal (son of Ur),
36. Hepher from Mekerah, Ahijah from Pelon,
37. Hezro from Carmel, Naarai (son of Ezbai),
38. Joel (brother of Nathan), Mibhar (son of Hagri),
39. Zelek from Ammon, Naharai from Beeroth (Joab's armor-bearer),
40. Ira and Gareb from Jattir,
41. Uriah the Hittite, Zabad (son of Ahlai),
42. Adina (son of Shiza from Reuben), chief of 30 men,
43. Hanan (son of Maakah), Joshaphat from Mithna,
44. Uzzia from Ashteroth, Shama and Jeiel from Aroer,
45. Jediael (son of Shimri), Joha (his brother), from Tiz,
46. Eliel from Mahavah, Jeribai and Joshaviah (sons of Elnaam), Ithmah the Moabite,
47. Eliel, Obed, and Jaasiel from Zobah.

1 Chronicles 12

Warriors Who Joined David

1. These are the men who joined David when he was hiding from Saul. They were brave fighters.
2. They could shoot arrows and throw stones with both hands. They were from Saul's family in Benjamin.
3. Their leader was Ahiezer, then Joash. They were sons of Shemaah from Gibeah. Then came Jeziel, Pelet, Beracah, Jehu from Anathoth,
4. Ishmaiah from Gibeon, a great warrior, and thirty men with him,
5. Jeremiah, Jahaziel, Johanan, Jozabad from Gederah,
6. Eluzai, Jerimoth, Bealiah, Shemariah, Shephatiah from Haruph,
7. Elkanah, Ishiah, Azarel, Joezer, and Jashobeam from Korah's family,
8. and Joelah and Zebadiah (sons of Jeroham) from Gedor.
9. Some strong warriors from Gad joined David in the wilderness. They were expert soldiers, like lions, and fast as deer.
10. Their leader was Ezer, then Obadiah, Eliab,
11. Mishmannah, Jeremiah,
12. Attai, Eliel,
13. Johanan, Elzabad,
14. Jeremiah, and Machbannai—11 in total.

15. They crossed the Jordan River when it was flooding and chased away enemies on both sides.

More Men Join David

16. Other men from Benjamin and Judah came to David at his camp.
17. David went to meet them and said, "If you come to help me, welcome. But if you're here to trick me, God will punish you."
18. God's Spirit came on Amasai, their leader. He said, "We are with you, David. Peace to you and all who help you." David welcomed them.
19. Some men from Manasseh joined David when he went to fight with the Philistines. But the Philistine rulers didn't trust David, so they sent him back.
20. These were the men from Manasseh who joined David: Adnah, Jozabad, Jediael, Michael, Jozabad, Elihu, and Zillethai—leaders of thousands.
21. They helped David fight enemy raiders. They were all strong warriors and leaders.
22. Every day more men joined David until he had a great army.

Soldiers Who Helped Make David King

23. These are the numbers of soldiers who came to David at Hebron to make him king, just as God had promised.
24. From Judah's family: 6,800 men armed for battle.
25. From Simeon's family: 7,100 brave soldiers.
26. From Levi's family: 4,600 men.
27. Jehoiada, leader from Aaron's family, brought 3,700 men.
28. Zadok, a brave young man, brought 22 officers.
29. From Benjamin, Saul's family: 3,000 men. Most of them had stayed loyal to Saul.
30. From Ephraim's family: 20,800 brave warriors, famous in their families.
31. From half of Manasseh's family: 18,000 came to make David king.
32. From Issachar's family: 200 leaders who understood the times and knew what Israel should do. Their families followed them.
33. From Zebulun's family: 50,000 trained soldiers who were loyal and ready to fight.
34. From Naphtali's family: 1,000 leaders and 37,000 men with shields and spears.
35. From Dan's family: 28,600 men ready for battle.
36. From Asher's family: 40,000 trained warriors.
37. From the east side of the Jordan (Reuben, Gad, and half of Manasseh): 120,000 men with all kinds of weapons.

Celebrating David's Kingship

38. All these men came with one purpose—to make David king. Everyone in Israel agreed.
39. They were with David for three days, eating and drinking. Their families had provided food.
40. People from nearby towns brought food—flour, cakes, wine, oil, cattle, and sheep. There was great joy in Israel.

1 Chronicles 13

The Sacred Chest (Ark) is Moved

1. David talked with his commanders and leaders.
2. He said, "If you agree, and if God is with us, let's ask the rest of Israel to join us, including priests and Levites in their towns."
3. "Let's bring back the Sacred Chest of our God. We didn't use it when Saul was king."
4. Everyone agreed.
5. So David gathered all Israel from the Shihor River in Egypt to Lebo

Hamath, to get the Sacred Chest from Kiriath Jearim.

6. David and all Israel went to Baalah (also called Kiriath Jearim) in Judah to bring back the Sacred Chest of God. The Lord sits above the winged creatures on the Chest.
7. They put the Sacred Chest on a new cart and took it from Abinadab's house. Uzzah and Ahio guided the cart.
8. David and all the people celebrated with all their strength. They played harps, lyres, tambourines, cymbals, and trumpets.
9. When they came to Kidon's threshing floor, the oxen stumbled. Uzzah reached out to stop the Sacred Chest.
10. God was angry because Uzzah touched the Sacred Chest. God struck him, and Uzzah died there.
11. David was upset that the Lord was angry with Uzzah. That place is still called Perez Uzzah.
12. David was afraid of God and said, "How can I bring the Sacred Chest to me?"
13. So he didn't move it to his city. He took it to the house of Obed-Edom of Gath.
14. The Sacred Chest stayed at Obed-Edom's house for three months, and the Lord blessed him and everything he owned.

1 Chronicles 14

David's Family Grows

1. King Hiram of Tyre sent messengers to David. They brought cedar wood, builders, and stone workers to build David a palace.
2. David knew God had made him king and made his kingdom strong for the good of Israel.
3. David married more women in Jerusalem and had more sons and daughters.
4. These are the names of the children born to him there: Shammua, Shobab, Nathan, Solomon,
5. Ibhar, Elishua, Elpelet,
6. Nogah, Nepheg, Japhia,
7. Elishama, Beeliada, and Eliphelet.

David Defeats the Philistines

8. When the Philistines heard David was king, they went to find him. David heard about it and went out to fight them.
9. The Philistines had raided the Valley of Rephaim.
10. David asked God, "Should I attack them? Will you help me win?" God said, "Yes. I'll help you win."
11. So David went to Baal Perazim and defeated them. He said, "God broke through my enemies like water breaking through a wall." That's why the place is called Baal Perazim.
12. The Philistines left their idols there. David had them burned.
13. Later, the Philistines came back to raid the valley again.
14. David asked God what to do. God said, "Don't attack them straight on. Go around and attack from the trees."
15. "When you hear marching in the treetops, attack right away. That means I've gone ahead of you to win the battle."
16. David did what God said and defeated the Philistines from Gibeon to Gezer.
17. David became famous, and all the nations were afraid of him because God made him powerful.

1 Chronicles 15

The Sacred Chest is Moved Correctly

1. David built houses for himself in Jerusalem. He also made a place for the Sacred Chest and set up a tent for it.

2. He said, "Only the Levites can carry the Sacred Chest. That's what the Lord chose them for."
3. David gathered everyone in Israel to bring the Sacred Chest to Jerusalem.
4. He called together Aaron's and Levi's families.
5. From Kohath's family: Uriel and 120 relatives.
6. From Merari's family: Asaiah and 220 relatives.
7. From Gershon's family: Joel and 130 relatives.
8. From Elizaphan's family: Shemaiah and 200 relatives.
9. From Hebron's family: Eliel and 80 relatives.
10. From Uzziel's family: Amminadab and 112 relatives.
11. David called the priests Zadok and Abiathar and the Levite leaders.
12. He said, "You are the family leaders. Make yourselves clean. Then bring the Sacred Chest to the place I prepared."
13. "Last time, we didn't do it right. We didn't ask God how to move it."
14. So the priests and Levites made themselves clean to carry the Sacred Chest.
15. The Levites carried it with poles, just as Moses had said by the Lord's command.
16. David told the Levite leaders to appoint singers to play lyres, harps, and cymbals and to sing with joy.
17. So the Levites chose Heman (son of Joel), Asaph (son of Berechiah), and Ethan (son of Kushaiah).
18. With them were Zechariah, Jaaziel, Shemiramoth, Jehiel, Unni, Eliab, Maaseiah, Benaiah,
19. and the musicians: Heman, Asaph, and Ethan. They played bronze cymbals.
20. Zechariah, Aziel, Shemiramoth, Jehiel, Unni, Eliab, Maaseiah, and Benaiah played harps.
21. Mattithiah, Eliphelehu, Mikneiah, Obed-Edom, Jeiel, and Azaziah played lyres.
22. Kenaniah led the singing because he was good at it.
23. Berekiah and Elkanah guarded the Sacred Chest.
24. Shebaniah, Joshaphat, Nethanel, Amasai, Zechariah, Benaiah, and Eliezer were priests. They blew trumpets in front of the Chest. Obed-Edom and Jehiah also guarded it.

The Sacred Chest Enters Jerusalem

25. David, the leaders, and the Levites went with joy to bring the Sacred Chest from Obed-Edom's house.
26. God helped the Levites carry it. They sacrificed seven bulls and seven rams.
27. David wore a linen robe, just like the Levites and singers. He also wore a linen priest's vest.
28. All Israel brought the Sacred Chest with shouts, trumpets, cymbals, harps, and lyres.
29. As the Chest came into Jerusalem, Saul's daughter Michal saw David dancing. She didn't respect him and felt ashamed of him.

1 Chronicles 16

The Sacred Chest Is Placed in the Tent

1. They brought the Sacred Chest of God and placed it in the tent David had set up. Then they offered burnt offerings and peace offerings.
2. After David finished the offerings, he blessed the people in God's name.
3. He gave every person in Israel, both men and women, a loaf of bread, a cake of dates, and a raisin cake.
4. He chose some Levites to serve before the Sacred Chest. They gave thanks and praise to the Lord.
5. Asaph was the leader, with Zechariah next. Then came Jeiel, Shemiramoth, Jehiel, Mattithiah, Eliab, Benaiah, and

Obed-Edom. They played harps and lyres. Asaph played the cymbals.

6. Benaiah and Jahaziel were priests who blew trumpets every day in front of the Sacred Chest.

David's Song of Thanks

7. That day, David gave this song to Asaph and the Levites to sing:
8. Thank the Lord. Call on Him. Tell the nations what He has done.
9. Sing to Him. Praise Him. Tell about the great things He has done.
10. Be proud of Him. Let those who follow God be happy.
11. Go to the Lord for help. Always seek Him.
12. Remember the great things He has done—His miracles and His decisions.
13. You are His people, His children, the family of Jacob.
14. He is the Lord our God. His rules are everywhere.
15. He keeps His promise forever—His word lasts for all people.
16. He made a promise to Abraham, and confirmed it with Isaac.
17. He gave it to Jacob as a law, to Israel as a lasting agreement:
18. "I will give you the land of Canaan."
19. At that time they were few in number and strangers in the land.
20. They traveled from one nation to another.
21. But God didn't let anyone hurt them. He warned kings not to harm them.
22. He said, "Don't touch my chosen people. Don't hurt my prophets."
23. Sing to the Lord, everyone on earth. Share the good news of His salvation.
24. Tell about His glory and miracles in all nations.
25. The Lord is great and deserves all praise. He is more powerful than all gods.
26. Other nations worship fake gods, but the Lord made the heavens.
27. Honor and power are with Him. Joy and strength fill His home.
28. Praise the Lord, all families of nations.
29. Give glory to the Lord. Bring an offering and come to worship Him.
30. Worship the Lord in holy beauty. Everyone should tremble before Him.
31. Let the earth be glad. Say among the nations, "The Lord rules!"
32. Let the sea roar with all that's in it. Let the fields be happy.
33. Then the trees will sing because the Lord is coming to judge the world.
34. Thank the Lord. He is good. His love lasts forever.
35. Say, "Lord, save us. Bring us back. Keep us safe so we can praise You."
36. Praise the Lord, the God of Israel, forever! Everyone said, "Amen!" and praised the Lord.

Worship Is Organized

37. David left Asaph and his group to serve daily before the Sacred Chest.
38. Obed-Edom and 68 others were assigned to help. Hosah and Obed-Edom were gatekeepers.
39. David also put Zadok and other priests at the Lord's altar in Gibeon to offer daily sacrifices,
40. as written in the Lord's law. They offered morning and evening sacrifices.
41. Heman, Jeduthun, and others were chosen to give thanks with the words, "His love lasts forever."
42. Heman and Jeduthun had trumpets and cymbals and played other instruments. Their sons were gatekeepers.
43. Then everyone went home. David also returned to bless his own family.

1 Chronicles 17

God's Promise to David

1. David said, "I live in a palace, but the Sacred Chest is in a tent."
2. Nathan the prophet said, "Do what's in your heart. God is with you."
3. But that night, God spoke to Nathan:
4. "Go tell David: You will not build me a house to live in.
5. I never lived in a house. I moved with the Israelites in a tent.
6. I never asked any leader, 'Why haven't you built me a house?'"
7. "Tell David: I chose you from the fields to lead My people.
8. I was with you. I defeated your enemies. I made you famous.
9. I will give My people a safe home.
10. I will give them peace. Evil people won't bother them anymore. I will make your family great.
11. When you die, I will raise up your son. He will rule after you.
12. He will build a house for Me, and I will make his kingdom last forever.
13. I will be his father, and he will be My son. I will never take My love from him.
14. I will put him over My people forever. His kingdom will never end."
15. Nathan told David everything God had said.

David's Prayer

16. David went into the tent and sat before God. He said, "Who am I, Lord, and what is my family, that You brought me this far?"
17. "You've made promises about my future and honored me. You treat me like I'm very important."
18. "What more can I say? You know me, Lord."
19. "You did all this to show Your greatness and keep Your promise."
20. "There's no one like You, Lord. No god but You."
21. "You chose Israel to be Your own. You saved them with miracles."
22. "You made them Your people forever. And You are their God."
23. "Now, Lord, do what You promised about my family. Keep Your word."
24. "Then people will always honor You and say, 'The Lord rules over Israel!' My family will stay strong before You."
25. "You have told me about these blessings, so I had the courage to pray."
26. "Lord, You are God. Your promises are true. You gave me this blessing."
27. "Please bless my family so we will always serve You. Lord, You have blessed, and it will last forever."

1 Chronicles 18

David Wins Many Battles

1. David defeated the Philistines and took Gath and its villages.
2. He also defeated Moab. The Moabites became his servants and paid him money.
3. David defeated Hadadezer, king of Zobah, as he tried to take control near the Euphrates River.
4. David captured 1,000 chariots, 7,000 chariot riders, and 20,000 foot soldiers. He kept 100 chariots and disabled the rest.
5. The Arameans of Damascus came to help Hadadezer. David killed 22,000 of them.
6. David set up guards in Damascus. The Arameans became his servants and paid money. God helped David win wherever he went.
7. David took the gold shields from Hadadezer's officers and brought them to Jerusalem.
8. He took a lot of bronze from Tebah and Cun, cities of Hadadezer. Solomon

later used it to make the bronze basin, pillars, and tools.

9. When King Tou of Hamath heard David had defeated Hadadezer,
10. he sent his son Hadoram to greet David and give him gifts of gold, silver, and bronze. Hadadezer had often fought Tou.
11. David gave the silver and gold to the Lord. He did this with all the treasure from Edom, Moab, Ammon, the Philistines, and Amalek.
12. Abishai (son of Zeruiah) defeated 18,000 Edomites in the Valley of Salt.
13. David set up guards in Edom. The people became his servants. The Lord helped David wherever he went.

David's Officials

14. David ruled Israel and did what was fair and right.
15. Joab (son of Zeruiah) was in charge of the army. Jehoshaphat (son of Ahilud) kept records.
16. Zadok and Ahimelek were priests. Shavsha was the royal secretary.
17. Benaiah (son of Jehoiada) led the bodyguards. David's sons were important officials.

1 Chronicles 19

War with the Ammonites

1. King Nahash of Ammon died. His son Hanun became king.
2. David said, "I'll be kind to Hanun, just as his father was kind to me." He sent messengers to comfort Hanun.
3. But Ammon's leaders said, "Do you think David really wants to honor your father? He sent spies!"
4. So Hanun shaved off half their beards, cut their clothes to show their backsides, and sent them away.
5. David heard what happened and sent word: "Stay in Jericho until your beards grow back."
6. The Ammonites knew they had made David angry. So they hired 32,000 chariot soldiers from Aram, along with troops from Maacah and Zobah.
7. They camped near Medeba. David sent Joab and the army.
8. The Ammonites lined up at their city gate. The other kings were in the fields.
9. Joab saw enemies in front and behind. He chose the best soldiers for battle with Aram.
10. The rest of the army, under Abishai, faced the Ammonites.
11. Joab said, "If Aram is too strong for me, help me. If the Ammonites are too strong for you, I'll help you."
12. "Be brave. Fight for our people and God's cities. May God do what He thinks is right."
13. Joab and his men attacked Aram. Aram ran away.
14. When the Ammonites saw Aram flee, they also ran. Abishai returned to Jerusalem.
15. Aram regrouped.
16. Hadadezer brought troops from the other side of the river. They came to Helam.
17. David gathered Israel and crossed the Jordan. He set up for battle at Helam. Aram fought him.
18. David defeated them. He killed 7,000 chariot drivers and 40,000 foot soldiers. He also killed their commander Shophak.
19. When Hadadezer's officers saw they were losing, they made peace with David and became his servants. Aram didn't help the Ammonites anymore.

1 Chronicles 20

David Takes Rabbah

1. In the spring, when kings go to war, Joab led the army and destroyed the Ammonites. He attacked Rabbah.

David stayed in Jerusalem. Later, David took the crown from their king.

2. David took the crown from the king's head. It weighed about 75 pounds and had precious stones. David put it on his own head. He also took many valuables from the city.
3. He made the people work with saws, picks, and axes. He did the same to all the Ammonite towns. Then he and the army went back to Jerusalem.

Giants Are Defeated

4. Later, there was a battle with the Philistines at Gezer. Sibbekai killed Sippai, a giant from the Rephaites.
5. In another battle with the Philistines, Elhanan killed Lahmi, the brother of Goliath. Lahmi's spear was huge.
6. In another battle at Gath, there was a man with six fingers on each hand and six toes on each foot—24 in all. He was also a giant.
7. He made fun of Israel, but Jonathan (David's nephew) killed him.
8. These men were descendants of giants in Gath. They were all killed by David and his men.

1 Chronicles 21

David Counts the People

1. Satan made David decide to count the people of Israel.
2. David told Joab, "Count everyone in Israel and Judah so I can know how many there are."
3. Joab said, "May God give you many people, but why do you want to do this? It will bring guilt on Israel."
4. But David insisted. So Joab went and counted all the people. Then he came back to Jerusalem.
5. Joab said there were 1.1 million men in Israel and 470,000 in Judah who could fight.
6. He didn't count the tribes of Levi or Benjamin because he disagreed with the king's command.
7. God was angry that David had counted the people, and He punished Israel.
8. David said to God, "I sinned. Please forgive me."
9. The Lord told the prophet Gad to give David a message.
10. "Tell David: I'm giving you three choices. Pick one punishment."
11. Gad came and said,
12. "You can choose: 3 years of famine, 3 months of losing battles, or 3 days of a plague sent by the Lord."
13. David said, "I'm in great trouble. Let God decide. I'd rather be punished by Him than by people."
14. So the Lord sent a plague. 70,000 people in Israel died.
15. God sent an angel to destroy Jerusalem, but He stopped. God told the angel, "Enough." The angel stood by the threshing floor of Araunah.
16. David looked up and saw the angel between earth and sky with a sword in his hand. David and the elders fell with their faces to the ground.
17. David said, "I'm the one who sinned. These people are innocent. Please punish me and my family, not them."

David Builds an Altar

18. The angel told Gad to tell David to build an altar to the Lord at Araunah's threshing floor.
19. David obeyed.
20. Araunah saw the angel and his four sons hid.
21. When David came, Araunah bowed before him.
22. David said, "Let me buy your threshing floor to build an altar, so the plague will stop."
23. Araunah said, "Take it! I'll even give you the oxen, wood, and grain."

24. David said, "No. I must pay the full price. I won't offer God something that costs me nothing."
25. David paid 600 gold coins for the place.
26. He built an altar and offered burnt and peace offerings. God answered with fire from heaven on the altar.
27. The Lord told the angel to put away his sword.
28. David saw that the Lord had answered him, so he offered more sacrifices there.
29. The Lord's altar and the Sacred Tent were still at Gibeon.
30. But David was afraid to go there because of the sword of the angel.

1 Chronicles 22

David Prepares for the Temple

1. David said, "This is where the Lord's Temple will be. This is where the altar for burnt offerings will go."
2. He told his workers to gather all the foreigners living in Israel. He put them to work cutting stones for the Temple.
3. David got large amounts of iron for nails and bronze for tools—so much he couldn't weigh it.
4. He also brought cedar logs. The people of Sidon and Tyre sent many logs to him.
5. David said, "My son Solomon is young. The Temple must be great and famous. So I'll get everything ready now." David gathered materials before he died.
6. Then he called Solomon and told him to build the Temple for the Lord.
7. David said, "My son, I wanted to build the Temple myself.
8. But God said, 'You've fought many wars and spilled blood. You will not build My Temple.'
9. 'But you will have a son who will have peace. He will build the Temple. His name will be Solomon, and I will give Israel peace during his life.'
10. 'He will build My Temple. I will be his father, and he will be My son. I will make his kingdom strong forever.'"
11. David said, "Now, my son, may the Lord help you and give you wisdom as you lead Israel and build the Temple."
12. "Obey God's laws and be strong and brave. Don't be afraid."
13. "If you follow the Lord's laws, you will succeed. Be strong and brave. Don't be scared."
14. "I've worked hard to prepare for this. I've saved 3,750 tons of gold and 37,500 tons of silver. I've gathered bronze and iron, too much to count. I've also gathered wood and stone. You can add more."
15. "You have many workers—stone cutters, builders, and craftsmen."
16. "You have gold, silver, bronze, and iron. Now get started. The Lord is with you."
17. David ordered all the leaders of Israel to help Solomon.
18. He said, "God has given you peace. He helped me defeat our enemies. He now rules the land."
19. "Now give your hearts to God. Build the Lord's Temple and bring the Sacred Chest and holy items there."

1 Chronicles 23

David Makes Solomon King

1. When David was old, he made his son Solomon the new king of Israel.
2. He gathered all the leaders, priests, and Levites.
3. They counted the Levites who were 30 years old or older. There were 38,000 of them.
4. David said, "24,000 will work at the Temple. 6,000 will be judges and officials.

5. 4,000 will be gatekeepers. 4,000 will praise the Lord with instruments I made."
6. David divided the Levites into three groups: Gershon, Kohath, and Merari.
7. Gershon's sons were: Ladan and Shimei.
8. Ladan's sons were: Jehiel (the leader), Zetham, and Joel—three in all.
9. Shimei's sons were: Shelomoth, Haziel, and Haran—three in all.
10. Shimei also had four more sons: Jahath, Zina, Jeush, and Beriah.
11. Jahath was the leader, and Zizah was second. Jeush and Beriah didn't have many sons, so they were counted as one group.
12. Kohath's sons were: Amram, Izhar, Hebron, and Uzziel—four sons.
13. Amram's sons were Aaron and Moses. Aaron and his sons served as priests and offered sacrifices.
14. Moses' sons were counted as part of the Levites.
15. Moses' sons were Gershom and Eliezer.
16. Gershom's son was Shebuel.
17. Eliezer's son was Rehabiah. He had many sons.
18. Izhar's son was Shelomith.
19. Hebron's sons were: Jeriah (the leader), Amariah (second), Jahaziel (third), and Jekameam (fourth).
20. Uzziel's sons were: Micah (leader) and Isshiah (second).
21. Merari's sons were: Mahli and Mushi. Mahli's sons were Eleazar and Kish.
22. Eleazar had no sons, only daughters. They married their cousins from Kish's family.
23. Mushi's sons were: Mahli, Eder, and Jeremoth—three sons.
24. These were all the Levites, listed by family and name. They were 20 years old or older and served at the Temple.
25. David said, "The Lord has given us peace and will live in Jerusalem forever."
26. "So the Levites won't need to carry the Sacred Chest or other items anymore."
27. David's last orders were to count the Levites 20 years old or older.
28. Their job was to help the priests in the Lord's Temple. They kept things clean and helped with all the work.
29. They also took care of the sacred bread, flour, and offerings.
30. Every morning and evening they stood and praised the Lord.
31. They also helped with all the special sacrifices during feasts and holy days.
32. They followed all the rules and helped the priests serve in the Meeting Tent and the Temple.

1 Chronicles 24

The Priests Are Divided Into Groups

1. Aaron's sons were Nadab, Abihu, Eleazar, and Ithamar.
2. Nadab and Abihu died before their father. They had no sons. So Eleazar and Ithamar served as priests.
3. David, with Zadok and Ahimelek, divided the priests into groups. Zadok's family came from Eleazar. Ahimelek's family came from Ithamar.
4. Eleazar's family had more leaders, so they got 16 groups. Ithamar's family got 8.
5. They used lots to divide the jobs, because both families had leaders.
6. Shemaiah the scribe wrote down the results in front of the king and leaders. He listed the groups from Eleazar and Ithamar.
7. The first group was Jehoiarib, second Jedaiah,
8. third Harim, fourth Seorim,
9. fifth Malkijah, sixth Mijamin,
10. seventh Hakkoz, eighth Abijah,

11. ninth Jeshua, tenth Shecaniah,
12. eleventh Eliashib, twelfth Jakim,
13. thirteenth Huppah, fourteenth Jeshebeab,
14. fifteenth Bilgah, sixteenth Immer,
15. seventeenth Hezir, eighteenth Happizzez,
16. nineteenth Pethahiah, twentieth Jehezkel,
17. twenty-first Jakin, twenty-second Gamul,
18. twenty-third Delaiah, twenty-fourth Maaziah.
19. These were their schedules to serve at the Temple. Aaron's family followed the Lord's commands, just as God told Moses.

Other Levite Families

20. These are the other Levites: From Amram's family—Shubael. From Shubael's family—Jehdeiah.
21. From Rehabiah's family—Isshiah.
22. From Izhar's family—Shelomoth. From Shelomoth's family—Jahath.
23. From Hebron's family—Jeriah, Amariah (second), Jahaziel (third), Jekameam (fourth).
24. From Uzziel's family—Micah. From Micah's family—Shamir.
25. Micah's brother was Isshiah. Isshiah's son was Zechariah.
26. From Merari's family—Mahli and Mushi. From Jaaziah's family—Beno.
27. From Merari's family (from Jaaziah)—Beno, Shoham, Zaccur, and Ibri.
28. From Mahli—Eleazar, who had no sons.
29. From Kish—Jerahmeel.
30. Mushi's sons were Mahli, Eder, and Jerimoth. These were the Levite families.
31. They used lots to choose their jobs, just like the priests. All were treated the same, no matter their age or rank.

1 Chronicles 25

Music Groups in the Temple

1. David and the army commanders chose men from Asaph, Heman, and Jeduthun's families to lead music in the Lord's Temple. They used harps, lyres, and cymbals.
2. Asaph's sons were Zaccur, Joseph, Nethaniah, and Asarelah. They were under Asaph's command, who worked for the king.
3. Jeduthun's sons were Gedaliah, Zeri, Jeshaiah, Shimei, Hashabiah, and Mattithiah. They played harps and sang praises to the Lord, under their father's direction.
4. Heman's sons were Bukkiah, Mattaniah, Uzziel, Shebuel, Jerimoth, Hananiah, Hanani, Eliathah, Giddalti, Romamti-Ezer, Joshbekashah, Mallothi, Hothir, and Mahazioth.
5. Heman was the king's prophet. God gave him 14 sons and 3 daughters.
6. All these men and their sons and relatives played music in the Lord's Temple. They served under Asaph, Jeduthun, and Heman.
7. They and their families were trained musicians. There were 288 skilled singers and players.
8. They used lots to decide the order of service. Everyone had an equal chance, whether they were young or old, teacher or student.

Groups by Lot

9. First lot: Joseph—his sons and relatives, 12 men.
10. Second: Gedaliah—his sons and relatives, 12 men.
11. Third: Zaccur—his sons and relatives, 12 men.
12. Fourth: Izri—his sons and relatives, 12 men.
13. Fifth: Nethaniah—his sons and relatives, 12 men.
14. Sixth: Bukkiah—his sons and relatives, 12 men.

15. Seventh: Jesharelah—his sons and relatives, 12 men.
16. Eighth: Jeshaiah—his sons and relatives, 12 men.
17. Ninth: Mattaniah—his sons and relatives, 12 men.
18. Tenth: Shimei—his sons and relatives, 12 men.
19. Eleventh: Azarel—his sons and relatives, 12 men.
20. Twelfth: Hashabiah—his sons and relatives, 12 men.
21. Thirteenth: Shubael—his sons and relatives, 12 men.
22. Fourteenth: Mattithiah—his sons and relatives, 12 men.
23. Fifteenth: Jeremoth—his sons and relatives, 12 men.
24. Sixteenth: Hananiah—his sons and relatives, 12 men.
25. Seventeenth: Joshbekashah—his sons and relatives, 12 men.
26. Eighteenth: Hanani—his sons and relatives, 12 men.
27. Nineteenth: Mallothi—his sons and relatives, 12 men.
28. Twentieth: Eliathah—his sons and relatives, 12 men.
29. Twenty-first: Hothir—his sons and relatives, 12 men.
30. Twenty-second: Giddalti—his sons and relatives, 12 men.
31. Twenty-third: Mahazioth—his sons and relatives, 12 men.
32. Twenty-fourth: Romamti-Ezer—his sons and relatives, 12 men.

1 Chronicles 26

Gatekeepers

1. These were the gatekeepers: From the Korahite family—Meshelemiah (son of Kore, son of Asaph).
2. Meshelemiah's sons were: Zechariah (first), Jediael (second), Zebadiah (third), Jathniel (fourth),
3. Elam (fifth), Jehohanan (sixth), and Eliehoenai (seventh).
4. Obed-Edom's sons were: Shemaiah (first), Jehozabad (second), Joah (third), Sacar (fourth),
5. Nethanel (fifth), Ammiel (sixth), Issachar (seventh), and Peullethai (eighth). God had blessed Obed-Edom.
6. His son Shemaiah had sons too. They became leaders because they were strong and capable.
7. Shemaiah's sons were: Othni, Rephael, Obed, Elzabad, and his brothers Elihu and Semakiah.
8. All these were sons and relatives of Obed-Edom. There were 62 in all—strong, skilled men.
9. Meshelemiah had 18 strong sons and relatives.
10. Hosah, from the Merari family, had sons too. Shimri was the leader, even though he wasn't the oldest.
11. Hilkiah was second, Tebaliah was third, Zechariah was fourth. Hosah had 13 sons and relatives.

Gate Assignments

12. These gatekeepers were divided into groups. They had different jobs at the Lord's Temple.
13. They used lots to decide which family would guard each gate.
14. The east gate went to Shelemiah. Zechariah, his wise son, got the north gate.
15. Obed-Edom got the south gate. His sons guarded the storehouse.
16. Shuppim and Hosah got the west gate and the Shalleketh Gate on the road that goes up. Their guards switched turns.
17. Each day there were six guards for the east gate, four for the north, four for the south, and two for the storerooms.

18. At the west gate, two guards stood by the road and two at the courtyard.
19. These were the gatekeeper groups from the families of Korah and Merari.

Treasuries and Holy Items

20. The Levites, led by Ahijah, were in charge of the treasuries and the holy items in God's Temple.
21. The descendants of Ladan (a Gershonite) included Jehieli and his sons.
22. Jehieli's sons Zetham and Joel were in charge of the Temple treasuries.
23. Others from Amram, Izhar, Hebron, and Uzziel's families also had jobs with the holy supplies.
24. Shebuel, a descendant of Moses and Rehabiah, was in charge of the treasuries.
25. Rehabiah's relatives helped him.
26. Shelomith and his family managed treasures taken from war and from leaders who had given things to the Lord.
27. These gifts were taken from the battles and used to keep up the Temple.
28. Samuel, Saul, Abner, Joab, and others had also given valuable things. Shelomith's family took care of them.

Other Leaders and Judges

29. Chenaniah and his sons (from Izhar's family) were judges and leaders over Israel outside the Temple.
30. From Hebron's family: Hashabiah and 1,700 strong men were in charge of things west of the Jordan River. They served the Lord and helped with government work.
31. In the 40th year of David's reign, records were checked, and strong leaders were found among the Hebronites in Jazer in Gilead.
32. Jeriah was their leader. There were 2,700 skilled leaders in his family. David put them in charge of religious and government work in the land east of the Jordan.

1 Chronicles 27

Army Divisions for Each Month

1. These are the army divisions that served the king each month. Each group had 24,000 men.
2. The first group served in the first month. Its leader was Jashobeam (from Perez's family).
3. He led all the commanders. His division had 24,000 men.
4. Second-month leader: Dodai the Ahohite. His group also had 24,000 men.
5. Third-month leader: Benaiah (son of Jehoiada, the priest). He was the commander of the king's personal guards.
6. He was a great warrior. His son Ammizabad became commander after him.
7. Fourth-month leader: Asahel (Joab's brother). After him came his son Zebadiah.
8. Fifth-month leader: Shamhuth the Izrahite.
9. Sixth-month leader: Ira (son of Ikkesh from Tekoa).
10. Seventh-month leader: Helez from Pelon (from Ephraim's family).
11. Eighth-month leader: Sibbekai from Hushah (from Zerah's family).
12. Ninth-month leader: Abiezer from Anathoth (from Benjamin).
13. Tenth-month leader: Maharai from Netophah (from Zerah's family).
14. Eleventh-month leader: Benaiah from Pirathon (from Ephraim).
15. Twelfth-month leader: Heldai from Netophah (from Othniel's family). (Each group had 24,000 men.)

Tribal Leaders

16. These were the family leaders from each part of Israel:
17. Reuben: Eliezer. Simeon: Shephatiah.
18. Levi: Hashabiah. Aaron: Zadok.

19. Judah: Elihu (David's brother). Issachar: Omri.
20. Zebulun: Ishmaiah. Naphtali: Jerimoth.
21. Ephraim: Hoshea. West Manasseh: Joel.
22. East Manasseh: Iddo. Benjamin: Jaasiel.
23. Dan: Azarel. These were the leaders of the families of Israel.
24. David didn't count everyone under 20, because the Lord promised to make Israel as many as the stars.
25. Joab started the count but didn't finish. God was angry, and that count was not recorded in the royal history.

Managers of the King's Property

26. Azmaveth was in charge of the royal storerooms.
27. Shimei managed the vineyards. Zabdi managed the wine supply.
28. Baal-Hanan took care of the olive trees. Joash managed the oil.
29. Shitrai managed cattle in Sharon. Shaphat managed cattle in valleys.
30. Obil managed camels. Jehdeiah managed donkeys. Jaziz managed sheep.
31. These were the people who managed King David's property.

David's Advisors

32. David's uncle Jonathan gave advice and taught him. Jehiel taught the king's sons.
33. Ahithophel gave advice. Hushai was the king's friend.
34. After Ahithophel died, Jehoiada (son of Benaiah) became the king's advisor. After Jehoiada died, Abiathar became advisor. Joab led the army.

1 Chronicles 28

David Tells the People About the Temple

1. David gathered all the leaders of Israel: commanders, judges, officers, and family leaders.
2. He stood and said, "My brothers and people, I wanted to build the Lord's Temple, where the Sacred Chest would stay."
3. "But God said to me, 'You will not build it, because you've fought many wars and shed blood.'"
4. "God chose me from my father's family to be king. He chose Judah, and from Judah, He chose my family. He picked me to be king over all Israel."
5. "Out of all my sons, the Lord chose Solomon to sit on Israel's throne."
6. "God said, 'Solomon will build My Temple. I will be his father, and he will be My son.'"
7. "'If he obeys My commands, I will make his kingdom strong forever.'"
8. "Now, all of you, follow God's commands so that you and your children will keep the land."
9. "Solomon, my son, know the God of your father. Serve Him with all your heart. If you seek Him, you will find Him. But if you turn away, He will reject you."
10. "The Lord chose you to build His Temple. Be strong and do it."
11. Then David gave Solomon the plans for the Temple—its rooms, storage areas, and upper levels.
12. He gave plans for everything: the courtyards, the rooms for the holy items, and all the work to be done.
13. He gave instructions for the priests and Levites, and the jobs they must do.
14. He gave the amounts of gold and silver for everything—tools, dishes, lampstands, and more.
15. He said how much gold and silver to use for each item.
16. He gave the amounts for the gold tables and silver tables.

17. He also listed the gold for the forks, bowls, and pitchers—and the silver for each kind.
18. He gave the amount of pure gold for the altar of incense and for the gold chariot of winged creatures that covered the Sacred Chest.
19. David said, "I wrote all of this with the Lord's help. He gave me understanding for the plans."
20. Then David told Solomon, "Be strong and brave. Do not be afraid. The Lord will be with you. He will help you until the Temple is finished."
21. "The priests and Levites are ready. Every skilled worker will help. God will be with you."

1 Chronicles 29

Gifts for the Temple

1. David said, "My son Solomon is young and needs help. The Temple will be great because it's for God, not for people."
2. "I gave all I could: gold, silver, bronze, iron, wood, stones, and more."
3. "I'm giving my own gold and silver too, because I love God's Temple."
4. "I'm giving 112 tons of gold and 262 tons of silver for the holy things."
5. "Now, who else will give gifts to the Lord today?"
6. The leaders of Israel, families, tribes, and commanders gave willingly.
7. They gave 188 tons of gold, 10,000 coins, 375 tons of silver, 675 tons of bronze, and 3,750 tons of iron.
8. People who had precious stones gave them to the Temple treasury.
9. Everyone was happy because the gifts were given freely to God. David was very happy too.

David Praises the Lord

10. David praised the Lord in front of everyone. He said:
11. "Lord, You are great, powerful, and full of glory. Everything in heaven and earth belongs to You. You rule over all."
12. "You give wealth and honor. You have power and strength in Your hands."
13. "Now we thank You and praise Your name."
14. "But who am I? And who are my people? We could only give You what You already gave us."
15. "We're only here for a short time, like shadows. We don't stay long."
16. "Lord, everything we gave came from You. It all belongs to You."
17. "I know You see our hearts. I gave with joy, and so did the people."
18. "Lord, keep this desire in our hearts forever. Help us always love You."
19. "Help Solomon follow Your commands and build the Temple."

Solomon Becomes King

20. David told everyone, "Praise the Lord!" They all praised God and bowed to the Lord and the king.
21. The next day, they made many offerings and sacrifices.
22. They ate and celebrated with joy. Then they made Solomon king a second time and poured oil on him to show he was chosen by God.
23. Solomon sat on the Lord's throne as king. All Israel obeyed him.
24. All the leaders and even David's other sons agreed to follow Solomon.
25. The Lord made Solomon very great. No king in Israel had ever been so respected.

David's Death

26. David was king of all Israel.
27. He ruled for 40 years—7 in Hebron and 33 in Jerusalem.
28. He died at an old age, full of years, riches, and honor. His son Solomon became king.

29. Everything David did is written in the books of Samuel, Nathan, and Gad.
30. Those books tell about his rule, power, and what happened to Israel and other nations.

– 2 Chronicles –

Covers Solomon's reign and the kings of Judah until the Babylonian exile.

2nd Chronicles 1

The Lord Makes Solomon Wise

1. Solomon became king, and the Lord made him strong and powerful.
2. He called all the leaders of Israel together.
3. They went to the Meeting Tent in Gibeon, the one Moses had made in the desert.
4. The Sacred Chest was in Jerusalem because David had brought it there from Kiriath Jearim.
5. But the bronze altar Bezalel made was still in front of the Lord's Meeting Tent in Gibeon. Solomon and everyone worshiped there.
6. Solomon offered 1,000 burnt offerings on that altar.
7. That night, God appeared to Solomon and asked, "What do you want?"
8. Solomon said, "You were kind to my father David. Now you've made me king.
9. Please keep your promise to David. I now rule a huge nation.
10. Give me wisdom and knowledge so I can be a good king."
11. God said, "You didn't ask for riches or to live long or to beat your enemies. You asked for wisdom.
12. So I'll give you wisdom. I'll also give you riches, fame, and honor like no other king ever had."
13. Then Solomon went back to Jerusalem and ruled Israel.

Solomon's Wealth

14. Solomon had 1,400 chariots and 12,000 horsemen, kept in cities and in Jerusalem.
15. He made silver and gold as common as rocks. Cedar was as common as fig trees.
16. His horses came from Egypt and Kue. His men bought them at market price.
17. Chariots cost 600 silver pieces, and horses 150. They also sold them to kings of the Hittites and Syria.

2nd Chronicles 2

Solomon Plans to Build the Temple

1. Solomon decided to build a Temple for the Lord and a palace for himself.
2. He chose 70,000 laborers, 80,000 stone cutters, and 3,600 supervisors.
3. He sent a message to King Hiram of Tyre: "Send me cedar wood like you did for my father David.
4. I'm building a Temple for God to burn incense, show the special bread, and offer sacrifices. This will happen daily, on Sabbaths, new moons, and festivals forever.
5. The Temple must be great because our God is greater than all others.
6. But who can build a Temple big enough for God? Even heaven can't hold Him. I just want a place to offer sacrifices.
7. Send me someone who knows how to work with gold, silver, bronze, iron, and colored cloth, and who can engrave designs. He'll work with the skilled workers David hired.
8. Send cedar, pine, and algum wood from Lebanon. Your men are the best woodcutters. My men will help.
9. I need a lot of wood. The Temple will be big and beautiful.

10. I'll give your workers 100,000 bushels of wheat, 100,000 of barley, 110,000 gallons of wine, and 110,000 gallons of oil."
11. Hiram replied, "The Lord loves Israel. That's why He made you king.
12. Praise the Lord, maker of heaven and earth! He gave David a wise son to build His Temple and a palace.
13. I'm sending Huram Abi. He's smart and skilled.
14. His mother was from Dan, and his father from Tyre. He can do all you ask and help your workers.
15. Send the food you promised.
16. We'll cut the wood, tie it into rafts, float it to Joppa, and you can take it to Jerusalem."

Solomon's Workers

17. Solomon counted all the foreigners in Israel. There were 153,600.
18. He assigned 70,000 as laborers, 80,000 as stone cutters, and 3,600 as supervisors.

2nd Chronicles 3

The Temple is Built

1. Solomon began building the Lord's Temple in Jerusalem on Mount Moriah, where the Lord appeared to David. It was built on the land David bought from Araunah.
2. He started building it on the second day of the second month in his fourth year as king.
3. The Temple was 90 feet long and 30 feet wide.
4. The entrance porch was 30 feet wide and 30 feet high. He covered the inside with gold.
5. He covered the main room with pine and pure gold. He decorated it with palm trees and chains.
6. He covered the room with beautiful jewels and gold from Parvaim.
7. He covered the beams, doorways, walls, and doors with gold and carved angels on the walls.
8. He made the Most Holy Place 30 feet wide and long. He covered it with 23 tons of gold.
9. He used 20 ounces of gold for each nail. He also covered the upper rooms in gold.
10. He made two large gold angels in the Most Holy Place.
11. Each angel's wings were 7 ½ feet long.
12. The wings touched each other and the walls.
13. The angels stood side by side, facing the main room.
14. He made a curtain of blue, purple, and red cloth and linen, with pictures of angels.
15. For the front of the Temple, he made 2 pillars, 27 feet tall, with 7 ½ foot caps.
16. He made chains and hung 100 pomegranates from them.
17. He put the pillars at the Temple entrance, one on the south named Jakin and the one on the north named Boaz.

2 Chronicles 4

Temple Furnishings

1. Solomon made a large bronze altar, 30 feet long, 30 feet wide, and 15 feet high.
2. He made a huge round bronze tank called the Sea. It was 15 feet across, 7 ½ feet deep, and 45 feet around.
3. Two rows of bronze bulls were under the rim. They were part of the Sea.
4. The Sea sat on 12 bronze bulls, 3 facing each direction.
5. The sides of the Sea were 3 inches thick. It held about 16,500 gallons of water.
6. He also made 10 smaller bowls to wash the tools for burnt offerings. 5 were

placed on the south side and 5 on the north. The priests used the Sea to wash.

7. He made 10 gold lampstands and put 5 on the south side and 5 on the north side of the Temple.
8. He made 10 tables and placed them 5 on each side, and made 100 gold bowls.
9. He built a courtyard for the priests and a large outer courtyard. The doors were covered with bronze.
10. He placed the Sea at the southeast corner of the Temple.
11. Huram made the pots, shovels, and bowls. He finished everything for Solomon's Temple:
12. The 2 pillars, 2 bowl-shaped tops, 2 chain decorations,
13. 400 pomegranates for the chains,
14. the carts and bowls,
15. the Sea and the 12 bulls under it,
16. and all the bronze tools—pots, shovels, and forks.
17. They were made in clay molds in the Jordan Valley between Succoth and Zarethan.
18. So much bronze was used they couldn't count it.
19. Solomon also had gold items made: the altar, the tables for the holy bread,
20. the gold lampstands to burn in front of the Most Holy Place,
21. the gold flowers, lamps, and tongs,
22. and the gold snuffers, bowls, ladles, and incense burners. Even the doors to the Most Holy Place and main room were covered in gold.

2 Chronicles 5

The Temple is Finished

1. Solomon put all the items his father David had dedicated into the Temple, including silver, gold, and other treasures.

The Sacred Chest is Moved to the Temple

2. Then Solomon called all the leaders of Israel to bring the Lord's Sacred Chest from the City of David to the Temple.
3. They came during the Festival of Shelters in the seventh month.
4. When the leaders arrived, the Levites picked up the Sacred Chest.
5. They brought the Sacred Chest, the Meeting Tent, and all the sacred items. The priests and Levites carried them.
6. Solomon and all Israel stood before the Sacred Chest. They sacrificed so many sheep, goats, and cattle that no one could count them.
7. The priests placed the Sacred Chest in the Most Holy Place under the wings of the angels.
8. The angels' wings were spread out over the Chest and its poles.
9. The poles were long enough to be seen from outside the Most Holy Place. They are still there today.
10. Inside the Sacred Chest were only the two stone tablets Moses had placed there at Mount Sinai when God made a promise with the Israelites.
11. When the priests came out of the Holy Place, all of them had made themselves clean.
12. The Levite musicians—Asaph, Heman, Jeduthun, their sons and relatives—stood east of the altar wearing fine linen. They played cymbals, harps, and lyres. 120 priests played trumpets.
13. The trumpet players and singers joined together to praise the Lord. They sang, "He is good! His love lasts forever!" Then a thick cloud filled the Temple.
14. The priests couldn't continue their work because the Lord's glory filled the Temple like a cloud.

2 Chronicles 6

1. Then Solomon said, "The Lord said He would live in a dark cloud."

2. "But I've built You a great Temple, a place for You to live forever."

3. Then he turned and blessed all the people of Israel, who were standing.

4. He said, "Praise the Lord, the God of Israel. He kept His promise to my father David. The Lord said it, and now He did it."

5. "Since He brought His people from Egypt, He hadn't chosen a city for a Temple or a king for Israel."

6. "But now He chose Jerusalem for His Temple, and He chose David to rule His people."

7. "My father David wanted to build the Temple for the Lord."

8. "But the Lord said, 'You want to build it, and that's good.'"

9. "But it will be your son who builds it, not you."

10. "And now that promise has come true. I am king, just like the Lord said. I built the Temple for Him."

11. "I put the Sacred Chest in it. It holds the agreement the Lord made with us."

12. Then Solomon stood in front of the Lord's altar in front of everyone and raised his hands.

13. He had made a bronze platform, 7½ feet long and wide, and 4½ feet high. He stood on it, knelt, raised his hands, and prayed.

14. "Lord, God of Israel, there is no God like You. You keep Your promises and show love to those who obey You."

15. "You kept Your promise to my father David. You spoke it and You did it."

16. "Now, Lord, keep Your other promise—that one of David's sons would always rule—if they obey You."

17. "Lord God of Israel, keep what You promised to David, my father."

18. "But can You really live on earth? Even heaven can't hold You. How can this Temple?"

19. "Still, hear my prayer and listen to what I'm asking."

20. "Watch over this Temple day and night. Hear me when I pray facing this place."

21. "Hear the prayers of Your people. Forgive them when they pray toward this place."

22. "If someone wrongs another person and swears to tell the truth in this Temple,"

23. "Then hear from heaven. Judge between them. Punish the guilty and show the innocent is right."

24. "If Israel sins and You let enemies beat them, but they turn back to You and pray,"

25. "Then hear from heaven and forgive them. Bring them back to the land You gave their ancestors."

26. "If there is no rain because they sinned, but they turn to You and pray at this Temple,"

27. "Then forgive and teach them to live right. Send rain on the land You gave them."

28. "If there is a famine, disease, or locusts, or enemies attack, or anything bad happens,"

30. "And someone prays and asks for help,"

31. "Then hear from heaven. Forgive and help. You know each person's heart."

32. "Then they will respect You and obey Your commands as long as they live."

33. "If a foreigner comes to pray toward this Temple,"

34. "Then hear their prayer too. That way, all people will know You and respect You."

35. "If Your people go to war and pray toward this city and Temple,"

36. "Then hear from heaven. Help them win."

37. "If they sin—and everyone sins—and You let enemies take them away,"

38. "But they are sorry and pray to You from the land where they were taken,"
39. "And if they turn to You with all their heart and soul and pray toward this land and city and Temple,"
40. "Then hear from heaven. Forgive them. Help them again."
41. "Now, God, please hear my prayer and be kind to this place."
42. "Come to Your Temple, You and the Sacred Chest. Let the priests be saved and the faithful be happy."
43. "Lord, don't forget Your promise to David. Remember Your love for him."

2 Chronicles 7

The Temple Is Dedicated

1. When Solomon finished praying, fire came down from heaven and burned up the offerings. The Lord's glory filled the Temple.
2. The priests couldn't enter because the Lord's glory filled it.
3. When the people saw the fire and God's glory, they knelt down, touched their faces to the ground, and worshiped. They said, "The Lord is good! His love lasts forever!"
4. Then the king and all the people offered sacrifices.
5. Solomon gave 22,000 cattle and 120,000 sheep to the Lord. The king and all the people dedicated the Temple.
6. The priests took their places, and so did the Levites with their instruments. They played music King David had made for worship. The priests blew trumpets across from them, and all the people stood.
7. Solomon set apart the central area of the courtyard in front of the Temple as holy. That's where he offered the burnt and grain offerings and the fat of peace offerings. The bronze altar was too small to hold them all.
8. Solomon and all Israel celebrated for 7 days. People came from as far north as Lebo Hamath and as far south as the Brook of Egypt.
9. On the 8th day they held a closing ceremony. They had spent 7 days dedicating the altar and 7 more days celebrating the Festival of Shelters.
10. On the 23rd day of the 7th month, Solomon sent everyone home. They were happy because the Lord had been good to David, Solomon, and His people.

The Lord Speaks to Solomon Again

11. Solomon finished the Lord's Temple and the palace. Everything he planned was done.
12. One night, the Lord appeared to Solomon and said: "I've heard your prayer. I chose this Temple to be My house of worship."
13. "If I close the sky and no rain falls, or send locusts or disease,
14. But My people, who are called by My name, are sorry and pray and obey Me again, then I will hear them, forgive them, and heal their land."
15. "I will watch and listen to every prayer made here."
16. "I chose and made this Temple holy. I will always live here. I will watch it and love it forever."
17. "If you, Solomon, follow Me like David did, and obey My commands,
18. Then I will keep My promise that someone from your family will always rule."
19. "But if you or your people turn away and worship other gods,
20. Then I will remove My blessing from this land. I will destroy this Temple, even though I made it holy. People will be shocked and make fun of it."
21. "They will ask, 'Why did the Lord destroy His own Temple?'"
22. "And the answer will be, 'Because they turned away from the Lord who saved

them and started worshiping other gods.'"

2 Chronicles 8

Solomon's Other Projects

1. It took Solomon 20 years to finish the Lord's Temple and his own palace.
2. He rebuilt the towns King Hiram gave him and sent Israelites to live there.
3. Then he attacked and captured Hamath Zobah.
4. He built up Tadmor in the desert and storage cities in Hamath.
5. He built cities in the upper and lower parts of Beth Horon.
6. He built other towns, including Baalath and cities for his chariots and horses. He built whatever he wanted in Jerusalem, Lebanon, and other places.
7. Solomon forced the people left in the land—like the Hittites, Amorites, Perizzites, Hivites, and Jebusites—to work as slaves.
8. These people were not Israelites, but descendants of the ones Israel had not destroyed.
9. Solomon didn't make Israelites slaves. They became his soldiers and commanders.
10. He had 250 officials in charge of the workers.
11. Solomon moved Pharaoh's daughter from the old city of David to the palace he built for her. He said, "She must not live where the Sacred Chest was."
12. Solomon offered sacrifices to the Lord on the altar in front of the Temple.
13. He did this daily, on Sabbaths, on New Moon days, and during the three main festivals—the Festival of Unleavened Bread, the Festival of Weeks, and the Festival of Shelters.
14. He assigned priests and Levites their duties, just like David had done.
15. They followed all the commands of David.
16. Solomon completed all the work for the Temple.
17. He went to Ezion Geber and Elath on the Red Sea in Edom.
18. Hiram sent ships with experienced sailors. They brought back 17 tons of gold from Ophir.

2 Chronicles 9

The Queen of Sheba Visits Solomon

1. The Queen of Sheba heard about Solomon's fame and came to test him with hard questions.
2. She brought large gifts and asked him everything she wanted. Solomon answered all her questions.
3. She saw his wisdom, the palace,
4. the food on his table, the way his officials served him, the clothes they wore, his cupbearers, and the steps to the Temple. She was amazed.
5. She said, "Everything I heard about you is true.
6. But I didn't believe it until I saw it. Your wisdom is even greater than I was told!
7. Your people and officials are lucky to be here.
8. Praise the Lord for making you king. He loves Israel and made you king to rule fairly."
9. She gave Solomon almost five tons of gold, spices, and jewels. No one ever brought spices like she did.
10. Hiram's men also brought gold and wood.
11. Solomon used the wood for steps to the Temple and instruments for the singers.
12. Solomon gave the queen anything she asked for. Then she went home.

Solomon's Wealth and Wisdom

13. Every year, Solomon received 25 tons of gold,
14. not counting the money from traders and kings nearby.
15. He made 200 large shields with 15 pounds of gold each,
16. and 300 smaller shields with almost 8 pounds each. He put them in the Forest Palace.
17. He made a great throne of ivory and covered it with pure gold.
18. It had 6 steps and a gold footstool. There were armrests with lions on both sides.
19. There were 12 lions on the steps. No other kingdom had anything like it.
20. All his cups were gold. Nothing was made of silver because it wasn't valuable then.
21. His ships went to Tarshish every 3 years and brought back gold, silver, ivory, apes, and peacocks.
22. Solomon was richer and wiser than any other king on earth.
23. Kings came from everywhere to hear his wisdom.
24. Each one brought gifts: gold, silver, clothes, weapons, spices, horses, and mules—every year.
25. Solomon had 4,000 stalls for horses and chariots and 12,000 horsemen.
26. He ruled over kings from the Euphrates River to Egypt.
27. He made silver as common as stones and cedar as common as sycamore trees.
28. Horses came from Egypt and other places.

Solomon's Death

29. Everything Solomon did is written in the records of Nathan, Ahijah, and Iddo the seer.
30. He ruled for 40 years in Jerusalem.
31. Then he died and was buried in David's City. His son Rehoboam became king.

2 Chronicles 10

Rehoboam Becomes King

1. Rehoboam went to Shechem because all Israel had gathered there to make him king.
2. Jeroboam (who had run to Egypt) heard about it and returned to Israel.
3. The people sent for Jeroboam. He and the rest of Israel came to Rehoboam and said:
4. "Your father made us work too hard. Please lighten the heavy load, and we will serve you."
5. Rehoboam said, "Come back in three days." So they left.
6. Rehoboam asked the older men who had advised his father, "What should I tell the people?"
7. They said, "If you're kind and speak nicely to them, they'll serve you forever."
8. But Rehoboam didn't listen to them. Instead, he asked the young men who had grown up with him.
9. He said, "What do you think I should tell them?"
10. The young men said, "Tell them, 'My little finger is thicker than my father's waist!'
11. 'My father made you work hard; I'll make it even harder!' 'He punished you with whips, I'll punish you with scorpions!'"
12. Three days later, Jeroboam and the people came back, as Rehoboam had told them.
13. But Rehoboam spoke harshly. He ignored the advice of the older men.
14. He told the people what the young men had said: "My father made you work hard. I'll make it worse! He

punished you with whips—I'll punish you with scorpions!"

15. The king refused to listen. This was all part of God's plan, just like He told Jeroboam through Ahijah.
16. When the people saw the king didn't listen, they shouted, "Why should we follow David's family? Let's go home, Israel! Take care of your own family, David!" So the people left.
17. Only the Israelites who lived in Judah still followed Rehoboam.
18. Rehoboam sent Adoniram, the man in charge of forced labor, but the people stoned him to death. Rehoboam barely escaped in his chariot and went back to Jerusalem.
19. Since that day, Israel has refused to be ruled by David's family.

2 Chronicles 11

Rehoboam Obeys God's Warning

1. Rehoboam returned to Jerusalem and gathered 180,000 trained soldiers from Judah and Benjamin to fight Israel and take back the kingdom.
2. But the Lord spoke to Shemaiah the prophet:
3. "Tell Rehoboam, king of Judah, and all the people of Judah and Benjamin:
4. 'Do not attack your brothers. Go home. This is My doing.'" So they obeyed and did not fight Jeroboam.

Rehoboam Builds Strong Cities

5. Rehoboam lived in Jerusalem and built strong cities in Judah.
6. He built Bethlehem, Etam, Tekoa,
7. Beth Zur, Soco, Adullam,
8. Gath, Mareshah, Ziph,
9. Adoraim, Lachish, Azekah,
10. Zorah, Aijalon, and Hebron. These were strong, walled cities in Judah and Benjamin.
11. He made them stronger with guards and storage places for food, olive oil, and wine.
12. He also put shields and spears in every city and made them very strong. He ruled over Judah and Benjamin.

Priests and Levites Move to Judah

13. The priests and Levites living in Israel left their towns and moved to Judah.
14. Jeroboam and his sons had fired them from serving as priests of the Lord.
15. Jeroboam chose his own priests for worshiping goat idols and the golden calves he had made.
16. People from every tribe of Israel who truly wanted to worship the Lord followed the priests and Levites to Jerusalem.
17. These people made Judah stronger. They supported Rehoboam, son of Solomon, for 3 years. During that time, they lived the way David and Solomon had.

Rehoboam's Family

18. Rehoboam married Mahalath. She was the daughter of David's son Jerimoth and Abihail, a daughter of Jesse's son Eliab.
19. They had three sons: Jeush, Shemariah, and Zaham.
20. Later, Rehoboam married Maacah, daughter of Absalom. They had four children: Abijah, Attai, Ziza, and Shelomith.
21. Rehoboam loved Maacah the most of all his wives and concubines. He had 18 wives and 60 concubines. He fathered 28 sons and 60 daughters.
22. He chose Abijah, son of Maacah, to be the next king.
23. Rehoboam was wise. He put his other sons in charge of different strong cities all over Judah and Benjamin. He gave them plenty of food and found wives for them.

2 Chronicles 12

1. After Rehoboam's kingdom became strong, he and all Israel turned away from the Lord.
2. In the fifth year of Rehoboam's rule, King Shishak of Egypt came to attack Jerusalem because the people had been unfaithful to the Lord.
3. Shishak came with 1,200 chariots, 60,000 horsemen, and countless soldiers from Egypt, including Libyans, Sukkites, and Ethiopians.
4. He captured the strong cities of Judah and marched to Jerusalem.
5. Then Shemaiah the prophet went to Rehoboam and the leaders of Judah who had gathered in Jerusalem and said, "This is what the Lord says: 'You abandoned Me, so I'm abandoning you to Shishak.'"
6. The leaders and Rehoboam humbled themselves and said, "The Lord is right."
7. When the Lord saw they had humbled themselves, He gave this message to Shemaiah: "Because they have humbled themselves, I will not destroy them. I will let them live. But they will be ruled by Shishak, so they learn the difference between serving Me and serving other rulers."
8. So they became servants of Shishak.
9. Shishak came and took the treasures from the Lord's Temple and from the royal palace. He took everything, even the gold shields Solomon had made.
10. Rehoboam made bronze shields instead and gave them to the guards at the palace gates.
11. When the king went to the Temple, the guards carried the shields, then put them back in the guardroom.
12. Because Rehoboam humbled himself, the Lord didn't destroy him completely. Things went better in Judah.
13. Rehoboam became king at 41 years old. He ruled 17 years in Jerusalem, the city the Lord had chosen from all the tribes of Israel. His mother's name was Naamah, and she was from Ammon.
14. Rehoboam did evil because he didn't really want to follow the Lord.
15. Everything Rehoboam did, from beginning to end, is written in the records of the prophet Shemaiah and the seer Iddo. Rehoboam and Jeroboam were always at war.
16. Rehoboam died and was buried in Jerusalem. His son Abijah became king after him.

2 Chronicles 13

1. Abijah became king of Judah in the 18th year of King Jeroboam of Israel.
2. He ruled for 3 years in Jerusalem. His mother was Micaiah, daughter of Uriel from Gibeah. There was war between Abijah and Jeroboam.
3. Abijah had 400,000 brave soldiers. Jeroboam had 800,000 strong soldiers from Israel.
4. Abijah stood on Mount Zemaraim in the hill country of Ephraim and shouted, "Listen to me, Jeroboam and all Israel!
5. Don't you know that the Lord God of Israel gave the kingdom to David and his sons forever by a covenant of salt?
6. But Jeroboam, son of Nebat, rebelled against Rehoboam, David's grandson.
7. Some worthless troublemakers helped Jeroboam fight Rehoboam when he was young and unsure of himself.
8. Now you're trying to fight the kingdom that belongs to the Lord's royal family. You have more soldiers and golden calves that Jeroboam made as gods.
9. You kicked out the priests of the Lord—the sons of Aaron—and the Levites. Instead, you made your own priests like the other nations. Anyone who brings a young bull and seven rams can become a priest of these fake gods.

10. But we still worship the Lord. Our priests are sons of Aaron, and the Levites help them.
11. Every morning and evening they offer burnt sacrifices and incense. They arrange the holy bread on the table and keep the golden lampstands lit. We follow the Lord our God. But you have turned away.
12. God is with us, and His priests are ready with the trumpets to call for help. Don't fight the Lord, God of your ancestors. You will lose."
13. Meanwhile, Jeroboam had secretly sent part of his army to attack from behind. Judah's army was trapped from the front and back.
14. The men of Judah saw the enemy on both sides. They cried out to the Lord, and the priests blew their trumpets.
15. The men of Judah shouted, and God defeated Jeroboam and Israel.
16. Israel ran away from Judah, and God gave Judah the victory.
17. Abijah and his army killed 500,000 of Israel's strongest soldiers.
18. The people of Judah won the battle because they trusted in the Lord, the God of their ancestors.
19. Abijah chased Jeroboam and took Bethel, Jeshanah, and Ephron with their surrounding villages.
20. Jeroboam never regained his power during Abijah's life. The Lord struck him, and he died.
21. Abijah became strong. He had 14 wives, 22 sons, and 16 daughters.
22. Everything else Abijah did is written in the story of the prophet Iddo.

2 Chronicles 14

Asa Trusts the Lord

1. Abijah died and was buried in the City of David. His son Asa became king. During his rule, the country had peace for 10 years.
2. Asa did what was right in the eyes of the Lord.
3. He removed the foreign altars and the shrines, smashed the sacred pillars, and cut down the Asherah poles.
4. He told the people of Judah to follow the Lord and obey His laws and commands.
5. He removed the pagan altars and incense places in every town in Judah. The kingdom had peace under his rule.
6. He built strong cities in Judah because the land was at peace and no one attacked them during those years. The Lord gave them rest.
7. He told the people, "Let's build these towns with walls, towers, gates, and bars while the land is still ours. We have followed the Lord, so He has given us peace." So they built and had success.
8. Asa had an army of 300,000 men from Judah with large shields and spears, and 280,000 men from Benjamin who carried small shields and bows. All of them were brave warriors.
9. Zerah the Ethiopian came to attack them with 1,000,000 men and 300 chariots. He reached Mareshah.
10. Asa went out to fight him. They met in the valley of Zephathah near Mareshah.
11. Asa prayed to the Lord: "Lord, only You can help the weak against the strong. Help us, Lord our God! We rely on You. We fight in Your name. Don't let anyone win against You!"
12. The Lord struck down the Ethiopians in front of Asa and Judah, and they ran.
13. Asa and his army chased them to Gerar. So many were killed that they couldn't fight back. The Lord destroyed them, and Judah carried away much treasure.
14. They also destroyed nearby towns because the people were afraid of the Lord. They took everything of value from those towns.

15. They raided camps and took many sheep, goats, and camels. Then they returned to Jerusalem.

2 Chronicles 15

Asa Destroys the Idols in Judah

1. God's Spirit came on Azariah son of Oded.
2. He went to Asa and said, "Listen! The Lord is with you when you are with Him. If you look for Him, you'll find Him. If you leave Him, He'll leave you.
3. For a long time, Israel had no true God, no teaching priests, and no law.
4. But in their trouble, they turned to the Lord and found Him.
5. In those days, it wasn't safe. There was trouble everywhere.
6. Nations and cities fought each other. God caused great suffering.
7. But you must be strong and not give up. Your hard work will be rewarded."
8. Asa was encouraged. He removed all the idols in Judah, Benjamin, and the towns he had captured in Ephraim. He repaired the Lord's altar in front of the Temple.
9. He gathered the people of Judah, Benjamin, and those from Ephraim, Manasseh, and Simeon who had moved to Judah after seeing that God was with him.
10. They all met in Jerusalem in the third month of Asa's 15th year as king.
11. That day they sacrificed 700 cattle and 7,000 sheep from what they had taken in battle.
12. Then they made a promise to follow the Lord with all their heart and soul.
13. Anyone who refused—no matter who—would be put to death.
14. They shouted their promise and blew trumpets and horns.
15. All Judah was happy because they had promised with all their heart and truly sought the Lord—and He gave them peace.
16. Asa removed his grandmother Maacah from her position as queen mother because she had made an Asherah idol. He cut it down and burned it in the Kidron Valley.
17. Although he didn't remove all the high places in Israel, Asa was faithful to the Lord all his life.
18. He brought into the Temple the silver, gold, and items he and his father had given.
19. There was no more war until Asa's 35th year as king.

2 Chronicles 16

Asa Stops Trusting the Lord

1. In Asa's 36th year, King Baasha of Israel came to attack Judah. He built up the town of Ramah to block anyone from entering or leaving Judah.
2. Asa took silver and gold from the Temple and palace and sent it to King Ben-Hadad of Syria in Damascus.
3. He said, "Let's make a peace agreement like our fathers did. I'm sending you a gift. Break your treaty with Baasha so he will leave me alone."
4. Ben-Hadad agreed and sent his army to attack cities in Israel. They took Ijon, Dan, Abel Maim, and towns in Naphtali.
5. When Baasha heard about it, he stopped building Ramah.
6. King Asa brought the people of Judah to carry away the stones and wood Baasha had used. They used them to build Geba and Mizpah.
7. At that time, the prophet Hanani went to Asa and said, "You trusted the king of Syria instead of the Lord. Now you missed your chance to defeat Syria.
8. Remember how huge the armies of Ethiopia and Libya were? But you trusted the Lord, and He helped you win.

9. The Lord watches everywhere to help those who trust Him. But you acted foolishly, so from now on, you will face war."
10. Asa was angry and put Hanani in prison. He also punished some of the people.
11. Everything Asa did, from beginning to end, is written in the Book of the Kings of Judah and Israel.
12. In his 39th year, Asa got a bad foot disease. Even then, he didn't ask the Lord for help—only doctors.
13. He died in the 41st year of his rule.
14. He was buried in the tomb he made for himself in the City of David. His body was lying on a bed covered in spices and perfumes, and a huge fire was burned in his honor.

2 Chronicles 17

Jehoshaphat Becomes King

1. Jehoshaphat, Asa's son, became king after him. He made Judah strong to guard against Israel.
2. He put soldiers in the strong cities of Judah and in the towns in Ephraim that Asa had taken.
3. The Lord was with Jehoshaphat because he followed David's good example and didn't worship the Baals.
4. He followed the God of his ancestors and obeyed His commands, not Israel's ways.
5. The Lord made his kingdom strong. All Judah brought him gifts, and he became rich and well-known.
6. He was proud to follow the Lord. He removed the idols and Asherah poles from Judah.
7. In his third year as king, he sent his officials Ben Hail, Obadiah, Zechariah, Nethanel, and Micaiah to teach in Judah.
8. With them were Levites: Shemaiah, Nethaniah, Zebadiah, Asahel, Shemiramoth, Jehonathan, Adonijah, Tobijah, and Tob-Adonijah. He also sent priests Elishama and Jehoram.
9. They went to every town in Judah and taught the people from the Lord's Book of Law.
10. The Lord made the nearby kingdoms afraid, so they didn't fight Judah.
11. Some Philistines brought Jehoshaphat gifts and silver. Some Arabs brought him 7,700 rams and 7,700 goats.
12. Jehoshaphat became stronger and built forts and cities with storage buildings.
13. He had large amounts of supplies and soldiers stationed in Jerusalem.
14. From Judah, the commanders were: Adnah with 300,000 soldiers,
15. Jehohanan with 280,000,
16. and Amasiah, who volunteered to serve the Lord, with 200,000.
17. From Benjamin, Eliada had 200,000 armed with bows and shields,
18. and Jehozabad had 180,000 ready for battle.
19. These men served the king and were stationed in the strong cities of Judah.

2 Chronicles 18

1. Jehoshaphat became rich and well-known. He made peace with Ahab by marriage.
2. A few years later, he visited Ahab in Samaria. Ahab gave him a big feast and asked him to help fight at Ramoth Gilead.
3. Ahab said, "Will you go to Ramoth Gilead with me?" Jehoshaphat said, "Yes, but let's ask the Lord first."
4. Jehoshaphat said, "Please ask the Lord what to do."
5. Ahab called 400 prophets and asked, "Should we fight?" They said, "Yes! God will give you victory."
6. Jehoshaphat asked, "Is there a prophet of the Lord we can ask?"

7. Ahab said, "Yes, one—Micaiah. But I hate him. He always says bad things about me." Jehoshaphat said, "Don't say that."
8. Ahab told an officer, "Bring Micaiah now."
9. The two kings sat on thrones in their royal robes at the city gate. The prophets spoke in front of them.
10. Zedekiah made iron horns and said, "God says you will crush the Syrians with these."
11. All the prophets said, "Go to battle! God will help you win!"
12. The messenger told Micaiah, "Everyone is saying good things. You should too."
13. Micaiah said, "I will say only what God tells me."
14. When he arrived, Ahab asked, "Should we go to battle?" Micaiah said, "Yes, go and win."
15. Ahab said, "Tell me the truth."
16. Micaiah said, "I saw Israel scattered on the hills like sheep with no shepherd. The Lord said, 'They have no leader. Let them go home.'"
17. Ahab said, "See? He never says anything good about me."
18. Micaiah said, "I saw the Lord on His throne with heaven's army around Him."
19. The Lord said, 'Who will trick Ahab into going to battle and dying there?'
20. One spirit said, 'I will.' God asked, 'How?'
21. The spirit said, 'I'll lie through the prophets.' God said, 'Go. It will work.'
23. Micaiah said, "Your prophets are lying. The Lord has decided you will fall."
24. Zedekiah slapped Micaiah and said, "When did God speak through you instead of me?"
25. Micaiah said, "You'll find out when you hide in a room."
26. Ahab ordered, "Take him to prison!"
27. "Give him only bread and water until I come back safely."
28. Micaiah said, "If you return safely, then the Lord didn't speak through me."
29. Ahab and Jehoshaphat went to Ramoth Gilead.
30. Ahab said, "You wear your royal robes. I'll disguise myself." Ahab went into battle in disguise.
31. The king of Aram told his chariot commanders, "Only fight the king of Israel."
32. When they saw Jehoshaphat, they thought he was the king of Israel and went to attack. Jehoshaphat called out, and the Lord helped him.
33. They saw he wasn't the king of Israel and stopped chasing him.
34. A soldier randomly shot an arrow. It hit Ahab between his armor. Ahab said, "I'm wounded! Get me out!"
35. The battle lasted all day. Ahab propped himself up in his chariot facing the Syrians. At sunset, he died.

2 Chronicles 19

1. Jehoshaphat returned safely to his palace in Jerusalem.
2. Jehu the prophet said, "Why did you help the wicked and love those who hate the Lord? Because of this, the Lord is angry with you.
3. But you did some good. You removed the idols and decided to follow the Lord."
4. Jehoshaphat went from Beersheba to the hill country of Ephraim and told the people to return to the Lord.
5. He appointed judges in each strong city of Judah.
6. He said, "Be careful in your decisions. You are judging for the Lord, not just for people. The Lord is with you."
7. "Respect the Lord. Be fair. The Lord does not accept bribes or show favoritism."

8. In Jerusalem, Jehoshaphat chose Levites, priests, and family leaders to judge cases involving the Lord's laws and other disagreements.
9. He told them, "Always respect the Lord and be honest in everything you do."
10. "When people come from their towns with hard cases—about God's law, commands, rules, or even murder—warn them not to sin. If you don't warn them, the Lord will be angry at you and them. Do this so you won't be guilty."
11. Amariah the high priest will be in charge of cases that involve the Lord. Zebadiah, leader from Judah's royal family, will handle the king's matters. The Levites will help you. Be strong. Do what is right. The Lord will be with you."

2 Chronicles 20

1. After that, the Moabites, Ammonites, and some Meunites came to fight Jehoshaphat.
2. A messenger told Jehoshaphat, "A large army is coming from Edom. They are already at Hazazon Tamar."
3. Jehoshaphat was afraid. He asked the Lord for help and told everyone in Judah to fast.
4. People from every town in Judah came to ask the Lord for help.
5. Jehoshaphat stood up in the Lord's Temple courtyard.
6. He prayed, "Lord, you are God of our ancestors. You rule all nations. No one can stop you."
7. "You drove out the people here and gave this land to Abraham's family forever."
8. "We live here and built a Temple to honor your name."
9. "We said, 'If trouble comes, we will stand here and ask you for help. You will hear and save us.'"
10. "Now people from Ammon, Moab, and Edom are coming to attack us."
11. "They want to push us out of the land you gave us."
12. "God, we are helpless. We don't know what to do. We look to you."
13. All the men, women, and children of Judah stood before the Lord.
14. The Lord's Spirit came on Jahaziel, a Levite from Asaph's family.
15. Jahaziel said, "Listen! The Lord says, 'Don't be afraid. This battle is not yours—it's mine.'"
16. "'Tomorrow, march down to meet them. They will come up the Ziz Pass and be at the end of the valley near Jeruel Desert.'"
17. "'You won't need to fight. Stand still and watch the Lord save you. Don't be afraid. I'll be with you.'"
18. Jehoshaphat bowed to the ground. Everyone else did too.
19. Levites from the Kohath and Korah families stood and praised the Lord loudly.
20. The next morning, they marched toward Tekoa. Jehoshaphat said, "Trust the Lord and you will stand strong. Believe His prophets and you will win."
21. He chose singers to walk in front of the army and sing, "Thank the Lord! His love lasts forever!"
22. As they sang, the Lord made the enemy armies attack each other.
23. The Ammonites and Moabites killed the people from Edom. Then they turned on each other.
24. When Judah's army arrived, they saw only dead bodies. No one had survived.
25. Jehoshaphat and his men took valuables and clothes from the dead. There was so much it took three days to collect it all.

26. On the fourth day, they met in the Valley of Berakah and praised the Lord.
27. They returned to Jerusalem, happy because the Lord had given them victory.
28. They entered Jerusalem with harps, lyres, and trumpets and went to the Temple.
29. When other nations heard what the Lord had done, they were afraid.
30. Jehoshaphat's kingdom had peace because God gave him rest.
31. Jehoshaphat became king at 35 and ruled 25 years in Jerusalem. His mother was Azubah, daughter of Shilhi.
32. He followed the ways of his father Asa and did what was right.
33. But the high places were not removed, and the people were not fully committed to God.
34. Everything else Jehoshaphat did is written in the records of Jehu, kept in the book of the kings of Israel.
36. Later, Jehoshaphat made an agreement with Ahaziah, king of Israel. Ahaziah did evil.
37. They agreed to build ships to sail to Tarshish. The ships were built at Ezion Geber.
38. Eliezer told Jehoshaphat, "Because you joined Ahaziah, the Lord will destroy your work." The ships were wrecked and never sailed.

2 Chronicles 21

1. Jehoshaphat died and was buried in the City of David. His son Jehoram became king.
2. Jehoram had six brothers: Azariah, Jehiel, Zechariah, Azariahu, Michael, and Shephatiah. They were all sons of Jehoshaphat, king of Judah.
3. Their father gave them gifts of silver, gold, and cities in Judah, but made Jehoram king because he was the oldest.
4. When Jehoram became king, he killed all his brothers and some of the leaders in Judah to keep his power.
5. Jehoram was 32 years old when he became king. He ruled in Jerusalem for 8 years.
6. He followed the evil ways of Ahab's family because he married Ahab's daughter. He did what the Lord said was wrong.
7. But the Lord didn't destroy Judah because of His promise to David. He promised to keep David's family on the throne.
8. During Jehoram's time, the people of Edom rebelled and chose their own king.
9. Jehoram took his army and attacked Edom at night. Even though he surrounded them, they escaped.
10. Edom stayed independent from Judah after that. Libnah also rebelled because Jehoram had turned away from the Lord.
11. Jehoram built pagan shrines in the hills of Judah. He led the people to sin and worship idols.
12. Elijah the prophet sent Jehoram a letter that said: "This is what the Lord, the God of David, says: You have not followed the good ways of your father Jehoshaphat or King Asa.
13. Instead, you acted like the evil kings of Israel. You led Judah and Jerusalem to worship idols, and you killed your own brothers who were better than you.
14. So now the Lord will strike your people, your children, your wives, and all your property.
15. You will suffer from a terrible disease in your intestines that will get worse day by day until they come out of you."
16. Then the Lord made the Philistines and Arabs angry at Jehoram, and they attacked Judah.
17. They broke into his palace, took all his treasures, his wives, and his sons. Only his youngest son Ahaziah was left.

18. After this, the Lord made Jehoram very sick in his intestines.

19. After two years, his intestines came out because of the disease, and he died in great pain. No one was sad when he died.

20. Jehoram was 32 when he became king. He ruled for 8 years in Jerusalem. No one honored him when he died. He was buried in the City of David, but not in the royal tombs.

2 Chronicles 22

1. The people of Jerusalem made Ahaziah king after Jehoram died. He was the youngest son because enemy raiders had killed his older brothers.

2. Ahaziah was 22 years old when he became king. He ruled in Jerusalem for 1 year. His mother was Athaliah, granddaughter of Omri.

3. Ahaziah followed Ahab's family and did evil because his mother told him to do wrong.

4. He did what was evil in the Lord's eyes, like Ahab's family. They gave him bad advice after his father died.

5. He went with Ahab's son, King Joram of Israel, to fight King Hazael of Syria at Ramoth Gilead. Joram was wounded.

6. Joram went to Jezreel to heal. Ahaziah went there to visit him.

7. God used this visit to bring Ahaziah down. While he was there, he met Jehu, who was chosen by the Lord to destroy Ahab's family.

8. While Jehu was punishing Ahab's family, he also found some of Ahaziah's relatives and killed them.

9. Jehu's men looked for Ahaziah. He was hiding in Samaria. They caught him and brought him to Jehu. He was killed. They buried him because he was the grandson of Jehoshaphat, who followed the Lord. No one was left in Ahaziah's family to rule.

10. When Athaliah, Ahaziah's mother, saw her son was dead, she killed all the rest of the royal family of Judah.

11. But Jehosheba, Ahaziah's sister, took his baby son Joash and hid him in a room with his nurse. She kept him safe from Athaliah.

12. Joash stayed hidden in the Lord's Temple for six years while Athaliah ruled the land of Judah.

2 Chronicles 23

1. In the seventh year, Jehoiada showed his strength. He made a secret agreement with five army commanders: Azariah son of Jeroham, Ishmael son of Jehohanan, Azariah son of Obed, Maaseiah son of Adaiah, and Elishaphat son of Zikri.

2. They traveled through Judah and gathered the Levites and leaders from all the families. They all came to Jerusalem.

3. In the Lord's Temple, the whole group made a covenant with the king. Jehoiada said, "The king's son must rule, just as the Lord promised David's family."

4. He gave this plan: "A third of you priests and Levites will guard the Temple doors on the Sabbath.

5. A third will guard the palace, and the rest will guard the Foundation Gate. All the people must stay outside the Temple.

6. Only the priests and Levites on duty may enter. The rest must stay out because the Temple is holy."

7. "The Levites must stay with the king. Each man must be armed. Kill anyone who enters the Temple. Stay with the king wherever he goes."

8. The Levites and army commanders did everything Jehoiada said. They brought their men, even those not on duty that week, because Jehoiada didn't let anyone go home.

9. Jehoiada gave the commanders the spears and large shields that had belonged to King David. These were kept in God's Temple.

10. The men stood with their weapons ready, from the south side to the north side of the Temple, in front of the altar and the Temple building.

11. Then they brought out the king's son Joash. They put the crown on him and gave him a copy of the law. Jehoiada and his sons anointed him and shouted, "Long live the king!"

13. When Athaliah heard the noise, she went to the Temple where the people were.

14. She saw the king standing by the pillar at the entrance. The officers and trumpeters were beside him. The people were rejoicing and blowing trumpets. Singers with instruments were leading the celebration. Athaliah tore her clothes and shouted, "Treason! Treason!"

15. Jehoiada the priest called the army commanders and said, "Take her out between the ranks. Kill anyone who follows her. Don't kill her in the Lord's Temple."

16. They seized her and took her to the entrance of the Horse Gate at the palace. There they killed her.

17. Jehoiada made a covenant with the Lord, the king, and the people that they would be the Lord's people.

18. Then the people went to Baal's temple and tore it down. They smashed the altars and idols and killed Mattan, Baal's priest.

19. Jehoiada put the priests and Levites in charge of the Lord's Temple, just as David had commanded. They offered sacrifices with joy and singing, as written in the Law of Moses.

20. He stationed guards at the Temple gates to keep out anyone who was not clean.

21. Then he and the commanders brought the king from the Temple. They entered the palace through the Upper Gate and seated the king on the royal throne.

22. All the people were happy, and the city was calm. Athaliah had been killed with the sword.

2 Chronicles 24

1. Joash was 7 years old when he became king. He ruled in Jerusalem for 40 years. His mother was Zibiah from Beersheba.

2. Joash did what pleased the Lord as long as Jehoiada the priest was alive.

3. Jehoiada chose two wives for Joash, and he had sons and daughters.

4. Later, Joash decided to repair the Lord's Temple.

5. He called the priests and Levites and told them, "Go to the towns of Judah and collect money each year for temple repairs. Do it quickly." But the Levites didn't hurry.

6. So Joash asked Jehoiada, "Why haven't you made the Levites collect the tax from Judah and Jerusalem? That money was commanded by Moses for the Lord's Tent."

7. Wicked Athaliah's sons had broken into the Temple and used holy items for worshiping Baal.

8. The king ordered a chest to be placed outside the Temple gate.

9. A message was sent through Judah and Jerusalem: "Bring the tax Moses gave in the desert for the Lord's Temple."

10. All the leaders and people gladly brought their money and put it in the chest until it was full.

11. When the chest was full, the Levites brought it to the king's officials. They emptied it, returned it, and kept doing this often. The people gave a lot of money.

12. The king and Jehoiada gave the money to the workers to repair the Temple. They hired stonecutters, carpenters, and metalworkers.

13. The workers were faithful, and the repairs were done well. They rebuilt it as it was before and made it stronger.

14. When the work was done, leftover money was used to make tools and bowls for the Temple. Burnt offerings were offered regularly during Jehoiada's life.

15. Jehoiada lived a long life. He died at 130 years old.

16. He was buried with the kings in the City of David because he had done good things for God and His Temple.

17. After Jehoiada died, the leaders of Judah came to the king and bowed down to him. The king listened to them.

18. They turned away from the Lord and started worshiping idols. This made the Lord angry with Judah and Jerusalem.

19. God sent prophets to warn them, but they didn't listen.

20. Then God's Spirit came on Zechariah, son of Jehoiada. He stood before the people and said, "This is what God says: Why have you turned away from the Lord? Because of this, you will not succeed."

21. The people made a plan to kill him. By the king's order, they stoned him in the courtyard of the Lord's Temple.

23. King Joash forgot how kind Zechariah's father had been to him. As Zechariah died, he said, "May the Lord see this and punish you."

24. At the end of that year, the Syrian army came and attacked Judah and Jerusalem. They killed the leaders and sent the loot back to their king in Damascus.

25. The Syrians had a small army, but the Lord let them win because Judah had turned against Him. That's how the Syrians punished Joash.

26. After the Syrians left, Joash was badly wounded. His own officials plotted against him and killed him on his bed because he had murdered Jehoiada's son.

27. The ones who killed him were Zabad, son of an Ammonite woman, and Jehozabad, son of a Moabite woman.

28. Joash's sons, the list of his many messages, and the rebuilding of the Temple are written in the book of the kings. His son Amaziah became king after him.

2 Chronicles 25

1. Amaziah was 25 years old when he became king. He ruled in Jerusalem for 29 years. His mother was Jehoaddan from Jerusalem.

2. He did what pleased the Lord, but not with his whole heart.

3. After his kingdom was secure, he killed the officials who had murdered his father.

4. But he didn't kill their children, because he obeyed the Lord's law written by Moses: "Parents must not be killed for their children's sins, and children must not be killed for their parents' sins."

5. Amaziah called together the men of Judah and put them into army groups by family. He chose commanders over 100 and 1,000. He found 300,000 strong, trained soldiers who could use spears and shields.

6. He also hired 100,000 strong soldiers from Israel for 7,500 pounds of silver.

7. But a prophet came and told him, "Don't take Israel's army with you. The Lord is not with Israel.

8. Even if you fight bravely, God will make you lose because He has the power to help or defeat."

9. Amaziah asked, "But what about the money I paid them?" The prophet said, "The Lord can give you much more than that."

10. So Amaziah sent the hired soldiers home. They were very angry with Judah and left in rage.

11. Amaziah led his army to the Salt Valley and killed 10,000 men from Edom.

12. Judah's army captured 10,000 more men alive and threw them off a cliff. They were all killed.

13. The soldiers Amaziah had sent home raided towns in Judah, killed 3,000 people, and stole many things.

14. When Amaziah returned from defeating Edom, he brought back the gods of Edom. He worshiped them and offered sacrifices to them.

15. The Lord was angry and sent a prophet who said, "Why do you worship gods who couldn't even save their own people from you?"

16. Amaziah interrupted the prophet, "Have I made you an advisor to the king? Stop talking or I'll kill you!" The prophet said, "I know God has decided to destroy you because you refused to listen."

17. Amaziah met with his advisors and sent a message to King Jehoash of Israel: "Come, let's fight face to face."

18. Jehoash replied, "A thistle in Lebanon told a cedar tree, 'Give your daughter to my son.' But a wild animal came by and crushed the thistle.

19. You are proud because you beat Edom. Be careful or you'll fall and drag Judah down with you."

20. But God wanted to punish Amaziah, so he refused to listen. Jehoash marched out and they met at Beth Shemesh in Judah.

21. Judah and Israel's armies faced each other. Amaziah's army was defeated.

22. The army of Judah ran away, and Amaziah was captured.

23. Jehoash brought Amaziah to Jerusalem. He broke down 600 feet of the city wall from the Ephraim Gate to the Corner Gate.

24. He took the gold, silver, and treasures from the Lord's Temple and the palace. He also took hostages and returned to Samaria.

25. Amaziah lived 15 more years after Jehoash died.

26. Everything else Amaziah did is written in the Book of the Kings of Judah and Israel.

27. After Amaziah turned away from the Lord, people made a plan to kill him. He fled to Lachish, but they sent men there and killed him.

29. His body was brought back on a horse and buried with his ancestors in Jerusalem.

2 Chronicles 26

1. All the people of Judah made Uzziah king after his father Amaziah died. Uzziah was 16 years old.

2. He rebuilt Elath and brought it back under Judah's control.

3. Uzziah was 16 when he became king. He ruled in Jerusalem for 52 years. His mother was Jekoliah from Jerusalem.

4. He did what pleased the Lord, like his father Amaziah.

5. He obeyed God while Zechariah was alive. Zechariah taught him to respect God. As long as Uzziah followed the Lord, God helped him.

6. Uzziah went to war against the Philistines. He tore down the walls of Gath, Jabneh, and Ashdod. Then he built towns near Ashdod and other places in Philistine land.

7. God helped him fight the Philistines, the Arabs in Gur-Baal, and the Meunites.

8. The Ammonites paid him taxes, and he became famous as far as Egypt.

9. Uzziah built towers in Jerusalem at the Corner Gate, Valley Gate, and the wall turn. He made them strong.

10. He also built towers in the desert and dug many wells. He had many cattle in the lowlands and valleys. He had farmers and vineyard workers in the hills and fertile lands because he loved farming.

11. Uzziah had an army ready to fight. They were grouped by families and led by commanders.
12. There were 2,600 strong leaders over the army.
13. They commanded 307,500 soldiers trained and ready to fight for the king.
14. Uzziah gave his army shields, spears, helmets, armor, bows, and slings.
15. In Jerusalem, skilled workers made machines that could shoot arrows and throw large stones from towers and corners. Uzziah became very famous and powerful because God helped him.
16. But when Uzziah became powerful, he became proud and unfaithful to the Lord. He went into the Lord's Temple to burn incense, something only priests should do.
17. Azariah the priest and 80 other brave priests followed him.
18. They told him, "Only priests should burn incense. Leave the Temple. You have sinned and the Lord will not honor you."
19. Uzziah got angry while holding the incense burner. Right then, leprosy appeared on his forehead in front of the priests.
20. Azariah and the priests saw the leprosy and rushed him out. He was eager to leave because the Lord had punished him.
21. King Uzziah had leprosy until he died. He lived in a separate house and was not allowed in the Temple. His son Jotham took care of the palace and ruled the people.
22. Everything else Uzziah did was written by the prophet Isaiah, son of Amoz.
23. Uzziah died and was buried near his ancestors in a field for those with leprosy. People said, "He had leprosy." His son Jotham became king after him.

2 Chronicles 27

1. Jotham was 25 years old when he became king. He ruled in Jerusalem for 16 years. His mother was Jerushah, daughter of Zadok.
2. Jotham did what pleased the Lord, just like his father Uzziah. But he didn't enter the Lord's Temple. The people kept doing wrong.
3. Jotham rebuilt the Upper Gate of the Lord's Temple and did a lot of work on the wall at the hill of Ophel.
4. He built towns in the hills of Judah and forts and towers in the forests.
5. He fought against the king of Ammon and won. The Ammonites gave him 7,500 pounds of silver, 62,000 bushels of wheat, and 62,000 bushels of barley each year for three years.
6. Jotham became powerful because he faithfully obeyed the Lord his God.
7. Everything else Jotham did, including his wars and other actions, is written in the book of the kings of Israel and Judah.
8. He was 25 years old when he became king and ruled for 16 years in Jerusalem.
9. Jotham died and was buried in Jerusalem. His son Ahaz became king after him.

2 Chronicles 28

1. Ahaz was 20 years old when he became king. He ruled in Jerusalem for 16 years. He did not follow the Lord like David had.
2. He followed the evil ways of the kings of Israel and even made idols for worshiping Baal.
3. He burned incense in the Valley of Hinnom and sacrificed his own sons with fire, copying the nations the Lord had removed.
4. He offered sacrifices and burned incense at every hill and under every tree.

5. So the Lord let the king of Syria defeat him. They captured many people and took them to Damascus. The king of Israel also defeated Ahaz and killed many soldiers.
6. Pekah, king of Israel, killed 120,000 soldiers from Judah in one day. These men had turned away from the Lord.
7. Zikri, a warrior from Ephraim, killed Maaseiah (the king's son), Azrikam (in charge of the palace), and Elkanah (second to the king).
8. Israel took 200,000 women and children as prisoners and brought them to Samaria. They also took much valuable property.
10. A prophet named Oded was in Samaria. He met the returning army and said, "The Lord let you defeat Judah because He was angry. But you went too far and killed without mercy.
11. Now you want to make these people your slaves? You have sinned against the Lord too.
12. Send the prisoners back. If you don't, the Lord will punish you in anger."
13. Some leaders of Ephraim—Azariah, Berechiah, Jehizkiah, and Amasa—agreed.
14. They told the soldiers, "You can't bring these prisoners here. You're guilty already, and the Lord's anger is on us."
15. So the soldiers gave up the prisoners and everything they took.
16. The leaders gave clothes and sandals to the prisoners, fed them, helped the sick, and brought the weak to Jericho. Then they returned to Samaria.
17. At that time, King Ahaz asked the king of Assyria for help.
18. The Edomites had attacked Judah and taken prisoners.
19. The Philistines had invaded towns in Judah and lived in them.
20. The Lord brought trouble on Judah because Ahaz had led the people away from God and had not been faithful.
21. The king of Assyria came to Ahaz, but didn't help him. Instead, he caused him more trouble.
22. Ahaz took treasures from the Lord's Temple, the palace, and the leaders, and gave them to the king of Assyria. But it didn't help.
23. Even when he was in trouble, Ahaz sinned even more.
24. He sacrificed to the gods of Syria, thinking they had helped them win. But this only brought more trouble.
25. He took the sacred items from the Lord's Temple and broke them. He shut the Temple doors and made altars on every street in Jerusalem.
26. He built altars in every town of Judah to worship other gods. This made the Lord very angry.
27. Everything else Ahaz did is written in the book of the kings of Judah and Israel.
28. Ahaz died and was buried in Jerusalem, but not in the tombs of the kings. His son Hezekiah became king after him.

2 Chronicles 29

1. Hezekiah was 25 years old when he became king. He ruled in Jerusalem for 29 years. His mother was Abijah, daughter of Zechariah.
2. He did what pleased the Lord, just like his ancestor David.
3. In the first month of his reign, he reopened the Temple doors and repaired them.
4. He called the priests and Levites to meet in the Temple courtyard.
5. He told them, "Clean yourselves and clean out the Temple. Remove everything unholy from God's Temple."
6. "Our ancestors were unfaithful. They turned their backs on God and abandoned His Temple."

7. "They shut the doors, put out the lamps, and stopped burning incense and giving offerings."

8. "That's why the Lord is angry with Judah and Jerusalem. Now we're feared, laughed at, and attacked."

9. "Many of our people died, and others were taken away as prisoners."

10. "Now I want to make a promise to the Lord so He will stop being angry with us."

11. "Don't ignore your duties. The Lord chose you to serve Him, offer sacrifices, and lead worship."

12. Then these Levites got to work: From the Kohath family: Mahath and Joel.

13. From the Merari family: Kish and Azariah. From the Gershon family: Joah and Eden

14. From the Elizaphan family: Shimri and Jeiel. From the Asaph family: Zechariah and Mattaniah

15. From the Heman family: Jehiel and Shimei. From the Jeduthun family: Shemaiah and Uzziel

16. These men gathered their brothers and purified themselves. Then they went to the Temple to clean it as the king commanded.

17. The priests went inside and brought out all the unclean items. The Levites carried them out to the courtyard, and others took them to the Kidron Valley.

18. They began cleaning on the first day of the first month. By the eighth day, they reached the Temple porch. It took eight more days to clean the Temple itself.

19. Then they went to King Hezekiah and said, "We've cleaned the entire Temple, the altar, the table, and everything that belongs to them."

20. "We also cleaned all the items King Ahaz threw away when he turned from God. They're ready for use again."

21. Early the next morning, Hezekiah gathered the city leaders and went to the Temple.

22. They brought seven bulls, seven rams, seven male lambs, and seven male goats to be sacrificed. These were for the nation, the Temple, and to remove their sins. The priests killed the animals and sprinkled the blood on the altar.

23. First, they killed the bulls, then the rams, then the lambs.

24. Then they brought the goats for the sin offering. The king and people laid their hands on them.

25. The priests killed the goats and sprinkled the blood on the altar to remove the sins of all Israel. The king had ordered this offering for everyone.

26. Hezekiah had the Levites play instruments made by King David. The priests blew trumpets as the music began.

27. The Levites stood with their instruments, and the priests stood with trumpets.

28. Hezekiah gave the order to offer the burnt offering. As it started, songs to the Lord began, with trumpets and instruments of David.

29. Everyone bowed down, the music played, and the singers sang until the sacrifice ended.

30. When it ended, the king and all the people knelt and worshiped.

31. Hezekiah and the leaders told the Levites to praise the Lord with songs of David and Asaph. They sang with joy and bowed in worship.

32. Hezekiah said, "Now you have dedicated yourselves to the Lord. Come bring sacrifices and offerings." The people brought many offerings, including burnt offerings.

33. They brought 70 bulls, 100 rams, and 200 lambs.

34. They also brought 600 cattle and 3,000 sheep as sacrifices.

35. There weren't enough priests to prepare all the offerings, so the Levites helped them until the work was done. The Levites were more eager to serve God than the priests were.

36. There were many burnt offerings, along with grain and drink offerings. So the Temple worship was restored.

37. Hezekiah and the people were happy that God had helped them do all this so quickly.

2 Chronicles 30

1. Hezekiah sent word to all Israel and Judah. He invited everyone to come to Jerusalem to celebrate the Passover to honor the Lord.

2. The king and his officials agreed to celebrate it in the second month.

3. They couldn't do it at the regular time because not enough priests were ready and the people hadn't gathered yet.

4. Everyone liked the king's plan.

5. So they sent messengers to all of Israel, from Beersheba to Dan, inviting them to Jerusalem to keep the Passover. Many had not followed God's instructions for years.

6. Messengers went out with letters from the king and his officials. It said, "People of Israel, return to the Lord your God. Then He will return to you."

7. "Don't be like your parents and family who turned away from the Lord. That's why they were ruined."

8. "Don't be stubborn. Obey the Lord and come to His Temple. Serve Him, and His anger will stop."

9. "If you return to God, He will be kind. Your relatives who were taken away will be allowed to return. The Lord is kind and merciful."

10. The messengers went to each town in Ephraim and Manasseh. Some people laughed at them and made fun.

11. But some people from Asher, Manasseh, and Zebulun humbled themselves and came to Jerusalem.

12. God helped the people in Judah stay united and obey the king's command.

13. A large crowd came to Jerusalem to celebrate the Festival of Unleavened Bread in the second month.

14. They removed all the altars and incense stands in Jerusalem and threw them into the Kidron Valley.

15. They killed the Passover lambs on the 14th day of the second month. The priests and Levites were ashamed and made themselves clean to do their duties.

16. They stood in their places and offered the sacrifices as written in the Law of Moses. The Levites helped the priests.

17. Many people had not purified themselves, so the Levites had to kill the lambs for them.

18. Many people from Ephraim, Manasseh, Issachar, and Zebulun ate the Passover without being fully clean. But Hezekiah prayed for them, asking the Lord to forgive them.

19. He said, "Lord, please forgive those who truly want to follow You, even if they aren't fully clean."

20. The Lord heard Hezekiah's prayer and healed the people.

21. The Israelites in Jerusalem celebrated with joy for seven days. The Levites and priests praised the Lord every day.

22. Hezekiah encouraged all the Levites who had served well. The people ate the festival food and gave thanks to God.

23. Then the whole group decided to keep celebrating for seven more days. They were full of joy.

24. Hezekiah gave 1,000 bulls and 7,000 sheep for the people. The leaders gave 1,000 bulls and 10,000 sheep. Many priests got ready to serve.

25. Everyone in Judah was happy. So were the priests, Levites, visitors from Israel,

and the people who had moved to Judah.

26. There was great joy in Jerusalem. Nothing like this had happened since the days of Solomon.

27. The priests and Levites stood and blessed the people. God heard their prayer, and His presence was felt in heaven.

2 Chronicles 31

1. After the Passover, everyone went to the towns of Judah. They broke down the stone pillars, cut down the Asherah poles, and destroyed the altars used for worshiping other gods. They did this in all of Judah, Benjamin, Ephraim, and Manasseh. Then they went back to their homes.

2. Hezekiah organized the priests and Levites into groups. Each group had its job—offering sacrifices and singing praises in the Lord's Temple, just as it was written in the Law.

3. The king gave his own money for the morning and evening offerings and for the special festivals listed in the Law.

4. He told the people in Jerusalem to give the priests and Levites their share so they could focus on their work for the Lord.

5. As soon as the people heard this, they gave the first part of their harvest—grain, wine, oil, honey, and everything from the fields. They brought a tenth of it all.

6. The people of Israel and Judah who lived in the towns also brought a tenth of their cattle and sheep and things dedicated to the Lord. They piled it all up.

7. They began in the third month and finished in the seventh.

8. When Hezekiah and the leaders saw the piles, they thanked the Lord and His people.

9. Hezekiah asked the priests and Levites about the piles.

10. Azariah the chief priest said, "Since the people started giving, we've had plenty. There's even a lot left over. The Lord has blessed His people."

11. Hezekiah ordered storerooms to be built in the Temple, and they were built.

12. They brought the offerings, tithes, and gifts into the storerooms. A Levite named Conaniah was in charge, and his brother Shimei was his helper.

13. The king appointed Jehiel, Azaziah, Nahath, Asahel, Jerimoth, Jozabad, Eliel, Ismakiah, Mahath, and Benaiah to help. They worked under Conaniah and Shimei by the order of King Hezekiah and Azariah the chief priest.

14. Kore, a Levite, was in charge of the East Gate and collected the freewill offerings for God.

15. He had helpers: Eden, Miniamin, Jeshua, Shemaiah, Amariah, and Shecaniah. They gave shares to the priests in their towns, by family.

16. They gave to all males over 3 years old who were listed in the Temple records for daily service.

17. The priests were listed by families, and the Levites aged 20 and up were listed by their duties.

18. Their wives and children were also listed, because they had all kept themselves holy for service.

19. Men were also appointed to give portions to every male priest and listed Levite living in the towns.

20. Hezekiah did all this throughout Judah. He did what was right, good, and faithful before the Lord.

21. Everything he did for God's Temple, the Law, and the commands—he did it all with all his heart. So he was successful.

2 Chronicles 32

1. After Hezekiah had faithfully served the Lord, King Sennacherib of Assyria attacked and destroyed the towns of

Judah and then planned to attack Jerusalem.

2. When Hezekiah saw that Sennacherib was coming to attack Jerusalem,
3. he and his officials decided to block the water springs outside the city.
4. Many people helped stop the water, saying, "Why should the king of Assyria find plenty of water?"
5. Hezekiah rebuilt the broken walls, added towers, built another wall outside, repaired the area around the city of David, and made weapons and shields.
6. He put army leaders in charge of the people and encouraged them.
7. He said, "Be strong and brave. Don't be afraid of the king of Assyria. There's a greater power with us than with him."
8. "He has only human strength, but we have the Lord our God to help us and fight for us." The people felt stronger after hearing Hezekiah.
9. While Sennacherib was attacking Lachish, he sent officers to Jerusalem with this message for Hezekiah and the people:
10. "Why are you trusting in Hezekiah, saying Jerusalem won't fall?"
11. "Hezekiah says the Lord will save you, but he's lying. You'll die from hunger and thirst."
12. "Didn't Hezekiah remove God's altars and say you can only worship at one altar?"
13. "Don't you know what I and other kings of Assyria have done to other nations? No gods saved them."
14. "Has any god saved a nation from me or my ancestors? Why would your God save you?"
15. "Don't let Hezekiah trick you. No god has saved a nation from me. Yours won't either."
16. Sennacherib's men continued insulting the Lord and Hezekiah.
17. He also wrote letters mocking the Lord, saying, "Other gods didn't help, and your God won't help either."
18. The officers shouted in Hebrew to the people on the walls to scare and confuse them.
19. They spoke of the God of Jerusalem like He was just another man-made idol.
20. Hezekiah and the prophet Isaiah prayed and cried out to heaven.
22. The Lord sent an angel who killed every officer and soldier in the Assyrian army. Sennacherib went home in shame. Some of his sons killed him in his own temple.
23. So the Lord saved Hezekiah and Jerusalem. He gave them peace.
24. People brought gifts to the Lord and presents to Hezekiah, and he became respected by many nations.
25. Later, Hezekiah became very sick and almost died. He prayed, and the Lord gave him a sign.
26. But he became proud and didn't thank God. So the Lord became angry.
27. Hezekiah and the people humbled themselves, and the Lord delayed His anger during Hezekiah's life.
28. Hezekiah became very rich. He built storerooms for silver, gold, spices, shields, and valuables.
29. He made storage places for grain, wine, oil, cattle, and sheep.
30. He built towns and had many animals. God gave him great wealth.
31. He blocked the upper spring of Gihon and brought the water down to the west side of Jerusalem. He succeeded in all he did.
32. When officials from Babylon came to ask about the miracle, God let Hezekiah be tested to show what was in his heart.
33. Everything else Hezekiah did is written in the book of the kings of Judah and Israel.

34. When he died, he was buried on the hill of the royal cemetery. Everyone in Judah honored him. His son Manasseh became king after him.

2 Chronicles 33

1. Manasseh was 12 years old when he became king, and he ruled from Jerusalem for 55 years.
2. He sinned against the Lord by doing the same evil things the nations did that the Lord had forced out of Israel's way.
3. He rebuilt the pagan shrines, altars to Baal, and Asherah poles his father Hezekiah had destroyed. He also worshiped the stars.
4. He built altars to false gods in the Lord's Temple, the place the Lord had said, "My name will be honored in Jerusalem forever."
5. He built those altars in both courtyards of the Temple.
6. Manasseh even sacrificed his sons in fire in the Hinnom Valley. He practiced magic and told fortunes. He used witchcraft and talked to spirits. This made the Lord very angry.
7. He even put a carved idol in God's Temple, where the Lord had said to David and Solomon, "I have chosen this Temple and Jerusalem for my name forever."
8. "I will never again remove my people from this land if they obey my commands and the Law I gave Moses."
9. But Manasseh led the people of Judah and Jerusalem to do even more evil than the nations the Lord had destroyed.
10. The Lord spoke to Manasseh and the people, but they didn't listen.
11. So the Lord sent the army commanders of Assyria. They captured Manasseh with hooks, tied him in chains, and took him to Babylon.
12. While in prison, Manasseh begged the Lord for help. He humbled himself and prayed.
13. The Lord heard him and brought him back to Jerusalem. Then Manasseh knew that the Lord was the true God.
14. After that, Manasseh rebuilt the outer wall of Jerusalem from the west of Gihon Spring, through the valley, to the Fish Gate, and around Ophel Hill. He made it very high. He also placed army commanders in every city in Judah.
15. He removed the foreign gods and idols from the Temple and threw away the altars he had built on the Temple hill and in the city.
16. He repaired the Lord's altar and offered peace and thanks offerings. He told Judah to worship only the Lord.
17. But the people still sacrificed at the shrines, though only to the Lord.
18. The rest of Manasseh's life, including his prayer and the words of the prophets who spoke in the Lord's name, are written in the records of the kings of Israel.
19. His prayer, how God answered him, all his sins, and how he humbled himself before he changed his ways are written in the records of the prophets.
20. When Manasseh died, he was buried at his palace. His son Amon became king.
21. Amon was 22 years old when he became king, and he ruled from Jerusalem for 2 years.
22. He did evil in the Lord's sight, just like his father Manasseh. He worshiped and offered sacrifices to the same idols.
23. But unlike his father, Amon didn't humble himself. Instead, he sinned even more.
24. His officials made a plan and killed him in the palace.
25. But the people of Judah killed those officials, and they made Amon's son Josiah the new king.

2 Chronicles 34

1. Josiah was 8 years old when he became king, and he ruled from Jerusalem for 31 years.
2. He did what pleased the Lord, and followed the example of King David, never turning away from what was right.
3. In his 8th year as king, while still young, Josiah began to seek the Lord. In his 12th year, he started destroying the shrines, Asherah poles, idols, and statues across Judah and Jerusalem.
4. He broke down the altars for Baal and cut down the incense altars above them. He smashed the idols and scattered the dust on the graves of those who had sacrificed to them.
5. He burned the bones of their priests on the altars. He did this across Judah to make it clean for the Lord.
6. He did the same in the towns of Manasseh, Ephraim, Simeon, and all the way to Naphtali.
7. He tore down altars and Asherah poles and crushed idols to dust everywhere. Then he returned to Jerusalem.
8. In his 18th year as king, after cleaning the land and the Temple, Josiah sent Shaphan, Maaseiah, and Joah to repair the Temple of the Lord.
9. They gave the money collected from the people of Judah and Israel to the priests and Levites at the Temple.
10. This money was given to the supervisors doing the work, and they paid workers to repair the Temple.
11. They also paid carpenters and builders to buy cut stone, wood, and beams to fix what earlier kings had damaged.
12. The workers did the job honestly. Their supervisors were Jahath and Obadiah, Levites from Merari's family, and Zechariah and Meshullam from Kohath's family. These men were all skilled musicians,
13. but they also supervised the workers and managed the different jobs and supplies. Some Levites were also secretaries and guards.
14. While the money was being brought to the Temple, Hilkiah the high priest found the Book of the Law that had been given through Moses.
15. Hilkiah said to Shaphan, "I found the Book of the Law in the Temple." Then he gave it to Shaphan.
16. Shaphan took the book to the king and said, "We've done everything you ordered.
17. The money collected in the Temple has been given to the workers and supervisors."
18. Then Shaphan said, "Hilkiah gave me a book," and read it to the king.
19. When Josiah heard the Law, he tore his clothes in sorrow.
20. Then he told Hilkiah, Ahikam, Abdon, Shaphan, and Asaiah,
21. "Go ask the Lord for me, and for all Israel and Judah, about what's written in this book. The Lord is very angry with us, because our ancestors didn't obey these laws."
22. Hilkiah and the others went to talk to the prophet Huldah, who lived in Jerusalem. Her husband Shallum was in charge of the royal clothes.
23. She told them, "The Lord says: I will bring disaster on this place and its people, just as written in the book.
24. They have turned away from Me and worshiped other gods, making Me very angry.
26. So I will punish this place and won't forgive them."
27. "But tell King Josiah,
28. because you were sorry, humbled yourself, and tore your clothes when you heard My words, I heard you.
29. I will let you die in peace. You won't see the disaster I'll bring." They took this message back to the king.
30. Then Josiah called together all the leaders of Judah and Jerusalem.

31. He went to the Temple with everyone—priests, Levites, and all the people. He read the entire Book of the Law out loud.
32. Standing by the pillar, Josiah made a promise to follow the Lord, obey His commands, and keep His covenant with all his heart and soul.
33. He had everyone in Jerusalem and Benjamin agree to this covenant too.
34. Josiah removed all the idols from all the lands that belonged to the Israelites. As long as he lived, he made sure everyone worshiped only the Lord their God.

2 Chronicles 35

1. Josiah celebrated the Passover in Jerusalem. The priests killed the Passover lambs on the 14th day of the first month.
2. He put the priests in their duties and encouraged them as they served in the Lord's Temple.
3. He told the Levites, who taught Israel and carried the Sacred Chest, "Put the Chest back in the Temple Solomon, son of David, built. Don't carry it on your shoulders anymore. Now serve the Lord and His people."
4. "Prepare yourselves by your family groups, as David and Solomon directed."
5. "Stand in the holy place with a group of Levites beside each family group of the people."
6. "Kill the Passover lambs, make yourselves clean, and help the people do the same."
7. Josiah gave 30,000 sheep and goats and 3,000 bulls from his own herds for the people to offer during the Passover.
8. His officials gave offerings too. Hilkiah, Zechariah, and Jehiel gave 2,600 Passover animals and 300 bulls to the priests.
9. The Levite leaders—Conaniah, Shemaiah, Nethanel, Hashabiah, Jeiel, and Jozabad—gave 5,000 Passover animals and 500 bulls for the Levites.
10. Everything was ready. The priests stood in their places. The Levites stood in their groups, just as the king had ordered.
11. The Passover lambs were killed. The priests sprinkled the blood, and the Levites skinned the animals.
12. They set aside the burnt offerings for each family group, just as written in the Law of Moses. They did the same with the bulls.
13. They roasted the Passover animals on the fire, as instructed. They boiled the other holy offerings in pots, kettles, and pans and gave it to the people.
14. Then the Levites got their own meal. The priests were busy offering sacrifices until nighttime, so the Levites prepared food for them too.
15. The musicians from Asaph's group were in their places, as David, Asaph, Heman, and Jeduthun had ordered. The guards were at the gates. They didn't leave their posts because the Levites prepared everything for them.
16. Everything was done that day just as Josiah commanded. The Passover was celebrated, and burnt offerings were made at the Lord's Temple.
17. The Israelites who were there celebrated the Passover and the Festival of Unleavened Bread for seven days.
18. The Passover had not been celebrated like this in Israel since the days of the prophet Samuel. None of the kings of Israel ever celebrated a Passover like Josiah did with the priests, Levites, and everyone from Judah and Israel.
19. This Passover was celebrated in Josiah's 18th year as king.
20. After all this, King Neco of Egypt came to fight at Carchemish. Josiah went out to fight him.
21. But Neco sent messengers saying, "This war isn't with you. I was sent by God to fight another nation. Don't get

in the way or you'll be going against God."

22. But Josiah didn't listen. He disguised himself and went to fight at Megiddo.
23. Archers shot King Josiah. He told his officers, "I'm badly hurt! Get me out!"
24. His men took him from his chariot, put him in another, and brought him to Jerusalem. He died and was buried in his family's tomb. Everyone in Judah and Jerusalem mourned.
25. Jeremiah wrote a funeral song for Josiah. Singers and musicians still sing sad songs about him. It became a tradition in Israel. These songs are written in the Book of Laments.
26. Everything else Josiah did—his devotion to the Lord and obedience to the Law—
27. is written in the book called the History of the Kings of Israel and Judah.

2 Chronicles 36

1. The people of Judah made Josiah's son Jehoahaz king in Jerusalem.
2. Jehoahaz was 23 years old when he became king, and he ruled in Jerusalem for 3 months.
3. Neco, the king of Egypt, removed Jehoahaz and forced Judah to pay 7,500 pounds of silver and 75 pounds of gold.
4. Neco made Jehoahaz's brother Eliakim king and changed his name to Jehoiakim. Then Neco took Jehoahaz back to Egypt as a prisoner.
5. Jehoiakim was 25 years old when he became king, and he ruled from Jerusalem for 11 years. He did what was evil in the Lord's eyes.
6. Then King Nebuchadnezzar of Babylon attacked and took Jehoiakim prisoner in chains.
7. Nebuchadnezzar also took valuable items from the Lord's Temple and put them in his palace in Babylon.
8. Everything else about Jehoiakim is written in the book called The History of the Kings of Israel and Judah. Then his son Jehoiachin became king.
9. Jehoiachin was 18 years old when he became king, and he ruled from Jerusalem for 3 months and 10 days. He also did what was evil in the Lord's eyes.
10. In the spring, King Nebuchadnezzar took Jehoiachin prisoner to Babylon along with more valuables from the Lord's Temple. He made Zedekiah, Jehoiachin's uncle, king over Judah and Jerusalem.
11. Zedekiah was 21 years old when he became king, and he ruled from Jerusalem for 11 years.
12. He did what was evil in the Lord's eyes and refused to humble himself when the prophet Jeremiah spoke to him from the Lord.
13. Zedekiah also broke his promise to Nebuchadnezzar, even though he swore in God's name to obey him. He was stubborn and refused to turn to the Lord.
14. All the leaders and priests became more sinful and did the same evil as the other nations. They disrespected the Temple the Lord had made holy.
15. The Lord had mercy and sent prophets to warn them over and over.
16. But the people made fun of God's messengers, ignored His words, and laughed at the prophets. So the Lord became very angry, and there was no way to stop His judgment.
17. He sent the king of Babylon. The Babylonian army killed their young men—even inside the Temple. They showed no mercy to anyone—young or old, man or woman.
18. The king took everything from the Lord's Temple and the king's palace, including treasures and sacred objects.
19. They burned down the Lord's Temple, destroyed Jerusalem's wall, burned all the palaces, and ruined everything valuable.

20. The few who survived were taken to Babylon as prisoners. They stayed there as servants until Persia took control.

21. This happened exactly as the Lord had said through the prophet Jeremiah. The land rested for 70 years to make up for the time the people had disobeyed.

22. In the first year of King Cyrus of Persia, the Lord caused him to make a public message. This fulfilled what the Lord had said through Jeremiah.

23. Cyrus said: "The Lord, the God of heaven, gave me all the kingdoms of the earth and told me to build Him a Temple in Jerusalem. If any of His people are here, may the Lord be with them. Let them go and rebuild His Temple."

– Ezra –

After exile, Jews return to rebuild the Temple and renew their commitment to God.

Ezra 1

Cyrus Lets the People Return Home

1. In Cyrus's first year as king of Persia, he made an announcement, just like the Lord said through Jeremiah.
2. "The Lord God of heaven gave me all the kingdoms on earth. He told me to build him a Temple in Jerusalem."
3. "His people can go to Jerusalem and rebuild it. May God be with you."
4. "Help them go back. Give them silver, gold, supplies, animals, and offerings."
5. The leaders, priests, and Levites who wanted to go got ready to leave.
6. Their neighbors gave them silver, gold, supplies, animals, and gifts.
7. King Cyrus gave back the things taken from the Temple.
8. He gave them to Mithredath, who counted them and gave them to Sheshbazzar.
9. Here is the list: 30 gold dishes, 1,000 silver dishes, 29 knives,
10. 30 gold bowls, 410 silver bowls, and 1,000 other items.
11. In total there were 5,400 gold and silver things. Sheshbazzar took them to Jerusalem.

Ezra 2

The People Who Returned to Jerusalem

1. These are the people King Nebuchadnezzar took as prisoners to Babylon. Now they returned to Jerusalem and their towns.
2. They were led by Zerubbabel, Jeshua, Nehemiah, Seraiah, Reelaiah, Mordecai, Bilshan, Mispar, Bigvai, Rehum, and Baanah. These are the men who returned:
3. Parosh's family – 2,172
4. Shephatiah's family – 372
5. Arah's family – 775
6. Pahath-Moab's family (descendants of Jeshua and Joab) – 2,812
7. Elam's family – 1,254
8. Zattu's family – 945
9. Zaccai's family – 760
10. Bani's family – 642
11. Bebai's family – 623
12. Azgad's family – 1,222
13. Adonikam's family – 666
14. Bigvai's family – 2,056
15. Adin's family – 454
16. Ater's family (descendants of Hezekiah) – 98
17. Bezai's family – 323
18. Jorah's family – 112
19. Hashum's family – 223
20. Gibbar's family – 95
21. People from Bethlehem – 123
22. Netophah – 56

23. Anathoth – 128
24. Azmaveth – 42
25. Kiriath Jearim, Kephirah, and Beeroth – 743
26. Ramah and Geba – 621
27. Michmash – 122
28. Bethel and Ai – 223
29. Nebo – 52
30. Magbish – 156
31. The other Elam – 1,254
32. Harim – 320
33. Lod, Hadid, and Ono – 725
34. Jericho – 345
35. Senaah – 3,630
36. Priests from Jedaiah's family (through Jeshua) – 973
37. Immer's family – 1,052
38. Pashhur's family – 1,247
39. Harim's family – 1,017
40. Levites from Jeshua and Kadmiel's family (descendants of Hodaviah) – 74
41. Musicians from Asaph's family – 128
42. Gatekeepers from Shallum, Ater, Talmon, Akkub, Hatita, and Shobai – 139
43. Temple servants: Ziha, Hasupha, Tabbaoth,
44. Keros, Siaha, Padon,
45. Lebanah, Hagabah, Akkub,
46. Hagab, Shalmai, Hanan,
47. Giddel, Gahar, Reaiah,
48. Rezin, Nekoda, Gazzam,
49. Uzza, Paseah, Besai,
50. Asnah, Meunim, Nephusim,
51. Bakbuk, Hakupha, Harhur,
52. Bazluth, Mehida, Harsha,
53. Barkos, Sisera, Temah,
54. Neziah, and Hatipha
55. Solomon's servants' descendants: Sotai, Hassophereth, Peruda,
56. Jaalah, Darkon, Giddel,
57. Shephatiah, Hattil, Pokereth-Hazzebaim, and Ami
58. Temple servants and Solomon's servants together – 392
59. These came from Tel Melah, Tel Harsha, Cherub, Addan, and Immer, but couldn't prove they were Israelites:
60. Delaiah, Tobiah, and Nekoda's families – 652
61. Priests from Hobaiah, Hakkoz, and Barzillai's families. Barzillai had married a woman from Barzillai of Gilead and took her name.
62. They looked for family records but couldn't find them, so they couldn't be priests.
63. The governor said they couldn't eat the priest's food until a priest with the Urim and Thummim could decide.
64. The total group who returned was 42,360 people.
65. They also had 7,337 servants and 200 male and female musicians.
66. They brought 736 horses and 245 mules.
67. They brought 435 camels and 6,720 donkeys.
68. When they arrived at the Temple in Jerusalem, some family leaders gave gifts to help rebuild it.
69. They gave 1,030 pounds of gold, 5,740 pounds of silver, and 100 robes for priests.
70. The priests, Levites, musicians, gatekeepers, Temple servants, and others moved into their towns.

Ezra 3

The First Offering on the New Altar

1. Seven months later, the Israelites had moved into their towns. They gathered in Jerusalem.

2. Jeshua son of Jozadak and Zerubbabel son of Shealtiel, with their relatives, built the altar of the God of Israel so they could offer burnt offerings, as the Law of Moses said.
3. They built the altar on its old spot, even though they were scared of the people around them. They gave burnt offerings every morning and evening.
4. They celebrated the Festival of Shelters and gave the right number of offerings each day.
5. They gave the daily offerings, the New Moon offerings, and the offerings for the yearly festivals. People also gave freewill offerings.
6. On the first day of the seventh month, they began to offer burnt offerings to the Lord, even though the Temple foundation wasn't built yet.

The Rebuilding of the Temple Begins

7. They hired stoneworkers and carpenters. They gave food, drink, and olive oil to the people of Sidon and Tyre, who brought cedar logs from Lebanon to Joppa, as Cyrus the king had allowed.
8. In the second month of the second year after returning, Zerubbabel, Jeshua, the priests, Levites, and others started rebuilding the Temple. Every Levite over 20 years old was put in charge.
9. Jeshua and his sons, Kadmiel and his sons, and Henadad's family and their sons worked together to supervise the work.
10. When the foundation was finished, the priests put on their robes and played trumpets. The Levites from Asaph's family played cymbals to praise the Lord, just like King David had said.
11. They sang to the Lord: "He is good! His love for Israel lasts forever!" Then everyone shouted loudly and praised the Lord because the foundation was done.
12. Many older priests, Levites, and leaders who had seen the first Temple cried loudly. But many others shouted with joy.
13. The noise was so loud, no one could tell the difference between the shouts and the crying.

Ezra 4

Others Try to Stop the Temple Work

1. The enemies of Judah and Benjamin heard that the people were rebuilding the Temple of the Lord, the God of Israel.
2. They went to Zerubbabel and the leaders and said, "Let us help you build. We worship your God and have offered sacrifices to him since King Esarhaddon of Assyria brought us here."
3. But Zerubbabel, Jeshua, and the leaders said, "No. Only we can rebuild the Temple for the Lord, the God of Israel. King Cyrus of Persia gave us this job."
4. So the people who were refused tried to make the builders afraid and stop the work.
5. They paid officials to block the work. This lasted during the time of King Cyrus until King Darius became king of Persia.

Trouble Rebuilding Jerusalem

6. When King Ahasuerus (Xerxes) became king, the enemies of Judah and Jerusalem wrote him false accusations.
7. Later, during the time of King Artaxerxes, Bishlam, Mithredath, Tabeel, and others wrote a letter in Aramaic that had to be translated.
8. Rehum the governor and Shimshai the secretary also wrote a letter to King Artaxerxes.
9. It was from Rehum, Shimshai, and their assistants—the judges and officials over the people from Persia, Erech, Babylon, Susa (the Elamites),

10. and from others King Ashurbanipal had brought to Samaria and the lands west of the Euphrates River.
11. This is what the letter said: "To King Artaxerxes, from your servants west of the Euphrates River:
12. The Jews who came here from Babylon are rebuilding Jerusalem. This city has been known to rebel. They have started fixing the walls and foundations.
13. If this city is rebuilt, they won't pay taxes, and your income will suffer.
14. We are loyal to you and don't want you to be hurt by this.
15. You can check the records. Jerusalem has always caused trouble for kings. That's why it was destroyed.
16. If this city is rebuilt, you'll lose control of the land west of the Euphrates River."
17. The king replied: "To Rehum, Shimshai, and your group in Samaria and west of the Euphrates. Greetings.
18. The letter you sent was read to me and translated.
19. I checked the records and found that Jerusalem has a history of rebelling against kings.
20. Strong kings once ruled there and collected taxes from people west of the Euphrates.
21. So I order the work to stop. The city must not be rebuilt unless I say so.
22. Do not ignore this. Stop the work right now."
23. When Rehum, Shimshai, and their group read the letter, they rushed to Jerusalem and stopped the work by force.
24. So the Temple work stopped. It stayed that way until the second year of King Darius of Persia.

Ezra 5

Work on the Temple Starts Again

1. The prophets Haggai and Zechariah spoke to the Jews in Judah and Jerusalem in the name of the God of Israel.
2. Zerubbabel and Jeshua began to rebuild the Temple again. The prophets helped them.
3. Tattenai, the governor west of the Euphrates River, Shethar Bozenai, and others came and asked, "Who gave you permission to rebuild this Temple and fix these walls?"
4. They also asked for the names of the men working on it.
5. But God was watching over the Jewish leaders, so they were not stopped. Tattenai waited to hear back from King Darius.
6. This is a copy of the letter Tattenai sent to King Darius:
7. "To King Darius. Greetings.
8. We went to Judah and saw the Temple of the great God being rebuilt. The people are working hard, and the walls are being repaired.
9. We asked the leaders, 'Who gave you permission to rebuild this Temple and fix the walls?'
10. We also asked for their names so we could report to you.
11. They said, 'We serve the God of heaven and earth. We are rebuilding the Temple that was built long ago by a great king of Israel.
12. But our ancestors made the God of heaven angry. He let King Nebuchadnezzar of Babylon destroy the Temple and take the people away.
13. In the first year of King Cyrus of Babylon, he gave an order to rebuild the Temple.
14. He gave back the gold and silver items that Nebuchadnezzar had taken. He gave them to Sheshbazzar, the governor.

15. He told Sheshbazzar to return everything and rebuild the Temple in Jerusalem on its old site.
16. Sheshbazzar laid the foundation of the Temple. The people have been working on it, but it is not finished yet.'
17. Please check the records to see if King Cyrus gave this order. Then let us know what to do."

Ezra 6

King Darius Finds the Order

1. King Darius gave an order to search the records in Babylon.
2. A scroll was found in Ecbatana in the province of Media. It said:
3. "In the first year of King Cyrus, he gave this order: Rebuild God's Temple in Jerusalem where sacrifices are offered. Make it 90 feet high and 90 feet wide.
4. Use three layers of large stones and one layer of wood. The king will pay for everything.
5. Return the gold and silver items Nebuchadnezzar took from the Temple. Put them back where they belong."

King Darius Gives a New Order

6. So King Darius sent this message to Tattenai, Shethar Bozenai, and others west of the Euphrates River:
7. "Stay away. Let the governor and the Jewish leaders rebuild the Temple.
8. Use money from taxes west of the Euphrates to pay for the work. Give them what they need right away.
9. Give them bulls, rams, sheep, wheat, salt, wine, and olive oil every day for the offerings.
10. Then they can offer sacrifices to please God and pray for me and my sons.
11. If anyone disobeys this order, tear a beam from his house, kill him on it, and destroy his house.
12. May God destroy any king or nation that tries to change or destroy this Temple. I, Darius, have given this order. It must be obeyed."

The Temple Is Finished and Dedicated

13. Tattenai, Shethar Bozenai, and their helpers obeyed the king.
14. The Jewish leaders kept building with help from the prophets Haggai and Zechariah. The Temple was finished, just as God had said and as Cyrus, Darius, and Artaxerxes had ordered.
15. The Temple was finished on the third day of the month of Adar in the sixth year of King Darius.
16. The Israelites, priests, and Levites were filled with joy and celebrated the Temple's dedication.
17. They gave 100 bulls, 200 rams, 400 lambs, and 12 goats—one for each tribe of Israel—as a sin offering.
18. The priests and Levites were given their duties at the Temple, just as the Law of Moses said.

The Passover and Festival

19. On the fourteenth day of the first month, they celebrated the Passover.
20. All the priests and Levites had made themselves clean. They killed the Passover lambs for everyone, including themselves.
21. The people who returned and those who left their sinful ways joined in the meal to honor the Lord.
22. They celebrated the Festival of Unleavened Bread for seven days. Everyone was happy because the Lord made the king of Assyria help them rebuild the Temple of God.

Ezra 7

Ezra Comes to Jerusalem

1. Years later, during the rule of King Artaxerxes of Persia, a man named Ezra came to Jerusalem. He was the son of Seraiah and grandson of Azariah.

2. His family line continued through Hilkiah, Shallum, Zadok, and Ahitub,
3. then Amariah, Azariah, Meraioth,
4. Zerahiah, Uzzi, Bukki,
5. Abishua, Phinehas, Eleazar, and Aaron the high priest.
6. Ezra came from Babylon. He was a teacher who knew the Law of Moses well. The king gave him everything he asked for because the Lord was with him.
7. Some Israelites, priests, Levites, musicians, gatekeepers, and Temple servants went to Jerusalem with Ezra in the seventh year of the king's rule.
8. Ezra arrived in Jerusalem in the fifth month of that same year.
9. He left Babylon on the first day of the first month and arrived on the first day of the fifth month. God helped him all the way.
10. Ezra had chosen to study, obey, and teach the Law of the Lord to Israel.

Artaxerxes Gives a Letter to Ezra

11. Ezra was a priest and teacher who knew the Lord's commands. King Artaxerxes gave him a letter. It said:
12. "From Artaxerxes, king of kings, to Ezra the priest and teacher of the Law of the God of heaven. Hello.
13. I allow any Israelites in my kingdom, including priests and Levites, to go with you to Jerusalem if they want to.
14. My advisors and I are sending you to check on Judah and Jerusalem. See if they are following your God's Law, which you teach.
15. Take the silver and gold we are freely giving to the God of Israel, who lives in Jerusalem.
16. Also take all the silver and gold you collect in Babylon, and the offerings from the people and priests for the Temple.
17. Use the money to buy bulls, rams, lambs, grain, and drink offerings to be sacrificed on God's altar in Jerusalem.
18. If you have silver or gold left over, use it in any way that pleases your God.
19. Take all the items given to you for worship in the Temple and deliver them to Jerusalem.
20. If you need anything else for the Temple, take it from the royal treasury.
21. I, King Artaxerxes, order all the treasurers west of the Euphrates River to give Ezra whatever he asks for.
22. Give up to 7,500 pounds of silver, 500 bushels of wheat, 550 gallons of wine, 550 gallons of olive oil, and unlimited salt.
23. Give everything the God of heaven needs for his Temple. We don't want to make him angry.
24. No one who works in the Temple—priests, Levites, musicians, gatekeepers, or servants—has to pay taxes.
25. Ezra, use your wisdom to choose judges and leaders for everyone west of the Euphrates River. Teach God's laws to anyone who doesn't know them.
26. Anyone who disobeys God's law or the king's law must be punished—by death, prison, losing property, or being sent away."

Ezra Praises God

27. Praise the Lord, the God of our ancestors! He made the king want to honor the Temple of the Lord in Jerusalem.
28. The Lord helped me and made the king, his advisors, and his officials support me. I gained courage and brought leaders of Israel with me to Jerusalem.

Ezra 8

The Families Who Returned with Ezra

1. These are the family leaders and the list of those who came with me from Babylon during King Artaxerxes's rule:
2. From Phinehas's family: Gershom. From Ithamar: Daniel. From David: Hattush.

3. From Shecaniah's family: a descendant. From Parosh: Zechariah and 150 others.
4. From Pahath Moab: Eliehoenai son of Zerahiah and 200 others.
5. From Zattu: Shecaniah son of Jahaziel and 300 others.
6. From Adin: Ebed son of Jonathan and 50 others.
7. From Elam: Jeshaiah son of Athaliah and 70 others.
8. From Shephatiah: Zebadiah son of Michael and 80 others.
9. From Joab: Obadiah son of Jehiel and 218 others.
10. From Bani: Shelomith son of Josiphiah and 160 others.
11. From Bebai: Zechariah son of Bebai and 28 others.
12. From Azgad: Johanan son of Hakkatan and 110 others.
13. From Adonikam, who came later: Eliphelet, Jeuel, Shemaiah, and 60 others.
14. From Bigvai: Uthai, Zaccur, and 70 others.

Ezra Finds Levites for the Temple

15. We gathered at the Ahava Canal and camped for 3 days. I checked the people and priests but found no Levites.
16. So I sent for these leaders: Eliezer, Ariel, Shemaiah, Elnathan, Jarib, another Elnathan, Nathan, Zechariah, and Meshullam. I also sent for the teachers Joiarib and Elnathan.
17. I sent them to Iddo, the leader in Casiphia. I told them to ask him and the Temple servants to send people to help at the Temple.
18. God helped us. They sent Sherebiah, a Levite from Mahli's family, and 18 relatives.
19. They also sent Hashabiah and Jeshaiah from Merari's family and 20 relatives.
20. They also brought 220 Temple servants. These were the ones King David had chosen to help the Levites. They were all listed by name.

Ezra Tells the People to Pray and Fast

21. At the Ahava Canal, I told everyone to fast and pray. We asked God to keep us, our children, and our things safe on the trip.
22. I was ashamed to ask the king for soldiers and horses to protect us because we told him, "Our God helps everyone who trusts him, but punishes those who turn away."
23. So we fasted and prayed. We asked God to protect us, and he answered.

Ezra Gives the Gifts to the Priests

24. I chose 12 leaders from the priests: Sherebiah, Hashabiah, and 10 others.
25. I gave them the silver, gold, and items the king, his advisors, officials, and Israelites had given for the Temple.
26. I weighed out 24 tons of silver, 7,500 pounds of silver items, and 7,500 pounds of gold.
27. I also gave 20 gold bowls worth 1,000 coins, and 2 fine polished bronze items as valuable as gold.
28. I told them, "You and these things are holy to the Lord. The silver and gold are gifts to God, the God of our ancestors.
29. Guard them carefully until you deliver them to the Temple in Jerusalem. The priests, Levites, and leaders will weigh everything there."
30. So the priests and Levites took the silver, gold, and items and carried them to Jerusalem.

They Arrive in Jerusalem

31. On the twelfth day of the first month, we left the Ahava Canal for Jerusalem. God protected us on the way.
32. We arrived in Jerusalem and rested for 3 days.
33. On the fourth day, we weighed the silver, gold, and items at the Temple.

Meremoth son of Uriah and Eleazar son of Phinehas received them. The Levites Jozabad son of Jeshua and Noadiah son of Binnui were with them.

34. Everything was counted, weighed, and recorded.
35. Then the people who returned offered sacrifices to the Lord: 12 bulls for Israel, 96 rams, 77 lambs, and 12 goats for sin offerings.
36. They gave the king's orders to the governors and officials west of the Euphrates. These leaders helped the people and supported the Temple.

Ezra 9

Ezra Is Upset About Mixed Marriages

1. Later, the leaders came to me and said, "Many Israelites, including priests and Levites, have married people from nearby nations. They follow the evil ways of the Canaanites, Hittites, Perizzites, Jebusites, Ammonites, Moabites, Egyptians, and Amorites.
2. The men of Israel married women from these nations. Our holy people have mixed with them. Even our leaders and officials have done this."
3. When I heard this, I tore my clothes, pulled out hair from my head and beard, and sat down shocked.
4. Everyone who feared God's warnings sat with me. I stayed there in shock until the evening sacrifice.

Ezra's Prayer

5. At the time of the evening sacrifice, I stood up with my clothes still torn. I knelt and lifted my hands to the Lord.
6. I prayed, "God, I'm too ashamed to look at you. Our sins are stacked up to the sky.
7. From the days of our ancestors until now, we've sinned. That's why we and our kings and priests have been ruled by other nations. We've been killed, taken, robbed, and shamed.
8. But now you've been kind to us. Some of us have survived. You gave us hope and safety at your Temple. You gave us new life after slavery.
9. We are still slaves, but you didn't leave us. You made the kings of Persia kind to us. You helped us rebuild your Temple and live in safety in Jerusalem.
10. But now, our God, what can we say? We disobeyed your commands again.
11. Your prophets warned us: 'The land you are giving us is filled with sin from the people who lived there before.'
12. They told us not to marry them or become close to them. If we obeyed, we could enjoy the land and pass it on to our children.
13. We are being punished, but not as much as we deserve. You still let us live.
14. Should we disobey again and marry people who do wrong? If we do, you will destroy us.
15. Lord, you are fair. We are guilty. But you have let us survive."

Ezra 10

The People Agree to End the Mixed Marriages

1. While Ezra was praying, crying, and bowing down in front of the Temple, a large crowd of Israelites gathered. They cried loudly too.
2. Shecaniah son of Jehiel, from Elam's family, said, "We have sinned. We married foreign women. But there is still hope for Israel.
3. Let's make a promise with God to send away all the foreign wives and their children. We will follow your advice and obey God's law.
4. Get up, Ezra. This is your job. We will support you. Be strong and do it."
5. Ezra stood up and made the priests, Levites, and all the people promise to do what Shecaniah said.

6. Then Ezra left the Temple and went to the room of Jehohanan son of Eliashib. He didn't eat or drink because he was still mourning about the people's sin.
7. A message was sent to all the returned people in Judah and Jerusalem to meet in Jerusalem.
8. Anyone who didn't come in 3 days would lose their property and be removed from the community.
9. On the 20th day of the 9th month, everyone from Judah and Benjamin came to Jerusalem. They sat in the Temple courtyard, scared because of the meeting and the heavy rain.
10. Ezra stood up and said, "You have been unfaithful. You married foreign women and added to Israel's guilt.
11. Now confess your sin to the Lord. Obey him. Separate yourselves from the foreign people and your foreign wives."
12. The whole crowd answered, "You are right! We will do what you said."
13. They added, "But there are many of us, and it is raining. We can't stay out here. This can't be done in one or two days.
14. Let our leaders handle this. Each man with a foreign wife can meet with the leaders and judges of his city until God's anger is gone."
15. Only Jonathan son of Asahel and Jahzeiah son of Tikvah opposed this. Meshullam and Shabbethai the Levite supported them.
16. The returned people agreed to the plan. Ezra chose family leaders to handle the matter. On the 1st day of the 10th month, they began to work.
17. By the 1st day of the 1st month, they finished questioning all the men who had married foreign wives.

The List of Men with Foreign Wives

18. These priests had married foreign wives: From Jeshua's family (son of Jozadak): Maaseiah, Eliezer, Jarib, and Gedaliah.
19. They promised to send their wives away and offered a ram for their sin.
20. From Immer's family: Hanani and Zebadiah.
21. From Harim's family: Maaseiah, Elijah, Shemaiah, Jehiel, and Uzziah.
22. From Pashhur's family: Elioenai, Maaseiah, Ishmael, Nethanel, Jozabad, and Elasah.
23. From the Levites: Jozabad, Shimei, Kelaiah (Kelita), Pethahiah, Judah, and Eliezer.
24. From the musicians: Eliashib. From the gatekeepers: Shallum, Telem, and Uri.
25. From Parosh's family: Ramiah, Izziah, Malkijah, Mijamin, Eleazar, Hashabiah, and Benaiah.
26. From Elam's family: Mattaniah, Zechariah, Jehiel, Abdi, Jeremoth, and Elijah.
27. From Zattu's family: Elioenai, Eliashib, Mattaniah, Jeremoth, Zabad, and Aziza.
28. From Bebai's family: Jehohanan, Hananiah, Zabbai, and Athlai.
29. From Bani's family: Meshullam, Malluch, Adaiah, Jashub, Sheal, and Jeremoth.
30. From Pahath Moab's family: Adna, Kelal, Benaiah, Maaseiah, Mattaniah, Bezalel, Binnui, and Manasseh.
31. rom Harim's family: Eliezer, Ishijah, Malkijah, Shemaiah, Shimeon,
32. Benjamin, Malluch, and Shemariah.
33. From Hashum's family: Mattenai, Mattattah, Zabad, Eliphelet, Jeremai, Manasseh, and Shimei.
34. From Bani's family: Maadai, Amram, Uel,
35. Benaiah, Bedeiah, Keluhi,
36. Vaniah, Meremoth, Eliashib,
37. Mattaniah, Mattenai, and Jaasu.
38. From Binnui's family: Shimei,
39. Shelemiah, Nathan, Adaiah,

40. Machnadebai, Shashai, Sharai,
41. Azarel, Shelemiah, and Shemariah,
42. Shallum, Amariah, and Joseph.
43. From Nebo's family: Jeiel, Mattithiah, Zabad, Zebina, Jaddai, Joel, and Benaiah.
44. All these men had married foreign wives. Some of them had children.

– Nehemiah –

Nehemiah rebuilds Jerusalem's walls and helps reform the people spiritually.

Nehemiah 1

Nehemiah's Prayer

1. These are the words of Nehemiah, son of Hacaliah: In the month of Chislev, during the 12th year of King Artaxerxes's reign, I was in the city of Susa.
2. Hanani, one of my brothers, came with some men from Judah. I asked them about the Jews who had returned from being prisoners and about Jerusalem.
3. They said, "Things are bad. The people are in trouble and feel ashamed. The wall of Jerusalem is torn down, and the gates have been burned."
4. When I heard this, I sat down and cried. For days, I mourned, didn't eat, and prayed to God.
5. I prayed, "Lord God of Heaven, you are great and powerful. You keep your promises to those who love you and obey your commands.
6. Please listen and see me praying. I pray day and night for your people, Israel. We have sinned, including me and my family.
7. We have disobeyed the laws and commands you gave through your servant Moses.
8. Remember what you told Moses: 'If you are unfaithful, I will scatter you among other nations.
9. But if you return to me and obey me, I will bring you back to the place I chose to be worshiped, even if you were scattered far away.'
10. These people are your servants. You saved them with your great power.
11. Lord, listen to my prayer and the prayers of those who worship you. Please help me when I ask the king for a favor. Let him say yes."

Nehemiah 2

Nehemiah Talks to the King

1. In the month of Nisan, during the 20th year of King Artaxerxes, I was serving him wine. I had never looked sad in front of him before.
2. He asked, "Why do you look so sad? You're not sick. Something must be bothering you." I was very afraid.
3. I said, "May the king live forever. How can I not be sad? The city where my ancestors are buried is in ruins, and its gates are burned."
4. The king asked, "What do you want?" I prayed to God before I answered.
5. I said, "If it pleases you, send me to Judah so I can rebuild the city where my ancestors are buried."
6. The king, with the queen beside him, asked, "How long will you be gone? When will you return?" I gave him a time, and he agreed.
7. I said, "Please give me letters for the governors west of the Euphrates River so I can travel safely to Judah.
8. And give me a letter to Asaph, the one in charge of your forest. I'll need wood for the Temple gates, the city wall, and my house." The king agreed because God was helping me.
9. I gave the letters to the governors. The king also sent army officers and horsemen with me.

10. When Sanballat the Horonite and Tobiah the Ammonite heard I came to help Israel, they were very upset.

Nehemiah Looks at the Walls

11. I arrived in Jerusalem and stayed three days.

12. Then I went out at night with a few men. I didn't tell anyone what God had put in my heart to do. I rode my own animal. No one else had one.

13. I went through the Valley Gate to the Jackal Well and the Dung Gate. I looked at the broken walls and burned gates.

14. I went to the Fountain Gate and the King's Pool, but there was no room to ride through.

15. I went up the valley, looked at the wall again, and came back through the Valley Gate.

16. The leaders, priests, and others didn't know where I had gone. I hadn't told anyone yet.

17. Then I said, "You see the trouble we're in. Jerusalem is destroyed and the gates are burned. Let's rebuild the wall so we won't be ashamed anymore."

18. I told them how God had helped me and what the king said. They said, "Let's start rebuilding!" So they began the good work.

19. But Sanballat, Tobiah, and Geshem laughed at us and said, "What are you doing? Are you rebelling against the king?"

20. I said, "God will help us succeed. We are his servants, and we will rebuild. You have no part in Jerusalem, no right to it, and no say in it."

Nehemiah 3

The Wall Is Rebuilt

1. The high priest Eliashib and other priests rebuilt the Sheep Gate. They put up the doors and dedicated it. Then they worked on the wall to the Tower of the Hundred and the Tower of Hananel.

2. The men of Jericho worked next to them. Next to them, Zaccur son of Imri worked.

3. The sons of Hassenaah rebuilt the Fish Gate. They set the doors, bolts, and bars.

4. Next to them, Meremoth son of Uriah worked. Then Meshullam son of Berekiah worked. Then Zadok son of Baana.

5. The people from Tekoa worked next, but their leaders refused to help.

6. Joiada son of Paseah and Meshullam son of Besodeiah repaired the Old Gate. They set the doors, bolts, and bars.

7. Melatiah of Gibeon and Jadon of Meronoth worked next, along with men from Gibeon and Mizpah.

8. Uzziel, a goldsmith, worked next. Hananiah, a perfume maker, worked beside him. They rebuilt part of the wall and reached the Broad Wall.

9. Rephaiah son of Hur, a leader in Jerusalem, repaired the next part.

10. Jedaiah son of Harumaph worked beside his own house. Hattush son of Hashabneiah worked beside him.

11. Malkijah son of Harim and Hasshub son of Pahath Moab fixed another section and the Tower of the Ovens.

12. Shallum son of Hallohesh, a leader in Jerusalem, worked with his daughters.

13. Hanun and the people of Zanoah repaired the Valley Gate. They set the doors, bolts, and bars, and rebuilt 1,500 feet of wall to the Dung Gate.

14. Malkijah son of Recab, leader of Beth Hakkerem, repaired the Dung Gate. He set the doors, bolts, and bars.

15. Shallun son of Kol-Hozeh, leader of Mizpah, repaired the Fountain Gate. He built the roof, set the doors, bolts, and bars. He also fixed the wall near the Pool of Siloam and the steps from the City of David.

16. Nehemiah son of Azbuk, leader of Beth Zur, repaired the wall near David's tomb and the army building.
17. Rehum son of Bani led the Levites who worked next. Hashabiah, leader of Keilah, repaired his section.
18. Binnui son of Henadad, leader of the other half of Keilah, worked next to him.
19. Ezer son of Jeshua, leader of Mizpah, repaired the section near the armory wall.
20. Baruch son of Zabbai worked very hard from the corner to the house of Eliashib the high priest.
21. Meremoth son of Uriah worked from the priest's house to the end of the next part.
22. Priests repaired the next section, each in front of his own house.
23. Benjamin and Hasshub worked beside their house. Azariah son of Maaseiah worked beside his.
24. Binnui son of Henadad repaired the wall next to Azariah's house and to the corner.
25. Palal son of Uzai worked near the tower at the king's palace. Pedaiah son of Parosh worked next to him.
26. Temple servants lived near the hill and the Water Gate. They worked on that part of the wall.
27. The people of Tekoa worked again from the big tower to the wall of Ophel.
28. The priests repaired the wall above the Horse Gate, each in front of his house.
29. Zadok son of Immer repaired across from his house. Shemaiah, gatekeeper of the East Gate, worked next to him.
30. Hananiah son of Shelemiah and Hanun, sixth son of Zalaph, worked next. Meshullam son of Berekiah worked across from his room.
31. Malkijah, a goldsmith, repaired the section near the Temple servants and traders. He worked up to the Inspection Gate and the upper room on the corner.
32. The goldsmiths and traders finished the wall from the corner to the Sheep Gate.

Nehemiah 4

Enemies Try to Stop the Work

1. When Sanballat heard we were rebuilding the wall, he got very angry and made fun of us.
2. He said to his friends and the army of Samaria, "What are these weak Jews doing? Will they finish the wall and offer sacrifices? Can they do this in one day? Can they bring these burned stones back to life?"
3. Tobiah the Ammonite said, "If a fox walked on their wall, it would fall down!"
4. I prayed, "God, hear how they insult us. Make them be hated. Let them be taken away as prisoners.
5. Don't forgive their sins or forget what they've done. They insulted the builders."
6. We kept building the wall, and soon it was halfway done. The people worked with all their hearts.
7. But when Sanballat, Tobiah, the Arabs, the Ammonites, and the men of Ashdod heard we were making progress, they got even angrier.
8. They planned to attack Jerusalem and stop the work.
9. But we prayed to God and set guards day and night.
10. The people of Judah said, "We are tired. There's too much rubble. We can't finish the wall."
11. Our enemies said, "We'll sneak in and kill them before they see us. That will stop the work."
12. The Jews who lived near them told us many times, "They will attack you from every direction."

13. So I put guards behind the wall in the low and open places. I gave swords, spears, and bows to the families.

14. I looked around and said, "Don't be afraid. Remember the Lord. He is great and powerful. Fight for your families, your sons, your daughters, your wives, and your homes."

15. When our enemies heard we knew their plan and that God ruined it, they left. So we went back to work on the wall.

16. From that day on, half the men worked, and the other half stood guard with weapons. The leaders stood behind the workers.

17. The workers carried building materials in one hand and held weapons in the other.

18. Each builder wore a sword at his side while he worked. The man with the trumpet stayed with me.

19. I said, "The work is spread out, and we are far apart on the wall.

20. If you hear the trumpet, come to us right away. God will fight for us."

21. We worked from sunrise until dark. Half the men stayed ready with weapons.

22. I told the people, "Everyone must stay in Jerusalem at night. We will work and stand guard night and day."

23. None of us, not me, my men, or the guards, took off our clothes. Each of us kept a weapon close, even when getting water.

Nehemiah 5

Nehemiah Helps the Poor

1. Some of the men and their wives complained against other Jews.

2. They said, "We have large families. We need more grain to have enough food to live."

3. Others said, "We had to sell our fields, vineyards, and homes to get food during the famine."

4. Some said, "We borrowed money to pay the king's taxes on our fields and vineyards.

5. We are just like the others. Our children are the same as theirs. But we've had to sell our sons and daughters as slaves. Some are already slaves, and we can't do anything because our fields and vineyards now belong to others."

6. When I heard this, I was very angry.

7. I thought about it, then I spoke against the officials and leaders. I said, "You are charging interest to your own people!" Then I called a large meeting to deal with this.

8. I said, "We have done our best to buy back our fellow Jews who were sold to foreigners. Now you are selling your own people again!" They had nothing to say.

9. I said, "What you're doing is wrong. You must show respect for God. Our enemies, the other nations, are watching us.

10. My family, my servants, and I have also loaned money and grain to the people. Let's stop charging interest.

11. Give back their fields, vineyards, olive trees, and houses. Return the money, grain, wine, and olive oil you took from them."

12. They said, "We will give everything back. We won't ask for anything more. We will do what you say." Then I called the priests and made them promise to keep this.

13. I shook out the folds of my robe and said, "If you don't keep your word, may God shake you out and leave you with nothing." Everyone said, "Amen," and praised God. The people did what they had promised.

Nehemiah Doesn't Take the Governor's Food Allowance

14. From the day I was made governor of Judah, during the 20th to the 32nd year of King Artaxerxes—12 years—I never took the food allowance that governors

usually get. My brothers didn't take it either.

15. The governors before me took food and silver from the people and had their servants act like rulers over them. But I didn't do that because I respect God.
16. I worked on the wall and didn't buy any land. All my men worked there too.
17. I fed 150 Jewish people and officials every day, along with people who came from other nations.
18. Every day I served one ox, six sheep, and many chickens. Every ten days I had all kinds of wine. But I never asked for the governor's food allowance, because the people were already struggling.
19. I said, "God, please remember everything I've done for these people."

Nehemiah 6

The Wall Is Finished

1. Sanballat, Tobiah, Geshem the Arab, and our other enemies heard we had rebuilt the wall. Only the gates weren't finished yet.
2. Sanballat and Geshem sent me a message: "Come meet us in one of the villages on the plain of Ono." But they were trying to trick me.
3. I sent a reply: "I'm doing important work. I can't stop. Why should I leave the work just to talk with you?"
4. They sent the same message four times, and I gave the same answer each time.
5. The fifth time, Sanballat sent his servant with an open letter.
6. It said: "People are talking. Geshem says it too. You and the Jews plan to rebel, and that's why you are rebuilding the wall. They say you want to be king.
7. They say you've appointed prophets to say this about you in Jerusalem: 'Nehemiah is king!' The king will hear about this. Come meet with us and talk."
8. I sent back: "That's a lie. You're making it all up."
9. They were trying to scare us and stop the work. But we kept working even harder.
10. Later, I went to visit Shemaiah. He said, "Let's meet in God's Temple and lock the doors. Someone is coming to kill you tonight!"
11. I said, "Should someone like me run away? I won't hide in the Temple."
12. I knew God had not sent him. He had been paid by Tobiah and Sanballat to scare me.
13. They hoped I would hide in the Temple and sin, so they could shame me.
14. I prayed, "God, remember Tobiah and Sanballat and what they did. Also remember Noadiah and the other prophets who tried to scare me."
15. The wall was finished on the 25th day of Elul. It took 52 days.
16. When our enemies heard it was finished, they were afraid and lost confidence. They knew this work was done with God's help.
17. During this time, the leaders of Judah kept sending letters to Tobiah, and he sent letters back.
18. Many in Judah were loyal to him because he was related to Shecaniah. His son had married the daughter of Meshullam.
19. People kept telling me good things about Tobiah, and they told him everything I said. Tobiah kept sending letters to scare me.

Nehemiah 7

List of the People Who Returned

1. After the wall was finished and the gates were set up, the guards, musicians, and Levites were given their jobs.

2. I put my brother Hanani and Hananiah, who was the palace commander, in charge of Jerusalem. Hananiah was honest and feared God more than most people.
3. I said, "Don't open the gates until the sun is hot. Lock the gates and assign guards—some at their posts, and others in front of their own houses."
4. The city was big, but not many people lived there yet, and the houses hadn't been rebuilt.
5. God put it in my heart to gather everyone and check their family records. I found the list of those who came back first, and this is what it said:
6. These are the people who came back from Babylon. King Nebuchadnezzar had taken them as prisoners, but they returned to their towns in Judah.
7. They came with Zerubbabel, Joshua, Nehemiah, Azariah, Raamiah, Nahamani, Mordecai, Bilshan, Mispereth, Bigvai, Nehum, and Baanah.
8. Descendants of Parosh – 2,172
9. Descendants of Shephatiah – 372
10. Descendants of Arah – 652
11. Descendants of Pahath-Moab (from Jeshua and Joab) – 2,818
12. Descendants of Elam – 1,254
13. Descendants of Zattu – 845
14. Descendants of Zaccai – 760
15. Descendants of Binnui – 648
16. Descendants of Bebai – 628
17. Descendants of Azgad – 2,322
18. Descendants of Adonikam – 667
19. Descendants of Bigvai – 2,067
20. Descendants of Adin – 655
21. Descendants of Ater (from Hezekiah) – 98
22. Descendants of Hashum – 328
23. Descendants of Bezai – 324
24. Descendants of Hariph – 112
25. Descendants of Gibeon – 95
26. From Bethlehem and Netophah – 188
27. From Anathoth – 128
28. From Beth Azmaveth – 42
29. From Kiriath Jearim, Kephirah, and Beeroth – 743
30. From Ramah and Geba – 621
31. From Michmash – 122
32. From Bethel and Ai – 123
33. From West Nebo – 52
34. From West Elam – 1,254
35. Descendants of Harim – 320
36. From Jericho – 345
37. From Lod, Hadid, and Ono – 721
38. From Senaah – 3,930
39. Priests: Descendants of Jedaiah (from Jeshua) – 973
40. Descendants of Immer – 1,052
41. Descendants of Pashhur – 1,247
42. Descendants of Harim – 1,017
43. Levites: Descendants of Jeshua (from Kadmiel and Hodaviah) – 74
44. Musicians: Descendants of Asaph – 148
45. Gatekeepers: Descendants of Shallum, Ater, Talmon, Akkub, Hatita, and Shobai – 138
46. Temple workers: Descendants of Ziha, Hasupha, Tabbaoth,
47. Keros, Sia, Padon,
48. Lebana, Hagaba, Shalmai,
49. Hanan, Giddel, Gahar,
50. Reaiah, Rezin, Nekoda,
51. Gazzam, Uzza, Paseah,
52. Besai, Meunim, Nephusim,
53. Bakbuk, Hakupha, Harhur,
54. Bazluth, Mehida, Harsha,
55. Barkos, Sisera, Temah,
56. Neziah, and Hatipha

57. Descendants of Solomon's servants: Sotai, Sophereth, Perida,
58. Jaala, Darkon, Giddel,
59. Shephatiah, Hattil, Pokereth-Hazzebaim, and Amon
60. Total Temple workers and Solomon's servants – 392
61. People from Tel Melah, Tel Harsha, Kerub, Addon, and Immer couldn't prove they were Israelites.
62. Descendants of Delaiah, Tobiah, and Nekoda – 642
63. Priests: Descendants of Hobaiah, Hakkoz, and Barzillai (who married a woman from Barzillai of Gilead and took her name)
64. These men couldn't find their names in the family records, so they couldn't be priests.
65. The governor said they couldn't eat priest food until a priest used the Urim and Thummim to decide.
66. Total people who returned – 42,360
67. Plus 7,337 male and female servants and 245 male and female musicians
68. They brought 736 horses, 245 mules,
69. 435 camels, and 6,720 donkeys
70. The leaders gave gifts for the Temple. The governor gave 1,000 gold coins, 50 bowls, and 530 robes for the priests.
71. Family leaders gave 20,000 gold coins and 2,750 pounds of silver.
72. The rest of the people gave 20,000 gold coins, 2,500 pounds of silver, and 67 robes for the priests.
73. The priests, Levites, gatekeepers, musicians, Temple workers, and all Israel settled in their towns. By the 7th month, everyone was in their hometowns.

Nehemiah 8

Ezra Reads the Law

1. All the people gathered in the courtyard by the Water Gate. They asked Ezra to bring the Book of the Law of Moses.
2. On the first day of the seventh month, Ezra brought out the Law and read it to the men, women, and all old enough to understand.
3. He read it from morning to noon. Everyone listened carefully.
4. Ezra stood on a wooden platform made for the event. On his right were Mattithiah, Shema, Anaiah, Uriah, Hilkiah, and Maaseiah. On his left were Pedaiah, Mishael, Malkijah, Hashum, Hashbaddanah, Zechariah, and Meshullam.
5. Ezra stood where everyone could see him. When he opened the book, everyone stood up.
6. Ezra praised the Lord, and the people raised their hands and said, "Amen! Amen!" Then they bowed down and worshiped the Lord.
7. The Levites—Jeshua, Bani, Sherebiah, Jamin, Akkub, Shabbethai, Hodiah, Maaseiah, Kelita, Azariah, Jozabad, Hanan, and Pelaiah—explained the Law to the people.
8. They read from the Law and explained it clearly so the people understood.
9. Nehemiah the governor, Ezra the priest, and the Levites said, "This is a holy day. Don't cry." The people were crying after hearing the Law realizing they had disobeyed.
10. Nehemiah said, "Go enjoy good food and sweet drinks. Share with those who have none. This is a holy day. Don't be sad. The Lord gives you strength."
11. The Levites said, "Calm down. This is a holy day. Don't be upset."
12. The people celebrated, ate, drank, and shared with others because they understood what was read.

Festival of Shelters

13. On the second day, the family leaders, priests, and Levites went to Ezra to learn more about the Law.

14. They found that the Lord had said the people must live in shelters during the Festival of Shelters.

15. They also saw it said to announce: "Go to the mountains and bring back branches from pine, olive, myrtle, palm, and other trees to make shelters."

16. So the people went and got branches and made shelters on their rooftops, in their yards, the Temple courtyard, and the town squares by the Water Gate and Ephraim Gate.

17. Everyone who had returned from captivity lived in these shelters. It hadn't been celebrated this way since Joshua's time. They were very happy.

18. Ezra read from the Book of the Law every day of the festival. On the eighth day, they held a closing ceremony, as the Law required.

Nehemiah 9

The People Confess Their Sins

1. On the 24th day of the same month, the Israelites gathered. They wore sackcloth, fasted, and put dirt on their heads.

2. They separated from foreigners and confessed their own sins and the sins of their ancestors.

3. They stood for 3 hours while the Law was read, then 3 more hours to confess their sins and worship the Lord.

4. On the Levite platform stood Jeshua, Bani, Kadmiel, Shebaniah, Bunni, Sherebiah, Bani, and Chenani. They cried out to the Lord.

5. Then the Levites—Jeshua, Kadmiel, Bani, Hashabneiah, Sherebiah, Hodiah, Shebaniah, and Pethahiah—said, "Stand and praise the Lord, your everlasting God! His name is greater than words can say."

The People's Prayer

6. "You alone are the Lord. You made the heavens, the stars, the earth, the seas, and everything in them. You give life to all, and the angels worship you.

7. You chose Abram and brought him from Ur. You named him Abraham.

8. You saw his heart was faithful and promised to give the land to his descendants. You kept your promise.

9. You saw our suffering in Egypt and heard us at the Red Sea.

10. You did miracles against Pharaoh and his people because they treated us badly. Your name became famous.

11. You split the sea so we could cross on dry ground. Then you drowned our enemies.

12. You led us with a cloud by day and fire by night.

13. You came down on Mount Sinai and gave us good laws.

14. You taught us to rest on the Sabbath and gave us your commands through Moses.

15. You gave us bread from heaven and water from a rock. You told us to take the land you promised.

16. But our ancestors were proud and refused to listen.

17. They ignored your miracles and chose a leader to go back to Egypt. But you forgave them. You are kind and full of love. You didn't leave them.

18. Even when they made a gold calf and said, "This is our god," you didn't leave them.

19. In your mercy, the cloud and fire still led them.

20. You gave your Spirit to teach them. You gave them food and water.

21. For 40 years, you took care of them. They had everything they needed.

22. You gave them kingdoms and land. They took the land of Sihon and Og.

23. You made their children as many as the stars and brought them to the promised land.

24. Their children went in and took the land. You defeated the people living there.
25. They took strong cities and good land. They had houses full of food, wells, vineyards, olive trees, and fruit trees. They had everything and were happy.
26. But they disobeyed you. They killed your prophets and sinned badly.
27. So you let their enemies rule them. But when they cried out, you saved them again.
28. Many times, they sinned, and many times you saved them. You warned them, but they wouldn't listen.
29. You told them to follow your laws, but they were stubborn.
30. For many years, you were patient. You warned them through your Spirit and prophets, but they wouldn't listen.
31. Still, you didn't destroy them. You are kind and full of love.
32. Now, our God, great and powerful, who keeps promises—don't forget all the trouble we've had since the time of the kings of Assyria.
33. You have been right in everything. We sinned.
34. Our kings, leaders, priests, and ancestors didn't obey your commands.
35. Even with a kingdom, rich land, and many blessings, they didn't serve you or stop doing evil.
36. Now we are slaves again in the land you gave us.
37. The land gives a lot of food, but it goes to the kings you put over us. We serve them and are in great trouble.
38. Because of all this, we made a written agreement. Our leaders, Levites, and priests signed and sealed it.

Nehemiah 10

The People Agree to Obey God

1. These are the names of the leaders who signed the agreement: Nehemiah the governor, son of Hacaliah, and Zedekiah,
2. Seraiah, Azariah, Jeremiah,
3. Pashhur, Amariah, Malkijah,
4. Hattush, Shebaniah, Malluch,
5. Harim, Meremoth, Obadiah,
6. Daniel, Ginnethon, Baruch,
7. Meshullam, Abijah, Mijamin,
8. Maaziah, Bilgai, and Shemaiah. These were the priests.
9. These were the Levites: Jeshua (son of Azaniah), Binnui (from the sons of Henadad), and Kadmiel.
10. Also Shebaniah, Hodiah, Kelita, Pelaiah, Hanan,
11. Mica, Rehob, Hashabiah,
12. Zaccur, Sherebiah, Shebaniah,
13. Hodiah, Bani, and Beninu.
14. These were the leaders of the people: Parosh, Pahath-Moab, Elam, Zattu, Bani,
15. Bunni, Azgad, Bebai,
16. Adonijah, Bigvai, Adin,
17. Ater, Hezekiah, Azzur,
18. Hodiah, Hashum, Bezai,
19. Hariph, Anathoth, Nebai,
20. Magpiash, Meshullam, Hezir,
21. Meshezabel, Zadok, Jaddua,
22. Pelatiah, Hanan, Anaiah,
23. Hoshea, Hananiah, Hasshub,
24. Hallohesh, Pilha, Shobek,
25. Rehum, Hashabnah, Maaseiah,
26. Ahiah, Hanan, Anan,
27. Malluch, Harim, and Baanah.

The People Promise to Obey

28. The rest of the people—the priests, Levites, gatekeepers, musicians, Temple workers, and all who had separated themselves from foreigners to follow God's Law—and their wives,

sons, and daughters (everyone who understood),

29. Promised to follow God's Law and obey all the commands He gave through Moses.
30. "We promise not to let our sons marry foreign women or let our daughters marry their sons.
31. We won't buy goods or food on the Sabbath or other holy days. We will let the land rest every seventh year and cancel all debts.
32. We will each give one-third of a silver coin every year for Temple expenses:
33. For the bread on the table, regular grain offerings, burnt offerings, sacrifices on special days, holy offerings, sin offerings, and all the duties of the Temple.
34. We drew lots to decide when each family would bring firewood for the Temple throughout the year.
35. We will bring the first part of our crops and fruit every year to the Lord's Temple.
36. We will bring the firstborn of our sons and animals to the priests at the Temple.
37. We will bring the first of our dough, gifts, fruit, wine, and **olive oil** to the priests and store them in the Temple rooms. We will give a tenth of our crops to the Levites, since they collect tithes.
38. A priest will go with the Levites when they collect tithes. The Levites will take a tenth of what they collect to the Temple storerooms.
39. The people of Israel and the Levites will bring their grain, **olive oil**, and wine to the storerooms. That's where the supplies for the priests, gatekeepers, and musicians are kept. We won't neglect the Temple of our God."

Nehemiah 11

Who Lived in Jerusalem

1. The leaders stayed in Jerusalem. The rest of the people cast lots. One out of every ten families had to move to Jerusalem. The other nine could stay in their towns.
2. The people praised everyone who willingly moved to Jerusalem.
3. These are the leaders who lived in Jerusalem. The rest of Israel, including priests, Levites, Temple workers, and descendants of Solomon's servants, lived in the towns of Judah on their own land.
4. From the tribe of Judah, living in Jerusalem were: Athaiah (son of Uzziah, son of Zechariah, son of Amariah, son of Shephatiah, son of Mahalalel, from Perez's family),
5. And Maaseiah (son of Baruch, son of Col-Hozeh, son of Hazaiah, son of Adaiah, son of Joiarib, son of Zechariah, from Shelah's family).
6. The total from the tribe of Judah in Jerusalem was 468 strong men.
7. From the tribe of Benjamin: Sallu (son of Meshullam, son of Joed, son of Pedaiah, son of Kolaiah, son of Maaseiah, son of Ithiel, son of Jeshaiah),
8. And after him: Gabbai and Sallai. They were 928 in total.
9. Joel (son of Zikri) was their leader. Judah (son of Hassenuah) was second in charge over the city.
10. From the priests: Jedaiah (son of Joiarib), Jakin,
11. Seraiah (son of Hilkiah, son of Meshullam, son of Zadok, son of Meraioth, son of Ahitub, who was the leader of God's Temple),
12. And their helpers: 822 men who worked in the Temple. Also, Adaiah (son of Jeroham, son of Pelaliah, son of Amzi, son of Zechariah, son of Pashhur, son of Malkijah),

13. And his relatives, 242 men. Also, Amashsai (son of Azarel, son of Ahzai, son of Meshillemoth, son of Immer),
14. And his relatives, 128 brave men. Zabdiel (son of Haggedolim) was their leader.
15. From the Levites: Shemaiah (son of Hasshub, son of Azrikam, son of Hashabiah, son of Bunni),
16. And Shabbethai and Jozabad, who were in charge of the outside work for the Temple.
17. Mattaniah (son of Mica, son of Zabdi, son of Asaph) led the songs of praise. Bakbukiah was second in charge. Also Abda (son of Shammua, son of Galal, son of Jeduthun).
18. The Levites in the holy city totaled 284.
19. The gatekeepers were Akkub, Talmon, and their relatives, who guarded the gates. There were 172 gatekeepers.
20. The rest of the Israelites, priests, and Levites lived in the other towns of Judah. Everyone lived on their family land.
21. The Temple workers lived on the hill of Ophel. Ziha and Gishpa were in charge of them.
22. The leader of the Levites in Jerusalem was Uzzi (son of Bani, son of Hashabiah, son of Mattaniah, son of Mica). He was from Asaph's family, who led the music in God's Temple.
23. The king had ordered that the singers be supported daily.
24. Pethahiah (son of Meshezabel, from the family of Zerah, son of Judah) worked for the king and helped the people.

People in the Villages

25. Some people from Judah lived in the towns of Kiriath Arba, Dibon, and Jekabzeel and nearby villages.
26. They also lived in Jeshua, Moladah, Beth Pelet,
27. Hazar Shual, Beersheba, and its villages,
28. Ziklag, Meconah, and its villages,
29. En Rimmon, Zorah, Jarmuth,
30. Zanoah, Adullam, and their villages, Lachish and its fields, and Azekah and its towns. They lived from Beersheba in the south up to the Valley of Hinnom in the north.
31. Some from the tribe of Benjamin lived in Geba, Michmash, Aija, and Bethel and its towns,
32. In Anathoth, Nob, Ananiah,
33. Hazor, Ramah, Gittaim,
34. Hadid, Zeboim, Neballat,
35. Lod, Ono, and the Valley of the Craftsmen.
36. Some Levites were sent from Judah to live with the tribe of Benjamin.

Nehemiah 12

List of Priests and Levites

1. These are the priests and Levites who came back with Zerubbabel (son of Shealtiel) and Jeshua:
   Seraiah, Jeremiah, Ezra,
2. Amariah, Malluk, Hattush,
3. Shecaniah, Rehum, Meremoth,
4. Iddo, Ginnethon, Abijah,
5. Mijamin, Maadiah, Bilgah,
6. Shemaiah, Joiarib, Jedaiah,
7. Sallu, Amok, Hilkiah, and Jedaiah. These were the priests and their helpers in Jeshua's time.
8. The Levites were Jeshua, Binnui, Kadmiel, Sherebiah, Judah, and Mattaniah. Mattaniah led the songs of thanks.
9. Bakbukiah and Unni stood next to them during the songs.
10. Jeshua was the father of Joiakim. Joiakim was the father of Eliashib. Eliashib was the father of Joiada.
11. Joiada was the father of Jonathan. Jonathan was the father of Jaddua.

Leaders During Joiakim's Time

12. These were the leaders of the priests in Joiakim's time:
From Seraiah's family – Meraiah
From Jeremiah's family – Hananiah

13. From Ezra's family – Meshullam
From Amariah's – Jehohanan

14. From Malluki's – Jonathan
From Shebaniah's – Joseph

15. From Harim's – Adna
From Meremoth's – Helkai

16. From Iddo's – Zechariah
From Ginnethon's – Meshullam

17. From Abijah's – Zicri
From Miniamin and Moadiah's – Piltai

18. From Bilgah's – Shammua
From Shemaiah's – Jehonathan

19. From Joiarib's – Mattenai
From Jedaiah's – Uzzi

20. From Sallai's – Kallai
From Amok's – Eber

21. From Hilkiah's – Hashabiah
From Jedaiah's – Nethanel

Records of Levites and Priests

22. The Levite leaders were listed during the time of Eliashib, Joiada, Johanan, and Jaddua. These records were kept during the rule of Darius the Persian king.

23. The family leaders of the Levites were listed in the official records up to Johanan, Eliashib's son.

24. The leaders of the Levites were: Hashabiah, Sherebiah, Jeshua (son of Kadmiel), and their helpers. They stood opposite each other to give praise and thanks, as David had said.

25. The gatekeepers were Mattaniah, Bakbukiah, Obadiah, Meshullam, Talmon, and Akkub. They guarded the storerooms at the gates.

26. These men lived during the time of Joiakim (Jeshua's son), Nehemiah the governor, and Ezra the priest.

Dedication of the Wall

27. When the wall was finished, the Levites came to Jerusalem to celebrate. They sang, played cymbals, harps, and lyres.

28. The singers came from nearby towns, from Netophathite villages,

29. From Beth Gilgal, and from the villages around Geba and Azmaveth. The singers had built their own villages near Jerusalem.

30. The priests and Levites made themselves and the people holy. They also cleaned the gates and the wall.

31. I brought the leaders up on the wall. I put together two large choirs. One walked on top of the wall to the right toward the Dung Gate.

32. Hoshaiah and half the leaders followed them.

33. Also Azariah, Ezra, Meshullam,

34. Judah, Benjamin, Shemaiah, and Jeremiah.

35. Some priests played trumpets. They were Zechariah (son of Jonathan, son of Shemaiah, son of Mattaniah, son of Micaiah, son of Zaccur, son of Asaph),

36. And his relatives Shemaiah, Azarel, Milalai, Gilalai, Maai, Nethanel, Judah, and Hanani. They had the instruments David used. Ezra the teacher led them.

37. At the Fountain Gate, they went straight up the stairs by the wall of David's City. They passed David's house and went to the Water Gate on the east side.

38. The second choir went to the left. I followed them with half the people. We walked on top of the wall past the Oven Tower to the Broad Wall,

39. Then over the Ephraim Gate, Jeshanah Gate, Fish Gate, Tower of Hananel, Tower of the Hundred, and the Sheep Gate. We stopped at the Guard Gate.

40. The two choirs went into God's Temple. I and half the leaders joined them.

41. The priests with trumpets were Eliakim, Maaseiah, Miniamin, Micaiah, Elioenai, Zechariah, and Hananiah.
42. Also Maaseiah, Shemaiah, Eleazar, Uzzi, Jehohanan, Malkijah, Elam, and Ezer. The singers sang loudly, led by Jezrahiah.
43. That day, many sacrifices were made. Everyone was happy. God made them happy. Even the women and children celebrated. People far away could hear the joy in Jerusalem.

Temple Officials

44. That day, men were chosen to be in charge of the rooms that stored gifts, first crops, and one-tenth offerings. They brought these from the farms to the Temple, as the Law required. The people of Judah were happy to support the priests and Levites.
45. The priests and Levites did their jobs. They kept everything clean and did the music and guard duties, just like David and Solomon had planned.
46. Long ago, in David's time, there were leaders for the singers and songs of praise.
47. In Zerubbabel's and Nehemiah's time, all Israel gave daily support to the singers and gatekeepers. They also gave holy gifts to the Levites, and the Levites gave a tenth to the priests.

Nehemiah 13

Nehemiah Fixes the Problems

1. That day, the people read from the Law of Moses. It said no Ammonite or Moabite should ever be allowed to join God's people.
2. These nations didn't give food and water to the Israelites. Instead, they paid Balaam to curse them. But God turned the curse into a blessing.
3. After hearing this, the people separated themselves from foreigners.
4. Before this, Eliashib the priest, who was in charge of the Temple rooms, was friends with Tobiah.
5. He let Tobiah use a large room in the Temple that had been used to store grain, incense, Temple tools, tithes of grain, new wine, olive oil, and gifts for the priests, Levites, singers, and gatekeepers.
6. I was not in Jerusalem when this happened. I had returned to King Artaxerxes in the 32nd year of his reign. Later, I asked the king to return and went back to Jerusalem.
7. When I got back, I learned what Eliashib had done for Tobiah. I was very upset.
8. I was so angry I threw all of Tobiah's things out of the room.
9. I ordered the room to be cleaned and brought back the Temple items, grain offerings, and incense.
10. I also found out the Levites hadn't received their food, so they had gone back to their farms.
11. I scolded the officials and said, "Why is God's Temple being neglected?" I brought the Levites and singers back and put them in their positions.
12. Then all the people of Judah brought a tenth of their grain, new wine, and olive oil to the storerooms.
13. I put Shelemiah the priest, Zadok the scribe, and Pedaiah the Levite in charge of the storerooms. Hanan (son of Zakkur, son of Mattaniah) helped them. They were honest men and were trusted to give out the supplies.
14. I prayed, "God, remember me for this. Don't forget how I helped your Temple and its work."
15. In those days, I saw people in Judah working on the Sabbath. They were treading winepresses, bringing in grain, loading donkeys with wine, grapes, figs, and all kinds of goods, and bringing them into Jerusalem on the Sabbath. I warned them not to sell food on that day.
16. Men from Tyre were bringing in fish and all kinds of goods and selling them in Jerusalem on the Sabbath.

17. I scolded the leaders of Judah and said, "Why are you doing evil by breaking the Sabbath?
18. Didn't our ancestors do the same thing? That's why God punished us and this city. Now you're making Him even angrier."
19. I ordered the city gates to be shut before the Sabbath and not opened until it ended. I put guards at the gates to stop goods from being brought in on the Sabbath.
20. Once or twice, traders and sellers camped outside the city.
21. I warned them, "If you do this again, I'll use force." After that, they didn't come back on the Sabbath.
22. I told the Levites to clean themselves and guard the gates to keep the Sabbath holy. I prayed, "God, remember me for this too. Be kind to me because of your great love."
23. I also saw that some Jews had married women from Ashdod, Ammon, and Moab.
24. Half of their children spoke the language of Ashdod or another group, but not the language of Judah.
25. I confronted them and cursed them. I hit some of them and pulled out their hair. I made them promise, "You will not let your daughters marry their sons or let their daughters marry your sons."
26. I said, "Wasn't it because of foreign women that Solomon sinned? No king was as great as him, but even he sinned by marrying women from other nations.
27. And now you're doing the same evil?"
28. One of Joiada's sons (Joiada was the son of Eliashib the high priest) had married Sanballat's daughter. I drove him away from me.
29. I prayed, "God, remember them for dishonoring the priesthood and your agreement with the Levites and priests."
30. I made sure everything was clean and organized. I assigned duties to the priests and Levites, just as they were supposed to do.
31. I made sure wood was brought for the altar at the right times, and that the first crops were offered. I prayed, "Remember me, my God, and be kind to me."

– Esther –

Queen Esther risks her life to save the Jews from destruction in Persia.

Esther 1

Queen Vashti Refuses the King

1. These events happened when King Xerxes ruled 127 provinces from India to Ethiopia.
2. At that time, he ruled from the fortress of Susa.
3. In the 3rd year of his reign, he had a big banquet for all his officials, military officers, governors, and leaders.
4. The celebration lasted 180 days. He showed off his riches and power.
5. When it ended, he held another banquet for everyone in Susa. It lasted 7 days and was held in the palace garden.
6. The courtyard had white, green, and blue curtains tied with purple ropes. The couches were gold and silver, sitting on floors made of colorful marble.
7. Drinks were served in gold cups, each cup was different. There was a lot of wine because the king was very generous.
8. The king told his servants everyone could drink as much as they wanted.
9. Queen Vashti also held a banquet for the women in the royal palace.
10. On the 7th day, after drinking a lot of wine, the king told his 7 eunuchs—

11. Mehuman, Biztha, Harbona, Bigtha, Abagtha, Zethar, and Carcas—
12. to bring Queen Vashti wearing her royal crown so he could show off her beauty.
13. But Queen Vashti refused to come. The king became very angry.
14. As usual, he asked his advisors what the law said.
15. His top advisors were Carshena, Shethar, Admatha, Tarshish, Meres, Marsena, and Memucan. They met with the king often.
16. The king asked, "What does the law say I should do about Queen Vashti not obeying me?"
17. Memucan said, "She didn't just insult you, she insulted all the officials and people in the kingdom.
18. When women hear she refused you, they'll start disobeying their husbands too.
19. By the end of the day, all the wives of the kingdom will be disrespecting their husbands. The men will be angry.
20. If it pleases you, make a law that Vashti can never come before you again. Pick a new queen better than her. This law can never be changed.
21. When this order is made known across the kingdom, all women will respect their husbands."
22. The king and his officials liked that idea and agreed.
23. Letters were sent to every province in its own language, saying every man should rule his own home and have the final say.

Esther 2

Esther Becomes Queen

1. Later, when King Xerxes calmed down, he remembered what Vashti had done and what was decided about her.
2. His servants said, "Let us find beautiful young virgins for the king.
3. Have officials in every province bring the most beautiful young virgins to the palace in Susa. Put them under Hegai, the king's eunuch, who is in charge of the women. He will give them beauty treatments.
4. The woman the king likes most will become queen instead of Vashti." The king agreed.
5. In Susa, there was a Jewish man named Mordecai, son of Jair, son of Shimei, son of Kish, from the tribe of Benjamin.
6. His family had been taken from Jerusalem as prisoners when King Nebuchadnezzar of Babylon took King Jehoiachin of Judah.
7. Mordecai was raising his cousin Hadassah (also called Esther). She had no parents. She was very beautiful and had a good figure. After her parents died, Mordecai raised her like his own daughter.
8. When the king's order was made public, many young women were brought to the palace. Esther was also taken and placed under Hegai's care.
9. Hegai liked her and gave her special attention. He gave her the best beauty treatments, seven servant girls, and moved her to the best room.
10. Esther didn't tell anyone she was Jewish because Mordecai told her not to.
11. Every day, Mordecai walked near the women's courtyard to find out how she was doing.
12. Each young woman had to complete 12 months of beauty treatments—6 months with oil of myrrh, and 6 months with perfumes and cosmetics—before going to the king.
13. When her turn came, she could take anything she wanted with her from the women's quarters.
14. In the evening, she went to the king. In the morning, she moved to another area under Shaashgaz, another eunuch. She stayed there unless the king asked for her by name.

15. Esther (daughter of Abihail, Mordecai's cousin) didn't ask for anything except what Hegai told her to take. Everyone who saw her liked her.
16. Esther was taken to King Xerxes in the 10th month (Tebeth) of the 7th year of his reign.
17. The king liked Esther more than any other woman. He put the royal crown on her head and made her queen instead of Vashti.
18. The king gave a big banquet to celebrate Esther. He invited all his officials and gave gifts to the provinces.

Mordecai Stops a Plot

19. When the young women were gathered again, Mordecai was sitting at the palace gate.
20. Esther still hadn't told anyone she was Jewish. She obeyed Mordecai just like she did when she lived with him.
21. One day while Mordecai was sitting at the gate, two of the king's guards—Bigthan and Teresh—got angry and planned to kill King Xerxes.
22. Mordecai found out and told Queen Esther. She told the king, giving Mordecai credit.
23. After the king investigated and found out it was true, the two men were hanged on a pole. This was all written in the official Book of the History of King Xerxes' Rule.

Esther 3

Haman's Evil Plan

1. Later, King Xerxes promoted Haman (son of Hammedatha the Agagite) and gave him a high position above all the other officials.
2. All the royal workers at the gate bowed to Haman, because the king had ordered it. But Mordecai didn't bow or show respect.
3. The workers at the gate asked Mordecai, "Why don't you obey the king's command?"
4. Day after day they asked him, but he wouldn't listen. So they told Haman to see if Mordecai's actions would be allowed, because Mordecai had said he was Jewish.
5. When Haman saw that Mordecai didn't bow or show respect, he became very angry.
6. But he didn't want to just punish Mordecai. He had been told that Mordecai was Jewish. So he planned to kill all the Jews in the kingdom.
7. In the 12th year of King Xerxes' reign, in the first month (the month of Nisan), they cast the lot (called "Pur") to choose a day and month to carry out the plan. The lot chose the 12th month, the month of Adar.
8. Haman went to King Xerxes and said, "There is a group of people in your kingdom who live differently from everyone else. They don't follow your laws. It's not right to let them stay.
9. If you agree, give the order to kill them. I'll give 10,000 large silver coins to the royal treasury."
10. The king took off his ring and gave it to Haman (the enemy of the Jews).
11. The king said, "You can keep the money and do whatever you want with those people."
12. On the 13th day of the first month, the royal secretaries were called. They wrote down everything Haman ordered. The orders were sent to the king's governors and leaders of each province in their own language. It was written in the name of King Xerxes and sealed with his ring.
13. Messengers were sent to all the provinces with the order to kill, destroy, and wipe out all the Jews—young and old, men and women—and to take their belongings. This was to happen in one day: the 13th day of Adar, the 12th month.
14. A copy of the order was sent out so everyone would be ready on that day.
15. The messengers left quickly, as the king commanded. The order was given in

the palace at Susa. The king and Haman sat down to drink, but the city of Susa was confused.

Esther 4

Mordecai Asks Esther for Help

1. When Mordecai learned everything that had happened, he tore his clothes, put on sackcloth and ashes, and went into the city crying loudly.
2. He stopped at the king's gate because no one wearing sackcloth was allowed to enter it.
3. In every province where the king's order was read, the Jews were very sad. They cried, fasted, and many wore sackcloth and laid in ashes.
4. Esther's servant girls and eunuchs told her what Mordecai was doing. She was very upset. She sent clothes for Mordecai to wear instead of sackcloth, but he wouldn't take them.
5. Esther called for Hathach, one of the king's eunuchs, and told him to go ask Mordecai what was wrong.
6. Hathach went to Mordecai in the city square in front of the gate.
7. Mordecai told him everything that had happened. He told him how much silver Haman promised to pay to kill the Jews.
8. He gave Hathach a copy of the order to kill the Jews. He told him to show it to Esther and explain everything. He told Hathach to tell Esther to go to the king and beg for mercy for her people.
9. Hathach went back and told Esther everything Mordecai said.
10. Esther sent a message back to Mordecai:
11. "Everyone knows that any man or woman who goes to the king without being called can be put to death—unless the king holds out his gold scepter. I haven't been called to see the king in 30 days."
12. Mordecai got the message.
13. He sent this reply: "Don't think you'll be safe just because you live in the palace.
14. If you stay quiet now, help will come for the Jews from somewhere else—but you and your family will die. Maybe you became queen for this exact reason."
15. Esther sent back this message to Mordecai:
16. "Tell all the Jews in Susa to fast for me. Don't eat or drink for three days, night or day. I and my servant girls will do the same. Then I'll go to the king, even though it's against the law. If I die, I die."
17. Mordecai went and did everything Esther told him to do.

Esther 5

Esther's Request Begins

1. On the third day, Esther put on her royal robes and stood in the inner courtyard of the palace. The king was sitting on his royal throne, facing the entrance.
2. When the king saw Esther, he was pleased. He held out his gold scepter, and she came close and touched the tip of it.
3. The king asked, "What do you want, Queen Esther? Ask anything—even half my kingdom—and I'll give it to you."
4. Esther said, "If it pleases you, let you and Haman come to a banquet I've prepared."
5. The king said, "Bring Haman right away!" So they went to the banquet.
6. While they were drinking wine, the king said, "Now tell me what you want. Ask anything—even half my kingdom—and I'll give it to you."
7. Esther answered, "This is my request:
8. If I have your favor, come again tomorrow with Haman to another

banquet. Then I'll tell you what I want."

9. Haman left the banquet happy and proud. But when he saw Mordecai at the gate—not standing or showing respect—he became very angry.
10. Still, he controlled himself and went home. He gathered his friends and his wife Zeresh.
11. He bragged about his wealth, his many sons, and how the king honored him and invited him to the queen's banquet.
12. He said, "I'm the only one Queen Esther invited to her banquet with the king—and I'm invited again tomorrow!
13. But all this means nothing while I still see Mordecai sitting at the gate."
14. His wife and friends said, "Build a pole 75 feet tall. Ask the king tomorrow to hang Mordecai on it. Then go to the banquet happy." Haman liked the idea and ordered the pole to be built.

Esther 6

Mordecai Is Honored

1. That night, the king couldn't sleep, so he asked for the Book of the History of His Rule to be read to him.
2. It told how Mordecai had warned the king about Bigthana and Teresh, two guards who had planned to kill him.
3. The king asked, "What reward or honor was given to Mordecai for this?" The servants replied, "Nothing was done for him."
4. The king said, "Who is in the courtyard?" Haman had just entered the outer courtyard to ask the king to hang Mordecai on the pole he had prepared.
5. The king's servants said, "Haman is here." The king said, "Bring him in."
6. When Haman came in, the king asked, "What should I do for a man I want to honor?" Haman thought, "He must be talking about me,"
7. so he said, "For the man the king wants to honor,
8. give him royal robes the king has worn and a horse the king has ridden. Place a royal crown on his head.
9. Let the robes and horse be given to one of the king's highest officials. Have that official dress the man and lead him on horseback through the city, shouting, 'This is what is done for the man the king wants to honor!'"
10. The king said, "Hurry! Get the robes and horse, just as you said. Do it for Mordecai the Jew who sits at the gate. Don't leave anything out."
11. So Haman got the robes and horse. He dressed Mordecai and led him through the city shouting, "This is what is done for the man the king wants to honor!"
12. Afterward, Mordecai returned to the king's gate, but Haman hurried home, sad and embarrassed.
13. He told his wife Zeresh and all his friends what happened. They said, "If Mordecai is Jewish, and you've started to fall before him, you will not win."
14. While they were still talking, the king's eunuchs arrived and quickly took Haman to Esther's second banquet.

Esther 7

Haman Is Hanged

1. So the king and Haman went to eat with Queen Esther.
2. On the second day, during the wine, the king asked Esther again, "What is your request? I will give it to you—even half my kingdom."
3. Queen Esther said, "If I have your favor, please let me live. That is what I ask. Please let my people live too.
4. My people and I have been sold to be destroyed, killed, and wiped out. If we were only being sold as slaves, I would have stayed quiet. But this is too terrible to ignore."

5. King Xerxes asked Queen Esther, "Who did this? Where is he?"

6. Esther said, "Our enemy is Haman—the evil man right here!" Haman was terrified in front of the king and queen.

7. The king got up in anger and went to the palace garden. Haman stayed to beg Queen Esther for his life. He saw the king had already decided to punish him.

8. When the king came back from the garden, Haman was falling on the couch where Esther was. The king shouted, "Will he attack the queen while I'm in the house?" As soon as the king said that, the servants covered Haman's face.

9. One servant named Harbona said, "There is a pole 75 feet tall standing at Haman's house. He made it for Mordecai, the man who saved your life." The king said, "Hang him on it!"

10. So they hanged Haman on the pole he had built for Mordecai. Then the king's anger went away.

Esther 8

The Jews Are Saved

1. That same day, King Xerxes gave Queen Esther everything that had belonged to Haman, the enemy of the Jews. Esther told the king that Mordecai was her cousin. So the king let Mordecai come in.

2. The king took back the ring he had given Haman and gave it to Mordecai. Esther put Mordecai in charge of Haman's property.

3. Again, Esther went to the king and begged him while crying. She asked him to stop Haman's evil plan to kill the Jews.

4. The king held out his gold scepter to Esther, and she got up and stood in front of him.

5. She said, "If it pleases you, and if I have your favor, please cancel Haman's letters. He sent orders to kill all the Jews in your kingdom.

6. I couldn't handle seeing my people destroyed. I would be heartbroken."

7. King Xerxes said, "I gave Esther Haman's property, and he was hanged for his plan.

8. Now you may write another letter in my name to help the Jews. Seal it with my ring. Once a letter is sealed with the king's ring, it cannot be changed."

9. On the 23rd day of the 3rd month (Sivan), the royal secretaries were called. Mordecai told them what to write to the Jews, the governors, the leaders, and the rulers in all 127 provinces from India to Ethiopia. The letters were written in every language and script. They were also written in Hebrew for the Jews.

10. Mordecai wrote the letters in the king's name and sealed them with the king's ring. Messengers on fast horses carried them.

11. The letters said that the king gave the Jews permission to gather and protect themselves. They could fight anyone who attacked them, destroy them, and take their things.

12. This would happen on the 13th day of the 12th month (Adar) in every province.

13. A copy of the letter was sent everywhere so that the Jews would be ready to fight on that day.

14. The messengers rode off quickly on the king's fast horses. The order was also read in the palace at Susa.

15. Mordecai left the king's presence wearing royal clothes—blue and white robes, a gold crown, and a purple robe. The city of Susa celebrated with joy.

16. The Jews were happy and full of joy.

17. In every province and city, the Jews celebrated with feasts and parties. Many people from other nations became Jews because they were afraid of the Jews.

Esther 9

The Jews Win and Celebrate Purim

1. On the 13th day of the 12th month (Adar), the day the enemies of the Jews had planned to destroy them, the opposite happened—the Jews defeated their enemies.
2. The Jews gathered in every city to protect themselves. No one could stand against them because people were afraid of them.
3. The governors, leaders, and royal officials helped the Jews because they were afraid of Mordecai.
4. Mordecai was now very powerful in the palace. Everyone knew about him, and his fame kept growing.
5. The Jews fought their enemies with swords and killed them. They did whatever they wanted to those who hated them.
6. In Susa, the Jews killed 500 men.
7. They also killed Parshandatha, Dalphon, Aspatha,
8. Poratha, Adalia, Aridatha,
9. Parmashta, Arisai, Aridai, and Vaizatha.
10. These were the 10 sons of Haman, the enemy of the Jews. But the Jews didn't take any of their things.
11. That day, the king was told how many were killed in Susa.
12. The king said to Esther, "The Jews have killed 500 men and Haman's 10 sons in Susa. What have they done in the rest of the provinces? What do you want now? I'll give it to you."
13. Esther said, "If it pleases you, let the Jews in Susa do the same thing tomorrow. And hang the bodies of Haman's sons on poles."
14. The king agreed. A law was made in Susa, and the bodies of Haman's sons were hanged.
15. On the 14th day of Adar, the Jews in Susa gathered again and killed 300 more men. But they didn't take anything.
16. In the other provinces, the Jews killed 75,000 of their enemies. But they didn't take anything.
17. This happened on the 13th day of Adar. On the 14th day, they rested and celebrated with a big feast.
18. The Jews in Susa had fought on both the 13th and 14th days. They rested on the 15th day and made it a day of joy and celebration.
19. That's why the Jews in the villages and small towns celebrate the 14th day of Adar with joy, food, and gifts for each other.
20. Mordecai wrote everything down and sent letters to all the Jews in every province.
21. He told them to celebrate every year on the 14th and 15th of Adar,
22. because those were the days when the Jews had rest from their enemies. Their sadness had turned into joy, and their mourning into celebration. So they should celebrate with feasts and send gifts to each other and to the poor.
23. The Jews agreed to do what Mordecai said and made it a yearly tradition.
24. Haman, the enemy of the Jews, had planned to destroy them and cast the lot (called "Pur") to choose a day.
25. But when Esther went to the king, he gave orders to stop Haman's evil plan. Haman and his sons were hanged on poles.
26. That is why the celebration is called Purim, from the word "Pur." Because of what was written in Mordecai's letter, the Jews continued to celebrate every year.
27. They promised to never forget these days and to celebrate them in every family and city, for all time.
28. The days of Purim were to be remembered by every generation of Jews, forever.
29. Queen Esther and Mordecai wrote a second letter about Purim to confirm the celebration.

30. Letters were sent to all 127 provinces with messages of peace and truth.
31. They told the Jews to keep the celebration every year at the right time, just as Mordecai and Esther had written.
32. The command from Esther made these rules about Purim official, and it was written down in the book.

Esther 10

Mordecai Is Honored

1. King Xerxes made the people in his kingdom, even on the islands, pay taxes.
2. Everything the king did, including how he honored Mordecai, is written in the Book of the History of His Rule.
3. Mordecai the Jew was the most powerful official under King Xerxes. He was respected by the Jews and worked hard to help and protect them.

– Job –

A man named Job suffers greatly but stays faithful, and God eventually restores him.

Job 1

Job and His Family

1. A man named Job lived in Uz. He always did what was right, respected God, and stayed away from evil.
2. He had 7 sons and 3 daughters.
3. He owned 7,000 sheep, 3,000 camels, 1,000 oxen, and 500 donkeys. He had many servants and was the richest man in the east.
4. His sons took turns having feasts at their homes and always invited their sisters.
5. After each feast, Job would get up early and offer a burnt sacrifice for each child. He did this because he thought they might have sinned or disrespected God in their hearts.

Angels, the Lord, and Satan

6. One day the angels came to stand before the Lord, and Satan came too.
7. The Lord asked Satan, "Where have you been?" Satan said, "I've been walking around on earth."
8. The Lord said, "Have you noticed my servant Job? No one on earth is like him. He does what is right, respects me, and avoids evil."
9. Satan replied, "Of course Job respects you.
10. You protect him, his house, and everything he owns. You've made him rich and successful.
11. But take away everything he owns, and he will curse you to your face!"
12. The Lord said, "Fine. You can take away everything he has, but don't hurt him." Then Satan left.

Job Loses Everything

13. One day Job's children were eating at the oldest brother's house.
14. A servant came and said, "Your oxen were plowing and the donkeys were eating nearby,
15. when the Sabeans attacked. They stole the animals and killed the workers. I'm the only one who escaped."
16. While he was still talking, another servant came and said, "Fire from God fell from the sky and burned up the sheep and the workers. I'm the only one who escaped."
17. While he was still talking, another servant came and said, "Three groups of Chaldeans attacked. They stole your camels and killed the workers. I'm the only one who escaped."
18. While he was still talking, another servant came and said, "Your children were eating at your oldest son's house,
19. when a strong wind came from the desert, hit the house, and it collapsed. All your children died. I'm the only one who escaped."

20. Job stood up, tore his robe, shaved his head, and fell to the ground to worship.

21. He said, "I was born with nothing, and I'll die with nothing. The Lord gave me everything, and now he's taken it away. Praise the Lord."

22. Even after all this, Job didn't sin or blame God.

Job 2

Job Becomes Sick

1. One day the angels came again to stand before the Lord, and Satan came too.

2. The Lord asked Satan, "Where have you been?" Satan answered, "I've been walking around on earth."

3. The Lord said, "Have you noticed Job? No one is like him. He does what is right, respects me, and avoids evil. He still follows me, even though you made me let you ruin him for no reason."

4. Satan replied, "People will give up anything to save their own lives.

5. But if you hurt his body, he'll curse you to your face."

6. The Lord said, "Fine. Do what you want with his body, but don't kill him."

7. So Satan left and gave Job painful sores all over his body.

8. Job sat in a pile of ashes and used a piece of broken pottery to scratch himself.

9. His wife said, "Are you still holding on to your faith? Just curse God and die."

10. Job said, "You're talking foolishly. Should we accept only good from God and not bad?" Even then, Job didn't sin.

Job's Three Friends

11. Job's 3 friends—Eliphaz the Temanite, Bildad the Shuhite, and Zophar the Naamathite—heard about his troubles and came to comfort him.

12. When they saw him from far away, they barely recognized him. They cried, tore their clothes, and threw dust on their heads.

13. They sat on the ground with him for 7 days and nights. No one said a word because they saw how much pain he was in.

Job 3

Erase the Day I Was Born

1. After this, Job spoke and cursed the day he was born.

2. He said:

3. "Erase the day I was born and the night I was conceived.

4. Let that day be dark. Let God forget it.

5. Cover it with a black cloud. Let it be terrifying.

6. Erase that night from the calendar.

7. Let it be empty, with no joy.

8. Let those who curse days curse it—those who know how to control the sea monster.

9. Keep its morning stars dark. Let it never see morning.

10. Curse that day for letting me be born to see this pain.

Why Didn't I Die at Birth?

11. Why didn't I die when I was born?

12. Why did my mother hold and feed me?

13. If I died then, I'd be resting in peace,

14. with kings and leaders who built big homes that now lie in ruins,

15. or with princes who had gold and silver.

16. Why wasn't I buried like a stillborn baby, like a child who never saw light?

17. In death, the wicked don't cause trouble, and the tired rest.

18. Prisoners are free, and no one shouts at them.

19. Rich and poor are the same there. Slaves are free from their masters.

Why Does God Let Me Live?

20. Why does God give life to those in pain, to people who are bitter?
21. They want to die, but it doesn't happen. They want death more than treasure.
22. They'll be happy when they die.
23. Why give life to people with no purpose, people God has cut off?
24. I cry instead of eating.
25. What I feared has come true.
26. I have no peace, no rest—only trouble."

Job 4

Be Patient and Listen

1. Then Eliphaz the Temanite said:
2. "Be patient and let me speak.
3. You've given strength to the weak.
4. Your words gave hope to those who were ready to give up.
5. But now that trouble has come to you, you panic with fear.
6. You trusted God—shouldn't that give you hope?
7. Think! Has anyone who did what was right ever been destroyed?
8. From what I've seen, people who do wrong end up suffering for it.
9. God breathes on them, and they die.
10. Lions may roar, but their teeth get broken.
11. The lion dies without food, and the cubs go hungry."

A Secret

12. "A secret message came to me.
13. I heard it in a dream.
14. Fear shook me to the bone.
15. A spirit passed by my face, and my hair stood on end.
16. It stopped, but I couldn't see what it was. Then I heard a voice:
17. 'Can a person be more right or pure than God?
18. God doesn't trust his angels; he sees faults in them.
19. He trusts people even less—they are made from dust and die like moths.
20. They wake up in the morning and are dead by night, and no one notices.
21. They die without wisdom.'"

Job 5

Ask for Help

1. "Cry for help—but who will answer? Which angel will help you?
2. Anger kills the foolish. Jealousy destroys the simple.
3. I've seen fools succeed, but their success was cursed.
4. Their children are never safe. They lose in court and no one helps them.
5. The hungry eat their crops, and others take what they have.
6. Trouble doesn't grow from the ground.
7. But people always have trouble.
8. If I were you, I'd ask God for help.
9. He does great things we can't understand—too many to count.
10. He sends rain and waters the land.
11. He lifts the humble and protects those who suffer.
12. He ruins the plans of the wicked.
13. He traps the clever in their own tricks.
14. They are confused in the daylight like it's night.
15. He saves the poor from the rich and powerful.
16. He gives the poor hope and stops evil people.

Consider Yourself Lucky

17. Be glad when God corrects you. Don't reject his discipline.
18. He hurts, but he also heals.
19. He will save you from trouble again and again.
20. He'll protect you during famine and war.
21. You'll be safe from lies and not afraid when destruction comes.
22. You'll laugh at destruction and hunger. You won't fear wild animals.
23. You'll be at peace with the land and the animals.
24. Your home will be safe and complete.
25. You'll have many children and grandchildren.
26. You'll live a long life and die well.
27. We've seen all this to be true. Listen and learn from it."

Job 6

It's Impossible

1. Then Job replied:
2. "If my pain could be weighed,
3. it would be heavier than all the sand. That's why I spoke harshly.
4. God has hit me with poison arrows. I feel attacked by him.
5. Does a donkey or an ox cry when it has food?
6. Who wants to eat tasteless food? Egg whites have no flavor.
7. I can't stand to eat. It makes me sick.
8. I wish God would give me what I ask—
9. I wish he would kill me.
10. That would comfort me. Even in pain, I haven't turned against him.
11. I have no strength left. I have no hope.
12. Am I made of stone or bronze?
13. I have no power left to help myself.

My Friends, I'm Desperate

14. A true friend is kind to someone in pain, even if they turn from God.
15. But my friends are not loyal.
16. You're like streams that freeze in winter—
17. and disappear in the heat.
18. Travelers search for water but die of thirst.
19. People from Sheba and Tema hope to find water,
20. but they arrive and are disappointed.
21. You see my troubles and are afraid to help.

What Have I Done Wrong?

22. Did I ask you for help?
23. Did I ask you to save me from enemies?
24. Just tell me what I did wrong, and I'll stay quiet.
25. Honest words hurt, but your words don't help.
26. You don't care what I say. You just argue.
27. You would sell out an orphan or betray a friend.
28. Look at me! Would I lie to your face?
29. Stop accusing me. I've done nothing wrong.
30. I know the difference between truth and lies."

Job 7

Why Is Life So Hard?

1. "Why is life so hard?
2. Like a servant begging for shade or a worker waiting for pay.
3. I've had months of suffering and nights of misery.
4. I lie in bed thinking, 'When will it be morning?' I toss and turn all night.

5. My body is full of sores and scabs. Pus leaks out of them.
6. My days fly by with no hope.

Don't Forget!

7. God, remember my life is short. I'll never be happy again.
8. You see me now, but soon I'll be gone.
9. Like a cloud that disappears, the dead don't return.
10. They're gone forever, never seen in their homes again.
11. So I won't stay quiet. I'll complain about my pain.
12. Am I the sea or a sea monster? Is that why you watch me?
13. When I try to sleep to escape my pain,
14. you scare me with dreams and nightmares.
15. I'd rather be strangled to death than live like this.
16. I hate my life. I won't live forever. Leave me alone. My life means nothing.
17. Why do people matter so much to you? Why do you care about them?
18. You check on us every morning and test us all the time.
19. Can't you just leave me alone for a second?
20. What have I done to you? Have I sinned? Why am I your target?
21. Why don't you forgive me? I'll soon be dead. You'll look for me, but I'll be gone."

Job 8

How Long Will You Talk?

1. Then Bildad the Shuhite replied:
2. "How long will you talk like this? You're not saying anything.
3. Does God ever do wrong? Does he ever judge unfairly?
4. If your children sinned, they got what they deserved.
5. But if you pray and ask God for help,
6. and if you are pure and honest, he will help you and give back what you lost.
7. You started small, but your future will be great.

Older People Are Wise

8. Ask the older generations and learn from them.
9. We haven't lived long and don't know much.
10. But they will teach you with their wisdom.
11. Can grass grow without water?
12. While it's still green, it dies faster than other plants.
13. That's what happens to people who forget God. The hopes of the wicked will die.
14. They trust in weak things that break easily.
15. They think they are safe, but they are not.
16. Evil people are like a plant in the sunshine that spreads across the garden.
17. Its roots wrap around stones,
18. but if you pull it out, it's gone and forgotten.
19. And other plants take its place.
20. But God won't reject good people or help evil ones.
21. He will make you smile again and fill your mouth with joy.
22. Your enemies will be ashamed, and their homes will be destroyed."

Job 9

What You're Saying Is True

1. Then Job replied:
2. "What you say is true, but how can anyone be right before God?

3. If someone argued with him, they couldn't answer one question out of a thousand.
4. God is wise and powerful. No one can stand against him and win.
5. He can move mountains.
6. He can shake the earth and make it tremble.
7. He can tell the sun not to rise and the stars not to shine.
8. He stretches out the sky and walks on the ocean waves.
9. He made the stars: the Dipper, Orion, the Pleiades, and the southern constellations.
10. He does amazing things we can't understand.
11. When he passes by, I can't see him.
12. If he takes something, who can stop him? Who can say, 'What are you doing?'
13. God doesn't hold back his anger. Even sea monsters fall before him.

Though I Am Innocent

14. So how could I argue with him? What would I say?
15. Even if I were innocent, I could only beg for mercy.
16. If I called out and he answered, I don't think he would listen.
17. He hits me again and again for no reason.
18. He won't let me rest. He fills my life with pain.
19. If strength matters, he's stronger. If justice matters, who can call him to court?
20. Even if I'm right, my own words make me guilty.
21. I'm innocent, but I hate my life.
22. Innocent or guilty—it doesn't matter. God destroys both.
23. When something terrible happens, he laughs.
24. The wicked control the land, and no one sees the truth. If it's not God allowing it, then who?

My Life Passes By So Fast

25. My days go by faster than a runner. I never see any joy.
26. They pass by like fast boats, like eagles diving for food.
27. If I say, 'I'll forget my problems and smile,'
28. I still fear what's coming. I know you won't see me as innocent.
29. If I'm already guilty, why try to defend myself?
30. Even if I wash with soap and clean my hands,
31. you would throw me into a filthy pit, and even my clothes would hate me.
32. God is not a person like me, so I can't argue with him or take him to court.
33. If only there were someone to stand between us and help us talk.
34. Someone to stop him from punishing me so I wouldn't be so afraid.
35. Then I could speak freely. But I can't do that alone."

Job 10

I Hate My Life

1. "I hate my life, so I'll speak freely.
2. God, don't just call me guilty—tell me what I did wrong.
3. Do you enjoy hurting me? Do you reject what you made and help the wicked?
4. Do you see things the way people do?
5. Do you live as short a life as we do?
6. Is that why you look for my sins and try to catch me doing wrong?
7. You know I'm not guilty, and no one can save me from you.
8. You made me with your hands. Now you want to destroy me?

9. Remember, you shaped me like clay. Will you turn me back to dust?
10. You poured me out like milk and thickened me like cheese.
11. You gave me skin, bones, and muscles.
12. You gave me life and kindness. You cared for me.

You Haven't Explained

13. But you were hiding your real plan.
14. You watched me closely, waiting for me to sin. You wouldn't forgive me.
15. If I'm guilty or innocent, I still suffer. I'm filled with shame and pain.
16. If I try to be strong, you crush me like a lion and show your power.
17. You keep bringing new trouble. You never stop attacking me.
18. Why let me be born at all? I wish I had died before anyone saw me.
19. It would be like I never existed, going from the womb straight to the grave.
20. I have only a few days left. Leave me alone so I can have a little peace.
21. Before I die and go to the land of darkness where I'll never return—
22. a dark land of death and confusion, where even light is dark."

Job 11

So Much Nonsense

1. Then Zophar the Naamathite replied:
2. "Should all your talking go unanswered? Do you think talking a lot makes you right?
3. Should we stay quiet while you lie? Shouldn't someone correct you when you mock God?
4. You say, 'I'm innocent. I'm pure in God's eyes.'
5. I wish God would speak and tell you the truth.
6. He would show you how deep his wisdom is. There's more than one side to the story. Know this—God has punished you less than you deserve.
7. Can you understand God's mysteries? Can you know everything about the Almighty?
8. His ways are higher than the sky and deeper than the grave. What can you do?
9. They are longer than the earth and wider than the sea.
10. If God arrests or judges someone, who can stop him?
11. He knows who's lying and sees everything.
12. A fool can't become wise any more than a wild donkey can give birth to a human.

Surrender Yourself to God

13. Surrender your heart to God and pray.
14. Stop sinning—both in public and in secret.
15. Then you will be confident and have no fear.
16. You'll forget your troubles.
17. Your life will shine brighter than the sun. Even darkness will feel like morning.
18. You'll feel safe and full of hope. You'll sleep peacefully.
19. You'll rest without fear, and many people will ask for your help.
20. But the wicked will go blind. They'll have no way to escape. Their only hope is death."

Job 12

You Think You're So Great

1. Then Job replied:
2. "You act like you know everything. I guess when you die, wisdom dies with you.
3. But I have a mind too. I know as much as you. Everything you've said, everyone already knows.

4. My friends laugh at me, even though I prayed and God answered. I'm honest and innocent, but now I'm a joke.
5. People laugh at those in trouble. They enjoy watching others fall.
6. But robbers live in peace, and those who make God angry live safely. God lets them.

If You Want to Learn

7. Ask the animals, and they'll teach you.
8. Ask the birds, the earth, or the fish, and they'll tell you.
9. Every living thing knows the Lord made this happen.
10. The life of every creature and the breath of every person is in his hands.
11. Just like the ear hears and the tongue tastes,
12. wisdom comes with age and understanding with long life.

Wisdom Belongs to God

13. But real wisdom, power, and understanding belong to God.
14. What he tears down can't be rebuilt. If he locks someone up, they can't be freed.
15. If he holds back water, there's drought. If he lets it loose, there's a flood.
16. He's in control of liars and those who believe lies.
17. He removes wise leaders and makes judges look foolish.
18. He takes power from kings and makes them prisoners.
19. He removes priests and top officials.
20. He makes trusted people silent and takes away wisdom from the old.
21. He brings shame to rulers and weakens the powerful.
22. He shows things hidden in darkness and brings light to deep secrets.
23. He makes nations rise and fall.
24. He makes leaders foolish and leaves them lost.
25. They stumble in the dark, like a drunk."

Job 13

I Know and Understand

1. "I've seen and heard all this. I understand it.
2. I know everything you know.
3. But I want to speak to God myself. I want to argue my case with him.
4. You are lying about God. You're like doctors who don't help.
5. Be quiet—that would be the smartest thing you've said.
6. Listen to me now.
7. Are you lying to protect God?
8. Are you trying to take his side?
9. What will happen when he checks you? Do you think you can fool him?
10. He'll punish you if you secretly take sides.
11. Doesn't his power scare you?
12. Your arguments are as weak as ashes and clay.

Be Quiet and Let Me Speak

13. Be quiet and let me speak. Whatever happens, happens.
14. I'll take the risk.
15. Even if he kills me, I'll still argue my case to him.
16. This is my only chance—because wicked people can't come before him.
17. Listen closely to what I say.
18. I've prepared my case. I know I'm right.
19. Who can prove me wrong? If you can, I'll stay silent and die.

I Only Ask 2 Things

20. God, I ask for 2 things—then I'll speak with you.
21. Stop punishing me and scaring me.

22. Then call me, and I'll answer—or let me speak, and you reply.
23. What have I done wrong? Show me my sins.
24. Why are you hiding from me? Why do you treat me like your enemy?
25. Would you crush a leaf blowing in the wind? That's all I am.
26. You accuse me of terrible things—even things I did as a child.
27. You chain my feet and watch my every step. You set limits on where I can go.
28. I'm falling apart like something rotten."

Job 14

Life Is Short and Full of Trouble

1. Life is short and full of trouble.
2. We grow like flowers, then die. We disappear like shadows.
3. So why focus on someone like me? Why bother judging me?
4. No one can be completely pure.
5. You already decided how long we live. We can't go beyond that time.
6. So leave us alone, so we can finish our days in peace.

When a Tree Is Cut Down

7. A tree has more hope than a person. If it's cut down, it can grow back.
8. Even if its roots grow old and the stump dies,
9. with just a little water, it will sprout again like a new plant.
10. But when a person dies, they're gone. Where do they go?
11. Like water dries up in a river,
12. people die and never come back. They won't wake up until the sky is gone.

Will We Humans Live Again?

13. I wish you'd hide me in the grave and forget me until your anger is over—but remember me later.
14. If someone dies, will they live again? I'd wait through this time, hoping for new life.
15. You would call, and I would answer. You would want me.
16. You'd count my steps but not watch for my sins.
17. You'd forgive and forget my wrongs.

No Hope Left

18. But just like mountains crumble and rocks fall,
19. and water wears away stone and washes away dirt, you destroy our hope.
20. You overpower us and send us away.
21. We never know what happens to our children.
22. We only feel our pain and sorrow."

Job 15

If You Had Any Sense

1. Then Eliphaz the Temanite said:
2. "A wise man wouldn't talk the way you do. You're full of hot air.
3. You talk just to hear yourself.
4. Your words turn people away from God and prayer.
5. Your sin shows in the way you speak.
6. You don't need me to judge you—your own words do that.
7. Were you the first person ever born? Were you alive before the mountains?
8. Did you hear God's secret plans? Do you think you're the only one who's wise?
9. What do you know that we don't?
10. Older and wiser men agree with us—older than your father!
11. Isn't God's comfort enough for you?
12. Why are you so upset?
13. You're angry with God and speak against him.
14. Can anyone be truly pure?

15. God doesn't even trust his angels. They're not pure to him.

16. So how can people be pure? We're sinful by nature.

Just Listen

17. Let me tell you what I've learned,

18. what wise men taught—truth passed down by their fathers,

19. who lived before foreigners came to this land.

20. Evil people suffer their whole lives.

21. Fear and trouble follow them constantly.

22. They don't feel safe and are afraid of being killed.

23. They search for food, knowing they're running out of time.

24. Fear and pain surround them like a king ready to attack.

25. This happens to those who fight against God,

26. who proudly attack him like a soldier with a shield.

27. Even if they are rich and powerful,

28. they will end up living in ruined houses,

29. because their wealth won't last. Everything they own will be gone.

30. They will live in darkness. God's breath will destroy them.

31. They trusted in worthless things, so they got nothing.

32. They'll die before their time.

33. Like grapes picked too early or a tree that drops its flowers,

34. evil people will have nothing. Their homes were built on lies and bribes.

35. They plan evil, do wrong, and live in dishonesty."

Job 16

I Hear This Often

1. Then Job replied:

2. "I've heard all this before. You are terrible at comforting me.

3. Will you ever stop talking?

4. If you were in my place, I could say the same things. I could point fingers and mock you.

5. But I would comfort you. I would try to ease your pain.

6. But even if I speak, my pain doesn't go away. If I stay quiet, it's still the same.

7. God has worn me out. He has destroyed my family.

8. I'm thin and weak. Everyone sees me and thinks I'm guilty.

9. God is angry with me and attacks me. He grinds his teeth and stares at me.

10. People mock me, slap me, and join together against me.

11. God lets evil people hurt me. He hands me over to the wicked.

Everything Was Good

12. I was living in peace, but God grabbed me and crushed me. He made me his target.

13. His arrows hit me again and again. My insides spill onto the ground.

14. He attacks me without stopping.

15. I wear sackcloth to show my sadness and sit in the dirt.

16. My face is red from crying. I have dark circles under my eyes.

17. But I've done nothing wrong. My prayers are honest.

18. Earth, don't hide my blood. Let my cry for help be heard forever.

19. Even now, I have a witness in heaven.

20. My friends have left me, but I cry to God.

21. I need someone to speak to God for me like a friend would.

22. Because soon I will die and never return."

Job 17

My Hope Is Dead

1. My hope is gone. My life is almost over. My grave is ready.
2. Everyone mocks me and makes fun of me.
3. God, please defend me. No one else will.
4. You kept them from understanding. Don't let them win.
5. Anyone who betrays a friend should have their children suffer.
6. God has made me an example to others. People spit in my face.
7. My eyes are weak from crying. My body is a shadow of what it was.
8. Good people are shocked by what's happened to me. They stand up against the wicked.
9. But good people will stay on the right path and grow stronger.

You Are No Help

10. But you, my friends—come back and try again. I still don't see one wise person among you.
11. My life is over. My plans are gone. My heart is broken.
12. You call night "day" and say light is near, but it's all darkness.
13. What hope do I have? My only hope is the grave.
14. I say to the grave, 'You are my father,' and to worms, 'You are my mother and sister.'
15. So where is my hope? Who can see any hope for me?
16. My hope will die with me to the grave."

Job 18

How Long Will You Keep Talking?

1. Then Bildad the Shuhite said:
2. "How long will you keep talking? Try using some sense—then we'll talk.
3. Do you think we're stupid?
4. You're so angry, but your anger won't shake the earth or move the rocks.
5. The light of the wicked will go out. Their fire won't burn anymore.
6. Their homes will be dark.
7. They used to walk with confidence, but now their own steps trip them up.
8. They walk into traps and fall into holes.
9. A trap grabs their heel and won't let go.
10. A rope is hidden on the ground, waiting for them.
11. Terrors are all around them, ready to attack.
12. They are weak with hunger, and disaster waits to destroy them.
13. Disease eats their skin. Their body rots away.
14. They're dragged out of their homes to die.
15. Fire burns down their house and everything they own.
16. Their roots dry up, and their branches die.
17. No one remembers them.
18. They're pushed out of the light into darkness.
19. They leave behind no children or family.
20. Everyone is shocked when they hear what happened.
21. This is what happens to wicked people—those who turn away from God."

Job 19

How Long Will You Torment Me?

1. Then Job replied:
2. "How long will you keep hurting me with your words?
3. You've insulted me ten times without shame.

4. Even if I did something wrong, it's my problem—not yours.
5. You think you're better than me because I'm suffering.
6. But it's God who trapped me.
7. I cry for help, but no one answers. There is no justice.
8. God blocks my path. I can't move forward.
9. He's taken away my honor and ruined my reputation.
10. He tears me down and destroys my hope.
11. He's angry and treats me like his enemy.
12. His army surrounds my home.

I'm Forgotten

13. My family has left me. My friends have turned against me.
14. My relatives are gone. My closest friends forgot me.
15. Guests and servants see me as a stranger.
16. I call my servant, but he ignores me.
17. My breath disgusts my wife. My own family wants nothing to do with me.
18. Even young children make fun of me.
19. My close friends hate me. Everyone I love has left me.
20. I'm skin and bones—barely alive.
21. Have mercy on me, my friends. God is already against me.
22. Why are you attacking me like God does? Haven't I suffered enough?

I Know My Savior Lives

23. I wish my words were written in a book,
24. or carved in stone forever!
25. I know my savior lives, and in the end, he will stand on earth.
26. After my body has decayed, I know I will see God again.
27. I will see him with my own eyes. I long for that moment.
28. You keep asking how to punish me, thinking I caused all this.
29. But you should fear punishment yourselves, because God judges everyone."

Job 20

Your Words Are Disturbing

1. Then Zophar the Naamathite replied:
2. "I have to speak. Your words upset me.
3. You insult me, so I have to respond.
4. Since the beginning of time,
5. the wicked have only been happy for a short time.
6. Even if they seem proud and powerful,
7. they disappear forever. People ask, 'Where did they go?'
8. They vanish like a dream.
9. Their homes won't remember them.
10. Their children will have to return what their parents stole.
11. The wicked die young.

Sinners Love Sinning

12. They enjoy doing wrong.
13. They hide it and hold onto it.
14. But it turns bitter and poisonous inside them.
15. They spit out the riches they took. God won't let them keep it.
16. They'll suck poison and still be killed by vipers.
17. They'll never enjoy rivers of milk and honey.
18. They'll lose everything they worked for.
19. They crushed the poor and stole their homes.
20. Their hunger was never satisfied.

21. When there's nothing left to take, their success ends.
22. At their highest moment, trouble strikes.
23. God's anger rains down on them.
24. If they run from one weapon, another strikes them.
25. An arrow sticks in their back, soaked in blood. Fear grips them.
26. Their treasures will be lost in darkness. A fire from God will burn them and everything they have.
27. Heaven will show their guilt. Earth will testify against them.
28. Their houses and wealth will be swept away on the day of God's judgment.
29. This is what God gives the wicked."

Job 21

If You Want to Offer Comfort

1. Then Job replied:
2. "Please listen to me.
3. Let me speak first—then you can mock me if you want.
4. My complaint is with God, not people. I have every right to be upset.
5. Look at me and be shocked.
6. I'm afraid even thinking about it.

Why Do the Wicked Succeed?

7. Why do the wicked live long lives, growing old and powerful?
8. They live to see their children and grandchildren.
9. Their homes are safe, and God doesn't punish them.
10. Their animals have no problems giving birth.
11. Their children play and dance.
12. They sing and enjoy music.
13. They live in comfort and die in peace.

Go Away!

14. They say to God, 'Leave us alone. We don't want to know your ways.
15. What do we gain by serving you or praying?'
16. They think their success comes from themselves, but I refuse to think like them.
17. How often do the wicked get punished? How often does God destroy them?
18. Are they blown away like straw in the wind?
19. You say, 'God saves punishment for their children.' But he should punish the wicked themselves,
20. so they can see their own destruction and feel God's anger.
21. Why should they care what happens to their family after they die?

Who Can Teach God?

22. Can anyone teach God? He judges the most powerful.
23. One person dies healthy and rich,
24. living a peaceful, easy life.
25. Another dies poor and bitter,
26. but both end up in the same grave, covered in worms.

Your Words Mean Nothing

27. I know what you're thinking and the lies you tell about me.
28. You ask, 'Where's the wicked man's house? Where is the home of the evil person?'
29. Haven't you asked travelers? Don't you know what they say?
30. Evil people escape trouble. They're spared on the day of judgment.
31. No one calls them out or punishes them.
32. They get fancy funerals, and guards watch over their graves.
33. Many people follow behind, and the ground is gentle on their body.

34. So how can your words comfort me? They're all lies."

Job 22

What Use Are We to God?

1. Then Eliphaz the Temanite said:
2. "Can a person really help God?
3. Does God gain anything if you're good or perfect?
4. Is God judging you because you respect him?
5. No—it's because of your sins. Your guilt has no end.
6. You took things from people without reason. You left them with nothing.
7. You refused water to the thirsty and food to the hungry.
8. You thought your power gave you the right to own everything.
9. You pushed away widows and crushed orphans.
10. That's why trouble surrounds you. That's why you live in fear.
11. That's why you're in the dark, drowning in problems.

God Lives in Heaven

12. God lives high above the stars.
13. But you say, 'God can't see me. He can't judge from up there.
14. He hides in the clouds and walks around in heaven.'
15. Are you following the path of wicked people from the past?
16. They were destroyed young.
17. They told God, 'Go away. What can the Almighty do to us?'
18. But it was God who gave them everything. I don't think like them.
19. Good people are glad when the wicked are destroyed.
20. They say, 'Look what's left of them—everything they had burned up.'

Surrender to God

21. Surrender to God, and you'll have peace and success.
22. Listen to his words and obey them.
23. Turn back to God. Stop doing wrong.
24. Throw away your love for gold.
25. Let God be your treasure instead.
26. Then you'll find joy in God and look up to him.
27. You'll pray, and he will hear you. You'll keep the promises you make.
28. Whatever you plan will succeed, and your future will shine.
29. If someone falls, and you say, 'Help them,' God will lift them up.
30. He'll even save guilty people—because of you."

Job 23

Today I Complain

1. Then Job replied:
2. "Today I'm complaining with a heavy heart.
3. If I knew where to find God, I'd go to him.
4. I would explain my case.
5. I would listen carefully to what he says.
6. Would he use his power against me? No, he would listen.
7. Honest people can speak with him, and he would prove me innocent forever.
8. But I can't find him anywhere—not in front or behind me,
9. not on my left or right. I look, but he's not there.
10. But he knows where I'm going. When he's done testing me, I'll come out like pure gold.
11. I've stayed on God's path. I've followed his ways.
12. I've kept his commands. His words mean more to me than food.

13. God always does what he wants. No one can change his mind.
14. He will do what he has planned for me—and more.
15. That's why I'm scared when I think about him.
16. God has made me weak. He terrifies me.
17. But even with all this darkness around me, I'm not silent."

Job 24

Why Doesn't God Set a Time?

1. God knows when judgment will happen, so why don't his people know?
2. Wicked people move property lines to steal land. They steal sheep with violence.
3. They take donkeys from orphans and oxen from widows as payment for debts.
4. They push the poor aside and force them to hide.
5. Like wild donkeys, the poor search for food for themselves and their children.
6. They gather food from fields and pick leftover grapes from the vineyards of the wicked.
7. They spend nights in the cold without clothes or blankets.
8. Soaking wet from rain, they hide among rocks.
9. The wicked take babies from poor mothers as payment for loans.
10. They leave the poor naked and hungry,
11. even though they press olives and make wine for others.
12. People cry out in the city, and the injured scream for help—yet God seems to ignore it.

Some Reject the Light

13. Some people reject the light. They avoid it and don't follow it.
14. Killers wake up early to murder the poor. At night, they become thieves.
15. Adulterers wait for darkness and cover their faces so no one sees them.
16. Thieves break into houses at night and hide during the day.
17. They love the night. It's when they feel safe.

Sinners Are Filthy

18. These sinners will disappear quickly. Everything they own is cursed. They won't enjoy their vineyards.
19. They'll die quickly, like heat melt snow.
20. Their mothers forget them. Worms eat their bodies. No one remembers them.
21. They abuse widows and hurt women without children.
22. God destroys the powerful. Even if they feel secure, they have no guarantee.
23. God may let them feel safe, but he is watching.
24. They may rise for a moment, but they'll soon be gone like everyone else.
25. Who can prove I'm wrong?"

Job 25

God is the One to Fear

1. Then Bildad the Shuhite replied:
2. "God is powerful and to be feared. He brings peace to everything.
3. He commands countless angels. His light reaches everywhere.
4. So how can a person be pure to God?
5. Even the moon and stars aren't pure to him.
6. So what is a human? Unpure-we're just worms."

Job 26

You've Been Helpful

1. Then Job replied:

2. "Wow, you've really helped the helpless!
3. You've given great advice to someone who knows nothing!
4. Who gave you these words? Who inspired you?
5. The dead tremble under the waters.
6. Hell is wide open to God. Destruction can't hide from him.
7. God hung the sky in the north and placed the earth in empty space.
8. He fills clouds with water, and they don't burst.
9. He covers the face of the moon.
10. He drew the line between day and night across the ocean.
11. Heaven shakes when God commands.
12. He calms the sea with his power.
13. His breath clears the skies. He crushed the fleeing sea monster.
14. These are just a small glimpse of God's power. Who can understand his full power?"

Job 27

I'm Not Going to Lie

1. Job kept speaking:
2. "I promise, as surely as God lives—the one who took away my rights and made me suffer—
3. as long as I'm alive, I won't lie.
4. I won't say anything wrong.
5. I'll never say you're right. I know I've done nothing wrong.
6. I will stay true to myself. I won't feel guilty.

Wicked People Have No Hope

7. My enemies should be treated like the wicked.
8. When God ends their life, what hope do they have?
9. Will God even listen when they cry out?
10. Do they really enjoy talking to him?

What Happens to the Wicked

11. I'll tell you what God does.
12. You've seen it too, so why keep talking nonsense?
13. This is what happens to evil people:
14. They might have many children, but most will die or go hungry.
15. Disease will take the rest. No one will mourn them.
16. They may save up piles of money and buy expensive things,
17. but they won't keep it. Others will take it.
18. Their houses are weak and fall apart.
19. They go to bed rich but wake up poor.
20. Fear sweeps in like a flood.
21. A storm wind carries them away.
22. It strikes without mercy.
23. People clap and laugh when they're gone."

Job 28

Gold and Silver Are Mined

1. People know where to find silver and how to refine gold.
2. They know where to find iron and how to melt copper.
3. They enter caves to find precious stones.
4. They dig deep tunnels into the earth. They rappel by ropes.
5. Above ground there's food, but below it's as hot as fire,
6. where they find sapphires and specks of gold.
7. No bird can get there.
8. No wild animal has been there.
9. People know how to remove rocks and cut into mountains at their base.

10. They tunnel through the rocks to see all their treasures.
11. They keeps the water from caving in and brings the treasuries out.

Where Is Wisdom Found?

12. But where is wisdom found?
13. No one can comprehend its value, no one knows where to find it.
14. It's not in the ocean or the sea.
15. It can't be bought with gold or silver.
16. Or precious stones.
17. Wisdom is worth more than anything, gold, crystal, jewels, nothing compares.
18. It's worth more than any gem.
19. All the topaz on earth couldn't buy it. It's worth more than the purest gold.
20. Then where does wisdom come from?
21. It is hidden from the eyes of all living things.
22. Death and destruction have only heard rumors.
23. Only God knows where to find wisdom.
24. He sees everything to the ends of the earth and under the sky.
25. God gives power to wind and water.
26. He set the limits for the rain and created the path for the lightning.
27. Then he saw wisdom, defined it, then made it known.
28. Then God said, "To fear the Lord is wisdom. To understand it, you must not do evil."

Job 29

Job Remembers His Good Life

1. Job continued:
2. "I wish I could go back to the way things were.
3. Back when God took care of me.
4. When His light helped me walk through the dark.
5. When God was with me and my children were around.
6. When I had plenty of food and life was easy.
7. When I walked to the city gate and sat with the leaders.
8. Young men stepped aside when I came near and the old stood up.
9. Officials stopped talking.
10. Leaders stayed quiet.
11. Everyone who heard or saw me praised me.
12. I helped the poor and the orphans.
13. People blessed me when I saved them from dying.
14. I wore justice and fairness like clothes.
15. I helped the blind see and the lame walk.
16. I took care of strangers.
17. I stopped evil people and saved their victims.
18. I thought I would live a long life and die in peace.
19. I was well connected and could call anyone at any time for help.
20. My power and glory never faded.
21. People respected me and listened to my advice.
22. When I spoke, they stayed quiet.
23. They listened and found my words refreshing.
24. When I smiled, they felt better. They looked for my approval.
25. I led them like a king. I helped those in trouble and comforted those who mourned."

Job 30

Now I Am Mocked

1. Now young men laugh at me—men whose fathers aren't good enough to watch a dog.

2. They were too worthless to be useful.
3. They were thin from hunger, living in empty, dry land.
4. They ate wild plants and tree roots.
5. They were driven out of society like thieves.
6. They lived in ditches and caves.
7. They screamed and hid under the bushes.
8. They were nobodies—fools with no name.
9. Now their sons make fun of me with songs.
10. They hate me and stay far away. They don't mind spitting at me.
11. God has made me weak, so they feel free to attack me.
12. Young men stand up against me. They push and attack me.
13. They block my path and try to hurt me.
14. They rush at me like soldiers breaking through a wall.
15. Fear has taken over me. My honor is gone, and hope has left me.
16. Now my life is full of pain.
17. My bones hurt at night, and the pain never stops.
18. God has grabbed my clothes and choked me with my own shirt.
19. He threw me in the dirt.
20. I cry to God, but He doesn't answer. I stand, but He doesn't look at me.
21. He is cruel to me and uses His power to crush me.
22. He throws me into the storm and tosses me around.
23. I know He will kill me.
24. No one should hurt someone who cries out for help.
25. I cried for those who were poor. I was sad for the suffering.
26. But when I waited for good, evil came. When I hoped for light, I got darkness.
27. My stomach turns from pain. I can't rest.
28. I walk around sad and crying.
29. I have become like wild animals.
30. My skin is burned and peeling. My body is hot with fever.
31. My harp is now used for sadness. My flute only plays funeral songs."

Job 31

Job Says He's Innocent

1. I made a promise not to look with lust at a young woman.
2. What does God give to people who sin?
3. Isn't trouble for the wicked and disaster for those who do wrong?
4. Doesn't God see everything I do and count every step?
5. Have I lied or tricked people?
6. Let God look at me. He will see I've been honest.
7. If I turned from the right path,
8. then let someone else eat my crops and tear up my fields.
9. If I desired another man's wife,
10. then let my wife be with another man.
11. Because what I would've done would 've been a terrible sin.
12. It would destroy everything.
13. If I was unfair to my workers,
14. what would I do when God judges me?
15. God made them just like He made me.
16. I never refused to help the poor.
17. I shared my food with orphans.
18. I helped orphans since I was young.
19. I gave clothes to people who were in need.
20. They thanked me for helping.
21. I never hurt orphans, even when I had power.

22. If I did, then let my arm fall off.
23. I feared God too much to do evil.
24. I never put my trust in money.
25. I didn't brag about my riches.
26. I didn't worship the sun or moon.
27. I never honored them.
28. That would be a sin. I would be lying to God.
29. I never celebrated when my enemies were hurt.
30. I didn't curse them.
31. My servants will say I always fed others.
32. I welcomed strangers in my home.
33. I didn't hide my sins like people do.
34. I wasn't afraid of people or hiding from them.
35. I wish someone would listen to me! I sign my name to prove I'm honest.
36. I would carry God's answer on my shoulder.
37. I would tell Him everything I've done.
38. If my land cries out because I've stolen,
39. or if I took it without paying,
40. then let weeds grow instead of crops."

Job 32

Elihu Gets Angry

1. Job's three friends stopped talking because Job insisted he was innocent.
2. A young man named Elihu got angry at Job for saying he was right and God was wrong.
3. He was also angry at the three friends for failing to prove Job wrong.
4. Elihu had waited because they were older.
5. But when he saw they had no answer, he got upset.
6. Elihu said, "I'm young, and you are older. That's why I waited.
7. I thought, 'Older people must be wise.'
8. But it is the spirit in people that gives understanding—God's breath inside them.
9. Wisdom doesn't always come with age.
10. So I will speak now. I will share my thoughts.
11. I listened to you and waited for your answers.
12. I paid close attention, but none of you proved Job wrong.
13. Don't say, 'We showed him he was wrong'—God, not people, must answer Job.
14. Job didn't argue with me, so I won't use your words.
15. They are shocked and quiet.
16. I waited, but no one said a word.
17. So I will speak. I have something to say.
18. I am full of words and can't hold them in.
19. I'm like wine in a bottle ready to burst.
20. I must speak so I can breathe.
21. I won't show favoritism or flatter anyone.
22. I don't know how to flatter, and if I did, God would punish me."

Job 33

Elihu Talks to Job

1. "Job, listen to me.
2. I will speak clearly.
3. I speak the truth.
4. God's Spirit made me. His breath gives me life.
5. If you can, answer me.
6. I am just like you. God made us both.
7. Don't be scared of me. I won't hurt you.
8. You said, 'I am innocent and have done nothing wrong.

9. I am clean and have no sin.
10. But God finds reasons to attack me.
11. He treats me like an enemy and watches everything I do.'
12. But you are wrong—God is greater than people.
13. Why do you argue with Him? He doesn't have to explain everything.
14. God speaks in many ways—even if people don't notice.
15. He speaks in dreams or at night in sleep.
16. He opens minds and warns people.
17. He keeps them from sin and pride.
18. He saves them from death.
19. Some are warned by pain and sickness.
20. They lose their appetite.
21. They become thin and weak.
22. They are close to death.
23. If there is an angel to help them,
24. God will be kind and save them from death.
25. Their body becomes healthy again.
26. They pray, and God listens.
27. They say, 'I sinned but it wasn't worth it.'
28. God saved me from death. Now I can live in the light.
29. God does this again and again.
30. He saves people and gives them light.
31. Listen to me, Job. Be quiet while I speak.
32. If you have something to say, speak up. If not, just listen.
33. I will teach you wisdom."

Job 34

Elihu Says God Is Fair

1. Elihu said:
2. "Listen to me you wise men!
3. Think hard about what I'm saying.
4. Let's judge what is right together.
5. Job says, 'I am innocent, but God is unfair.
6. I'm honest, but I'm being punished for no reason.
7. Who else talks like Job?
8. He speaks like evil people.'
9. Job said, 'There's no point in trying to please God.'
10. Listen to me—God never does wrong.
11. He gives people what they deserve.
12. God is fair. He doesn't do evil.
13. Who put Him in charge?
14. If God took away His Spirit, everyone would die.
15. All people would die and turn back to dust.
16. Listen, pay attention.
17. God is justice.
18. Can you call a king evil or a ruler wicked?
19. God doesn't favor the rich over the poor. He made them all.
20. People die in a instant—rich or poor, strong or weak.
21. God sees everything people do.
22. No one can hide in darkness.
23. God doesn't need to question people before judging them.
24. He destroys the powerful without asking.
25. He knows what they do, even at night.
26. He punishes them for their evil.
27. Because they turned away from Him
28. and made the poor cry out.
29. But if God chooses to do nothing, no one can criticize Him.
30. He keeps the godless from ruling.
31. Someone should say, 'I was wrong. I won't do it again.'

32. 'God, teach me what I don't see.'
33. Should God do what you say just to please you?
34. Smart people will say,
35. 'Job speaks without knowledge.'
36. I think Job should be tested more.
37. He adds rebellion to his sin and talks proudly against God."

Job 35

Elihu Says Job Is Wrong

1. Elihu continued:
2. "Do you think you're right to say, 'I'm right not God'?
3. You ask, 'What good is it to be innocent?'
4. I'll answer you and your friends.
5. Look at the sky—it's high above.
6. If you sin, does it hurt God?
7. If you're good, does it help Him?
8. Your actions only affect other people.
9. People cry out when they are hurt.
10. But no one says, 'Where is God, my Maker?'
11. He teaches us more than animals and birds.
12. But people cry and don't get answers because they are proud.
13. God doesn't listen to empty prayers.
14. You say you don't see God, but your case is before Him.
15. Job says God doesn't punish fast enough.
16. Job speaks without knowledge and says too much."

Job 36

Elihu Says God Is Powerful and Good

1. Elihu continued:
2. "Be patient. I have more to say about God.
3. I will speak the truth about Him.
4. My words are honest. I know what I'm saying.
5. God is strong but never cruel.
6. He doesn't let evil people live and gives justice to the poor.
7. He watches over the good and lifts them up.
8. If they are punished,
9. it's to show them their sins and pride.
10. He warns them to turn back.
11. If they obey, they will be blessed.
12. If not, they will die in pain without learning.
13. The wicked stay angry and never ask for help.
14. They die young in shame.
15. God helps those who suffer.
16. He wants to pull you out of trouble and bless you.
17. But you are full of judgment, not praise.
18. Don't let anger lead you to sin.
19. Your riches can't save you.
20. Don't wish for death in your pain.
21. Be careful—don't choose evil.
22. God teaches with His power.
23. No one tells Him what to do.
24. Remember to praise what He does.
25. Everyone sees His work.
26. God is greater than we can understand.
27. He makes rain from clouds.
28. He sends rain to the ground.
29. Who understands how clouds form or how thunders roar?
30. He spreads lightning over the sky.
31. This is how he judges people and provides food in abundance.

32. He controls the lightning.
33. The thunder announces the storm is coming and so do the animals."

Job 37

God's Power in the Storm

1. My heart pounds when I think about this.
2. Listen to the thunder in God's voice.
3. He sends the lightning across the sky..
4. After the lightning, thunder roars from His mouth.
5. God's voice is powerful and full of wonder.
6. He tells the snow and rain when to fall.
7. He stops people from working so they will notice Him.
8. Animals run and hide.
9. Storm winds come from the south.
10. God's breath makes ice and freezes water.
11. He fills the clouds with moisture.
12. They move in all directions by His command.
13. He sends them to bring punishment or show His love.
14. Job, stop and think about God's wonders.
15. Do you know how He makes the lightning flash?
16. Do you understand how clouds float in the sky?
17. When the air is still and hot, do you know why?
18. Can you help God spread out the sky?
19. Tell us what to say to Him. We are too ignorant to speak.
20. Should anyone speak to God? Would they die?
21. No one can look at the sun when it shines brightly.
22. But God comes in golden light from the north.
23. God is great and powerful. He is fair and never cruel.
24. So people should respect Him. He does not respect the arrogant.

Job 38

God Answers Job

1. Then the Lord spoke to Job from a storm:
2. "Who is this who speaks without knowledge?
3. Get ready to answer Me like a man.
4. Where were you when I made the earth?
5. Who decided its size?
6. What holds up its foundation?
7. Where were you when the morning stars sang?
8. Who closed the sea with doors when it burst out?
9. I covered it with clouds.
10. I set its limits and said,
11. 'You can come this far, no farther. Here your proud waves stop!'
12. Have you ever told the sun to rise or set?
13. Do you know how light reaches the ends of the earth?
14. As the light approaches, the earth takes shape, the mountains, valleys, waters.
15. Daylight restrains the wicked from doing violence.
16. Have you walked on the ocean floor?
17. Have you seen the gates of death?
18. Do you understand how big the earth is?
19. Where does light and darkness live?
20. Do you know how to get there?

21. Of course you know everything! You were born before it was all created, you are very old!
22. Do you know where snow and hail are kept?
23. I store them for times of trouble, for war and battle.
24. Where is the source of light, or of the east wind?
25. Who created the path for the rain and lightning?
26. Who sends rain to the desert?
27. Who makes grass grow in dry places?
28. Does the rain have a father?
29. Does ice and frost have a mother?
30. Water becomes hard like stone. The surface of water freezes.
31. Can you hold the stars in place?
32. Can you guide the constellations?
33. Do you know the laws of the sky?
34. Can you make it rain?
35. Can you send lightning and make it obey?
36. Who gives people wisdom and understanding?
37. Who is wise enough to count the clouds or tip over the rain jars?
38. When the dust becomes hard and clumps together?
39. Can you hunt food for lions?
40. Do you see them hiding in the bushes?
41. Who feeds baby ravens when they cry for food?"

Job 39

God Talks About Animals

1. Do you know when mountain goats give birth?
2. Do you count the months until deer have babies?
3. They bend down and give birth to their young.
4. The young grow strong and leave their mothers.
5. Who let the wild donkey go free?
6. I gave it the wilderness as its home.
7. It laughs at the noise of towns.
8. It searches the hills for food.
9. Will a wild ox work for you?
10. Can you make it plow your field?
11. Can you trust an ox?
12. Can you rely on it to bring in your grain?
13. The ostrich flaps her wings but can't fly.
14. She lays her eggs on the ground
15. and doesn't protect them.
16. She forgets the eggs could be crushed.
17. God didn't give her wisdom.
18. But she can run fast and outrun a horse.
19. Did you give horses strength?
20. Can you make them jump like grasshoppers?
21. They are ready for battle.
22. They laugh at fear.
23. They rush forward even when swords are flashing.
24. They race with excitement.
25. At the sound of the trumpet, they charge.
26. Do hawks fly south because of your wisdom?
27. Do eagles fly high at your command?
28. They build their nests on cliffs.
29. From there, they look for food.
30. Their young eat blood, and they go where there are dead bodies.

Job 40

God Challenges Job Again

1. The Lord said to Job:

2. "Will you argue with Me? Will you correct your Maker?"
3. Job answered:
4. "I am nothing. I can't answer You.
5. I have already said too much."
6. Then the Lord spoke to Job from a storm:
7. "Get ready to answer Me.
8. Will you say I'm wrong to make yourself right?
9. Do you have power like Mine? Can your voice thunder like Mine?
10. Put on honor and glory like clothes.
11. Show your anger and bring down the proud.
12. Look at the arrogant and humble them. Destroy the wicked.
13. Bury them in the ground.
14. Then I will praise you and say you're right.
15. Look at the massive beast. I made it like I made you. It eats grass like an ox.
16. It has strong muscles and bones like metal.
17. Its tail is strong like a tree.
18. Its bones are like iron bars.
19. It is one of My greatest creations. Only I can control it.
20. It eats in the hills with other animals.
21. It lies under trees and in tall grass.
22. The trees give it shade.
23. It's not afraid of a rushing river.
24. No one can capture it."

Job 41

God Describes Leviathan

1. Can you catch Leviathan (Sea Monster) with a hook?
2. Can you tie its mouth with a rope?
3. Will it beg you for mercy?
4. Will it promise to work for you?
5. Can you make it a pet?
6. Will people try to buy and sell it?
7. Can you hurt it with spears or harpoons?
8. If you try, you'll never forget it and won't try again.
9. You can't defeat it. Just seeing it is scary.
10. No one is brave enough to fight it. So who can stand against Me?
11. Everything under heaven belongs to Me.
12. I won't stay quiet about Leviathan's strength.
13. Who can strip off its armor?
14. Who can open its jaws full of sharp teeth?
15. Its back has rows of shields that are tightly sealed.
16. They are so close no air gets between them.
17. They stick together and won't come apart.
18. When it sneezes, light flashes out.
19. Fire comes from its mouth.
20. Smoke pours from its nose.
21. Its breath burns like hot coals.
22. Strength lives in its neck.
23. Its flesh is tight and strong.
24. Its heart is as hard as stone.
25. When it rises up, the mighty are afraid.
26. Swords, spears, and arrows do nothing.
27. Iron feels like straw, and bronze like wood.
28. Arrows don't scare it.
29. Clubs and stones bounce off.
30. Its underside is like sharp glass. It leaves a trail in the mud.
31. It makes the sea boil like a pot.
32. It leaves a shiny path in the water.

33. Nothing on earth is like it.
34. It looks down on the proud and rules over all animals."

Job 42

Job Responds and Is Blessed

1. Job replied to the Lord:
2. "I know You can do anything and can't be stopped.
3. I questioned your wisdom and spoke in ignorance.
4. You told me to listen and answer your questions.
5. I had only heard about You, but now I see You.
6. I hate myself. I take back everything I said.
7. After the Lord finished talking to Job, He said to Eliphaz:
   "You and your two friends were wrong. You didn't speak truthfully about Me like Job did.
8. So take seven bulls and seven rams. Go to Job and offer them. Job will pray for you, and I'll forgive you."
9. Eliphaz, Bildad, and Zophar did what God said, and God forgave them.
10. After Job prayed for his friends, the Lord made him successful again. He gave Job twice as much as before.
11. Job's brothers, sisters, and old friends visited him. They comforted him and gave him money and gold.
12. The Lord blessed Job more than ever. He had 14,000 sheep, 6,000 camels, 1,000 oxen, and 1,000 donkeys.
13. He had 7 sons and 3 daughters.
14. He named them Jemimah, Keziah, and Keren-Happuch.
15. They were the most beautiful women in the land. Job gave them land along with their brothers.
16. Job lived 140 more years. He saw his children, grandchildren, and great-grandchildren.
17. Then Job died, old and full of life.

– Psalms –

A collection of prayers, songs, and poems praising God

Psalm 1

1. People who don't listen to bad advice or copy bad people are blessed.
2. They love God's rules and think about them every day.
3. They are strong and do well.
4. Bad people are weak and fail.
5. They will be judged and lose.
6. God helps good people. Bad people are on the wrong path.

Psalm 2

1. Why are people planning to fight God?
2. Leaders join together to go against God and His chosen one.
3. They say, "Let's break free from God."
4. But God laughs at them from heaven.
5. He warns them and makes them afraid.
6. He says, "I have chosen my king in Zion."
7. The king says, "God told me I'm His Son."
8. God says, "Ask me, and I'll give you the whole world."
9. "You will rule and break your enemies."
10. So, kings, be smart.
11. Respect God and follow Him.
12. Accept His Son, or you will be destroyed.
    But anyone who trusts Him will be safe.

Psalm 3

1. Lord, so many people are against me.

2. They say, "God won't help him."
3. But You protect me and lift me up.
4. I call to You, and You answer me.
5. I lie down and sleep, and I wake up safe.
6. I'm not scared, even if many people are against me.
7. Lord, save me! Hit my enemies and stop them.
8. You bring victory and bless Your people.

Psalm 4

1. God, please answer me when I call.
2. People, why dyou lie and chase what's wrong?
3. God listens to good people.
4. Don't sin. Think before you speak.
5. Do what is right and trust God.
6. Many people ask, "Who will help us?"
7. But You make me happier than anyone.
8. I sleep in peace because You keep me safe.

Psalm 5

1. Listen to me, God.
2. Hear my cry for help.
3. Every morning, I pray to You.
4. You don't like evil.
5. Proud people can't stand near You.
6. You hate liars and those who hurt others.
7. But I can come to You because of Your love.
8. Lead me, Lord. Show me the right path.
9. My enemies lie and want to hurt me.
10. Punish them, God. They do wrong.
11. But let good people be happy and safe with You.
12. You bless them and protect them.

Psalm 6

1. Lord, don't be angry with me.
2. Help me. I am weak.
3. I'm very scared.
4. Please save me.
5. Dead people can't praise You.
6. I'm so sad, I cry all night.
7. I'm tired from crying.
8. Go away, bad people! God hears me.
9. He listens to my prayers.
10. My enemies will be ashamed and lose.

Psalm 7

1. Lord, I trust You. Save me from those chasing me.
2. If You don't, they'll tear me apart.
3. If I've done wrong,
4. If I've hurt someone or lied,
5. Then let my enemy catch me and win.
6. But get up, Lord! Stand against my enemies!
7. Judge them fairly.
8. You know what's right and wrong.
9. Stop the evil. Help good people.
10. You protect me.
11. You are fair and strong.
12. You judge evil every day.
13. If they don't stop, You will strike.
14. Bad people plan evil.
15. But they fall into their own traps.
16. Their plans will hurt themselves.
17. I will thank You, Lord. You do what is right.

Psalm 8

1. Lord, Your name is great everywhere!
2. Children praise You with power.
3. I see the sky, moon, and stars You made.
4. Why do You care about people?
5. You made us just a little lower than angels.
6. You gave us power over all things.
7. Animals, birds, fish,
8. everything on earth and in the sea.
9. Lord, Your name is great everywhere!

Psalm 9

1. I thank You, Lord, with all my heart.
2. I'm happy and sing about You.
3. You defeat my enemies.
4. You judge fairly.
5. You stop wicked people forever.
6. Their cities are gone.
7. But You, Lord, rule forever.
8. You judge everyone fairly.
9. You help people who are hurting.
10. Those who trust You are never alone.
11. Sing to God! Tell everyone what He's done.
12. He remembers the poor and listens to their cries.
13. Help me, Lord. I'm suffering.
14. Then I will praise You.
15. Evil people fall into their own traps.
16. God shows what is right.
17. Wicked people forget God and die.
18. But the poor will not be forgotten.
19. Rise up, Lord! Judge the earth.
20. Show the nations they are not stronger than You.

Psalm 10

1. Lord, why do You seem far away?
2. Evil people brag and hurt the poor.
3. They only care about money.
4. They ignore You.
5. They always win and think nothing can stop them.
6. They say, "I'll never fall."
7. Their words are full of lies and hate.
8. They hide and wait to attack the helpless.
9. Like a lion, they wait to catch the weak.
10. They think You don't see.
11. But You do see the pain.
12. Get up, Lord! Don't forget the poor.
13. Why do evil people think they can ignore You?
14. But You help orphans and the helpless.
15. Stop evil people from hurting others.
16. Lord, You rule forever.
17. You hear the prayers of the hurting.
18. You help the weak and stop cruel people.

Psalm 11

1. I trust the Lord. Why say, "Run away and hide"?
2. Bad people are ready to attack.
3. When laws are broken, what can good people do?
4. But God is in His temple. He sees everything.
5. He watches both good and bad people.
6. He will punish the wicked.
7. The Lord loves what is right. Good people will see Him.

Psalm 12

1. Lord, please help! All the good people are gone.

2. Everyone lies and says what others want to hear.
3. Stop their proud talk and lies.
4. They say, "We can say whatever we want!"
5. But God says, "I will help the poor and stop the cruel."
6. God's words are true and clean.
7. Lord, You keep us safe.
8. Evil people are everywhere.

Psalm 13

1. Lord, will You forget me forever?
2. How long will I feel alone and sad?
3. Look at me and answer me, Lord!
4. Don't let my enemies say, "We won!"
5. I trust Your love. I will be happy again.
6. I will sing to You because You are good to me.

Psalm 14

1. Fools say, "There is no God." They do bad things.
2. God looks down to see if anyone is good.
3. But no one does right. Not one.
4. Evil people hurt others and never pray.
5. But they will be scared when God shows up.
6. Good people are safe because God protects them.
7. I hope God saves His people. Then they will be happy again.

Psalm 15

1. Lord, who can live close to You?
2. People who do what is right and speak the truth.
3. They don't lie or gossip.
4. They keep their promises, even when it's hard.
5. They don't cheat or take bribes.
People like this will never be shaken.

Psalm 16

1. Keep me safe, God. I trust You.
2. You are all I need.
3. I love Your people.
4. I won't follow other gods.
5. You are my prize and my future.
6. You give me a good life.
7. I will follow Your advice.
8. I always remember You are with me.
9. So I'm glad and safe.
10. You won't let me rot in the grave.
11. You show me the way to live.
Being with You brings joy forever.

Psalm 17

1. Lord, please listen. I am being honest.
2. You know what is right.
3. You tested me and found nothing wrong.
4. I have not done evil like others.
5. I follow Your path and don't slip.
6. I call to You because You answer me.
7. Show Your love and save me.
8. Keep me safe like the apple of Your eye.
9. Hide me under Your wings.
10. My enemies are cruel and proud.
11. They chase me to hurt me.
12. They are like lions ready to attack.
13. Get up, Lord! Defeat them!
14. Don't let them win with their riches.
15. When I see You, I will be happy and feel full.

Psalm 18

1. I love You, Lord. You are my strength.
2. You are my rock and protector.
3. I call to You, and You save me.
4. I was in deep trouble.
5. I felt trapped and close to death.
6. I called for help, and You heard me.
7. The earth shook.
8. Smoke and fire came from You.
9. You came down from heaven.
10. You rode on clouds.
11. Darkness hid You.
12. Bright light flashed around You.
13. Your voice thundered.
14. You sent lightning and scattered enemies.
15. The sea opened by Your breath.
16. You reached down and pulled me out.
17. You saved me from strong enemies.
18. They attacked me, but You helped me.
19. You brought me to safety because You love me.
20. You gave me what I deserved.
21. I followed You.
22. I obeyed Your laws.
23. I tried to do what's right.
24. So You rewarded me.
25. You are kind to those who are kind.
26. You are good to the good.
27. You save the humble but crush the proud.
28. You light my way.
29. With You, I can face anything.
30. Your way is perfect. Your word is true.
31. No one is like You, God.
32. You make me strong.
33. You help me stand tall.
34. You teach me how to fight.
35. You protect me and help me win.
36. You hold me steady.
37. I chased my enemies and won.
38. I didn't stop until they were gone.
39. You made me strong in battle.
40. You made my enemies fall.
41. They called for help, but no one saved them.
42. I crushed them like dust.
43. You gave me victory over other nations.
44. People I didn't know now serve me.
45. They obey me quickly.
46. The Lord lives! He is my rock!
47. He gives me victory.
48. He saves me from enemies.
49. I will praise You, Lord.
50. You give great success to Your chosen king.

Psalm 19

1. The sky shows how great God is.
2. Every day and night speak about Him.
3. They don't use words, but everyone understands.
4. Their message goes all over the world.
5. The sun rises and shines everywhere.
6. It moves across the sky and nothing hides from it.
7. God's law is perfect. It helps us.
8. His rules are right. They make us glad.
9. His commands are clear. They help us see.
10. His words are better than gold and sweeter than honey.
11. They warn us and reward us.
12. Help me see my hidden sins.
13. Keep me from doing wrong on purpose.

14. Let my words and thoughts please You, Lord.

Psalm 20

1. May God answer you when you are in trouble.
2. May He help you and keep you safe.
3. May He remember your gifts and prayers.
4. May He give you what you ask for.
5. We will cheer when you win.
6. I know God saves His king.
7. Some trust in armies, but we trust God.
8. They fall, but we stand strong.
9. Lord, save the king! Hear us when we call.

Psalm 21

1. Lord, the king is happy because You gave him victory.
2. You gave him what he wanted.
3. You blessed him and put a crown on his head.
4. He asked to live, and You gave it.
5. You gave him honor and made him great.
6. You made him happy forever.
7. He trusts You and will not be shaken.
8. You will find Your enemies.
9. You will destroy them.
10. Their families will be gone.
11. They planned evil but failed.
12. You will strike them down.
13. We praise You, Lord, for Your power!

Psalm 22

1. God, why did You leave me?
2. I cry but You don't answer.
3. But You are holy. People praise You.
4. Our ancestors trusted You, and You saved them.
5. They called for help and You helped.
6. But I feel like nothing. People laugh at me.
7. They say, "If God loves him, He should help him."
8. You made me, God. You took care of me since birth.
9. Don't stay far away. I need help now.
10. Trouble is all around me.
11. Enemies surround me like wild animals.
12. I feel weak. My strength is gone.
13. My hands and feet hurt.
14. People stare and laugh.
15. They divide my clothes.
16. Lord, don't be far. Hurry and help me!
17. Save me from these enemies.
18. I will tell others how good You are.
19. Praise God, everyone who respects Him!
20. God helps the poor and listens to their cries.
21. I will praise You in front of everyone.
22. People everywhere will remember You.
23. Everyone will bow to You.
24. You rule over all.
25. Future people will hear about You.
26. They will be told what You have done.

Psalm 23

1. The Lord takes care of me. I have all I need.
2. He gives me rest and peace.
3. He gives me strength and shows me the right way.
4. Even when life is scary, I won't be afraid. You are with me.

5. You protect me and give me more than enough.
6. Your love will be with me forever. I will live with You always.

Psalm 24

1. The earth and everything in it belongs to God.
2. He made it all.
3. Who can be close to God?
4. Those who do right and speak the truth.
5. God will bless them.
6. They look for God and follow Him.
7. Open the gates! Let God come in!
8. Who is this King? It is the Lord!
9. Open the gates for the King of Glory!
10. The Lord is the King of Glory!

Psalm 25

1. Lord, I trust You.
2. Don't let me be ashamed. Don't let my enemies win.
3. People who trust You won't lose.
4. Show me Your ways. Teach me what to do.
5. Lead me in truth. You save me.
6. Remember Your love and kindness.
7. Forget the bad I did when I was young.
8. You are good and fair.
9. You teach humble people what's right.
10. Your way is full of love and truth.
11. Forgive me, Lord, even though my sin is big.
12. You teach people who respect You.
13. Their lives will be full and safe.
14. You share Your promise with those who follow You.
15. I keep my eyes on You, God.
16. Be kind to me. I'm alone and hurting.
17. My problems are big. Please help me.
18. See my pain and forgive me.
19. So many people hate me.
20. Protect me and keep me safe.
21. I trust You. Please don't let me fall.
22. God, save Your people.

Psalm 26

1. Lord, I've tried to live right.
2. Look at my heart and my thoughts.
3. I live by Your truth.
4. I don't spend time with liars.
5. I stay away from evil people.
6. I wash my hands to show I'm clean.
7. I thank You and tell people how great You are.
8. I love being in Your house.
9. Don't treat me like the wicked.
10. They do evil things.
11. But I try to live right. Be kind to me.
12. I stand on solid ground. I will praise You.

Psalm 27

1. The Lord is my light and my help. I won't be afraid.
2. Even if enemies come, they will fall.
3. If a whole army comes, I'll still trust God.
4. I only want to be with God and learn from Him.
5. He hides me when trouble comes.
6. He lifts me up above my enemies.
7. Lord, hear me when I call.
8. My heart says, "Come talk to God," so I do.
9. Don't hide from me. Don't leave me.

10. Even if my parents leave me, God won't.
11. Teach me the right way.
12. Don't let enemies win.
13. I believe I will see good things from God.
14. Wait for the Lord. Be strong.

Psalm 28

1. Lord, I call to You. Don't ignore me.
2. Hear my prayer for help.
3. Don't treat me like evil people who lie and hurt others.
4. Give them what they deserve.
5. They don't care about You. Destroy them.
6. Thank You, Lord, for hearing me.
7. You are my strength and shield. I trust You.
8. You give strength to Your people.
9. Save and bless us. Take care of us forever.

Psalm 29

1. Give praise to God!
2. Praise His power and glory.
3. God's voice is loud like thunder.
4. His voice is strong and full of power.
5. His voice breaks trees.
6. His voice shakes the land.
7. His voice flashes like fire.
8. His voice makes the desert shake.
9. His voice makes animals run and trees bend. Everyone shouts, "Glory!"
10. God rules over the storm.
11. He gives His people strength and peace.

Psalm 30

1. I praise You, Lord, because You saved me.
2. I cried to You, and You healed me.
3. You kept me alive.
4. Praise the Lord, you who follow Him!
5. His anger is short, but His love lasts forever.
6. I felt safe and thought nothing could go wrong.
7. But when You hid from me, I was scared.
8. I begged You for help.
9. I said, "What good is it if I die? Can dust praise You?"
10. Hear me, Lord. Help me!
11. You turned my sadness into dancing.
12. I will thank You forever.

Psalm 31

1. Lord, I trust You. Keep me safe.
2. Help me now! Be my rock and protector.
3. Guide me and keep me safe.
4. Save me from traps.
5. I put my life in Your hands.
6. I trust You, not fake gods.
7. I'm glad You care about me.
8. You saw my trouble and kept me safe.
9. Please help me. I'm sad and tired.
10. My life feels empty.
11. People make fun of me.
12. I feel forgotten.
13. People are planning to hurt me.
14. But I trust You, Lord.
15. My life is in Your hands.
16. Show me Your love.
17. Don't let me be ashamed.
18. Stop the liars.

19. You are kind to those who trust You.
20. You hide and protect them.
21. Thank You, Lord, for saving me.
22. I thought You left me, but You heard me.
23. Love the Lord, everyone who follows Him!
24. Be strong and trust Him.

Psalm 32

1. Happy is the one God forgives.
2. God doesn't count their sin.
3. When I hid my sin, I felt weak.
4. I had no strength left.
5. But I told You my sin, and You forgave me.
6. People should pray to You before trouble comes.
7. You protect and help me.
8. You teach me the right way.
9. Don't be stubborn like a horse.
10. Wicked people have trouble, but God loves those who trust Him.
11. Be happy and praise the Lord!

Psalm 33

1. Good people, praise the Lord!
2. Thank Him with music.
3. Sing a new song to Him.
4. God's words are true.
5. He loves what's right.
6. He made the skies and stars.
7. He made the oceans.
8. Everyone should respect Him.
9. He spoke, and it happened.
10. He stops evil plans.
11. But His plans last forever.
12. A nation is blessed when God is its Lord.
13. God sees everyone.
14. He watches all people.
15. He made their hearts and sees their actions.
16. Big armies don't save kings.
17. Strength can't save anyone.
18. God watches over those who trust Him.
19. He saves them in hard times.
20. We trust the Lord.
21. He makes us glad.
22. Show us Your love, Lord.

Psalm 34

1. I will always praise the Lord.
2. I will boast about Him.
3. Join me in praising God.
4. I asked God for help, and He answered.
5. When you look to Him, you shine with joy.
6. I was in trouble, and He saved me.
7. God's angel protects those who follow Him.
8. Try it—trust God and see how good He is.
9. Respect the Lord. He gives what you need.
10. Even lions go hungry, but God feeds His people.
11. Come, children, and listen—I'll teach you to respect God.
12. Want a good life?
13. Then don't lie or speak evil.
14. Turn from bad and do good.
15. God sees and hears good people.
16. He turns away from evil people.
17. He hears people in trouble.
18. He stays close to the brokenhearted.

19. Good people still have problems, but God saves them.
20. He protects their bodies.
21. Evil will destroy the wicked.
22. God saves His people who trust Him.

Psalm 35

1. Lord, fight against those who fight me.
2. Grab Your shield and help me.
3. Stop those chasing me.
4. Make my enemies fail.
5. Blow them away like dust.
6. Confuse and defeat them.
7. They tried to trap me for no reason.
8. Let their own traps catch them.
9. I will be glad because You saved me.
10. I'll say, "No one helps like God!"
11. Bad people lie about me.
12. They repay good with evil.
13. I prayed when they were sick.
14. I cared for them like a friend.
15. But they laughed when I was in trouble.
16. They made fun of me.
17. How long will You wait, Lord?
18. I will thank You in front of everyone.
19. Don't let my enemies win.
20. They speak lies.
21. They say, "We caught him!"
22. But You see everything, Lord.
23. Wake up and help me.
24. Judge me fairly.
25. Don't let them say, "We won!"
26. Let them be ashamed.
27. But let good people be happy.
28. I will keep talking about Your goodness.

Psalm 36

1. Evil people don't respect God.
2. They think too much of themselves.
3. Their words are lies.
4. They plan evil even in bed.
5. But Your love, Lord, reaches the sky.
6. Your truth stands tall.
7. Everyone can hide in Your care.
8. You give more than enough.
9. You are the source of life.
10. Keep loving those who know You.
11. Don't let pride or evil win.
12. Evil people will fall and never rise again.

Psalm 37

1. Don't be upset by evil people.
2. They won't last long.
3. Trust God and do good.
4. Love God, and He will give you good things.
5. Let God guide your life.
6. He will show your goodness.
7. Wait for God. Don't get angry at others.
8. Don't be mad—it leads to trouble.
9. Evil people will be gone.
10. Good people will live in peace.
11. The humble will be happy.
12. Evil people make plans,
13. but God laughs—they won't win.
14. They try to hurt others,
15. but their plans fail.
16. A little with God is better than a lot without Him.
17. God helps the good.
18. He takes care of them forever.
19. They won't be left with nothing.

20. But the wicked will disappear.
21. Evil people borrow and don't give back.
22. God blesses some and they get the land.
23. God helps good people stay steady.
24. They might fall, but won't stay down.
25. I've never seen the good go hungry.
26. They share and help others.
27. Stop doing bad. Do good.
28. God loves justice.
29. Good people will live in peace.
30. They speak with wisdom.
31. They follow God's ways.
32. Evil people watch,
33. but God won't let them win.
34. Wait for God. He will lift you up.
35. I've seen bad people look strong—
36. but they were gone the next day.
37. Look at the honest ones—they have peace.
38. But evil people are destroyed.
39. God saves the good.
40. He helps and protects them.

Psalm 38

1. Lord, don't punish me in anger.
2. I hurt badly.
3. My body is weak from my sin.
4. My guilt feels too heavy.
5. My wounds stink and hurt.
6. I'm bent over and sad.
7. I hurt all over.
8. I'm tired and broken.
9. You know all my pain.
10. My heart is weak.
11. Friends stay away.
12. Enemies try to trap me.
13. I'm like someone who can't speak.
14. I don't argue back.
15. I hope in You, Lord.
16. Don't let my enemies win.
17. I'm ready to fall.
18. I admit my sin.
19. My enemies hate me for no reason.
20. I try to do good, but they attack me.
21. Don't leave me, God.
22. Hurry to help me.

Psalm 39

1. I said, "I won't speak when evil people are near."
2. I was quiet, but it hurt inside.
3. I had to speak.
4. Lord, help me see how short life is.
5. Life is like a breath.
6. We rush around for nothing.
7. My hope is in You.
8. Save me from my sins.
9. I stay quiet because You are in control.
10. Please stop punishing me.
11. We disappear like dust.
12. Hear my prayer, Lord.
13. Let me have peace before I die.

Psalm 40

1. I waited for God, and He helped me.
2. He pulled me out of trouble and gave me a safe place to stand.
3. He gave me a new song to sing.
4. People who trust God are happy.
5. God has done so many great things.
6. You don't want just sacrifices—you want my heart.
7. I want to do what You want.
8. Your word is in my heart.

9. I tell others about You.
10. I don't hide what You've done.
11. Please keep showing me Your love.
12. I have many problems. My sins are too many to count.
13. Lord, please rescue me.
14. Let my enemies fail.
15. Let those who laugh at me be ashamed.
16. But let people who love You be glad.
17. I am weak, but You care for me. Hurry and help me, God.

Psalm 41

1. God blesses people who help the poor.
2. He protects them in hard times.
3. He gives them strength when they are sick.
4. I said, "Lord, please heal me."
5. My enemies talk bad about me.
6. They pretend to care, then lie.
7. They hope I die.
8. Even my friend turned against me.
9. But You help me, Lord.
10. You hold me up.
11. I know You love me because You keep me safe.
12. You let me stand tall forever.
13. Praise God forever!

Psalm 42

1. I want God like a deer wants water.
2. I'm sad because I feel far from Him.
3. I cry day and night.
4. I remember when I was happy with others at church.
5. Why am I sad? I will still trust God.
6. I feel low, but I remember You.
7. My pain feels deep.
8. But You show love and help me sing.
9. I say, "God, why have You forgotten me?"
10. My enemies hurt me and ask, "Where is your God?"
11. I'm sad, but I will still trust God.

Psalm 43

1. God, defend me. Help me against evil people.
2. You are my strength—why do I feel alone?
3. Send Your light to guide me.
4. I want to go to Your altar and praise You.
5. I feel sad, but I will trust You and praise You.

Psalm 44

1. God, we've heard how You helped our ancestors.
2. You gave them land and made their enemies lose.
3. They didn't win by their strength, but by Your power.
4. You are our King. Help us win.
5. With You, we beat our enemies.
6. I don't trust weapons—I trust You.
7. You saved us many times.
8. We praise You every day.
9. But now, You let us lose.
10. Our enemies beat us.
11. You let others take us.
12. You sold us for nothing.
13. Now people make fun of us.
14. We are laughed at by everyone.
15. I'm embarrassed and ashamed.
16. Enemies curse us and want to hurt us.
17. Even though we didn't forget You.
18. We stayed true to You.

19. But You let us suffer.
20. If we worshiped other gods, You would know.
21. You know everything.
22. We suffer and die for You.
23. Wake up, Lord! Help us!
24. Don't ignore us forever.
25. We are crushed.
26. Save us because You love us.

Psalm 45

1. My heart is full. I will speak of the king.
2. You are strong and kind.
3. Put on Your sword and show Your glory.
4. Ride out and win with truth and justice.
5. Your arrows are sharp—nations fall before You.
6. God's throne lasts forever.
7. God loves what's right and hates evil.
8. He has made You joyful.
9. You are dressed in fine clothes.
10. Listen, daughter—forget your old home.
11. The king wants you. He is your Lord.
12. People will bring you gifts.
13. You are beautiful inside and out.
14. You are brought to the king in joy.
15. Everyone is happy and singing.
16. Your sons will be leaders.
17. People will remember Your name forever.

Psalm 46

1. God is our protection and strength.
2. We won't be afraid, even if the earth shakes.
3. Even if mountains fall into the sea.
4. God's city is peaceful like a river.
5. God is there—it won't fall.
6. Nations fight, but God speaks and ends it.
7. God is with us. He protects us.
8. Come see what God has done.
9. He stops wars and breaks weapons.
10. "Be still and know I am God."
11. The Lord is with us.

Psalm 47

1. Clap your hands and shout to God!
2. He is the greatest King.
3. He rules over all people.
4. He chose land for us.
5. God goes up with shouts of joy.
6. Sing praises to God!
7. He is King over all.
8. God rules from His throne.
9. Leaders come together to worship Him.

Psalm 48

1. The Lord is great!
2. His city is strong and beautiful.
3. God keeps it safe.
4. Kings came to attack,
5. but they ran away in fear.
6. They shook like ships in a storm.
7. We saw how God protects the city.
8. He will do it forever.
9. We remember Your love, God.
10. People praise You everywhere.
11. Your justice makes us glad.
12. Look around the city. Count the towers.
13. See how strong it is.
14. God will be our guide forever.

Psalm 49

1. Listen, everyone—rich and poor.
2. I will speak wisely.
3. I will explain a riddle.
4. I listen to God while I play music.
5. I'm not afraid when trouble comes.
6. Rich people can't buy their way to heaven.
7. No one can pay God to save another person.
8. We all die.
9. Even wise people die.
10. Their money and homes don't last forever.
11. They name land after themselves, but they still die.
12. People die like animals.
13. This is what happens to fools.
14. Death is their future.
15. But God will save me from the grave.
16. Don't worry when others get rich.
17. They can't take anything with them.
18. They may look happy now,
19. but they will die.
20. People without understanding die like animals.

Psalm 50

1. God speaks to the whole earth.
2. He shines from His city.
3. He comes with fire and storms.
4. He judges His people.
5. He says, "Bring Me those who made promises to Me."
6. God is the judge.
7. He says, "I am your God.
8. I don't need your animals.
9. Every animal is already Mine.
10. I don't eat meat or drink blood.
11. I own the world.
12. I want your thanks, not just offerings.
13. Call Me when you're in trouble—I will help.
14. But to the wicked, He says,
15. 'Why talk about My laws when you ignore them?'
16. 'You lie, cheat, and hurt others.'
17. 'You thought I didn't see, but I did.'
18. 'Change your ways or face punishment.'
19. 'But those who thank Me and live right—I will save them.'"

Psalm 51

1. God, be kind to me.
2. Wash away all my sin.
3. I know I've done wrong.
4. I sinned against You.
5. I've been sinful since birth.
6. You want honesty.
7. Make me clean again.
8. Let me feel joy.
9. Don't look at my sins—erase them.
10. Make my heart clean.
11. Don't leave me, God.
12. Bring back my joy.
13. I'll teach others to follow You.
14. Forgive me so I can sing again.
15. Help me speak praise.
16. You don't want just sacrifices.
17. You want a humble heart.
18. Help Your city, God.
19. Then our offerings will please You.

Psalm 52

1. Why do you brag about hurting people?

2. Your words are sharp and mean.
3. You love lies more than truth.
4. You enjoy saying hurtful things.
5. But God will destroy you forever.
6. Good people will see it and laugh.
7. They'll say, "Look at him—he trusted money, not God."
8. But I trust God's love.
9. I will thank You forever, God.

Psalm 53

1. Fools say, "There is no God." They do what's wrong.
2. God looks to see if anyone does good.
3. But no one does what's right.
4. Evil people hurt others and never pray.
5. They should be scared—God is with the good.
6. I pray God saves His people. Then we will be glad again.

Psalm 54

1. God, save me by Your power.
2. Hear my prayer.
3. Strangers are attacking me.
4. But God helps me.
5. He will punish my enemies.
6. I will give You thanks, Lord.
7. You saved me from trouble.

Psalm 55

1. God, please listen to me.
2. I'm upset and scared.
3. My enemies are angry and full of hate.
4. My heart is pounding.
5. I'm afraid.
6. I wish I could fly away and rest.
7. I would run far away.
8. I would hide from the storm.
9. Lord, stop their evil plans.
10. I see trouble in the city.
11. There is lying and hurting everywhere.
12. It's not just enemies—it was my friend.
13. We used to go to church together.
14. That's why this hurts so much.
15. Let them face punishment.
16. But I will call to God.
17. I cry in the morning, afternoon, and night.
18. He hears me and saves me.
19. God never changes. He listens and helps.
20. My old friend broke his promise.
21. His words sounded nice but meant harm.
22. Give your worries to God—He will help.
23. Evil people won't last.
24. I trust You, Lord.

Psalm 56

1. God, people attack me all day.
2. Many fight against me.
3. When I'm afraid, I trust You.
4. I praise You and trust Your word.
5. My enemies twist my words.
6. They plan to hurt me.
7. Don't let them win, God.
8. You see my tears and remember them.
9. When I call You, my enemies run.
10. I trust You, God.
11. I'm not afraid of people.
12. I will thank You.
13. You kept me alive and safe.

Psalm 57

1. God, please help me. I hide in You.
2. I cry to You because You protect me.
3. You will send help from heaven.
4. My enemies are like lions.
5. God, You are the highest.
6. My enemies set traps, but they fell into them.
7. My heart is strong, Lord.
8. I will wake up early and sing.
9. I will praise You everywhere.
10. Your love and truth reach the skies.
11. You are greater than everything.

Psalm 58

1. You leaders don't judge fairly.
2. You plan evil and hurt others.
3. People lie from the start.
4. They are like snakes that don't listen.
5. Nothing can stop their poison.
6. God, break their teeth.
7. Let them disappear like water.
8. Let them melt away like wax.
9. Before they hurt anyone, stop them.
10. Good people will be glad when evil is punished.
11. Then everyone will know God is fair.

Psalm 59

1. God, save me from my enemies.
2. Keep me safe from people who want to hurt me.
3. They wait to attack me, but I did nothing wrong.
4. They rush to harm me. Please help!
5. You see it all, Lord.
6. Every night they come back like growling dogs.
7. They talk trash and think no one hears.
8. But You laugh at them, God.
9. You are my strength. I wait for You.
10. God loves me and protects me.
11. Don't kill them right away—let people learn.
12. Catch them in their lies.
13. Show Your power so people know You rule.
14. They come back every night like hungry dogs.
15. But I will sing about Your love every morning.
16. You are my safe place and my help.
17. I will sing to You, my strength and protector.

Psalm 60

1. God, You were angry and let us lose.
2. The earth shook. Please fix it.
3. You let us feel pain.
4. But You give help to those who respect You.
5. Save us and answer our prayers.
6. God said, "I will win and give My people land."
7. God owns all the land.
8. He rules over all nations.
9. Who will lead us to victory?
10. Have You left us, God?
11. Help us! Human help is useless.
12. With God, we will win.

Psalm 61

1. God, hear my cry.
2. I feel far away. Help me!
3. You are my safe place.
4. I want to stay close to You forever.
5. You heard my promises.

6. Give the king a long life.
7. Keep him safe with Your love and truth.
8. I will sing to You and keep my promises every day.

Psalm 62

1. I wait quietly for God.
2. He saves me. He is my rock.
3. How long will enemies try to bring me down?
4. They lie and act friendly but mean harm.
5. I will keep waiting for God.
6. He is my rock and safety.
7. He gives me strength and protection.
8. Trust God at all times. Tell Him everything.
9. People are weak, whether rich or poor.
10. Don't trust money or stealing.
11. God said power belongs to Him.
12. He loves us and gives us what we deserve.

Psalm 63

1. God, I need You.
2. I'm thirsty for You like dry land needs water.
3. Your love is better than life.
4. I will praise You always.
5. I feel full and happy when I think of You.
6. I remember You at night.
7. You help me and make me sing.
8. I stay close to You.
9. My enemies will be destroyed.
10. But I will be glad in God.

Psalm 64

1. God, please hear me and keep me safe.
2. Protect me from evil people.
3. They use words like weapons.
4. They hide and attack the innocent.
5. They make secret plans and think no one sees them.
6. But God will strike them down.
7. Their own words will hurt them.
8. Everyone will see and fear God.
9. Good people will be glad and trust Him.

Psalm 65

1. God, we praise You and keep our promises.
2. You hear our prayers.
3. When we sin, You forgive us.
4. You let us be close to You.
5. You answer us with power.
6. You made the mountains strong.
7. You calm the seas and stop big waves.
8. People far away respect You.
9. You take care of the land and give us food.
10. You water the land and make crops grow.
11. You give us good harvests.
12. The fields are full of grain.
13. The hills sing with joy.

Psalm 66

1. Everyone, shout for joy to God!
2. Sing about how great He is.
3. Say, "God, Your power is amazing!"
4. Everyone on earth worships You.
5. Come and see what God has done!
6. He split the sea, and people walked through.

7. He rules with power and watches us.
8. Thank Him, everyone!
9. He keeps us alive and safe.
10. God tested us like silver in fire.
11. We had hard times.
12. But You brought us to a better place.
13. I will give You offerings and keep my promises.
14. I will give what I said I would.
15. I bring gifts to honor You.
16. I will tell what God has done for me.
17. I cried to Him, and He listened.
18. If I had hidden sin, He would not have listened.
19. But He did listen.
20. Praise God—He didn't ignore my prayer.

Psalm 67

1. God, be kind and bless us.
2. Let everyone see Your ways.
3. Let all people praise You.
4. Let the nations be glad because You judge fairly.
5. Let everyone praise You.
6. The earth gives food because You bless us.
7. God blesses us, and everyone should respect Him.

Psalm 68

1. God gets up, and His enemies run away.
2. They disappear like smoke and melt like wax.
3. Good people are happy and sing to God.
4. Sing to the One who rides the clouds.
5. God helps orphans and widows.
6. He gives lonely people a home.
7. He led His people through the desert.
8. The earth shook when God came.
9. God sent rain and helped the land.
10. He gave poor people a home.
11. God gave a message, and many shared it.
12. Kings ran away.
13. God gave rest to His people.
14. He spread snow over the land.
15. God chose Mount Zion for His home.
16. He lives there forever.
17. God came with many angels.
18. He won and gave gifts to people.
19. Praise the Lord who helps us every day.
20. God saves us.
21. He will crush His enemies.
22. God will bring His people back.
23. Their enemies will be defeated.
24. We see God's power.
25. People sing and play music.
26. They praise God in the temple.
27. Israel's leaders praise Him.
28. God gives strength to His people.
29. Kings will bring Him gifts.
30. Stop those who want to fight.
31. Egypt and other lands will worship God.
32. All kingdoms, sing to God!
33. Praise the One who rides in the sky.
34. God is strong.
35. He gives strength to His people. Praise Him!

Psalm 69

1. God, save me! I'm drowning in trouble.
2. I'm sinking and have no help.
3. I'm tired from crying.

4. My enemies hate me for no reason.
5. You know my sins, God.
6. Don't let others be hurt because of me.
7. I've been insulted because of You.
8. Even my family stays away.
9. I care about Your house and get mocked for it.
10. I cry and fast, but they laugh.
11. I wear rough clothes, and they joke.
12. People talk badly about me.
13. But I keep praying to You, Lord.
14. Please save me from this mess.
15. Don't let me drown.
16. Answer me with Your love.
17. Don't hide from me. Hurry to help.
18. Come close and save me.
19. You see my pain and shame.
20. I looked for comfort but found none.
21. They gave me poison and sour drink.
22. Punish them.
23. Make them afraid.
24. Show them Your anger.
25. Make their homes empty.
26. They hurt people You punished.
27. Count their sins.
28. Erase their names.
29. I am hurting, but You can save me.
30. I will praise You with songs.
31. That pleases You more than sacrifices.
32. The poor will see this and be glad.
33. God listens to the needy.
34. Heaven and earth should praise Him.
35. God will save His people and give them land.
36. They will live there and praise Him.

Psalm 70

1. God, please help me now!
2. Let my enemies be confused and fail.
3. Let those who laugh at me be embarrassed.
4. Let all who look for You be happy.
5. I am poor and need You. Hurry, God! You are my help.

Psalm 71

1. Lord, I trust You. Don't let me be put to shame.
2. Save me and help me.
3. Be my rock and safe place.
4. Save me from cruel people.
5. I have trusted You since I was young.
6. You kept me safe since I was born.
7. People see how You protect me.
8. I praise You all day.
9. Don't leave me when I grow old.
10. My enemies say, "God has left him."
11. Don't be far, God—help me now.
12. Destroy those who want to hurt me.
13. Let them be ashamed.
14. But I will keep hoping and praising You.
15. I will talk about how You save me.
16. I will tell everyone how great You are.
17. You have taught me since I was young.
18. Even when I am old, let me tell others about You.
19. You do great things, God.
20. You let me suffer, but You give me life again.
21. You lift me up.
22. I will praise You with music.
23. I will sing because You saved me.
24. I will talk about You all day long.

Psalm 72

1. God, help the king do what is right.
2. Let him be fair to everyone.
3. Let the land have peace.
4. Help him protect the poor.
5. Let him be respected as long as the sun shines.
6. Let him bring life like rain on plants.
7. Let good people grow strong and have peace.
8. Let his kingdom go everywhere.
9. Let enemies bow down to him.
10. Kings will bring him gifts.
11. Everyone will serve him.
12. He helps the poor and helpless.
13. He cares for those in need.
14. He saves them from hurt and violence.
15. Let him live long.
16. Let the land grow lots of food.
17. May his name last forever.
18. Praise God, who does great things.
19. Let the whole earth be filled with His glory.
20. Amen!

Psalm 73

1. God is good to people who follow Him.
2. But I almost stopped believing.
3. I was jealous of people who do wrong but have good lives.
4. They seem healthy and happy.
5. They don't struggle like others.
6. They are proud and mean.
7. They only care about themselves.
8. They make fun of others.
9. They act like nothing can stop them.
10. People follow them and believe their words.
11. They say, "God doesn't see us."
12. These evil people live easy lives and get richer.
13. I wondered if I followed God for nothing.
14. Every day felt hard.
15. But if I had spoken those thoughts, I would've hurt others.
16. I didn't understand until I went to God's house.
17. Then I saw how it ends for them.
18. They will fall and be destroyed fast.
19. All their good life will disappear.
20. Like a bad dream, it will all be gone.
21. I was sad and confused.
22. I felt dumb.
23. But You stayed with me, God.
24. You guide me and will take me to glory.
25. I want nothing more than You.
26. My body and heart may fail, but God is my strength forever.
27. Those far from You will be lost.
28. But I'm safe because I stay close to You.

Psalm 74

1. God, why did You reject us?
2. Remember Your people.
3. Look at the damage enemies did to Your temple.
4. They shouted and broke everything inside.
5. They smashed the wood with axes.
6. They burned it down.
7. They ruined Your holy place.
8. They said, "Let's destroy them all."
9. We don't see miracles or prophets anymore.

10. How long, God? Will enemies mock You forever?
11. Why don't You stop them?
12. You have always been our King and Savior.
13. You made the sea and crushed sea monsters.
14. You fed animals with them.
15. You opened rivers and dried oceans.
16. You made day and night.
17. You created seasons and borders for the land.
18. Remember how enemies insult You.
19. Don't let Your people be forgotten.
20. Remember Your promise.
21. Don't let the poor be ignored.
22. Stand up, God, and defend Yourself.
23. Don't forget the noise of Your enemies.

Psalm 75

1. We thank You, God. We praise You.
2. You judge at the right time.
3. When the earth shakes, You hold it steady.
4. You tell the proud to stop bragging.
5. Don't think you are better than others.
6. No one lifts themselves up—God decides.
7. God brings some people down and lifts others up.
8. God gives the wicked a cup of punishment to drink.
9. I will praise God forever.
10. He will crush the power of evil and lift up the good.

Psalm 76

1. God is known in Judah and Israel.
2. His home is in Jerusalem.
3. He stopped weapons and war.
4. God is greater than strong mountains.
5. Brave soldiers ran away.
6. God spoke, and armies froze.
7. No one can stand before You when You are angry.
8. You gave judgment, and people feared You.
9. You saved the humble.
10. Even human anger brings You honor.
11. Keep your promises to God.
12. He brings down proud leaders and scares kings.

Psalm 77

1. I cry to God for help.
2. I reach out all night and can't rest.
3. I think about God and feel weak.
4. I can't sleep or speak.
5. I think about days long ago.
6. I remember songs and ask, "Has God left me?"
7. "Does He still love me?"
8. "Has He stopped being kind?"
9. "Has He forgotten to help?"
10. Then I said, "I will remember what God has done."
11. I will think about His miracles.
12. I will remember how great He is.
13. God, You are holy. No one is like You.
14. You do miracles and show power.
15. You saved Your people.
16. The sea saw You and shook.
17. Rain poured, and thunder roared.
18. Lightning lit up the world.
19. You led through the sea, but no one saw Your steps.
20. You led Your people like a shepherd.

Psalm 78

Listen to my teaching.

1. I will tell you stories from the past.
2. Things our parents told us.
3. We will tell our children about God's power.
4. God gave laws to Israel.
5. So each new generation would know.
6. Then they would trust and obey God.
7. Not like their stubborn ancestors.
8. Some warriors turned back in battle.
9. They didn't keep God's promise.
10. They forgot His miracles.
11. He did wonders in Egypt.
12. He split the sea and led them through.
13. He guided them with a cloud and fire.
14. He gave them water from rocks.
15. Water flowed like rivers.
16. But they kept sinning.
17. They tested God and wanted special food.
18. They said, "Can God give us food?"
19. He gave water, but can He give bread too?
20. God was angry but still gave them food.
21. He sent manna and meat.
22. He gave them all they wanted.
23. But they were greedy and ungrateful.
24. While eating, God punished them.
25. Many died.
26. Even then, they kept sinning.
27. They forgot His power.
28. He had saved them many times.
29. He turned rivers to blood.
30. Frogs, flies, locusts, and hail destroyed crops.
31. He killed animals and plants.
32. He struck Egypt with pain and sadness.
33. Still, Israel forgot.
34. They turned from God.
35. They lied to Him.
36. But He was patient and kind.
37. He forgave them many times.
38. He remembered they were weak.
39. But they kept testing Him.
40. They forgot all He did in Egypt.
41. He led them with a cloud and fire.
42. He gave water from rocks.
43. He fed them daily.
44. He brought them to the promised land.
45. He cleared out other nations.
46. He gave them homes and food.
47. Still, they turned to idols.
48. God was angry and let enemies win.
49. He left the temple.
50. He gave them over to war.
51. Then He chose David to lead them.
52. David cared for them like a shepherd.

Psalm 79

1. Enemies ruined Your temple, God.
2. They destroyed Jerusalem.
3. They left dead bodies everywhere.
4. We are laughed at by other nations.
5. How long, Lord? Will You stay angry forever?
6. Punish the nations that don't know You.
7. They destroyed Your people.
8. Don't hold our past sins against us. Help us now.
9. Save us and forgive us.
10. Show other nations that You are God.
11. Hear the cries of the prisoners.
12. Punish our enemies.

13. Then we, Your people, will praise You forever.

Psalm 80

1. Listen to us, God. You lead us like a shepherd.
2. Show Your power and save us.
3. Bring us back and show us Your kindness.
4. How long will You be angry when we pray?
5. You gave us tears instead of food.
6. Our neighbors fight us and laugh at us.
7. God, bring us back and help us.
8. You brought Israel out of Egypt like a vine.
9. You planted it and made it grow.
10. It spread across the land.
11. It reached the sea and the river.
12. But now it's broken down.
13. Animals and people destroy it.
14. God, please come back and help us.
15. Take care of Your people.
16. Enemies have burned everything.
17. Stay with the one You have chosen.
18. Then we will follow You.
19. Lord, bring us back and show us Your love.

Psalm 81

1. Sing for joy to God!
2. Praise Him with music.
3. Use the trumpet at the right time.
4. This is God's rule for Israel.
5. He gave this law when we left Egypt.
6. God took away our heavy load.
7. We called, and He saved us.
8. He tested us in the desert.
9. God said, "Listen to Me.
10. Don't worship other gods. I am the Lord who saved you."
11. But My people didn't listen.
12. So I let them go their own way.
13. If only they would follow Me.
14. I would stop their enemies.
15. I would punish those who hate Me.
16. But My people would have the best food and honey.

Psalm 82

1. God stands in the middle of the judges.
2. He says, "Why are you unfair?"
3. "Defend the poor and orphans."
4. "Help people who are weak and in trouble."
5. But they don't understand and walk in darkness.
6. God says, "I called you gods and sons,
7. but you will die like everyone else."
8. God, please judge the world. You rule over all.

Psalm 83

1. God, don't stay silent.
2. Your enemies are making noise.
3. They plan to destroy Your people.
4. They say, "Let's wipe them out so no one remembers Israel."
5. They all agree to fight You.
6. Many nations are joining together.
7. They want to take Your land.
8. God, stop them like You did before.
9. Defeat them like You did to other enemies.
10. Make them like dust in the wind.
11. Chase them with storms.
12. Make them afraid, so they turn to You.

13. Let them know You are the Most High over all the earth.

Psalm 84

1. Lord, Your house is a lovely place.
2. I want to be with You.
3. Even birds find a home near Your altar.
4. People who live near You are blessed.
5. People who trust You are strong.
6. When they pass through dry places, You give them water.
7. They grow stronger as they go.
8. God, listen to my prayer.
9. Be kind to our king.
10. One day in Your house is better than 1,000 anywhere else.
11. I'd rather stand at Your door than live in a rich home without You.
12. You give light, help, and blessings.
13. People who trust You are truly happy.

Psalm 85

1. Lord, You were kind to Your people.
2. You forgave their sins.
3. You stopped being angry.
4. Please help us again.
5. Don't stay angry forever.
6. Make us happy again.
7. Show us Your love.
8. I will listen to what God says.
9. He promises peace to those who follow Him.
10. Love and truth will meet.
11. Goodness will grow from the ground.
12. God gives good things.
13. His path is full of what is right.

Psalm 86

1. Lord, hear me—I need You.
2. I am faithful to You.
3. Be kind to me. I pray to You all day.
4. Make me glad, Lord.
5. You forgive and love everyone who calls to You.
6. Please listen to my prayer.
7. I call to You in trouble, and You help me.
8. No one is like You, God.
9. All nations will worship You.
10. You do great things.
11. Teach me to follow You.
12. I will praise You with all my heart.
13. Your love is great—you saved me from death.
14. Proud people attack me.
15. But You are kind and full of love.
16. Help me and show kindness.
17. Show my enemies that You help me.

Psalm 87

1. God built His city on a holy mountain.
2. He loves it more than any other place.
3. It's a special city.
4. People from many nations will be part of it.
5. Everyone will say, "This person was born in God's city."
6. The Lord writes down the names of those born there.
7. They all sing and say, "God is our home."

Psalm 88

1. Lord, I cry to You day and night.
2. Please listen to me.
3. I am very sad and feel close to death.

4. People treat me like I'm already dead.
5. I feel forgotten.
6. You put me in a dark place.
7. I feel crushed by Your anger.
8. My friends have left me.
9. I call to You, but nothing changes.
10. Do dead people praise You?
11. Can anyone in the grave tell about Your love?
12. Are Your miracles known in darkness?
13. But I keep praying to You, Lord.
14. Why do You turn away from me?
15. I've been hurting since I was young.
16. Your anger feels too heavy.
17. Trouble surrounds me all day.
18. Friends and family are gone. Darkness is my only friend.

Psalm 89

1. I will sing about Your love forever.
2. I will tell everyone how faithful You are.
3. You promised to bless David and his family forever.
4. You said his throne would never end.
5. All heaven praises You, Lord.
6. No one in heaven is like You.
7. You are powerful and deserve respect.
8. Lord, You are strong and faithful.
9. You calm the sea when it storms.
10. You crushed Your enemies.
11. You made the world and everything in it.
12. North and south belong to You.
13. Your arm is strong.
14. You do what is right and fair.
15. People who follow You are happy.
16. They praise You all day.
17. You make them strong.
18. You chose our king.
19. You picked David to lead.
20. You said, "I will protect him."
21. "No enemy will beat him."
22. "I will love him forever."
23. "His rule will last through his children."
24. But now it feels like You've turned away.
25. You let his enemies win.
26. You removed his crown.
27. He is weak and defeated.
28. How long will this last, God?
29. Remember how short life is.
30. Where is Your old love and promise?
31. Lord, please remember us.
32. Praise the Lord forever!

Psalm 90

A prayer by Moses

1. Lord, You have always been our home.
2. Before the world began, You were God.
3. You turn people back to dust.
4. A thousand years to You is like yesterday.
5. People are like a short dream.
6. We grow like grass and die by night.
7. Your anger ends our lives.
8. You see all our sins.
9. Life is short and full of trouble.
10. Most people live 70 or 80 years.
11. Help us respect You.
12. Teach us to use our time well.
13. Come back to us, Lord.
14. Fill us with Your love each morning.
15. Give us joy for all our sad days.

16. Show us Your work.
17. Bless what we do and make it strong.

Psalm 91

1. Whoever stays close to God is safe.
2. I trust God to protect me.
3. He saves you from danger.
4. He keeps you safe like a shield.
5. Don't fear day or night.
6. Don't fear sickness or attacks.
7. Others may fall, but you'll be safe.
8. You will see the wicked punished.
9. God is your shelter.
10. Nothing bad will happen to you.
11. God sends angels to guard you.
12. They will protect your steps.
13. You will not be hurt by wild things.
14. God says, "I will rescue you if you love Me."
15. "I will answer you and be with you."
16. "You will live long and see My help."

Psalm 92

1. It's good to thank You, Lord.
2. I sing to You in the morning and at night.
3. You make me glad.
4. Your works are amazing.
5. Only fools don't see Your greatness.
6. Evil people may grow in numbers fast,
7. but they will soon be gone.
8. You, Lord, will always rule.
9. Your enemies will fall.
10. You make me strong.
11. I see my enemies lose.
12. Good people grow strong like trees.
13. They stay strong when close to You.
14. Even when they are old, they will still grow.
15. They show that You are good and fair.

Psalm 93

1. The Lord rules. He is strong.
2. He has always been King.
3. The seas roar loudly.
4. But God is stronger than the sea.
5. Your rules are true.
6. Your house is holy forever.

Psalm 94

1. God, You punish evil. Show Yourself.
2. Stand up and judge the proud.
3. How long will evil people win?
4. They talk big and brag.
5. They hurt Your people.
6. They kill widows and orphans.
7. They think You don't see them.
8. But You made eyes and ears—You see and hear.
9. You teach people, so You know everything.
10. You correct nations and judge fairly.
11. You know all thoughts.
12. People are blessed when You teach them.
13. You give them peace during hard times.
14. You won't leave Your people.
15. Justice will return, and good people will follow it.
16. Who will stand with me against evil?
17. If You didn't help me, I would be dead.
18. When I feel weak, You support me.
19. You comfort me when I worry.
20. Evil rulers don't follow Your ways.

21. They hurt innocent people.
22. But You, Lord, are my protector.
23. You will punish the wicked.

Psalm 95

1. Let's sing to the Lord.
2. Let's shout to the One who saves us.
3. Let's thank Him and sing songs.
4. God is great and rules all gods.
5. He made the mountains and the sea.
6. Come, bow down and worship.
7. He is our God; we are His people.
8. Don't ignore Him like others did.
9. They tested Me, though they saw My power.
10. I was angry with them.
11. They didn't follow Me, so they didn't get rest.

Psalm 96

1. Sing a new song to the Lord.
2. Everyone, praise Him!
3. Tell the world about His greatness.
4. God is great and above all gods.
5. Other gods are fake.
6. God made the skies.
7. Praise Him with glory and strength.
8. Bring an offering and come to Him.
9. Worship the Lord.
10. Tell the nations: "God rules!"
11. Let the sky, sea, and land be happy.
12. Let trees and animals rejoice.
13. God is coming to judge the world. He will be fair.

Psalm 97

1. The Lord rules! Let everyone be happy!
2. He is fair and does what is right.
3. Fire goes before Him and burns His enemies.
4. Lightning lights up the world.
5. Mountains melt like wax before God.
6. The skies show His greatness.
7. People who worship idols are ashamed.
8. God's people are glad.
9. God is above all.
10. Love God and hate evil. He protects His people.
11. He gives light and joy to good people.
12. Be happy in the Lord and thank Him.

Psalm 98

1. Sing a new song to the Lord. He has done great things.
2. He showed His power and saved His people.
3. He remembered His love.
4. Everyone, shout and sing to God!
5. Play music to praise Him.
6. Blow trumpets and horns.
7. Let the sea and everything in it praise Him.
8. Let rivers clap and hills sing.
9. God is coming to judge the world fairly.

Psalm 99

1. The Lord rules! People should shake with fear.
2. He sits as King and is great.
3. Praise Him! He is holy.
4. He loves justice and fairness.
5. Worship Him! He is holy.
6. Moses, Aaron, and Samuel called to Him—and He answered.
7. He spoke to them and gave them laws.
8. God forgave them but punished their sins.

9. Praise the Lord! Worship Him. He is holy.

Psalm 100

1. Shout with joy to the Lord, everyone!
2. Worship Him with gladness.
3. Know that He is God. He made us, and we belong to Him.
4. Enter His gates with thanks.
5. The Lord is good. His love lasts forever.

Psalm 101

1. I will sing about love and fairness.
2. I will live a good life.
3. I won't look at evil things.
4. I will stay away from bad people.
5. I won't let anyone who gossips stay near me.
6. I will choose faithful people to help me.
7. Liars won't stay in my house.
8. I will stop evil every day.

Psalm 102

1. Lord, hear my prayer.
2. Don't hide from me.
3. I'm sad and weak.
4. I forget to eat.
5. My bones stick out.
6. I feel alone like a bird.
7. My enemies insult me every day.
8. I eat ashes like food.
9. I cry because You are angry.
10. My life is like a shadow.
11. But You, Lord, live forever.
12. Show kindness to Jerusalem again.
13. It's time to help Your city.
14. Even broken stones matter to us.
15. All nations will respect You.
16. You will rebuild Jerusalem.
17. You hear the cries of the poor.
18. Write this down for future people.
19. God looks down from heaven.
20. He hears prisoners and saves them.
21. People will praise Him.
22. My strength is weak.
23. Don't take me too soon, Lord.
24. You made everything long ago.
25. Heaven and earth will not last,
26. but You will never change.
27. Your people will live with You forever.

Psalm 103

1. I will praise the Lord with all my heart.
2. I won't forget what He has done.
3. He forgives my sins and heals me.
4. He saves me and shows me love.
5. He gives me good things.
6. God helps people who are treated badly.
7. He showed Moses and Israel what He can do.
8. God is kind and patient.
9. He doesn't stay angry forever.
10. He doesn't punish us as we deserve.
11. His love is huge for those who respect Him.
12. He removes our sins far away.
13. He cares for us like a good father.
14. He knows we are weak.
15. Our lives are short like grass.
16. We are gone quickly.
17. But God's love lasts forever.
18. He blesses those who follow His rules.
19. He rules from heaven.

20. Angels, praise Him!
21. Everyone who serves Him, praise Him!
22. Everything He made, praise Him!

Psalm 104

1. Lord, You are great!
2. You wear light like clothes.
3. You made the skies and clouds.
4. You ride the wind and use fire.
5. You made the earth strong.
6. Water once covered the land.
7. You moved it with Your voice.
8. Mountains rose, valleys formed.
9. You set borders for the sea.
10. You send water to rivers and streams.
11. Animals drink from them.
12. Birds sing in the trees.
13. You water the mountains.
14. You grow food for people and animals.
15. You give joy and strength.
16. Trees grow full and strong.
17. Birds make nests.
18. Goats live in the hills.
19. You made the moon and the sun.
20. Night comes, and animals move.
21. Lions roar and look for food.
22. Morning comes, and they hide.
23. People work during the day.
24. Lord, You made everything wisely.
25. The sea is big and full of life.
26. Ships sail there, and sea creatures swim.
27. Everything depends on You.
28. You give food, and they are full.
29. You hide, and they are afraid.
30. You give breath, and life begins.
31. May God be praised forever!
32. He touches the earth, and it shakes.
33. I will sing to God all my life.
34. Let my thoughts make Him happy.
35. Let sinners be gone. Praise the Lord!

Psalm 105

1. Thank the Lord! Call on Him!
2. Tell others what He has done.
3. Praise His name.
4. Look to God for strength.
5. Remember His miracles and laws.
6. You are His people.
7. He is our God.
8. He keeps His promise forever.
9. He made a promise to Abraham.
10. He gave land to his family.
11. He said, "This land is yours."
12. They were few and moved a lot.
13. God protected them.
14. No one could hurt them.
15. He warned kings not to harm them.
16. Then He sent hunger to the land.
17. He sent Joseph ahead.
18. Joseph was put in chains.
19. But God's plan came true.
20. The king let him go free.
21. He made Joseph a leader.
22. Joseph taught leaders and guided the king.
23. Then Israel moved to Egypt.
24. God made them strong.
25. But the Egyptians turned against them.
26. God sent Moses and Aaron.
27. They did miracles.
28. Darkness came.
29. Water turned to blood.
30. Frogs filled the land.
31. Flies and gnats came.

32. Hail and fire hit the land.
33. Plants were ruined.
34. Locusts ate everything.
35. Nothing green was left.
36. Then the oldest sons died.
37. God brought Israel out with gold and silver.
38. Egypt was glad they left.
39. God gave them shade and fire for light.
40. He gave food and water.
41. He split a rock and water came out.
42. He remembered His promise.
43. He brought His people with joy.
44. He gave them land.
45. So they would follow His ways. Praise the Lord!

Psalm 106

1. Praise the Lord! His love never ends.
2. No one can fully describe His power.
3. Happy are those who do right.
4. Lord, remember me and save me.
5. Let me share in Your blessings.
6. We have all sinned.
7. Our ancestors forgot Your power in Egypt.
8. But You saved them to show Your power.
9. You split the sea and led them through.
10. You saved them and drowned their enemies.
11. Then they believed—only for a while.
12. Soon they forgot again.
13. They wanted food their way.
14. You gave it, but they got sick.
15. They were jealous of Moses.
16. So the earth opened and swallowed people.
17. They made a gold calf and called it god.
18. They forgot God who saved them.
19. You wanted to destroy them,
20. but Moses prayed, and You stopped.
21. They didn't trust You in the land You gave.
22. They complained and didn't listen.
23. So You let them wander.
24. They worshiped other gods.
25. You let their enemies defeat them.
26. But You still heard their cries.
27. You saved them again and again.
28. They forgot and sinned more.
29. Yet You loved them and never gave up.
30. Thank You, Lord! Save us again!
31. We will thank You and praise You!
32. Praise the Lord forever!

Psalm 107

1. Thank the Lord! His love lasts forever.
2. He saved His people—tell everyone!
3. He brought them back from many places.
4. Some wandered in deserts.
5. They were hungry and tired.
6. They called to God, and He helped them.
7. He led them to safety.
8. Thank Him for His love!
9. He fills the hungry.
10. Some sat in darkness and chains.
11. They didn't listen to God.
12. They suffered, then cried out.
13. God saved them from the dark.
14. He broke their chains.
15. Thank Him for His love!
16. He sets people free.
17. Some were sick because of their sin.

18. They almost died.
19. They called to God, and He healed them.
20. Thank Him for His love!
21. Some sailed in big ships.
22. Storms scared them.
23. They called to God. He stopped the storm.
24. He brought peace.
25. Thank Him for His love!
26. God lifts up the poor.
27. He watches over everyone.
28. Be wise—see how much God loves.

Psalm 108

1. My heart is ready, God. I will sing to You.
2. I wake up early to praise You.
3. I will thank You among the nations.
4. Your love is great—it reaches the sky.
5. You are greater than everything.
6. Save us and answer our prayers.
7. God says, "I will give victory."
8. He owns every land.
9. He defeats every enemy.
10. Who will help us win?
11. Only You, God.
12. Human help is useless.
13. But with God, we win!

Psalm 109

1. God, please speak up for me.
2. People lie about me and speak hate.
3. They attack me for no reason.
4. I love them, but they accuse me.
5. I did good, but they gave back evil.
6. Let bad people be judged.
7. Let their lies be punished.
8. Let someone else take their place.
9. Let their children struggle.
10. Let their family be forgotten.
11. May they lose everything.
12. No one should help them.
13. Let their name be gone.
14. Let their sin not be forgotten.
15. God, remember what they did.
16. They were cruel to the poor.
17. They loved to curse—let it come back on them.
18. They wore hate like clothes—let it wrap them up.
19. Let these things happen to my enemies.
20. But You, Lord, help me!
21. You are kind and good.
22. I am poor and hurting.
23. I feel like a shadow at the end of the day.
24. I'm weak from not eating.
25. People laugh at me.
26. Help me, Lord!
27. Let everyone see You saved me.
28. Let them curse, but You bless me.
29. Let shame cover my enemies.
30. I will thank You loudly.
31. You stand beside the needy.

Psalm 110

1. The Lord said, "Sit at My right hand until I defeat your enemies."
2. God will give you power.
3. Your people will gladly follow You.
4. God made a promise: "You will be a priest forever."
5. God will crush kings on the day He judges.
6. He will rule over the nations.
7. He will stay strong to the end.

Psalm 111

1. I praise the Lord with all my heart.
2. Everything God does is great.
3. What He does shows His goodness.
4. He is kind and loving.
5. He gives food to those who respect Him.
6. He showed His people His power.
7. Everything He does is fair and true.
8. His rules will last forever.
9. He saved His people and made a promise forever.
10. Respect for God is the start of wisdom. Everyone who obeys Him has good understanding. Praise Him forever!

Psalm 112

1. Praise the Lord!
2. People who respect God and obey Him are happy.
3. Their children will be strong and blessed.
4. Good people have wealth and kindness.
5. They are kind and fair.
6. They will always be remembered.
7. They aren't afraid of bad news.
8. They trust God and stay calm.
9. They give to the poor and do what's right.
10. Wicked people will be angry when they see this.

Psalm 113

1. Praise the Lord!
2. Everyone should praise Him now and forever.
3. From sunrise to sunset, praise God.
4. He is greater than all nations.
5. No one is like our God.
6. He rules from above but cares about us.
7. He lifts up the poor.
8. He puts them with leaders.
9. He gives children to women with none. Praise the Lord!

Psalm 114

1. When Israel left Egypt,
2. God's people became a nation.
3. The sea moved away, and the river stopped.
4. Mountains jumped like animals.
5. Sea and river, why did you move?
6. Mountains, why did you jump?
7. Earth, shake before the Lord.
8. He turned rock into water.

Psalm 115

1. God, You deserve all the praise.
2. You are loving and faithful.
3. You live in heaven and do what You want.
4. Idols are silver and gold, made by people.
5. They have mouths but can't speak,
6. eyes but can't see,
7. ears but can't hear,
8. noses but can't smell,
9. hands but can't touch,
10. feet but can't walk.
11. People who make them are just like them.
12. Trust in the Lord—He helps and protects.
13. He blesses everyone who fears Him.
14. May God give you more and more.

15. You are blessed by the One who made heaven and earth.
16. Heaven belongs to God, but earth is for people.
17. Dead people don't praise Him—
18. but we will praise the Lord now and always!

Psalm 116

1. I love the Lord because He hears me.
2. He listens when I call.
3. I was close to death.
4. I called to God, and He saved me.
5. God is kind and full of love.
6. He protects simple people.
7. I can rest because He helped me.
8. He saved me from death and tears.
9. I will walk with Him while I live.
10. I believed, even when I was hurting.
11. I said, "Everyone lies!"
12. What can I give back to God?
13. I will thank Him and call on His name.
14. I will keep my promises to Him.
15. God cares when His people die.
16. I am Your servant—You set me free.
17. I will give You a thank offering.
18. I will keep my promises in front of everyone.
19. I will praise You in Your house.

Psalm 117

1. Everyone, praise the Lord!
2. His love is great, and His truth lasts forever! Praise the Lord!

Psalm 118

1. Thank the Lord! His love lasts forever.
2. Let Israel say, "His love lasts forever."
3. Let priests say, "His love lasts forever."
4. Let all who respect Him say, "His love lasts forever."
5. I was in trouble and called God. He helped me.
6. The Lord is with me—I won't be afraid.
7. He helps me win against my enemies.
8. It's better to trust God than people.
9. God is better than any ruler.
10. Many people were against me, but God helped me.
11. They surrounded me, but I destroyed them with God's help.
12. I was about to fall, but God caught me.
13. He is my strength and my song.
14. Good people shout with joy—they are safe.
15. God wins!
16. I will not die—I will live and speak about God.
17. God corrected me but didn't let me die.
18. Open the gate so I can thank the Lord.
19. I praise You because You answered me.
20. The stone that was rejected became the most important.
21. God did this—it's amazing!
22. This is the day God made—be glad!
23. Lord, save us!
24. Bless the one who comes in God's name.
25. God is our light.
26. Tie the offering and bring it to the altar.
27. You are my God—I praise You.
28. Thank the Lord! His love lasts forever!

Psalm 119

Aleph (1–8)

1. Happy are those who live by God's rules.
2. They seek Him with all their hearts.
3. They do no wrong.
4. God gave us laws.
5. I want to obey You fully.
6. I will not be ashamed if I follow Your word.
7. I will thank You and learn Your ways.
8. Please don't leave me.

Beth (9–16)

9. Young people stay pure by obeying You.
10. I seek You with all my heart.
11. I keep Your word in my heart.
12. Teach me, Lord.
13. I speak about Your laws.
14. I'm happy to follow them.
15. I think about them.
16. I will not forget Your word.

Gimel (17–24)

17. Be kind to me so I can live and obey.
18. Help me see wonderful things in Your law.
19. I am a stranger here—don't hide Your commands.
20. I want to know Your laws all the time.
21. You correct the proud.
22. Remove shame from me.
23. Even rulers talk against me, but I follow You.
24. Your laws bring me joy.

Daleth (25–32)

25. I feel low—give me life.
26. I told You my troubles.
27. Help me understand Your ways.
28. I am tired—give me strength.
29. Keep me away from lies.
30. I choose truth.
31. I hold on to You.
32. I will run to follow You.

He (33–40)

33. Teach me Your ways.
34. Help me understand and obey.
35. Make me want to follow You.
36. Turn my heart to You, not to things.
37. Help me focus on You.
38. Keep Your promises.
39. Take away my fear of shame.
40. I want to obey—give me life.

Waw (41–48)

41. Show me Your love.
42. Help me answer people who doubt me.
43. Let me keep speaking Your truth.
44. I will obey forever.
45. I walk in freedom because I follow You.
46. I will speak about You to leaders.
47. I love Your commands.
48. I will think about Your laws.

Zayin (49–56)

49. Lord, remember Your promise to me—it gives me hope.
50. When I suffer, Your word comforts me.
51. Proud people make fun of me, but I stay true to You.
52. I remember what You've done, and I'm comforted.
53. I get upset when people ignore Your word.
54. Your laws are like songs to me.
55. I think about You at night.
56. I follow Your rules and find peace.

Heth (57–64)

57. Lord, You are all I need. I promise to obey You.
58. I ask You to be kind to me.
59. I think about how I live and turn back to You.
60. I hurry to obey You.
61. Even when bad people try to trap me, I remember Your law.
62. I wake up at night to thank You.
63. I am friends with everyone who follows You.
64. Your love fills the earth—please teach me more.

Teth (65–72)

65. You have been good to me.
66. Teach me good judgment and knowledge.
67. I used to wander, but now I obey.
68. You are good, and what You do is good.
69. Proud people lie about me, but I stay true.
70. They don't care, but I enjoy Your law.
71. Trouble taught me to obey.
72. Your word is better than gold.

Yodh (73–80)

73. You made me—teach me to learn Your commands.
74. Others will see my faith and be glad.
75. I know You are right to correct me.
76. Let Your love comfort me.
77. I find life in Your word.
78. Let proud people be ashamed for lying.
79. Let others who respect You come to me.
80. Let me be honest and follow You.

Kaph (81–88)

81. I'm tired, waiting for You to save me.
82. I look for Your word.
83. I feel dry and weak, like an old bottle.
84. How long must I wait for You to punish the wicked?
85. Proud people set traps for me.
86. All Your commands are true—help me!
87. They almost destroyed me, but I didn't forget You.
88. Let me live by Your love. I will obey You.

Lamedh (89–96)

89. Lord, Your word lasts forever.
90. You are faithful to every generation.
91. Everything stands firm because You said so.
92. Your word gives me joy and keeps me going.
93. I won't forget it—it saved my life.
94. I belong to You—save me.
95. Evil people wait to destroy me, but I follow You.
96. Everything has limits—but not Your word.

Mem (97–104)

97. I love Your law—I think about it all day.
98. It makes me wiser than my enemies.
99. I understand more than my teachers.
100. I follow Your word better than the older people.
101. I stay away from wrong so I can obey You.
102. You teach me, and I listen.
103. Your word is sweeter than honey.
104. I learn what's right by knowing Your law.

Nun (105–112)

105. Your word is a light for my path.
106. I promised to follow You, and I will.
107. I'm hurting—please help me.
108. Accept my praise and teach me more.

109. My life is in danger, but I won't forget You.

110. Evil people set traps, but I stay on Your path.

111. Your word makes me happy.

112. I will obey You always.

Samekh (113–120)

113. I hate lies, but I love Your law.

114. You protect me—I trust You.

115. Go away, evil people—I follow God.

116. Hold me up, and I'll be safe.

117. Help me stand strong.

118. You reject those who turn from You.

119. You destroy liars like trash.

120. I respect and fear You.

Ayin (121–128)

121. I've done what is right—please protect me.

122. Don't let proud people hurt me.

123. I wait for You to save me.

124. Show love and teach me.

125. I want to understand Your word.

126. People ignore Your laws—it's time for You to act.

127. I love Your commands more than gold.

128. I follow all Your rules and hate every wrong path.

Pe (129–136)

129. Your laws are amazing.

130. Your word gives light and understanding.

131. I open my mouth and breathe it in.

132. Be kind to me.

133. Keep me from sin.

134. Save me from evil people.

135. Smile on me and teach me.

136. I cry when people disobey You.

Tsadhe (137–144)

137. Lord, You are fair and right.

138. Your rules are true.

139. I get upset when people forget You.

140. Your word is pure—I love it.

141. I may be small, but I follow You.

142. Your law is always right.

143. Even when life is hard, Your word gives me joy.

144. Your rules are right forever.

Qoph (145–152)

145. I call to You—please answer me.

146. I want to obey You.

147. I wake up early to pray.

148. I stay awake at night thinking about You.

149. Hear me in Your love.

150. Bad people are near, but they don't follow You.

151. But You are close, and Your word is true.

152. Your laws last forever.

Resh (153–160)

153. See my trouble and save me.

154. Stand up for me.

155. Wicked people don't follow You.

156. You are full of love—help me.

157. Many people are against me, but I stay true.

158. I hate those who reject You.

159. I love Your word—give me life.

160. Your word is truth from the beginning.

Shin (161–168)

161. Rulers attack me for no reason, but I respect You.

162. I rejoice over Your word like finding treasure.

163. I hate lies and love truth.

164. I praise You all day.
165. People who love Your law have peace.
166. I wait for You and obey Your commands.
167. I love Your word.
168. I follow all You say.

Taw (169–176)

169. Hear my cry and give me wisdom.
170. Let my prayer reach You—save me.
171. I praise You for teaching me.
172. I sing because Your rules are right.
173. Help me, because I choose Your way.
174. I long for You and love Your law.
175. Let me live and praise You.
176. I wandered like a lost sheep—please find me.

Psalm 120

1. I called to the Lord, and He answered me.
2. Lord, save me from lies and false people.
3. What will happen to liars?
4. Sharp arrows and hot coals will punish them.
5. I live in a place full of trouble.
6. I've lived too long among people who hate peace.
7. I want peace, but they want war.

Psalm 121

1. I look to the hills. Where does my help come from?
2. My help comes from the Lord, who made heaven and earth.
3. He won't let you fall. He never sleeps.
4. God watches over His people all the time.
5. He protects you.
6. The sun won't hurt you by day, nor the moon at night.
7. The Lord keeps you safe from all harm.
8. He watches over you now and forever.

Psalm 122

1. I was happy when they said, "Let's go to God's house!"
2. We are standing in Jerusalem!
3. The city is strong and united.
4. Tribes come there to praise the Lord.
5. That's where judges sit.
6. Pray for peace in Jerusalem.
7. May those who love the city be safe.
8. For my family and friends, I will say, "Peace be with you."
9. I will pray for good things to happen here because it is God's house.

Psalm 123

1. I look up to You, God in heaven.
2. Like servants watch their master, we look to You.
3. Show us kindness, Lord.
4. We've had enough of being laughed at and hated.

Psalm 124

1. If the Lord hadn't helped us—
2. enemies would have swallowed us alive.
3. Their anger was like a flood.
4. Water would have drowned us.
5. But God saved us!
6. We escaped like a bird from a trap.
7. The trap broke, and we got away.
8. Our help comes from the Lord, who made everything.

Psalm 125

1. People who trust God are strong, like mountains.
2. God surrounds His people forever.
3. Evil people won't rule the land of the good.
4. Lord, be good to those who do right.
5. But punish those who turn to evil. Let peace be with God's people.

Psalm 126

1. When God helped us, we were so happy.
2. We laughed and sang with joy.
3. People said, "God did great things for them!"
4. God, bring us back like flowing water.
5. People who cry now will laugh later.
6. Those who plant in tears will harvest with joy.

Psalm 127

1. If God doesn't build the house, the work is useless.
2. If God doesn't protect the city, guards are useless.
3. Children are a gift from God.
4. They are like arrows in a warrior's hand.
5. A man with many children is blessed.

Psalm 128

1. People who respect God and obey Him are blessed.
2. You will enjoy your work and be happy.
3. Your wife will be like a fruitful plant.
4. Your children will sit around your table.
5. God will bless you from Jerusalem.
6. You will live to see your grandchildren.

Psalm 129

1. People have hurt us since we were young—
2. but they never beat us.
3. They hurt us badly,
4. but the Lord set us free.
5. Let all who hate God's people be ashamed.
6. Let them be like dry grass.
7. Grass no one picks or blesses.
8. No one says, "God bless you" to them.

Psalm 130

1. Lord, I'm calling to You from deep trouble.
2. Please hear my cry.
3. If You counted all sins, no one could stand.
4. But You forgive—that's why we respect You.
5. I wait for You, Lord.
6. I wait like guards wait for morning.
7. Put your hope in the Lord—He always loves.
8. He will save His people from all sins.

Psalm 131

1. Lord, I'm not proud. I don't try to do big things.
2. I am calm and quiet, like a child with its mother.
3. People of Israel, trust the Lord now and always.

Psalm 132

1. Lord, remember how much David suffered.
2. He promised to build You a house.
3. He said he wouldn't rest until it was done.

4. We heard about the holy chest.
5. Let's go to the place where God is worshiped.
6. Let's bow down to Him.
7. Lord, come to Your resting place.
8. Let Your people sing with joy.
9. Keep Your promise to David.
10. You chose him and his family.
11. You said, "If his sons obey Me, they will rule."
12. You picked Zion as Your home.
13. You said, "This is My place forever."
14. "I will bless it and feed the poor."
15. "I will help the priests and make the people sing."
16. "David's family will grow strong."
17. "His enemies will be ashamed."

Psalm 133

1. It's good when people live in peace.
2. It's as refreshing as oil on a priest's head.
3. It's like dew on the mountains.
4. God blesses people who live in peace.

Psalm 134

1. Praise the Lord, all His servants.
2. Lift your hands and praise Him.
3. May God, who made everything, bless you.

Psalm 135

1. Praise the Lord!
2. Praise Him, all who serve in His house.
3. Praise Him—He is good!
4. God chose Israel as His people.
5. The Lord is great—greater than all gods.
6. He does whatever He wants.
7. He makes clouds, lightning, and rain.
8. He killed the oldest sons in Egypt.
9. He did great miracles.
10. He defeated strong kings.
11. He gave their land to Israel.
12. God's name lasts forever.
13. He defends His people.
14. Idols are just silver and gold—made by people.
15. They can't talk, see, or hear.
16. People who trust them are just as useless.
17. Everyone, praise the Lord!

Psalm 136

1. Thank the Lord—His love lasts forever!
2. He is the God of gods—His love lasts forever!
3. He does great wonders—His love lasts forever!
4. He made the sky, the sun, moon, and stars.
5. He rescued Israel from Egypt.
6. He split the Red Sea.
7. He led His people through it.
8. He defeated strong kings.
9. He gave Israel land.
10. He remembers us when we are weak.
11. He gives food to everyone.
12. Thank the God of heaven—His love lasts forever!

Psalm 137

1. By the rivers of Babylon, we sat and cried.
2. We remembered Jerusalem.
3. Our enemies wanted us to sing, but we couldn't.

4. How can we sing God's songs in a foreign land?
5. I will never forget Jerusalem.
6. If I forget, may I never sing again.
7. Lord, remember how Edom cheered when Jerusalem fell.
8. Babylon, you will fall too.
9. Those who destroy you will be happy.

Psalm 138

1. I thank You, Lord, with all my heart.
2. I sing praises to You.
3. You answered me when I called.
4. All kings will praise You when they hear Your words.
5. They will sing about how great You are.
6. You care for the humble but stay away from the proud.
7. Even when I'm in trouble, You protect me.
8. Lord, You will finish what You started in me. Your love never ends.

Psalm 139

1. Lord, You know everything about me.
2. You know when I sit and when I stand.
3. You see my thoughts from far away.
4. You know what I say before I say it.
5. You are all around me.
6. Your knowledge is too amazing for me.
7. I can't hide from You.
8. Wherever I go, You are there.
9. Even in the sky or under the sea, You are with me.
10. Your hand guides me.
11. Even darkness can't hide me from You.
12. Night is like day to You.
13. You made my body and put me together in my mother's womb.
14. I praise You because I am wonderfully made.
15. You saw me before I was born.
16. You wrote down all my days.
17. Your thoughts are so many!
18. If I tried to count them, they would be more than sand.
19. God, take away evil people.
20. They speak against You.
21. I hate those who hate You.
22. I stay away from people who fight against You.
23. Look into my heart, God.
24. Show me if I'm doing wrong and lead me in the right way.

Psalm 140

1. Lord, save me from evil people.
2. They plan to do wrong.
3. Their words are like sharp snakes.
4. Keep me safe from people who want to hurt me.
5. They set traps for me.
6. I say, "You are my God."
7. Lord, You protect me in battle.
8. Don't let evil people get what they want.
9. Punish those who lie.
10. Let trouble fall on them.
11. Don't let liars stay in power.
12. I know the Lord helps the poor.
13. Good people will praise You and live with You.

Psalm 141

1. Lord, I call to You. Please come quickly.
2. Hear my prayer like a sweet gift.

3. Help me watch what I say.
4. Don't let me do wrong things or hang out with evil people.
5. I want good people to do what is right—not praise from the wicked.
6. Their leaders will fall and learn Your truth.
7. My bones feel like they are scattered.
8. But I look to You for help.
9. Keep me safe from traps.
10. Let evil people fall into their own traps. I will escape.

Psalm 142

1. I cry out to the Lord.
2. I tell Him all my troubles.
3. He knows when I feel weak.
4. No one helps me—no one cares.
5. I say, "You are my safe place."
6. Hear my cry. I am low and tired.
7. Save me from those who chase me.
8. Bring me out of this prison so I can praise You.
9. Good people will gather around me because You are good to me.

Psalm 143

1. Hear my prayer, Lord. Answer me in Your goodness.
2. Don't judge me harshly—no one is perfect.
3. My enemy is crushing me.
4. I'm tired and afraid.
5. I remember all the good things You've done.
6. I reach out to You. I'm thirsty for You.
7. Answer me soon. Don't hide from me.
8. Show me Your love each morning. I trust You.
9. Show me the right path.
10. Teach me to do what You want.
11. Save me because You are good.
12. Stop those who hurt me. I belong to You.

Psalm 144

1. Praise the Lord! He teaches me how to fight.
2. He is my protector, my shield, and my help.
3. Lord, why do You care about people like us?
4. Life is short, like a breath.
5. Show Your power, God!
6. Flash lightning and scatter enemies.
7. Reach down and save me.
8. Enemies lie with their words.
9. I will sing a new song to You.
10. You give kings victory.
11. Save me from liars.
12. Let our sons grow strong.
13. Let our daughters be beautiful and wise.
14. Let our barns be full, and our animals grow.
15. Happy are the people whose God is the Lord.

Psalm 145

1. I will praise You, my King and God.
2. I will bless Your name every day.
3. The Lord is great and deserves all praise.
4. Each generation will tell the next about You.
5. I will talk about Your power and goodness.
6. Everyone will know about Your greatness.
7. They will celebrate Your kindness.

8. The Lord is patient and full of love.
9. He is kind to everyone.
10. All You made will praise You.
11. Your people will talk about Your kingdom.
12. They will tell how powerful You are.
13. Your kingdom lasts forever.
14. You lift up those who fall.
15. Everyone looks to You for food.
16. You open Your hand and feed all.
17. The Lord is always fair and kind.
18. He is close to those who call Him.
19. He helps those who respect Him.
20. He protects His people and destroys the wicked.
21. I will praise You, Lord. Let everyone praise You forever!

Psalm 146

1. Praise the Lord!
2. I will praise God as long as I live.
3. Don't trust people to save you.
4. When they die, their plans die too.
5. Happy are those who trust God.
6. He made everything.
7. He helps the poor and hungry.
8. He sets prisoners free.
9. He helps blind people see.
10. He lifts up those who are low.
11. He loves good people.
12. He protects strangers and helps orphans and widows.
13. The Lord will rule forever!

Psalm 147

1. Praise the Lord! It's good to sing to Him.
2. He rebuilds Jerusalem and brings back His people.
3. He heals broken hearts.
4. He knows every star by name.
5. God is powerful and wise.
6. He lifts up the humble and brings down the wicked.
7. Sing thanks to God.
8. He makes clouds, rain, and grass grow.
9. He feeds animals and baby birds.
10. He doesn't care about human strength.
11. He is happy with people who respect and trust Him.
12. Praise God, Jerusalem!
13. He keeps your city safe.
14. He gives you peace and food.
15. He sends out His word fast.
16. He covers the earth with snow and ice.
17. Then He sends heat to melt it.
18. He gives His word to His people.
19. He doesn't do this for other nations.
20. Praise the Lord!

Psalm 148

1. Praise the Lord from heaven!
2. Praise Him, angels and stars!
3. Praise Him, sun and moon!
4. Praise Him, sky and clouds!
5. He made everything.
6. He gave them their place forever.
7. Praise the Lord from the earth!
8. Praise Him, fire, hail, snow, wind, and mountains!
9. Praise Him, trees, animals, birds, and fish!
10. Praise Him, kings and all people!
11. Everyone should praise the Lord.
12. His name is greater than all.
13. He gives power to His people.
14. Praise the Lord!

Psalm 149

1. Praise the Lord! Sing a new song!
2. Be happy, people of Israel!
3. Dance and sing praises with music!
4. God is happy with His people.
5. Let them sing, even at night.
6. Let them praise and be ready to fight evil.
7. God will punish wicked nations.
8. He will bring justice.
9. This is honor for all His people. Praise the Lord!

Psalm 150

1. Praise God in His house!
2. Praise Him in heaven!
3. Praise Him for His power and greatness!
4. Praise Him with trumpets, harps, and drums!
5. Praise Him with dancing and flutes!
6. Praise Him with loud cymbals!
7. Let everything that breathes praise the Lord.

– Proverbs –

Wise sayings and advice for living a good, godly life.

Proverbs 1

1. These are Solomon's wise sayings.
2. They help you learn wisdom and know what's right.
3. They teach you how to live wisely and fairly.
4. They help simple people and young people make good choices.
5. Wise people can learn even more.
6. These sayings help you understand smart advice.
7. Respecting God is the start of wisdom. Fools hate wisdom.
8. Listen to your parents.
9. Their advice will help you.
10. Don't follow friends who want to do wrong.
11. If they say, "Let's hurt people and steal," don't go.
12. They say, "No one will stop us."
13. "We'll take everything for ourselves."
14. They say, "Join us."
15. But don't follow them. Stay away.
16. They rush to do bad things.
17. Don't walk into trouble like a bird into a trap.
18. People who hurt others will be trapped by their own actions.
19. Greedy people lose everything.
20. Wisdom shouts in the street.
21. She speaks in the town.
22. She says, "How long will you stay foolish?"
23. "Listen, and I will teach you."
24. "I called, but you ignored me."
25. "You didn't want my help."
26. "So when trouble comes, I won't help you."
27. "You'll be scared, but I won't answer."
28. "You'll look for me, but won't find me."
29. "You didn't respect me or want to learn."
30. "You laughed at my advice."
31. "Now you will suffer from your own choices."
32. "Fools are destroyed by turning away."
33. "But whoever listens to me will be safe."

Proverbs 2

1. My child, listen to my words.
2. Think hard about wisdom.
3. Ask for understanding.
4. Look for it like silver or treasure.
5. Then you will respect God and know Him.
6. The Lord gives wisdom.
7. He helps honest people.
8. He protects those who follow Him.
9. Then you will understand what is right and good.
10. Wisdom will fill your heart.
11. Good judgment will protect you.
12. Wisdom keeps you from bad people.
13. These people leave the right path.
14. They like doing wrong.
15. They lie and cheat.
16. Wisdom keeps you from unfaithful people.
17. They break promises and forget God.
18. Their path leads to death.
19. No one returns from it.
20. Stay on the good path.
21. Good people will live in the land.
22. Evil people will be removed.

Proverbs 3

1. My child, don't forget my teaching.
2. It will give you a long and peaceful life.
3. Always be kind and faithful.
4. Then people and God will respect you.
5. Trust God, not yourself.
6. Ask Him before you act—He'll guide you.
7. Don't think you know everything.
8. Respect God and turn from evil—this brings health.
9. Honor God with your money.
10. Then you'll always have enough.
11. Don't ignore God's correction.
12. He corrects you because He loves you.
13. Happy is the one who finds wisdom.
14. Wisdom is better than money or gold.
15. It's more valuable than anything.
16. Wisdom brings a long and good life.
17. It leads to peace.
18. It gives life and happiness.
19. God used wisdom to make the earth.
20. His knowledge made the skies.
21. Keep wisdom and good judgment.
22. They give life and safety.
23. You'll walk without fear.
24. You'll sleep well.
25. Don't fear sudden trouble.
26. God will protect you.
27. Help others when you can.
28. Don't delay help if you have it now.
29. Don't plan to hurt your neighbor.
30. Don't fight for no reason.
31. Don't be jealous of violent people.
32. God hates evil but is close to good people.
33. God blesses good homes but punishes the wicked.
34. He shows kindness to the humble.
35. Wise people are honored. Fools are ashamed.

Proverbs 4

1. Children, listen to your father's teaching.
2. I give good advice—follow it.
3. I was once a child too.
4. My father said, "Hold on to my words."

5. Get wisdom and understanding.
6. Don't ignore wisdom. She will protect you.
7. Wisdom is most important. Get it.
8. Love her, and she will honor you.
9. Wisdom brings respect.
10. Listen, and you will live long.
11. I teach you the right way.
12. You will walk without falling.
13. Hold on to my words—they bring life.
14. Don't follow evil people.
15. Avoid their path completely.
16. They can't sleep unless they do wrong.
17. They enjoy evil.
18. But the path of the good gets brighter and brighter.
19. The wicked walk in darkness.
20. My child, pay attention to me.
21. Keep my words in your heart.
22. They bring life and health.
23. Guard your heart—it controls your life.
24. Don't lie or speak badly.
25. Look straight ahead.
26. Think about where you're going.
27. Don't turn to evil.

Proverbs 5

1. My son, listen to my wisdom.
2. Use good sense and speak truth.
3. Wrong people may sound sweet,
4. but they lead to pain and death.
5. Stay far away from them.
6. They don't care about right and wrong.
7. Listen and don't turn away.
8. Don't go near their door.
9. Or you'll lose everything.
10. Strangers will take what's yours.
11. You'll regret it when it's too late.
12. You'll say, "Why didn't I listen?"
13. "Why did I ignore advice?"
14. "Now I'm ruined."
15. Be happy with your own wife.
16. Stay loyal.
17. Let her love be just for you.
18. Be glad with the wife you chose.
19. Enjoy her love always.
20. Don't love another woman.
21. God sees everything.
22. Sin traps people.
23. They die because they didn't listen.

Proverbs 6

1. Don't make promises you can't keep.
2. If you did, get out fast.
3. Don't wait—beg to be free.
4. Don't sleep until it's fixed.
5. Escape like a bird from a trap.
6. Be like an ant—work hard.
7. Ants don't need a boss.
8. They gather food in summer.
9. Don't be lazy.
10. A little sleep and poverty comes.
11. You'll be poor like a robber took everything.
12. Wicked people lie and cause trouble.
13. They use signs to trick others.
14. They stir up evil.
15. Trouble will destroy them fast.
16. God hates these six things (seven, really):
17. Pride, lying, hurting others,
18. evil thoughts, quick to do wrong,
19. lying in court, and causing fights.
20. Obey your parents' teaching.

21. Keep it in your heart.
22. It will guide you and protect you.
23. Their words are like a light.
24. They keep you from bad people.
25. Don't want what's not yours.
26. A bad choice can ruin your life.
27. Fire burns—sin does too.
28. You can't touch fire and not get burned.
29. You can't steal love and be safe.
30. A hungry thief may be forgiven,
31. but he still pays it back.
32. A cheater destroys himself.
33. He will face shame and pain.
34. Jealous people are dangerous.
35. They won't accept payment or forgive.

Proverbs 7

1. My son, follow my words.
2. Keep them safe like treasure.
3. Always remember them.
4. Love wisdom and understanding.
5. They protect you from wrong people.
6. I saw a foolish young man.
7. He walked near a bad woman's house.
8. It was dark outside.
9. She met him dressed to trap him.
10. She was loud and wild.
11. She didn't stay home.
12. She grabbed him and kissed him.
13. She said, "I came looking for you."
14. "Let's enjoy ourselves."
15. "My husband is gone."
16. "He won't be back for days."
17. She used sweet words.
18. He followed her right into danger.
19. Like an animal going to be killed.
20. Like a bird flying into a trap.
21. He didn't know it would cost his life.
22. Listen to me, sons.
23. Don't let your heart go to sin.
24. Many strong men have fallen this way.
25. Her house leads to death.

Proverbs 8

1. Wisdom calls out to everyone.
2. She speaks in public places.
3. She says, "Learn to be wise."
4. "I speak the truth."
5. "My words are fair and right."
6. "Nothing I say is tricky."
7. "My words help people live right."
8. "Wisdom is better than gold or silver."
9. "I hate pride and lies."
10. "I give good advice and knowledge."
11. "Wisdom is better than riches."
12. "I help people think clearly."
13. "Respecting God means hating evil."
14. "I give strength and understanding."
15. "Leaders rule well with wisdom."
16. "I love those who love me."
17. "I give riches and honor."
18. "My way leads to life."
19. "God made me first, before the world."
20. "I was there before the earth, oceans, and mountains."
21. "I was beside Him when He made everything."
22. "I was His delight, and I loved people."
23. "Listen to me and be blessed."
24. "Wait at my door and find life."
25. "Those who ignore me will hurt themselves."

Proverbs 9

1. Wisdom builds her house.
2. She prepares food and invites people in.
3. She says, "Come learn and live."
4. Leave foolish ways.
5. If you correct a mocker, they will hate you.
6. Correct the wise, and they will thank you.
7. Wisdom starts by respecting God.
8. Knowledge starts by knowing God.
9. Wisdom helps you live long.
10. Foolishness calls too, but she lies.
11. She says, "Come in and enjoy,"
12. but her path leads to death.

Proverbs 10

1. A wise son makes his parents glad. A foolish son brings sorrow.
2. Doing wrong doesn't help, but doing right saves.
3. God gives good things to good people.
4. Lazy people become poor.
5. Work hard at the right time.
6. Blessings come to good people.
7. People remember good people with joy.
8. Wise people accept commands.
9. Honest people are safe.
10. Crooked people will be found out.
11. Good words bring life.
12. Hate causes fights. Love makes peace.
13. Wisdom is found in smart people.
14. Wise people store knowledge.
15. Riches can protect, but poverty can destroy.
16. Good people work for life.
17. Listening to correction brings success.
18. Hiding hate or lying causes trouble.
19. Too much talk leads to sin.
20. Wise words are valuable.
21. Good people help others with their words.
22. God's blessing brings true wealth.
23. Fools enjoy doing wrong.
24. The wicked fear punishment.
25. Good people stand strong after trouble.
26. Lazy people are annoying to others.
27. Respecting God leads to long life.
28. Good people have joy. Wicked people lose hope.
29. God protects the honest.
30. Good people will not be moved.
31. Good words come from wise mouths.
32. Good people say what's helpful.

Proverbs 11

1. God hates cheating. He likes honesty.
2. Pride leads to shame. Humility leads to wisdom.
3. Good people make good choices.
4. Money won't save you, but doing right will.
5. Good people live safe lives.
6. Doing right saves honest people.
7. When bad people die, their hope dies too.
8. God rescues good people from trouble.
9. Evil people hurt others with words.
10. Cities are happy when good people succeed.
11. Cities fall when people are wicked.
12. A foolish person insults others.
13. A gossip shares secrets. A true friend stays quiet.
14. Plans fail without good advice.

15. Don't promise to pay someone else's debt.
16. A kind woman gains respect.
17. Being kind helps yourself. Being cruel hurts yourself.
18. Evil work is empty. Doing right brings reward.
19. Goodness brings life. Evil leads to death.
20. God hates crooked hearts. He loves honest ones.
21. Evil people won't win. Good people will be saved.
22. Beauty without wisdom is useless.
23. Good people want good things.
24. Some give freely and gain more. Others hold back and lose.
25. Helping others brings blessing.
26. People hate hoarders. They bless generous ones.
27. If you try to do good, you'll find favor.
28. Don't trust riches. Trust God.
29. Foolish people ruin their families.
30. Good people give life to others.
31. If the good are repaid, the wicked surely will be too.

Proverbs 12

1. Whoever loves correction is wise.
2. Good people please God.
3. Evil people won't stand strong.
4. A good wife makes her husband proud.
5. Honest people think good things.
6. Wicked people use words to harm.
7. Evil people fall. Good people stand.
8. A wise person is praised.
9. It's better to be simple than to pretend and go hungry.
10. Good people take care of animals.
11. Work your land, and you'll have food.
12. Wicked people chase bad things.
13. Bad people get trapped by their lies.
14. Good words bring good results.
15. Fools think they're always right.
16. Wise people stay calm.
17. Honest people speak truth.
18. Some words hurt, but wise words heal.
19. Truth lasts. Lies don't.
20. Peace brings joy.
21. No harm comes to the good.
22. God hates lies. He loves truth.
23. Wise people keep knowledge to themselves.
24. Hard workers become leaders.
25. Worry weighs you down. Kind words lift you up.
26. Good friends lead you right.
27. Lazy people don't finish the job.
28. Living right leads to life.

Proverbs 13

1. Wise children listen to their parents.
2. Good words bring good results.
3. Guard your mouth to stay out of trouble.
4. Lazy people get nothing. Hard workers get plenty.
5. Honest people hate lies.
6. Doing right protects you.
7. Some pretend to be rich but have nothing.
8. Rich people can pay to avoid trouble.
9. Good people shine bright.
10. Pride causes fights.
11. Quick money disappears. Steady work brings growth.
12. Hope that takes too long makes hearts sad.
13. Respecting rules brings reward.

14. Wise teaching saves lives.
15. Good sense brings success.
16. Smart people think before acting.
17. A good messenger brings help.
18. Lazy people end up poor.
19. A good goal brings joy.
20. Stay close to wise people and become wise.
21. Trouble chases sinners.
22. Good people leave blessings for their children.
23. Hard work brings food.
24. Loving parents correct their kids.
25. Good people always have enough.

Proverbs 14

1. A wise woman builds her home. A foolish one tears it down.
2. Good people respect God. Bad people don't.
3. Foolish words cause trouble.
4. Hard work brings results.
5. Honest people tell the truth.
6. Mockers find no wisdom.
7. Stay away from fools.
8. Wise people think before they act.
9. Fools laugh at sin.
10. No one can fully know someone else's heart.
11. The wicked will fall. The good will grow.
12. Some paths seem right but lead to death.
13. Laughing can hide sadness.
14. People get what they deserve.
15. Simple people believe anything.
16. Wise people avoid danger.
17. Quick-tempered people do foolish things.
18. Fools stay foolish. Wise people grow wiser.
19. Evil people must respect good people.
20. Poor people are ignored. Rich people have friends.
21. Being kind is better than judging.
22. Good plans lead to love and truth.
23. Hard work brings profit. Talk alone brings nothing.
24. Wise people are rewarded.
25. Honest people save lives.
26. Respect for God gives strength.
27. Respect for God protects you from danger.
28. A strong leader has many people.
29. Patient people are wise.
30. Peaceful hearts bring health.
31. Being cruel to the poor insults God.
32. Evil people fall. Good people are safe.
33. Wise people keep learning.
34. Doing right lifts a nation.
35. Kings reward good work.

Proverbs 15

1. A kind answer calms anger.
2. Wise words help. Foolish words hurt.
3. God sees everything.
4. Kind words heal.
5. Fools hate correction.
6. Good homes are blessed.
7. Wise people share knowledge.
8. God listens to the good.
9. He loves those who live right.
10. Ignoring correction leads to trouble.
11. God sees all hearts.
12. Mockers avoid wise people.
13. Happy hearts show on the face.
14. Wise people want to learn.

15. A cheerful heart is like a party.
16. It's better to fear God than be rich.
17. A simple meal with love is better than a feast with hate.
18. Angry people cause fights.
19. Lazy people make excuses.
20. Wise children make parents happy.
21. Foolish choices bring sadness.
22. Good advice brings success.
23. The right word brings joy.
24. Wise people stay away from death.
25. God protects the helpless.
26. He hates evil plans.
27. Greedy people bring trouble.
28. Good people think before they speak.
29. God is close to those who pray.
30. Good news makes people happy.
31. Correction helps you live longer.
32. Ignoring correction is self-harm.
33. Respect for God brings wisdom.

Proverbs 16

1. People make plans, but God decides.
2. God sees our true hearts.
3. Trust God with your plans.
4. God made everything for a reason.
5. God hates pride.
6. Love and truth remove sin.
7. God makes peace when people live right.
8. Honest money is better than lots of evil money.
9. We plan, but God leads.
10. Leaders should speak truth.
11. God cares about fairness.
12. Kings should hate evil.
13. Honest words please leaders.
14. A wise person calms anger.
15. A king's smile brings life.
16. Wisdom is better than gold.
17. Good people avoid evil.
18. Pride leads to a fall.
19. It's better to be humble than proud.
20. Listen to advice and do well.
21. Kind words help people learn.
22. Wisdom gives life.
23. Wise people choose good words.
24. Kind words are sweet and healing.
25. Some paths lead to death.
26. Hunger drives people to work.
27. Wicked people cause trouble.
28. Gossip breaks friendships.
29. Evil people lead others to sin.
30. Don't trust sneaky people.
31. Gray hair shows wisdom.
32. Patience is better than strength.
33. We throw dice, but God decides.

Proverbs 17

1. A dry crust with peace is better than a feast with fighting.
2. A wise servant can rule over a foolish son.
3. Fire tests gold; God tests hearts.
4. Evil people like listening to lies.
5. Making fun of the poor insults God.
6. Grandchildren are a joy.
7. Fools should not brag.
8. Some people think gifts are magical.
9. Forgiving a mistake keeps friends.
10. A wise person learns from correction.
11. Evil people always want to fight.
12. It's safer to meet a bear than a fool doing wrong.
13. People who return evil for good will always have trouble.

14. Stop fights before they escalate.
15. God hates when wrong is called right or right is called wrong.
16. Fools waste money on wisdom—they don't understand it.
17. A true friend always loves.
18. Don't make promises you can't keep.
19. People who love to argue cause trouble.
20. Twisted minds find no peace.
21. Parents are sad when their kids act foolish.
22. A happy heart is good for your health.
23. Bribes are wrong.
24. Wise people think ahead.
25. Foolish children bring parents sadness.
26. It's wrong to punish good people.
27. Wise people choose their words carefully.
28. Even quiet fools seem smart.

Proverbs 18

1. Selfish people hate advice.
2. Fools don't want to learn—they just talk.
3. Doing wrong brings shame.
4. Wise words are deep and helpful.
5. It's wrong to favor the guilty.
6. Fools cause fights.
7. Their words ruin them.
8. Gossip hurts people.
9. Lazy people are just like destroyers.
10. God is a safe place.
11. Rich people trust their money too much.
12. Pride comes before a fall.
13. Don't answer before listening.
14. A strong spirit helps in sickness.
15. Wise people want to learn.
16. A gift opens doors.
17. The first story sounds right until someone else speaks.
18. Some fights need help to settle.
19. A hurt brother is hard to win back.
20. Your words bring results.
21. Words can give life or death.
22. Finding a good spouse is a blessing.
23. Poor people beg; rich people speak harshly.
24. A true friend stays close.

Proverbs 19

1. It's better to be poor and honest than rich and foolish.
2. Rushing causes mistakes.
3. People ruin their lives and blame God.
4. Rich people have many friends.
5. Liars will be punished.
6. Everyone wants something from rich people.
7. Even family avoids the poor.
8. Love wisdom and you help yourself.
9. Witnesses who lie will be punished.
10. Fools shouldn't live like kings.
11. A wise person stays calm and forgives.
12. A king's anger is dangerous.
13. A foolish child brings pain.
14. A wise wife is from God.
15. Laziness leads to sleep and hunger.
16. Obey God and save your life.
17. Helping the poor honors God.
18. Correct your child while there's hope.
19. Angry people will keep getting into trouble.
20. Listen to advice and become wise.
21. People make plans, but God decides.
22. Loyalty matters more than money.

23. Respecting God leads to peace.
24. Lazy people won't even lift their food.
25. Punish mockers, and others will learn.
26. A child who hurts parents brings shame.
27. Stop listening to lies.
28. Wicked people enjoy wrong.
29. Mockers will be punished.

Proverbs 20

1. Wine makes people loud and foolish.
2. A king's anger is like a roar—don't make him mad.
3. Avoiding fights shows wisdom.
4. Lazy people don't work and end up hungry.
5. Good ideas are deep—wise people pull them out.
6. Many people say they're loyal, but few really are.
7. Good people live right. Their kids are blessed.
8. A king sees the truth and judges fairly.
9. No one is perfect.
10. God hates cheating.
11. Even kids show what kind of people they are by how they act.
12. God made eyes and ears—He sees and hears all.
13. Don't love sleep or you'll be poor.
14. Some people say, "It's no good," then buy it and brag.
15. Wisdom is better than gold.
16. Don't make promises for people you don't trust.
17. Stolen food might taste good but brings trouble.
18. Good plans need advice.
19. Gossips can't be trusted.
20. Respect your parents—or you'll lose everything.
21. Quick riches don't last.
22. Don't try to get even—let God handle it.
23. God hates cheating.
24. God guides our steps.
25. Don't make promises too fast.
26. Good leaders punish evil.
27. God sees deep inside us.
28. Love and truth keep a leader strong.
29. Young people have strength. Old people have wisdom.
30. Pain can teach a lesson.

Proverbs 21

1. God guides a king's heart like water in His hands.
2. People think they're right, but God sees the truth.
3. Doing right is better than sacrifice.
4. Proud hearts and evil thoughts are sin.
5. Careful plans bring success. Rushing brings failure.
6. Riches gained by lying will disappear.
7. Wicked people hurt themselves.
8. Guilty people walk crooked paths.
9. Better to live alone than with a nagging wife.
10. Evil people want to hurt others.
11. When mockers are punished, others get smarter.
12. God watches the wicked and brings justice.
13. Ignoring the poor leads to being ignored.
14. A secret gift can calm anger.
15. Doing right brings joy.
16. People who ignore wisdom will suffer.
17. Loving fun too much leads to poverty.
18. Wicked people fall into their own traps.

19. Better to live in the desert than with a mean wife.
20. Wise people save. Fools spend everything.
21. Doing right brings life.
22. Wisdom can beat strong cities.
23. Watch your words and stay out of trouble.
24. Proud people make trouble.
25. Lazy people want much but get little.
26. Good people give freely.
27. God hates offerings from wicked people.
28. Liars are ruined.
29. Wicked people pretend to be brave.
30. No plan works against God.
31. You can prepare for battle, but God gives victory.

Proverbs 22

1. A good name is better than riches.
2. God made both rich and poor.
3. Wise people see danger and avoid it.
4. Respect for God brings life, riches, and honor.
5. Trouble comes from bad choices.
6. Teach kids the right way—they'll remember.
7. Borrowers become servants.
8. Evil brings more trouble.
9. Generous people are blessed.
10. Kick out mockers, and peace will come.
11. God loves honest hearts.
12. God protects knowledge and blocks liars.
13. Lazy people make excuses.
14. Wrong people trap others.
15. Children need correction.
16. Hurting the poor or helping the rich just brings loss.
17. Listen and learn—this brings wisdom.
18. Keep these words in your heart.
19. Trust God with your life.
20. These sayings help you know truth.
21. They teach you to speak truth.
22. Don't cheat the poor or hurt the helpless.
23. God will defend them.
24. Don't be friends with angry people.
25. You might become like them.
26. Don't make promises you can't pay.
27. Or you'll lose everything.
28. Don't move boundary markers.
29. Skilled workers will serve leaders.

Proverbs 23

1. Don't eat too much when you're with important people.
2. Control yourself.
3. Don't want their fancy food—it may trick you.
4. Don't work just to get rich.
5. Money disappears quickly.
6. Don't eat with selfish people.
7. They may say "eat," but they don't mean it.
8. You'll regret it.
9. Don't waste wise words on fools.
10. Don't move boundary markers.
11. God defends the helpless.
12. Listen and learn.
13. Correct your children.
14. Discipline saves them from death.
15. A wise child makes parents happy.
16. I'm glad when you speak what's right.
17. Don't envy sinners. Respect God always.

18. Then your future will be good.
19. Be wise.
20. Don't hang out with drunkards or gluttons.
21. They become poor.
22. Respect your parents.
23. Buy truth and wisdom.
24. Good kids make parents proud.
25. Make your mom and dad glad.
26. Give God your heart.
27. Bad people are traps.
28. They lead to destruction.
29. Who has trouble? Those who drink too much.
30. Wine tricks people.
31. Don't be fooled by how it looks.
32. It will hurt you in the end.
33. You'll see strange things.
34. You'll feel out of control.
35. You'll be hurt and not remember it.
36. Then you'll want to drink again.

Proverbs 24

1. Don't envy evil people.
2. They plan violence.
3. A house is built with wisdom.
4. Knowledge fills it with good things.
5. Wise people are strong.
6. Get advice before you go to war.
7. Fools don't understand wisdom.
8. Evil people plan trouble.
9. Fools hate what's right.
10. Don't give up when it's hard.
11. Save people in danger.
12. God sees what you do.
13. Wisdom is sweet like honey.
14. It gives you a future.
15. Don't attack good people.
16. They get back up again.
17. Don't be glad when enemies fall.
18. God sees your heart.
19. Don't envy the wicked.
20. Evil people have no future.
21. Respect God and leaders.
22. Don't join rebels.
23. Don't judge unfairly.
24. People hate those who excuse the guilty.
25. But those who punish wrong are respected.
26. Honest words are good.
27. Finish your work before building your house.
28. Don't lie in court.
29. Don't say, "I'll get even."
30. I saw a lazy person's field—it was a mess.
31. It was full of weeds.
32. I learned something from it:
33. Lots of sleep and laziness brings poverty.

Proverbs 25

1. These are more proverbs from Solomon, copied by Hezekiah's men.
2. God hides some things; kings search for answers.
3. No one can fully understand a king's mind.
4. Remove trash from silver to make something pure.
5. Remove bad people from power to make a leader strong.
6. Don't brag in front of important people.
7. It's better to be invited up than told to go down.
8. Don't rush into fights.

9. Settle problems quietly.
10. Don't share secrets.
11. The right word at the right time is valuable.
12. Wise correction is like gold.
13. A good messenger brings peace.
14. Promises mean nothing if you don't keep them.
15. Patience can change minds.
16. Don't eat too much honey—you'll get sick.
17. Don't visit your neighbor too much—they'll get annoyed.
18. Lying about someone hurts them.
19. Trusting a bad person is like a broken tooth.
20. Singing to a sad person makes them feel worse.
21. Help your enemy if they're hungry or thirsty.
22. God will reward you.
23. Gossip causes anger.
24. Better to live on the roof than with a nagging wife.
25. Good news refreshes like cold water.
26. A good person who gives in to evil is like muddy water.
27. Too much honey isn't good.
28. A person with no self-control is like a broken wall.

Proverbs 26

1. Honor doesn't fit a fool.
2. A curse without cause won't stick.
3. Fools need correction.
4. Don't argue with fools, or you'll become like them.
5. Sometimes you must answer a fool to show truth.
6. Trusting a fool is asking for trouble.
7. A proverb means nothing to a fool.
8. Honoring a fool is like tying a rock to a sling.
9. A proverb in a fool's mouth is dangerous.
10. Hiring a fool is risky.
11. A fool repeats his mistakes.
12. A person who thinks they're wise when they're not is worse than a fool.
13. Lazy people make excuses.
14. Lazy people stay in bed.
15. Lazy people won't even feed themselves.
16. A lazy person thinks they're smarter than seven wise people.
17. Getting in other people's fights is foolish.
18. Joking about harm is wrong.
19. Don't say "I was only kidding" after causing pain.
20. No wood, no fire—no gossip, no fighting.
21. A troublemaker starts fights.
22. Gossip goes deep and hurts.
23. Kind words from a bad heart are fake.
24. Hateful people hide their hate.
25. Don't trust nice-sounding lies.
26. Hate will be exposed.
27. If you dig a trap for others, you'll fall in it.
28. Lies hurt others and ruin trust.

Proverbs 27

1. Don't brag about tomorrow—you don't know what will happen.
2. Let others praise you, not yourself.
3. A fool's anger is heavy and tiring.
4. Jealousy is worse than anger.
5. Honest correction is better than fake love.
6. A true friend tells the truth, even if it hurts.

7. A full person turns down even sweet food.
8. A person away from home feels lost.
9. Good friends bring joy.
10. Don't forget old friends.
11. Be wise and make your parents proud.
12. Wise people avoid danger.
13. Be careful when guaranteeing someone else's debt.
14. Too much talking early in the morning annoys people.
15. A nagging spouse is like constant dripping.
16. You can't stop them.
17. Friends help each other become better.
18. Care for your work, and you'll be rewarded.
19. People reflect what's in their hearts.
20. Death and desire are never full.
21. People are tested by praise.
22. A fool stays a fool, even after punishment.
23. Take care of your animals and work.
24. Money doesn't last forever.
25. Harvest comes in seasons.
26. Sheep and goats provide clothes and food.
27. They help feed your family.

Proverbs 28

1. Wicked people run even when no one's chasing.
2. A country with sin has lots of rulers.
3. A poor ruler hurts the poor.
4. People who break the law praise the wicked.
5. Evil people don't understand justice.
6. It's better to be poor and honest than rich and dishonest.
7. A wise child follows the law.
8. People who get rich by cheating will lose it.
9. God hates prayers from those who ignore Him.
10. Leading good people into sin is evil.
11. Rich people think they're smart, but the poor who see truth are wiser.
12. When good people win, everyone is happy.
13. Hiding sin leads to trouble. Confessing it brings mercy.
14. Respecting God keeps you safe.
15. A wicked ruler is like a roaring lion.
16. A greedy ruler ruins the land.
17. A guilty person will not rest.
18. Honest people stay safe.
19. Work hard to have food.
20. A faithful person is blessed.
21. Don't show favoritism.
22. Greedy people rush into poverty.
23. Honest correction helps more than flattery.
24. Stealing from family is wrong.
25. Greed causes fighting.
26. Don't trust yourself too much.
27. Help the poor and you'll lack nothing.
28. Hiding from the truth leads to ruin.

Proverbs 29

1. People who reject correction will suddenly fall.
2. When good people lead, everyone is happy.
3. A wise son makes his parents glad.
4. Fair rulers keep a country strong.
5. Flattery is a trap.
6. Evil people get trapped in their own sin.
7. Good people care about the poor.
8. Mockers stir up trouble.

9. Wise people don't win fights with fools.
10. Evil people hate honest people.
11. Fools speak without thinking.
12. A wicked leader gets bad advice.
13. God made both rich and poor.
14. Fair kings rule long.
15. Correction teaches children.
16. Wicked people cause trouble.
17. Correct your child, and they'll bring peace.
18. People without God's word run wild.
19. Words alone aren't enough—actions matter.
20. Quick words lead to trouble.
21. Spoiled servants bring sorrow.
22. Angry people start fights.
23. Pride brings you down.
24. Don't help a thief.
25. Fear traps people. Trusting God keeps you safe.
26. People seek approval, but God decides.
27. Good people hate evil.

Proverbs 30

Sayings of Agur

1. I am not wise on my own.
2. I don't know everything.
3. Only God fully understands.
4. No one but God controls heaven and earth.
5. God's word is always true.
6. Don't add to it.
7. I ask for two things:
8. Keep lies far from me, and
9. Give me just enough—not too much or too little.
10. Don't lie about others.
11. Some people disrespect parents.
12. Some think they are pure but are not.
13. Some are proud and look down on others.
14. Some hurt the poor.
15. Greed never stops.
16. Four things never get enough: the grave, a dry womb, land needing rain, and fire.
17. Disrespectful kids will be punished.
18. Four things amaze me:
19. an eagle in the sky, a snake on a rock, a ship on the sea, and a man with a woman.
20. Some people sin and think they've done nothing wrong.
21. Four things shake the earth:
22. a slave who becomes king, a fool who gets full,
23. a hated woman who marries, and a maid who replaces her boss.
24. Four small but wise creatures:
25. ants store food,
26. rock badgers make safe homes,
27. locusts work together,
28. lizards can go anywhere.
29. Four things move with confidence:
30. a lion, a rooster, a goat, and a king with his army.
31. Don't brag or act foolish—or you'll suffer.

Proverbs 31

Sayings of King Lemuel and the Wise Woman

1. These are words from King Lemuel's mother.
2. Don't waste your strength on women who destroy kings.
3. Don't get drunk—it makes leaders forget what's right.
4. Speak up for people who can't speak for themselves.

5. Help the poor and needy.
6. A strong woman is hard to find—she is worth more than jewels.
7. Her husband trusts her.
8. She works hard and provides food.
9. She gets up early.
10. She buys land and plants food.
11. She is strong and smart.
12. She helps the poor.
13. She prepares her family for every season.
14. She is not lazy.
15. Her words are wise and kind.
16. She teaches her kids well.
17. Her husband is proud of her.
18. Many women do great things, but she is the best.
19. Charm is tricky, and beauty fades.
20. But a woman who respects God should be praised.
21. Give her credit for her work.

– Ecclesiastes –

Life without God feels meaningless, but trusting Him brings purpose.

Ecclesiastes 1

1. These are the words of a wise teacher, son of David.
2. Everything feels empty and pointless.
3. What does a person gain from all their work?
4. People come and go, but the earth stays.
5. The sun rises and sets again.
6. The wind blows around in circles.
7. Rivers flow into the sea, but the sea never fills up.
8. Nothing ever feels finished.
9. What happened before will happen again.
10. Nothing is truly new.
11. People forget what happened long ago.
12. I, the teacher, ruled over Israel in Jerusalem.
13. I studied everything people do. It was tiring.
14. I saw that it's all chasing nothing.
15. What's broken can't be fixed.
16. I said, "I'm very wise, smarter than others before me."
17. So I studied wisdom and foolishness.
18. But more wisdom brings more sadness.

Ecclesiastes 2

1. I said, "I'll try fun and pleasure." But it felt empty.
2. Laughing didn't help.
3. I tried wine and foolish fun.
4. I built houses and planted gardens.
5. I made parks and planted trees.
6. I made lakes for watering plants.
7. I had workers, animals, and wealth.
8. I had silver, gold, singers, and everything I wanted.
9. I became great.
10. I tried everything fun.
11. But when I looked at all I did, it still felt pointless.
12. Then I thought about wisdom vs. foolishness.
13. Wisdom is better than foolishness.
14. But both wise and foolish people die.
15. So I thought, "What's the point?"
16. People forget both the wise and the foolish.
17. Life felt meaningless.
18. I hated my hard work. Someone else would get it all.

19. And they might waste it.
20. That made me feel hopeless.
21. You can work wisely, but someone else will take it.
22. What do people get for all their work?
23. Work brings pain, worry, and no rest.
24. The best thing is to eat, drink, and enjoy your work.
25. Only God makes that possible.
26. God gives wisdom and joy to good people.
27. But sinners gather things only to lose them.
28. It's all still meaningless.

Ecclesiastes 3

1. There's a right time for everything.
2. A time to be born and a time to die.
3. A time to plant and a time to harvest.
4. A time to cry and a time to laugh.
5. A time to keep and a time to throw away.
6. A time to be silent and a time to speak.
7. A time for love and a time for hate.
8. A time for war and a time for peace.
9. What does work really give us?
10. I saw that God gives us work to do.
11. He makes everything right at the right time.
12. People should enjoy life.
13. Enjoying your work is a gift from God.
14. What God does lasts forever.
15. What happens now has happened before.
16. I saw unfairness in court.
17. But I know God will judge all.
18. People and animals both die.
19. We all have the same breath.
20. All go to the same place—dust.
21. Who knows if our spirit goes up?
22. So enjoy your work, because that's what we get.

Ecclesiastes 4

1. I saw people suffering. No one helped them.
2. It's better to be dead than alive.
3. Better still is to never be born.
4. I saw people work hard just to compete. That's also pointless.
5. Lazy people destroy themselves.
6. Peace with less is better than stress with more.
7. I saw someone with no family working hard.
8. But who are they working for? It made no sense.
9. Two people are better than one.
10. If one falls, the other helps.
11. Two people stay warm together.
12. Two can fight off trouble better than one.
13. A poor wise child is better than a foolish old king.
14. Even if the child was in prison, he can still rise.
15. Many people follow the new leader.
16. But in time, they forget him too. That's also pointless.

Ecclesiastes 5

1. Be careful when you go to God's house.
2. Listen more than you speak.
3. Too many words mean nothing.
4. Don't make promises to God you won't keep.
5. It's better not to promise than to promise and not do it.

6. Don't say, "It was a mistake." God hears everything.
7. Too many words bring trouble. Respect God.
8. Don't be shocked if you see unfairness. Even rulers answer to higher ones.
9. A king still depends on the land.
10. Loving money never brings peace.
11. More money means more problems.
12. Workers sleep well; the rich often don't.
13. Some people lose everything by being greedy.
14. They leave nothing for their children.
15. You leave the world with nothing, just like you came.
16. So chasing riches is pointless.
17. Many live in darkness, pain, and anger.
18. It's best to enjoy your work and the life God gives.
19. If God gives you money, enjoy it.
20. You won't worry if you enjoy what God gives.

Ecclesiastes 6

1. I've seen something very sad.
2. God gives someone wealth, but they don't enjoy it. Others take it.
3. A man could have 100 kids and live long, but die unhappy—it's all meaningless.
4. It's better not to be born than to live a miserable life.
5. Even if you live 2,000 years but never enjoy it, what's the point?
6. We all end up dead.
7. People work to eat but are never full.
8. The wise don't gain more than the foolish.
9. Be happy with what you have.
10. You can't change what God has decided.
11. More words don't bring meaning.
12. No one knows what's best in life—it's short and unclear.

Ecclesiastes 7

1. A good name is better than nice perfume.
2. It's better to go to a funeral than a party.
3. Sadness can teach you more than laughter.
4. Wise people think about death.
5. Listen to wise people, not fools.
6. Fools laugh but say nothing helpful.
7. Money can help, but bribes ruin people.
8. Finishing something is better than starting.
9. Don't be quick to get angry.
10. Don't say, "Things were better back then."
11. Wisdom is good and protects you.
12. Wisdom gives life.
13. Accept what God does.
14. Be happy in good times. Learn in bad times.
15. I've seen good people suffer and bad people succeed.
16. Don't try to be too good or too wise.
17. Don't be too evil or foolish.
18. Respect God and stay balanced.
19. Wisdom gives strength.
20. No one on earth is perfect.
21. Don't listen to gossip—you might hear bad things.
22. You've spoken badly about others too.
23. I tried to be wise, but it's too deep.
24. No one can find out everything God has done.

Ecclesiastes 8

1. Wisdom makes you bright and kind.
2. Respect the king.
3. Do what the king says.
4. His word has power.
5. Wise people know the right time and way.
6. Every job has a proper time.
7. No one knows the future.
8. No one controls the wind or their own death.
9. People often hurt others.
10. Wicked people may get honor, but it won't last.
11. When punishment is slow, people keep doing wrong.
12. A sinner may live long, but it's better to fear God.
13. The wicked won't truly win.
14. Sometimes good people suffer, and bad people get rewarded. That's unfair.
15. So enjoy life—eating, drinking, and being happy are good gifts from God.
16. I tried to understand everything.
17. But I realized no one can fully understand what God does.

Ecclesiastes 9

1. Good people and bad people all face death.
2. Everyone shares the same fate—life ends.
3. That seems unfair.
4. But being alive is better than being dead.
5. The living know they'll die. The dead know nothing.
6. Their love, hate, and plans are gone.
7. So enjoy your food and drink.
8. Be happy.
9. Enjoy life with your wife.
10. Do your best while you're alive.
11. Life doesn't always go to the fastest or smartest.
12. No one knows when their time will come.
13. I saw a poor man save a city with his wisdom.
14. But no one remembered him.
15. Wisdom is better than strength,
16. even if people forget the wise.
17. Quiet wisdom is better than loud fools.
18. Wisdom is better than weapons—but one fool can ruin a lot.

Ecclesiastes 10

1. A little foolishness can ruin wisdom.
2. Wise people choose the right way.
3. Fools show they are foolish everywhere they go.
4. Stay calm when leaders are angry.
5. I've seen foolish people given power.
6. Servants may ride while leaders walk.
7. If you dig a pit, you might fall in.
8. If you break a wall, you might get hurt.
9. Work carefully, or you could be injured.
10. If the axe is dull, sharpen it—wisdom helps you succeed.
11. A snake bite does no good if you don't charm it first.
12. Wise words help; foolish words destroy.
13. Fools start with nonsense and end in madness.
14. Fools talk too much. No one knows the future.
15. Fools wear themselves out but don't know how to get home.
16. A country is in trouble with childish leaders.

17. A country is strong with wise, self-controlled leaders.
18. Lazy people ruin houses.
19. People enjoy food and drink, but money solves problems.
20. Don't curse the king, even in secret. Birds might tell him.

Ecclesiastes 11

1. Be generous—you don't know what good will come from it.
2. Share with others. Trouble might come.
3. Rain falls, and trees stay where they fall.
4. If you wait for perfect weather, you'll never plant.
5. You don't know how life starts or how God works.
6. So plant seeds in the morning and evening.
7. Light is good.
8. Enjoy your life, even if you live many years.
9. Be happy when you're young.
10. But remember—God will judge everything you do.

Ecclesiastes 12

1. Remember God while you are young.
2. Don't wait until life gets hard and you grow old.
3. Your body will grow weak.
4. Your eyes and ears won't work well.
5. You'll be afraid of falling.
6. Then you'll die and return to the dust.
7. Your spirit will go back to God.
8. Life can feel empty.
9. The teacher was wise and taught people knowledge.
10. He chose the best words to help people.
11. Wise words guide like a stick.
12. Be careful—there are too many books, and too much study is tiring.
13. Final message: Respect God and obey His commands.
14. God will judge everything, good or bad, even what's done in secret.

– Song of Songs –

A poetic love story celebrating marriage and romantic love.

Song of Songs 1

1. This is Solomon's song.
2. I love your kisses.
3. You smell good and your name is respected.
4. Take me with you. I'm happy to be with you.
5. I am dark-skinned but beautiful.
6. Don't stare at me because I'm dark.
7. Tell me where you take care of your sheep.
8. If you don't know, follow the tracks to the sheep.
9. You are beautiful, like a strong horse.
10. Your cheeks and neck look lovely.
11. We will make you pretty jewelry.
12. My king is near me; I smell perfume.
13. I keep your love close like perfume.
14. You are like flowers in a vineyard.
15. You are so beautiful, my love.
16. You are handsome too.
17. We sit together on soft grass and trees cover us.

Song of Songs 2

1. I am like a flower in a field.

2. You are more beautiful than all others.
3. You are strong and safe like a good tree.
4. You brought me to your home with love.
5. I feel weak with love.
6. Your arms are around me.
7. Wait for the right time for love.
8. I hear you coming, jumping over hills.
9. You are strong and quick.
10. You say, "Come with me."
11. Winter is gone.
12. Flowers are blooming.
13. Trees are growing fruit.
14. Let me see your face and hear your voice.
15. Stop little problems before they ruin our love.
16. I belong to you, and you belong to me.
17. Come back before the night is over.

Song of Songs 3

1. I looked for you at night and couldn't find you.
2. I went into the city to search.
3. I asked the guards, "Have you seen him?"
4. I found you and didn't let go.
5. Wait for the right time for love.
6. Look, here comes Solomon's carriage.
7. It is surrounded by strong guards.
8. Each guard has a sword.
9. Solomon made the carriage with silver and gold.
10. Inside is beautiful.
11. People celebrate the king and his wedding.

Song of Songs 4

1. You are very beautiful.
2. Your eyes are gentle.
3. Your hair is long and lovely.
4. Your smile is perfect.
5. Your lips are red and sweet.
6. Your neck is strong and proud.
7. You are perfect to me.
8. Come with me and be safe.
9. You make my heart happy.
10. Your love is better than anything.
11. Your kisses and words are sweet.
12. You are like a garden saved just for me.
13. You have the best smells and fruits.
14. Everything about you is lovely.
15. You are like a fresh spring of water.
16. Let the wind blow through your garden. Let your love be shared.

Song of Songs 5

1. I have come to be with you.
2. I was asleep, but my heart was awake.
3. You knocked on the door and said, "Let me in."
4. I didn't want to get up.
5. But I got up to open the door.
6. You were gone. I couldn't find you.
7. The city guards found me and hurt me.
8. I asked the women, "If you see him, tell him I miss him."
9. They asked, "Why is he so special?"
10. I said, "He is strong and handsome."
11. "His eyes and smile are gentle."
12. "He speaks kindly."
13. "He is everything I want."

Song of Songs 6

1. The women ask, "Where did he go?"

2. I say, "He went to the garden."
3. I belong to him, and he belongs to me.
4. He says, "You are beautiful."
5. "Your eyes shine."
6. "Your hair is long and pretty."
7. "Many women are lovely, but you are the best."
8. "Even queens praise you."
9. "You shine like the morning."
10. People look at you and are amazed.
11. I went to the garden to see the flowers.
12. I felt close to you without trying.

Song of Songs 7

1. He says, "You look beautiful from head to toe."
2. "Your legs are graceful."
3. "Your body is shaped with care."
4. "Your eyes are soft."
5. "Your hair flows like silk."
6. "You are lovely and kind."
7. "You stand tall and proud."
8. "Your love is like sweet fruit."
9. "Your kisses are like the best wine."
10. She says, "I belong to you, and you want me."
11. "Let's go out to the fields."
12. "We will rise early and enjoy the garden."
13. "The flowers are blooming."
14. "I have saved my love for you."

Song of Songs 8

1. I wish you were like my brother so I could hug you in public.
2. I would bring you home and care for you.
3. Your arm would hold me close.
4. Do not rush love. Wait for the right time.
5. "Who is this coming up from the desert?"
6. Keep me close to your heart forever.
7. Real love is strong and never ends.
8. We have a little sister. Let's protect her until she grows.
9. If she is good, we will reward her.
10. I am grown and feel strong. I bring peace to him.
11. Solomon had a vineyard.
12. He rented it to others. But my love belongs only to me.
13. He says, "I want to hear your voice."
14. She says, "Come quickly, like a deer running through the hills."

– Isaiah –

Isaiah warns of judgment but promises hope through a future Savior.

Isaiah 1

1. These are the words God gave Isaiah about Judah and Jerusalem.
2. God says, "I raised children, but they turned against Me."
3. Even animals know their owner. My people do not know Me.
4. They have done wrong and walked away from Me.
5. Why keep disobeying and getting punished?
6. You are hurt from head to toe.
7. Your land is ruined and taken by strangers.
8. Jerusalem is alone, like a small hut in a field.
9. If God hadn't saved a few people, we'd be destroyed like Sodom.
10. Listen, you leaders who act like Sodom.

11. God says, "I don't want your sacrifices. I'm tired of them."
12. "Stop bringing Me offerings. They mean nothing."
13. "I hate your gatherings and celebrations."
14. "I will not listen to your prayers."
15. "Your hands are full of sin."
16. "Wash yourselves. Do what's right."
17. "Help the weak. Be fair. Defend the helpless."
18. "Even if your sins are red like blood, I can make them clean."
19. "If you obey Me, you will have good things."
20. "If you refuse, you will be destroyed."
21. Jerusalem used to be good. Now it's full of evil.
22. What was pure is now dirty.
23. Your leaders love bribes and ignore the poor.
24. God says, "I will punish those who turned against Me."
25. "I will clean away your sins."
26. "I will give you good judges again."
27. People who return to Me will be saved.
28. Sinners will be crushed.
29. You loved false gods, but they will bring shame.
30. You will be like a dead tree with no water.
31. You and your idols will both burn, and no one will stop it.

Isaiah 2

1. This is another message Isaiah saw about Judah and Jerusalem.
2. One day, God's house will be the highest place, and people will come to it.
3. Nations will say, "Let's go to God so He can teach us."
4. God will settle arguments between countries.
5. People will stop making weapons and start making tools.
6. But Your people have turned to other gods.
7. They trust silver, gold, and armies.
8. They bow down to idols they made.
9. So people will be brought low.
10. Run and hide when God comes.
11. Proud people will be humbled. Only God will be honored.
12. God has a day to punish the proud.
13. He will bring down everything that seems strong.
14. Big mountains, high towers, strong walls—He will tear them down.
15. Ships and treasures will not matter.
16. All pride will be crushed.
17. Idols will be thrown away.
18. People will hide in caves from God's anger.
19. They'll throw away their idols made of silver and gold.
20. They'll run from God's power.
21. Don't trust people—they can't save you.

Isaiah 3

1. God will take away food, water, and leaders from Jerusalem.
2. There will be no soldiers, judges, or wise people.
3. No one will know what to do.
4. Children will rule, and people will fight.
5. Young people will disrespect older ones.
6. No one will want to lead.
7. They will say, "I can't help you."
8. Jerusalem has fallen because people speak and act against God.

9. Their sin is easy to see.
10. Tell good people they will be okay.
11. But evil people will suffer.
12. Children and women rule over the people.
13. God is ready to judge.
14. He will judge leaders who hurt others.
15. He says, "Why do you crush My people?"
16. Women in Jerusalem are proud and show off.
17. So God will make them bald and ashamed.
18. He will take away their fancy things.
19. Their jewelry, clothes, and perfume will be gone.
20. They will smell bad instead of nice.
21. They will wear ropes instead of belts.
22. They will be sad and hurt.
23. Their men will die in war.
24. The city will cry and sit alone.

Isaiah 4

1. Seven women will grab one man and say, "Let us be called by your name. We will take care of ourselves."
2. But the Lord will make His people beautiful again.
3. Those who survive will be called holy.
4. God will wash away all the evil.
5. God will protect His people like a cloud in the day and fire at night.
6. He will be like a shelter from heat and storm.

Isaiah 5

1. God had a vineyard (His people), and He took care of it.
2. He hoped for good grapes, but it gave bad ones.
3. God says, "What more could I have done?"
4. "I will stop caring for this vineyard."
5. "I won't protect it. Weeds will grow."
6. God wanted fairness, but saw violence and cries for help.
7. Trouble is coming to those who buy everything for themselves.
8. They will live alone in empty houses.
9. Their fields will grow nothing.
10. People party and forget God.
11. They don't see His work.
12. So they'll go into exile and suffer.
13. Only a few will be saved.
14. Many will die and be buried.
15. Proud people will be brought low.
16. God alone will be honored.
17. The land will be left for animals.
18. Some people run toward sin.
19. They dare God to act.
20. Some say wrong is right and right is wrong.
21. They think they're smart but aren't.
22. They brag about drinking.
23. They let the guilty go free for money.
24. But fire will destroy them.
25. God is angry because they rejected Him.
26. He will call in enemy nations.
27. They will come quickly and attack.
28. Their weapons are ready.
29. They will roar like lions and bring fear.
30. People will see only darkness and trouble.

Isaiah 6

1. Isaiah saw God on a high throne.
2. Angels called out, "Holy, holy, holy is the Lord!"

3. The place shook, and smoke filled the room.
4. Isaiah said, "I'm in trouble! I'm a sinner."
5. An angel touched his mouth with a hot coal and said, "Your sin is gone."
6. God asked, "Who will go for us?" Isaiah said, "I will go!"
7. God said, "Tell the people the truth, even if they don't listen."
8. Isaiah asked, "How long?"
9. God said, "Until the land is ruined."
10. A small part will be left, but even it will be burned.
11. Yet from that, something new will grow.

Isaiah 7

1. Enemies came to fight Jerusalem but failed.
2. The people were scared.
3. God told Isaiah, "Take your son and meet King Ahaz."
4. Say, "Don't be afraid. These enemies won't win."
5. "In 65 years, their land will be gone."
6. "If you don't believe, you won't stand strong."
7. God told Ahaz, "Ask Me for a sign."
8. Ahaz said, "I won't ask."
9. Isaiah said, "God will give a sign anyway."
10. "A young woman will have a baby named Immanuel (God is with us)."
11. "Before the child knows right from wrong, your enemies will be gone."
12. But hard times will come.
13. Foreign kings will take over.
14. People will suffer from hunger and pain.
15. The land will be empty and wild.

Isaiah 8

1. God told Isaiah, "Write this name: Maher-Shalal-Hash-Baz."
2. Isaiah's wife had a baby boy.
3. God said, "Before he says 'Mom' or 'Dad,' the enemy will be defeated."
4. The people refused God's way.
5. So God will bring a big army to flood the land.
6. But He will protect those who trust Him.
7. Isaiah was told not to fear what others fear.
8. Trust only in God.
9. God will be a safe place—but also a warning to many.
10. Some will trip over His truth.
11. Isaiah and his children are signs from God.
12. Don't ask dead people for answers.
13. Look to God's word instead.
14. People who ignore God will walk in darkness.

Isaiah 9

1. But there is hope. Light will come.
2. People in darkness will see a great light.
3. God will give joy and freedom.
4. He will break their chains.
5. Every soldier's gear will be burned.
6. A child will be born to lead us.
7. He will be called: Wonderful, Counselor, Mighty God, Prince of Peace.
8. He will rule forever with fairness.
9. God will make this happen.
10. But Israel was proud and didn't listen.
11. So God let enemies attack them.
12. The people still didn't turn back to Him.

13. So God cut off their leaders.
14. They misled others.
15. God didn't help them because they were all evil.
16. Everyone was hurting each other.
17. Even children and widows were not safe.
18. Evil was everywhere like a fire.
19. People turned against each other.
20. They were never satisfied.
21. They fought their own people.
22. This was God's judgment, and His anger was not over.

Isaiah 10

1. God says, "Trouble is coming to unfair leaders."
2. They hurt the poor and take from the weak.
3. When punishment comes, who will help you?
4. Nothing will stop God's judgment.
5. God used Assyria to punish His people.
6. But Assyria thought it won by its own power.
7. It planned to destroy many nations.
8. It said, "All kings are the same."
9. "We beat strong cities; Jerusalem will fall too."
10. But God says, "After I use Assyria, I will punish them for their pride."
11. They thought they were greater than God.
12. God says, "Can a tool brag over the one who uses it?"
13. God will stop the proud leaders.
14. A few people will survive.
15. Only those who trust God will return.
16. Don't be afraid of Assyria.
17. God will destroy them like fire.
18. He will burn up the enemy's power.
19. Only a few trees (people) will be left.
20. The people who remain will trust God.
21. A small group will return.
22. God said destruction is coming, but not all will die.
23. God will finish what He started.
24. So don't be afraid, even if the enemy strikes.
25. God's anger will soon end.
26. He will punish your enemies like He did in Egypt.
27. The burden will be lifted.
28. Assyria is getting closer to Jerusalem.
29. People are scared.
30. But God will stop them.
31. He will shake them.
32. He will cut them down like trees.
33. The proud will fall.

Isaiah 11

1. A new leader will come from Jesse's family.
2. God's Spirit will be with him—he will be wise and strong.
3. He will enjoy obeying God.
4. He will judge fairly and help the poor.
5. He will punish the wicked.
6. Wild animals will live in peace with each other.
7. Children will be safe with them.
8. There will be no harm in God's kingdom.
9. Everyone will know God.
10. The new leader will bring people together.
11. God will bring His people back from other lands.
12. He will gather them into one group again.

13. The tribes of Israel will stop fighting.
14. They will defeat their enemies together.
15. God will make a way for His people to return.
16. It will be like when He brought them out of Egypt.

Isaiah 12

1. You will say, "Thank You, God. You were angry, but now You comfort me."
2. "I trust You. I'm not afraid."
3. You will be happy to be saved.
4. Say, "Praise the Lord. Tell others what He's done."
5. "Sing to Him—He has done great things."
6. "Shout for joy! God is with us!"

Isaiah 13

1. This is a message about Babylon.
2. God calls soldiers to attack.
3. He gathers His army.
4. They come from far away to punish Babylon.
5. Everyone is scared—hearts melt with fear.
6. The day of the Lord is near.
7. People will cry and shake.
8. They will be weak and scared.
9. God's day will be full of anger.
10. The stars and sun will stop shining.
11. God will punish the world for its evil.
12. Many people will die.
13. The earth will shake.
14. People will run like scared animals.
15. Everyone caught will die.
16. Families will be torn apart.
17. God will send the Medes to attack.
18. They don't care about gold or people.
19. Babylon will be destroyed.
20. No one will live there again.
21. Wild animals will take over the land.
22. Babylon's time is almost over.

Isaiah 14

1. God will have mercy on Israel and bring them back home.
2. Foreign people will help and serve them.
3. God will give rest from pain and slavery.
4. You will say, "The king who hurt us is gone!"
5. God broke the power of evil rulers.
6. They crushed people with no mercy.
7. Now the whole earth is at peace.
8. Even trees are happy.
9. The grave is ready for the fallen king.
10. Others will say, "You are weak like us now."
11. You lost your power and pride.
12. You tried to rise high, but now you are brought low.
13. You said, "I will be like God."
14. But you were thrown down to the grave.
15. Others stare and say, "Is this the man who scared nations?"
16. He destroyed cities and locked people in.
17. But now he is alone and forgotten.
18. Other kings are buried with honor.
19. But you are left like trash.
20. Your children will not rule.
21. Their family will be destroyed.
22. God says, "I will rise up and wipe them out."
23. "Babylon will be empty, full of swamps and animals."

24. God has promised to destroy Assyria too.
25. He will crush them in His land.
26. This will happen everywhere.
27. No one can stop what God plans.
28. This message came when King Ahaz died:
29. Don't be happy when your enemy falls.
30. The poor will be safe.
31. But other cities will be destroyed.
32. What will happen to God's people? He will protect them.

Isaiah 15

1. God speaks about Moab:
2. Cities in Moab will be destroyed overnight.
3. People will run to high places and cry.
4. Everyone is scared and sad.
5. People flee, crying as they go.
6. The land is dry.
7. People carry what they can.
8. The whole land hears their cries.
9. Water is full of blood.
10. God will bring even more trouble.

Isaiah 16

1. Moab sends gifts to Jerusalem.
2. They ask for shelter and protection.
3. God says, "Be fair and help the people."
4. Hide the refugees.
5. A new king will rule with love and fairness.
6. But Moab is proud and full of itself.
7. So Moab will cry when it is destroyed.
8. Its fields will be ruined.
9. No more grapes or harvest.
10. No more joy in the farms.
11. My heart hurts for Moab.
12. They will pray, but it won't help.
13. This is what God said before.
14. Now He says, "In three years, Moab will be small and weak. Only a few people will be left."

Isaiah 17

1. This is a message about Damascus:
2. Damascus will become ruins.
3. Israel's cities will be empty.
4. Israel will lose its strength.
5. Only a few people will be left.
6. Like a tree with just a few olives.
7. Then people will turn back to God.
8. They will stop worshiping idols.
9. Cities will be empty like abandoned places.
10. This happened because you forgot God.
11. You plant gardens, but they won't grow.
12. Many enemies will come like rushing water.
13. But God will stop them.
14. In the morning, they will be gone.

Isaiah 18

1. This is a message for the land beyond the rivers of Cush (Africa).
2. You send people in boats to deliver messages.
3. Everyone on earth, watch what God will do.
4. God says, "I will wait and watch quietly."
5. Before the harvest, He will cut down the enemy.
6. Their bodies will be left for birds and animals.

7. After that, people will bring gifts to God in Jerusalem.

Isaiah 19

1. This is a message about Egypt:
2. God will come quickly.
3. Egypt will fall apart.
4. They will fight each other.
5. The Nile River will dry up.
6. Canals and plants will die.
7. Fishermen will be sad.
8. Workers will be hopeless.
9. Leaders will make bad choices.
10. Egypt will be confused.
11. The princes of Egypt don't understand.
12. Their wise men give bad advice.
13. God has made them foolish.
14. Egypt will fail in everything.
15. On that day, Egyptians will be afraid of Judah.
16. They will fear God.
17. People in five cities in Egypt will speak Hebrew and worship God.
18. One city will be called "City of the Sun."
19. There will be an altar to God in Egypt.
20. It will be a sign that God is watching.
21. God will show Himself to them.
22. They will turn to Him, and He will heal them.
23. Egypt, Assyria, and Israel will be united.
24. They will worship together.
25. God will bless them all.

Isaiah 20

1. God gave this message to Isaiah when King Sargon of Assyria sent his army to capture Ashdod.
2. God told Isaiah, "Take off your clothes and shoes." So Isaiah walked around like that.
3. God said, "Isaiah is a sign."
4. Just like Isaiah walked barefoot, Egypt and Cush will be taken away with no clothes.
5. People who trusted them will be ashamed.
6. They will say, "We hoped Egypt would help us, but they could not save us."

Isaiah 21

1. This is a message about Babylon:
2. Trouble is coming like a storm.
3. Isaiah was filled with fear and pain.
4. He was too scared to even look.
5. The enemy was getting ready to attack while Babylon partied.
6. God told Isaiah, "Set a guard to watch."
7. The guard said, "I see horses and soldiers."
8. Then he shouted, "Babylon has fallen!"
9. Her idols are broken.
10. Isaiah said, "My people, I told you what I heard from God."
11. This is a message about Edom:
12. Someone asks, "How much longer is the night?"
13. The answer: "Morning is coming, but more night too."
14. This is a message about Arabia:
15. Travelers must hide.
16. The people of Kedar will soon be gone.
17. Only a few soldiers will be left.

Isaiah 22

1. This is a message about Jerusalem:

2. Why are you on your rooftops, celebrating?
3. Your leaders ran away but were captured.
4. Isaiah said, "Don't try to comfort me. I am full of sorrow."
5. This is a day of trouble from God.
6. Enemies broke down the city gates.
7. They filled the valleys with soldiers.
8. You tried to prepare but didn't look to God.
9. You fixed the walls and stored water.
10. You broke houses to make the walls stronger.
11. But you didn't ask God for help.
12. God called for sadness and repentance.
13. But instead, people said, "Let's eat and drink, for tomorrow we die."
14. God said, "You will be punished for this."
15. God told Isaiah, "Go speak to Shebna, the palace manager."
16. "Why are you making a fancy tomb for yourself?"
17. "You will be taken away and die in a foreign land."
18. "You will lose your position."
19. God said, "I will replace you with Eliakim."
20. "I will give him your job and make him a father to Jerusalem."
21. "He will be like a strong key no one can break."
22. "But even strong things can fall when God says so."

Isaiah 23

1. This is a message about Tyre:
2. Ships from far away will cry when they hear Tyre is ruined.
3. The sea routes are quiet now.
4. Sidon is ashamed because its people depended on Tyre.
5. Egypt will be shocked too.
6. Everyone should cry—Tyre is gone.
7. This was once a happy city.
8. God planned this to stop human pride.
9. He wanted to humble the rich and strong.
10. Go to other lands if you must—but Tyre will still fall.
11. God raised His hand, and kingdoms shook.
12. Sidon will not escape either.
13. Look at Babylon—it was destroyed too.
14. Ships of Tarshish, your strong city is gone.
15. Tyre will be forgotten for 70 years.
16. After that, it will try to come back.
17. But its profits will go to God's people.

Isaiah 24

1. God will make the earth empty and ruined.
2. Everyone will suffer—rich, poor, servant, master.
3. The land will be completely destroyed.
4. The earth is sad and dry.
5. People broke God's laws.
6. So the earth is cursed, and many die.
7. Joy is gone.
8. Music and dancing have stopped.
9. No one drinks with joy.
10. Cities are broken and silent.
11. People cry for wine, but there's none.
12. Towns are in ruins.
13. Only a few people are left.
14. They praise God from far away.
15. They honor God everywhere.

16. Isaiah hears songs, but he says, "I am sad because people still do wrong."
17. Trouble and traps are coming for everyone.
18. The earth is shaking.
19. Everything is broken.
20. The earth falls and won't get up.
21. God will punish those in heaven and on earth.
22. He will lock them up.
23. God will rule from Jerusalem, and everyone will see His glory.

Isaiah 25

1. Lord, You are my God. I will praise You.
2. You destroyed strong cities.
3. Powerful nations will fear You.
4. You help the poor and needy.
5. You stop cruel people like a cloud blocks the sun.
6. God will make a great feast for all people.
7. He will remove sadness and death.
8. God will wipe away every tear.
9. People will say, "This is our God—we trusted Him, and He saved us!"
10. God's hand will protect His people.
11. But proud enemies will be crushed.
12. Their strong walls will be knocked down to the ground.

Isaiah 26

1. In that day, Judah will sing this song:
2. Our city is strong. God protects us.
3. God gives peace to those who trust Him.
4. Trust in God forever.
5. He brings down the proud.
6. The poor will walk on the ruins of the proud.
7. God makes a straight path for good people.
8. We wait for You, Lord.
9. We want to know You more.
10. Evil people do not learn, even when life is good.
11. Lord, Your hand is lifted high, but they don't see it.
12. You give us peace.
13. Others ruled us, but only You are our God.
14. Our old enemies are dead and gone.
15. You made our nation grow.
16. When we were in trouble, we prayed to You.
17. We were like a woman having a baby.
18. But we gave birth to nothing.
19. Yet Your people will rise again.
20. Go inside and wait for a little while.
21. God is coming to punish the earth.

Isaiah 27

1. God will punish the dragon-like enemy.
2. He will care for His vineyard—His people.
3. He will guard them day and night.
4. He is not angry with them.
5. Let them come to Him for peace.
6. His people will grow and bless the world.
7. God punished them, but not like He did others.
8. He punished them to make them better.
9. This removed their sin.
10. Empty cities will be destroyed.
11. People forgot God, so they will be left behind.

12. God will gather His people one by one.
13. A trumpet will sound, and His people will come back to worship Him.

Isaiah 28

1. This is a warning to Ephraim (northern Israel):
2. They are proud and drunk.
3. Their beauty will be crushed.
4. A powerful army is coming.
5. But God will be a crown for His people.
6. He will give strength to judges and soldiers.
7. But priests and prophets are drunk and confused.
8. Their tables are full of mess.
9. They think they are too smart to learn.
10. But they learn little by little.
11. God will speak to them in a way they don't understand.
12. He said, "Come rest," but they wouldn't listen.
13. So they will fall.
14. God says, "You rulers make deals with death."
15. "But I am putting a strong foundation in Zion."
16. "Trust in Me and you won't panic."
17. God will judge fairly.
18. Your deals with death won't work.
19. Trouble will come.
20. You won't find rest or safety.
21. God will act in a strange and surprising way.
22. Don't make fun of this. Your punishment will be worse.
23. Listen to this:
24. Farmers don't plow forever.
25. They plant when the ground is ready.
26. God teaches them what to do.
27. They use the right tools for each job.
28. God is wise and teaches us how to live.

Isaiah 29

1. This message is for Jerusalem (also called Ariel):
2. You celebrate every year, but I will bring trouble.
3. Your enemies will surround you.
4. You will be brought low and weak.
5. But the enemies will be blown away like dust.
6. God will come with power—earthquake, fire, storm.
7. The nations that attack Jerusalem will disappear like a dream.
8. Like a hungry person dreaming of food but waking up hungry.
9. You are blind to God's truth.
10. He has closed your eyes.
11. God's message is like a sealed book—you don't understand it.
12. Even if someone reads it, you can't understand.
13. God says, "People say they love Me, but their hearts are far away."
14. So He will do amazing things they won't understand.
15. Some try to hide from God, but He sees everything.
16. They act like God doesn't know best.
17. But soon, things will change.
18. The deaf will hear, the blind will see.
19. The poor will rejoice.
20. Evil people will be gone.
21. No more lies or unfair judges.
22. God says to Israel, "You won't be ashamed anymore."
23. Your children will respect Me, and you will fear Me again.

Isaiah 30

1. God says, "You make plans without Me."
2. You went to Egypt for help without asking Me.
3. But Egypt will not save you.
4. They will bring you shame.
5. Their promises are useless.
6. You carried gifts through the desert to bribe Egypt.
7. But Egypt is no help—it's a wasted effort.
8. Write this down so future people will know.
9. These people won't listen to God.
10. They tell prophets, "Don't tell us the truth."
11. "Speak nice things to us."
12. But God says, "Because you reject My word…"
13. "…You will fall suddenly."
14. Like a pot broken into pieces.
15. God says, "Come back and rest in Me."
16. But you said, "No! We'll escape on fast horses."
17. But your enemies will be faster.
18. God still waits to help you.
19. He will show you kindness.
20. You will go through trouble, but He will teach you.
21. You'll hear a voice say, "This is the way. Walk in it."
22. You'll throw away your idols.
23. God will send rain, and your land will grow food.
24. Your animals will have plenty.
25. Water will flow everywhere.
26. The light will be brighter than ever.
27. God is coming with fire and power.
28. He will punish His enemies.
29. But His people will sing and be happy.
30. God will strike the enemy with His voice.
31. Assyria will be destroyed by God.
32. Every strike will be with music.
33. Their leader will be thrown into fire.

Isaiah 31

1. God says, "You are wrong to trust Egypt's army instead of Me."
2. God is wise. He will bring disaster to those who ignore Him.
3. Egypt is human, not God.
4. God will protect Jerusalem like a lion protects its prey.
5. Like birds flying over a nest, God will protect and save it.
6. Turn back to God, people of Israel.
7. You will throw away your idols.
8. Assyria will fall by God's power, not human swords.
9. Their strong places will burn.
10. God's fire is in Jerusalem.

Isaiah 32

1. A good king will rule fairly.
2. He will protect people and bring peace.
3. Everyone will see and hear clearly.
4. People will understand and speak wisely.
5. Fools will not be called wise anymore.
6. Fools speak lies and hurt the poor.
7. They make evil plans.
8. Good people do good things.
9. Lazy women, listen—hard times are coming.
10. You will lose your homes and food.
11. Be afraid.
12. Cry for your fields and farms.

13. The land will grow weeds.
14. Cities will be empty.
15. But one day, God will send His Spirit.
16. Then there will be justice and peace.
17. People will live in safety.
18. They will rest without fear.
19. Even when trouble comes, God will keep you safe.
20. You will be blessed when you work and trust God.

Isaiah 33

1. You destroy others, but you will be destroyed.
2. Lord, be kind to us. Help us each day.
3. When You show up, enemies run.
4. Their treasures will be taken.
5. God lives high in heaven.
6. He keeps His people safe and gives them wisdom.
7. Brave people cry.
8. Peace is gone. Roads are empty.
9. The land is dry and sad.
10. God says, "Now I will act!"
11. Sinners will burn like fire.
12. Who can live near God if He is like fire?
13. Listen—only those who do right will be safe.
14. They speak truth and are fair.
15. They trust God, not money.
16. They will live safely and be fed.
17. You will see a great king.
18. You will remember the danger but feel safe.
19. You won't see cruel people anymore.
20. Look at Jerusalem! It will be strong.
21. God will be like a river of safety.
22. He is our judge, lawgiver, and king.
23. The enemy will fall apart.
24. No one will be sick, and sins will be forgiven.

Isaiah 34

1. Nations, listen!
2. God is angry with all nations.
3. Many people will die.
4. The sky will shake.
5. God will bring justice to Edom.
6. His sword is ready.
7. The land will be soaked with blood.
8. This is God's day of punishment.
9. The rivers will turn to tar.
10. The land will burn forever.
11. No one will live there again.
12. All leaders will be gone.
13. It will be full of wild animals.
14. Creatures will live in ruins.
15. Owls will rest there.
16. God's word has said this, and it will happen.

Isaiah 35

1. The desert will become a happy place.
2. Flowers will bloom. People will celebrate.
3. God will make weak people strong.
4. Tell the scared, "God is coming to save you!"
5. Then blind people will see.
6. Deaf people will hear. Crippled people will walk.
7. Water will flow in dry places.
8. A safe road will be there called the "Holy Road."
9. No lions or danger will be on it.
10. God's people will walk there and be full of joy.

Isaiah 36

1. King Sennacherib of Assyria sent his army to attack Jerusalem.
2. His commander stood outside the city and called out.
3. He said, "Tell King Hezekiah: Don't trust Egypt for help."
4. "Don't trust your God either."
5. "We are stronger than you."
6. "Make a deal with Assyria. We'll give you horses."
7. "Your God told us to attack you."
8. Hezekiah's officials said, "Speak in your language, not ours."
9. But the commander shouted in Hebrew so everyone could hear.
10. He said, "Don't trust Hezekiah. Don't trust your God."
11. "No god has saved any nation from us."
12. Hezekiah's people stayed silent.
13. Then they told the king everything the enemy said.

Isaiah 37

1. When King Hezekiah heard this, he tore his clothes and prayed.
2. He sent messengers to Isaiah.
3. They said, "We need help. Pray for us."
4. Isaiah said, "Don't be afraid. God will stop the enemy."
5. The enemy army had to leave because of a message from home.
6. But the king of Assyria sent a letter threatening Hezekiah again.
7. Hezekiah went to the temple and spread the letter out before God.
8. He prayed, "You alone are God. Save us."
9. God told Isaiah, "I have heard Hezekiah's prayer."
10. "I will protect this city."
11. That night, God sent an angel who killed many enemy soldiers.
12. The rest ran away.
13. Later, the king of Assyria was killed by his own sons.

Isaiah 38

1. King Hezekiah got very sick.
2. Isaiah told him, "You will die. Get ready."
3. Hezekiah prayed and cried to God.
4. God said, "I heard your prayer. I will give you 15 more years."
5. "I will also protect your city."
6. God gave Hezekiah a sign: the shadow moved backward.
7. Hezekiah wrote a message of thanks:
8. "I thought I would die, but You saved me."
9. "I will praise You all my life."

Isaiah 39

1. The king of Babylon sent letters and gifts to Hezekiah.
2. Hezekiah showed them everything in his palace.
3. Isaiah asked, "What did you show them?"
4. Hezekiah said, "Everything."
5. Isaiah said, "One day, Babylon will take all your treasures."
6. "Your family will become servants there."
7. Hezekiah said, "At least there will be peace while I live."

Isaiah 40

1. God says, "Comfort My people."
2. Tell them their punishment is over.
3. A voice says, "Prepare the way for God."

4. "Every valley will rise. Every mountain will lower."
5. "God's glory will be seen by everyone."
6. People are like grass. They die fast.
7. But God's word lasts forever.
8. Shout the good news: God is here!
9. God comes with power and kindness.
10. He takes care of His people like a shepherd.
11. God made everything.
12. No one taught Him anything.
13. Nations are small to Him.
14. Idols are nothing.
15. God sits high above the earth.
16. People are tiny compared to Him.
17. Don't compare God to anything.
18. He never gets tired.
19. He gives power to the weak.
20. Even young people get tired.
21. But those who trust God will be strong.
22. They will fly like eagles, run and not get tired.

Isaiah 41

1. Listen quietly, nations. God is speaking.
2. God gave power to a new leader in the east.
3. He defeats kings and nations.
4. God started it and controls it.
5. Nations are afraid and try to work together.
6. They build idols for help.
7. But God says to His people:
8. "You are My servant. I chose you."
9. "Don't be afraid. I am with you."
10. "I will help you and make you strong."
11. Your enemies will be ashamed and disappear.
12. You will look for them but not find them.
13. I, the Lord, hold your hand.
14. Don't be afraid. I will help you.
15. You will crush your enemies like dust.
16. You will praise God.
17. God will help the poor and thirsty.
18. He will make rivers in dry land.
19. He will plant trees in the desert.
20. People will see God's power.
21. God says to idols, "Prove your power."
22. But idols can't speak or do anything.
23. They are useless. God is the only true one.

Isaiah 42

1. God says, "Here is My servant. I chose him."
2. "He will bring justice. He won't yell or fight."
3. "He will help the weak and be gentle."
4. "He won't give up until he brings justice."
5. God created the world and gave life.
6. He says, "I called you to help others."
7. "You will open blind eyes and free prisoners."
8. "I am God. I won't share My glory."
9. What I said would happen is now coming true.
10. Sing a new song to God, everyone!
11. Let people in the desert and the sea praise Him.
12. Give God glory.
13. God will act with power.
14. He waited silently but now will move.
15. He will destroy mountains and rivers.
16. He will guide the blind safely.

17. Idols will be destroyed.
18. Listen, you who are blind and deaf.
19. My servant didn't obey Me.
20. He saw and heard but didn't care.
21. God wanted to show His goodness through him.
22. But His people were robbed and trapped.
23. Who will listen and learn?
24. God let them suffer because they didn't obey.
25. They were burned but didn't understand.

Isaiah 43

1. God says, "I created you. Don't be afraid. I saved you."
2. "When you face trouble, I'll be with you."
3. "I am your God. I give others for you."
4. "You are precious to Me. I love you."
5. "Don't be afraid. I will bring your people back."
6. "I will gather them from everywhere."
7. "Everyone I made will come to Me."
8. Bring out the people who are blind and deaf.
9. Let all nations come. Can their gods explain the past or predict the future?
10. "You are My witnesses," says God.
11. "I am the only God. There is no other."
12. "You saw Me save you. No one else can do that."
13. "No one can stop Me."
14. God will bring down Babylon.
15. He says, "I am your King and Creator."
16. He made a path through the sea.
17. He destroyed mighty armies.
18. "Forget the past—I'm doing something new."
19. "I will make roads in the desert and rivers in dry land."
20. Animals will honor God because He gives water.
21. He did it for His people.
22. But you stopped praying and honoring Me.
23. You didn't bring Me offerings.
24. You made Me tired with your sins.
25. "But I forgive you anyway."
26. "Tell Me if you're innocent."
27. Your leaders also sinned.
28. So I let trouble come, but I am still your God.

Isaiah 44

1. God says, "Listen, My chosen people."
2. "I made you and will help you."
3. "I will pour water on dry land and bless your children."
4. "They will grow strong like trees."
5. "They will proudly say, 'I belong to God.'"
6. God says, "I am the first and the last. I am the only God."
7. "No one else can tell the future like Me."
8. "Don't be afraid. You are My witnesses."
9. Idols are useless. Their makers are ashamed.
10. Why make a god that can't help you?
11. People who make idols will be embarrassed.
12. They work hard to shape the idol, but it's just a thing.
13. They make it look like a person.
14. They cut wood and use part of it to cook food.

15. Then they use the rest to make a god.
16. They bow down to a block of wood.
17. They don't stop to think, "This is silly."
18. They are blind to the truth.
19. They can't see how wrong it is.
20. They trust something fake.
21. God says, "Remember Me. I made you."
22. "I forgave your sins. Come back to Me."
23. The sky and earth should praise God.
24. God made everything.
25. He makes wise people look foolish.
26. He keeps His promises.
27. He says to the sea, "Be dry."
28. He will use Cyrus to rebuild Jerusalem and the temple.

Isaiah 45

1. God says to Cyrus, "I chose you to help My people."
2. "I will go ahead of you and make things easy."
3. "I will give you treasures and secrets."
4. "I do this for Israel, My chosen people."
5. "I am the only God."
6. "I give light and darkness. I make peace and hard times."
7. "I made the earth and people on it."
8. "Let goodness grow like plants from the earth."
9. Don't argue with God your Maker.
10. A child doesn't tell a parent how to do their job.
11. God says, "I made everything."
12. "I raised up Cyrus to do My work."
13. "People will bring wealth to you in peace."
14. Nations will know God is with you.
15. People will say, "God is the only Savior."
16. Idol worshipers will be ashamed.
17. But Israel will be saved forever.
18. God says, "I made the earth for people."
19. "I speak truth, not secrets."
20. Turn to Me and be saved, everyone.
21. There is no other God.
22. Every knee will bow to Me.
23. Only in God is strength and victory.
24. Everyone who hated Him will be ashamed.
25. God's people will be glad in Him.

Isaiah 46

1. The idols of Babylon are heavy and useless.
2. They can't save anyone.
3. God says, "I have carried you since birth."
4. "I will carry you and save you."
5. "No one is like Me."
6. Some people spend gold to make idols.
7. They bow down to it, but it cannot move or help.
8. Remember this and don't forget it.
9. God says, "I am the only God."
10. "I know the future."
11. "What I say will happen."
12. Listen, you who are stubborn.
13. "I am bringing salvation soon. I will save Israel."

Isaiah 47

1. Babylon, sit in the dirt. You lost your throne.
2. You are not called "Queen" anymore.
3. You will be punished and no one will stop it.

4. God is strong and holy—He is our Savior.
5. Babylon was proud, but now must be quiet.
6. God used Babylon to punish His people, but Babylon went too far.
7. Babylon said, "I'll always rule," but forgot about God.
8. They lived for pleasure and said, "Nothing bad will happen to me."
9. But in one day, everything will be gone.
10. They trusted in evil and thought they were safe.
11. But disaster is coming.
12. Magic and spells won't save them.
13. The stars won't help either.
14. Their helpers are weak like straw in a fire.
15. No one can save them.

Isaiah 48

1. Listen, people of Israel, who use God's name but don't mean it.
2. You say you follow God, but you don't live right.
3. God says, "I told you what would happen, and it did."
4. "I knew you were stubborn."
5. "That's why I told you ahead of time."
6. "Now I'm telling you new things too."
7. "You didn't know before because I didn't tell you."
8. "You've always disobeyed Me."
9. "But I wait to punish you because of My love."
10. "I made you clean through hardship."
11. "I do this for My name—not for you."
12. "I am the one true God."
13. "I made the earth and sky."
14. "I called Cyrus to help My people."
15. "I told him what to do, and he will succeed."
16. "God's Spirit sent Me to speak."
17. God says, "I teach you what is best."
18. "If you had listened, you would have had peace."
19. "Your children would be many."
20. Leave Babylon and shout with joy!
21. God gave water to His people in the desert.
22. But evil people won't have peace.

Isaiah 49

1. Listen, faraway lands—God chose Me before I was born.
2. He gave Me words like a sharp sword.
3. He said, "You are My servant, Israel."
4. I thought I worked for nothing, but God sees everything.
5. He chose Me to bring His people back.
6. God said, "You will bring light to the whole world."
7. People rejected God's servant, but kings will respect Him.
8. God says, "I will help You and bring My people back."
9. Prisoners will be free.
10. They will have food, water, and safety.
11. God will make a smooth road for them.
12. People will come from all over the world.
13. Heaven and earth will rejoice.
14. But Zion said, "God forgot me."
15. God says, "Can a mother forget her baby? I will never forget you."
16. "Your name is written on My hands."
17. Enemies will leave, and your children will return.
18. You will wear them like jewelry.

19. Your land once empty will be full again.
20. You will say, "There are too many people for this land!"
21. You will ask, "Where did all these children come from?"
22. God will call nations to bring your children home.
23. Kings will care for them.
24. Can anyone take back what's been stolen? Yes—God will do it.
25. God says, "I will fight for your children and save them."
26. Your enemies will destroy themselves. Then everyone will know I am the Lord, your Savior.

Isaiah 50

1. God says, "I didn't leave you. You left Me because of your sins."
2. "Why didn't you answer when I called?"
3. "I can dry the sea and cover the sky."
4. God gives Me the right words to help others.
5. I listen to Him and obey.
6. I let people hurt Me, but I did not quit.
7. God helps Me. I will not be ashamed.
8. God defends Me.
9. My enemies will fall.
10. Trust in God even when it's dark.
11. If you try to make your own light, you'll get burned.

Isaiah 51

1. Listen, all who want to do what's right.
2. Look back to Abraham. God blessed him and made him a great nation.
3. God will make your land full of joy again.
4. Pay attention—God's law will bring light to all people.
5. He will save and protect His people.
6. The sky and earth will not last forever, but God's help will.
7. Don't be afraid of what people say.
8. People die, but God's truth stays forever.
9. Wake up, Lord! Show Your power like before.
10. You defeated the sea monster and made a path through the sea.
11. Your people will come home singing with joy.
12. God says, "Don't be afraid of people—they are not forever."
13. "I made the sky and earth."
14. You will soon be free.
15. God stirs up the sea and keeps His people safe.
16. He covers you with His hand and puts His words in your mouth.
17. Wake up, Jerusalem! You have suffered enough.
18. No one could help you.
19. You lost your children and faced trouble.
20. Your children fainted in the streets.
21. But now God says, "You will not suffer more."
22. "I will punish those who hurt you."
23. "They will drink the cup of My anger instead."

Isaiah 52

1. Wake up, Jerusalem! Put on your strength and clean clothes.
2. Shake off the dust and stand tall.
3. God says, "You were sold for nothing; now I will save you for free."
4. Long ago, My people went to Egypt.
5. Now they suffer in Babylon and My name is disrespected.
6. But they will know My name again.

7. How beautiful are the feet of those who bring good news!
8. Watchmen shout with joy—God is bringing His people home.
9. Jerusalem will be happy again.
10. Everyone will see God save His people.
11. Leave Babylon! Don't touch anything unclean.
12. You won't leave in a hurry. God will lead you.
13. God's servant will succeed and be honored.
14. Many were shocked by His suffering.
15. But He will amaze nations, and kings will be silent before Him.

Isaiah 53

1. Many didn't believe the message about God's servant.
2. He grew up with nothing special.
3. People rejected Him and looked down on Him.
4. He carried our pain and sadness.
5. He was hurt for our sins. He was punished to bring us peace.
6. We all did wrong, but God put our punishment on Him.
7. He stayed quiet when He was hurt.
8. He was taken away and killed for our sins.
9. He was buried with the wicked, even though He did nothing wrong.
10. God planned this to save many people.
11. After His suffering, He will live again and see the results of His work.
12. He will be honored because He gave His life and took the blame for others.

Isaiah 54

1. Sing, woman with no children! Your family will grow.
2. Make your tent bigger—you'll need more space.
3. Your family will spread out everywhere.
4. Don't be afraid. You will not be ashamed anymore.
5. God, your Maker, is your husband.
6. He called you back, like a sad wife left alone.
7. For a moment, I left you—but now I bring you back with love.
8. My anger was short, but My kindness lasts forever.
9. Just like I promised Noah, I promise never to leave you.
10. Mountains may move, but My love will not.
11. You were hurting, but I will rebuild you strong.
12. Your children will be taught by God and have peace.
13. You will be safe and far from fear.
14. No weapon will win against you.
15. Anyone who tries to hurt you will fail.
16. I made the people and the tools.
17. You will win because you are My people.

Isaiah 55

1. Come, all who are thirsty! Come get water and food—even if you have no money.
2. Don't waste your time on things that don't help.
3. Listen to Me and live. I will make a promise like I did with David.
4. I made David a leader for the nations.
5. You will call people you don't know, and they will come to you because of God.
6. Seek God while you still can.
7. Turn from your sins. God will forgive.

8. "My thoughts are not like yours," says God.
9. "My ways are higher than your ways."
10. Just like rain helps plants grow,
11. God's word will do what He wants—it won't fail.
12. You will leave with joy and peace.
13. The land will sing, and trees will clap.
14. Instead of weeds, good trees will grow.
15. This will show God's power forever.

Isaiah 56

1. God says, "Do what is right. My help is coming soon."
2. People who obey God are blessed.
3. Foreigners and outsiders are welcome if they follow God.
4. Even people who can't have children are included.
5. God will give them a place and a name that lasts forever.
6. Anyone who loves God and keeps His ways will be accepted.
7. God's house will be a place of prayer for everyone.
8. God will gather more people into His family.
9. Bad leaders don't care. They are lazy and greedy.
10. They only care about themselves and never stop.

Isaiah 57

1. Good people die, but no one notices.
2. They are taken away to avoid trouble.
3. But sinful people are warned:
4. You make fun of others and do evil things.
5. You worship idols and hurt yourselves.
6. You follow false gods and forget the real God.
7. You look for help in the wrong places.
8. You try to make deals with many nations, but not with God.
9. You are tired of doing wrong, but you never stop.
10. You think your actions will save you.
11. God says, "Were you afraid of Me? Is that why you forgot Me?"
12. Your idols won't help you.
13. But whoever trusts Me will live safely.
14. God says, "Clear the path for My people."
15. God lives high above but stays close to the humble.
16. He will not stay angry forever.
17. God was angry because of sin but is ready to heal.
18. He will bring peace and comfort.
19. "Peace to those near and far," says God.
20. But wicked people are like a stormy sea—they have no peace.
21. "There is no peace for the wicked," says God.

Isaiah 58

1. God says, "Shout loudly! Tell My people their sins."
2. They act like they want to know Me, but they don't live right.
3. They ask, "Why doesn't God notice when we fast?"
4. But they fight and do wrong while fasting.
5. That's not the kind of fast God wants.
6. God wants you to stop injustice, set people free, and help others.
7. Share your food. Help the homeless.
8. Then your light will shine, and you'll be healed.
9. God will answer when you call.

10. If you help others, your light will shine in darkness.
11. God will guide you and give you strength.
12. You will rebuild broken places.
13. Respect the Sabbath.
14. Then you will enjoy the Lord, and He will bless you.

Isaiah 59

1. God can hear and save, but your sins block Him.
2. Your wrong choices have pushed God away.
3. You lie, hurt others, and do evil things.
4. No one tells the truth.
5. Your words cause pain and trouble.
6. Your actions can't bring peace.
7. You rush to do wrong.
8. You don't know the way to peace.
9. That's why justice and help are far away.
10. We feel around like blind people.
11. We growl like bears and cry like doves.
12. Our sins are many, and we know them.
13. We turned away from God and did wrong.
14. Justice is pushed away.
15. Truth is not welcome.
16. God saw there was no one to help, so He acted Himself.
17. He wore justice like armor.
18. He will repay evil with justice.
19. People everywhere will respect God.
20. A Savior will come and rescue those who turn from sin.
21. God says, "My Spirit and My words will never leave you or your children."

Isaiah 60

1. Shine bright, because God's light is here!
2. Darkness covers the earth, but God shines on you.
3. Nations and kings will come to your light.
4. Look around—your children are coming home.
5. You will be happy and amazed.
6. People will bring gold, gifts, and praise to God.
7. All the animals will be accepted at God's altar.
8. People will fly home quickly like birds.
9. Ships will bring your children and wealth.
10. Foreigners will help rebuild your city.
11. Your gates will always be open.
12. Nations that won't serve you will be destroyed.
13. Beautiful trees and treasures will honor God.
14. Those who hated you will bow down.
15. You were hated before, but now you will be loved forever.
16. You will be full and strong with God's help.
17. Instead of bronze, you'll have gold.
18. No more violence or destruction.
19. God will be your light forever.
20. You will never be sad again.
21. All your people will do right and own the land.
22. God will make this happen quickly.

Isaiah 61

1. God's Spirit is on Me—He sent Me to help people.
2. To bring good news to the poor, comfort the sad, and free the trapped.

3. To give beauty instead of ashes, joy instead of sadness.
4. People will rebuild old cities.
5. Others will help take care of your land.
6. You will be called priests of God.
7. Instead of shame, you'll get double blessings.
8. God loves justice and hates stealing.
9. Everyone will know you are blessed by God.
10. I am full of joy—God has saved and dressed Me in righteousness.
11. Just like seeds grow, God will grow justice and praise everywhere.

Isaiah 62

1. I won't stay quiet until Jerusalem is saved and shining.
2. All nations will see your goodness.
3. God will hold you like a crown in His hand.
4. You will no longer be called "Left Behind" or "Forgotten."
5. God will love you like a husband loves his bride.
6. I put watchmen on the walls to remind God of His promises.
7. Don't stop praying until He makes Jerusalem strong again.
8. God promises that enemies won't steal your food anymore.
9. You will enjoy what you worked for.
10. Prepare the road—God's people are coming home.
11. God says, "Tell everyone: Your Savior is coming!"
12. You will be called "God's Holy People," "Chosen," and "Loved."

Isaiah 63

1. "Who is this coming with power?" It is God, strong and ready to punish enemies.
2. His clothes are red like someone who stomped grapes.
3. God says, "I punished alone. No one helped Me."
4. "It was time to judge and save My people."
5. "I crushed enemies in My anger."
6. Then Isaiah remembered God's kindness:
7. God helped His people many times.
8. He said, "They are My children."
9. He saved them and carried them.
10. But they disobeyed, so God was sad and punished them.
11. They remembered the days of Moses and asked, "Where is God now?"
12. They cried, "God, You used to lead us and give us peace."
13. "Please come back and help us again."
14. "We are still Your people."

Isaiah 64

1. God, tear open the sky and come down!
2. Show Your power to everyone.
3. You've done amazing things before—do them again.
4. No one else can help like You.
5. You help those who do right, but we sinned.
6. We are all unclean, and even our good actions are like dirty clothes.
7. No one calls out to You like they should.
8. But You are our Father. We are the clay; You are the potter.
9. Don't stay angry forever.
10. Your cities are destroyed.

11. The temple is burned down.
12. Will You stay silent while we suffer?

Isaiah 65

1. God says, "I was ready to help, but no one asked."
2. "I reached out, but people ignored Me."
3. "They did what I hate. They worshiped false gods."
4. "They sat among graves and ate unclean food."
5. "They said, 'Stay away—I'm holier than you!'"
6. "But their actions make Me angry. I will not stay quiet."
7. "I will punish them and their fathers for their sins."
8. But God says, "I won't destroy everyone. Some are faithful."
9. "I will give the land to My chosen ones."
10. "They will have peace and safety."
11. "But those who forgot Me will be punished."
12. "When I called, you didn't answer. So you'll face trouble."
13. "My servants will eat, drink, and rejoice. You will be hungry, thirsty, and ashamed."
14. "My servants will sing with joy. You will cry in pain."
15. "Your name will be forgotten. My servants will get a new name."
16. "Whoever trusts Me will be blessed."
17. "I will make a new heaven and a new earth. You won't even think about the old one."
18. "Be happy! Jerusalem will be full of joy."
19. "No more crying there."
20. "People will live long lives."
21. "They will build homes and plant food—and enjoy them."
22. "They won't work for nothing."
23. "Their children will be blessed."
24. "I will answer before they call."
25. "Even wolves and lambs will live in peace. No more hurting or destroying."

Isaiah 66

1. God says, "Heaven is My throne, and earth is My footstool."
2. "I made everything. I care about humble people who respect Me."
3. But some people offer sacrifices but also do evil.
4. "I will punish them because they refused to listen."
5. God says to the faithful, "Your own people hate you—but I will help you."
6. God is coming with fire and power to punish the wicked.
7. Jerusalem will grow quickly and be full of joy.
8. It will happen all at once.
9. God says, "I won't stop halfway—I will finish what I started."
10. Be happy with Jerusalem.
11. You will be comforted and full of joy.
12. God says, "I will bring peace like a river."
13. "You will be comforted like a child with its mother."
14. You will see it and be glad.
15. God will come in fire to punish His enemies.
16. Many people will die.
17. Those who worship false gods will be destroyed.
18. But God will gather people from all nations.
19. He will show them His glory.

20. People from far away will come to worship Him.
21. God will choose new priests and servants.
22. "Just like the new heaven and earth will last, so will your children."
23. Every month and every week, people will worship God.
24. But those who disobey will be punished and remembered no more.

– Jeremiah –

Jeremiah pleads with Judah to repent, but they refuse and face exile.

Jeremiah 1

1. These are the words of Jeremiah. He was a priest from Benjamin.
2. God spoke to him during the 13th year of King Josiah of Judah.
3. God kept speaking through later kings until the 11th year of King Zedekiah, when Jerusalem was taken over.
4. God said to me,
5. "Before you were born, I chose you to be My prophet."
6. I said, "But I'm too young! I don't know what to say."
7. God said, "Don't say you're too young. Go where I send you and say what I tell you."
8. "Don't be afraid—I am with you to protect you."
9. God touched my mouth and said, "I am giving you the words to say."
10. "You will speak to nations and tell them what I will tear down and what I will build."
11. God said, "What do you see?" I said, "A branch from an almond tree."
12. God said, "That's right. I am watching My words come true."
13. Then God said, "What else do you see?" I said, "A pot of boiling water spilling from the north."
14. God said, "Trouble is coming from the north."
15. "Kings from the north will come and attack Judah."
16. "I will punish the people for worshiping false gods."
17. God said, "Get ready. Go tell them what I say."
18. "Don't be afraid, I will make you strong."
19. "They will fight you but not win. I am with you. I will keep you safe."

Jeremiah 2

1. God spoke to me again,
2. "Tell the people of Jerusalem: I remember how you used to love Me.
3. You were Mine. Anyone who hurt you was punished."
4. "But now My people have changed."
5. "What did I do wrong? Why did you leave me? Now they followed useless idols and became useless too."
6. "They forgot how I led them through the desert."
7. "I brought them to a good land, but they ruined it."
8. "The priests, leaders, and prophets stopped following Me and told lies."
9. "So, I will judge you," says God.
10. "No other nation changes its gods, but you changed Me for fake gods."
11. "The sky should be shocked by this."
12. "You did two wrong things: you left Me, and you made your own false gods."
13. "Can rivers forget where they come from?"
14. "Is Israel a slave? Why is he treated like one?"

15. "Enemies roared and destroyed the land."
16. "Your own leaders led you the wrong way."
17. "This happened because you left Me."
18. "You tried to get help from Egypt and Assyria."
19. "Your sins will punish you."
20. "Long ago, you broke away from Me."
21. "I planted you like a good vine, but you turned bad."
22. "Even soap can't wash away your guilt."
23. "You say, 'I haven't sinned,' but I see everything."
24. "You run around looking for help from others."
25. "You say, 'Egypt will save us!'"
26. "But just like a thief feels shame, so will you."
27. "You call wood and stone your gods."
28. "Let those fake gods save you—if they can."
29. "Why argue with Me? You all disobeyed."
30. "I tried to teach you, but you didn't listen."
31. "Why do you say I left you? I didn't."
32. "A girl doesn't forget her jewelry, but you forgot Me."
33. "You try to look good while doing wrong."
34. "I see the guilt on your hands."
35. "You say, 'I'm innocent!' But I will still judge you."
36. You change sides so easily—running to Egypt now?
37. You'll be disappointed there too."

Jeremiah 3

1. God says, "If a man divorces his wife and she marries someone else, should he take her back? No."
2. "But you have lived like a person with many lovers. Should I take you back?"
3. "You sinned everywhere."
4. "You act like nothing's wrong. You still call Me 'Father,' but don't mean it."
5. "You do wrong and expect forgiveness."
6. God said, "Have you seen what Israel did? She left Me and worshiped idols."
7. "I told her to come back, but she didn't."
8. "Then her sister Judah saw this and sinned too."
9. "They pretended to come back to Me."
10. "But their hearts weren't real."
11. God said, "Israel is better than Judah."
12. "Tell Israel: Come back to Me. I will not stay angry."
13. "Admit you did wrong. You left Me and worshiped idols."
14. "I am your husband. I will take you back."
15. "I will give you good leaders."
16. "You will grow and not need the old Ark of the Covenant anymore."
17. "People will come to Jerusalem to worship Me."
18. "Israel and Judah will come together."
19. "I wanted to give you good land, but you didn't obey."
20. "You were unfaithful like a cheating wife."
21. "I hear My people crying and begging to come back."
22. God says, "Come back and I will heal you."
23. The people say, "Other gods are lies."
24. "They only brought shame."

25. "We are sorry. We have sinned since childhood."

Jeremiah 4

1. God says, "If you come back to Me and stop worshiping idols, I will bless you."
2. "Be honest and true, and I will help all nations."
3. "It's time to change. Don't let sin grow."
4. "Open your hearts to me. Don't let my anger burn."
5. "Warn everyone: enemies are coming!"
6. "Tell people to run for safety."
7. "A lion is coming to destroy your land."
8. "Cry and be sad, because God's angry."
9. "Leaders, priests, and prophets will be scared."
10. I said, "God, You said we'd be safe—but now there's trouble!"
11. God says, "Bad times are coming."
12. "They are fast and strong."
13. "Jerusalem, change your heart, or you'll be destroyed."
14. "I hear enemy armies coming."
15. "They bring news of war."
16. "They surround cities and shout against Judah."
17. "This happens because of your sins."
18. "This is your own fault. You brought this on yourself."
19. My heart is in pain. I hear the sound of battle.
20. The land is being destroyed.
21. How long must I see this?
22. God says, "My people are foolish. They don't know Me."
23. I looked and saw the land empty and dark.
24. Mountains shook.
25. No people were left.
26. The cities were destroyed.
27. God said, "The land will be ruined, but not forever."
28. The earth is sad, the skies are dark.
29. People run and hide.
30. You try to look beautiful, but it won't save you.
31. I hear a woman in pain, crying like she's giving birth. It is Jerusalem, crying out.

Jeremiah 5

1. Go through the streets of Jerusalem. See if anyone is honest. If you find even one, I will forgive this city.
2. People say, "I live for God," but they're lying.
3. God, You see the truth. You punished them, but they didn't change.
4. The poor don't know better—but the rich still ignore You.
5. So I will punish both.
6. So a lion will attack them. A wolf will kill them at night. A leopard will watch the city and tear them apart.
7. God says, "Why should I forgive them? They left Me and sinned often."
8. They are full of desire and chase what is wrong.
9. God says, "Should I not punish them?"
10. Enemies will ravage the city but not destroy it completely.
11. My people Israel and Judah have turned against Me.
12. They say, "God won't do anything. Nothing bad will happen."
13. God says, "They lie in My name. I will punish them."
14. God's word will be like fire, and the people will be like wood—it will burn them.
15. A powerful nation is coming to attack.

16. Their arrows are deadly.
17. They will eat your food, animals, and children.
18. But I will not let them destroy you completely.
19. When you ask why, say, "Because you left God."
20. Tell this to everyone:
21. "You have eyes but don't see, ears but don't hear."
22. "God made the sea stop at the shore. He should be feared."
23. But the people are stubborn and rebel.
24. They don't thank God for the rain and harvest.
25. Your sins keep good things away.
26. Evil people lie in wait to trap others.
27. They grow rich by tricking people.
28. They ignore the poor and orphans.
29. God says, "Should I not punish this?"
30. Terrible things are happening.
31. Prophets lie, and people love it. But what will you do later?

Jeremiah 6

1. Run for safety, people of Benjamin. Trouble is coming from the north.
2. Jerusalem is beautiful, but it will be destroyed.
3. Enemies will surround Jerusalem.
4. They say, "Attack at noon!" But they keep fighting at a night.
5. The city is full of evil and hurt.
6. God says, "Cut down trees and build ramps to attack."
7. The city pours out sin like water.
8. God warns, "I will destroy you if you don't listen."
9. Enemies will take everything.
10. The people don't want to hear God's words.
11. God's anger is strong. He will punish everyone—young and old.
12. Houses and fields will be taken.
13. Everyone, from least to greatest, is greedy.
14. Leaders say, "Everything is fine," but it's not.
15. They're not even ashamed of their sin.
16. God says, "Ask for the good path. Walk in it." But they said, "No."
17. "I sent warnings, but they wouldn't listen."
18. So God will bring disaster.
19. "You rejected My word, so now face the results."
20. Your offerings don't please Me.
21. God says, "I will trip you up. You will fall."
22. A nation from the north is coming.
23. They are cruel and show no mercy.
24. We hear the news and feel afraid.
25. Don't go outside. There is danger everywhere.
26. Mourn and cry because punishment is coming.
27. God says, "I made you to test My people."
28. They are stubborn rebels.
29. No matter how hot the fire, they don't change.
30. They are rejects, useless to Me.

Jeremiah 7

1. God told Jeremiah to stand at the temple gate and speak:
2. "Hear God's word, all who come to worship."
3. God says, "Change your ways, and I will let you stay here."
4. Don't trust in the temple alone.
5. Do what is right. Help each other.

6. Don't hurt the helpless.
7. If you do what's right, I will let you stay.
8. But you lie and steal.
9. You worship other gods, then come here and think you're safe.
10. This house has become a place for robbers.
11. I see everything you do.
12. Go look at Shiloh. I used to live there, but I destroyed it.
13. I warned you, but you didn't listen.
14. So I will treat this temple like Shiloh.
15. I will throw you out like I did the people before you.
16. God says, "Don't pray for them. I won't listen."
17. Do you see what they're doing?
18. Families gather to worship false gods.
19. They hurt themselves, not Me.
20. So I will pour out My anger.
21. God says, "Your sacrifices mean nothing without obedience."
22. I wanted your hearts, not just offerings.
23. I said, 'Obey Me, and it will go well for you.'
24. But they didn't listen.
25. I sent prophets every day, but they ignored them.
26. They became even more stubborn.
27. They won't listen to you either, Jeremiah.
28. Tell them: "You are a nation that refuses to obey God."
29. Mourn for your people.
30. They did evil in God's house.
31. They even sacrificed children—something God never wanted.
32. So their land will become empty.
33. Bodies will be left for birds and animals.
34. Joy and singing will stop. The land will become silent.

Jeremiah 8

1. The bones of kings, leaders, and priests will be taken from their graves.
2. They will be left out under the sun and moon—the things they worshiped.
3. The people who survive will wish they were dead.
4. God says, "When people fall, they get back up. Why don't My people return to Me?"
5. They hold on to lies and don't turn back.
6. No one says, "What have I done?"
7. Birds know when to migrate, but My people don't know My ways.
8. You say you are wise and have My law, but you ignore it.
9. Wise people will be ashamed.
10. Everyone is greedy.
11. They say, "Everything is fine," when it's not.
12. They are not even ashamed of their sin.
13. There will be no harvest.
14. People ask, "Why is God punishing us?"
15. They hoped for peace but found fear.
16. The enemy is coming fast.
17. God says, "I will send snakes that can't be stopped."
18. Jeremiah says, "My heart is broken for My people."
19. "Isn't God still in Zion?"
20. "The harvest is over, and we are still not saved."
21. Jeremiah cries for his people.
22. He asks, "Is there no doctor to heal us?"

Jeremiah 9

1. Jeremiah wishes his eyes were a fountain to cry for his people.
2. He wants to leave because everyone lies and cheats.
3. They go from one sin to another.
4. Don't trust anyone—friends or family.
5. Everyone lies and tricks.
6. They refuse to know God.
7. God says, "I will test and punish them."
8. Their words are like arrows that hurt people.
9. Should I not punish them?
10. Jeremiah weeps for the mountains and destroyed cities.
11. The land is ruined and no one lives there.
12. Why did this happen? Because people left God's ways.
13. They followed idols and other gods.
14. God says, "I will feed them bitter food and scatter them."
15. They will cry and sing funeral songs.
16. Death is entering their windows.
17. Mothers and children will die.
18. Teach the women to cry.
19. A voice is heard crying, "We lost everything!"
20. Tell your daughters to cry.
21. Death has climbed through the windows.
22. Bodies will lie everywhere.
23. God says, "Don't brag about being wise, strong, or rich."
24. "Brag about knowing Me and doing what is right."
25. God will punish all people even those who think they are safe because of rituals.

Jeremiah 10

1. Listen to what God says.
2. Don't follow the ways of other nations.
3. They cut wood and decorate it like a god.
4. They use silver and gold, but it's just a statue.
5. Idols can't walk or talk. Don't fear them—they can't do anything.
6. No one is like God. He is great.
7. All nations should respect Him.
8. People who worship idols are foolish.
9. Idols are made by humans, not alive.
10. But God is real. He is the living King.
11. Idols will disappear when God acts.
12. God made the earth and the sky.
13. His voice brings thunder and rain.
14. People who make idols are foolish.
15. Idols are worthless and will be destroyed.
16. But God is not like them—He created everything.
17. Pack your bags—you are going into exile.
18. God says, "I will throw you out of your land."
19. Jeremiah says, "My people are hurt badly."
20. "Our homes are destroyed."
21. The leaders did not ask God for help.
22. The enemy is coming from the north.
23. Jeremiah says, "God, I know I can't control my life."
24. "Correct me gently, not in anger."
25. "Punish the nations that hurt Your people."

Jeremiah 11

1. God told Jeremiah,

2. "Remind the people about My agreement with them."
3. "I told them, 'Follow My commands, and you will be blessed. Cursed is anyone who does not obey'"
4. "I brought them out of Egypt and told them to obey Me."
5. "If they did, they would live in the land I gave them."
6. God said again, "Tell everyone in Judah to obey this agreement."
7. Jeremiah told the people everything God said.
8. But the people didn't listen.
9. They followed their stubborn hearts, so God punished them.
10. God told Jeremiah, "There is a secret plot among the people of Judah."
11. "They turned back to sin, like their ancestors."
12. "So I will bring disaster. They will cry, but I won't listen."
13. "Even if they pray, I won't help them."
14. "They have as many idols as cities."
15. God told Jeremiah, "Don't pray for them. I won't listen."
16. "They think they can still worship Me, but they keep doing wrong."
17. God once called them a beautiful olive tree, but now He will burn it down.
18. They brought this on themselves by worshiping other gods.
19. God showed Jeremiah the plot against him.
20. Jeremiah didn't know people were planning to kill him.
21. He said, "God, You judge fairly. Show them the truth."
22. Some men said, "Stop speaking in God's name or we'll kill you."
23. But God said, "They will be punished, and their children will die."

Jeremiah 12

1. Jeremiah said, "God, You are fair—but why do evil people succeed?"
2. "They look strong, but they don't really love You."
3. "You know me, God. Test me."
4. "The land is bad because of sin."
5. God said, "If small problems tire you, how will you handle big ones?"
6. "Even your own family has turned against you."
7. "I have left My house (My people). They turned on Me."
8. "My people roared at Me like a lion."
9. "Enemies attacked like wild birds."
10. "They ruined My vineyard."
11. "The land is empty and sad."
12. "Soldiers came and destroyed everything."
13. "The people planted wheat but harvested nothing."
14. God says, "I will punish the nations that hurt My people."
15. "But if they learn to follow Me, I will bless them too."
16. "If not, they will be destroyed."

Jeremiah 13

1. God told Jeremiah, "Buy a cloth belt and wear it. Don't wash it."
2. So Jeremiah did.
3. Later, God said, "Now take the belt and hide it in a crack in the rocks."
4. Jeremiah did.
5. After some time, God said, "Go get the belt."
6. Jeremiah found it ruined.
7. God said, "This is how I will ruin Judah's pride."
8. "They were close to Me like a belt, but they would not listen."

9. "They worshiped other gods and became useless."
10. "Tell them: every jar will be filled with wine."
11. "But I will fill them with confusion and make them crash into each other."
12. God says, "Don't be proud."
13. "Give God honor before it's too late."
14. "If you don't, you'll fall into darkness."
15. "You will cry, but I won't listen."
16. Jeremiah said, "Let my eyes cry for your people."
17. God says, "Tell the king and queen to step down. Their rule is ending."
18. "The cities are in danger."
19. "You hoped for peace, but war is coming."
20. "Look! The enemy is coming from the north."
21. "What will you do now?"
22. "Your pain will be like a woman giving birth."
23. "Can a person change their skin? No. You can't change your evil ways either."
24. "So I will scatter you like dust in the wind."
25. "This is what you get for forgetting Me."

Jeremiah 14

1. There was no rain.
2. People cried and their towns were empty.
3. Servants looked for water but found none.
4. The ground was dry.
5. Even animals left their babies.
6. Wild donkeys stood in the wind with no food.
7. The people said, "God, we sinned. Please help us anyway."
8. "You are our Savior—don't leave us."
9. But God said, "These people keep turning from Me. I won't accept their prayers."
10. "I will remember their sins and punish them."
11. God told Jeremiah, "Do not pray for them."
12. "If they fast, I won't listen. If they give offerings, I won't accept them."
13. Jeremiah said, "But false prophets say everything will be fine."
14. God said, "They lie. I didn't send them."
15. "Those prophets will die in the disaster they promised wouldn't come."
16. "Their followers will also die. No one will bury them."
17. God told Jeremiah, "Cry for My people."
18. People are wounded and dying everywhere.
19. The people ask, "God, have You left us?"
20. They admit, "We sinned. Please forgive us."
21. "Don't reject us. We are Your people."

Jeremiah 15

1. God said, "Even if Moses and Samuel stood here, I wouldn't change My mind."
2. "Tell the people: Some will die in war, some by hunger, others in exile."
3. "I will send four punishments: sword, dogs, birds, and animals."
4. "This is because of King Manasseh's evil."
5. "No one will feel sorry for Jerusalem."
6. "You left Me, so I will destroy you."
7. "I tried to teach you, but you kept doing wrong."

8. "Many of your people will die. Mothers will lose their children."
9. "Even strong people will be weak."
10. Jeremiah said, "I wish I were never born. Everyone hates me."
11. God said, "I will protect you."
12. "Can anyone break iron? No—and your enemies can't beat you without Me."
13. "I will give your treasures away as punishment for sin."
14. "You will serve others in a foreign land."
15. Jeremiah said, "God, remember me. Punish those who attack me."
16. "I love Your words. I belong to You."
17. "I sat alone because You told me to."
18. "Why is my pain never ending?"
19. God said, "If you return to Me, I will use you."
20. "You will be strong like a wall. They will fight you but lose."
21. "I will rescue and save you."

Jeremiah 16

1. God told Jeremiah, "Do not marry or have kids here."
2. "Children born here will die from war or sickness."
3. "No one will mourn or bury them."
4. "People will die like trash in the streets."
5. "Do not go to funerals."
6. "I have taken away peace, love, and mercy from these people."
7. "No one will comfort or feed the sad."
8. "Do not go to parties. I have taken away joy."
9. "I, the Lord, will make things silent."
10. When people ask, "Why is this happening?"
11. Say, "Because your ancestors and you disobeyed God."
12. "You have done worse than they did."
13. "So I will throw you out of this land."
14. But God says, "One day, I will bring My people back from other countries."
15. "It will be even greater than the time I brought them from Egypt."
16. "I will send people to find and bring them home."
17. "I see all their sins. Nothing is hidden."
18. "I will pay them back for their sins."
19. Jeremiah said, "God, You are my strength and shelter."
20. "Nations will come and say, 'Our idols are useless.'"
21. God said, "Then they will know my power, that I am the Lord."

Jeremiah 17

1. Judah's sins are carved in their hearts.
2. They worship idols even with their children.
3. God will take away their treasures and land and give it to their enemies.
4. They will lose the land I gave them.
5. God says, "Cursed is the one who trusts people, not Me."
6. "That person will be weak, like a dry bush."
7. "But blessed is the one who trusts Me."
8. "That person will be strong, like a tree near water."
9. People's hearts are tricky, full of sin, hard to understand.
10. God says, "I look at hearts and give people what they deserve."
11. A person who gets rich the wrong way will lose it all.
12. God's throne is the place of truth and power forever.

13. The Lord is hope. People who turn away from God will be ashamed.
14. Jeremiah says, "Heal me, God, and I'll be healed."
15. People mock Jeremiah and say, "Where's God's warning?"
16. Jeremiah says, "I didn't want to bring trouble—I spoke Your words."
17. "Don't scare me, God. You are my protection."
18. "Punish those who attack me."
19. God told Jeremiah, "Go to the city gate and tell people to obey Me."
20. "Tell the kings and people: Listen to God's word."
21. "Tell them not to carry loads on the Sabbath."
22. "Don't do any work on that day- keep it holy."
23. "Your ancestors didn't listen, but you still have a chance."
24. "If you obey, kings will sit on David's throne forever."
25. "But if you don't, this city will burn."

Jeremiah 18

1. God told Jeremiah, "Go to the potter's house."
2. "There I will give you a message."
3. So I went. The potter was making something with clay.
4. But the clay got messed up, so he shaped it into something else.
5. God said, "I can do the same with you, Israel."
6. "You are like clay in my hands."
7. "Sometimes I say I will destroy a nation. But if they stop doing evil, I won't destroy them."
8. "Other times I say I will bless a nation. But if they disobey, I will take back the blessing."
9. "Tell Judah I'm planning to punish them."
10. "But they'll say, 'It's no use. We'll do what we want.'"
11. So God says, "Ask the nations—who ever heard of such a thing?"
12. "My people forgot me. They made idols."
13. "They turned away from the good path."
14. "They made their land a desert."
15. "Everyone who passes by will be shocked."
16. "I will scatter them before their enemies."
17. Then the people said, "Let's attack Jeremiah! We won't listen to him."
18. Jeremiah said, "Lord, hear what they say!"
19. "Should good be paid back with evil? They dug a pit for me!"
20. "Remember how I prayed for them."
21. "Now let their children go hungry. Let them die in battle."
22. "Let their homes be empty. Let no one help them."
23. "Punish them. Don't forgive them."

Jeremiah 19

1. God said, "Buy a clay jar. Take leaders and priests with you."
2. "Go to the trash dump outside the city."
3. "Speak these words: God says He will bring disaster."
4. "Because the people left Me, burned incense to false gods, and killed innocent people."
5. "They even burned children as offerings."
6. "This place will be called 'The Valley of Death.'"

7. "The people will die here, and others will be shocked."
8. "There will be no more joy or weddings in Jerusalem."
9. "People will be so hungry they'll eat each other."
10. Then break the jar in front of them.
11. Say, "God will break this nation like this jar."
12. "They'll bury people in this dump because there will be no room left."
13. "All the houses in Jerusalem will be unclean like this place."
14. Jeremiah came back from the valley and told everyone in the temple:
15. "God says, 'I will bring every disaster I promised, because you won't listen.'"

Jeremiah 20

1. Pashhur the priest heard what I said and hit me and put me in jail.
2. The next day he let me go. I said, "God has changed your name. Now you are called 'Terror on Every Side.'"
3. "God says: I will hand you over to your enemies. You'll see your friends die.
4. Judah will be taken to Babylon. You'll die there and be buried with your friends."
5. "All the riches of Jerusalem will be taken by enemies."
6. "And you, Pashhur, and your family will go to Babylon and die there."
7. I said, "Lord, You tricked me. I said I wouldn't speak Your name, but I couldn't hold it in."
8. "Your message brings me nothing but shame and insults."
9. "Your words burn inside me. I have to speak."
10. "I hear people whispering, 'Let's trap him!' Even my friends want me to fall."
11. "But You are with me like a strong warrior. My enemies will fail."
12. "You see what people do. Show Your justice. I trust You."
13. "Sing to the Lord! He saves the helpless from the wicked!"
14. "But I curse the day I was born!"
15. "Curse the one who told my father, 'You have a son!'"
16. "Let that man be like a town God destroyed without pity."
17. "Why wasn't I killed at birth?"
18. "Why was I born, just to see pain and end my life in shame?"

Jeremiah 21

1. King Zedekiah sent messengers to ask Jeremiah,
2. "Will God help us against King Nebuchadnezzar of Babylon?"
3. Jeremiah answered, "No. God says He will fight against you."
4. "He will let the Babylonian army win."
5. "People in the city will die by sword, disease, or hunger."
6. "If you surrender, you will live. If you fight, you will die."
7. "I set life and death before you. Choose life."
8. "Tell the king of Judah: Do what is right."
9. "Help those being robbed. Stop evil. Or I will destroy your palace."

Jeremiah 22

1. God told Jeremiah: "Go to the king's house and say this—
2. Do what is right. Help the weak. Don't hurt the innocent."
3. "If you do this, your kingdom will last."
4. "But if you don't, your palace will become ruins."
5. "People will walk by and say, 'Why did God destroy this city?'"

6. “The answer: Because they left God.”
7. God says about King Shallum (Jehoahaz):
8. “He will be taken away and never return.”
9. “He will die in a foreign land.”
10. “Don’t cry for the dead king—cry for the one going into exile.”
11. About King Jehoiakim:
12. “You built a fancy palace, but you were cruel and unfair.”
13. “You didn’t help the poor. You only cared about yourself.”
14. “So you will die like a donkey—no funeral, no honor.”
15. About Jehoiachin (Coniah):
16. “Even if you were a ring on My finger, I would pull you off.”
17. “You and your mother will go into exile.”
18. “You will never return.”
19. “Write this man down as childless—none of his children will sit on David’s throne.”

Jeremiah 23

1. God says, “Bad leaders hurt My people. I will punish them.”
2. “I will bring My people back and give them good leaders.”
3. “A new king from David’s family will rule with wisdom.”
4. “His name will be ‘The Lord Makes Things Right.’”
5. People will say, “God brought us from all nations,” not just from Egypt.
6. God says, “My prophets are lying. They speak their own ideas.”
7. “They say everything will be fine, even when people are doing evil.”
8. “If they really heard from Me, they would warn people to stop sinning.”
9. Jeremiah says, “I am broken. God’s words shake me.”
10. “The land is full of sin. God’s judgment is near.”
11. Prophets and priests lie and do evil.
12. Their path is dark.
13. Prophets in Samaria led people to false gods.
14. Prophets in Jerusalem are even worse.
15. God says, “I will punish them. They are like poison.”
16. Don’t listen to their lies.
17. They say, “God said you’ll have peace,” but God did not say that.
18. No one stood in My council.
19. My anger is coming.
20. Later, you’ll understand clearly.
21. I didn’t send these prophets.
22. If they had heard Me, they would turn people from sin.
23. God says, “I see everything. No one can hide from Me.”
24. “I am near and far. I fill the whole earth.”
25. “I heard the prophets say they had dreams. They lie.”
26. “How long will they speak false words?”
27. “They make people forget Me.”
28. “Let them tell dreams, but My word is like fire and a hammer.”
29. “Don’t steal My words.”
30. “Stop saying, ‘This is God’s message,’ if I didn’t say it.”
31. “My word brings truth don’t twist my words.”
32. “Don’t say ‘God’s message’—I will punish those who do.”

Jeremiah 24

1. God showed Jeremiah two baskets of figs near the temple.

2. One basket had good figs. The other had rotten ones.
3. God said, "The good figs are like the people I sent into exile in Babylon."
4. "I will watch over them and bring them back."
5. "They will return to Me with all their heart."
6. "But the bad figs are like King Zedekiah and those left in Jerusalem."
7. "They will be a warning and a shame to others."
8. "They will die by war, hunger, or disease."

Jeremiah 25

1. God spoke to Jeremiah in the fourth year of King Jehoiakim. The first year of Babylon's King Nebuchadnezzar.
2. Jeremiah said, "For 23 years I've warned you, but you didn't listen."
3. "God sent many prophets, but you ignored them."
4. "They said, 'Turn from evil, and I'll let you stay in the land.'"
5. "But you didn't listen."
6. "So God says, 'I will send King Nebuchadnezzar of Babylon.'"
7. "He will destroy this land, and it will be empty."
8. "This will last for 70 years."
9. "After that, I will punish Babylon."
10. "Joy and happiness will end during those 70 years."
11. God gave Jeremiah a cup of wine and said, "Give it to all the nations."
12. "Make them drink and know My anger is coming."
13. Jeremiah gave it to Jerusalem, Judah, and surrounding kings.
14. He gave it to many nations far and near.
15. They all drank the cup of God's anger.
16. God said, "Warn all nations: I will punish everyone."
17. "Don't think you'll escape."
18. "People everywhere will die."
19. "The Lord will roar like a lion from heaven."
20. "The noise will shake the earth."
21. "The day of punishment has come."
22. "The dead will lie everywhere. No one will bury them."

Jeremiah 26

1. This message came during the beginning of King Jehoiakim's reign.
2. God told Jeremiah to speak at the temple.
3. He said, "Tell everyone everything I say. Don't leave anything out."
4. "Maybe they will change, and I won't punish them."
5. "If they don't listen, I will destroy this temple like I did Shiloh."
6. The priests and people heard him.
7. They said, "You must die for saying this!"
8. People came from everywhere to hear.
9. The leaders said, "He should be judged."
10. Jeremiah said, "God sent me. Change your ways, or He will punish you."
11. "I'm ready to die, but if you kill me, you'll be guilty of killing an innocent man."
12. Some leaders said, "This man does not deserve to die."
13. Others remembered how the prophet Micah warned Jerusalem long ago.
14. King Hezekiah listened to him and did not kill him.
15. Another man, Uriah, also spoke God's word.

16. But King Jehoiakim tried to kill him, so Uriah ran to Egypt.
17. The king brought him back and killed him.
18. Jeremiah was protected by Ahikam and was not killed.

Jeremiah 27

1. God told Jeremiah to make a yoke (a wooden bar for oxen) and wear it.
2. He said, "Send messages to the kings of Edom, Moab, Ammon, Tyre, and Sidon."
3. "Tell them to serve King Nebuchadnezzar of Babylon."
4. "If they do, they can stay in their land."
5. "If not, I will punish them with war, hunger, and disease."
6. "Don't listen to your false prophets who say, 'You won't serve Babylon.'"
7. "They are lying."
8. "Serve the king of Babylon and live."
9. "Even if you fight, you will lose."
10. Jeremiah gave the same message to King Zedekiah of Judah.
11. He said, "If you listen to God, you will live."
12. "Don't trust false prophets who say the temple treasures will return soon."
13. "They are lying. Those treasures will stay in Babylon until God brings them back later."

Jeremiah 28

1. A false prophet named Hananiah spoke in the temple.
2. He said, "God says Babylon's power will be broken in two years."
3. "The temple treasures and King Jehoiachin will come back."
4. Jeremiah said, "I hope that's true, but that's not what God told me."
5. "If a prophet says good things and they come true, then we know God sent him."
6. Hananiah took the yoke from Jeremiah and broke it.
7. He said, "God will break Babylon's power soon."
8. Later, God told Jeremiah,
9. "Go tell Hananiah: You broke a wooden yoke, but I will replace it with an iron one."
10. "Babylon will rule many nations."
11. God said, "Hananiah lied. He will die this year."
12. Two months later, Hananiah died.

Jeremiah 29

1. Jeremiah sent a letter to the people taken to Babylon.
2. He wrote it to the leaders, priests, and others in exile.
3. The letter said:
4. "God says: Build houses and live in them. Plant gardens and eat from them."
5. "Get married and have children. Help your families grow."
6. "Pray for Babylon to do well. If it has peace, you will too."
7. "Don't listen to the false prophets among you."
8. "They say things I didn't tell them."
9. "You will be in Babylon 70 years. Then I will bring you back."
10. "I know My plans for you—plans for good, not harm."
11. "You will call Me and pray to Me, and I will listen."
12. "You will find Me when you search with all your heart."
13. "I will bring you back from all the nations."

14. God also spoke about the people who stayed in Jerusalem:
15. "They will face war, hunger, and sickness."
16. "They will be a curse and an example of punishment."
17. Two false prophets, Ahab and Zedekiah, will be burned by the king of Babylon.
18. Another man, Shemaiah, sent a false message.
19. God said, "I did not send him. He will be punished."

Jeremiah 30

1. God told Jeremiah to write all these words in a scroll.
2. "A time of great trouble is coming for Israel."
3. "But I will save them."
4. "They will be afraid, but I will break their chains."
5. "They will serve Me and a new king from David's family."
6. "Don't be afraid. I will bring you back home."
7. "I will save you from far away."
8. "You were hurt, and no one helped—but I will heal you."
9. "I punished you for your sins, but I won't destroy you."
10. "Your enemies will be punished."
11. "One day, your land will be full again."
12. "I will bring back Jacob's people, and they will be safe."
13. "You will have joy, and I will punish those who hurt you."
14. "You will be Mine again. You will be My people, and I will be your God."

Jeremiah 31

1. God says, "I have always loved you. I will bring you back."
2. "You will plant vineyards and enjoy your land."
3. "People will return and sing with joy."
4. "I will turn tears into joy."
5. "I will comfort the hurting."
6. "Your work will be rewarded."
7. "Your children will come back."
8. "I will lead them home safely."
9. "They will not stumble—I will be like a Father to them."
10. "Nations, hear this: God is gathering His people."
11. "They were scattered, but now He brings them back."
12. "They will be like a watered garden."
13. "Young women and old men will dance together."
14. "I will give them joy instead of sadness."
15. God says, "A voice cries for lost children—but they will return."
16. "There is hope. They will come back."
17. God says, "I still care for Israel, My dear son."
18. "I heard him cry. I will bring him back."
19. "Put signs on the road to guide your return."
20. "I will do something new—a woman will protect a man."
21. God says, "I will make a new promise with Israel."
22. "It won't be like the old one they broke."
23. "I will write My law in their hearts. I will be their God."
24. "They will all know Me."
25. "I will forgive their sins forever."
26. God says, "As long as the sun, moon, and stars exist, I will keep My promise to Israel."

27. “Even if the sky could be measured, I will not reject My people.”
28. “Jerusalem will be rebuilt. It will be holy forever.”

Jeremiah 32

1. God spoke to Jeremiah while Jerusalem was under attack.
2. Jeremiah was in prison.
3. King Zedekiah put him there for saying the king would be captured.
4. God told Jeremiah, “Your cousin will ask you to buy his field.”
5. Soon after, his cousin came and asked.
6. Jeremiah bought the field and signed the papers.
7. He gave the papers to Baruch and said, “Store these in a safe place.”
8. Then Jeremiah prayed:
9. “God, You made everything. Nothing is too hard for You.”
10. “You show love but also judge sin.”
11. “You saved Israel from Egypt.”
12. “But now You are letting Babylon take the city.”
13. God replied, “Yes, I am giving the city to Babylon.”
14. “The people have sinned and worshiped idols.”
15. “They built altars to false gods, even for child sacrifice.”
16. “But one day, I will bring them back.”
17. “I will give them one heart to follow Me forever.”
18. “I will never stop doing good for them.”
19. “Fields will be bought again. This land has a future.”

Jeremiah 33

1. God spoke to Jeremiah again while he was still in prison.
2. God said, “Call to Me, and I will answer you.”
3. “You are trying to fix this city, but it will fall.”
4. “I will heal it and bring peace.”
5. “I will forgive their sin.”
6. “People everywhere will see and respect Me.”
7. “Joy will return to this place.”
8. “People will sing again: ‘Give thanks to God!’”
9. “In the future, My people will return.”
10. “Fields will be bought and owned again.”
11. “A good king from David’s line will rule fairly.”
12. “He will be called ‘The Lord Makes Things Right.’”
13. “David will always have someone on the throne.”
14. “The priests will always serve Me.”
15. “My promises to David and the priests will never end.”
16. “I will keep My people forever, just like the stars and sand never end.”

Jeremiah 34

1. God told Jeremiah to speak to King Zedekiah:
2. “Babylon will take this city.”
3. “You will see the king of Babylon and be taken there.”
4. “But you won’t die in battle. You will die in peace.”
5. The king listened, but the people did not.
6. The people had made a promise to free their slaves.
7. At first, they obeyed and let the slaves go.
8. But then they changed their minds and took them back.

9. God said, "You broke your promise."
10. "I will punish you with war, disease, and hunger."
11. "The king and his leaders will be captured by Babylon."

Jeremiah 35

1. God told Jeremiah, "Go to the Recabite family and bring them to the temple."
2. Jeremiah brought them and gave them wine to drink.
3. But they said, "We don't drink wine."
4. "Our ancestor Jonadab told us not to drink wine, build houses, or plant fields."
5. "We live in tents and obey everything he said."
6. Then God told Jeremiah,
7. "The Recabites obeyed their ancestor, but My people won't obey Me."
8. "I sent prophets, but they ignored them."
9. "The Recabites listened to a man. My people won't listen to God."
10. God said, "Disaster is coming to Judah."
11. But to the Recabites, God said, "You will always have descendants who serve Me."

Jeremiah 36

1. God told Jeremiah, "Write everything I told you on a scroll."
2. "Maybe the people will change when they hear it."
3. Jeremiah told Baruch to write the words.
4. Since Jeremiah couldn't go to the temple, Baruch read the scroll there.
5. People heard it and were afraid.
6. They told the king.
7. The king sent someone to read the scroll.
8. As it was read, the king cut off each part and burned it.
9. The king did not care.
10. God told Jeremiah, "Write it again."
11. God said the king would be punished.
12. Jeremiah and Baruch wrote everything again, and even added more.

Jeremiah 37

1. Zedekiah became king, but he and his people didn't listen to God.
2. He asked Jeremiah to pray for them.
3. Egypt's army came, and Babylon's army left for a while.
4. God told Jeremiah, "Babylon will return and destroy the city."
5. "Don't think Egypt will save you."
6. Jeremiah tried to leave the city but was arrested.
7. He was accused of trying to join the enemy.
8. Jeremiah said, "That's not true!" But they beat him and put him in a cell.
9. Later, King Zedekiah secretly asked him, "Is there a word from God?"
10. Jeremiah said, "Yes. You will be handed over to Babylon."
11. He asked the king not to send him back to the dungeon.
12. So the king put him in a safer place and gave him bread each day.

Jeremiah 38

1. Some officials heard Jeremiah saying, "Whoever stays in the city will die. Whoever surrenders will live."
2. The officials told the king, "He's hurting the people's hope."
3. The king said, "Do what you want with him."

4. So they lowered Jeremiah into a deep pit. There was no water—only mud.
5. He sank into the mud.
6. A man named Ebed-Melek told the king, "Jeremiah will die in that pit."
7. The king said, "Take 30 men and pull him out."
8. They lifted him out with old rags and ropes.
9. Jeremiah was put back in a safe prison.
10. King Zedekiah secretly met with him.
11. Jeremiah said, "If you listen to God and surrender, you will live."
12. "If you don't, the city will be burned."
13. The king was afraid of what people would say.
14. Jeremiah said, "God will protect you."
15. The king made Jeremiah promise not to tell anyone what they talked about.
16. When the officials asked, Jeremiah gave them a simple answer.
17. He stayed in prison until Jerusalem was captured.

Jeremiah 39

1. Babylon's army broke into Jerusalem.
2. King Zedekiah and his soldiers tried to escape at night.
3. The Babylonian army caught him.
4. They killed his sons and leaders.
5. Then they put out his eyes and took him to Babylon in chains.
6. Babylon's army burned the palace and the houses.
7. They tore down the city walls.
8. They took most people away as prisoners.
9. But they left the poor to take care of the land.
10. King Nebuchadnezzar told his officer, "Take care of Jeremiah. Do not hurt him."
11. Jeremiah was released from prison and lived safely.
12. God told Jeremiah to speak to Ebed-Melek, the man who helped him.
13. God said, "You will be safe during the trouble. You trusted Me."

Jeremiah 40

1. After Jeremiah was set free, the Babylonian captain told him,
2. "God gave this land to Babylon because of your people's sins."
3. "You can come with me or stay here—your choice."
4. Jeremiah chose to stay.
5. He went to live with Gedaliah, the new governor.
6. People who had left Judah heard Gedaliah was in charge.
7. They came back to Judah and lived there.
8. Gedaliah told them, "Don't be afraid. Live in the land and serve Babylon."
9. He promised they would be safe.
10. But a man named Ishmael secretly planned to kill him.

Jeremiah 41

1. Ishmael and ten men came to visit Governor Gedaliah.
2. They ate a meal together.
3. Then Ishmael killed Gedaliah and the men with him.
4. He also killed 70 travelers who came to worship God.
5. Ishmael threw their bodies in a pit.
6. He took others as captives and left.
7. Johanan and his army chased Ishmael.
8. When they found him, the captives ran to Johanan.
9. Ishmael escaped with eight men and got away.

10. Johanan led the rescued people toward Egypt.
11. They were afraid Babylon would punish them for Gedaliah's death.

Jeremiah 42

1. The leaders asked Jeremiah, "Pray to God for us. Tell us what to do."
2. They promised, "We will do whatever God says."
3. After 10 days, God gave Jeremiah an answer.
4. He said, "If you stay in Judah, I will protect you."
5. "Don't be afraid of Babylon. I will help you."
6. "But if you go to Egypt, you will die there."
7. "War, hunger, and disease will follow you."
8. "You said you'd listen to Me. So obey."
9. "If you leave, you will be punished."

Jeremiah 43

1. The leaders refused to listen.
2. They said, "Jeremiah is lying. God didn't tell you this."
3. They blamed Baruch for the message.
4. So they took everyone—including Jeremiah and Baruch—and went to Egypt.
5. When they got to Egypt, God gave Jeremiah another message:
6. "Take some stones and hide them where Pharaoh's palace is built."
7. "Say: Babylon's king will come here and set up his throne."
8. "He will burn the temples of Egypt's gods."

Jeremiah 44

1. God spoke to the people of Judah living in Egypt.
2. He said, "You saw how I destroyed Jerusalem because of sin."
3. "You kept worshiping false gods, even though I warned you many times."
4. "But you didn't listen, so I punished you."
5. "Now you are doing the same sins in Egypt."
6. "You are still burning incense to false gods."
7. "So I will punish you again. Most of you will die."
8. "Only a few will survive and return to Judah."
9. The people told Jeremiah, "We will keep doing what we want."
10. "We will worship the 'Queen of Heaven' like we did before."
11. "Back then, we had food and peace."
12. "Since we stopped, we have had trouble."
13. Jeremiah replied, "You brought this trouble on yourselves."
14. "God will punish you for your sins."
15. "You think false gods helped you, but they didn't."
16. "God will show you that He alone is in control."

Jeremiah 45

1. God gave a message to Baruch, Jeremiah's helper.
2. Baruch felt sad and tired.
3. God said, "Don't look for great things for yourself."
4. "I will bring trouble everywhere."
5. "But I will keep you safe wherever you go."

Jeremiah 46

Message about Egypt

1. God gave messages about other nations.
2. First, He spoke about Egypt.
3. He said, "Get your army ready, but you will lose."
4. "Your soldiers will run away."
5. "The day of punishment is coming."
6. "Egypt will fall, and its pride will be broken."
7. "They will cry for help, but no one will save them."
8. "Babylon's army is strong and will win."
9. "Even the best soldiers in Egypt will run."
10. Later, God said to His people:
11. "Don't be afraid, My people."
12. "I will bring you back from far away."
13. "I will punish the nations that hurt you."
14. "You won't be completely destroyed, but I will correct you."

Jeremiah 47

Message about the Philistines

1. God gave Jeremiah a message about the Philistines.
2. A flood of trouble is coming from the north.
3. The enemy's army is powerful—people will cry and run.
4. Cities will be destroyed.
5. Gaza and Ashkelon will suffer.
6. God's sword of judgment will not stop until His work is done.

Jeremiah 48

Message about Moab

1. God says, "Moab will be destroyed."
2. Towns will fall, and people will cry.
3. They trusted their strength and riches—but they will lose it all.
4. Moab's pride is too big.
5. People will run and cry in fear.
6. Judgment is coming to every city in Moab.
7. Moab was once powerful, but now it will be ashamed.
8. God says, "I know how proud they are—but it's all empty talk."
9. People will weep over the loss of their land and cities.
10. Those who escape will be few.
11. Moab had peace for a long time, but now they will be shaken.
12. God says, "I will send someone to pour them out like a jar."
13. They will be ashamed of their false god Chemosh.
14. Moab will be destroyed and mocked.
15. At the end, God says, "I will restore Moab's people later."

Jeremiah 49

Messages about Other Nations

About Ammon:

1. God says, "Why are you taking Israel's land?"
2. "Your land will be destroyed."
3. "But later I will bring you back."

About Edom:

4. God says, "No one can hide from My judgment."
5. "Edom will become a wasteland."
6. "Even the strong will be afraid."
7. "No one will live there again like before."

About Damascus (Syria):

8. "People are running in fear."
9. "The city will suffer and be weak. I will set fire to Damascus."

About Kedar and Hazor:

10. "Babylon will attack these desert people."
11. "They think they're safe, but they are not."
12. "Their land will become empty forever."

About Elam:

13. "Elam's army will be broken."
14. "They will be scattered across the world."
15. "But later I will restore Elam."

Jeremiah 50

Message about Babylon

1. God gave a message against Babylon.
2. He said, "Babylon's idols are fake. I will bring them down."
3. "A nation from the north will attack and destroy Babylon."
4. "My people, Israel and Judah, will return home and follow Me."
5. "They will look for the right path again."
6. "Their leaders led them the wrong way."
7. "Everyone who hurt them will be punished."
8. "Leave Babylon. Run from it."
9. "I will send many nations to fight against Babylon."
10. "They will defeat it."
11. "Babylon was happy when My people suffered—but I will punish them."
12. "Their city will be left empty."
13. "No one will want to live there."
14. "All nations will attack. Babylon has sinned against Me."
15. "The city will fall and never rise again."
16. "My people, leave Babylon and remember Me."
17. "Babylon crushed My people, but now I will crush Babylon."
18. "I will make their land dry and useless."
19. "Israel will return and have peace."
20. "Their sins will be forgiven."
21. "Babylon's army will be destroyed."
22. "The time for punishment has come."

Jeremiah 51

1. God says, "I will destroy Babylon for what it did to My people."
2. "Their city will be empty."
3. "Their idols will be broken."
4. "They were once powerful, but now they will fall."
5. "My people are not forgotten."
6. "Run from Babylon—don't stay there!"
7. "Babylon was like a golden cup, but it made nations crazy."
8. "Now it is broken."
9. "Nations tried to heal it, but they failed."
10. "God is punishing Babylon—tell everyone."
11. "God is using another nation to destroy it."
12. "Babylon's end is near."
13. "They were rich and proud, but it won't last."
14. "I will punish their army, kings, and people."
15. "God made the earth and controls everything."
16. "False idols are useless. They will be destroyed."

17. "God is the real King."
18. "Babylon burned Jerusalem, but now Babylon will burn."
19. "Jerusalem's people cried out, and God heard them."
20. "God says, 'You were My hammer, Babylon, but now I will destroy you.'"
21. "Babylon hurt many nations. Now I will hurt them."
22. "I will dry up their sea and their land."
23. "Their walls will fall."
24. "Jerusalem will be avenged."
25. Jeremiah told Seraiah to read this message in Babylon.
26. Then he said, "Tie a stone to the scroll and throw it in the river."
27. "Say, 'Babylon will sink and never rise again.'"

Jeremiah 52

The Fall of Jerusalem

1. Zedekiah was 21 when he became king. He ruled 11 years.
2. He did evil like the kings before him.
3. God became angry, and Babylon attacked.
4. After 2 years, Babylon broke into the city.
5. Zedekiah tried to escape but was caught.
6. They killed his sons and blinded him.
7. They took him to Babylon in chains.
8. Babylon burned the temple, palace, and houses.
9. They tore down the walls.
10. They took four thousands of people as prisoners.
11. They took gold, silver, and treasures from the temple.
12. Many items were listed: bowls, pans, basins, and more.
13. In total, thousands of valuable items were taken.
14. Babylon ruled over Judah.
15. Later, the king of Babylon released Jehoiachin from prison.
16. He gave him food and a place of honor.
17. Jehoiachin lived well for the rest of his life.

– Lamentations –

Poems mourning Jerusalem's destruction and the pain of exile.

Lamentations 1

1. Jerusalem used to be full of people. Now it is empty.
2. She cries all night. No one helps her.
3. Her people were taken away.
4. Her roads are empty. No one goes to the festivals.
5. Her enemies rule her.
6. Her children are gone.
7. Jerusalem remembers better days.
8. She sinned and was punished.
9. She did wrong and fell.
10. Her enemies took everything.
11. Her people are hungry.
12. Look at me and see my pain.
13. God sent fire into my bones.
14. I was tied up by my sins.
15. My young men were crushed.
16. I cry because I am alone.
17. No one helps Jerusalem.
18. God is fair. I sinned.
19. My friends left me.
20. I hurt deep inside.
21. People hear me cry, but no one helps.

22. God, punish them like you punished me.

Lamentations 2

1. God is angry. He destroyed Jerusalem.
2. He threw down the Temple.
3. He took away Israel's strength.
4. He killed people like an enemy.
5. God destroyed homes and palaces.
6. He stopped the festivals and Sabbath.
7. He left His Temple.
8. He planned to tear down the city.
9. The city gates are broken.
10. The leaders sit on the ground in silence.
11. I cry because of what I see.
12. Children beg for food and die.
13. No one can help Jerusalem.
14. The prophets lied.
15. People laugh and shake their heads.
16. Enemies shout, "We won!"
17. God did what He said.
18. Cry to the Lord.
19. Get up and pray at night.
20. Look, Lord. Children are dying.
21. Young and old lie dead.
22. You let the enemy kill everyone.

Lamentations 3

1. I have seen pain from God's anger.
2. He led me into darkness.
3. He turns against me again and again.
4. My body is broken.
5. He trapped me.
6. He left me in the dark.
7. He locked me in.
8. He won't hear my prayers.
9. My path is blocked.
10. He attacks like a lion.
11. He tore me apart.
12. He shot me with arrows.
13. I hurt inside.
14. People laugh at me.
15. I have no peace.
16. My hope is gone.
17. I remember my pain.
18. I said, "God is not helping me."
19. But I remember His love.
20. God's love never ends.
21. Every morning, He gives new mercy.
22. God is my hope.
23. Wait for God.
24. God is good to those who trust Him.
25. Be quiet and wait.
26. Accept suffering.
27. Let people hit you.
28. God will not stay angry forever.
29. He sees your pain.
30. He is fair.
31. He punishes, but He cares.
32. God knows when people are treated unfairly.
33. No one can go against God's plan.
34. Let us think about our sins.
35. Let us turn back to God.
36. Let us pray to Him.
37. We have sinned.
38. God has been angry.
39. He does not forgive right away.
40. People hunt us.
41. We are afraid.
42. I cry and cry.
43. I call to God.
44. He hears me.

45. He saves me.
46. Enemies tried to kill me.
47. I said, "I'm done."
48. But God heard me.
49. He came close.
50. He said, "Don't be afraid."
51. God helped me.
52. God judged my enemies.
53. God gave me justice.

Lamentations 4

1. Gold has lost its shine.
2. The people are treated like dirt.
3. Babies cry for food.
4. Mothers don't care for their children.
5. Rich people now eat garbage.
6. Punishment is worse than Sodom.
7. Leaders used to be strong and healthy.
8. Now they are weak and dirty.
9. Starving people die slowly.
10. Mothers cook their babies.
11. God showed His full anger.
12. No one thought Jerusalem would fall.
13. Prophets and priests did wrong.
14. They are dirty with blood.
15. People yell, "Go away!"
16. God does not accept them anymore.
17. We hoped for help, but none came.
18. The enemy chased us everywhere.
19. They were faster than us.
20. Our king was captured.
21. Edom, you laughed—but your turn is coming.
22. God will not punish us forever.

Lamentations 5

1. God, remember what happened to us.
2. Strangers took our land.
3. We are like orphans.
4. We must buy water and firewood.
5. We are tired.
6. We begged Egypt and Assyria for food.
7. Our parents sinned. We suffer for it.
8. Servants rule over us.
9. We risk our lives for bread.
10. Our skin is burned from hunger.
11. Women were attacked.
12. Leaders were hung.
13. Boys were forced to work.
14. Joy is gone.
15. Our hearts are sad.
16. We have sinned.
17. Our eyes are weak.
18. Mount Zion is ruined.
19. God, You rule forever.
20. Why do You forget us?
21. Bring us back to You.
22. Or have You rejected us forever?

– Ezekiel –

Ezekiel sees strange visions and tells exiles God will judge but also restore them.

Ezekiel 1

1. I was by a river in Babylon. I saw a vision from God.
2. It happened in the fifth year after King Jehoiachin was taken.
3. God spoke to me, Ezekiel.
4. I saw a big cloud and flashing fire.
5. Inside the fire were four living beings. They looked like people.
6. Each had four faces and four wings.
7. Their legs were straight, and their feet looked like shiny metal.

8. They had hands under their wings.
9. The wings touched each other. They moved straight ahead.
10. Each face looked like a man, a lion, an ox, and an eagle.
11. Their wings spread out.
12. They moved straight, wherever the wind took them.
13. They glowed like fire and lightning.
14. They moved quickly, like a flash of light.
15. I saw wheels beside each being.
16. The wheels looked like shiny crystals.
17. They could move in any direction.
18. The wheels were big and had many eyes.
19. When the beings moved, the wheels moved too.
20. The wind moved them together.
21. Wherever the beings went, the wheels went too.
22. I saw something like a glass dome above them.
23. Under the dome, their wings were stretched out.
24. Their wings made a loud sound.
25. When they stopped, they lowered their wings.
26. I saw a throne above the dome.
27. On the throne was someone who looked like a man. He glowed like fire and light.
28. It was bright like a rainbow. I knew this was God. I fell face down.

Ezekiel 2

1. God said, "Stand up. I want to speak to you."
2. His Spirit entered me and helped me stand.
3. He said, "I am sending you to Israel. They have turned against me."
4. "They are stubborn and don't listen."
5. "But they will know a prophet came to them."
6. "Don't be afraid of them, even if they fight you."
7. "Speak my words, even if they won't listen."
8. "Don't be like them. Listen to me."
9. I saw a scroll in God's hand.
10. He opened it. It was full of sad and scary words.

Ezekiel 3

1. God said, "Eat this scroll, then go speak to Israel."
2. I ate it. It tasted sweet.
3. He said, "Take my message to your people."
4. "I'm not sending you to people who speak a foreign language."
5. "I'm sending you to Israel. But they won't listen."
6. "They won't listen to me, so they won't listen to you either."
7. "They are stubborn."
8. "But I will make you just as strong."
9. "Don't be afraid of them."
10. "Listen carefully to everything I say."
11. "Go speak to the people. Tell them, whether they listen or not."
12. The Spirit lifted me up. I heard loud sounds around me.
13. I heard the sound of the wings and wheels moving.
14. The Spirit carried me away. I felt upset and angry, but God was with me.
15. I sat with the people for seven days. I was silent.
16. After seven days, God said,
17. "I made you a watchman for Israel. Listen to me and warn them."

18. "If I say someone will die and you don't warn them, they will die, and I will hold you responsible."
19. "But if you warn them and they ignore you, you are not responsible."
20. "If a good person turns bad and you don't warn them, they will die, and you'll be guilty."
21. "But if you warn them, you save yourself."
22. God told me to go to the valley.
23. I saw God's glory there. I fell face down.
24. The Spirit entered me and stood me up.
25. God said, "You will be tied up."
26. "I will make you silent. You won't speak unless I allow it."
27. "When I speak to you, you will say my words. If people won't listen, it's their choice."

Ezekiel 4

1. God said, "Take a brick. Draw the city of Jerusalem on it."
2. "Show it being attacked. Build walls, ramps, and camps around it."
3. "Put a metal pan between you and the city. This shows my anger."
4. "Lie on your left side for 390 days. That shows how long Israel sinned."
5. "Then lie on your right side for 40 days. That shows how long Judah sinned."
6. "Every day equals one year of sin."
7. "Face Jerusalem. Show that punishment is coming."
8. "I will tie you down so you can't move."
9. "Make bread from wheat, barley, beans, and other grains."
10. "Eat only a small amount each day."
11. "Drink only a little water each day."
12. "Cook your food over cow waste."
13. God said, "This shows how my people will eat unclean food in other nations."
14. I said, "God, I've never eaten unclean food."
15. God said, "Okay, use cow waste instead of human waste."
16. Then God said, "People in Jerusalem will have little food and water."
17. "They will be weak, sad, and scared."

Ezekiel 5

1. God said, "Take a sword. Use it to cut your hair and beard."
2. "Divide the hair into three parts. Burn one-third inside the city. Chop one-third with the sword. Throw one-third into the wind."
3. "Keep a few hairs. Then burn some of them too."
4. "This shows what will happen to the people in Jerusalem."
5. "I placed Jerusalem in the center of nations."
6. "But the people disobeyed more than the other nations."
7. "They rejected my laws."
8. "So I am against them. I will punish them."
9. "I will do things I've never done before."
10. "Parents will eat their own children. Children will eat their parents."
11. "I will leave few people alive. My Temple will no longer be honored."
12. "One-third will die from disease and hunger. One-third will die by the sword. One-third will be scattered."
13. "My anger will end. Then I will rest."
14. "I will ruin Jerusalem. People will see it and be shocked."
15. "When I punish you, other nations will watch and fear."

16. “I will send hunger, war, and disease.”
17. “I will kill people and animals.”

Ezekiel 6

1. God said,
2. “Speak to the mountains of Israel.”
3. “Say: God is angry. He will destroy the altars to false gods.”
4. “The people who worshiped them will die beside them.”
5. “I will scatter their bones around the altars.”
6. “Cities will be empty. Altars will be broken.”
7. “People will die. Then you will know I am God.”
8. “But I will let a few survive.”
9. “Those who escape will remember me. They will feel sorry for their sins.”
10. “They will know I punished them for a reason.”
11. God said, “Clap your hands and stomp your feet. Say, ‘They will die by sword, hunger, and disease.’”
12. “The far and the near will all be punished.”
13. “They will die near their idols.”
14. “Then they will know I am God.”

Ezekiel 7

1. God said,
2. “The end is coming for Israel.”
3. “I will punish you for your sins.”
4. “I will not show pity. You will get what you deserve.”
5. “Disaster is coming. It cannot be stopped.”
6. “The end is near.”
7. “Trouble is coming, not joy.”
8. “I will pour out my anger. I will judge you.”
9. “I will not show mercy.”
10. “The time has come. Your punishment is here.”
11. “Violence has taken over. Nothing good remains.”
12. “Buyers and sellers will lose everything.”
13. “They will not get their land back.”
14. “People will blow trumpets, but no one will fight.”
15. “Enemies are outside. Disease and hunger are inside.”
16. “Those who survive will hide in caves and cry.”
17. “Everyone will be scared.”
18. “They will wear rags and shave their heads.”
19. “They will throw away their silver and gold.”
20. “They used their money for idols. Now it means nothing.”
21. “I will give their treasures to enemies.”
22. “I will turn away from them. Enemies will destroy everything.”
23. “The land is full of violence.”
24. “I will bring the worst nations to take it.”
25. “Trouble is coming. No peace will come.”
26. “Disaster after disaster. No answers.”
27. “The king, the prince, and the people will all be afraid. Then they will know I am God.”

Ezekiel 8

1. Six years later, on the sixth month and fifth day, I sat in my house.
2. God’s power came on me. I saw a glowing figure like fire.
3. He grabbed me and lifted me between earth and heaven.
4. He showed me a vision of Jerusalem.

5. I saw a statue that made God angry.
6. God said, "Do you see this? You will see worse things."
7. He took me to a gate and showed me a hole in the wall.
8. He said, "Dig through." I did.
9. He said, "Go inside and look."
10. I saw drawings of animals and idols on the walls.
11. Seventy leaders of Israel were worshiping them.
12. God said, "They think I can't see them."
13. He said, "You will see worse."
14. He showed women crying for a false god.
15. He said, "You will see even worse than this."
16. I saw men at the Temple with their backs to God. They faced the sun and worshiped it.
17. God said, "They are doing terrible things."
18. "I will not show mercy. I will punish them."

Ezekiel 9

1. God called out, "Bring the guards with weapons."
2. Six men came. One man carried writing tools. They stood by the Temple.
3. God's glory moved to the entrance. He called the man with the tools.
4. God said, "Go through the city. Mark the people who are sad about the sins here."
5. Then He said to the others, "Follow him. Kill everyone who does not have the mark."
6. "Start at my Temple."
7. They began with the leaders.
8. I fell on my face and said, "God, will you destroy everyone?"
9. God said, "The people are full of sin. They say I don't see them."
10. "I will not pity them. They will get what they deserve."
11. The man with the tools came back and said, "I did what you told me."

Ezekiel 10

1. I saw a throne above the cherub angels.
2. God said to the man with the tools, "Take fire from between the wheels near the angels. Spread it over the city."
3. The man went in.
4. The cloud filled the Temple. God's glory was bright.
5. The sound of the wings was loud.
6. The man took fire and gave it to another.
7. The angels stood at the south side of the Temple.
8. Each angel had hands under its wings.
9. I saw four wheels. They looked shiny.
10. All four looked the same.
11. They moved in any direction without turning.
12. The angels and wheels were covered with eyes.
13. The wheels were called "whirling."
14. Each angel had four faces: man, lion, eagle, and ox.
15. These were the same beings I saw earlier.
16. When they moved, the wheels moved too.
17. They moved together, guided by the same Spirit.
18. God's glory moved to the Temple door.
19. Then the angels and wheels moved.
20. These were the same beings I saw by the river.

21. They each had four faces, four wings, and hands under the wings.
22. Their faces looked the same as before. They moved straight ahead.

Ezekiel 11

1. The Spirit lifted me up and took me to the east gate.
2. I saw 25 men. God said, "These men give bad advice."
3. "They say it's not time to build. But I will punish them."
4. God told me, "Speak against them."
5. The Spirit filled me. I said, "God knows your thoughts."
6. "You killed many people. You filled the city with death."
7. "So I will punish you."
8. "You are afraid of swords. But I will bring swords to you."
9. "I will take you out of the city and punish you."
10. "You will die. Then you will know I am God."
11. "This city will not protect you."
12. "You did not follow my laws."
13. As I spoke, one man died. I fell down and said, "God, will you destroy everyone?"
14. God said,
15. "Your relatives say you were sent away. But I will bring you back."
16. "I scattered you, but I will be with you."
17. "I will bring you home. You will remove idols and obey me."
18. "I will give you a new heart and new spirit."
19. "You will follow my rules."
20. "Then you will be my people, and I will be your God."
21. "But people who love idols will be punished."
22. The angels and wheels lifted up.
23. God's glory left the city.
24. The Spirit took me back to Babylon.
25. I told the people everything God showed me.

Ezekiel 12

1. God said,
2. "Ezekiel, the people see but don't understand. They hear but don't listen."
3. "Pack your things like someone going into exile."
4. "Leave your house during the day. Go somewhere else. Maybe they will listen."
5. "Dig through the wall and leave that way."
6. "Cover your face. Don't look at the land."
7. I did what God said.
8. The next morning, God said,
9. "The people are asking what you're doing."
10. "Tell them: This shows what will happen to the leader in Jerusalem."
11. "He will leave at night. He will dig through the wall."
12. "He will cover his face and won't look at the land."
13. "I will catch him and take him to Babylon. But he won't see it."
14. "I will scatter his people. Some will survive and tell others what happened."
15. "Then they will know I am God."
16. God also said,
17. "Eat your food shaking. Drink your water in fear."
18. "This shows how people in the land will eat when I punish them."
19. "Their cities will be destroyed."
20. "They will know I am God."

21. God said,
22. “The people say, ‘Prophecies never come true.’”
23. “Tell them: My words will happen soon.”
24. “No more delays. No more lies.”
25. “What I say will happen.”
26. God also said,
27. “People say, ‘The vision is for later.’”
28. “But I say: It will happen now.”

Ezekiel 13

1. God said,
2. “Speak against the fake prophets in Israel.”
3. “They speak lies from their own minds, not from me.”
4. “They are like foxes sneaking into broken walls.”
5. “They don’t help fix anything.”
6. “They lie and say, ‘God said,’ but I did not speak.”
7. “Their visions are fake.”
8. “I am against them.”
9. “Their names will be removed. They will not live in Israel.”
10. “They lied and said everything would be peaceful, but it wasn’t.”
11. “Their work is weak, like a wall covered in soft paint. Rain and wind will knock it down.”
12. “People will ask, ‘Where is the wall?’”
13. “I will destroy what they built.”
14. “They will know I am God.”
15. “I will destroy the wall and the people who painted it.”
16. “Those prophets gave false hope. I did not send them.”
17. “Now speak against the women who tell fake messages.”
18. “They sew charms and make magic to control people.”
19. “They lie to people for food and money.”
20. “I am against their magic. I will stop it.”
21. “I will save the people they were trapping.”
22. “They made good people sad and helped bad people feel safe.”
23. “I will stop their lies.”

Ezekiel 14

1. Some leaders came to sit with me.
2. God said,
3. “These men love idols. They shouldn’t ask me anything.”
4. “If people keep idols in their hearts but still ask me for help, I will answer with judgment.”
5. “They must turn away from idols.”
6. “Tell Israel: Stop worshiping false gods. Turn back to me.”
7. “If anyone keeps sinning and comes to me, I will answer with punishment.”
8. “I will turn against them.”
9. “If a prophet lies, I allowed it to test the people. I will punish that prophet.”
10. “Both the prophet and the person who asked will be punished.”
11. “Then Israel will stop sinning and follow me.”
12. God said,
13. “If a country sins, I will punish it by removing food.”
14. “Even if Noah, Daniel, and Job lived there, they could only save themselves.”
15. “If I send wild animals, the land will be empty.”
16. “Even if those three men lived there, they could not save their children.”
17. “If I send war, many people will die.”

18. "Only those three men would be saved."
19. "If I send disease, people will die."
20. "Again, only those three men would live."
21. "I may send war, hunger, wild animals, and disease."
22. "But I will let some people live."
23. "When you see how they live, you'll know I was right to punish them."

Ezekiel 15

1. God said,
2. "Is a grapevine better than other trees?"
3. "Can you use its wood for tools or furniture?"
4. "No. And after it burns, it's even more useless."
5. "If it was useless before the fire, it's worse after."
6. "That's what the people of Jerusalem are like. I will burn them."
7. "I will turn against them."
8. "The land will be destroyed because they turned against me."

Ezekiel 16

1. God said,
2. "Tell Jerusalem how sinful it is."
3. "You came from a land that didn't follow me."
4. "When you were born, no one cared for you. You were left alone."
5. "No one had pity. You were thrown away."
6. "I saw you and told you to live."
7. "You grew up and became strong."
8. "I saw you again and made you mine."
9. "I washed you and gave you clean clothes."
10. "I gave you fine jewelry and beautiful things."
11. "You looked like a queen."
12. "Your beauty was known everywhere."
13. "But you trusted in your beauty and turned against me."
14. "You acted badly with anyone who passed by."
15. "You gave away my gifts to win attention."
16. "You made false gods out of my silver and gold."
17. "You sacrificed your own children."
18. "You forgot me."
19. "You built fake altars in every place."
20. "You invited everyone to come to your altars."
21. "You even went after strangers and kings."
22. "You were not faithful to me."
23. "You were worse than other nations."
24. "You didn't remember where you came from."
25. "You acted worse than others, and it didn't even pay off."
26. "You gave yourself to other nations for nothing."
27. "You still were not satisfied."
28. "You did more evil than Sodom and Samaria."
29. "You did things even they didn't do."
30. "You acted like you had no shame."
31. "Your sisters, Sodom and Samaria, look better than you now."
32. "You looked down on them, but now you are worse."
33. "You will be punished like they were."
34. "But I will still remember my promise to you."
35. "You will be ashamed when you remember what you did."

36. "You will see how kind I am even when you don't deserve it."
37. "You will never brag again."

Ezekiel 17

1. God said,
2. "Tell this message to the people of Israel."
3. "A powerful king came to Israel. He took their king and leaders to his land."
4. "He made a promise with the new king of Israel to stay loyal."
5. "But the new king broke the promise."
6. "He sent messages to Egypt, asking for help."
7. "That king will not win. He broke his word."
8. "He will be punished."
9. "The king of Babylon will attack again."
10. "The king who broke the promise will die."
11. "He asked Egypt for help, but it won't work."
12. "He broke the oath. That's a sin."
13. "So he will be punished."
14. "But I will also plant a new leader."
15. "This new leader will grow strong."
16. "He will honor me."
17. "Then people will know I am God."
18. "I bring down the proud and raise up the humble."
19. "I keep my promises."

Ezekiel 18

1. God said,
2. "Why do you say, 'Children suffer for parents' sins?'"
3. "That saying is wrong. Everyone is responsible for their own actions."
4. "Every person belongs to me. The one who sins will die."
5. "A good person does what is right."
6. "He does not worship false gods."
7. "He helps others and is fair."
8. "He does not steal or cheat."
9. "He follows my rules. He will live."
10. "But if that man's son does wrong, he will be punished."
11. "If the son is violent, lies, or worships idols—"
12. "—he will not live. He will die for his sins."
13. "But if that man's grandson sees the evil and chooses to do good—"
14. "—he will not be punished for his father's sins."
15. "Each person is judged by what they do."
16. "If someone turns from sin, I forgive them."
17. "I don't want anyone to die. I want them to turn back to me."
18. "If a good person turns bad, he will die."
19. "If a bad person turns good, he will live."
20. "You say this isn't fair. But my way is fair."
21. "Your way is wrong."
22. "I will judge each person by what they do."
23. "So change your hearts. Stop doing evil."
24. "I don't want anyone to die. Please turn back and live."

Ezekiel 19

1. God said, "Sing a sad song for the leaders of Israel."
2. "Your mother was strong, like a lioness. She raised her cubs."

3. “One cub became strong, but he was captured and taken to Egypt.”
4. “She raised another cub. He also became strong.”
5. “But he attacked people, so they trapped him too.”
6. “He was taken in chains to Babylon.”
7. “Then the mother became like a dry vine, useless and burned.”
8. “This is a sad song, and it is true.”

Ezekiel 20

1. Some leaders of Israel came to ask me questions.
2. God said, “Don’t answer them. They don’t follow me.”
3. “Remind them what their ancestors did.”
4. “In Egypt, I told them to stop worshiping false gods.”
5. “I wanted to bring them to a good land.”
6. “But they disobeyed. They did not stop their sin.”
7. “So I was angry. I almost punished them in Egypt.”
8. “But I held back, so other nations would respect my name.”
9. “I brought them out of Egypt anyway.”
10. “In the desert, I gave them rules to live by.”
11. “I gave them a special day to rest—the Sabbath.”
12. “But they didn’t listen.”
13. “I thought about destroying them, but I didn’t.”
14. “I let their children live and gave them the same rules.”
15. “But they also disobeyed.”
16. “They followed idols.”
17. “Again, I held back from destroying them.”
18. “I warned their children not to live like their parents.”
19. “I told them to obey me.”
20. “They refused again.”
21. “So I let them follow their bad ways to learn a lesson.”
22. “But I did not destroy them all.”
23. “I told them I would scatter them to other countries.”
24. “They did not keep my laws.”
25. “They worshiped false gods.”
26. “I let them suffer because of their sins.”
27. “Tell them they made me angry with idols.”
28. “They worshiped statues on hills and offered sacrifices.”
29. “They called those places ‘high places,’ and the name stuck.”
30. “I asked them, ‘Why do you keep sinning like your fathers?’”
31. “You still worship false gods and sacrifice your children.”
32. “You think you can be like other nations. But you can’t.”
33. “I will punish you with strength and anger.”
34. “I will bring you back from the countries where you were taken.”
35. “I will judge you face to face.”
36. “Just like I judged your ancestors in the desert.”
37. “I will separate those who obey from those who don’t.”
38. “The rebels will not return to Israel.”
39. “You who love idols—go worship them! But later, you will listen to me.”
40. “One day, all of Israel will worship me on my holy mountain.”
41. “I will accept you again.”
42. “You will know I am God when I bring you home.”

43. "You will remember your sins and feel sorry."
44. "I will help you, even though you don't deserve it."

Ezekiel 21

1. God said,
2. "Turn toward Jerusalem. Speak against the Temple and the land of Israel."
3. "I am against you. I will punish good and bad people alike."
4. "Everyone will know I am the Lord."
5. "My sword is ready. It will not go back until the job is done."
6. "Cry out loud, Ezekiel, because terrible things are coming."
7. "People will fall. They will be scared."
8. God said,
9. "A sword is sharpened and polished."
10. "It is ready to be used."
11. "Be ready for war."
12. "Cry, because the leaders of Israel will die."
13. "I will test my people."
14. "The sword will strike again and again."
15. "People will be terrified."
16. "Use the sword in every direction."
17. "I will stop being angry after this."
18. God said,
19. "Mark two roads for the sword—one for the king of Babylon to go to Jerusalem and one to another city."
20. "The king will stand where the roads split. He will use magic to decide where to go."
21. "He will choose to attack Jerusalem."
22. "People in Jerusalem won't believe it. But it will happen."
23. "They broke their promise, so they will be punished."
24. "Their sins are known now."
25. "The king of Israel will lose his crown."
26. "Things will be changed. The low will be lifted up, and the proud will be brought down."
27. "The kingdom will not return until the right person comes."
28. God also said, "Speak against the Ammonites."
29. "They lied and used false visions."
30. "Their time to be punished has come too."
31. "I will pour out my anger."
32. "They will be destroyed and never remembered."

Ezekiel 22

1. God said,
2. "Ezekiel, judge Jerusalem. Tell the people their sins."
3. "You kill people and worship idols."
4. "Your time has come."
5. "Nations will laugh at you."
6. "Your leaders use power to kill."
7. "You are cruel to parents, immigrants, orphans, and widows."
8. "You treat my holy things as unimportant."
9. "You lie, murder, and do evil."
10. "You do not respect family or others."
11. "You commit terrible sins."
12. "You take money for violence. You forget me."
13. "I will punish you for these things."
14. "When I punish you, you will be too weak to fight back."
15. "I will scatter you to other nations."
16. "You will be ashamed. Then you will know I am God."
17. God said,

18. "The people of Israel are like dirty metal."
19. "I will put them in the fire and melt them like silver."
20. "They will feel my anger."
21. "I will pour it out until the sin is gone."
22. "They will know I am the one doing this."
23. God said,
24. "You are like a dry land with no rain."
25. "Your prophets lie and take money."
26. "Your priests break my laws."
27. "Your officials take from others and hurt people."
28. "Your prophets lie to cover up evil."
29. "The people steal, hurt the poor, and treat others unfairly."
30. "I looked for someone to stand for the land—but found no one."
31. "So I will punish them all. They will get what they deserve."

Ezekiel 23

1. God said,
2. "There were two sisters."
3. "They lived in Egypt and did wrong things from the start."
4. "The older sister was named Oholah. The younger was Oholibah. They were mine, but they acted badly."
5. "Oholah (Samaria) wanted other nations instead of me."
6. "She chased after powerful men in uniforms."
7. "She let herself be used by them."
8. "She never stopped the evil she started in Egypt."
9. "So I gave her to those nations she wanted."
10. "They took her clothes and killed her. People laughed at her."
11. "Her sister Oholibah (Jerusalem) saw this but did even worse."
12. "She chased after more powerful men."
13. "She was even more sinful than her sister."
14. "She saw pictures of men and wanted them."
15. "They wore belts and helmets. She chased them too."
16. "She sent messengers to bring them to her."
17. "They came, but she got tired of them."
18. "So I turned away from her too."
19. "She went back to her old evil ways from Egypt."
20. "She chased men like an animal in heat."
21. "She remembered her old sins and wanted more."
22. "So I will bring those men against you."
23. "They will come from all sides."
24. "They will attack you with weapons and rules."
25. "I will let them punish you. They will cut you and take everything."
26. "They will tear off your clothes and take your jewelry."
27. "Your sins will stop. You will not remember Egypt anymore."
28. "I will give you to the people you hated."
29. "They will treat you badly and take your things."
30. "You did this because you left me and chased others."
31. "You followed your sister's path, so you get the same punishment."
32. "You will suffer greatly."
33. "You will feel pain and shame."
34. "You will break into pieces and cry."

35. "You forgot me. That's why this is happening."
36. God said, "Judge Oholah and Oholibah. Tell them their sins."
37. "They committed evil, worshiped idols, and killed children."
38. "They did all this and still came to my Temple."
39. "They did these terrible things on the same day."
40. "They dressed up to meet foreign men."
41. "They sat on fancy couches and welcomed them."
42. "Drunk people and noise filled the room."
43. "These women should have been ashamed."
44. "They acted like prostitutes."
45. "They will be judged like criminals."
46. "I will bring people to punish them."
47. "They will be killed, robbed, and burned."
48. "This will teach others to stop sinning like them."
49. "You will be punished for what you did."

Ezekiel 24

1. God spoke to me on the tenth day of the tenth month.
2. He said, "Write down this day. The king of Babylon is attacking Jerusalem."
3. "Tell this story: A pot is placed on fire. Meat is added."
4. "They use the best meat."
5. "Let it boil."
6. God says, "The city is full of blood. It is like a dirty pot."
7. "Blood is everywhere, not even hidden."
8. "So I will punish them where all can see."
9. "Trouble is coming. I will make the fire hotter."
10. "Add more wood. Boil the meat. Burn the bones."
11. "Heat the pot until it glows. Burn away the rust."
12. "The rust is still there. It won't come off."
13. "Your sins are stuck on you. I tried to clean you, but you wouldn't change."
14. "I, the Lord, have spoken. I will not change my mind."
15. Then God said,
16. "Your wife will die suddenly. Do not cry. Do not mourn."
17. "Do not weep or eat funeral food. Do not act sad."
18. The next morning I told the people. That evening my wife died. I did what God said.
19. People asked, "Why are you not mourning?"
20. I said, "God has a message for you."
21. "God will destroy the Temple, which you love."
22. "You will do what I did. You will not mourn or cry."
23. "You will stay quiet and know God did this."
24. "I am a sign for you. What happened to me will happen to you."
25. "Soon you will lose everything. Your sons and daughters will die."
26. "You will hear the news."
27. "Then you will know I am the Lord."

Ezekiel 25

1. God said,
2. "Speak against the people of Ammon."
3. "They were happy when my people were hurt."

4. "I will give their land to other nations."
5. "Ammon will become a place for animals."
6. "I will punish them for laughing at Israel."
7. "Then they will know I am God."
8. "Moab also said Israel is nothing special."
9. "I will let others take Moab's cities."
10. "Moab will be punished and given to other people."
11. "Then they will know I am God."
12. "Edom took revenge on Judah."
13. "So I will punish Edom. Many will die."
14. "My people will carry out my anger."
15. "Philistines acted with hate and tried to destroy Judah."
16. "So I will punish them. They will suffer greatly."
17. "They will know I am God when I punish them."

Ezekiel 26

1. On the first day of the month, God said,
2. "Tyre laughed when Jerusalem fell. They hoped to get richer."
3. "So I am against Tyre. Many nations will attack you."
4. "They will break down your walls and destroy your towers."
5. "You will be flat like a rock where people dry fishing nets."
6. "Your towns will be destroyed."
7. "King Nebuchadnezzar of Babylon will attack you with horses, chariots, and soldiers."
8. "He will kill your people and destroy your towers."
9. "He will break your walls with his weapons."
10. "Dust from his horses will cover you."
11. "His horses will trample your streets."
12. "Your riches will be taken. Your buildings will be torn down."
13. "Your music will stop. No more singing or playing."
14. "You will be left like bare rock. A place to dry nets."
15. "The nations around you will shake in fear."
16. "Kings will step down from their thrones and be afraid."
17. "They will say, 'Tyre is ruined. Once powerful, now silent.'"
18. "The sea and coastal cities will be shocked."
19. "I will make you a deep ruin. You will never rise again."
20. "You will go down with the dead. You will not return."
21. "People will look for you, but you will be gone."

Ezekiel 27

1. God said,
2. "Sing a sad song for Tyre."
3. "You said you were perfect and beautiful."
4. "Your land was by the sea. You controlled trade."
5. "Your ships were made from the best wood."
6. "Your oars, decks, and sails were top quality."
7. "You had the best workers."
8. "Your sailors and builders were smart."
9. "Your ship was filled with treasure."
10. "Men from other lands worked as guards for you."
11. "Soldiers stood on your walls."
12. "You traded with many nations. You became rich."

13. "You traded goods and people."
14. "You got horses, clothes, and metals."
15. "You got ivory and more from far lands."
16. "You traded for gems, fabrics, and spices."
17. "You traded food and supplies with Israel and Judah."
18. "You traded wine and wool."
19. "You received iron and spices."
20. "You got blankets and robes."
21. "Arab traders brought animals."
22. "Other traders brought gold and perfumes."
23. "People from many lands came to you."
24. "They brought fine clothes and rugs."
25. "Your ships were filled with cargo."
26. "Your sailors took you far, but a storm destroyed you."
27. "All your riches and workers were lost."
28. "People cried when your sailors screamed."
29. "Everyone left their ships and stood on the shore."
30. "They cried loudly for you."
31. "They were sad and shocked."
32. "They sang a sad song: 'Who is like Tyre, now broken?'"
33. "You brought wealth to many."
34. "Now you are sunk in the sea."
35. "The world is shocked."
36. "You are gone, and people are afraid."

Ezekiel 28

1. God said,
2. "Tell the king of Tyre: You are proud. You think you are like a god."
3. "But you are only a man, not God."
4. "You became rich and wise, but your pride is your problem."
5. "You think money makes you smart."
6. "So I will bring strangers to attack you."
7. "They will destroy your beauty and power."
8. "You will die like any man."
9. "Will you still say you are a god when you die?"
10. "You will die like others."
11. Then God said,
12. "Sing a sad song for the king of Tyre."
13. "You were once great and full of beauty."
14. "You were in a perfect place. But you sinned."
15. "You became violent and greedy."
16. "So I removed you."
17. "You became proud and corrupt."
18. "Your greatness was ruined by your evil."
19. "Now people see your fall and are shocked."
20. God also said,
21. "Speak against Sidon."
22. "I am against you. People will know I am God."
23. "I will send sickness and war."
24. "Israel will no longer be hurt by neighbors like Sidon."
25. "I will bring my people home."
26. "They will live safely and know I am God."

Ezekiel 29

1. On the twelfth day of the tenth month, God said,
2. "Speak against Egypt and its king."
3. "Pharaoh, you act like you made the Nile River."

4. "But I will pull you out of the river like a fish."
5. "I will throw you in the desert. You will die there."
6. "Egypt will know I am God."
7. "You were like a weak stick. Israel leaned on you and got hurt."
8. "So I will bring a sword to Egypt."
9. "Egypt will become empty."
10. "From one end to the other, it will be a desert."
11. "No one will live there for 40 years."
12. "I will scatter Egyptians to other countries."
13. "After 40 years, I will bring them back."
14. "But Egypt will be weak. It won't rule over others again."
15. "Israel will never trust Egypt again."
16. "Then they will know I am God."
17. On the first day of the first month, God spoke again,
18. "Babylon's army worked hard attacking Tyre, but they got nothing."
19. "So I will give Egypt to Babylon as a reward."
20. "They will take its treasure."
21. "On that day, I will give strength to Israel and let Ezekiel speak again. Then they will know I am God."

Ezekiel 30

1. God said,
2. "Cry out. The day of punishment is near."
3. "It is a dark day. A day for judging nations."
4. "Egypt will be attacked. People will be afraid."
5. "Other nations will fall with Egypt."
6. "Egypt and its helpers will fall."
7. "It will be the worst time for Egypt."
8. "They will know I am God when I destroy them."
9. "Messengers will run to warn others."
10. "Babylon's king will destroy Egypt."
11. "His army will kill many people."
12. "The rivers will dry up. The land will be empty."
13. "I will destroy their idols and leaders."
14. "Towns like Pathros and Zoan will fall."
15. "People in cities like Sin will be afraid."
16. "The land will burn. People will die."
17. "Young men will fall. Cities will be taken."
18. "Darkness will cover the land."
19. "Egypt will know I am God."
20. On the seventh day of the first month, God said,
21. "I broke the arm of Pharaoh. It cannot hold a sword."
22. "I will not heal it. I will break it completely."
23. "I will send Egyptians to other nations."
24. "Babylon's king will grow stronger. Pharaoh will grow weaker."
25. "The people will see this clearly."
26. "They will know I am God."

Ezekiel 31

1. On the first day of the third month, God said,
2. "Tell Pharaoh: You are like a tall tree."
3. "You stood tall, with many branches and water around you."
4. "Your branches gave shelter to animals and birds."
5. "You were taller than other trees."
6. "Your roots went deep. Your limbs were strong."
7. "But you became proud."

8. "So I gave you to powerful people. They cut you down."
9. "You fell, and everything under you was scared."
10. "Foreign people left you on the ground."
11. "Birds sat on your branches. Animals walked over your trunk."
12. "This is what happens to proud leaders."
13. "Other nations saw and were afraid."
14. "No one should think they are too great."
15. "I made the ground shake when you fell."
16. "I brought you down to the place of the dead."
17. "Other nations went down too."
18. "Egypt, you are like this tree. You will fall too."

Ezekiel 32

1. On the first day of the twelfth month, God said,
2. "Sing a sad song for Pharaoh."
3. "You think you are strong like a lion, but you are just a sea monster."
4. "I will trap you and throw you on land."
5. "I will let birds and animals eat your body."
6. "I will cover the land with your blood."
7. "I will darken the skies above you."
8. "I will make the stars and moon go dark."
9. "Other nations will be afraid when you fall."
10. "They will shake in fear."
11. "Babylon's king will destroy you."
12. "Your people will die."
13. "No more animals will walk near your waters."
14. "Your rivers will stop flowing."
15. "The land will be empty."
16. "This is a sad song for Egypt."
17. On the fifteenth day of the same month, God said,
18. "Cry for Egypt and its people."
19. "Say to them: You will die like others."
20. "You will fall by the sword."
21. "The dead will welcome you."
22. "Assyria is there, surrounded by graves."
23. "Their people were killed in war."
24. "Elam is there too. They were shamed."
25. "They died and lie among the dead."
26. "Meshech and Tubal are there. They scared others but were killed."
27. "They died like everyone else."
28. "Pharaoh, you too will lie among the dead."
29. "Edom is there."
30. "Other kings are there. They all died."
31. "Pharaoh will see them and be comforted."
32. "I let Pharaoh scare others, but now he lies with the dead."

Ezekiel 33

1. God said,
2. "Tell the people: A watchman warns when danger comes."
3. "If the watchman blows the trumpet and people don't listen, they are responsible."
4. "If they listen, they save their lives."
5. "If the watchman stays silent and people die, it's his fault."
6. "You, Ezekiel, are my watchman. Warn the people."

7. "If I say someone will die for their sin, and you say nothing, they will die—and I will blame you."
8. "If you warn them and they don't listen, they will die—but you will be safe."
9. "If someone evil changes, they will live."
10. "If people say, 'Our sins are too big,' tell them: They can live if they turn back to me."
11. "I don't want anyone to die. Turn from sin and live."
12. "If good people start doing wrong, they will be punished."
13. "If bad people stop doing wrong, they will be saved."
14. "Don't trust in your past. What matters is what you do now."
15. "If a bad person does right and keeps my laws, they will live."
16. "Their past sins will be forgiven."
17. "People say, 'That's not fair!' But my way is fair."
18. "If a good person turns bad, they will die."
19. "If a bad person turns good, they will live."
20. "You say my way is unfair. I will judge everyone fairly."
21. On the fifth day of the tenth month, someone from Jerusalem came to me.
22. That morning, God opened my mouth. I could speak again.
23. God said,
24. "The people left in the land think they are safe."
25. "But they keep doing wrong."
26. "They murder and worship idols. They will not keep the land."
27. "I will punish them. The land will become empty."
28. "The mountains will be quiet. Cities will be ruined."
29. "Then they will know I am God."
30. "People sit and listen to your words but don't obey them."
31. "They like how you speak, but they won't change."
32. "You are like a singer to them—nice to hear but not followed."
33. "But soon, they will see that your words were true."

Ezekiel 34

1. God said,
2. "Speak against the leaders of Israel. They are like bad shepherds."
3. "They feed themselves but not the sheep."
4. "They don't help the weak or heal the sick."
5. "The people are lost. No one takes care of them."
6. "They wander everywhere. No one looks for them."
7. "So I am against these leaders."
8. "They let the people be taken and scattered."
9. "I will stop them from leading. I will take care of the people myself."
10. "I will look for my sheep and bring them back."
11. "I will bring them home from other countries."
12. "I will feed them in safe places."
13. "I will give them rest."
14. "I will look for the lost and heal the hurt."
15. "But I will punish the fat and greedy ones."
16. "I will be a fair judge for my people."
17. "I will remove those who hurt others."
18. "You eat the good grass and trample the rest."

19. "You drink clean water and make the rest muddy."
20. "I will save my people from you."
21. "You push and shove the weak."
22. "I will rescue my sheep."
23. "I will give them one good shepherd—my servant David."
24. "He will lead them and take care of them."
25. "I will make peace with the land. There will be no wild animals."
26. "The people will live in safety and be blessed."
27. "The land will grow food."
28. "They won't be afraid anymore."
29. "They will never go hungry again."
30. "They will know I am their God."
31. "They are my people. I care for them like a shepherd."

Ezekiel 35

Message against Edom

1. God said,
2. "Speak against Mount Seir. That's where Edom lives."
3. "Say: I am against you. I will destroy you."
4. "Your towns will be empty. You will know I am God."
5. "You hated Israel and helped when they were attacked."
6. "Because you loved violence, I will let you be killed."
7. "Your land will be ruined."
8. "People will die in the mountains and valleys."
9. "No one will live there again. Then you will know I am God."
10. "You said, 'These two nations will be ours.' But I was there."
11. "Because of your anger and hate, I will punish you."
12. "You will know I heard all your insults."
13. "You bragged and spoke against me. I heard it."
14. "The whole world will celebrate when you are destroyed."
15. "Just like you were happy when Israel fell, others will be happy when you fall."

Ezekiel 36

God promises to restore Israel

1. God said,
2. "Speak to the mountains of Israel. Say: Your enemies said, 'We will take this land.'"
3. "But I heard what they said."
4. "Now I speak to you, mountains and hills, rivers and valleys."
5. "I am angry with the nations that laughed at you."
6. "I promise they will be punished. But you will be blessed."
7. "You will no longer be laughed at."
8. "Your trees and crops will grow again."
9. "I will help you. People will live here again."
10. "The towns will be rebuilt."
11. "I will bring people and animals back. You will grow strong again."
12. "People will live on your land. You will never lose them again."
13. "You used to be blamed for others' deaths. That will stop."
14. "You will not make your people die anymore."
15. "No one will insult you again."
16. God said,
17. "The people of Israel sinned in their land. Their actions were disgusting."
18. "So I punished them and sent them to other nations."

19. "But in those nations, people insulted me because of them."
20. "They said, 'These are God's people, but they had to leave His land.'"
21. "I cared about my name. So I acted."
22. "Tell Israel: I am helping you—not because you deserve it, but to protect my name."
23. "I will show other nations I am holy."
24. "I will bring you back from the other countries."
25. "I will clean you from your sins."
26. "I will give you a new heart and a new spirit."
27. "I will help you obey me."
28. "You will live in your land again. You will be my people, and I will be your God."
29. "I will save you from sin and bless your crops."
30. "You won't be hungry again."
31. "You will remember your sins and be sorry."
32. "I do this for my name—not because you earned it."
33. "I will clean you and rebuild your cities."
34. "Your ruined land will grow again."
35. "People will say, 'This land looks like a garden again.'"
36. "Nations will see that I rebuilt what was destroyed."
37. "I will let my people grow in number."
38. "Like sheep in Jerusalem, people will fill the cities. Then everyone will know I am God."

Ezekiel 37

Dry bones come to life & Israel becomes one again

1. God took me to a valley full of bones.
2. He showed me the bones. They were very dry.
3. He said, "Can these bones live?" I said, "Only you know."
4. He said, "Speak to the bones. Say, 'Dry bones, listen to God's words.'"
5. "God says: I will make you alive again."
6. "I will cover you with skin and breathe life into you."
7. I spoke, and the bones moved and came together.
8. Muscles and skin appeared, but they had no breath.
9. God said, "Speak to the wind. Say, 'Breathe into these bones.'"
10. I spoke, and breath came. The bodies came alive and stood up.
11. God said, "These bones are like the people of Israel. They feel hopeless."
12. "Tell them: I will bring you out of your graves."
13. "You will know I am God."
14. "I will put my Spirit in you. You will live again."
15. God said,
16. "Take two sticks. Write 'Judah' on one and 'Israel' on the other."
17. "Hold them together in your hand like one stick."
18. "If people ask what this means, say,
19. 'God will make Judah and Israel one nation again.'"
20. "Hold the sticks so people can see them."
21. "Say: God will bring his people back from other lands."
22. "He will make them one nation with one king."
23. "They will stop worshiping idols."
24. "My servant David will be their king."
25. "They will live in the land I gave their ancestors."
26. "I will make a peace agreement with them that lasts forever."

27. "I will live with them. I will be their God."
28. "All nations will know I made Israel holy."

Ezekiel 38

God warns about Gog and future war

1. God said,
2. "Speak against Gog from the land of Magog."
3. "Say: I am against you, Gog, leader of Meshech and Tubal."
4. "I will turn you around and pull you out with your army."
5. "You will bring soldiers from Persia, Cush, and Put."
6. "Also Gomer and Beth Togarmah from the north."
7. "Get ready. Be prepared."
8. "Later, I will call you to attack a land that was once destroyed."
9. "You will come like a storm with many people."
10. "You will make an evil plan."
11. "You will say, 'Let's attack a peaceful land with no walls.'"
12. "You want to take things and control the land."
13. "Other nations will ask, 'Are you coming to steal?'"
14. "Tell Gog: When my people live in safety, you will attack."
15. "You will come from the far north with a big army."
16. "You will attack my people. But I will stop you so everyone sees my power."
17. "Long ago, prophets said you would come."
18. "When you attack, I will become very angry."
19. "There will be a huge earthquake."
20. "Animals, birds, and people will all feel it."
21. "Your army will panic and fight each other."
22. "I will punish you with disease, floods, and fire."
23. "Then everyone will know I am God."

Ezekiel 39

The end of Gog and God's promise to restore Israel

1. God said,
2. "Speak against Gog. Say: I am against you."
3. "I will knock your weapons out of your hands."
4. "You and your army will fall on the mountains of Israel."
5. "You will die in the open. I have spoken."
6. "I will send fire on your land and your allies."
7. "Then people will know I am God."
8. "What I said will happen. It will come true."
9. "People in Israel will use your weapons for firewood."
10. "They will not need to cut wood for seven years."
11. "Gog's army will be buried in Israel. The valley will be named after Gog."
12. "It will take seven months to bury all the dead."
13. "Everyone will help. It will be a big job."
14. "Men will be hired to search for bones."
15. "When bones are found, they will be marked for burial."
16. "The city nearby will be called Hamonah, meaning 'multitude.'"
17. God said, "Call the birds and wild animals."
18. "Tell them to come eat the bodies of Gog's army."

19. "Eat the meat and drink the blood."
20. "You will eat like at a big feast."
21. "Everyone will see my power."
22. "Israel will know I am their God from now on."
23. "Other nations will know Israel was punished for their sin."
24. "I let them be taken away, but I did not forget them."
25. "Now I will bring them back and show them kindness."
26. "They will live in peace and forget their shame."
27. "I will bring them home from other nations."
28. "Then they will know I am the Lord their God."
29. "I will never turn away from them again. I will put my Spirit in them."

Ezekiel 40

A man shows Ezekiel a new Temple

1. It was the 25th year of our exile.
2. God took me to Israel in a vision.
3. He set me on a high mountain. I saw a building like a city.
4. A man with a shiny face stood there. He had a measuring stick.
5. He said, "Watch closely. I will show you everything."
6. We came to the gate facing east. The man measured it.
7. Each doorway and room had the same size.
8. He measured the porch in front of the gate.
9. He measured the outer wall.
10. There were six guardrooms—three on each side of the gate.
11. He measured the entrance and the gate walls.
12. There were steps leading up.
13. He measured everything: the rooms, walls, and porch.
14. Then he took me to the outer courtyard.
15. There were rooms along the wall.
16. The pavement was around the courtyard.
17. He showed me more gates.
18. He measured each one. They matched the first gate.
19. We walked to the north gate.
20. He measured everything again—same size.
21. Each gate had steps, windows, and rooms.
22. We went to the south gate. It matched the others.
23. The same design was used everywhere.
24. Then he brought me to the inner courtyard.
25. The inner gate matched the outer gate.
26. There were steps and pillars.
27. We walked from gate to gate.
28. He measured the Temple itself.
29. The porch and walls had the same size.
30. He kept measuring—everything matched.
31. There were windows and decorations.
32. We looked at every side of the Temple.
33. Every entrance was measured.
34. All walls and rooms were the same.
35. The Temple was very exact and detailed.
36. The man showed me each area of the Temple.
37. He said, "This is God's house. Everything is holy."

Ezekiel 41

Inside the Temple building

1. He brought me to the main room of the Temple.
2. He measured the walls and doors.
3. He entered the inner room and measured it.
4. He said, "This is the Most Holy Place."
5. He measured the side walls.
6. He showed me three levels of side rooms built on the Temple.
7. Each level was wider than the one below it.
8. He measured the foundation.
9. He showed how the rooms were built into the walls.
10. There were 30 side rooms in total.
11. There were stairs and walkways between them.
12. On the west side, there was a large building.
13. He measured its size too.
14. He measured the front wall of the Temple.
15. He showed me the decorations on the walls—
16. carvings of palm trees and human figures.
17. These decorations covered all the walls.
18. Each carving showed a palm tree between two human shapes.
19. One face looked forward, the other to the side.
20. These carvings were everywhere.
21. The Temple doors were square.
22. There was a wooden altar.
23. The doors to the Most Holy Place were double doors.
24. They opened in the middle.
25. They also had palm tree carvings.
26. Windows and decorations were all around the Temple.

Ezekiel 42

Rooms for priests and Temple storage

1. The man took me to the outer courtyard.
2. He showed me rooms beside the Temple wall.
3. There were rooms on the north and south sides.
4. Each building had three floors.
5. The upper floors were smaller than the lower ones.
6. The rooms were used by priests.
7. There was a walkway between the buildings.
8. The man measured the whole area.
9. He said, "These rooms are holy. The priests will use them."
10. "They will store food and clothes used in worship."
11. "When they leave the holy area, they will change their clothes here."
12. The man measured the Temple's outer wall.
13. It formed a large square.
14. He said, "This wall separates what is holy from what is not."

Ezekiel 43

God's glory returns to the Temple

1. The man took me to the east gate.
2. I saw the glory of God coming from the east.
3. It was bright and powerful, like the vision I saw before.
4. God's glory entered the Temple through the east gate.
5. The Spirit lifted me up and took me inside.

6. God spoke to me from inside the Temple.
7. He said, "This is my throne. I will live here with my people forever."
8. "No more idols or sin near my holy name."
9. "I will live here with my people."
10. God said, "Show the Temple plan to Israel. Let them see their sins."
11. "Explain the design, laws, and rules."
12. "This Temple is holy. The top of the mountain is holy."
13. Then the man showed me the altar. He measured it.
14. It had three levels stacked like steps.
15. The top was square.
16. The whole altar had exact sizes.
17. Steps went up on the east side.
18. God said,
19. "Give a young bull for a sin offering."
20. "The priests must put blood on the altar corners."
21. "Burn the bull outside the Temple."
22. "The next day, offer a perfect goat."
23. "Then bring a bull and a ram."
24. "The priests will throw salt on them and offer them to God."
25. "Do this for seven days."
26. "Every day, give a goat to remove sin."
27. "After seven days, the altar will be ready."
28. "Then the people may offer sacrifices again."

Ezekiel 44

Rules for the Temple and priests

1. The man brought me back to the east gate.
2. God said, "Keep this gate shut. Only I, the Lord, have entered here."
3. "The prince may sit in it to eat, but only from the inside."
4. Then the man took me to the north gate. I saw God's glory in the Temple. I fell on my face.
5. God said, "Listen carefully. Watch everything in the Temple."
6. "Tell the rebels of Israel: Stop bringing in strangers and sinners."
7. "They ruined my Temple."
8. "You let others take care of my work instead of doing it yourselves."
9. "No stranger or sinner may enter my Temple."
10. "Levites who left me will still serve, but not in the most holy jobs."
11. "They will guard the gates and help in other ways."
12. "They will be ashamed for their past sins."
13. "They will not come near me or touch holy things."
14. "They will handle basic jobs only."
15. "But the priests from the family of Zadok stayed faithful."
16. "They may serve me at the altar and offer sacrifices."
17. "They must wear clean clothes when they serve."
18. "No wool clothing. Only linen."
19. "When they leave the holy place, they must change clothes."
20. "They must keep their hair neat—not too long, not shaved."
21. "They must not drink wine when serving."
22. "They may marry only virgins or widows of priests."
23. "They will teach people right from wrong."
24. "They will settle arguments using my laws."
25. "They must stay clean and follow my rules about purity."

26. "After being near the dead, they must wait seven days."
27. "Then they can return to serve in the Temple."
28. "I am their inheritance. They will not own land."
29. "They will eat offerings and holy food."
30. "They will receive the best of the harvest and gifts."
31. "They must not eat anything that dies on its own."

Ezekiel 45

Land for the Temple, priests, and rulers

1. God said, "When you divide the land, set aside a holy area."
2. "It must be large and square. This is for the Temple."
3. "Part of it is for the sanctuary."
4. "Another part is for the priests."
5. "Another part is for the Levites."
6. "Give land to the city next to this area."
7. "The ruler will get land on both sides of this holy area."
8. "He will no longer take land from the people."
9. "Leaders of Israel, stop being unfair. Follow my laws."
10. "Use honest scales, weights, and measures."
11. "Use one standard for dry and liquid goods."
12. "Use one standard for silver and money."
13. "Give part of your crops and animals as offerings."
14. "Give part of your oil and wheat."
15. "Give animals to use for sacrifices."
16. "Everyone must give to support the ruler's duties."
17. "The ruler must provide animals for sacrifices."
18. "On the first day of the first month, cleanse the Temple with a young bull."
19. "Put blood on the altar, Temple door, and gate corners."
20. "Do the same on the seventh day to remove sin."
21. "Celebrate Passover on the 14th day of the first month."
22. "The ruler must offer a bull for sin that day."
23. "For seven days, he must offer animals every day."
24. "Also give grain offerings and oil with each animal."
25. "Do the same in the seventh month for the festival."

Ezekiel 46

Temple worship and land rules

1. God said, "The east gate must stay closed during the week."
2. "But it must be opened on the Sabbath and the first day of each month."
3. "The ruler will enter through the gate and stand at the entrance."
4. "He must bring six lambs and one ram on the Sabbath."
5. "He must also bring a grain offering with oil."
6. "On the first day of the month, he must bring a young bull, six lambs, and one ram."
7. "He must bring grain and oil with each animal."
8. "The ruler must enter and leave through the same gate."
9. "The people must use opposite gates to enter and leave."
10. "The ruler will go in with the people and leave with them."
11. "During festivals, the same offerings must be brought."

12. "If the ruler brings a special gift, the gate must be opened for him."
13. "Every morning, offer a lamb to God."
14. "Also bring flour and oil with it."
15. "Do this every morning without fail."
16. "If the ruler gives land to his sons, it stays in the family."
17. "If he gives land to a servant, it goes back after the servant dies."
18. "The ruler must not take land from the people."
19. The man showed me a place behind the Temple.
20. He said, "This is where the priests cook the offerings."
21. He took me to four cooking rooms in the outer courtyard.
22. Each had a stone table for preparing sacrifices.
23. These were for the people to use.

Ezekiel 47

Water from the Temple and land boundaries

1. The man took me to the Temple door. I saw water flowing out from under the door.
2. The water flowed east, then south.
3. The man walked east with a measuring line. After 500 yards, the water was ankle deep.
4. After another 500 yards, the water was knee deep.
5. Then it was too deep to walk through—it became a river.
6. He said, "Do you see this?"
7. I saw many trees on both sides of the river.
8. He said, "This water flows to the Dead Sea. It will make the salt water fresh."
9. "Fish and life will fill the river."
10. "Fishermen will work from shore to shore."
11. "Swamps will remain salty."
12. "Fruit trees will grow along the river. They will never die or stop growing. Their fruit will be food, and their leaves will heal."
13. God said, "This is the land I am giving to the 12 tribes of Israel."
14. "Each tribe will get a part."
15. "These are the borders: On the north, from the sea to Hethlon and Hamath."
16. "Include towns like Zedad, Berothah, and Sibraim."
17. "The border continues to Hazar Enan."
18. "On the east, the border goes down from Hauran to the Dead Sea."
19. "The south border runs from Tamar to the river of Egypt."
20. "The west border is the Mediterranean Sea."
21. "Divide this land among the tribes."
22. "Strangers living among you will also get land."
23. "They must be treated like Israelites."

Ezekiel 48

The land is divided among the tribes

1. These are the tribes and the land each one will get:
2. Dan gets the land at the north border.
3. Next is Asher, just south of Dan.
4. Then Naphtali, south of Asher.
5. Then Manasseh, south of Naphtali.
6. Then Ephraim, south of Manasseh.
7. Then Reuben, south of Ephraim.
8. Then Judah, south of Reuben.
9. South of Judah is a special section for God.
10. This area is for the priests, Temple, and Levites.
11. The priests who stayed faithful will live near the Temple.

12. They get the best part of the land.
13. The Levites get land next to the priests.
14. They must not sell their land. It is holy.
15. Next to them is land for the city and workers.
16. The city will be a square—1.5 miles by 1.5 miles.
17. There will be open land around it.
18. The rest is for growing food.
19. People from all the tribes will work the land.
20. This entire section is square.
21. The ruler's land will be next to the holy area and the city.
22. The ruler's land goes from east to west.
23. South of this, the tribes continue:
24. Benjamin, then
25. Simeon, then
26. Issachar, then
27. Zebulun, then
28. Gad at the southern border.
29. This is how the land of Israel will be divided.
30. These are the city gates.
31. There are 12 gates, one for each tribe.
32. On the north: Reuben, Judah, and Levi.
33. On the east: Joseph, Benjamin, and Dan.
34. On the south: Simeon, Issachar, and Zebulun.
35. On the west: Gad, Asher, and Naphtali.
36. The city will be about 6 miles around.
37. The name of the city will be: "The Lord Is There."

– Daniel –

Daniel stays faithful in exile and receives visions of future kingdoms and God's rule.

Daniel 1

1. King Nebuchadnezzar of Babylon attacked Jerusalem.
2. He took King Jehoiakim and items from God's Temple.
3. He brought the items to his own god's temple.
4. He told his servant Ashpenaz to find smart young men from Israel.
5. They had to be healthy and handsome.
6. They had to learn Babylon's language and customs.
7. The king gave them food and training for three years.
8. Four of the boys were Daniel, Hananiah, Mishael, and Azariah.
9. The king gave them new names. Daniel became Belteshazzar.
10. Hananiah became Shadrach. Mishael became Meshach. Azariah became Abednego.
11. Daniel didn't want to eat the king's food.
12. He asked for vegetables and water instead.
13. The guard was worried they would look weak.
14. Daniel said, "Try us for 10 days."
15. After 10 days, they looked better than the others.
16. So the guard gave them only vegetables and water.
17. God gave them wisdom and knowledge.
18. Daniel could understand dreams.
19. After three years, they were brought to the king.
20. The king found them ten times wiser than his other advisors.
21. Daniel stayed in the palace until the next king ruled.

Daniel 2

The king's dream and Daniel's answer

1. King Nebuchadnezzar had dreams. He could not sleep.
2. He called his wise men to explain the dream.
3. He said, "Tell me what I dreamed and what it means."
4. The wise men said, "Tell us the dream, and we'll explain it."
5. The king said, "No. If you can't tell me the dream, I'll kill you."
6. "If you tell me, I'll reward you."
7. They said again, "Please tell us the dream first."
8. The king said, "You are stalling."
9. "Tell me the dream, or I'll know you are lying."
10. The wise men said, "No human can do this. Only the gods could."
11. The king got angry and ordered them all to be killed.
12. Daniel and his friends were in danger too.
13. Daniel asked the king for more time.
14. Daniel prayed with his friends.
15. God showed Daniel the dream and its meaning.
16. Daniel praised God.
17. He said, "God gives wisdom and controls kings."
18. Daniel went to the king and said, "Don't kill the wise men."
19. He said, "God showed me your dream."
20. The king asked, "Can you tell me my dream?"
21. Daniel said, "No man can—but God can."
22. "You saw a large statue in your dream."
23. "It had a gold head, silver chest, bronze stomach, iron legs, and clay feet."
24. "A rock hit the feet and broke the whole statue."
25. "The rock became a mountain that filled the earth."
26. "The statue means kingdoms."
27. "You are the gold head."
28. "Other kingdoms will come after you."
29. "The rock is God's kingdom. It will last forever."
30. "God showed you what will happen in the future."
31. The king bowed to Daniel.
32. He said, "Your God is the true God."
33. He made Daniel a high ruler.
34. Daniel asked for his friends to get jobs too.

Daniel 3

The fiery furnace

1. The king made a gold statue and told everyone to bow to it.
2. When the music played, all had to bow.
3. If anyone refused, they would be thrown into fire.
4. Shadrach, Meshach, and Abednego refused.
5. The king was angry. He called them in.
6. He said, "Bow now or be burned."
7. They said, "We won't bow. Our God can save us."
8. "Even if He doesn't, we will still not bow."
9. The king made the fire seven times hotter.
10. He threw them in. The fire killed the soldiers.
11. But the three men were not hurt.
12. The king saw four men walking in the fire.

13. He said, "The fourth looks like a son of a god."
14. He called them out. They were not burned.
15. He praised their God.
16. He said, "No other god can save like this."
17. He promoted the three men.

Daniel 4

The king becomes proud and is punished

1. King Nebuchadnezzar sent a message to all nations.
2. He said, "I want to tell you what God did for me."
3. "I had another dream. It scared me."
4. "I saw a big tree that reached the sky."
5. "It gave food and shelter to all."
6. "Then a messenger from heaven said, 'Cut down the tree.'"
7. "Leave the stump. Let the mind be changed to that of an animal."
8. "No one could explain the dream—except Daniel."
9. Daniel said, "The tree is you."
10. "You are great and powerful."
11. "But you will be driven away and live like an animal."
12. "You will eat grass for seven years."
13. "Then you will know that God is in control."
14. "But the stump means your kingdom will return when you learn this."
15. "So stop sinning. Do right. Maybe God will be kind."
16. One year later, the king was walking on his roof.
17. He said, "Look how great my kingdom is!"
18. A voice from heaven said, "Your power is gone."
19. The king became like an animal.
20. He lived outside and ate grass.
21. His hair grew like feathers. His nails grew like claws.
22. After seven years, he looked to heaven.
23. His mind came back.
24. He praised God and said, "God rules forever."
25. "He does what He wants."
26. The king got his kingdom back.
27. He said, "Now I praise the King of heaven."

Daniel 5

The writing on the wall

1. King Belshazzar gave a big party for 1,000 guests.
2. He used the gold cups taken from God's Temple.
3. They drank wine and praised fake gods.
4. Suddenly, a hand appeared and wrote on the wall.
5. The king turned pale and shook with fear.
6. He called his wise men to read the writing.
7. No one could explain it.
8. The queen said, "Call Daniel. He has wisdom from God."
9. The king said, "If you can read this, I'll give you riches and a high rank."
10. Daniel said, "I don't want your gifts, but I'll read it."
11. "Your father, Nebuchadnezzar, learned to honor God."
12. "But you, Belshazzar, did not."
13. "You used God's cups and praised idols."
14. "You did not honor God."
15. "So God sent this message."

16. "The writing says: Mene, Mene, Tekel, Parsin."
17. "Mene means: God has counted your days."
18. "Tekel means: You have been judged and failed."
19. "Parsin means: Your kingdom will be divided."
20. The king gave Daniel a robe, a gold chain, and made him third in command.
21. That night, the king was killed.
22. A new king, Darius, took over.

Daniel 6

Daniel in the lion's den

1. King Darius gave jobs to 120 leaders.
2. Daniel was one of the top three.
3. The king liked Daniel most because he was honest and wise.
4. Other leaders were jealous.
5. They couldn't find anything wrong with him.
6. So they made a plan.
7. They tricked the king into making a law:
8. "No one can pray to any god or person except the king for 30 days."
9. Anyone who breaks the law will be thrown into a den of lions.
10. Daniel kept praying to God three times a day.
11. The men caught him and told the king.
12. The king was sad but had to follow the law.
13. Daniel was thrown into the lion's den.
14. The king said, "I hope your God saves you."
15. The den was sealed with a stone.
16. The king could not sleep that night.
17. In the morning, he ran to the den.
18. He called out, "Daniel, are you alive?"
19. Daniel said, "Yes! God sent an angel to shut the lions' mouths."
20. The king was happy and pulled Daniel out.
21. Daniel had no injuries because he trusted God.
22. The king threw the men who tricked him into the den.
23. The lions killed them right away.
24. The king said, "Everyone must respect Daniel's God."
25. "He is the living God. He rescues and saves."
26. Daniel had success during the reign of Darius and the next king, Cyrus.

Daniel 7

Daniel's dream of four beasts and God's kingdom

1. Daniel had a dream in the first year of King Belshazzar.
2. He saw strong winds blowing over the sea.
3. Four big beasts came out of the water, each one different.
4. The first beast looked like a lion with wings. Its wings were pulled off. It stood like a man.
5. The second beast looked like a bear. It had three ribs in its mouth.
6. The third looked like a leopard with four wings and four heads.
7. The fourth beast was scary and strong. It had big teeth and crushed everything.
8. It had ten horns. Another small horn grew. Three old horns were pulled out. The new horn had eyes and a mouth.
9. Daniel saw thrones and God sitting to judge.
10. A river of fire flowed. Books were opened.

11. The beast with the mouth was destroyed.
12. The other beasts lost power.
13. Daniel saw someone like a man coming from the sky.
14. God gave him power over all people forever.
15. Daniel was confused.
16. He asked someone in the vision to explain it.
17. The four beasts mean four kingdoms will come.
18. But God's people will rule forever.
19. Daniel asked more about the fourth beast and the little horn.
20. The little horn spoke proudly and fought against God's people.
21. But God judged and gave power to His people.
22. The fourth beast means a strong kingdom will come.
23. It will crush everything.
24. Ten kings will come from it. Another king will rise and defeat three.
25. He will speak against God and hurt God's people for a time.
26. But God will take away his power forever.
27. God's people will rule all kingdoms forever.
28. Daniel was scared but kept the dream in his heart.

Daniel 8

Daniel's vision of a ram, a goat, and a future king

1. Daniel had another vision in the third year of King Belshazzar.
2. He saw himself in the city of Susa.
3. He saw a ram with two horns. One horn was higher than the other.
4. The ram charged west, north, and south. No one could stop it.
5. Then Daniel saw a goat come from the west.
6. It had one big horn on its head.
7. The goat ran fast and hit the ram. The ram was knocked down.
8. The goat became powerful, but its big horn broke. Four horns grew instead.
9. A small horn came from one of them. It grew very strong.
10. It grew so high it reached heaven. It stopped God's daily offerings.
11. It threw truth to the ground and succeeded for a while.
12. Daniel heard one angel ask another, "How long will this last?"
13. The other said, "2,300 evenings and mornings. Then the Temple will be clean again."
14. Gabriel came to help Daniel understand.
15. Daniel was scared and fell on his face.
16. Gabriel said, "This is for the end times."
17. The ram means Media and Persia.
18. The goat is Greece. The big horn is its first king.
19. The four horns are four kingdoms that will come after him.
20. The small horn is a later king. He will be tricky and evil.
21. He will destroy many people. He will fight against God.
22. But God will stop him without human hands.
23. Gabriel said, "Keep this vision secret for now."
24. Daniel was weak and sick for days.
25. Then he got up and went back to work.

Daniel 9

Daniel prays and gets a message

1. It was the first year of King Darius.

2. Daniel read in the Scriptures that Jerusalem would be empty for 70 years.
3. So Daniel prayed to God with fasting and sadness.
4. He said, "God, you are great and keep your promises."
5. "But we have sinned and done wrong."
6. "We did not listen to your prophets."
7. "You are right, and we are ashamed."
8. "We disobeyed and ignored your laws."
9. "You forgive, but we rebelled."
10. "We did not follow your commands."
11. "All Israel broke your law."
12. "You warned us this would happen."
13. "But we didn't turn back or ask for help."
14. "You are right to punish us."
15. "You saved us from Egypt. Please help us again."
16. "Don't be angry anymore. Jerusalem is your city."
17. "Please listen. Forgive us."
18. "We don't ask because we deserve it—but because you are kind."
19. "Lord, hear us. Please act now."
20. While Daniel was praying, Gabriel came.
21. He said, "God sent me to give you understanding."
22. "When you started praying, God answered."
23. "So listen carefully."
24. "There are 70 time periods to end sin and bring peace."
25. "From the command to rebuild Jerusalem until the chosen one comes, will be 7 periods and 62 more."
26. "Then he will be killed. The city will be destroyed again."
27. "A ruler will make a deal for one period. He will stop offerings. Then destruction will come."

Daniel 10

Daniel sees a vision and gets strength

1. In the third year of King Cyrus, Daniel had a vision.
2. It was true and very important.
3. Daniel did not eat fancy food or meat for three weeks.
4. On the 24th day, he stood by a river.
5. He saw a man in shining clothes with a gold belt.
6. His face was bright like lightning. His voice was loud.
7. Daniel was the only one who saw it. The others ran away.
8. Daniel became weak and pale.
9. He fainted when he heard the man speak.
10. A hand touched him and helped him up.
11. The man said, "Daniel, you are loved. Listen to me."
12. "God heard your prayer from the first day."
13. "But a spiritual enemy blocked me for 21 days."
14. "Michael, the archangel, came to help me."
15. Daniel bowed his head.
16. He said, "I am weak. I can't speak."
17. "I have no strength left."
18. The man touched him again and gave him strength.
19. He said, "Don't be afraid. Be strong."
20. He said, "I will fight the spiritual prince of Persia."
21. "Then the prince of Greece will come. But Michael helps me."

Daniel 11

Future wars between kings

1. The angel said, "I helped the king of Persia in the past."

2. “Three more kings will rise in Persia. The fourth will be rich and powerful.”
3. “Then a strong king will rise and rule a large empire.”
4. “But his kingdom will be divided into four parts.”
5. “One of his generals will become strong and rule another land.”
6. “The king of the south and the king of the north will fight.”
7. “One king will win, then lose. They will go back and forth for many years.”
8. “Armies will rise. Cities will be taken. Many people will die.”
9. “Some kings will make peace, then break it.”
10. “The north and south will keep fighting.”
11. “Sometimes the south will win. Sometimes the north will win.”
12. “One king will be proud and kill many people.”
13. “Later, another king will attack with a bigger army.”
14. “Many will join him, but they will fail.”
15. “The king of the north will take strong cities.”
16. “He will gain power and marry into the south’s family.”
17. “But the peace won’t last.”
18. “He will turn to other lands, but lose to a commander.”
19. “He will go home and fall.”
20. “The next king will collect taxes, then die suddenly.”
21. “A mean man will take over. He was not the rightful king.”
22. “He will trick people and take power.”
23. “He will make promises and break them.”
24. “He will surprise rich areas and defeat them.”
25. “He will fight the south with a strong army.”
26. “The south will be betrayed and fall.”
27. “Both kings will lie to each other. Their plans will fail.”
28. “The northern king will return home and attack God’s people.”
29. “Later, he will attack the south again but be stopped by ships.”
30. “He will go home angry and punish God’s people.”
31. “He will stop daily offerings and place a false god.”
32. “Many people will follow him. Others will stay faithful.”
33. “Wise people will teach others, but many will be killed.”
34. “God’s people will suffer for a while.”
35. “A proud king will come. He will say he’s greater than God.”
36. “He will succeed for a short time.”
37. “He won’t care about any god or family.”
38. “He will worship war and money.”
39. “He will reward those who follow him.”
40. “In the end, the king of the south will attack him.”
41. “He will enter many countries, including Israel.”
42. “He will take over Egypt and nearby lands.”
43. “He will become very rich.”
44. “But news from the east and north will scare him.”
45. “He will go to war again—but he will fall, and no one will help him.”

Daniel 12

The end and the promise of life after death

1. The angel said, “At that time, Michael will rise to protect your people.”

2. "There will be a time of great trouble—worse than ever before."
3. "But everyone whose name is written in God's book will be saved."
4. "Many people who have died will rise—some to life, some to shame."
5. "Wise people will shine like stars forever."
6. "Seal this message until the end."
7. "Many will search for answers. Knowledge will grow."
8. Daniel saw two angels. One asked, "How long until this ends?"
9. One said, "It will last a time, times, and half a time. When the trouble ends, all will be finished."
10. Daniel said, "I don't understand. What will happen next?"
11. The angel said, "Go your way. This is for the future."
12. "Some will be made pure. Others will keep doing wrong."
13. "The daily offering will stop. A false idol will be set up."
14. "There will be 1,290 days. Blessed are those who wait 1,335 days."
15. "Daniel, you will rest. Then you will rise to receive your reward."

– Hosea –

Hosea's broken marriage reflects Israel's unfaithfulness to God.

Hosea 1

1. God spoke to Hosea during the time of four kings in Judah and one king in Israel.
2. God told Hosea, "Marry a woman who will be unfaithful. This shows how Israel has turned away from me."
3. Hosea married Gomer. She had a son.
4. God said, "Name him Jezreel. I will punish Israel for what they did in Jezreel."
5. "I will break Israel's power."
6. Gomer had a daughter. God said, "Name her Lo-Ruhamah. I will not show love to Israel."
7. "But I will still love and help Judah."
8. Gomer had another son.
9. God said, "Name him Lo-Ammi. It means 'Not my people.' Israel is not my people anymore."
10. "But later, the people will be many again. They will be called 'Children of the Living God.'"
11. "Judah and Israel will come together. They will have one leader. Everything will be good again."

Hosea 2

1. Tell your people: "You are my brothers and sisters."
2. Tell your mother to stop being unfaithful.
3. If she doesn't, I will take away everything.
4. I won't help her children because they come from sin.
5. Their mother left me. She went after other men.
6. I will block her path so she can't find them.
7. She will look for them but not find them. Then she will say, "I should go back to my first husband."
8. She didn't know I gave her food, wine, and gold.
9. So I will take everything back.
10. I will shame her in front of others.
11. I will stop her joy, festivals, and celebrations.
12. I will destroy her vines and fig trees.
13. She used them to worship other gods.
14. So I will punish her.
15. But I will lead her into a quiet place and speak kindly.

16. I will give her back her land and make her happy again.
17. She will call me "my husband."
18. She will stop saying the names of other gods.
19. I will make peace for her with animals and people.
20. She will live safely.
21. I will be her God forever.
22. I will treat her with love, kindness, and fairness.
23. I will forgive her and accept her again.
24. I will say to 'Not my people,' "You are my people."
25. And they will say, "You are my God."

Hosea 3

Hosea takes his wife back

1. God said, "Love your wife again, even though she was unfaithful."
2. So I paid money to get her back.
3. I told her, "You must stay with me. Don't be with other men."
4. Israel will be without a king, leaders, or worship for a while.
5. But later, they will return to God and follow Him again.

Hosea 4

God's complaint about Israel

1. God says: "Listen, people of Israel. I have a complaint."
2. "There is no truth, no love, no knowledge of God."
3. "People lie, kill, steal, and cheat."
4. "That's why the land is sad. Animals and fish are dying."
5. "Don't argue. The priests are guilty too."
6. "My people are destroyed because they don't know me."
7. "The more priests there are, the more they sin."
8. "They want people to sin so they get more sacrifices."
9. "I will punish both priests and people."
10. "They will eat but still be hungry. They will sin but not grow."
11. "They love wine and false gods."
12. "They ask wooden idols for answers."
13. "They sacrifice on hilltops and under trees."
14. "Even the daughters sin, but I will not blame only them."
15. "Judah, don't follow Israel's sins."
16. "Israel is like a stubborn cow."
17. "They are joined to idols. Leave them alone."
18. "Their leaders love shame more than honor."
19. "A wind will carry them away. They will be ashamed."

Hosea 5

God warns Israel and Judah

1. Listen, priests and leaders. You have trapped the people.
2. You are deep in sin.
3. God says, "I know what you've done."
4. "You don't turn to me. You follow evil."
5. Israel is proud, but it will fall. Judah will fall too.
6. You bring offerings, but I won't accept them.
7. You have been unfaithful.
8. Blow the horn! Enemies are coming!
9. Israel will be punished. I told them but they didn't listen.
10. Judah's leaders have broken my laws.
11. Israel followed lies and was crushed.
12. I will be like rot to them.

13. They looked for help in other places, but not from me.
14. I will attack like a lion.
15. I will leave until they feel sorry and come back.

Hosea 6

God wants love, not fake worship

1. The people say, "Let's return to God. He hurt us, but He will heal us."
2. "In two or three days, He will raise us up."
3. "Let's try to know God. He comes like the rain."
4. But God says, "Your love disappears fast, like morning mist."
5. "I sent prophets to warn you."
6. "I want love, not sacrifices. I want people to know me, not just give gifts."
7. "But you broke the agreement like Adam did."
8. "Your cities are full of murder."
9. "Even the priests do evil."
10. "I see terrible things in Israel."
11. "Judah, your punishment is also coming."

Hosea 7

Israel's sin is deep

1. God says, "I tried to heal Israel, but I saw more sin."
2. "They lie and steal. They don't see that I remember everything."
3. "Their kings enjoy evil."
4. "They are full of desire and anger."
5. "On feast days, the leaders get drunk."
6. "Their hearts are full of evil."
7. "They burn with anger. Their leaders fall one by one."
8. "Israel mixes with other nations. They are weak now."
9. "Strangers take their strength, but they don't notice."
10. "Their pride shows, but they still don't return to me."
11. "They are like a bird flying to Egypt and Assyria for help."
12. "I will trap them and punish them."
13. "They ran away from me. They will be destroyed."
14. "They cry on their beds but don't pray to me."
15. "I gave them strength, but they used it to do wrong."
16. "They turned away from me. They will fall and be laughed at."

Hosea 8

Israel forgot God

1. "Sound the alarm! Enemies are coming because the people broke my agreement."
2. "They say they know me, but they don't obey me."
3. "They rejected what is good. So the enemy will chase them."
4. "They chose kings without asking me."
5. "Their idols make me angry."
6. "Those idols are made by people. They are worthless."
7. "They planted the wind, and now they get nothing back."
8. "Israel is swallowed up by the nations."
9. "They ran to Assyria like a wild donkey."
10. "They paid others for help. But I will gather them and punish them."
11. "Israel built many altars—but only sinned more."
12. "I gave them my laws, but they ignore them."
13. "They bring sacrifices, but I won't accept them."

14. "Israel forgot me and built palaces. Judah built strong cities. I will destroy them all."

Hosea 9

God is not pleased

1. God says, "Israel, don't be happy. You turned away from me."
2. "You gave your food and gifts to other gods."
3. "You will not stay in your land. You will go to Egypt or Assyria."
4. "You won't be able to worship me there."
5. "Your sacrifices won't mean anything."
6. "Everything you had will be ruined."
7. "The time for punishment is here."
8. "You think prophets are crazy, but they are warning you."
9. "You have sinned deeply."
10. "You used to be like good fruit, but now you follow shameful ways."
11. "Your children will be taken from you."
12. "Even if you have many kids, I will take them away."
13. "I see Israel in a good land, but I will still punish them."
14. "I will take away their children and end their blessings."
15. "All their evil started in Gilgal. I hate what they do."
16. "Their root is dry. They will have no fruit."
17. "They did not listen to me. They will be scattered."

Hosea 10

Israel will be judged

1. Israel was like a growing vine, but they only cared about themselves.
2. Their hearts are not right. They must be punished.
3. They will lose their king and leaders.
4. They make promises, but they lie.
5. People will cry for the idol at Beth Aven.
6. It will be taken to Assyria as a gift.
7. Their king will be gone like foam on water.
8. Their altars will be destroyed. They will be ashamed.
9. They have sinned for a long time. Now war will come.
10. They will be punished for their evil.
11. They liked easy work, but now they will work hard and be ruled.
12. God says, "Plant what is right. Follow me."
13. "But you planted evil and trusted lies."
14. "I will destroy your strong cities."
15. "Because of your great evil, you will be defeated."

Hosea 11

God still loves His people

1. God says, "I loved Israel like a child. I brought them out of Egypt."
2. "But the more I called, the more they ran away."
3. "I taught them how to walk. I carried them."
4. "I loved them, but they didn't understand."
5. "Now they will go back to slavery."
6. "Their cities will be destroyed by war."
7. "My people keep turning away from me."
8. "But I can't give up on them. I still care."
9. "I won't stay angry forever."
10. "They will follow me. I will bring them back."

11. "They will come home from far away."
12. "But Israel still lies and runs from me."

Hosea 12

Israel must turn back

1. Israel chases the wind. They lie and make deals with enemies.
2. God says He will punish them for what they've done.
3. Jacob fought in the womb. As a man, he wrestled with God.
4. He cried and begged for help. He met God at Bethel.
5. God is the Lord. His name is holy.
6. So come back to your God. Do what is right. Trust Him always.
7. But Israel is like a dishonest trader.
8. They say, "I'm rich. I don't need help."
9. But God says, "I am the one who helped you in the desert."
10. "I spoke through prophets to teach you."
11. "Your altars are useless."
12. Jacob ran to Aram and worked to get a wife.
13. A prophet led Israel out of Egypt and kept them safe.
14. But now they make God angry with their lies. They will be punished.

Hosea 13

Israel forgot God

1. Israel was once respected.
2. But they sinned by worshiping idols.
3. Now they will disappear like morning mist.
4. God says, "I am the Lord who brought you out of Egypt."
5. "I took care of you in the desert."
6. "But when you had food and safety, you forgot me."
7. "So I will attack you like a wild animal."
8. "You will be destroyed because you turned against me."
9. "I was the only one who could help you."
10. "You asked for a king. Now where is he?"
11. "I gave you a king, and I took him away."
12. "Your sins are stored up and will be judged."
13. "You refused to change when it was time."
14. "I could save you, but you won't listen."
15. "You are like a dry plant. Nothing good will grow."
16. "You will fall in battle because of your great evil."

Hosea 14

Return to God

1. God says, "Israel, come back to me. You have sinned."
2. "Say to me, 'Forgive us. We will praise you with our words.'"
3. "Don't trust other nations or idols. Only you, God, help us."
4. God says, "I will heal you and love you again."
5. "You will grow like flowers and trees."
6. "You will be strong and beautiful."
7. "You will live in peace and grow like grain and vines."
8. God says, "I am the one who gives you life. I am like a green tree."
9. "The wise will understand this. The foolish will ignore it."

– Joel –

A locust plague points to coming judgment, but God promises restoration.

Joel 1

1. This is the message God gave to Joel.
2. Listen, everyone. Has anything like this ever happened before?
3. Tell your children, so they can tell theirs.
4. Insects have eaten everything.
5. Wake up, you drunk people. The wine is gone.
6. A powerful enemy has come and destroyed the land.
7. They ruined the vines and trees.
8. Cry like someone who has lost everything.
9. There are no more offerings. The priests are sad.
10. The fields are ruined. No food is growing.
11. Farmers are upset. The wheat and barley are gone.
12. The vines and trees are dry. Joy has left the people.
13. Priests, put on sackcloth and cry.
14. Announce a day to fast. Call everyone to pray.
15. The day of the Lord is near. Trouble is coming.
16. There is no food or joy in the land.
17. Seeds rot in the ground. Barns are empty.
18. Animals are hungry. Even the sheep have no food.
19. God, I cry to you. Fires have burned the land.
20. Even the animals cry to you. The water is gone, and the land is burned.

Joel 2

1. Blow the trumpet! Warn everyone!
2. A dark and scary day is coming.
3. Enemies are burning everything in their path.
4. They look like soldiers ready to fight.
5. They run fast and climb walls.
6. People are scared and shake with fear.
7. The army stays in line and never stops.
8. They run into houses and jump on roofs.
9. The earth shakes. The sky goes dark.
10. God leads this powerful army.
11. His army is big and strong. Who can stand against it?
12. God says, "Come back to me with all your heart."
13. "Don't just tear your clothes—change your hearts."
14. "I am kind and ready to forgive."
15. Blow the trumpet! Call everyone together!
16. Bring the old and the young. Even babies.
17. Let the priests cry and pray.
18. Then God will care for the land again.
19. He will send food and stop the enemies.
20. The enemy will be pushed far away.
21. Don't be afraid. God will do great things.
22. Animals, don't be afraid. Grass will grow again.
23. People, be glad! God will send rain again.
24. The fields will be full of grain, wine, and oil.
25. God will give back what was lost.
26. You will have plenty to eat and be thankful.
27. You will know God is with you.

28. Later, God will pour out His Spirit on everyone.
29. Men and women will speak His words.
30. There will be signs in the sky and on earth.
31. The sun will go dark before the day of the Lord comes.
32. But anyone who calls on God will be saved.

Joel 3

1. God says, "I will bring back my people."
2. "I will judge the nations that hurt them."
3. "They sold my people as slaves. They gave away children for food and drinks."
4. "You will be paid back for what you did."
5. "You took my silver and gold and ruined my temple."
6. "You sold my people to faraway lands."
7. "But I will bring them back."
8. "You will be taken as slaves instead."
9. "Call the nations to get ready for war."
10. "Even weak people must prepare to fight."
11. "All nations, come and face me."
12. "I will sit and judge them all."
13. "They are full of sin. It is time to punish them."
14. Big decisions will be made that day.
15. The sun and moon will go dark.
16. God will speak loudly from Jerusalem.
17. Then you will know He is your God.
18. The mountains will drip with sweet wine.
19. Egypt and Edom will be destroyed.
20. But God's people will live forever.
21. God will forgive them.
22. The Lord will live in Jerusalem.

– Amos –

Amos condemns injustice and warns of God's judgment on Israel.

Amos 1

1. These are the words of Amos, a shepherd.
2. God gave him this message two years before an earthquake.
3. God says, "Damascus hurt others badly. I will punish them."
4. "I will burn their cities."
5. "I will break their gates and kill their king."
6. God says, "Gaza took people and sold them as slaves. I will punish them."
7. "I will burn their walls and destroy their leaders."
8. "No one will be left."
9. God says, "Tyre also sold people as slaves. I will punish them."
10. "I will burn their cities."
11. God says, "Edom chased his own brother with a sword. I will punish them."
12. "I will burn their cities and destroy their power."
13. God says, "Ammon hurt pregnant women in war. I will punish them."
14. "I will burn their capital city and kill their leaders."
15. "Their king will be taken away."

Amos 2

1. God says, "Moab burned the bones of a king. I will punish them."
2. "I will burn their cities and kill their leaders."

3. "Their rulers will die too."
4. God says, "Judah rejected my laws. I will punish them."
5. "I will burn their cities."
6. God says, "Israel sins again and again."
7. "They sell poor people for money or shoes."
8. "They hurt the weak and the helpless."
9. "They disrespect my holy name."
10. "They lie on clothes taken from others."
11. "They drink wine paid for by unfair fines."
12. "But I destroyed the enemy for them."
13. "I brought them out of Egypt and led them for 40 years."
14. "I gave them prophets and leaders."
15. "But you told the prophets to be quiet."
16. "I will crush you like a heavy cart."
17. "The fast won't escape. The strong will fall."
18. "The warriors and soldiers will all run away."

Amos 3

1. God says, "Listen, people of Israel. I brought you out of Egypt."
2. "You are the only nation I chose. So I will punish you for your sins."
3. Two people must agree to walk together.
4. A lion only roars if it catches something.
5. A trap only snaps if something triggers it.
6. A trumpet sounds when trouble comes.
7. God tells His plans to His prophets.
8. If God speaks, the prophet must speak too.
9. Shout this warning: Enemies will attack Israel.
10. The people store up violence in their homes.
11. God says, "An enemy will take your strength and rob your palaces."
12. "Only a few will survive, like a leg or piece of an ear."
13. "I will punish Israel for worshiping other gods."
14. "I will destroy their altars."
15. "I will tear down their houses, both big and small."

Amos 4

1. God says, "You rich women hurt the poor and demand more wine. You will be taken away."
2. "You will be dragged out of the city."
3. "You will be thrown out one by one."
4. "Go ahead, bring your sacrifices, but they don't mean anything to me."
5. "You love to show off your offerings."
6. "I gave you hunger, but you didn't return to me."
7. "I stopped the rain, but you didn't return to me."
8. "I sent drought and made you wander for water, but you didn't return to me."
9. "I ruined your crops with bugs and mold, but you didn't return to me."
10. "I sent sickness and war, but you didn't return to me."
11. "I destroyed cities like Sodom, but you didn't return to me."
12. "So now, get ready to meet your God."
13. "I made the mountains, the wind, and everything. I see your thoughts. I am the Lord."

Amos 5

1. "Listen to this sad song about Israel."
2. "The nation has fallen and will not rise."

3. "Only a few people will survive."
4. God says, "Come back to me and live."
5. "Don't go to your old places of worship. They won't help you."
6. "Seek God and live, or He will destroy you."
7. "You twist what is right and good."
8. "God made the stars and brings day and night."
9. "He gives strength and takes it away."
10. "You hate those who tell the truth."
11. "You cheat the poor. So you will not enjoy your fancy houses or wine."
12. "I know your many sins. You hurt the good people."
13. "The wise stay silent, because things are so bad."
14. "Do what is good so you may live."
15. "Hate evil, love good. Maybe God will show mercy."
16. God says, "People will cry in the streets."
17. "Even farms will be full of sadness."
18. "You want the day of the Lord, but it will be terrible for you."
19. "It will be a day of danger, not light."
20. "There will be no joy."
21. God says, "I hate your festivals. I will not accept your offerings."
22. "Take away your songs. I won't listen."
23. "Let justice flow like water."
24. "You brought me sacrifices in the desert, but you also worshiped fake gods."
25. "So I will send you far away to another land."

Amos 6

Warning to the rich

1. You think you're safe and important. But trouble is coming.
2. Look at other cities. They were strong too, but now they're gone.
3. You avoid thinking about danger.
4. You lie on soft beds and eat the best food.
5. You play music and drink too much wine.
6. You don't care that your nation is falling.
7. So you will be the first to go into exile.
8. God says, "I hate your pride. I will give your cities to enemies."
9. If ten people are left in one house, they will die.
10. A relative will come to take the bodies out.
11. God will destroy big and small houses.
12. You turn what is good into lies.
13. You brag for no reason.
14. God says, "I will bring a nation to crush you from one end of the land to the other."

Amos 7

Visions of judgment

1. God showed me a vision: He was sending locusts to eat the crops.
2. I said, "God, please don't do this. The people are too weak."
3. So God stopped the locusts.
4. Then God showed me fire that burned everything.
5. I said, "God, please stop. The people can't survive."
6. So God stopped the fire.
7. Then God showed me a wall and a tool to check if it was straight.
8. God said, "I am checking my people. I will not ignore their sin anymore."
9. The places of worship and the king's house will be destroyed.

10. Amaziah the priest told the king, "Amos is speaking against you."
11. He said, "Amos says you will die and Israel will go into exile."
12. Amaziah told Amos, "Go away. Speak somewhere else."
13. "Don't speak here at the king's place."
14. Amos said, "I'm not a prophet by trade. I take care of animals."
15. "But God told me to speak to Israel."
16. "So listen. You told me to stop speaking God's word."
17. "But here's what God says: Your wife will suffer. Your land will be taken. You will die in another country. And Israel will be taken away."

Amos 8

The end is near

1. God showed me a basket of ripe fruit.
2. He said, "The time is ripe. The end has come for Israel."
3. People will cry. There will be dead bodies everywhere.
4. Listen, you who crush the poor.
5. You say, "When will the Sabbath end so we can sell again?"
6. "We will cheat with false prices and lie about weights."
7. God says, "I see what you're doing. I will not forget."
8. The land will shake. People will cry.
9. The sun will go dark at noon.
10. Joy will turn to sadness.
11. A time is coming when people will hunger for God's word.
12. They will search but not find it.
13. Even strong young people will faint.
14. Those who worship idols will fall and never get up.

Amos 9

Final judgment and hope

1. I saw God standing by the altar.
2. He said, "Hit the top so the building falls. No one will escape."
3. "If they dig deep or climb high, I will find them."
4. "If they are taken away, I will send a sword after them."
5. God touches the earth, and it shakes.
6. He built the sky and made the earth.
7. God says, "You are not the only nation I brought out. I also brought others from far places."
8. "I will destroy the sinful people of Israel. But I will not destroy everyone."
9. "I will shake Israel like grain in a basket. The good will be saved."
10. All who think nothing bad will happen will die.
11. But later, I will rebuild the house of David."
12. "God's people will own what was taken from them."
13. "Crops will grow fast. The land will be full."
14. "I will bring my people back. They will rebuild and plant again."
15. "They will never be taken from their land again."

– Obadiah –

A short prophecy against Edom for its pride and cruelty toward Judah.

Obadiah 1

1. This is the message God gave to Obadiah.
2. God says, "I will punish Edom. Other nations will fight them."
3. "Edom is proud. They live high in the mountains and feel safe."

4. "But I will bring them down, no matter how high they go."
5. "Even thieves only take some things. But your land will be empty."
6. "Everything you hid will be taken."
7. "Your friends will trick and defeat you."
8. "I will destroy your wise men."
9. "Your soldiers will be afraid."
10. "You hurt your brother Jacob. You will be punished forever."
11. "You stood and watched as enemies attacked him."
12. "You laughed and stole what wasn't yours."
13. "You joined in when Judah was in trouble."
14. "You blocked people from escaping and handed them over."
15. "Now your turn has come. You will be judged."
16. "You hurt others. Now you will be hurt."
17. "But God's people will be saved on Mount Zion."
18. "They will destroy Edom like fire burns straw."
19. "They will take land back from the north and south."
20. "People from far away will return home."
21. "God will be King, and He will rule from Mount Zion."

– Jonah –

Jonah runs from God but is sent to help Nineveh repent.

Jonah 1

1. God told Jonah,
2. "Go to Nineveh. The people there are very evil."
3. But Jonah ran away. He went the other way.
4. He got on a ship heading for Tarshish.
5. God sent a big storm. The ship was about to break.
6. The sailors were scared. They each prayed to their gods.
7. They threw cargo into the sea to make the ship lighter.
8. Jonah was asleep below. The captain woke him up.
9. He said, "Pray to your God. Maybe He can help us."
10. The sailors cast lots to see who caused the trouble.
11. The lot fell on Jonah.
12. They asked, "Who are you? Where are you from?"
13. Jonah said, "I am a Hebrew. I worship the God who made the sea and land."
14. The men were afraid. They said, "Why did you run from God?"
15. The sea kept getting worse.
16. Jonah said, "Throw me into the sea. The storm will stop."
17. The men didn't want to, but the sea got worse.
18. So they prayed to God and threw Jonah overboard.
19. The sea became calm.
20. The men feared God and worshiped Him.
21. God sent a big fish to swallow Jonah.
22. Jonah was inside the fish for three days and three nights.

Jonah 2

Jonah prays inside the fish

1. Jonah prayed to God from inside the fish.
2. He said, "I called to you when I was in trouble."

3. "You heard me. You threw me into the sea."
4. "Waves covered me. I thought I was gone."
5. "But I looked to your Temple."
6. "Water closed over me. I sank down."
7. "Seaweed wrapped around my head."
8. "I was near death, but you saved me."
9. "I will thank you and do what I promised."
10. "Only you, God, can save."
11. Then God told the fish to spit Jonah out.
12. It did, and Jonah landed on dry land.

Jonah 3

Jonah goes to Nineveh

1. God spoke to Jonah again.
2. "Go to Nineveh. Give them my message."
3. Jonah obeyed. He went to the city.
4. Nineveh was a big city. It took three days to walk across.
5. Jonah walked one day in and said, "In 40 days, Nineveh will be destroyed!"
6. The people believed God. They stopped eating and put on rough clothes.
7. Even the king heard the message. He got off his throne.
8. He took off his robe, wore rough clothes, and sat in ashes.
9. He made a law: "Everyone must stop eating and pray to God."
10. "Stop doing wrong. Maybe God will forgive us."
11. God saw that they changed.
12. So He did not destroy them.

Jonah 4

Jonah gets angry

1. Jonah was angry that God did not destroy Nineveh.
2. He said, "God, this is why I ran. I knew you are kind and forgive people."
3. "Just let me die."
4. God said, "Is it right for you to be angry?"
5. Jonah went outside the city and waited.
6. God made a plant grow to give him shade.
7. Jonah was happy about the plant.
8. But the next day, God sent a worm to kill it.
9. Then the sun came up, and a hot wind blew. Jonah felt faint.
10. He said, "I want to die."
11. God said, "You care about a plant you didn't grow."
12. "Shouldn't I care about Nineveh, a city with thousands of people and animals?"

– Micah –

Micah warns of judgment but promises a coming ruler from Bethlehem.

Micah 1

1. This is the message God gave to Micah.
2. God says, "Listen, all people. I am speaking to you."
3. "I will come down and step on the earth."
4. "Mountains will melt. Valleys will split."
5. "This is because of the sins of Israel and Judah."
6. "Samaria will be destroyed. I will break its buildings."
7. "Its idols and treasures will be smashed."
8. Micah says, "I will cry and be sad."

9. "The wound is deep. The trouble has reached Judah."
10. "Don't tell others in Gath. Don't let them laugh."
11. "People in Shaphir will go away in shame."
12. "People in Zaanan will not come out to help."
13. "People in Lachish trusted in fast horses, not God."
14. "So you must give gifts to Moresheth Gath."
15. "Israel's kings will leave and go to Adullam."
16. "Cry loudly. You will lose your children. You will be taken away."

Micah 2

God warns those who do wrong

1. Trouble is coming to those who plan evil.
2. They take land and houses that are not theirs.
3. God says, "I will bring disaster on you."
4. "You will not be able to escape."
5. "Others will divide your land. You will lose it."
6. People tell the prophets, "Stop speaking bad news."
7. But God says, "My words are true for those who do right."
8. But you attack peaceful people.
9. You throw women out of their homes.
10. Get up and leave. This land is no longer safe.
11. You only want lies and false promises.
12. But I will bring my people back together.
13. I will lead them like a good shepherd.

Micah 3

God warns leaders and prophets

1. Micah says, "Leaders of Israel, you should know what is right."
2. "But you hate good and love evil."
3. "You hurt people instead of helping them."
4. "So when you call to God, He won't answer."
5. Prophets tell lies for money.
6. God says, "You will be left in darkness."
7. The false prophets will be ashamed.
8. But Micah says, "I am filled with God's power. I speak truth."
9. "Leaders twist justice. They build the city with sin."
10. "They take money to judge and teach."
11. "They say, 'God is with us.' But they still do evil."
12. So, because of them, Jerusalem will be destroyed.

Micah 4

Peace in the future

1. In the future, God's house will be the most important place.
2. People from all nations will come to learn from Him.
3. God will settle arguments between nations.
4. People will stop using weapons and live in peace.
5. Everyone will sit safely under their trees and vines.
6. God will bring back the weak and the outcasts.
7. He will be their king forever.
8. Jerusalem will be strong again.
9. But now, you cry like a woman in pain.
10. You will go to Babylon. But God will bring you back.

11. Many nations will gather against you.
12. But they don't know God's plan.
13. God will give you strength. You will win in the end.

Micah 5

A ruler will come from Bethlehem

1. Now your enemies attack you.
2. But a ruler will come from Bethlehem.
3. God's people will suffer for a time.
4. Then the ruler will lead with God's strength.
5. He will bring peace.
6. When Assyria attacks, God's people will fight back.
7. God's people will be like rain on the earth.
8. They will be strong and not afraid.
9. Their enemies will be destroyed.
10. God says, "I will take away your weapons and horses."
11. "I will destroy your cities and strong places."
12. "I will stop your magic and idols."
13. "You will no longer trust in false gods."
14. "I will punish the nations that do not obey me."

Micah 6

God tells what He wants

1. God says, "Listen. I have a case against you."
2. "Mountains and hills, hear my complaint."
3. "My people, what did I do wrong?"
4. "I brought you out of Egypt and gave you leaders."
5. "Remember how I protected you on the way to the Promised Land."
6. You ask, "What should I bring to God?"
7. "Should I bring animals or rivers of oil?"
8. God says, "I already told you what is good:
9. Do what is right, love kindness, and walk humbly with me."
10. But your city is full of lies and cheating.
11. I will not accept false weights and dishonest scales.
12. Rich people hurt others.
13. I will punish you.
14. You will eat but still be hungry.
15. You will plant but not harvest.
16. You follow bad examples. That's why you will be ruined.

Micah 7

Micah's sadness and hope

1. Micah says, "I feel sad. There are no good people left."
2. People lie and hurt others.
3. Leaders want money. Judges take bribes.
4. Even the best people are not honest.
5. Don't trust your neighbor.
6. Families fight. Children turn against parents.
7. But I will wait for God. He will hear me.
8. Enemies, don't laugh at me. I may fall, but I will get up.
9. I will accept God's punishment because I sinned.
10. But He will defend me and bring me into the light.
11. My walls will be rebuilt. My land will grow again.
12. People will come from many lands.
13. But the earth will suffer because of sin.

14. God, take care of your people like a shepherd.
15. Show us miracles like before.
16. Nations will be shocked and stop bragging.
17. They will fear God.
18. No one is like you, God. You forgive sin.
19. You will not stay angry. You love to show mercy.
20. You will keep your promises forever.

– Nahum –

God promises to judge the wicked city of Nineveh.

Nahum 1

1. This is the message about Nineveh. Nahum wrote it.
2. God gets angry at His enemies.
3. God is patient but powerful. He punishes the guilty.
4. He can dry up seas and rivers.
5. Mountains shake and the earth trembles when He comes.
6. No one can stand against His anger.
7. But God is good. He protects those who trust Him.
8. He will sweep away His enemies.
9. No one can fight against Him and win.
10. His enemies will be trapped and destroyed.
11. Someone from Nineveh planned evil against God.
12. God says, "They are strong, but I will break them."
13. "I will free you from their power."
14. God says to Nineveh, "You will be gone. No more children. Your idols will be destroyed."
15. Look! A messenger is coming to bring good news. "God's people, worship Him again."

Nahum 2

Nineveh will be attacked

1. Get ready! Your enemy is coming to attack.
2. God will bring back the glory of His people.
3. The enemy's shields are red. Soldiers are ready.
4. Chariots race through the streets.
5. The enemy rushes forward to break through.
6. The palace falls.
7. The queen is taken away. Her servants cry.
8. Nineveh is like a broken pool. People run away.
9. The enemy says, "Take the silver! Take the gold!"
10. Nineveh is empty and ruined.
11. Where is the lion's den now?
12. God says, "I am against you. I will destroy your power."
13. "Your chariots will burn. Your messengers will die.

Nahum 3

God will punish Nineveh

1. You are full of lies and violence.
2. You will hear the sound of whips and chariots.
3. Soldiers will charge. Many will die.
4. This is your punishment for evil and tricks.
5. God says, "I am against you. I will show everyone your shame."
6. "People will turn away in disgust."
7. "Everyone who sees you will say, 'Nineveh is destroyed!'"

8. You think you are better than Thebes? They fell too.
9. They had strong allies, but it didn't save them.
10. They were taken away as prisoners.
11. You will fall too. You will try to hide.
12. Your forts are weak like ripe fruit.
13. Your soldiers are like scared women.
14. Store up water. Prepare defenses.
15. But fire will destroy you.
16. You have many traders, but they won't help.
17. Your leaders are like bugs that fly away.
18. Your rulers sleep. Your people are scattered.
19. Nothing can heal you.
20. Everyone who hears about you will clap and cheer. You hurt many, and now it's your turn.

– Habakkuk –

Habakkuk questions God about evil, but learns to trust Him.

Habakkuk 1

1. This is the message God gave to Habakkuk.
2. Habakkuk said, "God, how long must I call for help?"
3. "Why do you let me see so much evil?"
4. "No one follows your law. Bad people win."
5. God said, "Watch what I will do. You won't believe it."
6. "I am sending the Babylonians. They are fast and cruel."
7. "They make their own rules and fear no one."
8. "Their horses are quick. Their soldiers are proud."
9. "They come to fight and destroy."
10. "They laugh at kings and walls."
11. "They move fast like the wind, then feel proud."
12. Habakkuk said, "God, you are forever. You are holy."
13. "Why do you let evil people win?"
14. "Why are people treated like fish with no ruler?"
15. "The enemy catches them all in nets."
16. "Then they worship their nets and brag about their success."
17. "Will they keep killing without being stopped?"

Habakkuk 2

God answers Habakkuk

1. I will wait and listen for God's answer.
2. God said, "Write down what I show you. Make it easy to read."
3. "The answer will come at the right time. Wait for it."
4. "Evil people are proud. Good people live by faith."
5. "The proud never stop wanting more."
6. "One day people will mock them and say, 'You stole from others!'"
7. "Now others will take from you."
8. "Because you hurt many people, you will be punished."
9. "You tried to stay safe by doing wrong."
10. "You hurt your own family by sinning."
11. "Even the stones in your walls will speak out."
12. "You built your city with violence."
13. "But all your work will be burned."
14. "One day, everyone will know about God."
15. "You tricked others and made them fall. Now shame will come to you."

16. "You will be punished. God sees what you did."
17. "The same pain you caused will come back on you."
18. "Idols can't help you."
19. "They can't speak or save anyone."
20. "But God is in His temple. Be quiet and respect Him."

Habakkuk 3

Habakkuk's prayer

1. This is a prayer from Habakkuk.
2. He said, "God, I have heard of your power. Do great things again."
3. "You came to help your people."
4. "You showed your power and glory."
5. "You brought sickness and fear to your enemies."
6. "You stood and shook the earth."
7. "You made nations afraid."
8. "You came to save your people, not to destroy the land."
9. "You used your power to stop your enemies."
10. "You crushed the leader of the wicked."
11. "You showed that you are in control."
12. "You came to rescue your people."
13. "You crushed the enemy king."
14. "You stopped the enemy army."
15. "You walked through the sea with power."
16. "I heard all this and shook with fear."
17. "Even if crops fail and animals die—
18. I will still be happy with God."
19. "God gives me strength. He helps me stand strong."

– Zephaniah –

God warns of coming judgment but offers hope for those who seek Him.

Zephaniah 1

1. This is the message God gave to Zephaniah.
2. God says, "I will wipe everything from the earth."
3. "I will destroy people, animals, birds, and fish."
4. "I will punish Judah and Jerusalem."
5. "I will remove all idols and false worship."
6. "I will punish those who turn away from me."
7. Be silent. The Lord's day is near.
8. "I will punish the leaders and their children."
9. "I will punish those who are violent and lie."
10. "People will cry all over the city."
11. "The market will be destroyed."
12. God says, "I will search the city."
13. "I will punish people who say, 'God won't do anything.'"
14. The Lord's day is near. It will be a terrible day.
15. It will be a day of trouble and fear.
16. A day of war and darkness.
17. God will bring pain to people for their sin.
18. Money will not save them.
19. God's anger will burn the whole land. No one will escape.

Zephaniah 2

God calls people to change

1. Come together before it's too late.
2. Turn to God before His anger comes.

3. All who want to do right—seek God. Maybe He will protect you.
4. God will punish cities like Gaza, Ashkelon, Ashdod, and Ekron.
5. The people near the sea will be judged.
6. Their land will become empty fields.
7. God's people will live there and rest.
8. God says, "I heard the insults from Moab and Ammon."
9. "They will be destroyed like Sodom and Gomorrah."
10. This will happen because they were proud.
11. God will show His power, and all people will worship Him.
12. God will also punish Cush and Assyria.
13. Nineveh will be empty and dry.
14. Animals will live there.
15. The proud city that thought it was safe will be gone.

Zephaniah 3

God judges and then forgives

1. Jerusalem is full of sin and refuses correction.
2. It does not listen to God or trust Him.
3. Its leaders are dangerous and greedy.
4. The prophets lie. The priests break the law.
5. But God is still right and fair every day.
6. He punished other nations, but His people didn't learn.
7. God said, "I thought they would change. But they kept sinning."
8. God says, "Wait for me. I will punish all nations."
9. "Then people everywhere will call on me and serve me."
10. "My people will return from far places."
11. "They will not be proud anymore."
12. "I will leave only humble and honest people."
13. "They will live in peace and be safe."
14. Sing and be happy, people of Israel!
15. God has taken away your punishment.
16. Don't be afraid. God is with you.
17. He will protect you and love you.
18. He will bring back those who are sad.
19. He will punish those who hurt you.
20. God will bring you home and give you honor.

– Haggai –

Haggai urges the people to rebuild the Temple after returning from exile.

Haggai 1

1. This message came from God in the second year of King Darius.
2. God said, "The people say, 'It's not time to rebuild the Temple.'"
3. But God said, "Why do you live in nice houses while my Temple is still broken?"
4. "Think about what you're doing."
5. "You plant but harvest little. You eat but are not full."
6. "You drink but stay thirsty. You earn money but it disappears."
7. God says, "Think about what you're doing."
8. "Go get wood and rebuild the Temple. I will be pleased."
9. "You hoped for much, but got little. I ruined your work."
10. "That's why the sky doesn't send rain, and the ground gives little food."
11. "I caused droughts on your land, food, animals, and all your work."
12. Then Zerubbabel and Joshua, with all the people, obeyed God.

13. Haggai gave them God's message: "I am with you."
14. God made them excited to work.
15. They started building the Temple on the 24th day of the month.

Haggai 2

1. God spoke again on the 21st day of the month.
2. He said, "Speak to Zerubbabel, Joshua, and the people."
3. "Some of you remember the old Temple. How does this one compare?"
4. "Don't be afraid. I am with you."
5. "I made a promise when you left Egypt. My Spirit is still with you."
6. "Soon I will shake the earth, sky, sea, and land."
7. "I will shake all nations. They will bring their treasures."
8. "Silver and gold belong to me."
9. "This new Temple will be greater than the old one. I will bring peace here."
10. On the 24th day of the ninth month, God spoke again.
11. He said, "Ask the priests this question."
12. "If holy meat touches other food, does that food become holy?" They said, "No."
13. "If someone touches something unclean and then touches food, does the food become unclean?" They said, "Yes."
14. God said, "It's the same with these people and their work. Everything they offer is unclean."
15. "Think about this: before you started building, things didn't go well."
16. "You expected much, but got little. I ruined your work."
17. "But from today on, I will bless you."
18. That same day, God gave a message to Zerubbabel.
19. He said, "I will shake the heavens and the earth."
20. "I will destroy kingdoms and armies."
21. "I will make Zerubbabel like a special ring. I have chosen him."

– Zechariah –

Zechariah encourages rebuilding and shares visions of God's future plans.

Zechariah 1

1. This message came from God in the second year of King Darius.
2. God said, "I was very angry with your ancestors."
3. "Tell the people: Come back to me, and I will come back to you."
4. "Don't be like your ancestors. They didn't listen to the prophets."
5. "Where are your ancestors now? Are they still alive?"
6. "But my words and commands came true. The people said, 'God was right to punish us.'"
7. On the 24th day of the 11th month, God gave Zechariah a vision.
8. He saw a man on a red horse standing among trees. Behind him were other horses.
9. Zechariah asked, "What do these horses mean?"
10. The angel said, "They were sent to check the earth."
11. The horses said, "We saw the earth. It is quiet and peaceful."
12. The angel asked God, "How long until you help Jerusalem?"
13. God answered with kind and good words.
14. The angel said, "God cares deeply about Jerusalem."
15. "He is angry at the nations that hurt it too much."

16. God says, "I will return to Jerusalem. My house will be rebuilt."
17. "Jerusalem will grow again. I will bless it."
18. Zechariah looked up and saw four horns.
19. He asked, "What are these?" The angel said, "They are the nations that scattered Judah."
20. Then he saw four workers.
21. He asked, "What are they doing?" The angel said, "They are coming to break the horns and stop those who hurt Judah."

Zechariah 2

God will protect His people

1. I looked up and saw a man with a measuring line.
2. I asked, "Where are you going?" He said, "To measure Jerusalem."
3. Another angel came and said,
4. "Tell him: Jerusalem will be too full for walls."
5. "God will protect it like a wall of fire."
6. God says, "People who are far away, come back home."
7. "Escape from the land of the north."
8. God says, "Anyone who hurts you hurts what I care about."
9. "I will punish the nations that took from you."
10. "Be happy, Jerusalem! I am coming to live with you."
11. "Many nations will join you. I will be your God."
12. "God will choose Jerusalem again."
13. Be quiet, everyone. God is moving.

Zechariah 3

God forgives His high priest

1. I saw the high priest Joshua standing in front of God.
2. Satan was there to accuse him.
3. God said, "I reject you, Satan."
4. Joshua was wearing dirty clothes.
5. God said, "Take off his dirty clothes."
6. Then God said to Joshua, "I forgive you. I will give you clean clothes."
7. They gave him clean robes and a clean hat.
8. God said, "If you obey me, you will lead my Temple."
9. "Look at this stone. I will remove sin in one day."
10. "On that day, people will sit together in peace."

Zechariah 4

God helps Zerubbabel

1. The angel came back and woke me up.
2. He said, "What do you see?"
3. I said, "A lampstand with a bowl on top. It has seven lamps and two olive trees next to it."
4. I asked, "What does this mean?"
5. The angel said, "Don't you know?" I said, "No."
6. He said, "This is God's message: Not by strength or power, but by My Spirit."
7. "Zerubbabel will finish the Temple. Nothing will stop him."
8. "People will see him lay the last stone and be happy."
9. "Zerubbabel started this work, and he will finish it."
10. "Don't make fun of small beginnings. God sees everything."
11. I asked, "What are the olive trees?"
12. "What are the branches pouring oil?"
13. He said, "Don't you know?" I said, "No."

14. He said, "They are the two people chosen to serve God."

Zechariah 5

God removes sin

1. I looked up and saw a big flying scroll.
2. The angel said, "It is 30 feet long and 15 feet wide."
3. He said, "This scroll has a curse written on it."
4. "It will punish those who steal and lie."
5. Then the angel showed me a basket.
6. I asked, "What is it?" He said, "It shows the sin of the people."
7. The basket had a lead cover. A woman was inside.
8. He said, "This is Wickedness." He pushed her back in.
9. Two women with wings lifted the basket into the air.
10. I asked, "Where are they taking it?"
11. He said, "To Babylon, where it belongs."

Zechariah 6

Four chariots and the crowning of Joshua

1. I looked up and saw four chariots coming between two mountains.
2. The first had red horses.
3. The second had black horses.
4. The third had white horses.
5. The fourth had spotted horses.
6. I asked the angel, "What are these?"
7. He said, "These are spirits sent by God to travel the earth."
8. The ones going north made God's Spirit rest there.
9. Then God said,
10. "Take silver and gold from the men who came from Babylon."
11. "Make a crown and put it on Joshua the high priest."
12. "Tell him: God says a man called the Branch will build His Temple."
13. "He will rule as both king and priest."
14. The crown will be kept in the Temple as a reminder."
15. "People from far away will help build. This will happen if you obey God."

Zechariah 7

God wants kindness, not just fasting

1. In the fourth year of King Darius, God gave another message.
2. People from Bethel asked the priests,
3. "Should we still fast like we have done every year?"
4. God said,
5. "When you fasted, was it really for Me?"
6. "When you eat or drink, isn't it for yourselves?"
7. "Remember what I said through the prophets?"
8. God said, "Be fair and kind to each other."
9. "Don't hurt widows, orphans, strangers, or the poor."
10. "But the people refused to listen. They were stubborn."
11. "So I didn't listen when they called out to Me."
12. "I scattered them far away."
13. "Their land was left empty and quiet."

Zechariah 8

God brings His people back

1. God said,
2. "I care deeply about Jerusalem. I will protect it."
3. "I will live there. It will be called the Faithful City."

4. "Old people will sit in peace. Children will play safely."
5. "This may seem hard to believe, but I can do it."
6. "I will bring my people home from far places."
7. "They will live in Jerusalem. They will be my people."
8. "Do not be afraid. Be strong and keep building."
9. "Before, there was no money and no safety."
10. "But I will not treat you the same way now."
11. "Seeds will grow. Rain will come. Crops will be full."
12. "I will bless you. Do not be afraid."
13. "You were a curse, but now you will be a blessing."
14. "I punished you before, but now I will do good."
15. "Speak truth. Judge fairly."
16. "Don't plan evil against others."
17. "I hate lies and fake promises."
18. "You fasted before, but now you will celebrate."
19. "Love truth and peace."
20. "People from many cities will come."
21. "They will say, 'Let's go ask God for help.'"
22. "Many nations will come to Jerusalem to worship God."
23. "Ten people from other lands will grab a Jew and say, 'Let us go with you. We heard God is with you.'"

Zechariah 9

God promises to protect

1. This is God's message: He sees all the people in the cities.
2. Cities like Hadrach, Damascus, Tyre, and Sidon are proud.
3. Tyre built strong walls and saved up riches.
4. But God will destroy it.
5. Ashkelon, Gaza, and Ekron will be afraid.
6. Foreigners will live in their land.
7. God will remove the evil from them.
8. He will guard His people. No one will hurt them again.
9. Be happy, Jerusalem! Your king is coming.
10. He will bring peace. His rule will go everywhere.
11. God says, "I will set your prisoners free."
12. "Come back to me. I will bless you again."
13. "I will protect my people in battle."
14. God will appear like lightning.
15. He will protect and save His people.
16. They will shine like jewels.
17. Their land will grow full of food and joy.

Zechariah 10

God helps His people

1. Ask God for rain. He is the one who sends it.
2. Idols and false teachers lie. They give no real answers.
3. God is angry at the leaders who mislead His people.
4. God will send a strong leader from Judah.
5. The people will fight and win with God's help.
6. God will make Judah and Joseph strong again.
7. They will be happy. Their children will rejoice.
8. God will call them, and they will come back.

9. Even if they were far away, they will remember Him.
10. God will bring them back from Egypt and Assyria.
11. They will pass through trouble, but God will protect them.
12. With God's help, they will be strong and walk in His ways.

Zechariah 11

God speaks about failed leaders

1. Open your doors, Lebanon—your trees will be burned.
2. Cry, trees and shepherds—your beauty is gone.
3. The shepherds cry because their fields are ruined.
4. God said, "Take care of the sheep that are ready to be killed."
5. Their buyers kill them and feel no guilt.
6. God said, "I will not help this land anymore."
7. So I cared for the sheep marked for slaughter.
8. I got rid of three bad shepherds in one month.
9. I became tired of the people, and they hated me.
10. I broke my staff called Favor, ending my agreement with them.
11. The sheep knew God's word was true.
12. I said, "If you want, pay me." They gave me 30 silver coins.
13. God said, "Throw it to the potter." So I did.
14. I broke my second staff called Union. This ended the unity of Judah and Israel.
15. God said, "Now act like a foolish shepherd."
16. "A bad shepherd will come. He won't care for the weak or help the injured."
17. He will only feed himself. He will be punished and lose his power.

Zechariah 12

God protects Jerusalem

1. This is a message from God about Israel.
2. God says, "I will make Jerusalem strong."
3. "All nations that attack it will hurt themselves."
4. "I will confuse their horses and riders."
5. The leaders of Judah will say, "God gives us strength."
6. God will make Judah strong like a fire.
7. God will save the homes of Judah first.
8. God will protect Jerusalem and its people.
9. God will destroy the nations that attack His people.
10. God will pour out His Spirit.
11. People will look at the one they hurt and cry for him.
12. Each family will cry separately.
13. The whole land will be sad.

Zechariah 13

God removes sin

1. A fountain will be opened to wash away sin.
2. God says, "I will remove all idols and false teachers."
3. Parents will stop their own children from lying in God's name.
4. False prophets will be ashamed and stop pretending.
5. They will say, "I'm not a prophet—I work the land."
6. If someone asks, "What are those wounds?" they will say, "I was hurt at home."

7. God says, "The shepherd will be struck, and the sheep will scatter."
8. Two-thirds of the people will die, but one-third will be saved.
9. God will test the survivors like silver and gold.
10. They will call to Him, and He will answer, "You are my people."

Zechariah 14

God wins in the end

1. A day is coming when your enemies will steal from Jerusalem.
2. God will let all nations fight against the city.
3. But then God will fight for His people.
4. He will stand on the Mount of Olives. The mountain will split in two.
5. People will run through the valley to escape.
6. On that day, there will be no light.
7. Only God knows the time. It will be one long day.
8. Living water will flow out from Jerusalem.
9. God will be King over the whole earth.
10. The land will be flat, and Jerusalem will stay safe and full.
11. People will live there. It will never be destroyed again.
12. God will strike the enemies with disease.
13. Panic will spread among the enemy armies.
14. Judah will fight too. The enemies' treasures will be taken.
15. Even the animals of the enemy will suffer.
16. Everyone left from the enemy nations will come to worship God every year.
17. Any nation that refuses will get no rain.
18. Egypt and others who don't join will face punishment.
19. This will happen to all who won't worship God.
20. On that day, even the bells on horses will say "Holy to the Lord."
21. All pots in Jerusalem will be special to God.
22. No one will come to the Temple to sell things ever again.

– Malachi –

God rebukes Israel's laziness in worship and promises a coming messenger.

Malachi 1

God speaks to His people

1. This is the message God gave to Israel through Malachi.
2. God says, "I have always loved you." But you ask, "How have you loved us?"
3. God says, "I chose Jacob, not Esau."
4. "Esau's land will stay ruined."
5. "You will see this and know I am great."
6. God says, "A son honors his father, but you do not honor Me."
7. "You offer bad food on My altar."
8. "You bring blind, sick, or hurt animals. Would your governor accept that?"
9. "Try giving him your leftovers and see what happens."
10. "I wish someone would shut the doors of the Temple."
11. "People from every nation respect Me—but you do not."
12. "You say, 'Serving God is too hard.'"
13. "You bring stolen and weak animals."
14. "I will punish anyone who promises a good gift but brings a bad one."
15. "I am a great King. All nations respect Me."

Malachi 2

God warns the priests and people

1. God says, "Priests, this warning is for you."
2. "If you don't listen, I will curse your blessings."
3. "I will make you and your family suffer."
4. "I made a promise with Levi to give life and peace."
5. "He honored Me and taught the truth."
6. "But now you priests have turned away."
7. "People should learn from priests, but you mislead them."
8. "So I made you look foolish in front of others."
9. God says, "We all have the same Creator."
10. "Why do we lie and break trust?"
11. "Judah has done wrong and married people who worship false gods."
12. "God will remove those who do this."
13. "You cry at the altar, but God doesn't listen."
14. You ask, "Why?"
15. "Because you broke your promise to your wife."
16. God hates divorce and violence.
17. You make God tired with your words. You say, "God thinks evil is good."

Malachi 3

God sends a messenger

1. God says, "I will send a messenger to prepare the way."
2. "The Lord will come suddenly, and who can stand before Him?"
3. "He will clean and test His people like fire tests gold."
4. "Then offerings will please God again."
5. "God will punish liars, cheaters, and those who hurt others."
6. God says, "I do not change, and that's why you are not destroyed."
7. "Return to Me, and I will return to you."
8. You ask, "How have we turned away?"
9. "You robbed Me by not bringing tithes and offerings."
10. "Bring the full tithe. I will bless you."
11. "Your crops will grow. I will protect you."
12. "People will call you blessed."
13. God says, "Your words have been hard against Me."
14. You say, "Serving God is useless."
15. "Evil people do wrong and still succeed."
16. But those who respect God talked to each other.
17. God wrote down their names.
18. He said, "They are My special people. I will reward them."

Malachi 4

The day of the Lord

1. God says, "The day is coming when the proud and evil will burn up."
2. "But for those who respect Me, joy and healing will rise like the sun."
3. "You will walk on the ashes of the wicked."
4. "Remember the laws I gave through Moses."
5. "I will send Elijah the prophet before the great day comes."
6. "He will help parents and children turn back to each other. If not, the land will be destroyed."

New Testament

– Matthew –

Jesus is the promised Messiah, teaching about God's kingdom and dying for sin.

Matthew 1

1. This is the list of Jesus' family. He came from David, who came from Abraham.
2. Abraham had Isaac. Isaac had Jacob. Jacob had Judah and his brothers.
3. Judah had Perez and Zerah (their mom was Tamar). Perez had Hezron. Hezron had Ram.
4. Ram had Amminadab. Amminadab had Nahshon. Nahshon had Salmon.
5. Salmon had Boaz (his mom was Rahab). Boaz had Obed (his mom was Ruth). Obed had Jesse.
6. Jesse had David. David became king. David had Solomon (his mom was Uriah's wife).
7. Solomon had Rehoboam. Rehoboam had Abijah. Abijah had Asa.
8. Asa had Jehoshaphat. Jehoshaphat had Joram. Joram had Uzziah.
9. Uzziah had Jotham. Jotham had Ahaz. Ahaz had Hezekiah.
10. Hezekiah had Manasseh. Manasseh had Amon. Amon had Josiah.
11. Josiah had Jeconiah and his brothers. This was before the people were taken to Babylon.
12. After Babylon, Jeconiah had Shealtiel. Shealtiel had Zerubbabel.
13. Zerubbabel had Abihud. Abihud had Eliakim. Eliakim had Azor.
14. Azor had Zadok. Zadok had Akim. Akim had Elihud.
15. Elihud had Eleazar. Eleazar had Matthan. Matthan had Jacob.
16. Jacob had Joseph. Joseph was Mary's husband. Mary gave birth to Jesus, who is called Christ.
17. So there were 14 generations from Abraham to David, 14 from David to Babylon, and 14 from Babylon to Jesus.
18. Here is how Jesus was born. Mary was engaged to Joseph, but before they married, she became pregnant by the Holy Spirit.
19. Joseph was a good man. He didn't want to shame Mary, so he planned to end things quietly.
20. While Joseph was thinking about this, an angel came in a dream. The angel said, "Joseph, don't be afraid to marry Mary. Her baby is from the Holy Spirit.
21. She will have a son. Name him Jesus. He will save his people from their sins."
22. This happened to fulfill what God had said through a prophet:
23. "A virgin will have a baby. He will be called Immanuel." (This means "God is with us.")
24. Joseph woke up and did what the angel said. He married Mary.
25. But he didn't sleep with her until after the baby was born. Joseph named the baby Jesus.

Matthew 2

1. Jesus was born in Bethlehem, in Judea, when Herod was king. Some wise men came from the east.
2. They asked, "Where is the baby born to be king of the Jews? We saw his star and came to worship him."
3. King Herod was upset. Everyone in Jerusalem was too.
4. Herod brought the priests and teachers together. He asked, "Where will the Messiah be born?"
5. They said, "In Bethlehem. That's what the prophet wrote."
6. "Bethlehem, you are not too small. A ruler will come from you who will lead my people."

7. Herod secretly met with the wise men. He asked when the star first appeared.
8. Then he sent them to Bethlehem. He said, "Find the child. When you do, tell me so I can worship him too."
9. The wise men followed the star. It led them to the place where the child was.
10. They were very happy when they saw the star.
11. They went into the house and saw the child with Mary. They bowed down and gave him gifts—gold, frankincense, and myrrh.
12. God warned them in a dream not to go back to Herod. So they went home a different way.
13. After they left, an angel told Joseph in a dream, "Get up! Take Mary and Jesus to Egypt. Stay there until I tell you. Herod wants to kill the child."
14. That night Joseph left for Egypt with Mary and Jesus.
15. They stayed there until Herod died. This fulfilled what God had said: "I called my son out of Egypt."
16. Herod was furious when the wise men didn't come back. He ordered all baby boys under age two in Bethlehem to be killed.
17. This fulfilled what the prophet Jeremiah said:
18. "A cry was heard in Ramah. Mothers were crying. They could not be comforted because their children were gone."
19. After Herod died, an angel spoke to Joseph in a dream in Egypt.
20. The angel said, "Get up. Take Jesus and Mary to Israel. The people who wanted to kill the child are dead."
21. So Joseph took Mary and Jesus back to Israel.
22. But Joseph was afraid to go to Judea because Herod's son was king. Then God warned him in another dream.
23. So he went to Galilee and lived in a town called Nazareth. This fulfilled what the prophets said: "He will be called a Nazarene."

Matthew 3

1. John the Baptist began preaching in the desert of Judea.
2. He said, "Turn back to God! His kingdom is near."
3. This is who the prophet Isaiah meant when he said, "A voice is calling in the desert: Get ready for the Lord!"
4. John wore clothes made of camel hair and a leather belt. He ate locusts and honey.
5. People from Jerusalem and all around came to hear him.
6. They confessed their sins and were baptized by him in the Jordan River.
7. When he saw some Pharisees and Sadducees coming, he said, "You snakes! Who warned you to run from God's anger?
8. Show by your actions that you really turned back to God.
9. Don't just say, 'We are Abraham's children.' God can make children for Abraham from these rocks.
10. The axe is ready. Trees that don't grow good fruit will be cut down and burned."
11. "I baptize you with water to show you turned back to God. But someone greater is coming. I'm not even good enough to carry his sandals. He will baptize you with the Holy Spirit and fire.
12. He will separate good people from bad, like wheat from husks. He will keep the wheat and burn the husks."
13. Then Jesus came from Galilee to be baptized by John.
14. John tried to stop him. He said, "You should baptize me! Why are you coming to me?"
15. Jesus said, "Let it happen. This is what God wants." So John baptized him.

16. As soon as Jesus came out of the water, heaven opened. He saw God's Spirit come down like a dove.
17. A voice from heaven said, "This is my Son. I love him. I am pleased with him."

Matthew 4

1. The Holy Spirit led Jesus into the desert to be tempted by the devil.
2. Jesus didn't eat for 40 days and nights. He was very hungry.
3. The devil said, "If you are God's Son, turn these stones into bread."
4. Jesus said, "People need more than bread. They need God's words."
5. Then the devil took Jesus to the top of the temple.
6. He said, "If you are God's Son, jump! The Bible says angels will catch you."
7. Jesus said, "Don't test God."
8. Then the devil took Jesus to a high mountain. He showed him all the world.
9. He said, "Bow down to me, and I will give you all this."
10. Jesus said, "Go away! The Bible says worship only God."
11. Then the devil left. Angels came and helped Jesus.
12. Jesus heard that John was put in prison, so he went to Galilee.
13. He moved to Capernaum, near the lake.
14. This fulfilled what the prophet Isaiah said.
15. "The land near the sea, in Galilee, where Gentiles live,
16. the people there were in darkness. Now they have seen a great light."
17. From then on, Jesus began to preach, "Turn back to God! His kingdom is near."
18. Jesus was walking by the lake. He saw two brothers, Simon (called Peter) and Andrew. They were fishing.
19. Jesus said, "Come with me. I will teach you to bring people to God."
20. Right away, they left their nets and followed him.
21. He saw two more brothers, James and John, in a boat with their father.
22. Jesus called them, and they left the boat and their father and followed him.
23. Jesus went around teaching, preaching, and healing people.
24. News about him spread. People brought the sick, and Jesus healed them all.
25. Large crowds followed him from Galilee, Jerusalem, and beyond the Jordan.

Matthew 5

1. Jesus saw the crowds. He went up a hill and sat down. His followers came close.
2. He began to teach them:
3. "God blesses those who know they need him. His kingdom belongs to them.
4. God blesses those who are sad. He will comfort them.
5. God blesses those who are gentle. They will have the earth.
6. God blesses those who want to do right. They will be filled.
7. God blesses those who are kind. He will be kind to them.
8. God blesses those with pure hearts. They will see God.
9. God blesses those who make peace. They will be called his children.
10. God blesses those who are hurt for doing right. His kingdom belongs to them.
11. God blesses you when people make fun of you or hurt you because of me.

12. Be happy! You will be rewarded in heaven. They hurt the prophets too.
13. You are like salt for the world. But if salt loses its taste, it's no good.
14. You are like light for the world. A city on a hill can't be hidden.
15. Don't hide a lamp. Put it where it gives light to everyone.
16. Let your light shine so people see your good deeds and praise God.
17. Don't think I came to end the law or prophets. I came to fulfill them.
18. Every part of God's law will last forever.
19. If you break God's commands and teach others to break them, you will be least in the kingdom. But if you obey and teach them, you will be great.
20. You must do better than the Pharisees, or you won't enter God's kingdom.
21. You've heard "Don't murder." But I say, don't even stay angry.
22. If you insult others, you will be judged.
23. If you're offering a gift to God and remember someone is mad at you,
24. leave your gift. Go make peace first, then come back.
25. Make peace quickly with anyone who accuses you.
26. If not, you may go to jail and stay until you pay everything.
27. You've heard "Don't cheat in marriage." But I say, don't even look at someone with desire.
28. That's the same as cheating in your heart.
29. If your eye makes you sin, get rid of it. It's better to lose one part than your whole body go to hell.
30. If your hand makes you sin, cut it off. Same reason.
31. You've heard, "You can divorce with papers." But I say,
32. if you divorce for no good reason, you cause cheating.
33. You've heard, "Keep your promises." But I say,
34. don't make promises at all. Not by heaven, earth, or anything.
35. Heaven is God's throne. Earth is his footstool. Jerusalem is his city.
36. Don't promise by your head. You can't make one hair white or black.
37. Just say "Yes" or "No." Anything more is from the devil.
38. You've heard, "An eye for an eye." But I say,
39. don't get back at people. If someone hits you, let them hit the other cheek too.
40. If someone takes your shirt, give them your coat.
41. If someone makes you walk a mile, walk two.
42. Give to those who ask. Help those who need it.
43. You've heard, "Love your neighbor. Hate your enemy." But I say,
44. love your enemies. Pray for them.
45. Then you'll be like God, who gives sun and rain to good and bad people.
46. If you love only those who love you, that's easy. Even bad people do that.
47. If you're kind only to friends, that's nothing special.
48. Be perfect, like your Father in heaven is perfect.

Matthew 6

1. Don't do good things just to be seen. God won't reward you for that.
2. When you give to the poor, don't show off. Don't be like those who want attention.
3. Instead, keep it private.
4. God sees what you do in secret and will reward you.
5. When you pray, don't try to impress people.

6. Go to your room, close the door, and pray in private. God will hear you.
7. Don't say the same thing over and over when you pray. God already knows.
8. Pray like this:
9. "Father in heaven, your name is holy.
10. Let your kingdom come. Let your will be done on earth like in heaven.
11. Give us the food we need today.
12. Forgive our sins, just like we forgive others.
13. Help us stay away from sin. Keep us safe from the devil."
14. If you forgive others, God will forgive you.
15. If you don't forgive, God won't forgive you.
16. When you fast, don't look sad like some people do.
17. Wash your face and smile.
18. Only God needs to know. He will reward you.
19. Don't save treasures on earth. They get ruined or stolen.
20. Save treasures in heaven. No one can take them.
21. Your heart will be where your treasure is.
22. Your eyes are like windows for your body. If they're good, your whole body is full of light.
23. If they're bad, you're full of darkness.
24. You can't serve two masters. You can't serve both God and money.
25. Don't worry about your life—what you'll eat or wear.
26. Look at the birds. They don't plant or store food, but God feeds them. You are worth more than birds.
27. Worrying can't add even one hour to your life.
28. Look at the flowers. They don't work, but they are beautiful.
29. Even King Solomon wasn't dressed as well as them.
30. If God takes care of grass and flowers, He'll take care of you.
31. So don't say, "What will we eat?" or "What will we wear?"
32. People who don't know God worry about that. God knows what you need.
33. Put God first, and He'll give you what you need.
34. Don't worry about tomorrow. Today has enough problems.

Matthew 7

1. Don't judge others, or you will be judged.
2. The way you judge is how you will be judged.
3. Don't point out someone's small mistake if you have a big one.
4. Fix yourself first.
5. Then you can help others.
6. Don't give what is holy to people who won't respect it.
7. Ask, and you'll get. Seek, and you'll find. Knock, and the door will open.
8. Everyone who asks, gets. Everyone who looks, finds. The door opens to those who knock.
9. Would you give your child a stone if they ask for bread?
10. Or a snake if they ask for fish?
11. If you, who aren't perfect, give good gifts, God will give even better to those who ask.
12. Treat others how you want to be treated. This is what the law and prophets teach.
13. The gate to life is narrow. Many take the easy way, but it leads to death.
14. The hard way leads to life, and only a few find it.
15. Watch out for false teachers. They look good but are dangerous.

16. You'll know them by what they do, like how you know trees by their fruit.
17. Good trees grow good fruit. Bad trees grow bad fruit.
18. A good tree can't grow bad fruit, and a bad tree can't grow good fruit.
19. Bad trees get cut down and burned.
20. So, look at what people do to know if they are true.
21. Not everyone who says "Lord" will enter heaven. Only those who obey God.
22. Some will say, "We did great things in your name!" But God will say,
23. "I never knew you. Go away."
24. A wise person hears God's words and obeys. That's like building a house on rock.
25. Rain and wind came, but the house stood strong.
26. A foolish person hears and ignores. That's like building a house on sand.
27. Rain and wind came, and the house crashed.
28. When Jesus finished teaching, the people were amazed.
29. He taught with real authority, not like their teachers.

Matthew 8

1. Large crowds followed Jesus down the hill.
2. A man with leprosy came and said, "Lord, if you want, you can heal me."
3. Jesus touched him and said, "I want to. Be healed." The man was healed right away.
4. Jesus said, "Don't tell anyone. Go show the priest and give the gift Moses said to give."
5. In Capernaum, a Roman officer came to Jesus and asked for help.
6. He said, "My servant is very sick and in pain."
7. Jesus said, "I will go heal him."
8. The officer said, "I'm not good enough for you to come. Just say the word and he will be healed.
9. I know how orders work. I give commands and people obey."
10. Jesus was amazed. He said, "I haven't seen faith like this in Israel."
11. "Many people from far away will be in God's kingdom.
12. But some who think they belong will be left out."
13. Jesus told the officer, "Go home. It's done." His servant was healed that moment.
14. Jesus went to Peter's house. Peter's mother-in-law was in bed with a fever.
15. Jesus touched her hand. The fever left. She got up and served them.
16. That evening, many people with demons came. Jesus cast out the spirits and healed the sick.
17. This fulfilled what Isaiah said: "He took our sickness and pain."
18. Jesus saw the crowd and told his followers to go to the other side of the lake.
19. A teacher of the law said, "I'll follow you anywhere."
20. Jesus said, "I don't even have a place to sleep."
21. Another man said, "Let me go bury my father first."
22. Jesus said, "Follow me now. Let the dead bury their dead."
23. Jesus and his followers got into a boat.
24. A big storm came. The waves covered the boat. Jesus was sleeping.
25. They woke him and said, "Lord, save us! We're going to die!"
26. Jesus said, "Why are you afraid? Where is your faith?" Then he told the storm to stop, and it became calm.
27. The men were amazed. "Even the wind and sea obey him!"

28. Jesus reached the other side. Two men with demons came from the tombs. They were so violent no one could pass by.
29. They shouted, "What do you want, Son of God? Don't torture us!"
30. Nearby, a large herd of pigs was feeding.
31. The demons begged, "Send us into the pigs."
32. Jesus said, "Go!" The demons went into the pigs. The pigs ran off a cliff and drowned.
33. The pig keepers ran into town and told everyone.
34. The whole town came to Jesus and begged him to leave.

Matthew 9

1. Jesus got back in the boat and went to his town.
2. Some people brought a paralyzed man to him. Jesus said, "Be happy. Your sins are forgiven."
3. Some teachers thought, "He's saying bad things against God!"
4. Jesus knew what they were thinking. He said, "Why do you think bad thoughts?
5. Is it easier to say 'Your sins are forgiven' or 'Get up and walk'?
6. I'll show you I have power to forgive sins." He said to the man, "Get up, take your mat, and go home."
7. The man got up and went home.
8. The crowd was amazed and praised God.
9. Jesus saw a man named Matthew sitting at a tax booth. He said, "Follow me." Matthew got up and followed.
10. Jesus ate dinner at Matthew's house. Many tax collectors and sinners came too.
11. Some Pharisees asked Jesus' followers, "Why does your teacher eat with sinners?"
12. Jesus heard and said, "Healthy people don't need a doctor. Sick people do.
13. I want kindness, not just rules. I came to help sinners, not the good people."
14. John's followers asked, "Why don't your followers fast like we do?"
15. Jesus said, "You don't fast when the groom is with you. You will fast when he is gone."
16. You don't patch old clothes with new cloth. It will tear more.
17. You don't put new wine in old skins. It will break. You use new skins for new wine."
18. A leader came and said, "My daughter just died. Please come and bring her back to life."
19. Jesus went with him. His followers came too.
20. A woman who had been bleeding for 12 years touched Jesus' clothes.
21. She thought, "If I just touch his clothes, I'll be healed."
22. Jesus turned and said, "Be brave. You are healed because you believed." She was healed right then.
23. Jesus reached the leader's house. People were crying loudly.
24. He said, "The girl isn't dead. She's just sleeping." They laughed at him.
25. Jesus sent the crowd away. He took the girl's hand, and she got up.
26. News spread everywhere.
27. Two blind men followed Jesus. They shouted, "Help us, Son of David!"
28. Jesus asked them, "Do you believe I can help you?" They said, "Yes."
29. He touched their eyes and said, "You will see because you believe."
30. Their eyes opened. Jesus said, "Don't tell anyone."
31. But they told everyone anyway.

32. Some people brought a man who couldn't speak and had a demon.
33. Jesus cast out the demon. The man spoke. People were amazed.
34. But the Pharisees said, "He uses the devil's power."
35. Jesus went to towns teaching, preaching, and healing.
36. He felt sad for the people. They were helpless like sheep without a shepherd.
37. He said, "The harvest is big, but the workers are few.
38. Pray for more workers to help bring people to God."

Matthew 10

1. Jesus called his 12 followers and gave them power to heal and cast out evil spirits.
2. These are their names: Simon (called Peter), Andrew, James, John,
3. Philip, Bartholomew, Thomas, Matthew, James (son of Alphaeus), Thaddaeus,
4. Simon (the Zealot), and Judas Iscariot (who later betrayed Jesus).
5. Jesus sent them out and said, "Go only to the people of Israel, not to other countries or Samaritans.
6. Help the lost people of Israel.
7. Tell them, 'God's kingdom is near!'
8. Heal the sick, raise the dead, cure skin disease, and cast out demons. You were given this power freely, so give freely.
9. Don't take money, gold, or silver with you.
10. Don't take extra clothes, shoes, or a walking stick. A worker should be given what they need.
11. When you enter a town, find someone good to stay with.
12. Greet the home with peace.
13. If they accept you, stay. If not, take your peace back.
14. If people won't listen, leave. Shake the dust off your feet as a warning.
15. On judgment day, it will be worse for them than for Sodom and Gomorrah.
16. I'm sending you out like sheep among wolves. Be wise and harmless.
17. Watch out. People will arrest you and take you to court.
18. You'll stand before leaders to tell them about me.
19. Don't worry about what to say. God will give you the right words.
20. It won't be you speaking. God's Spirit will speak through you.
21. Family members will turn on each other. Some will even be killed.
22. People will hate you because of me. But stay strong to the end and you will be saved.
23. If they chase you from one town, go to another. You won't finish going to all the towns before I return.
24. A student is not greater than the teacher. A servant is not greater than the master.
25. If they treated me badly, they will treat you badly too.
26. Don't be afraid. Everything hidden will be made known.
27. Speak the truth everywhere.
28. Don't fear people who can kill your body. Fear God who can judge forever.
29. Two sparrows are sold for a penny, but God sees each one.
30. God even knows how many hairs are on your head.
31. So don't be afraid. You are worth more than many birds.
32. If you say you follow me, I will say you belong to me in heaven.
33. If you deny me, I will deny you.

34. I didn't come to bring peace, but to divide. Some people will follow me, others won't.
35. Families will fight because of me.
36. Even your own family might become your enemies.
37. If you love anyone more than me, you aren't worthy of me.
38. If you don't accept the hard parts of following me, you're not worthy.
39. If you try to keep your life, you'll lose it. But if you give it up for me, you'll find it.
40. Whoever welcomes you, welcomes me. And whoever welcomes me, welcomes God.
41. If someone welcomes a prophet or a good person, they'll be rewarded.
42. If someone gives a drink of water to my followers, they won't lose their reward.

Matthew 11

1. After Jesus finished teaching his 12 followers, he went to teach in other towns.
2. John the Baptist was in prison. He heard what Jesus was doing and sent his followers to ask:
3. "Are you the one God promised, or should we wait for someone else?"
4. Jesus said, "Go tell John what you see:
5. The blind see. The lame walk. People with skin disease are healed. The deaf hear. The dead live again. The poor hear the good news.
6. God blesses those who believe in me."
7. After they left, Jesus talked about John. "What did you go to see in the desert? A weak man?
8. No. Did you see a rich man? No, those are in palaces.
9. You saw a prophet. Yes, and more than a prophet.
10. John is the one the Scriptures said would come before me.
11. No one ever born is greater than John. But the least in God's kingdom is greater than he is.
12. Since John started preaching, people have been trying hard to get into God's kingdom.
13. All the prophets and the law pointed to this time.
14. And if you believe it, John is Elijah, who was supposed to come.
15. If you can understand, listen!
16. What are people like today? Like kids in the market saying,
17. 'We played music, but you didn't dance. We cried, but you didn't care.'
18. John came and didn't eat or drink like others, and people said he had a demon.
19. I came eating and drinking, and people say I'm a friend of sinners. But wisdom is proven by actions."
20. Jesus warned the towns where he did miracles, but the people didn't turn to God.
21. "Woe to you, Chorazin and Bethsaida! If I had done these miracles in Tyre and Sidon, they would have turned to God.
22. It will be better for them than for you on judgment day.
23. Capernaum, do you think you'll go to heaven? No. You'll go down. If I had done these miracles in Sodom, it would still be here.
24. It will be better for Sodom than for you on judgment day."
25. Then Jesus prayed, "Father, thank you for hiding these things from the wise and showing them to children.
26. Yes, Father, this was your plan."
27. "My Father gave me everything. No one knows the Son except the Father. No one knows the Father except the Son and those the Son shows him to."

28. "Come to me if you're tired and carrying heavy burdens. I'll give you rest.
29. Follow me and learn from me. I am gentle and kind. You will find rest.
30. What I ask of you is easy, and my load is light."

Matthew 12

1. One day, Jesus was walking through grain fields on the Sabbath. His followers were hungry and picked some grain to eat.
2. Some Pharisees saw them and said, "It's against the law to pick grain on the Sabbath!"
3. Jesus said, "Haven't you read what David did when he was hungry? He ate the special bread in the temple, which isn't allowed for anyone but the priests.
4. The Sabbath was made for people, not people for the Sabbath.
5. I am greater than the temple.
6. If you understood what 'I want kindness, not sacrifice' means, you wouldn't judge these people.
7. The Son of Man is Lord of the Sabbath."
8. Jesus went into a synagogue.
9. A man with a paralyzed hand was there.
10. The Pharisees asked, "Is it against the law to heal on the Sabbath?"
11. Jesus said, "If your sheep falls into a hole, will you not help it on the Sabbath? A person is more valuable than a sheep. So it's right to do good on the Sabbath."
12. He told the man, "Stretch out your hand." The man did, and his hand was healed.
13. The Pharisees went out and made plans to kill Jesus.
14. Jesus knew about their plans and left. Many people followed him, and he healed them all.
15. He warned them not to tell others about him.
16. This fulfilled what the prophet Isaiah said:
17. "Here is my servant, whom I have chosen. He will not fight or shout. People will not hear his voice in the streets.
18. He will not break a bruised reed or put out a smoldering wick. He will bring justice.
19. He will not stop until he has made everything right."
20. The nations will trust in his name.
21. Then they brought a man who was blind and couldn't speak because of a demon.
22. Jesus healed him, and he could see and speak.
23. The crowds were amazed and said, "Could this be the Son of David?"
24. But the Pharisees said, "He drives out demons with the power of the devil."
25. Jesus knew what they were thinking. He said, "Every kingdom divided against itself will be destroyed. A city or house divided against itself won't stand.
26. If I drive out demons with the devil's power, then who do your followers use?"
27. "If I drive out demons by God's power, then God's kingdom has come to you."
28. "How can anyone enter a strong man's house and steal his things unless he first ties up the strong man?"
29. "Whoever is not with me is against me, and whoever does not gather with me scatters."
30. I tell you, people will be forgiven for any sin or bad thing they say. But if they speak against the Holy Spirit, they will not be forgiven.
31. A tree is known by its fruit. Good trees produce good fruit, and bad trees produce bad fruit.

32. You brood of vipers, how can you say anything good when you are evil? The mouth speaks what the heart is full of.
33. People will have to give account on the day of judgment for every careless word they say.
34. But by your words you will be justified, and by your words you will be condemned."
35. Then some Pharisees and teachers asked for a sign from heaven to prove who he was.
36. Jesus said, "A wicked and unfaithful generation asks for a sign, but no sign will be given except the sign of Jonah."
37. "Just as Jonah was three days and nights in the belly of a fish, the Son of Man will be three days and nights in the earth."
38. "On judgment day, the people of Nineveh will stand up and judge this generation because they repented when Jonah preached to them. And something greater than Jonah is here."
39. "The queen of the South will rise up and judge this generation because she came to listen to Solomon's wisdom. And something greater than Solomon is here."
40. When an evil spirit leaves a person, it goes through dry places looking for rest.
41. When it doesn't find any, it says, "I'll go back to the house I left."
42. When it returns, it finds the house empty, swept, and cleaned.
43. Then it brings seven other spirits more evil than itself, and they live there. The person is worse than before.
44. This is how it will be with this evil generation."
45. While Jesus was talking to the crowd, his mother and brothers stood outside, wanting to speak to him.
46. Someone said, "Your mother and brothers are outside, wanting to talk to you."
47. Jesus said, "Who is my mother, and who are my brothers?"
48. He pointed to his disciples and said, "Here are my mother and brothers.
49. Anyone who does the will of my Father in heaven is my brother and sister and mother."

Matthew 13

1. That same day, Jesus went out of the house and sat by the lake.
2. Large crowds gathered around him, so he got into a boat and sat down. The people stood on the shore.
3. Jesus told them many things in parables: "A farmer went out to plant seeds.
4. As he was scattering the seeds, some fell on the path, and the birds came and ate them up.
5. Some fell on rocky places, where the soil was shallow. They grew quickly but withered because they had no roots.
6. Other seeds fell among thorns, which grew up and choked the plants.
7. Still, other seeds fell on good soil, where they produced a crop—a hundred, sixty, or thirty times what was sown.
8. Whoever has ears, let them hear."
9. The disciples asked, "Why do you speak to the people in parables?"
10. Jesus replied, "The knowledge of the secrets of the kingdom of heaven has been given to you, but not to them.
11. Whoever has will be given more, and they will have an abundance. Whoever does not have, even what they have will be taken from them.
12. This is why I speak to them in parables: Though seeing, they do not see; though hearing, they do not hear or understand.
13. In them is fulfilled the prophecy of Isaiah:

14. 'You will be ever hearing but never understanding; you will be ever seeing but never perceiving.
15. For this people's heart has become calloused; they hardly hear with their ears, and they have closed their eyes. Otherwise, they might see with their eyes, hear with their ears, understand with their hearts and turn, and I would heal them.'
16. But blessed are your eyes because they see, and your ears because they hear.
17. For truly I tell you, many prophets and righteous people longed to see what you see but did not see it, and to hear what you hear but did not hear it."
18. "Listen then to what the parable of the sower means:
19. When anyone hears the message about the kingdom and does not understand it, the evil one comes and snatches away what was sown in their heart. This is the seed sown along the path.
20. The seed falling on rocky ground refers to someone who hears the word and at once receives it with joy.
21. But since they have no root, they last only a short time. When trouble or persecution comes because of the word, they quickly fall away.
22. The seed falling among the thorns refers to someone who hears the word, but the worries of this life and the deceitfulness of wealth choke the word, making it unfruitful.
23. But the seed falling on good soil refers to someone who hears the word and understands it. This is the one who produces a crop, yielding a hundred, sixty, or thirty times what was sown."

Matthew 14

1. King Herod heard about Jesus.
2. He said, "This must be John the Baptist, come back to life!"
3. Herod had arrested John, tied him up, and put him in prison because of Herodias, his brother's wife.
4. John had told Herod, "It's wrong for you to marry her."
5. Herod wanted to kill John, but he was afraid of the people, because they believed John was a prophet.
6. On Herod's birthday, Herodias's daughter danced for the guests, and Herod was very pleased.
7. He promised to give her anything she wanted.
8. She asked her mother what to ask for. Her mother said, "Ask for John the Baptist's head on a plate."
9. The king was upset, but he had made a promise in front of his guests.
10. So he sent soldiers to cut off John's head in prison.
11. They brought John's head on a plate and gave it to the girl, who gave it to her mother.
12. John's followers took his body and buried it. Then they told Jesus.
13. When Jesus heard this, he left by boat to be alone. But crowds followed him.
14. Jesus saw the crowd and felt sorry for them. He healed the sick.
15. That evening, his followers said, "It's getting late. Send the people away to buy food."
16. Jesus said, "They don't need to go. You give them something to eat."
17. They said, "We only have five loaves of bread and two fish."
18. Jesus said, "Bring them here."
19. He told the people to sit down. He took the food, looked up to heaven, and thanked God. Then he broke the bread and gave it to his followers to hand out.
20. Everyone ate and was full. They collected twelve baskets of leftovers.
21. About 5,000 men were fed, not counting women and children.
22. Right after that, Jesus made the disciples get into a boat and go ahead of him.

23. Then he went up on a mountain alone to pray. It got dark, and he was still there alone.
24. The boat was far from land and struggling against the wind.
25. Late at night, Jesus walked on the water toward them.
26. When they saw him, they were scared. They thought he was a ghost.
27. Jesus said, "Don't be afraid. It's me."
28. Peter said, "Lord, if it's you, let me come to you on the water."
29. Jesus said, "Come." So Peter got out and walked on the water toward Jesus.
30. But when he saw the wind and waves, he got scared and started to sink. He shouted, "Lord, save me!"
31. Jesus grabbed his hand and said, "You have little faith. Why did you doubt?"
32. They got in the boat, and the wind stopped.
33. The others worshiped him and said, "You really are God's Son."
34. They landed at Gennesaret.
35. People there recognized Jesus and told others.
36. They brought all the sick people. They begged to just touch his clothes. Everyone who touched him was healed.

Matthew 15

1. Some Pharisees and teachers came from Jerusalem to see Jesus.
2. They asked, "Why don't your followers follow our hand-washing rules?"
3. Jesus said, "Why do you break God's commands to follow your own rules?
4. God said, 'Honor your father and mother.' But you say, 'If you give money to God, you don't have to help your parents.' That's wrong.
5. You cancel God's word for your traditions.
6. You're hypocrites. Isaiah was right when he said:
7. 'These people honor me with words, but their hearts are far from me.
8. Their worship means nothing because they follow human rules.'"
9. Jesus called the crowd and said, "Listen and understand.
10. What goes into your mouth doesn't make you wrong. What comes out of your mouth shows what's in your heart."
11. The disciples said, "The Pharisees were upset by what you said."
12. Jesus said, "Don't worry. Every plant not planted by God will be pulled up.
13. Leave the Pharisees alone. They are blind leaders. If a blind man leads another blind man, both will fall."
14. Peter asked, "Explain that to us."
15. Jesus said, "Don't you understand yet?
16. Food goes into your stomach and then out of your body.
17. But words come from your heart. That's what makes you unclean.
18. Evil thoughts, murder, lying, and more come from the heart. These are the things that make a person wrong."
19. Then Jesus went to the area of Tyre and Sidon.
20. A woman from there shouted, "Lord, Son of David, help me! My daughter has a demon."
21. Jesus didn't answer her.
22. The disciples said, "Send her away. She keeps yelling."
23. Jesus said, "I was sent to help only the people of Israel."
24. But the woman came and begged, "Lord, help me!"
25. Jesus said, "It's not right to take children's food and give it to dogs."
26. She said, "Yes, Lord, but even dogs get crumbs from the table."

27. Jesus said, "You have great faith! Your daughter is healed." And she was healed at that moment.
28. Jesus left and went near a lake. He went up a mountain and sat down.
29. Large crowds came. They brought the blind, the crippled, and the sick. Jesus healed them all.
30. The people were amazed. They praised God.
31. Jesus called his disciples and said, "I feel sorry for the people. They've been with me for three days and have no food. I don't want to send them away hungry."
32. The disciples said, "Where can we get enough food for this crowd?"
33. Jesus asked, "How much food do you have?" They said, "Seven loaves and a few fish."
34. He told the people to sit.
35. He took the food, thanked God, and gave it to the disciples to share.
36. Everyone ate and was full. They picked up seven baskets of leftovers.
37. About 4,000 men ate, plus women and children.
38. After that, Jesus sent the people home and got into a boat.

Matthew 16

1. Some Pharisees and Sadducees came to test Jesus. They asked for a sign from heaven.
2. Jesus said, "You look at the sky and know what the weather will be.
3. But you don't understand the signs of what's happening now.
4. Evil people want signs, but the only sign you'll get is the sign of Jonah." Then Jesus left.
5. Later, Jesus' followers forgot to bring bread.
6. Jesus said, "Be careful of the yeast of the Pharisees and Sadducees."
7. The disciples talked and said, "He's upset we didn't bring bread."
8. Jesus knew what they were saying. He said, "Why are you talking about bread?
9. Don't you remember the 5,000 people I fed with five loaves and the 12 baskets of leftovers?
10. Or the 4,000 people I fed with seven loaves and the seven baskets left?
11. I'm not talking about bread. Watch out for the teachings of the Pharisees and Sadducees."
12. Then they understood—he meant their teachings, not real yeast.
13. Jesus asked his followers, "Who do people say I am?"
14. They said, "Some say John the Baptist. Others say Elijah or another prophet."
15. Jesus asked, "But who do you say I am?"
16. Peter said, "You are the Messiah, the Son of the living God."
17. Jesus said, "You are blessed, Peter. God showed this to you, not people.
18. You are Peter, and on this rock I will build my church. Even death won't stop it.
19. I will give you the keys to God's kingdom. What you allow on earth will be allowed in heaven."
20. Then Jesus told them not to tell anyone he was the Messiah.
21. From that time on, Jesus told his followers he would suffer, be killed, and rise after three days.
22. Peter said, "No, Lord! That will never happen!"
23. Jesus said to Peter, "Get away from me, Satan! You are thinking like people, not God."
24. Then Jesus told everyone, "If you want to follow me, give up what you want. Carry your cross and follow me.

25. If you try to save your life, you will lose it. But if you give up your life for me, you will find it.
26. What good is it to gain the world but lose your soul?
27. The Son of Man will come with angels and reward everyone for what they've done.
28. Some of you here won't die before you see the Son of Man in his kingdom."

Matthew 17

1. Six days later, Jesus took Peter, James, and John up a high mountain.
2. Jesus' face changed and shone like the sun. His clothes became bright as light.
3. Moses and Elijah appeared and talked with Jesus.
4. Peter said, "Lord, it's good we're here! Let's make three shelters—one for each of you."
5. While he was speaking, a bright cloud covered them. A voice said, "This is my Son. I love him. Listen to him!"
6. The disciples fell down in fear.
7. Jesus touched them and said, "Get up. Don't be afraid."
8. When they looked up, only Jesus was there.
9. As they went down the mountain, Jesus said, "Don't tell anyone what you saw until I rise from the dead."
10. The disciples asked, "Why do teachers say Elijah must come first?"
11. Jesus said, "Elijah already came, but people didn't recognize him. They hurt him, and they will hurt me too."
12. Then the disciples understood he meant John the Baptist.
13. They went back to the crowd. A man came and knelt before Jesus.
14. He said, "Lord, help my son! He has seizures and often falls into fire or water.
15. I brought him to your disciples, but they couldn't help."
16. Jesus said, "You people don't believe. How long must I stay and help you?" Then he said, "Bring the boy here."
17. Jesus told the demon to leave, and the boy was healed.
18. Later, the disciples asked Jesus, "Why couldn't we cast it out?"
19. Jesus said, "You didn't have enough faith. Even faith as small as a mustard seed can move a mountain."
20. "Nothing will be impossible if you believe."
21. [Some versions say: This kind only comes out with prayer and fasting.]
22. Later, Jesus told them again, "I will be handed over, killed, and rise on the third day." They were very sad.
23. They arrived in Capernaum. The tax men asked Peter, "Does your teacher pay the temple tax?"
24. Peter said, "Yes." Then he went into the house, and Jesus asked him first:
25. "Who do kings collect taxes from—their children or others?"
26. Peter said, "From others." Jesus said, "So the children don't have to pay.
27. But to avoid problems, go fish in the lake. The first fish you catch will have a coin in its mouth. Use it to pay the tax for both of us."

Matthew 18

1. The disciples asked Jesus, "Who is the greatest in God's kingdom?"
2. Jesus called a little child and said,
3. "You must become like this child to enter God's kingdom.
4. The most humble person is the greatest.
5. Anyone who welcomes a child like this welcomes me."
6. "If someone causes a child to sin, it would be better to tie a big rock

around their neck and throw them in the sea.

7. Bad things will happen in the world, but don't be the one who causes them.

8. If your hand or foot makes you sin, get rid of it. It's better to lose a body part than be thrown into fire.

9. If your eye causes you to sin, get rid of it too."

10. "Don't look down on children. Their angels always see God.

11. [Some versions say: The Son of Man came to save the lost.]

12. If a man has 100 sheep and one gets lost, he leaves the 99 and looks for the one.

13. When he finds it, he's happier about the one than the 99 who didn't get lost.

14. God doesn't want even one child to be lost."

15. "If someone sins against you, talk to them privately. If they listen, you've made peace.

16. If they don't, take one or two others to help.

17. If they still won't listen, tell the church. If they still refuse, treat them like someone outside your group."

18. "What you allow on earth will be allowed in heaven. What you don't allow will not be allowed."

19. "If two of you agree on something and pray for it, God will do it.

20. Where two or three come together in my name, I am there with them."

21. Peter asked, "How many times should I forgive someone? Seven times?"

22. Jesus said, "Not seven—seventy-seven times!"

23. "God's kingdom is like a king who wanted to settle debts.

24. One servant owed him millions but couldn't pay.

25. The king said to sell everything he had, even his family.

26. The servant begged, 'Please be patient! I'll pay it back!'

27. The king felt sorry and forgave the whole debt.

28. But that servant found another man who owed him a little. He grabbed him and said, 'Pay me now!'

29. The man begged, but the servant refused and threw him in jail.

30. Other people saw this and told the king.

31. The king was angry. He said, 'I forgave you. Shouldn't you forgive others?'

32. He sent the servant to be punished."

33. "God will do the same to you if you don't forgive from your heart."

Matthew 19

1. Jesus left Galilee and went to the area of Judea across the Jordan River.

2. Large crowds followed him, and he healed them there.

3. Some Pharisees came to test him. They asked, "Can a man divorce his wife for any reason?"

4. Jesus said, "God made people male and female.

5. A man will leave his parents, join with his wife, and they become one.

6. They are no longer two. What God joins together, no one should separate."

7. They asked, "Then why did Moses allow divorce?"

8. Jesus said, "Moses allowed it because people's hearts were hard. But it wasn't like that from the beginning.

9. Anyone who divorces his wife and marries another woman is wrong—unless she was unfaithful."

10. The disciples said, "Maybe it's better not to marry at all!"

11. Jesus said, "Not everyone can accept this. Some can live without marriage,

others are born that way, and some choose it for God's kingdom.

12. If you can accept this, do it."

13. People brought children to Jesus so he could bless them. The disciples told them to stop.

14. But Jesus said, "Let the children come. Don't stop them. God's kingdom belongs to them."

15. He placed his hands on them and blessed them.

16. A man came and asked Jesus, "What good thing must I do to have eternal life?"

17. Jesus said, "Only God is good. But if you want life, obey the commandments."

18. The man asked, "Which ones?"

19. Jesus said, "Don't kill, don't cheat, don't steal, don't lie, honor your parents, and love others."

20. The man said, "I already do all that. What else?"

21. Jesus said, "If you want to be perfect, sell everything, give the money to the poor, and follow me."

22. The man went away sad because he was very rich.

23. Jesus said to his disciples, "It's hard for rich people to enter God's kingdom.

24. It's easier for a camel to go through a needle than for a rich person to enter."

25. The disciples were shocked. "Then who can be saved?" they asked.

26. Jesus said, "With people, it's impossible. But with God, all things are possible."

27. Peter said, "We gave up everything for you. What will we get?"

28. Jesus said, "When everything is made new, you will sit on thrones and judge the tribes of Israel.

29. Anyone who gives up family or things for me will get much more—and eternal life.

30. But many who are first now will be last, and those who are last will be first."

Matthew 20

1. Jesus said, "God's kingdom is like a man who owned land. He went out early to hire workers.

2. He agreed to pay them one coin for the day and sent them to work.

3. At 9 a.m., he saw others standing around. He said, 'You can work too, and I'll pay you fairly.'

4. They went.

5. At noon and at 3 p.m., he did the same thing.

6. At 5 p.m., he found more people and asked, 'Why are you standing here all day?'

7. They said, 'No one hired us.' He said, 'Go work in my field too.'

8. At the end of the day, he told his manager, 'Pay everyone, starting with the last ones hired.'

9. The ones hired at 5 p.m. got one coin.

10. The ones hired early thought they'd get more, but they also got one coin.

11. They complained and said, 'We worked all day in the hot sun!'

12. The owner said, 'I paid you what we agreed. Can't I be generous?

13. It's my money. Don't be jealous because I'm kind.'

14. So the last will be first, and the first will be last."

15. Jesus was going to Jerusalem. He took the twelve disciples aside.

16. He said, "We are going to Jerusalem. I will be handed over, beaten, and killed. But after three days, I will rise again."

17. The mother of James and John came to Jesus with her sons.

18. She knelt and asked a favor.

19. Jesus asked, "What do you want?"

20. She said, "Let my sons sit beside you in your kingdom."
21. Jesus said, "You don't know what you're asking. Can they suffer like I will?"
22. They said, "Yes."
23. Jesus said, "You will suffer like me, but I can't choose who sits beside me. God will decide that."
24. The other ten disciples were upset.
25. Jesus said, "World leaders act like bosses. But not you.
26. Whoever wants to be great must serve others.
27. Whoever wants to be first must be a servant.
28. I came to serve and to give my life to save others."
29. Jesus and his followers were leaving Jericho. A big crowd followed.
30. Two blind men were sitting by the road. They shouted, "Jesus, Son of David, help us!"
31. The crowd told them to be quiet, but they shouted louder.
32. Jesus stopped and asked, "What do you want me to do?"
33. They said, "We want to see."
34. Jesus felt sorry for them. He touched their eyes, and they could see. They followed him.

Matthew 21

1. Jesus and his followers came near Jerusalem. He sent two of them ahead.
2. He said, "Go into the village. You'll find a donkey and her colt. Bring them to me.
3. If anyone asks, say, 'The Lord needs them.'"
4. This happened to fulfill the message from the prophet:
5. "Tell Jerusalem, your king is coming. He is gentle and riding on a donkey."
6. The followers went and did what Jesus said.
7. They brought the donkey and colt and put coats on them. Jesus sat on the colt.
8. A large crowd spread their coats and branches on the road.
9. The people shouted, "Hosanna to the Son of David! Blessed is he who comes in God's name!"
10. When Jesus entered Jerusalem, the whole city was stirred up. They asked, "Who is this?"
11. The crowd said, "This is Jesus, the prophet from Nazareth!"
12. Jesus went into the temple. He saw people buying and selling.
13. He overturned tables and said, "This is a house of prayer, but you made it a den of thieves!"
14. Blind and crippled people came to Jesus in the temple, and he healed them.
15. The priests saw the wonderful things he did and heard children shouting, "Hosanna to the Son of David!"
16. They were angry and asked Jesus, "Do you hear what these children are saying?"
17. Jesus said, "Yes. Haven't you read, 'From children's lips, God gets praise'?"
18. Jesus left and went to Bethany for the night.
19. The next morning, he was hungry. He saw a fig tree but found no fruit, only leaves.
20. He said, "May you never grow fruit again!" Right away, the tree dried up.
21. The disciples were amazed.
22. Jesus said, "If you believe and don't doubt, you can do more than this. You can even tell a mountain to move, and it will.
23. If you believe, you will receive what you ask for in prayer."

24. Jesus went back to the temple. The priests asked, "Who gave you the right to teach here?"

25. Jesus said, "I'll ask you a question. If you answer, I'll tell you. Who gave John the right to baptize—God or people?"

26. They talked and said, "If we say 'God,' he'll ask why we didn't believe John. But if we say 'people,' the crowd will be angry."

27. So they said, "We don't know." Jesus said, "Then I won't tell you who gave me authority."

28. Then Jesus told a story: "A man had two sons. He said to the first, 'Go work in the field.' The son said, 'No,' but later changed his mind and went.

29. The man told his second son. He said, 'Yes,' but didn't go.

30. Which son did what the father wanted?" They said, "The first."

31. Jesus said, "Sinners and tax collectors are entering God's kingdom before you. They believed John, but you didn't—even after seeing them change."

32. Jesus told another story: "A man planted a vineyard and let farmers take care of it. Then he went away.

33. At harvest time, he sent servants to get the fruit.

34. The farmers beat one, killed another, and threw stones at a third.

35. He sent more servants, but the same thing happened.

36. Last, he sent his son. He thought, 'They will respect my son.'

37. But the farmers said, 'Here comes the heir! Let's kill him and take everything!' So they did.

38. Jesus asked, "What will the owner do?" They said, "He will punish those farmers and give the vineyard to others."

39. Jesus said, "Haven't you read? 'The stone the builders didn't want became the most important.' That's what God did."

40. "God's kingdom will be taken from you and given to others who obey."

41. The priests knew Jesus was talking about them. They wanted to arrest him, but they were afraid of the people.

Matthew 22

1. Jesus told another story.

2. "A king had a wedding party for his son.

3. He sent servants to tell the guests it was time, but they didn't come.

4. He sent more servants: 'The food is ready. Come to the party!'

5. But the guests didn't care. One went to his farm. Another went to his job.

6. Others grabbed the servants and hurt them.

7. The king was angry. He punished them and burned their city.

8. Then he told his servants, 'The party is ready, but the guests didn't deserve it.

9. Go into the streets. Invite everyone you see.'

10. So the servants invited all kinds of people—good and bad. The wedding hall was full.

11. The king saw one man not wearing wedding clothes.

12. He asked, 'How did you get in without the right clothes?' The man had no answer.

13. The king said, 'Tie him up and throw him out!'"

14. "Many are invited, but few are chosen."

15. Then the Pharisees made a plan to trap Jesus with a question.

16. They sent some of their people with Herod's followers. They said, "Teacher, we know you are honest. Tell us: Should we pay taxes to Caesar?"

17. Jesus knew they were trying to trap him.
18. He said, "Why are you testing me? Show me a coin."
19. They gave him a coin. Jesus asked, "Whose picture is on this?"
20. They said, "Caesar's."
21. Jesus said, "Then give Caesar what belongs to Caesar, and give God what belongs to God."
22. They were amazed and left.
23. That same day, some Sadducees came. They didn't believe in life after death.
24. They said, "Moses said if a man dies without children, his brother should marry the wife and have a child for him.
25. There were seven brothers. The first married and died with no children.
26. The second married her and died. This happened with all seven.
27. Last, the woman died too.
28. At the resurrection, whose wife will she be?"
29. Jesus said, "You are wrong. You don't know the Scriptures or God's power.
30. When people rise from the dead, they won't marry. They'll be like angels.
31. God said, 'I am the God of Abraham, Isaac, and Jacob.' He's not the God of the dead, but the living."
32. The crowd was amazed at his answer.
33. A Pharisee who was an expert in the law asked Jesus a question to test him.
34. "Teacher, which command is the greatest?"
35. Jesus said, "'Love God with all your heart, soul, and mind.' This is the first and greatest command.
36. The second is like it: 'Love your neighbor like yourself.'
37. All God's laws come from these two commands."
38. Then Jesus asked them a question: "What do you think about the Messiah? Whose son is he?"
39. They said, "David's son."
40. Jesus said, "Why did David call him 'Lord'? If David calls him 'Lord,' how can he be his son?"
41. No one could answer. After that, no one dared to ask Jesus any more questions.

Matthew 23

1. Jesus spoke to the crowd and his disciples.
2. He said, "The teachers of the law and Pharisees sit in Moses' seat.
3. So do what they say, but don't do what they do. They don't practice what they preach.
4. They make rules for others but don't follow them themselves.
5. Everything they do is to be seen by others.
6. They want the best seats and to be honored in public.
7. They like being called 'Teacher.'
8. But you shouldn't try to be important. You are all equal. God is your only teacher and Father.
9. The greatest among you should be your servant.
10. Those who make themselves great will be humbled. Those who humble themselves will be made great."
11. "How terrible for you, teachers and Pharisees! You keep people out of God's kingdom.
12. You don't go in, and you stop others from going in.
13. You travel far to make one convert, then make them worse than before.
14. You say it's okay to lie if you don't swear by the temple, but if you swear by the gold in the temple, it matters. That's foolish.

15. What's more important—the gold or the temple that makes it holy?

16. You also say swearing by the altar doesn't matter, but swearing by the gift does. Wrong again!

17. You're missing the point."

18. "How terrible for you! You give a tenth of small things like spices but ignore justice, mercy, and faith.

19. You should do both.

20. You clean the outside of the cup but leave the inside full of greed.

21. Clean the inside, and the outside will be clean too.

22. You are like whitewashed tombs—nice outside, but full of death inside.

23. You look good to people, but inside you are full of lies and evil."

24. "You build graves for prophets and say, 'We wouldn't have killed them.'

25. But you prove you are just like those who did.

26. You are snakes! How will you escape judgment?

27. I will send prophets, but you will hurt and kill them too.

28. Because of this, you are guilty of all the innocent blood ever spilled.

29. All these things will come to this generation."

30. "Jerusalem, Jerusalem, you kill the prophets and reject those God sends!

31. I wanted to gather your people like a hen gathers her chicks, but you wouldn't let me.

32. Now your house is left empty.

33. You won't see me again until you say, 'Blessed is he who comes in the name of the Lord.'"

Matthew 24

1. Jesus left the temple. His followers pointed out the buildings.

2. Jesus said, "All of this will be destroyed. Not one stone will be left."

3. Later, they asked, "When will this happen? What are the signs before you return?"

4. Jesus said, "Don't let anyone fool you.

5. Many will say they are me. Don't believe them.

6. You'll hear about wars. Don't be afraid. These things must happen, but it's not the end yet.

7. Nations will fight. There will be famines and earthquakes.

8. These are only the beginning.

9. You will be arrested, hurt, and hated because of me.

10. Many will turn away from faith. People will hate each other.

11. False teachers will trick many.

12. Evil will grow, and love will grow cold.

13. But whoever stays true to the end will be saved.

14. This good news will be told all over the world. Then the end will come."

15. "You will see something terrible in the temple. That's the warning to run.

16. If you're in Judea, run to the mountains.

17. Don't go back inside for anything.

18. Don't even stop to get your coat.

19. It will be hard for pregnant women and mothers with babies.

20. Pray this doesn't happen in winter or on a Sabbath.

21. These will be the worst days ever.

22. If those days weren't shortened, no one would survive. But they will be shorter for God's people.

23. If someone says, 'Look, here is the Messiah,' don't believe it.

24. False messiahs will do fake miracles to trick people.

25. I'm warning you now.

26. If they say, 'He's in the desert!' don't go.
27. When I return, it will be as clear as lightning in the sky.
28. Where there's a dead body, vultures will gather."
29. "After the trouble, the sun will go dark. The moon won't shine. Stars will fall.
30. Then the Son of Man will appear in the sky. Everyone will see him.
31. He will send angels to gather his people."
32. "Learn from the fig tree. When it sprouts leaves, summer is near.
33. When you see these things, know the end is near.
34. This generation won't pass before all this happens.
35. Heaven and earth will end, but my words won't."
36. "No one knows the day or time—only God.
37. It will be like Noah's time. People were eating and drinking until the flood came.
38. That's how it will be when I return.
39. Two people will be in a field. One will be taken, one left.
40. Two women will be grinding grain. One will be taken, one left.
41. So stay ready.
42. You don't know when your Lord will come.
43. If a man knew when a thief would come, he'd stay awake.
44. Be ready. I will come when you don't expect me."
45. "A wise servant takes care of others while the master is gone.
46. That servant will be blessed when the master returns.
47. He will be given more responsibility.
48. But a bad servant says, 'My master won't be back soon.'
49. Then he starts hurting others and getting drunk.
50. That master will return when he's not expected.
51. He will punish the servant. That servant will be put with the unfaithful."

Matthew 25

1. "God's kingdom is like ten girls waiting for a wedding.
2. Five were wise and five were foolish.
3. The wise girls brought extra oil for their lamps.
4. The foolish ones did not.
5. The groom was late. They all got sleepy and fell asleep.
6. At midnight, someone shouted, 'The groom is here!'
7. They all woke up and got their lamps ready.
8. The foolish girls said, 'Give us some oil. Our lamps are going out!'
9. The wise girls said, 'No, there's not enough. Go buy some.'
10. While they were gone, the groom came. The wise girls went into the wedding. The door was shut.
11. Later, the others came and said, 'Let us in!'
12. But the groom said, 'I don't know you.'
13. So stay ready. You don't know the day or hour."
14. "It's like a man who left on a trip. He gave money to his servants.
15. One got five bags of gold. Another got two. Another got one. Each got what they could handle.
16. The one with five used it and earned five more.
17. The one with two earned two more.
18. But the one with one bag buried it.
19. After a long time, the master came back to see what they did.

20. The one with five said, 'I earned five more.' The master said, 'Well done! You were faithful. I'll trust you with more. Come celebrate!'
21. The one with two said, 'I earned two more.' The master said the same thing.
22. The one with one said, 'I was afraid and hid it. Here it is.'
23. The master said, 'You are lazy. You could have at least put it in the bank to earn interest.'
24. 'Take his money and give it to the one with ten.'
25. 'Those who use what they have will get more. But those who don't will lose even what they have.'
26. 'Throw the useless servant outside into the dark.'"
27. "When the Son of Man comes with his angels, he will sit on his throne.
28. All people will be gathered. He will separate them like a shepherd separates sheep and goats.
29. The sheep go on his right. The goats on his left.
30. He will say to the sheep, 'Come, you who are blessed. Take your place in the kingdom made for you.'
31. 'I was hungry and you fed me. I was thirsty and you gave me a drink. I was a stranger and you welcomed me.'
32. 'I was sick and in jail and you visited me.'
33. The people will ask, 'When did we do these things for you?'
34. The King will say, 'When you did it for others, you did it for me.'
35. Then he will say to the goats on his left, 'Go away. I was hungry and you didn't feed me. I was thirsty and you gave me nothing.'
36. 'I was a stranger and you didn't help. I was sick and in jail and you didn't visit.'
37. They will ask, 'When did we see you and not help?'
38. He will say, 'When you didn't help others, you didn't help me.'
39. Then they will be sent away. But the good people will have eternal life."

Matthew 26

1. Jesus finished teaching and told his followers,
2. "In two days, it will be Passover. I will be handed over and killed."
3. The priests and leaders met to plan how to arrest and kill Jesus.
4. They said, "Not during Passover, or the people might riot."
5. A woman came to Jesus with a jar of perfume. She poured it on his head while he was eating.
6. The disciples were upset and said, "This was a waste! The perfume could've been sold and given to the poor."
7. Jesus said, "Leave her alone. She did something good for me.
8. You will always have the poor, but not me.
9. She prepared my body for burial. People everywhere will remember what she did."
10. Then Judas went to the priests.
11. He asked, "What will you give me if I turn Jesus in?" They gave him 30 silver coins.
12. From then on, Judas looked for the right time to betray Jesus.
13. On Passover, Jesus told the disciples, "Go prepare the meal."
14. They asked, "Where should we go?"
15. Jesus said, "Go to this man's house. Say the teacher says, 'My time is near. I'll eat Passover with my followers there.'"
16. They did as Jesus said.
17. That evening, Jesus ate with the twelve.

18. While eating, he said, "One of you will betray me."

19. They were very upset. Each one asked, "Is it me?"

20. Jesus said, "The one who dips bread in the bowl with me will betray me.

21. It would be better if he had never been born."

22. Judas said, "Is it me, Teacher?" Jesus said, "Yes."

23. While they were eating, Jesus took bread, thanked God, broke it, and gave it to them. He said, "Take and eat. This is my body."

24. Then he took a cup, thanked God, and gave it to them. He said, "Drink this. It is my blood, poured out to forgive sins."

25. "I won't drink wine again until I drink it with you in my Father's kingdom."

26. They sang a song and went to the Mount of Olives.

27. Jesus said, "Tonight, you will all leave me. The Scriptures say the shepherd will be struck and the sheep will scatter."

28. "But after I rise, I'll meet you in Galilee."

29. Peter said, "Even if everyone leaves, I never will."

30. Jesus said, "Tonight, before the rooster crows, you will say three times you don't know me."

31. Peter said, "Even if I die, I'll never say that!" The others said the same.

32. Jesus went to a garden called Gethsemane. He told his followers, "Sit here while I pray."

33. He took Peter, James, and John with him. He was very sad.

34. He said, "Stay here. I feel like I'm dying inside."

35. Jesus walked a little away, fell to the ground, and prayed, "Father, if possible, don't let this happen to me. But I want your will, not mine."

36. He went back and found them asleep. He said to Peter, "You couldn't stay awake for one hour?"

37. "Pray so you won't fall into temptation."

38. He prayed again, "Father, if this must happen, I will do it."

39. He returned again and found them asleep.

40. He left and prayed a third time, saying the same thing.

41. Then he said, "Get up. It's time. The one who is turning me in is here."

42. Judas arrived with a crowd carrying swords.

43. He had told them, "The one I kiss is Jesus."

44. Judas kissed Jesus and said, "Hello, Teacher!"

45. Jesus said, "Friend, do what you came to do."

46. The men grabbed Jesus and arrested him.

47. One follower pulled out a sword and cut off a man's ear.

48. Jesus said, "Put the sword away. I could call angels to save me, but this must happen."

49. The followers ran away.

50. Jesus was taken to the high priest. Peter followed from far away.

51. People tried to find lies to use against Jesus.

52. Two men said, "He said he would destroy the temple and rebuild it in three days."

53. The high priest asked, "Are you the Son of God?"

54. Jesus said, "Yes. And you will see me sitting at God's side."

55. The priest tore his clothes and said, "He has spoken against God!"

56. They all said he should die.

57. They spit on him and hit him.

58. Peter was outside. A girl said, "You were with Jesus." He said, "No, I wasn't."

59. Another person said, "Yes, you were." Peter said, "I don't know him!"

60. A third person said, "You are one of them!" Peter shouted, "I don't know him!"

61. Right then, the rooster crowed. Peter remembered Jesus' words and cried.

Matthew 27

1. Early in the morning, the leaders decided to kill Jesus.

2. They tied him up and took him to the Roman ruler, Pilate.

3. Judas saw Jesus was condemned. He felt sorry and tried to return the money.

4. He said, "I did wrong! I turned in an innocent man!"

5. They said, "That's your problem." Judas threw the coins into the temple and hanged himself.

6. The leaders said, "We can't put this money in the temple. It's blood money."

7. So they used it to buy a field to bury strangers.

8. That's why it's still called the Field of Blood.

9. This fulfilled what was written by the prophet.

10. Jesus stood before Pilate. Pilate asked, "Are you the king of the Jews?" Jesus said, "You say so."

11. The priests accused him, but Jesus stayed silent.

12. Pilate was amazed.

13. Every year, Pilate let the people choose one prisoner to go free.

14. He asked, "Do you want Jesus or Barabbas?"

15. Pilate's wife sent him a message: "Don't harm this man. I had a bad dream about him."

16. The leaders told the crowd to ask for Barabbas and kill Jesus.

17. Pilate asked, "What should I do with Jesus?"

18. The crowd shouted, "Crucify him!"

19. Pilate asked, "Why? What has he done?" But they shouted louder.

20. Pilate washed his hands and said, "I'm not responsible for his death."

21. The people said, "Let his blood be on us and our children!"

22. Pilate set Barabbas free and had Jesus beaten and handed over to be killed.

23. The soldiers put a crown of thorns on Jesus' head and made fun of him.

24. They spit on him and hit him.

25. Then they led him away to be nailed to a cross.

26. A man named Simon was forced to carry Jesus' cross.

27. They gave Jesus wine with something bitter in it. He tasted it but didn't drink.

28. They nailed him to the cross and divided his clothes.

29. Above his head was a sign: "This is Jesus, the King of the Jews."

30. Two criminals were nailed to crosses beside him.

31. People walked by and made fun of Jesus.

32. The priests also mocked him: "He saved others but can't save himself!"

33. From noon to 3 p.m., it got dark.

34. Jesus cried out, "My God, why did you leave me?"

35. Some thought he was calling Elijah.

36. Someone gave him a sponge with wine to drink.

37. Jesus shouted again to God, and died.

38. The temple curtain tore in two. The earth shook. Rocks broke.
39. Tombs opened and many holy people were raised to life.
40. A soldier said, "This man really was the Son of God."
41. Many women watched from far away. They had followed Jesus and helped him.
42. That evening, a rich man named Joseph asked Pilate for Jesus' body.
43. He wrapped it in cloth and put it in a new tomb.
44. He rolled a big stone in front and left.
45. The next day, the leaders asked Pilate to guard the tomb.
46. They said, "His followers might steal the body and say he rose from the dead."
47. Pilate said, "Take guards and make it secure."
48. They sealed the stone and put soldiers in front of the tomb.

Matthew 28

1. Early Sunday morning, Mary Magdalene and the other Mary went to the tomb.
2. Suddenly, there was a big earthquake. An angel came down from heaven, rolled the stone away, and sat on it.
3. The angel looked bright like lightning. His clothes were white as snow.
4. The guards were so scared, they shook and fell down like dead men.
5. The angel said to the women, "Don't be afraid. I know you are looking for Jesus, who was killed.
6. He isn't here! He has risen, just like he said. Come see the place where he was.
7. Now go tell his followers, 'Jesus has risen from the dead. He is going to Galilee. You will see him there.'"
8. The women ran away quickly. They were scared but very happy. They ran to tell the others.
9. Suddenly, Jesus met them and said, "Hello!" They bowed down and held his feet.
10. Jesus said, "Don't be afraid. Go tell my brothers to go to Galilee. They will see me there."
11. Some of the guards went into the city and told the leaders everything that happened.
12. The leaders met and gave the soldiers a lot of money.
13. They said, "Tell people his followers stole the body while you were sleeping.
14. If the governor hears about this, we'll make sure you don't get in trouble."
15. The soldiers took the money and did what they were told. This story is still told today.
16. The eleven disciples went to Galilee, to the mountain Jesus had told them about.
17. They saw Jesus and worshiped him, but some still had doubts.
18. Jesus came to them and said, "All power in heaven and on earth has been given to me.
19. So go and teach people everywhere. Make them followers. Baptize them in the name of the Father, Son, and Holy Spirit.
20. Teach them to obey everything I taught you. I am with you always, to the end of time."

– Mark –

A fast-paced account showing Jesus as the powerful Son of God who suffers to save.

Mark 1

1. This is the beginning of the good news about Jesus, God's Son.

2. Long ago, God said, "I will send someone to get things ready."
3. "He will shout, 'Get ready! The Lord is coming!'"
4. That person was John the Baptist. He preached in the desert. He said, "Turn back to God and be baptized."
5. Many people came, admitted their sins, and were baptized in the Jordan River.
6. John wore camel hair clothes and a leather belt. He ate locusts and honey.
7. He said, "Someone more powerful is coming. I'm not even good enough to untie his sandals.
8. I baptize with water, but he will baptize you with the Holy Spirit."
9. Jesus came from Nazareth. John baptized him in the Jordan River.
10. As Jesus came out of the water, the sky opened. The Holy Spirit came down like a dove.
11. A voice from heaven said, "You are my Son. I love you. I am pleased with you."
12. Then the Spirit sent Jesus into the desert.
13. He was there for 40 days. Satan tempted him. Wild animals were there, but angels helped him.
14. After John was put in jail, Jesus went to Galilee. He said, "It's time. God's kingdom is near. Turn back to God and believe the good news."
15. Jesus was walking by the lake. He saw Simon and Andrew fishing.
16. He said, "Come with me. I will teach you to bring people to God."
17. Right away, they left their nets and followed him.
18. Jesus saw James and John, working with their father.
19. He called them too. They left their boat and followed Jesus.
20. Jesus went to Capernaum. On the Sabbath, he taught in the synagogue.
21. People were amazed. He taught with real authority.
22. A man with an evil spirit was there.
23. The spirit shouted, "What do you want with us, Jesus? Have you come to destroy us? I know who you are!"
24. Jesus said, "Be quiet! Come out!"
25. The spirit shook the man and came out.
26. Everyone was shocked. They asked, "What's this? Even evil spirits obey him!"
27. News about Jesus spread everywhere.
28. Jesus left the synagogue and went to Simon's house. Simon's mother-in-law was sick in bed.
29. Jesus touched her hand. She was healed and got up to serve them.
30. That evening, people brought the sick and those with demons.
31. The whole town came to the door.
32. Jesus healed many people and cast out many demons. He didn't let the demons speak because they knew who he was.
33. Early the next morning, Jesus went to a quiet place to pray.
34. Simon and others found him and said, "Everyone is looking for you!"
35. Jesus said, "Let's go to other towns. I must tell them the good news too."
36. He traveled through Galilee, preaching and casting out demons.
37. A man with leprosy came and begged, "If you want, you can heal me."
38. Jesus felt sorry for him. He touched the man and said, "I want to. Be healed."
39. The leprosy was gone right away.
40. Jesus said, "Don't tell anyone. Go show the priest and give the gift Moses said to give."
41. But the man told everyone.

42. Because of that, Jesus couldn't enter towns openly. He stayed in quiet places, but people still came from everywhere.

Mark 2

1. Jesus went back to Capernaum. People heard he was home.
2. A big crowd came. There was no room left.
3. Four men brought a paralyzed man to Jesus.
4. They couldn't get in, so they made a hole in the roof and lowered the man down.
5. Jesus saw their faith and said to the man, "Your sins are forgiven."
6. Some teachers of the law thought, "This is wrong! Only God can forgive sins!"
7. Jesus knew what they were thinking. He said, "Why are you thinking that?
8. Is it easier to say, 'Your sins are forgiven,' or 'Get up and walk'?
9. I'll show you I have power to forgive sins." He said to the man, "Get up, take your mat, and go home."
10. The man got up and walked out. Everyone was amazed.
11. Jesus walked by a tax booth. He saw Levi (Matthew) and said, "Follow me." Levi got up and followed him.
12. Later, Jesus ate at Levi's house. Many tax collectors and sinners were there.
13. The teachers asked the disciples, "Why does he eat with bad people?"
14. Jesus heard and said, "Healthy people don't need a doctor. I came to help sinners."
15. People asked, "Why don't your followers fast like John's?"
16. Jesus said, "Friends of a groom don't fast when he's with them. They will fast later."
17. "You don't put new cloth on old clothes. It will tear.
18. You don't put new wine in old skins. The skins will break."
19. One Sabbath, Jesus' followers picked grain. The Pharisees said, "That's against the law!"
20. Jesus said, "David ate special bread when he was hungry.
21. The Sabbath was made for people, not people for the Sabbath.
22. I am Lord of the Sabbath."

Mark 3

1. Jesus went to the synagogue. A man with a paralyzed hand was there.
2. Some people watched to see if Jesus would heal on the Sabbath.
3. Jesus said to the man, "Stand up."
4. He asked, "Is it right to do good on the Sabbath? Or to do harm?" No one answered.
5. Jesus was angry and sad. He said, "Stretch out your hand." The man did, and it was healed.
6. The Pharisees left and made plans to kill Jesus.
7. Jesus left with his followers. A large crowd followed him.
8. People came from all over to see him.
9. Jesus asked for a boat so the crowd wouldn't crush him.
10. He healed many, so people tried to touch him.
11. Evil spirits saw him and shouted, "You are God's Son!" But he told them to be quiet.
12. Jesus went up a mountain and chose twelve followers to be with him and to preach.
13. He gave them power to cast out demons.
14. Their names were: Simon (Peter), James, John, Andrew, Philip,

Bartholomew, Matthew, Thomas, James (son of Alphaeus), Thaddaeus, Simon the Zealot, and Judas Iscariot (who later betrayed him).

15. Jesus went home, but the crowd was too big to even eat.
16. Some said, "Jesus is out of his mind."
17. The teachers of the law said, "He gets his power from Satan!"
18. Jesus said, "How can Satan fight against himself?
19. A kingdom or house divided can't last."
20. "If I cast out demons by Satan's power, how can his kingdom stand?
21. No one can rob a strong man's house unless he ties him up first."
22. "All sins can be forgiven,
23. except saying bad things about the Holy Spirit. That sin will never be forgiven."
24. Jesus said this because people said he had an evil spirit.
25. Jesus' mother and brothers came. They waited outside.
26. People said, "Your family is looking for you."
27. Jesus said, "Who is my family?"
28. Then he said, "Anyone who does God's will is my family."

Mark 4

1. Jesus taught by the lake. A big crowd came, so he sat in a boat.
2. He taught them many things using stories.
3. He said, "A farmer went out to plant seeds.
4. Some seeds fell on the path. Birds ate them.
5. Some fell on rocky ground. They grew fast but had no roots and died in the sun.
6. Some fell in thorns. The thorns grew and choked the plants.
7. Some fell on good soil. They grew and made a big harvest."
8. Jesus said, "Whoever can understand, listen!"
9. Later, his followers asked what the story meant.
10. Jesus said, "You are allowed to understand. Others hear stories but don't understand."
11. Then he explained: "The seeds are God's message.
12. The path is people who hear the message but Satan takes it away.
13. The rocky ground is people who hear, get excited, but give up when things get hard.
14. The thorny ground is people who hear, but worries and money problems stop them.
15. The good soil is people who hear and obey. They grow and help others."
16. Jesus said, "You don't light a lamp and hide it. You put it where it shines."
17. "Everything hidden will be shown. If you listen and use what you learn, God will give you more."
18. Jesus said, "God's kingdom is like a man who plants seeds.
19. The seeds grow, but he doesn't know how. One day, it's ready to harvest."
20. "God's kingdom is like a tiny mustard seed. It grows into a big plant with branches for birds."
21. Jesus used many simple stories to teach.
22. He explained everything to his close followers.
23. That evening, Jesus said, "Let's go to the other side of the lake."
24. They left the crowd. Jesus was in the boat, sleeping.
25. A storm came. Waves crashed into the boat.

26. The followers woke him up and said, "Don't you care if we drown?"
27. Jesus got up and told the wind and waves to stop. It became calm.
28. He said, "Why are you afraid? Do you still have no faith?"
29. They were amazed. "Even the wind and sea obey him!"

Mark 5

1. Jesus and his followers reached the other side of the lake.
2. A man with an evil spirit came from the tombs.
3. He lived among the graves and couldn't be controlled.
4. People tried to tie him up, but he broke the chains.
5. Day and night, he screamed and hurt himself.
6. When he saw Jesus, he ran and bowed down.
7. He shouted, "Jesus, don't hurt me!"
8. Jesus had said, "Come out of this man!"
9. Jesus asked, "What is your name?" The spirit said, "Legion. There are many of us."
10. They begged Jesus not to send them far away.
11. A big herd of pigs was nearby.
12. The spirits begged, "Send us into the pigs." Jesus said, "Go."
13. The spirits went into the pigs. About 2,000 pigs ran off a cliff and drowned.
14. The pig herders ran into town and told everyone.
15. People came and saw the man sitting, dressed, and calm. They were afraid.
16. They asked Jesus to leave their area.
17. As Jesus got in the boat, the man asked to go with him.
18. But Jesus said, "Go home and tell your family what God did for you."
19. The man went and told people how Jesus helped him. Everyone was amazed.
20. Jesus crossed back to the other side. A crowd waited for him.
21. A man named Jairus came. He was a synagogue leader.
22. He begged Jesus, "My daughter is dying. Please come and heal her."
23. Jesus went with him. A large crowd followed.
24. A woman who had been bleeding for 12 years was there.
25. She had seen many doctors, but nothing helped.
26. She thought, "If I touch his clothes, I'll be healed."
27. She touched his coat, and the bleeding stopped.
28. Jesus felt power leave him. He asked, "Who touched me?"
29. The woman was scared but said, "It was me."
30. Jesus said, "Your faith healed you. Go in peace."
31. While he was speaking, someone came from Jairus's house. "Your daughter is dead," they said.
32. Jesus said, "Don't be afraid. Just believe."
33. He took Peter, James, and John and went to the house.
34. People were crying loudly.
35. Jesus said, "The girl is not dead. She's just asleep." They laughed at him.
36. Jesus took her hand and said, "Little girl, get up!"
37. She got up and walked. She was 12 years old.
38. Everyone was amazed.
39. Jesus said, "Don't tell anyone. Give her something to eat."

Mark 6

1. Jesus went to his hometown. His followers went with him.
2. On the Sabbath, he taught in the synagogue. People were shocked.
3. They asked, "Where did he get this power? Isn't he just a carpenter? Mary's son? Don't we know his brothers and sisters?"
4. They were offended. Jesus said, "A prophet is honored everywhere except his hometown."
5. He couldn't do many miracles there, only healed a few sick people.
6. He was amazed they had no faith.
7. Jesus went to other villages and taught.
8. He sent out the twelve disciples in pairs. He gave them power over evil spirits.
9. He told them, "Take only a walking stick. No bag, no money, no extra clothes."
10. "When someone welcomes you, stay in their home.
11. If people don't listen, leave and shake the dust off your feet."
12. The disciples went out and preached. They told people to turn back to God.
13. They cast out demons and healed many people.
14. King Herod heard about Jesus. Some thought Jesus was John the Baptist raised from the dead.
15. Others said he was Elijah or another prophet.
16. Herod said, "I killed John. This must be him come back."
17. Herod had arrested John because John told him it was wrong to marry his brother's wife.
18. Herodias, the wife, hated John and wanted him dead.
19. Herod protected John because he knew John was good and holy.
20. But at Herod's birthday party, Herodias's daughter danced. Herod was pleased.
21. He promised to give her whatever she wanted.
22. She asked her mother what to say. Her mother said, "Ask for John's head."
23. The girl said, "Give me John's head on a plate."
24. Herod was upset but kept his promise. He had John killed.
25. John's head was brought on a plate and given to the girl. She gave it to her mother.
26. John's followers took his body and buried it.
27. Jesus' disciples came back and told him what they did.
28. Many people kept coming, so they didn't even have time to eat.
29. Jesus said, "Let's go somewhere quiet and rest."
30. They got in a boat, but people saw them and ran ahead.
31. When Jesus saw the large crowd, he felt sorry for them. They were like sheep with no shepherd.
32. He taught them many things.
33. It got late. The disciples said, "Send the people away to buy food."
34. Jesus said, "You give them something to eat."
35. They said, "It would take a lot of money!"
36. Jesus asked, "How much food do you have?"
37. They said, "Five loaves of bread and two fish."
38. Jesus told the people to sit down.
39. He took the bread and fish, thanked God, and gave it to the disciples to hand out.
40. Everyone ate and was full. They picked up 12 baskets of leftovers.

41. About 5,000 men were fed.
42. Jesus told the disciples to get in the boat and go ahead while he sent the people home.
43. Then Jesus went up a mountain to pray.
44. That night, the boat was in the middle of the lake, and Jesus was alone on land.
45. He saw the disciples struggling with the wind.
46. He walked on the water toward them.
47. They thought he was a ghost and were scared.
48. Jesus said, "Don't be afraid. It's me!"
49. He got in the boat. The wind stopped. They were amazed.
50. They still didn't fully understand what Jesus had done.
51. They landed in Gennesaret. People saw Jesus and brought him the sick.
52. Wherever he went, people came and begged to touch even his clothes. All who touched him were healed.

Mark 7

1. Some Pharisees came to Jesus. They saw his followers eating without washing their hands.
2. The Pharisees always followed rules about washing.
3. They asked Jesus, "Why don't your followers follow our traditions?"
4. Jesus said, "Isaiah was right. You honor God with words, but your hearts are far away.
5. You follow human rules instead of God's commands."
6. "You cancel God's laws so you can keep your traditions.
7. For example, God said, 'Honor your father and mother.' But you say, 'I gave my money to God, so I don't have to help my parents.'
8. That's wrong. You cancel God's word with your rules."
9. Jesus called the crowd and said, "Listen. What goes into you doesn't make you wrong. What comes out of your heart does."
10. Later, the disciples asked about this.
11. Jesus said, "Food goes through your body and leaves. But evil thoughts, lies, greed, and hate come from your heart. That's what makes people wrong."
12. Jesus left and went to a non-Jewish area.
13. A woman came and begged Jesus to heal her daughter.
14. Jesus said, "I came for the children first." (He meant the Jews.)
15. She said, "Even dogs eat crumbs from the table."
16. Jesus said, "You have great faith. Your daughter is healed." And she was healed right then.
17. Jesus went to another area. People brought him a man who couldn't hear or speak well.
18. They begged Jesus to heal him.
19. Jesus took him aside, touched his ears, spit, and touched his tongue.
20. He looked up and said, "Be opened!"
21. The man could hear and speak clearly.
22. Jesus told them not to tell anyone, but they told everyone.
23. People were amazed. They said, "Jesus does everything well! He even makes the deaf hear and the mute speak!"

Mark 8

1. A big crowd followed Jesus. They had no food.
2. Jesus said, "I feel sorry for them. They've been with me for three days and have nothing to eat."
3. The disciples asked, "How can we feed them out here?"

4. Jesus asked, "How much food do you have?"
5. They said, "Seven loaves."
6. Jesus told the people to sit down. He thanked God and gave the bread to the disciples to pass out.
7. They also had a few small fish. Jesus thanked God and passed them out too.
8. Everyone ate and was full. They picked up seven baskets of leftovers.
9. About 4,000 people were fed.
10. Then Jesus got in a boat and left.
11. Some Pharisees came and asked for a sign from heaven.
12. Jesus sighed and said, "Why do you want a sign? No sign will be given."
13. He left them and got back in the boat.
14. The disciples forgot to bring enough bread. They only had one loaf.
15. Jesus said, "Watch out for the yeast of the Pharisees and of Herod."
16. The disciples said, "Is he talking about bread?"
17. Jesus said, "Why are you talking about bread? Don't you understand yet?"
18. "Remember when I fed 5,000? How many baskets were left?"
19. They said, "Twelve."
20. "And when I fed 4,000?" They said, "Seven."
21. Jesus said, "Don't you get it yet?"
22. Jesus came to Bethsaida. Some people brought a blind man and asked Jesus to touch him.
23. Jesus took the man out of the village, spit on his eyes, and asked, "Can you see anything?"
24. The man said, "I see people, but they look like trees walking."
25. Jesus touched his eyes again. The man looked carefully. Now he could see everything clearly.
26. Jesus said, "Go home, but don't go into the village."
27. Jesus asked his followers, "Who do people say I am?"
28. They said, "Some say John the Baptist, some say Elijah."
29. Jesus asked, "Who do you say I am?" Peter said, "You are the Messiah."
30. Jesus warned them not to tell anyone.
31. Then he said, "I must suffer, be rejected, be killed, and rise after three days."
32. Peter said, "No, Lord! That can't happen!"
33. Jesus said, "Get away, Satan! You are thinking like people, not God."
34. Jesus told the crowd, "If you want to follow me, give up your own way. Carry your cross and follow me."
35. "If you try to save your life, you'll lose it. But if you give up your life for me, you'll save it."
36. "What good is it to gain the world but lose your soul?"
37. "If you are ashamed of me, I'll be ashamed of you when I return."

Mark 9

1. Jesus said, "Some of you here won't die before you see God's kingdom come with power."
2. Six days later, Jesus took Peter, James, and John up a mountain.
3. Jesus' clothes became bright white.
4. Elijah and Moses appeared and talked with Jesus.
5. Peter said, "Let's build shelters for all three of you."
6. He didn't know what to say—he was scared.
7. A cloud covered them. A voice said, "This is my Son. Listen to him!"
8. When they looked again, only Jesus was there.
9. As they went down, Jesus said, "Don't tell anyone until I rise from the dead."

10. They wondered what he meant by "rise from the dead."
11. They asked, "Why do people say Elijah must come first?"
12. Jesus said, "Elijah has already come, and people hurt him just like the Scriptures said."
13. When they reached the others, a crowd was arguing with the disciples.
14. A man said, "Teacher, I brought my son to you. He has a spirit that makes him shake and fall. I asked your disciples to help, but they couldn't."
15. Jesus said, "You people have no faith! Bring the boy to me."
16. The boy was brought. The spirit made him shake and fall.
17. Jesus asked, "How long has he been like this?"
18. The father said, "Since he was little. If you can help, please do."
19. Jesus said, "Everything is possible if you believe."
20. The man said, "I believe! Help me believe more!"
21. Jesus told the spirit to leave and never come back. The spirit left, and the boy looked dead.
22. But Jesus took his hand and helped him up.
23. Later the disciples asked, "Why couldn't we help him?"
24. Jesus said, "This kind can only be cast out by prayer."
25. They left and passed through Galilee. Jesus said, "I will be handed over, killed, and rise after three days."
26. The disciples didn't understand but were afraid to ask.
27. On the road, they argued about who was the greatest.
28. Jesus asked, "What were you arguing about?"
29. They were silent.
30. Jesus said, "The greatest must be the servant of all."
31. He took a child and said, "Welcome a child, and you welcome me and God."
32. John said, "Someone is using your name to cast out demons, but he's not one of us."
33. Jesus said, "Don't stop him. If he's not against us, he's for us."
34. "If someone gives you a drink because you follow me, they will be rewarded."
35. "If you cause a child who believes in me to sin, it would be better to be thrown in the sea with a stone around your neck."
36. "If your hand, foot, or eye causes you to sin, get rid of it. It's better to lose a body part than to be thrown into fire."
37. "Be at peace with each other."

Mark 10

1. Jesus left and went to Judea. Crowds followed him, and he taught them.
2. Some Pharisees asked, "Can a man divorce his wife?"
3. Jesus asked, "What did Moses say?"
4. They said, "Moses let a man write a divorce paper and send her away."
5. Jesus said, "Moses allowed that because people were stubborn. But from the beginning, God made marriage to last."
6. "A man and woman become one. What God joins, no one should separate."
7. Later, the disciples asked more about this.
8. Jesus said, "Anyone who divorces and marries again is committing adultery."
9. People brought children to Jesus. The disciples told them to stop.
10. Jesus was upset and said, "Let the children come. God's kingdom belongs to them."
11. He hugged the children and blessed them.

12. A man ran up and asked, "Good teacher, what must I do to have eternal life?"
13. Jesus said, "Why call me good? Only God is good. You know the commandments."
14. The man said, "I've kept all of them since I was young."
15. Jesus looked at him with love and said, "You still need to do one thing. Sell your things, give to the poor, and follow me."
16. The man was sad and walked away because he was very rich.
17. Jesus said, "It's hard for rich people to enter God's kingdom."
18. The disciples were shocked.
19. Jesus said, "It's easier for a camel to go through a needle than for a rich person to enter heaven."
20. They asked, "Then who can be saved?"
21. Jesus said, "With people it's impossible, but not with God. With God, all things are possible."
22. Peter said, "We left everything to follow you."
23. Jesus said, "Anyone who gave up family or land for me will get more in this life—and in the next, eternal life.
24. But many who are first will be last. And many who are last will be first."
25. Jesus and his followers were heading to Jerusalem. He told them again,
26. "I will be arrested, hurt, and killed. After three days, I will rise again."
27. James and John said, "Let us sit next to you in heaven."
28. Jesus asked, "Can you suffer like I will?"
29. They said, "Yes."
30. Jesus said, "You will suffer like me, but I can't choose who sits beside me. God will decide."
31. The other ten were upset with James and John.
32. Jesus said, "In this world, rulers boss people around.
33. But not with you. If you want to be great, serve others.
34. I came to serve and to give my life to save many people."
35. Jesus and his followers went to Jericho. A blind man named Bartimaeus sat by the road.
36. He shouted, "Jesus! Help me!"
37. People told him to be quiet, but he shouted louder.
38. Jesus stopped and said, "Call him."
39. The man jumped up and came to Jesus.
40. Jesus asked, "What do you want?"
41. He said, "I want to see."
42. Jesus said, "Your faith has healed you." The man could see and followed Jesus.

Mark 11

1. Jesus came near Jerusalem. He told two followers,
2. "Go to the village. You'll find a young donkey. Untie it and bring it here.
3. If anyone asks why, say, 'The Lord needs it.'"
4. They found the donkey, untied it, and brought it to Jesus.
5. They put their coats on it, and Jesus sat on it.
6. People spread coats and branches on the road.
7. They shouted, "Hosanna! God bless the one who comes in His name!"
8. Jesus entered the temple and looked around. Then he left for Bethany with the twelve.
9. The next day, Jesus was hungry.
10. He saw a fig tree with leaves but no fruit. He said, "No one will eat from you again."
11. In Jerusalem, Jesus went to the temple. He saw people buying and selling.

12. He flipped tables and stopped people from using the temple like a store.
13. He said, "God's house should be for prayer, but you made it a den of thieves."
14. The leaders saw what he did and looked for a way to kill him.
15. That evening, Jesus and his followers left the city.
16. The next morning, they saw the fig tree was dead.
17. Peter said, "Look! The tree you cursed is dead!"
18. Jesus said, "Have faith in God.
19. If you believe and don't doubt, even a mountain can move.
20. When you pray, believe and you will receive.
21. Also, forgive others so God will forgive you."
22. Back in Jerusalem, the leaders asked, "Who gave you the right to do this?"
23. Jesus said, "I'll ask you a question too. Who gave John the power to baptize—God or people?"
24. They were afraid to answer. If they said "God," Jesus would ask why they didn't believe John.
25. If they said "people," the crowd might turn against them.
26. So they said, "We don't know."
27. Jesus said, "Then I won't tell you who gave me authority."

Mark 12

1. Jesus told a story: A man planted a vineyard and rented it to farmers.
2. At harvest, he sent a servant to get his share.
3. The farmers beat the servant and sent him away.
4. He sent more servants. Some were beaten. Some were killed.
5. Last, he sent his own son. He thought they would respect him.
6. But the farmers killed the son and said, "Now we get everything!"
7. Jesus asked, "What will the owner do?" He'll punish the farmers and give the vineyard to others.
8. Jesus said, "The stone the builders didn't want became the most important." (People didn't accept Jesus, but God made him the most important.)
9. The leaders knew Jesus was talking about them. They wanted to arrest him but were afraid of the crowd.
10. They sent people to trap Jesus with questions.
11. They asked, "Should we pay taxes to Caesar?"
12. Jesus said, "Show me a coin. Whose picture is on it?"
13. They said, "Caesar's."
14. Jesus said, "Give to Caesar what is his. Give to God what is God's."
15. They were amazed.
16. Some Sadducees, who didn't believe in life after death, asked a question.
17. They said, "A woman had seven husbands, one after the other. Whose wife will she be in heaven?"
18. Jesus said, "You don't understand. In heaven, people don't marry.
19. And yes, people do rise from the dead. God said, 'I am the God of Abraham, Isaac, and Jacob.' He's the God of the living, not the dead."
20. One teacher asked Jesus, "Which command is most important?"
21. Jesus said, "Love God with all your heart. That's the greatest.
22. The second is: Love others like yourself."
23. The teacher agreed. Jesus said, "You are close to God's kingdom."

24. After that, no one dared ask more questions.
25. Jesus asked, "Why do people say the Messiah is David's son?
26. David called him 'Lord.' So how can he be his son?"
27. The crowd listened gladly.
28. Jesus warned the people, "Watch out for teachers of the law. They love fancy clothes and praise.
29. But they cheat widows and pretend to be holy. They will be punished."
30. Jesus watched people put money in the temple box.
31. Rich people gave a lot.
32. A poor widow gave two small coins.
33. Jesus said, "She gave more than anyone. They gave extra. She gave everything she had."

Mark 13

1. One disciple said, "Look how big the temple buildings are!"
2. Jesus said, "One day every stone will be knocked down."
3. Later, Peter, James, John, and Andrew asked, "When will this happen?"
4. Jesus said, "Don't let anyone trick you.
5. Many will come and say they are me. Don't believe them.
6. You will hear about wars. Don't be afraid. These things must happen, but it's not the end.
7. Nations will fight. There will be earthquakes and famines. This is just the beginning."
8. "You will be arrested and taken to court. This will be your chance to tell people about me."
9. "Don't worry about what to say. God will help you speak."
10. "Families will turn against each other. People will hate you because of me. But stay strong, and you will be saved."
11. "When you see a terrible thing in the holy place, run to the mountains.
12. Don't go back for anything. Pray it's not winter or a Sabbath.
13. It will be the worst time ever."
14. "God will shorten those days to save his people.
15. If someone says, 'Look! The Messiah is here!'—don't believe it.
16. False teachers will do signs to trick people.
17. I'm warning you now—be ready."
18. "After that time, the sun and moon will go dark. Stars will fall.
19. Then everyone will see me coming with power and glory.
20. I will send angels to gather my people."
21. "Learn from the fig tree. When its leaves come out, you know summer is near.
22. When you see these things, know the end is near."
23. "This generation won't pass away before all this happens.
24. Heaven and earth will pass away, but my words won't."
25. "No one knows the day or time—only God."
26. "It's like a man who goes on a trip. He puts his servants in charge.
27. So stay alert. You don't know when the master will return."
28. "Don't fall asleep. Stay ready!"

Mark 14

1. It was almost Passover. The leaders were planning to kill Jesus.
2. They said, "Not during the holiday. The people might riot."
3. Jesus was eating at a house. A woman poured expensive perfume on his head.
4. Some said, "That's a waste! She could've sold it and helped the poor!"

5. Jesus said, "Leave her alone. She did a good thing. She prepared my body for burial."

6. "People will remember her wherever the good news is told."

7. Judas went to the priests. He promised to hand Jesus over. They paid him money.

8. On Passover, Jesus' disciples asked where to prepare the meal.

9. Jesus said, "Follow a man carrying water. Go to his house."

10. "Say, 'The teacher asks for the room to eat with his disciples.' He'll show you a room upstairs."

11. They did what Jesus said and prepared the meal.

12. That evening, Jesus sat with the twelve.

13. He said, "One of you will betray me."

14. They were sad and asked, "Is it me?"

15. Jesus said, "It's one of you eating with me now."

16. "I must suffer, but it would be better if that man were never born."

17. Jesus took bread, thanked God, broke it, and gave it to them.

18. He said, "This is my body."

19. Then he took a cup, gave thanks, and said, "This is my blood, poured out for many."

20. "I won't drink wine again until I drink it with you in God's kingdom."

21. They sang a song and went to the Mount of Olives.

22. Jesus said, "You will all leave me. But after I rise, I will meet you in Galilee."

23. Peter said, "I'll never leave you."

24. Jesus said, "Before the rooster crows twice, you'll say three times you don't know me."

25. Peter said, "Even if I die, I'll never say that." All the others said the same.

26. They went to a garden called Gethsemane. Jesus said, "Stay here while I pray."

27. He took Peter, James, and John. He said, "I feel very sad."

28. Jesus prayed, "Father, take this pain away—but I want your will, not mine."

29. He found the disciples sleeping. He said to Peter, "Couldn't you stay awake one hour?"

30. He prayed again, then found them sleeping again.

31. He prayed a third time, then said, "Get up. My betrayer is here."

32. Judas came with a crowd carrying swords.

33. Judas kissed Jesus. That was the signal.

34. The crowd arrested Jesus.

35. One follower cut off a man's ear.

36. Jesus said, "Why do you treat me like a criminal? I was with you every day."

37. The disciples ran away.

38. Jesus was taken to the high priest. Peter followed from far away.

39. People told lies about Jesus, but the stories didn't match.

40. The high priest asked, "Are you the Son of God?"

41. Jesus said, "I am."

42. The priest said, "You heard him! He spoke against God!"

43. They all said, "He must die."

44. Some spit on him and hit him.

45. Peter was outside. A girl said, "You were with Jesus!"

46. Peter said, "I don't know him."

47. Two more people said the same. Peter denied it again and again.

48. Then the rooster crowed twice.

49. Peter remembered Jesus' words and cried.

Mark 15

1. Early in the morning, the leaders took Jesus to Pilate.
2. Pilate asked, "Are you the king of the Jews?" Jesus said, "You say so."
3. The leaders made many charges, but Jesus stayed silent.
4. Pilate was surprised.
5. Every year, Pilate let the people choose one prisoner to go free.
6. A man named Barabbas was in jail for murder.
7. Pilate asked, "Do you want me to release Jesus?"
8. He knew the leaders were jealous.
9. But the leaders told the crowd to ask for Barabbas.
10. Pilate said, "What should I do with Jesus?"
11. The crowd shouted, "Crucify him!"
12. Pilate asked, "Why? What has he done?"
13. But they shouted louder. So Pilate gave them what they wanted.
14. He set Barabbas free. Jesus was beaten and taken to be killed.
15. Soldiers mocked Jesus. They dressed him in purple and put a crown of thorns on his head.
16. They hit him, spit on him, and made fun of him.
17. Then they led him away.
18. A man named Simon was forced to carry Jesus' cross.
19. They took Jesus to a place called Golgotha.
20. They offered him wine mixed with something bitter, but he didn't drink.
21. They nailed him to the cross.
22. Soldiers divided his clothes.
23. A sign above him said, "King of the Jews."
24. Two criminals were crucified with him.
25. People made fun of Jesus as they passed by.
26. At noon, the sky went dark for three hours.
27. At 3 p.m., Jesus shouted, "My God, why did you leave me?"
28. Someone gave him a drink. Then Jesus cried out and died.
29. The temple curtain tore from top to bottom.
30. A soldier said, "This man truly was God's Son."
31. Some women watched from a distance.
32. That evening, Joseph of Arimathea asked Pilate for Jesus' body.
33. Pilate let him take it.
34. Joseph wrapped Jesus in linen and laid him in a tomb.
35. He rolled a big stone in front of it.
36. Mary Magdalene and another Mary saw where Jesus was buried.

Mark 16

1. After the Sabbath, Mary Magdalene and two other women brought spices to the tomb.
2. They went early Sunday morning.
3. They asked, "Who will roll the stone away?"
4. But the stone was already rolled back.
5. They went inside and saw an angel in white.
6. He said, "Don't be afraid. Jesus is not here. He has risen!"
7. "Go tell his followers and Peter. He is going to Galilee. You will see him there alive."
8. The women were afraid and ran away. At first, they didn't say anything.
9. Later, Jesus appeared to Mary Magdalene. She told the others, but they didn't believe her.

10. Jesus appeared to two more followers. They told the others, but still no one believed.
11. Then Jesus appeared to the eleven disciples. He said, "Why don't you believe?"
12. "Go tell everyone the good news. Those who believe and are baptized will be saved."
13. "These signs will follow: they will cast out demons, speak new languages, heal the sick, and not be harmed."
14. After speaking, Jesus was taken up to heaven. He sat at God's right side.
15. The disciples went everywhere and told people the good news. God helped them.

–Luke –

Jesus brings salvation to all people, especially the poor and outcast.

Luke 1

1. Many people have written about what Jesus did.
2. They used eyewitness stories.
3. I studied everything carefully and decided to write it all down.
4. I'm writing to you, Theophilus, so you can be sure these things are true.
5. A priest named Zechariah and his wife Elizabeth lived during King Herod's time.
6. They obeyed God.
7. But they had no children, and both were old.
8. Zechariah was chosen to burn incense in the temple.
9. While he was inside, the people prayed outside.
10. An angel appeared near the altar.
11. Zechariah was scared.
12. The angel said, "Don't be afraid. God heard your prayer. Elizabeth will have a son. Name him John."
13. "He will bring you joy. Many will be happy he is born."
14. "He will be great. He must never drink wine. God's Spirit will be with him."
15. "He will turn many people back to God."
16. "He will prepare people for the Lord."
17. Zechariah said, "How can this be? We are old."
18. The angel said, "I am Gabriel. I stand with God. I came to give you good news."
19. "But since you didn't believe, you won't be able to talk until the baby is born."
20. The people outside were wondering why Zechariah was taking so long.
21. When he came out, he couldn't speak. They knew he had seen something.
22. He went home after his time at the temple.
23. Elizabeth became pregnant. She stayed quiet for five months.
24. She said, "God has blessed me. He has taken away my sadness."
25. In the sixth month, God sent Gabriel to a town called Nazareth.
26. He went to a young woman named Mary. She was engaged to Joseph.
27. Gabriel said, "Hello! God is with you!"
28. Mary was confused and wondered what the angel meant.
29. Gabriel said, "Don't be afraid. God is pleased with you."
30. "You will have a son. Name him Jesus."
31. "He will be great. He will be called the Son of God."
32. "He will be a king forever."
33. Mary said, "How can this happen? I'm not married."

34. Gabriel said, "God's Spirit will come to you. Nothing is impossible for God."
35. "Your cousin Elizabeth is pregnant, even though she is old."
36. Mary said, "I am God's servant. Let it happen as you say."
37. Then the angel left.
38. Mary hurried to visit Elizabeth.
39. When Mary greeted her, the baby jumped inside Elizabeth.
40. Elizabeth was filled with the Holy Spirit.
41. She said, "You are blessed, and your child is blessed!"
42. "You believed God's promise, and it will happen."
43. Mary said, "I praise God!"
44. "He has chosen me even though I am small."
45. "He has done great things for me."
46. "He is kind to those who respect him."
47. "He brings down the proud and lifts up the humble."
48. "He helps his people and keeps his promises."
49. Mary stayed with Elizabeth for three months, then went home.
50. Elizabeth had her baby. Everyone was happy.
51. On the eighth day, they came to name the baby Zechariah.
52. But Elizabeth said, "No. His name is John."
53. The people said, "No one in your family is named that."
54. They asked Zechariah. He wrote, "His name is John."
55. Right away, Zechariah could speak again.
56. He praised God.
57. Everyone was amazed. They wondered, "What will this child become?"
58. God's Spirit filled Zechariah. He said:
59. "Praise God! He came to save us."
60. "He kept his promise to send someone to prepare the way."
61. "You, John, will be that prophet."
62. "You will help people know they are forgiven."
63. "God will guide us and bring peace."
64. John grew up strong in spirit. He lived in the desert until his work began.

Luke 2

1. Caesar ordered everyone to be counted.
2. Each person had to go to their hometown to register.
3. Joseph went from Nazareth to Bethlehem, because it was his family's town.
4. He took Mary, who was pregnant.
5. While they were there, it was time for the baby to be born.
6. Mary had her first son. She wrapped him in cloth and laid him in a manger. There was no room in the inn.
7. Nearby, shepherds were watching their sheep at night.
8. An angel appeared. They were scared.
9. The angel said, "Don't be afraid. I bring good news for everyone.
10. Today in Bethlehem, a Savior was born. He is Christ the Lord."
11. "You'll find a baby in a manger, wrapped in cloth."
12. Suddenly, many angels appeared, praising God.
13. They said, "Glory to God! Peace to those He loves!"
14. The angels left. The shepherds said, "Let's go see this baby!"
15. They hurried to Bethlehem and found Mary, Joseph, and the baby.
16. They told everyone what the angel said.
17. People were amazed.

18. Mary remembered all these things.
19. The shepherds went back, thanking and praising God.
20. Eight days later, the baby was named Jesus, just like the angel said.
21. After 40 days, they took Jesus to the temple.
22. A man named Simeon was there. He loved God and was waiting for the Savior.
23. God told him he wouldn't die before seeing Jesus.
24. Simeon saw Jesus and praised God.
25. He said, "Now I can die in peace. I have seen your Savior."
26. "This child will bring light to the world."
27. Mary and Joseph were amazed.
28. Simeon told Mary, "He will help many, but many will fight against him. You will feel great pain."
29. A woman named Anna was also at the temple. She loved God and prayed every day.
30. She saw Jesus and thanked God.
31. Mary and Joseph returned to Nazareth.
32. Jesus grew strong and wise. God was with him.
33. When Jesus was 12, his family went to Jerusalem for Passover.
34. After the festival, they left, but Jesus stayed behind.
35. They didn't notice at first.
36. They searched for him for three days.
37. They found him in the temple, talking with teachers.
38. Everyone was amazed by what he said.
39. Mary asked, "Why did you stay behind?"
40. Jesus said, "Didn't you know I had to be in my Father's house?"
41. But they didn't understand.
42. Jesus went home and obeyed them. Mary remembered all these things.
43. Jesus grew in wisdom. He pleased God and people.

Luke 3

1. It was the time when many rulers and priests were in power.
2. God spoke to John, son of Zechariah, in the desert.
3. John preached near the Jordan River. He said, "Turn from your sins and be baptized."
4. He was the one the prophet wrote about: "A voice says, 'Get ready for the Lord.'"
5. Crowds came to hear John.
6. He said, "Change your ways! Don't think being Abraham's child is enough."
7. "God wants real change. A tree that doesn't grow good fruit will be cut down."
8. The people asked, "What should we do?"
9. John said, "Share your food and clothes."
10. Tax collectors asked, "What should we do?"
11. He said, "Don't cheat people."
12. Soldiers asked, "What about us?"
13. He said, "Be fair. Don't take money from people."
14. People wondered if John was the Messiah.
15. John said, "I baptize with water, but someone stronger is coming. I'm not even worthy to untie his sandals."
16. "He will baptize with the Holy Spirit."
17. John warned people and told them the good news.
18. He also told the ruler Herod that he was doing wrong.

19. Herod didn't like that and put John in prison.
20. Jesus was baptized too.
21. As he prayed, heaven opened.
22. The Holy Spirit came down like a dove.
23. A voice said, "You are my Son. I love you. I'm pleased with you."
24. Jesus was about 30 years old when he started his work.
25. Then the book lists Jesus' family tree—from Joseph back to Adam and to God.

Luke 4

1. Jesus was full of the Holy Spirit. He went into the desert.
2. For 40 days, the devil tested him. Jesus ate nothing and was hungry.
3. The devil said, "Turn this stone into bread."
4. Jesus said, "The Bible says people need more than bread."
5. Then the devil showed Jesus all the kingdoms and said, "I'll give you power if you worship me."
6. Jesus said, "The Bible says worship only God."
7. The devil took Jesus to the top of the temple and said, "Jump! The Bible says angels will protect you."
8. Jesus said, "Don't test God."
9. Then the devil left Jesus for a while.
10. Jesus went to Galilee. People heard about him.
11. He taught in synagogues. Everyone praised him.
12. He went to his hometown, Nazareth.
13. At the synagogue, he stood up to read.
14. He read from the prophet Isaiah: "God sent me to bring good news to the poor."
15. "To heal broken hearts. To free prisoners. To help the blind see."
16. Jesus said, "This has come true today."
17. Everyone was amazed. But then they said, "Isn't this Joseph's son?"
18. Jesus said, "Prophets are not accepted in their hometown."
19. The people got angry. They took him to a hill to throw him off.
20. But Jesus walked away safely.
21. Jesus went to Capernaum and taught on the Sabbath.
22. People were amazed by his teaching.
23. A man with an evil spirit shouted, "Jesus! Have you come to destroy us?"
24. Jesus said, "Be quiet. Come out!" The spirit left him.
25. People were amazed. They said, "Even evil spirits obey him!"
26. News about Jesus spread everywhere.
27. Jesus went to Simon's house. Simon's mother-in-law was sick.
28. Jesus healed her. She got up and served them.
29. That evening, many sick people came. Jesus healed them all.
30. He cast out demons. He told them not to speak because they knew he was the Messiah.
31. Early the next morning, Jesus went to a quiet place.
32. The people looked for him and begged him to stay.
33. But Jesus said, "I must tell others the good news too."
34. He traveled and preached in many towns.

Luke 5

1. Jesus was teaching near a lake. A big crowd came.
2. He got into Simon's boat and taught from there.
3. Afterward, Jesus said, "Let's go fish."

4. Simon said, "We tried all night and caught nothing—but we'll try again."
5. They caught so many fish the nets almost broke.
6. Simon said, "Lord, I'm a sinner. Go away from me!"
7. Jesus said, "Don't be afraid. From now on, you will bring people to God."
8. They left everything and followed him.
9. A man with a skin disease came and begged Jesus, "If you want to, you can heal me."
10. Jesus said, "I want to. Be healed!" The man was healed right away.
11. Jesus told him, "Don't tell anyone. Go show yourself to the priest."
12. More and more people came. Jesus often went away to pray.
13. Some men brought a paralyzed friend to Jesus.
14. They couldn't get through the crowd, so they made a hole in the roof and lowered him down.
15. Jesus saw their faith and said, "Your sins are forgiven."
16. The teachers were upset. "Only God can forgive sins!" they said.
17. Jesus said, "Is it easier to say, 'Your sins are forgiven' or 'Get up and walk'?"
18. Then he said to the man, "Get up, take your mat, and go home."
19. The man got up and walked. Everyone praised God.
20. Jesus saw a tax collector named Levi. He said, "Follow me."
21. Levi got up and followed Jesus.
22. Levi made a big dinner for Jesus. Many tax collectors came too.
23. Some teachers said, "Why does Jesus eat with sinners?"
24. Jesus said, "Healthy people don't need a doctor. I came to help sinners."
25. Some people asked, "Why don't your followers fast like others?"
26. Jesus said, "You don't fast at a wedding. You will fast later."
27. "No one puts new cloth on old clothes. No one puts new wine in old wine skins."

Luke 6

1. One Sabbath, Jesus' disciples picked grain to eat.
2. Some Pharisees said, "That's against the law!"
3. Jesus said, "Didn't you read what David did? He ate special bread only priests could eat."
4. "I am Lord of the Sabbath."
5. Another Sabbath, Jesus went to the synagogue. A man with a paralyzed hand was there.
6. The Pharisees watched to see if Jesus would heal him.
7. Jesus said, "Is it right to do good or bad on the Sabbath?"
8. He told the man, "Stretch out your hand." The man's hand was healed.
9. The Pharisees were very angry.
10. Jesus went to a mountain to pray all night.
11. The next day, he chose twelve disciples:
12. Simon (Peter), Andrew, James, John, Philip, Bartholomew,
13. Matthew, Thomas, James (son of Alphaeus), Simon (the Zealot),
14. Judas (son of James), and Judas Iscariot (who later betrayed him).
15. Jesus came down and stood with a big crowd.
16. People came from everywhere to hear him and be healed.
17. Jesus healed them all.
18. He looked at his disciples and said:

19. "You are blessed when you are poor. God's kingdom belongs to you."
20. "You are blessed when you are hungry. You will be full."
21. "You are blessed when you are sad. You will laugh."
22. "You are blessed when people hate you for following me."
23. "Be happy. You will be rewarded in heaven."
24. "But it will be bad for the rich. You've already had your good times."
25. "Bad for those who are full now. You will be hungry."
26. "Bad for those who laugh now. You will be sad."
27. "Love your enemies. Do good to those who hate you."
28. "Bless those who curse you. Pray for those who hurt you."
29. "If someone hits you, don't hit back. If someone takes your coat, don't stop them."
30. "Give to anyone who asks. Don't ask for things back."
31. "Treat others how you want to be treated."
32. "Even bad people love those who love them."
33. "Do good without expecting anything back."
34. "God will reward you. Be kind like God is kind."
35. "Don't judge others, and you won't be judged."
36. "Forgive, and you will be forgiven."
37. "Give, and God will give to you."
38. Jesus told a story: "Can a blind man lead another blind man? No. They will both fall."
39. "You must learn before teaching others."
40. "Don't look at a small fault in someone else when you have a big one yourself."
41. "Fix yourself first. Then help others."
42. "A good tree gives good fruit. A bad tree gives bad fruit."
43. "People are known by their actions."
44. "If you hear my words and obey, you are like a man who built his house on rock."
45. "If you hear and ignore, you are like a man who built on sand. The house will fall."

Luke 7

1. A Roman officer had a sick servant he cared about.
2. He sent Jewish leaders to ask Jesus to heal the servant.
3. They said, "This man is kind. He built our synagogue."
4. Jesus went with them.
5. Before Jesus got there, the officer sent friends to say, "I'm not worthy for you to come. Just say the word, and my servant will be healed."
6. Jesus was amazed. He said, "I haven't seen faith like this in all of Israel!"
7. When the friends got home, the servant was healed.
8. Jesus went to a town called Nain. A large crowd followed.
9. At the gate, a funeral was happening. A widow's only son had died.
10. Jesus felt sorry for her. He said, "Don't cry."
11. He touched the coffin and said, "Young man, get up!"
12. The man sat up and spoke. Jesus gave him back to his mother.
13. Everyone praised God. News spread everywhere.
14. John the Baptist's followers told him what Jesus did.
15. John sent two of them to ask Jesus, "Are you the one we've been waiting for?"

16. Jesus healed many people and said, "Tell John what you've seen. The blind see, the lame walk, and the poor hear the good news."
17. When they left, Jesus talked to the crowd.
18. He said, "John was more than a prophet."
19. "No one born is greater than John, but even the least in God's kingdom is greater."
20. Some people thanked God for John. Others rejected his message.
21. Jesus said, "You are like children who complain no matter what."
22. "John didn't eat or drink wine, and you said he had a demon."
23. "I eat and drink, and you say I'm a friend of sinners."
24. A Pharisee named Simon invited Jesus to eat.
25. A sinful woman came with perfume.
26. She cried and washed Jesus' feet with her tears, wiped them with her hair, kissed them, and poured perfume on them.
27. Simon thought, "If Jesus were a prophet, he'd know who she is."
28. Jesus told him a story: "Two men owed money. One owed a lot, the other a little. Both were forgiven. Who loved more?"
29. Simon said, "The one who was forgiven more."
30. Jesus said, "You're right."
31. Then he told the woman, "Your sins are forgiven. Your faith has saved you. Go in peace."

Luke 8

1. Jesus went from town to town, teaching the good news.
2. The twelve disciples were with him.
3. Some women followed too. They had been healed by Jesus.
4. A large crowd came. Jesus told a story:
5. "A farmer planted seeds.
6. Some fell on a path and were eaten by birds.
7. Some fell on rocks. They grew but died because they had no roots.
8. Some fell in thorns. The plants were choked.
9. Some fell on good soil and grew strong."
10. Jesus said, "Whoever can understand, listen!"
11. The disciples asked what the story meant.
12. Jesus said, "The seed is God's message.
13. The path is people who hear but forget because the devil takes it away.
14. The rocks are people who believe but give up when life gets hard.
15. The thorns are people who believe but care more about money and fun.
16. The good soil is people who hear and obey."
17. "Don't hide a light. Let it shine.
18. Listen carefully. If you use what you learn, God will give you more."
19. Jesus' mother and brothers came but couldn't get through the crowd.
20. Someone said, "Your family is outside."
21. Jesus said, "My real family is anyone who hears and obeys God."
22. One day, Jesus and his disciples were in a boat.
23. A big storm came. The boat started sinking.
24. The disciples said, "Help us!"
25. Jesus told the wind to stop, and it was calm. He asked, "Where is your faith?"
26. They reached a town called Gerasa.
27. A man with demons came to Jesus. He lived in the graveyard and had no clothes.

28. He shouted, "Jesus, don't hurt me!"
29. Jesus asked, "What is your name?" The man said, "Legion," because he had many demons.
30. The demons begged Jesus not to send them away.
31. They asked to go into a herd of pigs.
32. Jesus said yes. The demons entered the pigs, and the pigs ran off a cliff and died.
33. The people were scared. They asked Jesus to leave.
34. The man was healed and wanted to go with Jesus.
35. Jesus said, "Go home and tell what God did for you."
36. Jesus went back. A man named Jairus asked him to help his sick daughter.
37. On the way, a woman touched Jesus' coat. She had been bleeding for 12 years.
38. She was healed right away.
39. Jesus said, "Who touched me?" The woman came forward.
40. Jesus said, "Your faith healed you. Go in peace."
41. Then someone told Jairus, "Your daughter is dead."
42. Jesus said, "Don't be afraid. Just believe."
43. Jesus took the girl's hand and said, "Get up!"
44. She got up, and Jesus said, "Give her something to eat."

Luke 9

1. Jesus gave his twelve disciples power to heal and cast out demons.
2. He sent them out to preach and heal.
3. He said, "Take nothing with you. Stay in homes. If people won't listen, leave."
4. They went and told people about God's kingdom.
5. King Herod heard and was confused. He thought John the Baptist had come back to life.
6. The disciples returned and told Jesus everything.
7. A big crowd followed them. Jesus taught and healed the people.
8. The disciples said, "Send them away to get food."
9. Jesus said, "You give them something to eat."
10. They had five loaves of bread and two fish.
11. Jesus prayed, broke the bread, and gave it to the crowd.
12. Everyone ate and was full. There were 12 baskets of leftovers.
13. Jesus asked the disciples, "Who do people say I am?"
14. They said, "John, Elijah, or another prophet."
15. Jesus asked, "Who do you say I am?"
16. Peter said, "You are the Messiah."
17. Jesus warned them not to tell anyone.
18. He said, "I will suffer, die, and rise again on the third day."
19. "If you want to follow me, you must give up what you want and follow me."
20. "If you try to keep your life, you'll lose it. If you give it up for me, you'll find it."
21. "Don't be ashamed of me. I won't be ashamed of you when I return."
22. Jesus took Peter, James, and John up a mountain.
23. His face changed, and his clothes became bright.
24. Moses and Elijah appeared and talked with Jesus.
25. A cloud came. A voice said, "This is my Son. Listen to him!"
26. The disciples were afraid and didn't tell anyone what they saw.

27. The next day, a man said, "My son has a demon. Your disciples couldn't help."
28. Jesus healed the boy and gave him back to his father.
29. People were amazed.
30. Jesus said, "I will be handed over soon."
31. The disciples didn't understand and were afraid to ask.
32. They argued about who was greatest.
33. Jesus said, "The greatest must be like the least."
34. He put a child beside him and said, "Whoever welcomes a child welcomes me."
35. John said, "We stopped someone casting out demons in your name."
36. Jesus said, "Don't stop him. If he's not against us, he's for us."
37. Jesus decided to go to Jerusalem.
38. A village didn't welcome him.
39. James and John asked, "Should we call fire from heaven?"
40. Jesus said no and went to another village.
41. Someone said, "I'll follow you."
42. Jesus said, "Foxes have dens, but I have nowhere to sleep."
43. Another said, "Let me go bury my father first."
44. Jesus said, "Let the dead bury the dead. You go tell others about God."

Luke 10

1. Jesus chose 72 more followers and sent them out in pairs.
2. He said, "There are many people to reach, but few workers. Ask God to send more."
3. "Go! I'm sending you out like lambs among wolves."
4. "Don't take money or bags. Don't stop to talk on the road."
5. "When you enter a house, say, 'Peace to this house.' If they welcome you, stay and eat with them."
6. "Heal the sick and say, 'God's kingdom is near.'"
7. "If people don't welcome you, leave and say, 'We tried to help, but you wouldn't listen.'"
8. "Anyone who listens to you is listening to me. Anyone who rejects you rejects me."
9. The 72 followers came back happy. They said, "Even demons obey us!"
10. Jesus said, "I saw Satan fall like lightning. I've given you power. But be happy your names are written in heaven."
11. Then Jesus thanked God. He said, "You have shown these things to children, not just to wise people."
12. He told his disciples, "You are blessed to see and hear these things. Many wanted to, but didn't."
13. A teacher of the law asked Jesus, "What must I do to have eternal life?"
14. Jesus said, "What does the law say?"
15. The man said, "Love God and love your neighbor."
16. Jesus said, "You are right. Do this and you will live."
17. The man asked, "Who is my neighbor?"
18. Jesus told a story:
19. "A man was attacked and left hurt. A priest saw him but walked by."
20. "A helper from the temple also walked by."
21. "But a Samaritan stopped, helped him, and paid for his care."
22. Jesus asked, "Which one was a neighbor?" The man said, "The one who helped."
23. Jesus said, "Go and do the same."
24. Jesus visited Mary and Martha.

25. Martha was busy working. Mary sat and listened to Jesus.
26. Martha said, "Jesus, tell Mary to help me."
27. Jesus said, "Martha, you're worried about many things. Mary chose what's better."

Luke 11

1. Jesus was praying. When he finished, a disciple said, "Teach us to pray."
2. Jesus said, "Pray like this:
3. Father, your name is holy. Your kingdom come.
4. Give us food each day.
5. Forgive us, and help us forgive others.
6. Keep us safe from temptation."
7. Jesus said, "If a friend asks for food at midnight, even if you don't want to help, you will give it because he keeps asking."
8. "So keep asking, and you will receive. Keep knocking, and the door will open."
9. "If your child asks for a fish, would you give a snake? No!"
10. "If you give good things to your kids, God will give the Holy Spirit to those who ask."
11. Jesus cast out a demon. Some said, "He uses Satan's power."
12. Jesus said, "A kingdom divided can't stand. I use God's power, so God's kingdom has come."
13. "If a strong man guards his house, his things are safe. But if someone stronger attacks, he wins."
14. "If you're not with me, you're against me."
15. "When an evil spirit leaves a person, it looks for a place to rest. If it comes back and finds the person empty, it brings seven more evil spirits. That person ends up worse than before."
16. A woman shouted, "Your mother is blessed!"
17. Jesus said, "Better are those who hear God's word and obey."
18. People asked for a sign.
19. Jesus said, "The only sign will be the one from Jonah."
20. "Jonah was a sign to Nineveh. I am a sign to you."
21. "The queen of the south listened to Solomon. Someone greater than Solomon is here."
22. "The people of Nineveh turned to God. Someone greater than Jonah is here."
23. "Don't hide a lamp. Put it where it gives light."
24. "Your eyes are like a lamp. If they are good, your whole body is full of light. If not, your body is in darkness."
25. A Pharisee invited Jesus to eat.
26. The Pharisee was surprised that Jesus didn't wash first.
27. Jesus said, "You clean the outside, but inside you are full of greed."
28. "Give to the poor, and you will be truly clean."
29. "You Pharisees love the best seats and being praised. But inside, you are dead."
30. "You build tombs for the prophets, but your ancestors killed them."
31. "God will hold this generation responsible."
32. "You take away the key to knowledge. You don't enter, and you stop others."
33. The teachers got angry and tried to trap Jesus with questions.

Luke 12

1. A big crowd came. Jesus spoke to his disciples first.
2. He said, "Be careful of the Pharisees. They hide sin."

3. "Everything hidden will be seen. Every secret will be known."
4. "Don't fear people who can only kill your body. Fear God, who can judge forever."
5. "God sees every sparrow. You are worth much more than birds."
6. "If you speak up for me, I will speak up for you before God."
7. "If you deny me, I will deny you."
8. "You can be forgiven for speaking against me, but not for speaking against the Holy Spirit."
9. "Don't worry about what to say. The Holy Spirit will help you speak."
10. Someone in the crowd said, "Tell my brother to share the family money."
11. Jesus said, "I'm not a judge between you two."
12. Then he warned them, "Don't be greedy."
13. He told a story: "A rich man had a big harvest. He built bigger barns."
14. He said, 'Now I can relax and enjoy life.'"
15. "But God said, 'Tonight you will die. Then who gets your stuff?'"
16. "This is what happens to people who only care about money and not about God."
17. Jesus said, "Don't worry about your life, food, or clothes."
18. "Life is more than food. Your body is more than clothes."
19. "Look at birds. God feeds them. You are worth more."
20. "Worry doesn't help you. It can't add time to your life."
21. "Look at flowers. They don't work, but God dresses them beautifully."
22. "If God takes care of grass and birds, He'll take care of you too."
23. "Don't always think about food and drink. People who don't know God worry about these things."
24. "Put God first, and He will give you what you need."
25. "Give to the poor. Keep treasure in heaven."
26. "Where your treasure is, your heart will be."
27. "Be ready. Be like servants waiting for their master to come home."
28. "When he comes and finds them ready, he will be happy."
29. Peter asked, "Is this for us or for everyone?"
30. Jesus said, "A good servant takes care of others while the master is away."
31. "But if he says, 'My master won't come soon,' and acts badly, he will be punished."
32. "People who know what's right and don't do it will be punished more."
33. "I came to bring change. It may cause division, even in families."
34. "You know how to read the weather. Why not see what God is doing now?"
35. "Make peace with others before it's too late."

Luke 13

1. Some people told Jesus about others who were killed by Pilate.
2. Jesus said, "Do you think they were worse sinners? No. But if you don't turn to God, you will also be punished."
3. He told a story: "A man had a tree that gave no fruit."
4. "He said, 'Cut it down.' But the gardener said, 'Let me take care of it one more year.'"
5. "If it still gives no fruit, then cut it down."
6. On the Sabbath, Jesus saw a woman who had been bent over for 18 years.
7. He healed her. She stood up straight and praised God.

8. The synagogue leader was mad because it was the Sabbath.
9. Jesus said, "You untie your animals to drink on the Sabbath. Why not free this woman?"
10. His enemies were ashamed. The crowd was happy.
11. Jesus said, "God's kingdom is like a mustard seed. It starts small but grows big."
12. "It's also like yeast. A little bit makes a lot of dough rise."
13. Jesus went through towns, teaching as he traveled to Jerusalem.
14. Someone asked, "Will only a few be saved?"
15. Jesus said, "Try hard to enter through the narrow door. Many will try and fail."
16. "Once the door is closed, it's too late."
17. "You may say, 'We ate with you,' but I'll say, 'I don't know you.'"
18. "Some who are last now will be first later. And some who are first now will be last."
19. Some Pharisees said, "Leave here! Herod wants to kill you!"
20. Jesus said, "Tell that fox I will keep working. On the third day, I will finish."
21. "Jerusalem, you kill the prophets. I wanted to protect you, but you didn't want me."
22. "Now your house is empty. You won't see me again until you say, 'God bless the one who comes in His name!'"

Luke 14

1. One Sabbath, Jesus went to eat at a Pharisee's house. People watched him closely.
2. A man there was sick and swollen.
3. Jesus asked, "Is it right to heal on the Sabbath?"
4. No one answered. Jesus healed the man and sent him home.
5. He said, "If your animal falls in a hole on the Sabbath, you help it. Why not help a person?"
6. They had nothing to say.
7. Jesus noticed people picking the best seats.
8. He said, "Don't take the best seat at a wedding. Someone more important might come."
9. "Take the lowest seat. Then the host may invite you up front."
10. "Everyone who makes himself important will be made small. But those who stay humble will be honored."
11. Then Jesus told the host, "Don't invite only friends or rich people. They can invite you back."
12. "Invite the poor, the sick, and the blind. They can't pay you back. But God will reward you."
13. Someone at the table said, "How happy are those who eat in God's kingdom!"
14. Jesus told a story: "A man prepared a big dinner and invited many people."
15. When the food was ready, he sent a servant to tell them.
16. But they all made excuses. One said, 'I just bought land.'
17. Another said, 'I just bought oxen.'
18. Another said, 'I just got married.'
19. The servant told the master. The master was angry.
20. He said, "Go invite the poor, the blind, and the crippled."
21. After that, there was still room.
22. The master said, "Go out again and bring more people until the house is full."
23. "None of those who were invited first will get to eat."
24. Large crowds followed Jesus.

25. He said, "If you love your family more than me, you can't be my follower."
26. "You must carry your own cross and follow me."
27. "Think before you follow me. Like a man who plans before building a tower."
28. "Or a king who decides if he has enough soldiers for battle."
29. "You must give up everything to be my follower."
30. "Salt is good. But if it loses flavor, it's no good anymore."
31. "If you have ears, listen carefully."

Luke 15

1. Many tax collectors and sinners came to listen to Jesus.
2. The Pharisees said, "Why does he eat with sinners?"
3. So Jesus told them a story.
4. "If a man has 100 sheep and loses one, won't he leave the 99 to look for it?"
5. "When he finds it, he's happy and tells everyone."
6. "In the same way, heaven is happy when one sinner turns back to God."
7. Jesus told another story: "A woman has 10 coins and loses one."
8. "She lights a lamp, sweeps the house, and looks carefully until she finds it."
9. "Then she tells her friends, 'I found my lost coin!'"
10. "In the same way, angels are happy when one sinner turns back to God."
11. Jesus told a third story: "A man had two sons."
12. "The younger son said, 'Give me my share of the money.' So the father did."
13. "The son left and wasted all his money on bad living."
14. "He had nothing and got a job feeding pigs."
15. "He was so hungry, he wanted to eat the pig food."
16. "He said, 'I will go home and say I'm sorry.'"
17. He went home.
18. His father saw him and ran to him.
19. The son said, 'I'm not worthy to be your son.'
20. But the father said, 'Bring clean clothes and a ring. Kill the best animal. Let's celebrate!'"
21. "The older son was angry and didn't want to come in."
22. "The father said, 'You are always with me. But your brother was lost and now he's found.'"

Luke 16

1. Jesus told a story: A rich man had a manager who was wasting money.
2. The rich man said, "You can't be my manager anymore. Bring me the records."
3. The manager thought, "What should I do now? I'm not strong enough to work, and I don't want to beg."
4. Then he had an idea.
5. He called in people who owed the rich man money.
6. He said to one, "You owe 100 barrels of oil? Change it to 50."
7. He said to another, "You owe 100 bushels of wheat? Change it to 80."
8. The rich man praised the manager for being clever.
9. Jesus said, "Use your things wisely now so you will have reward later."
10. "If you are faithful with little, you will be faithful with much."
11. "If you can't be trusted with money, how can God trust you with true riches?"
12. "You can't serve both God and money."

13. The Pharisees loved money and made fun of Jesus.
14. Jesus said, "God knows your hearts. What people think is great is not always good to God."
15. "The law and the prophets came before John. Now the good news is preached."
16. "It's easier for the earth to disappear than for one small part of God's word to fail."
17. "If a man divorces his wife and marries another, he is committing adultery."
18. Jesus told another story: A rich man wore fine clothes and ate great food every day.
19. A poor man named Lazarus sat outside his gate. He was sick and hungry.
20. The dogs licked his sores.
21. The poor man died and went to heaven. The rich man died and went to a place of pain.
22. The rich man saw Abraham and Lazarus far away.
23. He said, "Father Abraham, send Lazarus to give me water!"
24. Abraham said, "You had good things in life. Lazarus had nothing. Now he is comforted and you are not."
25. "There's a big gap between us. No one can cross it."
26. The rich man said, "Then send Lazarus to warn my family."
27. Abraham said, "They have the Bible and the prophets."
28. The man said, "But if someone rises from the dead, they'll listen."
29. Abraham said, "If they won't listen to the Bible, they won't believe even if someone rises from the dead."

Luke 17

1. Jesus said to his disciples, "People will sin. But don't be the one who causes someone else to sin."
2. "If you hurt a child who believes in me, it would be better to be thrown in the sea."
3. "If someone sins, tell them. If they say sorry, forgive them."
4. "Even if they sin seven times in one day and say sorry, forgive them every time."
5. The disciples said, "Give us more faith!"
6. Jesus said, "If your faith is as small as a mustard seed, you can do big things."
7. "If a servant does his work, does the master say thank you? No. He expects it."
8. "You should say, 'We only did our duty.'"
9. Jesus traveled to Jerusalem. Ten men with leprosy met him.
10. They stood far away and shouted, "Jesus! Help us!"
11. Jesus said, "Go show yourselves to the priests."
12. As they went, they were healed.
13. One came back, praised God, and thanked Jesus. He was a Samaritan.
14. Jesus said, "Weren't ten healed? Where are the other nine?"
15. "This outsider came back, but the others did not."
16. Jesus told the man, "Your faith has made you well."
17. Some Pharisees asked, "When will God's kingdom come?"
18. Jesus said, "It's not something you can see with your eyes. God's kingdom is already here among you."
19. Jesus told his disciples, "Soon people will want to see me again but won't."
20. "Some will say, 'He's here!' or 'He's there!' Don't believe them."
21. "When I return, it will be like lightning flashing across the sky."
22. "But first I must suffer and be rejected."

23. "When I return, it will be like Noah's time. People were eating and drinking. Then the flood came."
24. "It will be like Lot's time. People were buying, selling, planting, building. Then fire came."
25. "Don't turn back like Lot's wife. You'll lose your life."
26. "Two people will be in one bed—one will be taken, the other left.
27. Two women will grind grain—one taken, one left."
28. The disciples asked, "Where will this happen?"
29. Jesus said, "Where there's a dead body, the vultures will gather."

Luke 18

1. Jesus told a story to show we should always pray and not give up.
2. He said, "A judge didn't care about people or God."
3. "A woman kept coming to him, saying, 'Help me!'"
4. "At first, he didn't care. But he got tired of hearing her."
5. "So he said, 'I'll help her so she'll stop bothering me.'"
6. Jesus said, "If a bad judge helps, won't God help you even more?"
7. "God hears those who cry out to Him day and night."
8. "But when the Son of Man comes, will he find people with faith?"
9. Then Jesus told a story for people who thought they were better than others.
10. "A Pharisee and a tax collector went to pray."
11. "The Pharisee said, 'Thank you, God, that I'm not a sinner like other people.'"
12. "'I fast and give money.'"
13. "But the tax collector said, 'God, forgive me. I'm a sinner.'"
14. "The tax collector was right with God. The Pharisee was not."
15. "Everyone who makes himself great will be brought low. But the humble will be lifted up."
16. People brought babies to Jesus. The disciples tried to stop them.
17. But Jesus said, "Let the children come to me. God's kingdom belongs to them."
18. A ruler asked Jesus, "What must I do to have eternal life?"
19. Jesus said, "You know the commandments."
20. He said, "I've obeyed them all."
21. Jesus said, "One thing is missing. Sell everything, give to the poor, and follow me."
22. The man was sad because he was very rich.
23. Jesus said, "It's hard for rich people to enter God's kingdom."
24. "It's easier for a camel to go through a needle than for a rich person to enter heaven."
25. The people said, "Then who can be saved?"
26. Jesus said, "With people, it's impossible. But with God, everything is possible."
27. Peter said, "We left everything to follow you."
28. Jesus said, "You will get much more in this life and eternal life in the next."
29. Jesus told the twelve, "We are going to Jerusalem. I will be handed over, hurt, and killed."
30. "But after three days, I will rise again."
31. They didn't understand what he meant.
32. Jesus came near Jericho. A blind man was sitting and begging.
33. He heard a crowd and asked what was happening.
34. They said, "Jesus is coming."

35. He shouted, "Jesus, help me!"
36. People told him to be quiet, but he shouted louder.
37. Jesus stopped and said, "Bring him to me."
38. Jesus asked, "What do you want?"
39. He said, "I want to see."
40. Jesus said, "Your faith has healed you."
41. The man could see and followed Jesus, praising God.

Luke 19

1. Jesus entered Jericho. A man named Zacchaeus lived there.
2. He was a rich tax collector.
3. He wanted to see Jesus but was too short to see over the crowd.
4. He climbed a tree to see him.
5. Jesus saw him and said, "Zacchaeus, come down! I'm staying at your house today."
6. Zacchaeus came down happy.
7. People said, "Jesus is staying with a sinner!"
8. Zacchaeus said, "I'll give half my money to the poor. If I cheated anyone, I'll pay back four times as much."
9. Jesus said, "Salvation has come to this house. I came to save the lost."
10. Jesus told a story: "A man went away to be made king. He gave ten servants money and said, 'Use this while I'm gone.'"
11. Some people hated him and didn't want him as king.
12. He returned as king and asked the servants what they did.
13. One said, "I made ten more coins." The king said, "Good job! Rule over ten cities."
14. Another said, "I made five more." The king said, "Rule over five cities."
15. Another said, "I hid your coin. I was scared."
16. The king said, "If you knew I was strict, why didn't you use the money wisely?"
17. "Take his coin and give it to the one with ten."
18. The people said, "He already has ten!"
19. The king said, "If you use what you have, you'll get more. But if you do nothing, you'll lose it."
20. Jesus went to Jerusalem. He sent two disciples ahead.
21. He said, "Go into the village. You'll find a donkey. Untie it and bring it here."
22. "If anyone asks why, say, 'The Lord needs it.'"
23. They brought the donkey. Jesus sat on it.
24. People put their coats on the road.
25. The crowd praised God and shouted, "Blessed is the King who comes in God's name!"
26. Some Pharisees said, "Tell them to stop!"
27. Jesus said, "If they are quiet, the rocks will shout."
28. Jesus saw the city and cried. He said, "You didn't see what would bring peace. Now trouble is coming."
29. "Enemies will surround you and destroy you because you didn't know God came to help you."
30. Jesus went into the temple. He saw people selling things.
31. He drove them out and said, "This is a house of prayer, but you made it a place for thieves!"
32. Every day Jesus taught in the temple. The leaders wanted to kill him.
33. But they couldn't, because all the people listened to him.

Luke 20

1. One day Jesus taught in the temple. The leaders asked, "Who gave you the right to do this?"
2. Jesus said, "I'll ask you a question. Was John's baptism from God or from people?"
3. They talked it over. "If we say 'from God,' he'll ask why we didn't believe John."
4. "If we say 'from people,' the crowd will be angry."
5. So they said, "We don't know."
6. Jesus said, "Then I won't tell you who gave me the right."
7. Jesus told a story: "A man planted a vineyard and rented it out."
8. "He sent a servant to collect his share. But the farmers beat him and sent him away."
9. "He sent another. They hurt him too."
10. "He sent a third. They also hurt him."
11. "Then he sent his own son. They killed him."
12. Jesus asked, "What will the owner do?"
13. "He will come, punish those farmers, and give the vineyard to others."
14. The people said, "No! That shouldn't happen!"
15. Jesus said, "The stone that was rejected became the most important."
16. "Anyone who falls on that stone will be broken."
17. The leaders knew Jesus was talking about them. They wanted to arrest him but were afraid of the crowd.
18. They sent spies to trick Jesus. They asked, "Should we pay taxes to Caesar?"
19. Jesus said, "Show me a coin. Whose picture is on it?"
20. They said, "Caesar's."
21. Jesus said, "Give Caesar what belongs to him, and give God what belongs to God."
22. They were amazed and couldn't trap him.
23. Some Sadducees, who didn't believe in life after death, asked about marriage in heaven.
24. They said, "A woman had seven husbands. In heaven, whose wife will she be?"
25. Jesus said, "There is no marriage in heaven."
26. "God said, 'I am the God of Abraham, Isaac, and Jacob.' He is the God of the living, not the dead."
27. Some teachers said, "Good answer, Teacher."
28. Jesus asked, "Why do people say the Messiah is David's son?"
29. "David called him 'Lord,' so how can he be his son?"
30. Jesus warned the people, "Watch out for teachers who love attention."
31. "They like the best seats and long prayers, but they hurt the poor."
32. "God will punish them more harshly."

Luke 21

1. Jesus saw rich people giving money at the temple.
2. He also saw a poor widow give two small coins.
3. Jesus said, "She gave more than anyone. Others gave from their extra. She gave all she had."
4. Some people talked about how beautiful the temple was.
5. Jesus said, "One day, every stone will be torn down."
6. They asked, "When will this happen?"
7. Jesus said, "Don't be fooled. Many will come and say, 'I'm the one!' Don't follow them."

8. "You'll hear about wars. Don't be afraid. These things must happen first."
9. "Nations will fight. There will be earthquakes and sickness."
10. "You'll be arrested and hurt. This will be your chance to tell others about me."
11. "Don't worry about what to say. I'll help you speak."
12. "Some of your family and friends will turn against you."
13. "People will hate you because of me. But not a hair on your head will be lost. Stay strong."
14. "When you see armies around Jerusalem, leave right away."
15. "Trouble will come. Many will die. The city will be taken over by other nations."
16. "You'll see signs in the sun, moon, and stars."
17. "People will be scared, not knowing what will happen next."
18. "Then you'll see the Son of Man coming in the clouds with power."
19. "When you see these things, stand tall! Your help is near."
20. He told them a story: "Look at a fig tree. When it grows leaves, you know summer is near."
21. "When you see these things, you'll know God's kingdom is near."
22. "This generation will see it happen. Heaven and earth will pass away, but my words won't."
23. "Be careful. Don't let your heart get heavy with partying or worry."
24. "Be ready. The Son of Man will come suddenly."
25. "Stay awake and pray so you can stand strong when that day comes."
26. Jesus taught every day in the temple.
27. At night, he stayed on a hill called the Mount of Olives.
28. Every morning, people came early to hear him teach.

Luke 22

1. It was almost time for Passover.
2. The leaders wanted to kill Jesus but were afraid of the people.
3. Satan entered Judas, one of the twelve disciples.
4. He went to the leaders and offered to betray Jesus.
5. They were happy and gave him money.
6. Judas looked for the right time to hand Jesus over.
7. Jesus sent Peter and John to prepare the Passover meal.
8. He said, "Follow a man carrying water. He'll show you a room."
9. "Prepare the meal there."
10. They found everything just like Jesus said.
11. When the time came, Jesus sat down with the twelve.
12. He said, "I wanted to eat this meal with you before I suffer."
13. "I won't eat again until it happens in God's kingdom."
14. He took a cup and gave thanks. He said, "Share this."
15. He took bread, gave thanks, broke it, and said, "This is my body given for you."
16. "Do this to remember me."
17. He took a cup and said, "This is my blood, poured out for you."
18. "But one of you will betray me."
19. They asked, "Who is it?"
20. They started arguing about who was the greatest.
21. Jesus said, "The greatest must be like the youngest. The leader must serve."
22. "I came to serve. I give you a place in my kingdom."

23. Jesus said, "Simon, Satan wants to test you. But I prayed for you."
24. Peter said, "I'll go to jail or die for you!"
25. Jesus said, "Before the rooster crows, you will say three times you don't know me."
26. Jesus told them to be ready for hard times.
27. Then he went to the Mount of Olives to pray.
28. He said, "Pray so you don't give in to temptation."
29. He went a little farther, knelt, and prayed, "Father, take this pain away—but your will, not mine."
30. An angel came to help him. He prayed harder. His sweat was like drops of blood.
31. He got up and found the disciples sleeping.
32. He said, "Get up and pray!"
33. A crowd came. Judas was with them.
34. Judas kissed Jesus to show them who he was.
35. The followers asked, "Should we fight?" One cut off a man's ear.
36. Jesus said, "Stop!" He healed the man.
37. They arrested Jesus and took him to the high priest's house. Peter followed.
38. A servant saw Peter and said, "You were with Jesus!"
39. Peter said, "No, I wasn't."
40. Two more times people asked, and Peter said, "I don't know him!"
41. Then the rooster crowed. Jesus looked at Peter.
42. Peter remembered what Jesus said and cried.
43. The guards beat Jesus and made fun of him.
44. In the morning, the leaders asked, "Are you the Messiah?"
45. Jesus said, "You won't believe me even if I say yes."
46. They said, "Are you God's Son?"
47. Jesus said, "Yes, I am."
48. They said, "We heard it from him ourselves!"

Luke 23

1. The leaders took Jesus to Pilate.
2. They said, "He's causing trouble and says he's a king."
3. Pilate asked, "Are you the king of the Jews?" Jesus said, "You say so."
4. Pilate said, "I find no reason to punish him."
5. They insisted, "He stirs up people all over!"
6. Pilate heard Jesus was from Galilee, so he sent him to Herod.
7. Herod was happy to see Jesus. He wanted to see a miracle.
8. He asked Jesus questions, but Jesus said nothing.
9. The leaders accused Jesus. The soldiers made fun of him.
10. Herod sent Jesus back to Pilate.
11. Pilate said, "Jesus has done nothing wrong."
12. "I will have him beaten and then let him go."
13. But the crowd shouted, "Kill him! Free Barabbas instead!"
14. Barabbas was in jail for murder.
15. Pilate wanted to release Jesus, but the crowd shouted louder.
16. So Pilate gave them what they wanted.
17. He let Barabbas go and gave Jesus to be killed.
18. They led Jesus away. Simon carried the cross.
19. Women cried for Jesus. He said, "Don't cry for me. Hard times are coming."

20. They nailed Jesus to a cross between two criminals.
21. Jesus said, "Father, forgive them. They don't know what they're doing."
22. The soldiers gambled for his clothes.
23. People made fun of Jesus. They said, "If you're the Messiah, save yourself!"
24. One criminal said, "Aren't you the Messiah? Save us!"
25. The other said, "We deserve this. But Jesus did nothing wrong."
26. He said, "Jesus, remember me."
27. Jesus said, "Today you will be with me in paradise."
28. Around noon, the sky turned dark.
29. At 3:00, Jesus said, "Father, I give you my spirit," and he died.
30. The temple curtain tore in two.
31. A Roman soldier said, "This man really was innocent."
32. People watched from a distance.
33. A man named Joseph asked Pilate for Jesus' body.
34. He wrapped it in cloth and laid it in a new tomb.
35. The women watched where he was buried.

Luke 24

1. Early Sunday morning, some women went to Jesus' tomb with spices.
2. They found the stone rolled away.
3. They went in, but Jesus' body was gone.
4. Two angels in bright clothes appeared.
5. The women were scared. The angels said, "Why are you looking for Jesus here? He has risen!"
6. "Remember? He said he would rise after three days."
7. The women remembered Jesus' words.
8. They ran to tell the disciples.
9. The women were Mary Magdalene, Joanna, Mary the mother of James, and others.
10. The men didn't believe them.
11. But Peter ran to the tomb. He saw the empty cloth and left, wondering what happened.
12. That same day, two followers were walking to a village called Emmaus.
13. Jesus came and walked with them, but they didn't recognize him.
14. He asked, "What are you talking about?"
15. They said, "Are you the only one who doesn't know what happened?"
16. "Jesus was a prophet. He was arrested and killed."
17. "We hoped he would save us."
18. "Some women said his body is gone and angels said he is alive."
19. Jesus said, "Don't you understand what the Scriptures said about the Messiah?"
20. He explained everything to them from the Bible.
21. When they got to the village, they asked Jesus to stay and eat.
22. As he broke the bread, they recognized him. Then he disappeared.
23. They said, "Our hearts felt something when he talked!"
24. They ran back to Jerusalem and told the others.
25. They said, "Jesus really is alive! He appeared to Peter!"
26. While they were talking, Jesus appeared and said, "Peace be with you."
27. They were scared, thinking he was a ghost.
28. Jesus said, "Look at my hands and feet. It's really me."
29. "Touch me. A ghost doesn't have a body like I do."
30. He showed them his hands and feet.

31. They were so happy they couldn't believe it.
32. Jesus said, "Do you have anything to eat?"
33. They gave him fish. He ate it in front of them.
34. Jesus said, "Everything written about me in the Bible had to happen."
35. He helped them understand the Scriptures.
36. He said, "It was written that the Messiah would suffer and rise again."
37. "Now tell people to turn to God and be forgiven. Start in Jerusalem."
38. "You saw all these things happen. I will send you what my Father promised."
39. He took them to Bethany, lifted his hands, and blessed them.
40. As he blessed them, he was taken up to heaven.
41. They worshiped him and went back to Jerusalem full of joy.
42. They stayed at the temple, praising God.

– John –

Jesus is the Son of God who gives eternal life to all who believe in Him.

John 1

1. In the beginning, the Word already existed.
2. The Word was with God, and the Word was God.
3. Everything was made through him.
4. He gave life to everything. His life gave people light.
5. The light shines in the darkness, and the darkness can't stop it.
6. God sent a man named John.
7. John came to tell people about the light, so they would believe.
8. John was not the light. He only told about the light.
9. The true light was coming into the world to help all people.
10. The Word was in the world. He made the world, but the world didn't know him.
11. He came to his own people, but they didn't accept him.
12. But anyone who did accept him became God's child.
13. These people were born from God, not from human parents.
14. The Word became Jesus and lived with us. We saw his glory.
15. John said, "This is the one I told you about. He came after me, but he is greater than me."
16. We have all received grace from him, more and more.
17. The law came through Moses. Grace and truth came through Jesus Christ.
18. No one has seen God, but Jesus made God known to us.
19. Jewish leaders sent priests to ask John, "Who are you?"
20. John said, "I am not the Messiah."
21. They asked, "Are you Elijah?" He said, "No."
22. "Are you the Prophet?" He said, "No."
23. They said, "Then who are you?" John said, "I am a voice calling in the desert. Get ready for the Lord."
24. They asked, "Why are you baptizing if you are not the Messiah?"
25. John said, "I baptize with water. But someone greater is here. You don't know him yet."
26. "He comes after me, but I'm not even worthy to untie his sandals."
27. This happened near the Jordan River.
28. The next day, John saw Jesus. He said, "Look! He takes away the world's sin!"
29. "This is the one I was talking about!"

30. "I didn't know who he was at first, but God showed me."
31. "I saw the Holy Spirit come down like a dove and rest on him."
32. "God told me, 'The one you see the Spirit rest on is the one who baptizes with the Holy Spirit.'"
33. "I saw it happen. He is God's Son."
34. The next day, John was with two of his followers.
35. He saw Jesus and said, "Look, the Lamb of God!"
36. The two followers followed Jesus.
37. Jesus turned and asked, "What do you want?"
38. They said, "Where are you staying?"
39. Jesus said, "Come and see." They stayed with him that day.
40. One of them was Andrew, Simon Peter's brother.
41. He told his brother, "We found the Messiah!"
42. He brought Simon to Jesus. Jesus said, "Your name is Simon. I will call you Peter."
43. The next day, Jesus found Philip and said, "Follow me."
44. Philip was from the same town as Andrew and Peter.
45. Philip found Nathanael and said, "We found the one Moses wrote about—Jesus from Nazareth."
46. Nathanael said, "Can anything good come from Nazareth?"
47. Philip said, "Come and see."
48. Jesus saw Nathanael coming and said, "Here is an honest man!"
49. Nathanael asked, "How do you know me?"
50. Jesus said, "I saw you under the fig tree before Philip called you."
51. Nathanael said, "You are the Son of God!"
52. Jesus said, "You believe because I told you that? You will see even greater things."

John 2

1. There was a wedding in Cana. Jesus' mother was there.
2. Jesus and his disciples were invited too.
3. They ran out of wine. Jesus' mother said, "They have no more wine."
4. Jesus said, "It's not time for me yet."
5. His mother told the servants, "Do whatever he says."
6. There were six large stone jars nearby.
7. Jesus said, "Fill the jars with water."
8. Then he said, "Now take some out and give it to the man in charge of the party."
9. He tasted it. It was now wine.
10. He didn't know where it came from, but the servants did.
11. The man said, "Most people serve the best wine first. But you saved the best for last."
12. This was Jesus' first miracle. His disciples believed in him.
13. After this, Jesus went to Capernaum with his family and disciples.
14. It was almost time for Passover, so Jesus went to Jerusalem.
15. In the temple, he saw people selling animals and exchanging money.
16. He made a whip and chased them out.
17. He said, "Don't turn my Father's house into a market!"
18. The leaders asked, "What sign can you show us for doing this?"
19. Jesus said, "Destroy this temple, and I'll raise it in three days."
20. They said, "It took 46 years to build it!"
21. But Jesus was talking about his body.

22. After he rose from the dead, his disciples remembered what he said.
23. Many people saw Jesus' miracles and believed in him.
24. But Jesus knew what people were really like.
25. He didn't need anyone to tell him what was in a person's heart.

John 3

1. A man named Nicodemus came to see Jesus at night.
2. He was a Pharisee and a Jewish leader.
3. He said, "We know God sent you. No one can do miracles like you without God."
4. Jesus said, "You must be born again to see God's kingdom."
5. Nicodemus asked, "How can a grown person be born again?"
6. Jesus said, "You must be born of water and the Spirit to enter Heaven."
7. Humans give birth to human life.
8. "The Spirit gives spiritual life. It's like the wind—you hear it but don't see it."
9. Nicodemus asked, "How is this possible?"
10. Jesus said, "You are Israel's teacher and don't understand?"
11. "We talk about what we know, but you don't believe."
12. "If you don't believe things on earth, how will you believe heavenly things?"
13. "No one has gone to heaven except the one who came from heaven—the Son of Man."
14. "Just like Moses lifted up a snake, the Son of Man must be lifted up."
15. "Then everyone who believes in him will have eternal life."
16. "God loved the world so much that he gave his only Son so that whoever believes in him will not die but have eternal life."
17. "God didn't send his Son to punish the world. He came to save it."
18. "People who believe are not judged. People who don't believe are already judged."
19. "Light came into the world, but people loved darkness more."
20. "People who do wrong hate the light."
21. "But those who do what's right come into the light."
22. After this, Jesus and his disciples went to the countryside.
23. He spent time with them and baptized people.
24. John was also baptizing in another place nearby.
25. His followers argued with someone about baptism.
26. They said, "Jesus is baptizing, and everyone is going to him!"
27. John said, "A person can only receive what God gives."
28. "I am not the Messiah. I was sent ahead of him."
29. "The bride belongs to the groom. I'm like the friend who is happy just to hear his voice."
30. "He must become greater. I must become less."
31. "Jesus comes from heaven and is greater than all."
32. "He tells what he has seen and heard, but many don't believe him."
33. "Whoever believes him agrees that God is true."
34. "Jesus speaks God's words. God gave him the Holy Spirit."
35. "God loves his Son and gave him everything."
36. "Whoever believes in the Son has eternal life. But those who reject him won't see life."

John 4

1. The Pharisees heard that Jesus was baptizing more people than John.
2. But it was really Jesus' disciples doing the baptizing.
3. Jesus left Judea and went back to Galilee.
4. He had to go through Samaria.
5. He came to a town called Sychar. He sat by a well. It was noon.
6. A Samaritan woman came to get water. Jesus said, "Give me a drink."
7. The woman was surprised. "You're a Jew, and I'm a Samaritan. Why ask me?"
8. Jesus said, "If you knew who I am, you'd ask me for living water."
9. She said, "You don't even have a bucket."
10. Jesus said, "If you drink this water, you'll get thirsty again."
11. "But if you drink my water, you'll never be thirsty again."
12. "It will become a spring inside you, giving eternal life."
13. The woman said, "Give me this water so I don't have to come here anymore."
14. Jesus said, "Go get your husband."
15. She said, "I don't have one."
16. Jesus said, "You're right. You've had five, and the man you're with now is not your husband."
17. The woman said, "You must be a prophet."
18. "Our people worship on this mountain, but Jews say we must worship in Jerusalem."
19. Jesus said, "A time is coming when true worshipers will worship the Father in spirit and truth."
20. The woman said, "I know the Messiah is coming."
21. Jesus said, "I am he."
22. The disciples came back. They were surprised Jesus was talking to a woman.
23. She left her jar and ran to town. She said, "Come see a man who told me everything I've done. Could he be the Messiah?"
24. The people came to see Jesus.
25. Meanwhile, the disciples said, "Eat something."
26. Jesus said, "My food is doing what God wants."
27. "Look, the fields are ready to harvest."
28. "Others planted, and now you can gather the crop."
29. Many Samaritans believed in Jesus because of the woman's words.
30. They asked him to stay. He stayed two days.
31. More people believed after hearing him themselves.
32. They told the woman, "Now we believe not just because of you, but because we heard him."
33. Jesus left for Galilee.
34. A prophet is not honored in his hometown.
35. But in Galilee, people welcomed him.
36. A government official came to Jesus. His son was sick in Capernaum.
37. He begged Jesus, "Please come and heal my son. He's about to die!"
38. Jesus said, "Go home. Your son will live."
39. The man believed and left.
40. His servants met him on the way and said, "Your son is better!"
41. He asked when it happened. They said, "Yesterday at 1:00."
42. That was the time Jesus had spoken.
43. He and his whole family believed.

John 5

1. Later, Jesus went to a festival in Jerusalem.
2. At a pool called Bethesda, many sick people lay there.
3. One man had been sick for 38 years.
4. Jesus asked, "Do you want to be healed?"
5. The man said, "No one helps me get in the pool. Others go in first."
6. Jesus said, "Get up! Pick up your mat and walk."
7. The man was healed right away. He picked up his mat and walked.
8. It was the Sabbath.
9. Some Jews said, "You can't carry your mat today!"
10. He said, "The man who healed me told me to."
11. They asked, "Who told you that?" But the man didn't know Jesus' name.
12. Later, Jesus found him and said, "Stop sinning or something worse may happen."
13. The man told the leaders it was Jesus.
14. The leaders were angry Jesus healed on the Sabbath.
15. Jesus said, "My Father is always working, and so am I."
16. They were even more angry. He was calling God his Father.
17. Jesus said, "The Son does what the Father shows him."
18. "The Father loves the Son and shows him everything."
19. "The Father raises the dead, and so does the Son."
20. "Whoever honors the Son honors the Father."
21. "If you believe in me, you have eternal life."
22. "The dead will hear my voice and rise."
23. "The Father has given me the power to judge."
24. "One day, all in the grave will hear my voice and come out—some to life, some to judgment."
25. Jesus said, "If I talk about myself, it means nothing. But John talked about me."
26. "You liked his light for a little while."
27. "But I have even better proof—my miracles."
28. "They show the Father sent me."
29. "The Scriptures talk about me, but you won't come to me."
30. "I don't need human praise."
31. "I know you don't really love God."
32. "Moses wrote about me. If you believed him, you'd believe me."
33. "But if you don't believe Moses' writings, you won't believe me either."

John 6

1. Jesus crossed over the lake.
2. A big crowd followed him because they saw his miracles.
3. Jesus went up a hill and sat down with his disciples.
4. It was almost time for Passover.
5. Jesus saw the crowd and asked Philip, "Where can we buy food?"
6. He was testing Philip. Jesus already knew what he would do.
7. Philip said, "Even a lot of money wouldn't buy enough bread for everyone."
8. Andrew said, "There's a boy with five loaves and two fish."
9. Jesus said, "Have the people sit down."
10. There were about 5,000 men.
11. Jesus took the bread and fish, gave thanks, and gave it to everyone.
12. They ate until they were full.

13. The disciples picked up twelve baskets of leftovers.
14. The people said, "This must be the Prophet God promised!"
15. Jesus knew they wanted to make him king, so he left.
16. That evening, the disciples got into a boat.
17. A storm came, and the water was rough.
18. They saw Jesus walking on the water.
19. He said, "Don't be afraid. It's me."
20. They let him in the boat, and they reached land right away.
21. The next day, people looked for Jesus.
22. They found him and said, "When did you get here?"
23. Jesus said, "You are looking for me because I gave you food, not because you understand."
24. "Don't work just for food that spoils. Work for food that gives eternal life."
25. They asked, "What must we do?"
26. Jesus said, "Believe in the one God sent."
27. They asked, "What sign will you show us?"
28. "Moses gave our ancestors bread from heaven."
29. Jesus said, "Moses didn't give the real bread. God gives the true bread."
30. "The bread from God gives life to the world."
31. They said, "Give us this bread always."
32. Jesus said, "I am the bread of life."
33. "Whoever comes to me will never be hungry or thirsty."
34. "But you still don't believe."
35. "Everyone the Father gives me will come to me, and I won't turn them away."
36. "I came down from heaven to do what God wants."
37. "God wants everyone who believes in me to have eternal life."
38. The Jews complained because Jesus said, "I came from heaven."
39. They said, "We know his father and mother."
40. Jesus said, "Stop complaining."
41. "Only people God draws can come to me."
42. "I will raise them to life on the last day."
43. "Everyone who listens and learns from God comes to me."
44. "I tell you the truth: whoever believes has eternal life."
45. "I am the bread of life."
46. "Your ancestors ate manna and died. But this bread gives life forever."
47. "This bread is my body, which I will give for the world."
48. The people argued, "How can he give us his body to eat?"
49. Jesus said, "If you don't eat my body and drink my blood, you won't have life."
50. "But whoever eats and drinks will have eternal life. I will raise them up."
51. "My body is real food. My blood is real drink."
52. Many followers said, "This is too hard to believe!"
53. Jesus knew they were complaining.
54. He said, "Does this upset you?"
55. "What if you saw me go back to heaven?"
56. "The Spirit gives life. The body is worth nothing."
57. "Some of you don't believe."
58. Many followers turned away and stopped following Jesus.
59. Jesus asked the twelve, "Do you want to leave too?"

60. Peter said, "Where would we go? You have the words of life."
61. "We believe you are the Holy One of God."
62. Jesus said, "I chose you, but one of you is a devil." He meant Judas.

John 7

1. Jesus stayed in Galilee because the leaders in Judea wanted to kill him.
2. His brothers said, "Go to the festival and show your miracles."
3. They didn't believe in him yet.
4. Jesus said, "It's not my time yet."
5. He stayed, but later went in secret.
6. At the festival, people looked for Jesus.
7. Some said, "He's a good man." Others said, "He fools people."
8. No one spoke openly because they were afraid.
9. Halfway through the festival, Jesus began teaching at the temple.
10. People were surprised. "How did he learn so much without going to school?"
11. Jesus said, "My teaching comes from God."
12. "If you want to do God's will, you'll know my teaching is true."
13. "Those who speak for themselves want praise. But I want to honor God."
14. "Moses gave you the law, but you don't keep it. Why do you want to kill me?"
15. The crowd said, "You're crazy! Who wants to kill you?"
16. Jesus said, "You're upset because I healed on the Sabbath."
17. "You circumcise on the Sabbath, but I made a man whole and you're angry."
18. "Stop judging by looks. Judge fairly."
19. Some said, "Isn't this the man they want to kill?"
20. "He's speaking openly, and no one stops him."
21. "When the Messiah comes, no one will know where he's from."
22. Jesus said, "You know me, and you know where I'm from. But I came from God."
23. "You don't know him, but I do."
24. They tried to arrest Jesus, but it wasn't time yet.
25. Many believed in him and said, "When the Messiah comes, will he do more miracles than this man?"
26. The Pharisees heard the crowd talking and sent guards to arrest him.
27. Jesus said, "I'll be with you a little longer. Then I'll go back to the One who sent me."
28. "You'll look for me but not find me. You can't go where I'm going."
29. The Jews asked, "What does he mean?"
30. On the last day of the festival, Jesus stood up and said, "If you're thirsty, come to me."
31. "Whoever believes in me will have rivers of living water inside."
32. He was talking about the Holy Spirit.
33. Some people said, "He must be the Prophet!"
34. Others said, "He's the Messiah."
35. Some asked, "Can the Messiah come from Galilee?"
36. "The Bible says he comes from David's family, from Bethlehem."
37. So the people were divided.
38. Some wanted to arrest him, but no one did.
39. The guards went back. The leaders asked, "Why didn't you bring him?"
40. They said, "No one ever spoke like him!"
41. The leaders said, "Have any of us believed in him?"

42. "Only the ignorant crowd believes him."
43. Nicodemus said, "Shouldn't we hear from him before judging?"
44. They said, "Are you from Galilee too? No prophet comes from Galilee!"

John 8

1. Early in the morning, Jesus went to the temple.
2. People came, and he sat down to teach them.
3. The teachers brought a woman who had sinned.
4. They said, "She was caught doing something wrong. The law says to stone her. What do you say?"
5. They were trying to trap Jesus.
6. Jesus bent down and wrote in the dirt.
7. They kept asking. He said, "If any of you has never sinned, throw the first stone."
8. Then he bent down again.
9. One by one, the people left.
10. Jesus said to the woman, "Where are they? Did no one condemn you?"
11. She said, "No one." Jesus said, "Then I don't condemn you either. Go and don't sin again."
12. Jesus said, "I am the light of the world. If you follow me, you won't walk in darkness."
13. The Pharisees said, "You can't talk about yourself. That means nothing."
14. Jesus said, "What I say is true because I know where I came from and where I'm going."
15. "You judge by human ways. I judge by God's truth."
16. "Even if I talk about myself, it's true—because the Father is with me."
17. They asked, "Where is your Father?"
18. Jesus said, "If you knew me, you would know my Father."
19. He said this while teaching at the temple.
20. No one arrested him because it was not yet time.
21. Jesus said, "I am going away. You will look for me but die in your sin."
22. "Where I go, you can't follow."
23. They asked, "Will he kill himself?"
24. Jesus said, "You are from this world. I am not."
25. "If you don't believe I am the one God sent, you will die in your sins."
26. They asked, "Who are you?"
27. Jesus said, "I have much to say, but I speak only what the Father tells me."
28. "When you lift up the Son of Man, then you will know who I am."
29. "I always do what pleases the Father."
30. Many believed in him.
31. Jesus said to those who believed, "If you obey my teaching, you are truly my followers."
32. "You will know the truth, and the truth will set you free."
33. They said, "We've never been slaves."
34. Jesus said, "Everyone who sins is a slave to sin."
35. "But if the Son sets you free, you are truly free."
36. "I know you are Abraham's children, but you are trying to kill me."
37. "You do what your father wants."
38. They said, "Abraham is our father!"
39. Jesus said, "If he were your father, you would do what he did. But you want to kill me."
40. "You are doing what your real father does."
41. They said, "We are not born from sin. God is our only Father!"
42. Jesus said, "If God were your Father, you would love me."

43. "But you don't understand because you don't want to hear me."
44. "Your father is the devil. He lies and causes sin."
45. "I speak the truth, and you don't believe me."
46. "Can any of you prove I've sinned? If not, why don't you believe me?"
47. The people said, "You're a Samaritan! You have a demon!"
48. Jesus said, "I don't have a demon. I honor my Father, and you dishonor me."
49. "If you obey my teaching, you will never die."
50. They said, "Now we know you have a demon! Even Abraham died!"
51. "Who do you think you are?"
52. Jesus said, "Abraham was happy to see my day coming."
53. They said, "You're not even 50! How can you have seen Abraham?"
54. Jesus said, "Before Abraham was born, I AM."
55. They picked up stones to throw at him, but Jesus hid and left the temple.

John 9

1. Jesus saw a man who was blind from birth.
2. His disciples asked, "Did this man or his parents sin?"
3. Jesus said, "Neither. This happened to show God's power."
4. "We must do God's work while it is day."
5. "I am the light of the world."
6. Jesus spit on the ground, made mud, and put it on the man's eyes.
7. He said, "Go wash in the pool of Siloam."
8. The man went, washed, and came back able to see.
9. His neighbors said, "Is this the same man?"
10. Some said, "Yes." Others said, "He just looks like him."
11. He said, "I'm the same man."
12. They asked, "How were your eyes opened?"
13. He said, "Jesus put mud on my eyes, I washed, and now I see."
14. They brought the man to the Pharisees.
15. It was the Sabbath when Jesus healed him.
16. The Pharisees asked, "How did he heal you?"
17. The man said, "He put mud on my eyes, I washed, and now I see."
18. Some Pharisees said, "This man is not from God. He worked on the Sabbath."
19. Others said, "How can a sinner do miracles?"
20. They were divided.
21. They asked the blind man again, "What do you say?"
22. He said, "Jesus is a prophet."
23. The Jews didn't believe he was blind before.
24. They called his parents and asked, "Is this your son?"
25. "Was he really born blind?"
26. His parents said, "Yes, but we don't know how he sees now. Ask him."
27. They were afraid of being kicked out of the synagogue.
28. So they asked the man again. He said, "I already told you. Why do you want to hear it again?"
29. "Do you want to follow him too?"
30. They got angry and said, "We follow Moses!"
31. The man said, "No one ever opened the eyes of a man born blind."

32. "If this man were not from God, he couldn't do it."
33. They said, "You were born in sin! Don't teach us!" And they threw him out.
34. Jesus found him and said, "Do you believe in the Son of Man?"
35. The man said, "Who is he?"
36. Jesus said, "You've seen him. It's me."
37. The man said, "I believe," and worshiped Jesus.
38. Jesus said, "I came to help the blind see and to show who is truly blind."
39. Some Pharisees said, "Are we blind too?"
40. Jesus said, "If you were blind, you wouldn't be guilty. But you claim to see—so your guilt remains."

John 10

1. Jesus said, "Anyone who doesn't enter the sheep pen through the gate is a thief."
2. "The one who enters through the gate is the real shepherd."
3. "The gatekeeper opens the gate for him. The sheep hear his voice."
4. "He calls each sheep by name and leads them out."
5. "The sheep follow him because they know his voice."
6. "They won't follow a stranger. They'll run away."
7. The people didn't understand, so Jesus said again:
8. "I am the gate for the sheep."
9. "All who came before were thieves. But the sheep didn't listen to them."
10. "I am the gate. If you enter through me, you'll be saved."
11. "You'll come in, go out, and find everything you need."
12. "A thief comes to steal and destroy. I came to give full life."
13. "I am the good shepherd. I give my life for the sheep."
14. "A hired man runs away when he sees danger. He doesn't care about the sheep."
15. "I know my sheep, and they know me."
16. "I also have other sheep not in this group. I must bring them too."
17. "They will listen, and there will be one group with one shepherd."
18. "The Father loves me because I give my life—and I will take it back."
19. "No one takes my life from me. I give it willingly."
20. The people were divided again.
21. Some said, "He has a demon! Don't listen to him!"
22. Others said, "Can a demon open blind eyes?"
23. Later, at a festival in Jerusalem, Jesus walked in the temple.
24. People asked, "How long will you keep us guessing? Are you the Messiah?"
25. Jesus said, "I told you, but you didn't believe."
26. "My miracles show who I am."
27. "But you don't believe because you're not my sheep."
28. "My sheep listen to me. I know them, and they follow me."
29. "I give them eternal life. They will never be lost."
30. "No one can take them from me."
31. "The Father and I are one."
32. The people picked up stones to throw at Jesus.
33. He said, "I've done many good things. Why are you trying to kill me?"
34. They said, "Not for your works, but because you claim to be God."
35. Jesus said, "The Scriptures call people gods whom God gave his message to."

36. "So why be angry at me for saying I'm God's Son?"
37. "If I don't do God's work, don't believe me."
38. "But if I do, believe the works, even if you don't believe me."
39. "Then you'll know the Father is in me, and I am in him."
40. They tried to arrest him, but he escaped.
41. He went across the Jordan River. Many followed him.
42. They said, "John the Baptist didn't do miracles, but everything he said about Jesus is true."
43. Many people there believed in Jesus.

John 11

1. A man named Lazarus was sick. He lived in Bethany with his sisters, Mary and Martha.
2. Mary was the one who poured perfume on Jesus' feet.
3. The sisters sent Jesus a message: "Lord, your friend is sick."
4. Jesus said, "This sickness won't end in death. It will show God's power."
5. Jesus loved Martha, Mary, and Lazarus.
6. But he stayed where he was for two more days.
7. Then he said, "Let's go to Judea."
8. The disciples said, "The people there want to kill you!"
9. Jesus said, "Our friend Lazarus is asleep, and I'm going to wake him up."
10. They said, "If he's sleeping, he'll get better."
11. Jesus said plainly, "Lazarus is dead."
12. "I'm glad I wasn't there, so you can believe."
13. Thomas said, "Let's go too, even if we die with him."
14. When Jesus arrived, Lazarus had been dead four days.
15. Many people were there to comfort Mary and Martha.
16. Martha went to meet Jesus. Mary stayed home.
17. Martha said, "Lord, if you had been here, he wouldn't have died."
18. "But I know God will give you whatever you ask."
19. Jesus said, "Your brother will rise again."
20. Martha said, "I know he will rise on the last day."
21. Jesus said, "I am the resurrection and the life."
22. "Anyone who believes in me will live, even after dying."
23. "Do you believe this?"
24. Martha said, "Yes, Lord. I believe you are the Son of God."
25. She went to get Mary. Mary ran to Jesus and fell at his feet.
26. She said, "Lord, if you had been here, he wouldn't have died."
27. Jesus saw her crying and was very sad.
28. He asked, "Where is he?"
29. They said, "Come and see."
30. Jesus cried.
31. The people said, "See how much he loved him."
32. Some said, "Couldn't he have saved him?"
33. Jesus went to the tomb. It was a cave with a stone in front.
34. He said, "Roll the stone away."
35. Martha said, "He's been dead four days. It will smell."
36. Jesus said, "Didn't I tell you? If you believe, you will see God's power."
37. They rolled the stone away.
38. Jesus prayed, "Father, thank you for hearing me."

39. "I know you always hear me, but I said this so others may believe."
40. Jesus shouted, "Lazarus, come out!"
41. Lazarus came out, still wrapped in cloth.
42. Jesus said, "Unwrap him and let him go."
43. Many people who saw this believed in Jesus.
44. Some told the Pharisees what happened.
45. The leaders met and said, "If we let him keep doing miracles, everyone will follow him."
46. "Then the Romans will come and take away our temple and our nation."
47. Caiaphas, the high priest, said, "It's better for one man to die than for the whole nation to be destroyed."
48. He didn't know he was speaking God's truth—Jesus would die for the people.
49. From that day, they planned to kill Jesus.
50. Jesus no longer walked openly among the people.
51. He left for a quiet town called Ephraim.
52. It was almost time for Passover.
53. People asked, "Will Jesus come to the festival?"
54. The leaders gave orders: "If anyone sees him, tell us so we can arrest him."

John 12

1. Six days before Passover, Jesus went to Bethany. Lazarus lived there.
2. They gave a dinner for Jesus. Martha served, and Lazarus was at the table.
3. Mary poured expensive perfume on Jesus' feet and wiped them with her hair.
4. Judas Iscariot said, "Why wasn't this sold and given to the poor?"
5. He didn't care about the poor. He was a thief.
6. Jesus said, "Leave her alone. She is getting me ready for my burial."
7. "You will always have the poor. You won't always have me."
8. A big crowd heard Jesus was there. They came to see him and Lazarus.
9. The leaders planned to kill Lazarus too.
10. Many Jews believed in Jesus because of him.
11. The next day, a large crowd took palm branches and went out to meet Jesus.
12. They shouted, "Blessed is the one who comes in God's name! He is the King of Israel!"
13. Jesus rode a young donkey, just as the Scriptures said.
14. At first, the disciples didn't understand. Later, they realized it was about Jesus.
15. People who saw Jesus raise Lazarus told others.
16. More people came because they heard about the miracle.
17. The Pharisees said, "The whole world is following him!"
18. Some Greeks came to see Jesus. They told Philip.
19. Philip told Andrew, and they told Jesus.
20. Jesus said, "The time has come for the Son of Man to be honored."
21. "A seed must die in the ground before it grows."
22. "Anyone who loves their life will lose it. But if you give your life to serve God, you will have eternal life."
23. "If you serve me, follow me. My Father will honor you."
24. Jesus said, "I am troubled, but I won't ask God to save me from this."
25. "This is why I came."
26. "Father, show your glory!"

27. A voice from heaven said, "I have shown it and will show it again."
28. The crowd heard it and was amazed.
29. Jesus said, "That voice was for you, not me."
30. "Now is the time for judgment."
31. "When I am lifted up, I will bring everyone to me."
32. He meant how he would die.
33. The crowd said, "We thought the Messiah would live forever."
34. "Who is the Son of Man?"
35. Jesus said, "Walk in the light while you have it. Then darkness won't take over you."
36. "Believe in the light."
37. After this, Jesus left and hid.
38. Even after so many miracles, many people still didn't believe.
39. This fulfilled Isaiah's prophecy.
40. Some leaders believed in him but didn't say it, because they were afraid of the Pharisees.
41. They wanted praise from people more than praise from God.
42. Jesus said, "If you believe in me, you believe in the one who sent me."
43. "I came as a light to the world."
44. "If you hear my words but don't obey, I won't judge you now. I came to save the world."
45. "But there is a judge—God's word will judge on the last day."
46. "I speak only what the Father told me to say."

John 13

1. Before Passover, Jesus knew his time had come.
2. He loved his followers and was ready to show them his love completely.
3. During dinner, the devil had already told Judas to betray Jesus.
4. Jesus got up, took off his outer clothes, and tied a towel around his waist.
5. He poured water into a bowl and began washing the disciples' feet.
6. Peter said, "Lord, are you washing my feet?"
7. Jesus said, "You don't understand now, but you will later."
8. Peter said, "You will never wash my feet!"
9. Jesus said, "If I don't, you have no part with me."
10. Peter said, "Then wash my hands and head too!"
11. Jesus said, "If you've had a bath, you only need to wash your feet."
12. "You are clean—but not all of you." He meant Judas.
13. After washing their feet, Jesus said, "Do you understand what I did?"
14. "I am your Lord and Teacher. If I wash your feet, you should wash each other's."
15. "I gave you an example. Do as I did."
16. "A servant is not greater than the master."
17. "Now that you know this, do it—and you'll be blessed."
18. Jesus said, "One of you will betray me."
19. He was troubled and said again, "One of you will turn against me."
20. The disciples were confused.
21. Peter signaled to John to ask who it was.
22. Jesus said, "It's the one I give bread to."
23. He dipped the bread and gave it to Judas.
24. After Judas took it, Satan entered him.
25. Jesus said, "Go do what you are going to do."
26. No one else knew what Jesus meant.

27. Judas left right away. It was night.
28. Jesus said, "Now the Son of Man is honored, and God is honored through him."
29. "Children, I'll be with you only a little longer."
30. "You will look for me, but you can't come where I'm going."
31. "I give you a new command: Love each other."
32. "As I have loved you, you must love one another."
33. "Everyone will know you follow me if you love each other."
34. Peter asked, "Where are you going?"
35. Jesus said, "You can't follow now, but you will later."
36. Peter said, "I'll give my life for you!"
37. Jesus said, "Will you? Before the rooster crows, you will say three times that you don't know me."

John 14

1. Jesus said, "Don't be worried. Trust in God and trust in me."
2. "There are many rooms in my Father's house. I'm going there to make a place for you."
3. "Then I'll come back and take you with me."
4. "You know the way to where I'm going."
5. Thomas said, "Lord, we don't know where you're going. How can we know the way?"
6. Jesus said, "I am the way, the truth, and the life. No one comes to the Father except through me."
7. "If you know me, you know my Father."
8. Philip said, "Show us the Father."
9. Jesus said, "If you've seen me, you've seen the Father."
10. "I speak God's words. God lives in me and does His work."
11. "Believe me, or believe because of the miracles you've seen."
12. "Anyone who believes in me will do what I've done—even greater things."
13. "If you ask anything in my name, I will do it."
14. "If you love me, you will obey my commands."
15. "I will ask the Father to send you a Helper—the Holy Spirit."
16. "He will stay with you forever."
17. "The world doesn't know Him, but you do. He lives with you and will be in you."
18. "I will not leave you alone. I will come back to you."
19. "Soon the world won't see me, but you will. You will live because I live."
20. "If you love me and obey me, my Father will love you."
21. Judas (not the betrayer) asked, "Why show yourself to us and not the world?"
22. Jesus said, "Anyone who loves me will obey me. We will live with them."
23. "But those who don't love me won't listen."
24. "These words come from the Father, not just from me."
25. "The Holy Spirit will teach you and remind you of everything I said."
26. "I give you peace. Don't be afraid."
27. "I'm going away now, but I will come back."
28. "If you really loved me, you'd be happy I'm going to the Father."
29. "I've told you all this before it happens, so you'll believe."
30. "The ruler of this world is coming, but he has no power over me."
31. "I do what the Father says so the world knows I love Him. Now, let's go."

John 15

1. Jesus said, "I am the true vine, and my Father takes care of it."
2. "He cuts off every branch that doesn't grow fruit."
3. "He trims every good branch so it grows more."
4. "You are already clean because of what I've told you."
5. "Stay close to me, and I'll stay close to you."
6. "A branch can't grow fruit by itself. You can't either without me."
7. "I am the vine, and you are the branches. Stay with me and you will grow fruit."
8. "If you don't stay with me, you are like a dead branch that's thrown away and burned."
9. "If you stay with me and obey me, ask for anything—it will be done."
10. "This brings glory to God—you will show you are my followers by growing fruit."
11. "I've loved you like the Father loves me. Stay in my love."
12. "You stay in my love when you obey me."
13. "I've told you this so your joy will be full."
14. "Here is my command: Love each other like I've loved you."
15. "The greatest love is to give your life for your friends."
16. "You are my friends if you obey me."
17. "I don't call you servants anymore. Servants don't know what their master is doing."
18. "You are my friends, because I've told you everything from the Father."
19. "You didn't choose me. I chose you to go and grow fruit that lasts."
20. "The Father will give you what you ask in my name."
21. "Love each other."
22. "If the world hates you, remember—it hated me first."
23. "If you were like the world, it would love you."
24. "But you are not like it. That's why the world hates you."
25. "Remember what I said: A servant is not greater than his master."
26. "If they hurt me, they will hurt you too."
27. "They don't know God who sent me."
28. "I showed them miracles. Now they have no excuse."
29. "They hate me and my Father too."
30. "This happened just like Scripture said: 'They hated me without reason.'"
31. "I will send the Helper from the Father. He will tell the truth about me."
32. "You must also tell others, because you've been with me from the start."

John 16

1. Jesus said, "I've told you all this so you won't give up."
2. "People will make you leave the synagogues. Some will even try to kill you, thinking they're serving God."
3. "They will do this because they don't know me or the Father."
4. "I didn't tell you earlier because I was with you. But now I'm going to the Father."
5. "None of you asked where I'm going. Your hearts are full of sadness."
6. "But it's good that I go. If I don't, the Helper won't come."
7. "When He comes, He will show the world what is wrong about sin, being right, and judgment."
8. "Sin is not believing in me."
9. "Being right is me going to the Father."

10. “Judgment is that the devil has already been judged.”
11. “There’s much more to say, but you can’t handle it now.”
12. “The Holy Spirit will come and lead you into all truth.”
13. “He won’t speak for himself—He will speak what He hears and tell you what’s coming.”
14. “He will bring me glory by telling you what I said.”
15. “Everything the Father has is mine. That’s why I said the Spirit will tell you what’s mine.”
16. “Soon, you won’t see me. But soon after, you will see me again.”
17. The disciples asked, “What does he mean, ‘a little while’?”
18. Jesus knew they were confused.
19. He said, “You will be sad, but your sadness will turn into joy.”
20. “When a woman gives birth, she has pain. But then she forgets the pain because she is happy.”
21. “You are sad now, but I will see you again. You will be full of joy, and no one can take it away.”
22. “Then you won’t need to ask me anything.”
23. “Ask the Father in my name, and He will give it to you.”
24. “Ask, and you will receive. Then your joy will be full.”
25. “I’ve used simple words, but soon I’ll speak plainly.”
26. “The Father Himself loves you because you love me.”
27. “I came from the Father and will return to Him.”
28. The disciples said, “Now we understand. You know everything!”
29. Jesus said, “Do you believe now?”
30. “The time is coming when you will all leave me alone.”
31. “But I’m not really alone—my Father is with me.”
32. “I’ve told you this so you’ll have peace.”
33. “In this world, you’ll have trouble. But be brave—I have won the victory!”

John 17

1. Jesus looked up to heaven and said, “Father, the time has come. Show your glory through me.”
2. “You gave me power over all people. I give eternal life to those you gave me.”
3. “Eternal life means knowing you, the only true God, and knowing me, the one you sent.”
4. “I brought you glory on earth by finishing what you gave me to do.”
5. “Now, Father, give me the glory I had with you before the world began.”
6. “I showed you to the people you gave me. They obeyed your word.”
7. “They know everything I have comes from you.”
8. “I gave them your words. They accepted them and believe you sent me.”
9. “I pray for them—not for the world—but for the ones you gave me.”
10. “They belong to you, just like I do.”
11. “I’m coming to you now. Keep them safe so they stay united, like we are.”
12. “While I was with them, I kept them safe. Only the one who chose to be lost was lost, just like Scripture said.”
13. “Now I’m coming to you. I’m saying this so they will have full joy.”
14. “I gave them your word, and the world hates them because they don’t belong to it.”
15. “I’m not asking you to take them out of the world, but to protect them from evil.”
16. “Make them pure with your truth. Your word is truth.”

17. "I send them into the world like you sent me."
18. "I make myself ready so they will be ready too."
19. "I pray not just for them, but also for everyone who will believe because of their words."
20. "I pray they will all be one—just like you and I are one."
21. "I want them to be one so the world will believe you sent me."
22. "I've given them the same glory you gave me, so they can be united."
23. "Let them be one, so the world knows you sent me and love them."
24. "Father, I want those you gave me to be with me and see my glory."
25. "You loved me before the world was made."
26. "I showed them what you're like. I will keep showing them, so your love will be in them, and I will be in them."

John 18

1. Jesus and his disciples went to a garden.
2. Judas knew the place and brought soldiers there.
3. Jesus went to meet them and said, "Who are you looking for?"
4. They said, "Jesus of Nazareth."
5. Jesus said, "I am he." They stepped back and fell down.
6. He asked again, "Who are you looking for?"
7. They said, "Jesus."
8. Jesus said, "I already told you. Let the others go."
9. Peter pulled out a sword and cut off a man's ear.
10. Jesus said, "Put your sword away. I must do what the Father wants."
11. They arrested Jesus and took him to the high priest.
12. Peter and another disciple followed.
13. Peter waited outside while the other disciple went in.
14. A servant girl said, "Aren't you one of his followers?"
15. Peter said, "No, I'm not."
16. He stood by a fire to warm himself.
17. Inside, the high priest questioned Jesus.
18. Jesus said, "I taught in public. Ask the people what I said."
19. One guard hit Jesus.
20. Jesus said, "If I was wrong, tell me how. If I wasn't, why hit me?"
21. They sent Jesus to another high priest, Caiaphas.
22. Meanwhile, someone else asked Peter, "Aren't you one of them?"
23. Peter said, "No, I'm not."
24. A third person said, "Didn't I see you with him?"
25. Peter said, "No!" Right then, a rooster crowed.
26. Jesus was taken to Pilate.
27. Pilate asked, "What's the charge?"
28. They said, "He's a criminal!"
29. Pilate said, "Judge him yourselves."
30. They said, "We can't put anyone to death."
31. Pilate asked Jesus, "Are you the king of the Jews?"
32. Jesus said, "My kingdom is not of this world."
33. Pilate asked, "So you are a king?"
34. Jesus said, "I was born to tell the truth."
35. Pilate asked, "What is truth?"
36. He told the crowd, "I find no fault in him."
37. But it was custom to free one prisoner at Passover.
38. Pilate said, "Do you want me to free Jesus?"

39. They shouted, "No! Free Barabbas!"

John 19

1. Pilate had Jesus whipped.
2. The soldiers made a crown of thorns and put it on Jesus' head.
3. They made fun of him and hit him.
4. Pilate brought Jesus out and said, "I find no reason to punish him."
5. The leaders shouted, "Crucify him!"
6. Pilate said, "You do it. I find no guilt."
7. They said, "He must die because he claimed to be God's Son."
8. Pilate was afraid. He asked Jesus, "Where are you from?"
9. Jesus didn't answer.
10. Pilate said, "Don't you know I have power to kill or free you?"
11. Jesus said, "You have power only because God let you."
12. Pilate tried to let Jesus go, but the people shouted, "If you let him go, you are no friend of Caesar!"
13. Pilate brought Jesus out and said, "Here is your king!"
14. They shouted, "Kill him!"
15. Pilate said, "Should I kill your king?"
16. They said, "We have no king but Caesar!"
17. Pilate handed Jesus over to be crucified.
18. Jesus carried his cross to a place called "The Skull."
19. They nailed him to the cross with two others.
20. Pilate put a sign above him: "Jesus of Nazareth, King of the Jews."
21. The leaders said, "Change the sign!"
22. Pilate said, "What I wrote, I wrote."
23. The soldiers took his clothes and cast lots for his robe.
24. Near the cross stood Jesus' mother and others.
25. Jesus said to his mother, "Here is your son," and to the disciple, "Here is your mother."
26. From then on, the disciple took care of her.
27. Jesus knew everything was finished.
28. He said, "I am thirsty."
29. They gave him vinegar on a sponge.
30. Jesus said, "It is finished." Then he died.
31. The soldiers broke the legs of the two others.
32. When they got to Jesus, he was already dead.
33. One soldier pierced his side. Blood and water came out.
34. This fulfilled Scripture: "None of his bones will be broken."
35. Joseph of Arimathea asked for Jesus' body.
36. He and Nicodemus wrapped the body and placed it in a new tomb.

John 20

1. Early Sunday, Mary Magdalene went to the tomb.
2. She saw the stone was moved.
3. She ran to Peter and another disciple and said, "They took the Lord's body!"
4. Peter and the other disciple ran to the tomb.
5. The other disciple got there first and looked in.
6. Peter went inside and saw the linen cloths.
7. The other disciple went in too. He saw and believed.
8. They still didn't understand Jesus had to rise.
9. They went home.
10. Mary stood outside crying.

11. She looked in the tomb and saw two angels.
12. They asked, "Why are you crying?"
13. She said, "They took my Lord, and I don't know where he is."
14. She turned and saw Jesus but didn't recognize him.
15. Jesus said, "Why are you crying?"
16. She thought he was the gardener. She said, "If you took him, tell me where."
17. Jesus said, "Mary." She knew it was him.
18. Jesus said, "Don't hold on to me. Go tell my followers I am going to the Father."
19. That evening, Jesus appeared to the disciples.
20. He said, "Peace be with you." He showed them his hands and side.
21. He said, "As the Father sent me, I'm sending you."
22. He breathed on them and said, "Receive the Holy Spirit."
23. Thomas wasn't there. He said, "I won't believe unless I see the holes in his hands."
24. A week later, Jesus appeared again.
25. He said to Thomas, "Look at my hands. Stop doubting."
26. Thomas said, "My Lord and my God!"
27. Jesus said, "You believe because you saw. Blessed are those who believe without seeing."
28. Jesus did many other miracles not written here.
29. These are written so you may believe Jesus is the Son of God and have life in his name.

John 21

1. Later, Jesus appeared to his disciples by the Sea of Galilee.
2. Peter, Thomas, and others were there.
3. Peter said, "I'm going fishing." They said, "We'll go too."
4. They caught nothing all night.
5. At dawn, Jesus stood on the shore. They didn't know it was him.
6. He said, "Throw your net on the right side." They did and caught many fish.
7. John said, "It's the Lord!"
8. Peter jumped into the water and swam to shore.
9. Jesus had a fire with fish and bread.
10. He said, "Bring some of the fish you caught."
11. They counted 153 fish, but the net didn't break.
12. Jesus said, "Come and eat."
13. This was the third time Jesus appeared after rising.
14. After breakfast, Jesus said, "Peter, do you love me?"
15. Peter said, "Yes, Lord."
16. Jesus said, "Feed my sheep." He asked two more times.
17. Peter felt sad but said, "You know I love you."
18. Jesus said, "When you were young, you dressed yourself. But when you're old, someone else will lead you."
19. He meant how Peter would die for him.
20. Peter saw John and asked, "What about him?"
21. Jesus said, "If I want him to stay alive until I return, what is that to you? You follow me."
22. People thought John would never die, but Jesus only said, "If I want him to stay, what is that to you?"
23. This book was written by the disciple who saw these things. His story is true.
24. Jesus did many more things. If all were written, the world couldn't hold the books.

– Acts –

The Holy Spirit empowers the apostles to spread the gospel from Jerusalem outward.

Acts 1

1. I wrote before about everything Jesus did and taught.
2. After he rose, he gave instructions through the Holy Spirit.
3. He showed the disciples many proofs that he was alive.
4. He stayed with them for 40 days and spoke about God's kingdom.
5. He told them, "Stay in Jerusalem. Wait for the Holy Spirit."
6. "John baptized with water. Soon you will be baptized with the Holy Spirit."
7. They asked, "Lord, will you bring the kingdom now?"
8. Jesus said, "Only the Father knows the time."
9. "But the Holy Spirit will come. You will receive power."
10. "You will tell people about me everywhere—in Jerusalem, in Judea, in Samaria, and all over the world."
11. After he said this, Jesus was lifted into the sky. A cloud hid him.
12. As they watched, two men in white clothes appeared.
13. They said, "Why are you staring at the sky? Jesus will come back the same way."
14. The disciples went back to Jerusalem from the Mount of Olives.
15. They stayed together in a house upstairs. They were:
16. Peter, John, James, Andrew, Philip, Thomas, Bartholomew, Matthew, James (son of Alphaeus), Simon, and Judas (son of James).
17. They kept praying with the women, with Mary the mother of Jesus, and with his brothers.
18. One day, Peter stood up with about 120 people.
19. He said, "Judas led the men who arrested Jesus."
20. "He was one of us, but he chose to betray Jesus."
21. "He died in a field. His place must be given to someone else."
22. "We must choose a man who was with us from the time of John's baptism until Jesus went to heaven."
23. Two men were suggested: Joseph (called Barsabbas) and Matthias.
24. They prayed, "Lord, you know every heart. Show us who you choose."
25. "Let this man take Judas's place."
26. They cast lots, and the lot fell to Matthias. He became one of the twelve apostles.

Acts 2

1. On the day of Pentecost, all the believers were together.
2. Suddenly, a sound came from heaven like a strong wind.
3. Flames of fire appeared over each person.
4. Everyone was filled with the Holy Spirit and spoke in different languages.
5. People from many nations were in Jerusalem.
6. They heard their own languages and were amazed.
7. They asked, "Aren't these people from Galilee?"
8. "How are they speaking our languages?"
9. "We hear them talking about the great things God has done."
10. Some people were confused. Others made fun of them.
11. Peter stood up with the other apostles and spoke.

12. He said, "Listen! These people are not drunk."
13. "This is what God said would happen."
14. "God said He would give His Spirit to all people."
15. "Young people will see visions. Old people will dream dreams."
16. "God will show signs in the sky and on the earth."
17. "Everyone who calls on the Lord will be saved."
18. Peter said, "Jesus did many miracles. God approved him."
19. "You killed him, but God raised him from the dead."
20. "We are witnesses. We saw him alive."
21. "Jesus is now in heaven, and he sent the Holy Spirit."
22. "This is what you are seeing and hearing today."
23. "God made Jesus both Lord and Messiah."
24. The people were sorry and asked, "What should we do?"
25. Peter said, "Turn from your sins. Be baptized in Jesus' name. You will be forgiven and receive the Holy Spirit."
26. About 3,000 people believed and were baptized that day.
27. The believers met often to learn, eat, and pray together.
28. They shared everything they had.
29. They praised God and helped each other.
30. More and more people joined them every day.

Acts 3

1. One day, Peter and John went to the temple to pray.
2. A man who couldn't walk was being carried there.
3. He sat at the temple gate and begged for money.
4. He saw Peter and John and asked them for help.
5. Peter said, "Look at us."
6. The man looked, hoping to get money.
7. Peter said, "I don't have money, but I will give you what I have. In Jesus' name, stand up and walk!"
8. Peter helped him up. His feet and legs became strong.
9. He jumped up, walked, and went into the temple with them.
10. He walked, jumped, and praised God.
11. People saw him and were amazed.
12. Peter said, "Why are you surprised? We didn't heal him ourselves."
13. "The God of Abraham, Isaac, and Jacob did this."
14. "You handed Jesus over to be killed, but God raised him."
15. "We are witnesses of this."
16. "Faith in Jesus made this man strong."
17. "You didn't know what you were doing, but God used it to fulfill His plan."
18. "Turn from your sins so your sins will be wiped away."
19. "God will send Jesus again at the right time."
20. "He must stay in heaven until everything is made new."
21. "Moses said God would raise up a prophet like him. That prophet is Jesus."
22. "Anyone who does not listen to him will be cut off."
23. "God sent Jesus first to bless you and turn you away from sin."

Acts 4

1. Peter and John were speaking to the people.

2. Some priests and guards were upset because they taught about Jesus rising from the dead.
3. They arrested Peter and John and put them in jail overnight.
4. But many people believed. Now there were about 5,000 believers.
5. The next day, the leaders asked, "By what power did you heal this man?"
6. Peter, filled with the Holy Spirit, said, "Jesus healed this man."
7. "You killed Jesus, but God raised him from the dead."
8. "Only Jesus can save us. There is no other name that can save."
9. The leaders saw Peter and John were bold, even though they were not trained teachers.
10. They also saw the healed man standing with them and didn't know what to say.
11. They told Peter and John to leave the room.
12. They said, "We can't deny a miracle happened."
13. "Let's tell them not to speak about Jesus anymore."
14. They called them back and warned them to stop.
15. But Peter and John said, "We must obey God, not you."
16. "We can't stop talking about what we saw and heard."
17. The leaders let them go because the people were praising God.
18. The healed man was over 40 years old.
19. Peter and John went back to the other believers and told them everything.
20. Everyone prayed together and asked God for boldness.
21. After they prayed, the place shook. They were all filled with the Holy Spirit.
22. They kept speaking God's message with courage.
23. The believers shared everything.
24. No one said, "This is mine."
25. Some sold land or houses and gave the money to help others.
26. A man named Barnabas sold land and gave the money to the apostles.

Acts 5

1. A man named Ananias and his wife Sapphira sold some land.
2. They kept part of the money and gave the rest, pretending it was all.
3. Peter said, "Ananias, you lied to the Holy Spirit!"
4. "You didn't lie to people—you lied to God!"
5. Ananias fell down and died.
6. Some young men buried him.
7. About three hours later, Sapphira came in.
8. Peter asked, "Did you sell the land for this amount?"
9. She said, "Yes."
10. Peter said, "Why did you agree to lie to God?"
11. She also fell down and died.
12. The same young men buried her next to her husband.
13. Everyone who heard about it was filled with fear.
14. The apostles did many miracles. More and more people believed.
15. Sick people were brought out hoping Peter's shadow would touch them.
16. Crowds came, and all the sick and troubled people were healed.
17. The high priest and Sadducees arrested the apostles and put them in jail.
18. That night, an angel opened the door and said, "Go back and keep teaching."
19. In the morning, they were in the temple teaching again.

20. The leaders were confused. The jail was locked, but the men were gone.
21. Someone said, "The men you jailed are teaching in the temple!"
22. The guards brought them in, but carefully, so the people wouldn't get angry.
23. The high priest said, "We told you not to teach about Jesus!"
24. Peter said, "We must obey God, not men."
25. "You killed Jesus, but God raised him."
26. "God made Jesus a leader and Savior. He gives forgiveness."
27. "We are witnesses, and so is the Holy Spirit."
28. The leaders were furious and wanted to kill them.
29. A Pharisee named Gamaliel stood up.
30. He said, "Be careful. Let them go."
31. "If their work is not from God, it will fail."
32. "If it is from God, you can't stop it."
33. They agreed and let the apostles go after beating them.
34. They ordered them not to speak about Jesus.
35. The apostles left happy to suffer for Jesus.
36. Every day, in the temple and in homes, they kept teaching about Jesus.

Acts 6

1. The number of believers kept growing.
2. Some widows were not getting enough food.
3. The apostles said, "We should not stop teaching to give out food."
4. "Choose seven good men full of the Spirit and wisdom."
5. "They will handle the food, and we will keep teaching and praying."
6. Everyone liked this idea. They chose Stephen, Philip, Procorus, Nicanor, Timon, Parmenas, and Nicolas.
7. The apostles prayed and laid hands on them.
8. God gave Stephen power to do miracles.
9. Some men argued with Stephen, but they couldn't win.
10. They paid people to lie and say Stephen spoke against God and Moses.
11. The people, leaders, and teachers got angry and grabbed Stephen.
12. They took him to the Jewish council.
13. The false witnesses said, "He talks against the law and the temple."
14. Everyone in the council looked at Stephen. His face looked like an angel.

Acts 7

1. The high priest asked, "Are these things true?"
2. Stephen said, "Listen! Long ago, God spoke to Abraham."
3. "God told Abraham to leave his country and go to a new land."
4. "God gave him no land right away, but promised it to his children."
5. "God said Abraham's family would be slaves in another country for 400 years."
6. "But God would free them and bring them back."
7. "God gave Abraham the covenant of circumcision. Then came Isaac, Jacob, and the 12 sons."
8. "The brothers were jealous of Joseph and sold him."
9. "But God helped Joseph in Egypt. He became ruler under Pharaoh."
10. "During a famine, Joseph's family came to Egypt."
11. "Their whole family moved there—75 people."

12. "Years passed. A new king didn't know Joseph."
13. "Our people became slaves and were treated badly."
14. "Then Moses was born. God saved him and helped him grow up in Pharaoh's house."
15. "When Moses was 40, he tried to help his people, but they rejected him."
16. "He ran away and lived in the desert for 40 years."
17. "Then God spoke to him from a burning bush."
18. "God said, 'I've seen my people's pain. Go lead them out of Egypt.'"
19. "God did miracles through Moses in Egypt and the desert."
20. "But the people still rejected Moses."
21. "They made a golden calf and worshiped it."
22. "God turned away and let them follow false gods."
23. "Later, God gave them the tent of worship."
24. "Then came Joshua, David, and Solomon, who built the temple."
25. "But God does not live in buildings made by people."
26. Stephen said, "You stubborn people! You resist the Holy Spirit!"
27. "Your ancestors hurt the prophets. Now you killed the One they talked about—Jesus!"
28. "You received God's law but didn't obey it!"
29. The leaders were furious.
30. Stephen looked up and saw Jesus standing in heaven.
31. He said, "I see heaven open and Jesus standing at God's right side!"
32. The people shouted, covered their ears, and ran at him.
33. They dragged him out and threw stones at him.
34. The witnesses put their coats at Saul's feet.
35. As they stoned Stephen, he prayed, "Lord Jesus, receive my spirit."
36. He said, "Lord, don't blame them." Then he died.

Acts 8

1. Saul agreed that Stephen should die.
2. That day, the church faced strong attacks. Many believers left Jerusalem.
3. Saul went house to house, dragging out believers and putting them in jail.
4. The believers who left kept sharing the good news.
5. Philip went to a city in Samaria and told people about Jesus.
6. Many listened and saw miracles. Evil spirits left, and sick people were healed.
7. The people were very happy.
8. A man named Simon did magic tricks and amazed people.
9. People said he had God's power.
10. But when Philip preached about Jesus, many believed and were baptized.
11. Simon believed too and followed Philip everywhere.
12. The apostles in Jerusalem heard Samaria had accepted God's word, so they sent Peter and John.
13. Peter and John prayed for the people to receive the Holy Spirit.
14. The Holy Spirit came when the apostles laid hands on them.
15. Simon saw this and offered money for that power.
16. Peter said, "You can't buy God's gift! Your heart is not right."
17. "Repent, or you will be punished."
18. Simon said, "Please pray for me so that won't happen."
19. Peter and John returned to Jerusalem, telling people about Jesus on the way.

20. An angel told Philip, "Go south on the road to Gaza."
21. Philip went and saw an Ethiopian man reading the Bible in a chariot.
22. The Holy Spirit said, "Go to that chariot."
23. Philip asked, "Do you understand what you're reading?"
24. The man said, "No, I need help."
25. Philip joined him. The man was reading about a sheep being led to be killed.
26. Philip explained it was about Jesus.
27. The man believed and said, "Here is water. Can I be baptized?"
28. They went into the water. Philip baptized him.
29. The Holy Spirit took Philip away. The man went home happy.
30. Philip appeared in another town and kept preaching the good news.

Acts 9

1. Saul was still trying to hurt Jesus' followers.
2. He asked the high priest for letters to arrest believers in Damascus.
3. As he neared Damascus, a bright light from heaven flashed around him.
4. He fell down and heard a voice: "Saul, why are you hurting me?"
5. Saul said, "Who are you?"
6. The voice said, "I am Jesus. Go into the city. You will be told what to do."
7. Saul got up, but he couldn't see. His friends led him to Damascus.
8. He was blind for three days and didn't eat or drink.
9. A man named Ananias was there. God told him in a vision to visit Saul.
10. Ananias was scared. "Saul hurts your people!"
11. But God said, "Go. I chose Saul to tell many people about me."
12. Ananias went and laid hands on Saul. "Jesus sent me to help you see and be filled with the Holy Spirit."
13. Something like scales fell from Saul's eyes. He could see again.
14. Saul was baptized and ate some food.
15. Right away, Saul preached in synagogues, saying, "Jesus is the Son of God!"
16. People were shocked. "Isn't this the man who arrested believers?"
17. But Saul grew stronger and confused those who didn't believe.
18. Some Jews planned to kill Saul.
19. His friends helped him escape by lowering him in a basket at night.
20. Saul went to Jerusalem. The disciples were afraid of him.
21. But Barnabas told them how Saul had met Jesus and preached bravely.
22. Saul spoke boldly about Jesus. Some people tried to kill him.
23. The believers helped Saul leave the city safely.
24. The church had peace and grew stronger.
25. Peter traveled and healed a man named Aeneas who couldn't walk for 8 years.
26. Peter said, "Jesus heals you. Get up!" And he did.
27. Many people turned to the Lord.
28. In another town, a good woman named Tabitha got sick and died.
29. The people asked Peter to come.
30. Peter prayed, and she came back to life!
31. Many people believed in the Lord.
32. Peter stayed in Joppa with a man named Simon.

Acts 10

1. A man named Cornelius lived in Caesarea. He was a Roman officer.
2. He loved God, prayed every day, and gave to the poor.
3. One afternoon, an angel came to him in a vision.
4. The angel said, "God has seen your prayers and gifts."
5. "Send men to Joppa to get a man named Peter."
6. Cornelius sent three men to Joppa.
7. The next day, Peter was on the roof praying.
8. He got hungry and had a vision.
9. He saw a large sheet coming down from heaven.
10. It had all kinds of animals on it.
11. A voice said, "Get up, Peter. Kill and eat."
12. Peter said, "No, Lord! I've never eaten unclean food."
13. The voice said, "Don't call anything unclean if God made it clean."
14. This happened three times. Then the sheet went back to heaven.
15. While Peter wondered what it meant, the men from Cornelius came to the house.
16. The Holy Spirit told Peter to go with them.
17. Peter went downstairs and said, "I am the one you are looking for."
18. The next day, Peter went with them to Cornelius' house.
19. Cornelius was waiting with his family and friends.
20. Peter said, "You know Jews usually don't visit Gentiles, but God showed me not to call anyone unclean."
21. Cornelius said, "An angel told me to send for you."
22. Peter began to speak: "God accepts people from every nation who respect Him and do what's right."
23. "God sent Jesus to bring peace. He healed people and did good things."
24. "Jesus was killed, but God raised Him."
25. "We ate and drank with Him after He came back to life."
26. "He told us to preach and say He will judge all people."
27. "Everyone who believes in Him will be forgiven."
28. While Peter was speaking, the Holy Spirit came on everyone there.
29. The Jewish believers were amazed.
30. Peter said, "Can anyone stop these people from being baptized?"
31. They were all baptized in Jesus' name.

Acts 11

1. The apostles and believers heard that Gentiles had accepted God's word.
2. When Peter returned to Jerusalem, some believers were upset.
3. They said, "You went into a Gentile's house and ate with him!"
4. Peter told them everything from the beginning.
5. He told them about the vision of the sheet and the voice from heaven.
6. He said, "Three men came for me. The Holy Spirit told me to go with them."
7. "Cornelius had a vision too and sent for me."
8. "I spoke, and the Holy Spirit came on them, just like He came on us."
9. "If God gave them the same gift, who am I to stop Him?"
10. The believers stopped arguing and praised God.
11. They said, "God has given life to the Gentiles too!"

12. Some believers had gone to other cities after Stephen died.
13. They told Jews about Jesus.
14. But some men from Cyprus and Cyrene went to Antioch and preached to Gentiles too.
15. God's power was with them, and many people believed.
16. The church in Jerusalem sent Barnabas to Antioch.
17. He was happy and encouraged them to stay true to the Lord.
18. Barnabas was a good man, full of the Holy Spirit and faith.
19. Many people were added to the church.
20. Barnabas went to Tarsus to find Saul.
21. He brought Saul to Antioch. They stayed for a year teaching many people.
22. In Antioch, the believers were first called "Christians."
23. Some prophets came from Jerusalem.
24. One prophet named Agabus said a famine was coming.
25. The disciples decided to help the believers in Judea.
26. They sent help through Barnabas and Saul.

Acts 12

1. King Herod started hurting some people in the church.
2. He had James, the brother of John, killed with a sword.
3. When he saw this made the people happy, he arrested Peter too.
4. It was during the Feast of Unleavened Bread.
5. Peter was put in jail, guarded by soldiers.
6. The church prayed hard for him.
7. One night, Peter was sleeping between two soldiers, chained up.
8. An angel came, and a light shined in the cell.
9. The angel woke Peter up and said, "Get up!" The chains fell off.
10. The angel said, "Get dressed and follow me."
11. Peter followed him, but he thought it was a dream.
12. They passed the guards, and the gate opened by itself.
13. They walked down the street, and the angel left.
14. Peter realized it was real. He said, "God sent an angel to rescue me!"
15. He went to Mary's house, where many were praying.
16. A girl named Rhoda answered the door, heard Peter's voice, and was so happy she forgot to open it.
17. She ran to tell the others, "Peter is at the door!"
18. They didn't believe her.
19. Peter kept knocking. They finally opened the door and were amazed.
20. He told them what happened and left for another place.
21. In the morning, the soldiers were confused.
22. Herod ordered a search and had the guards killed.
23. Later, Herod gave a speech. People shouted, "This is the voice of a god!"
24. Herod didn't praise God, but rather took the glorify for himself, so an angel killed him.
25. God's message kept spreading.
26. Barnabas and Saul finished their work and returned, taking John Mark with them.

Acts 13

1. In the church at Antioch, there were prophets and teachers: Barnabas, Simeon, Lucius, Manaen, and Saul.

2. While they prayed and fasted, the Holy Spirit said, "Set apart Barnabas and Saul for my work."
3. They fasted, prayed, laid hands on them, and sent them off.
4. They went to Cyprus and preached in Jewish synagogues.
5. John Mark helped them.
6. In Paphos, they met a sorcerer named Bar-Jesus.
7. He worked for a Roman leader named Sergius Paulus.
8. Sergius wanted to hear God's word, but Bar-Jesus tried to stop him.
9. Saul, now called Paul, filled with the Holy Spirit, said, "You are full of lies! God's hand is against you."
10. "You will be blind for a while." Bar-Jesus went blind immediately.
11. Sergius Paulus believed because he saw God's power.
12. Paul and his group sailed to Perga. John Mark left and went home.
13. Paul and Barnabas went to Antioch in Pisidia.
14. On the Sabbath, they went into the synagogue.
15. After the reading, the leaders asked them to speak.
16. Paul stood up and gave a message.
17. He told how God helped Israel, brought them out of Egypt, gave them leaders and kings.
18. He said David was a king after God's heart.
19. He said, "From David's family, God sent Jesus, our Savior."
20. "John the Baptist prepared the way."
21. "The leaders in Jerusalem didn't know Jesus was the Savior. They killed him."
22. "But God raised him from the dead. We saw him alive."
23. "Now we tell you the good news—Jesus brings forgiveness."
24. "The law of Moses could not free people from sin, but Jesus can."
25. Some people believed. Others were jealous and caused trouble.
26. Paul and Barnabas said, "We had to speak to Jews first, but now we will go to the Gentiles."
27. "God told us to be a light to all people."
28. The Gentiles were happy and believed.
29. God's word spread through the area.
30. But some Jews stirred up trouble and forced Paul and Barnabas to leave.
31. They shook the dust off their feet and went to the next town.
32. The believers were full of joy and the Holy Spirit.

Acts 14

1. In Iconium, Paul and Barnabas went to the synagogue.
2. They spoke so well that many Jews and Gentiles believed.
3. Some Jews refused and stirred up trouble.
4. The city was split—some sided with the Jews, others with the apostles.
5. A group planned to hurt and kill Paul and Barnabas.
6. They found out and left for Lystra and Derbe.
7. They kept preaching the good news.
8. In Lystra, a man who couldn't walk was sitting.
9. He listened to Paul.
10. Paul saw he had faith to be healed and said, "Stand up!"
11. The man jumped up and began to walk.
12. The crowd shouted, "The gods have come down to us!"
13. They called Barnabas "Zeus" and Paul "Hermes."

14. The priest of Zeus brought bulls to offer sacrifices.
15. Paul and Barnabas tore their clothes and shouted, "Stop! We are just people like you!"
16. "We came to tell you to turn from idols to the living God."
17. "God made the sky, earth, and sea. He gives rain and food."
18. Even then, the people barely stopped offering sacrifices.
19. Some Jews came from Antioch and Iconium and turned the crowd against Paul.
20. They stoned Paul and dragged him out of the city, thinking he was dead.
21. But he got up and went back into the city.
22. The next day, he and Barnabas went to Derbe.
23. They preached and many believed.
24. They went back to strengthen the believers and encourage them.
25. They warned that following Jesus brings hard times.
26. They chose leaders in each church, prayed, and trusted them to God.
27. Then they returned to Antioch, where they had started.
28. They told the church all that God had done and how many Gentiles had believed.

Acts 15

1. Some men came from Judea and said, "You must be circumcised to be saved."
2. Paul and Barnabas disagreed strongly.
3. The church sent them to Jerusalem to talk to the apostles and elders.
4. On the way, they told how God was saving Gentiles. Everyone was happy.
5. In Jerusalem, some believers said, "Gentiles must follow the law of Moses."
6. The apostles and elders met to talk about it.
7. After a lot of talking, Peter stood up.
8. He said, "God chose me to share the good news with the Gentiles."
9. "God gave them the Holy Spirit, just like us."
10. "God saved them by faith, not by law."
11. "We should not make it hard for them."
12. Paul and Barnabas told about the miracles God did through them.
13. Then James spoke.
14. He said, "The Scriptures said God would include the Gentiles."
15. "We should not make them follow all our laws."
16. "Just tell them to stay away from idols, sexual sin, meat from strangled animals, and blood."
17. The group agreed and wrote a letter to send to the Gentile churches.
18. They sent Paul, Barnabas, Judas, and Silas to deliver it.
19. The letter said: "You don't need to follow the law of Moses. Just stay away from idols, blood, and sexual sin."
20. The people were happy to get the letter.
21. Judas and Silas encouraged the believers.
22. After some time, Paul and Barnabas stayed in Antioch and kept teaching.
23. Later, Paul said to Barnabas, "Let's visit the churches again."
24. Barnabas wanted to take John Mark. Paul said no, because Mark had left them before.
25. They disagreed and separated.
26. Barnabas took Mark. Paul took Silas.

27. Both went out to share the good news in different places.

Acts 16

1. Paul went to Derbe and Lystra. A believer named Timothy lived there.
2. The believers spoke well of Timothy.
3. Paul wanted Timothy to go with him. So he circumcised him because of the Jews in the area.
4. They traveled from town to town, telling people what the apostles had decided.
5. The churches grew stronger and had more members every day.
6. The Holy Spirit didn't let them preach in Asia.
7. They tried to go to Bithynia, but the Spirit said no.
8. So they went to Troas.
9. That night, Paul had a vision. A man from Macedonia said, "Come help us!"
10. They believed God wanted them to go there and share the good news.
11. They sailed to Macedonia and arrived in Philippi.
12. On the Sabbath, they went outside the city to a place of prayer.
13. They talked to some women there.
14. One woman named Lydia listened. She sold purple cloth and worshiped God.
15. God opened her heart. She believed and was baptized.
16. She invited them to her house.
17. Later, they met a slave girl with an evil spirit. She told the future.
18. She made her owners a lot of money.
19. She followed Paul and shouted, "These men are servants of God!"
20. After many days, Paul turned and said, "In Jesus' name, come out!" The spirit left her.
21. Her owners were angry. They grabbed Paul and Silas and took them to court.
22. The crowd joined in. The officials beat them and put them in prison.
23. The jailer locked them in the deepest cell and chained their feet.
24. At midnight, Paul and Silas were praying and singing.
25. Suddenly, a strong earthquake shook the prison. All the doors opened, and the chains came off.
26. The jailer woke up and saw the doors open. He thought the prisoners had escaped and was going to kill himself.
27. Paul shouted, "Don't hurt yourself! We are all here!"
28. The jailer ran in and asked, "What must I do to be saved?"
29. Paul said, "Believe in Jesus, and you will be saved."
30. He and his family believed and were baptized.
31. The next day, the officials said, "Let them go."
32. But Paul said, "We are Roman citizens. You beat us without a trial."
33. The leaders were scared. They came and apologized.
34. Paul and Silas left the prison and visited Lydia's house before leaving the city.

Acts 17

1. Paul and Silas went to Thessalonica.
2. They went to the synagogue. Paul spoke for three Sabbaths.
3. He explained that the Messiah had to suffer and rise again.
4. Some Jews believed, along with many Greeks and women.
5. Some Jews were jealous. They started a riot and looked for Paul and Silas.
6. They grabbed a believer named Jason and took him to the leaders.

7. They shouted, "These men are causing trouble everywhere!"
8. "They say there is another king—Jesus!"
9. Jason had to pay money before they let him go.
10. That night, the believers sent Paul and Silas to Berea.
11. In Berea, they went to the synagogue.
12. The people there were eager to learn. They studied the Scriptures every day.
13. Many believed.
14. But Jews from Thessalonica came and stirred up trouble.
15. The believers sent Paul away, but Silas and Timothy stayed.
16. Paul went to Athens and waited for them.
17. He was upset by all the idols in the city.
18. He talked with people in the synagogue and marketplace every day.
19. Some teachers brought him to a meeting place called the Areopagus.
20. They said, "Tell us what you are teaching."
21. Paul stood up and said, "People of Athens, I see you are very religious."
22. "I saw an altar that said, 'To an Unknown God.' I want to tell you about Him."
23. "God made the world. He gives life to everyone."
24. "He doesn't live in temples or need anything."
25. "He wants people to look for Him."
26. "He is not far from anyone."
27. "He wants us to turn away from sin."
28. "He has set a day to judge the world by the man He raised—Jesus."
29. When Paul talked about rising from the dead, some laughed.
30. Others said, "We want to hear more."
31. Some believed, including a man named Dionysius and a woman named Damaris.

Acts 18

1. Paul left Athens and went to Corinth.
2. There he met Aquila and his wife Priscilla. They were tentmakers, just like Paul.
3. Paul stayed with them and worked.
4. Every Sabbath, he spoke in the synagogue and tried to convince Jews and Greeks.
5. When Silas and Timothy came, Paul focused fully on preaching.
6. Some Jews refused to believe. Paul said, "I'm going to the Gentiles now."
7. He went to stay at the house of a man named Titius Justus, who believed in God.
8. Crispus, the synagogue leader, believed in Jesus. Many others believed and were baptized.
9. One night, God spoke to Paul in a vision: "Don't be afraid. Keep speaking. I am with you."
10. So Paul stayed in Corinth for a year and a half, teaching.
11. Some Jews brought Paul to court and said, "He is teaching people to break the law!"
12. But the governor Gallio said, "This is about your own laws, not mine. Settle it yourselves."
13. He threw them out of court.
14. Then the people beat up the synagogue leader in front of Gallio, but he didn't care.
15. Paul stayed a little longer, then sailed to Syria with Priscilla and Aquila.
16. In Cenchrea, Paul shaved his head to show he had kept a promise to God.
17. They arrived in Ephesus. Paul preached in the synagogue.

18. The people wanted him to stay, but he said no.
19. He said, "I'll come back if God wants me to."
20. He sailed away and landed in Caesarea, then went to Antioch.
21. After some time, Paul left again and traveled from place to place, encouraging the churches.
22. A man named Apollos came to Ephesus. He knew the Scriptures well and spoke boldly about Jesus.
23. But he only knew about John's baptism.
24. Priscilla and Aquila taught him more about Jesus.
25. Apollos went to Achaia and helped many people believe.

Acts 19

1. Paul came back to Ephesus and met some believers.
2. He asked, "Did you receive the Holy Spirit when you believed?"
3. They said, "We haven't even heard of the Holy Spirit."
4. Paul asked, "What baptism did you receive?" They said, "John's."
5. Paul said, "John baptized to get ready for Jesus."
6. They believed and were baptized in Jesus' name.
7. When Paul laid hands on them, the Holy Spirit came, and they spoke in other languages and praised God.
8. Paul taught in the synagogue for three months.
9. Some people became stubborn and wouldn't believe.
10. Paul left and taught every day in a school for two years.
11. God gave Paul power to do miracles.
12. Even cloths that touched Paul healed people and cast out evil spirits.
13. Some men tried to copy Paul and said to a demon, "In Jesus' name, the one Paul preaches, come out!"
14. The demon said, "I know Jesus and Paul, but who are you?"
15. The man with the demon jumped on them and beat them up. They ran away naked and hurt.
16. People were afraid, and many believed in Jesus.
17. Some who practiced magic burned their scrolls in public. They were worth a lot of money.
18. The message about Jesus kept growing in power.
19. Paul planned to visit Macedonia, Achaia, Jerusalem, and then Rome.
20. A man named Demetrius made silver statues of a false god named Artemis.
21. He was upset because Paul was turning people away from idols.
22. Demetrius stirred up a crowd.
23. People shouted, "Great is Artemis of the Ephesians!"
24. The city was in chaos.
25. Paul wanted to go speak to the crowd, but his friends said no.
26. Some shouted one thing, others another. It was very confusing.
27. A city official calmed them down.
28. He said, "No one has robbed or spoken badly about our temple."
29. "If Demetrius has a problem, he should take it to court."
30. "Now go home before we all get in trouble."

Acts 20

1. After the trouble ended, Paul said goodbye and left for Macedonia.
2. He encouraged the believers in many places.
3. Then he went to Greece and stayed for three months.

4. Some Jews planned to hurt him, so he changed his travel plans.
5. He traveled with a group of helpers through different cities.
6. They all met up in Troas and stayed seven days.
7. On Sunday, the believers gathered to eat and listen to Paul.
8. He preached until midnight.
9. A young man named Eutychus sat in a window. He got sleepy and fell from the third floor.
10. He died, but Paul went down, hugged him, and said, "He is alive!"
11. Everyone was happy, and Paul kept talking until morning.
12. Then they all left.
13. Paul traveled by land while the others went by boat.
14. They met in Assos and sailed together.
15. They stopped at a few towns, trying to reach Jerusalem quickly.
16. Paul didn't stop in Ephesus because he wanted to be in Jerusalem by Pentecost.
17. From Miletus, he sent for the church leaders from Ephesus.
18. When they came, he said, "You know how I lived when I was with you."
19. "I served the Lord with all my heart, even during hard times."
20. "I taught you everything you needed to know."
21. "I told Jews and Gentiles to turn to God and believe in Jesus."
22. "Now I'm going to Jerusalem. I don't know what will happen there."
23. "But the Holy Spirit says I will face trouble."
24. "Still, I must finish the work Jesus gave me—to tell people the good news."
25. "I know you won't see me again."
26. "I taught you all of God's message. I am not guilty if anyone is lost."
27. "Be careful. Watch over yourselves and the church."
28. "Bad people will try to lead others away."
29. "I warned you for three years, day and night, with tears."
30. "Now I give you to God and His word."
31. "I didn't want anyone's money. I worked hard to help myself and others."
32. "It is better to give than to get."
33. After Paul said this, he prayed with them all.
34. They cried and hugged him because he said they would never see him again.

Acts 21

1. Paul and the others sailed to several cities on the way to Jerusalem.
2. In Tyre, they found believers and stayed with them for seven days.
3. The believers warned Paul not to go to Jerusalem.
4. When Paul left, they all prayed together on the beach.
5. They continued sailing and stopped in Caesarea.
6. They stayed at Philip's house. He was one of the first seven helpers.
7. He had four daughters who prophesied.
8. A prophet named Agabus came and tied his hands and feet with Paul's belt.
9. He said, "This is what will happen to Paul in Jerusalem."
10. Everyone begged Paul not to go.
11. Paul said, "I am ready to die for Jesus if needed."
12. So they said, "Let God's will be done."
13. They traveled on to Jerusalem.
14. The believers welcomed them happily.

15. Paul met with James and the church leaders.
16. He told them what God had done among the Gentiles.
17. They praised God but warned Paul that some Jews were angry.
18. They said, "Many believe you teach Jews to stop following Moses."
19. They had a plan: Paul would join some men in a temple ceremony to show he obeyed the law.
20. Paul agreed and went to the temple.
21. But some Jews saw him and shouted, "This man teaches against our people and our law!"
22. They grabbed Paul and dragged him out.
23. The whole city was in chaos.
24. Soldiers came and arrested Paul.
25. The crowd shouted, "Kill him!"
26. The commander ordered Paul to be taken to the fortress.
27. Paul asked, "Can I speak to the people?"
28. The commander was surprised that Paul spoke Greek.
29. Paul said, "I am a Jew from Tarsus. Please let me talk."
30. The commander let him.
31. Paul stood on the steps and quieted the crowd to speak.

Acts 22

1. Paul stood up and said, "Brothers, listen to me!"
2. When he spoke in their language, they got quiet.
3. Paul said, "I am a Jew. I was born in Tarsus but raised here in Jerusalem."
4. "I studied under Gamaliel and followed our laws."
5. "I once hurt believers. I arrested them and sent them to jail."
6. "One day, I was going to Damascus to arrest more believers."
7. "At noon, a bright light from heaven flashed around me."
8. "I fell down and heard a voice say, 'Saul, why are you hurting me?'"
9. "I asked, 'Who are you, Lord?' The voice said, 'I am Jesus of Nazareth.'"
10. "I was blind. My friends led me to Damascus."
11. "A man named Ananias came and healed my eyes."
12. "He said, 'God chose you to know His will and tell others about Jesus.'"
13. "I was baptized and called on Jesus' name."
14. "Later, in the temple, I had a vision. Jesus said, 'Leave Jerusalem. The people here won't believe you.'"
15. "I said, 'But Lord, they know I once hurt your followers!'"
16. "Jesus said, 'Go. I am sending you far away to the Gentiles.'"
17. The crowd became angry and shouted, "Kill him!"
18. The soldiers took Paul into the fortress.
19. They were about to whip him to make him talk.
20. Paul asked, "Is it legal to whip a Roman citizen who hasn't had a trial?"
21. The commander got scared when he heard Paul was a Roman.
22. The next day, the commander brought Paul before the Jewish leaders to find out why they were angry.

Acts 23

1. Paul looked at the leaders and said, "I have lived with a clean heart before God."
2. The high priest ordered someone to hit Paul in the mouth.

3. Paul said, "God will punish you! You sit here to judge me but break the law yourself!"
4. Someone said, "You insulted the high priest!"
5. Paul said, "I didn't know he was the high priest. The Bible says not to speak badly about your leaders."
6. Paul noticed some leaders were Sadducees and some were Pharisees.
7. He said, "I am a Pharisee. I am on trial because I believe in the resurrection of the dead!"
8. The leaders began to argue.
9. The Sadducees didn't believe in angels or resurrection. The Pharisees did.
10. The commander was afraid they would tear Paul apart, so he had soldiers take him away.
11. That night, Jesus appeared to Paul and said, "Be brave. You told people about me in Jerusalem. You will do the same in Rome."
12. The next morning, more than 40 men made a plan to kill Paul.
13. They promised not to eat or drink until they did.
14. They told the leaders, "Tell the commander to bring Paul again. We will kill him on the way."
15. But Paul's nephew heard the plan.
16. He went to the fortress and told Paul.
17. Paul called a soldier and said, "Take this boy to the commander."
18. The commander listened to the boy and told him not to tell anyone.
19. Then he called 200 soldiers, 70 horsemen, and 200 more with spears.
20. They took Paul to the governor in Caesarea that night to keep him safe.
21. The commander wrote a letter to Governor Felix saying Paul had done nothing wrong.
22. Paul arrived safely, and the governor promised to hear his case later.

Acts 24

1. Five days later, the high priest and some others came to see the governor, Felix.
2. They brought a lawyer named Tertullus.
3. The lawyer said, "Paul causes trouble everywhere."
4. "He is a leader of the Nazarene group."
5. "He tried to mess up the temple, so we arrested him."
6. "Ask him yourself—you'll see he's guilty."
7. Paul was allowed to speak.
8. He said, "I respect you, Governor. I will gladly defend myself."
9. "I was in Jerusalem only twelve days."
10. "I didn't cause trouble in the temple or argue in public."
11. "These men can't prove anything."
12. "I worship the God of our people, and I believe everything written in the law and prophets."
13. "I believe in the resurrection of the dead—both good and bad."
14. "I always try to do what's right before God and people."
15. "I brought gifts to the poor and offered sacrifices."
16. "Some Jews from other places started the trouble. They should be here if they have charges."
17. "These men here are mad because I said I believe in the resurrection."
18. Felix knew about the Way (the followers of Jesus), so he delayed the trial.
19. He said, "I'll decide later."
20. He let Paul have some freedom and visitors.
21. Later, Felix and his wife came to listen to Paul.

22. Paul talked about faith, right and wrong, and judgment.
23. Felix became afraid and said, "That's enough! I'll call you again later."
24. Felix hoped Paul would offer him money, so he kept calling him.
25. After two years, Felix was replaced by a new governor named Festus.
26. Felix left Paul in prison to please the Jews.

Acts 25

1. Festus became governor. Three days later, he went to Jerusalem.
2. The Jewish leaders told him about Paul and asked Festus to send Paul there.
3. They planned to kill Paul on the way.
4. But Festus said, "Paul is in Caesarea. I'm going there soon."
5. "Send your leaders with me, and we'll judge him there."
6. A few days later, Festus returned to Caesarea and held a trial.
7. The Jews made many false charges, but they had no proof.
8. Paul said, "I have done nothing wrong against the Jewish law, the temple, or Caesar."
9. Festus asked Paul, "Will you go to Jerusalem to be judged?"
10. Paul said, "No. I'm standing at Caesar's court. I should be judged here."
11. "If I'm guilty, I will accept death. But if I'm innocent, no one can give me to them."
12. "I appeal to Caesar!"
13. Festus talked with his advisors and said, "You asked to see Caesar. So you will."
14. A few days later, King Agrippa and Queen Bernice came to visit Festus.
15. Festus told the king about Paul.
16. He said, "The Jews wanted him dead, but I found no reason."
17. "Paul asked to go to Caesar, so I'm sending him."
18. "But I don't know what to write about him. Maybe you can help."
19. Agrippa said, "I want to hear him myself."
20. Festus said, "You will hear him tomorrow."

Acts 26

1. King Agrippa said to Paul, "You may speak for yourself."
2. Paul said, "I am happy to explain my case to you, King Agrippa."
3. "You know all about Jewish customs."
4. "The Jewish leaders know me. I followed the strictest Jewish group—the Pharisees."
5. "Now I am on trial because I believe God raises the dead."
6. "Why is it so hard to believe that God can raise the dead?"
7. "I once thought I should hurt the followers of Jesus."
8. "I put them in jail and voted to have them killed."
9. "I even chased them to other cities."
10. "On my way to Damascus, I saw a bright light from heaven."
11. "We all fell down. I heard a voice say, 'Saul, why are you hurting me?'"
12. "'I am Jesus. Get up. I have chosen you to tell people about me.'"
13. "So I obeyed the vision and preached to everyone—Jews and Gentiles."
14. "That's why the Jews arrested me."
15. "God helped me, and I'm still speaking the truth today."
16. "I am only saying what the prophets said would happen."
17. "That Christ would suffer, rise from the dead, and bring light to all."
18. Festus shouted, "Paul, you're crazy!"

19. Paul said, "I'm speaking the truth."
20. "King Agrippa, do you believe the prophets? I know you do!"
21. Agrippa said, "Are you trying to make me a Christian?"
22. Paul said, "I want everyone here to believe in Jesus!"
23. The king, the governor, and others got up.
24. They said, "Paul has done nothing wrong. He could be set free if he hadn't asked to go to Caesar."

Acts 27

1. Paul and other prisoners were handed to a Roman officer named Julius.
2. They boarded a ship heading toward Italy.
3. They stopped at several places on the way.
4. Julius was kind and let Paul visit his friends.
5. The winds were strong, and the trip was hard.
6. They reached a place called Fair Havens.
7. Paul warned them, "If we sail now, we'll face storms and danger."
8. But the captain and owner wanted to keep going.
9. A calm wind blew, so they set sail.
10. But soon, a terrible storm hit.
11. The ship was tossed by the wind and waves.
12. They tied ropes around the ship to hold it together.
13. They threw cargo overboard to lighten the ship.
14. They didn't see the sun or stars for many days.
15. They thought they would die.
16. Paul stood up and said, "You should have listened to me."
17. "But take courage. No one will die—only the ship will be lost."
18. "An angel told me that God will keep us safe."
19. "We must land on an island."
20. On the 14th night, the sailors sensed land nearby.
21. They let down anchors to slow the ship.
22. Some sailors tried to escape, but Paul said, "If they leave, we can't be saved."
23. So the soldiers cut the ropes and let the lifeboat go.
24. Paul told everyone to eat. "You need strength."
25. He gave thanks, broke bread, and they all ate.
26. There were 276 people on board.
27. After eating, they threw more cargo into the sea.
28. When it got light, they saw a bay with a beach.
29. They tried to steer the ship there.
30. But the ship hit a sandbar and got stuck.
31. The waves broke the back of the ship.
32. The soldiers wanted to kill the prisoners so they wouldn't escape.
33. But the officer wanted to save Paul, so he stopped them.
34. He told those who could swim to jump first.
35. The rest used boards and pieces of the ship.
36. Everyone made it safely to shore.

Acts 28

1. Everyone got to land safely. The island was called Malta.
2. The people there were kind. They made a fire because it was cold and raining.

3. Paul gathered sticks. A snake came out and bit his hand.
4. The people said, "This man must be a murderer."
5. But Paul shook the snake off into the fire and was not hurt.
6. They waited for him to swell up or die—but nothing happened.
7. They changed their minds and said, "He must be a god!"
8. A man named Publius let them stay at his house for three days.
9. His father was sick. Paul prayed, laid hands on him, and healed him.
10. Then others on the island came to be healed too.
11. The people gave Paul and his group everything they needed.
12. After three months, they got on another ship and sailed to Rome.
13. They stopped at a few places on the way.
14. Some believers heard Paul was coming and came to meet him.
15. Paul thanked God and felt encouraged.
16. In Rome, Paul was allowed to live in a house with a soldier guarding him.
17. After three days, Paul called the Jewish leaders together.
18. He said, "I was arrested in Jerusalem even though I did nothing wrong."
19. "I had to appeal to Caesar. That's why I'm here."
20. "I'm in chains because I believe in the hope of Israel."
21. They said, "We haven't heard anything bad about you, but we want to hear what you believe."
22. So they set a day to come back and listen.
23. Many came to Paul's house. He explained about God's kingdom and Jesus.
24. Some believed. Some did not.
25. Paul said, "Isaiah the prophet was right—some people will hear but not understand."
26. "God's salvation has been sent to the Gentiles, and they will listen."
27. Paul stayed in that house for two years.
28. He welcomed everyone and taught about Jesus without fear.

– Romans –

Paul explains how we're made right with God through faith, not the law.

Romans 1

1. This letter is from Paul. I serve Jesus and was chosen to preach God's message.
2. God promised this message long ago in the Scriptures.
3. It's about His Son, Jesus Christ, who came from David's family.
4. Jesus was shown to be God's Son when He rose from the dead.
5. Through Jesus, I was sent to tell all people to believe and obey Him.
6. You are included because you also belong to Jesus.
7. I'm writing to all of you in Rome who are loved by God. May God give you grace and peace.
8. First, I thank God for you. People everywhere talk about your faith.
9. I always pray for you.
10. I ask God to let me visit you soon.
11. I want to help make your faith stronger.
12. I also want to be encouraged by your faith.
13. I've tried to visit before, but I was stopped.
14. I must share the good news with all people, everywhere.

15. I am ready to preach to you in Rome too.
16. I am not ashamed of the good news. It saves everyone who believes.
17. This message shows how people can be made right with God—by faith.
18. God is angry when people do wrong and turn away from the truth.
19. People know the truth because God showed it to them.
20. Ever since the world was made, God's power has been clear.
21. No one has an excuse not to believe in Him.
22. They knew God but didn't thank or honor Him.
23. Their thinking became confused. Their hearts became dark.
24. They claimed to be wise but acted foolish.
25. They worshiped idols instead of God.
26. So God let them follow their sinful desires.
27. Women and men both started doing sexual things that were wrong.
28. Since they didn't want God, He let them live with evil minds.
29. They did wrong, were greedy, hated others, and were full of lies.
30. They were jealous, murderers, mean, and cruel.
31. They disobeyed their parents and didn't keep their promises.
32. They knew these things were wrong and deserved death, but they did them anyway—and even encouraged others to do them.

Romans 2

1. If you judge others but do the same wrong things, you are guilty too.
2. God judges people fairly.
3. You can't escape God's judgment just because you think you're better.
4. God is kind and patient, but that doesn't mean you should keep doing wrong.
5. If you keep sinning, you are building up God's anger against you.
6. God will give each person what they deserve.
7. People who do good and seek God will get eternal life.
8. People who are selfish and reject the truth will face God's anger.
9. Trouble will come to everyone who does evil—Jews first, then others.
10. But God will reward everyone who does good.
11. God treats all people the same.
12. People who don't know the law will be judged without it.
13. God wants people to obey, not just hear the law.
14. Some people do right even without knowing the law.
15. That shows God's law is written in their hearts.
16. God will judge everyone through Jesus.
17. If you call yourself a Jew and brag about knowing the law, be careful.
18. You say you know what's right.
19. You teach others and think you guide the blind.
20. But do you teach yourself?
21. You tell others not to steal—do you steal?
22. You say not to commit adultery—do you do it?
23. You brag about the law—but do you break it?
24. Because of you, people speak badly about God.
25. Being circumcised only matters if you obey the law.
26. If someone obeys the law but isn't circumcised, it's better than breaking the law while being circumcised.

27. A true Jew is one inwardly, and real circumcision is in the heart.

Romans 3

1. Is there any benefit in being a Jew? Yes—God gave them His words.
2. Some didn't believe, but God is always true.
3. Even if every person lies, God tells the truth.
4. Some people think, "If our sin shows how right God is, then He shouldn't punish us."
5. But if God didn't punish sin, how could He judge the world?
6. Some say, "Why not sin more so more good comes from it?"
7. That's wrong, and those who say it should be punished.
8. The truth is: No one is better than others.
9. Everyone—Jews and Gentiles—sins.
10. No one is right—not one.
11. No one understands or looks for God.
12. Everyone turns away and does wrong.
13. Their words are lies and curses.
14. They are quick to hurt and kill.
15. They don't know peace.
16. They don't fear God.
17. The law shows us what sin is.
18. No one can be made right with God by just following the law.
19. But now God has made a way to be right without the law.
20. The law and prophets told about this.
21. We are made right by trusting in Jesus.
22. This is for everyone who believes.
23. Everyone has sinned and fallen short of God's standard.
24. But God freely forgives because of Jesus.
25. Jesus gave His life to take the punishment for sin.
26. God is fair. He makes people right when they believe in Jesus.
27. No one can brag, because we are saved by faith, not by following rules.
28. We are made right with God by faith alone.
29. God is not just for Jews. He is also God of all people.
30. He makes both Jews and Gentiles right through faith.
31. Faith doesn't cancel the law. It shows the law is true.

Romans 4

1. Let's talk about Abraham, our ancestor.
2. If he was made right by his good actions, he could brag—but not before God.
3. The Bible says, "Abraham believed God, and God accepted him."
4. When people work, they earn money. But if God accepts someone because of faith, it's a gift—not something earned.
5. God accepts people who trust Him, not people who do everything perfectly.
6. King David also said people are blessed when God forgives them.
7. "Blessed are those whose sins are forgiven."
8. "Blessed is the one God doesn't count as guilty."
9. Was Abraham blessed because he was circumcised? No. He was blessed before that.
10. He was made right because of his faith, not because of a physical act.
11. Circumcision was a sign to show he already had faith.
12. He became the father of all who believe in God—circumcised or not.

13. God promised Abraham he would be blessed, not because he followed rules, but because he believed.
14. If only rule-followers are blessed, then faith doesn't matter.
15. But the law brings punishment because no one can keep it perfectly.
16. That's why God made it about faith—so the promise would be sure for everyone.
17. Abraham believed God could give life to the dead and make something out of nothing.
18. Even when there was no hope, Abraham hoped and believed.
19. He was about 100 years old, but still believed he would have a child.
20. He didn't doubt God. His faith made him strong.
21. He believed God would do what He promised.
22. That's why God accepted him.
23. These words weren't just written for Abraham.
24. They were written for us too—if we believe in God, who raised Jesus from the dead.
25. Jesus died for our sins and rose again to make us right with God.

Romans 5

1. We have been made right with God by faith. So now we have peace with Him through Jesus.
2. Jesus helps us stand strong and be happy about our hope.
3. We're also happy when we suffer, because suffering teaches us to be strong.
4. Being strong teaches us to never give up.
5. And never giving up helps us trust God more.
6. God's love has been poured into our hearts by the Holy Spirit.
7. Jesus died for us at just the right time—when we were still sinners.
8. People might die for a good person, but Jesus died for us while we were still doing wrong.
9. Now that we are right with God because of Jesus' blood, we will be saved from God's anger.
10. Jesus made us friends with God by His death. Now that He is alive, He keeps saving us.
11. We are happy because Jesus has made us right with God.
12. Sin came into the world through one man—Adam. And sin brought death.
13. Everyone sinned, so everyone died.
14. Even before the law, people sinned and died.
15. But what Jesus did is greater than what Adam did.
16. Adam's sin brought death. Jesus' gift brings life.
17. Adam's sin brought death to many. But Jesus brings grace and makes many people right with God.
18. One man's sin brought punishment to everyone.
19. But one man's obedience—Jesus—made many right with God.
20. The law showed people how bad sin is. But God's grace is even bigger.
21. Sin once ruled and brought death. Now God's grace rules and brings eternal life through Jesus.

Romans 6

1. Should we keep sinning so God can forgive us more?
2. No way! If we died to sin, we shouldn't keep living in it.
3. When we were baptized, we joined with Jesus in His death.
4. Just like Jesus rose from the dead, we now live a new life.

5. Our old self was put to death with Jesus so sin would lose its power.
6. Anyone who has died with Jesus is free from sin.
7. If we died with Him, we will also live with Him.
8. Jesus died once and will never die again.
9. Death has no power over Him.
10. He died to take away sin and now lives for God.
11. So you must think of yourselves as dead to sin but alive to God through Jesus.
12. Don't let sin control your body.
13. Don't use your body to do wrong. Use it to serve God.
14. Sin will not rule over you, because you live under grace, not law.
15. Should we sin because we are under grace? No!
16. If you obey sin, it becomes your master. But if you obey God, you become His servant.
17. You used to be slaves to sin, but now you follow God's way.
18. You are free from sin and now serve what is right.
19. Before, you used your body to do wrong. Now use it to do good for God.
20. When you served sin, you weren't free to do right.
21. What did that get you? Only shame and death.
22. Now you serve God, and you get eternal life.
23. The payment for sin is death, but God's free gift is eternal life through Jesus.

Romans 7

1. Don't you know, brothers and sisters, that the law rules over a person only while they are alive?
2. A married woman is tied to her husband by law until he dies.
3. But if he dies, she is free.
4. In the same way, you died to the law through Jesus.
5. Now you belong to Him and can live a new life.
6. We are free from the law and now serve God in a new way through the Spirit.
7. Is the law sinful? No! But the law shows us what sin is.
8. For example, without the law, I wouldn't know that wanting what others have is wrong.
9. Sin used the law to make me do wrong.
10. The law was meant to bring life, but sin used it to bring death.
11. Sin tricked me and used the law to kill me.
12. The law is holy. The commands are right and good.
13. Did the good law cause my death? No. Sin caused it.
14. The law is spiritual, but I am weak and sinful.
15. I don't understand myself. I do what I don't want to do, and I don't do what I should.
16. This shows that the law is good.
17. But sin lives in me and makes me do wrong.
18. I want to do what is right, but I can't do it perfectly.
19. I do the bad things I don't want to do.
20. It's not really me doing it—it's the sin inside me.
21. I find this rule: When I want to do good, evil is right there with me.
22. Deep down, I love God's law.

23. But another law fights inside me and makes me a prisoner of sin.
24. I feel trapped. Who will save me?
25. Thank God! Jesus Christ will rescue me.

Romans 8

1. If you belong to Jesus, God will not punish you.
2. The Holy Spirit sets you free from sin and death.
3. The law couldn't save us because we are weak.
4. So God sent His Son to deal with sin.
5. He did what the law could not do.
6. Now we can live by the Spirit, not by our old sinful ways.
7. People who live by sin think only about sin.
8. But people who live by the Spirit think about what the Spirit wants.
9. Sinful minds lead to death. Spirit-filled minds lead to life and peace.
10. A sinful mind fights against God.
11. If the Spirit lives in you, you belong to God.
12. If you don't have the Spirit of Christ, you don't belong to Him.
13. If Christ is in you, your body is dead because of sin, but your spirit is alive.
14. God's Spirit raised Jesus from the dead. He will raise you too.
15. So don't live by sin. You owe it nothing.
16. If you live by sin, you will die.
17. But if you live by the Spirit, you will live.
18. All who are led by God's Spirit are God's children.
19. You didn't receive fear. You received adoption.
20. You can call God, "Father."
21. The Spirit tells our spirit that we are God's children.
22. If we are God's children, we will receive everything He has for us.
23. Right now, we suffer with Jesus. Later, we will be glorified with Him.
24. The pain we feel now is nothing compared to the joy that's coming.
25. All of creation is waiting for that day.
26. Everything in the world is broken and waiting to be made new.
27. We wait too. We want our new bodies.
28. The Spirit helps us in our weakness.
29. We don't always know how to pray, but the Spirit prays for us.
30. God knows what the Spirit is saying.
31. God works everything for good for those who love Him.
32. God chose us before we were born.
33. He made us right with Him and will share His glory with us.
34. If God is for us, no one can be against us.
35. God gave His own Son for us. He will give us everything we need.
36. No one can accuse God's people. God has forgiven us.
37. Jesus died and rose again. He speaks to God for us.
38. Nothing can separate us from Jesus' love.
39. Not trouble, danger, hunger, or death.
40. In all things, we win through Jesus.
41. Nothing—life or death, angels or demons, today or tomorrow—can separate us from God's love.

Romans 9

1. I speak the truth. I'm not lying.
2. My heart is full of sorrow.
3. I would even give up my own salvation if it would help my people—the Jews.

4. They are God's chosen people.
5. God gave them the law, the promises, and the ancestors.
6. And Jesus came from them.
7. But not all who are born Jewish are truly God's people.
8. Being a child of Abraham doesn't make you saved.
9. God chose Isaac, not Ishmael.
10. Then God chose Jacob, not Esau.
11. God chose people before they were born—not because of what they did.
12. God shows mercy to whoever He wants.
13. This doesn't mean God is unfair.
14. God told Moses, "I will have mercy on who I want."
15. So it's not about how hard we try—it's about God's mercy.
16. God raised up Pharaoh to show His power.
17. God can show mercy or let hearts stay hard.
18. You may ask, "Why does God blame us if He controls everything?"
19. But who are we to argue with God?
20. A clay pot doesn't question the person who made it.
21. God is like the potter. He can do what He wants.
22. God has been patient even with those who reject Him.
23. He wants to show His glory to those He has chosen.
24. That includes Gentiles, not just Jews.
25. God said through Hosea, "People who were not mine will be called my people."
26. God also said only a few Israelites will be saved.
27. They tried to become right with God by following the law.
28. But they didn't reach it because they didn't believe.
29. They stumbled over Jesus, the one God sent to save them.

Romans 10

1. I want all my people, the Jews, to be saved.
2. They love God, but they don't understand His way.
3. They tried to make themselves right with God by keeping the law.
4. But Christ makes people right when they believe in Him.
5. Moses wrote that people must follow all the law to be right.
6. But being right by faith is different. It says:
7. "Don't say, 'Who will go up to heaven?' or 'Who will go down to the dead?'"
8. God's message is near. It's in your heart and mouth.
9. Say, "Jesus is Lord," and believe God raised Him. Then you'll be saved.
10. Believing in your heart makes you right with God. Saying it out loud saves you.
11. The Bible says, "Anyone who trusts in Him will not be disappointed."
12. It doesn't matter if you are a Jew or not. The same Lord blesses all who call on Him.
13. "Everyone who calls on the Lord will be saved."
14. But how can people call on Him if they don't believe?
15. And how can they believe if they never hear about Him?
16. People must be sent to tell the good news.
17. "How beautiful are the feet of those who bring good news!"
18. But not everyone listens to the good news.

19. Isaiah said, "Lord, who believed our message?"
20. Faith comes from hearing the message about Jesus.
21. But some heard and still didn't believe.
22. God says, "I reached out to people all day long, but they didn't listen."

Romans 11

1. Has God rejected the Jews? No way!
2. I am a Jew, and God has not rejected me.
3. Long ago, Elijah thought he was the only one left who followed God.
4. But God told him, "I have kept 7,000 people who have not worshiped idols."
5. In the same way, God still has a group of Jews who believe.
6. They were chosen by grace—not by earning it.
7. The others were stubborn and refused to believe.
8. The Scriptures say God let them be blind and deaf to the truth.
9. David said, "Their blessings became traps."
10. "Let them be unable to see."
11. But they didn't fall forever. Their fall helped the Gentiles believe.
12. One day, the Jews will come back, and it will bless the world even more.
13. I speak now to the Gentiles: I want my people to want what you have.
14. If they come back, it will be like life from the dead!
15. If part of a tree is holy, the whole tree is holy.
16. Some Jewish branches were broken off, and Gentiles were added like wild branches.
17. But don't brag. Remember, you are just a branch—God is the root.
18. Don't look down on the broken branches.
19. They were broken off because they didn't believe. You stand only by faith.
20. So don't be proud. Be humble.
21. If God didn't spare the natural branches, He won't spare you if you turn away.
22. God is kind, but He is also strict. He punishes those who fall but is kind to those who stay in faith.
23. If the Jews believe again, God can add them back.
24. If He added wild branches (Gentiles), He can easily add back the original ones (Jews).
25. I don't want you to be confused. Some Jews have hard hearts until all Gentiles come in.
26. Then all Israel will be saved.
27. God said, "I will take away their sins."
28. Right now, many Jews reject the good news, but God still loves them because of His promise to their ancestors.
29. God's gifts and His calling never change.
30. You Gentiles once disobeyed but now receive mercy.
31. The Jews disobey now, but they will receive mercy too.
32. God allowed all to disobey so He could show mercy to all.
33. God's wisdom is too deep to fully understand.
34. No one has given advice to God.
35. No one gave Him anything first.
36. Everything comes from Him, through Him, and for Him.
37. Glory to God forever. Amen.

Romans 12

1. Give your life to God like a living sacrifice. This pleases Him.

2. Don't live like the world. Let God change the way you think.
3. Be honest about who you are. Don't think you're better than others.
4. The body has many parts. Each part has a job.
5. We are like that in Christ. We all belong to each other.
6. God gave each of us different gifts.
7. If your gift is to teach, then teach.
8. If your gift is to encourage, then encourage.
9. If you give, give with joy. If you lead, lead well. If you help others, do it gladly.
10. Love must be real. Hate evil. Do what is good.
11. Love one another like family. Respect each other.
12. Work hard. Serve the Lord with energy.
13. Be happy because of hope. Be patient in trouble. Keep praying.
14. Share with people who need help. Be kind to strangers.
15. Bless those who hurt you. Don't curse them.
16. Be happy with happy people. Cry with sad people.
17. Treat everyone the same. Don't think you are better.
18. Don't pay back evil for evil. Do what is right.
19. If possible, live in peace with everyone.
20. Don't try to get revenge. Let God handle it.
21. If your enemy is hungry, feed him. If he's thirsty, give him a drink.
22. Don't let evil win. Win by doing good.

Romans 13

1. Obey the people in charge. God put them there.
2. If you fight against the law, you are fighting against what God made.
3. Good people don't need to be afraid of rulers—only wrongdoers do.
4. Do what is right, and you will be praised.
5. Rulers are God's servants to help you. But they also punish those who do wrong.
6. That's why you must obey—not just to avoid punishment but to have a clear heart.
7. Pay your taxes. Give respect and honor where it's due.
8. Don't owe anyone anything—except love.
9. If you love others, you follow the law.
10. The law says: Don't steal, don't kill, don't lie, don't want what isn't yours.
11. All of that is summed up by this: Love your neighbor as yourself.
12. Love does no harm to others. So love completes the law.
13. Do this because the time is short. Wake up! Salvation is closer than ever.
14. The night is almost over. The day is near.
15. Stop doing what is wrong. Live in the light.
16. Don't follow sinful desires. Live like Jesus.

Romans 14

1. Welcome people who are weak in faith. Don't argue about their opinions.
2. Some eat everything. Others eat only vegetables.
3. Don't look down on each other. God has accepted both.
4. Only God can judge His servants.
5. Some think one day is more special than others. Others think all days are the same.

6. Each person must decide what they believe is right.
7. If you do something for the Lord, honor Him.
8. Whether we live or die, we belong to the Lord.
9. Jesus died and rose to be Lord of everyone.
10. So don't judge or look down on others. We will all stand before God.
11. The Bible says, "Every knee will bow to Me, and every tongue will say I am God."
12. Each of us must answer to God.
13. So don't judge anyone. Instead, don't do things that might make someone fall.
14. Nothing is unclean by itself. But if someone believes it's wrong, then it is wrong for them.
15. If you hurt someone with what you eat, you are not acting in love.
16. Don't let your freedom ruin someone else's faith.
17. God's kingdom is not about food or drink. It's about living right, having peace, and joy in the Spirit.
18. If you serve Christ this way, God is pleased.
19. So let's try to live in peace and help each other grow in faith.
20. Don't ruin God's work for the sake of food.
21. It's better not to eat or drink anything that will make someone else fall.
22. Keep your beliefs between you and God.
23. If you do something you think is wrong, you are guilty. Whatever is not done in faith is sin.

Romans 15

1. We who are strong should help the weak, not just please ourselves.
2. Help others do what is right and build them up.
3. Even Christ didn't live to please Himself. He took the insults of others.
4. The Scriptures were written to teach us and give us hope.
5. Ask God to help you live in harmony with others.
6. Then you will all praise God together with one voice.
7. Accept each other like Christ accepted you.
8. Jesus came to help the Jews and to show that God keeps His promises.
9. He also came so the Gentiles would praise God too.
10. The Bible says, "Praise the Lord, all nations!"
11. And, "Rejoice, people from everywhere!"
12. Isaiah said, "The Root of Jesse (Jesus) will come, and He will give hope to the nations."
13. May God fill you with joy and peace as you trust Him.
14. I am sure you are full of goodness and knowledge. You can help each other.
15. I've written to remind you of some things because of God's grace to me.
16. God made me a servant to the Gentiles to tell them the good news.
17. I am proud of the work I've done for God.
18. I will only talk about what Christ has done through me.
19. Through miracles and the power of the Spirit, I preached from Jerusalem to Illyricum.
20. I tried to go where people had never heard about Christ.
21. The Bible says, "Those who never heard will understand."
22. That's why I was delayed in coming to you.

23. But now I plan to visit you on my way to Spain.
24. First, I'm going to Jerusalem to help the believers there.
25. The churches in Macedonia and Achaia gave money to help the poor believers in Jerusalem.
26. They were happy to give because they received spiritual blessings from the Jews.
27. After I deliver the gift, I'll come to you on my way to Spain.
28. I know I will come with God's blessing.
29. I ask you to pray for me.
30. Pray that I'll be safe from those who don't believe in Judea.
31. Pray that the believers in Jerusalem will welcome my help.
32. Then I can come to you with joy and rest with you.
33. May God give you peace. Amen.

Romans 16

1. I recommend our sister Phoebe to you. She is a servant in the church.
2. Welcome her and help her in any way she needs.
3. Say hello to Priscilla and Aquila. They worked with me for Christ.
4. They risked their lives to help me. All the churches thank them.
5. Say hello to the church that meets in their house.
6. Greet my dear friend Epenetus. He was one of the first to believe in Christ in Asia.
7. Greet Mary. She worked hard for you.
8. Say hello to Andronicus and Junia. They were in prison with me. They are respected among the apostles.
9. Greet Ampliatus, a dear friend in the Lord.
10. Say hello to Urbanus, a coworker for Christ, and to Stachys, my dear friend.
11. Greet Apelles. He stayed strong in faith.
12. Say hello to those who belong to the family of Aristobulus.
13. Greet Herodion, my relative.
14. Say hello to the believers in the household of Narcissus.
15. Greet Tryphena and Tryphosa, who work hard for the Lord.
16. Greet my dear friend Persis. She worked very hard for the Lord.
17. Say hello to Rufus, chosen by the Lord, and to his mother—who has also been like a mother to me.
18. Greet Asyncritus, Phlegon, Hermes, Patrobas, Hermas, and the other believers with them.
19. Say hello to Philologus and Julia, Nereus and his sister, and Olympas.
20. Greet all the believers with a holy kiss.
21. All the churches of Christ say hello.
22. Watch out for people who cause divisions. Stay away from them.
23. They don't serve Jesus. They serve themselves and use smooth talk to fool people.
24. Everyone knows about your faith, and I am glad.
25. I want you to be wise about good and stay away from evil.
26. God will soon crush Satan under your feet. May Jesus give you peace.
27. Timothy, my coworker, says hello.
28. So do Lucius, Jason, and Sosipater, my relatives.
29. I, Tertius, wrote this letter and send my greetings.
30. Gaius is hosting me and the whole church here. He says hello.
31. Erastus, the city's treasurer, and our brother Quartus say hello too.

32. Glory to God! He can make you strong by the good news about Jesus.
33. This message was kept secret for a long time.
34. But now it is made clear to all people.
35. Glory belongs to God forever through Jesus Christ. Amen.

– 1 Corinthians –

Paul corrects problems in the Corinthian church and teaches about love, worship, and resurrection.

1 Corinthians 1

1. This letter is from Paul, chosen by God to be an apostle of Jesus. Our brother Sosthenes is with me.
2. We're writing to God's church in Corinth. You are God's people, chosen to live for Jesus.
3. May God give you grace and peace.
4. I thank God for you because He gave you His kindness through Jesus.
5. You have been made rich in everything—speech, knowledge, and faith.
6. Your lives show that Jesus is real.
7. You have every spiritual gift while you wait for Jesus to return.
8. Jesus will keep you strong so you'll be guilt-free on judgment day.
9. God is faithful. He called you to share life with His Son, Jesus.
10. I ask you to all agree. Don't argue. Be united in heart and mind.
11. Some from Chloe's house told me there are fights among you.
12. Some say, "I follow Paul," or "I follow Apollos," or "I follow Peter," or "I follow Christ."
13. Christ isn't divided! Was Paul crucified for you? No.
14. Were you baptized in Paul's name? No.
15. I'm glad I didn't baptize many of you, so no one can say you belong to me.
16. I baptized Crispus, Gaius, and the family of Stephanas. That's it.
17. Christ didn't send me to baptize, but to preach the good news.
18. The message about the cross sounds silly to some, but to us it is God's power to save.
19. The Bible says, "God will destroy human wisdom."
20. Where are the wise people now? God made the world's wisdom look foolish.
21. People didn't find God through wisdom. Instead, God saves people through a message that sounds simple.
22. Jews want miracles. Greeks want smart answers.
23. But we preach Christ, who was killed. That's hard for Jews and foolish to others.
24. But to those God called, Jesus is God's power and wisdom.
25. God's way looks foolish to some, but it is stronger than anything people can do.
26. Think about yourselves. Most of you weren't wise or powerful or important.
27. But God chose the weak and simple to shame the strong and proud.
28. He chose what the world thinks is nothing to show what really matters.
29. No one can brag before God.
30. God put you in Christ. Jesus became our wisdom, goodness, and Savior.
31. So if you want to brag, brag about the Lord.

1 Corinthians 2

1. When I came to tell you about Jesus, I didn't use big or fancy words.
2. I decided to talk only about Jesus, who died on the cross.
3. I was nervous and weak when I spoke.

4. My words didn't try to impress anyone. I let God's Spirit show His power.
5. So your faith would not rest on human wisdom but on God's power.
6. We teach wisdom to those who are mature, but not the world's wisdom.
7. We speak God's secret wisdom—truth that was hidden but planned long ago.
8. The rulers of this world didn't understand it. If they had, they wouldn't have killed Jesus.
9. The Bible says, "No eye has seen, no ear has heard, and no mind has imagined what God has prepared for His people."
10. But God showed it to us by His Spirit.
11. Only a person's own spirit knows their thoughts. In the same way, only God's Spirit knows God's thoughts.
12. We received God's Spirit, not the world's, so we can understand what God gave us.
13. We teach this using Spirit-taught words, not human wisdom.
14. People without the Spirit don't accept what comes from God. It sounds foolish to them.
15. But spiritual people understand these things.
16. No one can fully know God's mind, but we have the mind of Christ.

1 Corinthians 3

1. Brothers and sisters, I couldn't talk to you like mature people.
2. You were like babies in Christ. I had to give you milk, not solid food.
3. You were still not ready because you were fighting and jealous.
4. When one of you says, "I follow Paul," and another says, "I follow Apollos," you're acting like regular people—not like God's people.
5. Who is Paul? Who is Apollos? We're just servants God used to help you believe.
6. I planted the seed, Apollos watered it, but God made it grow.
7. The one who plants and the one who waters are nothing without God.
8. Both workers will be rewarded for what they did.
9. We are working together for God. You are God's field. You are God's building.
10. God gave me a job like a wise builder. I laid the foundation, and someone else is building on it.
11. The only true foundation is Jesus Christ.
12. Each person must be careful how they build on that foundation.
13. If they use gold, silver, or straw, their work will be tested by fire.
14. If it survives, they get a reward.
15. If it burns up, they lose the reward—but they will still be saved.
16. You are God's temple. God's Spirit lives in you.
17. If anyone destroys God's temple, God will destroy that person. God's temple is holy—and you are that temple.
18. Don't fool yourself. If you think you're wise by the world's standards, become like a fool so you can be truly wise.
19. The world's wisdom is foolish to God.
20. The Bible says, "God catches the wise in their own tricks."
21. So no one should brag about people.
22. Everything belongs to you—Paul, Apollos, Peter, the world, life, death, the present, and the future.
23. You belong to Christ, and Christ belongs to God.

1 Corinthians 4

1. Think of us as servants of Christ and caretakers of God's truth.
2. A servant must be trustworthy.
3. I don't care if people judge me. I don't even judge myself.
4. My conscience is clear, but only God can judge me.
5. So don't judge others before the right time. God will bring everything to light.
6. Learn from us not to be proud or pick sides.
7. Everything you have is a gift from God, so why brag?
8. You already think you're rich and powerful—but you're not.
9. I think God has put us apostles last. We suffer, and people watch us like a show.
10. We are fools for Christ, but you think you're wise.
11. We are weak, but you feel strong.
12. We go hungry, get hurt, and have no homes.
13. When people curse us, we bless them. When they hurt us, we stay calm.
14. I'm not writing to shame you but to warn you like my own children.
15. You may have many teachers, but not many fathers. I became your father in Christ.
16. So follow my example.
17. I'm sending Timothy to remind you how I live and teach everywhere.
18. Some of you became proud and thought I wouldn't visit.
19. But I will come soon, if God lets me. Then I'll see what these proud people are really like.
20. God's kingdom is not just words—it's power.
21. Do you want me to come with kindness or correction?

1 Corinthians 5

1. I heard that someone in your church is sinning in a terrible way—even worse than what nonbelievers do.
2. A man is living with his father's wife.
3. You should be sad, but instead you are proud.
4. I'm not there, but I've already judged this sin.
5. You must remove this man and give him over to Satan so his spirit may be saved later.
6. Don't brag about this. Just a little sin can spread and ruin everything.
7. Get rid of the old sin, like old bread dough, and be new like fresh dough.
8. Celebrate life with honesty and truth, not with sin and lies.
9. I wrote before: Don't be close friends with people who call themselves believers but live in sin.
10. I didn't mean people outside the church—you'd have to leave the world to avoid all sinners.
11. I meant don't be close to believers who keep sinning—like those who are greedy, mean, or dishonest.
12. It's not our job to judge people outside the church.
13. But we must judge those inside. God will judge outsiders. So remove the evil person from among you.

1 Corinthians 6

1. If two believers argue, they shouldn't go to court. They should settle it in the church.
2. God's people will one day judge the world.
3. So why not handle small problems now?
4. Can't you find someone wise in the church to help?
5. It's a shame that believers are suing each other in front of nonbelievers.

6. It's better to be wronged than to take each other to court.
7. But instead, you hurt each other—even your own brothers and sisters.
8. Don't you know people who do wrong will not be part of God's kingdom?
9. People who sin sexually, worship idols, steal, or lie won't inherit God's kingdom.
10. Some of you used to live like that.
11. But now you've been washed clean. God made you holy and right through Jesus and the Holy Spirit.
12. Some say, "I'm free to do anything." But not everything is good.
13. "I can do what I want"—but I won't let anything control me.
14. Our bodies weren't made for sin. They were made to serve the Lord.
15. God will raise our bodies, just like He raised Jesus.
16. Your body is part of Christ. Don't join it to sin.
17. Anyone who is joined to the Lord is one with Him.
18. Run away from sexual sin. Other sins are outside the body, but sexual sin hurts your own body.
19. Your body is a temple of the Holy Spirit. God gave it to you.
20. You don't belong to yourself. God paid for you. So honor God with your body.

1 Corinthians 7

1. You asked about marriage. It's good to stay single.
2. But to avoid sexual sin, each man should have his own wife, and each woman her own husband.
3. Husbands and wives should care for each other.
4. A wife's body belongs to her husband, and a husband's body belongs to his wife.
5. Don't avoid each other, unless you both agree to focus on prayer.
6. Then come together again so Satan doesn't tempt you.
7. I wish everyone were single like me, but each person has their own gift from God.
8. If you are single or a widow, it's good to stay that way.
9. But if you can't control yourself, get married. It's better to marry than burn with desire.
10. Married people shouldn't leave their spouses.
11. If they do, they should stay single or go back to their spouse.
12. If a believer has a spouse who isn't a believer, and they agree to stay, then stay married.
13. The believing spouse helps the whole family be set apart for God.
14. But if the unbeliever wants to leave, let them go.
15. God has called us to live in peace.
16. Maybe you will help your spouse believe.
17. Everyone should live the life the Lord gave them.
18. If you were circumcised, stay that way. If not, don't get circumcised.
19. What matters is obeying God's commands.
20. Stay in the life God gave you.
21. If you were a slave when you became a Christian, don't worry. But if you can become free, do it.
22. A Christian slave is free in the Lord. A free Christian is a servant of Christ.
23. God paid for you, so don't become slaves of people.
24. Stay where you are with God.
25. About people who've never been married: I don't have a direct command, but I give advice as one who is trusted by God.

26. Because times are hard, it's good to stay single.
27. If you're married, stay married. If you're not, don't rush into it.
28. But if you do marry, you haven't sinned.
29. Time is short. Live in a way that puts God first.
30. Don't let anything in this world distract you from serving God.
31. This world is passing away.
32. Singles can focus on pleasing God.
33. Married people also have to think about pleasing their spouses.
34. I say this to help you, not trap you. I want you to serve the Lord fully.
35. If you're engaged and feel you must marry, go ahead. That's okay.
36. But if you decide to stay single, that's okay too.
37. Both choices are good, but staying single may be better.
38. A wife is tied to her husband while he lives.
39. If he dies, she can remarry, but only to a Christian.
40. In my opinion, she'll be happier if she stays single. And I believe God's Spirit is guiding me.

1 Corinthians 8

1. You asked about food offered to idols. We all know something, but love is more important than knowledge.
2. Anyone who thinks they know everything doesn't know as much as they think.
3. But anyone who loves God is known by God.
4. We know idols are not real gods. There is only one true God.
5. People may worship many "gods" or "lords," but we know the truth.
6. There is one God, the Father, who made everything. And one Lord, Jesus Christ, through whom we live.
7. But not everyone understands this. Some still think food offered to idols is wrong.
8. Food doesn't bring us closer to God. Eating or not eating doesn't change our standing with Him.
9. But be careful—your freedom should not hurt someone else's faith.
10. If someone weak in faith sees you eating idol food, they might copy you and feel guilty.
11. Then your knowledge would hurt them. And Jesus died for them too.
12. When you hurt others this way, you are also sinning against Christ.
13. So if food causes someone to fall, I'll never eat that food again.

1 Corinthians 9

1. Am I not free? Am I not an apostle? Haven't I seen Jesus? Aren't you proof of my work?
2. Even if others doubt me, you know I am an apostle to you.
3. This is my answer to anyone who questions me.
4. Don't I have the right to food and drink?
5. Don't I have the right to travel with a wife like the other apostles?
6. Or are Barnabas and I the only ones who must work for our own money?
7. Soldiers don't pay their own way. Farmers eat their crops. Shepherds drink the milk.
8. This isn't just human thinking. The law says it too.
9. Moses wrote, "Don't muzzle an ox while it's working."
10. This teaches us that workers deserve support.

11. If we gave you spiritual help, is it too much to ask for food in return?
12. Others get this help. Shouldn't we get it too? But we didn't use that right. We don't want to stop anyone from hearing the good news.
13. Temple workers eat from the temple. Preachers should be supported too.
14. The Lord said those who preach should be taken care of.
15. But I haven't used that right. I'd rather die than stop boasting about preaching for free.
16. Preaching the good news is something I must do. I can't brag about it.
17. If I do it willingly, that's good. But even if I don't, it's still my job.
18. My reward is preaching without asking for payment.
19. I'm free, but I make myself a servant to help more people believe.
20. I become like the Jews to help the Jews.
21. I become like someone without the law to help those people, though I still follow God's law.
22. I become weak to help the weak. I try to be like everyone so I can help save some.
23. I do all this to share in the blessings of the good news.
24. In a race, all runners run, but only one wins. Run to win!
25. Athletes train for a prize that won't last. We run for a prize that lasts forever.
26. So I run with purpose. I fight with control.
27. I train my body so I don't fail after teaching others.

1 Corinthians 10

1. Friends, remember what happened to our ancestors in the desert.
2. They all followed Moses. They all passed through the sea.
3. They all ate the same food from God and drank the same water.
4. That water came from a spiritual rock, and that rock was Christ.
5. But God was not pleased with most of them, so they died in the desert.
6. This teaches us not to want evil things like they did.
7. Don't worship idols like they did.
8. Don't sin sexually like they did. Many died because of it.
9. Don't test Christ. Some did, and snakes killed them.
10. Don't complain like some of them did. God punished them.
11. These things are written to warn us.
12. If you think you're strong, be careful not to fall.
13. Every temptation is something others have faced. God will help you. He'll give you a way out so you can stand.
14. So stay away from idol worship.
15. You are smart. Think about what I'm saying.
16. When we drink the cup at the Lord's Supper, we are sharing in Christ's blood.
17. When we eat the bread, we are sharing in His body. We are one body because we share one bread.
18. In old times, people who ate sacrifices were part of the altar.
19. I'm not saying idols or their food have power.
20. But idol worship is really worshiping demons. You can't share in both Christ and demons.
21. You can't drink from the Lord's cup and from demons' cup too.
22. Are we trying to make God angry? We can't fight against Him.

23. Some say, "I'm allowed to do anything," but not everything is good.
24. Don't just think about yourself. Think about others too.
25. You can eat meat sold in the market without worrying about it.
26. Everything belongs to the Lord.
27. If someone invites you to eat and you want to go, eat what's served.
28. But if someone says, "This food was offered to idols," then don't eat it—for their sake.
29. Your freedom is not a reason to make someone else fall.
30. If I thank God for food, why should I be judged?
31. Whatever you do—eat, drink, or anything—do it to honor God.
32. Don't cause others to sin—Jews, Gentiles, or anyone in the church.
33. I try to please everyone to help them be saved.

1 Corinthians 11

1. Follow my example like I follow Christ.
2. I praise you for remembering my teachings.
3. Christ is the head of every man. The man is the head of the woman. God is the head of Christ.
4. A man should not cover his head when he prays.
5. A woman should cover her head when she prays.
6. If she doesn't, it's the same as shaving her head. So she should cover it.
7. A man is made in God's image and reflects God's glory.
8. A woman reflects man's glory.
9. Man was not made for woman, but woman was made for man.
10. That's why a woman should show respect on her head.
11. But in the Lord, men and women need each other.
12. Woman came from man, but man is born from woman. And everything comes from God.
13. Judge for yourselves. Is it proper for a woman to pray uncovered?
14. Nature shows that long hair is a glory for a woman.
15. If anyone wants to argue, we don't have any other rule, and neither do the churches.
16. I can't praise you for your church meetings—they do more harm than good.
17. When you meet, there are divisions among you.
18. Some of you eat before others, and some go hungry.
19. Some even get drunk!
20. You're not really celebrating the Lord's Supper.
21. You shame those who have nothing.
22. I don't praise you for this.
23. I received from the Lord what I also passed on to you:
24. The night Jesus was betrayed, He took bread, gave thanks, broke it, and said, "This is My body. Remember Me when you eat it."
25. He took the cup and said, "This is My blood. Drink this to remember Me."
26. When you eat and drink, you show the Lord's death until He comes.
27. If you eat and drink in a wrong way, you are guilty of sin against the Lord's body and blood.
28. So examine yourself before you eat the bread and drink the cup.
29. If you eat and drink without respect, you bring judgment on yourself.
30. That's why many are weak and sick.
31. If we judged ourselves rightly, God wouldn't have to punish us.

32. But when God corrects us, it's to keep us from being judged with the world.
33. So wait for one another when you eat.
34. If you're hungry, eat at home. That way, your meeting won't bring judgment.
35. I'll give more instructions when I come.

1 Corinthians 12

1. Now I want to talk about spiritual gifts.
2. You used to follow false gods.
3. No one speaking by God's Spirit will say bad things about Jesus. And no one can say "Jesus is Lord" without the Holy Spirit.
4. There are different spiritual gifts, but they all come from the same Spirit.
5. There are different ways to serve, but the same Lord.
6. There are different ways God works, but it's still God doing everything.
7. The Spirit gives each person a gift to help others.
8. One person gets wisdom. Another gets knowledge.
9. Another gets faith. Another gets the power to heal.
10. Others get the power to do miracles, speak messages from God, know right from wrong spirits, speak different languages, or understand those languages.
11. The Spirit decides who gets what gift.
12. A body has many parts, but it's still one body.
13. In the same way, all believers were baptized into one body, no matter who we are.
14. The body has many parts, not just one.
15. The foot can't say, "I'm not part of the body because I'm not a hand."
16. The ear can't say, "I'm not part of the body because I'm not an eye."
17. If the whole body were an eye, how would we hear?
18. God put each part exactly where He wanted it.
19. If there was only one part, it wouldn't be a body.
20. But now there are many parts and one body.
21. The eye can't say to the hand, "I don't need you."
22. Every part is needed—even the ones that seem weaker.
23. We treat those parts with special care.
24. God put the body together so we care for each other.
25. If one part suffers, we all suffer. If one part is honored, we all share in the joy.
26. You are the body of Christ, and each of you is a part of it.
27. God gave the church first apostles, then prophets, then teachers, then those who do miracles, heal, help, lead, or speak different languages.
28. Not everyone has the same gifts.
29. Try your best to get the greater gifts.
30. But now I will show you the best way of all.

1 Corinthians 13

1. If I speak all languages but don't love, I'm just making noise.
2. If I can speak God's messages, know all things, and have great faith, but don't love, I am nothing.
3. If I give everything I have and even die for others, but don't love, it's worthless.
4. Love is patient and kind. Love is not jealous or proud.
5. Love is not rude or selfish. It doesn't get angry easily.
6. Love doesn't keep track of wrongs.
7. Love is happy with the truth, not with lies.

8. Love never fails. But messages from God will end. Speaking in other languages will stop. Knowledge will fade.
9. We only know a little now, and we speak only a little of God's truth.
10. But when the perfect comes, the partial will go away.
11. When I was a child, I talked and thought like a child. Now I've grown up and put childish things away.
12. Now we see things like looking in a cloudy mirror. One day we will see clearly.
13. Three things will last: faith, hope, and love. But the greatest is love.

1 Corinthians 14

1. Love is the most important. But also try to get spiritual gifts—especially speaking messages from God.
2. Speaking in another language helps only you unless someone understands it.
3. But speaking a message from God helps others grow, encourages them, and gives them hope.
4. Speaking in a different language helps yourself. Speaking a message from God helps the whole church.
5. It's better to speak words everyone can understand.
6. If I come to you speaking a language you don't know, it won't help.
7. Even instruments must play clear notes to make sense.
8. If a trumpet sounds unclear, who will get ready for battle?
9. It's the same if your words don't make sense. No one will understand you.
10. There are many languages in the world. All of them have meaning.
11. But if I don't understand, I'm like a stranger to the speaker.
12. So if you want spiritual gifts, aim to use them to help others.
13. If you speak in another language, pray to also explain it.
14. If I pray in another language, my spirit prays, but my mind doesn't understand.
15. I will pray and sing with both spirit and understanding.
16. If others can't understand you, they can't say "Amen."
17. You may be thankful, but they are not helped.
18. I thank God I speak in more languages than all of you.
19. But in church, I'd rather say 5 clear words than 10,000 unknown ones.
20. Don't be childish in your thinking. Be like babies when it comes to evil, but be grown-up in understanding.
21. The Bible says God used other languages to speak to people, but they still didn't listen.
22. So speaking in other languages is a sign for unbelievers. Speaking messages from God is for believers.
23. If everyone speaks in strange languages, visitors will think you're crazy.
24. But if everyone speaks messages from God, even strangers may feel God is speaking to them.
25. They might fall to their knees and worship God, saying, "God is really here!"
26. When you meet, each person may have a song, a teaching, or a message. But it must help the church.
27. If someone speaks in another language, only two or three should speak, one at a time, and someone must explain it.
28. If no one can explain, then stay silent.
29. Two or three people may speak messages from God. Others should listen and decide if it's true.

30. If someone else gets a message while another is talking, the first one should stop.
31. You can all take turns speaking, so everyone learns.
32. God's Spirit helps you control yourself.
33. God is not a God of confusion, but of peace.
34. Women should be respectful and listen during meetings, as the law says.
35. If they want to learn something, they should ask at home.
36. God's word didn't start with you, and it's not only for you.
37. If someone thinks they are a prophet or spiritual, they should agree with what I'm writing.
38. If they ignore this, they will be ignored.
39. So, want to speak God's messages, but also don't stop people from speaking in other languages.
40. Everything should be done in an orderly and respectful way.

1 Corinthians 15

1. I want to remind you of the good news I told you.
2. You are saved if you keep believing it—unless you believed for nothing.
3. Christ died for our sins, just as the Bible said.
4. He was buried and rose on the third day, just as the Bible said.
5. He appeared to Peter, then to the twelve.
6. Then He appeared to over 500 people at once.
7. Later, He appeared to James and then to all the apostles.
8. Last, He appeared to me, too.
9. I don't deserve to be called an apostle, because I once hurt God's church.
10. But God was kind to me. I worked hard for Him, and His grace wasn't wasted.
11. We all preach the same message, and that's what you believed.
12. If we say Christ rose from the dead, how can some of you say there is no resurrection?
13. If no one rises, then not even Christ rose.
14. And if Christ didn't rise, our message is useless, and so is your faith.
15. If Christ didn't rise, we are lying about God.
16. If no one rises from the dead, then Christ didn't rise either.
17. And if Christ didn't rise, your sins are not forgiven.
18. Then everyone who died believing in Jesus is lost.
19. If hope in Christ is only for this life, we are the most pitiful people.
20. But Christ really did rise from the dead! He's the first to rise, but not the last.
21. Death came through one man, Adam. Life came through one man, Jesus.
22. In Adam all die. In Christ all will be made alive.
23. But everyone in the right order: Christ first, then those who belong to Him when He returns.
24. Then the end will come. Christ will give the kingdom to God the Father.
25. He will rule until all enemies are under His feet.
26. The last enemy to be destroyed is death.
27. God put everything under Christ's control.
28. Then the Son will give everything back to God, and God will rule over all.
29. If the dead don't rise, why are some people baptized for them?
30. And why would we risk danger if there's no resurrection?

31. I face death every day.
32. If the dead don't rise, let's just eat and drink because tomorrow we die.
33. Don't be fooled. Bad friends ruin good behavior.
34. Wake up! Stop sinning. Some of you don't know God.
35. Some may ask, "How are the dead raised? What kind of body will they have?"
36. That's a foolish question. A seed must die before it grows.
37. The body you plant is not the body that grows.
38. God gives each kind of body as He chooses.
39. People, animals, birds, and fish all have different bodies.
40. There are also heavenly bodies and earthly bodies.
41. The sun, moon, and stars all shine differently.
42. It's the same with our bodies. Our earthly body dies, but it will be raised to live forever.
43. It is weak when buried, but powerful when raised.
44. It is natural now, but will be spiritual later.
45. The first man, Adam, became a living person. The last Adam (Jesus) became a life-giving spirit.
46. First comes the natural body, then the spiritual one.
47. The first man was from the earth. The second man is from heaven.
48. People are like the man they come from—earthly or heavenly.
49. One day, we'll have heavenly bodies like Jesus.
50. Flesh and blood can't enter God's kingdom.
51. Let me tell you a secret: Not all of us will die, but we will all be changed.
52. It will happen quickly, like a blink. The dead will rise, and we'll be changed.
53. We must put on bodies that never die.
54. Then it will come true: "Death has lost the fight!"
55. "Death, where is your victory? Where is your sting?"
56. Sin brings death. The law shows sin.
57. But thanks to God! He gives us victory through Jesus.
58. So, stand firm. Work hard for the Lord. Your work is never wasted.

1 Corinthians 16

1. Now about the money you're collecting to help others—I want you to do what I told the churches in Galatia.
2. On the first day of every week, each of you should set aside some money based on what you've earned. Save it ahead of time so I won't have to collect it when I visit.
3. When I come, I'll send your gift with trusted people to take it to Jerusalem.
4. If it seems right, I may go with them too.
5. I will come to you after I travel through Macedonia.
6. I might stay with you for a while—or even spend the winter.
7. I don't want to just stop by quickly. I hope to stay longer if the Lord allows it.
8. But I will stay in Ephesus until Pentecost.
9. There is a big opportunity to share the good news here, even though many are against me.
10. If Timothy comes, treat him kindly. He's doing God's work just like I am.
11. Don't let anyone look down on him. Help him continue his trip in peace. I'm waiting for him with the other believers.

12. I asked Apollos to visit you, but he didn't think it was the right time. He will come when he can.
13. Stay alert. Stand strong in your faith. Be brave and strong.
14. Do everything with love.
15. You know that Stephanas and his family were the first believers in Achaia. They have given their lives to help others.
16. Respect people like them and others who work hard for the Lord.
17. I was glad when Stephanas, Fortunatus, and Achaicus came. They helped me when you couldn't be here.
18. They encouraged me, and they also encouraged you. Respect people like them.
19. The churches in Asia say hello. Aquila and Priscilla say hello in the Lord, as well as the church that meets in their home.
20. All the believers here send their greetings. Greet each other with a holy kiss.
21. I, Paul, write this greeting with my own hand.
22. If anyone does not love the Lord, they are not part of us. Come, Lord!
23. May the grace of the Lord Jesus be with you.
24. My love to all of you who belong to Christ Jesus.

– 2 Corinthians –

Paul defends his ministry and urges the church to be generous and faithful.

2 Corinthians 1

1. This letter is from Paul, chosen by God to be an apostle of Jesus, and from Timothy. We're writing to God's church in Corinth and to all believers nearby.
2. May God our Father and Jesus give you grace and peace.
3. Praise God, the Father of Jesus. He is kind and comforts us.
4. He comforts us in our troubles so we can comfort others.
5. We share in Christ's suffering, and we also share in His comfort.
6. If we have trouble, it helps you. If we are comforted, it helps you too.
7. We know that if you suffer with Christ, He will also comfort you.
8. We had great trouble in Asia. We felt so much pressure that we thought we would die.
9. But this made us trust God, not ourselves. God raises the dead.
10. He saved us before and will do it again.
11. You help us when you pray. Then many will thank God when He answers.
12. We are proud that we lived with honesty and godly sincerity. We didn't rely on human wisdom but on God's grace.
13. We are writing only what you can read and understand. I hope you will fully understand us later.
14. Some of you already know and are proud of us, just as we are proud of you.
15. I planned to visit you first so I could bless you twice.
16. I wanted to visit on my way to Macedonia and again on the way back.
17. Was I unsure when I made these plans? No. I don't say "Yes" and "No" at the same time.
18. God is faithful. Our message to you is not "Yes and No."
19. Jesus, the Son of God, was preached to you by me, Silas, and Timothy. He is always "Yes."
20. All of God's promises are "Yes" in Christ. That's why we say "Amen" to God through Him.

21. God makes us strong and sure in Christ. He chose us.
22. He put His Spirit in our hearts as a promise that we belong to Him.
23. I call God as my witness—I didn't come back to Corinth because I didn't want to make you sad.
24. We don't control your faith. We want to help you grow in joy, because your faith is strong.

2 Corinthians 2

1. I decided not to visit you again if it would make you sad.
2. If I make you sad, who will cheer me up?
3. I wrote to you earlier so I wouldn't be sad when I came.
4. I was very upset when I wrote. I cried a lot. I didn't want to hurt you, but to show my deep love for you.
5. Someone has caused pain—not just to me but to all of you too.
6. That person has been punished enough.
7. Now forgive and comfort him. Don't let him feel too sad.
8. I ask you to show him love.
9. I wrote to see if you would obey and forgive.
10. If you forgive someone, I forgive them too.
11. We don't want Satan to trick us. We know how he works.
12. I went to Troas to preach about Jesus. The Lord gave me a good chance to do that.
13. But I was worried because I couldn't find my friend Titus. So I left and went to Macedonia.
14. Thanks to God, who always leads us in victory through Christ.
15. Our lives spread the message of Jesus like a sweet smell.
16. To some people, that smell brings life. To others, it brings death.
17. We don't twist God's message for money. We speak honestly before God, like people sent by Him.

2 Corinthians 3

1. Are we trying to prove ourselves again? Do we need letters of approval?
2. You are our letter—written on our hearts.
3. Everyone can read your lives and see we helped lead you to Christ.
4. You show that Christ sent us. God wrote the message on your hearts, not on stone.
5. We are not strong on our own. God gives us what we need.
6. He made us able to share His new promise—through the Spirit, not just written law.
7. The old law brought death. It was written on stone, but it still had glory.
8. The new way with the Spirit has even more glory.
9. If the old law, which brought punishment, had glory—how much more glory comes from being made right with God?
10. The old glory now seems small compared to the new one.
11. If the old way had glory, the new way will last forever.
12. We are bold because we have this hope.
13. Moses covered his face so people wouldn't see the fading glory.
14. But their minds became hard. Even now, when they read the old law, a veil covers their hearts.
15. That veil is taken away only in Christ.
16. When someone turns to the Lord, the veil is removed.
17. The Lord is the Spirit, and where the Spirit of the Lord is, there is freedom.

18. All of us, with open faces, reflect the Lord's glory and are being changed to be more like Him.

2 Corinthians 4

1. God gave us this work, and we won't give up.
2. We are honest. We don't lie or twist God's word. We speak the truth clearly before God.
3. Some people can't understand the good news—it's hidden from them because they don't believe.
4. Satan has blinded their minds. They can't see the light of the good news about Christ.
5. We don't preach about ourselves. We preach that Jesus is Lord.
6. God made light shine out of darkness. He shines in our hearts to help us show others the glory of Jesus.
7. We have this treasure in jars of clay. This shows that the power is from God, not us.
8. We are troubled but not crushed. We are confused but not hopeless.
9. We are hurt but not left alone. We are knocked down but not destroyed.
10. We carry Jesus' suffering in our bodies so His life can be seen in us.
11. We face death for Jesus so others can see His life in us.
12. We are always close to death, but you get to see life.
13. We believe, so we speak.
14. God raised Jesus and will also raise us to be with Him.
15. All this is for your benefit. More people will thank God as more receive His grace.
16. We don't give up. Even if our bodies are getting weak, our spirits are getting stronger every day.
17. Our troubles are small and temporary. They are preparing something great that will last forever.
18. We don't focus on what we see now. We focus on what we can't see yet. What we see now will soon be gone, but what we can't see will last forever.

2 Corinthians 5

1. Our bodies are like tents. One day they will die, but God has a forever home in heaven for us.
2. We are tired of living in these bodies and want our new heavenly bodies.
3. We want to be covered with our new life, not left with just this one.
4. While we are in these bodies, we struggle. We want to be with God and be made new.
5. God made us for this purpose, and He gave us the Holy Spirit to show us it's true.
6. So we are always confident. Even though we are still here on earth, we know God is with us.
7. We live by faith, not by what we see.
8. We would rather leave these bodies and be with the Lord.
9. So we try to please God whether we're here or with Him.
10. Everyone must stand before Jesus to be judged. We will each receive what we deserve for what we did—good or bad.
11. We know what it means to respect the Lord, so we try to tell people about Him.
12. We're not bragging. We hope you see our true hearts and can be proud of us.
13. If we seem crazy, it's for God. If we are thinking clearly, it's for you.
14. Christ's love controls us. He died for everyone.
15. So we no longer live for ourselves. We live for Him.

16. We don't look at people the way the world does. We used to see Christ that way, but not anymore.
17. Anyone who is in Christ is a new person. The old life is gone.
18. God made peace with us through Jesus, and now He wants us to help others make peace with Him too.
19. God doesn't count our sins against us if we believe in Jesus. And we are His messengers.
20. We speak for Christ. We ask you to make peace with God.
21. Jesus never sinned, but God put our sin on Him so we could be right with God.

2 Corinthians 6

1. We work together with God, and we beg you: Don't waste the gift God gave you.
2. God says, "Now is the time! Now is the day to be saved!"
3. We try not to do anything that would stop someone from believing.
4. We show we are true servants of God by being patient in trouble, pain, and hard times.
5. We are beaten, put in jail, attacked, tired, without sleep, and sometimes without food.
6. But we stay pure, wise, kind, and full of the Holy Spirit.
7. We tell the truth and trust God's power. We use God's tools to fight for what's right.
8. Some people honor us, others shame us. Some say we are liars, but we speak the truth.
9. We are known and unknown, almost dead but still alive, hurt but not killed.
10. We are sad but still full of joy. We are poor but make others rich. We have nothing but own everything.
11. Dear friends in Corinth, we have spoken freely to you. We love you with open hearts.
12. If you feel distant, it's not because of us—it's because of your own hearts.
13. Please open your hearts to us as well.
14. Don't join with people who don't follow Jesus. You don't belong together.
15. Good and evil don't mix. Light and darkness can't be friends.
16. God's people are His temple. God lives in us.
17. So, come out from among them. Be separate, says the Lord.
18. God says, "I will be your Father, and you will be my children."

2 Corinthians 7

1. Since we have these promises from God, let's stay away from sin and live in a way that pleases Him.
2. Make room in your hearts for us. We haven't hurt or tricked anyone.
3. I don't say this to blame you. We love you and would live or die for you.
4. I'm proud of you. I have great joy even during hard times.
5. When we came to Macedonia, we had no rest. We were attacked on the outside and afraid on the inside.
6. But God, who comforts the hurting, sent Titus to encourage us.
7. He told us how much you cared, how sorry you were, and how loyal you are to me. That made me very happy.
8. I made you sad with my letter, but I don't regret it—even if I did for a little while.
9. Now I'm glad, not because you were sad, but because your sadness made you change.
10. Sadness that comes from God leads to real change and salvation. But worldly sadness brings death.

11. Look at what your godly sadness did! You cared, you defended yourself, and you wanted to make things right.
12. I didn't write that letter to hurt you. I wanted you to see how much you care and to strengthen your love.
13. We were comforted. And even more, we were happy that Titus was encouraged by you.
14. I told him you would respond well, and you didn't disappoint.
15. He remembers how you welcomed him and respected him.
16. I'm glad I can trust you in everything.

2 Corinthians 8

1. Friends, we want to tell you how God helped the churches in Macedonia.
2. They were very poor and had many troubles, but they still gave with joy.
3. They gave all they could—and more.
4. They begged us to let them help God's people.
5. They gave themselves to the Lord first, then to us.
6. So we asked Titus to help you finish the giving you started.
7. You do well in everything—faith, speech, knowledge, love. Now do well in giving too.
8. I'm not forcing you, but I want to test your love by comparing it with others.
9. You know Jesus was rich, but He became poor to make you rich.
10. You were the first to give last year. Now finish what you started.
11. Give according to what you have.
12. If you're willing, your gift is accepted based on what you have, not what you don't.
13. I don't want you to suffer while others rest. I want fairness.
14. Right now, you have more. Later, they may have more. Help each other.
15. The Bible says, "The one who gathered much didn't have too much, and the one who gathered little didn't have too little."
16. Thanks to God for putting care in Titus's heart for you.
17. He agreed to come and wanted to help.
18. We are also sending another believer who is well known for preaching the good news.
19. He was chosen to help us take this gift to the needy.
20. We want to do everything right so no one can blame us.
21. We try to do what is right in God's eyes and in people's eyes.
22. We are also sending another brother who has proven he is trustworthy.
23. Titus is my partner. The others are messengers from the churches.
24. Show them your love so everyone sees that our pride in you is true.

2 Corinthians 9

1. I don't really need to write more about helping God's people.
2. I know you want to help. I've told others about your eagerness, and your example encouraged them.
3. But I'm sending these men to make sure your gift is ready.
4. If some Macedonians come with me and find out you're not ready, we'll be embarrassed—and so will you.
5. So I want your giving to be a willing gift, not something forced.
6. Remember this: Whoever plants a little gets a little. Whoever plants a lot gets a lot.
7. Each person should give what they decided in their heart. Don't give because you have to. God loves cheerful givers.
8. God can give you everything you need, so you can always help others.

9. The Scriptures say, "He gives to the poor, and his goodness lasts forever."
10. God gives seed to farmers and will give you what you need to give to others.
11. You will be made rich in every way so you can be generous.
12. Your gifts will help people and make them thank God.
13. When you give, it proves your faith is real.
14. The people you help will pray for you and thank God for you.
15. Thanks be to God for His amazing gift!

2 Corinthians 10

1. I, Paul, appeal to you with the gentleness of Christ.
2. Some think I am bold in my letters but weak in person. I ask that I won't have to be bold when I come.
3. We live in this world, but we don't fight the way the world does.
4. We use God's power to destroy strongholds—wrong thoughts and lies.
5. We destroy arguments and proud ideas that go against God. We make every thought obey Christ.
6. We are ready to correct disobedience once you obey fully.
7. Look at the facts. If someone thinks they belong to Christ, remember—we do too.
8. Even if I talk boldly about my authority, I'm not ashamed. God gave it to build you up, not tear you down.
9. I don't want to scare you with my letters.
10. Some say, "His letters are strong, but he's weak in person and not a good speaker."
11. Those people should know that what I write, I will also do when I come.
12. We won't compare ourselves to others who brag. They only measure themselves by each other.
13. We will stay within the work God gave us.
14. We were the first to bring you the good news about Jesus.
15. We're not taking credit for someone else's work.
16. We hope your faith grows so we can preach in new places.
17. "If anyone brags, they should brag about the Lord."
18. God is the one who approves people—not those who praise themselves.

2 Corinthians 11

1. I hope you'll be patient while I speak a little more. I care deeply for you.
2. I promised you to Christ like a bride to her husband.
3. But I'm afraid your minds will be tricked like Eve was by the devil.
4. Some people preach a different Jesus or a different message. You listen too easily.
5. I may not speak fancy words, but I do have knowledge.
6. I taught you the truth clearly.
7. I didn't take money from you when I preached. Was that wrong?
8. I accepted help from other churches so I wouldn't be a burden to you.
9. When I needed help, the believers from Macedonia helped me.
10. I'll keep doing this so no one can say I took advantage of you.
11. I do love you—God knows it.
12. I won't stop helping for free so false teachers can't pretend to be like us.
13. These people are fake apostles. They pretend to be from Christ.
14. Even Satan pretends to be an angel of light.

15. So it's no surprise his servants pretend to be good too.
16. I'll say this again—don't think I'm foolish. But even if I am, listen to me.
17. I'm speaking like a fool now, like someone who brags.
18. Others brag, so I'll brag a little too.
19. You put up with fools gladly—even though you are so wise.
20. You let people boss you around and hurt you.
21. I'm ashamed to say it, but I've been too weak for that.
22. Are they Jews? So am I. Are they from Abraham? So am I.
23. Are they servants of Christ? I am more. I've worked harder.
24. I've been in jail more, beaten more, and close to death many times.
25. Five times I got 39 lashes. Three times I was beaten with rods. Once I was stoned.
26. I was shipwrecked three times and once spent a night and day in the sea.
27. I've faced dangers from rivers, robbers, my own people, and strangers.
28. I've been hungry, cold, and without sleep. On top of that, I worry about all the churches.
29. When others are weak, I feel it too.
30. If I must brag, I'll brag about my weakness.
31. God knows I'm telling the truth.
32. In Damascus, the governor tried to arrest me.
33. But I escaped in a basket through a window in the wall.

2 Corinthians 12

1. I must go on bragging, though it doesn't help.
2. I know a man (he means himself) who was taken up to heaven.
3. It happened 14 years ago. Only God knows how it happened.
4. He heard things too amazing to explain.
5. I won't brag about that, only about my weakness.
6. Even if I did brag, I'd be telling the truth.
7. To keep me from being proud, God gave me a problem—a "thorn" in my body.
8. I begged God three times to take the pain away.
9. But God said, "My grace is enough. My power works best in weakness."
10. So I'm happy to be weak, so Christ's power can work in me.
11. That's why I'm okay with hard times, insults, and trouble—when I'm weak, I'm strong.
12. I've been a true apostle. I showed patience, miracles, and signs.
13. You were treated just like other churches—except I didn't ask you for money. Forgive me for that.
14. I'm ready to visit again. I still won't be a burden.
15. I will gladly spend everything I have—even myself—for you.
16. I never tricked you.
17. Did I take advantage of you through anyone I sent?
18. I asked Titus to visit. He didn't take anything from you, and we acted the same way.
19. You think we've been defending ourselves, but we speak before God. Everything we do is to help you.
20. I worry that when I come, I won't find you the way I hope.
21. I might have to mourn because some of you still live in sin and haven't changed.

2 Corinthians 13

1. This is my third visit. The Bible says two or three witnesses must agree to prove something.
2. I warned you before, and now I warn you again—if I come and find sin, I won't hold back.
3. You want proof that Christ speaks through me? You'll get it. He's not weak—He is powerful.
4. He was killed in weakness, but now He lives by God's power. We are weak, but we live with His power too.
5. Test yourselves. Make sure your faith is real. Jesus lives in you—unless your faith is fake.
6. I hope you'll see that our faith is real.
7. We pray you do what's right—not to prove we're right, but so you live right even if we seem weak.
8. We can't go against the truth—only for it.
9. We are glad when we are weak and you are strong.
10. That's why I'm writing this now, so I won't have to be harsh when I come.
11. Finally, be happy. Work to grow in faith. Encourage each other. Be united. Live in peace. Then God's love and peace will be with you.
12. Greet one another with a holy kiss.
13. All God's people say hello.
14. May Jesus' grace, God's love, and the Holy Spirit's friendship be with you all.

– Galatians –

Salvation is by grace through faith—not by following the law.

Galatians 1

1. This letter is from Paul. I was chosen by God, not by people, to be an apostle. God raised Jesus from the dead.
2. All the believers with me send greetings to the churches in Galatia.
3. May God the Father and our Lord Jesus Christ give you grace and peace.
4. Jesus gave His life for our sins, to rescue us from this evil world—just as God planned.
5. To God be glory forever. Amen.
6. I'm shocked that you are turning away from God so quickly.
7. You are believing a different message, but it's not really good news.
8. Even if we—or an angel—preach a different message, let them be punished.
9. I repeat: if anyone preaches a different message than the one you received, they should be punished.
10. Am I trying to please people or God? If I only wanted to please people, I wouldn't be Christ's servant.
11. I want you to know the good news I shared was not made up by people.
12. I didn't get it from anyone. Jesus Himself showed it to me.
13. You know how I used to live. I hurt God's church badly and tried to destroy it.
14. I followed the Jewish laws better than many others my age.
15. But God chose me before I was born. He showed me His Son so I could tell others about Him.
16. When God called me, I didn't ask people what to do.
17. I didn't go to Jerusalem to see the apostles. I went to Arabia, then came back to Damascus.
18. Three years later, I went to Jerusalem to visit Peter. I stayed with him for 15 days.
19. I didn't see any other apostles except James, the Lord's brother.
20. I promise I'm telling the truth.

21. Then I went to the areas of Syria and Cilicia.
22. The churches in Judea didn't know me personally.
23. They only heard, "The man who used to hurt us now tells people about the faith he tried to destroy."
24. And they praised God because of me.

Galatians 2

1. Fourteen years later, I went to Jerusalem again with Barnabas. I also brought Titus.
2. I went because God told me to go. I shared the message I preach to the Gentiles.
3. Even though Titus is not a Jew, no one made him get circumcised.
4. Some fake believers secretly came to spy on us and try to take away the freedom we have in Christ.
5. But we didn't give in to them for one minute. We wanted you to know the truth.
6. The leaders in Jerusalem didn't add anything to my message.
7. They saw that God had sent me to the Gentiles, just like He sent Peter to the Jews.
8. God gave both of us the power to do this work.
9. James, Peter, and John accepted Barnabas and me. They shook our hands to show we were partners.
10. They only asked us to help the poor, and we were already doing that.
11. When Peter came to Antioch, I had to correct him face to face.
12. At first, he ate with Gentiles. But when some Jews came, he stopped eating with them because he was afraid.
13. Other Jews followed Peter's example, even Barnabas.
14. I told Peter, "You are a Jew, but you live like a Gentile. So why are you trying to make Gentiles follow Jewish rules?"
15. We are Jews, not Gentile sinners.
16. But we know no one is made right with God by following the law. Only by faith in Jesus.
17. If we seek to be made right through Christ, does that make Christ a sinner? No way!
18. If I rebuild what I once destroyed, then I really am guilty.
19. The law showed me I was wrong, so I died to the law. Now I live for God.
20. I died with Christ. Now Christ lives in me. I live by faith in Him. He loved me and gave His life for me.
21. If we could be made right by the law, then Christ died for nothing.

Galatians 3

1. You foolish Galatians! Who tricked you? You saw Jesus clearly when I preached.
2. Did you receive the Holy Spirit by following the law? No—you received it by believing.
3. Are you so foolish? You started with the Spirit. Do you think you can finish by human effort?
4. Did you suffer for nothing?
5. Does God give you His Spirit and do miracles because you obey the law? No—it's because you believe.
6. Abraham believed God, and God accepted him.
7. Real children of Abraham are those who believe.
8. The Scriptures said long ago that God would bless the Gentiles too, because of their faith.
9. So all who believe like Abraham are blessed like him.
10. Those who try to follow the law are under a curse, because no one can keep it all.

11. The Bible says, "The right people live by faith."
12. The law is not based on faith. It says, "Do these things and live."
13. Christ took the curse for us when He died on the cross.
14. He did this so the blessing given to Abraham would come to the Gentiles, and we could receive the Spirit by faith.
15. Let me explain with an example. When a person makes a promise, no one can change it.
16. God made promises to Abraham and his "child"—that child is Christ.
17. The law came 430 years later. It doesn't cancel God's promise.
18. If the blessing depends on the law, then it doesn't depend on the promise. But God gave it to Abraham as a promise.
19. So why was the law given? It was added because of sin, until Christ came.
20. The law was given through angels and a mediator, but God made His promise directly.
21. Does the law go against God's promise? No. The law can't give life. Only faith in Jesus can do that.
22. The Scriptures show that all people are trapped in sin. The only way out is through faith in Jesus.
23. Before faith came, we were guarded by the law.
24. The law was like a teacher leading us to Christ so we would be made right by faith.
25. Now that faith has come, we don't need the law like that anymore.
26. You are all God's children through faith in Jesus.
27. All who were baptized into Christ are now clothed with Christ.
28. There is no Jew or Gentile, no slave or free, no man or woman. You are all one in Christ.
29. If you belong to Christ, then you are Abraham's children and part of God's promise.

Galatians 4

1. A child who will inherit everything is still like a servant until they grow up.
2. The child must follow rules set by guardians until the right time.
3. We were like that—stuck under the law.
4. But when the right time came, God sent His Son, born of a woman, under the law.
5. Jesus came to free us from the law so we could become God's children.
6. Because we are His children, God sent His Spirit into our hearts. We call Him "Father."
7. You are no longer a servant. You are a child of God. And if you are His child, you also receive His blessings.
8. Before, you didn't know God. You served false gods.
9. But now you know God—or better, God knows you. So why go back to weak and useless rules?
10. You follow special days, months, and years. That worries me.
11. I fear my work for you may have been wasted.
12. I beg you to be like me. I used to follow those rules too, but I stopped.
13. You remember when I first preached to you—even though I was sick.
14. You didn't treat me badly. You welcomed me like I was an angel or even Jesus.
15. What happened to your joy? You would have given me your own eyes!
16. Have I become your enemy because I tell you the truth?
17. Others are trying to win you over, but not for good reasons.

18. It's good to be eager for what's right—whether I'm with you or not.

19. My dear children, I feel pain again like a mother giving birth until Christ is fully in your hearts.

20. I wish I could be with you now and speak gently. I don't know what to do with you.

21. You who want to follow the law—do you know what the law really says?

22. Abraham had two sons—one by a slave woman and one by a free woman.

23. The slave woman's son was born by human effort. The free woman's son was born through God's promise.

24. This story shows two different agreements: One is from Mount Sinai and brings slavery. That is Hagar.

25. Hagar stands for Mount Sinai and the earthly Jerusalem, where people are still slaves.

26. But the heavenly Jerusalem is free, and she is our mother.

27. The Bible says the woman who couldn't have children will now have more than the one who had many.

28. Brothers and sisters, you are children of promise, just like Isaac.

29. Long ago, the son born by human effort picked on the son born by God's Spirit. It's the same now.

30. But what does the Bible say? "Send away the slave woman and her son."

31. So we are not children of the slave woman. We are children of the free woman.

Galatians 5

1. Christ set us free. So stay free. Don't go back to being slaves under the law.

2. If you get circumcised to be right with God, then Christ means nothing to you.

3. If you choose to follow the law, you must obey all of it.

4. If you try to be right by the law, you are separated from Christ and His grace.

5. But we wait for God to accept us because of faith and the Spirit.

6. In Christ, it doesn't matter if you're circumcised or not. What matters is faith that shows itself through love.

7. You were doing well. Who made you stop following the truth?

8. That idea didn't come from God.

9. A little wrong teaching can ruin everything.

10. I trust the Lord will help you stay on track. But the one confusing you will be punished.

11. If I still preached circumcision, I wouldn't be attacked. But I don't—so I am.

12. I wish those who are causing trouble would stop completely.

13. You were called to be free. But don't use freedom to do wrong. Instead, serve one another with love.

14. The whole law can be summed up like this: "Love your neighbor as yourself."

15. But if you fight and hurt each other, be careful—you might destroy one another.

16. Live by the Spirit, and you won't do what your sinful self wants.

17. Your sinful self fights the Spirit. They are against each other.

18. If the Spirit leads you, you're not under the law.

19. The things the sinful self does are clear: sexual sin, hate, jealousy, anger, selfishness, fighting, envy, and more.

20. People who keep doing these things will not be part of God's kingdom.

21. But the Spirit gives us love, joy, peace, patience, kindness, goodness, faithfulness, gentleness, and self-control.

22. There's no law against these things.

23. Those who belong to Christ have put their sinful ways to death.
24. Since we live by the Spirit, let's walk with the Spirit.
25. Let's not be proud, make trouble, or be jealous of each other.

Galatians 6

1. If another believer does something wrong, help them gently. But be careful not to fall into the same sin.
2. Help each other with your problems. That's how you obey Christ.
3. If you think you're better than others, you're fooling yourself.
4. Don't compare yourself to others. Look at your own actions.
5. Each person is responsible for their own life.
6. Anyone who is taught God's Word should share good things with their teacher.
7. Don't fool yourself. You can't trick God. You will get back what you plant.
8. If you live only to please yourself, you'll end up with nothing. But if you live to please the Spirit, you'll have life forever.
9. Don't get tired of doing good. At the right time, you'll be rewarded.
10. When you can, do good to everyone—especially to other believers.
11. Look! I'm writing this myself in big letters.
12. Some people want you to be circumcised so they can look good to others.
13. They don't even follow the whole law themselves.
14. I will only brag about one thing—Jesus dying on the cross. That's what matters most.
15. Being circumcised or not doesn't matter. What matters is becoming a new person in Christ.
16. Peace and mercy to everyone who follows this truth—and to God's people.
17. Don't let anyone give me trouble. I carry the marks of Jesus on my body.
18. My friends, may the grace of Jesus be with your spirit. Amen.

– Ephesians –

God unites all believers in Christ and calls them to live in love and unity.

Ephesians 1

1. This letter is from Paul. God chose me to be an apostle of Jesus. I'm writing to God's people in Ephesus who believe in Jesus.
2. I pray that God gives you grace and peace.
3. Praise God! He has blessed us through Christ with every spiritual blessing.
4. Before the world began, God chose us to be His holy people through Jesus.
5. He planned to adopt us as His children through Jesus. That made Him happy.
6. We thank God for His grace, which He gave us through Jesus.
7. Christ's blood paid for our sins. We are forgiven because of God's great grace.
8. God gave us so much wisdom and understanding.
9. He showed us His secret plan, which He wanted to do through Christ.
10. The plan was to bring everything together under Christ—things in heaven and things on earth.
11. In Christ, we were chosen to be God's people. That was always God's plan.
12. We who trusted Christ first should praise Him.
13. You also heard the truth and believed the good news that saved you. Then God gave you the Holy Spirit.

14. The Spirit is God's promise that we belong to Him. He guarantees our future until we receive everything He promised.
15. I've heard about your faith and love for all God's people.
16. I always thank God for you and pray for you.
17. I ask God to help you know Him better.
18. I pray that you see the amazing future God has for you.
19. God's power is very great for us who believe. It's the same power that raised Jesus from the dead.
20. God gave Jesus the highest place in heaven.
21. Jesus is above all leaders and powers, now and forever.
22. God put everything under Jesus' power and made Him the head of the church.
23. The church is Christ's body. He fills everything in every way.

Ephesians 2

1. You were once dead in your sins.
2. You used to live like the world, following the devil and doing wrong.
3. All of us once followed our selfish desires and were headed for punishment.
4. But God is full of mercy and love.
5. Even when we were dead in sin, He made us alive with Christ. This is a gift.
6. God raised us up with Christ and gave us a place with Him in heaven.
7. He did this to show His kindness through Christ forever.
8. You are saved by grace through faith. It's not your own doing.
9. You didn't earn it, so no one can brag.
10. God made us to do good things. He planned this long ago.
11. You used to be Gentiles. The Jews called you "uncircumcised."
12. At that time, you were without Christ. You were far from God.
13. But now, because of Jesus, you have been brought near.
14. Christ is our peace. He made Jews and Gentiles into one group.
15. He broke down the wall between us. He ended the law with its rules.
16. He made peace through the cross and joined us together.
17. Jesus brought the good news of peace to everyone—those far away and those near.
18. Through Him, we all have access to God by the Spirit.
19. You are no longer outsiders. You belong to God's family.
20. God's house is built on the teachings of the apostles and prophets. Jesus is the cornerstone.
21. The whole building is joined together in Christ.
22. And you are being built into a place where God lives by His Spirit.

Ephesians 3

1. I, Paul, am a prisoner because I serve Christ and help you Gentiles.
2. You've heard how God gave me this special job.
3. God showed me His secret plan, which I already wrote about briefly.
4. When you read it, you will understand what I know about Christ.
5. Long ago, people didn't know this plan. But now the Spirit has revealed it to the apostles and prophets.
6. The secret is this: Gentiles are part of the same family. They share in God's promises through Christ.
7. I became a servant of this message by God's gift and power.

8. Even though I am the least of God's people, He gave me the job of telling the Gentiles about Christ's riches.
9. I explain the plan that God kept hidden for ages.
10. Now His plan is being shown through the church.
11. This was always God's plan, made through Jesus.
12. Because of Jesus, we can come to God with confidence and faith.
13. So don't lose heart because I'm suffering. It's for your good.
14. I kneel before the Father.
15. All families in heaven and on earth come from Him.
16. I pray God gives you strength through His Spirit.
17. I pray Christ lives in your hearts through faith. I pray you are strong in love.
18. I want you to understand how wide, long, high, and deep His love is.
19. Christ's love is greater than we can fully know. But I pray you will experience it.
20. God can do more than we ask or imagine. His power works in us.
21. May He be praised in the church and in Christ forever. Amen.

Ephesians 4

1. I, Paul, a prisoner for the Lord, beg you to live the way God wants.
2. Be humble, gentle, and patient. Show love by putting up with each other.
3. Try hard to stay united and live in peace.
4. There is one body and one Spirit—just like you were called to one hope.
5. One Lord, one faith, one baptism.
6. One God and Father of all, who is over, through, and in everything.
7. Christ gave each of us a gift by His grace.
8. The Bible says, "He went up and gave gifts to people."
9. "He went up" means He also came down to earth.
10. The One who came down is the same One who went up higher than the heavens to fill everything.
11. Christ gave us leaders—apostles, prophets, preachers, and teachers.
12. Their job is to prepare God's people to serve and build up the church.
13. Then we will all be united in faith and grow to be more like Christ.
14. We won't be like babies anymore—easily tricked by lies.
15. Instead, we will speak the truth with love and grow to be like Christ in every way.
16. Christ makes the whole body work together. Each part helps, and the body grows stronger in love.
17. I tell you this: Don't live like unbelievers. Their thinking is empty.
18. They don't understand, and they are far from God because of their hard hearts.
19. They do whatever they want, and they don't care what's right.
20. But that's not how you learned about Christ.
21. You heard the truth about Jesus.
22. So leave your old life behind. That old life was full of sin and lies.
23. Let the Spirit change your thinking.
24. Put on your new self, made to be like God—full of goodness and truth.
25. Stop lying. Tell the truth, because we all belong to each other.
26. If you get angry, don't sin. Don't stay angry all day.
27. Don't give the devil a chance.
28. Anyone who stole must stop stealing and work hard so they can help others.

29. Don't say bad things. Speak words that help and build up.
30. Don't make the Holy Spirit sad. He marked you as God's own.
31. Get rid of anger, yelling, and mean talk. Don't be hateful.
32. Be kind and forgive each other, just like God forgave you.

Ephesians 5

1. Be like God, because you are His children.
2. Live with love, just like Christ loved us and gave Himself for us.
3. Don't even talk about sexual sin, greed, or other dirty things. These don't belong in your life.
4. Don't use bad language, jokes, or rude talk. Instead, thank God.
5. You can be sure: No one who is sexually sinful, greedy, or worships stuff instead of God will be in God's kingdom.
6. Don't let anyone fool you with empty words. These sins bring God's anger.
7. Don't be partners with people who do wrong.
8. You used to live in darkness, but now you are light in the Lord. So live like children of light.
9. The light brings goodness, right living, and truth.
10. Try to do what pleases the Lord.
11. Don't take part in bad things. Instead, show they are wrong.
12. People do shameful things in secret.
13. But the light shows what's really going on.
14. That's why it says, "Wake up! Rise from the dead, and Christ will shine on you."
15. Be careful how you live. Be wise, not foolish.
16. Use your time well, because the days are evil.
17. Don't be foolish. Learn what the Lord wants.
18. Don't get drunk. That leads to wrong choices. Instead, be filled with the Spirit.
19. Speak to each other with songs and praises to God.
20. Always give thanks to God the Father in the name of Jesus.
21. Respect and serve one another because you respect Christ.
22. Wives, follow your husbands like you follow the Lord.
23. The husband leads the wife like Christ leads the church.
24. The church follows Christ, so wives should follow their husbands in everything.
25. Husbands, love your wives like Christ loved the church. He gave His life for her.
26. He made the church holy by washing it with the Word.
27. He wanted the church to be beautiful, with no sin or fault.
28. Husbands should love their wives as they love their own bodies.
29. No one hates their own body. They feed and care for it—just like Christ does for the church.
30. We are part of His body.
31. The Bible says, "A man will leave his parents and be joined to his wife. The two will become one."
32. This is about Christ and the church.
33. Each of you must love your wife, and wives must respect their husbands.

Ephesians 6

1. Children, obey your parents because you belong to the Lord. This is the right thing to do.

2. "Honor your father and mother." This is the first command with a promise:
3. "If you honor them, you will have a good life and live a long time."
4. Fathers, don't make your children angry. Raise them to know and follow the Lord.
5. Servants, obey your masters with respect. Do it like you would obey Christ.
6. Don't just work hard when they're watching. Work from your heart like you're serving God.
7. Work with a good attitude, as if you are working for the Lord, not for people.
8. Remember, the Lord will reward everyone who does good—whether they are free or not.
9. Masters, treat your servants well. Don't threaten them. You both serve the same Master in heaven, and He treats everyone the same.
10. Be strong with the Lord's power.
11. Put on all of God's armor so you can stand against the devil's tricks.
12. We're not fighting people. We're fighting evil spirits and unseen powers.
13. So put on God's armor. Then when trouble comes, you'll stand strong.
14. Stand firm by:

– Wearing truth like a belt,
– Doing right like a chestplate,
– Being ready to share the good news of peace,

15. Use faith like a shield to stop the devil's attacks.
16. Wear salvation like a helmet. Use God's Word like a sword.
17. Pray all the time with the Spirit. Stay alert and keep praying for all God's people.
18. Pray for me too. Ask God to help me speak His message clearly and bravely.
19. I am in jail now because I preach this message, but I want to keep speaking it without fear.
20. Tychicus will tell you how I'm doing. He is a faithful brother in the Lord.
21. I'm sending him to encourage you and let you know everything.
22. Peace and love to all who believe in Jesus.
23. God's grace be with everyone who loves Jesus Christ with a true heart.

– Philippians –

Paul writes with joy, encouraging the church to stay strong and united in Christ.

Philippians 1

1. This letter is from Paul and Timothy. We serve Jesus. We're writing to all God's people in Philippi, including church leaders.
2. May God give you grace and peace.
3. I thank God every time I remember you.
4. I always pray for you with joy.
5. You have helped share the good news from the beginning until now.
6. I'm sure God will keep working in you until the job is finished when Jesus returns.
7. It's right for me to feel this way because I love you. We've shared God's grace—even while I'm in jail and defending the good news.
8. God knows how much I care about you with the love of Jesus.
9. I pray your love grows more and more with knowledge and understanding.
10. I want you to know what's best and to live clean lives until Jesus returns.
11. May your lives be full of good things that come from Jesus, bringing praise to God.
12. I want you to know that my time in jail has helped spread the good news.

13. Everyone here knows I'm in jail for Christ.
14. Most believers are now more brave to speak about Jesus because of my chains.
15. Some preach about Christ with good hearts. Others do it with jealousy or to cause trouble for me.
16. The first group loves me and knows I'm here to defend the good news.
17. The others preach for selfish reasons, hoping to make things worse for me.
18. But I don't care. Christ is being talked about, and that makes me happy. I will keep rejoicing.
19. I know your prayers and the help from the Spirit of Jesus will lead to my freedom.
20. I hope I won't be afraid, but that I'll be bold. I want Christ to be honored in my life or death.
21. To me, living means serving Christ, and dying is even better.
22. If I stay alive, I can do more work for God. I don't know which is better.
23. I want to leave and be with Christ, which is better for me.
24. But staying alive is better for you.
25. I believe I will stay and help you grow in joy and faith.
26. Then you will be even more thankful for me when I visit again.
27. Live in a way that honors Jesus. Whether I see you or hear about you, I hope to know you're standing strong together.
28. Don't be afraid of those who fight against you. That shows they will lose and you will win—with God.
29. God gave you the gift of believing in Christ, and also the gift of suffering for Him.
30. You are going through the same struggle you saw me face, and now you know I'm still facing it.

Philippians 2

1. If Christ has helped you, if His love comforts you, if you share in the Spirit, then…
2. Make me happy by working together, loving one another, and being united.
3. Don't be selfish. Don't try to look better than others. Be humble.
4. Care about others, not just yourself.
5. Think and act like Jesus.
6. Even though He was God, He didn't try to stay equal with God.
7. He gave that up and became a servant. He was born as a man.
8. He obeyed God completely—even when it meant dying on a cross.
9. So God gave Him the highest place and the name above all names.
10. One day, everyone will bow to Jesus.
11. And everyone will say, "Jesus Christ is Lord," to bring glory to God.
12. My friends, obey God just like you did when I was with you. Keep doing it now when I'm not there.
13. God is working in you, helping you want to do what pleases Him.
14. Do everything without complaining or arguing.
15. Be pure and innocent, like God's children, shining like lights in the world.
16. Hold tightly to the word of life. Then I will be proud I didn't work for nothing.
17. Even if I give my life for you, I am glad and full of joy.
18. You should be happy too and rejoice with me.
19. I hope to send Timothy to you soon. He will bring back good news.
20. He really cares about you.
21. Most people only care about themselves, not Jesus.
22. But you know Timothy has helped me like a son.

23. I hope to send him soon, as soon as I know what will happen to me.
24. I trust the Lord will let me come too.
25. I also think I should send Epaphroditus back to you. He is my brother and helper.
26. He misses you and was very upset that you heard he was sick.
27. He was really sick—almost died. But God healed him.
28. I'm sending him back so you will be happy and I will worry less.
29. Welcome him with joy. Respect people like him.
30. He almost died helping me. He risked his life to serve Christ when you couldn't.

Philippians 3

1. My brothers and sisters, always be joyful in the Lord.
2. Watch out for people who try to make you follow rules to be saved.
3. True believers worship by the Spirit, not by religious rituals.
4. If anyone could brag about following the rules, it would be me.
5. I was circumcised on the eighth day, a true Israelite, from the tribe of Benjamin.
6. I followed all the Jewish laws. I even tried to stop the church.
7. But everything I used to think was important, I now think is worthless.
8. Knowing Jesus is more valuable than anything else. I gave up everything for Him.
9. I don't try to be right by following the law. I am right with God because I trust in Christ.
10. I want to know Jesus. I want to share in His suffering and rise from the dead like Him.
11. I haven't reached my goal yet, but I keep trying.
12. I keep running to win the prize Jesus promised me.
13. I forget what's behind and reach for what's ahead.
14. I run toward the goal to win the prize God calls me to through Jesus.
15. Mature people should think this way. If not, God will show you.
16. Let's keep living by what we've already learned.
17. Follow my example. Watch those who live the way we taught you.
18. Many people live like enemies of the cross. It makes me cry.
19. They think only about this life. Their end is destruction.
20. But we are citizens of heaven. We are waiting for Jesus to return.
21. He will change our weak bodies to be like His glorious body.

Philippians 4

1. My dear brothers and sisters, I love you. Stay strong in the Lord.
2. I ask Euodia and Syntyche to agree in the Lord.
3. Help them—they worked hard with me to share the good news.
4. Always be joyful in the Lord. I say it again—be joyful!
5. Be kind to everyone. The Lord is near.
6. Don't worry. Pray about everything. Thank God, and ask Him for what you need.
7. Then God's peace will guard your hearts and minds through Christ.
8. Think about what is true, noble, right, pure, lovely, and good.
9. Do what you learned and saw from me. God's peace will be with you.
10. I'm so happy you care about me again. I know you always did, but had no chance to help.

11. I'm not saying this because I need anything. I've learned to be content.
12. I know how to live with a little or a lot. I've learned the secret of being content in any situation.
13. I can do everything through Christ who gives me strength.
14. Still, thank you for helping me when I was in trouble.
15. You were the only church that helped me when I left Macedonia.
16. Even when I was in Thessalonica, you sent help again and again.
17. I'm not asking for more. I want you to be rewarded for giving.
18. I have everything I need now. Your gift was like a sweet-smelling offering to God.
19. My God will meet all your needs through Jesus.
20. Glory to God forever and ever. Amen.
21. Say hello to every believer. The people with me say hello too.
22. All God's people here send greetings—especially those from Caesar's house.
23. May the grace of Jesus be with you all.

– Colossians –

Jesus is above all, and believers are complete in Him.

Colossians 1

1. This letter is from Paul, chosen by God to be an apostle, and from Timothy our brother.
2. We're writing to God's people in Colossae, who trust in Christ. May God give you grace and peace.
3. We always thank God when we pray for you.
4. We've heard about your faith in Jesus and your love for others.
5. You have this hope because you know what's waiting for you in heaven.
6. The good news is spreading all over the world. It's changing lives—just like it changed yours.
7. Epaphras taught you this. He is our friend and a faithful servant of Christ.
8. He told us about the love you have through the Spirit.
9. Since we heard about you, we haven't stopped praying for you.
10. We ask God to help you know His will and to live in a way that pleases Him.
11. May you do good, know God better, and have His strength and patience.
12. Always thank the Father. He made you ready to share in His blessings.
13. He saved us from darkness and brought us into His Son's kingdom.
14. His Son, Jesus, forgives our sins.
15. Jesus shows us what God is like. He is over all things.
16. Everything in heaven and on earth was made through Him.
17. He existed before everything and holds it all together.
18. He is the head of the church. He rose from the dead first. He is the most important one.
19. God was pleased to live fully in Jesus.
20. Through Jesus, God brought peace by the blood Jesus shed on the cross.
21. You were once far from God. You did wrong and were His enemies.
22. But now, Jesus has brought you close through His death to make you holy and clean.
23. But you must keep your faith strong and not move away from the good news.
24. I'm glad to suffer for you. I do this to help the church, which is Christ's body.
25. God gave me this job to help you by sharing His message fully.
26. The message was hidden for a long time but is now shown to His people.

27. God wanted everyone to know that the riches of this mystery include the Gentiles too. And the mystery is this: Christ lives in you.
28. So we tell everyone about Christ, teaching them to be wise so they can be complete in Him.
29. I work hard and struggle for this, using the strength Christ gives me.

Colossians 2

1. I want you to know how hard I've worked for you, for the people in Laodicea, and for others who haven't met me.
2. I want you to be encouraged and united in love, with full understanding of God's truth.
3. All the treasures of wisdom and knowledge are found in Christ.
4. I tell you this so no one tricks you with smooth words.
5. I'm not there with you, but I'm happy to see your strong faith and order.
6. Keep living in Christ, just like you started.
7. Stay rooted in Him. Keep growing. Be strong in faith and always thankful.
8. Don't let anyone fool you with empty ideas based on human thinking instead of Christ.
9. All of God lives fully in Christ in a human body.
10. Christ is in charge of everything. You have everything you need in Him.
11. In Christ, you were changed inside. This is not like regular circumcision. It's a new life.
12. When you were baptized, you were buried with Christ and raised to new life through faith.
13. You were dead in your sins, but God made you alive with Christ. He forgave all your sins.
14. He erased the record of rules against us by nailing it to the cross.
15. He defeated evil powers and showed His victory over them.
16. So don't let anyone judge you about food, drink, or special days.
17. These things were only shadows. Christ is the real thing.
18. Don't let anyone trick you by acting super humble or worshiping angels.
19. Those people don't hold on to Christ, the head. The whole body grows when it's connected to Him.
20. You died with Christ to the world's rules, so don't live by them anymore.
21. Don't follow rules like "Don't touch this" or "Don't eat that."
22. These are human commands that don't last.
23. These rules seem wise, but they don't really help stop sinful desires.

Colossians 3

1. You were raised with Christ. So think about what's in heaven, not just on earth.
2. Keep your mind on things above.
3. Your old life is gone. Your new life is hidden with Christ in God.
4. When Christ appears, you will appear with Him in glory.
5. So get rid of sinful things—sexual sin, greed, and wrong desires.
6. God is angry about these things.
7. You used to do them, but not anymore.
8. Now put away anger, hate, lies, and dirty language.
9. Don't lie to each other. You took off your old self and put on the new self.
10. The new self is being made to be like God.
11. It doesn't matter if you are Jew or Gentile, rich or poor. Christ is what matters.

12. You are God's chosen people. Be kind, humble, gentle, patient, and forgiving.
13. Forgive others as God forgave you.
14. Love is the most important thing. It brings everything together.
15. Let the peace of Christ rule your heart. Be thankful.
16. Let Christ's message live in you. Teach and encourage each other with wisdom, songs, and thanks to God.
17. Whatever you do or say, do it in the name of Jesus and give thanks to God.
18. Wives, follow your husbands.
19. Husbands, love your wives and don't be harsh.
20. Children, obey your parents. This pleases the Lord.
21. Fathers, don't make your children angry.
22. Workers, obey your bosses and do your best even when they're not watching. Do it for God.
23. Work hard like you're working for the Lord, not for people.
24. The Lord will reward you.
25. But anyone who does wrong will be punished fairly. God treats everyone the same.

Colossians 4

1. Masters, be fair and kind to your workers. You have a Master in heaven too.
2. Never stop praying. Be thankful and stay alert.
3. Pray for us too, that God will open doors for the message of Christ.
4. Pray that I can speak clearly.
5. Be wise with people who don't believe. Use your time well.
6. Speak kindly and wisely. Know how to answer everyone.
7. Tychicus will tell you all about me. He is a dear brother and faithful servant.
8. I'm sending him to encourage you.
9. Onesimus is coming too. He is one of you and a faithful friend.
10. Aristarchus, who is in jail with me, sends greetings. So does Mark, Barnabas's cousin.
11. Jesus (called Justus) also sends greetings. These are the only Jews working with me for God's kingdom.
12. Epaphras, one of you, prays hard for you. He wants you to be strong and do what God wants.
13. I know how hard he works for you and for people in Laodicea and Hierapolis.
14. Luke, the doctor, and Demas say hello.
15. Greet the believers in Laodicea and at Nympha's house church.
16. After reading this letter, share it with the Laodicean church. Read their letter too.
17. Tell Archippus: Finish the work the Lord gave you.
18. I, Paul, am writing this final part myself. Remember that I'm in jail. May grace be with you.

– 1 Thessalonians –

Paul encourages believers to stay faithful and look forward to Jesus' return.

1 Thessalonians 1

1. This letter is from Paul, Silas, and Timothy. We are writing to the church in Thessalonica. You belong to God the Father and the Lord Jesus Christ. May God give you grace and peace.
2. We always thank God for you and pray for you.
3. We remember your faith, your love, and your hope in Jesus.
4. God loves you and chose you.
5. When we told you the good news, it came with power, the Holy Spirit, and

6. full confidence. You saw how we lived among you.
7. You followed our example and the Lord's. Even in hard times, you welcomed the message with joy from the Holy Spirit.
8. You became examples to all the believers in Macedonia and Achaia.
9. Your faith in God is known everywhere. We don't need to say anything more.
10. People talk about how you turned away from idols and began to serve the one true God.
11. They say you are waiting for His Son, Jesus, who came back to life. He will rescue us from the coming judgment.

1 Thessalonians 2

1. Friends, you know our visit to you was not a waste of time.
2. We had already suffered in Philippi, but God gave us the courage to speak to you anyway.
3. We didn't trick you. We didn't lie. We didn't try to fool anyone.
4. God trusted us with His message, and we spoke to please Him—not people. He knows our hearts.
5. We didn't use flattery or try to get your money. God is our witness.
6. We didn't ask for praise from you or anyone else.
7. We were gentle with you, like a mother caring for her baby.
8. We loved you so much, we were happy to share not just the good news, but our lives too.
9. You remember how we worked hard so we wouldn't be a burden. We preached the good news day and night.
10. You saw how we lived right and fairly and in a way that honored God.
11. We treated each of you like a father helps his children.
12. We encouraged and guided you to live in a way that pleases God.
13. We thank God because when you heard His message, you accepted it not as human words, but as God's truth.
14. You suffered like the churches in Judea. They were hurt by their own people, and so were you.
15. The Jews killed the Lord Jesus and the prophets. They forced us to leave. They try to stop us from helping the Gentiles.
16. They keep sinning and will face God's anger.
17. Friends, we were taken away from you for a short time. We missed you and wanted to come back.
18. We tried again and again, but Satan stopped us.
19. You are our hope, our joy, and our reward when Jesus returns.

1 Thessalonians 3

1. When we couldn't wait any longer, we decided to stay in Athens alone.
2. We sent Timothy to help you stay strong in your faith.
3. We didn't want you to give up when things got hard. You know suffering comes with following Christ.
4. We told you before that trouble would come, and it did.
5. I was worried that Satan had tempted you, and our work might be wasted.
6. But now Timothy is back with good news. He says you still have strong faith and love. You remember us kindly and want to see us.
7. That news gave us comfort and strength during our own hard times.
8. We feel alive again knowing your faith is strong.
9. We thank God with joy for all the good we hear about you.

10. We pray night and day to see you again and help your faith grow.
11. We ask God to clear the way for us to come to you.
12. May the Lord make your love grow more and more—for each other and for everyone.
13. Then your hearts will be strong and clean when Jesus comes with all His people.

1 Thessalonians 4

1. Friends, we taught you how to live in a way that pleases God. Now keep doing it even more.
2. You know the rules we gave you from Jesus.
3. God wants you to live a clean life. Stay away from sexual sin.
4. Learn to control your body in a way that honors God.
5. Don't live with lust like people who don't know God.
6. Don't take advantage of or hurt others in these matters. God will punish those who do.
7. God didn't call us to live in sin but to live a clean life.
8. If you ignore this, you're not ignoring people—you're ignoring God, who gave you His Spirit.
9. You don't need us to teach you to love others. God already taught you.
10. You already love God's people. Now love them even more.
11. Try to live a quiet life. Mind your own business and work with your hands.
12. Then people who don't believe will respect you, and you won't have to depend on anyone.
13. We want you to understand what happens to believers who have died. Don't be sad like people who have no hope.
14. We believe Jesus died and rose again. We also believe He will bring with Him those who died believing in Him.
15. We tell you what the Lord said: When Jesus returns, those still alive won't go first.
16. The Lord will come from heaven with a loud shout. The dead in Christ will rise first.
17. Then those still alive will be taken up with them to meet the Lord in the air.
18. So we will be with the Lord forever. Encourage each other with this truth.

1 Thessalonians 5

1. You don't need me to write about when the Lord will come.
2. You know it will happen like a thief in the night.
3. People will say, "Everything is fine," and then sudden trouble will come.
4. But you are not in the dark. That day won't surprise you.
5. You are children of light and day—not darkness or night.
6. So stay awake and be ready. Don't live like people in the dark.
7. People sleep and get drunk at night.
8. But we live in the day. Stay clear-headed. Trust God, love others, and wear hope like armor.
9. God didn't choose us to face His anger but to be saved through Jesus.
10. Jesus died so we can live with Him, whether we're alive or dead.
11. So encourage each other and build each other up.
12. Respect your church leaders. They work hard and help guide you.
13. Show them love and respect. Live in peace with everyone.
14. Help those who struggle. Encourage the shy. Be patient with everyone.

15. Don't try to get even. Always try to do good to everyone.
16. Always be joyful.
17. Never stop praying.
18. Be thankful in everything. This is what God wants.
19. Don't ignore the Holy Spirit.
20. Don't ignore messages from God.
21. Test everything. Keep what is good.
22. Stay away from all evil.
23. May God make your whole life holy—your spirit, soul, and body—until Jesus returns.
24. God is faithful. He will do it.
25. Friends, pray for us.
26. Greet each other with love.
27. Read this letter to everyone in the church.
28. May Jesus give you grace.

– 2 Thessalonians –

Paul corrects confusion about Jesus' return and warns against laziness.

2 Thessalonians 1

1. This letter is from Paul, Silas, and Timothy. We are writing to the church in Thessalonica, to those who belong to God our Father and the Lord Jesus Christ.
2. May God give you grace and peace.
3. We always thank God for you. Your faith and love keep growing.
4. We tell other churches how strong you are when you suffer and stay faithful.
5. Your troubles show that God is making you worthy of His kingdom.
6. God will punish those who hurt you.
7. He will give rest to you and to us when Jesus comes from heaven with His powerful angels.
8. He will punish those who don't know God and those who don't obey the good news about Jesus.
9. They will be separated from the Lord forever.
10. This will happen when Jesus comes. Everyone who believed will honor Him. You believed our message, so you will be there.
11. We always pray that God will help you live the life He called you to. We pray that He will give you power to do good.
12. Then Jesus will be honored because of you, and you will be honored because of Him. This is possible through God's grace.

2 Thessalonians 2

1. Now, about Jesus coming again and us being gathered to Him…
2. Don't get scared or confused by people saying that the Lord has already come.
3. Don't let anyone fool you. That day won't come until there's a big turning away from God and the "man of sin" appears.
4. He fights against God, puts himself above God, and even sits in God's temple, saying he is God.
5. Remember, I told you all this when I was with you.
6. Something is holding him back right now. He will be revealed at the right time.
7. Evil is already working, but it's being held back until the one who holds it back is taken away.
8. Then the evil one will come, and Jesus will destroy him with His breath when He comes.
9. The evil one will come with Satan's power—fake miracles, lies, and tricks.
10. He will fool those who refuse to love the truth and be saved.

11. God lets them believe the lies, because they didn't want the truth.
12. So they will be judged for enjoying evil instead of believing the truth.
13. But we thank God for you. You were chosen to be saved through the Spirit and by believing the truth.
14. God called you through our message, so you could share in Jesus' glory.
15. So stay strong and hold on to what we taught you—by word or letter.
16. May Jesus and God our Father comfort your hearts and make you strong to do good.

2 Thessalonians 3

1. Pray for us. Ask God to spread His message fast and clearly.
2. Pray that we will be kept safe from evil people. Not everyone has faith.
3. But the Lord is faithful. He will make you strong and protect you.
4. We are sure you are doing and will keep doing what we taught.
5. May the Lord help you love others and be strong like Christ.
6. Stay away from believers who are lazy and won't follow the teachings we gave you.
7. You know you should follow our example. We were not lazy when we were with you.
8. We worked hard day and night so we wouldn't be a burden.
9. We had the right to ask for help, but we chose to work to show you how to live.
10. We gave this rule: If someone doesn't want to work, they shouldn't eat.
11. We hear some of you are lazy and cause problems.
12. We tell those people: In the name of Jesus, settle down and work quietly.
13. Don't get tired of doing what is right.
14. If someone doesn't obey this letter, don't associate with them so they feel ashamed.
15. But don't treat them like enemies. Warn them as a brother or sister.
16. May the Lord of peace give you peace always, in every way.
17. I, Paul, write this last part myself. This is my sign in every letter.
18. May the grace of the Lord Jesus be with you all.

– 1 Timothy –

Paul gives instructions to Timothy about leading the church well.

1 Timothy 1

1. This letter is from Paul. God and Jesus chose me to be an apostle.
2. I'm writing to Timothy, my true son in the faith. May God give you grace, mercy, and peace.
3. When I left for Macedonia, I asked you to stay in Ephesus to stop people from teaching wrong things.
4. Tell them not to waste time on stories or long family lists. These things bring confusion, not faith.
5. The goal is love—from a clean heart, good conscience, and real faith.
6. Some people have turned away from this and now talk about useless things.
7. They want to teach the law but don't understand it themselves.
8. The law is good if it's used the right way.
9. The law is not for good people. It's for lawbreakers, sinners, and those who don't respect God.
10. It's for people who do wrong, hurt others, lie, or do anything that goes against God's truth.
11. This teaching agrees with the good news that God trusted me to share.

12. I thank Christ Jesus for giving me strength and trusting me to serve Him.
13. I used to speak against Jesus, hurt His people, and act badly. But God showed me mercy because I didn't understand.
14. Jesus gave me grace, faith, and love.
15. This is a true and important saying: Jesus came to save sinners—and I'm the worst one.
16. But God was patient with me to show that Jesus can save anyone.
17. Honor and glory to God forever. He is the only true King.
18. Timothy, I'm giving you this command. Use what the prophets said about you to fight the good fight.
19. Keep your faith and a clean conscience. Some people rejected this and ruined their faith.
20. Hymenaeus and Alexander are two of them. I gave them over to God's discipline so they would learn not to speak against Him.

1 Timothy 2

1. First, I ask you to pray for everyone. Ask God to help them. Thank Him for them.
2. Pray for kings and all leaders so we can live in peace and godliness.
3. This makes God happy. He wants everyone to be saved and know the truth.
4. There is one God and one way to reach Him—through Jesus Christ.
5. Jesus gave His life to save everyone. This message came at the right time.
6. I was chosen to share it with all people.
7. I'm telling the truth—I'm a teacher of faith and truth to non-Jews.
8. I want men everywhere to pray with clean hearts, free from anger or arguing.
9. Women should dress modestly and respectfully—not just to get attention.
10. Women should focus on doing good, which is proper for people who follow God.
11. A woman should learn quietly and respectfully.
12. I do not allow a woman to teach or have authority over a man. She should be quiet.
13. Adam was made first, then Eve.
14. Adam was not tricked, but Eve was.
15. But women will be saved by having children, living in faith, love, and holiness, with self-control.

1 Timothy 3

1. Here's a true saying: If someone wants to be a church leader, that's a good goal.
2. A church leader must be a good person. He must be faithful to his wife, be self-controlled, wise, honest, respectful, kind, and able to teach.
3. He should not get drunk, fight, or love money.
4. He must lead his family well, with respectful children.
5. If he can't manage his own family, he can't care for the church.
6. He must not be a new believer or he might get proud and fall.
7. He must have a good reputation with outsiders, so he won't be trapped by the devil.
8. Church helpers must be honest, not greedy or addicted to wine.
9. They must hold tightly to the truth with a clear heart.
10. Test them first. If they pass, then let them serve.
11. Women helpers must also be respected, not gossip, and be faithful in everything.
12. Helpers must have one wife and lead their children and home well.

13. Those who serve well earn respect and grow strong in faith.
14. I hope to visit you soon, but I'm writing this in case I'm delayed.
15. Then you'll know how to live in God's family—the church of the living God, which teaches the truth.
16. The truth about Jesus is great:
    He came as a man,
    Was made right by the Spirit,
    Was seen by angels,
    Was preached to all people,
    Was believed in,
    And taken up to heaven.

1 Timothy 4

1. The Spirit clearly says that in the last days, some people will leave the faith and follow evil spirits and lies.
2. These liars pretend to be holy, but their hearts are hard.
3. They say people must not marry or eat certain foods. But God made these things to be enjoyed by those who believe the truth.
4. Everything God made is good. Nothing should be refused if it is accepted with thanks.
5. It is made holy by God's word and prayer.
6. Remind the people about this. Then you will be a good servant of Jesus, growing in faith and truth.
7. Don't waste time on silly stories. Train yourself to follow God.
8. Physical training helps a little. Training to follow God helps for this life and the next.
9. This is a true and important teaching.
10. We work hard and trust in the living God, who saves everyone—especially those who believe.
11. Teach these things and tell people to obey them.
12. Don't let anyone look down on you because you are young. Show them how to live with your words, actions, love, faith, and purity.
13. Until I come, keep reading the Scriptures, encouraging people, and teaching them.
14. Don't forget the gift God gave you when the church leaders prayed for you.
15. Practice these things so everyone can see your progress.
16. Be careful how you live and what you teach. Keep doing it. Then you'll save yourself and your listeners.

1 Timothy 5

1. Don't be harsh with older men. Treat them like your father. Treat younger men like brothers.
2. Treat older women like mothers, and younger women like sisters. Be pure in how you act.
3. Take care of widows who truly need help.
4. If a widow has children or grandchildren, they should take care of her. That pleases God.
5. A true widow is alone and trusts God. She prays day and night.
6. But a widow who only lives for pleasure is spiritually dead.
7. Teach these things so people live right.
8. Anyone who doesn't take care of their family is worse than someone who doesn't believe in God.
9. Only put a widow on the care list if she is over 60, faithful to her husband,
10. and known for doing good, raising children, helping others, and showing kindness.
11. Don't put younger widows on the list. They may want to marry again and leave their promise to Christ.
12. That would be wrong.
13. They may also become lazy and gossip or get into trouble.

14. So it's better for young widows to marry, raise children, and manage their homes.
15. Some have already turned away from the faith.
16. If a woman believer has widows in her family, she should care for them. Then the church can help those who truly need it.
17. Leaders who do their job well should be respected, especially those who teach and preach.
18. The Scriptures say, "Don't stop an ox from eating while it works," and, "A worker deserves pay."
19. Only listen to complaints against a leader if two or three people agree.
20. Correct those who sin, so others will be warned.
21. Obey these instructions fairly. Don't pick favorites.
22. Don't be quick to choose leaders. Don't share in other people's sins. Keep your life clean.
23. Stop drinking only water. Drink a little wine to help your stomach and sickness.
24. Some people's sins are clear now. Others will be seen later.
25. Good works are also easy to see. Even the ones that are hidden will be known someday.

1 Timothy 6

1. Slaves should respect their masters so people won't say bad things about God's name or His teaching.
2. If their master is a believer, they should still respect him because he is a brother in Christ. Help him even more because he is part of God's family.
3. If someone teaches something different and does not agree with the true teaching about Jesus,
4. that person is proud and doesn't really understand. They love to argue and
5. fight about words. This causes jealousy, anger, insults, and lies.
6. These people are always fighting and never know the truth. They think being godly will make them rich.
7. True godliness with contentment is great wealth.
8. We brought nothing into this world, and we can take nothing out.
9. If we have food and clothes, we should be happy.
10. People who want to get rich fall into traps and do foolish, harmful things. These things ruin and destroy them.
11. Loving money is the root of all kinds of evil. Some people want money so much they leave the faith and hurt themselves.
12. But you, man of God, run from these things. Follow what is right. Have faith, love, patience, and kindness.
13. Fight the good fight of faith. Hold tightly to eternal life. God called you to this when you chose to follow Him in front of others.
14. God gives life to all, and Jesus told the truth before Pontius Pilate. I tell you to obey this command
15. until Jesus returns. Keep your life clean and without blame.
16. At the right time, God will show Jesus, the blessed and only King of all kings and Lord of all lords.
17. He alone never dies and lives in light no one can approach. No one has seen Him. To Him be honor and power forever. Amen.
18. Tell rich people not to be proud or to trust in money. It doesn't last. They should trust in God, who gives us everything to enjoy.
19. Tell them to do good, be rich in good works, and be generous.
20. This way, they will store up true treasure in heaven and have a strong future.

21. Timothy, guard what God has given you. Stay away from useless talk and lies that pretend to be knowledge.
22. Some who followed that have wandered from the faith.
May God's grace be with you.

– 2 Timothy –

Paul's final letter urges Timothy to stay strong and faithful to the gospel.

2 Timothy 1

1. This letter is from Paul. God chose me to be an apostle of Jesus. He promised life through Christ.
2. I'm writing to Timothy, my dear child. May God give you grace, mercy, and peace.
3. I thank God when I pray for you. I serve Him with a clean heart, like my ancestors did.
4. I remember your tears. I want to see you so I can be happy again.
5. I remember your strong faith. Your grandmother Lois and your mother Eunice had it too. I believe you do as well.
6. I remind you to keep using the gift God gave you when I laid my hands on you.
7. God did not give us fear. He gave us power, love, and self-control.
8. Don't be ashamed of telling others about Jesus or of me, His prisoner. Be ready to suffer with me for the good news, using God's power.
9. God saved us and chose us to live a holy life—not because we earned it, but because He planned it long ago.
10. That plan became clear when Jesus came. He broke the power of death and brought life through the good news.
11. God chose me to share that message as a preacher, apostle, and teacher.
12. That's why I suffer, but I'm not ashamed. I know the One I trust. He will keep safe what I've given Him until the end.
13. Follow the truth I taught you. Keep it with faith and love in Jesus.
14. Protect the good things God gave you with the help of the Holy Spirit.
15. You know everyone in Asia left me, including Phygelus and Hermogenes.
16. May God bless Onesiphorus. He often helped me and wasn't ashamed that I was in prison.
17. When he came to Rome, he looked hard until he found me.
18. I hope the Lord shows him kindness on the day He returns. You know how much he helped me in Ephesus.

2 Timothy 2

1. Timothy, be strong through the grace that comes from Jesus.
2. Share what I taught you with others who will also teach more people.
3. Be like a good soldier of Christ. Be ready to suffer.
4. A soldier doesn't get tied up in daily life. He tries to please his leader.
5. Athletes must follow the rules to win.
6. Farmers who work hard should get the first share of crops.
7. Think about this. God will help you understand.
8. Remember Jesus Christ—He came from David's family and rose from the dead. This is the good news I preach.
9. I suffer for it and am even in chains. But God's message is not chained.
10. I keep going for the sake of God's people, so they can be saved through Jesus.
11. Here is a true saying:
If we died with Him, we will live with Him.
If we stay strong, we will rule with

12. Him.
If we turn away, He will turn away from us.
Even if we are not faithful, He stays faithful.
13. Remind people of these things. Warn them not to argue about words—it only hurts people.
14. Do your best to please God. Be a good worker who teaches truth clearly.
15. Stay away from foolish talk. It leads to more sin.
16. This kind of talk spreads like a disease. Hymenaeus and Philetus do this.
17. They left the truth and say the resurrection has already happened. They are ruining some people's faith.
18. But God's truth stands strong. He knows who belong to Him. And everyone who belongs to Him must turn away from evil.
19. In a big house, there are all kinds of dishes—some for special use, some for everyday use.
20. If you keep yourself clean, you'll be ready for special use—useful to God.
21. Run away from sinful desires. Follow what is right. Have faith, love, and peace with others who follow the Lord.
22. Don't get into silly arguments. They only start fights.
23. The Lord's servant must not fight but be kind, a good teacher, and patient.
24. Be gentle when correcting others. Maybe God will help them change and know the truth.
25. Then they can escape the devil's trap and be free.

2 Timothy 3

1. You should know that in the last days, things will be very hard.
2. People will love only themselves and money. They will be proud, rude, and disobedient to parents. They won't be thankful or holy.
3. They won't love others or forgive. They'll lie, lose control, be mean, and hate what's good.
4. They'll turn against friends, be reckless, and love pleasure more than God.
5. They will act religious but reject God's power. Stay away from them.
6. Some of them sneak into homes and trick weak people who are full of sin and confusion.
7. These people are always learning but never understand the truth.
8. Just like Jannes and Jambres fought against Moses, these people fight the truth. Their minds are ruined, and they fail in faith.
9. But they won't get far. Everyone will see their foolishness.
10. You know how I live—my teaching, my goals, my faith, my patience, my love, and my strength.
11. You know about the trouble I faced and how God rescued me from it all.
12. Everyone who wants to live for Jesus will have trouble.
13. Evil people will get worse. They'll trick others and be tricked themselves.
14. But you must keep living by what you've learned and believe. You know who taught you.
15. Since you were a child, you've known the Scriptures. They help you trust Jesus and be saved.
16. All Scripture comes from God. It teaches us what is true, shows us what is wrong, helps us change, and trains us to do what's right.
17. Then God's servant is ready and fully prepared to do good.

2 Timothy 4

1. Before God and Jesus—who will judge everyone—I give you this command:
2. Preach the message. Be ready all the time. Help people with patience and clear teaching.

3. A time is coming when people won't listen to true teaching. They'll find teachers who say what they want to hear.
4. They'll stop listening to the truth and believe lies.
5. But you must stay steady. Don't give up when things are hard. Do the work of spreading the good news. Finish the job God gave you.
6. My life is almost over. I'm like a drink being poured out. My time is almost done.
7. I have fought the good fight. I have finished the race. I have kept the faith.
8. Now a crown of reward is waiting for me. The Lord will give it to me on the day He returns—and not just to me, but to everyone who loves Him.
9. Try to come see me soon.
10. Demas left me. He loved the world more and went to Thessalonica. Crescens went to Galatia. Titus went to Dalmatia.
11. Only Luke is with me. Bring Mark with you. He's helpful to me.
12. I sent Tychicus to Ephesus.
13. When you come, bring the coat I left with Carpus, and also the books—especially the scrolls.
14. Alexander the metalworker did me great harm. The Lord will pay him back.
15. Watch out for him. He fought hard against what we said.
16. At my first trial, no one helped me. Everyone left me. I hope God forgives them.
17. But the Lord stood with me and gave me strength so I could fully share the message. All people heard it.
18. The Lord saved me from danger, and He will keep me safe. He will bring me safely to His heavenly kingdom. Praise Him forever. Amen.
19. Say hello to Priscilla and Aquila and to the family of Onesiphorus.
20. Erastus stayed in Corinth. Trophimus was sick, so I left him in Miletus.
21. Try to come before winter. Eubulus, Pudens, Linus, Claudia, and all the brothers and sisters send greetings.
22. May the Lord be with you. May His grace be with you all.

– Titus –

Paul tells Titus how to lead churches with good teaching and godly living.

Titus 1

1. This letter is from Paul, a servant of God and an apostle of Jesus. I help God's chosen people believe and know the truth.
2. This truth leads to godly living and gives hope of eternal life. God promised this life long ago, and He always keeps His promises.
3. At the right time, He showed this message to us. He trusted me to share it.
4. I'm writing to Titus, my true son in the faith. May God the Father and Jesus give you grace and peace.
5. I left you in Crete so you could finish what we started and choose leaders for each church.
6. A church leader must be a good man. He should have only one wife and children who respect him and believe in God.
7. A leader takes care of God's work, so he must live right. He must not be proud, angry, a drinker, a fighter, or greedy.
8. He should be kind to strangers, love what is good, be wise, fair, and self-controlled.
9. He must stick to true teaching so he can teach others and correct those who are wrong.

10. There are many people who refuse to obey. They talk nonsense and trick others, especially among the Jews.
11. Their mouths must be stopped. They ruin whole families by teaching lies for money.
12. One of their own prophets said, "Cretans are always liars, evil people, and lazy."
13. This is true. So correct them strongly, so their faith will be strong.
14. Don't let them listen to Jewish stories or commands from people who turn away from the truth.
15. To those who are pure, everything is clean. But to those who are corrupt and don't believe, nothing is clean. Their minds and hearts are dirty.
16. They say they know God, but their actions show they don't. They are disobedient and unfit for doing anything good.

Titus 2

1. Teach what is right and true.
2. Older men should be self-controlled, respectful, wise, and strong in faith, love, and patience.
3. Older women should live in a way that shows respect for God. They should not gossip or drink too much. They should teach what is good.
4. They must teach younger women to love their husbands and children.
5. Younger women should be wise, pure, take care of their homes, be kind, and obey their husbands. Then no one will speak badly about God's word.
6. In the same way, tell young men to control themselves.
7. Always be a good example. Do what is right. Teach clearly and seriously.
8. Use clean, strong words that no one can criticize. Then anyone against you will be ashamed because they won't have anything bad to say.
9. Slaves must obey their masters and try to please them. They should not talk back
10. or steal. They must be honest and faithful so they show how good God's teaching is.
11. God's grace has come. It brings salvation to all people.
12. It teaches us to say no to evil and to live with self-control, doing what is right.
13. We wait for the hope of Jesus to come again. He is our great God and Savior.
14. He gave Himself for us to save us from sin and make us His special people—eager to do good.
15. Teach these things. Correct and encourage with authority. Don't let anyone ignore you.

Titus 3

1. Remind people to obey rulers and authorities. Be ready to do good.
2. Don't speak badly about anyone. Be peaceful, kind, and gentle to everyone.
3. We were once foolish and disobedient. We were tricked and slaves to many desires. We were jealous and hated others.
4. But then the kindness and love of God appeared.
5. He saved us—not because of anything we did—but because of His mercy. He washed us clean and gave us new life through the Holy Spirit.
6. God poured out the Spirit through Jesus our Savior.
7. Because of His grace, we are made right with God and will live forever.
8. This is a true message. Teach it strongly. Encourage believers to do good. These things are good and helpful.
9. Stay away from foolish arguments, family lists, fights, and debates about the law. These are useless.

10. If someone keeps causing division, warn them once, then again. After that, don't have anything to do with them.
11. Such people are twisted and sinning. They know they're wrong.
12. When I send Artemas or Tychicus to you, do your best to meet me in Nicopolis. I plan to stay there for the winter.
13. Help Zenas the lawyer and Apollos. Make sure they have everything they need.
14. Our people must learn to do good by helping with real needs. Then they won't be useless.
15. Everyone with me sends greetings. Greet those who love us in faith. Grace be with you all.

– Philemon –

Paul asks a Christian master to forgive and welcome back his runaway slave.

Philemon 1

1. This letter is from Paul, a prisoner for Jesus, and from Timothy. We're writing to Philemon, our dear friend and worker for Christ.
2. Also to Apphia, our sister, Archippus, our fellow soldier, and the church that meets in your home.
3. May God our Father and Jesus Christ give you grace and peace.
4. I always thank God when I pray for you.
5. I hear about your love and your faith in the Lord Jesus and for all believers.
6. I pray your faith will show in your good actions and help you understand all the good things we have in Christ.
7. Your love has made me very happy and encouraged me. You have helped the hearts of God's people.
8. Because of Christ, I could command you to do the right thing,
9. but instead, I'm asking you with love. I, Paul, am an old man and now a prisoner for Jesus.
10. I'm asking you for my son Onesimus. I became like a father to him while I was in jail.
11. He wasn't helpful to you before, but now he is helpful to both of us.
12. I'm sending him back to you. He is very dear to me.
13. I wanted to keep him here to help me while I'm in jail for preaching the good news.
14. But I didn't want to do anything without your permission. I want you to help because you want to, not because you have to.
15. Maybe he left you for a short time so you could have him back forever—
16. no longer as a slave, but as more than a slave—a dear brother in Christ.
17. If you think of me as your friend, welcome him like you would welcome me.
18. If he has done anything wrong or owes you anything, charge it to me.
19. I, Paul, am writing this with my own hand: I will pay it back. (And don't forget—you owe me your very life!)
20. Yes, my brother, please do this for me in the Lord. Make me happy in Christ.
21. I'm writing knowing you will do what I ask—and even more.
22. Also, get a room ready for me. I hope to visit you soon if God allows it.
23. Epaphras, who is in jail with me for Christ, sends you greetings.
24. So do Mark, Aristarchus, Demas, and Luke, my helpers.
25. May the grace of the Lord Jesus be with your spirit.

– Hebrews –

Jesus is the perfect high priest and final sacrifice who fulfills the Old Covenant.

Hebrews 1

1. Long ago, God spoke to people through the prophets in many ways.
2. But now, in these last days, He has spoken to us through His Son. God made everything through Him and gave Him control over everything.
3. The Son shows exactly what God is like. He keeps everything going with His powerful word. He cleaned away our sins and now sits beside God in heaven.
4. He is much greater than the angels. God gave Him a greater name than theirs.
5. God never said to an angel, "You are my Son. Today I have become your Father."
6. When God brought His firstborn Son into the world, He said, "Let all God's angels worship Him."
7. God says angels are His servants, like wind and fire.
8. But about His Son, He says, "Your throne, O God, will last forever. You rule fairly."
9. "You loved what is right and hated evil. So God chose You and gave You great joy."
10. He also says, "Lord, You made the earth and the skies in the beginning."
11. "They will not last, but You will. They will wear out like clothes."
12. "You will roll them up like a robe and change them. But You stay the same. Your life never ends."
13. God never said to an angel, "Sit at my right side until I defeat your enemies."
14. Angels are spirits sent to help those who will be saved.

Hebrews 2

1. We must pay close attention to what we've heard so we don't drift away from it.
2. The message given through angels was true, and anyone who disobeyed it was punished.
3. So how can we escape if we ignore such a great way to be saved? This message came from Jesus and was confirmed by those who heard Him.
4. God also showed it was true by doing miracles and giving the Holy Spirit.
5. God didn't give control of the world to angels.
6. In the Bible, it says, "What is man that You care for him?"
7. "You made him a little lower than angels for a short time, then crowned him with glory."
8. God put everything under people's control. But we don't see that fully yet.
9. But we do see Jesus. He was made a little lower than angels, and He suffered and died. Now He is crowned with glory. He died so that everyone could be saved.
10. It was right for God to make Jesus suffer to save many people. That's how Jesus became the perfect leader.
11. Jesus and those He saves are all part of one family. That's why He's not ashamed to call them brothers and sisters.
12. He says, "I will tell others about You and praise You."
13. He also says, "I will trust God," and "Here I am with the children God gave me."
14. Since people are human, Jesus became human too. He died to break the power of the devil, who had the power over death.
15. He set free all who lived in fear of dying.
16. Jesus didn't come to help angels, but to help people.

17. He had to be like us in every way. He became a priest who could be kind and faithful and take away our sins.

18. Since He suffered and was tempted, He can help us when we're tempted too.

Hebrews 3

1. Friends, you share in God's heavenly call. Think about Jesus, the one we believe in and follow. He is our high priest.

2. He was faithful to God, just like Moses was faithful to God's house.

3. But Jesus deserves more honor than Moses, like a builder is more important than the house he builds.

4. Every house is built by someone, but God built everything.

5. Moses was a servant in God's house. He spoke about things that were coming later.

6. But Christ is the Son over God's house. And we are His house—if we stay strong in our faith and hope.

7. The Holy Spirit says: "Today, if you hear His voice,

8. don't harden your hearts like people did in the desert.

9. Your ancestors tested Me and saw what I did for 40 years.

10. I was angry with them. They always went the wrong way and didn't understand My ways.

11. So I said, 'They will never enter My rest.'"

12. So, brothers and sisters, be careful. Make sure none of you turns away from God with an evil heart.

13. Instead, encourage each other every day while it's still "today," so no one is tricked by sin.

14. We belong to Christ if we hold on to our faith until the end.

15. The Bible says again: "Today, if you hear His voice, don't harden your hearts."

16. Who were the people who heard and still rebelled? It was those Moses led out of Egypt.

17. God was angry with them for 40 years. They sinned and died in the desert.

18. God said they would not enter His rest.

19. So we see they couldn't enter because they didn't believe.

Hebrews 4

1. God promised us a place of rest. We must be careful not to miss it.

2. The good news was shared with us and with them, but they didn't believe it, so it didn't help them.

3. We who believe will enter God's rest. God said, "They will never enter My rest," even though His work was finished long ago.

4. In the Bible it says, "On the seventh day, God rested from all His work."

5. But some didn't believe and didn't enter that rest.

6. That promise still stands for others. Those who didn't believe were the ones who missed it.

7. God set another day—"Today." He said this through David long after Moses.

8. If Joshua had given them rest, God wouldn't have spoken about another day.

9. So a special rest still waits for God's people.

10. Anyone who enters God's rest also rests from their own work, just like God did.

11. Let's try hard to enter that rest, so we don't fall like those who didn't believe.

12. God's word is alive and powerful. It cuts deep, showing what's in our hearts.

13. Nothing is hidden from God. Everything is clear to Him. We must answer to Him.

14. We have a great high priest—Jesus, the Son of God. He has gone to heaven. So let's hold on to our faith.
15. Jesus understands our weaknesses. He was tempted in every way but didn't sin.
16. So we can come boldly to God's throne. There we will find mercy and grace to help us.

Hebrews 5

1. Every high priest is chosen from people and is appointed to help others by offering gifts and sacrifices to God.
2. He can be gentle with those who are ignorant or going the wrong way, because he also has weaknesses.
3. He must offer sacrifices for his own sins too, not just for others.
4. No one takes this honor for himself. He must be chosen by God, like Aaron was.
5. Christ didn't make Himself high priest. God said to Him, "You are My Son. Today I have become Your Father."
6. He also said, "You are a priest forever."
7. While Jesus was on earth, He prayed with loud cries and tears to God, who could save Him. God heard Him because He trusted Him.
8. Even though Jesus was God's Son, He learned obedience by suffering.
9. After He was made perfect, He became the source of eternal salvation for everyone who obeys Him.
10. God called Him a high priest.
11. We have a lot more to say about this, but it's hard to explain because you aren't trying to understand.
12. By now, you should be teachers. But you still need someone to teach you the basics of God's word again.
13. You still need milk, not solid food. Anyone who lives on milk is like a baby and doesn't understand right from wrong.
14. Solid food is for grown-ups, who train themselves to know the difference between good and evil.

Hebrews 6

1. Let's move past the basic teachings about Christ and grow up in our faith.
2. We shouldn't have to keep learning again about turning from sin, trusting God, baptisms, laying on hands, rising from the dead, and final judgment.
3. If God allows, we will move forward.
4. Some people hear the truth, share in the Holy Spirit,
5. and know the good things of God. But if they turn away,
6. it's impossible to bring them back. They would be rejecting Jesus again.
7. Land that drinks the rain and grows crops is blessed by God.
8. But land that only grows thorns is worthless. It will be burned.
9. Dear friends, even though we say these things, we are sure of better things for you—things that bring salvation.
10. God is fair. He won't forget the love you've shown by helping His people.
11. We want each of you to keep showing this same effort until the end.
12. Don't be lazy. Be like those who trust God and receive what He promised.
13. When God made a promise to Abraham, He swore by Himself because no one is greater than Him.
14. He said, "I will bless you and give you many descendants."
15. Abraham waited patiently and received what God promised.
16. People swear by someone greater. That ends an argument.
17. God wanted to make His promise very clear, so He made an oath.

18. These two things—God's promise and oath—never change. God cannot lie. We can trust Him and feel safe.
19. This hope is strong and steady, like an anchor for our souls. It leads us into God's presence.
20. Jesus went there ahead of us. He is our high priest forever.

Hebrews 7

1. Melchizedek was king of Salem and priest of God. He met Abraham and blessed him.
2. Abraham gave him a tenth of everything. Melchizedek's name means "king of righteousness," and he was also king of peace.
3. We don't know his father, mother, or when he was born or died. He is like the Son of God and is a priest forever.
4. Think how great he was—Abraham gave him a tenth of what he had.
5. The law says that priests from Levi's family collect tithes from others, even though those others are family too.
6. But Melchizedek was not from Levi, and he still got a tithe from Abraham and blessed him.
7. The one who blesses is greater than the one who is blessed.
8. Levi's priests die, but Scripture says Melchizedek lives.
9. It's like Levi gave a tenth to Melchizedek through Abraham.
10. Levi was not yet born, but he was still part of Abraham.
11. If perfection came through Levi's priesthood, we wouldn't need another priest like Melchizedek.
12. But since the priesthood changed, the law had to change too.
13. Jesus came from a different tribe—not from Levi but from Judah. Moses never said priests would come from Judah.
14. It's clear Jesus came from Judah, and He became a priest like Melchizedek.
15. Jesus didn't become a priest because of a rule about family.
16. He became a priest through the power of a life that never ends.
17. The Bible says, "You are a priest forever, like Melchizedek."
18. The old rule was set aside because it was weak and couldn't save anyone.
19. The old law made nothing perfect. But now we have a better hope—one that brings us close to God.
20. Jesus also became a priest with God's oath.
21. Other priests became priests without an oath. But God said to Jesus: "The Lord has sworn and will not change His mind: You are a priest forever."
22. Because of this, Jesus brings a better agreement between God and people.
23. There were many priests before, because they died.
24. But Jesus lives forever. He will never stop being priest.
25. So He can save everyone who comes to God through Him. He always lives to speak for them.
26. Jesus is the kind of high priest we need—holy, perfect, and pure. He is in heaven and not like other people.
27. He doesn't need to offer sacrifices every day for His own sins and then for others'. He did this once for all when He gave Himself.
28. The law made weak people priests. But God's oath came after the law and made His perfect Son the priest forever.

Hebrews 8

1. The main point is this: We have a high priest like Jesus. He is sitting next to God in heaven.
2. He serves in the true place of worship that God made—not people.

3. Every high priest gives gifts and sacrifices. So Jesus must also offer something.
4. If He were on earth, He wouldn't be a priest, since others already offer gifts by the old law.
5. But those priests serve only a copy of the real thing in heaven. God told Moses to follow the pattern exactly when he built the tent.
6. But Jesus has a better job. He gives us a better promise from God.
7. If the first promise had worked, we wouldn't need a second one.
8. But God said His people broke the first promise. So He said, "I will make a new promise with My people."
9. "It won't be like the old one they broke."
10. "This is the new promise: I will put My laws in their minds and hearts. I will be their God, and they will be My people."
11. "No one will need to teach others about God. Everyone will know Me."
12. "I will forgive their sins and forget the wrongs they did."
13. When God said "new," He made the first promise old. And what is old will soon disappear.

Hebrews 9

1. The first agreement had rules for worship and a holy place on earth.
2. A tent was set up. The first room had a lampstand, table, and bread. This was the Holy Place.
3. Behind the curtain was another room called the Most Holy Place.
4. It had the gold altar for incense and the Ark of the Covenant. Inside the Ark were a gold jar of manna, Aaron's staff that budded, and the stone tablets of the law.
5. Above the Ark were the angels of glory. But we won't talk more about that now.
6. The priests went into the first room often to do their work.
7. But only the high priest went into the second room, and only once a year. He offered blood for his own sins and the sins of the people.
8. The Holy Spirit was showing that the way to God was not open while the first tent still stood.
9. This was a picture for that time. The gifts and sacrifices couldn't fully clean the hearts of the people.
10. These were just rules about food, drink, and washing. They were only for a short time.
11. But when Christ came, He was the high priest of good things. He entered the greater, more perfect tent—not made by humans.
12. He entered the Most Holy Place once, not with animal blood but with His own. He gave us forever salvation.
13. Animal blood and ashes made people clean on the outside.
14. But the blood of Christ cleans our hearts so we can serve the living God. His Spirit offered Himself without sin.
15. That's why He made a new agreement. His death freed people from sins done under the old one. Now they can get what God promised—eternal life.
16. When someone makes a will, it only works after they die.
17. A will means nothing while the person is still alive.
18. That's why the first promise also needed blood.
19. When Moses gave the law, he used animal blood, water, red wool, and a branch to sprinkle the book and the people.
20. He said, "This is the blood of the agreement God made with you."

21. He also sprinkled the tent and everything used in worship.
22. The law says nearly everything must be made clean with blood. Without blood, there is no forgiveness.
23. The things on earth were just copies of the real things in heaven. They had to be cleaned with animal blood, but heavenly things needed better sacrifices.
24. Christ didn't enter a holy place made by people. He went into heaven itself to stand before God for us.
25. He didn't have to offer Himself many times like the high priest does every year.
26. If He had, He would have had to suffer many times since the world began. But He came once, at the end of time, to remove sin by His sacrifice.
27. People die once and then face judgment.
28. Christ was offered once to take away many sins. He will come again—not to deal with sin but to save those waiting for Him.

Hebrews 10

1. The law was only a shadow of good things to come. It couldn't make people perfect.
2. If it could, sacrifices would have stopped. People would be clean and feel no guilt.
3. But every year, those sacrifices reminded people of their sins.
4. Animal blood can't take away sins.
5. That's why Christ said, "You didn't want sacrifices. You gave Me a body instead."
6. "You weren't pleased with burnt offerings."
7. "So I said, 'Here I am, God. I've come to do what You want.'"
8. First He said, "You don't want offerings." Then He said, "I came to do what You want." So God ended the old way and started the new.
9. By this, we are made holy because Jesus gave His body once and for all.
10. Priests offer the same sacrifices every day, but they don't take away sins.
11. But Jesus offered one sacrifice for all time and then sat down by God.
12. Now He waits until His enemies are defeated.
13. By one offering, He made His people perfect forever.
14. The Holy Spirit also tells us this.
15. He says, "This is the promise I will make: I will put My laws in their hearts."
16. "I will not remember their sins anymore."
17. If sins are forgiven, there's no need for more sacrifices.
18. So, friends, we can go into God's presence with confidence because of Jesus.
19. His blood opened a new and living way through the curtain—His body.
20. We have a great priest over God's house.
21. So let's come close to God with honest hearts and strong faith.
22. Our hearts have been cleaned. Our bodies have been washed with water.
23. Let's hold on to our hope. God keeps His promises.
24. Let's think about how to help each other love and do good.
25. Don't stop meeting together. Encourage each other more as the day gets closer.
26. If we keep sinning on purpose after knowing the truth, there is no more sacrifice.
27. Only fear of judgment and fire will remain.
28. Anyone who broke Moses' law died without mercy.

29. How much worse will it be for someone who rejects Jesus and insults God's Spirit?
30. God says, "I will punish. I will repay."
31. It is a fearful thing to fall into God's hands.
32. Remember when you first believed. You suffered, but stayed strong.
33. Some of you were insulted or attacked. Others helped those who were treated badly.
34. You had sympathy for people in jail. You even accepted losing your stuff with joy, knowing you had something better in heaven.
35. So don't throw away your confidence. It will bring a reward.
36. You need patience so you can do what God wants and get what He promised.
37. "In a little while, the One who is coming will come."
38. "My righteous people will live by faith."
39. We are not people who give up. We believe and are saved.

Hebrews 11

1. Faith means being sure of what we hope for and knowing something is real even if we don't see it.
2. People in the past were praised because of their faith.
3. By faith, we understand that God made the world from nothing.
4. By faith, Abel gave a better offering than Cain. God was pleased with him.
5. By faith, Enoch was taken to heaven without dying. He pleased God.
6. Without faith, it's impossible to please God. You must believe He exists and rewards those who seek Him.
7. By faith, Noah built a boat to save his family. He trusted God's warning.
8. By faith, Abraham obeyed God and moved to a new land.
9. He lived in tents, waiting for the city God built.
10. He looked forward to a place God designed.
11. By faith, Sarah had a child, even though she was old. She believed God would keep His promise.
12. From one man, Abraham, came many people—like the stars or sand—too many to count.
13. These people died still trusting God. They didn't see the promises fulfilled, but they knew they were coming.
14. People who live by faith know this world is not their real home.
15. If they were thinking about the place they left, they could have gone back.
16. But they wanted a better place—a heavenly home. So God is not ashamed to be their God.
17. By faith, Abraham offered Isaac to God, even though Isaac was the promised son.
18. Abraham believed God could raise the dead.
19. He received Isaac back, in a way.
20. By faith, Isaac blessed Jacob and Esau about their future.
21. By faith, Jacob blessed Joseph's sons.
22. By faith, Joseph spoke about the future and gave instructions about his bones.
23. By faith, Moses' parents hid him as a baby. They weren't afraid of the king.
24. By faith, Moses chose to suffer with God's people instead of enjoying sin for a short time.
25. He saw Christ as more valuable than Egypt's riches.
26. He looked forward to God's reward.
27. By faith, he left Egypt, not fearing the king.
28. By faith, he kept the Passover and put blood on doorways so the people would be safe.

29. By faith, the Israelites crossed the Red Sea. The Egyptians drowned trying to follow.
30. By faith, the walls of Jericho fell after the people marched for seven days.
31. By faith, Rahab welcomed the spies and wasn't killed with the others.
32. What more can I say? I don't have time to talk about Gideon, Barak, Samson, Jephthah, David, Samuel, and the prophets.
33. By faith, they won battles, ruled fairly, and saw God's promises come true.
34. They shut the mouths of lions, escaped fire, and were made strong again.
35. Women got their dead back to life. Others were beaten and refused to give up their faith.
36. Some were mocked, beaten, chained, and put in jail.
37. Some were stoned or cut in two. Others were killed by the sword. Some were poor and mistreated.
38. The world was not worthy of them.
39. They were praised for their faith, but they didn't receive everything God promised.
40. God had something better planned for us, so they would not be made perfect without us.

Hebrews 12

1. We have a big crowd of people who lived by faith watching us. So let's get rid of sin and run the race with strength.
2. Keep your eyes on Jesus. He started our faith, and He makes it complete. He didn't give up when He had to suffer on the cross.
3. Think about Jesus and how He stayed strong when people hated Him. That will help you not give up.
4. You haven't had to suffer and die for your faith like He did.
5. Remember what God says: "My child, don't ignore the Lord's discipline. He corrects the one He loves."
6. God teaches us like a good father teaches his children.
7. If you're being corrected, it means you're His child.
8. If you're not corrected, you're not really His child.
9. We respected our parents when they disciplined us. Shouldn't we respect God even more?
10. Our parents trained us for a short time. God does it for our good, to make us holy.
11. Discipline doesn't feel good at the time. But later, it helps us live better lives.
12. So stand tall. Be strong.
13. Walk in a straight path, so your weak legs will heal and not get worse.
14. Try to live in peace and be holy. Without holiness, no one will see the Lord.
15. Don't let bitterness grow. It will cause trouble and hurt many.
16. Don't be like Esau, who sold his blessing for one meal.
17. Later, he wanted the blessing back but it was too late, even though he cried.
18. You have not come to a mountain full of fire, darkness, and fear like the people in Moses' time.
19. They heard a voice so loud they begged it to stop.
20. They couldn't follow what was commanded—they were too scared.
21. Even Moses said, "I'm shaking with fear."
22. You have come to Mount Zion, the city of God, with angels and people of faith.
23. Their names are written in heaven. God is their judge. Jesus made all this possible with His blood.

24. His blood brings forgiveness, not fear.
25. Don't ignore God's warning. If people didn't escape when He warned them on earth, we won't escape if we ignore His voice from heaven.
26. His voice shook the earth once. He will shake heaven and earth again.
27. This shows that what can be shaken will go away. What can't be shaken will stay forever.
28. So let's be thankful. We are part of a kingdom that will never be shaken. Let's worship God with respect and awe.
29. Our God is a consuming fire.

Hebrews 13

1. Keep loving each other like family.
2. Don't forget to show kindness to strangers. Some people have helped angels without knowing it.
3. Remember those in jail as if you were in jail too. Think of those suffering as if it were you.
4. Honor marriage. Keep it pure. God will judge those who are unfaithful.
5. Don't love money. Be happy with what you have. God said, "I will never leave you."
6. So we can say, "The Lord helps me. I won't be afraid. No one can really hurt me."
7. Remember your leaders who taught you God's word. Think about how they lived, and follow their faith.
8. Jesus Christ is the same yesterday, today, and forever.
9. Don't be fooled by strange teachings. It's better to be made strong by God's grace than by rules about food.
10. We have an altar that those who follow the old law have no right to use.
11. The blood of animals is taken into the holy place, but their bodies are burned outside the camp.
12. In the same way, Jesus suffered outside the city to make us holy.
13. So let's go to Him, even if it means being rejected.
14. This world is not our real home. We are waiting for our forever home.
15. Through Jesus, let's always offer praise to God—giving thanks with our words.
16. Don't forget to do good and share with others. God is pleased with that.
17. Obey your leaders. They watch over your souls and must answer to God. Make their job joyful, not hard.
18. Pray for us. We want to live right in every way.
19. I especially ask you to pray so I can come back to you soon.
20. May the God of peace, who brought Jesus back from the dead, help you do everything good.
21. May He give you everything you need to do His will. May Jesus work in us. To Him be glory forever. Amen.
22. Please listen to what I've written. It's short but important.
23. I want you to know that Timothy has been set free. If he comes soon, we will come see you together.
24. Greet all your leaders and all God's people. The believers from Italy say hello.
25. May God's grace be with you all.

– James –

True faith shows in actions—like controlling the tongue and helping others.

James 1

1. This letter is from James, a servant of God and of Jesus. I'm writing to the twelve tribes scattered around the world. Hello!
2. Be happy when you have hard times. These test your faith.

3. Testing makes you stronger.
4. Let it grow your patience so you'll be complete and not lacking anything.
5. If you need wisdom, ask God. He gives freely to everyone.
6. But ask with faith. Don't doubt. Doubters are like waves pushed around by the wind.
7. People who doubt shouldn't expect to get anything from God.
8. They are unsure and change all the time.
9. Believers who are poor should be glad that God honors them.
10. Rich people should be glad when they're made humble. Their riches won't last.
11. Rich people fade away like flowers in the sun.
12. Blessed are those who keep going during hard times. They will receive a crown of life from God.
13. When you are tempted, don't say, "God is tempting me." God doesn't do wrong or tempt anyone.
14. We are tempted by our own desires.
15. Desire leads to sin. Sin leads to death.
16. Don't be tricked, dear friends.
17. Every good thing comes from God. He never changes.
18. He chose to give us life through His word so we could be His special people.
19. Listen first, think before you speak, and don't rush to get angry.
20. Anger does not please God.
21. Stop doing wrong. Accept the word God put in you. It can save you.
22. Don't just listen to God's word. Do what it says.
23. If you hear but don't do it, it's like looking in a mirror and then forgetting what you look like.
24. You saw yourself, but then forgot.
25. But if you look closely into God's perfect word and keep doing it, you will be blessed.
26. If you think you are religious but can't control your tongue, your religion is useless.
27. Real religion that God accepts is this: Help orphans and widows, and stay away from the world's sin.

James 2

1. Don't treat people better just because they're rich.
2. Suppose someone comes in wearing fancy clothes and jewelry, and another person comes in wearing old, dirty clothes.
3. If you give the rich person a good seat but make the poor person stand or sit on the floor,
4. you're showing favoritism and judging people unfairly.
5. Listen, dear friends: God chose the poor to be rich in faith and to be part of His kingdom.
6. But you insult the poor. Aren't the rich the ones who take you to court?
7. They are the ones who speak badly about Jesus.
8. The Bible says, "Love your neighbor as yourself." That is the right thing to do.
9. But if you treat some people better than others, you're sinning.
10. If you follow the whole law but break one rule, you're guilty of breaking all of it.
11. God said, "Do not commit adultery," and, "Do not kill." Breaking either one is still sin.
12. Speak and act like people who will be judged by the law that gives freedom.
13. If you don't show mercy, God won't show you mercy. But mercy wins over judgment.
14. What good is it to say you have faith if you don't show it by your actions?

15. Suppose someone needs food and clothes.
16. If you say, "Good luck! Stay warm and fed," but don't help—what good is that?
17. Faith without action is dead.
18. Someone might say, "You have faith, I have action." Show me your faith without action, and I'll show you my faith by my actions.
19. You believe in one God. Good! Even demons believe that—and they shake with fear.
20. Faith without action is useless.
21. Abraham showed his faith by offering his son Isaac to God.
22. His faith and actions worked together. His faith was made complete by what he did.
23. The Bible says, "Abraham believed God, and it was counted as righteousness."
24. So you see, people are made right with God by what they do, not just by what they believe.
25. Rahab the prostitute was also made right with God by helping the spies escape.
26. Just as the body without the spirit is dead, so faith without action is dead.

James 3

1. Not many of you should become teachers. Teachers will be judged more strictly.
2. We all make mistakes. If someone never says anything wrong, they're perfect and can control their whole body.
3. We use bits to control horses.
4. Ships are huge, but small rudders guide them wherever the captain wants—even in strong winds.
5. In the same way, the tongue is small but can do big things. A tiny spark can start a big fire.
6. The tongue is like a fire. It can mess up your whole life. It can come from hell.
7. People can tame animals—birds, reptiles, and sea creatures.
8. But no one can tame the tongue. It's wild and full of poison.
9. We use it to praise God and curse people made in His image.
10. Praises and curses come from the same mouth. This should not happen.
11. Can fresh water and salty water come from the same spring?
12. Can a fig tree grow olives? Or a grapevine grow figs? No. A salty spring can't give fresh water.
13. Are you wise and understanding? Then show it by living right and doing good with a humble heart.
14. But if you're jealous or selfish, don't brag. That's not wisdom from God.
15. That kind of wisdom comes from the earth—it's unspiritual and from the devil.
16. Where there's jealousy and selfishness, there's disorder and every kind of evil.
17. But wisdom from God is pure, peaceful, gentle, kind, full of mercy and good actions. It's sincere and fair.
18. People who make peace will plant seeds of peace and gather what is right and good.

James 4

1. Why do you fight and argue? It's because you want things and don't get them.
2. You want something but don't get it, so you fight. You don't ask God.
3. And when you do ask, you don't get it because you ask for selfish reasons.
4. You can't be friends with the world and with God. Loving the world means being God's enemy.
5. God wants our full love and is jealous for us.

6. But God gives more grace. The Bible says, "God opposes the proud but gives grace to the humble."
7. So obey God. Say no to the devil, and he will run from you.
8. Come close to God, and He will come close to you. Wash your hands and clean your hearts.
9. Be sorry for your sins. Cry and be serious.
10. Be humble, and God will lift you up.
11. Don't speak badly about others. If you judge others, you're judging God's law.
12. God is the only judge. Don't take His place.
13. Don't say, "Today or tomorrow we will go here or there to make money."
14. You don't even know what will happen tomorrow. Your life is like a mist—it's here for a short time, then gone.
15. You should say, "If the Lord wants, we will live and do this or that."
16. But you brag and act proud. That is wrong.
17. If you know the right thing to do but don't do it, you are sinning.

James 5

1. Listen, rich people. Cry and be sad for the trouble that's coming.
2. Your riches are rotting. Your clothes are full of holes.
3. Your gold and silver are rusted. The rust will be a witness against you.
4. You didn't pay the workers who mowed your fields. Their cries have reached God.
5. You lived in luxury and pleased yourself. You fattened yourselves for the day of judgment.
6. You judged and killed innocent people who didn't fight back.
7. Be patient, brothers and sisters, until the Lord comes. Farmers wait for rain and their crops.
8. You must wait too. Stay strong. The Lord is coming soon.
9. Don't complain about each other, or you will be judged.
10. Look at the prophets who spoke for God. They were patient in suffering.
11. We say they were blessed. You've heard of Job's patience. And you've seen how kind God is.
12. Don't swear by heaven or earth. Just say "Yes" or "No." Anything more is wrong.
13. If you're suffering, pray. If you're happy, sing.
14. If you're sick, call the church leaders. Let them pray and anoint you with oil in Jesus' name.
15. The prayer of faith will heal the sick, and God will raise them up. If they've sinned, they'll be forgiven.
16. Tell your sins to each other and pray for each other so you'll be healed. The prayer of a good person is powerful.
17. Elijah was a human like us. He prayed for no rain, and it didn't rain for 3½ years.
18. He prayed again, and it rained, and the earth grew crops.
19. If someone wanders from the truth and another brings them back,
20. remember this: Whoever turns a sinner back will save that person from death and cover many sins.

– 1 Peter –

Peter encourages believers to stand firm through suffering and live holy lives.

1 Peter 1

1. This letter is from Peter, an apostle of Jesus. I'm writing to God's people who had to leave their homes and are scattered across many places.
2. God the Father chose you. The Spirit made you holy. You obeyed Jesus and

3. were made clean by His blood. May God give you more grace and peace.
4. Praise God! Because of His mercy, He gave us new life through Jesus' resurrection. Now we have real hope.
5. God has a gift waiting for you in heaven. It will never spoil or fade away.
6. Through faith, God's power protects you until your full salvation comes.
7. Be happy about this, even though now you may have to suffer for a little while.
8. These troubles test your faith, just like fire tests gold. When your faith passes the test, it brings praise and honor when Jesus returns.
9. You haven't seen Jesus, but you love Him. You believe in Him and are filled with joy.
10. Your faith will bring you the reward—your full salvation.
11. The prophets talked about this salvation. They searched carefully to understand it.
12. God's Spirit showed them that the Christ would suffer and then be honored. They wrote it down for you.
13. They learned that what they were saying wasn't for themselves but for you. Now it has been told to you by those who shared the good news. Even angels want to understand these things.
14. So get ready. Think clearly. Put all your hope in the gift you'll get when Jesus comes back.
15. Obey God like children who want to please Him. Don't go back to your old ways.
16. Be holy in all you do, just like God is holy.
17. The Scriptures say, "Be holy, because I am holy."
18. If you call God your Father, respect Him. He judges everyone fairly.
19. You were saved from an empty life. Not with silver or gold,
20. but with the precious blood of Jesus, the perfect Lamb.
21. God chose Him before the world began, but He came at the right time for you.
22. Because of Jesus, you believe in God, who raised Him from the dead. So your faith and hope are in God.
23. You made your hearts clean by obeying the truth. So love each other deeply.
24. You've been born again—not from something that dies, but from God's living word.
25. People and their glory fade like grass and flowers.
26. But God's word lasts forever. And this is the word that was shared with you.

1 Peter 2

1. Stop doing wrong things. Don't lie, be jealous, or speak badly about others.
2. Like babies want milk, you should want to learn God's word so you can grow strong.
3. You have already tasted how good the Lord is.
4. Come to Jesus. He is the living stone. People rejected Him, but God chose Him and loves Him.
5. You are also like living stones. God is building you into a spiritual house. You will serve God like priests.
6. The Scriptures say, "I am placing a stone in Zion. The one who trusts in Him will never be disappointed."
7. This is good news for believers. But for those who don't believe, the stone they rejected has become the most important one.
8. For them, Jesus is a rock that makes them trip. They fall because they don't obey God.
9. But you are chosen. You are special to God. He saved you so you can tell others how great He is.

10. You were once not a people. Now you are God's people. You didn't have mercy. Now you do.
11. Friends, stay away from sinful desires. They fight against your soul.
12. Live good lives. Then even if people say bad things about you, they will see your good works and praise God.
13. Obey people in power, like kings and governors. God wants us to do this.
14. They are sent to punish those who do wrong and praise those who do right.
15. God wants you to live right and stop foolish people from speaking against you.
16. Live as free people, but don't use your freedom to do wrong. Live as God's servants.
17. Respect everyone. Love believers. Honor God. Respect the king.
18. Servants, obey your masters—even if they are unfair.
19. It pleases God when you suffer for doing good because you follow Him.
20. It's no big deal if you suffer for doing wrong. But if you suffer for doing right, that pleases God.
21. Jesus suffered for you. Follow His example.
22. He never sinned or lied.
23. When people hurt Him, He didn't fight back. He trusted God to judge fairly.
24. He took our sins on Himself so we can live right. By His wounds, we are healed.
25. You were like lost sheep. Now you've returned to your Shepherd.

1 Peter 3

1. Wives, follow your husbands. Even if they don't believe, your good behavior can help them turn to God.
2. They will see your pure and respectful life.
3. Don't focus on fancy hair, jewelry, or clothes.
4. Instead, have a gentle and quiet spirit. That is what God values.
5. Long ago, holy women who trusted God made themselves beautiful this way.
6. Sarah obeyed Abraham. You are her children if you do what is right and don't give in to fear.
7. Husbands, treat your wives with respect. They share the gift of life with you. Then nothing will block your prayers.
8. Finally, love each other. Be kind, humble, and work together.
9. Don't pay back evil with evil. Instead, bless others. God will bless you.
10. The Scriptures say, "If you want a good life, keep your tongue from speaking evil."
11. "Turn away from evil and do good. Try to live in peace."
12. "God watches over the good. But He turns away from those who do evil."
13. Who will hurt you if you always try to do what's right?
14. But even if you suffer for doing good, you are blessed. Don't be afraid.
15. Keep Christ as Lord in your heart. Be ready to explain your hope, but do it gently and with respect.
16. Keep your conscience clear. Then if people speak against you, they will be ashamed.
17. It's better to suffer for doing good than for doing wrong—if that's God's plan.
18. Christ also suffered once for sins. He was right, and He died for those who were wrong to bring us to God.
19. After He died, He preached to the spirits in prison.
20. These were people from Noah's time, who didn't listen. Only a few were saved through water in the ark.

21. That water is like baptism. Baptism doesn't just wash dirt off. It shows that you've given your heart to God.
22. Jesus went to heaven and is now at God's right side. Angels and powers are under His control.

1 Peter 4

1. Since Jesus suffered, you should be ready to suffer too. Suffering helps you stop sinning.
2. Don't live for your own desires. Live for what God wants.
3. In the past, you lived in sin—doing wrong things, getting drunk, partying, and worshiping idols.
4. Now that you don't do those things anymore, others are surprised and may insult you.
5. But they will have to answer to God.
6. The good news was preached even to those who have died, so they could live with God.
7. The end is near. Be careful and stay calm so you can pray.
8. Most of all, love each other deeply. Love covers many sins.
9. Be kind and welcome others into your homes without complaining.
10. Use the gifts God gave you to serve each other.
11. If you speak, speak God's words. If you help, do it with God's strength. Then God will be praised through Jesus.
12. Friends, don't be surprised when you have to suffer. It's a test.
13. Be glad when you suffer like Christ did. You'll be even happier when He returns.
14. If people insult you because you follow Jesus, you are blessed. God's Spirit is with you.
15. Don't suffer because you did wrong—like stealing or hurting others.
16. But if you suffer for being a Christian, don't be ashamed. Praise God.
17. It's time for God's judgment to begin, starting with His people.
18. If it's hard for the godly to be saved, how much worse will it be for those who reject God?
19. If you suffer for doing right, trust your life to God. He made you and will take care of you.

1 Peter 5

1. I'm also a church leader, and I saw Christ suffer. I'll also share in His glory.
2. I say to other leaders: Take care of God's people like a shepherd cares for sheep. Do it because you want to, not for money.
3. Don't boss people around. Be a good example.
4. When the Chief Shepherd (Jesus) comes, you'll get a crown that never fades.
5. Young people, follow your leaders. Everyone, be humble with each other. "God opposes the proud but gives grace to the humble."
6. Stay humble under God's hand. He will lift you up at the right time.
7. Give all your worries to Him. He cares for you.
8. Be alert. Your enemy the devil is like a lion, looking for someone to attack.
9. Stay strong in your faith. Remember that other believers everywhere are also suffering.
10. After you suffer a little, God will make you strong again. He called you to share in His glory forever.
11. To God be power forever. Amen.
12. I've written this short letter with the help of Silas. Stay strong in God's grace.
13. The church in Babylon sends greetings. So does Mark, my son in Christ.

14. Greet each other with love. Peace to all of you who are in Christ.

–2 Peter –

Peter warns against false teachers and reminds Christians of Jesus' return.

2 Peter 1

1. This letter is from Simon Peter, a servant and apostle of Jesus. I'm writing to those who trust Jesus like we do. God made you right with Him.
2. May you have more grace and peace as you learn about God and Jesus.
3. God gave us everything we need to live a godly life through knowing Him.
4. He gave us great promises so we can live like Him and stay away from sin.
5. So try hard to add to your faith: goodness,
6. then knowledge, self-control, patience, godliness,
7. kindness, and love.
8. If you grow in these, you will be useful and strong in knowing Jesus.
9. But if you don't, you are blind and forget that God forgave your sins.
10. So work hard to show you really belong to God. Then you won't fall.
11. God will welcome you into Jesus' eternal kingdom.
12. I'll keep reminding you of these things, even though you already know them.
13. As long as I'm alive, I want to help you remember.
14. I know I will die soon, as Jesus told me.
15. I'll do my best to help you remember these things even after I'm gone.
16. We didn't make up stories when we told you about Jesus. We saw His greatness.
17. God the Father gave Him honor. He said, "This is My Son, and I love Him."
18. We heard this voice from heaven when we were with Jesus on the mountain.
19. We also have the prophets' messages. You should pay attention to them—they shine like a light in the dark.
20. First, remember this: no prophecy in Scripture came from someone's own idea.
21. These messages came from God. The Holy Spirit helped people speak His words.

2 Peter 2

1. False teachers will come. They will secretly teach lies and even deny Jesus. This will destroy them.
2. Many people will follow their wrong ways. Because of them, others will speak badly about the truth.
3. These teachers only want money. They tell lies to get rich. But they will be punished.
4. God didn't let the angels get away with sin. He sent them to a dark prison.
5. God destroyed the world with a flood but saved Noah and seven others.
6. He burned Sodom and Gomorrah to warn people. But He saved Lot, a good man.
7. Lot was upset by the evil around him every day.
8. The Lord knows how to rescue people who follow Him and punish those who don't.
9. This is especially true for people who live to please their sinful desires and hate authority.
10. They are bold and proud. They insult heavenly beings without respect.
11. Even angels don't speak badly about them before the Lord.
12. These people speak without understanding. They act like animals that don't think. They will be destroyed.
13. They do evil openly. They love to sin.

14. Their eyes are full of sin. They never stop doing wrong. They trick weak people. They are greedy.
15. They left the right path and followed the way of Balaam, who loved money.
16. But Balaam was stopped by a donkey that spoke with a human voice.
17. These people are like dry wells and dark clouds. God has a place of darkness ready for them.
18. They brag and speak nonsense. They trick people who are just escaping sin by promising freedom.
19. But they are slaves to sin. People are slaves to whatever controls them.
20. If someone escapes sin through Jesus but then goes back to sin, they are worse off than before.
21. It would've been better if they never knew the truth.
22. They are like dogs that go back to what they threw up or pigs that get dirty again.

2 Peter 3

1. This is now my second letter to you. I want to help you remember what the prophets and apostles taught.
2. In the last days, people will make fun of the truth. They will follow their own evil desires.
3. They'll say, "Where is Jesus? He promised to come!"
4. They will forget that long ago God made the world and sent a flood.
5. But God's word made the heavens and the earth.
6. Then the world was flooded and destroyed.
7. Now, by that same word, the world is being kept for fire and judgment.
8. Don't forget this: To the Lord, one day is like a thousand years, and a thousand years is like one day.
9. The Lord isn't slow to keep His promise. He's being patient, giving everyone time to turn back to Him.
10. But the day of the Lord will come like a thief. The sky will disappear, and everything will be destroyed by fire.
11. So think about how you should live—holy and godly lives.
12. Look forward to the day of God. That day will bring fire, and everything will melt.
13. But we are waiting for a new heaven and a new earth where everything is right.
14. So, friends, try to live in peace and do what's right.
15. Remember: God's patience means salvation.
16. Paul also wrote about this. Some of his letters are hard to understand, and people twist them—just like they twist other Scriptures.
17. So, be careful. Don't get tricked and fall from your strong faith.
18. Grow in the grace and knowledge of Jesus.
    To Him be glory now and forever. Amen.

– 1 John –

True believers live in love, truth, and obedience to God.

1 John 1

1. We are telling you about the One who existed from the beginning. We heard Him, we saw Him, and we even touched Him. He is the Word of life.
2. This life was shown to us, and now we share it with you. It comes from God and lasts forever.
3. We are sharing what we saw and heard, so you can be part of our group. And our group is joined with God the Father and Jesus His Son.
4. We write this so our joy can be full.

5. This is the message we heard from Jesus: God is light, and there is no darkness in Him.
6. If we say we are joined with Him but still live in darkness, we're lying.
7. But if we live in the light, like God does, then we share life with each other. And the blood of Jesus cleans us from all sin.
8. If we say we don't have sin, we are fooling ourselves.
9. But if we tell the truth about our sins, God will forgive us and make us clean.
10. If we say we've never sinned, we are saying God is a liar, and His word isn't in us.

1 John 2

1. My children, I'm writing this so you won't sin. But if you do sin, Jesus speaks to the Father for us.
2. Jesus died to take the punishment for our sins—and for the whole world.
3. If we obey His commands, we know we really know Him.
4. If someone says, "I know God," but doesn't obey Him, that person is lying.
5. If we obey God, we truly love Him, and we live in Him.
6. If we say we live in Him, we should live like Jesus did.
7. I'm not giving you a new rule, but an old one you've had from the start: love one another.
8. Still, I'm writing it again, because the darkness is leaving and the true light is shining.
9. If someone says, "I'm in the light," but hates others, they are still in darkness.
10. If you love others, you're living in the light, and you won't fall.
11. But if you hate others, you're in darkness and don't know where you're going.
12. I write to you, children: Your sins are forgiven because of Jesus.
13. I write to you, parents: You know the One who was from the beginning.
    I write to you, young people: You have defeated the evil one.
14. I say it again:
    Children—you know the Father.
    Parents—you know the One from the beginning.
    Young people—you are strong, and God's word lives in you. You defeated the evil one.
15. Don't love the world or the things in it. If you do, you don't truly love God.
16. The world gives us sinful desires, pride, and greed—but these don't come from God.
17. The world and its desires are passing away, but those who do God's will live forever.
18. Dear children, the end is near. Many enemies of Christ have come—just like you heard they would.
19. They left us, showing they never really belonged with us.
20. But you have the Holy Spirit, and you know the truth.
21. I'm writing because you do know the truth—not because you don't.
22. A liar is someone who denies Jesus is the Christ. That person is against Christ.
23. Whoever denies the Son doesn't have the Father either. But if you accept the Son, you have the Father too.
24. Keep the truth you heard from the start. If you do, you will stay joined with the Son and the Father.
25. God promised us eternal life.
26. I'm writing to warn you about those who try to trick you.
27. But the Holy Spirit teaches you everything. So stay with what He taught you.
28. Stay joined with Jesus. Then you can be confident when He comes back.

29. If you know Jesus always does what's right, you know His children do too.

1 John 3

1. See how much the Father loves us! He calls us His children—and we really are!
2. Dear friends, we are already God's children. But we don't yet know what we'll be like. We do know we will be like Jesus.
3. Everyone who hopes in Jesus tries to stay pure, just like Him.
4. Everyone who sins is breaking God's law. Sin is lawlessness.
5. Jesus came to take away sins. He never sinned.
6. If you stay joined with Him, you won't keep sinning. But if you keep sinning, you don't really know Him.
7. Don't be fooled. If you do what's right, you're righteous like Jesus.
8. But if you keep sinning, you belong to the devil. The devil has sinned from the beginning. Jesus came to destroy his work.
9. God's children don't keep on sinning, because God's life is in them.
10. This is how we know who are God's children and who are the devil's: Anyone who doesn't do what is right or doesn't love others doesn't belong to God.
11. This is the message you heard from the beginning: Love one another.
12. Don't be like Cain. He belonged to the devil and killed his brother. Why? Because Cain did evil and Abel did good.
13. Don't be surprised if the world hates you.
14. We know we've passed from death to life because we love others. Those who don't love are still dead.
15. If you hate someone, it's like murder in your heart. And murderers don't have eternal life.
16. We know what love is because Jesus gave His life for us. We should give our lives for others.
17. If you have plenty and see someone in need but don't help, how can God's love be in you?
18. Children, don't just say you love people—show it by what you do.
19. That's how we know we belong to the truth, and it will make us confident before God.
20. Even if we feel guilty, God is greater than our feelings and knows everything.
21. If we don't feel guilty, we can be bold when we pray.
22. We receive what we ask for because we obey God and do what pleases Him.
23. This is His command: Believe in Jesus and love each other.
24. Those who obey stay joined with God, and He lives in them. We know this because of the Spirit He gave us.

1 John 4

1. Dear friends, don't believe everyone who says they speak for God. Test them to see if they are true, because many false teachers have gone out.
2. This is how you know if someone has God's Spirit: They say Jesus came in a real human body.
3. If they don't say that, they don't have God. They have the spirit of the enemy of Christ.
4. But you belong to God. You have already won, because God in you is greater than the enemy in the world.
5. People who belong to the world speak like the world, and the world listens to them.
6. But we belong to God. People who know God listen to us. That's how we

know the Spirit of truth and the spirit of lies.

7. Dear friends, let us love one another. Love comes from God. Everyone who loves is born of God and knows God.

8. Whoever doesn't love doesn't know God, because God is love.

9. God showed His love by sending His only Son so we could have life through Him.

10. This is real love—not that we loved God, but that He loved us and sent Jesus to take away our sins.

11. Dear friends, since God loved us that much, we should love each other.

12. No one has ever seen God, but if we love each other, God lives in us.

13. We know we live in Him because He gave us His Spirit.

14. We saw and now tell others that the Father sent His Son to save the world.

15. If you say Jesus is God's Son, God lives in you and you live in God.

16. We know and believe God's love for us. God is love. If we live in love, we live in God.

17. Love makes us brave on judgment day. We live like Jesus in this world.

18. Real love takes away fear. If you're afraid, your love isn't complete.

19. We love because God loved us first.

20. If someone says, "I love God," but hates others, they're lying. If you can't love people you see, you can't love God you can't see.

21. God gave us this command: Anyone who loves God must also love others.

1 John 5

1. Everyone who believes that Jesus is the Christ is a child of God. If you love the Father, you will love His children too.

2. We know we love God's children if we love God and obey His commands.

3. Loving God means obeying Him. And His commands are not hard.

4. Everyone born of God wins against the world. Our faith gives us this victory.

5. Who wins against the world? Only those who believe Jesus is God's Son.

6. Jesus came by water and blood—not just water, but both. The Spirit says this is true.

7. There are three that tell us the truth:

8. the Spirit, the water, and the blood. They all agree.

9. We believe people's words, but God's words are greater. He tells us Jesus is His Son.

10. If you believe in God's Son, you know this is true. If you don't believe, you're saying God is a liar.

11. Here's the truth: God gave us eternal life, and this life is in His Son.

12. If you have the Son, you have life. If you don't, you don't have life.

13. I'm writing to you who believe in Jesus, so you'll know you have eternal life.

14. We can be confident when we pray. If we ask for what pleases God, He hears us.

15. If we know He hears us, we know we'll get what we asked for.

16. If you see another believer sin, pray for them. God will give them life. But some sins lead to death. I'm not saying you should pray for that.

17. All wrongdoing is sin, but not every sin leads to death.

18. We know that God's children don't keep on sinning. God protects them, and the evil one can't harm them.

19. We belong to God, but the world is under the power of the evil one.

20. We know God's Son came and gave us understanding. Now we know the true God and have life in His Son.

21. Dear children, keep away from idols.

– 2 John –

A short letter warning against false teachers and urging love and truth.

2 John

1. This letter is from the elder. I'm writing to a special lady and her children, whom I love in truth. Everyone who knows the truth loves you too.
2. We love you because the truth lives in us and stays with us forever.
3. Grace, mercy, and peace will be with us from God the Father and Jesus His Son.
4. I was very happy to find out that some of your children are living by the truth, just as the Father told us to.
5. Dear lady, I'm asking you to love each other. This isn't a new rule—it's what we had from the beginning.
6. Loving each other means living the way God wants us to. That's the command we were given from the start.
7. Many people who deny that Jesus came in a real body have gone out into the world. They are liars and enemies of Christ.
8. Be careful! Don't lose what you've worked for. Stay strong and receive your full reward.
9. Anyone who goes too far and doesn't follow Christ's teaching does not have God. But if you follow Christ's teaching, you have both the Father and the Son.
10. If someone comes to you and doesn't teach the truth about Christ, don't welcome them into your home or encourage them.
11. If you do, you're sharing in the wrong they're doing.
12. I have much more to say, but I don't want to write it with pen and paper. I hope to come and talk to you in person so we can be truly happy.
13. The children of your chosen sister send their love.

– 3 John –

A personal note praising a faithful believer and warning against prideful leaders.

3 John

1. This letter is from the elder. I'm writing to my dear friend Gaius. I love you in the truth.
2. Dear friend, I hope you are doing well and staying healthy, just like your soul is doing well.
3. I was very happy when some believers came and told me how faithful you are and how you live by the truth.
4. Nothing makes me happier than hearing my children are living by the truth.
5. Dear friend, you are showing love when you help other believers, even if they are strangers.
6. They told the church about your love. Please keep helping them in a way that pleases God.
7. They travel for Jesus and don't take help from people who don't believe.
8. So we should help them too, so we can work together for the truth.
9. I wrote a letter to the church, but Diotrephes, who loves to be in charge, will not accept us.
10. If I come, I'll talk about what he's doing. He talks badly about us, refuses to welcome other believers, and even stops others who try to help.
11. Dear friend, don't copy what is bad. Do what is good. People who do good belong to God. People who do evil don't know God.
12. Everyone speaks well of Demetrius, and the truth agrees. We speak well of

13. him too, and you know we tell the truth.
14. I have more to say, but I don't want to write it down with pen and ink.
15. I hope to see you soon. Then we can talk face to face.
16. Peace to you. Your friends here send greetings. Please greet each of our friends there by name.

– Jude –

Jude urges believers to fight for the faith and reject false teachers.

Jude

1. This letter is from Jude, a servant of Jesus and brother of James. I'm writing to those who are loved by God, called by Him, and kept safe by Jesus.
2. May you have more mercy, peace, and love.
3. Friends, I wanted to write about how we all share in salvation. But now I must urge you to fight for the true faith, which was given once for all.
4. Some people have secretly joined your group. They are evil and twist God's message. They say God's grace means
5. we can sin. They refuse to follow Jesus Christ.
6. You already know this, but remember: God saved His people from Egypt, but later destroyed those who didn't believe.
7. He punished angels who didn't stay in their place. They are locked up in darkness until judgment day.
8. Sodom and Gomorrah were full of sin. They are an example of what happens to people who reject God.
9. These false teachers do the same. They live sinful lives, reject authority, and insult heavenly beings.
10. Even the archangel Michael didn't insult the devil. He said, "The Lord rebuke you!"
11. But these people insult things they don't understand. They act like animals and destroy themselves.
12. Trouble to them! They are like Cain, who killed his brother. They are greedy like Balaam. They rebel like Korah.
13. They are like hidden dangers at your gatherings. They only care about themselves. They are clouds with no rain, trees with no fruit, pulled up and dead.
14. They are like wild waves, throwing up shame like foam. They are like stars that wander, doomed to darkness.
15. Enoch, the seventh from Adam, warned about them: "The Lord is coming with thousands of holy ones."
16. He will judge everyone and punish all who do evil.
17. These people complain, follow their own desires, brag, and flatter others to get what they want.
18. Friends, remember what the apostles said:
19. "In the last days, people will make fun of God and live however they want."
20. These people cause divisions. They don't have the Spirit.
21. But you, friends, build your faith and pray in the Holy Spirit.
22. Stay in God's love and wait for Jesus to bring you eternal life.
23. Be kind to those who doubt.
24. Help save others from the fire. Show mercy, but be careful. Hate sin, even when it looks tempting.
25. God can keep you from falling and bring you to Him with great joy.
26. To God, our only Savior through Jesus—glory, power, and authority forever! Amen.

–Revelation –

John sees visions of spiritual battles, judgment, and Jesus' final victory.

Revelation 1

1. This book shows what God gave Jesus to tell His people—what will happen soon. Jesus sent an angel to tell it to John.
2. John told everything he saw. It came from God and Jesus.
3. Anyone who reads this book, listens to it, and obeys it will be blessed. The time is near.
4. This is from John to the seven churches in Asia.
Grace and peace to you from God, who was, who is, and who is coming. And from the seven spirits before His throne.
5. And from Jesus, the faithful one, who rose from death, and rules over all kings.
He loves us. He freed us from our sins with His blood.
6. He made us into a group of priests to serve God His Father.
To Jesus be glory and power forever!
7. Look! He is coming in the clouds. Everyone will see Him—even those who hurt Him.
8. All people will cry when they see Him. This will happen!
9. God says, "I am the beginning and the end. I am the one who was, who is, and who is coming. I have all power."
10. I am John, your brother. I also suffer like you and wait for God's kingdom. I was sent to an island called Patmos because I told people about Jesus.
11. On the Lord's Day, I was filled with the Holy Spirit. I heard a loud voice behind me, like a trumpet.
12. It said, "Write what you see and send it to the seven churches."
13. I turned to see who was speaking. I saw seven golden lampstands.
14. In the middle of them was someone like a Son of Man. He wore a long robe with a gold band around His chest.
15. His head and hair were white like wool, white as snow. His eyes were like fire.
16. His feet were like glowing metal. His voice was loud like rushing water.
17. He held seven stars in His right hand. A sharp sword came from His mouth. His face was bright like the sun.
18. When I saw Him, I fell at His feet like I was dead. He put His right hand on me and said, "Don't be afraid. I am the First and the Last."
19. "I am the Living One. I was dead, but now I'm alive forever. I have the keys to death and the grave."
20. "Write what you have seen, what is now, and what will happen later."
21. "The seven stars you saw in My hand are the angels of the seven churches. The seven lampstands are the seven churches."

Revelation 2

Message to the church in Ephesus:

1. This is what Jesus says—the one who holds the seven stars and walks among the seven lampstands:
2. "I know what you do. You work hard and don't give up. You don't let evil people stay. You test those who say they are apostles but are not. You found they were lying.
3. You have been patient and strong for Me.
4. But I have this against you: You don't love Me or others like you did at first.
5. Remember how things used to be. Turn back. Do what you did before. If not, I'll take away your lampstand.
6. But you hate what the Nicolaitans do. I hate it too.
7. Listen to what the Spirit says. To the one who wins, I'll give the right to eat from the tree of life in God's garden."

Message to the church in Smyrna:

8. Jesus says this—the First and the Last, the one who died and came back to life:

9. "I know your troubles. I know you are poor—but you are rich in faith. I know people lie about you.

10. Don't be afraid. Some of you will be put in jail to test you. Be strong, even to death. I will give you a crown of life.

11. Listen to the Spirit. Whoever wins will not be hurt by the second death."

Message to the church in Pergamum:

12. Jesus says this—the one with the sharp double-edged sword:

13. "I know where you live—where Satan rules. You stayed strong. You didn't say 'no' to Me, even when My faithful follower Antipas was killed.

14. But I have some things against you: Some of you follow Balaam's teaching. He led people into sin.

15. Others follow the Nicolaitans, who teach wrong things.

16. Turn back now! If you don't, I will come and fight them with My sword.

17. Listen to the Spirit. Whoever wins will get hidden manna and a white stone with a secret name on it."

Message to the church in Thyatira:

18. Jesus says this—the Son of God with fire in His eyes and feet like bronze:

19. "I know what you do—your love, faith, service, and patience. You are doing more now than before.

20. But I have something against you. You let that woman Jezebel lead people into sin.

21. I gave her time to turn away from her sin, but she won't.

22. So I will bring suffering to her and those who follow her.

23. I will punish them, and everyone will know I see hearts and minds. I will give each of you what you deserve.

24. But some of you have not followed her ways. I won't put more on you.

25. Just hold on until I come.

26. Whoever wins and obeys Me will rule nations with power.

27. They will rule with strength, just like I received from My Father.

28. I will also give them the morning star.

29. Listen to what the Spirit says to the churches."

Revelation 3

Message to the church in Sardis:

1. Jesus says this—the one with the seven spirits and seven stars:

"I know what you do. People think you are alive, but you are dead.

2. Wake up! Make what little you have left strong before it dies completely.

3. Remember what you learned. Obey it. Turn back. If not, I'll come like a thief, and you won't know when.

4. Some in Sardis haven't done wrong. They will walk with Me in white clothes.

5. Whoever wins will be dressed in white. I won't erase their name from the book of life. I'll say their name in front of My Father and angels.

6. Listen to the Spirit."

Message to the church in Philadelphia:

7. Jesus says this—the true and holy one who holds the key of David:

8. "I know what you do. I opened a door for you, and no one can close it. You have little strength but obeyed Me and didn't say 'no' to Me.

9. Some people say they are Jews but are lying. I will make them bow at your feet and know I love you.

10. You obeyed Me when times were hard. I will keep you safe during the big test coming to the world.

11. I am coming soon. Hold on to what you have.
12. Whoever wins will be a strong pillar in God's house. I will write God's name, the city's name, and My new name on them.
13. Listen to the Spirit."

Message to the church in Laodicea:

14. Jesus says this—the Amen, the true and faithful witness:
15. "I know what you do. You are not hot or cold. I wish you were one or the other.
16. But because you are lukewarm, I will spit you out.
17. You say, 'I'm rich and need nothing,' but you don't know you're really poor, blind, and naked.
18. I tell you to buy from Me gold that's been tested, white clothes to cover your shame, and medicine for your eyes so you can see.
19. I correct those I love. So be serious and turn back to Me.
20. I stand at the door and knock. If anyone opens the door, I will come in and eat with them.
21. Whoever wins will sit with Me on My throne, just like I won and sat with My Father.
22. Listen to what the Spirit says to the churches."

Revelation 4

1. After this, I saw a door open in heaven. A voice like a trumpet said, "Come up here. I will show you what must happen next."
2. Right away, the Spirit took me there. I saw a throne in heaven, and someone was sitting on it.
3. The one sitting on the throne was shining like jewels. A rainbow, green like an emerald, was around the throne.
4. Around the throne were 24 other thrones with 24 elders sitting on them. They wore white clothes and gold crowns.
5. Lightning and thunder came from the throne. Seven torches were burning in front. These are the seven spirits of God.
6. In front of the throne was something like a sea of glass, clear like crystal. Around the throne were four living beings, full of eyes front and back.
7. The first looked like a lion. The second looked like an ox. The third had a face like a man. The fourth looked like a flying eagle.
8. Each being had six wings and was covered in eyes. Day and night they said:
   "Holy, holy, holy is the Lord God, who was, who is, and who is coming."
9. When they praise God, the one on the throne, who lives forever,
10. the 24 elders bow down. They put their crowns in front of the throne and say:
11. "Our Lord and God, You deserve all praise, honor, and power.
    You made everything. Everything exists because You wanted it."

Revelation 5

1. Then I saw a scroll in the right hand of the one on the throne. It had writing inside and out and was sealed with seven seals.
2. A strong angel said loudly, "Who is worthy to open the scroll and break the seals?"
3. No one in heaven, on earth, or under the earth could open it or even look at it.
4. I cried because no one could open the scroll.
5. One of the elders said, "Don't cry! Look! The Lion from Judah's tribe, from David's family, has won! He can open the scroll."
6. Then I saw a Lamb standing near the throne. He looked like He had been

killed. He had seven horns and seven eyes, which are the seven spirits of God sent into all the earth.

7. He went and took the scroll from the one on the throne.

8. When He took it, the four living beings and the 24 elders fell before Him. Each had a harp and gold bowls full of incense, which are the prayers of God's people.

9. They sang a new song:
"You are worthy to take the scroll and open it,
because You were killed,
and with Your blood You bought people for God
from every tribe, language, people, and nation.

10. You made them a kingdom and priests to serve our God.
They will rule on the earth."

11. I looked again and saw thousands and millions of angels around the throne. They said loudly:

12. "The Lamb who was killed is worthy to receive power, riches, wisdom, strength,
honor, glory, and praise!"

13. Then I heard every creature in heaven, on earth, under the earth, and in the sea say:

"To the One on the throne and to the Lamb,
be praise, honor, glory, and power forever and ever!"

14. The four living beings said, "Amen!" And the elders bowed down and worshiped.

Revelation 6

1. The Lamb opened the first seal. I heard one of the four living beings say, "Come!"

2. I saw a white horse. The rider had a bow and was given a crown. He went out to win battles.

3. The Lamb opened the second seal. The second living being said, "Come!"

4. I saw a red horse. Its rider was given power to take peace from the earth. He had a big sword.

5. The Lamb opened the third seal. The third living being said, "Come!"
I saw a black horse. Its rider held a scale in his hand.

6. I heard a voice say, "A small amount of food costs a full day's pay! But don't harm the oil or wine."

7. The Lamb opened the fourth seal. The fourth living being said, "Come!"

8. I saw a pale horse. Its rider was named Death, and the grave followed behind. They were given power to kill a fourth of the earth with war, hunger, and wild animals.

9. The Lamb opened the fifth seal. I saw under the altar the souls of those killed for speaking God's word.

10. They shouted, "Lord, how long until You judge and punish those who killed us?"

11. Each one was given a white robe. They were told to wait a little longer until more followers were killed like they were.

12. The Lamb opened the sixth seal. There was a big earthquake. The sun turned black, the moon turned red,

13. and stars fell to earth like figs from a tree in the wind.

14. The sky rolled up like a scroll, and mountains and islands were moved.

15. Everyone—kings, leaders, rich, strong, and even slaves—hid in caves.

16. They shouted to the mountains, "Fall on us! Hide us from the One on the throne and from the Lamb's anger!"

17. "The great day of His anger has come. Who can stand?"

Revelation 7

1. After this, I saw four angels standing at the four corners of the earth. They held back the winds.

2. I saw another angel coming from the east with God's seal. He called to the four angels.

3. He said, "Don't hurt the earth, sea, or trees until we mark God's servants on their foreheads."

4. I heard how many were marked—144,000 people from all the tribes of Israel.

5. 12,000 from Judah,
12,000 from Reuben,
12,000 from Gad,

6. 12,000 from Asher,
12,000 from Naphtali,
12,000 from Manasseh,

7. 12,000 from Simeon,
12,000 from Levi,
12,000 from Issachar,

8. 12,000 from Zebulun,
12,000 from Joseph,
12,000 from Benjamin.

9. After this, I saw a huge crowd from every nation and language—too many to count. They stood before the throne and the Lamb, wearing white robes and holding palm branches.

10. They shouted, "Salvation comes from our God and the Lamb!"

11. All the angels stood around the throne, the elders, and the living beings. They fell on their faces and worshiped God.

12. They said, "Amen! Blessing, glory, wisdom, thanks, honor, power, and strength belong to God forever!"

13. One of the elders asked me, "Who are these in white robes, and where did they come from?"

14. I said, "Sir, you know."
He said, "They came out of great trouble. They washed their robes in the Lamb's blood and made them clean.

15. That's why they stand before God and serve Him day and night. He lives among them.

16. They will never be hungry or thirsty again. The sun won't hurt them.

17. The Lamb will be their shepherd. He will lead them to springs of living water.
God will wipe every tear from their eyes."

Revelation 8

1. The Lamb opened the seventh seal. There was silence in heaven for about half an hour.

2. I saw seven angels standing before God. They were given seven trumpets.

3. Another angel came with a golden bowl. He stood at the altar and was given a lot of incense to mix with the prayers of God's people.

4. The smoke from the incense and prayers went up to God.

5. Then the angel took fire from the altar, put it in the bowl, and threw it to the earth. There was thunder, lightning, and an earthquake.

6. The seven angels got ready to blow their trumpets.

7. The first trumpet sounded. Hail and fire mixed with blood were thrown to earth. A third of the earth, trees, and grass burned up.

8. The second trumpet sounded. Something like a big burning mountain was thrown into the sea. A third of the sea turned to blood.

9. A third of the sea creatures died. A third of the ships were destroyed.

10. The third trumpet sounded. A big star, burning like a torch, fell on a third of the rivers and springs.

11. The star was called Wormwood. A third of the water became bitter, and many people died from it.

12. The fourth trumpet sounded. A third of the sun, moon, and stars were darkened. A third of the day and night had no light.

13. Then I saw an eagle flying in the sky. It shouted, "Trouble is coming! Trouble

for the people on earth when the last three trumpets sound!"

Revelation 9

1. The fifth trumpet sounded. A star fell from the sky to earth. It was given the key to the deep hole.
2. The star opened the hole, and smoke came out like from a giant furnace. The sky and sun were darkened.
3. From the smoke came locusts. They were told to hurt only people who didn't have God's mark on their foreheads.
4. They couldn't kill, only hurt for five months. Their sting was like a scorpion.
5. During those days, people will want to die, but they won't be able to.
6. The locusts looked like horses ready for battle. They had gold-like crowns, human faces,
7. hair like women, teeth like lions,
8. breastplates like iron, wings that sounded like rushing chariots,
9. and tails with stingers like scorpions. Their power to hurt people lasted five months.
10. Their king was the angel of the deep pit. His name means "Destroyer."
11. The first trouble is over. Two more are coming.
12. The sixth trumpet sounded. A voice came from the golden altar before God.
13. It told the sixth angel, "Let loose the four angels tied at the great river Euphrates."
14. These four angels had been kept ready for this hour, day, month, and year to kill a third of the people.
15. The army they led had 200 million riders.
16. In my vision, the horses and riders wore red, blue, and yellow armor. The horses had heads like lions, and fire, smoke, and sulfur came from their mouths.
17. A third of the people died from the fire, smoke, and sulfur.
18. The horses' power was in their mouths and tails. Their tails were like snakes that could hurt people.
19. But the rest of the people didn't turn away from their sins. They still worshiped demons and idols made of gold, silver, bronze, stone, and wood—things that can't see or move.
20. They didn't stop their murders, magic, bad behavior, or stealing.

Revelation 10

1. I saw another strong angel come from heaven. He was surrounded by a cloud, had a rainbow above his head, a shining face, and legs like fire.
2. He held a small scroll that was open. He put one foot on the sea and one on land.
3. He shouted loudly like a lion. When he shouted, seven voices spoke like thunder.
4. I was about to write what they said, but a voice from heaven said, "Don't write it. Keep it secret."
5. The angel raised his hand to heaven
6. and said, "There will be no more waiting! When the seventh angel blows his trumpet, God's plan will be finished—just like He said to the prophets."
7. Then the voice I heard from heaven spoke again: "Go take the scroll from the angel standing on the sea and land."
8. I went to the angel and asked for the scroll. He said, "Take it and eat it. It will taste sweet but upset your stomach."
9. I took the scroll and ate it. It tasted sweet like honey but made my stomach hurt.

10. Then I was told, "You must speak again about many people, nations, languages, and kings."

Revelation 11

1. I was given a stick like a ruler and told, "Measure God's temple and the altar. Count the people worshiping there.
2. But don't measure the outer area. It's been given to other people. They will control the city for 42 months."
3. "I will give My two witnesses power to speak for 1,260 days. They will wear rough clothes."
4. These two are like two olive trees and two lampstands standing before the Lord.
5. If anyone tries to hurt them, fire comes from their mouths and destroys their enemies.
6. They have power to stop the rain, turn water into blood, and send plagues whenever needed.
7. After they finish their message, a beast will come from the deep and kill them.
8. Their bodies will lie in the street of the great city where the Lord was killed.
9. People from every group will see their bodies for three and a half days. They won't allow them to be buried.
10. People will be happy about their death, even sending gifts to each other, because the two prophets had caused them trouble.
11. But after three and a half days, God gave them life. They stood up, and everyone was terrified.
12. A loud voice from heaven said, "Come up here." They went up in a cloud, and their enemies watched.
13. At that moment, there was a strong earthquake. A tenth of the city fell, and 7,000 people died. The others were scared and gave glory to God.
14. That was the second trouble. The third is coming soon.
15. The seventh angel blew his trumpet. Loud voices in heaven said, "The kingdom of the world now belongs to our Lord and His Christ! He will rule forever!"
16. The 24 elders bowed down and worshiped God.
17. They said, "Lord God Almighty, You are the One who is and was. We thank You, because You have begun to rule with great power.
18. The nations were angry, but Your anger has come. It's time to judge the dead and reward Your servants—prophets, holy people, and all who respect You."
19. Then God's temple in heaven was opened. The ark of His promise was seen. There was lightning, thunder, an earthquake, and large hail.

Revelation 12

1. A great sign appeared in the sky. It was a woman. She was about to have a baby.
2. She cried out in pain, ready to give birth.
3. Then another sign appeared—a big red dragon with seven heads and ten horns. Each head had a crown.
4. Its tail swept a third of the stars out of the sky. It stood in front of the woman, ready to eat her baby.
5. She gave birth to a boy who will rule all nations. God took the child up to His throne.
6. The woman ran into the desert where God prepared a place for her. She stayed there 1,260 days.
7. Then war broke out in heaven. Michael and his angels fought the dragon.
8. The dragon lost and was thrown out of heaven.
9. This dragon is the devil, also called Satan. He was thrown to earth with his angels.

10. A loud voice said, "Now God has won! Satan has been thrown down! He accused God's people day and night."
11. "They won by the blood of Jesus and by telling the truth. They didn't give up, even when it meant death."
12. "So rejoice, heaven! But trouble to the earth, because the devil is angry and knows he has little time."
13. When the dragon saw he was thrown to earth, he chased the woman who gave birth to the child.
14. She was given wings to fly to safety in the desert, where God would care for her for a time.
15. The dragon tried to flood her out, but the earth helped her by swallowing the water.
16. Then the dragon got even more angry and went to fight the rest of her children—those who obey God and believe in Jesus.

Revelation 13

1. The dragon stood by the sea. A beast came out of the sea. It had ten horns and seven heads. Each horn had a crown, and each head had a name that insulted God.
2. The beast looked like a leopard, with feet like a bear and a mouth like a lion. The dragon gave the beast power.
3. One of the beast's heads looked wounded, but it was healed. Everyone was amazed and followed the beast.
4. They worshiped the dragon for giving power to the beast. They said, "Who is like the beast? Who can fight it?"
5. The beast was allowed to speak proud words and say bad things about God. It ruled for 42 months.
6. It said bad things about God, His name, His home, and His people in heaven.
7. It was allowed to fight and defeat God's people. It ruled over every group and nation.
8. Everyone on earth worshiped it—except those whose names were written in the Book of Life.
9. Whoever has ears, listen:
10. If you're meant to be captured, you'll be captured. If you're meant to be killed, you'll be killed.
    God's people must be patient and stay faithful.
11. Then I saw another beast coming from the earth. It had two horns like a lamb but spoke like a dragon.
12. It used the first beast's power and made the world worship the first beast, whose wound was healed.
13. It did great miracles, even making fire come from the sky.
14. It tricked people and told them to make a statue of the first beast.
15. It was allowed to give life to the statue so it could speak. Anyone who refused to worship it would be killed.
16. It forced everyone—rich, poor, free, or slave—to get a mark on their right hand or forehead.
17. No one could buy or sell unless they had the mark: the name of the beast or its number.
18. Here is a clue: The number is 666. It stands for a person's name.

Revelation 14

1. I saw the Lamb standing on Mount Zion. With Him were 144,000 people. They had His name and His Father's name written on their foreheads.
2. I heard a sound from heaven like rushing water and loud thunder. It also sounded like people playing music.
3. The 144,000 sang a new song in front of God's throne. Only they could learn the song. They were saved from the earth.
4. They had kept themselves pure. They followed the Lamb wherever He went. They were the first ones saved for God and the Lamb.

5. No lies were found in them. They did what was right.
6. Then I saw another angel flying in the sky. He had the good news to tell everyone on earth.
7. He said loudly, "Respect God and give Him glory! The time has come for Him to judge. Worship the One who made the skies, earth, sea, and water springs!"
8. A second angel said, "The great city of Babylon has fallen! She made all nations sin with her evil ways."
9. A third angel said loudly, "If anyone worships the beast or gets its mark,
10. they will drink the full anger of God. They will be punished with fire before the angels and the Lamb.
11. They will have no rest, day or night. This is for anyone who worships the beast or takes its mark."
12. God's people must be strong. They keep God's commands and stay faithful to Jesus.
13. Then I heard a voice from heaven say, "Write this: Blessed are those who die in the Lord from now on."
"Yes," said the Spirit. "They will rest, and their good works will follow them."
14. I looked and saw a white cloud. On it sat someone like a Son of Man with a gold crown and a sharp sickle.
15. Another angel came and said, "Use your sickle. The time to harvest has come!"
16. The one on the cloud swung his sickle, and the earth was harvested.
17. Another angel came from the temple with a sharp sickle.
18. Yet another angel came with power over fire. He said, "Use your sickle! Cut the grapes from the earth. They are ready!"
19. The angel did it and threw the grapes into a big winepress of God's anger.
20. The grapes were crushed outside the city. Blood flowed like a river, very deep and far.

Revelation 15

1. I saw another great and amazing sign in heaven. Seven angels had the last seven plagues. These would finish God's anger.
2. I saw something like a glass sea mixed with fire. Those who had won against the beast stood beside it. They held harps from God.
3. They sang the song of Moses and the Lamb:
"Lord God, You are powerful and amazing!
Your ways are right and true.
You are King over all!
4. Everyone will respect You. All people will worship You.
You alone are holy. Your right actions are now seen."
5. Then I looked and saw the temple in heaven opened.
6. The seven angels came out, wearing clean, bright clothes with gold bands.
7. One of the four living beings gave each angel a gold bowl filled with God's anger.
8. The temple was filled with smoke from God's glory and power. No one could enter the temple until the seven plagues were finished.

Revelation 16

1. I heard a loud voice from the temple say to the seven angels, "Go and pour out the seven bowls of God's anger on the earth."
2. The first angel poured out his bowl. Painful sores broke out on people who had the beast's mark and worshiped it.
3. The second angel poured out his bowl into the sea. The water turned to blood and everything in the sea died.

4. The third angel poured out his bowl into the rivers and springs. They also turned to blood.
5. The angel in charge of water said, "God, You are fair. You gave them blood because they spilled the blood of Your people."
6. Another voice said, "Yes, Lord God! What You did is right!"
7. The fourth angel poured out his bowl on the sun. It became so hot it burned people.
8. They cursed God and did not turn back to Him.
9. The fifth angel poured out his bowl on the beast's throne. His kingdom became dark. People bit their tongues in pain.
10. They cursed God for their pain and sores. But they still didn't turn from their sins.
11. The sixth angel poured out his bowl on the Euphrates River. Its water dried up to prepare the way for kings from the east.
12. Then I saw three evil spirits that looked like frogs come out of the dragon, the beast, and the false prophet.
13. They were demons and did miracles. They went to gather all the kings of the world for a great battle.
14. "Look," Jesus said, "I'm coming like a thief. Blessed is the one who stays ready."
15. The spirits gathered the kings at a place called Armageddon.
16. The seventh angel poured out his bowl into the air. A loud voice from the temple said, "It is done!"
17. There was lightning, thunder, and the biggest earthquake ever.
18. The great city split into three parts. Cities all over the world fell. God remembered Babylon and gave her the cup of His anger.
19. Every island disappeared. Mountains were gone.
20. Huge hailstones fell from the sky. People cursed God because the hail was so terrible.

Revelation 17

1. One of the seven angels came to me and said, "Come, I'll show you the punishment of the evil woman who sits over many waters."
2. The kings of the world sinned with her. People on earth got drunk from her evil actions.
3. Then the angel took me to a desert in the Spirit. I saw a woman sitting on a red beast. The beast had seven heads and ten horns and was full of bad names.
4. The woman wore purple and red clothes. She had gold, jewels, and pearls. She held a gold cup full of evil.
5. On her forehead was a name: "Babylon the Great, Mother of Evil, Queen of Sin."
6. She was drunk with the blood of God's people. When I saw her, I was amazed.
7. The angel said, "Why are you surprised? I'll explain the woman and the beast she rides."
8. "The beast you saw was alive, then not, and will come again from the deep pit. People whose names are not in the Book of Life will be amazed when they see it."
9. "Here is what the seven heads mean: They are seven hills and seven kings.
10. Five are gone, one is now, and one is yet to come and will stay only a short time.
11. The beast who was and is not is an eighth king. He belongs to the seven and is going to be destroyed."
12. "The ten horns are ten kings who haven't ruled yet. They will rule with the beast for a short time.

13. They all agree to give their power to the beast.
14. But they will fight the Lamb, and the Lamb will win. He is Lord of all. His people are the called and faithful ones."
15. The angel said, "The waters the woman sits on are people from every land and language.
16. The beast and the ten horns will hate the woman. They will take everything from her and burn her.
17. God put it in their hearts to do His will. They will give the beast their power until what God said is finished."
18. "The woman you saw is the great city that rules over the kings of the earth."

Revelation 18

1. After this, I saw another angel come down from heaven. He had great power, and the earth lit up from his glory.
2. He shouted, "Babylon the Great has fallen! She has become a home for demons and evil spirits."
3. "All nations sinned with her. The kings sinned with her. The merchants got rich from her wealth."
4. I heard another voice say, "Come out of her, My people. Don't share in her sins. Don't be punished with her."
5. "Her sins are stacked up to heaven. God remembers what she has done."
6. "Give her what she gave others. Pay her back double."
7. "She was proud and lived in luxury. Now give her pain and sadness."
8. "She says, 'I'm a queen! I'll never be sad!' But in one day, her plagues will come. She will die, and fire will burn her. God has judged her."
9. The kings who sinned with her will cry when they see the smoke from the fire.
10. They will stand far away and say, "Oh no! The great city is destroyed in one hour!"
11. The merchants will cry too. No one will buy their goods anymore.
12. They sold gold, silver, jewels, fine clothes, wood, spices, wine, oil, animals, and even people.
13. Everything they loved is now gone.
14. Merchants who got rich from her will stand far away in fear and cry.
15. They'll say, "Oh no! The great city is gone in one hour!"
16. Ship captains, sailors, and all who worked at sea will cry too.
17. They'll say, "Was there ever a city like this?"
18. They'll throw dust on their heads and cry, "She is gone in one hour!"
19. But heaven, saints, apostles, and prophets—be glad! God has judged her for what she did to you.
20. Then a mighty angel threw a big stone into the sea and said, "This is how Babylon will be thrown down. It will never be found again."
21. No music, work, or light will ever be found there again.
22. The merchants were powerful, but they fooled the world.
23. Babylon was full of the blood of prophets, saints, and all who were killed on earth.

Revelation 19

1. After this, I heard a loud sound in heaven. A large crowd said, "Hallelujah! Salvation and glory and power belong to God!"
2. "He judged the evil woman who ruined the earth. He punished her for killing His people."
3. They shouted, "Hallelujah! Her smoke goes up forever!"
4. The 24 elders and the four living beings fell down and worshiped God. They said, "Amen! Hallelujah!"

5. A voice from the throne said, "Praise our God, all who serve Him, great and small!"

6. Then I heard a huge crowd. It sounded like rushing water and loud thunder. They shouted, "Hallelujah! The Lord God rules!"

7. "Let's be glad and happy! The wedding of the Lamb has come! His bride is ready."

8. She was given clean, white clothes to wear. These clothes are the good things God's people do.

9. The angel said, "Write this: Blessed are those invited to the Lamb's wedding feast." He added, "These words are true."

10. I bowed to worship him, but he said, "Don't do that! I'm a servant like you. Worship God!"

11. Then I saw heaven opened. A white horse came out. Its rider is called Faithful and True. He judges fairly and makes war.

12. His eyes were like fire. He wore many crowns. He had a name no one knew but Himself.

13. He wore a robe dipped in blood. His name is the Word of God.

14. The armies of heaven followed Him on white horses, wearing white clothes.

15. From His mouth came a sharp sword to strike the nations. He will rule them with strength. He brings God's anger.

16. On His robe and thigh was written: "KING OF KINGS AND LORD OF LORDS."

17. Then I saw an angel standing in the sun. He shouted, "Come, birds! Come eat the flesh of kings, generals, strong men, horses, and all people!"

18. The beast, the kings, and their armies came to fight the rider on the white horse.

19. But the beast was captured, along with the false prophet who did miracles and tricked people into worshiping the beast.

20. They were thrown alive into the lake of fire.

21. The rest were killed by the sword from the rider's mouth. Birds ate all their flesh.

Revelation 20

1. I saw an angel come down from heaven. He had the key to the bottomless pit and a big chain.

2. He grabbed the dragon (Satan) and tied him up for 1,000 years.

3. The angel threw him into the pit and locked it so he couldn't trick the nations again until the 1,000 years were over. After that, he would be let out for a short time.

4. I saw thrones and people sitting on them who were given power to judge. I also saw the souls of people who were killed for following Jesus. They had not worshiped the beast or taken its mark. They came back to life and ruled with Christ for 1,000 years.

5. The rest of the dead didn't come back to life until the 1,000 years were over. This is the first resurrection.

6. Blessed are the people in this first resurrection. The second death has no power over them. They will be priests of God and Christ and will rule with Him for 1,000 years.

7. After the 1,000 years, Satan will be set free.

8. He will trick the nations and gather them for war. There will be so many it's like counting grains of sand.

9. They will surround God's people and the holy city, but fire will come down and destroy them.

10. The devil, who tricked them, will be thrown into the lake of fire with the beast and false prophet. They will be punished forever.

11. Then I saw a great white throne. The earth and sky ran away from it.

12. I saw the dead, big and small, standing before God. Books were opened. Another book—the Book of Life—was also opened. People were judged by what they had done.
13. The sea gave up its dead. Death and the grave gave up their dead too. Everyone was judged.
14. Death and the grave were thrown into the lake of fire. This is the second death.
15. If anyone's name was not in the Book of Life, they were thrown into the lake of fire.

Revelation 21

1. I saw a new heaven and a new earth. The old heaven and earth were gone. There was no sea.
2. I saw the holy city, the new Jerusalem, coming down from heaven like a beautiful bride.
3. I heard a loud voice say, "Now God lives with His people! They will be His people, and He will be their God."
4. God will wipe away every tear. There will be no more death, sadness, crying, or pain.
5. The one on the throne said, "I am making everything new." He said, "Write this down. These words are true."
6. Then He said, "It is done! I am the beginning and the end. I will give the thirsty water from the spring of life—for free."
7. "Those who win will get all this. I will be their God, and they will be My children."
8. "But people who are afraid, don't believe, do evil, murder, sin sexually, follow idols, or lie—they will be thrown into the lake of fire. This is the second death."
9. One of the seven angels said to me, "Come! I'll show you the Lamb's bride."
10. He took me up to a high mountain and showed me the holy city, coming down from heaven.
11. It shined with God's glory. It sparkled like a jewel.
12. It had a big wall with twelve gates. Each gate had the name of one of the twelve tribes of Israel.
13. There were three gates on each side—north, south, east, and west.
14. The wall had twelve foundation stones with the names of the twelve apostles.
15. The angel had a measuring stick to measure the city, its gates, and its walls.
16. The city was square—just as wide as it was long and high. It was huge.
17. The wall was thick and tall. Everything was measured in God's own scale.
18. The wall was made of jasper. The city was pure gold, clear like glass.
19. The foundations were decorated with precious stones—like jasper, sapphire, emerald, and more.
20. The twelve gates were twelve pearls. Each gate was made from a single pearl. The streets were gold and clear like glass.
21. I didn't see a temple there. The Lord God and the Lamb are the temple.
22. The city didn't need the sun or moon. God's glory was its light, and the Lamb was its lamp.
23. The nations will walk in its light. The kings will bring their glory to it.
24. The gates will never be shut. There will be no night there.
25. People will bring their best into the city.
26. But nothing bad or sinful will enter—only those whose names are in the Lamb's Book of Life.

Revelation 22

1. The angel showed me a river of life. It was clear like crystal and flowed from God's throne and the Lamb.
2. It went down the middle of the city street. On each side of the river was the tree of life. It gave 12 kinds of fruit, one for each month. Its leaves healed the nations.
3. Nothing bad will be there. God and the Lamb will be on the throne. God's people will serve Him.
4. They will see His face, and His name will be on their foreheads.
5. There will be no more night. They won't need a lamp or the sun. The Lord will give them light, and they will rule forever.
6. The angel said, "These words are true. The Lord sent His angel to show His servants what must happen soon."
7. Jesus says, "Look, I am coming soon! Blessed are those who obey the words of this book."
8. I, John, heard and saw these things. When I saw them, I bowed to worship the angel.
9. But the angel said, "Don't do that! I am a servant like you. Worship God!"
10. Then he said, "Don't hide these words. The time is near.
11. Let those who do wrong keep doing wrong, and those who do right keep doing right."
12. Jesus says, "Look, I am coming soon! I will reward everyone for what they have done.
13. I am the First and the Last, the Beginning and the End."
14. "Blessed are those who obey God's commands. They can eat from the tree of life and enter the city."
15. "Outside the city are those who do evil—like liars, murderers, and idol worshipers."
16. "I, Jesus, sent My angel to give you this message. I am the Root of David and the bright morning star."
17. The Spirit and the Bride say, "Come!" Let the one who hears say, "Come!" Whoever is thirsty, come and take the water of life—it's free.
18. I warn anyone who hears this book: Don't add to these words or take away from them. If you do, you will face God's punishment.
19. If you take away from this book, you will lose your share in the tree of life and the holy city.
20. Jesus says, "Yes, I am coming soon." Amen! Come, Lord Jesus!
21. May the grace of the Lord Jesus be with everyone. Amen.

* 9 7 9 8 9 9 9 3 5 3 4 0 5 *

20250729185530